Canadian Literature Index

A Guide to Periodicals and Newspapers
Cumulative Index to 1987 Publications

Canadian Literature Index

A Guide to Periodicals and Newspapers

CUMULATIVE INDEX TO 1987 PUBLICATIONS

Janet Fraser, BA, MA, MLS, *Editor*
Richard Hanson, BA, MA, *Managing Editor*
Allan Weiss, BA, MA, PhD, *Indexer*

ECW PRESS

Canadian Cataloguing in Publication Data

Fraser, Janet, 1954 –

ISBN 1-55022-084-5

1. Canadian literature – 20th century – Periodicals - Indexes. 2. Canadian literature – 20th century – History and Criticism – Periodicals – Indexes.
1. Title.

Z1375.F72 1990   016.81   C87-93440-6

This index was compiled for publication using AUTHEX, a microcomputer-based indexing program developed by Gordon Ripley of *Reference Press*. The publisher is grateful to Mr. Ripley for his assistance.
Processing, post-processing, design & imaging by ECW Type & Art, Oakville, Ontario.
Cover design by Bette Davies.

Published by ECW PRESS, 307 Coxwell Avenue, Toronto, Ontario M4L 3B5

Table of Contents

Background and Objectives of the Index

The *Canadian Literature Index: A Guide to Periodicals and Newspapers* was created in response to the need for comprehensive access to the vast amount of Canadian literature and literary criticism published on a periodical basis. Up to this point there has been no Canadian reference guide to literary periodical publishing. Therefore, the mandate of the *Canadian Literature Index* is to provide scholars, students and general readers of Canadian literature with a periodicals guide devoted exclusively to their interests.

In order to meet the mandate of the *Canadian Literature Index*, I have researched all Canadian periodicals, international periodicals and Canadian newspapers that deal significantly with Canadian literature, and have selected over one hundred sources. The core of the sources collection is the Canadian literary periodical. There are over 150 Canadian literary periodicals and I have generously selected all those that meet my criteria of quality and reliability. I have then selected general-interest Canadian periodicals and newspapers and international periodicals on the basis of literary content, quality and circulation.

The *Canadian Literature Index* has dual objectives: one, to access all Canadian primary materials (poems, short stories, novels, plays and literary essays), and two, to access all Canadian secondary materials (critical articles, book reviews, interviews and bibliographies), in the field of Canadian literature. To this end, primary materials are carefully checked to ensure that the author published is Canadian, while secondary materials are carefully checked to ensure that the books and authors covered are Canadian. For example, a Canadian writer publishing a poem would be included in *CLI*, while a Canadian writer publishing a book review of an American novel would be excluded. Conversely, an American publishing a poem would be excluded from *CLI*, while an American publishing a book review of a Canadian novel would be included. Extensive author and subject authority files are maintained to ensure consistent, reliable headings in the Author Index and the Subject Index.

The 1985 edition of the *Canadian Literature Index* was the first volume of an annual series. With new editions, periodicals will be added for indexing and refinements of *CLI* will be made.

Any suggestions or questions can be addressed to Janet Fraser, Editor, *Canadian Literature Index*, in care of ECW PRESS.

Janet Fraser, February 17, 1987.

Arrangement of the Index

The *Canadian Literature Index* is comprised of two main sections, the Author Index and the Subject Index, supplemented by appendices which include publication and availability information for the indexed periodicals and newspapers.

The *Author Index: Guide to Contributors, Critical and Creative* is an alphabetical listing by name of all Canadians who have published poems, short stories, plays and other original material in the indexed sources and of all literary critics and scholars who have published articles and reviews of Canadian literary books in the indexed sources.

Author headings have been standardized according to the correct form of name most commonly used for the author, in other words, the name the author seems to use for himself/herself. Generally, the most complete information available for the name is used. Variants in lettering and punctuation are not followed, with a couple of notable exceptions, (for example: Nichol, bp).

The *Subject Index: Guide to Critical Coverage of Canadian Writers, Books and Themes* is an alphabetical listing of subject headings and author and book headings, inter-filed in the manner of a 'mixed' library catalogue. Therefore, there are three distinct types of headings within the Subject Index: the author, the book title, and the subject, or 'keyword.'

The book title as heading is intended to provide direct access to all reviews and critical articles dealing significantly with that book. The author and full title of the book are provided, as well as the enhancement or 'descriptive cataloguing' which designates the genre of the book. As an added feature, the title as heading also includes titles of Canadian literary periodicals.

The author as heading is intended to provide direct access to all reviews, articles, interviews and bibliographies dealing significantly with that author. Author headings have been standardized according to the correct form by which the author is most commonly known. Generally, the most complete information available for the name is used. Pseudonymous authors appear under their pseudonyms, with a cross reference from their real names. There is one exception: Pierre Berton, who used the pseudonym Lisa Kroniuk for *one* of his books. There are several collective authors included, mostly theatre collectives who have co-written plays.

The subject heading is intended to provide access to both broad subject areas of Canadian literary history and criticism and specific areas of thematic and formal criticism. Geographically, broad areas of Canadian criticism may be found under **CANADIAN LITERATURE . . .** , and broad areas of regional criticism can be found under the specific regions. Ethnic groups of writing and writers within Canada may be accessed directly (for example, **JEWISH-CANADIAN, UKRAINIAN-CANA-DIAN**), or under the more general heading, **ETHNIC-CANADIAN WRITING**.

An added feature are the subject headings which serve purely as comprehensive listings of book reviews. For the researcher or librarian interested in certain types of publications in Canada (for example, anthologies or first novels), headings such as **ANTHOLOGIES: BOOK REVIEWS** and **FIRST NOVELS: BOOK REVIEWS** provide a complete list. A list of subject headings is appended to this section.

BILINGUALISM

The *Canadian Literature Index* is designed to provide coverage of Canadian authors writing in any language. Since the vast majority of Canadian authors write in English and/or French, the Index covers primarily English and French-language literature. However, *CLI* is *not* a bilingual index in that the language used to access French authors and titles is English. The only French-language information is that of the actual literature, in other words, the title of the entry or the book title as subject heading. In the case of a translated book title as subject heading, the language of the original work is used, followed by the translation (for example, **BEAUX GESTES/ BEAUTIFUL DEEDS**). When a bilingual book is reviewed, the title enhancement area designates which version is being reviewed (for example: review of *Beaux Gestes*, or, review of *Beautiful Deeds*).

ANNOTATIONS

In the Author Index, entries under headings are comprised of title and publication information, while in the Subject Index, entries under headings are comprised of title, author, and publication information. An added feature of entries for both indexes of *CLI* is the title enhancement or 'annotation' area, which follows the title entry area. 'Annotations' are used to describe and clarify the genre and content of the entry, since often the actual titles provide no clues. In the Author Index, the researcher can identify the genre in which a literary contributor is working or the critical area in which a scholarly contributor is working. In the Subject Index, the researcher can more easily identify the books and authors being discussed, the generic type of entry, or the content of an article.

KEYWORDS

In the Subject Index, subject headings or 'keywords' appear at the end of entries for which there are other headings. The 'keywords' area is designed to describe the entry further as well as lead researchers to other subject areas of interest.

ABBREVIATIONS

The abbreviations and full titles of periodicals and newspapers indexed are provided in another section. The following is a key to the abbreviations used in the bibliographic area of the entries to designate additional information (for example, illustrations or photographs included with an entry) and publication information.

Key to Abbreviations

Aug	• August
Books	• Books Section
bibliog	• bibliography
biog	• biography
Dec	• December
Feb	• February
illus	• illustration
Jan	• January
[n.p.]	• no page number given
No	• number
Nov	• November
Oct	• October
p	• page
photo	• photograph
pseud	• pseudonym
SM	• Saturday Magazine
Sept	• September
trans	• translation
Vol	• Volume

CLI Update

STYLE CHANGES

The style of French-language book and periodical titles has been changed to international style. Therefore, only the first significant letter of a title is capitalized.

CROSS REFERENCES

In 1986 cross references have been made from a translated book title subject heading to the title subject heading in the original language (for example: *The Tin Flute See* **BONHEUR D'OCCASION/THE TIN FLUTE/Novel by Gabrielle Roy).**

PERIODICALS

Four periodicals have been added for indexing in 1986: *Journal of Canadian Poetry, Room of One's Own, The Toronto South Asian Review* and *Writing. Room of One's Own* first appeared in the *First Quarter Supplement; The Toronto South Asian Review* and *Writing* in the *Second Quarter Supplement* and *Journal of Canadian Poetry* in the *Third Quarter Supplement*.

ACKNOWLEDGEMENTS

At this time, the staff of the *Canadian Literature Index* would like to thank all those who have helped us with the project since it began in 1985. First, we would like to thank the editors and business managers of the periodicals chosen for indexing for their generous support in sending us their publications regularly. We would also like to thank Jane Cooper and the staff of the John P. Robarts Library Current Periodicals Reading Room and Microtext Room for their helpful and courteous assistance and the use of office space. Finally, we would like to thank all those who contributed their informed opinions and enthusiasm for the *Canadian Literature Index*, and in particular, Patricia Fleming, Richard Landon and Francess Halpenny of the University of Toronto and Wendy Craig, Librarian.

How to Use CLI

In this section one sample search will illustrate how *CLI* works. In the sample search, a researcher wants to know everything that has been written by and about the Canadian author, **Timothy Findley**, in literary periodicals and newspapers in 1986.

To find out what has been written *by* Timothy Findley, the researcher turns to the *Author Index*. Entries include:

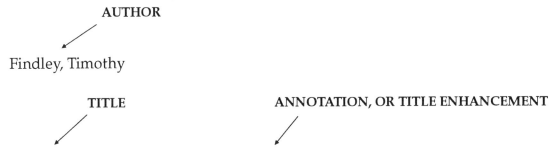

AUTHOR

Findley, Timothy

TITLE   **ANNOTATION, OR TITLE ENHANCEMENT**

Focal point; excerpt from a novel in progress. illus · *Can Forum* Feb 1986; Vol 65 No [756]: p26-30.

Growing up together; article about the Canadian Authors Association. photo · *Can Auth & Book* Spring 1986; Vol 61 No 3: p6.

[Untitled]; review of *The Whole Night, Coming Home. J of Can Poetry* 1986; Vol 1: p10-12.

A writer's craft; essay. *Grain* Feb 1986; Vol 14 No 1: p6-10.

PERIODICAL

The researcher discovers that Timothy Findley has published essays, book reviews, articles and an excerpt from a novel in progress in various Canadian literary periodicals.

To find out what has been written *about* Timothy Findley, the researcher begins with a particular review of Findley's novel, *The Telling of Lies*, in which he is interested. This review is written by fellow novelist Aritha van Herk, so he looks up van Herk in the *Author Index*.

AUTHOR

van Herk, Aritha
Mystery novel's political subplot blurs its strength; review of *The Telling of Lies*. CH Nov 17, 1986: pC1.

At this point the researcher would like to find out more about Findley's *The Telling of Lies* so he looks up the book heading in the *Subject Index*. Entries include:

SUBJECT   DESCRIPTIVE CATALOGUING

THE TELLING OF LIES/Novel by Timothy Findley

Image of body out in open in beach in Maine sparked story; article. Joel Yanofsky. *MG* Oct 25, 1986: pB8.

Murder & mayhem: the refined art of a storyteller; review of *The Telling of Lies*. Margaret Cannon. *G&M* Oct 25, 1986: pE19.

Mystery novel's political subplot blurs its strength; review of *The Telling of Lies*. Aritha van Herk. *CH* Nov 17, 1986: pC1.

Sharing the guilt; review of *The Telling of Lies*. Wayne Grady. *Books in Can* Nov 1986; Vol 15 No 8: p16-17.

AUTHOR   BOOK REVIEWS

The researcher finds a number of reviews as well as background articles related to *The Telling of Lies* in newspapers and periodicals. The review by Margaret Cannon is part of a regular column reviewing mystery novels. The reviews by Aritha van Herk and Wayne Grady are written from a more literary perspective.

Now the researcher wants to see everything that has been written *about* Timothy Findley so he looks him up in the *Subject Index*. He finds a variety of entries which include:

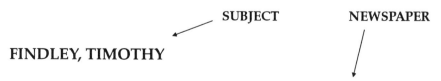

SUBJECT   NEWSPAPER

FINDLEY, TIMOTHY

Findley novel wins talking book award; article. *TS* April 29, 1986: pE1.
[AWARDS, LITERARY]

INTERVIEW

Interview with Timothy Findley. Eugene Benson. *World Lit in Eng* Spring 1986; Vol 26 No 1: p107-115.

PERIODICAL   ARTICLE

"It could not be told": making meaning in Timothy Findley's *The Wars*; article. Diana Brydon. *J of Common Lit* 1986; Vol 21 No 1: p75-84.

Memoirs of the Great War: Graves, Sassoon and Findley; article. Sister M.L. McKenzie. *U of Toronto Q* Summer 1986; Vol 55 No 4: p395-411.
[GREAT BRITAIN-CANADA LITERARY RELATIONS]

Timothy Findley's Gnostic parable; article. George Woodcock. *Can Lit* Winter 1986; No 111: p232-237.
[BIBLICAL MYTHS AND MYTHOLOGY]   KEYWORDS

The researcher discovers many articles, reviews and interviews which deal with Findley's novels *The Telling of Lies*, *The Wars*, and *Not Wanted on the Voyage* in Canadian and international periodicals and newspapers. The types of entries range from news articles about awards Findley has won to general interviews with Findley to in-depth critical articles.

The researcher is particularly interested in George Woodcock's article and through examination of the keywords becomes further interested in the subject of **BIBLICAL MYTHS AND MYTHOLOGY**. He finds other critical articles:

SUBJECT

BIBLICAL MYTHS AND MYTHOLOGY
The riddle of concentric worlds in Obasan; article. Erika Gotlieb. *Can Lit* Summer 1986; No 109: p34-53.
[THE APOCALYPSE; MYTHS AND LEGENDS IN LITERATURE]

FRENCH-LANGUAGE ARTICLE   **KEYWORDS**

Ashini: contradictions messianiques ou messianisme impossible?; article. Guy Lecomte. abstract · *Etudes can* Dec 1986; No 21 (part one): p257-262.
[NATIVE CANADIANS IN LITERATURE]

The researcher decides to write an article comparing aspects of biblical mythology in Timothy Findley's *Not Wanted on the Voyage* and Joy Kogawa's *Obasan*.

List of Keyword Subject Headings

Acadian Writing and Writers **X** French-Canadian Literature
Agents, Literary
Animal Imagery
Animal Stories
Anthologies: Book Reviews
The Apocalypse
Arctic Canada
Artist Figure
Atlantic Provinces as Setting **X** Maritime Provinces Writing
Atlantic Provinces Drama **X** Maritime Provinces Writing
Atlantic Provinces Literature: Bibliography **X** Maritime Provinces Writing
Atlantic Provinces Writing and Writers **X** Maritime Provinces Writing
Audio-Visuals and Canadian Literature
Australia-Canada Literary Relations
Authors, Canadian
Autobiographical Writing *see also* Confessional Writing
Avant-Garde Writing *see* Postmodernist Writing and Criticism
Awards, Literary *see also* Governor General's Awards
Belgium-Canada Literary Relations
Biblical Myths and Mythology **XX** Myths and Legends in Literature
Book Reviewing
Book Trade in Canada
British Columbia Writing and Writers
Canadian Drama: History and Criticism
Canadian Fiction: History and Criticism
Canadian Identity *see* Cultural Identity
Canadian Imagination
Canadian Landscape and Landmarks
Canadian Literary Periodicals
Canadian Literary Publishing **XX** Publishing and Publishers in Canada
Canadian Literature (18th Century): History and Criticism
Canadian Literature (19th Century): History and Criticism
Canadian Literature (20th Century): History and Criticism
Canadian Literature: Bibliography
Canadian Literature: Biography
Canadian Literature: History and Criticism

List of Abbreviations and Titles of Periodicals and Newspapers Indexed

All periodicals and newspapers are interfiled in this list. Please note that newspapers are differentiated from periodicals by single letter abbreviations (for example, *WFP* signifies *The Winnipeg Free Press*). For further information on the periodicals, please turn to the appendix.

ABBREVIATION • Title

Afram • Afram Newsletter
Alpha • Alpha
Amer R of Can Studies • The American Review of Canadian Studies
Antigonish R • The Antigonish Review
Arc • Arc: A Magazine of Poetry and Criticism
Ariel • Ariel: A Review of International English Literature
Atlan Insight • Atlantic Insight
Atlan Prov Book R • The Atlantic Provinces Book Review
Atlantic • The Atlantic
Atlantis • Atlantis: A Women's Studies Journal

Books in Can • Books in Canada
Border Cross • Border Crossings
Brick • Brick
British J of Can Studies • The British Journal of Canadian Studies

Can Auth & Book • Canadian Author & Bookman
Can Child Lit • Canadian Children's Literature
Can Drama • Canadian Drama
Can Fic Mag • Canadian Fiction Magazine
Can Forum • The Canadian Forum
Can Lit • Canadian Literature
Can Poet • Canadian Poetry
Can Theatre R • Canadian Theatre Review
Capilano R • The Capilano Review
CH • The Calgary Herald
Chatelaine • Chatelaine
CRNLE Reviews J • The CRNLE Reviews Journal
Cross Can Writ Q • Cross-Canada Writer's Quarterly

CV 2 • Contemporary Verse 2
Dalhousie R • The Dalhousie Review
Dandelion • Dandelion
Descant • Descant
Dino R • The Dinosaur Review

Ellipse • Ellipse
Eng Studies in Can • English Studies in Canada
Essays on Can Writ • Essays on Canadian Writing
Estuaire • Estuaire
Études can • Études canadiennes
Études fran • Études françaises
Études lit • Études littéraires
Event • Event: Journal of the Contemporary Arts
Exile • Exile: A Literary Quarterly

Fiddlehead • The Fiddlehead
Fin Post • The Financial Post
Fireweed • Fireweed: A Feminist Quarterly

G&M • The Globe and Mail
Germination • Germination
Grain • Grain

Idler • The Idler
Island • Island

J of Can Culture • Journal of Canadian Culture
J of Can Fic • Journal of Canadian Fiction
J of Can Poetry • Journal of Canadian Poetry
J of Can Studies • Journal of Canadian Studies
J of Common Lit • Journal of Commonwealth Literature
Jeu • Jeu: cahiers de théâtre

Lettres québec • Lettres québécoises
Liberté • Liberté

Maclean's • Maclean's
Malahat R • The Malahat Review
Matrix • Matrix
MD • Le Devoir
MG • The Gazette
Moebius • Moebius
Mosaic • Mosaic
New Q • The New Quarterly
New York R of Books • The New York Review of Books
New Yorker • The New Yorker
NeWest R • The NeWest Review
North Light • Northern Light

Northward J • Northward Journal: A Quarterly of Northern Arts
La Nouvelle barre du jour • La Nouvelle barre du jour
NYT Book R • The New York Times Book Review

Open Letter • Open Letter

Poetry Can R • Poetry Canada Review
Pottersfield P • The Pottersfield Portfolio
Prairie Fire • Prairie Fire
Prairie J of Can Lit • The Prairie Journal of Canadian Literature
Prism • Prism International

Quarry • Quarry
Queen's Q • Queen's Quarterly
Quill & Quire • Quill & Quire

Room of One's Own • Room of One's Own
Rubicon • Rubicon

Sat Night • Saturday Night
Studies in Can Lit • Studies in Canadian Literature

Theatre Hist in Can • Theatre History in Canada
Times Lit Supp • The Times Literary Supplement
Tor Life • Toronto Life
Tor South Asian R • The Toronto South Asian Review
TS • The Toronto Star

U of Toronto Q • The University of Toronto Quarterly
U of Windsor R • The University of Windsor Review

Voix et images • Voix et images

Wascana R • Wascana Review
Waves • Waves
West Coast R • West Coast Review
WFP • The Winnipeg Free Press
World Lit in Eng • World Literature Written in English
Writing • Writing

Yale French Studies • Yale French Studies

Zeitschrift Kanada-Studien • Zeitschrift der Gesellschaft für Kanada-Studien

Author Index: *Guide to Contributors, Critical and Creative*

Aagaard, I.

Margaret Laurence left a wonderful legacy; letter to the editor. *TS* Jan 10, 1987: pB3.

Abbey, Lloyd

At Lions Gate Hospital; poem. *Event* Summer 1987; Vol 16 No 2: p56–57.

Abeles, Susan

[Untitled]; letter to the editor. *G&M* Jan 21, 1987: pA7.

Abley, Mark

Detective with the blues; review of *The Mournful Demeanor of Lieutenant Boruvka*. photo · *Maclean's* Sept 14, 1987; Vol 100 No 37: pT12.

George Woodcock's glassy prose banishes pain, passion; review of *Beyond the Blue Mountains*. photo · *MG* Dec 31, 1987: pB7.

The girl she never was; biographical article. photo · *Sat Night* Nov 1987; Vol 102 No 11: p52–54, 56, 58–59.

Heartbreak road; review article about *Heartbreaks Along the Road*. illus · *Sat Night* Oct 1987; Vol 102 No 10: p59–62.

Hugh Hood artfully rewrites history of Italian renaissance; review of *Five New Facts About Giorgione*. *MG* Nov 7, 1987: pK12.

Jack Hodgins is famous for his extravagant tales about the unpredictable characters of Vancouver Island. . . .; review of *The Honorary Patron*. photo · *MG* Sept 26, 1987: pJ9.

Return of the native son; film review of *In the Shadow of the Wind*. photo · *Maclean's* Jan 26, 1987; Vol 100 No 4: p54.

[Untitled]; theatre review of *Fire*. photo · *Maclean's* Jan 26, 1987; Vol 100 No 4: p55.

Acheson, James

[Untitled]; review of *Dreams of Speech and Violence*. *Amer R of Can Studies* Autumn 1987; Vol 17 No 3: p352–353.

Ackerman, Marianne

Bold style masks some flimsy ideas; theatre review of *This Is What Happens In Orangeville*. *MG* June 5, 1987: pD2.

Book store aims to please the theatre and movie crowd; article. *MG* Feb 17, 1987: pE8.

Check out drama fest for new theatre talent; article. photo · *MG* April 25, 1987: pH7.

A critic takes a final bow: some general reflections on Quebec theatre scene; essay. photo · *MG* July 4, 1987: pC10.

Director, cast work wonders; theatre review of *Ce qui reste du désir*. photo · *MG* March 18, 1987: pD3.

Don't get the wrong idea – writer Ward's an original; article. photo · *MG* Feb 11, 1987: pB7.

Drama fest heads for grand finale; theatre reviews of *Jack of Hearts* and *Collideoscope*. photo · *MG* May 1, 1987: pD3.

Dubois: Toronto's playwright-of-the-hour; theatre reviews. photo · *MG* May 5, 1987: pB6.

Einstein a moving piece of theatre; theatre review. photo · *MG* May 1, 1987: pD4.

English theatre in spotlight; article. *MG* May 2, 1987: pH1.

Experimental theatre: only some works; theatre review of *Nouvelles pour le théâtre*. *MG* Feb 5, 1987: pE6.

Festival focus on multi-media events; article. *MG* April 8, 1987: pF1.

Festival of Americas: a rare feast of imaginative theatre; article. photo · *MG* May 23, 1987: pH9.

Gabrielle Roy travelled from an impoverished household in Manitoba. . . .; review of *Enchantment and Sorrow*. illus · *MG* Nov 28, 1987: pJ9.

Lament for a nation; review of *Death-Watch*. *Maclean's* Oct 19, 1987; Vol 100 No 42: p60a.

Michel Tremblay's 19th play superbly crafted – call it even a masterpiece; theatre review of *Le Vrai monde?*. photo · *MG* April 18, 1987: pC1.

Momentum picks up for Week 2 of theatre fest; article. photo · *MG* June 1, 1987: pD7.

Native actress returns to roots for inspiration; article. photo · *MG* May 29, 1987: pD2.

New play at Centaur is strong medicine – and a strange mixture; theatre review of *Somebody Somebody's Returning*. *MG* Feb 6, 1987: pD1.

Le Night Cap Bar a minor thriller that tries to be more; theatre review. *MG* April 9, 1987: pE8.

Off-stage drama in awards; article. *MG* May 4, 1987: pB9.

Piggery kicks off '87 seasons with warm and witty winner; theatre review of *Artichoke*. *MG* June 29, 1987: pD9.

Political themes heavy in theatre fest; article. *MG* Feb 4, 1987: pB6.

Prepare for sincerely ridiculous as new-look Carmen is unveiled; article. photo · *MG* April 23, 1987: pE3.

Le Printemps cool flash but no sizzle; theatre review of *Le Printemps, monsieur Deslauriers*. photo · *MG* April 14, 1987: pB8.

The Quebec invasion: French connection has 'le tout Toronto' abuzz; article. photo · *MG* May 5, 1987: pB6.

Sam Gesser tries again with Lily; article. photo · *MG* Feb 21, 1987: pD1.

Sense of guilt driving force behind thinly sketched Lily; theatre review of *Lily of the Mohawks*. *MG* Feb 27, 1987: pC2.

Stage version of early Radio-Canada drama works well; theatre review of *Florence*. *MG* April 1, 1987: pD8.

Theatre fest fever is spreading fast; article. photo · *MG* May 30, 1987: pC9.

Theatrefest: images and memories; article. photo · *MG* June 6, 1987: pH10.

Three openings in a week for busy young playwright; article. photo · *MG* April 4, 1987: pG1.

TNE's Mao charming highly visual theatre; theatre review of *Mao Tsé Toung, ou soirée de musique au consulat*. *MG* Feb 28, 1987: pG5.

[Untitled]; theatre review of *Mao Tse Toung ou soirées de musique au consulat*. *MG* March 20, 1987: pC7.

[Untitled]; theatre review of *Le Vrai monde?*. *MG* April 24, 1987: pD8.

[Untitled]; theatre review of *Le Vrai monde?*. *MG* May 1, 1987: pD6.

[Untitled]; theatre review of *Einstein*. *MG* May 15, 1987: pD6.

[Untitled]; article. *MG* June 5, 1987: pD4.

[Untitled]; theatre review of *Artichoke*. *MG* July 3, 1987: pC10.

Zany Toupie Wildwood an escape story made to measure for its outdoor space; theatre review. photo · *MG* July 2, 1987: pE5.

Acorn, Milton

Captain Neal MacDougal in nineteen-fourteen; poem. *Grain* Spring 1987; Vol 15 No 1: p9.

The genesis of MacDougal; essay. *Grain* Spring 1987; Vol 15 No 1: p7–9.

I am the real Irving Layton; poem. *Poetry Can R* Spring 1987; Vol 8 No 1–2: p7.

In memoriam; poem. *Poetry Can R* Spring 1987; Vol 8 No 1–2: p6.

It's all in mother's head; poem. *Poetry Can R* Spring 1987; Vol 8 No 1–2: p6.

On learning that Big Steel has finally taken over Mine Mill's principal local; poem. *Poetry Can R* Spring 1987; Vol 8 No 1–2: p7.

Rusty nail metaphor; poem. *Poetry Can R* Spring 1987; Vol 8 No 1–2: p6.

Seadancers; poem, includes essay. *Grain* Spring 1987; Vol 15 No 1: p10.

Sonnets of Martin Dorion (XI); poem. *Poetry Can R* Spring 1987; Vol 8 No 1–2: p7.

[Untitled]; letter · *Brick (special issue)* Summer 1987; No 30: p58.

Adachi, Ken

10 Canadian writers talk shop; review of *Canadian Writers at Work*. *TS* Dec 13, 1987: pE7.

Albee reads from first play in last act of great festival; column. *TS* Oct 26, 1987: pD5.

Anne's author faced darkness; review of *The Selected Journals of Lucy Maud Montgomery, Volume Two*. *TS* Dec 6, 1987: pC8.

Authors, booksellers angry over sale plan; article. *TS* Feb 12, 1987: pF4.

Authors' festival organizer coy about this year's lineup; column. photo · *TS* Aug 24, 1987: pB1.

Authors ham it up on TV special; column. photo · *TS* Oct 12, 1987: pB5.

An autobiography like few you've read; review of *My Father's House*. photo · *TS* Sept 27, 1987: pA23.

B.C. writer deliberately jars Jell-O minds; article. biog photo · *TS* March 7, 1987: pM4.

Brave novel needs power of a narrative; review of *Cage*. *TS* June 21, 1987: pA23.

But will Black respect Saturday Night on Sunday morning?; column. *TS* June 19, 1987: pD23.

Choice of 1987: fiction out front in 10 of the 'best'; reviews. photo · *TS* Dec 5, 1987: pM6.

Clever novelist confuses the critics; column. *TS* Oct 22, 1987: pB4.

Dancing Chicken more of a turkey, reviewer finds; review. *TS* Nov 8, 1987: pA19.

Dorothy Livesay: a rare breed of woman; biographical article. photo · *TS* June 28, 1987: pA19.

English novelist praises Toronto festival; column. *TS* March 30, 1987: pF4.

Everything's coming up roses for busy Canadian publishers; article. photo · *TS* Sept 22, 1987: pC2.

Fact and fiction make an impressive novel; review of *In the Skin of a Lion*. photo · *TS* May 30, 1987: pM4.

Feminist quarterly honors Laurence; column. *TS* Nov 16, 1987: pC5.

The fight for love and truth hampered by riddle of past; reviews of *Between Men* and *Getting Married in Buffalo Jump*. photo · *TS* Oct 17, 1987: pM4.

Findley novel a sell-out in London despite critical vitriol; article. *TS* April 6, 1987: pB1.

Firings at McClelland unsettle book community; column. *TS* Jan 19, 1987: pD1.

A flowering spring and a simplistic guide; reviews of *Northern Spring* and *A Reader's Guide to the Canadian Novel* (second edition). photo · *TS* Aug 1, 1987: pM4.

Frye finally wins elusive award for best non-fiction book of '86; article. photo · *TS* May 28, 1987: pH1.

Frye in good position to take Governor-General's prize; column. photo · *TS* April 30, 1987: pH1.

The gofers are gaining control; article about women publishers. photo · *TS* March 21, 1987: pM3.

Harbourfront's authors festival opens with intriguing weekend; article, includes schedule. photo · *TS* Oct 16, 1987: pD12.

In ordinary life we don't assume we know anyone; article. *TS* Sept 19, 1987: pM5.

Inspector Salter of Green Gables; review of *A Body Surrounded by Water*. *TS* July 12, 1987: pA19.

It's good to see and hear feisty Callaghan; television review of *Morley Callaghan: First Person Singular*. photo · *TS* March 24, 1987: pC6.

"I've done what I set out to do; I have nothing to regret"; essay. photo · *CH* Jan 7, 1987: pD3.

J.D. Salinger's biography too tame to cause ripples; column. *TS* Feb 2, 1987: pD2.

Jane Urquhart's stand-up talent; review of *Storm Glass*. *TS* June 7, 1987: pG11.

Kinsella finds the pathos in ordinary lives; review of *Red Wolf, Red Wolf*. *TS* Sept 6, 1987: pA19.

L'Actualite picks up six magazine awards; article. *TS* May 22, 1987: pE21.

Latecomer to fiction-writing a talent to watch; column. photo · *TS* Oct 19, 1987: pC5.

A lesson in how to look at life and virtues of love and courage; review of *Enchantment and Sorrow*. photo · *TS* Nov 14, 1987: pM4.

Lowry links Greek myth with cautionary tale; reviews of *Malcolm Lowry: Vancouver Days* and *Hear Us O Lord from Heaven Thy Dwelling Place*. photo · *TS* July 11, 1987: pM4.

Magazine to have face lift; column. photo · *TS* Dec 15, 1987: pG4.

Margaret Atwood's new anthology food for thought; column. photo · *TS* April 13, 1987: pB1.

Margaret Laurence dead at 60: revered writer remembered for her humanity as well as books; article. biog photo · *TS* Jan 6, 1987: pD1-D2.

McClelland quits publishing with characteristic class; column. photo · *TS* Feb 20, 1987: pD23.

Memoirs major theme in this fall's line-up but enough variety to suit everyone's taste; preview of fall book list. photo · *TS* Aug 29, 1987: pM4.

A momentous day for writers; column. *TS* March 16, 1987: pB1.

A new and nervy short story writer; review of *Inspecting the Vaults*. *TS* Feb 1, 1987: pB7.

New jewel in Canada's literary crown; review of *Tales from Firozsha Baag*. photo · *TS* April 18, 1987: pM4.

New novel moves into realism; review of *The Honorary Patron*. photo · *TS* Oct 3, 1987: pM4.

A newcomer to Canadian crime fiction; review of *Gallows View*. *TS* April 19, 1987: pA19.

No blockbusters in spring lists; preview of spring book list. *TS* Feb 15, 1987: pA19.

On the street where they lived; review of *The Oxford Illustrated Literary Guide to Canada*. photo · *TS* Nov 29, 1987: pA21.

Ondaatje's latest novel winning raves in Britain; column. photo · *TS* Aug 31, 1987: pB5.

Outcome of Bell Jar libel suit closely monitored by publishers; column. *TS* Jan 26, 1987: pD4.

Page on places and things pure pleasure; review of *Brazilian Journal*. photo · *TS* June 27, 1987: pM4.

Poet Gwendolyn MacEwen dead; obituary. photo · *TS* Dec 1, 1987: pH1.

Poet's triumphant ascent presented with grace, insight; review of *E.J. Pratt: The Master Years*. photo · *TS* Dec 19, 1987: pM4.

Portrait of an extraordinary man: a vibrant and influential presence in our intellectual and political life; review of *The Politics of the Imagination*. photo · *TS* Nov 21, 1987: pM4.

Quebec native son sums up his feelings on la belle province; review of *Heartbreaks Along the Road*. photo · *TS* Oct 24, 1987: pM4.

Quebec nurses its surrealists; review of *Intimate Strangers*. photo · *TS* June 13, 1987: pM4.

Ranging from colored bleakness to breeziness; reviews of novels by Paulette Jiles. photo · *TS* Feb 28, 1987: pM4.

Risk-taking writer off to a good start; review of *The Butterfly Chair*. *TS* Nov 22, 1987: pC9.

Saturday Night film dispiriting; column. photo · *TS* Sept 7, 1987: pB2.

Saturday Night loses a guy who loves his craft; column. *TS* June 25, 1987: pF1.

Something gravely missing in Brian Moore's last novel; review of *The Color of Blood*. photo · *TS* Sept 5, 1987: pM4.

Stephen Spender a highlight of authors' festival; article. *TS* Sept 24, 1987: pC1.

Take a look at a 'little' magazine; review of *Descant*. *TS* July 19, 1987: pA21.

Tears flow as piper's lament eulogizes Margaret Laurence; article. photo · *TS* Jan 10, 1987: pA6.

There are times when you must go home again; review of *Beyond the Blue Mountains*. photo · *TS* Nov 28, 1987: pM4.

Two novels offer pain – and incidental pleasures; reviews of *Death-Watch* and *Five Facts about Giorgione*. *TS* Aug 30, 1987: pA19.

Wiseman wrote a moving memoir; review of *Memoirs of a Book-Molesting Childhood*. *TS* Nov 15, 1987: pA23.

World's waiting for second Walshe novel; column. *TS* July 20, 1987: pB7.

Writers in prison benefit from gala; column. photo · *TS* Nov 9, 1987: pC1.

Writers' Union lets off steam; column. *TS* June 1, 1987: pD2.

Writing program a splendid notion; column. photo · *TS* July 6, 1987: pD5.

Written word celebrated at National Book Festival; column. photo · *TS* April 20, 1987: pD2.

Year in books had a familiar ring; survey article. photo · *TS* Dec 27, 1987: pE19.

Adams, B.K.

[Untitled]; review of *Rue du Bac*. *Books in Can* Oct 1987; Vol 16 No 7: p24.

Adams, James

At 75, Canada's 'worrier poet' still scorns restraint; article. photo · *CH* Dec 29, 1987: pC9.

Adams, John Coldwell

Blind men and elephants; essay. illus · *Can Auth & Book* Spring 1987; Vol 62 No 3: p7–8.

Sir Charles G.D. Roberts: post biography; article. *Can Poet* Fall-Winter 1987; No 21: p77–80.

Adamson, Arthur

The river; poem. *Prairie Fire* Autumn 1987; Vol 8 No 3: p78.

The weight of the potatoes; poem. illus · *Prairie Fire* Autumn 1987; Vol 8 No 3: p76.

Writing life; reviews of *Hired Hands* and *What Feathers Are For*. *Can Lit* Winter 1987; No 115: p230–232.

Adilman, Mona Elaine

Brain-death; poem. *Cross Can Writ Q* 1987; Vol 9 No 1: p25.

Pammy; poem. *Can Auth & Book* Summer 1987; Vol 62 No 4: p22.

Adilman, Sid

Arts awards lack flash and glamour; column. *TS* Oct 17, 1987: pH2.

Atlantis in The Twilight Zone; column. *TS* Oct 20, 1987: pH1.

Carlton's closing for major renovations; column. *TS* Dec 29, 1987: pE1.

CBC variety keeps smiling despite budget cuts; column. *TS* Feb 26, 1987: pB1.

Devil, angel: Alliance has it covered; column. *TS* May 16, 1987: pG3.

Domingo gave opera company a $40,000 break; column. *TS* March 13, 1987: pC19.

Expansion blamed for red ink at CBC's sales division; column. *TS* Nov 2, 1987: pC4.

Getting ready for the Calgary Olympics; reviews of children's books. *TS* Dec 5, 1987: pM10.

Juicy real-life crime tales heat up fall book lists; column. *TS* Oct 3, 1987: pJ1.

Radio's Scales of Justice seen as possible CTV series; column. *TS* Dec 30, 1987: pB1.

Too much of a good thing is wonderful; reviews of children's books. illus · *TS* Dec 5, 1987: pM4.

Toronto firm dramatizes U.S. tales; column. *TS* Jan 7, 1987: pF1.

Ahmad, Iqbal

The birth of faith; short story. *Descant* Fall 1987; Vol 18 No 3: p92–97.

Queen of the hills; short story. *Descant* Fall 1987; Vol 18 No 3: p81–91.

Ahmad, Manzur

The door; short story. *Tor South Asian R* Spring 1987; Vol 5 No 3: p71–80.

Ainsworth, Lynne

Play retells story of 1837 rebellion; article. photo · *TS (Neighbours)* June 30, 1987: p19.

Aird, Paul

My legacy; poem. *Waves* Spring 1987; Vol 15 No 4: p95.

Alaton, Salem

Firings at M&S puzzle executives; article. *G&M* Jan 20, 1987: pD9.

Mixed reviews for Tamara; article. *G&M* Dec 4, 1987: pD9.

Alford, Edna

Art of darkness; review of *Inspecting the Vaults*. *Books in Can* May 1987; Vol 16 No 4: p26–27.

Allard, Jacques

D'où vient Voix et images?; article. *Voix et images* Winter 1987; No 35: p294–303.

Allard-Lacerte, Rolande

Chagall, Plante et Mercier. . . .; essay. *MD* Dec 21, 1987: p6.

Claude, Clemence. . . .et qui d'autre?; editorial. *MD* July 27, 1987: p6.

De la fronde au bazooka; editorial. *MD* Jan 19, 1987: p14.

Allemang, John

Australian writer staying on for fall; article. *G&M* Oct 26, 1987: pC11.

Authors outraged by fire sale prices; article. *G&M* Feb 13, 1987: pC11.

Friends bring poet back to life at wake; article. photo · *G&M* March 23, 1987: pC12.

Interviews, literary 'gossip' slated for authors' festival; article. photo · *G&M* Sept 24, 1987: pD6.

Last-minute readers and party-bound writers; article. photo · *G&M* Oct 21, 1987: pC9.

Literary stock shows strong rate of return; article. *G&M* Oct 23, 1987: pD9.

No lack of food for thought; article. photo · *G&M* Oct 29, 1987: pD3.

Raising their glasses at the write angles; article. *G&M* Oct 17, 1987: pC14.

The secret of her success; article about Anna Porter. photo · *G&M (Toronto Magazine)* Aug 1987; Vol 2 No 5: p36–39, 63, 65, 67.

Some go to the Falls, Sariola goes to the 'burbs; article. *G&M* Oct 22, 1987: pD5.

Allen, Robert

The Gaza Strip; short story. *Matrix* Fall 1987; No 25: p50–52.

Allentuck, Andrew

All this and quality, too; review of *The Last White Man in Panama*. *WFP* Oct 24, 1987: p54.

Allison, Gay

Night life; poem. *Dandelion* Fall-Winter 1987; Vol 14 No 2: p28.

Winter night in Peterborough; poem. *Dandelion* Fall-Winter 1987; Vol 14 No 2: p26–27.

Almon, Bert

Cultural revolutions; poem. *Cross Can Writ Q* 1987; Vol 9 No 2: p13.

In the parking lot; poem. *New Q* Winter 1987; Vol 6 No 4: p51.

A night of the full moon; poem. *Can Forum* Oct 1987; Vol 67 No 772: p32.

Reading the census; poem. *U of Windsor R* Fall-Winter 1987; Vol 20 No 1: p53.

A symposium; poem. *New Q* Winter 1987; Vol 6 No 4: p52.

Trial by experience; reviews of *Letters from Some Islands* and *Private Properties*. *Can Lit* Winter 1987; No 115: p206–208.

[Untitled]; review of *It Takes All Kinds*. *Poetry Can R* Spring 1987; Vol 8 No 2–3: p44–45.

[Untitled]; review of *Silk Trail*. *Poetry Can R* Spring 1987; Vol 8 No 2–3: p62.

[Untitled]; review of *The Collected Poem*. *Poetry Can R* Summer 1987; Vol 8 No 4: p32.

Alonzo, Anne-Marie

Brune orchidée noire; poem. *Estuaire* Autumn 1987; No 46: p55–56.

Self-portrait as a self imitator; prose poem. *Estuaire* Summer 1987; No 45: p33.

[Untitled]; review of *Chambres*. *Estuaire* Winter 1986–87; No 43: p75–76.

[Untitled]; review of *Textures en textes*. *Estuaire* Spring 1987; No 44: p79.

Alton, Don

The bet; short story. photo · *TS* Aug 11, 1987: pH7.

Amabile, George

Don't get stuck in the snow and if you do, why not?; prose poem. *Prairie Fire* Autumn 1987; Vol 8 No 3: p57.

Inventing Nogales; poem. *Arc* Fall 1987; No 19: p43–44.

This business of getting through the night; poem. *Prairie Fire* Autumn 1987; Vol 8 No 3: p31.

Ambrose, Mary

Portrait of a society whose vision is shaped by television; review of *Cambodia*. *G&M* July 25, 1987: pC15.

Amirault, Peggy

Books in motion; article. *Quill & Quire* Aug 1987; Vol 53 No 8: p24.

Amprimoz, Alexandre

Cognitive science; poem. *New Q* Winter 1987; Vol 6 No 4: p53–54.

Exiled in the west; poem. *Prairie J of Can Lit* 1987; No 8: p28–29.

Faiblesses d'un roman ambitieux; review of *Les Griffes de l'empire*. *Can Child Lit* 1987; No 47: p86–87.

Les Îles de la nuit d'Alain Grandbois: clôture du monde et ouverture du verbe; article. *Can Lit* Spring 1987; No 112: p64–70.

The poet builds; review of *À la façon d'un charpentier*. *Prairie Fire* Autumn 1987; Vol 8 No 3: p118–119.

La poétique de la mort: la poésie italo-canadienne et italo-québécoise aujourd'hui; article. *Studies in Can Lit* 1987; Vol 12 No 2: p161–176.

Prochain épisode: notes de re-cherche; article. *Studies in Can Lit* 1987; Vol 12 No 1: p129–145.

Solution; poem. *Poetry Can R* Summer 1987; Vol 8 No 4: p4.

Sonnet; poem. *Prairie J of Can Lit* 1987; No 8: p29.

Valeurs ludiques et valeurs fonctionelles: Le Visiteur du soir de Robert Soulières; article. *Can Child Lit* 1987; No 45: p6–13.

Why order pizza under a volcano; poem. *New Q* Winter 1987; Vol 6 No 4: p55.

Andel, Mark

A farm at Raraba; letter to the editor. *Atlantic* May 1987; Vol 259 No 5: p14.

Andersen, Marguerite

Blanche colombe; short story. *Moebius* Winter 1987; No 31: p61–69.

Chronique: Bouraoui, Cahiers blues; reviews of *Reflet pluriel* and French periodical featuring French-Canadian literature. *Poetry Can R* Fall 1987; Vol 9 No 1: p16.

Chronique: reflets et signes; review of *Bouquet de signes*. *Poetry Can R* Summer 1987; Vol 8 No 4: p23.

Chronique: soliloques; reviews of poetry books. *Poetry Can R* Spring 1987; Vol 8 No 2–3: p23–24.

Discours-fleuve; reviews of *Le Coupeur de têtes* and *Les Deux soeurs*. *Can Lit* Winter 1987; No 115: p182–184.

International P.E.N.: a world association of writers; article. *Poetry Can R* Spring 1987; Vol 8 No 2–3: p27.

Anderson, Ann Leger

Prairie love; review of *Prairie Women*. *Can Lit* Winter 1987; No 115: p249–251.

Anderson, Bill

Anne sequel likely to outdraw original; article. photo · *WFP* Dec 1, 1987: p34.

Anderson, Gaëtan

Entretien-fiction avec Victor-Lévy Beaulieu; fictional essay. photo · *Moebius* Winter 1987; No 31: p5–21.

Anderson, Mia

Advent; poem. *Fiddlehead* Winter 1987; No 154: p68–69.

The apotheosis; poem. *Malahat R* Sept 1987; No 80: p66–75.

City snow song; poem. *Northward J* 1987; No 42: p33–34.

The sign; prose poem. *Matrix* Fall 1987; No 25: p29–31.

Anderson, Rod

Circles; poem. *Germination* Fall 1987; Vol 11 No 1: p36.

Control; poem. *Germination* Fall 1987; Vol 11 No 1: p35.

Subrisive activities; poem. *CV 2* Spring 1987; Vol 10 No 3: p23–24.

Suitor; poem. *Germination* Spring 1987; Vol 10 No 2: p34.

Sunday; poem. *Germination* Spring 1987; Vol 10 No 2: p35.

[Untitled]; review of *In the Spirit of the Times*. *Poetry Can R* Spring 1987; Vol 8 No 2–3: p43.

[Untitled]; review of *Wordseed*. *Poetry Can R* Spring 1987; Vol 8 No 2–3: p50.

[Untitled]; review of *Poets Who Don't Dance*. *Poetry Can R* Spring 1987; Vol 8 No 2–3: p58.

Word entropy; poem. *Matrix* Fall 1987; No 25: p53–54.

Anderson-Jones, Teruko

The pearl; poem. *Can Auth & Book* Winter 1987; Vol 62 No 2: p21.

Andrès, Bernard

Littérature et recherche universitaire: la question des revues; introduction. *Voix et images* Winter 1987; No 35: p266.

La littérature québécoise à Voix et images: créneau ou ghetto?; article. *Voix et images* Winter 1987; No 35: p303–312.

De Voix et images du pays à Voix et images: 20 ans déjà; editorial. *Voix et images* Autumn 1987; Vol 13 No 1: p5–6.

Andrew, Ruby

Frontier women: two tales in search of the perfect marriage; reviews of *Between Men* and *Getting Married in Buffalo Jump*. photo · *Quill & Quire* Sept 1987; Vol 53 No 9: p76.

Gabrielle Roy: a compelling glimpse of an enchanting life; review of *Enchantment and Sorrow*. photo · *Quill & Quire* Dec 1987; Vol 53 No 12: p23.

[Untitled]; review of *A Stone Watermelon*. *Quill & Quire* April 1987; Vol 53 No 4: p28–29.

[Untitled]; review of *Brazilian Journal*. *Quill & Quire* May 1987; Vol 53 No 5: p22, 24.

[Untitled]; review of *A Body Surrounded by Water*. *Quill & Quire* Oct 1987; Vol 53 No 10: p22–23.

Andrews, Audrey

Canadian Quixote flogs death; review of *Canadian Sunset*. *CH* April 18, 1987: pE5.

Roy's candid memoirs recall joy and sorrow; review of *Enchantment and Sorrow*. photo · *CH* Dec 20, 1987: pE6.

[Untitled]; review of *The Garden of Eloise Loon*. *Dandelion* Spring-Summer 1987; Vol 14 No 1: p89–91.

[Untitled]; review of *The Self-Completing Tree*. *CH* Sept 27, 1987: pE6.

Andrews, Caroline

Butterfly man; short story. photo · *TS* July 10, 1987: pA14.

Andrews, Jancis M.

A thing of beauty; short story. illus · *Can Auth & Book* Summer 1987; Vol 62 No 4: p17–19.

Womanning the lifeboat; short story. *Room of One's Own* April 1987; Vol 11 No 3: p39–49.

Andrishak, Ruth

A woman's touch; short story. *Prairie Fire* Summer 1987; Vol 8 No 2: p43–45.

Andrus, David

Walls; short story. illus · *Can Auth & Book* Spring 1987; Vol 62 No 3: p18–20.

Andrychuk, Kristin

Births; poem. *New Q* Spring-Summer 1987; Vol 7 No 1–2: p202.

Dirty tricks; poem. *Quarry* Winter 1987; Vol 36 No 1: p12–13.

Gone to ground; poem. *Quarry* Winter 1987; Vol 36 No 1: p13–14.

Wringer washer; poem. *New Q* Spring-Summer 1987; Vol 7 No 1–2: p203.

Angenot, Marc

"J'aime mieux vivre que me définir"; article. *Liberté* Feb 1987; Vol 29 No 1: p46–50.

Angus, Douglas

The cross fox; short story. illus · *Queen's Q* Spring 1987; Vol 94 No 1: p43–56.

Angus, William

Emily Carr play; letter to the editor. *G&M* Sept 29, 1987: pA6.

Annharte

Banana moon; poem. *Prairie Fire* Autumn 1987; Vol 8 No 3: p14.

Jumper moon; poem. illus · *Prairie Fire* Autumn 1987; Vol 8 No 3: p15.

Appell, M.R.

Wintery procession; poem. *Can Auth & Book* Winter 1987; Vol 62 No 2: p21.

Archambault, Gilles

Et si on éteignait?; essay. *MD* April 11, 1987: pC2.

Ma vie littéraire: manuels très scolaires; essay. *MD (Livre d'ici)* Sept 12, 1987: p16.

Les plaisirs de la mélancholie: éloge du conférencier; essay. *MD* July 4, 1987: pC3.

Les plaisirs de la mélancolie: ce soir, on déguste; essay. *MD* Aug 22, 1987: pC5.

Les plaisirs de la mélancolie: imbéciles, je vous aime; essay. *MD* Dec 19, 1987: pC2.

Archer, Anne

[Untitled]; reviews of poetry books. *Queen's Q* Winter 1987; Vol 94 No 4: p1042–1043.

Archibald, E. Jane

Books for librarians; review of *Subject Index to Canadian Poetry in English for Children and Young People*. *Atlan Prov Book R* Feb-March 1987; Vol 14 No 1: p15.

Armitage, Christopher

[Untitled]; review of *Sir Charles God Damn*. *Amer R of Can Studies* Winter 1987–88; Vol 17 No 4: p439–440.

Armstrong, David

Saderdaynight (ritual); poem. *Matrix* Spring 1987; No 24: p29.

Armstrong, Jane

Staunch few attend Laurence memorial; article. photo · *WFP* Jan 11, 1987: p2.

Armstrong, Jeannette C.

The awakening; short story. *Can Fic Mag* (special issue) 1987; No 60: p40–51.

Armstrong, Julian

Atwood anthology ranges from tart to tangy; article. illus · *MG* Nov 11, 1987: pE2.

Arnason, David

Artesian; prose poem. *Prairie Fire* Winter 1987–88; Vol 8 No 4: p21–23.

Arnold, Ivor A.

Diachronie des styles de la poésie québécoise, 1960–80; article. *Studies in Can Lit* 1987; Vol 12 No 1: p3–14.

Arnott, Joanne

In my dance class; poem. *Fireweed* Fall 1987; No 25: p63.

Arrand, Ellen

Whom among ye feareth the Lord?; short story. *Room of One's Own* April 1987; Vol 11 No 3: p17–25.

Arrell, Doug

Bruce McManus, playwright; introduction to play excerpt from *Schedules*. *Prairie Fire* Spring 1987; Vol 8 No 1: p50.

Winnipeg theatre in the eighties: moving towards a theatrical culture; article. *Prairie Fire* Autumn 1987; Vol 8 No 3: p52–57.

Arsenault, Paula

Creation; poem. *Alpha* Winter 1987; Vol 11: p35.

Ascherson, Neal

Polish nightmares; review of *The Color of Blood*. illus · *New York R of Books* Dec 17, 1987; Vol 34 No 20: p44, 46, 48.

Ashby, Adele

Make way for a fine crop of picture-books; reviews of children's books. *Quill & Quire* (Books for Young People) Aug 1987; Vol 53 No 8: p6.

A trio of poets to tickle a child's fancy; reviews of children's poetry books. *Quill & Quire* (Books for Young People) June 1987; Vol 53 No 6: p10.

[Untitled]; reviews of *Come into My Room* and *Hey World, Here I Am!*. *Quill & Quire* (Books for Young People) April 1987; Vol 53 No 4: p5.

[Untitled]; reviews of *Katie's Alligator Goes to Daycare* and *Tom Doesn't Visit Us Any More*. *Quill & Quire* (Books for Young People) Dec 1987; Vol 53 No 12: p8–9.

[Untitled]; review of *Monica's Mother Said No!*. *Quill & Quire* (Books for Young People) Dec 1987; Vol 53 No 12: p9.

Atherton, Stanley S.

On strategies; review of *Gaining Ground*. *Can Lit* Winter 1987; No 115: p184–186.

Atkinson, David W.

From city to country; review of *Sandy*. *Can Child Lit* 1987; No 46: p89–90.

Atwood, Margaret

Atwood: let's not rush into free trade; essay. *TS* Nov 5, 1987: pA30.

In a Caribbean taxi; prose excerpt from *Bodily Harm*. *G&M* Dec 24, 1987: pA6.

Margaret Atwood talks to Margaret Drabble; interview. photo · *Chatelaine* April 1987; Vol 60 No 4: p73, 124, 126, 130.

The Mermaid Inn: the return of the asterisk; essay. photo · *G&M* June 27, 1987: pD6.

Profiting by our wilderness; essay. photo · *TS* Aug 8, 1987: pM1.

[Untitled]; biographical articles. *Brick* (special issue) Summer 1987; No 30: ppassim.

[Untitled]; essay. photo · *Chatelaine* May 1987; Vol 60 No 5: p50.

Who created whom? Characters that talk back; essay. photo · *NYT Book R* May 31, 1987: p36.

Aubert, Rosemary

[Untitled]; reviews of *My Round Table* and *Everything Happens at Once*. *Poetry Can R* Spring 1987; Vol 8 No 2–3: p48.

Aubin, Benoit

Le Matou author used radio journalism for artistic ends; review of *Du sommet d'un arbre*. photo · *MG* Jan 3, 1987: pB7.

Springtime, and some more Malouins; review of *Il y a toujours des printemps en Amérique*. photo · *MG* Oct 31, 1987: pJ11.

Audet, Noël

De la poésie à la prose; review of *L'Hiver de Mira Christophe*. photo · *Lettres québec* Winter 1986–87; No 44: p26–28.

Une épopée des Caraïbes; review of *La Discorde aux cent voix*. *Lettres québec* Spring 1987; No 45: p24–26.

Les Héritiers (prix Robert Cliche) et L'Écrit-vent; reviews. photo · *Lettres québec* Autumn 1987; No 47: p19–21.

L'homme à éclipses; short story. *Moebius* Summer 1987; No 33: p29–35.

Auf der Maur, Nick

Literary language turns inflammatory at glossy benefit dinner; article. *MG* Nov 9, 1987: pA2.

Little literary magazine packs loads of pleasure; article. *MG* June 19, 1987: pA2.

The rumor mill grinds: Chrétien to the NDP?; column. *MG* March 4, 1987: pA2.

There's more at stake than military balance; column. *MG* April 29, 1987: pA2.

Aust, Edward

[Untitled]; biographical articles. *Brick (special issue)* Summer 1987; No 30: ppassim.

Austen, Lorelei

In your house; poem. *Fiddlehead* Spring 1987; No 151: p18–19.

The occasion; poem. *Fiddlehead* Spring 1987; No 151: p20.

Scene 1; poem. *Fiddlehead* Spring 1987; No 151: p19.

Austin, Allan

[Untitled]; review of *The Progress of Love. World Lit in Eng* Spring 1987; Vol 27 No 1: p58–59.

Austin, Diana

The country of the human heart; review of *Goodbye Harold, Good Luck. Fiddlehead* Spring 1987; No 151: p107–110.

Avis, Nick

[Untitled]; poem. *Cross Can Writ Q* 1987; Vol 9 No 3–4: p8.

Avison, Margaret

[Untitled]; review of *Names of God. Books in Can* May 1987; Vol 16 No 4: p23.

Axelson, John

You taught me well; short story. photo · *TS* July 5, 1987: pD5.

Ayim, Maryann

[Untitled]; review of *Dancing in the Dark. Atlantis* Fall 1987; Vol 13 No 1: p189–191.

Babby, Ellen Reisman

Des Nouvelles d'Edouard: Michel Tremblay's fugal composition; article. *Amer R of Can Studies* Winter 1987–88; Vol 17 No 4: p383–394.

A fitting homage; review of *Études littéraire* (special issue). *Essays on Can Writ* Spring 1987; No 34: p190–195.

Babineau, Guy

Kanada: the miniseries; humourous essay. *Can Forum* Feb 1987; Vol 66 No 766: p41–42.

Badoux, Patricia

Pourquoi a-t-on peur de Maude?; theatre review of *"JAMMÉE, les nerfs! les nerfs!"*. photo · *MD* May 7, 1987: p13.

Baglow, John

Babel; poem. *Prism* Summer 1987; Vol 25 No 4: p76.

Babel; poem. *Capilano R* 1987; No 44: p46.

Between friends; poem. *Poetry Can R* Fall 1987; Vol 9 No 1: p9.

Body politic; poem. *Can Forum* Nov 1987; Vol 67 No 773: p9.

Cyborg; poem. *Prism* Summer 1987; Vol 25 No 4: p75.

Homecoming; poem. *Arc* Fall 1987; No 19: p46.

How to understand what is happening in South Africa; poem. *Can Lit* Summer-Fall 1987; No 113–114: p27.

Letter; poem. *Poetry Can R* Fall 1987; Vol 9 No 1: p9.

Mediated view; poem. *Capilano R* 1987; No 44: p48.

Memory; poem. *Capilano R* 1987; No 44: p47.

Political poetry – a rejoinder; essay. *Arc* Spring 1987; No 18: p72–74.

Specialist; poem. *Arc* Fall 1987; No 19: p45.

Winter solstice; poem. *Poetry Can R* Fall 1987; Vol 9 No 1: p9.

Bailey, Bruce

Dancing In The Dark: what happens when a homemaker cracks; film review. photo · *MG* Jan 17, 1987: pD4.

The Genies: Le Déclin rises to the occasion; article. photo · *MG* March 19, 1987: pB5.

John and the Missus is slow, but sincere; film review. *MG* April 18, 1987: pC3.

Newfoundland on the back burner; article. photo · *MG* April 18, 1987: pC3.

Organizers up against a wall to get art fest off the ground; article. photo · *MG* June 5, 1987: pD1.

A piece of the rock; film review of *In the Shadow of the Wind*. photo · *MG* Jan 10, 1987: pG3.

Some method to madness in hiring of Fraticelli as new NFB women's studio head; article. photo · *MG* May 11, 1987: pB5.

Bailey, Don

The diviner; essay. *Brick* Winter 1987; No 29: p6–9.

Letter of intent; short story. *Prairie Fire* Spring 1987; Vol 8 No 1: p23–31.

Bailey, Ian

Professional writers aid aspiring authors from Ontario libraries; article. *WFP* Nov 20, 1987: p38.

Saturday Night editor envisions moe changes; article. photo · *WFP* Dec 21, 1987: p35.

Saturday Night's new editor champing at bit; article. photo · *CH* Dec 22, 1987: pD8.

Bailey, Nancy

Ours as daughters; reviews of *Duet for Three* and *Flitterin' Judas. Can Lit* Spring 1987; No 112: p143–145.

[Untitled]; review of *Sub / version. World Lit in Eng* Autumn 1987; Vol 27 No 2: p262–264.

Bain, George

Telling tales on Saturday Night; column. *Maclean's* July 27, 1987; Vol 100 No 30: p44.

Baird, Elizabeth

Recipes to dispel bad taste of food in Canadian fiction; article. *TS* Nov 25, 1987: pC6.

Baker, Brian

Small talk with the lover of the woman you love; poem. *Can Auth & Book* Summer 1987; Vol 62 No 4: p22.

Baker, Winona

Extended care; poem. *New Q* Spring-Summer 1987; Vol 7 No 1–2: p204–205.

Prairie set; poem. *New Q* Spring-Summer 1987; Vol 7 No 1–2: p206–209.

Baldridge, Mary Humphrey

The high level bridge (1960); short story. *Room of One's Own* April 1987; Vol 11 No 3: p81–97.

The house on 95th Street (1950); short story. *New Q* Spring-Summer 1987; Vol 7 No 1–2: p85–105.

Ball, J. Leslie

Short stories lay bare peoples' foibles, passions; review of *Tales from Firozsha Baag*. *CH* July 5, 1987: pF7.

Ball, Vincent

Leo Petroff poet, pressman fought for czar; obituary. photo · *TS* Jan 25, 1987: pA20.

Ballinger, Karen

Disneyland; poem. *Fireweed* Fall 1987; No 25: p81.

Baltensperger, Peter

Educating a pink flamingo; poem. *New Q* Winter 1987; Vol 6 No 4: p56–57.

First snow; poem. *Germination* Spring 1987; Vol 10 No 2: p24.

Bancroft, George W.

Treasured memoir; letter to the editor. *Tor Life* July 1987; Vol 21 No 10: p8.

Banks, Lorna

"Ladies" in waiting; poem. *Atlantis* Fall 1987; Vol 13 No 1: p124.

Bannerji, Himani

Between sound and meaning; poem. *Tor South Asian R* Spring 1987; Vol 5 No 3: p22.

Midnight; poem. *Tor South Asian R* Spring 1987; Vol 5 No 3: p26.

Mother, do you have a will?; poem. *Tor South Asian R* Spring 1987; Vol 5 No 3: p25–26.

'Paki go home'; poem. *Tor South Asian R* Spring 1987; Vol 5 No 3: p23–24.

To Sylvia Plath; poem. *Maclean's* Jan 19, 1987; Vol 100 No 3: p27.

Bantin, Mark

Summer; poem. *Alpha* Winter 1987; Vol 11: p7.

Banting, Pamela

Fred Wah: poet as theor(h)et(or)ician; article. *Open Letter* Spring 1987; Vol 6 No 7: p5–20.

The[eye]or[I]y; essay. *Prairie Fire* Summer 1987; Vol 8 No 2: p33–39.

Barbour, Douglas

Antipodean travels with Robert Kroetsch; essay. *Prairie Fire* Winter 1987–88; Vol 8 No 4: p24, 26–32.

Future and past histories: repeating winning formulae simply not on the cards; review of *Burning Chrome*. *TS* March 7, 1987: pM4.

SF for survival; review of *Tesseracts*. *Can Lit* Spring 1987; No 112: p141–143.

[Untitled]; review of *The Darkest Road*. *Malahat R* June 1987; No 79: p160–161.

[Untitled]; poem. *Cross Can Writ Q* 1987; Vol 9 No 3–4: p12.

Barclay, Byrna

Anything Elsie's truck stop; short story. *New Q* Fall 1987; Vol 7 No 3: p7–15.

Speak under covers; short story. *Event* March 1987; Vol 16 No 1: p41–51.

Barclay, Paul

Two ways of making poetry; reviews of *The Prismatic Eye* and *Walking Slow*. *Prairie Fire* Summer 1987; Vol 8 No 2: p56–59.

Barfoot, Joan

The official truth; letter to the editor. *Books in Can* Aug-Sept 1987; Vol 16 No 6: p39.

Barker, Christine

A new love; poem. *Antigonish R* 1987; No 69–70: p126.

Barnes, Mike

Accident; poem. *Waves* Winter 1987; Vol 15 No 3: p77.

Working in the O.R.; poem. *Waves* Winter 1987; Vol 15 No 3: p76.

Barnet, David

Out of the collectives; article. photo · *Can Theatre R* Winter 1987; No 53: p5–6.

Barratt, Harold

A Somali voice in cold Canada; review of *The Bottle and the Bushman*. *Fiddlehead* Summer 1987; No 152: p89–91.

Barreto-Rivera, Rafael

Dr. Sadhu's semi-optics, or how to write a virtual-novel by the book: Steve McCaffery's Panopticon; article. *Open Letter (special issue)* Fall 1987; Vol 6 No 9: p39–47.

Barrett, Caroline

[Untitled]; review of *La Corrida de l'amour*. *Voix et images* Winter 1987; No 35: p348–349.

Barry, Dave

Chapter 1: Carter Crater strides into the Oval Office. . . .; short story. *MG* April 4, 1987: pH9.

Barry, Sandra

Before a solar eclipse; poem. *Antigonish R* 1987; No 69–70: p181–182.

Bartlett, Brian

A distant stream on Mount Madonna; poem. *Rubicon* Fall 1987; No 9: p101–102.

From the upriver bus; poem. *Rubicon* Fall 1987; No 9: p100–101.

"Les nouvelles de cousin Emmanuel": varieties of salvation and imagination in Ferron's Cotnoir; article. *Studies in Can Lit* 1987; Vol 12 No 2: p177–186.

Bartlett, Donald R.

Childhood experiences in The Loved and the Lost; article. *New Q* Spring-Summer 1987; Vol 7 No 1–2: p294–300.

Barton, Ellie

[Untitled]; review of *Relations. Quarry* Fall 1987; Vol 36 No 4: p86–87.

Barton, John

Excerpt from a travel journal; poem. *Queen's Q* Summer 1987; Vol 94 No 2: p309–311.

Jack-in-the-pulpit remembered; poem. *U of Windsor R* Fall-Winter 1987; Vol 20 No 1: p81.

We were the lovers; poem. *Queen's Q* Summer 1987; Vol 94 No 2: p311.

Base, Ron

Empire strikes 8 Genies; article. photo · *TS* March 19, 1987: pE1.

John And The Missus misses despite commendable acting; film review. photo · *TS* Feb 6, 1987: pD8.

Basmajian, Shaunt

The parting; poem. *Poetry Can R* Fall 1987; Vol 9 No 1: p39.

Small press reviews; reviews of poetry books. *Cross Can Writ Q* 1987; Vol 9 No 1: p25.

[Untitled]; reviews of poetry books. *Cross Can Writ Q* 1987; Vol 9 No 2: p22.

[Untitled]; poem. *Cross Can Writ Q* 1987; Vol 9 No 3–4: p4.

[Untitled]; reviews of *Squid Inc. 86* and *The Buda Books Poetry Series. Cross Can Writ Q* 1987; Vol 9 No 3–4: p43.

[Untitled]; reviews of poetry books. *Cross Can Writ Q* 1987; Vol 9 No 3–4: p44, 49.

Bastien, Mark

Cards; short story. *New Q* Winter 1987; Vol 6 No 4: p15–20.

Satirist courts 'humorless' Toronto; article. photo · *TS* July 13, 1987: pC3.

[Untitled]; letter to the editor. *New Q* Fall 1987; Vol 7 No 3: p104.

Batt, Sharon

[Untitled]; reviews of *Housebroken* and *Private Properties. Room of One's Own* Sept 1987; Vol 11 No 4: p109–112.

Batten, Jack

A new wave of sleuths; article. photo · *Maclean's* Nov 23, 1987; Vol 100 No 47: pT10–T11.

The plot thickens; review of *Equinox. Books in Can* May 1987; Vol 16 No 4: p27–28.

Battler, Lesley

The aleph; poem. *Writing* Dec 1987; No 20: p3–12.

Batty, Nancy

[Untitled]; reviews of *Through the Nan Da Gate* and *Death Is an Anxious Mother. Dandelion* Spring-Summer 1987; Vol 14 No 1: p84–87.

Bauer, Jan

Life in the sun; short story. *Waves* Winter 1987; Vol 15 No 3: p30–32.

Baum, Rosalie Murphy

Snow as reality and trope in Canadian literature; article. *Amer R of Can Studies* Autumn 1987; Vol 17 No 3: p323–333.

Bawden, Jim

Anne of Green Gables – the Sequel; television review. photo · *TS* Dec 5, 1987: pF1, F12.

Atwood at the cottage; column. *TS* April 2, 1987: pG2.

Benny bumbles into a murder in the wilds; television review of *Murder Sees the Light*. photo · *TS* March 14, 1987: pJ6.

Fine script moves Heaven On Earth right to heart; television review. photo · *TS* Feb 28, 1987: pF1.

Hockey drama kicks off new Canadian TV season; column. photo · *TS* Jan 2, 1987: pD21.

Bayard, Caroline

Choisir la poésie: une tentative mitigée; review of *Choisir la poésie. Lettres québec* Spring 1987; No 45: p42–43.

La démarche de François Charron; review of *Le Fait de vivre ou d'avoir vécu. Lettres québec* Winter 1986–87; No 44: p48–49.

Les géographies et le souffle chez Madeleine Gagnon; reviews of *Les Fleurs du Catalpa* and *L'Infante immémoriale*. photo · *Lettres québec* Winter 1986–87; No 44: p46–47.

Le récit à la NBJ; review of *La Nouvelle barre du jour. Lettres québec* Summer 1987; No 46: p34–35.

La relève poétique en Acadie?; review of *Requiem en saule pleureur. Lettres québec* Spring 1987; No 45: p43.

Beardsley, Doug

The good and evil angels; poem. *Can Forum* Nov 1987; Vol 67 No 773: p27.

Heaven's graces; poem. *New Q* Spring-Summer 1987; Vol 7 No 1–2: p222.

Opus one; poem. *New Q* Spring-Summer 1987; Vol 7 No 1–2: p221.

Small person; poem. *New Q* Spring-Summer 1987; Vol 7 No 1–2: p220.

Beauchamp, Hélène

René-Daniel Dubois: the generous word; article. photo trans · *Can Theatre R* Spring 1987; No 50: p29–36.

Les trois saisons de la Maison Théâtre: bilan critique de la programmation de la Maison québécoise du Théâtre pour article. photo · *Can Child Lit* 1987; No 48: p77–84.

With passion, intensity and style; review of *Les Petits pouvoirs*. *Can Child Lit* 1987; No 45: p65–68.

Beauchemin, Yves

L'affichage français; essay. *Liberté (special issue)* 1987: p37–43.

Surmenage: le dernier filon; essay. *Liberté* June 1987; Vol 29 No 3: p32–35.

Sweat; short story. trans · *Dandelion* Fall-Winter 1987; Vol 14 No 2: p110–135.

[Untitled]; prose excerpts from *Du sommet d'un arbre*. *Lettres québec* Spring 1987; No 45: p9–11.

Beaudet, Marie-Andrée

André Roy ou l'invention d'un littéral métaphysique; introduction. *Estuaire* Spring 1987; No 44: p63–66.

Beaudoin, Réjean

Benito, vierge et rêveur de profession; review of *Benito*. *Liberté* Oct 1987; Vol 29 No 5: p163.

La culture de la confusion; reviews of *Extase et déchirure* and *L'Amour de la carte postale*. *Liberté* Dec 1987; Vol 29 No 6: p107–113.

Ici, maintenant et autrement; review of *Ni le lieu ni l'heure*. *Liberté* Aug 1987; Vol 29 No 4: p125–126.

À la recherche du lieu perdu; essay. *Liberté* Oct 1987; Vol 29 No 5: p21–30.

L'étrangeté du quotidien; review of *Le Surveillant*. *Liberté* June 1987; Vol 29 No 3: p104–105.

Le malin plaisir de déplaire; review of *L'Obsèdante obèse*. *Liberté* Oct 1987; Vol 29 No 5: p161–162.

Le métier d'écrire; review of *L'Hiver au coeur*. *Liberté* Aug 1987; Vol 29 No 4: p110–114.

Mon p'tit change; essay. *Liberté* Dec 1987; Vol 29 No 6: p157–158.

Les noeuds sacrés de l'âme, de la terre et du sang; reviews of novels. *Liberté* Oct 1987; Vol 29 No 5: p106–114.

Pas d'atout mais du coeur; review of *SoirS sans AtouT*. *Liberté* Feb 1987; Vol 29 No 1: p153–154.

La passion cuisinée; review of *La Passion selon Galatée*. *Liberté* June 1987; Vol 29 No 3: p90–94.

Le salut de Pierre Vallières; review of *Noces obscures*. *Liberté* April 1987; Vol 29 No 2: p139–140.

La statue de François Hertel; review of *Hertel, l'homme et l'oeuvre*. *Liberté* Feb 1987; Vol 29 No 1: p100–104.

La ville toute verte, bordée de montagnes enneigées; review of *L'Hiver de Mira Christophe*. *Liberté* April 1987; Vol 29 No 2: p118–124.

Beaulieu, Carole

Les Québécois boudent les Africains; article. *MD* Sept 4, 1987: p16.

Beaulieu, Germaine

Comme un fantôme à l'appartment zéro; poem. *Estuaire* Spring 1987; No 44: p15–17.

Beaulieu, Victor-Lévy

L'Héritage ou le rêve d'écrire; prose excerpt from *L'Héritage*. photo · *MD* Nov 7, 1987: pD1-D2.

Victor-Lévy Beaulieu: pour lire et pour voir; essay. photo · *MD* Nov 14, 1987: pD20.

Beaumont, Alison

She thinks about drowning; poem, includes essay. biog photo · *Cross Can Writ Q* 1987; Vol 9 No 1: p16.

Beauregard, Micheline

L'inscription du littéraire dans Le Matou d'Yves Beauchemin; article. abstract · *Études lit* Spring-Summer 1987; Vol 20 No 1: p131–147.

Beausoleil, Claude

[Untitled]; review of *SoirS sans AtouT*. *Estuaire* Winter 1986–87; No 43: p77.

[Untitled]; review of *Quarante voiles pour un exil*. *Estuaire* Spring 1987; No 44: p82.

Beck, David J.

Tatterdemalion; short story. *Waves* Spring 1987; Vol 15 No 4: p18–20.

Beckett, Sandra

Le retour de Jiji et Pichou; review of *Je boude*. *Can Child Lit* 1987; No 47: p77–78.

Beddoes, Julie

Country manners; reviews of *The Progress of Love* and *Goodbye Harold, Good Luck*. *Brick* Winter 1987; No 29: p24–27.

Sandor, Alex and the rest: multiplication of the subject in John Marlyn's Under the Ribs of Death; article. *Open Letter* Summer 1987; Vol 6 No 8: p5–14.

Beggs, Mike

Oakville poet, 21, carves career out of experiences on the road; article. photo · *TS (Neighbors)* Aug 4, 1987: p13.

Behrens, Peter

To the dead girl; short story. *Rubicon* Fall 1987; No 9: p148–149.

Belcher, Margaret

Castles of childhood; review of *A Forest for Zoe*. *Can Lit* Winter 1987; No 115: p208–209.

Bélisle, Marie

Seconde avancée; poem. illus · *La Nouvelle barre du jour* May 1987; No 200: p9–14.

Bell, Blair

Atwood offers rich Canadian perspective; letter to the editor. *Fin Post* Nov 30, 1987: p15.

Bell, Celina

A brutal inheritance; review of *The Butterfly Chair*. *Maclean's* Dec 7, 1987; Vol 100 No 49: pT8.

Bell, J.E. Maureen

A sacred duty; short story. photo · *TS* July 3, 1987: pA16.

Bell, John

Chain reaction; poem. *CV 2* Spring 1987; Vol 10 No 3: p31.

Santa Claws; poem. *New Q* Spring-Summer 1987; Vol 7 No 1–2: p199.

Shells; poem. *New Q* Spring-Summer 1987; Vol 7 No 1–2: p200–201.

Bell, Nancy

Gone with the Fringe: being there: a flying look at the 1987 Edmonton Fringe Theatre Festival; article. photo · *NeWest R* Oct 1987; Vol 13 No 2: p9–11.

Bellamy, Connie

Matrimony; review of *Mother and Daughter Relationships in the Manawaka Works of Margaret Laurence*. *Essays on Can Writ* Winter 1987; No 35: p93–99.

Belleau, André

La passion de l'essai; essay. *Liberté* Feb 1987; Vol 29 No 1: p92–97.

Belleau, Jacques

Au revoir et à samedi matin. . . .; essay. *Liberté* Feb 1987; Vol 29 No 1: p58–60.

Bemrose, John

The ambassador's wife; review of *Brazilian Journal*. illus · *Maclean's* Aug 10, 1987; Vol 100 No 32: p51.

Angel with a lariat; review of *Caprice*, includes profile. photo · *Maclean's* June 29, 1987; Vol 100 No 26: p49–50.

A clash of crimsons; review of *The Color of Blood*. *Maclean's* Oct 19, 1987; Vol 100 No 42: p60f.

Daddy's little girl; review of *My Father's House*. *Maclean's* Oct 26, 1987; Vol 100 No 43: p52h.

Domestic drama that hits home; article, includes theatre reviews. photo · *Maclean's* Aug 17, 1987; Vol 100 No 33: p49.

Drama's daring new voice; theatre review of *Pericles Prince of Tyre by William Shakespeare*. photo · *Maclean's* April 27, 1987; Vol 100 No 17: p61.

A garden of adult verse; review of *The Difficulty of Living on Other Planets*. *Maclean's* Nov 16, 1987; Vol 100 No 46: p64b.

Love among the ruins; theatre review of *I Am Yours*. *Maclean's* Nov 30, 1987; Vol 100 No 48: p65.

Marriage of true minds; theatre review of *Tête à tête*. photo · *Maclean's* Sept 21, 1987; Vol 100 No 38: p50.

Portraits of patriarchs; television review of *First Person Singular*. photo · *Maclean's* March 30, 1987; Vol 100 No 13: p63.

Revenge of the native; review of *A Dream Like Mine*. photo · *Maclean's* Nov 9, 1987; Vol 100 No 45: p64g.

Satan with a sword; article. photo · *Maclean's* May 25, 1987; Vol 100 No 21: p55.

[Untitled]; review of *Southeasterly*. *Books in Can* Oct 1987; Vol 16 No 7: p26–27.

[Untitled]; theatre review of *Beautiful City*. photo · *Maclean's* Oct 19, 1987; Vol 100 No 42: p70.

[Untitled]; theatre review of *Royalty Is Royalty*. *Maclean's* Oct 19, 1987; Vol 100 No 42: p70.

[Untitled]; review of *Detaining Mr. Trotsky*. *Maclean's* Nov 9, 1987; Vol 100 No 45: p70.

View from the bridge; review of *In the Skin of a Lion*. *Maclean's* June 8, 1987; Vol 100 No 23: pU10.

Benazon, Michael

An interview with Mordecai Richler. photo · *Matrix* Spring 1987; No 24: p39–49.

Bennett, Donna

On the margin: looking for a literary identity; article. illus · *Can Forum* April 1987; Vol 67 No 768: p17–25.

The review review; review of *The Anthology Anthology*. *Essays on Can Writ* Spring 1987; No 34: p119–126.

Bennett, Julia

Writers for dinner; article. photo · *Maclean's* Dec 7, 1987; Vol 100 No 49: pS1.

Benson, Mark

Cycles; reviews of *L'Oeil interrompu* and *Poison*. *Can Lit* Spring 1987; No 112: p136–138.

Maniaques depressifs; reviews of poetry books. *Can Lit* Spring 1987; No 112: p138–141.

Une voix ontarienne; review of *Chroniques du Nouvel-Ontario*. *Can Lit* Winter 1987; No 115: p251–253.

Bentley, D.M.R.

A New Brunswick Roberts; review of *The Collected Poems of Sir Charles G.D. Roberts*. *Can Lit* Spring 1987; No 112: p133–136.

Preface; editorial. *Can Poet* Fall-Winter 1987; No 21: pv–vii.

Beran, Carol L.

George, Leda, and a poured concrete balcony: a study of three aspects of the evolution of Lady Oracle; article. *Can Lit* Spring 1987; No 112: p18–28.

Beray, Patrice

Ailleurs, au monde; poem. *Estuaire* Autumn 1987; No 46: p39–40.

Beresford, Claire

Coach; short story. *Quarry* Fall 1987; Vol 36 No 4: p35–41.

Berg, Jeff

Cambodia: whose idea is this?; review article about *Cambodia*. *West Coast R* Spring 1987; Vol 21 No 4: p73–77.

Berg, Maggie

[Untitled]; review of *(f.)Lip*. *Rubicon* Fall 1987; No 9: p194–195.

Berg, Sharon

The dream; poem. *New Q* Spring-Summer 1987; Vol 7 No 1–2: p165–167.

Making strange; poem. *New Q* Spring-Summer 1987; Vol 7 No 1–2: p163–164.

Overdue; poem. *New Q* Fall 1987; Vol 7 No 3: p67–70.

[Untitled]; review of *Given Names*. *Poetry Can R* Spring 1987; Vol 8 No 2–3: p46.

Berger, Maxianne

Window; poem. *Poetry Can R* Spring 1987; Vol 8 No 1–2: p13.

Berger, Thomas

[Untitled]; biographical articles. *Brick (special issue)* Summer 1987; No 30: ppassim.

Bergeron, Bertrand

Cette nuit ou une autre; short story. *La Nouvelle barre du jour* April 1987; No 198: p56–58.

L'effet transparence; short story. *La Nouvelle barre du jour* April 1987; No 198: p59–63.

Relais; short story sequence. illus · *La Nouvelle barre du jour* April 1987; No 198: p56–63.

Bergeron, Sylvie-L.

Lettre à mon père; short story. *Moebius (special issue)* Spring 1987; No 32: p55–59.

[Untitled]; review of *Les Voyants*. *Moebius* Summer 1987; No 33: p137–139.

Bernier, Sylvie

L'illustration de Maria Chapdelaine: les lectures de Suzor-Côté et Clarence Gagnon; article. illus · *Can Lit* Summer-Fall 1987; No 113–114: p76–90.

Bernier, Yvon

Benito ou la confirmation d'un talent de romancier; review of *Benito*. photo · *Lettres québec* Autumn 1987; No 47: p24–25.

"Ce morceau de chair inexpliqué qu'il faut bien appeler le coeur. . . ."; review of *La Coeur découverte*. photo · *Lettres québec* Spring 1987; No 45: p26–27.

Deux fictions sur fond d'histoire; reviews of *La Fin de l'histoire* and *L'Amour de Jeanne*. photo · *Lettres québec* Winter 1986–87; No 44: p31–33.

Un roman historique remarquable: Katana; review. photo · *Lettres québec* Summer 1987; No 46: p18–19.

Le "Spécial Québec 86" du Magazine littéraire: une carte de visite pour les Français; review. *Lettres québec* Spring 1987; No 45: p67.

Bernstein, Charles

Panoptical artifice; article. *Open Letter (special issue)* Fall 1987; Vol 6 No 9: p9–15.

Berrouët-Oriol, Robert

[Untitled]; review article about *L'Hiver de Mira Christophe*. *Moebius* Winter 1987; No 31: p143–148.

Bersianik, Louky

Pré-liminaire; essay. illus · *La Nouvelle barre du jour (special issue)* March 1987; No 196: p68–80.

Berton, Pierre

Saturday Night intriguing tale of intrigue; letter to the editor. *TS* July 8, 1987: pA18.

Writers' forum; letter to the editor. *WFP* Nov 29, 1987: p6.

Bertrand, Huguette

Suite hallucinante; poem. *Moebius* Winter 1987; No 31: p77–79.

Surimpression; poem. *Moebius* Summer 1987; No 33: p37–38.

Bertrand, Pierre

L'utopie comme refus de la réalité; essay. *Moebius* Summer 1987; No 33: p65–69.

Les métamorphoses masquées de la censure; essay. *Moebius (special issue)* Spring 1987; No 32: p87–95.

Bérubé, Georges L.

La forêt dans l'oeuvre de Louis Caron: une puissance libératrice; article. abstract · *Études can* 1987; No 23: p123–133.

Bérubé, Renald

Du sommet d'un arbre ou le regard en plongée et en quatre temps; article. *Voix et images* Spring 1987; Vol 12 No 3: p404–415.

Berzins, Rai

Assault on your nonchalance; poem. *Arc* Fall 1987; No 19: p47.

Breakfast; poem. *Waves* Winter 1987; Vol 15 No 3: p65.

Frankenstein on the lawn; poem. *Matrix* Fall 1987; No 25: p26.

The guy who deified gravity; poem. *Fiddlehead* Spring 1987; No 151: p71.

The hall of the broadloom king; short story. *Quarry* Spring 1987; Vol 36 No 2: p66–69.

I have not decided what the snake means; poem. *New Q* Winter 1987; Vol 6 No 4: p58.

The neighbour; poem. *Arc* Fall 1987; No 19: p48.

Quiz; poem. *Fiddlehead* Spring 1987; No 151: p70.

Bessai, Diane

[Untitled]; review of *Robertson Davies, Playwright*. *Ariel* April 1987; Vol 18 No 2: p101–104.

Bessette, Gérard

Anita; prose excerpt from *The Cycle*. trans · *Exile* 1987; Vol 12 No 2: p27–56.

Bettis, Paul

Michael Hollingsworth: making history; interview. photo · *Can Theatre R* Fall 1987; No 52: p36–44.

Beugnot, Bernard

Analyse spectrale d'Études françaises; article. *Voix et images* Winter 1987; No 35: p278–284.

Bevis, Richard

Voice of one's own; review of *Cocktails at the Mausoleum*. *Can Lit* Winter 1987; No 115: p186–188.

Beyers, Joanna

A poem with pits in it; poem. *Room of One's Own* Jan 1987; Vol 11 No 2: p72.

Bhaggiyadatta, Krisantha Sri

Eight poems; poem. *Tor South Asian R* Spring 1987; Vol 5 No 3: p35–38.

Winter '84; poem. *Tor South Asian R* Spring 1987; Vol 5 No 3: p38–39.

Bibeau, Paul-André

Les aveux indiscrets d'un robot dormant; short story. *Moebius* Winter 1987; No 31: p83–96.

Biggs, Chuck

An unsolvable maze; review of *Time Pressure*. *WFP* Dec 12, 1987: p50.

Bildfell, Laurie

From box to book; reviews of *Lisa Makes the Headlines* and *Griff Makes a Date*. *Can Child Lit* 1987; No 46: p93–94.

What you see is what you buy: new directions in mass-market promotion; article. *Quill & Quire* Dec 1987; Vol 53 No 12: p4, 6.

Billings, Robert

[Untitled]; poetry excerpts from *White City Poems*. *Malahat R* June 1987; No 79: p143–148.

Bilodeau, Paul

Paul Hiebert author wrote Sarah Binks; obituary. photo · *TS* Sept 7, 1987: pA7.

Bilson, Geoffrey

[Untitled]; letter to the editor. *Can Child Lit* 1987; No 45: p98.

Binchy, Maeve

[Untitled]; review of *You Can't Catch Me!*. *NYT Book R* March 1, 1987: p31.

Binder, Mary Ellen

The Canadian north; review of *Very Last First Time*. *Can Child Lit* 1987; No 45: p82–86.

Binns, Ronald

Lowry's mouths; review of *Confabulations*. *Can Lit* Spring 1987; No 112: p85–87.

Binyon, T.J.

Criminal proceedings; review of *Fool's Gold*. *Times Lit Supp* April 17, 1987; No 4385: p411.

Criminal proceedings; review of *A City Called July*. *Times Lit Supp* July 17, 1987; No 4398: p778.

Criminal proceedings; review of *Sleep While I Sing*. *Times Lit Supp* Aug 21, 1987; No 4403: p910.

Criminal proceedings; review of *Sleep While I Sing*. *Times Lit Supp* Oct 9, 1987; No 4410: p1124.

Biondi, Ferdinand

Nouvel élan; letter to the editor. *MD* Sept 18, 1987: p10.

Birchard, Guy

Coup de hache; poem. *West Coast R* Spring 1987; Vol 21 No 4: p11.

Destroyed after something delicious; poem. *West Coast R* Spring 1987; Vol 21 No 4: p11.

Monograph: Leo Mirau, carver, painter; poem. *West Coast R* Spring 1987; Vol 21 No 4: p5–7.

Palliser's triangle; poem. *West Coast R* Spring 1987; Vol 21 No 4: p8–9.

Scrying; poem. *West Coast R* Spring 1987; Vol 21 No 4: p10.

Bird, Florence

[Untitled]; biographical articles. *Brick (special issue)* Summer 1987; No 30: ppassim.

Bird, Michael

Heuresis: the mother-daughter theme in A Jest of God and Autumn Sonata; article. *New Q* Spring-Summer 1987; Vol 7 No 1–2: p267–273.

Birdsell, Sandra

An excerpt from Act One of *The Revival*. *Prairie Fire* Spring 1987; Vol 8 No 1: p44–49.

The missing child; prose excerpt from *The Missing Child*. illus · *Prairie Fire* Autumn 1987; Vol 8 No 3: p32–50.

The sermon; prose excerpt from *The Missing Child*. illus · *Prairie Fire* Autumn 1987; Vol 8 No 3: p16, 18–21.

Birney, Earle

For George Johnston; poem. *Malahat R (special issue)* March 1987; No 78: p147.

Bishop, Neil B.

Conservatisme; reviews of novels. *Can Lit* Winter 1987; No 115: p169–172.

Le livre d'Abel; review of *Steven le Hérault*. *Can Lit* Spring 1987; No 112: p126–128.

Le personnage français dans quelques romans québécois contemporains; article. *Voix et images* Autumn 1987; Vol 13 No 1: p82–103.

Bishop, Scot

[Untitled]; review of *Adult Entertainment*. *Rubicon* Fall 1987; No 9: p196–197.

bissett, bill

The silver hors; poem. *Cross Can Writ Q* 1987; Vol 9 No 3–4: p12.

Splintrs the virgin mary is popular in a poplar tree in th sault; poem. *Cross Can Writ Q* 1987; Vol 9 No 3–4: p13.

Bissoondath, Neil

Elegant living for a select few; essay. illus · *Idler* May-June 1987; No 13: p51–54.

Bitar, Walid

Carnavale; poem. *Prism* Autumn 1987; Vol 26 No 1: p24.

Nias; poem. *Arc* Spring 1987; No 18: p9.

Our new leader; poem. *Arc* Spring 1987; No 18: p10.

A survivor recalls the pleasure of suburbs; poem. *Arc* Spring 1987; No 18: p8.

Xian; poem. *Prism* Autumn 1987; Vol 26 No 1: p22–23.

Black, Barbara

Anglos, Ukrainians, Indians mesh cultures in novel set in Alberta; review of *Getting Married in Buffalo Jump*. *MG* Aug 29, 1987: pJ3.

Anthony Hyde follows Red Fox; article. photo · *MG* May 23, 1987: pJ9.

Brian Moore's Jesuit priest travels into heart of darkness; reviews of novels. *MG* March 7, 1987: pH11.

Burgess touch refreshes yet another Roman tale; reviews of *Dancing in the Dark* and *John and the Missus*. *MG* April 11, 1987: pG7.

Comic novel about the North is as sharp as frostbite; review of *Contact Prints*. *MG* June 13, 1987: pJ8.

(French) fun at the fair; article. *MG* Nov 28, 1987: pJ11.

How English rose, prospered and begat new tongues; review of *The Telling of Lies*. *MG* Dec 19, 1987: pJ13.

Immigrant experience yields stream of interesting tales; reviews of *Tales from Firozsha Baag* and *The Fencepost Chronicles*. *MG* May 30, 1987: pJ9.

Kinsella should stretch his fancy; review of *Red Wolf, Red Wolf*. photo · *MG* Sept 12, 1987: pI6.

Lieut. Boruvka Czechs in to the case; review of *The Mournful Demeanor of Lieutenant Boruvka*. photo · *MG* Oct 17, 1987: pJ13.

Montreal needle trade is setting for comic tale about working girl; review of *Damaged Goods*, includes profile. photo · *MG* July 18, 1987: pJ9.

Montreal poets inspired by travel in hot countries; reviews of poetry books. *MG* March 28, 1987: pE9.

Montreal spy connection adds spice to the latest Mackenzie King novel; article. photo · *MG* April 11, 1987: pG6.

Sainty, beloved bishop relives past as he lies dying; review of *The Bishop*. *MG* Sept 19, 1987: pJ8.

South African journalist finds a tragic answer to question of apartheid; reviews of *Intimate Strangers* and *After the Fact*. *MG* Feb 7, 1987: pB9.

This famous Montreal writer keeps a low profile; article. photo · *MG* May 16, 1987: pJ7.

Tune in, turn on, drop out: truckin' back to the '60s with Esquire; reviews of *Lime Street at Two* and *The Next Best Thing*. *MG* July 4, 1987: pJ9.

Black, J. David

Bareskin; poem. *Waves* Winter 1987; Vol 15 No 3: p74.

Black, Larry

Bright lights, Big Apple; article. photo · *Maclean's* Dec 7, 1987; Vol 100 No 49: p69–70.

Blackburn, William

Even parents are people; review of *The Quarter-Pie Window*. *Can Child Lit* 1987; No 46: p76–77.

Blackstone, Mary

Freud, Dora and Ibsen; theatre review of *Dora: A Case of Hysteria*. photo · *NeWest R* Summer 1987; Vol 12 No 10: p17.

Blades, Joe

Found synthetic adventure clues; poem. *Cross Can Writ Q* 1987; Vol 9 No 3–4: p9.

Blagrave, Mark

"O brave new world": colonialism in Hunter Duvar's De Roberval; article. *Can Drama* 1987; Vol 13 No 2: p175–181.

Blaikie, Dave

Retain subsidies, publisher urges; article. *G&M* April 29, 1987: pC8.

Blaise, Clark

Stories of the medieval in the present day; reviews of *Beneath the Western Slopes* and *Medieval Hour in the Author's Mind*. *Quill & Quire* June 1987; Vol 53 No 6: p34.

Blake, Peter

Dog in the attic; review of *Different Dragons*. *Times Lit Supp* May 15, 1987; No 4389: p529.

Blakey, Bob

Actor hopes Rubbish exudes innocent joy; biographical article. photo · *CH* April 3, 1987: pC11.

ATP experiment pleased insiders; article. photo · *CH* Feb 14, 1987: pG1.

ATP's Postman Rings Once is a risk within a larger risk; article. *CH* Jan 30, 1987: pC1.

Lacrosse road trips inspired Bolt's play; article. photo · *CH* Jan 24, 1987: pA11.

P.E.I.'s spirited redhead returns; article. photo · *CH* Dec 2, 1987: pD1.

Playrites '87: ATP wades into new wave in theatre; article. photo · *CH* Jan 10, 1987: pB3.

Playwright finds fodder in crisis-centre duty; article. photo · *CH* Jan 16, 1987: pF1.

Pollock's Egg won't be done in time for festival; article. photo · *CH* June 18, 1987: pD7.

Sweatshops give budding poets shot at Olympic gold; article. *CH* Aug 18, 1987: pD7.

Three-act comedy goes on too long; theatre review of *Getting Mama Married. CH* March 8, 1987: pE2.

Writers want out of OCO festival; article. *CH* March 20, 1987: pC3.

Blanchard, Lynn

Cashman trades size for liveliness; article. photo · *G&M* Dec 14, 1987: pC12.

Blanchard, Sylvain

Le Duvernay à Gérald Godin, le Victor-Morin à André Brassard; article. *MD* Oct 9, 1987: p13–14.

Les maisons de la culture de Montréal accueillent la Quinzaine ontaroise; article. *MD* Nov 4, 1987: p14.

Le prix David va à Fernand Ouellette; article. photo · *MD* Nov 5, 1987: p15.

Blissett, William

Three talks with George Johnston; interview. biog · *Malahat R (special issue)* March 1987; No 78: p37–51.

Block, Laurie

Peanuts, here; poem. *Grain* Fall 1987; Vol 15 No 3: p31.

Bloom, Michael

[Untitled]; review of *Bloodsong. NYT Book R* Aug 23, 1987: p16.

Blostein, David

Fargo North Dakota; short story. *Wascana R* Spring 1987; Vol 22 No 1: p22–32.

On Chiemsee; short story. *New Q* Fall 1987; Vol 7 No 3: p31–38.

Blouin, Louise

[Untitled]; review of *L'Hydre à deux coeurs. Estuaire* Summer 1987; No 45: p57.

[Untitled]; review of *L'Audace des mains. Estuaire* Autumn 1987; No 46: p83.

Blue Cloud, Peter

Winter crow; short story. *Can Fic Mag (special issue)* 1987; No 60: p144–145.

Body, Marjorie

P.K. Page: traveller, conjuror, journeyman; article. photo · *Cross Can Writ Q* 1987; Vol 9 No 2: p4–5, 28.

Body, Marjory

History comes alive; review of *The Nine Days Queen. Can Child Lit* 1987; No 48: p85–86.

Boettcher, Monika

The funeral; prose poem. *Waves* Winter 1987; Vol 15 No 3: p70.

The statue; poem. *Waves* Winter 1987; Vol 15 No 3: p70.

Bogaards, Winnifred M.

[Untitled]; reviews of *Probable Fictions* and *The Art of Alice Munro. Eng Studies in Can* March 1987; Vol 13 No 1: p115–119.

Boire, Gary

Canadian (tw)ink: surviving the white-outs; article. *Essays on Can Writ* Winter 1987; No 35: p1–16.

Twice-told tales; review of *The Montreal Story Tellers. Can Lit* Spring 1987; No 112: p130–131.

Wheels on fire: the train of thought in George Ryga's The Ecstasy of Rita Joe; article. *Can Lit* Summer-Fall 1987; No 113–114: p62–74.

Boisvert, Nathalie

La femme de sable; short story. *Estuaire* Spring 1987; No 44: p35–36.

Boisvert, Yves

De nos jours je prends la résolution de penser à quelque chose; poem. *Estuaire* Summer 1987; No 45: p11–13.

Boivin, Jean-Roch

Au rayon de la nouvelle: l'écriture sur commande; reviews of *Qui a peur de?. . . .* and *L'Aventure, la mésaventure.* photo · *MD* Dec 24, 1987: pC11.

Auprès de ma blonde, qu'il fait bon, fait bon. . . .; review of *La Blonde d'Yvon. MD* Oct 17, 1987: pD3.

Le complexe de Jonas; review of *La Vie à rebours.* photo · *MD* Dec 19, 1987: pD3.

Un coup d'essai qui est aussi un coup de ma[i]tre!; review of *Le Père de Lisa. MD* Nov 28, 1987: pD11.

De la drogue, de la passion de l'absolu et de l'amour dont toujours tout reste à dire; review of *Les Grands désordres.* photo · *MD* Oct 24, 1987: pD5.

De l'Italie, de l'art et de la civilisation; review of *Lettres d'Italie.* photo · *MD* Sept 19, 1987: pD3.

Délivrez-nous de Claude Jasmin!; letter to the editor. *MD* Oct 6, 1987: p8.

"Donner naissance à des choses grandes et imparfaites"; review of *Des Cailloux blancs pour les forêts obscures.* photo · *MD* Oct 31, 1987: pD3.

En poche, le premier roman de Yolande Villemaire: un thriller gigogne; review of *Meurtres à blanc.* photo · *MD* May 2, 1987: pD3.

Une enfant du siècle au "monde merveilleux du kitsch du coeur"; review of *Rose-Rouge. MD* Aug 29, 1987: p11–12.

Esther Rochon: une écriture "cool"; review of *Le Traversier.* photo · *MD* April 18, 1987: pD3.

Gilles Archambault et l'art de la sourdine; review of *L'Obsédante obèse et autres agressions*. photo · *MD* June 20, 1987: pD3.

Un jeune couple de Québécois en quête du "ginseng de l'âme"; review of *Nichan*. photo · *MD* Sept 12, 1987: pD2.

L'histoire d'un homme qui voulait la paix; review of *Benito*. photo · *MD* May 16, 1987: pD3.

L'imagination au pouvoir, la grammaire en déroute; review of *L'Ergastule*. *MD* July 11, 1987: pC7.

L'impossible fuite et les tragiques exigences de l'amour entre deux frères; review of *Le Premier mouvement*. *MD* Aug 8, 1987: pC7.

Littérature sur mesure: de la nouvelle à la page; review of *XYZ*. *MD* Oct 10, 1987: pD2-D3.

Madeleine Ferron au sommet de son talent; review of *Un Singulier amour*. photo · *MD* Sept 26, 1987: pD3.

Micheline La France et les fils de sa trame; interview. photo · *Lettres québec* Summer 1987; No 46: p32–33.

Une mystique du désir; review of *Marcher dans Outremont ou ailleurs*. photo · *MD* June 13, 1987: pD3.

Par-delà la mort, le docteur Ferron continue de soigner nos âmes; review of *La Conférence inachevée*. photo · *MD* June 27, 1987: pC8.

Un polar polyphonique à la recherche du temps perdu; review of *Notre-Dame du colportage*. *MD* Dec 5, 1987: pD3.

Pour l'amour des grand-mères, des petites filles et des petits garçons, de l'art, de Montréal et pour l'amour tout court; review of *Myriam première*. photo · *MD* Dec 12, 1987: pD3.

Un roman à la gloire de l'Hydro-Québec; review of *Blizzard sur Québec*. *MD* Nov 21, 1987: pD3.

Un roman bâclé qui fera fureur dans les supermarchés; review of *Probablement l'Espagne*. *MD* Nov 14, 1987: pD15.

Un roman biparental lourd de bonnes intentions; review of *Les Trains d'exils*. *MD* July 25, 1987: pC7.

Sous le signe du Scorpion, Andrée-A. Michaud nous convie aux confins de l'obsession; review of *La Femme de Sath*. *MD* June 6, 1987: pD3.

Le suicide comme métaphore; review of *Beaux draps*. *MD* May 30, 1987: pD3.

Boivin, Jean-Roch [*sic*]

Un roman d'érudition au souffle immense; review of *Katana*. photo · *MD* March 28, 1987: pD3.

Boivin, Mario

[Untitled]; letter to the editor. *Jeu* 1987; No 43: p181.

Bolender, Keith

The Last Real Summer a 'warm,' faded memory; article. *TS (Neighbours)* Jan 27, 1987: p20.

Bolin, John S.

The very best of company: perceptions of a Canadian attitude towards war and nationalism in three contemporary plays; article. *Amer R of Can Studies* Autumn 1987; Vol 17 No 3: p309–322.

Bolt, Carol

DOT DOT DOT. . . .or some notes on notation in playscripts; essay. *Open Letter* Spring 1987; Vol 6 No 7: p51–56.

Female leads: search for feminism in the theatre; essay. illus · *Can Forum* June-July 1987; Vol 67 No 770: p37–40.

Bomais, Marie-France

War Babies: du théâtre féroce; theatre review. photo · *MD (L'Express de Toronto)* March 17, 1987: p4.

Bonanno, Giovanni

Italian-made; review of *Contrasts*. *Can Lit* Winter 1987; No 115: p178–182.

Bond, Carolyn

[Untitled]; review of *The Power to Move*. *Quarry* Fall 1987; Vol 36 No 4: p83–86.

Bonenfant, Réjean

L'innomable païen; short story. *Moebius* Autumn 1987; No 34: p35–37.

[Untitled]; review of *Pris de présence*. *Estuaire* Autumn 1987; No 46: p84–85.

Bonheim, Helmut

The aporias of Lily Littel: Mavis Gallant's "Acceptance of Their Ways"; article. *Ariel* Oct 1987; Vol 18 No 4: p69–78.

Boone, Laurel

The Anchorage series proceedings: the Sir Charles G.D. Roberts and Joseph Howe symposia; reviews of *The Sir Charles G.D. Roberts Symposium* and *The Joseph Howe Symposium*. *Essays on Can Writ* Spring 1987; No 34: p196–201.

Home from the sea; article. photo · *Books in Can* June-July 1987; Vol 16 No 5: p3.

In principio; reviews. *Can Lit* Winter 1987; No 115: p209–211.

Perfect hindsight; review of *Sounding the Iceberg*. *Books in Can* April 1987; Vol 16 No 3: p38–39.

Boone, Mike

Anne II: Canadians' love affair resumes; article. photo · *MG* Dec 4, 1987: pC1.

Brilliantly crafted Green Gables sequel Follows naturally; television review. *MG* Dec 4, 1987: pC8.

Geminis are sad reminder of TV's glory days; column. *MG* Dec 9, 1987: pF3.

Heaven On Earth: TV drama at its best; television review. *MG* Feb 27, 1987: pC7.

Murder Sees The Light best left in dark; television review. *MG* March 13, 1987: pD6.

Shakespeare meets the Butterfly in rerun heaven; column. *MG* April 29, 1987: pH2.

Booth, David

[Untitled]; review of *One Thousand Cranes*. *Quill & Quire (Books for Young People)* June 1987; Vol 53 No 6: p11.

Booth, Rod

An exaggeration; letter to the editor. *Maclean's* Nov 30, 1987; Vol 100 No 48: p4.

Booth, William T.

Landscape with politicians; review of *Northrop Frye: A Vision of the New World. Essays on Can Writ* Winter 1987; No 35: p117–122.

Borovoy, A. Alan

Librarians have cause for porn bill concern; essay. photo · *TS* Nov 21, 1987: pA2.

Borsky, Mary

Snowed in; short story. *Quarry* Spring 1987; Vol 36 No 2: p8–13.

Borson, Roo

[Untitled]; essay. *Poetry Can R* Summer 1987; Vol 8 No 4: p15.

Botting, Gary

A trophy of sorts; short story. illus · *Queen's Q* Autumn 1987; Vol 94 No 3: p580–586.

Bouchard, Claude

Le kalpa de Sandou Manqual ou la raison de l'univers; short story. *Liberté* Aug 1987; Vol 29 No 4: p5–16.

Bouchard, Gilbert

A cool one after a day in the field; poem. *NeWest R* Sept 1987; Vol 13 No 1: p4.

Boucher, Denise

Et le fruit; essay. illus · *La Nouvelle barre du jour (special issue)* March 1987; No 196: p53–55.

Boucher, Yvon

Certaine courtisane blonde au soleil dans une robe noire principalement; short story. *Moebius (special issue)* Spring 1987; No 32: p69–73.

Boudreau, Solange

Quand un ours polaire dérive vers le sud; reviews of children's stories by Cécile Gagnon. *Can Child Lit* 1987; No 47: p62–63.

Boulton, Marsha

People; column. *Maclean's* Aug 10, 1987; Vol 100 No 32: p43.

Bourassa, Alan

Hearing of Nakasone's apology in the UN for Japanese involvement in World War Two; poem. *Quarry* Summer 1987; Vol 36 No 3: p37.

A medieval nobleman travels from Paris to Orleans; poem. *Quarry* Summer 1987; Vol 36 No 3: p36.

Small towns; poem. *Germination* Fall 1987; Vol 11 No 1: p49.

Thinking of white magic I hear reports of fighting in South Yemen; poem. *Quarry* Summer 1987; Vol 36 No 3: p37.

Bourassa, André-G.

Deux pièces en forme d'interrogatoire; reviews of *Being at Home with Claude* and Fragments d'une lettre d'adieu lus par des géologues. photo · *Lettres québec* Spring 1987; No 45: p50–51.

Masques, personnages et personnes; reviews of plays. photo · *Lettres québec* Summer 1987; No 46: p51–52.

Paul-Marie Lapointe chez Seghers; review of *Paul-Marie Lapointe. Lettres québec* Summer 1987; No 46: p77–78.

Bourassa, Lucie

[Untitled]; review of *Rock desperado. Estuaire* Winter 1986–87; No 43: p77.

[Untitled]; review of *Jusqu'à la moëlle des fièvres. Estuaire* Summer 1987; No 45: p58–59.

Bourgeois, Alin

Il s'avança (premier mouvement); poem. illus · *La Nouvelle barre du jour* April 1987; No 198: p6–19.

Bourne, Lesley

The voice says in such a way; poem. *Event* March 1987; Vol 16 No 1: p30–31.

Bourne, Lesley-Anne

Voices; poem. *Tor Life* Nov 1987; Vol 21 No 17: p186.

Wading; poem. *CV 2* Spring 1987; Vol 10 No 3: p34.

Woman dying; poem. *CV 2* Spring 1987; Vol 10 No 3: p33.

Boutin, Richard

[Untitled]; reviews of *Lascaux* and *Catégoriques un deux trois. Estuaire* Summer 1987; No 45: p52–54.

Bouygues, C.

La vue comparatiste; review of *Le Pays natal. Can Lit* Winter 1987; No 115: p211–213.

Bouzek, Don

In the neighbourhood of my heart; essay. photo · *Can Theatre R* Winter 1987; No 53: p20–25.

Bowering, George

Conversations about Caprice; prose excerpt from *Caprice. Descant (special issue)* Spring-Summer 1987; Vol 18 No 1–2: p108–111.

The Elks come to town; prose excerpt from *Caprice.* photo · *Descant (special issue)* Spring-Summer 1987; Vol 18 No 1–2: p104–107.

Errata; column. *Brick* Winter 1987; No 29: p52–53.

Further adventures of errata; essay. illus · *Brick* Fall 1987; No 31: p48–50.

I would even wear one of their hats if it wasn't so dumb; essay. *Descant (special issue)* Spring-Summer 1987; Vol 18 No 1–2: p101–103.

Milton Acorn (1923–1986); obituary. *Can Lit* Spring 1987; No 112: p216–218.

A rifle in deep centre; prose excerpt from *Caprice*. *Descant (special issue)* Spring-Summer 1987; Vol 18 No 1–2: p113–116.

Selections from Errata; essay. *Prairie Fire* Winter 1987–88; Vol 8 No 4: p6, 8.

Bowering, Marilyn

Christmas in Prague, 1986; poem. *Can Forum* Nov 1987; Vol 67 No 773: p17.

The dead appear; poems. *Can Forum* Nov 1987; Vol 67 No 773: p16–17.

I have been dreaming about the wife; poem. *Can Forum* Nov 1987; Vol 67 No 773: p17.

My dear friends; poem. *Can Forum* Nov 1987; Vol 67 No 773: p16–17.

Native land; poem. *Can Forum* Nov 1987; Vol 67 No 773: p16.

The red factory; poem. *Can Forum* Nov 1987; Vol 67 No 773: p16.

Boyd, Steve

[Untitled]; review of *One Out of Four*. *CH* Jan 25, 1987: pE4.

Bradbury, Patricia

Jane Urquhart's short stories in the landscape of the poet; review of *Storm Glass*. photo · *Quill & Quire* July 1987; Vol 53 No 7: p64.

Moore shatters illusion in the search for spiritual survival; review of *The Color of Blood*. photo · *Quill & Quire* Aug 1987; Vol 53 No 8: p29.

Stories painful and fresh; review of *The Old Dance*. *Quill & Quire* Jan 1987; Vol 53 No 1: p28.

[Untitled]; review of *Autobiographies*. *Quill & Quire* Nov 1987; Vol 53 No 11: p27.

Braden, Christopher

Behind that mournful face there truly is a sad person; review of *This One's on Me*. photo · *TS* Nov 14, 1987: pM4.

Brady, Elizabeth

Airing Canlit chestnuts; review of *After the Fact*. *Fiddlehead* Autumn 1987; No 153: p103–106.

Braganza, Brian

Desolation; poem. *Waves* Spring 1987; Vol 15 No 4: p26.

Braid, Kate

Class conscious; poem. *Fireweed* Fall 1987; No 25: p20.

Brandis, Marianne

A different "somewhere" – the lives of working children; essay. photo · *Can Child Lit* 1987; No 48: p62–64.

Brannagan, Ruth M.

Eternity ring; short story. photo · *TS* June 29, 1987: pA8.

Brant, Beth

Turtle gal; short story. *Can Fic Mag (special issue)* 1987; No 60: p61–73.

Brass, Lorne

Lorne Brass: enfant de la télé; essay. photo · *Jeu* 1987; No 44: p124–125.

Brault, Jacques

Bonheur caché; essay. *Voix et images* Winter 1987; No 35: p185.

Comme une visitation; essay. *Voix et images* Winter 1987; No 35: p183.

Une conversation dans le noir; essay. *Liberté* Feb 1987; Vol 29 No 1: p61–62.

Hommage à Ghislaine Legendre; poem. *MD* Sept 12, 1987: pD5.

Un lieu d'écriture; essay. photo · *Voix et images* Winter 1987; No 35: p182.

Mine rien: tout; essay. *Voix et images* Winter 1987; No 35: p184.

La voix minimale; article. *Voix et images* Autumn 1987; Vol 13 No 1: p66–69.

Braux, Clara

The Canadian lady; short story. illus · *Cross Can Writ Q* 1987; Vol 9 No 2: p10–11, 30.

Sleeping beauty; short story. *Waves* Winter 1987; Vol 15 No 3: p33–40.

Bray, Rosemary L.

[Untitled]; review of *A Candle for Christmas*. *NYT Book R* Dec 6, 1987: p81.

Brazao, Dale

Vandals' $150,000 rampage trashes home; article. photo · *TS* Oct 13, 1987: pA2.

Brazier, John

The disappearances of Guevara; poem. *West Coast R* Spring 1987; Vol 21 No 4: p23–26.

Brebner, Diana

All for the burning bodies; poem. *Grain* Winter 1987; Vol 15 No 4: p22.

The dark ages; poem. *Grain* Winter 1987; Vol 15 No 4: p23.

Grandmother remembers her wars; poem. *New Q* Winter 1987; Vol 6 No 4: p59.

A migratory gift; poem. *Malahat R* Sept 1987; No 80: p35.

Pauper sum ego; poem. *Malahat R* Sept 1987; No 80: p36.

Pink hearts with no teeth; poem. *Event* March 1987; Vol 16 No 1: p32.

Brenna, Dwayne

Loss and renewal: Changes of State by Gary Geddes; review. *NeWest R* Sept 1987; Vol 13 No 1: p18.

Brennan, Anthony S.

Zig-zag management; reviews of *Nadine* and *A Hero Travels Light*. *Fiddlehead* Winter 1987; No 154: p91–95.

Brennan, Brian

B-Movie wins laughs with gags, old lines; theatre review of *B-Movie, the Play*. *CH* Sept 19, 1987: pD6.

Broadway's grip on theatre deceiving; column. *CH* Aug 6, 1987: pC2.

Canadian troupes will command the spotlight in '88; article. *CH* April 28, 1987: pC8.

Canadians on Broadway; article. photo · *CH* April 4, 1987: pB4.

City thespian lands role in HMS Pinafore; column. *CH* Sept 22, 1987: pC9.

Critics agree on one thing: peace is paramount; article. photo · *CH* Dec 10, 1987: pF1.

Critics cite play festival's possibilities; article. *CH* Feb 14, 1987: pG4.

Fare can't be taken at face value; theatre review of *Possibly Yours*. photo · *CH* March 10, 1987: pC7.

Festival features Alberta playwrights; article. *CH* Feb 19, 1987: pD4.

Hackneyed pot-boiler contains few surprises; theatre review of *And When I Wake*. photo · *CH* March 15, 1987: pE2.

Late Blumer's a step behind; theatre review. photo · *CH (Sunday Magazine)* Jan 13, 1987: pD5.

Lunchbox hopes farce will score; article. photo · *CH* Sept 25, 1987: pF1.

Murder mystery hatched in eerie isolated farmhouse; article. *CH* March 13, 1987: pC1.

Musical Fire is a damp sparkler; theatre review. photo · *CH* Feb 14, 1987: pG4.

Persistence pays off for determined actor-writer; article. photo · *CH* March 6, 1987: pF1.

Pinsent's presence overshadows film; film review of *John and the Missus*. photo · *CH* May 15, 1987: pE8.

Play examines porn issues; theatre review of *Intimate Invasion*. *CH* Nov 6, 1987: pE8.

Play lacks clear plot; theatre review of *Winning*. photo · *CH* Jan 26, 1987: pB6.

Play needs time to be digested; theatre review of *Today I Am a Fountain Pen*. *CH* Dec 1, 1987: pD3.

Playwright's debut shows promise; theatre review of *Penumbra*. photo · *CH* Jan 20, 1987: pA10.

Pollock is tops again; article. photo · *CH* May 27, 1987: pA1.

Pollock play makes debut on TC stage in '88 season; article. photo · *CH* April 23, 1987: pD1.

Promising comedy weighed down by serious issues; theatre review of *The Melville Boys*. *CH* April 11, 1987: pF2.

Season's greetings: companies take cues from holidays past; article. photo · *CH* Nov 22, 1987: pA11.

Sex Tips tastefully, cleverly staged; theatre review of *Sex Tips for Modern Girls*. photo · *CH* Sept 29, 1987: pD7.

Sex Tips to open Lunchbox season; article. *CH* Aug 8, 1987: pF2.

Small, nostalgic play is an unexpected delight; theatre review of *Salt-Water Moon*. photo · *CH* Jan 18, 1987: pE1.

The state of theatre: avant-garde advances bewilder actors, critics; article. photo · *CH* Oct 18, 1987: pC4.

Tame gay play marked by low-camp theatrics; theatre review of *The Postman Rings Once*. photo · *CH* Feb 1, 1987: pC6.

Theatre notes; column. *CH* May 11, 1987: pC6.

Weekend blitz will be ATP's litmus test; column. *CH* Feb 3, 1987: pF9.

Brennan, Pat

Saturday Night branches out in search of publishing profits; article. photo · *TS* Jan 6, 1987: pE1.

Breton, Gaétan

[Untitled]; review of *Le Traversier*. *Moebius* Summer 1987; No 33: p135–136.

Brewster, Elizabeth

Cold lunch; short story. illus · *Can Forum* April 1987; Vol 67 No 768: p28–32.

Collage; short story. *New Q* Spring-Summer 1987; Vol 7 No 1–2: p14–35.

Fiction class: exercise one (with credit to John Gardner); poem. *Event* March 1987; Vol 16 No 1: p70–71.

George Johnston's poems: letters of a friend; article. *Malahat R (special issue)* March 1987; No 78: p136–146.

Letter to T.S. Eliot; poem. *Event* March 1987; Vol 16 No 1: p72–74.

[Untitled]; reviews of *The Paris-Napoli Express* and *White of the Lesser Angels*. *Event* March 1987; Vol 16 No 1: p103–104.

Well-meant advice; short story. illus · *NeWest R* Oct 1987; Vol 13 No 2: p14–15, 17.

Winter images; poem. *Poetry Can R* Spring 1987; Vol 8 No 2–3: p22.

Brière, Eloise A.

[Untitled]; review of *Littérature canadienne francophone. Amer R of Can Studies* Winter 1987–88; Vol 17 No 4: p449–450.

Bringhurst, Robert

Bodhidharma; poem. *Rubicon* Spring 1987; No 8: p105.

Conversations with a toad; poetry excerpt from a work in progress. *Border Cross* Spring 1987; Vol 6 No 2: p32.

Conversations with a toad; poem. *Descant* Winter 1987; Vol 18 No 4: p7–14.

Hóng Zìchéng; poem. *Rubicon* Spring 1987; No 8: p103–104.

Sengzhaò; poem. *Rubicon* Spring 1987; No 8: p106.

The starlight is getting steadily dimmer; poetry excerpt from *The Lyell Island Variations*. *Rubicon* Spring 1987; No 8: p107.

Brink, D.A.

TC performance gave entertainment; letter to the editor. *CH* April 7, 1987: pA6.

Brisset, Annie

Votre leçon d'humanité; essay. *Liberté* April 1987; Vol 29 No 2: p106–107.

Brochu, André

De quoi mourir en beauté?; article. *Études fran* Autumn-Winter 1987; Vol 23 No 1–2: p119–129.

La fiction du réel / le réel de la fiction; reviews of poetry books. *Voix et images* Winter 1987; No 35: p322–330.

Jacques Brault: le quotidien transfiguré; introduction. illus · *Voix et images* Winter 1987; No 35: p187.

L'interrogation totale de la mort; reviews of poetry books. *Voix et images* Autumn 1987; Vol 13 No 1: p165–174.

La poésie dans la prose, ou le clochard illuminé; article. illus · *Voix et images* Winter 1987; No 35: p212–220.

Usages du poème; reviews of poetry books. *Voix et images* Spring 1987; Vol 12 No 3: p539–547.

Brochu, Jean-Claude

Témoinage: la leçon des choses; article. illus · *Voix et images* Winter 1987; No 35: p250–254.

Brockwell, Stephen

[Untitled]; review of *Out of the Willow Trees*. *Rubicon* Spring 1987; No 8: p225–226.

[Untitled]; review of *Landslides*. *Rubicon* Fall 1987; No 9: p182–184.

Brooks, Eunice

Your place; poem. *Room of One's Own* Sept 1987; Vol 11 No 4: p99.

Brossard, Nicole

Aroused; poem. trans · *Exile* 1987; Vol 12 No 1: p105–124.

Brost, Carole

Beyond repair; poem. *Prairie Fire* Spring 1987; Vol 8 No 1: p33.

Moral support; poem. *New Q* Spring-Summer 1987; Vol 7 No 1–2: p216.

Offspring; poem. *New Q* Spring-Summer 1987; Vol 7 No 1–2: p214–215.

Spring is born; poem. *Prairie Fire* Spring 1987; Vol 8 No 1: p32.

Broten, Delores

After the fall; poem. *New Q* Spring-Summer 1987; Vol 7 No 1–2: p225–226.

Ties that bind; poem. *New Q* Spring-Summer 1987; Vol 7 No 1–2: p223–224.

Brouwer, Sigmund

Sparrows fall uncounted; short story. *Queen's Q* Summer 1987; Vol 94 No 2: p376–382.

Brown, Allan

Eyes; the dark; poem. *Quarry* Winter 1987; Vol 36 No 1: p114.

Pause; poem. *Quarry* Winter 1987; Vol 36 No 1: p113.

Brown, Andrew

Laughing in the air; poem. *New Q* Spring-Summer 1987; Vol 7 No 1–2: p217.

Magician; poem. *New Q* Spring-Summer 1987; Vol 7 No 1–2: p218–219.

Brown, Edna

Play review endorsed; letter to the editor. *CH* Feb 8, 1987: pB4.

Brown, Heather

Scenario; poem. *Prism* Autumn 1987; Vol 26 No 1: p25–26.

Brown, Lindsay

Michael Ondaatje gives Toronto its early voice; review of *In the Skin of a Lion*. photo · *MG* June 20, 1987: pJ9.

Oak tree is weak base of H.R. Percy's tangled tales; review of *Tranter's Tree*. photo · *MG* July 25, 1987: pJ8.

Brown, Louise

Librarians fear 'censorship' in new porn law; article. photo · *TS* Nov 16, 1987: pA1, A8.

Brown, Ronnie R.

Bus stations; poem. *Arc* Spring 1987; No 18: p11–12.

Having a wonderful time. . . .; poem. *Arc* Spring 1987; No 18: p13–14.

Brown, Russell

[Untitled]; reviews of *Robert Kroetsch* and *Another Country*. *U of Toronto Q* Fall 1987; Vol 57 No 1: p161–166.

Brown, Sylvia M.

Kicking against the pricks; review of *A Mazing Space*. *Books in Can* Dec 1987; Vol 16 No 9: p36–37.

Brownstein, Bill

Culture Shock: not enough substance for two-act play; theatre review. *MG* July 13, 1987: pB9.

Nightspots: storytellers unite at La Ricane; column. *MG* Jan 24, 1987: pD6.

This poetic winner could rhyme on a dime anytime; column. *MG* July 25, 1987: pD12.

Versifiers rhyme for gold at first poetry Olympics; article. *MG* July 21, 1987: pD1.

Bruce, Harry

Personal fallacy be damned!; column. *Atlan Insight* Dec 1987; Vol 9 No 12: p16.

Bruised Head, Shirley

An afternoon in bright sunlight; short story. *Can Fic Mag* (special issue) 1987; No 60: p33–39.

Brulotte, Gaétan

Le fulgurante ascension de Bou; short story. *Moebius* Autumn 1987; No 34: p17–22.

Le poète des rues; short story. *Estuaire* Summer 1987; No 45: p19–21.

Bryan, Jay

Writer won't let blindness slow him down; article. photo · *MG* July 2, 1987: pC1.

Brydon, Diana

Shallow griefs; review of *Back on Tuesday. Can Lit* Winter 1987; No 115: p194–195.

Buchanan, Roberta

Elemental poem; poem. *Atlantis* Spring 1987; Vol 12 No 2: p101–102.

Stuffed with legends; review of *The Devil Is Loose!. Can Lit* Winter 1987; No 115: p213–214.

Buckley, Joanne

Living to tell the tale: survival guides for adolescent readers; reviews of *Can You Promise Me Spring?* and *We're Friends, Aren't We?. Can Child Lit* 1987; No 46: p78–79.

Buday, Grant

That old time religion; short story. *Event* Summer 1987; Vol 16 No 2: p45–50.

Buhasz, Laszlo J.

Life slices; review of *Night Driving. G&M* June 6, 1987: pC19.

Muscular idea; review of *The Dream Auditor. G&M* May 9, 1987: pC21.

Rough gems; review of *The Dream Auditor. G&M* June 20, 1987: pC19.

Buitenhuis, Peter

Scott Symons and the strange case of Helmet of Flesh; article. *West Coast R* Spring 1987; Vol 21 No 4: p59–72.

[Untitled]; reviews of *Varieties of Exile* and *Prairie Women. Queen's Q* Summer 1987; Vol 94 No 2: p467–470.

Bullock, Michael

The grey fleece; poem. *Can Lit* Winter 1987; No 115: p106.

The well; short story. *Matrix* Spring 1987; No 24: p33–35.

Burgess, Anthony

Nobel sentiments; article. illus · *Sat Night* Dec 1987; Vol 102 No 12: p15–16.

Burgess, John

The mission for three-fifty; short story. photo · *TS* July 13, 1987: pD7.

Burke, Anne

Introduction; editorial article. *Prairie J of Can Lit* 1987; No 9: p4–6.

"Look homeward, angel" – an irreverent look at grants; poem. *Cross Can Writ Q* 1987; Vol 9 No 3–4: p29.

Margaret Laurence 1926–1987: prairie, ancestors, woman; article. *Cross Can Writ Q* 1987; Vol 9 No 2: p16–17, 29.

The small press; editorial. *Prairie J of Can Lit* 1987; No 8: p4.

That painting; short story. *Prairie J of Can Lit* 1987; No 9: p47–53.

Thunder Creek Publishing Co-op; article. *Cross Can Writ Q* 1987; Vol 9 No 2: p32.

[Untitled]; review of *Wittgenstein Elegies. Poetry Can R* Spring 1987; Vol 8 No 2–3: p47.

[Untitled]; review of *Dark Galaxies. Poetry Can R* Spring 1987; Vol 8 No 2–3: p51.

[Untitled]; reviews of poetry books. *Poetry Can R* Summer 1987; Vol 8 No 4: p38.

[Untitled]; essay. photo · *Cross Can Writ Q* 1987; Vol 9 No 3–4: p22–23.

Burke, Brian

The day I killed Joseph Mengele; short story. *Waves* Spring 1987; Vol 15 No 4: p11–14.

Margaret Atwood Island; poem. *Northward J* 1987; No 42: p35–36.

Martinique; short story. *Prism* Summer 1987; Vol 25 No 4: p122–125.

The undiscovered country; short story. *Prism* Spring 1987; Vol 25 No 3: p7–16.

Burnard, Bonnie

Editorial. 22 · *Grain* Summer 1987; Vol 15 No 2.

Burnett, Murdoch

Red Deer Press series champions western writers; reviews of poetry books. *CH* Dec 13, 1987: pC11.

Burnett, Virgil

Wandering Gentiles; short story. *Descant (special issue)* Spring-Summer 1987; Vol 18 No 1–2: p174–178.

Burnham, Clint

[Untitled]; review of *Cambodia. Malahat R* June 1987; No 79: p156–157.

Burns, Cliff

The cattletruck; short story. *Rubicon* Fall 1987; No 9: p72–75.

Burrs, Mick

The prairies: AltaSaskMan; regional column. *Poetry Can R* Fall 1987; Vol 9 No 1: p22.

The prairies: numb Canadian poets; regional column. *Poetry Can R* Summer 1987; Vol 8 No 4: p24.

The prairies: poetry as ingrown toenail; regional column. *Poetry Can R* Spring 1987; Vol 8 No 2–3: p19.

Simple journeys to other planets; prose poem. *Grain* Summer 1987; Vol 15 No 2: p20.

Burt, Robert

Riding summer; poem. *New Q* Winter 1987; Vol 6 No 4: p60–64.

[Untitled]; poetry excerpt from *The Boys of Summer*. *Fiddlehead* Summer 1987; No 152: p28–29.

Bushkowsky, Aaron

Another way we remember; poem. *Prairie Fire* Spring 1987; Vol 8 No 1: p17.

At bay; poem. *Antigonish R* 1987; No 69–70: p49.

Dusting; poem. *Antigonish R* 1987; No 69–70: p48.

E i e i o; poem. *Antigonish R* 1987; No 69–70: p51–52.

The fabled wind; poem. *Antigonish R* 1987; No 69–70: p52–53.

Part about parting; poem. *Prairie Fire* Spring 1987; Vol 8 No 1: p18.

The same wait; poem. *Antigonish R* 1987; No 69–70: p50–51.

She insisted she wasn't; poem. *Prairie Fire* Spring 1987; Vol 8 No 1: p16.

[Untitled]; poem. *Prairie Fire* Spring 1987; Vol 8 No 1: p19.

Butterfield, Martha

Inuit woman; poem. *Quarry* Fall 1987; Vol 36 No 4: p70.

Monarch; poem. *Quarry* Fall 1987; Vol 36 No 4: p69–70.

Butts, Richard

Tiger killer; short story. illus · *Queen's Q* Winter 1987; Vol 94 No 4: p829–839.

Buxton, Bonnie

Dead man's valley; short story. photo · *TS* Aug 27, 1987: pF7.

Bye, Cristine

Author's heritage provides fuel for stories; article. photo · *CH (Sunday Magazine)* July 19, 1987: p9.

Byers, Mary

A bad poet rates title; letter to the editor. *G&M* July 29, 1987: pA7.

Byrnes, Michael Allen

Bacon and eggs; short story. *Waves* Spring 1987; Vol 15 No 4: p21–26.

Cabray, Paul

[Untitled]; reviews of *Doubtful Motives* and *A Body Surrounded by Water*. *MG* Aug 15, 1987: pL2.

Caccia, Fulvio

Soyons francs; essay. illus · *Liberté (special issue)* 1987: p50–53.

Cahill, Jack

Street cop Chuck Konkel is also K.G.E. Konkel, novelist; article. photo · *TS* Oct 18, 1987: pD7.

Calhoun, Sue

La Sagouine: home to stay; article. photo · *Atlan Insight* April 1987; Vol 9 No 4: p19–21.

Callaghan, Barry

Au revoir; poem. *Tor Life* Dec 1987; Vol 21 No 18: p66.

Bread alone; poem. *Tor Life* Dec 1987; Vol 21 No 18: p66.

Grace; poem. *Tor Life* Dec 1987; Vol 21 No 18: p66.

Margaret Laurence in England; essay. photo · *Books in Can* March 1987; Vol 16 No 2: p9–12.

Mirror mirror; poem. *Tor Life* Dec 1987; Vol 21 No 18: p67.

Now it will rain; poem. *Tor Life* Dec 1987; Vol 21 No 18: p66.

On the death of his mother; poem. *Tor Life* Dec 1987; Vol 21 No 18: p66.

The queen of heaven; poem. *Tor Life* Dec 1987; Vol 21 No 18: p67.

The sleepwalker; poem. *Tor Life* Dec 1987; Vol 21 No 18: p67.

Stone blind love; poems. illus · *Tor Life* Dec 1987; Vol 21 No 18: p66–67.

Treasured island; essay. illus · *Tor Life* April 1987; Vol 21 No 5: pH7-H8,H10,H12-H13.

[Untitled]; prose excerpt from *Promise of Rain*. *Exile* 1987; Vol 12 No 1: p5–55.

The way the heart is; short story. illus · *Tor Life* June 1987; Vol 21 No 9: p62, 100, 102–107.

Callaghan, Morley

Morley Callaghan's Cabbagetown; essay. photo · *TS* April 2, 1987: pA6.

Callendar, Newgate

Crime; review of *To an Easy Grave*. *NYT Book R* Jan 18, 1987: p23.

Crime; review of *A City Called July*. *NYT Book R* March 8, 1987: p29.

Crime; review of *The Hollow Woman*. *NYT Book R* March 29, 1987: p25.

Callwood, June

Misery of incest drove novelist to divide her personality; column. *G&M* Sept 30, 1987: pA2.

Problem of perception distorts debate on pornography bills; column. *G&M* July 1, 1987: pA2.

Camerlain, Lorraine

"O.K. on change!"; article. photo · *Jeu* 1987; No 45: p83–97.

Questions sur des questions; essay. photo · *Jeu* 1987; No 45: p164–168.

Cameron, Anne

As you wish, she said....; short story. *Room of One's Own* Jan 1987; Vol 11 No 2: p3–8.

Cameron, Hamish

Bertelsmann deals Doubleday to Porter; article. photo · *Quill & Quire* Feb 1987; Vol 53 No 2: p8.

CBA '87; article. photo · *Quill & Quire* Sept 1987; Vol 53 No 9: p6, 10, 12.

CBPC mission looking to long-term China trade; article. photo · *Quill & Quire* Nov 1987; Vol 53 No 11: p11.

Export sales depend on Frankfurt presence; article. photo · *Quill & Quire* Dec 1987; Vol 53 No 12: p10.

Federal book program finally official; article. *Quill & Quire* Jan 1987; Vol 53 No 1: p13.

Gloves off as book industry assails feds; article. photo · *Quill & Quire* Jan 1987; Vol 53 No 1: p12.

Making the rights move: why publishers are paying so much more; article. photo · *Quill & Quire* March 1987; Vol 53 No 3: p8, 10.

McClelland retires, no more encores; article. photo · *Quill & Quire* April 1987; Vol 53 No 4: p14.

Opening the book on China: contacts before contracts on the Far Eastern front; article. photo · *Quill & Quire* Nov 1987; Vol 53 No 11: p10–11.

The price of rights: the role of the literary agent; article. photo · *Quill & Quire* April 1987; Vol 53 No 4: p4–5.

Seal added to Porter acquisitions; article. *Quill & Quire* April 1987; Vol 53 No 4: p14.

The spring lists: prices holding steady in a shaky world; preview of spring book list. photo · *Quill & Quire* Feb 1987; Vol 53 No 2: p5–6.

Cameron, Silver Donald

Income averaging is essential for writer; letter to the editor. *Fin Post* Oct 19, 1987: p15.

Cameron, Stevie

New publishing career takes Clarkson 'beyond adrenalin'; column about Adrienne Clarkson. *G&M* July 23, 1987: pA2.

Saturday Night editor has few regrets as new career opens; column. *G&M* Aug 20, 1987: pA2.

Campbell, Don

Toronto team wants poetry back in Olympic Games lineup; article. photo · *WFP* July 25, 1987: p46.

Campbell, Donald

Anne to be adapted for ballet; article. *WFP* Nov 26, 1987: p83.

Arts crowd feels chill: cultural community lines up against pact; article. *WFP* Dec 19, 1987: p44.

Author spent prize money early; article. photo · *WFP* June 24, 1987: p27.

Author unaware latest book mystery; article. photo · *WFP* Sept 29, 1987: p29.

Author's crimes behind him, but emotional ghosts remain; article. *WFP* Dec 26, 1987: p20.

Birdsell says she's touched by her own film; article. photo · *WFP* Oct 30, 1987: p29.

Books break cultural silence, look at fumbled conversation; article. photo · *WFP* Dec 7, 1987: p16.

French writers survive here, Quebecers told; article about Les Éditions du blé. photo · *WFP* July 22, 1987: p36.

Funding fuss shocks writer-in-residence; article. photo · *WFP* Oct 6, 1987: p32.

Kinsella promotes book, but slips into baseball; article. photo · *WFP* Sept 15, 1987: p29.

Sculptor to help shape women's festival; article. *WFP* July 28, 1987: p28.

Soloist's view of Rita Joe grows; article. photo · *WFP* Oct 2, 1987: p21.

Successful local novel to be made into film; article. *WFP* Sept 26, 1987: p30.

W.O. Mitchell's creative thoughts turn to plays; article. photo · *WFP* Oct 8, 1987: p42.

Campbell, Maida

Anne sequel takes too many liberties; letter to the editor. photo · *G&M* Dec 26, 1987: pD7.

Campbell, Randy

[Untitled]; poetry excerpts from *Crossing the Barrens. Fiddlehead* Autumn 1987; No 153: p27–31.

Campbell, Richard

The man who made Ontario Orange; review of *The Orangeman*. photo · *TS* Feb 8, 1987: pG8.

Campeau, Françine

Les indomptés; short story. *Moebius* Winter 1987; No 31: p35–47.

Candelaria, Fred

Honest man; poem. *Antigonish R* 1987; No 69–70: p127.

Caniparoli, Walter

Down and out in Toronto and Buffalo; short story. *Fiddlehead* Autumn 1987; No 153: p41–47.

Cannon, Margaret

Black Sheep time; review of *Mortal Sins*. photo · *G&M* Nov 14, 1987: pE4.

Crime writers who use the macabre to maximum effect; review of *Whisperland*. photo · *G&M* Nov 21, 1987: pC23.

A decade of great thrillers continues with two treasures; reviews of *Swann: A Mystery* and *The Last White Man in Panama*. *G&M* Sept 26, 1987: pC23.

Fatalities and feminism in Lotus Land; reviews of *Fieldwork* and *The Goldfish Bowl*. *G&M* Aug 29, 1987: pC17.

Murder & mayhem: plot and details in a cop's life; reviews of *Gallows View* and *Equinox*. photo · *G&M* May 23, 1987: pC23.

Murder & mayhem: Spenser's clones; review of *Crang Plays the Ace*. photo · *G&M* April 25, 1987: pC19.

Murder & mayhem: the English style of the whodunits; reviews of *A Body Surrounded by Water* and *Doubtful Motives*. photo · *G&M* July 18, 1987: pC17.

Murder & mayhem: tough guys on clean street; reviews of crime novels. *G&M* Jan 3, 1987: pE15.

Surprising weight from the newcomers; reviews of *The Glorious East Wind* and *Ripper*. *G&M* Nov 7, 1987: pC23.

Three new faces deserving discovery; reviews of crime novels. photo · *G&M* Oct 17, 1987: pE4.

Three new twists on old and favorite spy themes; review of *Rue du Bac*. *G&M* Sept 12, 1987: pC19.

Carbray, Paul

Slain hitchhiker doesn't live up to writer's promise; reviews of *Sleep While I Sing* and *Sherlock Holmes and the Case of the Raleigh Legacy*. *MG* Feb 21, 1987: pB8.

Cardy, Michael

Decline of faith; poem. *New Q* Winter 1987; Vol 6 No 4: p65.

Gentle advice to a young lady with literary aspirations for later on; poem. *Can Auth & Book* Fall 1987; Vol 63 No 1: p22.

The legacy of Margaret Laurence; article. *Can Auth & Book* Summer 1987; Vol 62 No 4: p3.

Prufrock redivivus; poem. *New Q* Fall 1987; Vol 7 No 3: p98.

Wall poster; poem. *New Q* Fall 1987; Vol 7 No 3: p99.

Carey, Barbara

Archives; poem. *New Q* Winter 1987; Vol 6 No 4: p68.

Explaining ourselves to ourselves; poem. *CV 2* Spring 1987; Vol 10 No 3: p8.

In the garden for the last time; poem. *Cross Can Writ Q* 1987; Vol 9 No 1: p21.

In the name of the Mother; review of *SP/ELLES*. *Books in Can* Jan-Feb 1987; Vol 16 No 1: p20–21.

The mutability of memory: Rhea Tregebov's No One We Know; review. *Quarry* Summer 1987; Vol 36 No 3: p70–75.

Observation; poem. *CV 2* Spring 1987; Vol 10 No 3: p9.

The peanut butter wars; poem. *New Q* Winter 1987; Vol 6 No 4: p66–67.

Spectacles; poem. *Arc* Fall 1987; No 19: p49–50.

[Untitled]; reviews of poetry books. *Cross Can Writ Q* 1987; Vol 9 No 1: p23–24.

[Untitled]; review of *Night Light*. *Quill & Quire* Jan 1987; Vol 53 No 1: p26–27.

[Untitled]; review of *A Long Night of Death*. *Books in Can* Jan-Feb 1987; Vol 16 No 1: p25.

[Untitled]; review of *Children of Abel*. *Books in Can* March 1987; Vol 16 No 2: p27.

[Untitled]; review of *Through the Nan Da Gate*. *Books in Can* March 1987; Vol 16 No 2: p27–28.

[Untitled]; review of *The Power to Move*. *Books in Can* May 1987; Vol 16 No 4: p23–24.

[Untitled]; review of *China Shockwaves*. *Books in Can* June-July 1987; Vol 16 No 5: p23.

[Untitled]; review of *How to Read Faces*. *Books in Can* June-July 1987; Vol 16 No 5: p25.

[Untitled]; reviews of *The Proper Lover* and *Above the Tilted Earth*. *Poetry Can R* Summer 1987; Vol 8 No 4: p34.

[Untitled]; letter to the editor. *New Q* Fall 1987; Vol 7 No 3: p103.

[Untitled]; review of *Selected Poems*. *Books in Can* Dec 1987; Vol 16 No 9: p29–30.

[Untitled]; review of *Poems Released on a Nuclear Wind*. *Books in Can* Dec 1987; Vol 16 No 9: p30–31.

The view from here; poem. *Can Forum* Nov 1987; Vol 67 No 773: p40.

Carey, Pauline

Age and the masters of short fiction; review of *Night Light*. *G&M* Jan 10, 1987: pE14.

Cruel events; review of *A Hero Travels Light*. *G&M* Jan 24, 1987: pE18.

The gaucherie and confusion of early manhood; review of *The Year of Fears*. *G&M* Oct 17, 1987: pE4.

Introspection; review of *Standing Flight*. *G&M* Jan 31, 1987: pE18.

Is this the ultimate CanLit novel?; review of *Canadian Sunset*. *G&M* Feb 28, 1987: pE20.

Latin terror; review of *A Long Night of Death*. *G&M* Aug 22, 1987: pC14.

[Untitled]; reviews of *The Swell Season* and *A Model Lover*. *Cross Can Writ Q* 1987; Vol 9 No 1: p19–20.

[Untitled]; reviews of short story collections. *Cross Can Writ Q* 1987; Vol 9 No 3–4: p46–47.

Carin, Michael

Montrealer's 'time bus' tours superpowers' war zone; review of *The Moon Goddess and the Son*. *MG* Feb 14, 1987: pB8.

These 'night drivers' travel stark roads that enjoy neither beginning nor an end; review of *Night Driving*. photo · *MG* April 25, 1987: pH12.

Carley, Dave

The auntie goes down under; short story. photo · *TS* Aug 30, 1987: pD5.

Carley, James P.

The romance of the Far East; review of *The Moneylenders of Shahpur*. *G&M* July 25, 1987: pC15.

Carman, Candace

[Untitled]; review of *A Hero Travels Light*. *Books in Can* Jan-Feb 1987; Vol 16 No 1: p25.

Carpenter, David

What we talk about when we talk about Carver; essay. photo · *Descant (special issue)* Spring-Summer 1987; Vol 18 No 1–2: p20–43.

Carpentier, André

Portrait bougé d'André B. (extraits de journal); journal excerpts. *Liberté* Feb 1987; Vol 29 No 1: p63–65.

Carr, Brenda

Litany; poem. *CV 2* Summer 1987; Vol 10 No 4: p14–15.

Carr, Graham

"All we North Americans": literary culture and the continentalist ideal, 1919–1939; article. *Amer R of Can Studies* Summer 1987; Vol 17 No 2: p145–157.

Dated lives: English-Canadian literary biography; article. *Essays on Can Writ* Winter 1987; No 35: p57–73.

[Untitled]; review of *Spider Blues*. *Poetry Can R* Spring 1987; Vol 8 No 2–3: p61–62.

Carrier, Denis

[Untitled]; review of *Theatre and Politics in Modern Quebec*. *Theatre Hist in Can* Fall 1987; Vol 8 No 2: p243–245.

Carrier, Roch

Québec 10 / 10: bientôt 100 titres; essay. photo · *MD* Nov 14, 1987: pD20.

Carrington, Ildikó de Papp

A Swiftian sermon; review of *The Handmaid's Tale*. *Essays on Can Writ* Spring 1987; No 34: p127–132.

Carson, Ann

Straining credulity; review of *Le Coupeur de têtes*. *Prairie Fire* Summer 1987; Vol 8 No 2: p75–76.

Carson, Judith

[Untitled]; reviews of *Flight Against Time* and *The Late Great Human Road Show*. *Can Forum* Aug-Sept 1987; Vol 67 No 771: p48–49.

Carson, Susan

Clarkson: I want to make book publishing pay; interview with Adrienne Clarkson. photo · *MG* Dec 7, 1987: pB12.

Carver, Peter

Major's realistic epistles to Springsteen; review of *Dear Bruce Springsteen*. photo · *Quill & Quire (Books for Young People)* Aug 1987; Vol 53 No 8: p4.

Past and present merge in painful, haunting tales; reviews of *False Face* and *Who Is Frances Rain?*. photo · *Quill & Quire (Books for Young People)* Oct 1987; Vol 53 No 10: p10.

Salmonberry Wine a rare concoction of complex issues and gutsy realism; review. photo · *Quill & Quire (Books for Young People)* April 1987; Vol 53 No 4: p3.

[Untitled]; review of *Jacob Two-Two and the Dinosaur*. *Quill & Quire (Books for Young People)* April 1987; Vol 53 No 4: p9.

[Untitled]; review of *Hidden Gold Mystery*. *Quill & Quire (Books for Young People)* June 1987; Vol 53 No 6: p10.

Casas, Maria

Chit chat; column. *Quill & Quire (Books for Young People)* April 1987; Vol 53 No 4: p3.

Chit chat; column. *Quill & Quire (Books for Young People)* June 1987; Vol 53 No 6: p3.

Chit chat; column. *Quill & Quire (Books for Young People)* Aug 1987; Vol 53 No 8: p3.

Chit chat; column. *Quill & Quire (Books for Young People)* Oct 1987; Vol 53 No 10: p8.

Casey, Jane

Editorial. *CV 2* Spring 1987; Vol 10 No 3: p6–7.

Castelo, Adelle

[Untitled]; review of *The Life of Helen Alone*. *Quill & Quire* Jan 1987; Vol 53 No 1: p27–28.

[Untitled]; review of *Dzelarhons*. *Quill & Quire* March 1987; Vol 53 No 3: p73.

[Untitled]; review of *Brazilian Journal*. *Idler* Sept-Oct 1987; No 14: p49.

Castro, Ginette

[Untitled]; review of *La Nouvelle barre du jour* (special issue). *Études can* June 1987; No 22: p131.

Cathers, Ken

Devon; poem. *Arc* Spring 1987; No 18: p16.

The end; poem. *Arc* Spring 1987; No 18: p15.

These are the houses; poem. *Event* Summer 1987; Vol 16 No 2: p102.

Cauchon, Paul

Anne Hébert, Wilfrid Lemoyne, Ginette Anfousse reçoivent les premiers prix Fleury-Mesplet; article. photo · *MD* Nov 20, 1987: p13–14.

Arlette Cousture obtient le Prix du public; article. photo · *MD* Nov 24, 1987: p11.

La Bibliothèque Nationale fait sensation au Salon du livre; article. photo · *MD* Nov 21, 1987: pA7.

Cause toujours ma Clémence. . . .; article. photo · *MD* April 10, 1987: p13.

Ceux et celles qui nous disent qui lire; article. *MD* May 2, 1987: pD1, D8.

Godin, lauréat de la ville de Montréal; article. photo · *MD* Nov 20, 1987: p12.

Marie Cardinal: la drogue comme révélateur; article. photo · *MD* Nov 14, 1987: pD13, D19.

Même Proust y trouve son compte; article. photo · *MD* Nov 24, 1987: p11.

Ne s'improvise pas improvisateur qui veut!; column. *MD* Jan 21, 1987: p7.

On se marche sur les pieds au Salon; article. photo · *MD* Nov 23, 1987: p1, 8.

Le Salon du livre le plus populaire depuis dix ans; article. photo · *MD* Nov 25, 1987: p11.

Le Salon du livre se veut montréalais; article. photo · *MD* Nov 6, 1987: p13.

Solitaire, voyeuse et voyante; article. photo · *MD* Nov 6, 1987: p15.

[Untitled]; notice. photo · *MD* Oct 9, 1987: p15.

[Untitled]; notice. *MD* Dec 4, 1987: p15.

[Untitled]; notice. *MD* Dec 11, 1987: p13.

Les Voisins: scènes de la vie de banlieue; article. photo · *MD* Sept 25, 1987: p15.

Voyage théâtral dans la francophonie; article. photo · *MD* Aug 29, 1987: pC3.

Caulder, Colline

Proof that poetry is not dead; review of *Diary of Desire*. *TS* Oct 25, 1987: pA18.

TV's generation suffers detachment; reviews of *The Blue House* and *Not Noir*. *TS* Nov 28, 1987: pM5.

Cavell, Richard

Demon of analogy; review of *L'Itinerario del senso nella narrativa di Malcolm Lowry*. *Can Lit* Spring 1987; No 112: p87–88.

Cay, Marilyn

Cold morning; poem. *NeWest R* Sept 1987; Vol 13 No 1: p15.

Chamberlain, Adrian

Neepawa mourns Laurence; article. photo · *WFP* Jan 6, 1987: p1, 4.

Chamberlain, Timothy

[Untitled]; review of *Margaret Atwood's CanLit Foodbook*. *Books in Can* Dec 1987; Vol 16 No 9: p27.

Chamberland, Paul

Le Dieu argent: l'aveuglement des riches; letter to the editor. *MD* Nov 16, 1987: p7.

Chamberland, Roger

Bibliographie de Jacques Brault; bibliography. *Voix et images* Winter 1987; No 35: p256–264.

Champagne, Lyse

Fifi; short story. *Room of One's Own* Sept 1987; Vol 11 No 4: p90–98.

Same-day return; short story. illus · *Antigonish R* 1987; No 69–70: p77–86.

Chan, Weyman

Another man's shoes; short story. illus · *CH (Sunday Magazine)* July 19, 1987: p6–10.

[Untitled]; review of *Black Swan*. *Dandelion* Spring-Summer 1987; Vol 14 No 1: p87–89.

Chanin, Lawrence

[Untitled]; review of *The Secret Journal of Alexander Mackenzie*. *Can Auth & Book* Summer 1987; Vol 62 No 4: p24.

Chapman, Geoff

Danger! A trained assassin at work; review of *The Next Best Thing*. *TS* June 14, 1987: pA18.

I say, a hero too prim, too precious, eh wot?; review of *No Holds Barred*. *TS* May 9, 1987: pM4.

One slick thriller – and another that's not so slick; review of *The Last White Man in Panama*. *TS* Oct 18, 1987: pC8.

Charach, Ron

And the shoeshine man dreams; poem. *Descant* Winter 1987; Vol 18 No 4: p30.

The cage dweller; poem. *Prism* Summer 1987; Vol 25 No 4: p98–99.

Dagwood at seven A.M.; poem. *Grain* Fall 1987; Vol 15 No 3: p34–35.

A final celebration; poem. *Matrix* Spring 1987; No 24: p35.

Funny poem with a pun; poem. *New Q* Winter 1987; Vol 6 No 4: p70–71.

Him, men; poem. *New Q* Winter 1987; Vol 6 No 4: p69.

I kill the afternoon; poem. *Poetry Can R* Fall 1987; Vol 9 No 1: p28.

In search of Mr Green; poem. *Queen's Q* Summer 1987; Vol 94 No 2: p442–443.

In the room of airtight windows; poem, includes essay. biog photo · *Cross Can Writ Q* 1987; Vol 9 No 1: p17.

In the station of echoes; poem. *New Q* Spring-Summer 1987; Vol 7 No 1–2: p181.

Julius Dithers in the morning; poem. *Grain* Fall 1987; Vol 15 No 3: p36–37.

Labour and delivery; poem. *Queen's Q* Autumn 1987; Vol 94 No 3: p641–642.

Listen: it is Dagwood; poem. *Grain* Fall 1987; Vol 15 No 3: p32–33.

My new mouth; poem. *Arc* Fall 1987; No 19: p51.

So Dad got the suits; poem. *New Q* Spring-Summer 1987; Vol 7 No 1–2: p182–183.

Someone else's fire; poem. *Poetry Can R* Fall 1987; Vol 9 No 1: p28.

To see my friends; poem. *Descant* Winter 1987; Vol 18 No 4: p27–28.

The versatile body; poem. *Arc* Fall 1987; No 19: p52.

A walk through the one lung; poem. *Poetry Can R* Fall 1987; Vol 9 No 1: p28.

A welder's dream; poem. *Descant* Winter 1987; Vol 18 No 4: p29.

You would have to live with it; poem. *Poetry Can R* Fall 1987; Vol 9 No 1: p28.

Charbonneau, Frédéric

Hésitation; review of *Clara*. *Lettres québec* Autumn 1987; No 47: p70.

Virgile; short story. *Moebius* Autumn 1987; No 34: p49–57.

Charney, Ann

Leaving; short story. illus · *Can Auth & Book* Winter 1987; Vol 62 No 2: p18–20.

Men need heroes; short story. *Descant (special issue)* Spring-Summer 1987; Vol 18 No 1–2: p147–154.

Charron, Claude

Probablement l'Espagne, le premier roman de Claude Charron; excerpt. photo · *MD* Oct 31, 1987: pD1, D8.

Charron, François

Le châssis du rêveur; poem. *Estuaire* Winter 1986–87; No 43: p9.

Une chose très calme; poem. *Estuaire* Winter 1986–87; No 43: p10.

Une ligne noire; poem. *Estuaire* Winter 1986–87; No 43: p8.

L'obstacle est inséparable du temps; poem. *Estuaire* Winter 1986–87; No 43: p7.

Le mensonge lèche nos yeux; poem. *Estuaire* Winter 1986–87; No 43: p8.

La sensation de mon corps; poem. *Estuaire* Winter 1986–87; No 43: p9.

Chase, Gillean

Obituaries; poem. *Fireweed* Winter 1987; No 24: p74–75.

Chassay, Jean-François

Les bienfaits de la bombe; review of *Les Samourailles*. *MD* Dec 5, 1987: pD4.

Personnages en quête d'eux-mêmes; review of *Le Sexe des étoiles*. photo · *MD* Dec 12, 1987: pD4.

Radiographie urbaine; review of *Au milieu, la montagne*. photo · *MD* Oct 24, 1987: pD3.

Chast, Roz

A girl's best friend is her skate; review of *I Want a Dog*. *NYT Book R* Nov 8, 1987: p32.

Chenier, Ray

The legend of the raccoon; short story. *Can Fic Mag (special issue)* 1987; No 60: p158–159.

Cherry, Frances

January sales; short story. *Room of One's Own* Sept 1987; Vol 11 No 4: p80–84.

Cherry, Zena

'Great literary dinner' attracts 17 authors; column. *G&M* Oct 29, 1987: pA20.

Leacock celebration honors medal winner; column. *G&M* May 26, 1987: pD12.

London dinner honors authors from Canada; column. *G&M* Jan 22, 1987: pA17.

Chisvin, Sharon

Promise of spring; short story. photo · *TS* July 16, 1987: pF7.

Chittick, Kathryn

Putrefying sore; reviews of fictional works. *Can Lit* Spring 1987; No 112: p128–129.

Chodakowski, K.

Is it in question; poem. *Alpha* Winter 1987; Vol 11: p10.

Chodan, Lucinda

Erika Ritter: a shlep as bewildered as her audience; article. photo · *MG* Oct 31, 1987: pD13.

Hidden in prairies are little oddities, large truths; review of *Beyond Forget*. photo · *MG* Jan 31, 1987: pB8.

The Philadelphia experiment: a disaster in Canada, Duddy tries again in U.S.; article. photo · *MG* Sept 29, 1987: pB5.

Unlikely characters populate realistic Calgary urbanscape; review of *Between Men*. photo · *MG* Oct 24, 1987: pJ13.

Choyce, Lesley

The conjugal visit; poem. *New Q* Spring-Summer 1987; Vol 7 No 1–2: p151.

A degree in nothingness; poem. *Germination* Fall 1987; Vol 11 No 1: p31.

East coast report: BS is alive and well in Halifax; regional column. *Poetry Can R* Summer 1987; Vol 8 No 4: p16.

East Coast report: Labrador and the gift of tongues; regional column. *Poetry Can R* Spring 1987; Vol 8 No 1–2: p14–15.

The mermaid inn: catching up with old ideas; essay. photo · *G&M* Dec 5, 1987: pD6.

My brother's Winnebago; poem. *New Q* Spring-Summer 1987; Vol 7 No 1–2: p150.

One small step; essay. *Books in Can* May 1987; Vol 16 No 4: p4–6.

President Marcos and the 3000 pairs of shoes; poem. *Germination* Fall 1987; Vol 11 No 1: p30.

Seasonal adjustments; poem. *New Q* Winter 1987; Vol 6 No 4: p72.

This poem; poem. *Germination* Fall 1987; Vol 11 No 1: p32–34.

[Untitled]; essay. photo · *Cross Can Writ Q* 1987; Vol 9 No 3–4: p25–26.

Wildcat strike at the angst mine; poem. *New Q* Winter 1987; Vol 6 No 4: p73–74.

Christakos, Margaret

Not Egypt; poem. *Writing* Dec 1987; No 20: p20–24.

Christensen, Peter

The war against money; short story. *Event* Summer 1987; Vol 16 No 2: p83–85.

Christie, Linda

A series of filth; poem. *Antigonish R* 1987; No 69–70: p203.

Christy, Jim

The mermaid inn: history in the underground; essay. photo · *G&M* July 11, 1987: pD6.

Chryssoulakis, Mary

Sisters; poem. *Can Auth & Book* Winter 1987; Vol 62 No 2: p22.

Cimon, Anne

Beachcomber; poem. *Waves* Winter 1987; Vol 15 No 3: p67.

Literary funding in Quebec; article. *Cross Can Writ Q* 1987; Vol 9 No 3–4: p31, 64.

[Untitled]; reviews of *Noman's Land* and *Queen of the Headaches*. *Cross Can Writ Q* 1987; Vol 9 No 1: p20–21.

[Untitled]; reviews of poetry books. *Poetry Can R* Spring 1987; Vol 8 No 2–3: p62.

[Untitled]; review of *Woman in the Woods*. *Rubicon* Spring 1987; No 8: p215–216.

[Untitled]; review of *Cloud Gate*. *Rubicon* Spring 1987; No 8: p221–222.

[Untitled]; letter to the editor. *Books in Can* Jan-Feb 1987; Vol 16 No 1: p38.

[Untitled]; reviews. *Cross Can Writ Q* 1987; Vol 9 No 3–4: p47–48.

Clark, Eliza

Cameo; short story. illus · *Fireweed* Winter 1987; No 24: p71–72.

Clark, Hilary

Autumn ghazal; poem. *Writing* 1987; No 18: p30.

Natural history; poem. *Writing* 1987; No 18: p30.

Winter ghazal; poem. *Writing* 1987; No 18: p29.

Clark, Joan

War stories; short story. *Fiddlehead* Winter 1987; No 154: p28–38.

Clark, Philip

Franco-Manitoban satire translates sense of deja vu; theatre review of *Avant qu'les autres le fassent*. *WFP* Oct 17, 1987: p34.

French play tackles social problems; theatre review of *Les Tremblay 2*. *WFP* April 4, 1987: p23.

Letinsky Cafe dishes out fantasy play focusing on ghost of Marilyn Monroe; theatre review. *WFP* Feb 7, 1987: p23.

Clark, Ron

Obit(e)uary; poem. *NeWest R* Sept 1987; Vol 13 No 1: p16.

Ray Lull's biggest regret; poem. *NeWest R* Sept 1987; Vol 13 No 1: p16.

[Untitled]; review of *Pieces of Map, Pieces of Music*. *Wascana R* Spring 1987; Vol 22 No 1: p92–95.

Clark, William

'Grand old man' Voaden sees play revived at 84; article. photo · *TS* April 5, 1987: pD6.

Clarke, George Elliott

How exile melts to a hundred roses: postscript; prose poem. *Germination* Fall 1987; Vol 11 No 1: p15.

Look homeward, anti-hero, and be enraged; poem, includes note. *Germination* Fall 1987; Vol 11 No 1: p10.

Love poem / song regarding Weymouth Falls: postscript; poem. *Germination* Fall 1987; Vol 11 No 1: p14.

Monologue for Selah bringing spring to Weymouth Falls; poem. *Germination* Fall 1987; Vol 11 No 1: p12.

Night train to Weymouth Falls; poem. *Germination* Fall 1987; Vol 11 No 1: p11.

Passion without precision; review of *The Uncollected Acorn*. *Atlan Prov Book R* May-June 1987; Vol 14 No 2: p11.

Proverbs of Weymouth Falls; poem. *Germination* Fall 1987; Vol 11 No 1: p13.

Clegg, Sherri

Actors' message not lost on kids; article. photo · *CH* April 2, 1987: pD11.

Legg pulls off one-man show; theatre review of *A Terrible Beauty*. *CH* April 4, 1987: pB6.

New troupe doesn't shun controversy; article. *CH* April 10, 1987: pE1.

Clément, Louis-Maxime

[Untitled]; poetry excerpt from *Nekuia (traces des morts)*. *Estuaire* Winter 1986–87; No 43: p27–31.

Clenman, Donia

Children on a swing; poem. *Poetry Can R* Summer 1987; Vol 8 No 4: p33.

The crystal chandelier; poem. *Poetry Can R* Summer 1987; Vol 8 No 4: p33.

The dead umbrella; poem. *Poetry Can R* Summer 1987; Vol 8 No 4: p33.

My hands smell of sap; poem. *Poetry Can R* Summer 1987; Vol 8 No 4: p33.

The newspaper girl; poem. *Poetry Can R* Summer 1987; Vol 8 No 4: p33.

On the island; poem. *Poetry Can R* Summer 1987; Vol 8 No 4: p33.

Poverty; poem. *Poetry Can R* Summer 1987; Vol 8 No 4: p33.

Clenman, Donia Blumenfeld

Crete; poem. *Can Forum* March 1987; Vol 66 No 767: p31.

The eclipse; poem. *Can Forum* March 1987; Vol 66 No 767: p30–31.

Greek landscape; poem. *Can Forum* March 1987; Vol 66 No 767: p31.

In Vancouver with Emily; poem. *Can Forum* March 1987; Vol 66 No 767: p30.

A spark of the divine; poems. *Can Forum* March 1987; Vol 66 No 767: p30–31.

Stratford at night; poem. *Can Forum* March 1987; Vol 66 No 767: p31.

Clery, Val

Musicians jazz up Ondaatje poetry; column. *TS* Nov 26, 1987: pB3.

Cleverley, Fred

Rohmer spins good yarn; review of *Rommel and Patton*. *WFP* Jan 10, 1987: p66.

Cliche, Anne Élaine

Paradigme, palimpseste, pastiche, parodie dans Maryse de Francine Noël; article. *Voix et images* Spring 1987; Vol 12 No 3: p430–438.

Cliche, Élène

[Untitled]; review of *L'Oeuvre romanesque de Marie-Claire Blais*. *Voix et images* Winter 1987; No 35: p318–321.

Clifford, Wayne

[Untitled]; poetry excerpt from On Abducting the Cello. *Quarry* Winter 1987; Vol 36 No 1: p109–111.

Cloutier, Cécile

De poetica; essay. *MD (L'Express de Toronto)* March 17, 1987: p5.

L'esthétique de "Jolis deuils"; article. *Can Lit* Spring 1987; No 112: p40–47.

Clute, John

Embracing the wilderness; reviews of *The Oxford Book of Canadian Short Stories in English* and *Bluebeard's Egg*. *Times Lit Supp* June 12, 1987; No 4393: p626.

Coates, Carrol F.

Theatre encore; reviews of *L'Ours et le kangourou* and *Au septième ciel*. *Can Lit* Winter 1987; No 115: p255–257.

Coates, Donna

Hodgins still has the knack; review of *The Honorary Patron*. photo · *CH* Nov 8, 1987: pE6.

Cochrane, Michael G.

Divorce picnic; short story. photo · *TS* July 9, 1987: pA16.

Coffey, Michael

Grammatology & economy; article. photo · *Open Letter (special issue)* Fall 1987; Vol 6 No 9: p27–38.

Cogswell, Fred

Comes back to spoil my rest; poem. *Poetry Can R* Summer 1987; Vol 8 No 4: p29.

Inside the chapel: Villa Madonna; poem. *Fiddlehead* Winter 1987; No 154: p70–73.

The jay; poem. *Poetry Can R* Summer 1987; Vol 8 No 4: p29.

Wordsworth county; poem. *Antigonish R* 1987; No 69–70: p164.

Cohen, Leonard

[Untitled]; essay. *Brick (special issue)* Summer 1987; No 30: p56.

Cohen, Matt

Emotional arithmetic; prose excerpt from a work in progress. illus · *Books in Can* Aug-Sept 1987; Vol 16 No 6: p11–12.

Cohn, Martin

Copyright law would fine pirates $1 million; article. *TS* May 28, 1987: pA1, A4.

How to sell free trade? Bash Ontario, Richler says; article. photo · *TS* Nov 19, 1987: pA1, A8.

Cole, Norma

[Untitled]; poetry excerpt from *Mace Hill Remap*. *Writing* Dec 1987; No 20: p35–43.

Coleman, Bob

The Yankee devils!; review of *The Alley Cat*. *NYT Book R* Jan 11, 1987: p14.

Coleman, J. Winnett

Killing him softly; short story. *Room of One's Own* Sept 1987; Vol 11 No 4: p73–79.

Coleman, Patrick

Settling with style; review of *The Blue Ontario Hemingway Boat Race*. *Essays on Can Writ* Winter 1987; No 35: p152–155.

Collet, Paulette

De l'ouest, des nouvelles et de l'histoire; reviews of short story books. photo · *Lettres québec* Summer 1987; No 46: p68–70.

Racisme et complexes dans l'ouest; review of *Sans bon sang*. photo · *Lettres québec* Autumn 1987; No 47: p68–69.

La Sagouine: un regard perçant et lucide, source d'espoir; article. *Can Drama* 1987; Vol 13 No 1: p43–49.

Collin, Solange

. . . .Le Théâtre des Cuisines 1; essay. illus · *La Nouvelle barre du jour (special issue)* March 1987; No 196: p29–31.

Collins, Chris

37 volumes in a shoebox; poem. *NeWest R* Sept 1987; Vol 13 No 1: p11.

My brother, in light; poem. *NeWest R* Sept 1987; Vol 13 No 1: p11.

Collins, Sean

War play pokes fun at military, politicians; article. photo · *TS (Neighbours)* May 5, 1987: p24.

Collins, Suzanne

Bomber princess; poem. *Poetry Can R* Spring 1987; Vol 8 No 1–2: p15.

Cats; poem. *Poetry Can R* Spring 1987; Vol 8 No 1–2: p15.

Old spice; poem. *Poetry Can R* Spring 1987; Vol 8 No 1–2: p15.

Collins, Terry

Boxing; poem. *Arc* Fall 1987; No 19: p53.

Comeau, Paul-André

À l'heure du glasnost comment exorciser le social-réalisme. . . .; article. photo · *MD* Aug 1, 1987: pC5.

Le primat et le patriote; review of *La Couleur du sang*. *MD* Dec 12, 1987: pD8.

Qui a peur des héritiers de Papineau?; review of *La Fin de l'histoire*. *MD* March 14, 1987: pD7.

Comensoli, Viviana

Transculture; reviews of poetry books. *Can Lit* Spring 1987; No 112: p120–123.

Conant, Oliver

[Untitled]; review of *Entering Fire*. *NYT Book R* June 7, 1987: p30.

[Untitled]; review of *The Ring Master*. *NYT Book R* Nov 1, 1987: p24.

Conlogue, Ray

Appealing performer wasted in aimless ghost town saga; theatre review of *Tag in a Ghost Town*. photo · *G&M* May 15, 1987: pD10.

Bat Masterson deals with words and how they can shape identity; theatre review of *Bat Masterson's Last Regular Job*. photo · *G&M* Oct 10, 1987: pC6.

Best food forward in the theatre world; article. *G&M* Jan 10, 1987: pE3.

Black Bonspiel presents a devil of a problem; theatre review of *The Black Bonspiel of Wullie MacCrimmon*. photo · *G&M* April 18, 1987: pC7.

Clashes of tone mute play's voice; theatre review of *Precipice*. photo · *G&M* Jan 14, 1987: pC8.

Comedy with a clever twist; theatre review of *The Melville Boys*. photo · *G&M* Feb 27, 1987: pD11.

Destinations strays off course despite strong cast, director; theatre review of *All Other Destinations Are Cancelled*. photo · *G&M* Feb 25, 1987: pC10.

Dilemma in Bordertown; theatre review of *Bordertown Cafe*. photo · *G&M* July 4, 1987: pC9.

Evocative, but laced with ennui; theatre review of *Opium*. photo · *G&M* Jan 14, 1987: pC7.

Family drama lacks depth; theatre review of *South of Heaven*. photo · *G&M* Nov 23, 1987: pC12.

Farmer's Rebellion stands test of time; theatre review of *1837: The Farmers' Revolt*. *G&M* Dec 8, 1987: pD7.

Flaws show in Beautiful City; theatre review. photo · *G&M* Oct 1, 1987: pD5.

French version of Walker play riddled with extra problems; theatre review of *L'Amour en deroute*. photo · *G&M* Nov 16, 1987: pD12.

From profound and provocative to simplistic and obscure; article. photo · *G&M* Dec 26, 1987: pC3.

Gifted playwright never lost sense of compassion, outrage; article. photo · *G&M* Nov 20, 1987: pD5.

Girls a slick, witty musical; theatre review of *Girls in the Gang*. photo · *G&M* July 2, 1987: pD3.

Gonna take a sentimental journey; theatre review of *Africa Solo*. photo · *G&M* Nov 18, 1987: pC7.

Horror spoof keeps audience on edge; theatre review of *The Vile Governess & Other Psychodramas*. photo · *G&M* Sept 10, 1987: pD3.

I Am Yours wages a comedy war of women; theatre review. photo · *G&M* Nov 18, 1987: pC6.

Intimate Admiration has few insights, wooden dialogue; theatre review. photo · *G&M* July 1, 1987: pC5.

Jacob Two-Two meets The Fang in zippy musical; theatre review. photo · *G&M* Oct 26, 1987: pC11.

Jewel shines with unexpected qualities; theatre review of *Jewel*. photo · *G&M* April 27, 1987: pC12.

Kids speak on their own behalf; theatre review of *Forever Young*. photo · *G&M* Jan 3, 1987: pE8.

Making saint of Trotsky pays off for play; theatre review of *Detaining Mr. Trotsky*. photo · *G&M* Oct 23, 1987: pD13.

Mikado, B-Movie big Dora winners; article. photo · *G&M* June 23, 1987: pD8.

Mixing spirits, bingo and genius; article. photo · *G&M* Nov 21, 1987: pC5.

Much to do with very little; theatre review of *Tragedy of Manners*. *G&M* Oct 5, 1987: pD11.

Mystifying show looks at nature of art, magic; theatre review of *Pericles Prince of Tyre by William Shakespeare*. photo · *G&M* April 10, 1987: pC6.

Neptune cooks up a delicious satire; theatre review of *Tartuffe*. photo · *G&M* April 17, 1987: pC7.

Palmer play shows surprising sweetness; theatre review of *A Day at the Beach*. photo · *G&M* Dec 12, 1987: pC8.

Playwright avoids 'giving answers'; article. photo · *G&M* March 2, 1987: pD9.

The Postman Rings Once too often; theatre review. photo · *G&M* Oct 8, 1987: pD5.

Premieres spice Tarragon season; column. photo · *G&M* April 23, 1987: pC1.

Puppetry the great strength of this Peter and the Wolf; theatre review of *Loving You Is Like Trying to Sing Along with Frank Sinatra*. *G&M* April 24, 1987: pC7.

Reed remembered for 'wonderful' work; column. *G&M* Sept 22, 1987: pD7.

The Rez Sisters lacks a satisfying resolution; theatre review. photo · *G&M* Nov 26, 1987: pA29.

Rollicking rock and old-time religion stoke Fire; theatre review. photo · *G&M* Jan 13, 1987: pC7.

Shuttling between layers of reality; theatre review of *War Babies*. photo · *G&M* March 4, 1987: pC8.

A singular scrubwoman; article about Viola Leger. photo · *G&M* May 2, 1987: pC1, C5.

Some advances, some retreats in theatre season selections; column. photo · *G&M* Aug 28, 1987: pD8.

Some good moments in Cradle Pin despite awkward direction; theatre review. photo · *G&M* Sept 17, 1987: pD5.

'Squowse' sparkles for kids; theatre review of *Willie the Squowse*. photo · *G&M* Dec 11, 1987: pD6.

Story of hit play's fade-out reads like a B-Movie script; article. photo · *G&M* April 16, 1987: pD1.

Tete-a-Tete worthwhile for its wit and elegance; theatre review. photo · *G&M* Nov 13, 1987: pD13.

Theatre Direct probes urban kids' reality; theatre reviews of *The Snake Lady* and *Thin Ice*. *G&M* April 29, 1987: pC7.

Tired dreams and holy fools; theatre review of *Unexpected Moves*. photo · *G&M* Oct 28, 1987: pC7.

'Titanic encounter' typifies rising star's style; theatre review of *Le Printemps, monsieur Deslauriers*. photo · *G&M* April 16, 1987: pD3.

Toronto, Mississippi is well worth a visit; theatre review. photo · *G&M* Oct 7, 1987: pC8.

Tragic truth in Being at Home; theatre review of *Being at Home with Claude*. photo · *G&M* April 8, 1987: pC8.

Tremblay looks in the mirror and doesn't like what he sees; theatre review of *Le Vrai monde?*. photo · *G&M* Oct 2, 1987: pD10.

A triumph of Gothic comedy; theatre review of *Zastrozzi*. photo · *G&M* May 14, 1987: pC3.

Turtle Jazz excruciating; theatre review. photo · *G&M* June 27, 1987: pE8.

Uneven but energetic look at life as a native woman; theatre review of *Aria*. *G&M* March 12, 1987: pC7.

Up Your Alley is a jangle of conflicting styles; theatre review. photo · *G&M* Jan 15, 1987: pD4.

Vanity Press experiences first-play problems; theatre review. *G&M* March 14, 1987: pE10.

Walker has left the city but the city hasn't left him; article. photo · *G&M* Sept 19, 1987: pC1, C4.

Conn, Jan

Correll; poem. *Prairie Fire* Summer 1987; Vol 8 No 2: p41–42.

Farm-aid, Champaign-Urbana, September, 1985; poem. *Prairie Fire* Summer 1987; Vol 8 No 2: p40.

Connor, H.W.

From mind to mind; reviews of *Night Studies* and *Wishbones*. *Can Lit* Spring 1987; No 112: p118–120.

Conolly, L.W.

Dramatic trilogies; review of *The Power Plays*. *Can Lit* Spring 1987; No 112: p110–112.

[Untitled]; review of *Five from the Fringe*. *World Lit in Eng* Spring 1987; Vol 27 No 1: p56–58.

[Untitled]; review of *Canadian Literature in English*. *Theatre Hist in Can* Fall 1987; Vol 8 No 2: p247–249.

[Untitled]; review of *All the Bright Company*. *Can Drama* 1987; Vol 13 No 2: p231–233.

Conway, Anne-Marie

Under the red robe; review of *The Color of Blood*. *Times Lit Supp* Oct 2, 1987; No 4409: p1073.

Cook, Gregory M.

Implication by omission; letter to the editor. *Quill & Quire* April 1987; Vol 53 No 4: p3.

Cookshaw, Marlene

The Queen of Burnaby; poem. *Prism* Autumn 1987; Vol 26 No 1: p54.

Roulette; poem. *Prism* Autumn 1987; Vol 26 No 1: p56–57.

Sammy explains evolution; poem. *Prism* Autumn 1987; Vol 26 No 1: p55.

Cooley, Dennis

Amusement park; poem. *Prism* Summer 1987; Vol 25 No 4: p27–28.

April showers; poem. *NeWest R* April 1987; Vol 12 No 8: p8.

Breaking & entering (thoughts on line breaks); essay, includes poem. *Open Letter* Spring 1987; Vol 6 No 7: p77–99.

The Canadian was in the frosting house; poem. *NeWest R* Sept 1987; Vol 13 No 1: p19.

Driving home; poem. *Cross Can Writ Q* 1987; Vol 9 No 1: p27.

The muse of absence; poem. *Prairie Fire* Winter 1987–88; Vol 8 No 4: p34.

Parchment; poem. *Prairie Fire* Winter 1987–88; Vol 8 No 4: p35.

[Untitled]; poetry excerpt from *Planting*. *Prairie Fire* Winter 1987–88; Vol 8 No 4: p33.

The vernacular muse in prairie poetry (conclusion); article. *Prairie Fire* Autumn 1987; Vol 8 No 3: p88–94.

The vernacular muse in prairie poetry (Part 3); article. *Prairie Fire* Summer 1987; Vol 8 No 2: p49–53.

The vernacular muse in prairie poetry (Part Two); article. *Prairie Fire* Spring 1987; Vol 8 No 1: p60–70.

Cooper, Allan

The bee leaves the deep flower reluctantly; poem. *Fiddlehead* Summer 1987; No 152: p46–47.

A note on political poems; editorial. *Germination* Fall 1987; Vol 11 No 1: p25.

The orchard; poem. *Germination* Spring 1987; Vol 10 No 2: p52–53.

The poem stalking; essay. *Germination* Fall 1987; Vol 11 No 1: p53–56.

The poems of Edward Gates; introduction. *Germination* Spring 1987; Vol 10 No 2: p27–28.

The poems of George El[l]iott Clarke; introduction. *Germination* Fall 1987; Vol 11 No 1: p7–8.

The poems of Lorraine Vernon; introduction. *Germination* Fall 1987; Vol 11 No 1: p41.

A presence in the earth; essay. *Germination* Spring 1987; Vol 10 No 2: p48–49.

A presence in the earth; poem. *Germination* Spring 1987; Vol 10 No 2: p50.

Ten yellow daffodils; poem. *Germination* Spring 1987; Vol 10 No 2: p51.

Cooper, Richard W.

Bruce Hutchison – senior scribe; biographical article. photo · *Can Auth & Book* Spring 1987; Vol 62 No 3: p5–6.

Copeland, Ann

Another Christmas; short story. *Fiddlehead* Winter 1987; No 154: p75–86.

Another country; short story. *New Q* Spring-Summer 1987; Vol 7 No 1–2: p133–145.

Parting; short story. *U of Windsor R* Spring-Summer 1987; Vol 20 No 2: p31–49.

Copithorne, Judith

Signature ligature significate; poem. *Cross Can Writ Q* 1987; Vol 9 No 3–4: p11.

West coast recollections; article. *Cross Can Writ Q* 1987; Vol 9 No 3–4: p10.

Coppens, Patrick

Etiquette rouge où se reproduisent les étoiles; prose poem. *Moebius (special issue)* Spring 1987; No 32: p63–64.

Coppolino, Andrew

A Canadian in the Garsington circle: Frank Prewett's literary friendships; biographical article. *Studies in Can Lit* 1987; Vol 12 No 2: p273–289.

Corcoran, Dennis

A prose experiment; review of *Cambodia: A Book for People Who Find Television Too Slow. TS* Feb 15, 1987: pA18.

Corcoran, James Dennis

Brian Fawcett; interview. photo · *Books in Can* May 1987; Vol 16 No 4: p38–40.

Corner, Virginia

Nurturing a romantic spirit; article. illus photo · *TS* July 6, 1987: pC1.

Cornish, Mary Lou

[Untitled]; review of *Miss Abigail's Part. Cross Can Writ Q* 1987; Vol 9 No 3–4: p49.

Corrigall, Melodie

The spider; short story. *Room of One's Own* Sept 1987; Vol 11 No 4: p86–89.

Corrigan, Maureen

[Untitled]; review of *Miss Abigail's Part. NYT Book R* March 1, 1987: p20.

Corriveau, Hugues

Dominique Lauzon ou une étonnante vivacité; introduction. *Estuaire* Spring 1987; No 44: p51–52.

Les lieux; prose excerpt from *Mobiles*. illus · *La Nouvelle barre du jour* Feb 1987; No 193: p53–62.

[Untitled]; review of *Vivre n'est pas clair. Estuaire* Spring 1987; No 44: p83.

[Untitled]; review of *Astrales jachères. Estuaire* Summer 1987; No 45: p51–52.

[Untitled]; review of *Écrire la lumière. Estuaire* Summer 1987; No 45: p59.

Cosier, Tony

Driving fallowfield; poem. *Germination* Spring 1987; Vol 10 No 2: p21.

Lodgepole; poem. *Germination* Spring 1987; Vol 10 No 2: p20.

New Year meditation; poem in English and in French translation. *Antigonish R* Winter 1987; No 68: p34–35.

Cosseboom, Ray

The archer; prose poem. *Grain* Spring 1987; Vol 15 No 1: p45.

Back there; prose poem. *Grain* Spring 1987; Vol 15 No 1: p45.

Beyond Hollyhock Hill; prose poem. *Grain* Spring 1987; Vol 15 No 1: p48.

The cosmic woman; prose poem. *Grain* Spring 1987; Vol 15 No 1: p48.

Hieroglyphics; prose poem. *Grain* Spring 1987; Vol 15 No 1: p46.

Laurie; prose poem. *Grain* Spring 1987; Vol 15 No 1: p49.

Quickly sketched; prose poem. *Grain* Spring 1987; Vol 15 No 1: p47.

The subway; prose poem. *Grain* Spring 1987; Vol 15 No 1: p47.

Waiting; prose poem. *Grain* Spring 1987; Vol 15 No 1: p46.

Costopoulos, Olga

Migraine / buzz-saw; poem. *Arc* Spring 1987; No 18: p17.

Côté, Diana-Jocelyne

Toutes les femmes sont fatales; series of linked prose poems. *La Nouvelle barre du jour (special issue)* 1987; No 197: p7–59.

Côté, Lucie

Éclats d'existence; review of *L'Hiver de Mira Christophe. MD* April 28, 1987: p17.

Côté, Marc

Remembrance of things past; review of *Doc. Books in Can* March 1987; Vol 16 No 2: p1718.

Stage fright; article. *Books in Can* June-July 1987; Vol 16 No 5: p3, 5.

[Untitled]; review of *Ha! Ha!. Books in Can* March 1987; Vol 16 No 2: p25.

[Untitled]; review of *Becoming Light. Books in Can* Dec 1987; Vol 16 No 9: p31.

[Untitled]; review of *Islands*. *Books in Can* Dec 1987; Vol 16 No 9: p31.

Côté, Michelle

Artemisia tridentata; essay. *Moebius* Summer 1987; No 33: p71–76.

Cotnoir, Louise

Sous l'angle de la provocation ou quand la théorie imagine; essay. bibliog biog · *La Nouvelle barre du jour (special issue)* 1987; No 201–202: p81–94.

La traversée des miroirs; essay. illus · *La Nouvelle barre du jour (special issue)* March 1987; No 196: p20–25.

With the desire to die; prose excerpt from a work in progress. illus · *La Nouvelle barre du jour* Feb 1987; No 193: p9–18.

Cotterell, Ann

Listings; annotations. *British J of Can Studies* June 1987; Vol 2 No 1: p191–193.

Cottrell, Barbara

Meta's story; poem. *Arc* Fall 1987; No 19: p54.

Priorities; poem. *Arc* Fall 1987; No 19: p56.

A very fine lady; poem. *Arc* Fall 1987; No 19: p55–56.

Couillard, Marie

L'art pictural dans les derniers romans de Marie-Claire Blais; article. *Can Lit* Summer-Fall 1987; No 113–114: p268–272.

Courchesne, Georges-A.

Rapport du jury de composition française; essay, includes introduction. *Études lit* Spring-Summer 1987; Vol 20 No 1: p174–183.

Courtemanche, Gil

Katana, épopée fascinante dont le héros est le Japon; article. photo · *MD* March 28, 1987: pD1, D8.

Cowan, Bert

[Untitled]; review of *The Fisherman's Revenge*. *Books in Can* March 1987; Vol 16 No 2: p25.

[Untitled]; review of *Papers*. *Books in Can* March 1987; Vol 16 No 2: p26.

Cowan, Cindy

[Untitled]; review of *Doc*. *Can Theatre R* Fall 1987; No 52: p95–96.

Cowan, Judith

Autonomie; poem. *Liberté* June 1987; Vol 29 No 3: p51.

Évasion sociale; poem. *Liberté* June 1987; Vol 29 No 3: p53.

À la mémoire de Samuel de Champlain; poem. *Liberté* June 1987; Vol 29 No 3: p52.

News photo; poem. *Matrix* Spring 1987; No 24: p17.

Seacoast; poem. *Arc* Fall 1987; No 19: p57.

Cowan, Teresa

[Untitled]; review of *There's a Dragon in My Closet*. *Quill & Quire (Books for Young People)* April 1987; Vol 53 No 4: p5.

Cox, Yvonne

People: the Genie Awards; column. photo · *Maclean's* March 30, 1987; Vol 100 No 13: p44–45.

People; column. *Maclean's* Jan 12, 1987; Vol 100 No 2: p29.

People; column. photo · *Maclean's* Jan 26, 1987; Vol 100 No 4: p48.

People; column. photo · *Maclean's* Feb 2, 1987; Vol 100 No 5: p32.

People; column. *Maclean's* March 9, 1987; Vol 100 No 10: p48.

People; column. *Maclean's* May 4, 1987; Vol 100 No 18: p54.

People; column. photo · *Maclean's* June 8, 1987; Vol 100 No 23: p46.

People; column. *Maclean's* May 18, 1987; Vol 100 No 20: p36.

People; column. *Maclean's* Aug 17, 1987; Vol 100 No 33: p44.

People; column. photo · *Maclean's* Oct 5, 1987; Vol 100 No 40: p56.

People; column. photo · *Maclean's* Oct 26, 1987; Vol 100 No 43: p34.

People; column. photo · *Maclean's* Nov 2, 1987; Vol 100 No 44: p48.

People; column. *Maclean's* Nov 16, 1987; Vol 100 No 46: p64.

People; column. *Maclean's* Nov 23, 1987; Vol 100 No 47: p46.

People; column. *Maclean's* Dec 21, 1987; Vol 100 No 51: p30.

Crabb, Michael

Troupe's translation of Atwood promises more than it delivers; review of dance based on *Murder in the Dark*. *TS* June 7, 1987: pG2.

Craggs, R.S.

Payment to writers; letter to the editor. *Can Auth & Book* Spring 1987; Vol 62 No 3: p2.

Craig, Terrence

Noticing three poets; reviews of poetry books. *Atlan Prov Book R* May-June 1987; Vol 14 No 2: p10.

Recent poetry; reviews of poetry books. *Atlan Prov Book R* Feb-March 1987; Vol 14 No 1: p18.

Cram, W.A.

Bicycles, shiny birds, and other things that glitter; short story. *Prism* Winter 1987; Vol 25 No 2: p21–28.

Cramer, Abigail

[Untitled]; review of *Can You Catch Josephine?*. *CH* Dec 6, 1987: pD9.

Craven, Joan

Book captures emotional moment for child; reviews of *Big Sarah's Little Boots* and *A Difficult Day*. *CH (Neighbors)* Oct 28, 1987: pA18.

Books offer children world of adventure; reviews. *CH (Neighbors)* April 1, 1987: pA7.

Experts recommend books for children; column. *CH (Neighbors)* Aug 26, 1987: pA4.

Legend of Calgary no ordinary tall tale; column. *CH (Neighbors)* July 8, 1987: pA8.

Perfect time to buy child a favorite book; column. *CH (Neighbors)* Nov 25, 1987: pA12.

Crawford, Trish

The raconteur of the day-care set; article. photo · *TS* Aug 9, 1987: pD1-D2.

Crew, Robert

B-Movie the play gets flood of offers; column. photo · *TS* Feb 11, 1987: pF1.

B-Movie's devilish wit proves nothing succeeds like excess; theatre review of *B-Movie, The Play*. photo · *TS* Jan 23, 1987: pD18.

Barrie audiences responding to Pinsent play; column. photo · *TS* July 27, 1987: pD1.

Bat Masterson keeps on and on; theatre review of *Bat Masterson's Last Regular Job*. photo · *TS* Oct 11, 1987: pC3.

Blyth's Cafe dishes up cliches; theatre review of *Bordertown Cafe*. *TS* June 26, 1987: pE4.

Cabarets, readings, workshops have Stratford in full swing; theatre review of *Miss Balmoral of the Bayview*. photo · *TS* July 19, 1987: pC2.

Conversing with spirits of the dead; survey article. photo · *TS* Dec 26, 1987: pE3.

A Day at the Beach still has a way to go; theatre review. *TS* Dec 7, 1987: pC4.

Dubois' Pericles not perfect but impressive nonetheless; theatre review of *Pericles Prince of Tyre by William Shakespeare*. photo · *TS* April 10, 1987: pD20.

Emily Carr paints a bland wash; theatre review. photo · *TS* Nov 25, 1987: pB5.

The Fabulous Kelley fails to fulfil promise; theatre review. *TS* April 30, 1987: pH3.

Feminists launch festival; article. *TS* Jan 16, 1987: pD17.

Gem of a Jewel needs strong actress; theatre review of *Jewel*. photo · *TS* April 28, 1987: pG3.

Get set for double shot of Dubois; article. photo · *TS* April 4, 1987: pF1, F8.

Heart-warming tale limited but likeable; theatre review of *The Melville Boys*. *TS* Feb 27, 1987: pD21.

Here are the highlights of biggest stage season; column. photo · *TS* Sept 25, 1987: pE3, E6.

Hosanna on high to the queen; theatre review. photo · *TS* May 27, 1987: pE3.

Intelligent writer lost in translating to drama; theatre review of *War Babies*. photo · *TS* March 4, 1987: pB3.

Intimate Admiration one big bore; theatre review. photo · *TS* June 28, 1987: pC2.

Italian troupe offers a touch of class; theatre review of *Together / Ensemble*. *TS* May 13, 1987: pB3.

It's tragic but there goes old Queen St. neighborhood; theatre review of *Tragedy of Manners*. photo · *TS* Oct 4, 1987: pC2.

Lethbridge writer's play to be staged at Stratford; article. photo · *TS* March 2, 1987: pB3.

Like a chameleon Kliest breathes life into Aria's women; theatre review of *Aria*. photo · *TS* March 6, 1987: pD11.

Main course: murder; article about murder-mystery weekends. photo · *TS* Aug 1, 1987: pE1, E3.

The Mikado hits a high note with seven Dora Awards; article. photo · *TS* June 23, 1987: pE3.

Murrell wins top theatre award; article. photo · *TS* Jan 30, 1987: pD21.

Musical circus in tune with children's festival; column. *TS* April 2, 1987: pG3.

Neville to extend stay at Stratford for a year; column. *TS* June 24, 1987: pF1.

New Canadian drama needs leaner approach; theatre review of *All Other Destinations Are Cancelled*. photo · *TS* Feb 25, 1987: pF3.

One-man Bethune show to tour China; column. *TS* March 19, 1987: pE3.

Paula Wing's Lydia is filled with love, joy and rich spirit; column. *TS* Nov 8, 1987: pC2.

Play dares to add levity to legacy; theatre review of *Tête à tête*. photo · *TS* Nov 15, 1987: pC2.

Play talks to handicapped via Elvis; article. photo · *TS* Oct 2, 1987: pE12.

Play's memorable but its production is rather less so; theatre review of *Play Memory*. photo · *TS* July 3, 1987: pD21.

Play's premise unfulfilled; theatre review of *Bachelor-Man*. *TS* Nov 13, 1987: pE26.

Play's real anger diluted: potential George Walker firecracker fizzles into sentimentality; theatre review of *Beautiful City*. photo · *TS* Oct 1, 1987: pE1.

Portrait of Bethune strong on passion; theatre review of *Gone the Burning Sun*. photo · *TS* March 27, 1987: pD22.

PUC stops here for cabaret night; article. *TS* April 24, 1987: pE12.

Space crunch may kill Solar Stage; column. *TS* Aug 9, 1987: pC3.

Spoof of Canadian history a riot of fun; theatre review of *The Mackenzie / Papineau Rebellion*. photo · *TS* April 16, 1987: pC15.

Talented comediennes energetic and funny; theatre review of *Fertility*. *TS* March 6, 1987: pD21.

Talented young writer fails to take off this time; theatre review of *South of Heaven*. photo · *TS* Nov 20, 1987: pE26.

Tamara, Tamara, they'll love it Tamara; column. *TS* Dec 4, 1987: pD27.

Tamara gets a rave in New York Times; column. *TS* Dec 3, 1987: pB1.

Tamara producers work on Casa Loma '88; article. *TS* Dec 2, 1987: pB4.

Taut Trotsky play an intelligent debut; theatre review of *Detaining Mr. Trotsky*. *TS* Oct 22, 1987: pB1.

Theatre people censure censorship; column. photo · *TS* Dec 19, 1987: pK2.

Theatrelife exposes raw side of the stage; theatre review. photo · *TS* March 30, 1987: pB3.

Theatrelife takes typecasting to the limit; article about Graham Harley. photo · *TS* March 27, 1987: pD14.

Thompson play true to form; theatre review of *I Am Yours*. photo · *TS* Nov 18, 1987: pB1.

Three Toronto plays premiere at Calgary fest; article, includes theatre reviews. photo · *TS* Feb 10, 1987: pB4.

Toronto, Mississippi a heartfelt new play; theatre review. *TS* Oct 7, 1987: pD1.

Unexpected Moves jaunty little comedy; theatre review. photo · *TS* Oct 28, 1987: pE2.

Valentine Browne launching 'world tour'; column. photo · *TS* Oct 15, 1987: pE1.

Wacky Cathy Jones returns; theatre review of *Wedding in Texas and Other Stories*. photo · *TS* Feb 18, 1987: pE3.

Weak play an aberration for theatre; theatre review of *Precipice*. photo · *TS* Jan 14, 1987: pF4.

Wild, wacky Vile Governess a delicious spoof of Ibsen angst; theatre review of *The Vile Governess & Other Psychodramas*. photo · *TS* Sept 11, 1987: pE11.

Wrestling tale grip quite easy to slip; theatre review of *Cradle Pin*. photo · *TS* Sept 18, 1987: pD16.

Young Quebec writer pens remarkable play; theatre review of *Being at Home with Claude*. photo · *TS* April 8, 1987: pD3.

Zastrozzi returns in splended form; theatre review. photo · *TS* May 14, 1987: pF3.

Crittenden, Danielle

Typist to the stars; essay. illus · *Idler* Sept-Oct 1987; No 14: p39–44.

Crittenden, Max

Was this book written with Ollie in mind?; review of *Booby Trap*. *TS* July 19, 1987: pA20.

Cronyn, Hume

Bushes could be trees; poem. *Waves* Spring 1987; Vol 15 No 4: p64–65.

Crosta, Suzanne

[Untitled]; review of *Le Pouvoir des mots, les maux du pouvoir*. *U of Toronto Q* Fall 1987; Vol 57 No 1: p212–214.

Crozier, Lorna

Cat, French class, grocery list, etc.; poem. *Malahat R* Sept 1987; No 80: p87.

Cat named desire; poem. *Dandelion* Spring-Summer 1987; Vol 14 No 1: p27.

Cat named solitaire; poem. *Dandelion* Spring-Summer 1987; Vol 14 No 1: p26.

The Goldberg variations; poem. *Can Lit* Spring 1987; No 112: p59.

Not a Berryman (for J.R.); poem. *Border Cross* Summer 1987; Vol 6 No 3: p20.

The Pacific; poem. *Malahat R* Sept 1987; No 80: p88.

Picture: a window, a woman, night; poem. *Poetry Can R* Spring 1987; Vol 8 No 2–3: p25.

Quitting smoking; prose poem. illus · *Border Cross* Summer 1987; Vol 6 No 3: p59.

Crusz, Rienzi

Elegy; poem. *Tor South Asian R* Summer 1987; Vol 6 No 1: p38.

Love poem; poem. *Tor South Asian R* Summer 1987; Vol 6 No 1: p37.

Ode to the muse; poem. *Tor South Asian R* Summer 1987; Vol 6 No 1: p36.

Talking for myself; essay. *Tor South Asian R* Summer 1987; Vol 6 No 1: p29–35.

Csamer, Mary Ellen

Another goodbye; poem. *Matrix* Fall 1987; No 25: p72.

The official truth; letter to the editor. *Books in Can* June-July 1987; Vol 16 No 5: p40.

When the heart goes; poem. *Arc* Fall 1987; No 19: p58.

Cude, Wilfred

Cleverness will prevail; review of *Tales Until Dawn*. photo · *Atlan Prov Book R* Nov-Dec 1987; Vol 14 No 4: p7.

[Untitled]; review of *The Telling of Lies*. *Antigonish R* Winter 1987; No 68: p55–60.

Cuerrier

PSSST; prose poem. illus · *La Nouvelle barre du jour* Feb 1987; No 193: p20–24.

Cuerrier, Yves

Becs électriques (sûrement post-moderne); prose poem. *Estuaire* Spring 1987; No 44: p9–10.

Cuff, John Haslett

Ambitious hockey saga fails to score; television review of *The Last Season*. photo · *G&M* Jan 3, 1987: pE5.

'Compelling' stories from Mrs. Gouzenko; television review of *Voices on the Water*. *G&M* Oct 17, 1987: pC3.

Film draws engaging portrait; column. photo · *G&M* July 23, 1987: pD3.

Fun and games with sharp-tongued Tracey; column. *G&M* May 2, 1987: pC4.

Gambles hedged with returns. article. *G&M* May 30, 1987: pC3.

Kingsley triumphs in Silas Marner; television review of *Murder Sees the Light*. photo · *G&M* March 14, 1987: pE5.

Mini-series bred from Davies' novel; article. photo · *G&M* April 8, 1987: pC7.

Slick Anne sequel takes no chances with success; television review. photo · *G&M* Dec 5, 1987: pC5.

Tramp takes the safe route; television review of *Tramp at the Door*. photo · *G&M* Jan 1, 1987: pC1.

Culík, Jan

Josef Skvorecky; letter to the editor. *Times Lit Supp* Feb 6, 1987; No 4375: p137.

Culley, Peter

Crocodile sweat; poem. *Writing* 1987; No 18: p26–28.

Cumming, Peter

Elizabeth's signs; short story. *U of Windsor R* Spring-Summer 1987; Vol 20 No 2: p68–74.

Curle, Howard

[Untitled]; review of *A Stone Watermelon*. *Border Cross* Summer 1987; Vol 6 No 3: p21.

Curran, Peggy

Jack the Ripper is wealthy MD in thriller with social conscience; review of *Ripper*. *MG* Nov 7, 1987: pK13.

Romantic novel set in India is typical of Canadian writer's British penchant; review of *The Moneylenders of Shahpur*. *MG* Aug 8, 1987: pJ3.

Currie, Ellen

I pledge allegiance to myself; review of *The Elizabeth Stories*. *NYT Book R* July 12, 1987: p11.

Currie, Robert

[The Bones of Their Occasion]; review. photo · *NeWest R* Dec 1987; Vol 13 No 4: p15.

Currie, Rod

Funny theatre piece says life imitates movie life; article. *CH* Jan 24, 1987: pA11.

Hostess fumes over no-shows; article about the Great Literary Dinner Party. photo · *G&M* Aug 28, 1987: pD10.

Incest victim recounts anguish, horror in novel; article. photo · *WFP* Nov 9, 1987: p19.

Laurence clung to roots; obituary. photo · *WFP* Jan 6, 1987: p21.

Margaret Laurence dead at 60; obituary. photo · *CH* Jan 6, 1987: pD5.

Saturday Night observes 100th birthday; article. *WFP* Jan 6, 1987: p26.

Tough publisher tackles new mystery; article. photo · *WFP* Dec 1, 1987: p32.

Currie, Sheldon

Ken Harvey's very short stories; review of *No Lies. Atlan Prov Book R* Feb-March 1987; Vol 14 No 1: p16.

Curry, J.W.

4 poems & 2 collages; poems. *Poetry Can R* Spring 1987; Vol 8 No 2–3: p17.

Defying linear deification – contemporary Toronto visual poetry; article. illus · *Cross Can Writ Q* 1987; Vol 9 No 3–4: p6–8.

Curtis, Brian

Laurence service; letter to the editor. photo · *WFP* Jan 26, 1987: p6.

Cyr, Paul Albert

[Untitled]; review of *Voices of Deliverance. Amer R of Can Studies* Autumn 1987; Vol 17 No 3: p354–355.

Czarnecki, Mark

Believing is seeing; review of *Canadian Sunset. Books in Can* Jan-Feb 1987; Vol 16 No 1: p19–20.

Going down the road; article. biog photo · *Books in Can* March 1987; Vol 16 No 2: p13.

Czaykowski, Bogdan

Race to the limit; poem. *Prism* Spring 1987; Vol 25 No 3: p69–70.

Dabby, Victor

Jacob Two-Two returns with pet dinosaur and new villain; article. *CH* June 14, 1987: pE1.

Dabydeen, Cyril

Methuselah; short story. *Northward J* 1987; No 42: p16–19.

The private poet as public servant; essay. photo · *Can Auth & Book* Spring 1987; Vol 62 No 3: p9.

Dafoe, Christopher

Saturday Night's first century; editorial. *WFP* Jan 18, 1987: p6.

Dagenais, Angèle

La "Coalition de 1%" rencontrera Bourassa; article. photo · *MD* Dec 4, 1987: p13.

Coeur à coeur en plein coeur du parc Lafontaine; theatre review. photo · *MD* Sept 25, 1987: p14.

Du théâtre comme dans un moulin; article. photo · *MD* Nov 11, 1987: p11.

Les étudiants du secondaire préfèrent Les Filles de Caleb; article. *MD* Nov 4, 1987: p14.

Fernande Saint-Martin: une "grammaire" du langage visuel; article. photo · *MD* April 4, 1987: pC1, C8.

Francine d'Amour, prix Guérin; article. photo · *MD* Nov 5, 1987: p13.

Le milieu artistique encouragé par les intentions libérales; article. photo · *MD* Dec 15, 1987: p11.

Pour en finir une fois pour toutes avec la réforme; article. *MD* Oct 16, 1987: p13–14.

Le Sous-sol des anges ou les années de braise; theatre review. photo · *MD* Dec 15, 1987: p11.

Sylvain Trudel remporte le Prix Molson; article. photo · *MD* Nov 11, 1987: p11.

Tandis qu'on négocie au sommet, un millier d'oiseaux chantent la paix; theatre review of *Un Millier d'oiseaux*. photo · *MD* Dec 11, 1987: p11.

Dahlie, Hallvard

[Untitled]; review of *All the Way Home. Queen's Q* Summer 1987; Vol 94 No 2: p480–482.

[Untitled]; review of *Encounters and Explorations. U of Toronto Q* Fall 1987; Vol 57 No 1: p156–158.

Dahms, Moshie

[Untitled]; bibliography. *J of Common Lit* 1987; Vol 22 No 2: p43–60.

Dales, Kim

[Untitled]; play excerpt from *Dora: A Case of Hysteria. Grain* Summer 1987; Vol 15 No 2: p67–75.

D'Alfonso, Antonio

La chambre; poem. *Estuaire* Autumn 1987; No 46: p11–16.

Désamour; essay. *Estuaire* Summer 1987; No 45: p15–16.

Quebec: festival national de la poésie; regional column. *Poetry Can R* Spring 1987; Vol 8 No 2–3: p22.

[Untitled]; review of *Tequila Sunrise. Poetry Can R* Spring 1987; Vol 8 No 2–3: p36–37.

[Untitled]; review of *Le Chemin brulé. Estuaire* Winter 1986–87; No 43: p77–78.

[Untitled]; review of *Nous passions. Estuaire* Summer 1987; No 45: p49.

[Untitled]; review of *L'Infante immémoriale. Estuaire* Summer 1987; No 45: p54–55.

[Untitled]; review of *La Voix de Carla. Estuaire* Autumn 1987; No 46: p89–90.

Dalley, Jan

Directional devices; review of *Once: A Lullaby. Times Lit Supp* April 3, 1987; No 4383: p356.

Dalton, Sheila

Friends / conversation; poem. *Poetry Can R* Summer 1987; Vol 8 No 4: p27.

To the boy with the onyx elephant; poem. illus · *Poetry Can R* Summer 1987; Vol 8 No 4: p27.

[Untitled]; letter to the editor. *Cross Can Writ Q* 1987; Vol 9 No 3–4: p64.

Damato, Jacqueline

[Untitled]; review of *The Bottle and the Bushman. Can Auth & Book* Winter 1987; Vol 62 No 2: p24.

Dambrofsky, Gwen

Young man goes west, again; review of *Beyond Forget*. photo · *TS* Feb 14, 1987: pM4.

Daniels, Barry

With friends like these. . . .; short story. illus · *TS* June 28, 1987: pA16.

Daniels, L.G.

Boadicea; short story. *Tor South Asian R* Spring 1987; Vol 5 No 3: p15–21.

Dansereau, Estelle

A sophisticated, compelling dialogue; review of *Configuration. Essays on Can Writ* Spring 1987; No 34: p174–179.

[Untitled]; reviews of *Blind Painting* and *All the Polarities. Quarry* Summer 1987; Vol 36 No 3: p82–86.

Danys, Milda

[Untitled]; poem. *Fireweed* Winter 1987; No 24: p27.

Daoust, Jean-Paul

Les ailleurs amoureux; editorial. *Estuaire* Autumn 1987; No 46: p5–6.

André Roy: on n'écrit pas impunément; interview. *Estuaire* Spring 1987; No 44: p71–78.

Sexe chauve; poem. *Estuaire* Summer 1987; No 45: p31.

Un star system au Québec?; article. photo · *Jeu* 1987; No 43: p47–49.

Suite contemporaine; poem. *Estuaire* Winter 1986–87; No 43: p51–52.

[Untitled]; review of *Terroristes d'amour. Estuaire* Spring 1987; No 44: p80.

Daran, Morris

T.V.; poem. *Alpha* Winter 1987; Vol 11: p31.

Darling, Michael

A pair of grey eyes; poem. *CV 2* Summer 1987; Vol 10 No 4: p37.

Whose woods these are; poem. *Can Lit* Winter 1987; No 115: p104–105.

Why I have to stop reading poetry; poem. *CV 2* Summer 1987; Vol 10 No 4: p36.

Darnell, Gary

Intersection; poem. *New Q* Winter 1987; Vol 6 No 4: p75.

Dault, Gary Michael

At the cafe; poem. *Tor Life* Dec 1987; Vol 21 No 18: p25.

Barker Fairley 1887–1986; obituary. *Can Lit* Summer-Fall 1987; No 113–114: p273–274.

Branch line; poem. *Tor Life* Nov 1987; Vol 21 No 17: p47.

New for spring; poem. *Tor Life* May 1987; Vol 21 No 7: p83.

Daurio, Beverley

Between; poem. *Prism* Spring 1987; Vol 25 No 3: p47.

Book was fiction and piece fictitious too; letter to the editor. *TS* Dec 27, 1987: pB2.

Chorus of many voices; essay. *Cross Can Writ Q* 1987; Vol 9 No 1: p7, 28–29.

Editorial. *Poetry Can R* Spring 1987; Vol 8 No 1–2: p2.

Editorial. *Poetry Can R* Summer 1987; Vol 8 No 4: p2.

I have my doubts; poem. *Prism* Spring 1987; Vol 25 No 3: p47.

Lust; poem. *Matrix* Fall 1987; No 25: p54.

Supply and demand; editorial. *Poetry Can R* Fall 1987; Vol 9 No 1: p2.

[Untitled]; reviews of fictional works. *Cross Can Writ Q* 1987; Vol 9 No 1: p18–19.

[Untitled]; review of *From the Dark Wood*. *Poetry Can R* Spring 1987; Vol 8 No 2–3: p47.

[Untitled]; reviews. *Cross Can Writ Q* 1987; Vol 9 No 2: p23.

[Untitled]; reviews of novels. *Cross Can Writ Q* 1987; Vol 9 No 3–4: p45–46.

When you are young; poem. *Prism* Spring 1987; Vol 25 No 3: p47.

Davey, Frank

Fort and forest: instability in the symbolic code of E.J. Pratt's Brebeuf and His Brethren; article. abstract · *Études can* 1987; No 23: p183–194.

Daviau, Diane-Monique

Une anthologie d'auteurs canadiens traduits en allemand; review of *Erkundungen, 26 kanadische Erzähler*. *Lettres québec* Summer 1987; No 46: p72–73.

David, Carole

Moebius ou les vertus paradoxales de l'athéisme; column. photo · *MD* April 11, 1987: pD3.

La nouvelle, le clip de l'écriture; review of *XYZ*. *MD* March 7, 1987: pB2.

Un numéro d'Études françaises explore les rapports de la littérature et des médias; review. *MD* May 9, 1987: pD2.

Qui de neuf du côté universitaire?; reviews of periodicals. *MD* Jan 17, 1987: pB5, B7.

Les revues se font voir pour être lues; article. *MD* March 14, 1987: pD3.

David, Gilbert

[Untitled]; review of *Le Théâtre pour enfants au Québec: 1950–1980. Jeu* 1987; No 42: p176–179.

Davidson, Arnold E.

[Untitled]; review of *Perspectives on Mordecai Richler*. *Amer R of Can Studies* Summer 1987; Vol 17 No 2: p257–259.

Davies, Hilary

Christmas 1918; poem. *Poetry Can R* Fall 1987; Vol 9 No 1: p25.

Davies, Richard A.

Clockmaker; review of *Recollections of Nova Scotia: The Clockmaker*. *Can Lit* Spring 1987; No 112: p123–124.

Davies, Robertson

Decorating the place; prose excerpt from *The Table Talk of Samuel Marchbanks*. *G&M* Dec 24, 1987: pA6.

The strange and rewarding life of a writer; essay. photo · *TS* March 21, 1987: pM2.

[Untitled]; essay. photo · *Chatelaine* May 1987; Vol 60 No 5: p52.

We must sing with the voices God gave us; essay. photo · *TS* Sept 19, 1987: pM1.

Davis, Frances

Spring at St. Jovite; poem. *Can Auth & Book* Spring 1987; Vol 62 No 3: p23.

To my father; poem. *Waves* Winter 1987; Vol 15 No 3: p71.

Davis, Richard C.

Fluid landscape / static land: the traveller's vision; article. *Essays on Can Writ* Spring 1987; No 34: p140–156.

An important animal story; review of *Red Fox*. *Can Child Lit* 1987; No 47: p82–84.

Davis, Robert

1837 revolt hits centre stage; article. photo · *TS (Neighbors)* Aug 11, 1987: p16.

Blood Relations script at fault; theatre review. photo · *TS (Neighbours)* April 7, 1987: p16.

Insight Theatre shows get better and better; theatre review of *Whispers of Moonlight*. *TS (Neighbors)* Aug 11, 1987: p16.

Teenage amateur theatre group produces play at 'real' theatre; article. photo · *TS (Neighbours)* Feb 10, 1987: p26.

Wanted! One detective show; theatre review of *Wanted!*. photo · *TS (Neighbors)* May 26, 1987: p19.

Dawber, Diane

Break; poem. *Quarry* Winter 1987; Vol 36 No 1: p16.

Pull cord; poem. *Quarry* Winter 1987; Vol 36 No 1: p15.

[Untitled]; essay. *Quill & Quire (Books for Young People)* Oct 1987; Vol 53 No 10: p3.

Dawe, Tom

Humour from the heart; review of *A Collection of Stories*. *Atlan Prov Book R* Sept-Oct 1987; Vol 14 No 3: p13.

Dawson, Eric

Cowboys don't cry. . . .except on a movie set; article. photo · *TS* Aug 26, 1987: pD1.

Poet tries to capture true cadence of China; article. photo · *CH* Dec 10, 1987: pF5.

Rewrites upset author; article. *CH* Aug 27, 1987: pC2.

Day, Moira

Fringe '87: the state of the art; article. photo · *NeWest R* Oct 1987; Vol 13 No 2: p12–13.

Taking the "kiddie stuff" seriously: the 1987 Edmonton International Children's Festival; article. photo · *NeWest R* Oct 1987; Vol 13 No 2: p6–8.

Day, Sandy

Roses; poem. *U of Windsor R* Spring-Summer 1987; Vol 20 No 2: p87.

Daymond, Douglas

[Untitled]; review of *The Impossible Sum of Our Traditions*. *World Lit in Eng* Autumn 1987; Vol 27 No 2: p264–269.

Daziron, Héliane

Symbols of transformation: Alice Munro's "Mrs. Cross and Mrs. Kidd"; article. *Open Letter* Summer 1987; Vol 6 No 8: p15–24.

[Untitled]; review of *Autobiographical and Biographical Writing in the Commonwealth*. *Afram* Jan 1987; No 24: p75.

de Bellefeuille, Normand

L'avant-dernier poème au monde!; essay. *Estuaire* Summer 1987; No 45: p43–45.

Pratiques: douze hypothèses; essay. illus · *La Nouvelle barre du jour* Feb 1987; No 193: p83–94.

de Billy, Hélène

Le 16e Salon du livre de Québec: la francophonie est au rendez-vous; article. photo · *MD* April 25, 1987: pD1, D6.

Christine comme un poison dans l'eau; article. *MD* April 30, 1987: p13.

À l'affiche du Salon du livre de Québec; article. photo · *MD* April 27, 1987: p11–12.

Mais Anne Hébert était là; article. *MD* May 4, 1987: p9–10.

Le Salon du livre de Québec: c'est parti!; article. photo · *MD* April 29, 1987: p13.

de Grandpré, Chantal

Les clichés du futur; review of *Les Géants de Blizzard*. *Can Child Lit* 1987; No 46: p68–70.

de Montbrun, Nicole

[Untitled]; review of *Madelaine*. *Quill & Quire* June 1987; Vol 53 No 6: p32–33.

De Roo, Harvey

Happy Enough: the poetry of George Johnston; article. *Malahat R (special issue)* March 1987; No 78: p106–131.

de Villiers, Marq

[Untitled]; editorial. *Tor Life* June 1987; Vol 21 No 9: p6.

de Vries, Patricia

Every old person is Somebody: the image of aging in Canadian children's literature; article. *Can Child Lit* 1987; No 46: p37–44.

Deahl, James

Ars poetica; poem. *Poetry Can R* Spring 1987; Vol 8 No 2–3: p26.

Four pieces for my marriage; poem sequence. *Poetry Can R* Spring 1987; Vol 8 No 2–3: p26.

Island trilogy; poem. *Waves* Winter 1987; Vol 15 No 3: p72.

Milton Acorn: in memoriam; obituary. photo · *Poetry Can R* Spring 1987; Vol 8 No 1–2: p6.

Whiteway's export; poem. *Poetry Can R* Spring 1987; Vol 8 No 2–3: p26.

Dearden, Carolyn

Red Deer College Arts Centre: life after hockey?; article. photo · *NeWest R* Feb 1987; Vol 12 No 6: p15–16.

Décarie, François

Le geste barbare; poem. *Moebius* Winter 1987; No 31: p132.

Intérieur; poem. illus · *Moebius* Autumn 1987; No 34: p80–84.

La question suscite la censure; poem. *Moebius (special issue)* Spring 1987; No 32: p83–86.

Décarie, Nicole

[Untitled]; review of *Felix Leclerc, le roi heureux*. *Moebius* Spring 1987; No 32: p125–127.

[Untitled]; review of *L'Hiver au coeur*. *Moebius* Summer 1987; No 33: p133.

Dedora, B.

Fantasy no. 1: I wanted to be famous in the world of letters: real famous; poem. *Cross Can Writ Q* 1987; Vol 9 No 3–4: p10.

Deer, Glen

Miracle, mystery, and authority: rereading The Double Hook; article. *Open Letter* Summer 1987; Vol 6 No 8: p25–43.

Delimal, H.-Paul

Des Boches à Fridolin; letter to the editor. *MD* Jan 17, 1987: pB2.

Delisle, Michael

Les changeurs de signes; prose poem. *La Nouvelle barre du jour (special issue)* 1987; No 192: p9–29.

Mélancolie; series of linked prose poems. illus · *La Nouvelle barre du jour (special issue)* 1987; No 192: p35–57.

Demers, Dominique

Les 10 ans de La Courte Échelle; article. photo · *MD* Sept 26, 1987: pD6.

Chouette: des livres, des jeux, des jouets; article. photo · *MD* Dec 5, 1987: pD6.

Des contes pour guérir; article. photo · *MD* May 30, 1987: pD6.

Dix années de littérature pour jeunes Québécois; article. photo · *MD* Nov 14, 1987: pD10.

Ginette Anfousse: il fallait une nouvelle héroïne et Rosalie est née; article. photo · *MD* April 11, 1987: pD1.

Un grand voyage. . . .; essay. *MD* Nov 28, 1987: pD6.

L'embarras du choix; review of *Un Chien, un vélo et des pizzas*. *MD* Nov 28, 1987: pD6.

Littérature jeunesse; reviews of children's books. *MD* Oct 10, 1987: pD6.

Littérature jeunesse; reviews of children's books. *MD* Nov 21, 1987: pD6.

La magie du livre pour enfants; review of *Quel est ce bruit?*. *MD* July 4, 1987: pC5.

Les malheurs de Rosalie ou l'éloge de l'enfance; reviews of children's books. *MD* May 2, 1987: pD3.

Pour les adolescents: quatre mains et deux solitudes; reviews of young adult novels. photo · *MD* Dec 19, 1987: pD6-D7.

La vague-jeunesse sera choyée; article. photo · *MD* Nov 14, 1987: pD10.

Demers, Jeanne

Liminaire; editorial. illus · *La Nouvelle barre du jour (special issue)* March 1987; No 196: p7-9.

L'inframanifeste illimité; article. *La Nouvelle barre du jour (special issue)* 1987; No 194: p7-18.

Tableau chronologique des interventions à portée manifestaires qui ont marqué l'évolution du féminisme au Québec; bibliography. *La Nouvelle barre du jour (special issue)* 1987; No 194: p21-94.

Dempster, Barry

Domanski, Harris, Hutchman; reviews of poetry books. *Poetry Can R* Summer 1987; Vol 8 No 4: p31.

In search of Mary; poem. *Matrix* Spring 1987; No 24: p31-32.

Jacobs, Lever, Marriott; reviews of poetry books. *Poetry Can R* Spring 1987; Vol 8 No 2-3: p35.

MacEwen and McKay; reviews of *Afterworlds* and *Sanding Down This Rocking Chair on a Windy Night*. *Poetry Can R* Fall 1987; Vol 9 No 1: p29-30.

The man in the centre of the candle; poem. *Matrix* Spring 1987; No 24: p30.

A prairie state of mind; review of *The Garden of Eloise Loon*. *Can Forum* April 1987; Vol 67 No 768: p40.

Somewhere in time; review of *Century*. illus · *Can Forum* Aug-Sept 1987; Vol 67 No 771: p45-46.

[Untitled]; essay. *Poetry Can R* Summer 1987; Vol 8 No 4: p15.

Writing home; short story. *Dandelion* Fall-Winter 1987; Vol 14 No 2: p72-87.

Denham, Paul

The best part of going out; editorial. *NeWest R* Oct 1987; Vol 13 No 2: p1.

The elephant: a federal or provincial responsibility?; review of *What We Bring Home*. illus · *NeWest R* Summer 1987; Vol 12 No 10: p14.

Getting physical; reviews of *Dance of the Particles* and *Playing with Fire*. *Essays on Can Writ* Spring 1987; No 34: p44-47.

Paul Hiebert, 1892-1987; obituary. *NeWest R* Oct 1987; Vol 13 No 2: p1.

Possessing the promised land; editorial. *NeWest R* Nov 1987; Vol 13 No 3: p1.

Standing up for himself; reviews of *The Uncollected Acorn* and *Whiskey Jack*. *Books in Can* June-July 1987; Vol 16 No 5: p30, 32.

[Untitled]; review of *Flicker and Hawk*. *Books in Can* June-July 1987; Vol 16 No 5: p24.

[Untitled]; review of *A Time for Loving*. *Books in Can* June-July 1987; Vol 16 No 5: p24-25.

Denis, Jean-Luce

Questions sur une démarche; essay. photo · *Jeu* 1987; No 45: p159-163.

Denoon, Anne

No need to explain; review of *Visitations*. *Books in Can* Aug-Sept 1987; Vol 16 No 6: p21, 24.

Women with a past; review of *The Indigo Dress*. *Books in Can* May 1987; Vol 16 No 4: p16.

Deorksen, Leona M.

Ernest Buckler's holy family; article. *New Q* Spring-Summer 1987; Vol 7 No 1-2: p232-239.

Déry, Francine

Au noir de l'oeuvre; essay. illus · *La Nouvelle barre du jour (special issue)* March 1987; No 196: p88-93.

Déry, Pierre-Justin

[Untitled]; review of *Les Heures*. *Estuaire* Summer 1987; No 45: p55-57.

Desautels, Denise

La mémoire amnésique; poem. *Estuaire* Summer 1987; No 45: p9-10.

Desgreniers, Paul

[Untitled]; review of *Quarante voiles pour un exil*. *Moebius* Winter 1987; No 31: p142-143.

Désiront, André

Déclin de l'enseignement de notre littérature; article. illus · *MD (Livre d'ici)* Sept 12, 1987: p16-17.

Desjardins, Louise

Coupe-circuit; poem. *Estuaire* Autumn 1987; No 46: p49-51.

Le défilé; prose excerpt from *La Minutie de l'araignée*. illus · *La Nouvelle barre du jour* April 1987; No 198: p31-39.

M'étamper violette; essay. *La Nouvelle barre du jour (special issue)* 1987; No 191: p25-39.

Pour l'effet sur ma grand-mère qui me surveillait d'en haut quand j'étais petite; prose poem. *Estuaire* Spring 1987; No 44: p27-28.

Desrosiers-Bonin, Diane

André Belleau, lecteur de Rabelais; article. *Liberté* Feb 1987; Vol 29 No 1: p51-53.

Desruisseaux, Pierre

[Untitled]; poem. *Estuaire* Winter 1986-87; No 43: p11-14.

Deveson, Richard

Early espièglerie; review of *The Papers of Samuel Marchbanks*. *Times Lit Supp* Oct 16, 1987; No 4411: p1137.

Dew, Robb Forman

A magnificent greed; review of *Duet for Three*. *NYT Book R* April 5, 1987: p19.

Dewdney, Christopher

Command; prose poem. *Prism* Summer 1987; Vol 25 No 4: p34.

Incriminating knowledge; prose poem. *Prism* Summer 1987; Vol 25 No 4: p34.

The uncanny; prose poem. *Prism* Summer 1987; Vol 25 No 4: p34.

di Giorgio, Anna

I heard you might be dying Charles; poem. *CV 2* Spring 1987; Vol 10 No 3: p38.

di Michele, Mary

Between the sexes; reviews of poetry books. *Books in Can* March 1987; Vol 16 No 2: p31–32.

Down the tube; review of *Cambodia*. *Books in Can* Jan-Feb 1987; Vol 16 No 1: p23.

Dreaming for our children; column. *Poetry Can R* Fall 1987; Vol 9 No 1: p19.

The many words for snow; poem. *Poetry Can R* Summer 1987; Vol 8 No 4: p14–15.

A South American education; essay. illus · *Books in Can* Aug-Sept 1987; Vol 16 No 6: p3.

Speculations: cosmology and language: the new priests and the old; article. *Poetry Can R* Spring 1987; Vol 8 No 2–3: p25.

Speculations: Les Deux maggots at the end of the universe; column. *Poetry Can R* Summer 1987; Vol 8 No 4: p9.

[Untitled]; review of *The Deepening of the Colours*. *Books in Can* May 1987; Vol 16 No 4: p23.

[Untitled]; review of *Delayed Mercy*. *Books in Can* June-July 1987; Vol 16 No 5: p23–24.

[Untitled]; essay. *Poetry Can R* Summer 1987; Vol 8 No 4: p14.

[Untitled]; review of *Travelling Light*. *Poetry Can R* Summer 1987; Vol 8 No 4: p35.

Difalco, Salvatore

Not marked on the map; poem. *Tor Life* Oct 1987; Vol 21 No 1[5]: p37.

Too late to cancel it now; poem. *New Q* Fall 1987; Vol 7 No 3: p90–91.

Valentine; poem. *Tor Life* Feb 1987; Vol 21 No 2: p31.

Whatever blows your skirt away; poem. *Tor Life* Oct 1987; Vol 21 No 1[5]: p114.

Dilworth, Thomas

[Untitled]; review of *Ashbourn*. *U of Windsor R* Spring-Summer 1987; Vol 20 No 2: p88–90.

DiManno, Rosie

Dear Bruce Springsteen one author's fan letter; article. *TS* Oct 2, 1987: pE23.

Lee's whimsy cuts into heavy issues; article. photo · *TS* Nov 1, 1987: pC2.

Literary celebrities featured on menu; article. *TS* Sept 25, 1987: pE28.

Rez Sisters inviting you out for bingo; article. photo · *TS* Nov 20, 1987: pE3.

Dionne, André

Le théâtre qu'on joue; theatre reviews. photo · *Lettres québec* Winter 1986–87; No 44: p53–54.

Le théâtre qu'on joue; theatre reviews. illus photo · *Lettres québec* Spring 1987; No 45: p47–48.

Le théâtre qu'on joue; theatre reviews. photo · *Lettres québec* Summer 1987; No 46: p47–48.

Le théâtre qu'on joue; theatre reviews of *Le Printemps, monsieur Deslauriers* and *Le Vrai monde?*. photo · *Lettres québec* Autumn 1987; No 47: p49–50.

Dionne, René

La Revue d'histoire littéraire du Québec et du Canada français; article. *Voix et images* Winter 1987; No 35: p287–294.

Ditsky, John

A blues; poem. *Antigonish R* 1987; No 69–70: p125.

Fruits & vegetables; poem. *Antigonish R* 1987; No 69–70: p125.

Postcard from Sparta; poem. *Can Auth & Book* Fall 1987; Vol 63 No 1: p16.

Dixon, Michael F.N.

Fiction; survey review article. *U of Toronto Q* Fall 1987; Vol 57 No 1: p1–7.

Dixon, Roslyn

Paulette Jiles' fictional strategies; reviews of Sitting in the Club Car Drinking Rum and Karma-Kola and *The Late Great Human Road Show*. *Event* Summer 1987; Vol 16 No 2: p127–130.

Dobbins, Jan

[Untitled]; review of *Moira's Birthday*. *CH* Dec 6, 1987: pD9.

Dobbs, Kildare

Lovat Dickson, 1902–1987 obituary. *Books in Can* March 1987; Vol 16 No 2: p21.

Dobson, Debby

A story mostly about my mother; short story. *Grain* Spring 1987; Vol 15 No 1: p57–60.

Doerksen, Gerald

[Untitled]; review of *Blue Riders*. *Rubicon* Spring 1987; No 8: p222–223.

[Untitled]; review of *Open Windows*. *Rubicon* Spring 1987; No 8: p223–224.

Donaldson, Jeffery

Circumvallation; poem. *Rubicon* Fall 1987; No 9: p51.

Come spring; poem. *Rubicon* Fall 1987; No 9: p52.

Exchange rate; poem. *Rubicon* Fall 1987; No 9: p53.

In place of maps; poem. *Rubicon* Fall 1987; No 9: p49–50.

Spending part of the winter; poem. *Rubicon* Fall 1987; No 9: p50.

[Untitled]; review of *Ashbourn*. *Rubicon* Fall 1987; No 9: p169–170.

Vitruvius; poem. *Exile* 1987; Vol 12 No 2: p57–63.

Donlan, John

Apples; poem. *Arc* Fall 1987; No 19: p60.

Chasing the terminator; poem. *Arc* Fall 1987; No 19: p59.

Communication deluxe; review of *In the Second Person*. *CV 2* Spring 1987; Vol 10 No 3: p58–60.

Domestic economy; poem. *CV 2* Spring 1987; Vol 10 No 3: p45.

Donnell, David

Cagney, George Raft, & Elisha Cook, Jnr.; poem. *Can Forum* June-July 1987; Vol 67 No 770: p34–36.

Chocolate; poem. *Malahat R* Sept 1987; No 80: p63–65.

Potato head; poem. *Malahat R* Sept 1987; No 80: p57–59.

Rowing; poem. *Malahat R* Sept 1987; No 80: p60–62.

U.S. report: political poems & personal visions; comparative column. *Poetry Can R* Summer 1987; Vol 8 No 4: p26.

The U.S.: foundation poets & personal views; comparative column. *Poetry Can R* Fall 1987; Vol 9 No 1: p25.

The U.S.: regions & districts as labels; comparative column. *Poetry Can R* Spring 1987; Vol 8 No 2–3: p29.

[Untitled]; essay. *Poetry Can R* Summer 1987; Vol 8 No 4: p15.

Donnelly, Pat

Ageless Fridolin skits leave crowd euphoric; theatre review of *Les Fridolinades*. photo · *MG* Nov 27, 1987: pC1.

A box that could have stayed closed; theatre review of *Pandora*. *MG* March 18, 1987: pD3.

Child's play? Far from it; article. photo · *MG* July 31, 1987: pC1.

Community theatre in festival limelight; article. *MG* July 6, 1987: pB9.

Coup De Soleil isn't great theatre, but it's a nice winter break; theatre review. *MG* Jan 23, 1987: pC5.

'Coward' classy but disappoints as theatre; theatre review of *Noel Coward: A Portrait*. photo · *MG* Nov 26, 1987: pH5.

The effort is there but results disappoint; theatre review of *Jack of Hearts*. *MG* July 18, 1987: pD8.

Empty seats a shame as theatre fest hits midway point; article. *MG* July 10, 1987: pD4.

From English to French to English; article. photo · *MG* Sept 5, 1987: pC6.

Gélinas and Oligny: a match made in theatrical heaven; theatre review of *La Passion de Narcisse Mondoux*. photo · *MG* Jan 20, 1987: pD11.

Help! Kirk! Star Trek image being tarnished!; theatre review of *Gilles Vachon: Indendiaire*. *MG* Aug 13, 1987: pE16.

Homosexual passion, religious theatre crux of Les Feluettes; theatre review. *MG* Sept 12, 1987: pD13.

Imaginative kids' plays hit the spot; theatre reviews of *The Knocks* and *Coeur à coeur*. *MG* April 9, 1987: pE8.

Kingston editor retains theatre critics' award; article. *MG* Oct 5, 1987: pB15.

Last Voyage appeals to all; theatre review of *The Last Voyage of the Devil's Wheel*. photo · *MG* Dec 16, 1987: pF3.

Lepage play romps away with festival Grand Prize; article. *MG* June 8, 1987: pD7.

Lightweight Tête-à-Tête an evening of intimacy; theatre review. *MG* Sept 10, 1987: pC14.

Linda Griffiths gives NTS reading tonight; article. photo · *MG* Nov 2, 1987: pB13.

Marilyn situation poignant but where's the drama?; theatre review of *Marilyn (journal intime de Margaret Macpherson)*. photo · *MG* Oct 15, 1987: pE12.

Murder for Sale turns mystery into song and dance; theatre review. *MG* June 6, 1987: pH10.

Music, theatre union needs fine tuning; theatre reviews of *Le Dernier quatuor d'un homme sourd* and *La Goutte*. *MG* Nov 18, 1987: pD3.

New Maillet play slow getting off the mark; theatre review of *Margot la Folle*. *MG* Oct 7, 1987: pH4.

No Cycle is a deeply searching celebration of life in the 1980s; theatre review. photo · *MG* Dec 12, 1987: pD20.

NTS's Dog Day a hazard in more ways than one; theatre review. *MG* Dec 19, 1987: pE6.

Oiseaux makes nuclear point without traumatizing kids; theatre review of *Un Millier d'oiseaux*. *MG* Dec 19, 1987: pE9.

One-man Vinci tour de force for Lepage; theatre review. *MG* June 5, 1987: pD2.

Oublier could have been a lot of things but misses chance; theatre review. photo · *MG* Nov 4, 1987: pB9.

Piggery production circumvents Salt Water Moon pitfalls; theatre review. *MG* Aug 15, 1987: pE15.

The Piggery scores a direct hit with scary-funny Canadian play; theatre review of *I'll Be Back Before Midnight*. *MG* July 21, 1987: pD2.

Playing linguistic musical chairs; article. *MG* June 2, 1987: pD11.

A plea to understand adults; theatre review of *Coup de Fil*. *MG* Feb 10, 1987: pB7.

Plenty of life left in this classic; theatre review of *Le Temps d'une vie*. *MG* Sept 18, 1987: pC10.

Poetic, spell-binding Caryopse is theatre for thinking person; theatre review of *Caryopse ou le monde entier*. *MG* Oct 30, 1987: pC2.

A rare glimpse at our multiculturalism; theatre review of *Baba Jacques Dass and Turmoil at Côte des Neiges Cemetery*. *MG* Oct 17, 1987: pD9.

La Sagouine shows drawing power of good story well-told; theatre review. *MG* Nov 6, 1987: pC1.

See Bob Run dark ride into subconscious; theatre review. *MG* Oct 1, 1987: pE7.

Stratford ahead of the game – and it's no overnight miracle; column. *MG* Dec 10, 1987: pD6.

Stylish direction freshens Bonjour; theatre review of *Bonjour, là, bonjour*. photo · *MG* Nov 25, 1987: pH4.

Summer theatre: there's lots of it and some has substance; article. photo · *MG* Aug 1, 1987: pE5.

Syndrome obscure yet polished; theatre review of *Le Syndrome de Cézanne*. *MG* March 5, 1987: pD13.

Talk-rock musical sizzles with energy and staging is slick; theatre review of *Heavy Minou*. photo · *MG* Nov 17, 1987: pE7.

Talky treatment for Chekhov's life; theatre review of *Tchekov Tchekova*. photo · *MG* Jan 24, 1987: pC8.

Theatre for young people on the upswing in Montreal; article. photo · *MG* Oct 23, 1987: pC3.

Tightrope Time a poetic one-man show that spans black history of Nova Scotia; theatre review. photo · *MG* Sept 10, 1987: pC14.

[Untitled]; theatre review of *I'll Be Back Before Midnight*. *MG* July 24, 1987: pC10.

[Untitled]; theatre review of *Gilles Vachon: Incendiaire*. *MG* Aug 14, 1987: pC8.

[Untitled]; theatre reviews. *MG* Sept 11, 1987: pC8.

[Untitled]; theatre reviews of *Tête à tête* and *Les Feluettes*. *MG* Sept 18, 1987: pC8.

[Untitled]; theatre reviews. *MG* Nov 27, 1987: pC7.

[Untitled]; theatre reviews. *MG* Dec 4, 1987: pC6.

V.S.O.P. pale imitation of a play; theatre review. *MG* Oct 16, 1987: pC7.

Donohue, Patrick

Baptism; short story. photo · *TS* July 26, 1987: pD5.

Donovan, Rita

Meddling with time; review of *Landslides*. *Fiddlehead* Summer 1987; No 152: p100–104.

Doolan, Maureen

Tell it slant; short story. *Room of One's Own* Jan 1987; Vol 11 No 2: p73–79.

Doolittle, Joyce

Rites returns ATP to its roots; article. photo · *NeWest R* April 1987; Vol 12 No 8: p16.

Doran, Marlene

Nightmare; short story. photo · *TS* July 27, 1987: pD7.

Doré, Jean-François

Une littérature qui flatte l'oreille; article. *MD* Dec 10, 1987: p13.

La poésie québécoise dénaturée dans la capitale française; essay. *MD* Dec 5, 1987: pC2.

Quatre musiciens à la rescousse de Francoeur; article. photo · *MD* June 11, 1987: p17.

Dorion, Hélène

[Untitled]; review of *L'Usage du réel*. *Estuaire* Winter 1986–87; No 43: p79.

[Untitled]; poetry and prose excerpt from *Les Retouches de l'intime*. illus · *Estuaire* Spring 1987; No 44: p29–32.

[Untitled]; review of *Poèmes*. *Estuaire* Spring 1987; No 44: p83–84.

[Untitled]; reviews of *Le Fait de vivre ou d'avoir vécu* and *La Chambre des miracles*. *Estuaire* Summer 1987; No 45: p50–51.

Le visage de la ville; prose poem. *Estuaire* Autumn 1987; No 46: p17–19.

Dorscht, Susan Rudy

A deconstructive narratology; reading Robert Kroetsch's Alibi; article. *Open Letter* Summer 1987; Vol 6 No 8: p78–83.

Tellings; reviews of poetry books. *Can Lit* Winter 1987; No 115: p257–260.

Dorsey, Candas Jane

English poverty parlayed into perfect prose; biographical article. photo · *Quill & Quire* May 1987; Vol 53 No 5: p23.

Doucet, Clive

The gift of humorous bifocals; review of *Stephen Leacock: A Reappraisal*. photo · *G&M* Aug 1, 1987: pC16.

Doucette, L.E.

[Untitled]; reviews of *Theatre and Politics in Modern Quebec* and *French-Canadian Theater*. *U of Toronto Q* Fall 1987; Vol 57 No 1: p186–189.

[Untitled]; review of *La Vitalité littéraire de l'Ontario français*. *U of Toronto Q* Fall 1987; Vol 57 No 1: p206–207.

[Untitled]; review of *Langues et littératures au Nouveau-Brunswick*. *U of Toronto Q* Fall 1987; Vol 57 No 1: p207–209.

Douglas, Marion

Acting just the same; short story. *Prairie J of Can Lit* 1987; No 9: p24–28.

Andrew and the beasts; short story. *Capilano R* 1987; No 42: p10–16.

No falling stars; short story. *Room of One's Own* Sept 1987; Vol 11 No 4: p63–70.

Dowd, Jean-François

Des échappées de lumière. . . .; review of *Apparence*. *MD* April 28, 1987: p17.

Dowding, Martin

The fall line-up: political pundits, literary lore, and sports strategies; previes of fall book list. photo · *Quill & Quire* July 1987; Vol 53 No 7: p10, 12, 14, 16.

Title tattle; column. *Quill & Quire (Books for Young People)* Dec 1987; Vol 53 No 12: p3.

[Untitled]; review of *Gallows View*. *Quill & Quire* March 1987; Vol 53 No 3: p71.

[Untitled]; review of *The Great War of Words*. *Quill & Quire* Nov 1987; Vol 53 No 11: p25.

Writers-in-libraries program well under way; article. *Quill & Quire* July 1987; Vol 53 No 7: p62–63.

Dowling, David

Languages of exile; review of *Varieties of Exile*. *Can Lit* Winter 1987; No 115: p216–218.

Downes, Gwladys V.

Breathing in tune and time; review of *Pieces of Map, Pieces of Music*. *Event* Summer 1987; Vol 16 No 2: p115–118.

Downey, Donn

Library doors closed as porn bill ridiculed; article. photo · *G&M* Dec 11, 1987: pD18.

Writer's women among most memorable in Canadian fiction; obituary. photo · *G&M* Jan 6, 1987: pA11.

Downie, Glen

Diagnosis: heart failure; poem. *Waves* Winter 1987; Vol 15 No 3: p46.

Living in sin: 1; poem. *Waves* Winter 1987; Vol 15 No 3: p48.

The Marias Mexico City; poem. *Waves* Winter 1987; Vol 15 No 3: p47.

Private screening; poem. *CV 2* Summer 1987; Vol 10 No 4: p16.

Downie, Mary Alice

The son of the evening star; short story. *Quarry* Winter 1987; Vol 36 No 1: p104–108.

Doyle, Donna

[Untitled]; letter to the editor. *Cross Can Writ Q* 1987; Vol 9 No 3–4: p64.

Doyle, Margaret

Van lit; reviews of *Vancouver: Soul of a City* and *Vancouver Poetry*. *Can Lit* Winter 1987; No 115: p188–190.

Drache, Sharon

Esoteric callings; review of *A.M. Klein: Literary Essays and Reviews*. *G&M* May 16, 1987: pC19.

Macabre parade of masks; review of *Our Hero in the Cradle of Confederation*. *G&M* July 11, 1987: pC14.

Meaning and craft; review of *Le Repos et l'oubli*. photo · *G&M* May 30, 1987: pC21.

Drage, Margaret

[Untitled]; review of *Wordseed*. *Cross Can Writ Q* 1987; Vol 9 No 2: p22.

Dragland, Stan

Scott and Indian Affairs; review of *A Narrow Vision*. *Can Poet* Fall-Winter 1987; No 21: p103–109.

Drainie, Bronwyn

A megalomania for radio drama; reviews of *All the Bright Company* and *Image in the Mind*. photo · *G&M* Nov 28, 1987: pC19.

Draper, Gary

Style and substance; review of *The Family Romance*. *Books in Can* May 1987; Vol 16 No 4: p29–31.

[Untitled]; reviews of *The Revels* and *Northern Poems: Where the Heart Catches Its Breath*. *Poetry Can R* Spring 1987; Vol 8 No 2–3: p37.

Dubé, Marcel

"Tout ici doit être reconquis"; essay. *MD* March 2, 1987: p11.

Dubé, Pierrette

Une petite fille qui ne manque pas de courage; review of *Le Testament de Madame Legendre*. *Can Child Lit* 1987; No 48: p86–87.

Dublin, Max

Arranged around mountains; poem. *U of Windsor R* Spring-Summer 1987; Vol 20 No 2: p29.

Spring fever; poem. *U of Windsor R* Spring-Summer 1987; Vol 20 No 2: p30.

Dubois, Jacques

Le Québec à Liège; article. *Voix et images* Spring 1987; Vol 12 No 3: p566–567.

Dubois, Michelle

Cela s'appelle vivre; poem. *Estuaire* Winter 1986–87; No 43: p34.

Espace soie sauvage; poem. *Estuaire* Winter 1986–87; No 43: p33.

L'or des dimanches dormait dans nos ventres; poem. *Estuaire* Winter 1986–87; No 43: p35.

Murmure mouvant; poem. *Estuaire* Winter 1986–87; No 43: p34.

Poème poison; poem. *Estuaire* Winter 1986–87; No 43: p36.

Tissus; poems. *Estuaire* Winter 1986–87; No 43: p33–36.

Dubois, René-Daniel

Being at home with Claude; play. photo trans · *Can Theatre R* Spring 1987; No 50: p40–58.

Dubois, Roger

[Untitled]; letter to the editor. *Lettres québec* Spring 1987; No 45: p7.

Ducas, Marie-Claude

Réalité Jeunesse 87: de l'énergie à revendre; article. photo · *MD* Aug 10, 1987: p9.

Duchêne, Anne

Respect for the facts; review of *The Progress of Love*. *Times Lit Supp* Jan 30, 1987; No 4374: p109.

Duciaume, Jean-Marcel

La forêt dans l'oeuvre littéraire et picturale d'Emily Carr; article. abstract biog · *Études can* 1987; No 23: p135–145.

Ducrocq-Poirier, Madeleine

Introduction par Marie Le Franc de la forêt en littérature québécoise; article. abstract · *Études can* 1987; No 23: p87–92.

Dudek, Louis

The monument; review of *The Politics of the Imagination*. illus · *G&M* Nov 21, 1987: pC23.

[Untitled]; biographical articles. *Brick (special issue)* Summer 1987; No 30: ppassim.

Duffy, Carol Ann

Miles away; poem. *Poetry Can R* Summer 1987; Vol 8 No 4: p28.

Practising being dead; poem. *Poetry Can R* Summer 1987; Vol 8 No 4: p28.

Duffy, Dennis

Calling attention to the Maritimes; review of *Under Eastern Eyes*. *G&M* Nov 21, 1987: pC23.

More than forty-nine parallels; review of *Recovering Canada's First Novelist*. *Essays on Can Writ* Spring 1987; No 34: p170–173.

[Untitled]; reviews of *Blind Zone* and *Wenkchemna*. *Poetry Can R* Spring 1987; Vol 8 No 2–3: p45.

[Untitled]; reviews of *Archibald Lampman* and *John Metcalf*. *Eng Studies in Can* Sept 1987; Vol 13 No 3: p355–357.

A voyage into the countries of the mind; review of *Inspecting the Vaults*. photo · *G&M* Feb 21, 1987: pE19.

Dufresne, Curtis Dean

You can always use a little support; short story. photo · *TS* July 22, 1987: pD6.

Dufresne, Jean-V.

[Untitled]; review of *La Détresse et l'enchantement*. *MD* Nov 28, 1987: pD8.

Duguid, Lindsay

Capital appreciation; review of *Overhead in a Balloon*. *Times Lit Supp* Sept 25, 1987; No 4408: p1052.

Duhaime, André

Instants; poem. *Estuaire* Spring 1987; No 44: p33–34.

[Untitled]; poem in French and in English translation. *Cross Can Writ Q* 1987; Vol 9 No 3–4: p9.

Dumas, Evelyn

Fadette, de Saint-Hyacinthe à Toronto; article. *MD* June 6, 1987: pD7.

Traduire c'est trahir, disent les Italiens; mais certains le font avec un tel bonheur!; article. photo · *MD* June 6, 1987: pD1, D8.

Dumas, Hélène

Triangular play development; article about Le Centre d'essai des auteurs dramatiques. photo trans · *Can Theatre R* Spring 1987; No 50: p66–69.

Dumas, Jacqueline

Love and art; letter to the editor. *Books in Can* June-July 1987; Vol 16 No 5: p40.

Dumont, François

Anthologies de poésie québécoise; survey article. *Voix et images* Spring 1987; Vol 12 No 3: p486–492, 494–496.

Dumont, Marilyn

Beyond recognition; poem. *CV 2* Summer 1987; Vol 10 No 4: p26.

"One day in May"; poem. *CV 2* Summer 1987; Vol 10 No 4: p27.

Duncan, Ann

Children's-book artists love their work; article. photo · *MG* Nov 14, 1987: pD1.

There's not much money in kids' books; article. photo · *MG* Nov 14, 1987: pD1.

Duncan, Frances

Female images in some (mostly Canadian) children's books; article. *Room of One's Own* Sept 1987; Vol 11 No 4: p11–24.

[Untitled]; review of *Dzelarhons*. *Room of One's Own* Sept 1987; Vol 11 No 4: p112–115.

Duncan, Mark

[Untitled]; review of *The Old Dance*. *Border Cross* Spring 1987; Vol 6 No 2: p29–30.

[Untitled]; review of *The Fencepost Chronicles*. *Border Cross* Summer 1987; Vol 6 No 3: p23–24.

Dunford, Warren

Moment's glory; short story. photo · *TS* July 29, 1987: pD7.

Dunlap, Thomas R.

"The old kinship of earth": science, man and nature in the animal stories of Charles G.D. Roberts; article. abstract · *J of Can Studies* Spring 1987; Vol 22 No 1: p104–120.

Dunn, Sonja

Gordon Korman: entertaining as ever; review of *Don't Care High*. *Can Child Lit* 1987; No 46: p83.

Dunwoody, Michael

Eyeless in Babylon; poem. *Event* March 1987; Vol 16 No 1: p8–11.

Litany; poem. *Waves* Spring 1987; Vol 15 No 4: p40–43.

Dupré, Louise

Lettre retrouvée; essay. *Estuaire* Summer 1987; No 45: p35–37.

Dupuis, Gilbert

Le pompier et l'immigrant; short story. *Moebius* Winter 1987; No 31: p119–126.

Duquette, Jean-Pierre

Colloque de l'Académie Québec / Francophonie; article. *Lettres québec* Spring 1987; No 45: p69.

Durcan, Paul

Doris fashions; poem. *Antigonish R* 1987; No 69–70: p205.

Nora dreaming of Kilcash; poem. *Antigonish R* 1987; No 69–70: p204.

Dussault, Danielle

L'impolie; short story. *Moebius* Winter 1987; No 31: p71–76.

Dussault, Jean-Claude

Requiem pour l'utopie; essay. *Moebius* Summer 1987; No 33: p25–28.

Duthie, Beth

[Untitled]; review of *Frogs. CH* Jan 25, 1987: pE4.

Dutton, Paul

Else; poem. *Cross Can Writ Q* 1987; Vol 9 No 3–4: p13.

Royal George schedule, June 17 – September 29 Shaw Festival, 1985; poem. *Poetry Can R* Summer 1987; Vol 8 No 4: p13.

The sonic graffitist: Steve McCaffery as improvisor; article. photo · *Open Letter (special issue)* Fall 1987; Vol 6 No 9: p17–25.

[Untitled]; review of *The Weight of Oranges. Quill & Quire* Jan 1987; Vol 53 No 1: p32.

[Untitled]; review of *SP / ELLES. Quill & Quire* Feb 1987; Vol 53 No 2: p20.

Dwyer, Deirdre

Questions for my father; poem. *Event* March 1987; Vol 16 No 1: p61–63.

Summer's gone south; poem. *Germination* Spring 1987; Vol 10 No 2: p22–23.

Dyba, Ken

Backstage; short story. *Prairie J of Can Lit* 1987; No 9: p29–35.

Dyck, Betty

[Untitled]; review of *Can You Promise Me Spring?. Can Auth & Book* Spring 1987; Vol 62 No 3: p25.

Dyck, E.F.

The critical art of Eli Mandel; review of *The Family Romance. Prairie Fire* Autumn 1987; Vol 8 No 3: p98–101.

Looking beyond the landscape; review of *Heading Out. Books in Can* April 1987; Vol 16 No 3: p34.

The rhetoric of the prairie formula-poem; article. *Prairie Fire* Spring 1987; Vol 8 No 1: p71–77.

Trope as topos in the poetry of Robert Kroetsch; review article about *Advice to My Friends. Prairie Fire* Winter 1987–88; Vol 8 No 4: p86, 88–93.

Dyck, Murray J.

La croix d'Emilie; short story. photo · *TS* Aug 15, 1987: pM5.

Dyens, Ollivier

[Untitled]; poetry excerpts from *Légendes.* illus · *La Nouvelle barre du jour* April 1987; No 198: p42–51.

Dyment, Margaret

Poetry's eye; review of *Dark Galaxies. Arc* Spring 1987; No 18: p18–22.

[Untitled]; review of *Shaking the Dreamland Tree. Arc* Fall 1987; No 19: p61–65.

Early, Len

Blewointment: rites of passage; review of *The Last Blewointment Anthology: Volume One. Essays on Can Writ* Winter 1987; No 35: p178–181.

Earnshaw, Lee

The landscape artist; poem. *Alpha* Winter 1987; Vol 11: p18.

The miracle; poem. *Alpha* Winter 1987; Vol 11: p18.

Eason, Bruce

The Appalachian Trail; short story. *Fiddlehead* Spring 1987; No 151: p84.

Meeting you; prose poem. *Fiddlehead* Spring 1987; No 151: p85.

Eaton, Brian

Phyrric victory; poem. *Alpha* Winter 1987; Vol 11: p29.

Edel, Leon

[Untitled]; biographical articles. *Brick (special issue)* Summer 1987; No 30: ppassim.

Edinborough, Arnold

Dispatches from the arts world, east and west; column. *Fin Post* Oct 26, 1987: p21.

A fond look back at the books of autumn; reviews of *The Honorary Patron* and *Swann: A Mystery. Fin Post* Nov 2, 1987: p24.

Summer stock theatre sets stage for winter; column. photo · *Fin Post* Sept 21, 1987: p34.

Edwards, Brian

Novelist as trickster: the magical presence of Gabriel García Márquez in Robert Kroetsch's What The Crow Said; article. *Essays on Can Writ* Spring 1987; No 34: p92–110.

Representation and celebration: Stephen Scobie's rain songs; review of *Expecting Rain*. *Essays on Can Writ* Spring 1987; No 34: p33–38.

Egan, Bessie Condos

Formulaic mysteries to attract unenthusiastic readers; reviews of *The Ghost Ships That Didn't Belong* and *The Secret of Sunset House*. *Quill & Quire (Books for Young People)* June 1987; Vol 53 No 6: p6.

Eisenkraft, Harriet

Bright lights of the city; article. photo · *Tor Life* May 1987; Vol 21 No 7: p54–58, 78, 80–81, 83.

The top 50; article. *Tor Life* May 1987; Vol 21 No 7: p50–53, 72, 74, 77.

Elderkin, Susan Huntley

[Untitled]; reviews of *Stoning the Moon* and *The Deepening of the Colours*. *Quarry* Summer 1987; Vol 36 No 3: p76–79.

Elgaard, Elin

Celia's long weekend; short story. *Grain* Winter 1987; Vol 15 No 4: p76–91.

Ellenwood, Ray

The automatist movement of Montreal: towards non-figuration in painting, dance, and poetry; article. illus · *Can Lit* Summer-Fall 1987; No 113–114: p11–27.

Elliot, Ian

Wouldn't this make one hell of a suicide note?; poem. *Can Auth & Book* Fall 1987; Vol 63 No 1: p16.

Elliot, Patricia

In the eye of abjection: Marie Cardinal's The Words to Say It; article. *Mosaic* Fall 1987; Vol 20 No 4: p71–81.

Ellis, Sarah

Romance and rebellion in young adult fiction; reviews of *Nobody Asked Me* and *Storm Child*. *Can Child Lit* 1987; No 46: p87–89.

Ellison, Victoria

[Untitled]; letter to the editor. *Books in Can* Nov 1987; Vol 16 No 8: p40.

Emmott, Kirsten

Deep underground; poem. *Waves* Spring 1987; Vol 15 No 4: p62–63.

Endicott, Marina

Being Mary; short story. *Grain* Spring 1987; Vol 15 No 1: p74–80.

Engel, Howard

A shot in the park; essay. illus · *G&M* March 14, 1987: pE1.

English, Kathy

Edmonton author's a hit in England; article. photo · *TS* March 8, 1987: pD5.

Enright, Robert

Fiducious says: He who tax reading, will sit on reader's attacks; editorial. *Border Cross* Spring 1987; Vol 6 No 2: p4.

A mazing grace: the writings of Robert Kroetsch; article. *Border Cross* Summer 1987; Vol 6 No 3: p29–30.

Epstein, Ronald

God's chosen people / God's frozen people; poem. *Alpha* Winter 1987; Vol 11: p33.

Subway by night; poem. *Alpha* Winter 1987; Vol 11: p33.

Essar, Dennis

Un beau roman historique; review of *Les Initiés de la Pointe-aux-Cageux*. *Can Child Lit* 1987; No 48: p98–100.

Estok, Michael

Disappearing solitudes; review of *Invisible Fictions*. *Atlan Prov Book R* Sept-Oct 1987; Vol 14 No 3: p12.

[Untitled]; letter to the editor. *New Q* Fall 1987; Vol 7 No 3: p103.

Éthier-Blais, Jean

Andrée Maillet: bien écrire dans la fierté des origines; column. photo · *MD* Sept 19, 1987: pD8.

"La belle inconnue qui déambule depuis des siècles. . . ."; review of *La Fée calcinée*. *MD* Nov 28, 1987: pD14.

Bernard Valiquette, éditeur: "le vin, le vent, la vie. . . ."; column. *MD* June 20, 1987: pD8.

Blizzard. . . .: un sommet dans l'art d'Alice Parizeau; review of *Blizzard sur Québec*. *MD* Dec 5, 1987: pD10.

Cette fleur qui veut occuper tout la place; review of *La Poursuite*. *MD* May 23, 1987: pD8.

Défense (et illustration?) de la langue française; essay. *Liberté (special issue)* 1987: p44–49.

Des mythes canadiens comme les Français les aiment; review of *Tchipayuk ou le chemin du loup*. photo · *MD* Dec 19, 1987: pD10.

Une famille dévorée par l'ennui et le néant de vie inutiles; review of *Les Dimanches sont mortels*. *MD* Nov 21, 1987: pD12.

François Hertel (1905–1985); obituary. *Can Lit* Spring 1987; No 112: p218–221.

Guy Delahaye, un gamin mélancolique, sourire aux lèvres; column. *MD* Sept 12, 1987: pD8.

Un homme dont les semelles étaient de vent; review of *L'Écrit-vent*. *MD* May 16, 1987: pD8.

Hubert Aquin: un héros extérieur à nous mêmes; column. photo · *MD* March 14, 1987: pD5.

Un Italien au Québec: cet autre rivage jamais atteint; column. *MD* Oct 24, 1987: pD8.

J'ai surpris la voix d'un érudit aimable; column. *MD* April 18, 1987: pD8.

Jean Larose: un dialogue entre l'Écrit et l'Oral; column. *MD* Sept 26, 1987: pD8.

Un livre comme Hémon: secret, magique, introuvable; column. *MD* May 30, 1987: pD8.

Menaud prophète: et si Joson n'était pas mort. . . .; column. photo · *MD* Oct 3, 1987: pD8.

Ne restent que ces témoins irrécusables et lumineux; column. *MD* March 21, 1987: pD8.

Le Nelligan de Wyczynski: un si beau cadeau; review. photo · *MD* Dec 24, 1987: pC13.

Ouellette et Royer: depuis la mort jusqu'à l'amour. . . .; reviews of *Les Heures* and *Depuis l'amour*. *MD* June 27, 1987: pC9.

À Saint-Tite, la saga d'un patrimoine secret et sacré; column. photo · *MD* May 2, 1987: pD8.

Un univers peuplé d'éternels voyageurs sans bagages; column. photo · *MD* Nov 14, 1987: pD19.

La vie est bien faite, dit Vendredi, et juste en somme!; column, includes prose excerpt from *L'Hiver au coeur*. *MD* April 4, 1987: pD8.

Le vrai penseur, un beau matin, prend son bâton de pèlerin; review of *Essais inactuels*. *MD* May 9, 1987: pD8.

Étienne, Gérard

Dyane Léger, l'enfant terrible d'Acadie; reviews of *Graines de fées* and *Sorcière du vent!*. photo · *MD* July 4, 1987: pC7.

Evans, Gwyneth

History lessons; review of *White Mist*. *Can Child Lit* 1987; No 45: p55–57.

Evans, Lynne McIlvride

In the morning that is still; poem. *Waves* Winter 1987; Vol 15 No 3: p49.

Wormpickers (illegal immigrants work the night shift); poem. *Waves* Winter 1987; Vol 15 No 3: p49.

Evason, Greg

[Untitled]; poem. *Cross Can Writ Q* 1987; Vol 9 No 3–4: p13.

[Untitled]; poetry excerpt from *Symptoms of Collage*. *Cross Can Writ Q* 1987; Vol 9 No 3–4: p13.

Evasuk, Stasia

Age of reason: play with eight senior actors seeks to dispel myths on aging; article. photo · *TS* Aug 31, 1987: pC3.

Age of reason: she's a giant among storytellers; column about Alice Kane. photo · *TS* March 23, 1987: pC2.

Everard, Mark

[Untitled]; review of *Overlooking the Red Jail*. *Books in Can* June-July 1987; Vol 16 No 5: p22.

Everest, Beth

Hakone; poem. *Quarry* Summer 1987; Vol 36 No 3: p28.

Thru an open window; poem. *Quarry* Summer 1987; Vol 36 No 3: p29.

Everett-Green, Robert

Musical morality tales with a touch of magic; article. *G&M* May 12, 1987: pC10.

Evetts, Josephine

Cycle; poem. *Dandelion* Fall-Winter 1987; Vol 14 No 2: p5–14.

Jacob wrestling; poem. *Dandelion* Spring-Summer 1987; Vol 14 No 1: p22.

Fabre, Michel

Nouvelles du centre; article. *Afram* June 1987; No 25: p1–2.

[Untitled]; review of *The Handmaid's Tale*. *Études can* June 1987; No 22: p136–138.

[Untitled]; review of *The Handmaid's Tale*. *Afram* Jan 1987; No 24: p54–56.

Fagan, Cary

Joanne on Poros; poem. *Antigonish R* 1987; No 69–70: p88.

Magog; poem. *Antigonish R* 1987; No 69–70: p88.

The Paris letters; short story. illus · *Cross Can Writ Q* 1987; Vol 9 No 2: p12–13.

Poetic license: down and out and happy in London; column. *Poetry Can R* Spring 1987; Vol 8 No 2–3: p23.

Poetic license: the great Seymour Thrid; column. *Poetry Can R* Summer 1987; Vol 8 No 4: p12.

The reel stuff; essay. *Books in Can* May 1987; Vol 16 No 4: p3–4.

Something in common; reviews of poetry books. *Prairie Fire* Spring 1987; Vol 8 No 1: p83–87.

To make a short story long; review of *On Middle Ground*. *Books in Can* Aug-Sept 1987; Vol 16 No 6: p19–20.

[Untitled]; review of *The Alligator Report*. *Books in Can* April 1987; Vol 16 No 3: p24.

[Untitled]; review of *The Dream Auditor*. *Books in Can* June-July 1987; Vol 16 No 5: p22.

[Untitled]; reviews of *Standing Flight* and *The Legacy*. *Cross Can Writ Q* 1987; Vol 9 No 2: p24–25.

Women and things; review of *Melancholy Ain't No Baby*. *Prairie Fire* Summer 1987; Vol 8 No 2: p70–71.

A wonderful way to go; review of *Memoirs of a Book-Molesting Childhood*. *Books in Can* Dec 1987; Vol 16 No 9: p32–33.

Faiers, Chris

After work on a small rock in Ashbridge's Bay; poem. *Poetry Can R* Summer 1987; Vol 8 No 4: p17.

Chalk players; poem. photo · *Cross Can Writ Q* 1987; Vol 9 No 2: p3.

Sick day; poem. *Poetry Can R* Summer 1987; Vol 8 No 4: p17.

Fairley, Anne Rockwell

Willie – the fisherman; poem. *Can Auth & Book* Spring 1987; Vol 62 No 3: p21.

Fairweather, Scott

[Untitled]; letter to the editor. *TS* Dec 4, 1987: pD10.

Falk, David

The descent into hell of Jacques Laruelle: chapter I of Under The Volcano; article. *Can Lit* Spring 1987; No 112: p72–83.

Farber, Michael

Canada's a hit with this group; article. *MG* Oct 9, 1987: pA3.

Farkas, Endre

[Untitled]; poem. *Poetry Can R* Fall 1987; Vol 9 No 1: p17.

Farmiloe, Dorothy

The best in poetry; letter to the editor. photo · *G&M* Jan 17, 1987: pD7.

Farrant, M.A.C.

The "we used to be middle-class" cookbook; short story. *Waves* Spring 1987; Vol 15 No 4: p15–17.

Farrell, Dan

It was like being hundreds of miles from a tachometer; poem. *Writing* 1987; No 18: p36–37.

Faulkner, Paul

[Untitled]; review of *The Night Workers of Ragnarök*. *Quarry* Spring 1987; Vol 36 No 2: p116–117.

Fawcett, Brian

The human comedy; review of *Farewell Tour*. *Books in Can* April 1987; Vol 16 No 3: p18.

McFadden's dilemma; article. illus · *Books in Can* March 1987; Vol 16 No 2: p3–5.

Ste[ph]en Reid's Jackrabbit Parole; review. *West Coast R* Spring 1987; Vol 21 No 4: p78–80.

[Untitled]; review of *Virgin Science*. *Books in Can* Jan-Feb 1987; Vol 16 No 1: p28.

Fay, Michael

Copyright worries; letter to the editor. *G&M* Oct 19, 1987: pA6.

Federici, Corrado

[Untitled]; review of *The Other Shore*. *Poetry Can R* Spring 1987; Vol 8 No 2–3: p45–46.

[Untitled]; review of *The Centaur's Mountain*. *Poetry Can R* Summer 1987; Vol 8 No 4: p33.

[Untitled]; review of *Liturgy of Light*. *Poetry Can R* Summer 1987; Vol 8 No 4: p36.

Fee, Margery

Stephen Scobie; interview. biog · *Can Lit* Winter 1987; No 115: p81–102.

Story postponed; review of *Goodbye Harold, Good Luck*. *Can Lit* Winter 1987; No 115: p218–220.

Fensom, Lydia

Dark galaxies: the poetry of Susan McMaster; interview. *Quarry* Fall 1987; Vol 36 No 4: p78–82.

Féral, Josette

Face to face with the actor; theatre review of *La Tour*. photo trans · *Can Theatre R* Spring 1987; No 50: p78–81.

Ferguson, Derek

Olympic Arts Festival unveiled; article. *TS* April 28, 1987: pG1.

Ferguson, Eva

Award-winning writer marches to own beat; article. photo · *CH* Nov 22, 1987: pG8.

Ferguson, Jean

Médiocrité; letter to the editor. *MD* Feb 24, 1987: p8.

Ferguson, Ted

An author in search of a title; essay. photo · *G&M* Feb 14, 1987: pD6.

The hiding place; short story. biog photo · *TS* July 17, 1987: pD7.

Ferguson, Trevor

Getting on a literary roulette wheel; reviews of fictional works. *MG* Nov 14, 1987: pJ11.

Quebec fiction writers dwell in realm of dreams, madness, surrealism; review of *Invisible Fictions*. *MG* July 18, 1987: pJ9.

Spleen may write the poem, but Layton's heart will speak tomorrow; reviews of poetry books. *MG* Sept 26, 1987: pJ11.

Zane Grey heroine turns Western novel upside down; review of *Caprice*. *MG* May 9, 1987: pI9.

Ferland, Guy

Dans les poches; reviews of *Dictionnaire de moi-même* and *Mon cheval pour un royaume*. *MD* May 30, 1987: pD2.

Dans les poches; reviews. *MD* Sept 26, 1987: pD6.

Dans les poches; reviews of paperback books. *MD* Oct 31, 1987: pD6.

Les débuts parisiens d'un jeune Manitobain; article. photo · *MD* Nov 21, 1987: pD1, D12.

La domination française préoccupe davantage les éditeurs; article. photo · *MD* Nov 24, 1987: p13.

Monique Proulx: comme un gratte-ciel; article. photo · *MD* Dec 31, 1987: pC9.

Promenade au Salon du livre; article. *MD* Nov 24, 1987: p13.

La règne du genre mort; article. *MD* Oct 26, 1987: p11.

La revue des revues; reviews of periodicals. *MD* Sept 19, 1987: pD6.

La revue des revues; reviews of periodicals. *MD* Oct 17, 1987: pD6.

La revue des revues; reviews of periodicals. *MD* Dec 5, 1987: pD6.

Le trou de la serrure; review of *Tremblements du désir*. *MD* May 30, 1987: pD3.

La vitrine du livre; review of *Aaa, aâh, ha ou les amours malaisés*. *MD* Jan 3, 1987: pC2.

La vitrine du livre; review of *Saint Cooperblack*. *MD* Jan 31, 1987: pB2.

La vitrine du livre; reviews of *À double sens* and *Le Fils d'Ariane*. *MD* Feb 14, 1987: pC2.

La vitrine du livre; reviews. *MD* March 7, 1987: pB2.

La vitrine du livre; review of *Beaux draps*. *MD* May 16, 1987: pD4.

La vitrine du livre; reviews. *MD* May 9, 1987: pD4.

La vitrine du livre; reviews. *MD* May 2, 1987: pD4.

La vitrine du livre; reviews. *MD* May 23, 1987: pD4.

La vitrine du livre; reviews. *MD* May 30, 1987: pD4.

La vitrine du livre; reviews. *MD* June 6, 1987: pD4.

La vitrine du livre; review of *Le Premier mouvement*. *MD* June 13, 1987: pD4.

La vitrine du livre; reviews. *MD* June 20, 1987: pD4.

La vitrine du livre; reviews of *Trois* and *Vice Versa*. *MD* July 4, 1987: pC6.

La vitrine du livre; reviews of *Retour II: journal d'émotions* and *N'eût été cet été nu*. *MD* July 11, 1987: pC6.

La vitrine du livre; review of *Sprotch et le tuyau manquant*. *MD* July 18, 1987: pC6.

La vitrine du livre; review of *Guy Delahaye et la modernité littéraire*. *MD* July 25, 1987: pC6.

La vitrine du livre; reviews of *Le Jeu illocutoire* and *XYZ*. *MD* Aug 1, 1987: pC6.

La vitrine du livre; review of *Gabrielle Roy et Margaret Laurence: deux chemins, une recherche*. *MD* Aug 8, 1987: pC6.

La vitrine du livre; reviews. *MD* Aug 29, 1987: pC12.

La vitrine du livre; reviews of periodicals. *MD* Sept 5, 1987: pC8.

La vitrine du livre; reviews. *MD* Sept 12, 1987: pD4.

La vitrine du livre; reviews. *MD* Sept 19, 1987: pD4.

La vitrine du livre; review of *Peux-tu attraper Joséphine*. *MD* Sept 26, 1987: pD4.

La vitrine du livre; reviews of *Poètes québécois contemporains* and *Comparaison et raison*. *MD* Oct 10, 1987: pD4.

La vitrine du livre; reviews of *Hommes* and *Heureusement, ici il y a la guerre*. *MD* Oct 17, 1987: pD4.

La vitrine du livre; review of *Tchipayuk ou le chemin du loup*. *MD* Oct 31, 1987: pD4.

La vitrine du livre; reviews. *MD* Nov 7, 1987: pD4.

La vitrine du livre; reviews. *MD* Nov 14, 1987: pD16.

La vitrine du livre; reviews. *MD* Nov 21, 1987: pD4.

La vitrine du livre; reviews of *Le Québec en poésie* and *L'-Aventure, la mésaventure*. *MD* Nov 28, 1987: pD11.

La vitrine du livre; reviews of fictional works. *MD* Dec 5, 1987: pD4.

La vitrine du livre; review of *ô solitude!*. *MD* Dec 19, 1987: pD6.

Ferns, Chris

Growing up in the saddle; review of *Boss of the Namko Drive*. *Can Child Lit* 1987; No 47: p81–82.

Ferns, John

[Untitled]; review of *The Atlantic Anthology*. *British J of Can Studies* June 1987; Vol 2 No 1: p184–185.

[Untitled]; review of *The Northern Imagination*. *British J of Can Studies* June 1987; Vol 2 No 1: p187–188.

Versions of St. Hope; review of *The Life of Hope*. *Can Lit* Spring 1987; No 112: p114–115.

Ferrell, Sarah

Realpolitik of the spirit; article. photo · *NYT Book R* Sept 27, 1987: p11.

Ferres, John H.

[Untitled]; review of *Robertson Davies*. *Amer R of Can Studies* Winter 1987–88; Vol 17 No 4: p450–452.

Ferri, John

First World War propaganda undermined truth about second; article. photo · *CH* Nov 11, 1987: pA5.

Propagandists had huge impact; article. *TS* Nov 8, 1987: pA16.

Ferron, Jacques

[Untitled]; prose excerpt from *Quince Jam*. *Brick (special issue)* Summer 1987; No 30: p57.

Fetherling, Doug

The end of Fulford's era; article. *Maclean's* July 6, 1987; Vol 100 No 27: p53.

F.R. Scott: just portrayal of a poetic humanist; review of *The Politics of the Imagination*. photo · *Quill & Quire* Sept 1987; Vol 53 No 9: p80.

Mandel's two minds and Woodcock's single purpose; reviews of *The Family Romance* and *Northern Spring*. photo · *Quill & Quire* May 1987; Vol 53 No 5: p20.

Memoirs of the Renaissance; short story. *Quarry* Summer 1987; Vol 36 No 3: p38–44.

Fiamengo, Marya

Destinations; reviews of *Essential Words* and *Voix-Off*. *Can Lit* Spring 1987; No 112: p112–114.

Fieber, Glenn

A private enterprise; poem. *Event* Summer 1987; Vol 16 No 2: p100–101.

Filewod, Alan

The hand that feeds; article. photo · *Can Theatre R* Summer 1987; No 51: p9–15.

The ideological formation of political theatre in Canada; article. abstract · *Theatre Hist in Can* Fall 1987; Vol 8 No 2: p254–263.

The political dramaturgy of the Mummers Troupe; article. *Can Drama* 1987; Vol 13 No 1: p60–71.

Popular theatre; editorial. *Can Theatre R* Winter 1987; No 53: p3.

Filewod, Ian

Underdeveloped alliance; essay. photo · *Can Theatre R* Winter 1987; No 53: p39–42.

Filip, Raymond

Another brick in the wall; article. *Books in Can* Aug-Sept 1987; Vol 16 No 6: p4–5.

Dada processing; essay. *Books in Can* Nov 1987; Vol 16 No 8: p4–5.

Flashes of mortality; review of *Zembla's Rocks*. *Books in Can* April 1987; Vol 16 No 3: p36.

Kid's stuff; essay. *Books in Can* Dec 1987; Vol 16 No 9: p6–7.

No respect; letter to the editor. *Books in Can* April 1987; Vol 16 No 3: p40.

Skin deep; review of *Other Voices*. *Books in Can* Oct 1987; Vol 16 No 7: p28–29.

Speculations: honk: American and Canadian vernacular; column. *Poetry Can R* Summer 1987; Vol 8 No 4: p19.

Speculations: roots & other treasures; column. *Poetry Can R* Spring 1987; Vol 8 No 2–3: p21.

Speculations: the ethnic music in Canadian poetry; column. *Poetry Can R* Fall 1987; Vol 9 No 1: p18.

[Untitled]; review of *Behind the Orchestra*. *Books in Can* Nov 1987; Vol 16 No 8: p26.

Filson, Bruce K.

The lawless spirit; short story. *Quarry* Summer 1987; Vol 36 No 3: p20–24.

A unicorn's invention; short story. *Prairie J of Can Lit* 1987; No 9: p7–13.

Filter, Reinhard

Dreammaker; short story. *Prism* Winter 1987; Vol 25 No 2: p55–57.

Finch, Roger

Essentials of set design; poem. *Waves* Spring 1987; Vol 15 No 4: p56.

The origin of fire; poem. *Wascana R* Fall 1987; Vol 22 No 2: p28–29.

Papermaking; poem. *Antigonish R* 1987; No 69–70: p68.

Findley, Timothy

Bragg and Minna; short story. *Malahat R* Sept 1987; No 80: p5–22.

A life of eloquence and radicalism; obituary. photo · *Maclean's* Jan 19, 1987; Vol 100 No 3: p52–53.

My final hour: an address to the Philosophy Society, Trent University, Monday, 26 January 1987; essay. abstract · *J of Can Studies* Spring 1987; Vol 22 No 1: p5–16.

The name's the same; short story. *Grain* Spring 1987; Vol 15 No 1: p16–24.

Through the looking glass; review of *Storm Glass*. *Books in Can* June-July 1987; Vol 16 No 5: p14.

Writing: the pain & the pleasure; essay. illus · *TS* March 21, 1987: pM1,M5.

Fines, Beatrice

Wanted: dead or alive; editorial. *Can Auth & Book* Winter 1987; Vol 62 No 2: pii.

Fink, Howard

CKUA: radio drama and regional theatre; article. abstract · *Theatre Hist in Can* Fall 1987; Vol 8 No 2: p221–233.

Finley, David

Kahlua bath; short story. *New Q* Winter 1987; Vol 6 No 4: p21–24.

Witch hazel; short story. illus · *NeWest R* Nov 1987; Vol 13 No 3: p12, 17.

Finnigan, Joan

[Untitled]; poetry excerpt from *Songs from Both Sides of the River*. *Quarry* Summer 1987; Vol 36 No 3: p59–61.

Fisette, Jean

La poésie de Paul-Marie Lapointe; review of *Paul-Marie Lapointe*. *Voix et images* Autumn 1987; Vol 13 No 1: p174–178.

La poésie du point de vue de la réception; review of *Pragmatique de la poésie québécoise*. *Voix et images* Winter 1987; No 35: p314–318.

Fisher, Randy

Geologists find gold in arts; article. photo · *Fin Post* May 4, 1987: p22.

Fitzgerald, John

Young writer explores time-honored themes; theatre review of *Young Art*. photo · *G&M* Jan 17, 1987: pE13.

Fitzgerald, Judith

Bill Percy turns his back on the sea; biographical article. photo · *TS* June 21, 1987: pD8.

A body of love; poem. *Cross Can Writ Q* 1987; Vol 9 No 1: p27.

Desperately seeking Susan; essay. photo · *TS* June 18, 1987: pD1, D4.

Does one need a passport for Arcadia?; essay. *TS* July 26, 1987: pA21.

February; poem. *Can Forum* May 1987; Vol 67 No 769: p26–27.

In the home of your hands; poems. illus · *Can Forum* May 1987; Vol 67 No 769: p26–29.

January; poem. *Can Forum* May 1987; Vol 67 No 769: p26.

June; poem. *Can Forum* May 1987; Vol 67 No 769: p27–28.

Kelly's taut, grim narrative; review of *A Dream Like Mine*. *TS* Nov 22, 1987: pC9.

November; poem. *Can Forum* May 1987; Vol 67 No 769: p28–29.

October; poem. *Can Forum* May 1987; Vol 67 No 769: p28.

Oh, for the good old days; letter to the editor. *Quill & Quire* July 1987; Vol 53 No 7: p6.

Poetic licence: G-G's list: what? No women poets?; column. *TS* May 10, 1987: pA23.

Poetic licence: poetry is dead, so why do we need reviews?; column. *TS* June 28, 1987: pA19.

Poetic licence: with best wishes, to Irving Layton; column. *TS* May 31, 1987: pA23.

Poetic licence: yes, you can discuss literature and bend an elbow here; essay. illus · *TS* Aug 9, 1987: pA21.

So you think poetry no longer exists for readers?; reviews of *Afterworlds* and *Sanding Down This Rocking Chair on a Windy Night*. photo · *TS* May 3, 1987: pA24.

With these older poets, the strengths are intrinsic; reviews of poetry books. photo · *TS* Dec 20, 1987: pE6.

Flaherty, Kathleen

[Untitled]; letter to the editor. *TS* Nov 27, 1987: pD11.

Fleck, Polly

Coyote's last trick; poem. *Dandelion* Spring-Summer 1987; Vol 14 No 1: p28.

Flomen, Marty

City of caves; poem. *Can Auth & Book* Fall 1987; Vol 63 No 1: p16.

Flood, Cynthia

Tabletalk; short story. *Event* Summer 1987; Vol 16 No 2: p25–32.

Twoscore and five; short story. *Room of One's Own* April 1987; Vol 11 No 3: p3–16.

A young girl-typist ran to Smolny: notes for a film; short story. *Prism* Winter 1987; Vol 25 No 2: p40–50.

Flood, John

Editor's notebook; editorial. *Northward J* 1987; No 41: p2.

Editor's notebook; editorial. *Northward J* 1987; No 42: p2.

Floyd, Donald

Stories strange, disturbing; review of *Inspecting the Vaults*. *WFP* April 18, 1987: p50.

Flynn, Andrew

[Untitled]; reviews of *In the Spirit of the Times* and *One Night*. *Rubicon* Spring 1987; No 8: p202–205.

Flynn, David M.

Duel; short story. photo · *TS* July 31, 1987: pD6.

Fogg, Lea

Frankie get your gun!; short story. photo · *TS* July 28, 1987: pC5.

Folch-Ribas, Jacques

Amérique, utopie; review of *Les Matins du Nouveau Monde*. *Liberté* June 1987; Vol 29 No 3: p106–107.

Architecture et Éros: la théorie et la pratique; essay. illus · *Liberté* Oct 1987; Vol 29 No 5: p36–47.

Le fragment de Nadine; essay. *Liberté* Feb 1987; Vol 29 No 1: p66–67.

L'épormyable élan; article. *Liberté* Aug 1987; Vol 29 No 4: p128–129.

Le Prince Anar; play. *Liberté* Dec 1987; Vol 29 No 6: p57–89.

Regardage: à bon regardeur, salut; essay. *Liberté* June 1987; Vol 29 No 3: p19–22.

Suzanne Lamy; obituary. *Liberté* June 1987; Vol 29 No 3: p103.

Folsom, Eric

A man shopping; poem. *Arc* Fall 1987; No 19: p66.

The March snow; poem. *Arc* Fall 1987; No 19: p67.

The old road to Sydenham; poem. *Quarry* Winter 1987; Vol 36 No 1: p112.

Foote, Peter

How it strikes a philologist: George Johnston's translation of saga prose; article. *Malahat R (special issue)* March 1987; No 78: p92–97.

Foran, Charles

Flag; short story. *Rubicon* Fall 1987; No 9: p7–29.

[Untitled]; review of *The Alley Cat*. *Rubicon* Spring 1987; No 8: p176–178.

Forbes, Greg

By Lago Atitlan; poem. *Quarry* Winter 1987; Vol 36 No 1: p98–101.

An unmarked car; poem. *Quarry* Winter 1987; Vol 36 No 1: p97–98.

Ford, Catherine

Moore didn't finish his suspense novel; review of *The Color of Blood*. *CH* Sept 5, 1987: pH7.

Forest, Luc

Dipalindrome: l'été buté, tu, bétel, le té bu, te tube tel; poem. *La Nouvelle barre du jour* Feb 1987; No 193: p29.

La mer à boire; poem. *La Nouvelle barre du jour* Feb 1987; No 193: p30.

Palindrome 7035 lettres: la brève muse rude du résumé verbal; poem. *La Nouvelle barre du jour* Feb 1987; No 193: p31–44.

Tétraholorime: sa rime s'arrime; poem. illus · *La Nouvelle barre du jour* Feb 1987; No 193: p27–28.

Tétrapalindrome; poem. *La Nouvelle barre du jour* Feb 1987; No 193: p30.

Forint, Alexander

Short stories dwell on death and dying; letter to the editor. *TS* July 14, 1987: pA12.

Forman, Gideon

[Untitled]; review of *Black Swan. Books in Can* May 1987; Vol 16 No 4: p20–21.

[Untitled]; review of *Ashbourn. Books in Can* June-July 1987; Vol 16 No 5: p24.

[Untitled]; review of *Mother I'm So Glad You Taught Me How to Dance. Books in Can* Aug-Sept 1987; Vol 16 No 6: p28.

Where it's near; review of *Remembering Summer. Books in Can* April 1987; Vol 16 No 3: p22.

Forsey, Eugene

[Untitled]; biographical articles. *Brick (special issue)* Summer 1987; No 30: ppassim.

Forst, Graham

Zarathustran; review of *Waiting for the Messiah. Can Lit* Spring 1987; No 112: p109–110.

Forsyth, Louise H.

Les femmes dans le théâtre du Québec et du Canada / Women in the theatre of Quebec and Canada; introduction. *Theatre Hist in Can (special issue)* Spring 1987; Vol 8 No 1: p3–7.

Forth, Steven

Winter yellow; poem. *Writing* Nov 1987; No 19: p30–36.

Foster, Deborah

STARR: teaching responsible sex; article. photo · *Can Theatre R* Winter 1987; No 53: p76–78.

Foster, Jim

What would you do as PM?; article. *TS* Nov 8, 1987: pD7.

Fotheringham, Allan

Farley Mowat gets U.S. again; column. *CH* Oct 29, 1987: pA8.

Fournier, Carol Ann

The silver frame; short story. *Room of One's Own* Sept 1987; Vol 11 No 4: p100–107.

Fournier, Marcel

Le "médecin de Nelligan"; review of *Guy Delahaye et la modernité littéraire. MD* Aug 29, 1987: pC14.

Fox, Sandra

Zelda Zelda; poem. *CV 2* Summer 1987; Vol 10 No 4: p38–39.

Fraser, Graham

[Untitled]; biographical articles. *Brick (special issue)* Summer 1987; No 30: ppassim.

Fraser, Keath

Damages; short story. *Prism* Spring 1987; Vol 25 No 3: p55–64.

Fraser, Matthew

Death theme recurs in Maillet play; theatre review of *Margot la Folle.* photo · *G&M* Oct 12, 1987: pC9.

Fridolin's as funny as ever; theatre review of *Les Fridolinades.* photo · *G&M* Jan 27, 1987: pC5.

Hyde is named Author of the Year; article. photo · *G&M* Nov 17, 1987: pD7.

Leaping in triumph across cultural frontiers; article. photo · *G&M* Dec 26, 1987: pC10.

National Library acquires 'a real treasure trove'; article. photo · *G&M* Oct 7, 1987: pC7.

Neptune Theatre's Barometer Rising too faithful to book; theatre review. *G&M* Nov 9, 1987: pD9.

Night of Little Knives aims its barbs at cults; theatre review of *La Nuit des p'tits couteaux.* photo · *G&M* Jan 19, 1987: pC9.

Ouzounian finds a niche in Halifax; article. photo · *G&M* Dec 21, 1987: pC9.

A playwright bares his soul; theatre review of *Le Vrai monde?.* photo · *G&M* April 25, 1987: pC5.

Six days of praise for the printed page; article about the Salon du livre de Montréal. photo · *G&M* Nov 7, 1987: pC13.

Taken for granted?; article about the Canada Council. illus photo · *G&M* Feb 28, 1987: pE1, E5.

Translating words into action; article about literary translation. illus · *G&M* Feb 7, 1987: pE1, E4.

A work of power, imagination; article. photo · *G&M* Nov 30, 1987: pC9.

Fraser, Sharon

Taking the measure of Maxine; article. photo · *Atlan Insight* Sept 1987; Vol 9 No 9: p16–18.

Fraticelli, Marco

Poetry in motion – new dimensions in creating with computers; article. illus · *Cross Can Writ Q* 1987; Vol 9 No 3–4: p19–20.

Fraumeni, Paul

The southbound; short story. photo · *TS* July 20, 1987: pA14.

Frazer, Frances

Wars with internal dragons; reviews of *Lost and Found* and *Different Dragons. Can Child Lit* 1987; No 45: p91–93.

Fréchette, Carole

Grandeur et misère: le retour du père sur la scène québécoise; article. photo · *Jeu* 1987; No 45: p17–35.

"L'arte è un veicolo": entretien avec Robert Lepage; interview. photo · *Jeu* 1987; No 42: p109–126.

À l'écoute du texte; introduction. *Jeu* 1987; No 45: p15.

Thèmes et formes; article. photo · *Jeu* 1987; No 42: p40–48.

Freedman, Benjamin

The doctor-patient relationship; poem. *Prism* Summer 1987; Vol 25 No 4: p90–91.

Freiberg, Stanley K.

To Goya; poem. *Ariel* April 1987; Vol 18 No 2: p12–13.

Freir, Pam

Arthur's legacy; short story. photo · *TS* July 30, 1987: pH7.

French, D.

[Untitled]; review of *Homecoming*. *Books in Can* Nov 1987; Vol 16 No 8: p24.

[Untitled]; review of *The Port Dalhousie Stories*. *Books in Can* Nov 1987; Vol 16 No 8: p25.

French, William

Anti-smoking message is right on target; column. *G&M* April 14, 1987: pC7.

Booking time for the issues; column. *G&M* April 21, 1987: pD7.

Buoyant mood at booksellers' annual meeting; column. *G&M* June 30, 1987: pD7.

Canadian authors spend spare time reading each other; article. photo · *G&M* Feb 17, 1987: pC7.

Canadian readers may be all booked up this fall; preview of fall book list. photo · *G&M* Aug 20, 1987: pC1.

Canadian writers make headlines in France; column. photo · *G&M* Dec 22, 1987: pD5.

Celebrity status leaves Maillet 'street-wise'; column. *G&M* Aug 13, 1987: pD1.

Change is in the wind; column. photo · *G&M* May 19, 1987: pC9.

Columns prompt readers to write; column. *G&M* April 7, 1987: pC7.

Conflicting memories of a friend about to self-destruct; review of *Malcolm Lowry: Vancouver Days*. photo · *G&M* June 18, 1987: pD1.

A corporate romp in Adland, N.Y.; review of *No Holds Barred*. *G&M* March 14, 1987: pE19.

Czech detective a belated delight; review of *The Mournful Demeanor of Lieutenant Boruvka*. *G&M* Sept 10, 1987: pD1.

Disasters, memoirs, news headline spring book list; preview of spring book list. *G&M* March 12, 1987: pC1.

The driven writer; review of *Beyond the Blue Mountains*. *G&M* Nov 21, 1987: pC21.

Fiction, women writers preferred by readers, survey finds; column. photo · *G&M* April 28, 1987: pC5.

Fiction's favorites show their colors for fall; preview of fall book list. *G&M* Aug 21, 1987: pC9.

Food for thought and literature; review of *The CanLit Foodbook*. *G&M* Nov 14, 1987: pE3.

Free-fall fiction; review of *In the Skin of a Lion*. *G&M* May 23, 1987: pC21.

Gators, jugglers and the gerbil that ate L.A.; review of *The Alligator Report*. illus · *G&M* Feb 19, 1987: pC1.

Getting an early start in the book game; column. *G&M* Nov 24, 1987: pD5.

Ghosts, gondolas and some fantastical imagining; review of *Five New Facts About Giorgione*. photo · *G&M* Sept 1, 1987: pD7.

The grisly trade in animals; column. *G&M* Sept 29, 1987: pD5.

A gritty tale of a teacher's turmoil among the Cree; review of *Contact Prints*. photo · *G&M* April 9, 1987: pC1.

High performance; review of *87: Best Canadian Stories*. *G&M* Dec 19, 1987: pC21.

Historical novel starring oak tree a shade too slow; review of *Tranter's Tree*. photo · *G&M* June 11, 1987: pD1.

The holy murder; review of *The Color of Blood*. *G&M* Sept 5, 1987: pC13.

It's CanLit's turn on literary assembly line; review of *Canadian Writers Since 1960 (First Series)*. *G&M* Jan 20, 1987: pD9.

Jolts suggest that publishing is no longer a trade for the gentle folk; article. photo · *G&M* Dec 26, 1987: pC21.

King Leary is a type of literary hat trick; review. photo · *G&M* Oct 20, 1987: pD5.

The likeable poet; review of *E.J. Pratt: The Master Years*. *G&M* Dec 5, 1987: pC21.

Literary minutiae; review of *The Oxford Illustrated Literary Guide to Canada*. *G&M* Nov 28, 1987: pC19.

Making short work of an award winner; column. *G&M* Dec 8, 1987: pD5.

Marriage and violence Western-Canadian style; reviews of *Getting Married in Buffalo Jump* and *The Dancing Chicken*. photo · *G&M* Nov 19, 1987: pA25.

Mawkish history; review of *Between Men*. *G&M* Sept 26, 1987: pC21.

McClelland's exit ends chapter in Canadian publishing; article. photo · *G&M* Feb 20, 1987: pD5.

Memories of Malcolm Lowry; column. illus · *G&M* Aug 18, 1987: pD7.

Middle class under fire; review of *Red Wolf, Red Wolf*. photo · *G&M* Sept 3, 1987: pC1.

Mired in reality; review of *The Honorary Patron*. *G&M* Sept 19, 1987: pC17.

A moving tribute to a great writer; article. photo · *G&M* Jan 10, 1987: pE6.

New award celebrates Commonwealth writers; column. photo · *G&M* Nov 17, 1987: pD7.

Novel about family tragedy a powerful debut; review of *The Butterfly Chair*. illus · *G&M* Dec 3, 1987: pA25.

Poetry sweatshops add a new twist to Olympic tradition; column. *G&M* March 3, 1987: pC7.

Polished prose from diplomat; biographical article. photo · *G&M* Jan 27, 1987: pC5.

Prairie writer displays poise and assurance in book of short stories; review of *A Stone Watermelon*. photo · *G&M* March 5, 1987: pD1.

Promotion ordeal inspires Berton to do even more; column. *G&M* Sept 15, 1987: pA21.

Public Lending Right debate takes new twist; column. *G&M* Nov 10, 1987: pD7.

Raising two worthy books from the dead; reviews of *Kicking Against the Pricks* and *Incognito*. photo · *G&M* Feb 24, 1987: pD7.

Recapturing flower-power days; review of *Remembering Summer*. *G&M* Feb 12, 1987: pC1.

A red-letter day for Canadian writers; column. *G&M* March 10, 1987: pD7.

A reminder 'of the covenant that binds man to moth and star'; review of *Dancing on the Shore*. *G&M* Sept 17, 1987: pD1.

The road to evil; review of *Heartbreaks Along the Road*. *G&M* Oct 17, 1987: pE3.

A salute to a writer of rare integrity; article. photo · *G&M* Jan 6, 1987: pC5.

Saturday Night changes will take time to implement; column. photo · *G&M* Dec 15, 1987: pD5.

A shimmering crop of short stories from 'other' places; review of *Storm Glass*. *G&M* June 25, 1987: pD1.

There's still room for the Great Mall Novel; review of *The Promised Land*. photo · *G&M* March 19, 1987: pD1.

Timely celebrations of women's achievements; column. photo · *G&M* Dec 1, 1987: pD5.

Translators feast on Pheasant; column. illus · *G&M* Sept 22, 1987: pD5.

The tribulations of these teens are a trial for readers; review of *The Port Dalhousie Stories*. illus · *G&M* April 23, 1987: pC1.

Tropical dreaming; review of *Brazilian Journal*. *G&M* June 27, 1987: pE17.

U.S. school bans use of Farley Mowat book; column. *G&M* May 12, 1987: pC7.

Wacky novel competition hits bottom with a thud; review of *Hardwired Angel*. *G&M* Aug 25, 1987: pD7.

Writers lend their expertise; column. *G&M* June 23, 1987: pD5.

Fretwell, Kathy

Summer hiatus; poem. *Quarry* Fall 1987; Vol 36 No 4: p34.

Frey, Cecelia

Apocalyptic consumers; review of *The Late Great Human Road Show*. photo · *CH* March 15, 1987: pE5.

Cats and tea leaves; short story. illus · *Antigonish R* 1987; No 69–70: p169–177.

The man who heard things; short story. *Matrix* Spring 1987; No 24: p50–57.

Morbid stories confront human spirit; review of *Medieval Hour in the Author's Mind*. *CH* June 21, 1987: pE5.

New author weaves poetic stories into magical fantasy; review of *Beneath the Western Slopes*. *CH* Sept 20, 1987: pE6.

Novel loses its energy in whirlpool; review of *The Whirlpool*. *CH* Jan 11, 1987: pF4.

Rollicking tale captures spirit of Acadian life; review of *Mariaagélas*. photo · *CH* Jan 4, 1987: pE4.

Shields fashions mystery; review of *Swann: A Mystery*. photo · *CH* Nov 22, 1987: pA16.

Sitting; poem. *NeWest R* Sept 1987; Vol 13 No 1: p15.

[Untitled]; review of *The Promised Land*. *CH* May 17, 1987: pE5.

[Untitled]; review of *Some of Eve's Daughters*. *CH* June 7, 1987: pE6.

Victims left poised, petrified; review of *A Stone Watermelon*. *CH* April 12, 1987: pF7.

Women make difference in prairie family; review of *Under the House*. *CH* July 19, 1987: pE4.

Wriggling into the light; poem. *NeWest R* Sept 1987; Vol 13 No 1: p15.

Fricke, Gitta

Delightful play; letter to the editor. photo · *WFP* Oct 20, 1987: p6.

Friedlander, Mira

B-Movie could extend run but 'that would be suicide'; article. photo · *TS* March 13, 1987: pC11.

Friedman, Thomas B.

Realizing Kroetsch's poetry; reviews of *Excerpts from the Real World* and *Seed Catalogue*. *Prairie Fire* Winter 1987–88; Vol 8 No 4: p95–98.

Friesen, Patrick

Albert Street mirror for Carol; poem. *CV 2* Spring 1987; Vol 10 No 3: p35.

Dream of the black river; poem. *CV 2* Spring 1987; Vol 10 No 3: p36–37.

Friesen, Sofiah

Teenage eating problems; review of *I Was a 15-Year-Old Blimp*. *Can Child Lit* 1987; No 46: p84.

Frost, Helen

Mud, sticks, food; poem. *Fiddlehead* Winter 1987; No 154: p15.

Fry, August J.

[Untitled]; review of *Varieties of Exile*. *British J of Can Studies* June 1987; Vol 2 No 1: p180–181.

Fuchs, Barbara

Definitions; poem. *NeWest R* Sept 1987; Vol 13 No 1: p13.

Today I raked leaves; poem. *NeWest R* Sept 1987; Vol 13 No 1: p13.

Fulford, Robert

Alone at the microphone, Jack McClelland takes a final bow; article. photo · *Sat Night* June 1987; Vol 102 No 6: p56.

Anne's secret quality keeps her coming back; column. *TS* Dec 5, 1987: pF1.

Brilliant comic leaves us gasping; column. photo · *TS* June 20, 1987: pM5.

Day the book world changed forever; column. *TS* Aug 1, 1987: pM7.

Insulting an author; letter to the editor. *G&M* July 17, 1987: pA6.

Nearly 30 years and still promising; column. *TS* May 2, 1987: pM5.

Old heck; column. illus · *Sat Night* Nov 1987; Vol 102 No 11: p7–8, 10–11.

Orphan from Neepawa; editorial article. illus · *Sat Night* May 1987; Vol 102 No 5: p5–6.

Sound ship in a sea of malice; column about the Canada Council. photo · *TS* March 28, 1987: pM5.

A unique way of seeing the world; column. *TS* Sept 26, 1987: pM5.

Fuller, Guy M.

Liturgies; poetry excerpt from *Fathers*. *NeWest R* Sept 1987; Vol 13 No 1: p4.

Fullerton, Mimi

Wrong network; letter to the editor. *G&M* Oct 19, 1987: pA6.

Gabriel, Barbara

Fairly good times: an interview with Mavis Gallant. *Can Forum* Feb 1987; Vol 66 No 766: p23–27.

Gagné, René

Du réel à l'imaginaire; review of *Planéria*. *Can Child Lit* 1987; No 47: p94–95.

Le roman policier désarmé; review of *Vol à retardement*. *Can Child Lit* 1987; No 46: p85–86.

Gagné, Sylvie

Extrait de naissance; prose poem. illus · *La Nouvelle barre du jour* May 1987; No 200: p53–60.

Gagnon, André

Translations of children's books in Canada; article. bibliog · *Can Child Lit* 1987; No 45: p14–53.

Gagnon, Andrée

[Untitled]; letter to the editor. *Lettres québec* Spring 1987; No 45: p7.

Gagnon, Daniel

Les archipels; short story. *Liberté* Dec 1987; Vol 29 No 6: p28–30.

Le corps de l'âme; letter to the editor. *MD* May 25, 1987: p8.

Gagnon, Jean

Strip-tease; essay. *Moebius* Autumn 1987; No 34: p39–47.

Gagnon, Jean Chapdelaine

L'industrie du livre y trouve son compte; article. *MD* Nov 14, 1987: pD8.

Le livre de poche au Québec: la grande histoire de petits livres; article. photo · *MD* Oct 24, 1987: pD1, D8.

[Untitled]; review of *Poèmes 1*. *Estuaire* Spring 1987; No 44: p79–80.

[Untitled]; review of *Depuis l'amour*. *Estuaire* Summer 1987; No 45: p57–58.

[Untitled]; letter to the editor. *MD* Oct 10, 1987: pD4.

[Untitled]; reviews of *Les Noms du père* and *Coq à deux têtes*. *Estuaire* Autumn 1987; No 46: p85–86.

Gagnon, Madeleine

A la mémoire d'André Belleau; essay. *Liberté* Feb 1987; Vol 29 No 1: p68–69.

[Untitled]; poem. *Liberté* Feb 1987; Vol 29 No 1: p69.

Gailliot, Jean-Hubert

Trente-six chandelles; prose poem. illus · *La Nouvelle barre du jour* May 1987; No 200: p77–85.

Gajdel, Edward

Stars of the city, year two; photographic portfolio. *Tor Life* Oct 1987; Vol 21 No 1[5]: p89–95.

Galef, David

Night ward; short story. *Prism* Winter 1987; Vol 25 No 2: p7–15.

Gallagher, S.F.

[Untitled]; review of *Robertson Davies, Playwright*. *Eng Studies in Can* June 1987; Vol 13 No 2: p234–237.

Gallant, Mavis

Dédé; short story. *New Yorker* Jan 5, 1987; Vol 62 No 46: p28–34.

Let it pass; short story. *New Yorker* May 18, 1987; Vol 63 No 13: p38–50, 52–53, 56–58,

Men were all she needed; excerpt from *Overhead in a Balloon*. *NYT Book R* March 15, 1987: p7.

Gallays, François

Faut-il brûler Clavel?; reviews of novels by Bernard Clavel. photo · *Lettres québec* Autumn 1987; No 47: p27–29.

Galt, George

Giant steps; review of *Collected Poems*. *Books in Can* Jan-Feb 1987; Vol 16 No 1: p16–17.

The poet in the pink palace; review article about *Brazilian Journal*. photo · *Sat Night* Sept 1987; Vol 102 No 9: p61–63.

Gamache, Chantal

André Belleau et le Cercle Bakhtin; article. *Liberté* Feb 1987; Vol 29 No 1: p54–57.

"Un blessé qui se sauve"; review of *Le Pouvoir des mots, les maux du pouvoir. Lettres québec* Winter 1986–87; No 44: p83.

Des personnages et un langage qui se déchirent; review of *Un Oiseau vivant dans la gueule.* photo · *MD* Oct 24, 1987: pD3.

Des regards qui s'attardent; review of *Plages. MD* April 4, 1987: pD3.

En toute simplicité; review of *Voix et images.* photo · *MD* Nov 7, 1987: pD3.

Une histoire de jeunesse; review of *Tableau de jeunesse. MD* May 23, 1987: pD3.

L'intérêt de Voix & images pour les aventures culturelles de notre société; review. *MD* April 25, 1987: pD3.

Lire et relire Marie-Claire Blais; review of *L'Oeuvre romanesque de Marie-Claire Blais. Lettres québec* Spring 1987; No 45: p52.

La route sinue fortement; review of *Extrême livre des voyages. Lettres québec* Autumn 1987; No 47: p70.

Les voix des Amériques; review of *Voix et images* (special issue). *MD* March 21, 1987: pD2.

Gamache, Donna

Paper plates; short story. photo · *TS* Aug 9, 1987: pD5.

Gambi, Vincent

Haiku; poem. *Tor Life* March 1987; Vol 21 No 4: p17.

Haiku; poem. *Tor Life* March 1987; Vol 21 No 4: p27.

Haiku; poem. *Tor Life* May 1987; Vol 21 No 7: p33.

Haiku; poem. *Tor Life* May 1987; Vol 21 No 7: p70.

Haiku; poem. *Tor Life* May 1987; Vol 21 No 7: p71.

Haiku; poem. *Tor Life* Sept 1987; Vol 21 No 13: p36.

Haiku; poem. *Tor Life* Oct 1987; Vol 21 No 15: p52.

Haiku; poem. *Tor Life* Nov 1987; Vol 21 No 17: p105.

Haiku; poem. *Tor Life* Dec 1987; Vol 21 No 18: p116.

Three haiku; poems. *Tor Life* Sept 1987; Vol 21 No 13: p74.

Gamester, George

CNE goers always knew that Chuck was a hustler; biographical article. *TS* Sept 3, 1987: pA2.

Fingers was a real wizard at keyboards, not smalltalk; biographical article. *TS* Nov 12, 1987: pA2.

How Newfie named Porky just died for TV fame; biographical article. *TS* June 25, 1987: pA2.

Professor loved booze but had sense of humor; biographical article. *TS* Sept 17, 1987: pA2.

Rob had presence as student in the '20s; biographical article. *TS* Oct 15, 1987: pA2.

Garand, Dominique

Des contes et des nouvelles pour rêver; reviews of short story books. *Voix et images* Spring 1987; Vol 12 No 3: p551–555.

Entretien; interview with Paul Chamberland. *Moebius* Summer 1987; No 33: p5–24.

Entrevue de Pierre Vallières; interview. *Moebius (special issue)* Spring 1987; No 32: p5–21.

Le mal-à-l'oeuvre; short story. *Moebius* Autumn 1987; No 34: p65–72.

Ostentation / présentation / tentation; editorial. *Moebius* Autumn 1987; No 34: p1–5.

Gard, Peter

The company he keeps; review of *Ned 'n' Me. Atlan Prov Book R* Sept-Oct 1987; Vol 14 No 3: p13.

Gardner, Susan

Manicure; poem. *Can Auth & Book* Winter 1987; Vol 62 No 2: p22.

Garebian, Keith

Drama of failed pole trek unfulfilled; reviews of *Flight of the Falcon* and *Poems New and Selected. TS* Oct 31, 1987: pM5.

Enter stage centre: can Toronto build a national theatre?; article. *Can Forum* Aug-Sept 1987; Vol 67 No 771: p24–29.

Examining the blight of solitude; review of *Bring Me Your Passion. TS* Dec 27, 1987: pE19.

Gender aside, a strong collection of stories by Canadian women; review of *More Stories by Canadian Women. TS* Oct 31, 1987: pM11.

Poets in search of praise; reviews of *One Night at the Indigo Hotel* and *The Bones of Their Occasion. TS* May 16, 1987: pM4.

Slight drag but Cormorant takes off; reviews of *Slow Mist* and *Exile Home / Exilio En la Patria.* photo · *TS* March 28, 1987: pM4.

Stories of the West best when satirical; review of *The Unsettling of the West.* photo · *TS* May 24, 1987: pA19.

[Untitled]; review of *Skelton at 60. Quill & Quire* Feb 1987; Vol 53 No 2: p18.

[Untitled]; review of *Prague. Quill & Quire* June 1987; Vol 53 No 6: p31.

[Untitled]; review of *Dreams of Speech and Violence. Quill & Quire* June 1987; Vol 53 No 6: p35.

[Untitled]; theatre review of *Intimate Admiration. Queen's Q* Autumn 1987; Vol 94 No 3: p753–755.

[Untitled]; theatre review of *Play Memory. Queen's Q* Autumn 1987; Vol 94 No 3: p755–757.

[Untitled]; review of *North of Intention. Quill & Quire* July 1987; Vol 53 No 7: p66.

[Untitled]; review of *Private and Fictional Words. Quill & Quire* Oct 1987; Vol 53 No 10: p23–24.

Garland, Shelagh

[Untitled]; review of *Afternoon Tea. Books in Can* May 1987; Vol 16 No 4: p20.

[Untitled]; review of *Cage. Books in Can* Oct 1987; Vol 16 No 7: p24.

[Untitled]; review of *Malcolm Lowry: Vancouver Days. Books in Can* Dec 1987; Vol 16 No 9: p26.

Garneau, Hector de Saint-Denys

Angoisse / Anguish; poem in French and in English translation. *Ellipse* 1987; No 37: p18–19.

[Au lecteur] / [For you, my reader. . . .]; poem in French and in English translation. *Ellipse* 1987; No 37: p16–17.

[Les cheveux châtains] / [Auburn hair]; poem in French and in English translation. *Ellipse* 1987; No 37: p30–31.

[Et cependant dressé en nous] / [And yet there stands within us. . . .]; poem in French and in English translation. *Ellipse* 1987; No 37: p18–19.

[Et j'évoque au retour] / [I call up once again. . . .]; poem in French and in English translation. *Ellipse* 1987; No 37: p18–19.

[Faible oripeau] / [Tattered finery]; poem in French and in English translation. *Ellipse* 1987; No 37: p32–33.

[J'avais son bras] / [Her arm of cool water]; poem in French and in English translation. *Ellipse* 1987; No 37: p24–25.

[Le jour, les hymnes] / [That day, the hymns]; poem in French and in English translation. *Ellipse* 1987; No 37: p42–45.

Mains / Hands; poem in French and in English translation. *Ellipse* 1987; No 37: p22–23.

Mains / Hands; poem in French and in English translation. *Ellipse* 1987; No 37: p36–37.

[Mes paupières en se levant] / [As my eyelids ascend]; poem in French and in English translation. *Ellipse* 1987; No 37: p24–25.

[Mon cher François] / [My dear François]; poem in French and in English translation. *Ellipse* 1987; No 37: p26–27.

[Nous allons détacher nos membres] / [We shall detach our limbs]; poem in French and in English translation. *Ellipse* 1987; No 37: p20–21.

[Nous avons attendu de la douleur][We had come to expect pain]; poem in French and in English translation. *Ellipse* 1987; No 37: p22–23.

[Nous avons trop pris garde] / [We cared too much]; poem in French and in English translation. *Ellipse* 1987; No 37: p34–35.

[Nous des ombres] / [We, shadows]; poem in French and in English translation. *Ellipse* 1987; No 37: p20–21.

[Nous n'avait pas fini] / [We were not done]; poem in French and in English translation. *Ellipse* 1987; No 37: p46–53.

Pins / Pines; poem in French and in English translation. *Ellipse* 1987; No 37: p16–17.

Les pins / Pines; poem in French and in English translation. *Ellipse* 1987; No 37: p28–29.

[Quand on est réduit à ses os] / [When one is reduced to his bones]; poem in French and in English translation. *Ellipse* 1987; No 37: p16–17.

[Quitte le monticule] / [Leave this impossible mound]; poem in French and in English translation. *Ellipse* 1987; No 37: p38–41.

Réponse à des critiques / In response to criticism; poem in French and in English translation. *Ellipse* 1987; No 37: p54–55.

Garvey, Pete

The angel and the devil; children's poem. illus · *TS* Dec 27, 1987: pC18.

Asteroids on toast; children's poem. illus · *TS* April 5, 1987: pC12.

Attack of the washing machine!; children's poem. illus · *TS* Dec 6, 1987: pE6.

The baby & the rattlesnake; children's poem. illus · *TS* July 19, 1987: pH6.

Be my Valentine!; children's poem. illus · *TS* Feb 15, 1987: pA17.

The clever daffodil; children's poem. illus · *TS* July 12, 1987: pH6.

The cloud and the crocodile; children's poem. illus · *TS* March 8, 1987: pH6.

The door; children's poem. *TS* Aug 9, 1987: pH6.

Edward the Easter Egg; children's poem. illus · *TS* April 19, 1987: pH6.

Fishes' birthday parties; children's poem. illus · *TS* May 31, 1987: pE6.

The genius; children's poem. illus · *TS* Oct 11, 1987: pH6.

The giant and the fairy; children's poem. illus · *TS* Nov 15, 1987: pG8.

The great tippity-bird; children's poem. illus · *TS* Feb 1, 1987: pA20.

How to be a poet; children's poem. illus · *TS* Nov 22, 1987: pG10.

A hundred million years ago; children's poem. illus · *TS* Dec 13, 1987: pG10.

I can fly!; children's poem. illus · *TS* Aug 2, 1987: pH6.

I wanna be hairy!; children's poem. illus · *TS* Nov 8, 1987: pG8.

Katy's killer caterpillar!; children's poem. illus · *TS* March 22, 1987: pH6.

King of the world!; children's poem. illus · *TS* March 15, 1987: pH6.

Lazybones; children's poem. illus · *TS* Dec 20, 1987: pE8.

Legs!; children's poem. illus · *TS* Aug 30, 1987: pH6.

Little tiny us!; children's poem. illus · *TS* Sept 6, 1987: pC6.

Long John Silver!; children's poem. illus · *TS* April 26, 1987: pC10.

The magician; children's poem. illus · *TS* Jan 25, 1987: pA18.

Mean Mickey MacKay!; children's poem. illus · *TS* July 26, 1987: pH6.

Mixed-up toys!; children's poem. illus · *TS* Jan 11, 1987: pG8.

Mother's Day!; children's poem. illus · *TS* May 10, 1987: pA18.

Mud pies; children's poem. illus · *TS* Sept 13, 1987: pC8.

My favorite breakfast; children's poem. illus · *TS* Nov 29, 1987: pG15.

My favorite foods; children's poem. illus · *TS* Jan 18, 1987: pC8.

My favorite foods; children's poem. illus · *TS* Sept 27, 1987: pC8.

My monster Dad!; children's poem. illus · *TS* June 21, 1987: pH6.

My old graddad!; children's poem. illus · *TS* Aug 16, 1987: pA18.

My pet blob; children's poem. illus · *TS* March 29, 1987: pH6.

My snail, Lightening; children's poem. illus · *TS* March 1, 1987: pA17.

The other Paddington; children's poem. illus · *TS* April 12, 1987: pH6.

OUCH!!; children's poem. illus · *TS* Feb 22, 1987: pA21.

The Queen and I; children's poem. illus · *TS* June 14, 1987: pA21.

The sky; children's poem. illus · *TS* May 17, 1987: pA18.

The sock and the shoe; children's poem. illus · *TS* Feb 8, 1987: pC8.

The spider web; children's poem. illus · *TS* Oct 18, 1987: pH7.

Test time; children's poem. illus · *TS* Sept 20, 1987: pA23.

The thing!; children's poem. illus · *TS* June 7, 1987: pC8.

Uncle Dingbat; children's poem. illus · *TS* Aug 23, 1987: pA16.

Wendy, the pretty witch; children's poem. illus · *TS* Nov 1, 1987: pG10.

What I do best!; children's poem. illus · *TS* Oct 25, 1987: pH6.

What if. . . .; children's poem. illus · *TS* Oct 4, 1987: pH6.

Willy Walrus's toothache; children's poem. illus · *TS* July 5, 1987: pH6.

Yo ho ho and a bottle of pop; children's poem. illus · *TS* May 3, 1987: pC10.

Gasparini, Len

Poem; poem. *Waves* Spring 1987; Vol 15 No 4: p57.

Gaston, Bill

Heaven, Earth and Aikman; short story. *Event* Summer 1987; Vol 16 No 2: p77–82.

Heaven on Earth; short story. *Matrix* Spring 1987; No 24: p10–14.

Six modern poems; poem. *Prism* Summer 1987; Vol 25 No 4: p23–24.

Texada quarry; poem. *Prism* Summer 1987; Vol 25 No 4: p22.

Gatenby, Greg

[Untitled]; essay. *Poetry Can R* Summer 1987; Vol 8 No 4: p15.

Gates, Edward

Five ghazals; poem sequence. *Germination* Spring 1987; Vol 10 No 2: p29–33.

Gaudet, Gérald

André Roy, "l'écouteur des choses tristes"; review of *L'Accélérateur d'intensité*. photo · *MD* Dec 5, 1987: pD9.

Le corps vibrant de désir; interview with Fernand Ouellette. photo · *Lettres québec* Winter 1986–87; No 44: p16–21.

Dominique Lauzon: "Dans une zone si fragile de lui-même"; interview. *Estuaire* Spring 1987; No 44: p57–60.

François Charron: "la précieuse leçon de la tendresse"; review of *La Chambre des miracles*. photo · *MD* May 16, 1987: pD2.

Jean Chapdelaine Gagnon: dans l'apprentissage des langues; review of *Dans l'attente d'une aube*. *MD* Oct 3, 1987: pD3.

Marcel Dubé: la tragédie de l'homme blessé; interview, includes introduction. photo · *Lettres québec* Summer 1987; No 46: p41–46.

Les mots retrouvent tous leurs pouvoirs; review of *C'est encore le solitaire qui parle*. photo · *MD* Sept 5, 1987: pC9.

Un sens de la voix à retrouver; interview with Paul Zumthor. photo · *Estuaire* Winter 1986–87; No 43: p65–73.

La violence de la mort; review of *Sursis*. *MD* Dec 12, 1987: pD3.

Vivre de sa plume au Québec; interview with Madeleine Ouellette-Michalska. photo · *Lettres québec* Spring 1987; No 45: p12–14.

Vivre de sa plume au Québec; interview with François Charron. photo · *Lettres québec* Autumn 1987; No 47: p11–13.

Gaudreau, Claude

Théâtre (désir critique) 1; essay. *Moebius* Autumn 1987; No 34: p99–110.

Gaulin, Michel

Leçons du monde animal; review of *La Ménagerie*. *Can Child Lit* 1987; No 45: p86–87.

Gault, Connie

The news; prose excerpt from a work in progress. *Grain* Summer 1987; Vol 15 No 2: p49–55.

Gauthier, Guy

A spokesman for his time; review of *Journal de bord du gamin des ténèbres*. *Prairie Fire* Autumn 1987; Vol 8 No 3: p113–115.

Gauvin, Lise

La question des journaux intimes; article. *Études fran* Winter 1987; Vol 22 No 3: p101–115.

Gawthrop, Dan

[Untitled]; letter to the editor. *G&M* Nov 21, 1987: pD7.

Gay, Marie-Louise

Hockey sweaters and picture books: matching the external image with the inner content; review of *The Hockey Sweater*. *Can Child Lit* 1987; No 45: p90–91.

Gay, Michel

Y inclus / Including; poem in French and in English translation. *Writing* 1987; No 18: p42–51.

Geauvreau, M. Cherie

Concertino; poem. *Prism* Autumn 1987; Vol 26 No 1: p67.

Shut your hole honey, mine's making money; poem. *Prism* Autumn 1987; Vol 26 No 1: p68–69.

Gebbia, Alessandro

Reading Robert Kroetsch in Italy; article. *Prairie Fire* Winter 1987–88; Vol 8 No 4: p83–85.

Geddes, Gary

The dream bed; poem. *Capilano R* 1987; No 44: p4–10.

The dump; poem. illus · *Queen's Q* Spring 1987; Vol 94 No 1: p114–115.

Gee, Estelle

Books program; letter to the editor. *G&M* Oct 29, 1987: pA6.

Gee, Tom

At the intersection with Mitty; poem. *Can Auth & Book* Fall 1987; Vol 63 No 1: p17.

When I am old; poem. *Can Auth & Book* Spring 1987; Vol 62 No 3: p23.

Geitzler, Fran

[Untitled]; review of *The Green Gables Detectives*. *CH* Dec 6, 1987: pD9.

Gellert, James

Bugs, battles & ballet; reviews of *On Stage, Please* and *Redcoat*. *Can Lit* Winter 1987; No 115: p220–223.

How I spent my summer mystery; reviews of young adult novels by J. Robert Janes. *Can Child Lit* 1987; No 48: p93–95.

Gellis, Willard

Backslidn Kenworth / sonet; poem. *Prairie J of Can Lit* 1987; No 8: p33.

Geminder, Kathleen

Cosmogony; poem. *CV 2* Summer 1987; Vol 10 No 4: p42–44.

Genest, Françoise

À la mecque du livre, des bibliophiles et des femmes; article. *MD* Nov 14, 1987: pD8.

Pour tous les goûts; article, include schedule of events. photo · *MD* Nov 14, 1987: pD6-D7.

Sept autres Salons dont on néglige souvent l'impact; article. *MD* Nov 14, 1987: pD8.

Genuist, Monique

Idéologie féministe dans Le Temps sauvage et C'était avant la guerre à l'Anse à Gilles; article. abstract · *Theatre Hist in Can (special issue)* Spring 1987; Vol 8 No 1: p49–58.

Gérin, Pierre

Sus aux trafiquants de stupéfiants!; review of *Le Secret de Lamorandière*. *Can Child Lit* 1987; No 48: p90–91.

Gerry, Thomas

A choice of codes; reviews of poetry books. illus · *NeWest R* Nov 1987; Vol 13 No 3: p16–17.

Native dramas; review of *The Land Called Morning*. *Can Child Lit* 1987; No 46: p97–98.

The north and its artistic images: a provocative view; review of *Ice Swords*. *Can Child Lit* 1987; No 45: p59–61.

Rare / fear; reviews of *Green Eyes, Dukes & Kings* and *The Book of Fears*. *Can Lit* Spring 1987; No 112: p107–108.

[Untitled]; review of *August Nights*. *Rubicon* Spring 1987; No 8: p208–210.

Violence and narrative metalepsis in Guy Vanderhaeghe's fiction; article. *Studies in Can Lit* 1987; Vol 12 No 2: p199–211.

Gerson, Carole

[Untitled]; reviews of short story collections. *Queen's Q* Summer 1987; Vol 94 No 2: p483–484.

Gervais, André

"L'écriture réside en ce lieu que la rature désire"; essay. *La Nouvelle barre du jour (special issue)* 1987; No 191: p7–21.

Post-scriptum vite; editorial. *La Nouvelle barre du jour (special issue)* 1987; No 191: p63.

Sans titre; essay. *Moebius (special issue)* Spring 1987; No 32: p61–62.

Gervais, Jocelyne

Devant la porte; prose poem. *Liberté* Dec 1987; Vol 29 No 6: p31–32.

Ghai, Gail

Just desserts; poem. *New Q* Spring-Summer 1987; Vol 7 No 1–2: p161–162.

Trilingual; poem. *New Q* Spring-Summer 1987; Vol 7 No 1–2: p157–158.

Twin; poem. *New Q* Spring-Summer 1987; Vol 7 No 1–2: p159–160.

Gibbs, Robert

Flyovers / stopovers; poem. *Can Lit* Winter 1987; No 115: p102–104.

For a sketch of lovers by Bruno Bobak; poem. illus · *Fiddlehead* Spring 1987; No 151: p5.

Hearing again from the earth earthy; poem. *Germination* Fall 1987; Vol 11 No 1: p38.

My turn at the ballet; poem. *Germination* Fall 1987; Vol 11 No 1: p37.

[Untitled]; poem. *Germination* Fall 1987; Vol 11 No 1: p39.

[Untitled]; review of *Changes of State*. *Poetry Can R* Fall 1987; Vol 9 No 1: p33–34.

Waking with the groundhog; poem. *Poetry Can R* Spring 1987; Vol 8 No 2–3: p19.

Watching the watchers in the reptile house; poem. *Can Lit* Winter 1987; No 115: p65.

Gibson, Jim

No claims to priority; letter to the editor, includes poem. *CH* Sept 9, 1987: pA6.

Gibson, Sally

Colonel South looks north; short story. *Can Forum* Nov 1987; Vol 67 No 773: p40–41.

Giffen, Peter

Voyages of the mind; article, includes review of *The Darkest Road*. photo · *Maclean's* March 23, 1987; Vol 100 No 12: p66–67.

Gignac-Pharand, Elvine

Une analyse éclairante du théâtre pour enfants; review of *Le Théâtre pour enfants au Québec*. *Can Child Lit* 1987; No 46: p95–96.

Giguère, Richard

Le réel et la fiction du réel; reviews of *Les Soirs rouges* (reprint) and *La Fiction du réel*. photo · *Lettres québec* Winter 1986–87; No 44: p38–40.

La tentation du romanesque; reviews of poetry books. photo · *Lettres québec* Autumn 1987; No 47: p37–39.

Gilbert, Gerry

Volume; poem. *Writing* 1987; No 18: p17–21.

Gilbert, John

To tell the truth; review of *Prague*. *Books in Can* March 1987; Vol 16 No 2: p17.

Gilbert, William A.

Laurence's hour; letter to the editor. *G&M* Feb 2, 1987: pA6.

Gillese, John Patrick

Sward draws blood; letter to the editor. *Can Auth & Book* Spring 1987; Vol 62 No 3: p2.

Gillet, Jean-Noël

Le Sourd dans la ville, de Mireille Dansereau, est bien accueilli à la Mostra de Venise; article. *MD* Sept 9, 1987: p13.

Gillies, John

The illusion principle; poem. *Antigonish R* 1987; No 69–70: p128–129.

Gillmor, Don

Alcoholic vet's story drives home the horror; review of *Unknown Soldier*. photo · *MG* Oct 17, 1987: pJ12.

Gilroy, James P.

Comme un vent; reviews of poetry books. *Can Lit* Winter 1987; No 115: p260–261.

Giltrow, Janet

Narrative authority and the economy of secrets; review of *The Indigo Dress*. *Event* Summer 1987; Vol 16 No 2: p121–124.

Gingell, Susan

Solecki's Ondaatje; review of *Spider Blues*. *Can Lit* Summer-Fall 1987; No 113–114: p214–217.

Giroux, Robert

[Untitled]; review of *L'Amour de la carte postale*. *Moebius* Summer 1987; No 33: p146–148.

Givner, Joan

A conversation with Ernst Havemann; interview. biog · *Wascana R* Fall 1987; Vol 22 No 2: p41–52.

Nelly's place; short story. *U of Windsor R* Fall-Winter 1987; Vol 20 No 1: p32–43.

The trade; short story. illus · *Can Auth & Book* Fall 1987; Vol 63 No 1: p18–22.

Glaap, Albert-Reiner

Noises Off and Jitters: two comedies of backstage life; article. *Can Drama* 1987; Vol 13 No 2: p210–215.

Glassco, David

Fighting words; review of *The Great War of Words*. *Can Forum* Nov 1987; Vol 67 No 773: p36–37.

Glenday, John

The apple ghost; poem. *Fiddlehead* Autumn 1987; No 153: p10.

Glickman, Susan

"All in war with time": the poetry of Don Coles; article. *Essays on Can Writ* Winter 1987; No 35: p156–170.

Anarchy and afterthoughts; review of *Afterworlds*. *Books in Can* June-July 1987; Vol 16 No 5: p26.

Camera obscura; series of linked poems. *Rubicon* Spring 1987; No 8: p39–51.

Country music; poem. *Malahat R* Dec 1987; No 81: p16–17.

Dark room; poem. *Rubicon* Spring 1987; No 8: p48–50.

Families; poem. *Malahat R* Dec 1987; No 81: p18–19.

Giovanni Battista Della Porta: 1540–1615; poem. *Rubicon* Spring 1987; No 8: p43–44.

Heavy weather; poem. *Malahat R* Dec 1987; No 81: p20–21.

Johann Kepler: 1571–1630; poem. *Rubicon* Spring 1987; No 8: p45.

Leonardo da Vinci: 1452–1519; poem. *Rubicon* Spring 1987; No 8: p42.

Metafiction I: bon voyage; prose poem. *Event* March 1987; Vol 16 No 1: p34.

Metafiction II: a familiar story; prose poem. *Event* March 1987; Vol 16 No 1: p35.

Mo Ti; fl. 400 B.C.; poem. *Rubicon* Spring 1987; No 8: p39.

Muhammad ibn al-Hasan, known as 'Alhazen': 965–1039; poem. *Rubicon* Spring 1987; No 8: p40.

Poem about your laugh; poem. *Malahat R* Dec 1987; No 81: p22.

"Proceeding before the amorous invisible": Phyllis Webb and the Ghazal; article. *Can Lit* Winter 1987; No 115: p48–61.

Roger Bacon: 1214?-1294; poem. *Rubicon* Spring 1987; No 8: p41.

Stone poem; poem. *Can Lit* Summer-Fall 1987; No 113–114: p107–108.

[Untitled]; review of *Candy from Strangers. Poetry Can R* Spring 1987; Vol 8 No 2–3: p42–43.

[Untitled]; reviews of *Who's to Say?* and *Shaking the Dreamland Tree. Poetry Can R* Summer 1987; Vol 8 No 4: p32.

Who's there?; poem. *Malahat R* Dec 1987; No 81: p15.

Glinsky, Joseph

The last supper; short story. *Prairie J of Can Lit* 1987; No 9: p36–46.

Gloin, Lew

College guide leaves no term unstoned; review of *All the Bright Company. TS* Sept 13, 1987: pA22.

Maple Leaf memories in print; reviews of *The Bishop* and *The Glassy Sea. TS* July 12, 1987: pA18.

Summer reading for quiet times; review of *Illusions.* photo · *TS* Aug 9, 1987: pA21.

Thanks to Robertson Davies; article. *TS* May 10, 1987: pA22.

Glover, Douglas

For God's sake; review of *The Color of Blood. Books in Can* Oct 1987; Vol 16 No 7: p18.

The lady of the boathouse; prose excerpt from a work in progress. *Books in Can* June-July 1987; Vol 16 No 5: p11–12.

Lost horizons; review of *Beyond Forget. Books in Can* Jan-Feb 1987; Vol 16 No 1: p20.

Wedding in wheat; review of *Getting Married in Buffalo Jump. Books in Can* Oct 1987; Vol 16 No 7: p32, 34.

Glover, Patrick

Greys; poem. *Alpha* Winter 1987; Vol 11: p32.

Gnarowski, Michael

[Untitled]; biographical articles. *Brick (special issue)* Summer 1987; No 30: ppassim.

Goar, Carol

Flora MacDonald has librarians in a huff; article. photo · *TS* Dec 3, 1987: pA27.

Ottawa struggles to ensure authors get their due; article. illus · *MG* Dec 4, 1987: pB3.

Goarke, Louis

Pigeons; poem. *Can Auth & Book* Winter 1987; Vol 62 No 2: p22.

Gobeil, Pierre

[Untitled]; review of *Probablement l'Espagne. Moebius* Autumn 1987; No 34: p123–125.

Godard, Barbara

Robertson Davies' dialogic imagination; article. *Essays on Can Writ* Spring 1987; No 34: p64–80.

Taking to the woods: of myths, metaphors and poets; article. abstract · *Études can* 1987; No 23: p159–171.

Telling it over again: Atwood's art of parody; article. *Can Poet* Fall-Winter 1987; No 21: p1–30.

Translations; survey review article. *U of Toronto Q* Fall 1987; Vol 57 No 1: p77–98.

Godbout, Jacques

La peine capitale; essay. *Liberté* Feb 1987; Vol 29 No 1: p70–74.

Godbout, Patricia

Avant-propos / Forward; editorial article in French and in English translation. *Ellipse* 1987; No 38: p4–7.

Goddard, John

Cons and prose; biographical article. photo · *Books in Can* May 1987; Vol 16 No 4: p8–11.

Crossing the bar; review of *Bloodsong. Books in Can* Dec 1987; Vol 16 No 9: p33, 35.

Duncan Campbell Scott: a poet who put down Indians; review of *A Narrow Vision.* photo · *MG* Aug 1, 1987: pJ7.

Personal recollections of controversy that made Margaret Laurence weep; article. photo · *MG* Jan 10, 1987: pB8.

Songs of the sea-witch; article. photo · *Sat Night* July 1987; Vol 102 No 7: p23–29.

Tale of eternal triangle reads like a tract; review of *Memory Board. MG* Nov 14, 1987: pJ10.

[Untitled]; article. *Maclean's* April 27, 1987; Vol 100 No 17: p61.

Goddard, Peter

Authors talk about books as movies; article. *TS* Oct 20, 1987: pH4.

Poetry videos trying to tap youth market; column. photo · *TS* Jan 21, 1987: pD3.

Priest is Toronto's pied piper of poetry; article. illus · *TS* Jan 9, 1987: pD3.

Saturday Night celebrates sobriety; article. photo · *TS* Jan 6, 1987: pD4.

Tamara New York; article. photo · *TS* Nov 22, 1987: pC1, C4.

Godfrey, John

The peril of Mexico; article. *Fin Post* Nov 30, 1987: p14.

Godfrey, Stephen

Aboriginal issue takes centre stage; theatre review of *No' Xya'.* photo · *G&M* Nov 7, 1987: pC3.

Ambitious drama falls short of the mark; theatre reviews of *Penguins* and *Sliding for Home*. photo · *G&M* Nov 26, 1987: pA25.

Another playwright foiled by Emily Carr; theatre review of *Song of This Place*. photo · *G&M* Sept 18, 1987: pD11.

At home in left field; article. photo · *G&M* April 25, 1987: pC1, C5.

Back to the earth with baby, Mr. Big and the Fat Lady; theatre reviews of *The Good Baby* and *The Enchanted Forest*. photo · *G&M* July 18, 1987: pC1, C4.

Brides in Space launched on a mission impossible; theatre review of *Brides in Space*. photo · *G&M* Jan 15, 1987: pD1.

Charming comedy toys with the work ethic; theatre review of *The Idler*. photo · *G&M* Sept 29, 1987: pD5.

Contrived character flaws Zaydok; theatre review. photo · *G&M* Oct 28, 1987: pC5.

Customs detains book recounting Indian legends; article. *G&M* June 22, 1987: pC9.

Daredevil dramatist slips out of focus; theatre review of *Dixieland's Night of Shame*. photo · *G&M* May 9, 1987: pC5.

Dubois' Bedouins run riot through prairie theatre; theatre review of *Don't Blame the Bedouins*. photo · *G&M* Dec 3, 1987: pA25.

Extravaganzas, close calls and chaos, with imaginative windows on the arts; article. photo · *G&M* Dec 26, 1987: pC10.

Festival One plays singularly successful; theatre reviews. photo · *G&M* May 8, 1987: pF9.

Glick clicks at last; article. photo · *G&M* Dec 5, 1987: pC1, C5.

Hodgins brings his island into the literary limelight; article. photo · *G&M* Sept 19, 1987: pC1.

A madcap journey out to the Backyard; theatre review of *Backyard Beguine*, includes profile. photo · *G&M* April 8, 1987: pC7.

Melody Farm feels like two plays trying to be one; theatre reviews of *Melody Farm* and *Biting Nails*. photo · *G&M* Feb 18, 1987: pC7.

A new horizon; biographical article. photo · *G&M* May 16, 1987: pC1.

New-play festival deserves a curtain call; theatre reviews. photo · *G&M* Feb 10, 1987: pC5.

Play born out of obsession; article. photo · *G&M* Sept 12, 1987: pC9.

The play's the thing, despite thieves, greed and flops; article. photo · *G&M* Aug 8, 1987: pC1.

Quirks, interruptions don't deflate festival; article. photo · *G&M* Sept 22, 1987: pD5.

Smooth ride on The Last Bus; theatre review. photo · *G&M* Feb 16, 1987: pD9.

Subsidies and writers: two views are debated; article. *G&M* April 29, 1987: pC5.

A success story for children; article. photo · *G&M* May 18, 1987: pD9.

TV evangelism thriller merits rerun on radio; theatre review of *The 101 Miracles of Hope Chance*. *G&M* Dec 7, 1987: pD9.

Typical folks tell powerful internment story; theatre review of *Another Morning*. photo · *G&M* April 24, 1987: pC5.

UBC plans Lowry symposium; article. *G&M* April 30, 1987: pC1.

Vancouver Fringe springs surprises; article. photo · *G&M* Sept 15, 1987: pA21.

Godin, Deborah

Noon, above the General; poem. *Prairie J of Can Lit* 1987; No 8: p34–35.

Godin, Jean Cléo

Un texte dense et beau; theatre review of *Le Testament*. photo · *Jeu* 1987; No 44: p191–192.

Théâtre; survey review article. *U of Toronto Q* Fall 1987; Vol 57 No 1: p74–77.

Goding, William E.

Underdog; poem. *Tor South Asian R* Spring 1987; Vol 5 No 3: p68.

Goedhart, Bernie

From giant snakes to punk pigeons: escapism at its best; reviews of children's stories. *Quill & Quire (Books for Young People)* June 1987; Vol 53 No 6: p5.

Morgan, May, Melinda: new heroines offer humour and fantasy; reviews of children's books. *Quill & Quire (Books for Young People)* Oct 1987; Vol 53 No 10: p24.

Renaissance man Donn Kushner a delightful challenge for children; article. photo · *Quill & Quire (Books for Young People)* Dec 1987; Vol 53 No 12: p1, 3.

Stéphane Poulin's sensitive approach to life and art; article. photo · *Quill & Quire (Books for Young People)* Aug 1987; Vol 53 No 8: p1, 8.

[Untitled]; review of *A Tail Between Two Cities*. *Quill & Quire (Books for Young People)* Dec 1987; Vol 53 No 12: p9.

Goetz-Stankiewicz, Marketa

A literary scherzo; review of *Dvorak in Love*. illus · *Can Forum* Aug-Sept 1987; Vol 67 No 771: p41–43.

Gold, Artie

R.W. 11; poem. *Poetry Can R* Fall 1987; Vol 9 No 1: p17.

Gold, Gary

Definitions; essay. *Prairie J of Can Lit* 1987; No 8: p41.

Gold, Jack

Forgive him, Lord, he's just a bit confused; letter to the editor. *MG* March 17, 1987: pB2.

Goldbloom, Michael

Le privilège exigeant d'être Québécois; essay. photo · *MD* March 19, 1987: p11.

Goldie, Terry

Collective concern; theatre reviews of *The Daily News* and *The Fishwharf and Steamboat Men*. photo · *Can Theatre R* Spring 1987; No 50: p81–83.

The impossible dream; review of *A Dream Like Mine*. *Books in Can* Nov 1987; Vol 16 No 8: p30–31.

Mixed doubles; review of *Memory Board*. *Books in Can* Nov 1987; Vol 16 No 8: p19–20.

Goldsmith, Annette

[Untitled]; review of *A Handful of Time*. *Quill & Quire (Books for Young People)* April 1987; Vol 53 No 4: p10.

Golfman, Noreen

A question of taste; reviews of *After Six Days* and *Mario*. *Can Lit* Spring 1987; No 112: p104–107.

[Untitled]; review of *The Montreal Story Tellers*. *Amer R of Can Studies* Spring 1987; Vol 17 No 1: p118–119.

Golland-Lui, Della

Authors group fought for public lending right; letter to the editor. *TS* April 6, 1987: pA16.

Gom, Leona

Après aerobics; poem. *Queen's Q* Spring 1987; Vol 94 No 1: p71.

Guilt; poem. *Queen's Q* Spring 1987; Vol 94 No 1: p70–71.

The neighbour; poem. *Ariel* April 1987; Vol 18 No 2: p45.

Sue's story; poem. *Queen's Q* Spring 1987; Vol 94 No 1: p70.

Goodman, Rod

Of headlines, AIDS causes, Lindbergh, and Atwood; article. *TS* May 2, 1987: pB2.

Gordon, Alison

She's living exactly the way she wants; article. photo · *TS* May 24, 1987: pD1-D2.

Gordon, Annette

For the sake of Clarity; letter to the editor. *Books in Can* Nov 1987; Vol 16 No 8: p40.

Gordon, E.J.

Garden tale helps cancer children; article. photo · *MG* Aug 25, 1987: pC6.

Gordon, King

[Untitled]; biographical articles. *Brick (special issue)* Summer 1987; No 30: ppassim.

Gordon, Ruth

[Untitled]; biographical articles. *Brick (special issue)* Summer 1987; No 30: ppassim.

Gorman, LeRoy

Haiku; poem. *Cross Can Writ Q* 1987; Vol 9 No 2: p23.

Into another winter; poem. *Tor South Asian R* Summer 1987; Vol 6 No 1: p49–51.

Making the grade; poem. *Can Forum* Feb 1987; Vol 66 No 766: p8.

[Untitled]; review of *Foot Through the Ceiling*. *Poetry Can R* Summer 1987; Vol 8 No 4: p32–33.

[Untitled]; poem. *Cross Can Writ Q* 1987; Vol 9 No 3–4: p2.

Gorse, Oliver

The latest novels; review of *Dvorak in Love*. *Idler* March-April 1987; No 12: p58.

[Untitled]; review of *The Progress of Love*. *Idler* March-April 1987; No 12: p59–60.

[Untitled]; review of *Adult Entertainment*. *Idler* March-April 1987; No 12: p60.

Gosselin, Michel

[Untitled]; review of *Le Coeur découvert*. *Moebius* Winter 1987; No 31: p141–142.

Gough, Patrick

Atwood displays talent for fiction; letter to the editor. *G&M* Nov 21, 1987: pD7.

Gould, Elliott

Playwright reaps laughs from reality; article. photo · *CH* May 22, 1987: pF1.

Gould, Maria

Baby; short story. *Event* March 1987; Vol 16 No 1: p56–59.

Gould, Martha

Mademoiselle in the tropics with whales; poem. *NeWest R* Sept 1987; Vol 13 No 1: p10.

Prayer; poem. *NeWest R* Sept 1987; Vol 13 No 1: p11.

Gourdeau, Gabrielle

Les connivences implicites entre le texte et l'image: le cas Maria Chapdelaine; article. *Can Lit* Summer-Fall 1987; No 113–114: p93–107.

Gourlay, Elizabeth

The discipline; poem. *Event* Summer 1987; Vol 16 No 2: p106.

Govier, Katherine

Book reviewing is operating in a closed shop; essay. photo · *CH* Dec 9, 1987: pF1-F2.

The mermaid inn: when BritLit meets CanLit; essay. photo · *G&M* Jan 17, 1987: pD6.

Trouble with reviews – is reviewers, writer says; essay. photo · *TS* Dec 6, 1987: pC9.

Gowan, Elsie Park

The last caveman; play. *Theatre Hist in Can (special issue)* Spring 1987; Vol 8 No 1: p83–121.

Grace, Sherrill

Confabulation; review of *Confabulations*. illus · *Essays on Can Writ* Spring 1987; No 34: p18–23.

Drama views / perspectives dramatiques: Herman Voaden's Murder Pattern: 1936 and 1987; article. *Can Drama* 1987; Vol 13 No 1: p117–119.

Home rituals; review of *Noman's Land*. *Can Lit* Spring 1987; No 112: p102–104.

Grace-Warrick, Christa

Notes from the Fringe / 1; article. photo · *Can Theatre R* Summer 1987; No 51: p79–80.

Grady, Wayne

From Ahmadabad to Tennessee; reviews of *86: Best Canadian Stories* and *Coming Attractions 4*. *Books in Can* March 1987; Vol 16 No 2: p29–30.

Literary heist; article. illus · *Sat Night* Nov 1987; Vol 102 No 11: p61–64.

To be continued; review of *Steven, le hérault*. *Books in Can* June-July 1987; Vol 16 No 5: p20.

Graham, Barbara Florio

[Untitled]; review of *On Stage with Maara Haas*. *Can Auth & Book* Spring 1987; Vol 62 No 3: p24.

Graham, Gord

Can computers take on the task of translating?; article. *Quill & Quire* March 1987; Vol 53 No 3: p68.

The ears have it: audio cassettes selling soundly in stores; article. photo · *Quill & Quire* April 1987; Vol 53 No 4: p6, 8.

Graham, Neile

Settled in Montana for winter; poem. *Descant* Winter 1987; Vol 18 No 4: p18.

Sleeping with lambs; poem. *Descant* Winter 1987; Vol 18 No 4: p19.

Grandbois, Alain

Quand Alain Grandbois écrivait des lettres bouleversantes à Lucienne; prose excerpt from *Lettres à Lucienne*. *MD* Nov 28, 1987: pD1-D2.

Grandfield, Cathi

The harbour; poem. *Fiddlehead* Spring 1987; No 151: p79.

A sudden flash; poem. *Fiddlehead* Spring 1987; No 151: p79.

Granfield, Linda

[Untitled]; review of *Four Seasons for Toby*. *Quill & Quire (Books for Young People)* April 1987; Vol 53 No 4: p9.

[Untitled]; review of *A House Far from Home*. *Quill & Quire (Books for Young People)* June 1987; Vol 53 No 6: p10.

[Untitled]; reviews of *The Green Gables Detectives* and *The Loon Lake Murders*. *Quill & Quire (Books for Young People)* Aug 1987; Vol 53 No 8: p5–6.

Grant, Craig

Sally's last breakfast; short story. *New Q* Fall 1987; Vol 7 No 3: P45–53.

Grant, Shelagh

Irked by criticism; letter to the editor. *G&M* Aug 6, 1987: pA6.

Graves, Warren

The Mermaid Inn: whither pornography?; essay. photo · *G&M* June 13, 1987: pD6.

Gray, Martin

Snow fell all night; poem. *Poetry Can R* Fall 1987; Vol 9 No 1: p11.

Green, Mary Jean

Laure Conan and Madame de La Fayette: rewriting the female plot; article. *Essays on Can Writ* Spring 1987; No 34: p50–63.

[Untitled]; review of *Anne Hébert: architexture romanesque*. *Amer R of Can Studies* Spring 1987; Vol 17 No 1: p115–116.

Green, Richard G.

The last raven; short story. *Can Fic Mag (special issue)* 1987; No 60: p160–167.

Green, Terence M.

Andrew Weiner; interview. photo · *Books in Can* Oct 1987; Vol 16 No 7: p38–40.

Win some, lose some; letter to the editor. *Books in Can* Aug-Sept 1987; Vol 16 No 6: p40.

Greene, Elizabeth

Intrigue; short story. *Quarry* Fall 1987; Vol 36 No 4: p23–28.

Greene, Richard

English December; poem. *Poetry Can R* Spring 1987; Vol 8 No 1–2: p13.

Utopia; poem. *Poetry Can R* Spring 1987; Vol 8 No 1–2: p13.

Waking; poem. *Poetry Can R* Spring 1987; Vol 8 No 1–2: p13.

Greenstein, Michael

Other Americas; reviews of *The Light in the Piazza* and *Voyage to the Other Extreme*. *Can Lit* Spring 1987; No 112: p97–100.

Greenwood, Barbara

Somewhere – in the Canadian past; essay. photo · *Can Child Lit* 1987; No 48: p66–68.

Greenwood, G.P.

Collection highlights neglected genre; review of *On Middle Ground*. *CH* Oct 4, 1987: pE6.

Western Canadian poets display talents in new volume; reviews of poetry books. *CH* July 5, 1987: pF7.

Greenwood, Gail

[Untitled]; review of *Cage*. *CH* Sept 27, 1987: pE6.

Greer, Sandy

[Untitled]; review of *The Native in Literature*. *Quill & Quire* June 1987; Vol 53 No 6: p35.

Greffard, Madeleine

Au coeur de l'imaginaire; theatre review of *Le Vrai monde?*. photo · *Liberté* Dec 1987; Vol 29 No 6: p146–147.

Greggs, Nancy

The subway mouse; short story. *TS* Aug 28, 1987: pH11.

Gregory, John

[Untitled]; review of *Steven, Le Herault. Quill & Quire* April 1987; Vol 53 No 4: p28.

Greig, Jean B.

[Untitled]; letter to the editor. *Can Auth & Book* Spring 1987; Vol 62 No 3: p2.

Griffin, John

Cohen's spirit everywhere during tribute by Warnes; article about Jennifer Warnes. *MG* June 19, 1987: pC1.

Jennifer Warnes brings home the songs of Leonard Cohen; article. photo · *MG* June 11, 1987: pG1.

Griffin, Joseph

Interviews with Canadian fiction writers; review of *Speaking for Myself. Atlan Prov Book R* May-June 1987; Vol 14 No 2: p11.

Griggs, Terry

A bird story; short story. *Malahat R* Dec 1987; No 81: p30–38.

Grigsby, Wayne

Aubry play superb theatre; theatre review of *La Nuit des p'tits couteaux. MG* Jan 16, 1987: pD2.

Carbone 14 does it again; theatre review of *Opium. MG* Jan 12, 1987: pB8.

Cultural epic is must-see theatre; theatre review of *La Trilogie des dragons. MG* Jan 17, 1987: pC5.

Curtain rises on new play, new theatre; theatre review of *Up Your Alley. MG* Jan 12, 1987: pB5.

Fire bites off a lot, chews most of it; theatre review of *Fire. MG* Jan 10, 1987: pH7.

[Untitled]; theatre reviews of *Fire* and *Opium. MG* Jan 16, 1987: pD10.

Grills, Barry

Marathon; short story. *Quarry* Fall 1987; Vol 36 No 4: p42–49.

Grimes, William

[Untitled]; review of *The Mournful Demeanour of Lieutenant Boruvka. NYT Book R* Sept 6, 1987: p16.

Grisé, Yolande

La forêt dans le roman "ontarois"; article. abstract · *Études can* 1987; No 23: p109–122.

Un oeil ouvert sur le monde, l'autre fermé sur soi; review of *Hertel, l'homme et l'oeuvre*. photo · *Lettres québec* Winter 1986–87; No 44: p60–61.

Les quarante ans d'un écrivain québécois; review of *Journal 2, août 1985 – avril 1986*. photo · *Lettres québec* Spring 1987; No 45: p54–55.

Le testament d'un artiste; review of *La Conférence inachevée*. photo · *Lettres québec* Autumn 1987; No 47: p35–36.

Une vie de Patachon bien sympathique; reviews of *D'ailleurs et d'ici* and *Contes gouttes ou le pays d'un reflet*. photo · *Lettres québec* Summer 1987; No 46: p59–60.

Groen, Rick

Wit, wisdom and tall tales take centrestage; article. photo · *G&M* Oct 22, 1987: pD6.

Groening, Laura

Emily Nasrallah's first novel; review of *Flight Against Time. Atlan Prov Book R* May-June 1987; Vol 14 No 2: p9.

Groleau, Alain

Fête macabre; prose poem. *Estuaire* Spring 1987; No 44: p24.

I'm only sleeping (au feu des jours); prose poem. *Estuaire* Spring 1987; No 44: p23.

L'abattement du soleil; prose poem. *Estuaire* Spring 1987; No 44: p26.

Lettre folle à cousine; prose poem. *Estuaire* Spring 1987; No 44: p26.

Grove-White, Elizabeth

Editorial. photo · *Brick (special issue)* Summer 1987; No 30: p51.

Growe, Sarah Jane

Relating the newcomers' pain; article. photo · *TS* Jan 8, 1987: pD1, D4.

Gruending, Dennis

Writing Saskatchewan – a literary symposium; article. photo · *NeWest R* Nov 1987; Vol 13 No 3: p9–11.

Guillaume, Pierre

[Untitled]; review of *L'Avénement de la modernité culturelle au Québec. Études can* June 1987; No 22: p132.

Gunn, Genni

Dead mail; poem. *CV 2* Summer 1987; Vol 10 No 4: p24.

Gunnars, Kristjana

Making draft horses out of the gods: an interview with Robert Bringhurst. photo · *Prairie Fire* Spring 1987; Vol 8 No 1: p4–15.

'Meditation on a snowy morning': a conversation with Robert Kroetsch. photo · *Prairie Fire* Winter 1987–88; Vol 8 No 4: p54–62.64–67.

Gur-Arie, Alice

[Untitled]; review of *Small Regrets. Quill & Quire* Jan 1987; Vol 53 No 1: p28.

[Untitled]; review of *The Alligator Report. Quill & Quire* May 1987; Vol 53 No 5: p20.

Gustafson, Ralph

Beethoven as an example of the unconditional; poem. *Can Lit* Summer-Fall 1987; No 113–114: p178.

A dozen more profound stanzas; poem. *Can Lit* Winter 1987; No 115: p45–47.

Exhibition; poem. *Can Lit* Summer-Fall 1987; No 113–114: p90–91.

Final disquisition on the giant tube-worm; poem. *Dandelion* Spring-Summer 1987; Vol 14 No 1: p24.

Lest violence be misunderstood; poem. *Dandelion* Spring-Summer 1987; Vol 14 No 1: p23.

The question of priority for the moment; poem. *Dandelion* Spring-Summer 1987; Vol 14 No 1: p25.

[Untitled]; biographical articles. *Brick (special issue)* Summer 1987; No 30: ppassim.

Gutteridge, Don

Old photographs and the documentary imperative; essay. *Can Lit* Summer-Fall 1987; No 113–114: p253–258.

[Untitled]; reviews of critical works. *Queen's Q* Summer 1987; Vol 94 No 2: p464–467.

Gwyn, Richard

Conrad Black deal to buy Saturday Night said up in air; article. *TS* July 3, 1987: pA1, A4.

H., Iain Arthur

Passport jungle; poem. *Alpha* Winter 1987; Vol 11: p30.

Haas, Maara

For Lani; poem. *Can Auth & Book* Winter 1987; Vol 62 No 2: p21.

Hadekel, Peter

Authors paying for book tariff; column. *MG* Feb 17, 1987: pC1.

Haderlein, Konrad

[Untitled]; review of *Deutsches schriftum in Kanada 1835–1984. Zeitschrift Kanada-Studien* 1987; Vol 7 No 1: p255–263.

Haeck, Philippe

Figures, summaries, questions; article. trans · *Ellipse* 1987; No 37: p6–15.

L'apprentissage de Saint-Denys Garneau; article. *Voix et images* Autumn 1987; Vol 13 No 1: p115–122.

La table rouge; essay. *La Nouvelle barre du jour (special issue)* 1987; No 191: p43–48.

Haensel, Regine

Cultural heritage; review of *Pieces of the Jigsaw Puzzle. Prairie Fire* Autumn 1987; Vol 8 No 3: p120–122.

Halam-Andres, Joan

Take books off CBC's shelf; letter to the editor. *G&M* Oct 17, 1987: pD7.

Hale, Amanda

Ballrooms and boardroom tables; essay. photo · *Can Theatre R* Winter 1987; No 53: p29–32.

Halewood, Peter

[Untitled]; review of *Another Country. Rubicon* Spring 1987; No 8: p218–219.

[Untitled]; review of *Dvorak in Love. Rubicon* Fall 1987; No 9: p165–166.

Hall, Lynda

Shaman; short story. illus · *CH (Sunday Magazine)* July 26, 1987: p24–29.

Hall, Phil

1953; poem. *Can Forum* Feb 1987; Vol 66 No 766: p28.

Colonial imperative; essay. *Books in Can* Oct 1987; Vol 16 No 7: p4–5.

Five minutes; poem. *Germination* Spring 1987; Vol 10 No 2: p25.

Heart and anchor; poem. *Can Forum* Feb 1987; Vol 66 No 766: p29.

Hell; poem. *Can Forum* Feb 1987; Vol 66 No 766: p28.

Narrative tendencies; reviews of poetry books. *Waves* Winter 1987; Vol 15 No 3: p84–88.

Old enemy juice; poems. illus · *Can Forum* Feb 1987; Vol 66 No 766: p28–29.

Pioneers; poem. *Can Forum* Feb 1987; Vol 66 No 766: p29.

The self-completing poet; review of *The Self-Completing Tree.* illus · *Can Forum* Aug-Sept 1987; Vol 67 No 771: p37–39.

Song debris; poem. *Can Forum* Feb 1987; Vol 66 No 766: p28.

Swoop; poem. *Can Forum* Feb 1987; Vol 66 No 766: p28–29.

[Untitled]; review of *Sometimes They Sang. Books in Can* June-July 1987; Vol 16 No 5: p21–22.

[Untitled]; review of *Anyone Can See I Love You. Books in Can* Aug-Sept 1987; Vol 16 No 6: p27–28.

[Untitled]; review of *Letters from the Equator. Books in Can* Aug-Sept 1987; Vol 16 No 6: p28.

[Untitled]; reviews of *Canada Gees Mate for Life* and *Zygal. Poetry Can R* Fall 1987; Vol 9 No 1: p34.

Waiting for Wayman to get off work; article. *Quarry* Fall 1987; Vol 36 No 4: p73–77.

Hall, Roger

Literary 'docudrama' captures the essence; review of *The Orangeman.* photo · *G&M* Feb 14, 1987: pE19.

Hall, Shannon

Audience plays out dilemmas in drama; article. photo · *CH* Nov 22, 1987: pG8.

Halliday, David

I am a landscape painter; prose poem. illus · *Cross Can Writ Q* 1987; Vol 9 No 3–4: p9.

On Atwood; essay. *Waves* Spring 1987; Vol 15 No 4: p51–54.

[Untitled]; letter to the editor. *Waves* Spring 1987; Vol 15 No 4: p92–93.

[Untitled]; essay. photo · *Cross Can Writ Q* 1987; Vol 9 No 3–4: p23.

Halmy, Nijola

The lonely crowd; short story. photo · *TS* July 4, 1987: pM5.

Halpin, Susan

[Untitled]; letter to the editor. *TS* Nov 27, 1987: pD11.

Hamilton, Alice

[Untitled]; poems. *Prism* Winter 1987; Vol 25 No 2: p37–39.

Hamilton, Janet

Moving tales of homelands left behind; reviews of *Bloodsong* and *Tales from Firozsha Baag*. photo · *Quill & Quire* June 1987; Vol 53 No 6: p32.

Musgrave makes it with love, sex, death; review of *The Dancing Chicken*. photo · *Quill & Quire* Oct 1987; Vol 53 No 10: p22.

Repressing abuse: the crime against Sylvia; review of *My Father's House*. photo · *Quill & Quire* Aug 1987; Vol 53 No 8: p33.

[Untitled]; review of *Coming Attractions 5*. *Quill & Quire* Dec 1987; Vol 53 No 12: p22.

Hamilton, John

Film's end; review of *The Disposables*. *G&M* June 13, 1987: pC20.

Hamilton, K.N.

Sound effects; short story. photo · *TS* Aug 22, 1987: pM5.

Hamilton, Mary G.

Passionate and practical; review of *Michele Landsberg's Guide to Children's Books*. *Can Child Lit* 1987; No 46: p64–65.

Hamilton, Richard

[Untitled]; review of *Economic Sex*. *Rubicon* Spring 1987; No 8: p226.

Hamilton, Seymour

Probing horror with footnotes; review of *Cambodia*. *CH* May 17, 1987: pE5.

Hamm, Eugene L.

Early morning hunter; poem. *Alpha* Winter 1987; Vol 11: p7.

Grandmother; poem. *Alpha* Winter 1987; Vol 11: p7.

Hancock, Geoff

Canada's short fiction shortchanged here; reviews of *87: Best Canadian Stories* and *Coming Attractions 5*. *TS* Dec 27, 1987: pE19.

A dazzling novel that attempts to be masterpiece; review of *Selakhi*. *TS* Nov 29, 1987: pA21.

Dissension in the backyard of Canada's frozen near north; review of *Contact Prints*. photo · *TS* May 3, 1987: pA24.

A monument to folly; review of *Dustship Glory*. *Can Forum* Feb 1987; Vol 66 No 766: p39–40.

Mystery that truly mystifies; review of *Swann: A Mystery*. *TS* Oct 18, 1987: pC9.

A rich, feminist novel from Quebec; reviews of *A Forest for Zoe* and *After the Fact*. *TS* Feb 15, 1987: pA19.

A sensitive tale focusing on aging; review of *Memory Board*. photo · *TS* Nov 21, 1987: pM4.

Hanley, Patricia

After all; poem. *Dandelion* Fall-Winter 1987; Vol 14 No 2: p17.

Somewhere south of here; poem. *Dandelion* Fall-Winter 1987; Vol 14 No 2: p16.

Hanns, Genine

A reflection; poem. *Can Auth & Book* Fall 1987; Vol 63 No 1: p17.

Hanson, Hart

Beautiful boy fades; short story. *Malahat R* Dec 1987; No 81: p86–93.

Harder, Naomi

Confession to a friend; poem. *Quarry* Fall 1987; Vol 36 No 4: p29–31.

Harding-Russell, Gillian

Amnesia: for Claude Jutra; poem. *Capilano R* 1987; No 43: p17.

Archibald; poem. *Dandelion* Fall-Winter 1987; Vol 14 No 2: p38–40.

B.C. international – in search of new subjects and forms; reviews. *Event* Summer 1987; Vol 16 No 2: p125–127.

Claude Jutra's note; poem. *Capilano R* 1987; No 43: p18–19.

The folly of acting in anger; review of *The Falcon Bow*. *Can Child Lit* 1987; No 46: p74–75.

"Footprints in the snow which stop"; review of *The Immaculate Perception*. *Event* March 1987; Vol 16 No 1: p105–106.

Jack rabbits; poem. *NeWest R* Sept 1987; Vol 13 No 1: p9.

The jogger; poem. *Capilano R* 1987; No 43: p22–23.

The living house; poem. *Capilano R* 1987; No 43: p24–25.

A note on Ondaatje's "Peter": a creative myth; article. *Can Lit* Spring 1987; No 112: p205–211.

Nursery rhyme, myth and dream; reviews of *Shaking the Dreamland Tree* and *Eleusis*. *NeWest R* Sept 1987; Vol 13 No 1: p17–18.

The old man in the vacant lot; poem. *Event* Summer 1987; Vol 16 No 2: p60–61.

The timber wolves; poem. *NeWest R* Sept 1987; Vol 13 No 1: p9.

[Untitled]; review of *Spider Blues*. *U of Toronto Q* Fall 1987; Vol 57 No 1: p166–168.

You have a wart; poem. *Capilano R* 1987; No 43: p20–21.

Harley, Kathryn

[Untitled]; review of *My Darling Judith*. *Maclean's* Oct 19, 1987; Vol 100 No 42: p70.

[Untitled]; review of *McClure*. *Maclean's* Nov 9, 1987; Vol 100 No 45: p70.

Harmon, Joan

Afterthought; poem. *Fiddlehead* Spring 1987; No 151: p58.

Her beauty; poem. *Fiddlehead* Spring 1987; No 151: p59.

The long game; poem. *Fiddlehead* Spring 1987; No 151: p57.

The walk to Westfield; poem. *Fiddlehead* Spring 1987; No 151: p56.

Harris, Beverly

[Untitled]; review of *Excerpts from the Real World*. *Dandelion* Spring-Summer 1987; Vol 14 No 1: p81–84.

Harris, C.K.

Conception of winter; poem. *Queen's Q* Autumn 1987; Vol 94 No 3: p542.

Harris, Claire

Against the blade; poem. illus · *Can Forum* Aug-Sept 1987; Vol 67 No 771: p14–17.

Litany; poem. *Ariel* Oct 1987; Vol 18 No 4: p21.

Harris, Ethel

Doppelganger; poem. *Matrix* Fall 1987; No 25: p18.

Grave robber; poem. *Matrix* Fall 1987; No 25: p17.

Jerusalem; poem. *Can Auth & Book* Summer 1987; Vol 62 No 4: p23.

Mummy; poem. *Matrix* Fall 1987; No 25: p80.

Harris, Marjorie

More in anger than in sorrow; letter to the editor. *Quill & Quire* April 1987; Vol 53 No 4: p3.

Harris, Neil

Child subversion reigns in delightful play; theatre review of *Jacob Two-Two Meets the Hooded Fang*. *WFP* Nov 13, 1987: p37.

Children's fantasy fails to fulfil promise; theatre review of *A Princess Comes of Age*. *WFP* Nov 21, 1987: p22.

Co-op's Texas offers hot night of theatre; theatre reviews of *Laundry and Bourbon* and *Lone Star*. *WFP* June 17, 1987: p27.

Harrison, James

Janet Lunn's time / space travellers; article. *Can Child Lit* 1987; No 46: p60–63.

The rhythms of ritual in Margaret Laurence's The Tomorrow-Tamer; article. *World Lit in Eng* Autumn 1987; Vol 27 No 2: p245–252.

Harrison, Jeanne

Blue irises; poem. *Quarry* Winter 1987; Vol 36 No 1: p30.

Bouquet; poem. *Quarry* Winter 1987; Vol 36 No 1: p31.

The sacrifice of Actaeon; poem. *Quarry* Winter 1987; Vol 36 No 1: p29.

Harrison, Keith

Rain in the Laurentians; short story. *Fiddlehead* Autumn 1987; No 153: p5–9.

Harrison, Richard

Pinocchio as a man; poem. *Quarry* Fall 1987; Vol 36 No 4: p55–56.

Harry, Margaret

Dreamers; poem. *CV 2* Summer 1987; Vol 10 No 4: p41.

Fiction and racial attitudes; review of *Racial Attitudes in English-Canadian Fiction, 1905–1980*. *Atlan Prov Book R* Nov-Dec 1987; Vol 14 No 4: p10.

Hart, Bill

Rohmer brews mystery from fact and fiction; review of *Rommel and Patton*. *CH* March 22, 1987: pF5.

Hart, Jonathan

Dream songs; poem. *Grain* Winter 1987; Vol 15 No 4: p30.

Letter to India; poem. *Grain* Winter 1987; Vol 15 No 4: p31.

Lost in the telling; poem. *Grain* Winter 1987; Vol 15 No 4: p30.

Hart, Matthew

How green is thy valley; humourous essay. *G&M (Toronto Magazine)* April 1987; Vol 2 No 1: p96.

What's bred in the Bono; humourous essay. illus · *G&M (Toronto Magazine)* June 1987; Vol 2 No 3: p88.

Hart, William

Hyacinth; short story. *Prairie J of Can Lit* 1987; No 8: p42–46.

Hartling, Christina

Censors, reviews hot topics at Writers Union AGM; article. photo · *Quill & Quire* Aug 1987; Vol 53 No 8: p22–23.

Hartog, Diana

Basho sets forth on his autumn journey; poem. *Malahat R* June 1987; No 79: p45.

The family eyes; poem. *Malahat R* June 1987; No 79: p43–44.

Hieroglyphics; poem. *Brick* Fall 1987; No 31: p64.

The mother inside; poem. *Event* Summer 1987; Vol 16 No 2: p97.

Tender buttons; poem. *Malahat R* June 1987; No 79: p46.

Two poems about rain, one written after Chernobyl, one before; poem. *Malahat R* June 1987; No 79: p47.

Hartsfield, Carla

Applause; poem. *Waves* Winter 1987; Vol 15 No 3: p63.

Bone; poem. *Arc* Spring 1987; No 18: p25–26.

Cathedral; poem. *Rubicon* Fall 1987; No 9: p97.

Edith; poem sequence. illus · *Poetry Can R* Spring 1987; Vol 8 No 2-3: p16.

Fog; poem. *Arc* Spring 1987; No 18: p23–24.

Green; poem. *Tor Life* Sept 1987; Vol 21 No 13: p33.

Him; poem. *Arc* Spring 1987; No 18: p27–28.

Marriage of two trees; poem. *Arc* Spring 1987; No 18: p29–30.

Pearl and Jack; poem. *Antigonish R* 1987; No 69–70: p157–158.

Playing; poem. *Arc* Spring 1987; No 18: p31.

Speeding; poem. *Tor Life* Sept 1987; Vol 21 No 13: p78.

To Mozart: a birthday; poem. *Malahat R* Dec 1987; No 81: p84–85.

Harvey, Ken J.

Carnival monster; poem. *Antigonish R* 1987; No 69–70: p180.

Little bones; poem. *Matrix* Spring 1987; No 24: p58–59.

Long, delicate procession; poem. *Prism* Spring 1987; Vol 25 No 3: p79.

The magic of belief: or The birth of cubism; poem. *Fiddlehead* Summer 1987; No 152: p39.

Harvey, Roderick W.

Comic solutions; review of *A City Called July*. *Can Lit* Winter 1987; No 115: p214–216.

Harvor, Beth

To supper in the morning and to bed at noon; short story. *Fiddlehead* Summer 1987; No 152: p5–18.

Hashmi, Alamgir

Captain Kirk in Karachi; poem. *Tor South Asian R* Summer 1987; Vol 6 No 1: p64–65.

The man who worked the nights; poem. *Tor South Asian R* Summer 1987; Vol 6 No 1: p63–64.

Notice inviting quotations; poem. *Tor South Asian R* Summer 1987; Vol 6 No 1: p63.

Postcard from Switzerland; poem. *Tor South Asian R* Summer 1987; Vol 6 No 1: p66.

So what if I live in a house made by idiots?; poem. *Tor South Asian R* Summer 1987; Vol 6 No 1: p66.

Hatch, Ronald B.

Confederation poets; reviews. *Can Lit* Winter 1987; No 115: p223–225.

Poetry; survey review article. *U of Toronto Q* Fall 1987; Vol 57 No 1: p33–50.

The power of love; review of *The Honorary Patron*. *Can Forum* Oct 1987; Vol 67 No 772: p39–40.

Underwing; reviews of *In the Shadow of the Vulture* and *The Quarter-Pie Window*. *Can Lit* Spring 1987; No 112: p95–97.

[Untitled]; reviews of critical works. *Eng Studies in Can* March 1987; Vol 13 No 1: p107–115.

Hauser, Gwen

Literary prizes exclude minorities; letter to the editor. *TS* May 22, 1987: pA18.

La vie quotidienne; poem. *Waves* Spring 1987; Vol 15 No 4: p73.

Women of the whole world; poem. *CV 2* Spring 1987; Vol 10 No 3: p50–51.

Havemann, Ernst

The exiles; short story. illus · *Atlantic* Nov 1987; Vol 260 No 5: p103–106.

My father's son; short story. illus · *Atlantic* June 1987; Vol 259 No 6: p48–52.

[Untitled]; letter to the editor. *Atlantic* May 1987; Vol 259 No 5: p14.

Hayes, David

What's Black and White and may or may not be read all over?; article. photo · *Tor Life* Dec 1987; Vol 21 No 18: p54–60, 108, 110–111.

Hayes, Elliott

Midnight: the arrest; poem. illus · *Can Forum* Jan 1987; Vol 66 No 765: p20.

Hayes, Glenn

[Untitled]; review of *Into Nests, Each Perfect as an Inner Ear!*. *Poetry Can R* Spring 1987; Vol 8 No 2–3: p57–58.

[Untitled]; review of *Meditations*. *Poetry Can R* Spring 1987; Vol 8 No 2–3: p58–59.

[Untitled]; review of *Vancouver Poetry*. *Poetry Can R* Fall 1987; Vol 9 No 1: p36–37.

Hayne, David M.

[Untitled]; review of *Arthur de Bussières, poète, et l'École littéraire de Montréal*. *U of Toronto Q* Fall 1987; Vol 57 No 1: p178–179.

Haynes, Dave

Film stars stage celebrity bashes; column. *WFP* June 19, 1987: p21.

Remembrance Day spurs London terror memories; article. photo · *CH* Nov 11, 1987: pB1.

Hayward, Annette

[Untitled]; review of *L'Oeuvre romanesque de Marie-Claire Blais*. *U of Toronto Q* Fall 1987; Vol 57 No 1: p183–184.

Hazell, Tim

Rock of ages; poem. *Can Auth & Book* Spring 1987; Vol 62 No 3: p22.

Healy, Thomas

[Untitled]; review of *Home Truths*. *British J of Can Studies* June 1987; Vol 2 No 1: p183–184.

Heath, Terrence

The alibis of Kroetsch and Butler; introduction to Alibi Drawings. *Border Cross* Summer 1987; Vol 6 No 3: p31–32.

On rescuing some old poems; essay. *Grain* Summer 1987; Vol 15 No 2: p11–13.

Hébert, Anne

[Untitled]; letter. photo · *Brick (special issue)* Summer 1987; No 30: p41–42.

Hébert, François

Autour de notre langue (dans ma langue); essay. illus · *Liberté (special issue)* 1987: p25–31.

Isidore, Imelda, mais qui vous prie encore?; fictional essay. illus · *Liberté* Dec 1987; Vol 29 No 6: p98–106.

Opinions d'un mauvais philosophe ou d'un mauvais écrivain sur la question des rapports de la pensée et de l'écriture; essay. *Liberté* April 1987; Vol 29 No 2: p54–61.

Présentation; editorial. *Liberté* Feb 1987; Vol 29 No 1: p2.

Pretentieux? Idéalistes? Elitistes?; article. *Liberté* Feb 1987; Vol 29 No 1: p159–160.

Reportage: les adorateurs de la Danseuse nue; essay. *Liberté* June 1987; Vol 29 No 3: p23–31.

Hébert, Pierre

Après les mille et une nuits; review of *Le Huitième jour*. photo · *Lettres québec* Winter 1986–87; No 44: p29–30.

Ce qui arrive, quant on écrit pour communiquer; review of *Le Cri de l'oie blanche*. photo · *Lettres québec* Summer 1987; No 46: p24–25.

Être adolescent, aujourd'hui; review of *La Poursuite*. photo · *Lettres québec* Spring 1987; No 45: p28–29.

Jalons pour une narratologie du journal intime: le statut du récit dans le Journal d'Henriette Dessaulles; article. *Voix et images* Autumn 1987; Vol 13 No 1: p140–156.

À l'impossible certains sont tenus; reviews of *Benito* and *Aaa, Aâh, Ha ou les amours malaisées*. *Voix et images* Autumn 1987; Vol 13 No 1: p192–194.

Pourquoi le manque de croyances peut vous faire mourir de soif; review of *Le Souffle de l'Harmattan*. photo · *Lettres québec* Autumn 1987; No 47: p22–23.

Romans; survey review article. *U of Toronto Q* Fall 1987; Vol 57 No 1: p22–32.

Heffron, Dorris

Writers rank high in Chinese society; article. photo · *Quill & Quire* Nov 1987; Vol 53 No 11: p11.

Heft, Harold Jack

For Pelle Lindbergh, goaltender; poem. *Rubicon* Fall 1987; No 9: p103.

[Untitled]; review of *Children of Abel*. *Rubicon* Fall 1987; No 9: p176–177.

[Untitled]; review of *Dance with Desire*. *Rubicon* Spring 1987; No 8: p184–185.

Heighton, Steven

Downing's fast; short story. *New Q* Winter 1987; Vol 6 No 4: p36–47.

English cemetery, Gaspésie; poem. *Arc* Spring 1987; No 18: p34.

Entrophy; poem. *Fiddlehead* Autumn 1987; No 153: p50–51.

Holiday; poem. *Arc* Spring 1987; No 18: p33.

Josef Stalin: later works; poem. *Quarry* Winter 1987; Vol 36 No 1: p102.

Sailing, Gulf Islands; poem. *Arc* Spring 1987; No 18: p32.

Sky burial; poem. *Grain* Fall 1987; Vol 15 No 3: p62.

Unfinished Buddha, Samed Island; poem. *Queen's Q* Summer 1987; Vol 94 No 2: p443.

Heine-Koehn, Lala

ΣΕΛΑ, the bearing stool; poem. *Dandelion* Fall-Winter 1987; Vol 14 No 2: p22–23.

The art of hospitality; poem. *New Q* Spring-Summer 1987; Vol 7 No 1–2: p192–194.

The hands of mothers are holy; poem. *New Q* Spring-Summer 1987; Vol 7 No 1–2: p190–191.

In the small hours; poem. *Arc* Fall 1987; No 19: p68.

May I ask for the hand of your sister; poem. *Prairie Fire* Summer 1987; Vol 8 No 2: p46.

The recalled hours; poem. *Arc* Fall 1987; No 19: p68.

Whoever he is; poem. *Prairie Fire* Summer 1987; Vol 8 No 2: p47.

Heinricks, Geoff

[Untitled]; review of *Cambodia*. *Quill & Quire* June 1987; Vol 53 No 6: p31–32.

[Untitled]; review of *The Last White Man in Panama*. *Quill & Quire* Sept 1987; Vol 53 No 9: p79.

Hekkanen, Ernest

Hidden in the flesh near her heart; poem. *Matrix* Spring 1987; No 24: p37.

The Last Rites Hotel; poem. *Ariel* April 1987; Vol 18 No 2: p80.

Today a flight of tongues; poem. *Matrix* Spring 1987; No 24: p37.

Heller, Liane

The poetry sweatshop; article. photo · *Cross Can Writ Q* 1987; Vol 9 No 1: p5–6, 28.

Summer swelled, whirred; poem. *Tor Life* June 1987; Vol 21 No 9: p36.

[Untitled]; review of *Dance with Desire*. *Cross Can Writ Q* 1987; Vol 9 No 1: p22–23.

Weightlifter; poem. *Tor Life* Jan 1987; Vol 21 No 1: p23.

Helm, Michael

Memory & words; reviews of *Fables of Brunswick Avenue* and *Bottled Roses*. *Can Lit* Spring 1987; No 112: p92–95.

[Untitled]; review of *A Model Lover*. *Rubicon* Spring 1987; No 8: p224–225.

Helwig, David

Ceramic horses; short story. *Quarry* Winter 1987; Vol 36 No 1: p77–90.

Starting over; reviews of *The Late Great Human Road Show* and *Sitting in the Club Car Drinking Rum and Karma-Kola*. *Books in Can* Jan-Feb 1987; Vol 16 No 1: p15.

[Untitled]; reviews of short story collections. *Queen's Q* Winter 1987; Vol 94 No 4: p1022–1024.

Helwig, Maggie

Acorn: swept up in imagery; review of *Whiskey Jack*. photo · *TS* Feb 8, 1987: pG8.

Bowering's capricious Western; review of *Caprice*. *TS* May 17, 1987: pA17.

Childhood endured across frontiers; review of *A Hero Travels Light*. *TS* Feb 21, 1987: pM6.

Cliched veter[a]n profoundly human; review of *Unknown Soldier*. *TS* Oct 10, 1987: pM8.

Collection charms despite certain bias; review of *Farewell Tour*. *TS* May 9, 1987: pM10.

Common language in private words; reviews of poetry books. *TS* Aug 8, 1987: pM10.

I scali santi; poem. *Can Forum* Oct 1987; Vol 67 No 772: p27.

Magnificent voice of the poetic mad; review of *Names of God*. *TS* April 11, 1987: pM4.

Moving pictures; review of *Cambodia*. illus · *Can Forum* Aug-Sept 1987; Vol 67 No 771: p39–41.

Poor George and Jessie, poor reader; review of *Afternoon Tea*. *TS* Feb 28, 1987: pM6.

Powerful imagery impresses; review of *Medieval Hour in the Author's Mind*. *TS* June 28, 1987: pA18.

The Prospero figure: Northrop Frye's magic criticism; article. *Can Forum* Oct 1987; Vol 67 No 772: p28–32.

'Romance' a record by which poet puts theory into practice; review of *The Family Romance*. photo · *TS* May 23, 1987: pM4.

Some beautiful moments but all too fleeting; reviews of poetry books. *TS* Aug 15, 1987: pM6.

Unkind but true: little skill in first novel; review of *Counterpoint*. *TS* June 20, 1987: pM7.

Henderson, Brian

The cut delphiniums; poem. *Rubicon* Fall 1987; No 9: p60.

Dreambody; poem. *Rubicon* Fall 1987; No 9: p58.

Gravity feel; poem. *Rubicon* Fall 1987; No 9: p59.

The night imagines; poem. *Rubicon* Fall 1987; No 9: p60.

Seeing in Frobisher Bay; poem. *Rubicon* Fall 1987; No 9: p57.

[Untitled]; poem. *Rubicon* Fall 1987; No 9: p61.

Henderson, Helen Drummond

[Untitled]; biographical article. *Brick (special issue)* Summer 1987; No 30: p19.

Henderson, Mark

The hardware store; poem. *Fiddlehead* Summer 1987; No 152: p20.

Saturday afternoon I; poem. *Fiddlehead* Summer 1987; No 152: p21.

Saturday afternoon II; poem. *Fiddlehead* Summer 1987; No 152: p21–22.

Saturday afternoon III; poem. *Fiddlehead* Summer 1987; No 152: p22.

The wad of bills; poem. *Fiddlehead* Summer 1987; No 152: p23.

Henry, Eileen Cameron

Puppet; poem. *Antigonish R* Winter 1987; No 68: p37.

Hentsch, Thierry

René-Daniel Dubois: the generous word; article. photo trans · *Can Theatre R* Spring 1987; No 50: p29–36.

Herman, Peter

[Untitled]; review of *Waiting for the Messiah*. *Rubicon* Spring 1987; No 8: p181–183.

[Untitled]; review of *The Skin of a Song*. *Rubicon* Fall 1987; No 9: p198–199.

Heron, Kim

Do we really escape?; article. photo · *NYT Book R* July 12, 1987: p11.

Herzberg Lister, Rota

[Untitled]; review of *English-Canadian Theatre*. *Can Drama* 1987; Vol 13 No 2: p227–228.

Hesbois, Laure

Schéma actantiel d'un pseudo-récit: le Torrent d'Anne Hébert; article. *Voix et images* Autumn 1987; Vol 13 No 1: p104–114.

Hewett, G.A.

Nowhere o'er the pears; poem. *Prism* Autumn 1987; Vol 26 No 1: p93–94.

Heyer, Paul

Algonkian snowshoes; poem. *Poetry Can R* Fall 1987; Vol 9 No 1: p11.

Hicks, Anne

Red crayon; review of *The Need of Wanting Always*. *Can Lit* Spring 1987; No 112: p91–92.

Hicks, John V.

Beast without; poem. *Antigonish R* 1987; No 69–70: p208.

Cling; poem. *Can Lit* Spring 1987; No 112: p31.

A matter of form; essay. *Grain* Summer 1987; Vol 15 No 2: p7–8.

On having to thumb through pages to find Ciardi; poem. *Grain* Summer 1987; Vol 15 No 2: p10.

Out of this dream; poem. *Antigonish R* 1987; No 69–70: p207.

Sonnet for a small girl; poem. *Grain* Summer 1987; Vol 15 No 2: p8.

Statement on an early unpublished poem; essay. *Grain* Summer 1987; Vol 15 No 2: p9.

Telltale; poem. *Grain* Summer 1987; Vol 15 No 2: p6.

Winter zero; poem. *Wascana R* Spring 1987; Vol 22 No 1: p34.

Hiebert, Paul

About Sarah Binks; essay. *Grain* Fall 1987; Vol 15 No 3: p9.

A dedication; prose excerpt from *Sarah Binks*. *Grain* Fall 1987; Vol 15 No 3: p9.

Hi, Sooky, ho, Sooky; poem, includes essay. *Grain* Fall 1987; Vol 15 No 3: p10–11.

Sweet songstress; prose and poetry excerpt from *Sarah Binks*. *G&M* Dec 24, 1987: pA6.

Higgins, Iain

"Every force evolves a form"; poem. *Prism* Spring 1987; Vol 25 No 3: p54.

The love song of Ceyx; poem. *Prism* Spring 1987; Vol 25 No 3: p54.

Highet, Alistair

Manifold destiny: metaphysics in the poetry of Christopher Dewdney; article. *Essays on Can Writ* Spring 1987; No 34: p2–17.

Hildebrandt, Gloria

[Untitled]; review of *Vigil*. *Books in Can* May 1987; Vol 16 No 4: p21.

Hill, Beth Munroe

Connection; poem. *NeWest R* Feb 1987; Vol 12 No 6: p9.

My father is a fireman; poem. *NeWest R* Feb 1987; Vol 12 No 6: p14.

[Untitled]; poem. *NeWest R* Feb 1987; Vol 12 No 6: p9.

Hill, Douglas

Fiction for slow days when reading is the happiest sport; review of *Murder Sees the Light*. *G&M* Aug 1, 1987: pC15.

Fine short stories examine contemporary domestic life; reviews of *Dzelarhons* and *Afternoon Tea*. *G&M* Jan 24, 1987: pE17.

How short story writers can gain their literary credibility; review of *Goodbye Harold, Good Luck*. *G&M* April 18, 1987: pC17.

A humanistic vision of the lives of churchmen and women; reviews of *The Glassy Sea* and *The Bishop*. *G&M* Sept 12, 1987: pC17.

The latest reports from the exotic worlds of fantasy; review of *The Summer Tree*. *G&M* July 11, 1987: pC13.

Publishers meet the demand with reissued crime classics; reviews of *The Night the Gods Smiled* and *One-Eyed Merchants*. *G&M* Feb 28, 1987: pE19.

Small regional presses as saviors of cultural information; reviews of fictional works. *G&M* Oct 10, 1987: pC21.

Today's assignment: short fiction that's worth a long look; reviews of short story books. *G&M* March 14, 1987: pE19.

Top flight practitioners of the craft of writing mysteries; review of *The Telling of Lies*. *G&M* Nov 21, 1987: pC21.

[Untitled]; review of *The Letter*. *Books in Can* Jan-Feb 1987; Vol 16 No 1: p24.

[Untitled]; review of *Looking for the Last Big Tree*. *Books in Can* Jan-Feb 1987; Vol 16 No 1: p25–26.

A wealth of provocative and inspiring literary criticism; reviews. *G&M* Sept 5, 1987: pC13.

The wonders and pleasures of fictional empire-building; reviews of novels by Matt Cohen. photo · *G&M* Jan 3, 1987: pE15.

Hill, Gerald

437–1825: the new number; poem. *Prairie J of Can Lit* 1987; No 8: p40.

Appearance vs. reality: taking possession; poem. *Prairie J of Can Lit* 1987; No 8: p38–39.

Beginning; poem. *Malahat R* Sept 1987; No 80: p85.

Desire; poem. *Malahat R* Sept 1987; No 80: p86.

Grass; poem. *Malahat R* Sept 1987; No 80: p86.

Picking rock; poem. *NeWest R* Nov 1987; Vol 13 No 3: p15.

A slow and painful debt: the purchase; poem. *Prairie J of Can Lit* 1987; No 8: p37–38.

Solution at Bell's Beach; poem. *Poetry Can R* Fall 1987; Vol 9 No 1: p11.

[Untitled]; review of *The Natural History of Water*. *Poetry Can R* Spring 1987; Vol 8 No 2–3: p45.

[Untitled]; review of *The Face of Jack Munro*. *Poetry Can R* Spring 1987; Vol 8 No 2–3: p46–47.

[Untitled]; review of *Open Windows*. *Poetry Can R* Fall 1987; Vol 9 No 1: p37.

Watch; poem. *Malahat R* Sept 1987; No 80: p86.

Wood; poem. *Malahat R* Sept 1987; No 80: p85.

Hill, Heather

Book fair to expand, offers new prizes; article. photo · *MG* Sept 4, 1987: pC2.

Celebs help publishing house launch fall season; article. *MG* Aug 28, 1987: pC1.

Fall books: raft of recycles on wave of high advances; preview of fall book list. photo · *MG* July 4, 1987: pJ7.

First electronic novel hits computer screens; article. photo · *MG* Aug 1, 1987: pJ9.

French book fair aims for more anglophones; article. *MG* Nov 6, 1987: pC1.

French literary prize falls because of budget cuts; article. *MG* Sept 9, 1987: pH1.

'Great Literary Dinner Party' proceeds start trickling out to deserving writers; article. *MG* May 30, 1987: pJ8.

Library gets 19th-century windfall featuring Canadian literary legend; article. illus · *MG* Aug 7, 1987: pA1, A4.

MacLennan, the lion of CanLit, turns 80; article. biog photo · *MG* March 20, 1987: pA1, A5.

May Cutler wins publishing award; article. *MG* June 23, 1987: pC10.

Montreal's Eden Press has impressive spring book list; article. photo · *MG* March 13, 1987: pG7.

N.Y. honor for Robertson Davies; article. *MG* Feb 11, 1987: pB5.

Now M&S wants a profit on its books; article. photo · *MG* Feb 28, 1987: pB4.

Quebec author Lemay gets exhibit; article. *MG* March 17, 1987: pC10.

Richler lays aside sharp stiletto to write Jacob Two-Two; article. photo · *MG* May 25, 1987: pF5.

Toronto author praises three of 'God's good men'; review of *Three Lives in Mine.* photo · *MG* March 28, 1987: pE8.

Tundra turns 20; article. photo · *MG* May 2, 1987: pH13.

Underground arts surfacing for festival; article. *MG* Sept 2, 1987: pH1.

Visionary author retains warmth and wit at 80; article. photo · *CH* March 24, 1987: pD1.

The write stuff in Toronto: literary fesival is world's largest; article. photo · *MG* Oct 20, 1987: pE6.

Hilles, Robert

Everything living; poem. *Poetry Can R* Fall 1987; Vol 9 No 1: p7.

Flin Flons; review of *Headframe. Prairie Fire* Autumn 1987; Vol 8 No 3: p109–112.

Hell and some notes on a piano; prose poem. *Quarry* Summer 1987; Vol 36 No 3: p18.

Morning is an invisible thing that passes; poem. *NeWest R* Sept 1987; Vol 13 No 1: p12.

Outlasting the landscape; poem. *Malahat R* Sept 1987; No 80: p37–38.

A poem is a machine for making choices; prose poem. *Prairie Fire* Summer 1987; Vol 8 No 2: p32.

Promise of the rising sun; poem. *Poetry Can R* Fall 1987; Vol 9 No 1: p7.

Something dangerous; prose poem. *Quarry* Summer 1987; Vol 36 No 3: p19.

A tender man; poem. *Malahat R* Sept 1987; No 80: p39.

[Untitled]; reviews of *The Beekeeper's Daughter* and *Midnight Found You Dancing. Poetry Can R* Spring 1987; Vol 8 No 2–3: p41.

Walking across a graveyard to mail a postcard; prose poem. *Quarry* Summer 1987; Vol 36 No 3: p17.

A warm place in winter; poem. *CV 2* Spring 1987; Vol 10 No 3: p32.

When transforms flesh; prose poem. *Quarry* Summer 1987; Vol 36 No 3: p18.

Words contain sleep; poem. *Prairie Fire* Summer 1987; Vol 8 No 2: p31.

Hillis, Doris

Interview with Barbara Sapergia: her plays, her concerns, her influences. photo · *NeWest R* Oct 1987; Vol 13 No 2: p2–4.

Interview with Mick Burrs. bibliog biog photo · *Prairie J of Can Lit* 1987; No 8: p5–19.

Interview with Sharon Butala. *Wascana R* Spring 1987; Vol 22 No 1: p37–53.

Hillis, Rick

Blue; short story. *Prism* Summer 1987; Vol 25 No 4: p100–115.

Girl dreaming blue machines; poem. *Border Cross* Summer 1987; Vol 6 No 3: p48.

Hunted citizens; poem. *Can Lit* Winter 1987; No 115: p125.

Old man 1: life in a one-way mirror; poem. *Arc* Spring 1987; No 18: p35.

Old man 2: timesmoke; poem. *Arc* Spring 1987; No 18: p36.

Old man 3: if you look close his smile is rubber; poem. *Arc* Spring 1987; No 18: p37.

Old man 4: down & dirty; poem. *Arc* Spring 1987; No 18: p38–39.

Old man 5: the night is chill; poem. *Arc* Spring 1987; No 18: p39.

Hinchcliffe, Peter

Lost innocents; reviews of *Nothing So Natural* and *Flavian's Fortune. Can Lit* Spring 1987; No 112: p90–91.

Hinz, Evelyn J.

The religious roots of the feminine identity issue: Margaret Laurence's The Stone Angel and Margaret Atwood's Surfacing; article. abstract · *J of Can Studies* Spring 1987; Vol 22 No 1: p17–31.

Hjartarson, Paul

Discourse of the other; review of *Advice to My Friends. Can Lit* Winter 1987; No 115: p135–138.

Hluchy, Patricia

[Untitled]; article. *Maclean's* Nov 2, 1987; Vol 100 No 44: p52f.

Hoban, Russell

The bear in Max Ernst's bedroom or the magic wallet; essay. photo · *Brick* Fall 1987; No 31: p8–14.

Hochbruck, Wolfgang

Oral Wiebe; interview with Rudy Wiebe. *Zeitschrift Kanada-Studien* 1987; Vol 7 No 1: p251–254.

Hodge, A. Trevor

[Untitled]; letter to the editor. *G&M* Nov 21, 1987: pD7.

Hoffman, Eva

A soft spot for sousaphones; review of *Dvorak in Love.* illus · *NYT Book R* Feb 22, 1987: p11.

Hohtanz, Marie

Passionate playwright; interview with Sharon Pollock. photo · *CH (Sunday Magazine)* Nov 29, 1987: p6–10.

Holland, Clifford G.

[Untitled]; reviews of *The Bridge Out of Town* and *A Model Lover*. *Queen's Q* Summer 1987; Vol 94 No 2: p472–474.

Hollingshead, Greg

Under the whip; short story. *Matrix* Spring 1987; No 24: p60–70.

Hollingsworth, Margaret

The day I killed the Pope; short story. *Writing* Jan 1987; No 17: p42–47.

Margarita; short story. *Malahat R* June 1987; No 79: p48–60.

Holloway, Ann

Relevant writing; reviews of *Private and Fictional Words* and *More Stories by Canadian Women*. *G&M* Nov 28, 1987: pC22.

Holloway, Anne

Echoes of a tin flute; review of *Enchantment and Sorrow*. *Maclean's* Nov 23, 1987; Vol 100 No 47: p54d,54f.

Holmes, Nancy

The last entry; short story. *New Q* Fall 1987; Vol 7 No 3: p39–44.

Riding lesson; poem. *Antigonish R* Winter 1987; No 68: p39.

Yseult at 100 KPH; poem. *West Coast R* Spring 1987; Vol 21 No 4: p51.

Holt, Bruce D.

[Untitled]; letter to the editor. *G&M* April 22, 1987: pA7.

Winning story first-class work; letter to the editor. *CH* Aug 15, 1987: pA6.

Homel, David

Editions Fides: keeping the faith at 50; article. photo · *Quill & Quire* April 1987; Vol 53 No 4: p18.

Films in Fortin's future; article. *Quill & Quire* Oct 1987; Vol 53 No 10: p6.

Fresh names on the Quebec literary front; article. photo · *Quill & Quire* Oct 1987; Vol 53 No 10: p4, 6.

The good fight; article about May Cutler. photo · *Books in Can* Dec 1987; Vol 16 No 9: p8–10.

The name of Roseau grows in Quebec book market; article. *Quill & Quire* March 1987; Vol 53 No 3: p58.

New lines, Lévesque make for lively Salon du Livre; article. photo · *Quill & Quire* Jan 1987; Vol 53 No 1: p14–15.

[Untitled]; review of *Farewell Tour*. *Quill & Quire* April 1987; Vol 53 No 4: p28.

Hood, Wharton

[Untitled]; poem. *Cross Can Writ Q* 1987; Vol 9 No 3–4: p12.

Hoogland, Joan

Sumas prairie; poem. *Prairie J of Can Lit* 1987; No 8: p30.

Ties; poem. *Prairie J of Can Lit* 1987; No 8: p31.

Horn, Michiel

[Untitled]; biographical articles. *Brick (special issue)* Summer 1987; No 30: ppassim.

Horne, Lewis

The claims of summer; poem. *Queen's Q* Spring 1987; Vol 94 No 1: p14.

January; poem. *Wascana R* Spring 1987; Vol 22 No 1: p33.

Horner, Jan

A design-conscious guy; reviews of *Settlements* and *The Natural History of Water*. *CV 2* Spring 1987; Vol 10 No 3: p61–66.

Editorial. *CV 2* Summer 1987; Vol 10 No 4: p6–7.

Hornosty, Cornelia C.

Discovery; poem. *Waves* Winter 1987; Vol 15 No 3: p61.

The iron; poem. *Atlantis* Fall 1987; Vol 13 No 1: p52.

Pioneer; poem. *Can Auth & Book* Spring 1987; Vol 62 No 3: p22.

Horowitz, Anthony

Uncertain futures; review of *This Place Has No Atmosphere*. *Times Lit Supp* Oct 30, 1987; No 4413: p1205.

Hospital, Janette Turner

Knots of age and sex; review of *Memory Board*. *G&M* Oct 17, 1987: pE5.

Howells, Coral Ann

LMM: finding a voice; review of *The Selected Journals of L.M. Montgomery*. *Can Child Lit* 1987; No 45: p79–81.

Up in the air; review of *Time in the Air*. *Can Lit* Winter 1987; No 115: p150–152.

Howells, Robin

Pélagie-la-Charrette and the carnivalesque; article. *British J of Can Studies* June 1987; Vol 2 No 1: p48–60.

Hryciuk, Marshall

Strand 44; poem. *Cross Can Writ Q* 1987; Vol 9 No 3–4: p15.

Hubbell, Sue

Love with the right farm hand; review of *Getting Married in Buffalo Jump*. *NYT Book R* Aug 16, 1987: p22.

Hudson, Nicholas

Magpie mind; review of *The Papers of Samuel Marchbanks*. *Can Lit* Spring 1987; No 112: p88–90.

Huggan, Isabel

[Untitled]; review of *A Stone Watermelon*. *Books in Can* April 1987; Vol 16 No 3: p25.

Hughes, Helena

Writer's obit upstaged by Reagan's operation; letter to the editor. *TS* Jan 8, 1987: pA12.

Hughes, Monica

Canadian content in England; essay. *Quill & Quire (Books for Young People)* April 1987; Vol 53 No 4: p4.

My search for Somewhere; essay. photo · *Can Child Lit* 1987; No 48: p15–28.

Hulan, Renée

Part one: emptiness; poem. *Alpha* Winter 1987; Vol 11: p18.

Part two: revenge; poem. *Alpha* Winter 1987; Vol 11: p18.

Hulse, Michael

Worlds in collision; review of *In the Skin of a Lion. Times Lit Supp* Sept 4, 1987; No 4405: p948.

Hume, Christopher

Award-winning children's story lights up stage; article. photo · *TS* Dec 3, 1987: pB5.

Delightfully tiny Willie makes a big impression; theatre review of *Willie the Squowse.* photo · *TS* Dec 11, 1987: pD14.

Drawing power; article. illus photo · *TS* Nov 1, 1987: pC1, C5.

Fast-paced kids' tale is simply irresistible; theatre review of *Jacob Two-Two Meets the Hooded Fang.* photo · *TS* Oct 23, 1987: pE8.

Funny British play praises non-conformity; theatre reviews of *Comment devenir parfait en trois jours* and *Coeur à coeur. TS* May 14, 1987: pF7.

The humor saves Lolita, but it's strained; theatre review of *The Last Will and Testament of Lolita. TS* June 5, 1987: pE19.

Jacob meets Dippy the dinosaur; article. *TS* May 26, 1987: pG1.

Matinee Idol winner a model mother of 2; article. photo · *TS* June 19, 1987: pD23.

Munsch tells it like it is for kids; article. *TS* Feb 6, 1987: pD19.

'Natural writer' mourned; article. *TS* Jan 6, 1987: pD1.

Today's model; article. photo · *TS* Jan 9, 1987: pD4.

Hummell, Steven

Spike; short story. *Quarry* Spring 1987; Vol 36 No 2: p70–88.

Tulugaaq; short story. *Exile* 1987; Vol 12 No 2: p121–127.

Humphreys, Helen

What if forever only lasts until Tuesday?; poem. *Poetry Can R* Spring 1987; Vol 8 No 2–3: p54–55.

Hunt, Nigel

. . . .Lest ye be judged; article. photo · *Can Theatre R* Summer 1987; No 51: p17–23.

Hillar Liitoja: chaos and control; article. photo · *Can Theatre R* Fall 1987; No 52: p45–49.

Hunt, Sharon J.

[Untitled]; review of *Memory Board. Quarry* Fall 1987; Vol 36 No 4: p87–88.

Hunt, Stephen

"Weekend people"; short story. photo · *NeWest R* Summer 1987; Vol 12 No 10: p7–9.

Hunter, Bruce

Creative writing teachers – reflections and advice; article. photo · *Cross Can Writ Q* 1987; Vol 9 No 1: p3–4.

Light against light; poem. *Dandelion* Fall-Winter 1987; Vol 14 No 2: p34–35.

Lilacs; poem. *Dandelion* Fall-Winter 1987; Vol 14 No 2: p36–37.

[Untitled]; reviews of poetry books. *Cross Can Writ Q* 1987; Vol 9 No 3–4: p40–42.

Hunter, Catherine

The poet's double gift; review of *The Garden Going On without Us. Prairie Fire* Spring 1987; Vol 8 No 1: p78–82.

[Untitled]; review of *The Telling of Lies. Malahat R (special issue)* March 1987; No 78: p148–151.

Hunter, Lynette

[Untitled]; review of *The Blue Notebook. British J of Can Studies* June 1987; Vol 2 No 1: p188–189.

Hunter, Martin

Cheque mates; article about the Ontario Arts Council. illus · *Tor Life* June 1987; Vol 21 No 9: p52, 86–90, 93, 95–96.

Hurley, Michael

[Untitled]; review of *Northrop Frye: A Vision of the New World. Queen's Q* Spring 1987; Vol 94 No 1: p219–222.

Hurley, Theresa

[Untitled]; review of *With a Sudden & Terrible Clarity. Quarry* Spring 1987; Vol 36 No 2: p109–111.

[Untitled]; review of *Suburbs of the Arctic Circle. Quarry* Spring 1987; Vol 36 No 2: p111–113.

Hurst, W.G.

Misadventures in the word trade; short story. *Quarry* Spring 1987; Vol 36 No 2: p89–93.

Hurwitz, Anita

[Untitled]; reviews of poetry books. *Poetry Can R* Spring 1987; Vol 8 No 2–3: p38–39.

[Untitled]; reviews of poetry books. *Poetry Can R* Spring 1987; Vol 8 No 2–3: p50–51.

Husband, Elaine

A last column, and a farewell to a great friend; article. photo · *CH* Dec 16, 1987: pA8.

Laurence kept finger on pulse of humanity; column. *CH* Jan 21, 1987: pA8.

NFB films spark memories of Margaret Laurence; column. *CH* Jan 28, 1987: pA10.

Hussey, Charlotte

[Untitled]; review of *A Dialogue with Masks*. *Rubicon* Spring 1987; No 8: p205–208.

[Untitled]; review of *The Fabulous Disguise of Ourselves*. *Rubicon* Fall 1987; No 9: p163–164.

Hutcheon, Linda

Murder & lies; reviews of *A Single Death* and *The Telling of Lies*. *Can Lit* Winter 1987; No 115: p225–227.

Shape shifters: Canadian women novelists challenge tradition; article. illus · *Can Forum* Jan 1987; Vol 66 No 765: p26–32.

Hutcheson, John

A very public life; review of *The Politics of the Imagination*. *Can Forum* Oct 1987; Vol 67 No 772: p40–41.

Hutchison, Sandra

Diamond panes; review of *The Glass Air*. *Can Lit* Summer-Fall 1987; No 113–114: p247–249.

Hutchman, Laurence

Still lifes; reviews of poetry books. *Can Lit* Winter 1987; No 115: p263–264.

Ultrasound; poem. *Can Lit* Summer-Fall 1987; No 113–114: p75.

[Untitled]; review of *Changes of State*. *Rubicon* Spring 1987; No 8: p190–193.

[Untitled]; review of *The Collected Poems*. *Rubicon* Fall 1987; No 9: p179–182.

Hye, Allen E.

Diamond & daydream; review of *The Iowa Baseball Confederacy*. *Can Lit* Winter 1987; No 115: p162–164.

Hykin, Susan

Co-operation; poem. *Event* Summer 1987; Vol 16 No 2: p58.

Convergence; poem. *Event* Summer 1987; Vol 16 No 2: p59.

Hyland, Gary

Hammel reads from the Persian; poem. *NeWest R* Sept 1987; Vol 13 No 1: p5.

Hammel's soliloquy at the herbalist's; poem. *NeWest R* Sept 1987; Vol 13 No 1: p5.

The honest singing; poem. *Prairie J of Can Lit* 1987; No 8: p35.

The imposter syndrome; poem. *NeWest R* Sept 1987; Vol 13 No 1: p5.

The old song; poem. *Prairie J of Can Lit* 1987; No 8: p36.

Play by play; poem. *New Q* Fall 1987; Vol 7 No 3: p62–63.

Public square, Buenos Aries; poem. *New Q* Fall 1987; Vol 7 No 3: p61.

South America; prose poem. *Grain* Summer 1987; Vol 15 No 2: p21.

Imbert, Patrick

De la sociologie des cultures à la bibliologie; review of *Québec Canada France*. *Lettres québec* Winter 1986–87; No 44: p78.

Le prolétariat montréalais écrasé; review of *Au milieu la montagne*. photo · *Lettres québec* Winter 1986–87; No 44: p63–64.

Tout texte fondateur en cache un autre!; reviews of *Les Révélations du crime* and *L'Influence d'un livre*. *Lettres québec* Autumn 1987; No 47: p58–60.

Inbar, Lavinia

The space of images; reviews of poetry books. *Can Lit* Summer-Fall 1987; No 113–114: p245–247.

[Untitled]; reviews of poetry books. illus · *Poetry Can R* Spring 1987; Vol 8 No 2–3: p51–53.

Innes, Eva

Geologists find gold in arts; article. photo · *Fin Post* May 4, 1987: p22.

Ioannou, Susan

Art for art & and truth; editorial. *Cross Can Writ Q* 1987; Vol 9 No 3–4: p37, 64.

Dawn snow; poem. *Dandelion* Fall-Winter 1987; Vol 14 No 2: p33.

Dysmenorrhea; poem. *Poetry Can R* Summer 1987; Vol 8 No 4: p39.

Echocardiogram; poem. *Prism* Summer 1987; Vol 25 No 4: p92.

Fiction and poetry: a question of size; essay. illus · *Can Auth & Book* Summer 1987; Vol 62 No 4: p4–5.

In your light; poem. *Poetry Can R* Summer 1987; Vol 8 No 4: p39.

My favourite Canadian poem; article. *Cross Can Writ Q* 1987; Vol 9 No 1: p11, 21.

Of time & the writer; essay. *Cross Can Writ Q* 1987; Vol 9 No 2: p27.

A ruffle between friends; short story. photo · *TS* Aug 3, 1987: pD7.

Sea deep; poem. *Dandelion* Fall-Winter 1987; Vol 14 No 2: p32.

When; poem. *Ariel* Jan 1987; Vol 18 No 1: p26.

Irie, Kevin

Chronology, the pond; poem. *Cross Can Writ Q* 1987; Vol 9 No 1: p10.

Denial; poem. *Northward J* 1987; No 43: p32.

Estrangement; poem. *Poetry Can R* Summer 1987; Vol 8 No 4: p22.

The fishing line; poem. *Northward J* 1987; No 43: p32.

Hearts; poem. *Poetry Can R* Fall 1987; Vol 9 No 1: p19.

In hiding; poem. illus · *Cross Can Writ Q* 1987; Vol 9 No 1: p10.

The muskellunge; poem. *Northward J* 1987; No 43: p33.

The specimen carp; poem. *Northward J* 1987; No 43: p34.

The swan's nest, winter; poem. *Germination* Fall 1987; Vol 11 No 1: p22.

Irish, Paul

Arts Scarborough will sponsor workshop for novice writers; article. *TS (Neighbours)* May 12, 1987: p10.

Creative Workshops for Children encourage young writers to produce; article. *TS (Neighbours)* May 5, 1987: p18.

Drama festival holds showcase; article. *TS (Neighbours)* April 7, 1987: p21.

Lizzie Borden story staged in Pickering; article. *TS (Neighbours)* March 24, 1987: p14.

Scarborough authors to sign books; article. *TS (Neighbours)* April 21, 1987: p13.

Scarborough librarian turns children's author; article. photo · *TS (Neighbors)* Dec 8, 1987: p10.

Irvine, Lorna

Parody & legacy; reviews. *Can Lit* Winter 1987; No 115: p264–267.

Sailing the oceans of the world; article. *New Q* Spring-Summer 1987; Vol 7 No 1–2: p284–293.

[Untitled]; review of *Dorothy Livesay. Amer R of Can Studies* Winter 1987–88; Vol 17 No 4: p452–453.

Irwin, Joan

A wealth of fine films lies waiting in Canadian novels; column. *TS* Jan 17, 1987: pG7.

Iserman, Bruce

Anxiety above; poem. *Cross Can Writ Q* 1987; Vol 9 No 2: p15.

The green house on Spruce; poem. *Fiddlehead* Spring 1987; No 151: p17.

Sex in high summer's dream; poem. *Matrix* Fall 1987; No 25: p27.

Sitting for a portrait; poem. *Prism* Autumn 1987; Vol 26 No 1: p8.

[Untitled]; poem. *CV 2* Summer 1987; Vol 10 No 4: p25.

[Untitled]; poem. *Prism* Autumn 1987; Vol 26 No 1: p7.

Israel, Callie

Horse stories tell of struggles to achieve personal worth; reviews of *Storm Rider* and *Summer Goes Riding*. photo · *Quill & Quire (Books for Young People)* Oct 1987; Vol 53 No 10: p16.

There's a lot more here than a little by Little; review of *Little by Little*. photo · *Quill & Quire (Books for Young People)* Dec 1987; Vol 53 No 12: p3.

[Untitled]; review of *The Dream Catcher. Quill & Quire (Books for Young People)* June 1987; Vol 53 No 6: p4, 6.

Israel, Inge

The caretaker; poem. *Quarry* Summer 1987; Vol 36 No 3: p32.

Cosine; poem. *Quarry* Summer 1987; Vol 36 No 3: p31.

Legato; poem. *Quarry* Summer 1987; Vol 36 No 3: p30.

Sanri matsubara; poem. *Quarry* Summer 1987; Vol 36 No 3: p31.

Israelson, David

Atwood urges stop to plans for road in wilderness area; article. *TS* Feb 17, 1987: pC14.

Issenhuth, Jean-Pierre

Autour d'une "noyade orchestrale"; review of *La Mort aurorale. Liberté* Dec 1987; Vol 29 No 6: p154–155.

Brault, Fischer, Liscano; review of *Poèmes 1. Liberté* June 1987; Vol 29 No 3: p74–79.

De Bellefeuille, Nepveu, Lemaire, Royer; reviews of poetry books. *Liberté* Aug 1987; Vol 29 No 4: p78–87.

Jardinage: la hardiesse du jardinier; essay. *Liberté* June 1987; Vol 29 No 3: p14–18.

L'obsession de l'impossible; review of *Mouvement sans fin. Liberté* June 1987; Vol 29 No 3: p105–106.

Marie Uguay, Mandelstam, Luzi; review of *Poèmes. Liberté* April 1987; Vol 29 No 2: p86–94.

Reconnaissance à André Roy; review of *Vagabondages. Liberté* Oct 1987; Vol 29 No 5: p162–163.

À six heures et demie du matin, dans le bruit des conversations. . . .; essay. *Liberté* Dec 1987; Vol 29 No 6: p22–25.

Vues anachroniques sur les bâtisses; essay. *Liberté* Oct 1987; Vol 29 No 5: p61–64.

Itani, Frances

A season of mourning; poem sequence. *Room of One's Own* Sept 1987; Vol 11 No 4: p3–10.

White butterfly; short story. illus · *Can Forum* Jan 1987; Vol 66 No 765: p21–23.

Ito, Sally

Frogs in the rain barrel; poem. *Matrix* Fall 1987; No 25: p32.

Jews in old China; poem. *Capilano R* 1987; No 43: p4.

Kyoto; poem. *Capilano R* 1987; No 43: p6–8.

On meeting the prophet: five stages; poem. *Capilano R* 1987; No 43: p9.

Sansei; poem. *Dandelion* Spring-Summer 1987; Vol 14 No 1: p17.

Upon seeing a sculpture of Maitreya, the future Buddha; poem. *Capilano R* 1987; No 43: p5.

Jackson, J.R. de J.

[Untitled]; review of *Studies in Literature and the Humanities. Eng Studies in Can* June 1987; Vol 13 No 2: p229–234.

Jackson, Lawrence

[Untitled]; review of *We're Friends, Aren't We. Can Auth & Book* Winter 1987; Vol 62 No 2: p24.

Jackson, Marni

Ondaatje fuses poetry & history; review of *In the Skin of a Lion*. photo · *Chatelaine* Sept 1987; Vol 60 No 9: p10.

Jackson, Martha

Heartfelt service; letter to the editor. *G&M* Jan 27, 1987: pA6.

Jacob, Suzanne

[Untitled]; essay. *Estuaire* Summer 1987; No 45: p17–18.

Jacobs, Maria

Home's in the eye; poem. *Poetry Can R* Fall 1987; Vol 9 No 1: p24.

John at eighty; poem. *Poetry Can R* Summer 1987; Vol 8 No 4: p18.

Territorial; poem. *Poetry Can R* Summer 1987; Vol 8 No 4: p18.

This small matter of eternity; poem. *Poetry Can R* Summer 1987; Vol 8 No 4: p18.

Trimming the tree; poem. *Poetry Can R* Summer 1987; Vol 8 No 4: p18.

[Untitled]; essay. *Poetry Can R* Summer 1987; Vol 8 No 4: p14.

You do not need to love a man to mourn him in December; poem. *Poetry Can R* Summer 1987; Vol 8 No 4: p18.

Jacquot, Martine

Anne of Green Gables in translation; review of *Anne. . . la Maison aux pignons verts*. *Atlan Prov Book R* Feb-March 1987; Vol 14 No 1: p13.

An interview with Jeannine Landry-Theriault. biog photo · *Fiddlehead* Summer 1987; No 152: p72–75.

Mystery for young readers; review of *Le Secret de Lamorandière*. *Atlan Prov Book R* Sept-Oct 1987; Vol 14 No 3: p7.

Two illustrated Acadian books; reviews of *Pépère Goguen loup de mer*. *Atlan Prov Book R* Nov-Dec 1987; Vol 14 No 4: p11.

Jager, Manfred

Canadian books for kids gain fame; article. photo · *WFP* Oct 20, 1987: p33.

Manitoba writers gather for literary conference; article. *WFP* Oct 22, 1987: p46.

James, Caryn

The last time I smelled Paris; article. photo · *NYT Book R* March 15, 1987: p7.

James, Peter D.

Dropout plans to drop in; letter to the editor. photo · *G&M* Aug 29, 1987: pD7.

[Untitled]; review of *The Orangeman*. *Quill & Quire* Feb 1987; Vol 53 No 2: p17.

James-French, Dayv

After the blade; poem. *Grain* Fall 1987; Vol 15 No 3: p29.

Cats; poem. *Fiddlehead* Summer 1987; No 152: p41.

Making believe; poem. *Quarry* Summer 1987; Vol 36 No 3: p54.

Night vision; poem. *Quarry* Summer 1987; Vol 36 No 3: p53.

Pro / choice / life; poem. *Quarry* Summer 1987; Vol 36 No 3: p55.

Sourdough; poem. *Fiddlehead* Summer 1987; No 152: p40.

Spoons; poem. *Grain* Fall 1987; Vol 15 No 3: p28.

Jansen, Ann

[Untitled]; review of *Illusions*. *Quill & Quire* June 1987; Vol 53 No 6: p32.

Jansen, Walfried

Only the raven; poem. *NeWest R* Sept 1987; Vol 13 No 1: p7.

Janzen, Harold R.

Spirits fishing in the night; poem. *Prairie Fire* Autumn 1987; Vol 8 No 3: p51.

Jarman, Mark

Flaws, good work mark collections; reviews of *The Slidingback Hills* and *Heading Out*. *CH* April 26, 1987: pE5.

Interesting stories reach into dark depths; review of *Night Driving*. *CH* May 31, 1987: pF5.

Structure eludes Ondaatje's imagination; review of *In the Skin of a Lion*. *CH* Aug 23, 1987: pE4.

Jasmin, Claude

"Adieu Albert, je t'aimais bien, tu sais!"; letter to the editor. *MD* Feb 14, 1987: pA10.

Le ghetto homosexuel; essay. *MD* Sept 30, 1987: p11.

Jasper, Pat

Black tie dinner; poem. *Waves* Winter 1987; Vol 15 No 3: p69.

First spring away from home; poem. *Event* March 1987; Vol 16 No 1: p64–65.

March: vernal equinox; poem. *Can Lit* Winter 1987; No 115: p43–44.

Missing snapshot; poem. *Quarry* Fall 1987; Vol 36 No 4: p32–33.

The morning after; poem. *Waves* Winter 1987; Vol 15 No 3: p68.

Jeffrey, Scott

Songs of innocence and experience – the hometown in us all; reviews of *Headframe* and *No Fixed Address*. *NeWest R* Summer 1987; Vol 12 No 10: p13.

Jenkinson, Dave

Pacific coast adventure; review of *Cry to the Night Wind*. *Can Child Lit* 1987; No 47: p67–68.

Jensen, Jack

Win some, lose some more; letter to the editor. *Books in Can* Nov 1987; Vol 16 No 8: p40.

Jensen, Margaret

Past formula; review of *The Deep End*. *Can Lit* Winter 1987; No 115: p176–178.

Jernigan, Kim

Foreward. *New Q* Spring-Summer 1987; Vol 7 No 1–2: p11–13.

Jewinski, Ed

Psychic violence: The Stone Angel and modern family life; article. *New Q* Spring-Summer 1987; Vol 7 No 1–2: p255–266.

Jewison, D.B.

[Untitled]; review of *Varieties of Exile. U of Toronto Q* Fall 1987; Vol 57 No 1: p151–154.

Jirgens, Karl

Landscapes & eyes; reviews of poetry books. *Can Lit* Spring 1987; No 112: p192–193.

[Untitled]; review of *Total Refusal. Books in Can* June-July 1987; Vol 16 No 5: p21.

Zendmark; review of *Oab 1. Can Lit* Summer-Fall 1987; No 113–114: p217–219.

Jobe, Ronald A.

The effect of the international children's book industry on Canadian publishing endeavours for children and young people; article. *Can Child Lit* 1987; No 47: p7–11.

Joe, J.B.

In the loony bin; short story. *Can Fic Mag (special issue)* 1987; No 60: p52–57.

Window; short story. *Can Fic Mag (special issue)* 1987; No 60: p58–60.

Johnson, Brian D.

Anne of Green Gables grows up; article. photo · *Maclean's* Dec 7, 1987; Vol 100 No 49: p46–48, 50.

Hockey's puckish wit; review of *King Leary. Maclean's* Nov 9, 1987; Vol 100 No 45: p64h.

Jacob Two-Two in love; review of *Jacob Two-Two and the Dinosaur.* photo · *Maclean's* June 1, 1987; Vol 100 No 22: p52.

Pages for the powerful; article. photo · *Maclean's* Jan 19, 1987; Vol 100 No 3: p62.

The restless dreamer from the Rock; article. photo · *Maclean's* Feb 2, 1987; Vol 100 No 5: p76–78.

Johnson, George

New & noteworthy; review of *The Progress of Love. NYT Book R* Aug 30, 1987: p34.

New & noteworthy; review of *Bluebeard's Egg. NYT Book R* Nov 22, 1987: p50.

Notable paperbacks; checklist. *NYT Book R* Dec 6, 1987: p90–93.

Johnson, Linda Wikene

Aquarius; poem. *New Q* Fall 1987; Vol 7 No 3: p72.

Gemini; poem. *New Q* Fall 1987; Vol 7 No 3: p73.

The moon; poem. *New Q* Fall 1987; Vol 7 No 3: p71.

Johnson, Marion

O dear!; letter to the editor. *Books in Can* Jan-Feb 1987; Vol 16 No 1: p38.

Johnson, Phil

Aspiring writers take their books to the library; article. photo · *TS (Neighbors)* Sept 22, 1987: p20.

Author-playwright shares wealth of experience; article. photo · *TS (Neighbors)* Sept 29, 1987: p14.

Indian culture dying fast; article. photo · *TS (Neighbors)* Oct 13, 1987: p16.

Lickety split! He's hoping kids' books will zoom him to top; article. *TS (Neighbors)* Nov 3, 1987: p8.

Roots, new country put author, lecturer on tug-of-war path; article. photo · *TS (Neighbours)* Feb 3, 1987: p14.

Visually impaired tread the boards; article. photo · *TS (Neighbors)* July 28, 1987: p16.

Writers must be critical of own work, novelist says; article. photo · *TS (Neighbors)* Sept 22, 1987: p20.

Johnson, Quendrith

Photographs of urban living; short story. *Rubicon* Fall 1987; No 9: p76–80.

[Untitled]; review of *Schizotexte. Rubicon* Spring 1987; No 8: p186–187.

Johnson, Sandi

July the twelfth, and sunny; poem. *New Q* Fall 1987; Vol 7 No 3: p65.

A small wedding, in the spring; poem. *New Q* Fall 1987; Vol 7 No 3: p64.

To a bright blue sky; poem. *New Q* Fall 1987; Vol 7 No 3: p66.

Johnson, William

Threat or inspiration?; essay. photo · *MG* Nov 14, 1987: pB3.

Johnston, Basil H.

Summer holidays in Spanish; short story. *Can Fic Mag (special issue)* 1987; No 60: p146–153.

The truth, the whole truth; short story. *Can Fic Mag (special issue)* 1987; No 60: p154–157.

Johnston, Donald

[Untitled]; biographical articles. *Brick (special issue)* Summer 1987; No 30: ppassim.

Johnston, Fred

Not another Belfast poem; poem. *Fiddlehead* Autumn 1987; No 153: p78–79.

Portavogie; poem. *Fiddlehead* Autumn 1987; No 153: p80–81.

Johnston, George

Bed-time; poem. *Malahat R (special issue)* March 1987; No 78: p25.

Bee seasons; short story. *Malahat R (special issue)* March 1987; No 78: p57–66.

Crow's nests in court metres; poem. *Malahat R (special issue)* March 1987; No 78: p76.

Domestic; poem. *Malahat R (special issue)* March 1987; No 78: p22.

Home again; poem. *Malahat R (special issue)* March 1987; No 78: p26.

Home free; poem. *Malahat R (special issue)* March 1987; No 78: p24.

In it; poem. *Malahat R (special issue)* March 1987; No 78: p23.

John Olaf; poem. *Malahat R (special issue)* March 1987; No 78: p133.

Jonathan; poem. *Malahat R (special issue)* March 1987; No 78: p132–133.

Life; poem. *Malahat R (special issue)* March 1987; No 78: p134.

O moonlight; poem. illus · *Malahat R (special issue)* March 1987; No 78: p33.

Poems about the wind; poem. *Malahat R (special issue)* March 1987; No 78: p135.

Restored; poem. *Malahat R (special issue)* March 1987; No 78: p132.

Snowfall in still weather; poem. *Malahat R (special issue)* March 1987; No 78: p134.

Johnston, Susan

From somewhere to the left of you; poem. *Capilano R* 1987; No 44: p61.

The rain goddess; poem. *Capilano R* 1987; No 44: p62.

Unable to make a poem I defy language; poem. *Capilano R* 1987; No 44: p60.

Johnstone, J.K.

The Lafreniere family of Agassiz; reviews of *Night Travellers* and *Ladies of the House*. illus · *NeWest R* April 1987; Vol 12 No 8: p12.

Jolly, Clive

Writers are serious; letter to the editor. *CH* Sept 9, 1987: pA6.

Jolly, Grace

The purple silk; short story. *Grain* Spring 1987; Vol 15 No 1: p81–83.

Jonas, Christina

Two ceremonies planned to honor Guelph author of Flanders poem; article. *TS* Nov 9, 1987: pD34.

Jones

[Untitled]; review of *Helmet of Flesh. Rubicon* Spring 1987; No 8: p199–202.

Jones, Ben

Lazarovitch to Layton; review of *Irving Layton: A Portrait. Can Lit* Winter 1987; No 115: p160–162.

Jones, D.G.

Leonardo at the end; poem. *Poetry Can R* Spring 1987; Vol 8 No 1–2: p4.

Le mérite d'Archibald Lampman; article. trans · *Ellipse* 1987; No 38: p89–95.

Nancy C. and Norman D.; poem. *Poetry Can R* Spring 1987; Vol 8 No 1–2: p5.

St. Al and the heavenly bodies; review of *The Collected Poems. Brick* Winter 1987; No 29: p14–20.

[Untitled]; biographical articles. *Brick (special issue)* Summer 1987; No 30: ppassim.

Jones, Deborah

Fiery 'disaster' forces publisher to retrace steps; article. photo · *G&M* July 21, 1987: pC7.

'It hurts' to leave Halifax, writer discovers; article. photo · *G&M* June 24, 1987: pC5.

Jones, Donald

City's first and only 'poet laureate' died a pauper on Elm St.; biographical article. illus · *TS* Nov 21, 1987: pM3.

Fishing tales made all Canada laugh; biographical article. photo · *TS* July 18, 1987: pM3.

Priest became Canada's 'Poet Laureate'; biographical article. photo · *TS* Dec 26, 1987: pK3.

Jones, Dorothy

The spider and the rose: Aritha van Herk's No Fixed Address; article. *World Lit in Eng* Spring 1987; Vol 27 No 1: p39–56.

Jones, Frank

Atwood, Newman taped for Yule; article. photo · *TS* Nov 21, 1987: pM6.

A fox shows off its cunning; review of tape version of *The Red Fox. TS* Sept 26, 1987: pM4.

Jones, Kathy

Disappearing into Japan; review of *Almost Japanese. NYT Book R* Aug 16, 1987: p23.

Jones, Miriam

[Untitled]; review of *Sandinista. Rubicon* Fall 1987; No 9: p197–198.

Jongkind, Nenke

[Untitled]; letter to the editor. *G&M* Jan 27, 1987: pA6.

Jory, Rosi

The New World and the Old World for children; review of *The Green Gables Detectives. Atlan Prov Book R* Nov-Dec 1987; Vol 14 No 4: p4.

Journeaux, Andrea

Margaret Laurence's legacy; letter to the editor. *Maclean's* March 9, 1987; Vol 100 No 10: p6.

Joy, Arthur R.

High grade on the fifth shot; short story. photo · *TS* July 24, 1987: pH7.

Joyce, Dianne

High tension wires – a postwar incident; poem. *U of Windsor R* Spring-Summer 1987; Vol 20 No 2: p10–11.

The way it must have been; poem. *U of Windsor R* Spring-Summer 1987; Vol 20 No 2: p12.

Julien, Jacques

Machine romanesque; review of *Les Silences du corbeau*. *Can Lit* Winter 1987; No 115: p227–229.

Kadar, Marlene

Convincing and colourful; review of *Tales of a Gambling Grandma*. *Can Child Lit* 1987; No 47: p91–92.

Kahn, Elaine

Love and sin in Rosedale; review of *Adele at the End of the Day*. *TS* April 19, 1987: pA18.

Kalbfuss, Elisabeth

Children's author enjoys growing readership; interview with Dayal Kaur Khalsa. photo · *MG* Dec 24, 1987: pL2.

Kallasmaa-Davis, Ester

Last lap; short story. photo · *TS* Aug 13, 1987: pD10.

Kamboureli, Smaro

How do you make love in a new country?; poem. *Can Forum* Jan 1987; Vol 66 No 765: p38.

Stealing the text: George Bowering's Kerrisdale Elegies and Dennis Cooley's Bloody Jack; article. *Can Lit* Winter 1987; No 115: p9–23.

Translating the gender of silence; essay. *CV 2* Spring 1987; Vol 10 No 3: p52–57.

Kaminskas, Jurate

Rêverie sur l'eau; review of *Au pays des gouttes*. *Can Child Lit* 1987; No 47: p75–76.

Kanaganayakam, C.

Politics & paradise; review of *Sandinista*. *Can Lit* Winter 1987; No 115: p270–272.

Kapica, Jack

No conflict of interest in Globe book review; letter to the editor. *TS* Dec 21, 1987: pA14.

What business do publishers think they're in?; article. illus · *G&M* Nov 14, 1987: pE1.

Kapiczowski, Mike

Book's author original talent; letter to the editor. *CH* Oct 13, 1987: pA6.

Kappler, Brian

Plotting against the royals; reviews of *Broken English* and *Merlin's Web*. *MG* Nov 7, 1987: pK13.

Kareda, Urjo

A whole lotta scribblin' goin' on; article about Poetry Sweatshop. photo · *G&M (Toronto Magazine)* March 1987; Vol 1 No 12: p12–13.

Kastner, Susan

Author O'Brien plays to win; article. *TS* Oct 11, 1987: pD1.

Katre, Pierre

[Untitled]; poem. *Estuaire* Spring 1987; No 44: p11–14.

Kattan, Naïm

Célébration de la différence; essay. *Liberté* Feb 1987; Vol 29 No 1: p75–76.

Du jardin à la forêt; essay. abstract · *Études can* 1987; No 23: p65–70.

Kay, Guy Gavriel

Arrow; poem. *Prism* Summer 1987; Vol 25 No 4: p45.

Kaye, Frances W.

Understanding zero; review of *The Garden Going On without Us*. *Can Lit* Winter 1987; No 115: p138–139.

Kealy, Kieran

It's how it should have happened; review of *The Singing Stone*. *Can Child Lit* 1987; No 47: p71–72.

Kearley, W.O.R.

Delirium tea; poem. *Fiddlehead* Spring 1987; No 151: p14–15.

Kearns, Janet

The blessed? event; short story. illus · *Fireweed* Winter 1987; No 24: p31–35.

Keefer, Janice Kulyk

[Untitled]; review of *Paris Notebooks*. *U of Toronto Q* Fall 1987; Vol 57 No 1: p168–170.

Keeler, Julia

Chores; poem. *Waves* Spring 1987; Vol 15 No 4: p48–49.

The late paintings at the Phillips; poem. *Matrix* Spring 1987; No 24: p49.

Keeshig-Tobias, Lenore

[Untitled]; review of *The Fencepost Chronicles*. *Books in Can* Jan-Feb 1987; Vol 16 No 1: p25.

Keith, Julie Houghton

Falling; short story. *Fiddlehead* Spring 1987; No 151: p49–55.

Keith, Margaret

[Untitled]; review of *What's Bred in the Bone*. *Northward J* 1987; No 43: p43–46.

Keith, W.J.

A.J.M. Smith; poem. *Can Lit* Summer-Fall 1987; No 113–114: p92.

Apocalyptic imaginations: notes on Atwood's The Handmaid's Tale and Findley's Not Wanted on the Voyage; article. *Essays on Can Writ* Winter 1987; No 35: p123–134.

Dates and details in Mavis Gallant's "Its Image On The Mirror"; article. *Studies in Can Lit* 1987; Vol 12 No 1: p156–159.

For my parents; poem. *Antigonish R* Winter 1987; No 68: p114.

Jack Hodgins and the sources of invention; article. *Essays on Can Writ* Spring 1987; No 34: p81–91.

Keeping tabs on the poetry explosion; review of *Canadian Poetry Chronicle (1984)*. *Essays on Can Writ* Winter 1987; No 35: p100–104.

On death and shelter; poem. *Antigonish R* Winter 1987; No 68: p114–115.

Penelope; poem. *Antigonish R* Winter 1987; No 68: p116.

"To hell with the family!": an open letter to The New Quarterly; letter to the editor. *New Q* Spring-Summer 1987; Vol 7 No 1–2: p320–324.

Tom Thomson; poem. *Can Lit* Summer-Fall 1987; No 113–114: p144.

"Uncertain Flowering" an overlooked short story by Margaret Laurence; article. *Can Lit* Spring 1987; No 112: p202–205.

[Untitled]; reviews of *Studies in Literature and the Humanities* and *The Impossible Sum of Our Traditions* · *U of Toronto Q* Fall 1987; Vol 57 No 1: p145–148.

W.O. Mitchell from The Alien to The Vanishing Point; article. *World Lit in Eng* Autumn 1987; Vol 27 No 2: p252–262.

Kellar, Sally Ann

Researching Elizabeth Smart; letter to the editor. *TS* July 5, 1987: pD3.

Keller, Betty C.

Game over; short story. *Matrix* Fall 1987; No 25: p56–72.

Kelley, Paul

[Untitled]; prose poem. *CV 2* Spring 1987; Vol 10 No 3: p10.

[Untitled]; prose poem. *CV 2* Spring 1987; Vol 10 No 3: p11.

[Untitled]; prose poem. *CV 2* Spring 1987; Vol 10 No 3: p12.

[Untitled]; prose poem. *CV 2* Spring 1987; Vol 10 No 3: p13.

[Untitled]; prose poem. *CV 2* Spring 1987; Vol 10 No 3: p14.

[Untitled]; prose poem. *CV 2* Spring 1987; Vol 10 No 3: p15.

[Untitled]; prose poem. *CV 2* Spring 1987; Vol 10 No 3: p16.

[Untitled]; prose poem. *CV 2* Spring 1987; Vol 10 No 3: p17.

Kelly, Deirdre

Anne's back home, safe and sound; theatre review of *Anne of Green Gables*. photo · *G&M* June 29, 1987: pC9.

'Best theatre in America' aim of festival; article. *G&M* May 28, 1987: pD1.

Playful poetry for adults, 'what a subversive idea'; article. photo · *G&M* Nov 3, 1987: pD8.

Ragweed publisher goes against the PEI tide; article about Libby Oughton. photo · *G&M* July 14, 1987: pC5.

To Sir Noel, with affection; theatre review of *Noel Coward: A Portrait*. photo · *G&M* July 3, 1987: pD9.

Trying to crack the big time; article. photo · *G&M* April 7, 1987: pC7.

Warnes warm to Cohen's material; column. *G&M* May 30, 1987: pC18.

Kelly, Kathy

[Untitled]; review of *Time in the Air*. *Quarry* Winter 1987; Vol 36 No 1: p133–135.

Kelly, M.T.

Canada the way it used to be; review of *Canadian Crusoes*. *G&M* Jan 10, 1987: pE17.

Impressive; review of *Under the House*. *G&M* Feb 14, 1987: pE20.

Intense tale; review of *Slash*. *G&M* June 6, 1987: pC19.

MacEwen possessed a talent that was fragile, precocious; article. photo · *G&M* Dec 2, 1987: pC5.

The mermaid inn: let the Lady Evelyn be; essay. photo · *G&M* July 25, 1987: pD6.

An obsession for B.C.'s trees; review of *Looking for the Last Big Tree*. photo · *G&M* Feb 7, 1987: pE19.

Kemp, Penny

Inside out; poem. *New Q* Spring-Summer 1987; Vol 7 No 1–2: p210–211.

Re solution; poem. *Poetry Can R* Fall 1987; Vol 9 No 1: p13.

Simple as a planet; poem. *Poetry Can R* Spring 1987; Vol 8 No 2–3: p21.

Sin tax; poem. *Poetry Can R* Fall 1987; Vol 9 No 1: p13.

[Untitled]; poetry excerpts from *The Red Convertible*. *Cross Can Writ Q* 1987; Vol 9 No 2: p9.

[Untitled]; poetry excerpt from *What the Ear Hears Last(s)*. *Poetry Can R* Fall 1987; Vol 9 No 1: p13.

Won; poem. *Poetry Can R* Fall 1987; Vol 9 No 1: p13.

Kendall, Robert

From the bank; poem. *Can Lit* Winter 1987; No 115: p63.

Kennedy, Alan

Surya's companion; poem. *Arc* Spring 1987; No 18: p40.

Kennedy, Janice

Baby of the family gets respect raising flock of Canada geese; reviews of children's books. *MG* Oct 3, 1987: pJ13.

Gabrielle Roy manuscript discovered posthumously is gentle fable of peace; reviews of children's books. *MG* Jan 31, 1987: pB9.

Gammer Gurton leaps from early English stage into the 20th century; reviews of children's books. *MG* Nov 21, 1987: pJ13.

Getting a head start on Christmas; reviews of children's books. *MG* Dec 12, 1987: p112.

Jacob Two-Two returns in another grand adventure; review of *Jacob Two-Two and the Dinosaur*. *MG* May 30, 1987: pJ7.

Kids' entertainer Penner plans three shows here; article. photo · *MG* Nov 19, 1987: pE7.

Midsummer doldrums are relieved with engaging, artful activity book; review of *Log Jam*. *MG* Aug 1, 1987: pJ9.

Nation-wide book festival opens this weekend; article. *MG* Nov 14, 1987: pD1.

Native heritage is displayed in three timely books; reviews of children's books. *MG* April 4, 1987: pH11.

Robert Munsch readying sore tonsils for Montreal shows; article. photo · *MG* Oct 22, 1987: pC1.

Sam McGee leads the way in showing the potential of poetry; reviews of children's poetry books. *MG* March 7, 1987: pH10.

School's out, and books are in; reviews of children's books. *MG* July 4, 1987: pJ9.

Kennedy, Paul

Paul Quarrington: a good sport in life and letters; article, includes review of *King Leary*. photo · *Quill & Quire* Sept 1987; Vol 53 No 9: p77.

Kennedy, Ronnie

A delightful anthology; review of *Prairie Jungle*. *Can Child Lit* 1987; No 45: p57–58.

Kennedy, Rosemary

[Untitled]; review of *Big Sarah's Little Boots*. *CH* Dec 6, 1987: pD9.

Kent, Jane

1988; article. photo · *CH* Dec 29, 1987: pB4.

Tales for teenagers feature strong, viable family units; reviews of *The Baby Project* and *Payment in Death*. *CH* April 12, 1987: pF7.

Kent, Peter

Two women parables; short story. *Quarry* Winter 1987; Vol 36 No 1: p19–25.

Kenter, Robert

Father; poem. *Antigonish R* 1987; No 69–70: p87.

Kentfield, Beverley

The trouble with Dawn; short story. photo · *TS* Aug 1, 1987: pM5.

Kenyon, Linda

Hybrid; short story. *New Q* Spring-Summer 1987; Vol 7 No 1–2: p53–63.

Kenyon, Michael C.

It is after all winter; short story. *Dandelion* Spring-Summer 1987; Vol 14 No 1: p55–56.

Parallel rivers; short story. *Grain* Fall 1987; Vol 15 No 3: p19–27.

[Untitled]; review of *Storm Glass*. *Malahat R* Sept 1987; No 80: p137–138.

Kernaghan, Eileen

Tales from the holograph woods; poem. *Prism* Summer 1987; Vol 25 No 4: p61.

Kerner, Fred

CAA opposes pornography bill; article. *Quill & Quire* Aug 1987; Vol 53 No 8: p24.

Kerr, Don

At the margins of disaster; review of *Man at Stellaco River*. *Prairie Fire* Spring 1987; Vol 8 No 1: p88–90.

Domestic play; short story. *New Q* Spring-Summer 1987; Vol 7 No 1–2: p50–52.

European ice berg, Ontario Art Gallery; poem. *Quarry* Fall 1987; Vol 36 No 4: p61–62.

Jig saw Constable; poem. *Poetry Can R* Spring 1987; Vol 8 No 2–3: p63.

A love for the land in the west that once was; review of *Beyond Forget*. photo · *Quill & Quire* Jan 1987; Vol 53 No 1: p31.

My wonderful longing; short story. *Waves* Winter 1987; Vol 15 No 3: p41–44.

[Untitled]; play excerpt from *Talking Back*. *NeWest R* May 1987; Vol 12 No 9: p14.

VAG rant; poem. *Quarry* Fall 1987; Vol 36 No 4: p59–60.

Kerr, Luella

M M arm; poem. *Arc* Fall 1987; No 19: p70.

Radiation; poem. *Arc* Fall 1987; No 19: p69.

[Untitled]; review of *Distances*. *Poetry Can R* Fall 1987; Vol 9 No 1: p35–36.

Kerr, R.

What a field archaeologist is supposed to do; poem. *Matrix* Fall 1987; No 25: p73.

Kerslake, Susan

Providing; excerpt from a novel in progress. *New Q* Spring-Summer 1987; Vol 7 No 1–2: p106–112.

Kertzer, Adrienne

Meaningful nonsense; reviews of children's books. *Can Lit* Winter 1987; No 115: p165–167.

Kertzer, Jon

Against the reasoning mind; reviews of *In the Village of Alias* and *Vibrations in Time*. *Fiddlehead* Autumn 1987; No 153: p97–100.

Kessler, Deirdre

Home for Christmas; children's story. illus · *Atlan Insight* Dec 1987; Vol 9 No 12: p29.

Kevan, Martin

St. Agnes' Eve; or, criticism becomes part of literature; fictional essay. *Essays on Can Writ* Winter 1987; No 35: p37–56.

Khalsa, Dayal Kaur

[Untitled]; prose excerpt from *I Want a Dog*. illus · MG Dec 24, 1987: pL1.

Kidd, Kenneth

Conrad Black purchases Saturday Night magazine; article. *TS* June 19, 1987: pF1.

Megamergers rock book publishers; article. photo · *TS* June 14, 1987: pF1-F2.

Kidney, David

A brief encounter; short story. *Quarry* Spring 1987; Vol 36 No 2: p62–63.

Kiesners, Diana

This is your pilot speaking; short story. *New Q* Fall 1987; Vol 7 No 3: p16–19.

Kim, Sabina

The house of Babi Yaga; poem. *Grain* Winter 1987; Vol 15 No 4: p72–73.

Kimball, Arthur

Recognition; poem. *Queen's Q* Autumn 1987; Vol 94 No 3: p608.

Kind, Deborah

[Untitled]; review of *Red Fox*. *TS* Oct 25, 1987: pH6.

King, Annabelle

Restaurant dining room evokes early Quebec era; article. *MG* Nov 28, 1987: pI5.

King, Thomas

Bingo Bigbear and the tie-and-choker bone game; short story. *Can Fic Mag (special issue)* 1987; No 60: p89–98.

Introduction: an anthology of Canadian Native fiction; editorial article. *Can Fic Mag (special issue)* 1987; No 60: p4–10.

Joe the painter and the Deer Island massacre; short story. *Can Fic Mag (special issue)* 1987; No 60: p99–112.

Not counting the Indian, there were six; short story. *Malahat R* Sept 1987; No 80: p76–81.

Kingcaid, Renee A.

La place de l'humain; review of *Ram le Robot*. *Can Child Lit* 1987; No 45: p87–90.

Kingsley, V. Victor

Untimely demise of a sonata; short story. photo · *TS* July 7, 1987: pA11.

Kingwell, Mark

[Untitled]; review of *Northrop Frye: A Vision of the New World*. *Rubicon* Spring 1987; No 8: p193–195.

Kinsella, W.P.

Elvis bound; short story. *Descant (special issue)* Spring-Summer 1987; Vol 18 No 1–2: p127–139.

Homer; short story. *Matrix* Fall 1987; No 25: p19–26.

A hundred dollars worth of roses; short story. *New Q* Winter 1987; Vol 6 No 4: p25–35.

Katmandu; short story. *Waves* Winter 1987; Vol 15 No 3: p14–15.

Kirchhoff, H.J.

Author of exotic Asian thriller isn't your average Toronto cop; article. photo · *G&M* Nov 7, 1987: pC14.

Author's ready to hand out advice; article. photo · *G&M* May 6, 1987: pC6.

Chilling view; review of *Dreams of an Unseen Planet*. *G&M* June 13, 1987: pC20.

Darkness casts a powerful spell; theatre review of *Darkness on the Edge of Town*. photo · *G&M* May 15, 1987: pD8.

Deneau Publishers seeks reorganization; column. *G&M* Dec 29, 1987: pC8.

Experiments and flat yarns; review of *Pure Fiction*. *G&M* Jan 17, 1987: pE18.

Eye for detail key to authors' festival; article. photo · *G&M* Oct 16, 1987: pB1-B2.

Foster's life even richer than the stories he writes; article. photo · *G&M* Nov 19, 1987: pA31.

Going to the fair? Take along a page of your best writing; article. illus · *G&M* May 1, 1987: pC8.

Isolation helps nurture Keefer's writing; article. photo · *G&M* Oct 28, 1987: pC5.

Methuen staffers go in all directions; column. *G&M* Dec 24, 1987: pC3.

Novel shelved for sharp scrutiny of the sixties; column. *G&M* Dec 19, 1987: pC17.

Olympic festival to open with Wheeler film; article. photo · *G&M* Dec 8, 1987: pD5.

Prize-winning writer basks in attention; article. photo · *G&M* April 18, 1987: pC7.

Richler revels in kidlit success; article. photo · *G&M* June 10, 1987: pC5.

'Severance Santa' visits Methuen 'wake'; article. *G&M* Dec 12, 1987: pC3.

Strength from Quebec; review of *Intimate Strangers*. photo · *G&M* Jan 31, 1987: pE18.

Kirk, Heather

The fairy-tale elements in the early work of Mazo de la Roche; article. *Wascana R* Spring 1987; Vol 22 No 1: p3–17.

Tom Arnett: portrait of a pro; biographical article. photo · *Cross Can Writ Q* 1987; Vol 9 No 2: p14–15, 30.

Kirkwood, Hilda

The diviner's gift: in celebration of Margaret Laurence; essay. *Can Forum* Feb 1987; Vol 66 No 766: p5–6.

A kind of education; short story. *Waves* Winter 1987; Vol 15 No 3: p25–29.

Matter-of-fact visions; reviews of *Learning by Heart* and *Queen of the Headaches*. *Can Forum* Jan 1987; Vol 66 No 765: p39.

Remembering the beginning: Barker Fairley on the origins of the Forum; interview. illus · *Can Forum* Jan 1987; Vol 66 No 765: p6–8.

A true voice; review of *Black Swan*. *Waves* Spring 1987; Vol 15 No 4: p74–76.

Uneven gaps; review of *Small Regrets*. *Waves* Spring 1987; Vol 15 No 4: p77–79.

Varied and valuable; review of *Pure Fiction*. *Waves* Spring 1987; Vol 15 No 4: p76–77.

Kirsch, Fritz Peter

[Untitled]; review of *The French Novel of Quebec*. *Zeitschrift Kanada-Studien* 1987; Vol 7 No 1: p265–266.

Kitcher, W.H.C.

The dawn; short story. *Quarry* Spring 1987; Vol 36 No 2: p60–61.

Kizer, Carolyn

Mr. Small isn't here. Have an iguana!; review of *In the Skin of a Lion*. illus · *NYT Book R* Sept 27, 1987: p12–13.

Kizuk, Alex

The case of the forgotten Electra: Pickthall's apostrophes and feminine poetics; article. *Studies in Can Lit* 1987; Vol 12 No 1: p15–34.

One man's access to prophecy: the sonnet series of Frank Oliver Call; article. *Can Poet* Fall-Winter 1987; No 21: p31–41.

Quilting – a spiral of experience; review of *Dorothy Livesay*. *Can Poet* Fall-Winter 1987; No 21: p110–115.

Religion, place, & self in early twentieth-century Canada: Robert Norwood's poetry; article. *Can Lit* Winter 1987; No 115: p66–77.

[Untitled]; review of *The Bumper Book*. *U of Toronto Q* Fall 1987; Vol 57 No 1: p150–151.

Klassen, Sarah

Cataract; poem. *CV 2* Spring 1987; Vol 10 No 3: p46.

Lilac Street; poem. *CV 2* Spring 1987; Vol 10 No 3: p47.

[Untitled]; poem. *Poetry Can R* Fall 1987; Vol 9 No 1: p23.

Klatte, Ross

Inside South Africa, fictionally; article, includes review of *Bloodsong*. photo · *CH* July 26, 1987: pE5.

Klein, A.M.

The break-up / La débâcle; poem in English and in French translation. *Ellipse* 1987; No 37: p82–83.

Grain elevator / Le silo à céréales; poem in English and in French translation. *Ellipse* 1987; No 37: p84–85.

Heirloom / Hoirie; poem in English and in French translation. *Ellipse* 1987; No 37: p70–71.

Indian reservation: Caughnawaga / Caughnawaga: réserve indienne; poem in English and in French translation. *Ellipse* 1987; No 37: p72–75.

Montreal / Montréal; poem in English and in French translation. *Ellipse* 1987; No 37: p112–115.

Out of the pulver and the polished lens / Induit de la poudre et du verre poli; poem in English and in French translation. *Ellipse* 1987; No 37: p88–97.

Prophet in our midst: a story for Passover; short story in English and in French translation. *Ellipse* 1987; No 37: p104–111.

Psalm XXVII: a psalm to teach humility / Psaume XXVII: une leçon d'humilité; poem in English and in French translation. *Ellipse* 1987; No 37: p86–87.

The rocking chair / La berceuse; poem in English and in French translation. *Ellipse* 1987; No 37: p76–77.

The sugaring / Les érables de la passion; poem in English and in French translation. *Ellipse* 1987; No 37: p80–81.

[Untitled]; poetry excerpt from *The Hitleriad* in English and in French translation. *Ellipse* 1987; No 37: p98–99.

[Untitled]; prose excerpt from *Beyond Sambation* in English and in French translation. *Ellipse* 1987; No 37: p100–103.

Winter night: Mount Royal; poem in English and in French translation. *Ellipse* 1987; No 37: p78–79.

Kline, Valerie

China beach in winter; poem. *Antigonish R* 1987; No 69–70: p9.

Old woman who paints; poem. *Antigonish R* 1987; No 69–70: p8.

Knelman, Martin

Authors' festival revisited; article. *Tor Life* Oct 1987; Vol 21 No 1[5]: p17.

Brian Moore: this is your life; article. *Tor Life* June 1987; Vol 21 No 9: p19.

Chain letter; article. illus · *Tor Life* May 1987; Vol 21 No 7: p11.

From the Frye pen into the foyer; article. photo · *Tor Life* Aug 1987; Vol 21 No 11: p10.

Hits and Missus; article. biog photo · *Tor Life* Feb 1987; Vol 21 No 2: p29–31.

Jack: the sequel; article about Jack McClelland. photo · *Tor Life* May 1987; Vol 21 No 7: p13.

John Fraser: child star; article. photo · *Tor Life* Dec 1987; Vol 21 No 18: p12.

[Untitled]; theatre review of *Zastrozzi*. *Tor Life* June 1987; Vol 21 No 9: p115.

[Untitled]; television review of *Anne of Green Gables – The Sequel*. photo · *Tor Life* Dec 1987; Vol 21 No 18: p131.

Knight, Ann

[Untitled]; review of *The Carpenter of Dreams*. *Poetry Can R* Spring 1987; Vol 8 No 2–3: p44.

Knister Givens, Imogen

Death by drowning; letter to the editor. *Books in Can* Aug-Sept 1987; Vol 16 No 6: p38.

Knowles, Richard Paul

Atlantic theatre: a review article. *J of Can Studies* Spring 1987; Vol 22 No 1: p135–140.

Sharon Pollock: personal frictions; review of *Doc*. *Atlan Prov Book R* Feb-March 1987; Vol 14 No 1: p19.

"The truth must out": the political plays of John Krizanc; article. *Can Drama* 1987; Vol 13 No 1: p27–33.

Knowles, Stanley

[Untitled]; biographical articles. *Brick (special issue)* Summer 1987; No 30: ppassim.

Kogawa, Joy

April Christmas tree; poem. *Cross Can Writ Q* 1987; Vol 9 No 2: p7.

The campaign; poem. illus · *Cross Can Writ Q* 1987; Vol 9 No 2: p7.

The rebirth of Baby Anna; excerpt from a novel in progress. illus · *Books in Can* Oct 1987; Vol 16 No 7: p11–14.

[Untitled]; excerpt from a novel in progress. illus · *Fireweed* Winter 1987; No 24: p60–62.

[Untitled]; essay. photo · *Chatelaine* May 1987; Vol 60 No 5: p52.

Kohn, Anna

Joy Kogawa: a need to reach out. . . .; biographical article. photo · *Cross Can Writ Q* 1987; Vol 9 No 2: p6–7, 28.

Kokotailo, Philip

[Untitled]; review of *Arriving at Night*. *U of Windsor R* Spring-Summer 1987; Vol 20 No 2: p90–92.

Koller, Katherine

Inside the giant: Fringe for kids; article. photo · *NeWest R* Oct 1987; Vol 13 No 2: p13.

Kolybaba, Kathie

Portrait; short story. *Border Cross* Spring 1987; Vol 6 No 2: p23–24.

Red shoes / a city I've never lived in; prose poem. *Prairie Fire* Autumn 1987; Vol 8 No 3: p22.

Sandy; short story. *Room of One's Own* April 1987; Vol 11 No 3: p67–70.

Komori, Leslie

Interview with Joy Kogawa. *Fireweed* Winter 1987; No 24: p63–66.

Konrad, Victor A.

Current Canadian studies; column. *Amer R of Can Studies* Autumn 1987; Vol 17 No 3: p360–366.

Current Canadian studies; column. *Amer R of Can Studies* Winter 1987–88; Vol 17 No 4: p464–469.

Konyves, Tom

Poet's block; poem. *Poetry Can R* Fall 1987; Vol 9 No 1: p17.

Korp, Maureen

Brown bed; poem. *Arc* Spring 1987; No 18: p41.

The business lunch; poem. *Antigonish R* 1987; No 69–70: p209.

Melting ice; poem. *Arc* Spring 1987; No 18: p42.

Köster, Patricia

Seeing voices; reviews of *Voices and Visions* and *Voices of Deliverance*. *Can Lit* Summer-Fall 1987; No 113–114: p239–241.

Kouznétsova, Irina

La littérature du Québec en URSS; article. photo · *Lettres québec* Summer 1987; No 46: p71–72.

Kramer, Lotte

Amoeba; poem. *Poetry Can R* Fall 1987; Vol 9 No 1: p27.

Knowledge; poem. *Poetry Can R* Fall 1987; Vol 9 No 1: p27.

Kreisel, Henry

Columns of dark; review of *Selected Poems*. *Can Lit* Winter 1987; No 115: p272–275.

Kremberg, Rudy

Balls; short story. illus · *Queen's Q* Spring 1987; Vol 94 No 1: p154–163.

Kritsch, Holly

Baptism; poem. *Arc* Spring 1987; No 18: p43.

"The bump" – Springhill – 1958; poem. *Arc* Spring 1987; No 18: p44.

Carnival man; poem. *Arc* Spring 1987; No 18: p45.

When I was fifteen; poem. *Arc* Spring 1987; No 18: p46.

Women's ward; poem. *Arc* Spring 1987; No 18: p47.

Kroetsch, Robert

After paradise; poem. *Prairie Fire* Winter 1987–88; Vol 8 No 4: p68–77.

From the upstate New York journals; journal. *Border Cross* Summer 1987; Vol 6 No 3: p41–47.

[Untitled]; review of *The Family Romance*. *Dandelion* Fall-Winter 1987; Vol 14 No 2: p145–147.

Kroha, Lucienne

[Untitled]; review of *Contrasts*. *Queen's Q* Spring 1987; Vol 94 No 1: p206–208.

Kröller, Eva-Marie

Roy Kiyooka's The Fontainebleau Dream Machine: a reading; article. *Can Lit* Summer-Fall 1987; No 113–114: p47–58.

Trieste and George Bowering's Burning Water; article. *Open Letter* Summer 1987; Vol 6 No 8: p44–54.

[Untitled]; review of *Anne. . . .La Maison aux pignons verts*. *Can Lit* Winter 1987; No 115: p290.

Krysinski, Wladimir

Avec André Belleau et Bakhtine en Sardaigne; essay. *Liberté* April 1987; Vol 29 No 2: p108–110.

Kubicek, J.L.

.618034 to 1; poem. *Ariel* July 1987; Vol 18 No 3: p66.

Kuester, Martin

ReTracing prairie voices: a conversation with Birk Sproxton. photo · *Prairie Fire* Summer 1987; Vol 8 No 2: p4–10.

The Twayning of Robert Kroetsch; review of *Robert Kroetsch*. *Prairie Fire* Winter 1987–88; Vol 8 No 4: p101–105.

[Untitled]; review of *Essays on Saskatchewan Writing*. *Zeitschrift Kanada-Studien* 1987; Vol 7 No 1: p267–269.

[Untitled]; review of *Trace*. *Zeitschrift Kanada-Studien* 1987; Vol 7 No 1: p272–274.

Kulyk Keefer, Janice

Cheap thrills; reviews of *The Last Hunter* and *Gallows View*. *Books in Can* June-July 1987; Vol 16 No 5: p37–38.

Cirrus; poem. *Quarry* Fall 1987; Vol 36 No 4: p63.

Col tempo; poem. *Quarry* Fall 1987; Vol 36 No 4: p64.

For Michael, 37; poem. *Descant* Winter 1987; Vol 18 No 4: p20–21.

Fort Anne and four Acadians; poem. *Rubicon* Fall 1987; No 9: p98–99.

God's little acreage; review of *Dancing on the Shore*. *Books in Can* Dec 1987; Vol 16 No 9: p23–24.

Heart of darkness; reviews of first novels. *Books in Can* Dec 1987; Vol 16 No 9: p37–39.

James de Mille's strange manuscript; review of *A Strange Manuscript Found in a Copper Cylinder*. *Atlan Prov Book R* May-June 1987; Vol 14 No 2: p12.

The lesson; short story. *Matrix* Spring 1987; No 24: p71–79.

Local heroes; reviews of first novels. *Books in Can* Nov 1987; Vol 16 No 8: p35, 37.

Me, myself, and I; reviews of first novels. *Books in Can* Oct 1987; Vol 16 No 7: p35–36, 38.

Transfigurations; short story. illus · *Can Forum* Nov 1987; Vol 67 No 773: p18–21.

[Untitled]; review of *In the Feminine*. *U of Toronto Q* Fall 1987; Vol 57 No 1: p201–203.

Urban scrawl; reviews of first novels. *Books in Can* Aug-Sept 1987; Vol 16 No 6: p33–34.

World of wonders; reviews of first novels. *Books in Can* May 1987; Vol 16 No 4: p37–38.

Kurt, Ronald

Fidgeting in the sun; poem. *NeWest R* Oct 1987; Vol 13 No 2: p19.

Lacey, Liam

Author, actor combine to make Sun a success; theatre review of *Gone the Burning Sun*. photo · *G&M* March 27, 1987: pD9.

B-Movie features Grade-A laughs; theatre review. photo · *G&M* Jan 22, 1987: pC3.

Bachelor uses intriguing techniques; theatre review of *Bachelor-Man*. photo · *G&M* Nov 14, 1987: pC8.

Beyond the Fringe: Stewart Lemoine's off-the-wall humor has finally moved east; article. photo · *G&M* Sept 23, 1987: pC10.

Book industry groups protest anti-porn bill; article. *G&M* Sept 17, 1987: pD6.

Book review editors take the hot seat at writers' conference; article. photo · *G&M* May 30, 1987: pC5.

CBC explores impact of AIDS on the arts; article. *G&M* April 11, 1987 pE3.

Crowded theatres indicate success of Edmonton Fringe; article. *G&M* Aug 17, 1987: pC9.

Ernest and Ernestine are funny and familiar; theatre review of *The Anger of Ernest and Ernestine*. photo · *G&M* May 28, 1987: pD6.

Flashes of gold among the dross at Fringe festival; theatre reviews. *G&M* Aug 19, 1987: pC5.

Force of evil unveiled in play about murder; theatre review of *This Is What Happens in Orangeville*. photo · *G&M* Jan 31, 1987: pE4.

A funny look at a bad girl; theatre review of *See Bob Run*. photo · *G&M* July 22, 1987: pC6.

Gay murder explored, unexplained; theatre review of *Steel Kiss*. *G&M* Oct 5, 1987: pD11.

Glass's Play Memory is sober look at alcoholism; theatre review. photo · *G&M* July 3, 1987: pD11.

His historical send-up is 10-year project; article. photo · *G&M* May 2, 1987: pC5.

Historical satire highly original, funny; theatre review of *The Mackenzie / Papineau Rebellion*. photo · *G&M* April 16, 1987: pD6.

Hosanna ages with grace and style; theatre review. photo · *G&M* May 27, 1987: pC10.

Ideas sheds light on eclectic career; radio review. *G&M* April 7, 1987: pC7.

Less is Moore for Brian; article. photo · *G&M* Oct 20, 1987: pD5.

Looking back at a tragedy; theatre review of *The Komagata Maru Incident*. *G&M* April 2, 1987: pC5.

A marriage of fact and fiction; article. photo · *G&M* Jan 19, 1987: pC9.

The Mikado paces Dora nominees; article. *G&M* May 27, 1987: pC8.

More history lesson than drama; theatre review of *The African Roscius*. photo · *G&M* July 15, 1987: pC6.

Pythagoras's problem; theatre review of *Pythagoras – The Mystery*. photo · *G&M* July 23, 1987: pD5.

Radio job 'a chance to fulfil a fantasy'; article. photo · *G&M* June 29, 1987: pC9.

Robert Fulford resigns as editor of Saturday Night; article. photo · *G&M* June 25, 1987: pD1.

Roll 'em, cowboys; article. photo · *G&M* Aug 29, 1987: pC1.C3.

A salute to detective stories; article. photo · *G&M* Dec 8, 1987: pD7.

Saturday Night sale unsure, search for editor continues; article. *G&M* July 4, 1987: pC4.

Tall tales and home truths; article. photo · *G&M* Aug 22, 1987: pC3.

Theatre life stylish, ingenious; theatre review. photo · *G&M* April 1, 1987: pC5.

Trotsky 'tough act to follow' for playwright; article. photo · *G&M* Nov 12, 1987: pA31.

TWP to take Bethune show to China; column. photo · *G&M* March 20, 1987: pD10.

The world according to Munsch; article. biog photo · *G&M* Jan 24, 1987: pE1.

Writers revive censorship-pornography debate; article. photo · *G&M* June 1, 1987: pC9.

Lachance, Ginette

L'accident; short story. *Moebius (special issue)* Spring 1987; No 32: p43–45.

Lachapelle, Côme

Point de chute; poem. illus · *La Nouvelle barre du jour* May 1987; No 200: p69–74.

Lacombe, Michèle

Francophones on writing; review of *Voices of Deliverance*. *Essays on Can Writ* Winter 1987; No 35: p105–110.

The other Montrealers; review of *The Mysteries of Montreal*. *Essays on Can Writ* Spring 1987; No 34: p180–184.

Lacroix, Benoit

Ah! les Beaucerons!; review of *Les Grandes corvées beauceronnes*. *MD* Sept 19, 1987: pD2.

Cris et silences des poètes d'automne; review of *Éclats d'âme*. *MD* Dec 19, 1987: pD3.

Les sentiers de la peur; review of *La Fille de Thomas Vogel*. *MD* Nov 7, 1987: pD3.

Lacroix, Jean-Michel

Revue des revues; annotated list of periodicals. *Études can* June 1987; No 22: p141–175.

Lacroix, Yves

Entrevue avec Yves Beauchemin; interview. *Voix et images* Spring 1987; Vol 12 No 3: p376–382.

Yves Beauchemin, en toute simplicité: présentation; editorial. *Voix et images* Spring 1987; Vol 12 No 3: p358.

Ladky, Mary S.

[Untitled]; review of *Black Swan*. *Rubicon* Fall 1987; No 9: p200–201.

[Untitled]; review of *Learning by Heart*. *Rubicon* Fall 1987; No 9: p201–202.

Lafleur, Françoise

Les artistes ontarois débarquent à Montréal; article. *MD* Nov 12, 1987: p13.

Une fête autour d'un conte; article. photo · *MD* Dec 16, 1987: p11.

À l'écoute de la poésie d'ici; article. *MD* Dec 19, 1987: pD10.

L'édition ontaroise: un monde à découvrir; article. *MD* Nov 19, 1987: p13.

Second début; article. photo · *MD* Nov 14, 1987: pD11.

Lafuste, France

Les auteurs québécois habillés de cuir....; article. photo · *MD* June 8, 1987: p9.

Carole Levert: pas besoin de s'appeler Maggie pour être éditrice; article. photo · *MD* Dec 31, 1987: pC9-C10.

Claire Harrison plaide en faveur des romans Harlequin; article. photo · *MD* Dec 12, 1987: pD1, D12.

Francine d'Amour ou le plaisir d'écrire à l'état pur; article. photo · *MD* Dec 5, 1987: pD1.

Gilles Vigneault: que nos ma[i]tres redeviennent des ma[i]tres à penser; article. photo · *MD* Dec 19, 1987: pC1, C12.

Noël, période bénie pour les libraires; article. photo · *MD* Nov 28, 1987: pD1.

Le Salon fait la fête et se donne un objectif: conquérir les jeunes; article. *MD* Nov 14, 1987: pD3.

Laing, Bonnie

Strays; short story. *Fiddlehead* Spring 1987; No 151: p37–43.

Lamartine, Thérèse

Quand le politique est privé: ou la face privée du politique; essay. illus · *La Nouvelle barre du jour (special issue)* March 1987; No 196: p59–65.

Lambton, Gwen

A room of my own; short story. illus · *Fireweed* Fall 1987; No 25: p103–114.

Lamont-Stewart, Linda

Lilly & Willie; review of *Lily: A Rhapsody in Red*. *Can Lit* Winter 1987; No 115: p275–277.

Lamothe, Raymonde

Les fruits de mon imagination; letter to the editor. *MD* Aug 19, 1987: p8.

Lamoureux, Johanne

[Untitled]; poem. illus · *Estuaire* Summer 1987; No 45: p47.

Lampman, Archibald

At the Long Sault: May, 1660 / Long Sault: Mai 1660; poem in English and in French translation. *Ellipse* 1987; No 38: p54–61.

The City of the End of Things / La Cité de la fin des choses; poem in English and in French translation. *Ellipse* 1987; No 38: p76–81.

The frogs / Les grenouilles; poem in English and in French translation. *Ellipse* 1987; No 38: p66–71.

Heat / Chaleur; poem in English and in French translation. *Ellipse* 1987; No 38: p62–65.

A January morning / Matin de janvier; poem in English and in French translation. *Ellipse* 1987; No 38: p74–75.

Late November / Fin novembre; poem in English and in French translation. *Ellipse* 1987; No 38: p70–71.

Morning on the lievre / Matin sur la lièvre; poem in English and in French translation. *Ellipse* 1987; No 38: p72–75.

On the companionship with nature / En communion avec la nature; poem in English and in French translation. *Ellipse* 1987; No 38: p84–85.

A sunset at Les Éboulements / Soleil couchant sur les éboulements; poem in English and in French translation. *Ellipse* 1987; No 38: p86–87.

To a millionnaire / À un millionnaire; poem in English and in French translation. *Ellipse* 1987; No 38: p82–83.

Winter uplands / Des hauts plateaux d'hiver; poem in English and in French translation. *Ellipse* 1987; No 38: p60–61.

Lamy, Mario-Gabriel

Genèse; poem. *Moebius* Autumn 1987; No 34: p73–79.

Lamy, Suzanne

De l'érudition: l'esprit et la lettre; reviews of periodicals. *Voix et images* Winter 1987; No 35: p342–346.

Du privé au politique: la Constellation du Cygne de Yolande Villemaire; article. *Voix et images* Autumn 1987; Vol 13 No 1: p18–28.

Radom (Pologne); essay. *Voix et images* Autumn 1987; Vol 13 No 1: p9–17.

Landale, Zoë

Newborn; poem. *Fireweed* Fall 1987; No 25: p74.

Only movement of your needle; poem. *Prism* Autumn 1987; Vol 26 No 1: p70.

Sister, blessing; poem. *Prism* Autumn 1987; Vol 26 No 1: p71–72.

Still life: hearth keeper with frenzy; poem. *Fireweed* Fall 1987; No 25: p72–73.

What about a valentine?; poem. *Fireweed* Fall 1987; No 25: p75.

Landry-Theriault, Jeannine

[Untitled]; prose excerpt from *Un Soleil mauve sur la baie*. trans · *Fiddlehead* Summer 1987; No 152: p75–76.

Lane, Jr., Lauriat

[Untitled]; review of *Northrop Frye: A Vision of the New World*. *Eng Studies in Can* Sept 1987; Vol 13 No 3: p349–352.

Lane, M. Travis

Coming home; poem. *New Q* Fall 1987; Vol 7 No 3: p78.

Field; poem. *Can Lit* Spring 1987; No 112: p29.

Ministries of grace; review of *A Sacrifice of Fire*. *Fiddlehead* Spring 1987; No 151: p110–115.

Pelagic; poem. *Arc* Spring 1987; No 18: p48.

The red king dreamed me; poem. *New Q* Fall 1987; Vol 7 No 3: p76–77.

Tiger poems; reviews of poetry books. *Fiddlehead* Autumn 1987; No 153: p88–91.

You ask me what I'm thinking; reviews of poetry books. *Fiddlehead* Winter 1987; No 154: p95–104.

You want your truths told of you; poem. *Arc* Spring 1987; No 18: p49.

Lane, Patrick

Brothers; poem. *Malahat R* Sept 1987; No 80: p30–31.

Dominion Day dance; poem. *Malahat R* Sept 1987; No 80: p32.

The exact shape of distance; article. *NeWest R* Sept 1987; Vol 13 No 1: p2–3, 19.

How do you spell beautiful?; short story. *Grain* Summer 1987; Vol 15 No 2: p57–60.

Night; poem. *Malahat R* Sept 1987; No 80: p33.

Nunc dimittis; poem. *Malahat R* Sept 1987; No 80: p34.

Lang, Allen A.

Layton's Holocaust view nonsense; letter to the editor. *MG* March 17, 1987: pB2.

Langevin, Donna

Looking over the water; poem. *Poetry Can R* Fall 1987; Vol 9 No 1: p11.

Langlois, Christian

Les arts de la scène à l'heure de l'expérimentation vidéographique; article. photo · *Jeu* 1987; No 44: p126–132.

Lanoie, Richard

[Untitled]; review of *Mobile Homes*. *Rubicon* Spring 1987; No 8: p215.

[Untitled]; review of *Other Selves*. *Rubicon* Spring 1987; No 8: p221.

Lanthier, Philip

Harnessing poetry; reviews of *Blind Painting* and *Small Horses & Intimate Beasts*. *Can Lit* Winter 1987; No 115: p140–142.

An interview with Robert Allen. biog bibliog photo · *Matrix* Fall 1987; No 25: p34–49.

A note on The Hawryliw Process; article. *Matrix* Fall 1987; No 25: p39–40.

Parlour pump organs and prairie cafes; reviews of *Waiting for Saskatchewan* and *The Louis Riel Organ & Piano Company*. *NeWest R* April 1987; Vol 12 No 8: p13, 15.

Lapalme, Michel

[Untitled]; prose excerpt from *Le Crime de Jérimadeth*. photo · *MD* Dec 5, 1987: pD1, D8.

Lapham, Lewis H.

Theatre of Future would lack only stage and script; theatre review of *Tamara*. photo · *G&M* Dec 12, 1987: pC12.

Lapierre, René

Dix autoportraits à la gomme; short story sequence. *Liberté* Dec 1987; Vol 29 No 6: p8–19.

Présentation; introduction. *Liberté* Aug 1987; Vol 29 No 4: p4–5.

Sur un concept de Bakhtine; essay. *Liberté* Feb 1987; Vol 29 No 1: p77–78.

Lapp, Claudia

Ashes; poem. *Poetry Can R* Fall 1987; Vol 9 No 1: p17.

Laprade, Louise

Autour du Théâtre expérimental des femmes; essay. illus · *La Nouvelle barre du jour (special issue)* March 1987; No 196: p82–86.

Large, Kathy

Looking for Lucy Maud; article. *Atlan Insight* June 1987; Vol 9 No 6: p48–49.

La Rue, Monique

Entre France et Québec: des lieux, des liens, une voix; article. *Voix et images* Autumn 1987; Vol 13 No 1: p42–45.

Latham, David

From the hazel bough of Yeats: Birney's masterpiece; article. *Can Poet* Fall-Winter 1987; No 21: p52–58.

Lives of the poet; review of *The Self-Completing Tree*. *Books in Can* April 1987; Vol 16 No 3: p27–28.

Latif-Ghattas, Mona

Pavane sur un ailleurs flottant; prose poem. *Estuaire* Autumn 1987; No 46: p53–54.

Latouche, Daniel

Des personnages qui s'imposent aussi bien à Londres qu'à Montréal; article. photo · *MD* Sept 5, 1987: pC4.

Latta, William

Rune-writer; review of *Eye of the Father*. *Can Lit* Winter 1987; No 115: p191–193.

Lau, Evelyn

An autumn photograph; poem. *Prism* Spring 1987; Vol 25 No 3: p81.

Protest; poem. *Alpha* Winter 1987; Vol 11: p33.

The quiet room; poem. *Prism* Spring 1987; Vol 25 No 3: p80.

The quiet room; poem. *Can Auth & Book* Fall 1987; Vol 63 No 1: p16.

Streets; essay. *Can Auth & Book* Summer 1987; Vol 62 No 4: p19–21.

Laurence, Margaret

If I had one hour to live. . . .; essay. photo · *G&M* Jan 10, 1987: pD1, D8.

My final hour; essay. illus photo · *TS* Jan 17, 1987: pM1,M9,M17-M18.

Laurendeau, Francine

Une belle et dense histoire difficile à porter à l'écran; article. photo · *MD* Oct 24, 1987: pC1, C12.

Laurendeau, Paul

Censurer, verbe. Ne dites pas censurer dans. *Moebius (special issue)* Spring 1987; No 32: p41–42.

Laurier, Marie

La 55e saison du Club musical et littéraire; article. photo · *MD* Oct 21, 1987: p14.

Antoine Gallimard, petit-fils de Gaston et fils de Claude; article. photo · *MD* Dec 14, 1987: p9.

Arlette Cousture, arrière-petite-fille de Caleb et vedette malgré elle; article. photo · *MD* Sept 12, 1987: pD1.

De bien belles rencontres chez Hermès; article. photo · *MD* Dec 31, 1987: pC9-C10.

Le demi-siècle de Fides; article. *MD* March 10, 1987: p11.

Le deuxième roman de Francine Noël; article. photo · *MD* Nov 18, 1987: p11.

Fides a 50 ans; article. photo · *MD* March 14, 1987: pD1-D2.

Fides édite la liste de ses livres depuis 1937; article. photo · *MD* March 23, 1987: p3.

Une fournée de nouveaux micro-livres chez Stanké; article. photo · *MD* Sept 26, 1987: pD3.

Une immense "auberge espagnole" prête à accueillir ses 80,000 visiteurs; article. photo · *MD* Oct 31, 1987: pD1, D8.

"Un jour, j'écrirai un livre sur le Québec": Louis-Martin Tard a tenu sa promesse; article. photo · *MD* Oct 3, 1987: pD1, D8.

L'Académie canadienne française accueille Félix; article. photo · *MD* Dec 24, 1987: pA7.

Lévesque s'oppose vigoureusement à une surtaxe pour les biens culturels; article. *MD* April 11, 1987: pA3.

Paul Wyczynski signe une "somme nelliganienne"; review of *Nelligan*. photo · *MD* Nov 28, 1987: pD11.

Le Seuil diffusera des auteurs du Boréal; article. photo · *MD* Oct 1, 1987: p13.

Laurin, Benoît

Érosion; poem. *Estuaire* Autumn 1987; No 46: p29–32.

Lâcher les rênes; poem. *Estuaire* Spring 1987; No 44: p19–22.

Lautens, Gary

Writer who can't come in from the cold; article. *TS* Nov 30, 1987: pA3.

Lauzon, Dominique

Le triangle; prose poem. illus · *La Nouvelle barre du jour* April 1987; No 198: p23–25.

[Untitled]; poetry excerpts from *Portraits du souffle possible*. *Estuaire* Spring 1987; No 44: p53–56.

Lavallée, Marcel

Gustave Lamarche; letter to the editor. *MD* Oct 30, 1987: p10.

Lavoie, Pierre

Le complexe de Quichotte; article. illus photo · *Jeu* 1987; No 44: p8–13.

Des voix á découvrir; article. photo · *Jeu* 1987; No 44: p79–87.

Du hasard et de la nécessité: genèse de l'oeuvre; essay. photo · *Jeu* 1987; No 45: p169–170.

Parutions récentes; list of recent publications. *Jeu* 1987; No 44: p219–221.

Points de repère: entretiens avec les créateurs; interview with the Théâtre Repère collective. photo · *Jeu* 1987; No 45: p177–208.

[Untitled]; theatre review of *Bain public*. photo · *Jeu* 1987; No 42: p168–169.

Law, Alex

Angel Star a sweet treat but not much substance; theatre review of *Merry Christmas Angel Star*. *TS (Neighbors)* Dec 1, 1987: p19.

Brampton, Etobicoke schools make it to drama festival finals; article. *TS (Neighbours)* May 5, 1987: p24.

Breakout's only strength is in its message; theatre review. photo · *TS (Neighbours)* March 31, 1987: p18.

Cedarbrae Collegiate's play to compete at Ontario finals; article. *TS (Neighbours)* May 5, 1987: p9.

Comedy enjoyable despite bad acoustics, set changes; theatre review of *The Fourposter*. *TS (Neighbours)* March 10, 1987: p14.

Curtain Club play needs to show more emotional thigh; theatre review of *A Spider in the House*. *TS (Neighbors)* Dec 1, 1987: p19.

Etobicoke, Brampton students win Sears drama festival honors; article. photo · *TS (Neighbours)* May 19, 1987: p19.

Maritime Song has promise, lacks cohesion; theatre review. photo · *TS (Neighbors)* Sept 22, 1987: p13.

Maritime Song needs a tune-up; theatre review. *TS (Neighbors)* Sept 22, 1987: p26.

'Memory play' takes woman to childhood; article. *TS (Neighbors)* Nov 24, 1987: p16.

Pickering crime writer hopes to steal award; article. photo · *TS (Neighbours)* May 19, 1987: p17.

Production of Blood Relations offers electric performances; theatre review. photo · *TS (Neighbours)* April 7, 1987: p16.

Scarborough publisher banking on audio books; article. photo · *TS (Neighbors)* Sept 22, 1987: p6.

Scarborough schools compete in Sears drama festival regionals; article. *TS (Neighbours)* April 14, 1987: p14.

Sinners' cast in over its head; theatre review. *TS (Neighbours)* June 16, 1987: p22.

This play doesn't come to life; theatre review of *The Last Real Summer*. *TS (Neighbors)* Dec 8, 1987: p19.

World of fantasy important to kids Oshawa writer says; article. photo · *TS (Neighbours)* Feb 24, 1987: p16.

Lawlor, Carol

Milk International Children's Festival; article. *Tor Life* May 1987; Vol 21 No 7: p107.

Lawlor, Patty

[Untitled]; reviews of *Edythe With a Y* and *It Isn't Easy Being Ms. Teeny Wonderful*. *Quill & Quire (Books for Young People)* April 1987; Vol 53 No 4: p8.

[Untitled]; review of *Outta Sight*. *Quill & Quire (Books for Young People)* Aug 1987; Vol 53 No 8: p7.

[Untitled]; review of *Me and Luke*. *Quill & Quire (Books for Young People)* Oct 1987; Vol 53 No 10: p22.

Lawrence, P. Scott

Romantic adventure set in Panama City is as thin as the celluloid it's written for; review of *The Last White Man in Panama*. photo · *MG* Nov 7, 1987: pK12.

Tapestry times three; review of *The Darkest Road*. photo · *MG* March 7, 1987: pH11.

These roads lead to Roch; review of *Heartbreaks Along the Road*. photo · *MG* Dec 19, 1987: pJ12.

Vivid imagination drives novel's slender plot line; review of *Adele at the End of the Day*. photo · *MG* April 11, 1987: pG5.

Writer leads us on his Mexican magical mystery tour; review of *Beneath the Western Slopes*. photo · *MG* July 18, 1987: pJ8.

Lawrence, Robert G.

Hitler's letter; review of *The Letter*. *Can Lit* Winter 1987; No 115: p229–230.

Layton, Irving

Inter-view; poem. *Cross Can Writ Q* 1987; Vol 9 No 2: p13.

Socrates at the Centaur; poem. *Can Lit* Spring 1987; No 112: p16–17.

[Untitled]; biographical articles. *Brick (special issue)* Summer 1987; No 30: ppassim.

Layton, Max

Much hard sledding through the North; review of *The Ice Eaters*. *G&M* Nov 14, 1987: pE3.

Leacock, Stephen

A Christmas letter; prose excerpt from *Literary Lapses*. *G&M* Dec 24, 1987: pA6.

Leahy, David

[Untitled]; reviews of *Small Horses & Intimate Beasts* and *Blind Painting*. *Queen's Q* Spring 1987; Vol 94 No 1: p189–191.

[Untitled]; reviews of *The Uncollected Acorn* and *A Stand of Jackpine*. *Rubicon* Fall 1987; No 9: p167–168.

Lebel, Maurice

Prenez et lisez. . . .; review of *Le Repos et l'oubli. MD* Dec 5, 1987: pD4.

[Untitled]; review of *Autobiography of Oliver Goldsmith. Études can* June 1987; No 22: p134–136.

Leblanc, Gérald

Vancouver avec tes yeux; poem. *Estuaire* Autumn 1987; No 46: p9.

Leblanc, Marie-Louise

[Untitled]; theatre review of *La Danse du diable.* photo · *Jeu* 1987; No 45: p214–216.

Le Blanc, Danièle

[untitled]; theatre review of *Opium.* photo · *Jeu* 1987; No 43: p155–156.

Lebowitz, Andrea

Family continuum; review of *Miss Abigail's Part. Can Lit* Winter 1987; No 115: p152–155.

Lebuis, Claude

La censure éditoriale: quelques repères; article. *Moebius (special issue)* Spring 1987; No 32: p23–31.

Leckie, Barbara

Circle games; reviews of fictional works. *Can Lit* Winter 1987; No 115: p278–280.

An interview with Josef Skvorecky. bibliog biog photo · *Rubicon* Fall 1987; No 9: p106–127.

[Untitled]; review of *Spring Tides. Rubicon* Spring 1987; No 8: p195–197.

Ledger, Brent

Dead end; review of *Heartbreaks Along the Road. Books in Can* Dec 1987; Vol 16 No 9: p21–22.

Elizabeth Smart's journals: dress rehearsal for a novel; review of *Necessary Secrets.* photo · *Quill & Quire* Feb 1987; Vol 53 No 2: p16.

Excellent illusions, cloying clichés in short-story collections; reviews of *Afternoon Tea* and *Inspecting the Vaults.* photo · *Quill & Quire* March 1987; Vol 53 No 3: p72.

Fighting words; biographical article. photo · *Books in Can* April 1987; Vol 16 No 3: p9–10, 12–14.

Humorous Hodgins takes a conventional turn; review of *The Honorary Patron.* photo · *Quill & Quire* Aug 1987; Vol 53 No 8: p30.

Katherine Govier; interview. photo · *Books in Can* Nov 1987; Vol 16 No 8: p39–40.

Poetic justice; review of *Swann: A Mystery. Books in Can* Oct 1987; Vol 16 No 7: p15–16.

Shadows of a dream; review of *A Forest for Zoe. Books in Can* June-July 1987; Vol 16 No 5: p17–18.

Story anthologies: the tried, the true, and the best of the new; reviews of short story anthologies. photo · *Quill & Quire* Jan 1987; Vol 53 No 1: p29.

[Untitled]; review of *Intimate Strangers. Quill & Quire* Feb 1987; Vol 53 No 2: p17.

[Untitled]; review of *The Bumper Book. Quill & Quire* March 1987; Vol 53 No 3: p73–74.

[Untitled]; review of *Alberta Bound. Quill & Quire* April 1987; Vol 53 No 4: p27–28.

[Untitled]; review of *Contact Prints. Quill & Quire* May 1987; Vol 53 No 5: p20.

Leduc, Daniel

Des livres et nous; short story. *Moebius (special issue)* Spring 1987; No 32: p33–39.

Entre deux chats pitres; short story. *Moebius* Autumn 1987; No 34: p87–90.

L'instinct de l'occident; poem. *Moebius* Summer 1987; No 33: p61–64.

Ledwell, Frank J.

People and P.E.I.; review of *The Governor of Prince Edward Island. Atlan Prov Book R* Feb-March 1987; Vol 14 No 1: p9.

Lee, John B.

Haircut; poem. *New Q* Winter 1987; Vol 6 No 4: p79–80.

The hollow dark; poem. *Poetry Can R* Fall 1987; Vol 9 No 1: p11.

I hear there's money in basketball; poem. *Poetry Can R* Summer 1987; Vol 8 No 4: p17.

Longpig contemplates his inclinations; poem. *New Q* Winter 1987; Vol 6 No 4: p81–82.

Looking at the In-Memoriam issue of Writers' Quarterly; poem. photo · *Cross Can Writ Q* 1987; Vol 9 No 2: p3.

The old cow blues; poem. *Arc* Fall 1987; No 19: p71.

Origami; poem. *Arc* Fall 1987; No 19: p72.

Some people are just lucky; poem. *Arc* Spring 1987; No 18: p50.

What goes round comes round; poem. *Poetry Can R* Summer 1987; Vol 8 No 4: p17.

Why women don't wear girdles any more; poem. *Arc* Spring 1987; No 18: p51.

Leedahl, Shelley A.

Calendar years; poem. *NeWest R* Sept 1987; Vol 13 No 1: p8.

Leeper, Muriel

Anne of Green Gables opens with lively spirit; theatre review. *TS (Neighbours)* April 28, 1987: p14.

Group brings back Anne of Green Gables; article. *TS (Neighbours)* April 7, 1987: p21.

Play is sheer magic; theatre review of *The Unicorn Moon. TS (Neighbors)* Nov 17, 1987: p14.

Unicorns and princesses hit Scarborough stage; article. photo · *TS (Neighbors)* Oct 27, 1987: p10.

Lefebvre, Paul

Dennis O'Sullivan: la disjonction entre la vie et l'écran; article. photo · *Jeu* 1987; No 44: p142–143.

Heureusement pour le théâtre, l'argent n'a pas d'odeur; article. photo · *MD* March 14, 1987: pC3.

L'envers de l'abandon; theatre review of *Coup de fil.* photo · *Jeu* 1987; No 44: p192–193.

Mao, sa révolution et nous; theatre review of *Mao Tsé-toung ou soirées de musique au consulat.* photo · *MD* March 3, 1987: p5.

Mécanique violente et masques aimables; theatre review of *Le Syndrome de Cézanne.* photo · *MD* Feb 23, 1987: p10.

Robert Lepage: new filters for creation; interview, includes introduction. photo · *Can Theatre R* Fall 1987; No 52: p30–35.

Sainte Kateri et le mythe du bon sauvage; theatre review of *Lily of the Mohawks.* photo · *MD* March 4, 1987: p6.

Théâtre et adolescence; article. photo · *MD* March 7, 1987: pB1, B7.

[Untitled]; theatre review of *Le Syndrome de Cézanne. MD* Feb 27, 1987: p7.

Lefler, Peggy

[Untitled]; poem. *Cross Can Writ Q* 1987; Vol 9 No 3–4: p14.

Lefurgey, Dawn

What Mrs. Simpson did; short story. photo · *TS* July 11, 1987: pM8.

Légaré, Huguette

La mort du récit muet; short story. *Moebius* Autumn 1987; No 34: p59–60.

Légaré, Yves

Un rôle méconnu pour l'Uneq; letter to the editor. *MD* Oct 10, 1987: pD4.

Legendre, B.A.

Image juxtaposition in A Jest Of God; article. *Studies in Can Lit* 1987; Vol 12 No 1: p53–68.

Leggett, John

Death with the proper shaman; review of *The Bishop. NYT Book R* Jan 11, 1987: p23.

Leggo, Carl

Dispelling the dog day; poem. *Fiddlehead* Spring 1987; No 151: p26–29.

Innocence; poem. *Fiddlehead* Spring 1987; No 151: p29–30.

Theology; poem. *CV 2* Spring 1987; Vol 10 No 3: p48.

Le Huenen, Roland

Le récit de voyage: l'entrée en littérature; article. abstract · *Études lit* Spring-Summer 1987; Vol 20 No 1: p45–61.

Leigh-Lizotte, Dorothy

Un laboratoire d'écriture ludique; review of *Popcorn. MD* April 28, 1987: p17.

Leiren-Young, Mark

Definite Jessie material; article. photo · *Can Theatre R* Summer 1987; No 51: p32–35.

Entrances and exits; column. photo · *Can Theatre R* Fall 1987; No 52: p91–94.

Leith, Linda

Serendipity; review of *In the Skin of a Lion.* illus · *Can Forum* Aug-Sept 1987; Vol 67 No 771: p35–37.

Lemaire, Michel

Jacques Brault essayiste; article. *Voix et images* Winter 1987; No 35: p222–238.

Rapts; prose poem. *Liberté* June 1987; Vol 29 No 3: p49–50.

LeMesurier, Glen

The crane (a study of flight); poem. *Alpha* Winter 1987; Vol 11: p21.

Under the influence of magnetic migration pathways down the Appalachian ridge. Québec 1985; poem. *Queen's Q* Spring 1987; Vol 94 No 1: p172.

Lemire, Maurice

L'autonomisation de la "littérature nationale" au XIXe siècle; article. abstract · *Études lit* Spring-Summer 1987; Vol 20 No 1: p75–98.

Lemm, Richard

Abuse of copyright; letter to the editor. *G&M* Dec 1, 1987: pA6.

Exile & belonging: two Maritime poets; reviews of *White of the Lesser Angels* and *Tiger in the Skull. Atlan Prov Book R* May-June 1987; Vol 14 No 2: p10.

Lemoine, Wilfrid

André Belleau: entretien autobiographique; interview. *Liberté* Feb 1987; Vol 29 No 1: p4–27.

L'étonnement Belleau; essay. *Liberté* Feb 1987; Vol 29 No 1: p79–81.

Lennox, John

Carnivalesque and parody in Le Jardin des délices; article. *Can Lit* Spring 1987; No 112: p48–58.

Lenoski, Daniel

Charting discoveries; review of *The Need of Wanting Always.* photo · *NeWest R* Nov 1987; Vol 13 No 3: p13, 17.

Lent, John

Artifice of eternity; poem. *Prairie Fire* Summer 1987; Vol 8 No 2: p54–55.

Ghost in the vortex; poem. *Event* Summer 1987; Vol 16 No 2: p103–105.

Looking for the face of Saturday night; review of *The Face of Jack Munro. CV 2* Summer 1987; Vol 10 No 4: p52–54.

Leonard, Paul

[Untitled]; letter to the editor. *Can Theatre R* Winter 1987; No 53: p4.

Leonard, Veronica

Three stories for children; reviews of children's books. *Atlan Prov Book R* Nov-Dec 1987; Vol 14 No 4: p1.

Lepage, Gilles

The Price Is Right; short story. *Moebius* Autumn 1987; No 34: p9–16.

Lepage, Yvan G.

Prendre possession de nos biens; article about La Bibliothèque du Nouveau Monde. photo · *Lettres québec* Spring 1987; No 45: p60–61.

Lépine, Stéphane

[Untitled]; theatre review of *La Visite des sauvages*. photo · *Jeu* 1987; No 42: p141–147.

[Untitled]; theatre review of *Tchekhov Tchekhova*. photo · *Jeu* 1987; No 42: p161–164.

Lerch, Renate

Could be disaster story for children's magazine; article. *Fin Post* Oct 5, 1987: p3.

Direct marketing writes Harlequin's own happy ending to romance wars; article. illus photo · *Fin Post* Oct 26, 1987: p23.

Lesage, Claudine

Mini-comptes rendus; reviews of *Legs et Bizou / Legs and Bizou* and *Une Journée de Sophie Lachance*. *Can Child Lit* 1987; No 46: p110.

Lesage, Gilles

Mais Félix a préféré rester dans son [i]le. . . .; article. photo · *MD* Jan 28, 1987: p1, 10.

Le Scouarnec, Jean-Louis

La vertige de ma liberté; essay. *Moebius (special issue)* Spring 1987; No 32: p47–53.

Letarte, Geneviève

Ailleurs de pacotille; short story. *Estuaire* Autumn 1987; No 46: p43–47.

Létourneau, Michel

Sommeil; poem. illus · *La Nouvelle barre du jour* May 1987; No 200: p47–50.

Lett, Dan

Course helps teenagers hone writing skills; article. photo · *WFP* July 22, 1987: p32.

Neepawa forgives its most famous citizen; article. photo · *TS* Oct 18, 1987: pD5.

Léveillé, J.R.

De la littérature franco-manitobaine: being a very short history of Franco-Manitoban writing; survey article. illus · *Prairie Fire* Autumn 1987; Vol 8 No 3: p58–69.

Levene, Mark

Fiction; survey review article. *U of Toronto Q* Fall 1987; Vol 57 No 1: p7–21.

Levenson, Christopher

The art of the impossible: two recent versions of translation; review of *Exile Home*. *Arc* Fall 1987; No 19: p38–42.

Colonist; poem. *Antigonish R* 1987; No 69–70: p46.

The editor replies; · *Arc* Spring 1987; No 18: p75–77.

The other side of the coin; editorial. *Arc* Spring 1987; No 18: p4–7.

Verse translation in Canada; editorial article. *Arc* Fall 1987; No 19: p4–6.

Lever, Bernice

Chap-book award; notice. *Waves* Winter 1987; Vol 15 No 3: p89.

Congratulations!; notice. *Waves* Winter 1987; Vol 15 No 3: p89.

Editor's note. *Waves* Spring 1987; Vol 15 No 4: p94.

The Milton Acorn People's Award; notice. *Waves* Winter 1987; Vol 15 No 3: p89.

[Untitled]; essay. photo · *Cross Can Writ Q* 1987; Vol 9 No 3–4: p26.

Lévesque, Gaétan

Prix et distinctions; list of award winners. photo · *Lettres québec* Autumn 1987; No 47: p7.

Voix et images 36; review. *Lettres québec* Autumn 1987; No 47: p66.

Lévesque, Micheline

Tellement me hantent parfois; prose poem. *Estuaire* Winter 1986–87; No 43: p37–38.

Lévesque, Richard

Le retour magistral de Tremblay; theatre review of *Le Vrai monde?*. photo · *MD* April 16, 1987: p15.

Lévesque, Robert

27 mars, journée mondiale du théâtre; column. photo · *MD* March 24, 1987: p11.

André Brassard prend congé de mise en scène; column. *MD* May 5, 1987: p11.

Les anges dans nos campagnes; article. *MD* June 4, 1987: p13.

Une apocalypse du désassorti; theatre review of *Bonjour, là, bonjour*. photo · *MD* Nov 24, 1987: p11.

Avis aux consommateurs; theatre review of *V.S.O.P.* photo · *MD* Oct 16, 1987: p15.

Bouchard et les feux de Roberval; theatre review of *Les Feluettes*. photo · *MD* Sept 25, 1987: p13.

Bouleversante Patricia Nolin; theatre review of *Tchekhov Tchekhova*. photo · *MD* Jan 29, 1987: p5.

Büchner, Marivaux, Shephard, Gélinas: un mois théâtral chargé; column. photo · *MD* Jan 6, 1987: p4.

Ça manque d'esprit(s) dans la maison!; theatre review of *Les Fantômes de Martin*. *MD* Nov 26, 1987: p13.

Le Café de la Place se bilinguise; article. photo · *MD* May 22, 1987: p15.

Une centième au Café de la Place; article. photo · *MD* Dec 3, 1987: p13.

Dany Laferrière: "le talent ça m'irait!"; article. photo · *MD* Oct 10, 1987: pD3.

Denise Filiatrault revient au théâtre; column. *MD* April 28, 1987: p14.

Des dramaturges ayant en commun l'usage du français; theatre review of *Fragments d'une lettre d'adieu lus par des géologues*. *MD* Sept 9, 1987: p13.

Des estivants sans été; theatre review of *La Société de Métis*. *MD* Sept 29, 1987: p13.

Des Fridolinades sorties de leur temps; theatre review of *Les Fridolinades*. photo · *MD* Jan 14, 1987: p6.

Dragons, Feluettes et Vrai monde; survey article. photo · *MD* Dec 31, 1987: pC1, C12.

Du côté du rococo. . . .; theatre review of *Le Troisième fils du professeur Yourolov*. *MD* Sept 23, 1987: p11.

Dubois chez Duceppe: les années de plomb de l'après-référendum; article. photo · *MD* April 25, 1987: pC1, C10.

Les fantômes devront attendre. . . .; column. *MD* Nov 10, 1987: p13, 15.

Félix Leclerc aux soins coronariens; article. photo · *MD* Nov 9, 1987: p1, 10.

Félix Leclerc reste toujours chancelant; article. *MD* Nov 10, 1987: p1, 12.

Les Feluettes seront en France en 1988; article. photo · *MD* Nov 5, 1987: p13.

La fièvre du lundi matin; theatre review of *Toupie Wildwood*. *MD* June 25, 1987: p13.

Les Fous de Bassan se cassent le bec sur un vrai mur; article. *MD* Feb 25, 1987: p1, 12.

Le grand prix va à Robert Lepage; article. photo · *MD* June 8, 1987: p1, 8.

Le grand règlement de comptes de Michel Tremblay; theatre review of *Le Vrai monde?*. photo · *MD* April 6, 1987: p11.

Le grand retour de Murielle Dutil dans Le Temps d'une vie; column. *MD* April 7, 1987: p12.

La grande virée à Wildwood; column. photo · *MD* June 16, 1987: p13.

Gratien Gélinas: le retour de Fridolin; article. illus photo · *MD* Jan 10, 1987: pB1, B4.

La guerre de religion de Denise Boucher; column. photo · *MD* Jan 13, 1987: p6.

Ionesco soufflera ses 75 chandelles à Montréal; column. *MD* May 12, 1987: p14.

Japrisot à La Licorne, Strauss à Fred-Barry; column. *MD* Feb 3, 1987: p7.

Je serai Robert Thomas ou rien. . . .; theatre review of *Le Night Cap Bar*. photo · *MD* April 9, 1987: p13.

Jour un pour le 2e Festival des Amériques; column. photo · *MD* May 26, 1987: p13.

Le Laferrière nouveau; article. photo · *MD* Sept 30, 1987: p13.

Limoges, principale vitrine du théâtre québécois en Europe; column. photo · *MD* Sept 29, 1987: p13.

L'insoutenable dureté de l'être; theatre review of *Oublier*. photo · *MD* Nov 4, 1987: p13.

Michel-Marc Bouchard: Roberval, 1912, j'avais 19 ans. . . .; article. photo · *MD* Sept 12, 1987: pC1-C2.

Moisson d'avril; column. photo · *MD* March 31, 1987: p17.

Montréal au centre des Amériques; article. photo · *MD* May 23, 1987: pC1.

"Nouvelles pour le théâtre"; column. *MD* Jan 27, 1987: p5.

Oublier ou ne pas oublier; article. photo · *MD* Oct 31, 1987: pC1, C3.

Un parc, quelques rues et deux quartiers; article. photo · *MD* Nov 14, 1987: pD1, D3.

Les pièges de l'esthétique; theatre review of *Opium*. photo · *MD* Jan 16, 1987: p7.

Quatre personnages en quête d'une pièce; theatre review of *Le Dernier quatuor d'un homme sourd*. photo · *MD* Nov 20, 1987: p13.

Le Québec sera très présent au 2e Festival de théâtre des Amériques; article. photo · *MD* April 8, 1987: p13.

Québec: Alexandre Hausvater quitte la Quinzaine théâtrale; column. *MD* April 14, 1987: p12.

Quelque chose d'Aurore. . . .; theatre review of *Gilles Vachon, incendiaire*. *MD* Aug 19, 1987: p11.

Qui sera le directeur artistique du TPQ?; column. *MD* Nov 17, 1987: p11.

Rachel Lortie prend les choses en mains; article. *MD* Oct 2, 1987: p13.

La rentrée théâtrale; article. photo · *MD* Sept 12, 1987: pC1-C2.

Le retour du "Chien mexicain"; column. *MD* June 9, 1987: p11.

Robert Lalonde: un théâtre de risques et sans compromis; article. photo · *MD* April 4, 1987: pC1, C8.

Robert Lepage, de Nyon en Avignon; article. photo · *MD* Aug 6, 1987: p11.

Robert Lepage, globe-trotter; column. photo · *MD* Oct 20, 1987: p13, 15.

Robert Lepage impose son Vinci dans la Ville lumière; column. photo · *MD* Dec 8, 1987: p11.

Ronfard et les traces de Mao, Nadon et les frasques de Lorenzaccio; column. *MD* Feb 17, 1987: p7.

La Russie de Basile, le Québec de Dubois; review of *Le Printemps, monsieur Deslauriers*. photo · *MD* Oct 10, 1987: pD6.

Le sourd dans la ville, de Mireille Dansereau: près du roman mais loin de l'inspiration; film review. *MD* Sept 19, 1987: pA7.

Suspense à la Quinzaine de Québec; column. *MD* Sept 22, 1987: p11.

Le théâtre du Rire joue gagnant; column. *MD* Oct 13, 1987: p11.

Théâtre ouvert et théâtre intime; theatre review of *Marilyn (journal intime de Margaret Macpherson)*. *MD* Oct 14, 1987: p14.

Le théâtre québécoise triomphe maintenant dans les grandes salles; column. photo · *MD* Dec 1, 1987: p11.

Les théâtres d'été: au petit bonheur la blague; article. photo · *MD* June 13, 1987: pC1, C10.

Tremblay chez les plus grands; article. photo · *MD* Oct 8, 1987: p13.

[Untitled]; theatre review of *Tchekhov Tchekhova*. *MD* Jan 30, 1987: p7.

[Untitled]; theatre review of *Tchekhov Tchekhova*. *MD* Feb 6, 1987: p7.

[Untitled]; theatre reviews. photo · *MD* March 13, 1987: p15.

[Untitled]; notice. *MD* May 22, 1987: p15.

[Untitled]; theatre review of *Le Troisième fils du professeur Yourolov*. *MD* Oct 2, 1987: p15.

[Untitled]; theatre reviews of *Oublier* and *Tête à tête*. *MD* Nov 6, 1987: p15.

[Untitled]; theatre review of *Oublier*. photo · *MD* Nov 13, 1987: p15.

[Untitled]; theatre review of *Les Feluettes*. *MD* Nov 27, 1987: p15.

[Untitled]; theatre reviews. *MD* Dec 4, 1987: p15.

Yvette Brind'amour reçoit le prix Molson du Conseil des arts; column. *MD* Nov 3, 1987: p13.

Yvon Rivard et Northrop Frye parmi les lauréats des prix du gouverneur général; article. photo · *MD* May 28, 1987: p13.

Lévesque, Solange

Harmonie et contrepoint; article. photo · *Jeu* 1987; No 42: p100–108.

Une histoire cousue de fils araignées; theatre review of *Gilles Vachon, incendiaire*. photo · *Jeu* 1987; No 45: p216–217.

Opéra-fête: the power of the image; article. photo trans · *Can Theatre R* Spring 1987; No 50: p20–25.

Ouvrir la boîte à maux; theatre review of *Pandora*. photo · *Jeu* 1987; No 44: p177–180.

Un printemps clair-obscur; theatre review of *Le Printemps, monsieur Deslauriers*. photo · *Jeu* 1987; No 44: p180–182.

Tenir l'univers dans sa main; article. photo · *Jeu* 1987; No 45: p111–120.

[Untitled]; theatre reviews of *La Tour* and *Les Objets parlent*. photo · *Jeu* 1987; No 43: p145–147.

[Untitled]; theatre review of *Tête à tête*. photo · *Jeu* 1987; No 43: p167–168.

Levine, Allan

CanHistory?; review of *Sounding the Iceberg*. *G&M* Feb 28, 1987: pE20.

The poet who ran Indian Affairs; review of *A Narrow Vision*. photo · *G&M* Feb 28, 1987: pE17.

Lewis, David

[Untitled]; review of *The Collected Poems of George Whalley*. *Queen's Q* Winter 1987; Vol 94 No 4: p1045–1047.

Lewis, Justin

Car to California; short story. *Malahat R* June 1987; No 79: p104–110.

Leznoff, Glenda

Potato dreams; short story. *Room of One's Own* April 1987; Vol 11 No 3: p27–34.

Light, Joanne

Maxine Tynes' first book of poems; review of *Borrowed Beauty*. photo · *Atlan Prov Book R* Sept-Oct 1987; Vol 14 No 3: p14.

Prayer for a young child; poem. *Alpha* Winter 1987; Vol 11: p14.

To my neighbours; poem. *Alpha* Winter 1987; Vol 11: p14.

Lilburn, Tim

Thoughts towards a Christian poetics; essay. illus · *Brick* Winter 1987; No 29: p34–36.

Trip to Ossossane; essay. *Brick* Fall 1987; No 31: p41–42.

Lillard, Charles

100 Mile house; poem. *Antigonish R* Winter 1987; No 68: p25.

Canyon City; poem. *Fiddlehead* Spring 1987; No 151: p33.

Iskut; poem. *Fiddlehead* Spring 1987; No 151: p32.

Jones Creek; poem. *Antigonish R* Winter 1987; No 68: p24.

Kitsumkalum; poem. *Waves* Spring 1987; Vol 15 No 4: p67.

The mermaid inn: the silent voices of the past; essay. photo · *G&M* Sept 12, 1987: pD6.

Meziadin; poem. *Event* Summer 1987; Vol 16 No 2: p11.

St. Anne's crossing; poem. *Can Lit* Spring 1987; No 112: p47.

Williams Lake; poem. *Antigonish R* Winter 1987; No 68: p26.

Liman, Claude

Arks (July / August, 1984); poem. *Northward J* 1987; No 43: p30.

Palimpsest of an early frost (September, 1984); poem. *Northward J* 1987; No 43: p31.

Recipe for spring (May, 1984); poem. *Northward J* 1987; No 43: p29.

Riding the winter bus (January, 1984); poem. *Northward J* 1987; No 43: p29.

Linder, Norma West

September rose; poem. *Can Auth & Book* Fall 1987; Vol 63 No 1: p16.

Lindquist, Vernon R.

[Untitled]; review of *The Impossible Sum of Our Traditions*. *Amer R of Can Studies* Autumn 1987; Vol 17 No 3: p353–354.

Linehan, Don

Allspice; poem. *Waves* Spring 1987; Vol 15 No 4: p68.

And the students asked, "What does the poem mean?"; poem. *Germination* Spring 1987; Vol 10 No 2: p19.

Frog Lake July '84; poem. *Fiddlehead* Summer 1987; No 152: p49–50.

Letters to young poets; essay. *Germination* Spring 1987; Vol 10 No 2: p18.

Poem in the old Gaelic style; poem. *Waves* Spring 1987; Vol 15 No 4: p68.

Sidney; poem. *Fiddlehead* Summer 1987; No 152: p48.

Lintula, Douglas

Copyright groups no threat to free flow of information; letter to the editor. *G&M* Oct 21, 1987: pA7.

Lipovenko, Dorothy

A good book blurb helps a lot. Is it right?; article. *G&M* Dec 26, 1987: pB1-B2.

Lisitza, Lorinda

Tough dancing; poem. *Grain* Winter 1987; Vol 15 No 4: p65.

Little, C.H.

[Untitled]; review of *A Model Lover*. *Can Auth & Book* Winter 1987; Vol 62 No 2: p23.

Little, George

Sophie's song; short story. *Fiddlehead* Summer 1987; No 152: p84–88.

Little, Jean

A key to the garden; essay. photo · *Can Child Lit* 1987; No 48: p64–66.

Littler, William

Applebaum spooks score for Davies' ghost story; review of *The Harper of the Stones*. *TS* May 12, 1987: pF4.

Davies conjures a musical ghost for children; article about *The Harper of the Stones*. photo · *TS* May 9, 1987: pJ12.

Livesay, Dorothy

Death by drowning; essay. illus · *Books in Can* April 1987; Vol 16 No 3: p15–16.

The initiation; short story, includes essay. *Grain* Fall 1987; Vol 15 No 3: p12–18.

[They Shall Inherit the Earth]; review. *Brick* Winter 1987; No 29: p47–48.

Lobb, Edward

Imagining history: the romantic background of George Bowering's Burning Water; article. *Studies in Can Lit* 1987; Vol 12 No 1: p112–128.

Lochhead, Douglas

Vigils & mercies; poem sequence. photo · *Antigonish R* Winter 1987; No 68: p61–76.

Loewen, Rob

[Untitled]; poem. *CV 2* Spring 1987; Vol 10 No 3: p49.

[Untitled]; poem. *NeWest R* Summer 1987; Vol 12 No 10: p6.

[Untitled]; poem. *NeWest R* Summer 1987; Vol 12 No 10: p9.

[Untitled]; poem. *NeWest R* Oct 1987; Vol 13 No 2: p19.

Lomax, Dave

Isn't it nice to think so; poem. *Waves* Spring 1987; Vol 15 No 4: p55.

Long, Catherine

The horn player; short story. *Waves* Spring 1987; Vol 15 No 4: p35–38.

Longchamps, Renaud

Aventure; essay. *La Nouvelle barre du jour (special issue)* 1987; No 191: p51–60.

La cédraie; poem. *Estuaire* Winter 1986–87; No 43: p17.

Le ciel; poem. *Estuaire* Winter 1986–87; No 43: p21.

Description du territoire; poems. *Estuaire* Winter 1986–87; No 43: p16–22.

Faune et flore; poem. *Estuaire* Winter 1986–87; No 43: p20.

Le héron bleu; poem. *Estuaire* Winter 1986–87; No 43: p21.

L'arbre; poem. *Estuaire* Winter 1986–87; No 43: p16.

L'eau; poem. *Estuaire* Winter 1986–87; No 43: p20.

L'or et les graviers; poem. *Estuaire* Winter 1986–87; No 43: p19.

Le marais; poem. *Estuaire* Winter 1986–87; No 43: p19.

Pour en finir avec le XXIe siècle ou poème à pou; poem. *Estuaire* Summer 1987; No 45: p27–30.

Le pré; poem. *Estuaire* Winter 1986–87; No 43: p18.

La rivière; poem. *Estuaire* Winter 1986–87; No 43: p18.

Le ruisseau; poem. *Estuaire* Winter 1986–87; No 43: p17.

Le sentier; poem. *Estuaire* Winter 1986–87; No 43: p22.

La terre; poem. *Estuaire* Winter 1986–87; No 43: p16.

La voie ferrée; poem. *Estuaire* Winter 1986–87; No 43: p18.

Longfield, Kevin

Not overpaid; letter to the editor. *WFP* Sept 19, 1987: p7.

Longo, Louise

Infinite song; review of *The Self-Completing Tree*. *Waves* Spring 1987; Vol 15 No 4: p84–87.

[Untitled]; review of *Changes of State*. *Books in Can* Jan-Feb 1987; Vol 16 No 1: p27–28.

[Untitled]; review of *Excerpts from the Real World. Books in Can* Jan-Feb 1987; Vol 16 No 1: p28.

[Untitled]; review of *Hammerstroke. Quill & Quire* March 1987; Vol 53 No 3: p74–75.

[Untitled]; review of *The Immaculate Perception. Quill & Quire* March 1987; Vol 53 No 3: p75.

[Untitled]; interview with Paul Quarrington, includes introduction. illus · *Waves* Spring 1987; Vol 15 No 4: p5–10.

Lord, Michel

Aaa! Aâh! Ha! que de belles catastrophes narratives!; reviews. photo · *Lettres québec* Spring 1987; No 45: p32–35.

D'abominables délices; review of *L'Envoleur de chevaux et autres contes. Lettres québec* Winter 1986–87; No 44: p81.

Entre la réussite et l'échec; reviews of science fiction books. photo · *Lettres québec* Autumn 1987; No 47: p33–34.

L'effet science-fiction tous azimuts: la SF québécoise en 1986–1987; reviews of science fiction books and periodicals. *Voix et images* Autumn 1987; Vol 13 No 1: p180–189.

La quête de la pensée la pensée de la quête; review of *Le Traversier.* photo · *Lettres québec* Summer 1987; No 46: p28–29.

Lorimer, James

Gordon Pinsent reminds us of our sense of place; editorial. *Atlan Insight* May 1987; Vol 9 No 5: p3.

Loucks, Randee

[Untitled]; review of *Doc. Dandelion* Fall-Winter 1987; Vol 14 No 2: p147–150.

Louis, M.K.

[Untitled]; review of *The Glass Air. Malahat R (special issue)* March 1987; No 78: p156–158.

[Untitled]; review of *Brazilian Journal. Malahat R* June 1987; No 79: p162–164.

Louise, Sarah

Dick and Jane and me; short story. *Quarry* Winter 1987; Vol 36 No 1: p42–57.

Louttit, Neil

A spot of skulduggery with an Asian flavor; review of *The Glorious East Wind. WFP* Dec 19, 1987: p51.

LoVerso, Marco P.

Dialectic, morality, and the Deptford trilogy; article. *Studies in Can Lit* 1987; Vol 12 No 1: p69–89.

Lovesey, Oliver

Mine talk; poem. *Fiddlehead* Summer 1987; No 152: p70–71.

Lowey, Mark

Poetry to stuff into a stocking; reviews of poetry books. photo · *CH* Dec 13, 1987: pC8.

Virgin on the high board; poem. *Poetry Can R* Fall 1987; Vol 9 No 1: p11.

The writer's short story (the characters' harangue); short story. illus · *Cross Can Writ Q* 1987; Vol 9 No 3–4: p21, 52–53.

Lowndes, Colin

Into the depths of Milton Acorn's passion; review of *Milton Acorn: The Uncollected Acorn.* photo · *G&M* March 21, 1987: pE18.

Lozeau, Albert

Les amitiés / Friendships; poem in French and in English translation. *Ellipse* 1987; No 38: p12–13.

Bonheur malheureux / Unhappy happiness; poem in French and in English translation. *Ellipse* 1987; No 38: p38–39.

Bonheur rêvé / Dream of happiness; poem in French and in English translation. *Ellipse* 1987; No 38: p24–25.

Charme dangereux / Dangerous attraction; poem in French and in English translation. *Ellipse* 1987; No 38: p30–31.

Dernière flamme / Final flame; poem in French and in English translation. *Ellipse* 1987; No 38: p10–11.

Effets de neige et de givre / Effects of snow and frost; poem in French and in English translation. *Ellipse* 1987; No 38: p16–17.

Érable rouge / Red maple; poem in French and in English translation. *Ellipse* 1987; No 38: p32–33.

Intimité / Intimacy; poem in French and in English translation. *Ellipse* 1987; No 38: p8–9.

L'attente / The sweet pain of waiting; poem in French and in English translation. *Ellipse* 1987; No 38: p22–23.

À l'automne / To autumn; poem in French and in English translation. *Ellipse* 1987; No 38: p28–29.

Lumière / Light; poem in French and in English translation. *Ellipse* 1987; No 38: p36–37.

Mars / March; poem in French and in English translation. *Ellipse* 1987; No 38: p20–21.

Le matin / Morning; poem in French and English translation. *Ellipse* 1987; No 38: p18–19.

Mauvaise solitude / Gloomy loneliness; poem in French and in English translation. *Ellipse* 1987; No 38: p34–35.

Nocturnes; poem in French and in English translation. *Ellipse* 1987; No 38: p14–15.

Par la fenêtre / Through the window; poem in French and in English translation. *Ellipse* 1987; No 38: p42–43.

La poussière du jour / The dust of the day; poem in French and in English translation. *Ellipse* 1987; No 38: p26–27.

Le rêve mort / The dead dream; poem in French and in English translation. *Ellipse* 1987; No 38: p40–41.

Lucas, Andrew J.

Real estate; poem. *Alpha* Winter 1987; Vol 11: p19.

The reaper pales; poem. *Alpha* Winter 1987; Vol 11: p22.

Lush, Laura

The diver; poem. *Event* March 1987; Vol 16 No 1: p36–37.

Luxton, Stephen

Semiotic song; review of *North of Intention*. *Matrix* Fall 1987; No 25: p77–79.

Lynch, Gerald

One's company; short story. *Capilano R* 1987; No 42: p56–62.

Lynch, Marguerite

In the shadow of the cathedral; short story. photo · *TS* Aug 4, 1987: pB7.

Lynde, Denyse

The dowser character in the plays of Gwen Pharis Ringwood; article. *Ariel* Jan 1987; Vol 18 No 1: p27–37.

Lynes, Jeanette

Magnolia; short story. *Malahat R* Dec 1987; No 81: p70–73.

Mac, Kathy

Family hysteria; poem. *New Q* Spring-Summer 1987; Vol 7 No 1–2: p212–213.

Symptom; poem. *Prism* Summer 1987; Vol 25 No 4: p89.

What is this thing called, Love?; poem. *Antigonish R* Winter 1987; No 68: p132.

MacAndrew, Barbara

Anne of Green Gables grows up; article. photo · *Maclean's* Dec 7, 1987; Vol 100 No 49: p46–48, 50.

MacCormack, Karen

Forgeries; prose poem. *Writing* Nov 1987; No 19: p37–38.

Macdonald, Claudia

[Untitled]; poem. *Fireweed* Fall 1987; No 25: p26–27.

Macdonald, Cyril

1–416–964–6362; prose poem. *Alpha* Winter 1987; Vol 11: p29.

Macdonald, Don

TV reporter in Winnipeg suddenly a hit with historical novel on Metis in French; article. photo · *G&M* Dec 21, 1987: pC10.

Macdonald, Hugh

Sunset; poem. *Can Auth & Book* Spring 1987; Vol 62 No 3: p22.

MacDonald, Larry

The Sunday School Christmas Tree caper; humourous essay. *NeWest R* Dec 1987; Vol 13 No 4: p19.

MacDonald, Lorne

Creon's revenge; poem. *Wascana R* Fall 1987; Vol 22 No 2: p64–65.

MacDonald, Roger

Short short stories by Kent Thompson; review of *Leaping Up Sliding Away*. *Atlan Prov Book R* Feb-March 1987; Vol 14 No 1: p18.

MacDuff, Pierre

Le projet de loi C-54 sur la pornographie: une menace potentielle pour les arts; essay. photo · *Jeu* 1987; No 45: p10–12.

MacEwen, Gwendolyn

1958; poem. *Can Forum* Jan 1987; Vol 66 No 765: p24–25.

Absences; poem. *Poetry Can R* Summer 1987; Vol 8 No 4: p21.

Elemental; poem. *Poetry Can R* Summer 1987; Vol 8 No 4: p21.

Fireworks; poem. *Can Forum* Jan 1987; Vol 66 No 765: p25.

In the garden of the Chelsea Arts Club; poem. *Poetry Can R* Summer 1987; Vol 8 No 4: p20.

Marino Marini's horses and riders; poem. *Poetry Can R* Summer 1987; Vol 8 No 4: p21.

The name of the night; poem. *Can Forum* Jan 1987; Vol 66 No 765: p24.

Niagara daredevil, 37, buried near the Falls; poem. *Poetry Can R* Summer 1987; Vol 8 No 4: p21.

The park, 20 years later; poem. *Can Forum* Jan 1987; Vol 66 No 765: p24.

The Tao of physics; poem. *Poetry Can R* Summer 1987; Vol 8 No 4: p20.

An unconditional kingdom; poems. illus · *Can Forum* Jan 1987; Vol 66 No 765: p24–25.

[Untitled]; essay. photo · *Cross Can Writ Q* 1987; Vol 9 No 3–4: p22.

Vacuum genesis; poem. photo · *Poetry Can R* Summer 1987; Vol 8 No 4: p20.

The Wah Mai Cafe; poem. *Can Forum* Jan 1987; Vol 66 No 765: p24.

You can study it if you want; poem. *Poetry Can R* Summer 1987; Vol 8 No 4: p21.

MacEwen, John

The making of the weapon; short story. *Fiddlehead* Autumn 1987; No 153: p69–74.

MacGillivray, Royce

[Untitled]; review of *The Orangeman*. *Books in Can* Jan-Feb 1987; Vol 16 No 1: p27.

Machowski, Zenon

Majutsusha; short story. photo · *TS* July 15, 1987: pG10.

MacInnis, Craig

Bongo and McToots play along when Boinks bop in on our galaxy; article. photo · *TS* Jan 9, 1987: pD3.

Lightweight vets replacing Ritter on CBC Dayshift; column. *TS* Aug 20, 1987: pF1.

MacIntyre, Jean

Language and structure in Billy Bishop Goes To War; article. *Can Drama* 1987; Vol 13 No 1: p50–59.

MacIsaac, Dan

Foundations of cages; poem. *Antigonish R* 1987; No 69–70: p28.

MacKay, Barbara

Daddy's girl; article. photo · *Books in Can* Oct 1987; Vol 16 No 7: p3.

Mackay, Claire

[Untitled]; essay. photo · *Cross Can Writ Q* 1987; Vol 9 No 3–4: p24.

MacKay, Gillian

Under the Nazi shadow; review of *Mortal Sins*. *Maclean's* Nov 23, 1987; Vol 100 No 47: p54a.

MacKay, Samm

Paper flowers; poem. *New Q* Spring-Summer 1987; Vol 7 No 1–2: p173–176.

Mackay, Scott

On that night; short story. *Fiddlehead* Spring 1987; No 151: p73–78.

MacKendrick, Louis K.

Trimly clipped and barboured; reviews of *Visible Visions* and *The Harbingers*. *Essays on Can Writ* Spring 1987; No 34: p39–43.

[Untitled]; review of *Tales from Firozsha Baag*. *Books in Can* Aug-Sept 1987; Vol 16 No 6: p25–26.

Mackenzie, Nancy

At Strome Glen farm; poem. *Capilano R* 1987; No 43: p86.

Psalmistry; poem. *Capilano R* 1987; No 43: p84–85.

The yarn; poem. *Capilano R* 1987; No 43: p82–83.

MacKinnon, Donna Jean

Contemplating dens; article. photo · *TS* Oct 18, 1987: pC1, C6.

Macklem, Katherine

Authors' earnings: account books talk; article. *MG* Sept 28, 1987: pB9.

It's tougher in French, too; article. photo · *MG* Sept 28, 1987: pB9.

Writers confront publishing odds; article. photo · *MG* Sept 28, 1987: pB9.

MacLennan, Hugh

An orange from Portugal; essay. illus · *TS* Dec 5, 1987: pM1,M10-M11,M15.

[Untitled]; biographical articles. *Brick (special issue)* Summer 1987; No 30: ppassim.

Macleod, Catherine

A lesson from myths: live in harmony; review of *Dzelarhons*. *TS* April 5, 1987: pA22.

MacLeod, Robert

Home of Toronto writer ransacked; article. photo · *G&M* Oct 14, 1987: pA15.

MacLeod, Sue

Women to watch in the Maritimes; article. photo · *Chatelaine* April 1987; Vol 60 No 4: p114, 116, 118, 120.

MacLulich, T.D.

Thematic criticism, literary nationalism, and the critic's new clothes; article. *Essays on Can Writ* Winter 1987; No 35: p17–36.

MacMillan, Carrie

Maritime letters; reviews. *Can Lit* Spring 1987; No 112: p189–192.

MacPhee, Dianne

Aggie; poem. *Alpha* Winter 1987; Vol 11: p34.

November; poem. *Alpha* Winter 1987; Vol 11: p34.

Macpherson, Jay

GJ at Victoria: from Acta to Auk; article. *Malahat R (special issue)* March 1987; No 78: p52–56.

MacSween, R.J.

Crime; poem. *Antigonish R* Winter 1987; No 68: p51.

The fault; poem. *Antigonish R* Winter 1987; No 68: p49.

Flying; poem. *Antigonish R* 1987; No 69–70: p139.

That country; poem. *Antigonish R* Winter 1987; No 68: p50.

Madoff, Mark S.

Erasures; review of *A Tale of Two Countries*. *Can Lit* Spring 1987; No 112: p185–186.

Maggs, Randall

Four poets; reviews of poetry books. *Can Lit* Winter 1987; No 115: p280–284.

Magnuson, Judy

[Untitled]; review of *The Lucky Old Woman*. *CH* Dec 6, 1987: pD9.

Magnuson, Wayne J.

[Untitled]; letter to the editor. *NeWest R* April 1987; Vol 12 No 8: p1.

Maguire, Dianne

The sanitary inspector; short story. illus · *Queen's Q* Autumn 1987; Vol 94 No 3: p622–629.

Mailhot, Laurent

André Belleau; obituary. *Études fran* Winter 1987; Vol 22 No 3: p3–5.

Études françaises, vingt ans après; article. *Voix et images* Winter 1987; No 35: p284–287.

A poet at his window: Albert Lozeau; article. trans · *Ellipse* 1987; No 38: p45–53.

Mailhot, Michèle

De Montréal à Kingsbury: un circuit intérieur; prose excerpt from *Notes de parcours,* includes introduction. photo · *Lettres québec* Summer 1987; No 46: p62–63.

Mailloux, Louise

Trou d'insomnie; short story. *Liberté* Dec 1987; Vol 29 No 6: p33–38.

Main, Hannah J.

White; poem. *Poetry Can R* Summer 1987; Vol 8 No 4: p9.

You call out promises; poem. *Poetry Can R* Summer 1987; Vol 8 No 4: p9.

Major, Alice

Aging I. . . .; poem. *New Q* Spring-Summer 1987; Vol 7 No 1–2: p180.

Happy endings; poem. *Can Auth & Book* Fall 1987; Vol 63 No 1: p17.

Palliative care; poem. *Event* March 1987; Vol 16 No 1: p75.

Phone calls I; poem. *New Q* Spring-Summer 1987; Vol 7 No 1–2: p177–178.

Phone calls II; poem. *New Q* Spring-Summer 1987; Vol 7 No 1–2: p179.

Rainy morning; poem. *Wascana R* Spring 1987; Vol 22 No 1: p57.

Major, Robert

Faire de la terre ou faire la guerre? L'intertexte napoléonien dans le roman de défrichement québécois; article. abstract · *Études can* 1987; No 23: p71–86.

L'instinct territorial; review of *Le Roman du territoire. Voix et images* Autumn 1987; Vol 13 No 1: p162–165.

[Untitled]; review of *Hertel, l'homme et l'oeuvre. U of Toronto Q* Fall 1987; Vol 57 No 1: p185–186.

Malak, Amin

Margaret Atwood's The Handmaid's Tale and the dystopian tradition; article. *Can Lit* Spring 1987; No 112: p9–16.

Malarte, Claire-Lise

Un sapristi de bon livre; review of *Les Catastrophes de Rosalie. Can Child Lit* 1987; No 48: p102–104.

Malcolm, Andrew H.

[Untitled]; review of *Beyond Forget. NYT Book R* July 5, 1987: p15.

Malcolm, Douglas

Grime and punishment; review of *Crang Plays the Ace. Books in Can* April 1987; Vol 16 No 3: p35.

Smooth skating; review of *King Leary. Books in Can* Oct 1987; Vol 16 No 7: p27.

Through a lens darkly; review of *Contact Prints. Books in Can* May 1987; Vol 16 No 4: p28.

[Untitled]; review of *The Queen's Secret. Books in Can* Jan-Feb 1987; Vol 16 No 1: p26.

[Untitled]; review of *Rommel and Patton. Books in Can* April 1987; Vol 16 No 3: p24–25.

[Untitled]; review of *A Body Surrounded by Water. Books in Can* Aug-Sept 1987; Vol 16 No 6: p25.

Malden, Peter

[Untitled]; review of *Blind Painting. Rubicon* Fall 1987; No 9: p170–173.

Malenfant, Paul Chanel

Coqs à deux têtes; series of linked poems. *La Nouvelle barre du jour (special issue)* 1987; No 195: p7–58.

Icônes; prose poem. *Moebius (special issue)* Spring 1987; No 32: p65–68.

[Untitled]; poetry excerpt from *Tirées au clair.* illus · *La Nouvelle barre du jour* May 1987; No 200: p17–26.

Mallam, Teresa

Quilted patch; reviews of poetry books. *Can Lit* Spring 1987; No 112: p176–179.

Mallet, Gina

Morley Callaghan, past & present; television review of *Morley Callaghan: First Person Singular.* photo · *Chatelaine* April 1987; Vol 60 No 4: p22.

[Untitled]; theatre reviews. *G&M (Toronto Magazine)* Nov 1987; Vol 2 No 8: p29.

Mallinson, Jean

Green thumb; short story. *Wascana R* Spring 1987; Vol 22 No 1: p68–76.

Mallory, J.R.

[Untitled]; biographical articles. *Brick (special issue)* Summer 1987; No 30: ppassim.

Maloney, Elizabeth

[Untitled]; review of *Showcase Animals. Rubicon* Fall 1987; No 9: p186–187.

Malterre, Elona

Thriller mired in words; review of *Merlin's Web. CH* Nov 8, 1987: pE6.

Maltman, Kim

The technology of reverie; poem. *Tor Life* Oct 1987; Vol 21 No 1[5]: p43.

[Untitled]; essay. *Poetry Can R* Summer 1987; Vol 8 No 4: p14.

Malyon, Carol

Children in tree; poem. *Poetry Can R* Summer 1987; Vol 8 No 4: p8.

Milk truck; poem. *Poetry Can R* Summer 1987; Vol 8 No 4: p8.

Queen car; poem. *Tor Life* June 1987; Vol 21 No 9: p25.

Seated figure; poem. *Tor Life* Aug 1987; Vol 21 No 11: p44.

Summer in town; poem. *Poetry Can R* Summer 1987; Vol 8 No 4: p8.

To Prince Edward Island; poem. *Poetry Can R* Summer 1987; Vol 8 No 4: p8.

Woman, man and boat; poem. *Poetry Can R* Summer 1987; Vol 8 No 4: p8.

Mandel, Charles

The allure of Alberta in history and contemporary life; review of *The Best of Alberta.* photo · *Quill & Quire* Dec 1987; Vol 53 No 12: p27.

Edmonton winners in Pulp contest; article. *Quill & Quire* Jan 1987; Vol 53 No 1: p18.

Horsing around; review of *Caprice. G&M* May 23, 1987: pC23.

Poetry Sweatshop moves west; article. photo · *Quill & Quire* Oct 1987; Vol 53 No 10: p10.

Seized books spark assistance; article. *Quill & Quire* April 1987; Vol 53 No 4: p15–16.

Manguel, Alberto

Brevity, soul and wit; article. photo · *Maclean's* Sept 21, 1987; Vol 100 No 38: p53–54.

A change of climate; review of *A Shapely Fire. Books in Can* Nov 1987; Vol 16 No 8: p33–34.

The fixed point of love; review of *Memory Board. Maclean's* Oct 19, 1987; Vol 100 No 42: p60b.

A framework for history; review of *The Ring Master.* photo · *G&M* Nov 14, 1987: pE1.

The Kipling Play in two parts (an excerpt); play excerpt, includes introduction. illus · *Descant* Fall 1987; Vol 18 No 3: p31–40.

Laurels in literature; article. *Maclean's* Nov 2, 1987; Vol 100 No 44: p52a–52b.

A literary smorgasbord; review of *The CanLit Foodbook.* photo · *Maclean's* Nov 23, 1987; Vol 100 No 47: p54b.

Lost in translation; review of *The Mournful Demeanor of Lieutenant Boruvka. Books in Can* June-July 1987; Vol 16 No 5: p13–14.

The mermaid inn: the poor relation of the arts; essay. photo · *G&M* Oct 3, 1987: pD6.

Out of this world; review of *Le Coeur découvert. Books in Can* April 1987; Vol 16 No 3: p31–32.

The secret sharer; article. illus · *Sat Night* July 1987; Vol 102 No 7: p39–41.

Sweet are the uses of anthology; essay. *NYT Book R* Aug 23, 1987: p1, 22–23.

Too little too late; review of *The Honorary Patron. Books in Can* Aug-Sept 1987; Vol 16 No 6: p14.

[Untitled]; review of *The Darkest Road. Tor Life* March 1987; Vol 21 No 4: p93, 95.

[Untitled]; review of *Albertine, in Five Times. Books in Can* May 1987; Vol 16 No 4: p22.

[Untitled]; review of *In the Skin of a Lion. Tor Life* May 1987; Vol 21 No 7: p105.

[Untitled]; review of *Le Poison dans l'eau. Books in Can* Nov 1987; Vol 16 No 8: p24–25.

[Untitled]; letter to the editor. *G&M* Oct 17, 1987: pD7.

Manicom, David

Anchor post; poem. *Fiddlehead* Spring 1987; No 151: p60–61.

Broken homes; poem. *Prism* Autumn 1987; Vol 26 No 1: p17–18.

December evening, Montréal; poem. *Fiddlehead* Spring 1987; No 151: p62.

In a station of the Montréal Metro; poem. *Event* March 1987; Vol 16 No 1: p66–67.

An interview with Roo Borson. biog photo · *Rubicon* Spring 1987; No 8: p53–85.

Love alight; poem. *Grain* Winter 1987; Vol 15 No 4: p33.

Lunacy; poem. *Grain* Winter 1987; Vol 15 No 4: p32.

The names are black, winged insects; poem. *Matrix* Spring 1987; No 24: p36.

Passing by; poem. *Poetry Can R* Spring 1987; Vol 8 No 1–2: p15.

Prochaine épisode; poem. *Can Forum* June-July 1987; Vol 67 No 770: p33.

[Untitled]; review of *In Transit. Rubicon* Spring 1987; No 8: p173–176.

[Untitled]; review of *Saturday Nights at the Ritz. Rubicon* Spring 1987; No 8: p216–217.

[Untitled]; review of *Inspecting the Vaults. Rubicon* Fall 1987; No 9: p150–152.

[Untitled]; review of *Sanding Down This Rocking Chair on a Windy Night. Rubicon* Fall 1987; No 9: p184–185.

[Untitled]; review of *The Night the Dog Smiled. Rubicon* Fall 1987; No 9: p199–200.

Worked out; poem. *Prism* Summer 1987; Vol 25 No 4: p116–117.

Manley, Frank

Noah's birds; poem. *Can Lit* Spring 1987; No 112: p59.

[Untitled]; review of *Downfall People. Books in Can* Jan-Feb 1987; Vol 16 No 1: p24–25.

Mansbridge, Francis

[Untitled]; reviews of *Singing Against the Wind* and *A Time for Loving. Poetry Can R* Fall 1987; Vol 9 No 1: p30.

Manseau, Pierre

Les bonnes oeuvres du frère Quiet; short story. *Moebius* Summer 1987; No 33: p39–46.

Manson, Jane

In control; short story. photo · *TS* Aug 10, 1987: pD7.

Manson, Ruth

Best picks of feminism; review of *Fireworks. G&M* May 2, 1987: pC18.

Escapes into feminine victimization; review of *Illusions. G&M* July 25, 1987: pC16.

[Untitled]; review of *The Bridge Out of Town. Quill & Quire* March 1987; Vol 53 No 3: p71.

Manthorpe, Jonathan

Sale of magazine stalled over debt; article. *CH* July 4, 1987: pC6.

Marchamps, Guy

[Untitled]; review of *Indigo nuit. Estuaire* Winter 1986–87; No 43: p76–77.

Marchand, Blaine

After all; poem. *Arc* Fall 1987; No 19: p74.

Breaking the myths about the Canada Council: literary officer Robert Richard's inside view of Council operations; article. *Cross Can Writ Q* 1987; Vol 9 No 3–4: p28–29, 57.

Emblem; poem. *Arc* Fall 1987; No 19: p73–74.

Marchand, Clément

[Untitled]; prose poem. *Estuaire* Autumn 1987; No 46: p7.

[Untitled]; prose poem. *Estuaire* Autumn 1987; No 46: p8.

Marcotte, Gilles

Poésie de novembre; article. illus · *Voix et images* Winter 1987; No 35: p239–249.

Pour mémoire; article. *Liberté* Feb 1987; Vol 29 No 1: p39–45.

Margoshes, Dave

Anthology samples Prairie writing; review of *The Old Dance. CH* Feb 22, 1987: pE6.

Arguing with science; poem. *Can Lit* Summer-Fall 1987; No 113–114: p91–92.

The ballad of the man who shat snakes; short story. *Grain* Winter 1987; Vol 15 No 4: p36–41.

Delicacy, humor mark wry novel; review of *Getting Married in Buffalo Jump. CH* Oct 11, 1987: pE6.

A different kind of Quebec; review of *Invisible Fictions. G&M* July 18, 1987: pC15.

Fascinating trio comes to grips with aging; review of *Memory Board. CH* Nov 29, 1987: pE6.

I am a gateman; short story. *Matrix* Spring 1987; No 24: p18–29.

Turning back the clock; poem. *Poetry Can R* Summer 1987; Vol 8 No 4: p19.

Marin, Richard

CanLit's queen gets one cold shoulder from U.S.; article. illus · *MG* Jan 31, 1987: pB7.

Marken, Ron

[Untitled]; theatre review of *Melody Farm. Maclean's* Feb 23, 1987; Vol 100 No 8: p55.

Markin, Allan

[Untitled]; review of *Dancing Visions. Poetry Can R* Spring 1987; Vol 8 No 2–3: p60.

[Untitled]; review of *Out of the Willow Trees. Poetry Can R* Fall 1987; Vol 9 No 1: p33.

Markle-Craine, Sylvia

One miss, one hit; reviews of *And I'm Never Coming Back* and *Madam Piccolo and the Craziest Pickle Party Ever. Can Child Lit* 1987; No 48: p100–102.

Marlatt, Daphne

Channel time; poem. *Cross Can Writ Q* 1987; Vol 9 No 3–4: p14.

River run; poem. *Cross Can Writ Q* 1987; Vol 9 No 3–4: p15.

[Untitled]; prose excerpt from *Ana Historic*. illus · *Can Forum* June-July 1987; Vol 67 No 770: p27–33.

[Untitled]; prose excerpt from *Ana Historic. West Coast R* Spring 1987; Vol 21 No 4: p12–22.

[Untitled]; poetry excerpts from *Double Negative. Writing* Nov 1987; No 19: p21–29.

[Untitled]; prose excerpt from *Ana Historic,* includes introduction. *Prairie Fire* Winter 1987–88; Vol 8 No 4: p36–41.

Marmier, Jean

[Untitled]; review of *Anne Hébert: architexture romanesque. Études can* June 1987; No 22: p133–134.

Marnoch, J.D.

Roots; letter to the editor. photo · *WFP* Jan 16, 1987: p6.

Marple, Vivian

[Untitled]; poetry excerpts from *Trading Pictures for Stories. Alpha* Winter 1987; Vol 11: p11.

Marquis, André

26 ans d'écriture, deux trajectoires opposées; reviews of *L'Écouté* and *SoirS sans AtouT*. photo · *Lettres québec* Winter 1986–87; No 44: p42–43.

Des livres ou des poètes?; reviews of *La Chevelure de Bérénice* and *Ces étirements du regard*. photo · *Lettres québec* Summer 1987; No 46: p35–36.

Deuxième festival national de la poésie 1986; article. photo · *Lettres québec* Winter 1986–87; No 44: p6.

La métamorphose du quotidien; reviews of poetry books. photo · *Lettres québec* Autumn 1987; No 47: p41–43.

La répétition de l'intime; reviews of poetry books. photo · *Lettres québec* Spring 1987; No 45: p44–46.

[Untitled]; review of *Un Homme et son péché. Moebius (special issue)* Spring 1987; No 32: p119–120.

Marriott, Anne

Death in the Cariboo; poem sequence. *Poetry Can R* Fall 1987; Vol 9 No 1: p15.

Temporaries; short story. *Room of One's Own* Jan 1987; Vol 11 No 2: p44–58.

Marshall, Beverley

He loves me. . . .he loves me not; short story. photo · *TS* Aug 12, 1987: pD6.

Marshall, Joyce

Blood and bone; short story. illus · *Can Forum* Aug-Sept 1987; Vol 67 No 771: p18–23.

Jake's leaps; short story. *Dandelion* Spring-Summer 1987; Vol 14 No 1: p62–71.

Marshall, Scott

The first time; poem. *Alpha* Winter 1987; Vol 11: p31.

Folded; poem. *Alpha* Winter 1987; Vol 11: p31.

Marshall, Tom

Missed connections; review of *In the Skin of a Lion. Books in Can* June-July 1987; Vol 16 No 5: p16.

[Untitled]; reviews of poetry books. *Cross Can Writ Q* 1987; Vol 9 No 1: p24–25.

[Untitled]; review of *Selected Poems II. Poetry Can R* Spring 1987; Vol 8 No 2–3: p40.

[Untitled]; review of *Acadian Poetry Now / Poésie acadienne contemporaine. Poetry Can R* Spring 1987; Vol 8 No 2–3: p48–49.

[Untitled]; prose excerpt from Voices on the Brink. *Quarry* Winter 1987; Vol 36 No 1: p32–39.

[Untitled]; review of *White of the Lesser Angels. U of Windsor R* Fall-Winter 1987; Vol 20 No 1: p94–95.

[Untitled]; poetry excerpt from *Summer Variations. Queen's Q* Summer 1987; Vol 94 No 2: p412–414.

[Untitled]; review of *Collected Poems. Queen's Q* Summer 1987; Vol 94 No 2: p474–475.

[Untitled]; review of *The Collected Poems. Queen's Q* Summer 1987; Vol 94 No 2: p475–477.

[Untitled]; poetry excerpt from *Summer Variations. Poetry Can R* Summer 1987; Vol 8 No 4: p5.

[Untitled]; essay. *Cross Can Writ Q* 1987; Vol 9 No 3–4: p24.

Marteau, Robert

Philosophales; fictional essay. *Liberté* April 1987; Vol 29 No 2: p71–82.

Martens, Debra

The pip; short story. *Room of One's Own* Jan 1987; Vol 11 No 2: p14–21.

[Untitled]; review of *Theatre and Politics in Modern Quebec. Rubicon* Fall 1987; No 9: p177–179.

[Untitled]; review of *Time in the Air. Room of One's Own* Sept 1987; Vol 11 No 4: p115–118.

Martens, Doreen

Choreographer's dance fantasy pieces dramatic, sensuous; column. *WFP* March 23, 1987: p17.

Expect the unexpected in off-beat murder mystery; television review of *Murder Sees the Light. WFP* March 13, 1987: p31.

Greek immigrants populate collection; article. *WFP* Oct 23, 1987: p32.

Loquacious Layton a joy to hear; television review of *Poet: Irving Layton Observed*. photo · *WFP* July 25, 1987: p47.

Manitobans get month in spotlight on CBC TV, radio; column. *WFP* Feb 23, 1987: p14.

Tammy saw cats on wings; column. *WFP* Aug 12, 1987: p21.

Washing Machine gives hilarious twist to technophobia tale; television review. photo · *WFP* March 21, 1987: p25.

A Way Out may not thrill residents of Beausejour; column. *WFP* March 14, 1987: p23.

Martin, André

[Untitled]; essay. *Estuaire* Summer 1987; No 45: p23–24.

Martin, Eva

Pulp science fiction: slick adventures in a moral void; reviews of *Clone Patrol* and *Satellite Skyjack. Quill & Quire (Books for Young People)* June 1987; Vol 53 No 6: p8.

Traditional tales made new again with super illustrations; reviews of *The Dragon* and *The Lucky Old Woman. Quill & Quire (Books for Young People)* Aug 1987; Vol 53 No 8: p7.

[Untitled]; reviews of *Orca's Song* and *Raven Returns the Water. Quill & Quire (Books for Young People)* Oct 1987; Vol 53 No 10: p23.

Martin, Norma

Catharine Parr Traill; letter to the editor. *G&M* Feb 28, 1987: pD7.

Martin, Raymond

[Untitled]; reviews. *Moebius* Winter 1987; No 31: p164–166.

Martin, Robert

The Gipper and The Jaw spice up Tartuffe; article. photo · *G&M* April 10, 1987: pC9.

Martin, Sandra

The big menace; reviews of *I'll Make You Small* and *Mischief City. G&M* Jan 17, 1987: pE18.

Inventive illustrator works magic with a rainy day; article. illus photo · *G&M* July 4, 1987: pC5.

Writers of the 'foul literature of glory'; review of *The Great War of Words. G&M* Oct 24, 1987: pC19.

Martin, W.R.

Family relations in Alice Munro's fiction; article. *New Q* Spring-Summer 1987; Vol 7 No 1–2: p247–254.

Martindale, Sheila

[Untitled]; reviews of poetry books. *Cross Can Writ Q* 1987; Vol 9 No 2: p20–21.

Martiniuk, Lorraine

Far enough down any road; poem. *Dandelion* Spring-Summer 1987; Vol 14 No 1: p18.

Martino, Mauro

Tonight it's my grandfather; poem. *Cross Can Writ Q* 1987; Vol 9 No 2: p15.

Marty, Sid

At the breaking of drought; poem. *Malahat R* Sept 1987; No 80: p110.

First rain of summer; poem. *NeWest R* Sept 1987; Vol 13 No 1: p14.

Funny how things go on; poem. *Prairie Fire* Summer 1987; Vol 8 No 2: p21.

Hunting elk; poem. *NeWest R* Sept 1987; Vol 13 No 1: p14.

Lane is chained to rock of reality; review of *Selected Poems*. *CH* Dec 13, 1987: pC8.

Medicine; poem. *Grain* Winter 1987; Vol 15 No 4: p74–75.

Sky humour; poem. *Malahat R* Sept 1987; No 80: p111.

Sweatshop atmosphere wrong place to encourage real poetry; letter to the editor. photo · *CH* Aug 30, 1987: pB4.

You had to be there; poem. *Prairie Fire* Summer 1987; Vol 8 No 2: p20.

Mason, Michael A.

Canadian servicemen's memoirs of the Second World War; article. *Mosaic* Fall 1987; Vol 20 No 4: p11–22.

Massel, Dona Paul

The burning of toast; poem. *New Q* Spring-Summer 1987; Vol 7 No 1–2: p184.

The eyes of the future; poem. *New Q* Spring-Summer 1987; Vol 7 No 1–2: p185–186.

Massoutre, Guylaine

À propos de Jean Tétreau, Hertel l'homme et l'oeuvre; review. *Voix et images* Spring 1987; Vol 12 No 3: p527–530.

Mastai, Judith

Now more than ever; article. photo · *Can Theatre R* Winter 1987; No 53: p7–10.

Masters, John

New video law keeps Vancouver's accent on lust; column. *TS* Jan 10, 1987: pK4.

Matchan, Linda

Author calls free-trade deal a disaster; article. photo · *CH* Oct 11, 1987: pE7.

Matheson, Sue

Problems; review of *Small Horses and Intimate Beasts*. *Prairie Fire* Summer 1987; Vol 8 No 2: p68–69.

Matheson, Tracy Shepherd

[Untitled]; review of *Masques of Morality*. *Books in Can* Oct 1987; Vol 16 No 7: p21.

Mathews, Lawrence

Pissing in the parking lot; review of *Felice: A Travelogue*. *Essays on Can Writ* Winter 1987; No 35: p147–151.

Matson, Patricia

Everything by thought waves; reviews of short story collections. *Event* March 1987; Vol 16 No 1: p97–100.

Mattson, Nancy

Maria does the ironing; poem. *NeWest R* Sept 1987; Vol 13 No 1: p6.

Maria sews a wedding dress; poem. *NeWest R* Sept 1987; Vol 13 No 1: p6.

Talisman; poem. *NeWest R* Sept 1987; Vol 13 No 1: p6.

Maudsley, Marla

Book about a funny dog; review of *The Dog Who Wouldn't Be*. *TS* March 1, 1987: pA17.

Maviglia, Joseph

Carlo's dream; poem. *Can Forum* April 1987; Vol 67 No 768: p42.

The job is God; poem. *Can Forum* Jan 1987; Vol 66 No 765: p40.

The light bounce; poem. *Arc* Fall 1987; No 19: p75.

Navigation; poem. *Event* March 1987; Vol 16 No 1: p40.

May, Cedric

Dire l'exode: l'oeuvre d'A.M. Klein; article. *Ellipse* 1987; No 37: p57–69.

Mayer, Ian

Recalling the best of CBC radio drama; article. *G&M* Nov 14, 1987: pC20.

Maynard, Rona

Canada's queen of crime fiction; biographical article. photo · *Chatelaine* April 1987; Vol 60 No 4: p108–109.

Mayne, Seymour

[Untitled]; biographical articles. *Brick (special issue)* Summer 1987; No 30: ppassim.

Mays, John Bentley

Fraser to be editor of Saturday Night; article. photo · *G&M* July 17, 1987: pD11.

Solving the perfect culture crime; article. photo · *G&M* Jan 1, 1987: pC3.

Splash of grey heralds Saturday Night centenary; article. photo · *G&M* Jan 5, 1987: pC9.

McAdam, Rhona

The family hour; poem. *New Q* Spring-Summer 1987; Vol 7 No 1–2: p155–156.

TV 1; poem. *New Q* Spring-Summer 1987; Vol 7 No 1–2: p152–154.

Viewing the new world; poem. *Antigonish R* Winter 1987; No 68: p111.

McAllister, Lesley

Acorn's poems pro-life; review of *The Uncollected Acorn*. *TS* June 13, 1987: pM4.

All about women and relationships; reviews of *Housebroken* and *Frogs*. *TS* Jan 3, 1987: pM6.

Each to her own rhythm; reviews of poetry books. *TS* July 25, 1987: pM5.

Random musings of a middle-aged middle-class male; reviews of poetry books. *TS* Oct 10, 1987: pM4.

Seasons, time and memory; reviews of poetry books. *TS* March 21, 1987: pM5.

Under dark cover of stark militarism; review of *A Long Night of Death*. *TS* April 25, 1987: pM7.

[Untitled]; reviews of *August Nights* and *Jokes for the Apocalypse*. *Cross Can Writ Q* 1987; Vol 9 No 2: p24.

[Untitled]; reviews of *Under the House* and *A Forest for Zoe*. *Cross Can Writ Q* 1987; Vol 9 No 3–4: p48–49.

Women are the root of all change; reviews of *The Unravelling* and *The Merzbook*. photo · *TS* Nov 14, 1987: pM4.

Words move unrestrained and with joy across pages; review of *The Martyrology* (Book Six). *TS* June 20, 1987: pM4.

McAteer, Michael

A priest taking life one day at a time; article. photo · *TS* May 23, 1987: pM17.

Reaching out to little children through books; article. photo · *TS* Dec 12, 1987: pM15.

McAuley, John

Paradox; poem. *Poetry Can R* Fall 1987; Vol 9 No 1: p17.

McBride, Daniel

[Untitled]; review of *Sacrifices*. *Tor South Asian R* Summer 1987; Vol 6 No 1: p83–85.

McBurney, Margaret

A bad poet rates title; letter to the editor. *G&M* July 29, 1987: pA7.

McCaffery, Steve

[Untitled]; poetry excerpt from *What Else Should a Rubber Stamp Say?*; · *Open Letter (special issue)* Fall 1987; Vol 6 No 9: p59–66.

McCallion, Jean

Algoma; poem. *Northward J* 1987; No 40: p57.

Circus performer; poem. *Northward J* 1987; No 40: p57.

Colour it granite; poem. *Northward J* 1987; No 40: p54.

Glacier stones; poem. *Northward J* 1987; No 40: p55.

Northern autumn morning; poem. *Northward J* 1987; No 40: p56.

The oak; poem. *Northward J* 1987; No 40: p57.

To gather stones; poem. *Northward J* 1987; No 40: p55.

Tough roots; poem. *Northward J* 1987; No 40: p56.

McCallum, Paddy

Close-up magic; poem. *Can Lit* Winter 1987; No 115: p24–25.

Gifts; poem. *Can Lit* Winter 1987; No 115: p24.

The lost son; poem. *Can Lit* Winter 1987; No 115: p25–26.

The poetry of George Jehoshaphat Mountain; poem. *Can Lit* Winter 1987; No 115: p26–27.

McCann, Peggy

The palace; short story. *New Q* Fall 1987; Vol 7 No 3: p20–30.

McCarthy, Dermot

The dying generations; reviews of poetry books. *Essays on Can Writ* Spring 1987; No 34: p24–32.

On the beach at Bayfield, with Jacques, August '83; poem. *CV 2* Spring 1987; Vol 10 No 3: p43.

McCarthy, Richard

Entertaining; letter to the editor. *WFP* Nov 7, 1987: p7.

McCartney, Sharon

Barrhead; poem. *New Q* Fall 1987; Vol 7 No 3: p84.

In the Blood reserve; poem. *New Q* Fall 1987; Vol 7 No 3: p85.

Not now; poem. *Prism* Spring 1987; Vol 25 No 3: p66.

Sunkist; poem. *Prism* Spring 1987; Vol 25 No 3: p65.

McCaw, Kim

"The missing story"; introduction to play excerpt from *The Revival*. *Prairie Fire* Spring 1987; Vol 8 No 1: p42–43.

McCawley, Mark

Tapestry; poem. *Fiddlehead* Spring 1987; No 151: p21.

McClelland, Jack

Margaret Laurence; essay. bibliog photo · *Quill & Quire* Feb 1987; Vol 53 No 2: p9.

McClelland, Maggie D.

Cool tale captures mystique of North; review of *The Cremation of Sam McGee*; · *CH* Feb 25, 1987: pE1.

McColl, Len

Go gentle into that good diary; short story. photo · *TS* Aug 17, 1987: pC28.

McComb, Pat

The spring Krista went to the park; short story. photo · *TS* Aug 23, 1987: pD5.

McConnel, Frances Ruhlen

[Untitled]; review of *Learning by Heart*. illus · *NYT Book R* Aug 2, 1987: p16.

McCormack, Eric

Home; short story. *Descant* Winter 1987; Vol 18 No 4: p51–54.

Peace comes dropping slow; short story. *Descant* Winter 1987; Vol 18 No 4: p55–58.

McCormack, Thelma

Body & language; review of *In the Feminine. Can Lit* Winter 1987; No 115: p142–144.

[Untitled]; review of *Subversive Elements. Atlantis* Fall 1987; Vol 13 No 1: p191–193.

McCormick, Marion

Border voices speak language of literature; article. illus · *MG* July 10, 1987: pJ5.

Elizabeth Smart: love left her battered, but not wrecked; review of *Necessary Secrets.* photo · *MG* Jan 10, 1987: pB8.

Literary 'exiles' came to Canada from choice, not need; review of *Varieties of Exile. MG* Jan 3, 1987: pB8.

The mystery of Mary Swann, poet, farmwife and murder victim, is more like a comedy of manners; review of *Swann: A Mystery.* photo · *MG* Oct 31, 1987: pJ12.

Reporter trips over angles of 'light' Indian story; review of *A Dream Like Mine. MG* Nov 21, 1987: pJ12.

The restoration of CanLit; article, includes review. photo · *MG* March 7, 1987: pH10.

Sylvia Fraser frees the Minotaur at the heart of her own labyrinth; review of *My Father's House.* photo · *MG* Oct 3, 1987: pJ11.

McCormick, Patrick

A Christmas poem for our times; poem. illus · *TS* Dec 24, 1987: pC1.

McCutchan, Don

[Untitled]; letter to the editor. *G&M* Nov 20, 1987: pA6.

McDonald, Larry

Beyond the merely competent; reviews of critical works. *Atlan Prov Book R* Sept-Oct 1987; Vol 14 No 3: p11.

Politics, playwriting and Zero Hour; interview with Arthur Milner. photo · *Can Theatre R* Winter 1987; No 53: p43–48.

McDougall, Lori

Annick launches classroom kits; article. *Quill & Quire (Books for Young People)* Oct 1987; Vol 53 No 10: p23–24.

Ragweed still adding up cost of fire; article. *Quill & Quire* Sept 1987; Vol 53 No 9: p71.

McDougall, R.L.

Reappraisals; review of *The Thomas Chandler Haliburton Symposium. Can Lit* Spring 1987; No 112: p186–188.

McDougall, Robert L.

Dear George; essay. *Malahat R (special issue)* March 1987; No 78: p27–32.

McDougall, Tom

Canadian content updates classic 17th-century satire; theatre review of *Tartuffe.* photo · *CH* April 13, 1987: pF3.

McElroy, Gil

Building a background of understanding; poem. *Northward J* 1987; No 41: p33–34.

Humans, in manipulating possible dimensions; poem. *Northward J* 1987; No 41: p34.

Targets; poem. *Northward J* 1987; No 41: p35.

Young diamonds; poem. *Northward J* 1987; No 41: p34.

McElroy, James

[Untitled]; reviews of poetry books. *Poetry Can R* Fall 1987; Vol 9 No 1: p36.

McEwen, Alec

Author deserves a fair hearing; letter to the editor. photo · *Fin Post* Nov 23, 1987: p19.

McEwen, Barbara

[Untitled]; review of *Études littéraires. Theatre Hist in Can* Fall 1987; Vol 8 No 2: p234–237.

McFadden, David

Blue irises; poem. *Malahat R* Sept 1987; No 80: p29.

Elephants; poem. *Malahat R* Sept 1987; No 80: p25.

The inchworm; poem. *Malahat R* Sept 1987; No 80: p27.

Love's like milk; poem. *Malahat R* Sept 1987; No 80: p23.

Shantideva; poem. *Malahat R* Sept 1987; No 80: p26.

Terrible storm on Lake Erie; poem. *Malahat R* Sept 1987; No 80: p28.

Torn between love and loyalty; reviews of *Sir Charles God Damn* and *Sir Charles G.D. Roberts: A Biography.* photo · *Brick* Fall 1987; No 31: p55–59.

A visit to the zoo; poem. *Malahat R* Sept 1987; No 80: p24.

McGauley, Laurie-Ann

Super(stack) inspiration; essay. photo · *Can Theatre R* Winter 1987; No 53: p35–38.

McGehee, Peter

The ballad of Hank McCaul; poem. *Event* March 1987; Vol 16 No 1: p86–91.

Goldfish; short story. *Waves* Spring 1987; Vol 15 No 4: p31–34.

Goldfish; short story. photo · *TS* June 30, 1987: pA16.

McGillivray, Mary

[Untitled]; reviews of *The Collected Poems of Sir Charles G.D. Roberts* and *Sir Charles God Damn. Queen's Q* Winter 1987; Vol 94 No 4: p1039–1042.

McGoogan, Kenneth

100-year-old magazine filled with literary gems; column. *CH* Jan 25, 1987: pE4.

Alberta foundation a boon to the arts; article. *Quill & Quire* Feb 1987; Vol 53 No 2: p10–11.

Alberta writers to fight 'censorship' bill; column. *CH* Nov 29, 1987: pE6.

Ancestors inspire novelist; column. biog photo · *CH* May 31, 1987: pF5.

As for me and my horse; review of *Caprice*. *Books in Can* June-July 1987; Vol 16 No 5: p15–16.

Author interviews hit airwaves; column. *CH* April 18, 1987: pE5.

Author's favorite comic pieces 'came in an unbidden moment'; article. photo · *CH* Oct 23, 1987: pF1.

Autumn promises Canadian book bonanza; preview of fall book list. *CH* June 21, 1987: pE5.

Banff Centre lands novelist; column. *CH* Feb 22, 1987: pE6.

Big day for literary fund-raisers; column. *CH* Oct 18, 1987: pC7.

Bizarre tale dark, quirky and Rendell; review of *Rue du Bac*. *CH* Oct 4, 1987: pE6.

Book beat's busy next week; article. *CH* Feb 4, 1987: pF4.

Book puts Calgary on literary map; review of *Between Men*. photo · *CH* Sept 5, 1987: pH7.

Calgary attracting superstars to Olympic literary festival; article. photo · *Quill & Quire* Oct 1987; Vol 53 No 10: p9.

Calgary poets dominate nationwide competition; article. *CH* July 30, 1987: pC2.

Calgary project makes kids published writers; article. *Quill & Quire (Books for Young People)* June 1987; Vol 53 No 6: p4.

Calgary writers clean up; article. photo · *CH* May 10, 1987: pE2.

Calgary writers take top honors; column. *CH* April 9, 1987: pE7.

Canadian crime fiction emerges from the shadows; article. illus · *CH* April 13, 1987: pF1.

Culture director's tribute to author captured sentiment; column. photo · *CH* Jan 27, 1987: pB6.

Dandelion uncovers new voice; column. photo · *CH* Feb 1, 1987: pC8.

Daring diner date jogs writer; column. photo · *CH* Dec 20, 1987: pE6.

Daring novel rewarding read; review of *Adele at the End of the Day*. *CH* April 26, 1987: pE5.

Editor's ethnic tale wins short-story event; article. *CH* June 27, 1987: pA8.

Experts offered the write advice; article. photo · *CH* April 6, 1987: pD6.

Fall promises plethora from publishers; preview of fall book list. photo · *CH* July 14, 1987: pB6.

Fantasy becomes winning author's reality; article. photo · *CH* March 17, 1987: pC7.

Festival attracts glitterati; column. *CH* Sept 27, 1987: pE6.

Festival attracts kids' writers; column. *CH* Sept 20, 1987: pE6.

Festival winds bring W.O. home; column. *CH* March 1, 1987: pC8.

Fiery MacLennan defends late Margaret Laurence; article. *CH* May 31, 1987: pF2.

Fine art of writing: Banff Centre nurtures authors, playwrights, screenwriters; article. photo · *CH* May 16, 1987: pC1.

Firm has an ear for kids' books; article. *CH* Feb 17, 1987: pC7.

First novel turned into TV movie; column. *CH* May 3, 1987: pE6.

Foundaion awards new round of grants; article. *CH* Dec 10, 1987: pF2.

Francis has winner in new whodunit; review of *The Last White Man in Panama*. *CH* Nov 1, 1987: pE6.

Free trade imperils identity; column. *CH* Dec 13, 1987: pC9.

From P.E.I. to Big Apple; review of *A Body Surrounded by Water*. *CH* Aug 2, 1987: pC8.

Heart of the city; review of *Between Men*. *Books in Can* Aug-Sept 1987; Vol 16 No 6: p18–19.

Hot money and grizzly tales hit the presses this spring; preview of spring book list. *CH* Feb 6, 1987: pD1.

J.P. Donleavy here in '88; column. *CH* July 26, 1987: pE5.

Kinsella displays new range; review of *Red Wolf, Red Wolf*. photo · *CH* Aug 30, 1987: pE4.

Lee cooks up Alligator Pie for adults; review of *The Difficulty of Living on Other Planets*. *CH* Nov 8, 1987: pE6.

Legendary Leaf proved inspiration to Toronto novelist; article. *CH* Dec 7, 1987: pB6.

Libraries given bulk of grants; article. *CH* Aug 27, 1987: pC5.

Literary arts at Calgary Olympics; article. *Quill & Quire* Feb 1987; Vol 53 No 2: p11.

Literary arts foundation doles out another $190,000; article. *CH* March 11, 1987: pD2.

Literary extravaganza goes national; column. *CH* April 5, 1987: pE5.

Literary giants got rotten reviews; column. *CH* Jan 18, 1987: pE4.

Literary world loses a champion; column. *CH* July 12, 1987: pE4.

Manitoban attracts nationwide attention; column. photo · *CH* April 12, 1987: pF7.

McClelland's retirement marks end of an era; article. photo · *CH* Feb 24, 1987: pF5.

McDonald scores with Canada's booksellers; article. *CH* June 30, 1987: pE1.

Metcalf chairs debate; column. *CH* March 8, 1987: pE5.

More surprises from Kinsella; column. *CH* Sept 13, 1987: pE5.

Mother and son; review of *Adele at the End of the Day*. *Books in Can* April 1987; Vol 16 No 3: p20.

Noted authors to attend; article. *CH* April 28, 1987: pC7.

Novel tourney nears; article. illus · *CH* Aug 28, 1987: pC1.

Oilpatch geologist mines for literary success; article. photo · *CH* April 3, 1987: pC1.

Olympic readings scheduled; article. *CH* Oct 1, 1987: pD1.

Paperback PIs battle crime; review of *A City Called July*. photo · *CH* Sept 6, 1987: pE7.

Paperny takes giant step with new novel; biographical article. photo · *CH* Feb 21, 1987: pG1.

Poets fare best under payment scheme, says chairman; article. *CH* May 1, 1987: pE4.

Poets help celebrate Dandelion; column. *CH* June 28, 1987: pF8.

Poets propelled by Thistledown; article. *CH* April 12, 1987: pF2.

Promising literary debut made by young mother; review of *The Woman Upstairs*. biog photo · *CH* May 10, 1987: pE5.

Putting pen to paper could reap $1,000; article. *CH* Feb 4, 1987: pF1.

Red Deer Press lauches series; column. photo · *CH* Nov 22, 1987: pA16.

Short-story prize doubled for winner; column. *CH* May 24, 1987: pE6.

Smart-aleck of Can-Lit scores again; review of *Caprice*. photo · *CH* May 17, 1987: pE5.

Storm brewing in literary heaven; column. *CH* Jan 11, 1987: pF4.

Successful Alberta children's writers pen new works; article. photo · *CH* Dec 18, 1987: pE7.

Third time lucky for rising author; article. photo · *CH* Nov 16, 1987: pB3.

Tribute to author planned; article. photo · *CH* Jan 16, 1987: pF1.

U of A alumna wins novel contest; column. *CH* April 2, 1987: pD14.

Vancouver man wins pulp prize; article. *CH* Nov 11, 1987: pA18.

Western voice strengthened in publishers association; article. photo · *CH* March 24, 1987: pD1.

Whodunits hit bookshelves in big way; review of *Gallows View*. *CH* June 7, 1987: pE6.

Writers, publishers, libraries rejoice; column. *CH* June 14, 1987: pE6.

Writers' event grows on young people; column. *CH* March 29, 1987: pE5.

Writers plan on doing it with style; column. *CH* March 22, 1987: pF5.

Writers' union condemns censorship bill; article. photo · *CH* June 2, 1987: pF6.

Youth writers flourish in Alberta; article. photo · *CH* Feb 21, 1987: pG1.

McGrath, Carmelita

Avondale; poem. *Waves* Spring 1987; Vol 15 No 4: p69.

Spring?; poem. *Waves* Spring 1987; Vol 15 No 4: p70.

Western Cove revisited; poem. *Waves* Spring 1987; Vol 15 No 4: p70–71.

McGrath, Joan

Beatrix Potter better than ever; reviews of *Nobody Said It Would Be Easy* and *Log Jam*. *TS* April 25, 1987: pM4.

Big responsibilities theme of tall tale and growing-up story; reviews of *The Doll* and *Jacob's Little Giant*. photo · *Quill & Quire (Books for Young People)* Aug 1987; Vol 53 No 8: p11.

Current crop of kids' books is brighter than spring gardens; reviews of *Pop Bottles* and *A Handful of Time*. *TS* May 24, 1987: pA19.

A dragon stands on guard; review of *A Book Dragon*. *TS* Dec 20, 1987: pE5.

Family ties and mysteries; reviews of children's novels. *Quill & Quire (Books for Young People)* Dec 1987; Vol 53 No 12: p10.

Freeman and Crook offer adventure and mystery in serial form; reviews of *Danger on the Tracks* and *Payment in Death*. photo · *Quill & Quire (Books for Young People)* April 1987; Vol 53 No 4: p9.

Heartless violence of terrorism explored in this numbing novel; review of *Equinox*. *TS* June 13, 1987: pM4.

The jolly fireplace's darker side; reviews of children's books. *TS* Nov 22, 1987: pC8.

Literary lions linger in libraries; reviews of children's books. *TS* Dec 20, 1987: pE5.

A little help on the dull days; reviews of children's books. *TS* Aug 2, 1987: pC11.

Little's achievements simply huge; reviews of *Little by Little* and *Her Special Vision*. *TS* Nov 29, 1987: pA21.

Lively story of immigrants needs a sequel; review of *Tuppence Ha'penny Is a Nickel*. *TS* Aug 30, 1987: pA19.

A lovely, polished tree tale; review of *Tranter's Tree*. *TS* June 7, 1987: pG11.

Readers, writers of tomorrow; column. *TS* July 5, 1987: pA18.

Tales that will tempt tots of all ages; review of *Mad Queen of Mordra*. *TS* Sept 19, 1987: pM6.

Thrills and chills: hints for Hallowe'en reading; reviews of children's books. illus · *Quill & Quire (Books for Young People)* Oct 1987; Vol 53 No 10: p8.

A title that will grab teenagers; reviews of children's books. *TS* Oct 25, 1987: pA18.

[Untitled]; review of *The Perfect Circus*. *Quill & Quire* March 1987; Vol 53 No 3: p72–73.

[Untitled]; review of *Nobody Said It Would Be Easy*. *Quill & Quire (Books for Young People)* April 1987; Vol 53 No 4: p10.

[Untitled]; review of *The Butterfly Chair*. *Quill & Quire* Sept 1987; Vol 53 No 9: p78–79.

[Untitled]; review of *Greenapple Street Blues*. *Quill & Quire (Books for Young People)* Oct 1987; Vol 53 No 10: p19, 22.

McGrath, Leslie

[Untitled]; reviews of *The Fusion Factor* and *Zanu*. *Quill & Quire (Books for Young People)* June 1987; Vol 53 No 6: p9–10.

McGrath, Robin

Down in the crisper; poem. *Northward J* 1987; No 43: p35.

McGraw, Margaret

[Untitled]; review of *Private and Fictionalized Words. Books in Can* Nov 1987; Vol 16 No 8: p24.

McGuirk, Kevin

People walk my street at evening; poem. *Matrix* Fall 1987; No 25: p74.

Snowy night; poem. *Antigonish R* 1987; No 69–70: p10.

McIlroy, Randal

Acting sparkles in insulting play; theatre review of *Letter from Wingfield Farm. WFP* Nov 26, 1987: p79.

Anne of Green Gables bland as porridge; theatre review. *WFP* Dec 20, 1987: p20.

Bear gives lesson in keeping identity; theatre review of *I Am a Bear! WFP* Oct 10, 1987: p48.

Bedouins voluminous toy chest filled with witty, wordy delight; theatre review of *Don't Blame the Bedouins. WFP* Nov 13, 1987: p35.

Black comedy neither dark nor funny; theatre review of *Mum. WFP* March 6, 1987: p20.

Children's play provides dizzy gaiety, excitement; theatre review of *Snowsuits, Birthdays, & Giants! WFP* Dec 20, 1987: p21.

Dinner theatre play leaves bland aftertaste; theatre review of *The Melville Boys. WFP* Nov 4, 1987: p43.

Evangelical lampoon offers lightweight fun; theatre review of *The 101 Miracles of Hope Chance. WFP* Nov 20, 1987: p35.

Indecisive play fails to elicit empathy for young characters; theatre review of *Rock Is Dead. WFP* July 25, 1987: p48.

Intriguing idea poses performance problems; review of *Anna. WFP* June 28, 1987: p24.

Play lacks strong shape; theatre review of *Bordertown Cafe. WFP* Oct 2, 1987: p19.

McInnes, Nadine

Loss; poem. *Fireweed* Winter 1987; No 24: p67.

McKay, Ally

Call night; short story. *Quarry* Spring 1987; Vol 36 No 2: p14–24.

Fire; short story. *Grain* Winter 1987; Vol 15 No 4: p24–29.

Necessary Orpheus; short story. *Event* Summer 1987; Vol 16 No 2: p16–24.

McKay, Don

Domestic animals; poem. *Malahat R* Dec 1987; No 81: p28–29.

Ink Lake; poem. *Dandelion* Spring-Summer 1987; Vol 14 No 1: p29–35.

Luke & co.; poem. *Malahat R* Dec 1987; No 81: p23–25.

Plantation; poem. *Malahat R* Dec 1987; No 81: p26–27.

McKay, Sharon E.

Ingenuity needed to encourage kids to read; article. *TS (Neighbors)* Dec 8, 1987: p21.

McKellar, Hugh

Adventure in corners of Canada; reviews of *St. Vitus Dance* and *Our Hero in the Cradle of Confederation. TS* Aug 23, 1987: pA20.

Enduring a thankless existence with father; reviews of *Black Swan* and *Small Regrets. TS* Jan 31, 1987: pM4.

Reader left with agreeable sense of déjà vu; reviews of *Beneath the Western Slopes* and *The Woman Upstairs. TS* Aug 9, 1987: pA21.

Top felon worth troop of bumblers; review of *The Hollow Woman. TS* April 18, 1987: pM4.

McKenzie-Porter, Patricia

Space of white; poem. *Poetry Can R* Fall 1987; Vol 9 No 1: p19.

McKie, Paul

All Sales Final subtle family drama focusing on lost romance, death; column. photo · *WFP* Oct 17, 1987: p30.

Anne sequel wonderfully fresh fare amid TV drudgery; television review of *Anne of Green Gables: The Sequel.* photo · *WFP* Dec 4, 1987: p35.

Get new year off to good start with Dancing In The Dark; film review. photo · *WFP* Jan 4, 1987: p14.

Moliere's farce gets modern twist; television review of *Tartuffe.* photo · *WFP* Oct 1, 1987: p40.

Niagara Falls boring television; television review. photo · *WFP* Nov 9, 1987: p22.

Pinsent tells touching story; film review of *John and the Missus.* photo · *WFP* April 19, 1987: p15.

Selling doesn't mean selling out; article. photo · *WFP* Oct 24, 1987: p22.

Winkler catches Layton on film; article. photo · *WFP* Feb 27, 1987: p33.

McKinney, Christine

Barren grounds; poem. *Northward J* 1987; No 40: p58.

Lost in white; poem. *Northward J* 1987; No 40: p59.

The swan; poem. *Northward J* 1987; No 40: p59.

McKinney, Louise

Dubois' dramatic debut; article. *Tor Life* April 1987; Vol 21 No 5: p18.

Roman heartbeat; reviews of *The Other Shore* and *Moving Landscape. Can Lit* Winter 1987; No 115: p232–234.

McLean, Anne

I married the father of the neutron bomb; short story. *Quarry* Spring 1987; Vol 36 No 2: p43–57.

McLean, Celia

Forward. *New Q* Spring-Summer 1987; Vol 7 No 1–2: p229–231.

McLeod, Bruce

Margaret Laurence slaked a human thirst; column. *TS* Jan 13, 1987: pA15.

McManus, Bruce

An excerpt from Act 2 of Schedules. *Prairie Fire* Spring 1987; Vol 8 No 1: p51–55.

McMaster, Susan

[Untitled]; poem. *Cross Can Writ Q* 1987; Vol 9 No 3–4: p18.

Word-music: notation for the spoken voice; essay. illus · *Quarry* Summer 1987; Vol 36 No 3: p62–69.

McMurray, Line

Le corps extrême de l'esprit-machine; essay. bibliog biog · *La Nouvelle barre du jour (special issue)* 1987; No 201–202: p97–111.

McMurtry, Jim

Laurence deserves honor; letter to the editor. *G&M* Jan 21, 1987: pA7.

McNamara, Eugene

Adagio; poem. *U of Windsor R* Fall-Winter 1987; Vol 20 No 1: p9.

In the springhouse; poem. *U of Windsor R* Fall-Winter 1987; Vol 20 No 1: p10.

Ordinary time; short story. *Fiddlehead* Autumn 1987; No 153: p20–25.

Sailboats; short story. *U of Windsor R* Fall-Winter 1987; Vol 20 No 1: p3–8.

McNamara, Tim

Generous and open; letter to the editor. photo · *G&M* Dec 19, 1987: pD7.

Three Desks: a turning point in James Reaney's drama; article. *Queen's Q* Spring 1987; Vol 94 No 1: p15–32.

McPheron, William

Steve McCaffery's Panopticon; article. photo · *Open Letter (special issue)* Fall 1987; Vol 6 No 9: p49–54.

McPherson, Christopher

Nightmare in parentheses; short story. *Wascana R* Fall 1987; Vol 22 No 2: p30–37.

Paranoia; short story. *Wascana R* Spring 1987; Vol 22 No 1: p58–64.

McRobbie, Kenneth

The acacias of Columbus; poem. *Queen's Q* Winter 1987; Vol 94 No 4: p866–867.

McSween, Donald

[Untitled]; biographical article. *Brick (special issue)* Summer 1987; No 30: p61.

McSweeney, Kerry

Sorceries; review of *Black Robe. Essays on Can Writ* Spring 1987; No 34: p111–118.

Meadwell, Kenneth W.

Italian-Canadian voices; review of *Contrasts. Prairie Fire* Summer 1987; Vol 8 No 2: p72–74.

Simplicité et dynamisme; review of *Alerte ce soir à 22 heures. Can Child Lit* 1987; No 45: p70–71.

Medwid, Angela Marie

[Untitled]; poem. *CV 2* Summer 1987; Vol 10 No 4: p28–29.

We have to shout; review of *Mr Spock Do You Read Me?. CV 2* Summer 1987; Vol 10 No 4: p55–58.

Meier, Ellen Bick

Northern magus; letter to the editor. *Books in Can* June-July 1987; Vol 16 No 5: p40.

Meigs, Mary

[Untitled]; prose excerpt from *La Tête de Méduse*. photo · *MD* Dec 12, 1987: pD1, D10.

Meindl, Dieter

Die Depression der dreiBiger Jahre im amerikanischen und kanadischen Roman; article. abstract · *Zeitschrift Kanada-Studien* 1987; Vol 7 No 1: p193–204.

Meinema, Clarence

Shades of love; poem. *New Q* Spring-Summer 1987; Vol 7 No 1–2: p187.

Melady, Michele

[Untitled]; review of *Flight Against Time. Books in Can* May 1987; Vol 16 No 4: p21.

Melançon, Joseph

L'autonomisation de la littérature: sa taxinomie, ses seuils, sa sémiotique; article. abstract · *Études lit* Spring-Summer 1987; Vol 20 No 1: p17–43.

Melançon, Robert

Belleau; review of *Surprendre les voix. Liberté* April 1987; Vol 29 No 2: p137–139.

De la poésie et de quelques circonstances: entretien avec Jacques Brault; interview. illus · *Voix et images* Winter 1987; No 35: p188–211.

Devenez mécène, abonnez-vous!; reviews of periodicals. *Liberté* June 1987; Vol 29 No 3: p80–87.

Ding et Dong; reviews of periodicals. *Liberté* Dec 1987; Vol 29 No 6: p122–129.

La littérature est inactuelle; reviews of *La Nouvelle barre du jour* and *Le Beffroi. Liberté* Aug 1987; Vol 29 No 4: p102–108.

Ph.D., écrivain; article. *Liberté* Feb 1987; Vol 29 No 1: p32–3.

Trois premiers numéros: Le Beffroi, Filigrane, Kérosène; reviews. *Liberté* April 1987; Vol 29 No 2: p125–128.

Melfi, Mary

Life sentence; poem. *Antigonish R* Winter 1987; No 68: p94.

Melmoth, John

The off-the-wall writing on the wall; review of *Famous Last Words*. *Times Lit Supp* April 24, 1987; No 4386: p435.

Melnyk, George

[Untitled]; review of *Beyond Forget*. photo · *NeWest R* Nov 1987; Vol 13 No 3: p14.

Mendes, Errol P.

Death of a dancer (dead from corporate PCBs); poem. *Can Auth & Book* Summer 1987; Vol 62 No 4: p23.

Méndez, Javier García

Le silence de Trente arpents; article. *Voix et images* Spring 1987; Vol 12 No 3: p452–469.

Mendis, Ranjini

Betrayal runs through short story collection; review of *Home-coming*. *CH* Dec 6, 1987: pD8.

Mennie, James

First novels set to different literary keys; reviews of *Crang Plays the Ace* and *Gallows View*. photo · *MG* April 11, 1987: pG6.

This international thriller is like a long, winding and ultimately pointless safari; review of *Rue du Bac*. *MG* Oct 3, 1987: pJ13.

Menzies, Diane

Foodbook combines recipes, dash of prose; article. photo · *WFP* Nov 18, 1987: p38.

Recipes, poetry, prose a tasty concoction; article. photo · *TS* Dec 2, 1987: pC1, C9.

Merasty, Billy

Beaded, flower-designed wrist-band; prose poem. *Prairie Fire* Autumn 1987; Vol 8 No 3: p86.

Reindeer Lake; prose poem. *Prairie Fire* Autumn 1987; Vol 8 No 3: p87.

Worry; poem. *Prairie Fire* Autumn 1987; Vol 8 No 3: p87.

Merivale, Patricia

Black lyricist; review of *Gilbert La Rocque: l'écriture du rêve*. *Can Lit* Spring 1987; No 112: p124–126.

On both hands; review of *All the Polarities*. *Can Lit* Summer-Fall 1987; No 113–114: p207–212.

Merrett, Robert James

Kinetic space; reviews of poetry books. *Can Lit* Summer-Fall 1987; No 113–114: p241–243.

Merril, Judith

C-54, what are you? Proposed censorship legislation is loony; essay. photo · *Quill & Quire* Dec 1987; Vol 53 No 12: p16–17.

Merrill, Joan

Bank teller; poem. *Room of One's Own* Sept 1987; Vol 11 No 4: p57.

Branch in the water; poem. *Room of One's Own* Sept 1987; Vol 11 No 4: p58–59.

The bum god sits down to supper; poem. *Room of One's Own* Sept 1987; Vol 11 No 4: p60–62.

Messier, Judith

Breaking; short story. *Moebius* Winter 1987; No 31: p111–117.

Sparkolloïd; short story. *Moebius* Summer 1987; No 33: p53–60.

Metcalf, John

Freedom from culture: liberating the Canadian literary world from the subversion of government subsidy; essay. photo · *Cross Can Writ Q* 1987; Vol 9 No 3–4: p27, 53–57.

Metcalfe, Robin

Cats; poem. *Can Forum* Nov 1987; Vol 67 No 773: p42.

Sharon Pollock; interview. photo · *Books in Can* March 1987; Vol 16 No 2: p39–40.

Meyer, Bruce

Two windows: an interview with D.G. Jones. bibliog biog photo · *Poetry Can R* Spring 1987; Vol 8 No 1–2: p3–5.

Meyer, Wm.

Anne Bradstreet: boxing with Beelzebub; poem. *Fiddlehead* Autumn 1987; No 153: p57.

Arriving; poem. *Fiddlehead* Autumn 1987; No 153: p59.

Misunderstood rain; poem. *Fiddlehead* Autumn 1987; No 153: p58.

Michalska, BethMarie

Peaches and war; poem. *Quarry* Winter 1987; Vol 36 No 1: p26.

Michaud, Ginette

Le cru et le cuit; review of *Toute la terre à dévorer*. *Liberté* Aug 1987; Vol 29 No 4: p115–120.

Philosophie et littérature en revue(s): genres et styles mêlés; reviews of *Le Beffroi* and *Sédiments*. *Liberté* April 1987; Vol 29 No 2: p129–133.

Michon, Jacques

Une Amérique d'arrière-cour; review of *Américane*. *MD* Oct 17, 1987: pD3-D4.

Couples; reviews of novels. *Voix et images* Autumn 1987; Vol 13 No 1: p189–192.

Écrire l'histoire ou histoire d'écrire; reviews of novels. *Voix et images* Spring 1987; Vol 12 No 3: p548–550.

Les enfants du déclin; reviews of novels. *Voix et images* Winter 1987; No 35: p331–334.

L'inquiétante étrangeté des récits de Jacques Brossard; review of *Le Sang du souvenir*. *MD* Sept 5, 1987: pC7.

Une rêverie à deux voix; review of *La Cavée*. photo · *MD* June 20, 1987: pD3.

Un roman de jeunesse de Pierre Vallières; review of *Noces obscures*. *MD* May 16, 1987: pD3, D8.

Micros, Marianne

When is a book not a book? The novels of Welwyn Wilton Katz; article. *Can Child Lit* 1987; No 47: p23–28.

Middlebro', Sylvia

Two sensitive poets; reviews of *Some Talk Magic* and *An Armadillo Is Not a Pillow*. *Can Child Lit* 1987; No 46: p99–100.

Middleton, Christopher

Cybele; poem. *Poetry Can R* Summer 1987; Vol 8 No 4: p26.

Mierau, Maurice

The difference between a martyr and a suicide; poem. *Border Cross* Summer 1987; Vol 6 No 3: p20.

Soldiers; poem. *Border Cross* Summer 1987; Vol 6 No 3: p20.

[Untitled]; review of *Visitations*. *Rubicon* Spring 1987; No 8: p217–218.

[Untitled]; review of *Melancholy Ain't No Baby*. *Rubicon* Spring 1987; No 8: p220–221.

Mietkiewicz, Henry

The artist behind Irving Layton's bravado; television review of *Poet: Irving Layton Observed*. photo · *TS* July 30, 1987: pH5.

Berton's memoirs due out in the fall; column. *TS* June 25, 1987: pF3.

'Brightly woven' the right words; review of *The Darkest Road*. *TS* April 5, 1987: pA22.

Bringing sci-fi down to Earth; article. illus · *TS* May 24, 1987: pC1.

David Suzuki set to tell his story in Metamorphosis; column. *TS* April 12, 1987: pC3.

Disciplined acting shines in play etched in despair; theatre review of *Darkness on the Edge of Town*. *TS* May 12, 1987: pF4.

Documentary profiles witty author; television review of *The Lonely Passion of Brian Moore*. photo · *TS* July 22, 1987: pD3.

Dora Awards still waiting for stardom; column. photo · *TS* June 20, 1987: pJ6.

Fulford leaves his Saturday Night post; article. photo · *TS* June 25, 1987: pA2.

Inspired comic shares sharp observations; theatre review of *Dixieland's Night of Shame*. photo · *TS* June 2, 1987: pG3.

John Fraser new Saturday Night editor; column. *TS* July 17, 1987: pE23.

Lolita grows up to get last laughs; article. *TS* May 29, 1987: pE13.

Michael Ondaatje's new novel rocks its way to market; column. *TS* May 21, 1987: pF2.

Movie makers focusing on Canadian authors; column. photo · *TS* July 28, 1987: pC2.

Of fantasies and those magical visits; reviews of science fiction and fantasy books. *TS* Dec 5, 1987: pM19.

Playwright torn between two countries; article. photo · *TS* June 30, 1987: pE2.

Poignancy compensates for failure to comment; theatre review of *Song for Nisei Fishermen*. photo · *TS* May 8, 1987: pD11.

Publisher to cut Sauve anecdote in book of gossip; column. *TS* July 10, 1987: pE23.

Pythagoras mystery makes audience play archeologist; theatre review of *Pythagoras – The Mystery*. *TS* July 24, 1987: pE9.

Rubinek to write novel on escape from Nazis; column. photo · *TS* June 2, 1987: pG3.

Star-spangled shows high-stepping to T.O.; article. photo · *TS* June 26, 1987: pE1, E3.

Sword plays: it's fight for the right to parry; article. photo · *TS* May 8, 1987: pD3.

Tag makes your hair stand on end; theatre review of *Tag in a Ghost Town*. *TS* May 15, 1987: pD11.

Tale hampered by small stage; theatre review of *Young Art*. photo · *TS* Jan 18, 1987: pG3.

Teen hitchhikes back to childhood horror; theatre review of *See Bob Run*. photo · *TS* July 23, 1987: pB4.

Temptonga doesn't let audience in on the plot; theatre review. photo · *TS* April 10, 1987: pD12.

Toronto's busy theatres merit superior magazine; column. *TS* May 20, 1987: pE3.

Well-wrought Anger comedy marred only by false-note finale; theatre review of *The Anger in Ernest and Ernestine*. photo · *TS* May 29, 1987: pE12.

Writers praise Robert Fulford; article. photo · *TS* June 26, 1987: pE25.

Miles, Angela

[Untitled]; review of *Love's Sweet Return*. *Atlantis* Fall 1987; Vol 13 No 1: p185–187.

Miles, Ron

Eyes of children; poem. *Queen's Q* Spring 1987; Vol 94 No 1: p132.

Fine lines & fractures; review of *Immune to Gravity*. *Can Lit* Spring 1987; No 112: p183–185.

Millar, Dianne

[Untitled]; review of *Jacob's Little Giant*. *CH* Dec 6, 1987: pD9.

Millar, Mary

[Untitled]; review of *Miss Abigail's Part*. *Queen's Q* Summer 1987; Vol 94 No 2: p477–478.

[Untitled]; review of *The Progress of Love*. *Queen's Q* Winter 1987; Vol 94 No 4: p1015–1017.

[Untitled]; review of *Adult Entertainment*. *Queen's Q* Winter 1987; Vol 94 No 4: p1024–1026.

Millard, Peter

The Abbotsford; short story. illus · *NeWest R* Dec 1987; Vol 13 No 4: p12–13, 18.

[Untitled]; review of *Beyond Forget*. photo · *NeWest R* Nov 1987; Vol 13 No 3: p15.

Miller, Judith

Rummaging in the sewing basket of the gods: Sheila Watson's "Antigone"; article. *Studies in Can Lit* 1987; Vol 12 No 2: p212–221.

She came through the door; poem. *New Q* Winter 1987; Vol 6 No 4: p83.

The writer-as-a-young-woman and her family: Montgomery's Emily; article. *New Q* Spring-Summer 1987; Vol 7 No 1–2: p301–319.

Miller, Kathleen

Crows; short story. *Capilano R* 1987; No 42: p37–42.

In the blood; short story. *Capilano R* 1987; No 42: p51–55.

The lure; short story. *Capilano R* 1987; No 42: p43–50.

Miller, Mark

Musicians breathe life into poems; review. photo · *G&M* Nov 30, 1987: pC11.

Milliken, Barry

Run; short story. *Can Fic Mag (special issue)* 1987; No 60: p138–143.

Mills, Allen

Evolution of an intellectual; review of *The Politics of the Imagination*. photo · *WFP* Nov 14, 1987: p50.

Mills, John

Fear and loathing in Yucatan; review of *Tourists*. *Essays on Can Writ* Spring 1987; No 34: p133–135.

Stories vivid, unpleasant – and memorable; reviews of short story books. *Fiddlehead* Autumn 1987; No 153: p91–95.

[Untitled]; prose excerpt from *A Place of Disaffection*. *West Coast R* Spring 1987; Vol 21 No 4: p27–47.

Mills, Sparling

At seventeen; poem. *New Q* Spring-Summer 1987; Vol 7 No 1–2: p189.

If Mother gets sick; poem. *New Q* Spring-Summer 1987; Vol 7 No 1–2: p188.

Shakespeare loved violas; poem. *Can Auth & Book* Summer 1987; Vol 62 No 4: p22.

[Untitled]; review of *The Top of the Heart*. *Poetry Can R* Spring 1987; Vol 8 No 2–3: p41–42.

[Untitled]; review of *Deep North*. *Poetry Can R* Spring 1987; Vol 8 No 2–3: p59–60.

[Untitled]; review of *Schizotexte*. *Poetry Can R* Summer 1987; Vol 8 No 4: p38.

[Untitled]; review of *Robert Lovelace: An Examination of the Individual Mind and Its Limits*. *Poetry Can R* Summer 1987; Vol 8 No 4: p38.

[Untitled]; review of *Precious Stones*. *Poetry Can R* Fall 1987; Vol 9 No 1: p30.

Writing a poem; poem. *Prairie J of Can Lit* 1987; No 8: p49.

Millway, Betty

Hubert Evans – elder of the tribe; article. photo · *Can Auth & Book* Winter 1987; Vol 62 No 2: p2–3.

Milne, Heather

Eyes down; short story. photo · *TS* Aug 21, 1987: pA21.

Milner, Arthur

Zero hour; play. illus photo · *Can Theatre R* Winter 1987; No 53: p50–69.

Milnes, Irma McDonough

Saltman's superior guide good news about Canadian books; review of *Modern Canadian Children's Books*. photo · *Quill & Quire (Books for Young People)* April 1987; Vol 53 No 4: p1, 3.

Milot, Louise

Études littéraires est-elle indispensable?; essay. *Voix et images* Winter 1987; No 35: p267–271.

Léonce, Léonil. . . .et Sept fois Jeanne; reviews of *Cette fois, Jeanne. . . .* and *La Double vie de Léonce et Léonil*. photo · *Lettres québec* Autumn 1987; No 47: p17–18.

Une passion d'auteure; review of *La Passion selon Galatée*. photo · *Lettres québec* Summer 1987; No 46: p21–23.

Quand la "réalité" risque de l'emporter sur la fiction; review of *Toute la terre à dévorer*. photo · *Lettres québec* Autumn 1987; No 47: p15–16.

Savoir garder ses distances; review of *Les Silences du corbeau*. photo · *Lettres québec* Spring 1987; No 45: p22–23.

Le second déclin de l'empire américain; review of *Une Histoire américaine*. photo · *Lettres québec* Winter 1986–87; No 44: p22–25.

Milot, Pierre

Qui a peur de l'intellectuel in 1987?; reviews. *Voix et images* Spring 1987; Vol 12 No 3: p530–534.

Minni, C.D.

For the record; letter to the editor. *Books in Can* Jan-Feb 1987; Vol 16 No 1: p38.

Minsos, Susan

[Another Season's Promise]; theatre review. *NeWest R* Dec 1987; Vol 13 No 4: p17.

[Fire]; theatre review. *NeWest R* April 1987; Vol 12 No 8: p17.

[The Last Bus]; theatre review. *NeWest R* April 1987; Vol 12 No 8: p17.

Miraglia, Anne Marie

Poulin; review of *Études françaises (special issue)*. *Can Lit* Spring 1987; No 112: p152–154.

Mirolla, Michael

Author reveal's book's skeleton; review of *Century*. *CH* Jan 4, 1987: pE4.

The cantina; short story. *Matrix* Fall 1987; No 25: p2–16.

Explosive debut made by writer; review of *Fire Eyes*. photo · *CH* Sept 13, 1987: pE5.

Hostile Earth Mother insidiously subdues human colony; review of *Dreams of an Unseen Planet*. photo · *MG* April 4, 1987: pH10.

Lycanthropy; short story. *Capilano R* 1987; No 44: p67–72.

Point I; short story. *Capilano R* 1987; No 43: p60–71.

Quebec's literary lights shed old traditions; review of *Intimate Strangers*. *CH* March 8, 1987: pE5.

The singular man; short story. *Capilano R* 1987; No 43: p72–81.

Spider Robinson's time traveller lands in rural N.S.; review of *Time Pressure*. *MG* Dec 24, 1987: pL8.

Stories by Quebec writers cover magical terrain; review of *Invisible Fictions*. *CH* Oct 25, 1987: pE5.

Strangers; short story. *Dandelion* Spring-Summer 1987; Vol 14 No 1: p50–54.

[Untitled]; review of *Alberta Bound*. *Dandelion* Fall-Winter 1987; Vol 14 No 2: p143–145.

Miron, Gaston

Les génocides; poem. *Liberté (special issue)* 1987: p36.

L'espoir; poem. *Liberté (special issue)* 1987: p36.

Mistry, Rohinton

Facing the precipice; short story. illus · *Can Forum* March 1987; Vol 66 No 767: p19–29.

The new epoch; short story. *Descant* Fall 1987; Vol 18 No 3: p5–18.

Mitcham, Allison

Acadians in English; review of *Mariaagélas*. *Fiddlehead* Spring 1987; No 151: p120–122.

Mitcham, Linda

Writer fears free trade will kill her career; article. photo · *WFP* Oct 9, 1987: p36.

Mitchell, Beverley

Anti-drug play goes to school; article. photo · *MG* Nov 18, 1987: pE7.

Mitchell, Constantina

Beauchemin's The Alley Cat as modern myth; article. *Amer R of Can Studies* Winter 1987–88; Vol 17 No 4: p409–418.

Mitton, Jennifer

The Parker pen; short story. *Fiddlehead* Winter 1987; No 154: p5–11.

Mock, Irene

Ernst Havemann; interview. photo · *Books in Can* Dec 1987; Vol 16 No 9: p39–40.

Mockevïciuté, Dana

[Untitled]; review of *La Nuit émeraude*. *Moebius* Summer 1987; No 33: p139.

Mogensen, Ejler

Bella; short story. photo · *TS* July 18, 1987: pM5.

Moisan, Clément

Présentation; editorial. *Études lit* Spring-Summer 1987; Vol 20 No 1: p9–16.

Moisan, Roger

Pauvre choix; letter to the editor. *MD* Feb 7, 1987: pA18.

Mombourquette, Michael J.

The gate-keeper; short story. *Fiddlehead* Winter 1987; No 154: p49–57.

Monkman, Leslie

Canadian historical fiction; review article about *Sounding the Iceberg*. *Queen's Q* Autumn 1987; Vol 94 No 3: p630–640.

Monoré-Johnson, Ghislaine

Un livre tendre; review of *Crac!* *Can Child Lit* 1987; No 48: p97–98.

Monsen, Jocelyn G.

Beach walk; poem. *Prairie Fire* Autumn 1987; Vol 8 No 3: p71.

Bush pilot; poem. *Prairie Fire* Autumn 1987; Vol 8 No 3: p71.

Spring of the high water; poem. *Prairie Fire* Autumn 1987; Vol 8 No 3: p70.

Montagnes, Ramona

Canadian children's literature 1983/Bibliographie de la littérature canadienne pour la jeunesse: 1983; bibliography. *Can Child Lit* 1987; No 47: p29–56.

Montero, Gloria

A temporary state of grace; short story. *Room of One's Own* Sept 1987; Vol 11 No 4: p49–56.

Monzano, Guido

[Untitled]; review of *Paris Notebooks*. *Idler* March-April 1987; No 12: p60–61.

Mooers, Vernon

The new neighbours; poem. *Alpha* Winter 1987; Vol 11: p34.

Mooney-Jardine, Brenda

Reconciliation; poem. *Poetry Can R* Fall 1987; Vol 9 No 1: p31.

Moore, John

[Untitled]; review of *Remembering Summer. Quill & Quire* June 1987; Vol 53 No 6: p33.

Moore, Lynn

Credit Valley's Artichoke has lots of heart; theatre review. photo · *TS (Neighbours)* Feb 24, 1987: p16.

Moore, Mavor

Arts enrich lives as well as pockets; column. *G&M* Aug 15, 1987: pC3.

A smoking gun response from Salutin; column. *G&M* Aug 8, 1987: pC3.

Why has the wheel been reinvented so often? I forget; column. *G&M* July 11, 1987: pC1.

Moore, Roger

Army worms; poem. *Fiddlehead* Winter 1987; No 154: p43.

Barnfather; poem. *Poetry Can R* Fall 1987; Vol 9 No 1: p24.

Bears; poem. *Fiddlehead* Winter 1987; No 154: p44.

Brecon beacons; poem. *Ariel* Jan 1987; Vol 18 No 1: p38.

Death and the maiden; poem. *Antigonish R* 1987; No 69–70: p154.

El Greco's house; poem. *Arc* Fall 1987; No 19: p76.

Family portrait; poem. *Waves* Spring 1987; Vol 15 No 4: p72.

Unfinished symphony; poem. *Arc* Fall 1987; No 19: p76.

Velasquez; poem. *Fiddlehead* Winter 1987; No 154: p45.

Moore, Stewart

Flight 210; short story. *Fiddlehead* Summer 1987; No 152: p31–38.

It could be the ocean; short story. *Waves* Spring 1987; Vol 15 No 4: p27–30.

Moran, Angelin

The tryst; poem. *Waves* Spring 1987; Vol 15 No 4: p61.

Upon learning of a high suicide rate among dentists; poem. *Waves* Spring 1987; Vol 15 No 4: p60.

Morch, Karen

Atwood not disappointed at losing Commonwealth Prize; article. photo · *CH* Dec 3, 1987: pF3.

Writer from Jamaica wins literary award; article. *G&M* Dec 2, 1987: pC6.

Moreau, Anne

[Untitled]; biographical articles. *Brick (special issue)* Summer 1987; No 30: ppassim.

Morin, Marc

Bozo et les bas-culottes; theatre review of *La Waitress*. photo · *MD* Feb 25, 1987: p8.

Les ondes littéraires; list of radio and television programs. *MD* Oct 31, 1987: pD2.

Les ondes littéraire; list of radio and television programs. *MD* Nov 7, 1987: pD2.

Les ondes littéraires; list of radio and television programs. *MD* Nov 14, 1987: pD14.

Les ondes littéraires; list of radio and television programs. *MD* Nov 21, 1987: pD2.

Les ondes littéraires; list of radio and television programs. *MD* Nov 28, 1987: pD12.

Les ondes littéraires; list of radio and television programs. *MD* Dec 5, 1987: pD2.

Les ondes littéraires; list of radio and television programs. *MD* Dec 12, 1987: pD2.

Les ondes littéraires; list of radio and television programs. *MD* Dec 19, 1987: pD2.

Les ondes littéraires; list of radio and television programs. *MD* Dec 24, 1987: pC10.

Les ondes littéraires; list of radio and television programs. *MD* Dec 31, 1987: pC10.

Le phénomène des best-sellers au Québec; article. photo · *MD* Nov 21, 1987: pD1, D12.

Sir Noël Pringle ou Sir Noël Coward?; theatre review of *Noel Coward: A Portrait*. photo · *MD* Nov 26, 1987: p15.

[Untitled]; review of *La Servante écarlate*. *MD* Nov 28, 1987: pD8.

La vie littéraire; column. *MD* Oct 31, 1987: pD2.

La vie littéraire; column. *MD* Nov 14, 1987: pD14.

La vie littéraire; column. *MD* Nov 21, 1987: pD2.

La vie littéraire; column. photo · *MD* Nov 28, 1987: pD12.

La vie littéraire; column. *MD* Dec 5, 1987: pD2.

La vie littéraire; column. *MD* Dec 12, 1987: pD2.

La vie littéraire; column. photo · *MD* Dec 19, 1987: pD2.

La vie littéraire; column. *MD* Dec 24, 1987: pC10.

Walter Borden en 12 temps. . . .; theatre review of *Tightrope Time*. *MD* Sept 15, 1987: p11.

Moritz, A.F.

Our unemployment; poem. *Queen's Q* Winter 1987; Vol 94 No 4: p986.

Morley, Patricia

[Untitled]; review of *Dreams of Speech and Violence. Books in Can* Aug-Sept 1987; Vol 16 No 6: p25.

Morrell, A.C.

The I and the eye in the desert: the political and philosophical key to Dave Godfrey's The New Ancestors; article. *Studies in Can Lit* 1987; Vol 12 No 2: p264–272.

Images of motherhood; review of *The Paris-Napoli Express*. *Fiddlehead* Summer 1987; No 152: p91–95.

Morris, Roberta

Arctic vs Toronto clash of cultures; review of *The Ice Eaters*. *TS* Dec 20, 1987: pE6.

[Untitled]; reviews of *Candy from Strangers* and *Second Nature*. *Cross Can Writ Q* 1987; Vol 9 No 3–4: p42.

Morrison, Ardith

Structures; short story. photo · *TS* July 12, 1987: pD5.

Morrison, Thelma M.

Words Stratford-style; poem. *Can Forum* June-July 1987; Vol 67 No 770: p26.

Morrissey, Stephen

Feel nothing; poem. *Antigonish R* 1987; No 69–70: p39–40.

The middle of a life; poem. *Poetry Can R* Fall 1987; Vol 9 No 1: p16.

Preludes; poem. *Poetry Can R* Summer 1987; Vol 8 No 4: p25.

[Untitled]; review of *The Night the Dog Smiled*. *Poetry Can R* Spring 1987; Vol 8 No 2–3: p36.

[Untitled]; reviews of poetry books. *Poetry Can R* Spring 1987; Vol 8 No 2–3: p49.

[Untitled]; reviews of poetry books. *Poetry Can R* Fall 1987; Vol 9 No 1: p32.

Morritt, Hope

Porn bill will fling us back to 19th century; letter to the editor. *TS* May 26, 1987: pA20.

Robertson Davies shows he's a sexist; letter to the editor. *TS* Oct 15, 1987: pA24.

Morrow, Martin

Architecture offers author comic design; article. photo · *CH* Dec 31, 1987: pD1.

Playwright goes to war on conservative theatre; article. *CH* Oct 31, 1987: pH4.

Tried-and-true still packs punch in stage thriller; theatre review of *The Mark of Cain*. photo · *CH* Nov 3, 1987: pF11.

Morton, Colin

Auditory camouflage; poem. *Can Lit* Spring 1987; No 112: p31.

First books from five regional presses; reviews of poetry books. *Arc* Spring 1987; No 18: p52–59.

London, certainly; poem. *Can Lit* Spring 1987; No 112: p30.

Sticks and stones; letter to the editor. *Books in Can* June-July 1987; Vol 16 No 5: p39.

That's true; poem. *Cross Can Writ Q* 1987; Vol 9 No 3–4: p17.

Morton, Desmond

Hyping the good fight; review of *The Great War of Words*. *Books in Can* Nov 1987; Vol 16 No 8: p14–15.

Moser, Marie

All the fallen sparrows; short story. photo · *TS* Aug 20, 1987: pF6.

Moser-Verrey, Monique

Deux échos québécois de grands romans épistolaires du dix-huitième siècle français; article. *Voix et images* Spring 1987; Vol 12 No 3: p512–514, 516–522.

Moses, Daniel David

The chain; poem. *Arc* Spring 1987; No 18: p60–61.

Gramma's doing; short story. *Can Fic Mag (special issue)* 1987; No 60: p77–82.

King of the raft; short story. *Can Fic Mag (special issue)* 1987; No 60: p74–76.

The moon in early Upper Canada; poem. *Poetry Can R* Fall 1987; Vol 9 No 1: p18.

Our lady of the glacier; poem. *Antigonish R* 1987; No 69–70: p11–12.

An oval moon; poem. *Waves* Spring 1987; Vol 15 No 4: p66.

The trickster theatre of Tomson Highway; article. biog · *Can Fic Mag (special issue)* 1987; No 60: p83–88.

Moss, Jane

Drama summary; review of *Theatre and Politics in Modern Québec*. *Can Lit* Winter 1987; No 115: p175–176.

Sexual games: hypertheatricality and homosexuality in recent Quebec plays; article. *Amer R of Can Studies* Autumn 1987; Vol 17 No 3: p287–296.

Théâtre au masculin; reviews of plays. *Can Lit* Spring 1987; No 112: p180–183.

Moss, John

[Untitled]; letter to the editor. *Books in Can* June-July 1987; Vol 16 No 5: p39–40.

Motoi, Ina

[Untitled]; poem. *Fireweed* Winter 1987; No 24: p28.

[Untitled]; poem. *Fireweed* Winter 1987; No 24: p28.

Moulton-Barrett, Donalee

Women to watch in the Maritimes; article. photo · *Chatelaine* April 1987; Vol 60 No 4: p114, 116, 118, 120.

Mouré, Erin

The arbitrary; poem. *Writing* 1987; No 18: p39.

The beauty of furs; prose poem. *CV 2* Summer 1987; Vol 10 No 4: p30.

The calf; poem. *Writing* 1987; No 18: p40.

Corrections to muddy thinking; poem. *Poetry Can R* Spring 1987; Vol 8 No 2–3: p33.

Corrections to the beauty of furs: a site glossary; prose poem. *CV 2* Summer 1987; Vol 10 No 4: p31.

The coupling; poem. *Writing* 1987; No 18: p40.

The curious; poems. *Writing* 1987; No 18: p38–41.

The curious; poem. *Writing* 1987; No 18: p38.

The force of; poem. *Writing* 1987; No 18: p41.

Gorgeous; poem. *Poetry Can R* Spring 1987; Vol 8 No 2–3: p32.

A history of Vietnam & Central America as seen in the paintings of Leon Golub; poem. *Poetry Can R* Fall 1987; Vol 9 No 1: p24.

Muddy thinking; poem. *Poetry Can R* Spring 1987; Vol 8 No 2–3: p33.

The new; poem. *Writing* 1987; No 18: p38.

Palm Sunday; poem. *Poetry Can R* Spring 1987; Vol 8 No 2–3: p32.

The pressure; poem. *Writing* 1987; No 18: p39.

The producers; poem. *Matrix* Spring 1987; No 24: p9.

Rose; poem. *Poetry Can R* Spring 1987; Vol 8 No 2–3: p33.

Thrushes; poem. biog photo · *Poetry Can R* Spring 1987; Vol 8 No 2–3: p32–33.

[Untitled]; review of *Waiting for Saskatchewan*. *Rubicon* Spring 1987; No 8: p187–189.

Mouré, Ken

[Untitled]; review of *Paris Notebooks*. *Rubicon* Fall 1987; No 9: p155–157.

Mousseau, Heather

Just good fun; letter to the editor. *WFP* Dec 6, 1987: p6.

Muchison, Carol

Writer another victim of tobacco industry; letter to the editor. *TS* Jan 14, 1987: pA14.

Mueller, Martha Ann

[Untitled]; review of *Dislocations*. *Queen's Q* Autumn 1987; Vol 94 No 3: p692–694.

Muench, Heidi

Dream trap; poem. *CV 2* Summer 1987; Vol 10 No 4: p33.

The lake; poem. *CV 2* Summer 1987; Vol 10 No 4: p32.

Reply; poem. *CV 2* Summer 1987; Vol 10 No 4: p34.

Tattooed man: a Diane Arbus photo; poem. *CV 2* Summer 1987; Vol 10 No 4: p35.

Muir, Fran

Dreamer; short story. *Event* Summer 1987; Vol 16 No 2: p63–69.

Mulvihill, James

The Rebel Angels: Robertson Davies and the novel of ideas; article. *Eng Studies in Can* June 1987; Vol 13 No 2: p182–194.

Mummers Theatre Collective

Buchans: a mining town; play. *Can Drama* 1987; Vol 13 No 1: p73–116.

Munro, Alice

Oh, what avails; short story. *New Yorker* Nov 16, 1987; Vol 63 No 39: p42–52, 55–56, 58–59, 62.

Sin of omission; letter to the editor. *Books in Can* April 1987; Vol 16 No 3: p40.

[Untitled]; essay. photo · *Chatelaine* June 1987; Vol 60 No 6: p84.

[Untitled]; letter to the editor. *Books in Can* Aug-Sept 1987; Vol 16 No 6: p38–39.

Munro, Jane

[Untitled]; review of *Double Standards*. *Poetry Can R* Spring 1987; Vol 8 No 2–3: p44.

[Untitled]; review of *Melancholy Ain't No Baby*. *Poetry Can R* Summer 1987; Vol 8 No 4: p34.

Munro, Karen

A brief case of love; short story. photo · *TS* Aug 19, 1987: pB6.

Munton, Ann

Livesay's selected seasons – a heady brew; review of *The Self-Completing Tree*. *Event* Summer 1987; Vol 16 No 2: p133–137.

Muretich, James

Chileans fight militarism with poetry, music; article. photo · *CH* July 24, 1987: pF1.

Fresh jazz flowing in clubs; article. photo · *CH* June 25, 1987: pD1.

Murphy, Sarah

No exorcism yet, father; short story. *Grain* Winter 1987; Vol 15 No 4: p56–64.

Murray, Lachlan

Antigonish summer; poem. *Can Lit* Winter 1987; No 115: p61–62.

For Miss Cooke; poem. *Can Lit* Winter 1987; No 115: p123.

Musgrave, Susan

Custer Sloat's Christmas dinner; short story. illus · *G&M* Dec 24, 1987: pA7.

Rolling boil; poem. *Event* Summer 1987; Vol 16 No 2: p51–55.

Musselwhite, Bill

Bumbling Benny takes new case; television review of *Murder Sees the Light*. photo · *CH* March 14, 1987: pF6.

Laurence tribute deserved better from The Journal; television review. *CH* Jan 7, 1987: pD4.

Myhr, Gail

Disease of the soul; short story. *Room of One's Own* April 1987; Vol 11 No 3: p99–109.

Nadezhdin, Daniel

Bells on the necks of cows; poem. *Arc* Fall 1987; No 19: p77.

Eternity; poem. *Arc* Fall 1987; No 19: p77.

Nash, Roger

Banking by mirrors; short story. *Queen's Q* Summer 1987; Vol 94 No 2: p303–308.

Cleaning the brasses; poem. *Wascana R* Spring 1987; Vol 22 No 1: p65–66.

The coppery weathercock; poem. *Antigonish R* 1987; No 69–70: p200.

The dream of the rood; poem. *Antigonish R* 1987; No 69–70: p201.

Evening; poem. *Can Auth & Book* Summer 1987; Vol 62 No 4: p23.

The mandarin of morning; poem. *Can Forum* April 1987; Vol 67 No 768: p5.

One day; poem. *Prism* Summer 1987; Vol 25 No 4: p20.

A rare gramophone recording: my father-in-law the conductor; poem. *Prism* Summer 1987; Vol 25 No 4: p18.

The shaking; poem. *Prism* Summer 1987; Vol 25 No 4: p19.

The tea ceremony; poem. *Ariel* Jan 1987; Vol 18 No 1: p16.

This is my mother's camera; poem. *Can Lit* Summer-Fall 1987; No 113–114: p167.

Voyages of a garden shed; poem. *Quarry* Fall 1987; Vol 36 No 4: p57–58.

Nasrallah, Emily

The final signature; short story. trans · *Dandelion* Fall-Winter 1987; Vol 14 No 2: p88–93.

Naudin, Marie

Plus adulte que les adultes; review of *Ani Croche*. *Can Child Lit* 1987; No 45: p61–62.

Necakov, Lillian

[Untitled]; poem. *Cross Can Writ Q* 1987; Vol 9 No 3–4: p2.

Nelken, Harry

Not so easy; letter to the editor. *WFP* Oct 18, 1987: p6.

Nelson, Hugh

Accommodations; poem. *Fiddlehead* Summer 1987; No 152: p64.

Last words; essay. *Fiddlehead* Summer 1987; No 152: p65–67.

Pictures of fine doctors; poem. *Fiddlehead* Summer 1987; No 152: p62–63.

Nepveu, Pierre

Le retranchement; essay. *Liberté* Oct 1987; Vol 29 No 5: p70–72.

Nettell, Stephanie

Paperbacks in brief; review of *Lost and Found*. *Times Lit Supp* May 15, 1987; No 4389: p529.

Neveu, Louise

Quand le politique est privé: ou la face privée du politique; essay. illus · *La Nouvelle barre du jour (special issue)* March 1987; No 196: p59–65.

Nevill, Sue

Cold front; short story. illus · *Room of One's Own* April 1987; Vol 11 No 3: p36–38.

New, W.H.

Introduction; survey article. *J of Common Lit* 1987; Vol 22 No 2: p30–43.

Making connections; review of *More Stories by Canadian Women*. *Books in Can* Oct 1987; Vol 16 No 7: p31–32.

Margaret Laurence 1926–1987; obituary. *Can Lit* Spring 1987; No 112: p221–223.

Otherworlds; editorial. *Can Lit* Winter 1987; No 115: p3–6.

Pour enfants; reviews of children's books. *Can Lit* Summer-Fall 1987; No 113–114: p275.

[Untitled]; review of *Dictionnaire des oeuvres littéraires du Québec*. *Can Lit* Spring 1987; No 112: p223–224.

Newcombe, George

Autumn beings; poem. *Fiddlehead* Winter 1987; No 154: p58.

Lessons about consonants perish like dust; poem. *Fiddlehead* Winter 1987; No 154: p59.

A long and silent world; poem. *Fiddlehead* Winter 1987; No 154: p61.

Once; poem. *Fiddlehead* Winter 1987; No 154: p60.

Newlove, John

Don't give me any; poem. *Quarry* Summer 1987; Vol 36 No 3: p57.

Pages of illustrations; poem. *Quarry* Summer 1987; Vol 36 No 3: p56.

River; poem. *Quarry* Summer 1987; Vol 36 No 3: p58.

[Untitled]; essay. *Brick (special issue)* Summer 1987; No 30: p58.

Newman, Frank

The bet; short story. photo · *TS* Aug 24, 1987: pB5.

Newman, S.A.

[Untitled]; reviews of *The Need of Wanting Always* and *The Paris-Napoli Express*. *Cross Can Writ Q* 1987; Vol 9 No 1: p20.

Newton, Robbie

[Untitled]; letter to the editor. *NeWest R* Summer 1987; Vol 12 No 10: p1.

Nichol, bp

The annotated, anecdoted, beginnings of a critical checklist of the published works of Steve McCaffery; bibliography, includes introduction. *Open Letter (special issue)* Fall 1987; Vol 6 No 9: p67–92.

Horizon #11; poem. *Can Lit* Summer-Fall 1987; No 113–114: p61.

Introduction. *Open Letter (special issue)* Fall 1987; Vol 6 No 9: p7.

The lungs: a draft; prose excerpt from *Organ Music*. *Prairie Fire* Winter 1987–88; Vol 8 No 4: p47–49.

Sine (horizon no. 17); poem. *Cross Can Writ Q* 1987; Vol 9 No 3–4: p2.

Single letter translation of Basho's "Frog / Pond / Plop"; poem. *Cross Can Writ Q* 1987; Vol 9 No 3–4: p2.

St. Anzas: basis / bases; poetry excerpt from *The Martyrology*. *Writing* Dec 1987; No 20: p27–32.

Water poem #5; poem. *Can Lit* Summer-Fall 1987; No 113–114: p61.

Nichols, Philip

Haida war dance; poem. *Tor Life* April 1987; Vol 21 No 5: p36.

Nicholson, Mervyn

Food and power: Homer, Carroll, Atwood and others; article. *Mosaic* Summer 1987; Vol 20 No 3: p37–55.

Niechoda, Irene

Listening for space; review of audio tapes by Norbert Ruebsaat. *Event* Summer 1987; Vol 16 No 2: p130–132.

Niskala, Brenda

The shine has gone out of the apples; poem. *NeWest R* Sept 1987; Vol 13 No 1: p11.

Nixon, Rosemary

Allowances; short story. illus · *CH (Sunday Magazine)* Aug 9, 1987: p16–18.

Noble, Peter S.

[Untitled]; review of *Voices of Deliverance. British J of Can Studies* June 1987; Vol 2 No 1: p181–182.

[Untitled]; review of *Spring Tides. British J of Can Studies* June 1987; Vol 2 No 1: p182.

[Untitled]; review of *All the Way Home. British J of Can Studies* June 1987; Vol 2 No 1: p182–183.

Nodelman, Billie

Six weeks; short story. *Prairie Fire* Summer 1987; Vol 8 No 2: p13–19.

Noizet, Pascale

Bibliographie de Suzanne Lamy; bibliography. *Voix et images* Autumn 1987; Vol 13 No 1: p70–80.

Nolan, Patricia

Death mask; short story. *Capilano R* 1987; No 44: p11–15.

Hide and seek; prose poem. *Capilano R* 1987; No 44: p16.

Nold, John

Crows on the cornfield; poem, includes introduction. *Quarry* Summer 1987; Vol 36 No 3: p5–12.

Implications of the scarlet tanager; poem. *Poetry Can R* Spring 1987; Vol 8 No 2–3: p34.

My shadow falls in the dream of a fox; poem. *Arc* Spring 1987; No 18: p64.

Secrets we keep; poem. *Poetry Can R* Spring 1987; Vol 8 No 2–3: p34.

Souvenir; poem. *Poetry Can R* Spring 1987; Vol 8 No 2–3: p34.

To hold a hawk; poem. *Arc* Spring 1987; No 18: p63.

Village Christmas; poem. *Poetry Can R* Spring 1987; Vol 8 No 2–3: p34.

Wildflowers; poem. *Poetry Can R* Spring 1987; Vol 8 No 2–3: p34.

Noonan, Gerald

Not a job to cry at; poem. *New Q* Spring-Summer 1987; Vol 7 No 1–2: p168–170.

Tenth of Peel; poem. *New Q* Spring-Summer 1987; Vol 7 No 1–2: p171–172.

Noonan, James

Dramatic fringe; reviews of *Five from the Fringe* and *Politics and the Playwright: George Ryga. Can Lit* Winter 1987; No 115: p235–238.

Norman, Chad

Movement within the mustard seed; poem. *Waves* Winter 1987; Vol 15 No 3: p58–59.

Normandeau, Régis

Du désir à l'écriture ou vice versa; review of *Lignes de nuit. Lettres québec* Summer 1987; No 46: p70.

Écrire sur l'écrire; review of *L'Usage du réel. Lettres québec* Spring 1987; No 45: p64.

Mort, vie et écriture; review of *Le Tombeau d'Adélina Albert.* photo · *Lettres québec* Autumn 1987; No 47: p69.

Norrie, Helen

Excellent books for the very young; review of *Have You Seen Josephine?. WFP* July 11, 1987: p57.

Funny books are a joy to find; reviews of *An Armadillo Is Not a Pillow* and *Tales of a Gambling Grandma. WFP* Feb 14, 1987: p60.

A mystery in Manitoba; review of *Who Is Frances Rain? WFP* Dec 5, 1987: p57.

Novels deal with family breakup; reviews of *The Doll* and *Dear Bruce Springsteen. WFP* Dec 5, 1987: p57.

Paperbacks offer good value; review of *Nicole's Boat. WFP* May 23, 1987: p74.

Struggles of adolescence; review of *The Empty Chair. WFP* April 11, 1987: p60.

Time travel series maintains quality; review of *Me, Myself and I. WFP* Dec 5, 1987: p57.

Youngsters get choice of beautiful books; reviews. *WFP* Dec 5, 1987: p57.

Norris, Ken

The agony of being an Expos fan; essay. *Descant (special issue)* Spring-Summer 1987; Vol 18 No 1–2: p140.

Andre Dawson, at the height of his career; poem. *Descant (special issue)* Spring-Summer 1987; Vol 18 No 1–2: p141.

Deep water; prose poem. *Poetry Can R* Summer 1987; Vol 8 No 4: p29.

The former Véhicule poets; introduction. *Poetry Can R* Fall 1987; Vol 9 No 1: p17.

Guam; prose poem. *Poetry Can R* Fall 1987; Vol 9 No 1: p17.

[Untitled]; poem. *Descant (special issue)* Spring-Summer 1987; Vol 18 No 1–2: p142.

[Untitled]; poem. *Descant (special issue)* Spring-Summer 1987; Vol 18 No 1–2: p143.

Norris, Nanette

Short shrift for novel's art; review of *Penumbra. Essays on Can Writ* Spring 1987; No 34: p136–139.

Norskey, Carolellen

[Untitled]; review of *Fireweed. Quill & Quire (Books for Young People)* June 1987; Vol 53 No 6: p6, 9.

[Untitled]; review of *Albertine, in Five Times. Quill & Quire* June 1987; Vol 53 No 6: p31.

[Untitled]; review of *The Tiger's Daughter. Quill & Quire* July 1987; Vol 53 No 7: p65.

[Untitled]; review of *Counterpoint. Quill & Quire* Aug 1987; Vol 53 No 8: p30.

[Untitled]; review of *On Middle Ground. Quill & Quire* Sept 1987; Vol 53 No 9: p78.

[Untitled]; reviews of *Doubtful Motives* and *Fieldwork. Quill & Quire* Sept 1987; Vol 53 No 9: p79.

North, John

Mysteries to feed the mind with varying tastes; reviews of *Crang Plays the Ace* and *To an Easy Grave.* photo · *Quill & Quire* March 1987; Vol 53 No 3: p74.

[Untitled]; review of *The Letter. Quill & Quire* Jan 1987; Vol 53 No 1: p27.

[Untitled]; review of *Jericho Falls. Quill & Quire* Feb 1987; Vol 53 No 2: p17.

[Untitled]; review of *The Hollow Woman. Quill & Quire* June 1987; Vol 53 No 6: p32.

[Untitled]; review of *Booby Trap. Quill & Quire* July 1987; Vol 53 No 7: p65.

[Untitled]; review of *Children of the Shroud. Quill & Quire* Sept 1987; Vol 53 No 9: p79.

[Untitled]; review of *Merlin's Web. Quill & Quire* Sept 1987; Vol 53 No 9: p79.

[Untitled]; review of *Mortal Sins. Quill & Quire* Oct 1987; Vol 53 No 10: p22.

[Untitled]; review of *Broken English. Quill & Quire* Nov 1987; Vol 53 No 11: p24.

Notar, Clea

[Untitled]; review of *Voices & Visions. Rubicon* Spring 1987; No 8: p214.

Nothof, Anne

Collective creativity – working Odd Jobs; article. photo · *Can Drama* 1987; Vol 13 No 1: p34–42.

David French and the theatre of speech; article. *Can Drama* 1987; Vol 13 No 2: p216–223.

Nouch, Kathleen E.

Another world; poem. *NeWest R* Nov 1987; Vol 13 No 3: p19.

Novak, Barbara

Confetti summer; short story. *Malahat R* Sept 1987; No 80: p116–124.

Noyes, Steve

Herb Schellenberg; poem. *Malahat R* June 1987; No 79: p81–82.

Them that sleep; short story. *Fiddlehead* Autumn 1987; No 153: p83–87.

[Untitled]; review of *The Other Shore. Rubicon* Spring 1987; No 8: p219.

Nutting, Leslie

[Untitled]; review of *Correct in This Culture. Poetry Can R* Fall 1987; Vol 9 No 1: p38.

Oberman, Sheldon

Somewhere between; poem. *CV 2* Spring 1987; Vol 10 No 3: p39–40.

O'Brien, Peter

[Untitled]; review of *The Immaculate Perception. Rubicon* Fall 1987; No 9: p187–190.

[Untitled]; review of *Pieces of Map, Pieces of Music. Rubicon* Fall 1987; No 9: p203–204.

O'Connell, Dorothy

Options; short story. illus · *Fireweed* Fall 1987; No 25: p39–44.

O'Connor, Patricia T.

New & noteworthy; reviews of *The Voice at the Back Door* and *Fire in the Morning. NYT Book R* Feb 1, 1987: p32.

New & noteworthy; review of *The Handmaid's Tale.* photo · *NYT Book R* Feb 8, 1987: p38.

New & noteworthy; review of *Home Truths.* photo · *NYT Book R* Feb 22, 1987: p34.

New & noteworthy; review of *Borderline. NYT Book R* May 10, 1987: p34.

Notable paperbacks; checklist. *NYT Book R* Dec 6, 1987: p90–93.

O'Donnell, Kathleen M.

The poetry of Alphonse Piché 1946–1982; article. *U of Windsor R* Spring-Summer 1987; Vol 20 No 2: p75–81.

O'Flaherty, Patrick

Fish killer; short story. *Fiddlehead* Winter 1987; No 154: p64–66.

O'Flanagan, Robert

A green spot; short story. *Grain* Summer 1987; Vol 15 No 2: p23–24.

O'Grady, Jane

Imprecise intertwinings; review of *This Is Not for You. Times Lit Supp* June 26, 1987; No 4395: p698.

O'Grady, Thomas B.

Frank Ledwell's colloquial ease; review of *The North Shore of Home. Atlan Prov Book R* Feb-March 1987; Vol 14 No 1: p17.

O'Leary, Véronique

.... Le Théâtre des Cuisines 2; essay. illus · *La Nouvelle barre du jour (special issue)* March 1987; No 196: p34–49.

Olenick, Roberta

Mrs. Isfeld; short story. illus · *Fireweed* Fall 1987; No 25: p77–80.

Oleson, Tom

Flaws mar a major fantasy; review of *The Darkest Road*. photo · *WFP* June 13, 1987: p58.

Moore's latest disappointing; review of *The Color of Blood*. photo · *WFP* Sept 5, 1987: p58.

Taking a survey of the world; review of *The Oxford Illustrated Literary Guide to Canada*. *WFP* Dec 12, 1987: p50.

Oliva, Peter S.

The exhumation; short story. illus · *CH (Sunday Magazine)* Aug 2, 1987: p18–21.

Oliver, Michael Brian

Poor bastard; poem. *Can Lit* Spring 1987; No 112: p71.

Olscamp, Marcel

British Railways; poem. illus · *La Nouvelle barre du jour* Feb 1987; No 193: p47–50.

Ondaatje, Michael

Little seeds; prose excerpt from *In the Skin of a Lion*. *Malahat R* June 1987; No 79: p17–22.

O'Neill, John

Beluga whale birth; poem. *Malahat R* June 1987; No 79: p128.

Her fear is whale; poem. *Malahat R* June 1987; No 79: p127.

Inuit hunters; poem. *Antigonish R* Winter 1987; No 68: p40.

Moose II; poem. *Malahat R* June 1987; No 79: p126.

The moose; poem. *Malahat R* June 1987; No 79: p125.

Pigeon-toed; poem. *Queen's Q* Summer 1987; Vol 94 No 2: p287.

The river's window; poem. *Fiddlehead* Spring 1987; No 151: p80.

Still life, Taylor River; poem. *Fiddlehead* Spring 1987; No 151: p83.

Storm warning; poem. *Fiddlehead* Spring 1987; No 151: p82.

Theology at Robson Bite; poem. *Fiddlehead* Spring 1987; No 151: p81.

O'Neill, Juliet

Richler toasts any deal that puts it to Ontario; article. photo · *CH* Nov 19, 1987: pA18.

Oore, Irène

Comme il vous plaira; review of *Le Complot*. *Can Child Lit* 1987; No 46: p90–92.

La forêt dans l'oeuvre imaginaire de Marie-Claire Blais; article. abstract · *Études can* 1987; No 23: p93–108.

Oppel, Kenneth

[Untitled]; review of *Lisa*. *Quill & Quire (Books for Young People)* Dec 1987; Vol 53 No 12: p6.

Orange, John

[Untitled]; review of *Canadian Literature in English*. *U of Windsor R* Spring-Summer 1987; Vol 20 No 2: p92–94.

O'Regan, James

Making image theatre; article. *Can Theatre R* Spring 1987; No 50: p10–13.

O'Reilly, Magessa

Grignon plurilingue; article. *Voix et images* Autumn 1987; Vol 13 No 1: p123–139.

Orenstein, Leo

Separation; short story. photo · *TS* Aug 5, 1987: pB11.

O'Riordan, Robert G.

Lady Godiva; short story. biog photo · *Cross Can Writ Q* 1987; Vol 9 No 1: p12–13, 26–27.

Ormsby, E.

Starfish; poem. illus · *Antigonish R* 1987; No 69–70: p7.

O'Rourke, David

On the carpet: a memoir of Layton and Callaghan; column. photo · *Poetry Can R* Fall 1987; Vol 9 No 1: p14–15.

Osachoff, Margaret Gail

Prairie spaces in the big city: western theatre in Toronto; theatre reviews. *NeWest R* Oct 1987; Vol 13 No 2: p18–19.

[Untitled]; review of *A Public and Private Voice*. *U of Windsor R* Spring-Summer 1987; Vol 20 No 2: p94–97.

[Untitled]; letter to the editor. *NeWest R* Dec 1987; Vol 13 No 4: p1.

Osadchuck, Robert

Mirages; short story. *Moebius* Winter 1987; No 31: p103–107.

Osborne, Anne

A question of age; poem. *Can Auth & Book* Fall 1987; Vol 63 No 1: p17.

The view from here; editorial. *Can Auth & Book* Summer 1987; Vol 62 No 4: p2.

Oskaboose, Gilbert

The serpent's eggs; short story. *Can Fic Mag (special issue)* 1987; No 60: p168–171.

Ostendorf, Doris

For a moment; poem. *Can Auth & Book* Winter 1987; Vol 62 No 2: p22.

Ostick, Stephen

Dramaturge bridges theatre gap; article about Per Brask. photo · *WFP* Jan 21, 1987: p31.

Oswald, Brad

Actor drawn to play by novelty, challenge of playing a bear; article. *WFP* Oct 7, 1987: p39.

Actors explore effects of porn; article. photo · *WFP* Sept 9, 1987: p36.

Border play proves timely; article. photo · *WFP* Sept 30, 1987: p41.

Cercle tries for last laugh first; article. photo · *WFP* Oct 16, 1987: p33.

Child power injects fun into play; article. photo · *WFP* Nov 13, 1987: p37.

Children's play not child's play; article. *WFP* Dec 16, 1987: p38.

Comedy hits Canadian vein; article. photo · *WFP* Nov 25, 1987: p43.

Gas Station to stage breezy theatre fare for summer crowd; article. *WFP* June 27, 1987: p31.

New troupe's motto: laugh with Leacock; article about the Leacock Players. *WFP* Sept 1, 1987: p26.

Play likely to be tough viewing; article. photo · *WFP* Nov 7, 1987: p23.

PTL debacle timely for writer; article. photo · *WFP* Nov 19, 1987: p49.

Theatre company faces stiff test; article. photo · *WFP* Sept 23, 1987: p44.

O'Toole, Lawrence

Elegy for a dying village; film review of *John and the Missus*. photo · *Maclean's* Feb 2, 1987; Vol 100 No 5: p78.

Ouaknine, Serge

Le réel théâtral et le réel médiatique; essay. photo · *Jeu* 1987; No 44: p94–111.

Ouellet, Pierre

[Untitled]; review of *Extrême livre des voyages*. *Estuaire* Autumn 1987; No 46: p87–88.

Ouellette, Fernand

André Belleau (1930–1986); essay. *Liberté* Feb 1987; Vol 29 No 1: p28–31.

La pensée de la poésie; essay. *Liberté* April 1987; Vol 29 No 2: p83–84.

Ouellette-Michalska, Madeleine

André Vachon: le rappel d'une fable ancienne; review of *Toute la terre à dévorer*. photo · *MD* May 23, 1987: pD3.

Aquin et Hypatie filant le parfait amour en Paganie; review of *Renaissance en Paganie*. photo · *MD* June 13, 1987: pD3.

École buissonnière; review of *L'Académie du désir*. *MD* Oct 31, 1987: pD3.

Une écriture qui se cherche encore; review of *L'Écran brisé*. *MD* July 25, 1987: pC6.

Un fil d'Ariane habilement tendu; review of *Le Fils d'Ariane*. photo · *MD* March 28, 1987: pD3.

Une fille bien de son siècle; review of *Cette fois, Jeanne. . . .* *MD* Sept 5, 1987: pC9.

France Ducasse: l'â d'or de l'enfance; review of *La Double vie de Léonce et Lénoil*. photo · *MD* May 9, 1987: pD3.

L'institution littéraire ou la transparence voilée; prose excerpt from *L'Amour de la carte postale*. *Lettres québec* Autumn 1987; No 47: p55–57.

Mourir comme un chat?; reviews of *Mourir comme un chat* and *Facéties*. *MD* July 4, 1987: pC6.

Pour l'amour d'un puzzle; review of *La Passion selon Galatée*. *MD* March 14, 1987: pD3.

La reconstitution de tableaux d'époque; review of *Du soufre dans les lampions*. photo · *MD* April 25, 1987: pD3.

Si Ringuet n'avait pas regardé l'atlas; review of *Le Choix de Jean Panneton dans l'oeuvre de Ringuet*. photo · *MD* Sept 19, 1987: pD3.

Oughton, John

Industrial arts dream; poem. *Prism* Summer 1987; Vol 25 No 4: p30–31.

Lord of the wings; review of *Sanding Down This Rocking Chair on a Windy Night*. *Books in Can* June-July 1987; Vol 16 No 5: p12–13.

Outram, Richard

Around and about; poem. *Exile* 1987; Vol 12 No 2: p116.

Barbed wire; poem. *Exile* 1987; Vol 12 No 2: p118.

Full circle; poem. *Exile* 1987; Vol 12 No 2: p120.

My grandmother; poem. *Exile* 1987; Vol 12 No 2: p117.

Remark; poem. *Exile* 1987; Vol 12 No 2: p119.

Owen, I.M.

Bred in the bark; review of *Tranter's Tree*. *Books in Can* May 1987; Vol 16 No 4: p19.

Children of the world; review of *Intimate Strangers*. *Books in Can* Jan-Feb 1987; Vol 16 No 1: p17–18.

Entering infinity; review of *Enchantment and Sorrow*. *Books in Can* Dec 1987; Vol 16 No 9: p17–18.

Part six of twelve; review of *The Motor Boys in Ottawa*. *Idler* Jan-Feb 1987; No 11: p47–49.

Owen, Margaret

The essence of the prairies; review of *Queen of the Headaches*. *Prairie Fire* Summer 1987; Vol 8 No 2: p63–65.

Owens, Suzanne

Mites vs. pee wees; poem. *Fiddlehead* Summer 1987; No 152: p26–27.

Rapid appearance on mirrors and moons; poem. *Wascana R* Spring 1987; Vol 22 No 1: p67.

Ower, John

Poet-confessor; review of *Archibald Lampman*. *Can Lit* Winter 1987; No 115: p167–169.

The story of an affinity: Lampman's "The Frogs" and Tennyson's "The Lotos-Eaters"; article. *Can Lit* Winter 1987; No 115: p285–289.

Oxendine, Pamela

Getting even; poem. *Fireweed* Winter 1987; No 24: p12–13.

The men I know; poem. *Fireweed* Winter 1987; No 24: p14–15.

[Untitled]; poem. *Fireweed* Winter 1987; No 24: p15.

Pacey, Michael

Garden; poem. *Fiddlehead* Summer 1987; No 152: p80.

Kent County orchestra; poem. *Fiddlehead* Summer 1987; No 152: p82.

The quarrel; poem. *Fiddlehead* Summer 1987; No 152: p81.

Packer, Miriam

The nest; play. *Quarry* Fall 1987; Vol 36 No 4: p5–22.

Padolsky, Enoch

Grove's "Nationhood" and the European immigrant; article. abstract · *J of Can Studies* Spring 1987; Vol 22 No 1: p32–50.

Page, Malcolm

Notes from the Fringe / 2; article. photo · *Can Theatre R* Summer 1987; No 51: p80–82.

Three new political plays; theatre reviews. *Can Drama* 1987; Vol 13 No 2: p224–226.

[Untitled]; review of *Sextet*. *Theatre Hist in Can (special issue)* Spring 1987; Vol 8 No 1: p129–133.

Page, P.K.

Crow's nest; poem. *Malahat R (special issue)* March 1987; No 78: p73–74.

Mme Bourgé dreams of Brazil; short story. *Cross Can Writ Q* 1987; Vol 9 No 2: p5.

Notes on re-reading George Johnston; article. *Malahat R (special issue)* March 1987; No 78: p67–72.

Remembering George Johnston reading; poem. *Malahat R (special issue)* March 1987; No 78: p75.

[Untitled]; biographical articles. *Brick (special issue)* Summer 1987; No 30: ppassim.

Winter morning; poem. *Can Lit* Summer-Fall 1987; No 113–114: p45.

Paikeday, Thomas M.

Bad form in the grammar war; letter to the editor. *G&M* April 22, 1987: pA7.

Paquette, Jean-Marcel

Constantes et ruptures en recherche littéraire: le cas d'Études littéraires; article. *Voix et images* Winter 1987; No 35: p271–277.

Paquin, Jacques

[Untitled]; reviews of *Langues d'aimer* and *Le Tant-à-coeur*. *Estuaire* Summer 1987; No 45: p49–50.

[Untitled]; reviews of *Les Mémoires artificielles* and *Les Changeurs de signes*. *Estuaire* Autumn 1987; No 46: p83–84.

Parameswaran, Uma

Quilted patch; reviews of poetry books. *Can Lit* Spring 1987; No 112: p176–179.

Paratte, Henri-Dominique

Masks; prose poem. *Alpha* Winter 1987; Vol 11: p13.

Paré, François

Mini-comptes rendus; review of *L'Arbre mort*. *Can Child Lit* 1987; No 45: p96–97.

Mini-comptes rendus; review of *Contes du pays de l'orignal*. *Can Child Lit* 1987; No 47: p100–101.

Poèmes et rimes pour émerveiller; review of *Mon ami Pierrot*. *Can Child Lit* 1987; No 46: p100–101.

Paré, Isabelle

Claude Charron, complice de la liberté; article. photo · *MD* Nov 14, 1987: pD13.

Paré, Line

Échos des rêveries enfantines; review of *Dans mon petit violon*. *Can Child Lit* 1987; No 46: p101–102.

Paré, Margaret

Mini-reviews; reviews of children's books. *Can Child Lit* 1987; No 45: p93–96.

Parent, Dominique

L'avenir du français au Québec; article. *Lettres québec* Summer 1987; No 46: p9.

Parizeau, Alice

Un beau roman; review of *L'Héritage*. photo · *MD* Dec 12, 1987: pD5.

Une famille, un coin du monde, un pays; review of *Il y aura toujours des printemps en Amérique*. *MD* Oct 3, 1987: pD3.

À la recherche de tendresse; review of *Les Vingt-quatre heures du clan*. *MD* Dec 24, 1987: pC11.

À la rencontre des huguenots de Namur; review of *Le Feu des souches*. *MD* Dec 12, 1987: pD4.

Quand Alice Parizeau imagine une tentative de corruption au Devoir; prose excerpt from *Blizzard sur Québec*. photo · *MD* Nov 14, 1987: pD1, D12.

Le syndrome du best-seller; review of *Sous la griffe du sida*. photo · *MD* Dec 19, 1987: pD4.

[Untitled]; reviews of novels. *MD* Nov 28, 1987: pD9.

Parker, Susan

Silk purse; poem. *Poetry Can R* Fall 1987; Vol 9 No 1: p9.

Parkin, Andrew

Spitting on the fire; poem. *Antigonish R* 1987; No 69–70: p165–166.

[Untitled]; reviews. *Poetry Can R* Summer 1987; Vol 8 No 4: p36–37.

[Untitled]; reviews of poetry books. *Poetry Can R* Fall 1987; Vol 9 No 1: p37.

Parks, Joy

Rhymes to grow by; poem. *Fireweed* Fall 1987; No 25: p97–101.

[Untitled]; poem. *Fireweed* Fall 1987; No 25: p25.

Parr, John

Engaging stories by newcomer; review of *A Stone Watermelon. TS* March 29, 1987: pA19.

Lively collection; review of *Alberta Bound. TS* June 7, 1987: pG11.

Pass, John

A clue; poem. *Event* Summer 1987; Vol 16 No 2: p99.

A drink of water; poem. *Event* Summer 1987; Vol 16 No 2: p98.

Paterson, Janet M.

[Untitled]; review of *Hubert Aquin ou la quête interrompue. U of Toronto Q* Fall 1987; Vol 57 No 1: p182–183.

Pattinson, Chris

[Untitled]; review of *Nos amis, robots. TS* Feb 8, 1987: pC8.

Paulson, Ron

[Untitled]; short story. *Quarry* Winter 1987; Vol 36 No 1: p103.

Pavlovic, Diane

Cartographie: l'Allemagne québécoise; article. bibliog photo · *Jeu* 1987; No 43: p77–110.

Du décollage à l'envol; article. illus photo · *Jeu* 1987; No 42: p86–99.

Figures: portraits en dix tableaux; article. photo · *Jeu* 1987; No 45: p141–158.

Gilles Maheu: corps à corps; article. photo trans · *Can Theatre R* Fall 1987; No 52: p22–29.

L'être et le para[i]tre: une question du XVIIe siècle posée aujourd'hui; article. photo · *Jeu* 1987; No 44: p154–168.

Reconstitution de "La Trilogie"; article. photo · *Jeu* 1987; No 45: p40–82.

Le sable et les étoiles; article. photo · *Jeu* 1987; No 45: p121–140.

La scène peuplée d'écrans; introduction. photo · *Jeu* 1987; No 44: p91–92.

Splendeurs et misères; article. photo · *Jeu* 1987; No 42: p27–39.

Théâtrographie illustrée; list of plays. photo · *Jeu* 1987; No 44: p169–174.

Thèmes et formes; article. photo · *Jeu* 1987; No 42: p40–48.

[Untitled]; theatre review of *Bilico.* photo · *Jeu* 1987; No 42: p149–151.

[Untitled]; theatre review of *À la recherche de M..* photo · *Jeu* 1987; No 42: p167–168.

[Untitled]; theatre review of *Rien à voir. Jeu* 1987; No 42: p170.

[Untitled]; theatre review of *Le Facteur réalité.* photo · *Jeu* 1987; No 44: p112–113.

[Untitled]; theatre review of *Montréal, série noire.* photo · *Jeu* 1987; No 44: p139–141.

[Untitled]; theatre review of *Fiction.* photo · *Jeu* 1987; No 44: p151–153.

Payne, Rhonda

Via Newfoundland and Africa; essay. photo · *Can Theatre R* Winter 1987; No 53: p26–28.

Peake, Linda M.

[Untitled]; review of *Willful Acts. Theatre Hist in Can (special issue)* Spring 1987; Vol 8 No 1: p126–129.

[Untitled]; review of *The Melville Boys. Books in Can* March 1987; Vol 16 No 2: p25.

[Untitled]; review of *Odd Jobs. Books in Can* March 1987; Vol 16 No 2: p25–26.

Péan, Stanley

À l'index; short story. *Moebius* Winter 1987; No 31: p97–101.

Pearce, Jon

The idea of a poem: an interview with Milton Acorn. *Can Poet* Fall-Winter 1987; No 21: p93–102.

Pearse, Linda

Print power, a book for children; review of *Jeremy Gates and the Magic Key. Atlan Prov Book R* Feb-March 1987; Vol 14 No 1: p14.

A quality spin-off; review of *The Anne of Green Gables Storybook. Atlan Prov Book R* Nov-Dec 1987; Vol 14 No 4: p4.

Pedersen, Stephen

Death on the waterfront; theatre review of *Barometer Rising,* includes profile. photo · *Maclean's* Nov 23, 1987; Vol 100 No 47: p57.

Pedoe, William

A date with Joan; short story. photo · *TS* July 2, 1987: pB6.

Pell, Barbara

Introductory; review of *Canadian Writers and Their Works. Can Lit* Spring 1987; No 112: p179–180.

Pelletier, Claude

Dossiers de presse sur les écrivains québécois: un instrument de recherche unique pour les bibliothèques et les chercheurs; article. *Lettres québec* Summer 1987; No 46: p74–76.

Pelletier, Francine

Atwood keeps high profile among Québécois readers; article. photo · *MG* May 26, 1987: pD9.

Caleb's juggernaut; article. photo · *MG* Oct 31, 1987: pJ11.

Dany's destiny; article. photo · *MG* Dec 24, 1987: pL8.

'Oiseau' feeds on violent love – 'Neruda' long 2-hour stretch; theatre reviews of *Un Oiseau vivant dans la gueule* and *Off Off Off*. *MG* June 3, 1987: pB4.

Stark theatrical visions lose focus in pile of sordid detail; theatre review of *Overground*. *MG* May 26, 1987: pD11.

Pelletier, Jacques

Constitution d'une avant-garde littéraire; article. abstract · *Études lit* Spring-Summer 1987; Vol 20 No 1: p111–130.

L'air du temps; review of *Sédiments 1986*. *Voix et images* Spring 1987; Vol 12 No 3: p524–527.

Pemmy

Wanted: homemaker; poem. *Atlantis* Fall 1987; Vol 13 No 1: p86.

Pengilly, Gordon

[Untitled]; poetry excerpts from *The Cow Poems*. *Dandelion* Spring-Summer 1987; Vol 14 No 1: p5–16.

Penman, Margaret

A cogent view of Canadian theatre; review of *English-Canadian Theatre*. photo · *TS* Dec 27, 1987: pE18.

Magic of popular play is lost in translation; theatre review of *L'Amour en DeRoute*. *TS* Nov 16, 1987: pB6.

Reality, fiction mix in new Tremblay play; theatre review of *Le Vrai monde?*. *TS* Oct 4, 1987: pC4.

Penny, Michael

Pellagra, geophysicist; poem. *Malahat R* Sept 1987; No 80: p109.

Penrod, Lynn

Un conte philosophique; review of *Non, je ne suis pas né*. *Can Child Lit* 1987; No 45: p81–82.

Structure sociale, stratégie textuelle: l'univers narratif de Monique Corriveau; article. *Can Child Lit* 1987; No 46: p45–59.

Penz, K.M.

Eating; poem. *Room of One's Own* Sept 1987; Vol 11 No 4: p85.

Pereira, Helen

Green and gold; short story. illus · *Antigonish R* Winter 1987; No 68: p117–128.

Perel, Shloime

[Untitled]; review of *Essential Words*. photo · *Cross Can Writ Q* 1987; Vol 9 No 2: p18–19.

Perkel, Colin N.

Sticks and stones; short story. photo · *TS* July 6, 1987: pA15.

Perkins, Don

[Five from the Fringe]; review. *NeWest R* April 1987; Vol 12 No 8: p18.

Last of the makeovers; theatre review of *The Thin Edge*. *NeWest R* Feb 1987; Vol 12 No 6: p17.

Scenes from a relationship; theatre review of *Schedules*. *NeWest R* Dec 1987; Vol 13 No 4: p17.

[Ten Lost Years]; theatre review. *NeWest R* Summer 1987; Vol 12 No 10: p18.

Perkyns, Dorothy

Fiction for children: history and mystery; reviews of *Rats in the Sloop* and *Shivers in Your Nightshirt*. *Atlan Prov Book R* Feb-March 1987; Vol 14 No 1: p14.

Perkyns, Richard

Atlantic alternatives in theatre; review of *Canadian Theatre Review*. *Atlan Prov Book R* Feb-March 1987; Vol 14 No 1: p11.

Perren, Susan

Annabel and Goldie go to the sea, Josephine goes to school; reviews of *Can You Catch Josephine?* and *Goldie and the Sea*. *Quill & Quire (Books for Young People)* Oct 1987; Vol 53 No 10: p18–19.

Snoring, smuggling, and snuggling; reviews of children's stories. *Quill & Quire (Books for Young People)* Dec 1987; Vol 53 No 12: p8.

[Untitled]; review of *The Wart on My Finger*. *Quill & Quire (Books for Young People)* June 1987; Vol 53 No 6: p11.

[Untitled]; review of *Mrs. Dunphy's Dog*. *Quill & Quire (Books for Young People)* Aug 1987; Vol 53 No 8: p6–7.

Perrot-Bishop, Annick

Le grand vide; short story. *Moebius* Winter 1987; No 31: P49–59.

Perry, Richard

Asimov robotics. . . .orchestral overtures. . . .marvellous Munsch; reviews of tape versions of children's books. photo · *Quill & Quire (Books for Young People)* Aug 1987; Vol 53 No 8: p10.

Magical wishes. . . .old tales to savour. . . .musical rainbow; review of tape version of *The Three and Many Wishes of Jason Reid*. *Quill & Quire (Books for Young People)* Dec 1987; Vol 53 No 12: p6.

Pair of thrillers. . . .giving the Devil his due. . . .sci-fi fare; review of tape version of *The Red Fox*. photo · *Quill & Quire* Aug 1987; Vol 53 No 8: p38.

Revolting teddies. . . .time-travelling tot. . . .rhymes macabre; reviews of tape versions of *The Olden Days Coat* and *Auntie's Knitting a Baby*. photo · *Quill & Quire (Books for Young People)* Oct 1987; Vol 53 No 10: p14.

Petch, Steve

Another morning; play. photo · *Can Theatre R* Fall 1987; No 52: p59–81.

Petchanatz, Christophe

Elles se sont installées aux fenêtres. . . .; short story. illus · *La Nouvelle barre du jour* May 1987; No 200: p63–65.

Peterman, Michael

New ventures; editorial article. *J of Can Studies* Winter 1987–88; Vol 22 No 4: p3–4.

Passing observations upon the Canadian literary scene, 1985–1987; article. *J of Can Studies* Spring 1987; Vol 22 No 1: p3–4, 160.

Resident & alien; review of *Sheila Watson and The Double Hook*. *Can Lit* Winter 1987; No 115: p144–146.

[Untitled]; review of *Robertson Davies, Playwright*. *Theatre Hist in Can* Fall 1987; Vol 8 No 2: p249–252.

[Untitled]; review of *Canadian Crusoes*. *U of Toronto Q* Fall 1987; Vol 57 No 1: p160–161.

Peters, Dexter

[Untitled]; review of *Whale Waddleby*. *TS* Feb 1, 1987: pA20.

Petersen, Karen

Autocalypse; poem. *U of Windsor R* Fall-Winter 1987; Vol 20 No 1: p54.

Cynicism: last resort of the idealist; poem. *New Q* Winter 1987; Vol 6 No 4: p84.

Dumb luck; poem. *Rubicon* Spring 1987; No 8: p109.

The lost Pleiad; poem. *New Q* Fall 1987; Vol 7 No 3: p93.

November; poem. *New Q* Fall 1987; Vol 7 No 3: p92.

Perception : definition; poem. *New Q* Winter 1987; Vol 6 No 4: p85.

Scapegoat; poem. *New Q* Winter 1987; Vol 6 No 4: p87.

Touched; poem. *New Q* Winter 1987; Vol 6 No 4: p88–89.

Waiting for Odysseus; poem. *Rubicon* Spring 1987; No 8: p108–109.

Wild Winnebagos on the rampage; poem. *New Q* Winter 1987; Vol 6 No 4: p86.

Peterson, Michel

La baguette; short story. illus · *La Nouvelle barre du jour* April 1987; No 198: p67–76.

Le bénévolat au théâtre: un concours obligé: entretien avec Madeleine Rivest, de la Maison Théâtre; interview. photo · *Jeu* 1987; No 42: p135–139.

Les grands explorateurs; short story. *Moebius* Winter 1987; No 31: p127–130.

Petrowski, Nathalie

En attendant la bombe; column. *MD* Oct 3, 1987: pC2.

Plume: écrire pour sauver sa peau; article. photo · *MD* Feb 20, 1987: pB1, B7.

Pett, Alex

The Wife of Bath today – games of love; review of *The Old Dance*. *Event* March 1987; Vol 16 No 1: p100–102.

Phenix, Patricia

The marriage bed; poem. *Wascana R* Spring 1987; Vol 22 No 1: p56.

Philip, Marlene

Hard time, maximum time; reviews of *The Only Minority Is the Bourgeoisie* and *Doing Time*. *Tor South Asian R* Spring 1987; Vol 5 No 3: p28–34.

Philips, Anne

Continuity of immigrants; poem. *NeWest R* Oct 1987; Vol 13 No 2: p16.

Phillips, Edward

How my novel of manners won the prize for crime; essay. illus · *MG* June 27, 1987: pI3.

Phillips, Louis

Naming day in Eden; poem. *Queen's Q* Autumn 1987; Vol 94 No 3: p551.

Picard, Anne-Marie

[Untitled]; review of *Féminins singuliers*. *U of Toronto Q* Fall 1987; Vol 57 No 1: p200–201.

Picton, John

Sue just knew she was going to win – and she did; article. photo · *TS* June 28, 1987: pA17.

Pierce, D.

Death is a riot; poem. *Fiddlehead* Winter 1987; No 154: p18.

Meadowlark; poem. *Fiddlehead* Winter 1987; No 154: p19.

Unimagined child; poem. *Fiddlehead* Winter 1987; No 154: p16–17.

Pierce, Lorne

[Untitled]; interview with Sir Charles G.D. Roberts. *Can Poet* Fall-Winter 1987; No 21: p63–76.

Pierson, Ruth Roach

Wars and roses; poem. *Atlantis* Spring 1987; Vol 12 No 2: p23.

Pierssens, Michel

La nuit transfigurée; essay. *Liberté* Feb 1987; Vol 29 No 1: p82–84.

Piette, Alain

Avatars d'un pacte amoureux; article. *Voix et images* Autumn 1987; Vol 13 No 1: p46–51.

Focalisation, voyeurisme et scène originaire dans Serge d'entre les morts; article. *Voix et images* Spring 1987; Vol 12 No 3: p497–511.

Pilon, Jean-Guy

Un collaborateur éclairé; essay. *Liberté* Feb 1987; Vol 29 No 1: p85.

Pinsent, Gordon

Doubts and fears of a writing actor; essay. photo · *TS* Jan 24, 1987: pG1.

Pitavy, Danièle

La forêt chez les écrivains anglophones; article. abstract · *Études can* 1987; No 23: p147–157.

Pitfield, Michael

[Untitled]; biographical articles. *Brick (special issue)* Summer 1987; No 30: ppassim.

Pitman, Teresa

Girls like me; short story. photo · *TS* Aug 7, 1987: pD22.

Piuze, Simone

Andrée Ferretti: "je ne peux être que politique, puisque je veux agir sur le monde"; article. photo · *MD* July 25, 1987: pC5.

La passion de Louise Courteau; article. photo · *MD* March 21, 1987: pD1, D8.

Plant, Richard

[Untitled]; review of *Whittaker's Theatre*. *Can Theatre R* Winter 1987; No 53: p79–80.

Plantos, Ted

From known to invention; editorial. *Cross Can Writ Q* 1987; Vol 9 No 3–4: p2.

The literary editor: unsung cultural hero; editorial. *Cross Can Writ Q* 1987; Vol 9 No 1: p2.

Literary life-support systems & the Ontario Arts Council; article. photo · *Cross Can Writ Q* 1987; Vol 9 No 3–4: p30–31, 59–60.

Literary Ontario: a regional irony; editorial. *Cross Can Writ Q* 1987; Vol 9 No 2: p2.

The Milton Acorn Memorial People's Poetry Award; article. illus · *Poetry Can R* Summer 1987; Vol 8 No 4: p17.

Pocknell, Pauline

Rus in urbe: un concept classique pour enfants modernes; review of *Si l'herbe poussait sur les toits*. *Can Child Lit* 1987; No 47: p79–81.

Poetker, Audrey

The adulterers: trying to say love; poem. *CV 2* Spring 1987; Vol 10 No 3: p29–30.

Everything here is a poem; poem. *CV 2* Spring 1987; Vol 10 No 3: p26–28.

Poissant, Claude

[Untitled]; theatre review of *Le Petit univers de R.P.* photo · *Jeu* 1987; No 42: p148–149.

Polson, Don

Another straw; poem. *Antigonish R* 1987; No 69–70: p47.

Distances; poem. *U of Windsor R* Spring-Summer 1987; Vol 20 No 2: p82.

Two nights; poem. *U of Windsor R* Spring-Summer 1987; Vol 20 No 2: p83.

Pomer, Bella

Not meant to be a thriller; letter to the editor. *Quill & Quire* June 1987; Vol 53 No 6: p4.

Pond, Marilyn

Duff's house; short story. *Descant* Winter 1987; Vol 18 No 4: p62–69.

Pontbriand, Jean-Noël

La ville; poem. *Estuaire* Winter 1986–87; No 43: p39–48.

Poonia, Gurtek

Proud father; short story. *New Q* Spring-Summer 1987; Vol 7 No 1–2: p64–76.

Pope, Dan

Expiation of an untraced murder; short story. *Descant* Winter 1987; Vol 18 No 4: p44–50.

Remembering the river; poem. *New Q* Winter 1987; Vol 6 No 4: p90.

Porteous, Timothy

[Untitled]; biographical articles. *Brick (special issue)* Summer 1987; No 30: ppassim.

Porter, Anna

None of the above; letter to the editor. *Books in Can* May 1987; Vol 16 No 4: p40.

Porter, Deborah

Criticism misdirected; letter to the editor. *G&M* Oct 28, 1987: pA6.

Porter, Helen

[Untitled]; review of *The Tiger's Daughter*. *Books in Can* Aug-Sept 1987; Vol 16 No 6: p29.

Portman, Jamie

Actor studies each role with director's eye; article. photo · *CH* Oct 8, 1987: pF5.

Alberta play bombs at Blyth festival; theatre review of *Border-town Cafe*. *CH* July 2, 1987: pF1.

Alberta playwright's work squanders talent; theatre review of *Intimate Admiration*. *CH* June 29, 1987: pC1.

Canada Council 30 years old; article. *TS* Dec 17, 1987: pC2.

Council funds fostered arts across nation; article about the Canada Council. *CH* Dec 15, 1987: pC1.

Government sabotaging its own cultural initiatives; article. photo · *CH* Aug 8, 1987: pF3.

Halifax blast commemorated in effective stage production; theatre review of *Barometer Rising*. *CH* Nov 12, 1987: pD2.

History turning to dust: institute races time to microfilm ravaged literature; article. *CH* Oct 28, 1987: pD1.

Minister insists postal subsidies crucial to periodicals; article. *CH* Sept 25, 1987: pF2.

Munro wins third Governor General's Award; article. photo · *CH* May 28, 1987: pC9.

Murrell to write play for Stratford; article. *CH* Oct 7, 1987: pD2.

Neville to don makeup for new Canadian play; article about John Neville. photo · *CH* June 23, 1987: pB6.

Short fiction is thriving; review of *86: Best Canadian Stories*. *CH* Jan 18, 1987: pE4.

Summer-stock circuit rises to new heights in southern Ontario; article. photo · *CH* July 7, 1987: pC8.

W.O. Mitchell's Crocus cronies shine on stage; theatre review of *Royalty Is Royalty*. *CH* Oct 15, 1987: pF1.

Posesorski, Sherie

The absurd majesty of desires; review of *Small Claims*. *G&M* Jan 31, 1987: pE20.

A friendship; review of *A Forest for Zoe*. *G&M* Jan 10, 1987: pE17.

Hard memory; review of *Isle of Joy*. *G&M* Aug 22, 1987: pC14.

Novel's heroine searches for life after divorce; review of *The Life of Helen Alone*. *MG* Jan 24, 1987: pB8.

Sardonic commentary; review of *The Parrot Who Could*. *G&M* Aug 8, 1987: pC18.

[Untitled]; review of *The Whirlpool*. *Books in Can* Jan-Feb 1987; Vol 16 No 1: p26.

[Untitled]; review of *Dzelarhons*. *Books in Can* June-July 1987; Vol 16 No 5: p22.

Potter, Robin

A day at the office; poem. *Can Forum* April 1987; Vol 67 No 768: p32.

I want our talk to be safe; poem. *Room of One's Own* April 1987; Vol 11 No 3: p35.

Pottier, Anna

Poetical protest; letter to the editor. *G&M* July 27, 1987: pA6.

Publishers serve up some dismal fare; letter to the editor. photo · *G&M* July 8, 1987: pA7.

Potvin, Elizabeth

The Bell Jar and Mrs. Blood: portraits of the artist as divided woman; article. abstract · *Atlantis* Fall 1987; Vol 13 No 1: p38–46.

"The eternal feminine" and the clothing motif in Grove's fiction; article. *Studies in Can Lit* 1987; Vol 12 No 2: p222–238.

Potvin, Luc

Retour; letter to the editor. *MD* March 28, 1987: pA10.

Poulin, Jeanne

Quebec publishers meet English Canada at Frankfurt; article. *Quill & Quire* Dec 1987; Vol 53 No 12: p11.

Pouliot, Joséphine

D'autres classiques; letter to the editor. *MD* June 16, 1987: p10.

Powe, B.W.

If the book ends; essay. illus · *G&M* June 13, 1987: pC17.

Powell, Barbara

[Untitled]; reviews of *Afterworlds* and *Sanding Down This Rocking Chair on a Windy Night*. *Wascana R* Fall 1987; Vol 22 No 2: p88–91.

Powell, David A.

Sex and Politics: parody in the bedrooms of the province; theatre review. *NeWest R* Nov 1987; Vol 13 No 3: p18.

Power, Nicholas

[Untitled]; poem. illus · *Cross Can Writ Q* 1987; Vol 9 No 3–4: p12.

Pozier, Bernard

De l'amour comme ailleurs; poem. *Estuaire* Autumn 1987; No 46: p23–24.

Du mauvais dans le poème; essay. *Estuaire* Summer 1987; No 45: p39–41.

[Untitled]; review of *L'Écouté*. *Estuaire* Winter 1986–87; No 43: p75.

[Untitled]; review of *Le Prix du lait*. *Estuaire* Summer 1987; No 45: p58.

Pratt, Brian

From the back of the bus; poem. *Waves* Winter 1987; Vol 15 No 3: p62.

Precosky, Don

Of poets and hackers: notes on Canadian post-modern poets; article. *Studies in Can Lit* 1987; Vol 12 No 1: p146–155.

Preece, Katrina

[Untitled]; review of *Dislocations*. *Malahat R* (special issue) March 1987; No 78: p151–152.

Préfontaine, Yves

La littérature en perte de vitesse!; letter to the editor. *MD* Aug 12, 1987: p8.

Pollen; poem. trans · *Arc* Fall 1987; No 19: p12–13.

Prayer in simple prose; poem. trans · *Arc* Fall 1987; No 19: p10–11.

Prest, Harry

"Give me melancholy or give me death"; reviews of *Children of Abel* and *The Moving Light*. *U of Windsor R* Fall-Winter 1987; Vol 20 No 1: p95–98.

Prince, Heather

Carvings; short story. *Fiddlehead* Autumn 1987; No 153: p62.

Church break; short story. *Fiddlehead* Autumn 1987; No 153: p63.

Lunch break; short story. *Fiddlehead* Autumn 1987; No 153: p64.

Supper break; short story. *Fiddlehead* Autumn 1987; No 153: p66.

Wallpaper stories; short story. *Fiddlehead* Autumn 1987; No 153: p65.

Pritchard, Mary

There and back again; review of *Blaine's Way*. *Can Child Lit* 1987; No 46: p66–67.

Procyk, C.P.

Responsibi[li]ty; poem. *NeWest R* Sept 1987; Vol 13 No 1: p15.

Prokosh, Kevin

Artist colony; article. *WFP* Aug 4, 1987: p27.

Canadian playwrights give urban life short shrift, says one writer who didn't; article. *WFP* Jan 22, 1987: p35.

The great Canadian dream; article. photo · *WFP* March 18, 1987: p35.

Plays probe evils of prejudice; article. photo · *WFP* Feb 3, 1987: p32.

Playwright, 37, credits absurd inquisitiveness for surrealistic drama; article. photo · *WFP* March 6, 1987: p20.

Prairie playwright: Kelly Rebar's characters have roots in Canadian soil; article. photo · *WFP* Sept 19, 1987: p29.

Riel play aims to right wrongs; article. photo · *WFP* March 5, 1987: p36.

Writer turns back on Bach; biographical article. photo · *WFP* Oct 31, 1987: p21, 31.

Young bards suffer image problem; article. photo · *WFP* Sept 5, 1987: p29–30.

Prose, Francine

[Untitled]; review of *Jacob Two-Two and the Dinosaur*. *NYT Book R* Oct 18, 1987: p38.

Proulx, Sylvain

La mort sera tentée; poem. illus · *La Nouvelle barre du jour* May 1987; No 200: p29–33.

Provencher, Richard

Fort Louisbourg; poem. *Can Auth & Book* Winter 1987; Vol 62 No 2: p21.

Purdy, Al

An arrogance; poem. *Poetry Can R* Fall 1987; Vol 9 No 1: p21.

Crimes of the heart; reviews of *Gothic* and *The Animals Within*. *Books in Can* April 1987; Vol 16 No 3: p32, 34.

Flying over Vancouver Island; poem. *Malahat R* June 1987; No 79: p113–114.

The gossamer ending; poem. *Malahat R* June 1987; No 79: p111–112.

How I wasted Canada Council money – and wrote a thousand poems; essay. photo · *Cross Can Writ Q* 1987; Vol 9 No 3–4: p34–35, 58–59.

"Irving Layton speaking"; interview. photo · *Waves* Winter 1987; Vol 15 No 3: p5–13.

Jalopies; poem. photo · *Poetry Can R* Fall 1987; Vol 9 No 1: p20.

Maybe fish; poem. *Poetry Can R* Fall 1987; Vol 9 No 1: p20.

The mermaid inn: permanently Canadian; essay. photo · *G&M* Nov 14, 1987: pD6.

On the death of F.R. Scott, January 31, 1985; poem. illus · *Books in Can* Nov 1987; Vol 16 No 8: p11.

Questions; poem. *Books in Can* Nov 1987; Vol 16 No 8: p11.

Riding west; poem. *Poetry Can R* Fall 1987; Vol 9 No 1: p21.

[Untitled]; biographical articles. *Brick (special issue)* Summer 1987; No 30: ppassim.

[Untitled]; letter to the editor. *Cross Can Writ Q* 1987; Vol 9 No 3–4: p64.

Purdy, Anthony

Une bibliographie indispensable; review of *Bibliographie analytique d'Yves Thériault, 1940–1984*. *Can Child Lit* 1987; No 45: p54–55.

Quarrington, Paul

Home opener, 1908; excerpt from a novel in progress. *Descant (special issue)* Spring-Summer 1987; Vol 18 No 1–2: p117–126.

Tight to something; short story. *Descant (special issue)* Spring-Summer 1987; Vol 18 No 1–2: p12–19.

Quednau, Marion

Family; prose excerpt from *The Butterfly Chair*. *Malahat R* Sept 1987; No 80: p95–108.

Those accidents of truth that sneak up; review of *Memoirs of a Book-Molesting Childhood*. *G&M* Dec 26, 1987: pC23.

Quélen, Dominique

Un carnet noir et autres textes; poems. illus · *La Nouvelle barre du jour* May 1987; No 200: p37–44.

Lucernaires; poem. *La Nouvelle barre du jour* May 1987; No 200: p43–44.

[Untitled]; poetry excerpts from *Un Carnet noir*. *La Nouvelle barre du jour* May 1987; No 200: p37–38.

[Untitled]; poetry excerpts from *Cela*. *La Nouvelle barre du jour* May 1987; No 200: p39–40.

Vers des jours moins bien; poem. *La Nouvelle barre du jour* May 1987; No 200: p41–42.

Querengesser, Neil

Waves; poem. *Dandelion* Fall-Winter 1987; Vol 14 No 2: p24.

Quickenden, Robert

Chapbooks range from good to silly; reviews of poetry books. *WFP* Jan 31, 1987: p55.

Mandel makes a sure-footed guide; review of *The Family Romance*. *WFP* July 18, 1987: p54.

Poets exhibit vast differences; reviews of *Flicker and Hawk* and *Skrag*. *WFP* May 16, 1987: p70.

Poets view China, Dada; reviews of *China: Shockwaves* and *The Merzbook*. *WFP* Dec 5, 1987: p56.

Young poets on display; reviews of poetry books. photo · *WFP* March 14, 1987: p52.

Quigley, Theresia

A crowded Eden; review of *Spring Tides*. *Fiddlehead* Autumn 1987; No 153: p102–103.

Two Quebec novels in translation; reviews of *Standing Flight* and *The Legacy*. *Fiddlehead* Summer 1987; No 152: p95–98.

Quill, Greg

Copyright Act opponents called 'irresponsible'; article. *TS* Dec 29, 1987: pE1, E5.

Decline rises to top Genie nominations; article. photo · *TS* Feb 5, 1987: pF1.

Poets train for Winter Olympics in Calgary; article. *TS* May 13, 1987: pB5.

Toronto honors the best with annual arts awards; article. photo · *TS* Sept 23, 1987: pF1.

Quinn, Joseph A.

Editor's introduction. photo · *U of Windsor R* Fall-Winter 1987; Vol 20 No 1: p2.

Quinnet, Paul

[Untitled]; letter to the editor. *Atlantic* May 1987; Vol 259 No 5: p14.

Rabinovitch, Sandra

CBC's Vanishing Point; letter to the editor. *G&M* Nov 3, 1987: pA6.

Racine, Bernard

Au sommet, l'univers littéraire francophone; article. *MD* Aug 15, 1987: pC2.

Radford, F.L.

[Untitled]; review of *Another Country*. *World Lit in Eng* Spring 1987; Vol 27 No 1: p60–62.

Radison, Garry

Figures; poem. *Ariel* Oct 1987; Vol 18 No 4: p52.

Radkewycz, Alexandra

Robert Billings, 38, poet, critic, teacher; obituary. photo · *TS* June 29, 1987: pA23.

Radu, Kenneth

4.5 on the Richter scale; short story. *Rubicon* Spring 1987; No 8: p149–156.

Auto-da-fé; poem. *CV 2* Summer 1987; Vol 10 No 4: p40.

A bird in the hand; short story. *Prism* Winter 1987; Vol 25 No 2: p59–68.

Sleep; poem. *Event* March 1987; Vol 16 No 1: p92–94.

Treading water; poem. *Fiddlehead* Spring 1987; No 151: p46–47.

Rae, Lisbie

Tremblay at P'tit Bonheur, 1982–1985; article. photo · *Can Drama* 1987; Vol 13 No 1: p1–26.

[Untitled]; reviews. *Can Drama* 1987; Vol 13 No 2: p229–231.

Raeburn, Charles A.

For T.S. Eliot; poem. *Alpha* Winter 1987; Vol 11: p29.

Rafelman, Rachel

[Untitled]; review of *A Long Night of Death*. *Quill & Quire* Feb 1987; Vol 53 No 2: p17.

[Untitled]; review of *Under the House*. *Quill & Quire* April 1987; Vol 53 No 4: p29.

Rajic, Negovan

A gaol for innocents; short story. illus trans · *Idler* Sept-Oct 1987; No 14: p24–27.

A winter evening; short story. illus trans · *Idler* Jan-Feb 1987; No 11: p14–16.

Randle, Doug

A field guide to the generations passing; short story. *Quarry* Spring 1987; Vol 36 No 2: p32–42.

Rapoport, Janis

Letter to Don Domanski; poem. *Poetry Can R* Spring 1987; Vol 8 No 1–2: p11.

Letters to Douglas Donegani; poem. *Poetry Can R* Spring 1987; Vol 8 No 1–2: p11.

Mog the poet; poem. *Poetry Can R* Fall 1987; Vol 9 No 1: p39.

Night: Ridge Road, Wolfville, Nova Scotia; poem. *Poetry Can R* Fall 1987; Vol 9 No 1: p39.

Post cards from Nova Scotia; poem sequence. *Poetry Can R* Spring 1987; Vol 8 No 1–2: p11.

[Untitled]; essay. photo · *Cross Can Writ Q* 1987; Vol 9 No 3–4: p24–25.

Rasmussen, Tamara

'Toes; poem. *Antigonish R* 1987; No 69–70: p206.

Raspa, Anthony

Imperfect conquests; reviews of *The Manor House of De Villeray* and *Le Tour du Québec par deux enfants*. *Can Lit* Winter 1987; No 115: p172–174.

Ratapopoulos, Almanzor

Du char: petit manuel à l'usage du FAD1001F; humourous essay. illus · *Liberté (special issue)* 1987: p63–73.

Raymond, M.H.

Jesus of the aerials; short story. *Prism* Autumn 1987; Vol 26 No 1: p90–92.

Reed, Alison

Stimulus; poem. *Queen's Q* Autumn 1987; Vol 94 No 3: p571.

Regan, Stephen

[Untitled]; review of *Fables of Brunswick Avenue*. *British J of Can Studies* June 1987; Vol 2 No 1: p185–187.

[Untitled]; review of special Canadian issue of *Lines Review*. *British J of Can Studies* June 1987; Vol 2 No 1: p189–190.

Regan, Tom

A sound beyond hearing; article. photo · *Atlan Insight* Dec 1987; Vol 9 No 12: p19–21.

Regush, Nicholas

Feeding on glimmers of hope; article. photo · *MG* May 30, 1987: pB1.

Montreal poet hopes for second shot at surgery; article. *MG* Oct 28, 1987: pA6.

Parkinson's victim: new hope for survival; article. photo · *MG* April 24, 1987: pA1, A5.

Poet Hertz too weak for surgery in Mexico; article. photo · *MG* May 28, 1987: pA1, A5.

Poet still hoping for last-chance surgery; article. *MG* June 1, 1987: pA3.

Victim of Parkinson's is too weak for surgery; article. *MG* May 21, 1987: pA1.

Reid, D.C.

Aberdaron; short story. *Quarry* Spring 1987; Vol 36 No 2: p59.

Dear Aldous; poem. *Antigonish R* 1987; No 69–70: p202.

Somewhere out of Abersoch; short story. *Quarry* Spring 1987; Vol 36 No 2: p58.

Reid, David A.

[Untitled]; review of *The Devil Is Innocent*. *Quill & Quire* Jan 1987; Vol 53 No 1: p27.

Reid, Monty

Specimen; poem. *NeWest R* Feb 1987; Vol 12 No 6: p18.

Touchscreen; poem. *NeWest R* Feb 1987; Vol 12 No 6: p4.

Reimer, Dolores

My aunt's house; poem. *NeWest R* Sept 1987; Vol 13 No 1: p12.

No return on investment; poem. *NeWest R* Sept 1987; Vol 13 No 1: p12.

Reimer, Douglas

Witty plenitude; review of *Afternoon Starlight*. *Prairie Fire* Spring 1987; Vol 8 No 1: p91–93.

Reimer, Mavis

[Untitled]; reviews of *The Fusion Factor* and *Zanu*. *Border Cross* Spring 1987; Vol 6 No 2: p25.

Reiter, David

Our bones get stiff; poem. *Dandelion* Fall-Winter 1987; Vol 14 No 2: p31.

The snow in us; poem. *Dandelion* Fall-Winter 1987; Vol 14 No 2: p30.

Summer before winter; short story. *Wascana R* Fall 1987; Vol 22 No 2: p69–81.

Relke, Diana M.A.

Demeter's daughter: Marjorie Pickthall & the quest for poetic identity; article. *Can Lit* Winter 1987; No 115: p28–43.

Killed into art: Marjorie Pickthall and The Wood Carver's Wife; article. biog · *Can Drama* 1987; Vol 13 No 2: p187–200.

Rémillard, Jean-Robert

Une auteure qui se découvrira; theatre review of *Overground*. *Liberté* Dec 1987; Vol 29 No 6: p156.

Du déjà goûté quelque part; theatre review of *Le Vrai monde?*. *Liberté* Dec 1987; Vol 29 No 6: p145–146.

Renaud, André

Un beau livre de réflexions; review of *L'Univers est fermé pour cause d'inventaire*. *Lettres québec* Summer 1987; No 46: p64–65.

Le dualisme de Naïm Kattan; review of *Le Repos et l'oubli*. photo · *Lettres québec* Autumn 1987; No 47: p52–53.

Renaud, Linda

Hollywood: some call it Quebec South; article. photo · *MG* Dec 19, 1987: pE7.

Retzleff, Marjorie

A frog he would a-wooing go; review of *Frogs*. *Matrix* Fall 1987; No 25: p75–76.

Rhead, Valerie

The spider plant; short story. photo · *TS* Aug 6, 1987: pH6.

Rhenisch, Harold

Brushwork; poem. *Grain* Fall 1987; Vol 15 No 3: p52–57.

The light in the fingers; poem. *Event* Summer 1987; Vol 16 No 2: p14–15.

Michael Rhenisch, graveur; poem. *Fiddlehead* Winter 1987; No 154: p20–26.

Ten years after planting the house field; poem. *Ariel* April 1987; Vol 18 No 2: p63–64.

The threshing floor; poem. *Event* Summer 1987; Vol 16 No 2: p12–13.

[Untitled]; poetry excerpt from *The Koan*. *Antigonish R* 1987; No 69–70: p61–67.

We will not be read; poem. *Grain* Fall 1987; Vol 15 No 3: p58–61.

Ricard, François

Le destinataire privilégié; essay. *Liberté* Feb 1987; Vol 29 No 1: p86–87.

Notes à chaud; essay. *Liberté (special issue)* 1987: p60–62.

Riccio, Joan

Fragment on a Greek island; poem. *Poetry Can R* Spring 1987; Vol 8 No 1–2: p13.

Rice, Bruce

Wedding picture; poem. *Grain* Summer 1987; Vol 15 No 2: p19.

Rice, Nicholas

Mistaken identity; letter to the editor. *G&M* Oct 9, 1987: pA6.

Richar, Gustav A.

Cloud Lake; short story. *Northward J* 1987; No 42: p20–27.

Richardson, Keith

[Untitled]; biographical articles. *Brick (special issue)* Summer 1987; No 30: ppassim.

Riches, Brenda

The breeding ground; short story. *Capilano R* 1987; No 43: p10–16.

Editorial. *Grain* Winter 1987; Vol 15 No 4: p5.

Imprint; prose poem. *Rubicon* Fall 1987; No 9: p54.

Open invitation; prose poem. *Rubicon* Fall 1987; No 9: p55.

Time pieces; prose poem. *Capilano R* 1987; No 44: p55–59.

The wheel; short story. biog photo · *Cross Can Writ Q* 1987; Vol 9 No 1: p14–15, 27.

Ricou, Laurie

Triptych; editorial article. *Can Lit* Summer-Fall 1987; No 113–114: p4–6.

[Untitled]; reviews of foreign books and periodicals about Canadian literature. *Can Lit* Summer-Fall 1987; No 113–114: p274–275.

[Untitled]; review of *Prairie Women. U of Toronto Q* Fall 1987; Vol 57 No 1: p154–156.

Riddell, John

Now wise will expect; poem. *Cross Can Writ Q* 1987; Vol 9 No 3–4: p15.

Ridout, John S.

Authors and libraries; letter to the editor. *G&M* Nov 4, 1987: pA6.

Rigelhof, T.F.

A gringo's view of Mexico; review of *Cage. G&M* July 18, 1987: pC17.

Ray Smith's world; reviews of *Century* and *The Montreal Story Tellers. Atlan Prov Book R* Feb-March 1987; Vol 14 No 1: p17.

The real story behind the story; review of *A Dream Like Mine.* photo · *G&M* Oct 24, 1987: pC19.

The thrill of reading intoxicating stories; review of *Telling the Tale. G&M* Sept 5, 1987: pC13.

Unlikely romantic; review of *Unknown Soldier. G&M* Dec 12, 1987: pE5.

Rile, Karen

[Untitled]; review of *Nadine. NYT Book R* Aug 9, 1987: p20.

Rioux, Hélène

Sisyphe; short story. *Moebius* Winter 1987; No 31: p25–30.

[Untitled]; review of *La Poursuite. Moebius* Winter 1987; No 31: p135–137.

Riskin, Mary W.

A mating of east and west; review of *Between Men. Maclean's* Oct 12, 1987; Vol 100 No 41: p56h.

Ritter, Erika

In spite of alienation, Acorn did go home again; essay. photo · *TS* Sept 12, 1987: pM2.

It's more which than what; review of *The CanLit Foodbook. TS* Dec 5, 1987: pM14.

Writing a book the perfect gift; review of *The CanLit Foodbook. CH* Dec 6, 1987: pB1.

Rivard, Ken

On an empty sidewalk; poem. *Poetry Can R* Summer 1987; Vol 8 No 4: p16.

Sawmill baseball; short story. *Waves* Spring 1987; Vol 15 No 4: p39.

When Gina looks straight; poem. *Wascana R* Spring 1987; Vol 22 No 1: p91.

The year I was born; poem. *CV 2* Spring 1987; Vol 10 No 3: p25.

Rivard, Yvon

La première ou la dernière; essay. *Liberté* Dec 1987; Vol 29 No 6: p20–21.

Le roman sans qualités; review of *L'Hiver de Mira Christophe. Liberté* June 1987; Vol 29 No 3: p103.

Voyage: l'oiseau le plus rapide; essay. *Liberté* June 1987; Vol 29 No 3: p35–38.

Robb, Nancy

Kulyk Keefer's rising star: five books in three genres in one year; article, includes reviews. photo · *Quill & Quire* July 1987; Vol 53 No 7: p69–70.

Pitt on Pratt: a match made in Newfoundland; article. photo · *Quill & Quire* Aug 1987; Vol 53 No 8: p31.

Robert, Lucie

Hommage à David Hayne; review of *Solitude rompue.* photo · *Lettres québec* Spring 1987; No 45: p68.

Les jeunes loups; reviews. *Voix et images* Spring 1987; Vol 12 No 3: p561–564.

Misères de l'édition théâtrale; reviews of plays. *Voix et images* Winter 1987; No 35: p339–342.

La naissance d'une parole féminine autonome dans la littérature québécoise; article. abstract · *Études lit* Spring-Summer 1987; Vol 20 No 1: p99–110.

Théâtre didactique; reviews of *Mademoiselle Autobody* and *Sortie de secours*. *Voix et images* Autumn 1987; Vol 13 No 1: p196–198.

Robert, Suzanne

La conscience comme trame de vie; essay. *Liberté* Feb 1987; Vol 29 No 1: p88–89.

Magasinage: un délice culturel; essay. *Liberté* June 1987; Vol 29 No 3: p10–13.

Nues-propriétés ou L'insidieux pouvoir de l'architecture; essay. *Liberté* Oct 1987; Vol 29 No 5: p4–7.

Sisyphe, Virgile et Dracula; essay. *Liberté* Dec 1987; Vol 29 No 6: p4–7.

Roberts, David

Writer's earnings questioned; article. *WFP* Sept 9, 1987: p1, 4.

Roberts, Dorothy

A home on Needham Street; poem. *Fiddlehead* Summer 1987; No 152: p24–25.

The snowflakes; poem. *Antigonish R* 1987; No 69–70: p167.

Roberts, Kevin

101 south s.f.; poem. *Can Lit* Summer-Fall 1987; No 113–114: p206.

San Francisco sonnet; poem. *Can Lit* Summer-Fall 1987; No 113–114: p144.

Where is here?; poem. *Can Lit* Summer-Fall 1987; No 113–114: p206.

Roberts, Paul

Bowering's western: woolly post-modernist chic; review of *Caprice*. photo · *Quill & Quire* May 1987; Vol 53 No 5: p19.

Copper-plating a strange fantasy; review of *A Strange Manuscript Found in a Copper Cylinder*. *TS* July 4, 1987: pM10.

Poetry of love at its purest; reviews of poetry books. *TS* Aug 15, 1987: pM10.

Robidoux, Réjean

Nelligan n'était pas fou, il acceptait seulement de passer pour ce fou qui s'appelait Nelligan. review of *Nelligan n'était pas fou!*. *Lettres québec* Winter 1986–87; No 44: p74–76.

Robinson, Harry

An Okanagan Indian becomes a captive circus showpiece in England; poem. *Can Fic Mag (special issue)* 1987; No 60: p11–32.

Robinson, Michelle

Lots of tribulations in doing translation; letter to the editor. *G&M* March 4, 1987: pA7.

Robinson, Peter

[Untitled]; review of *The Mournful Demeanor of Lieutenant Boruvka*. *Quill & Quire* June 1987; Vol 53 No 6: p33.

[Untitled]; review of *The Glorious East Wind*. *Quill & Quire* Sept 1987; Vol 53 No 9: p79.

Robson, Barbara

Award nomination 'petrifies' Prairie storyteller; article. photo · *WFP* May 23, 1987: p21–22.

Library-use payments not trumpeted; article. *WFP* April 1, 1987: p35.

Local playwright wins literary tripleheader; article. photo · *WFP* Feb 25, 1987: p34.

Name power: local poet wrestles with words, increase in feminist knowledge; article. photo · *WFP* Oct 13, 1987: p33.

Novelist, poet Kroetsch receives top payment under library fee plan; article. *WFP* April 22, 1987: p38.

Prairie Publishers Group disbanding after five years; article. *WFP* March 4, 1987: p33.

Tale of tales; article about Kay Stone. photo · *WFP* Dec 6, 1987: p18.

Winnipeg poet envisages role as quiet healer; article. photo · *WFP* April 3, 1987: p30.

Rocard, Marcienne

[Untitled]; review of *Time in the Air*. *Études can* June 1987; No 22: p138–139.

Rochon, Lisa

Innovation and athletic interpretation mingle in Dutch treatment of Atwood; review of dance based on *Murder in the Dark*. *G&M* June 8, 1987: pC10.

Munro wins top literary prize; article. photo · *G&M* May 28, 1987: pD1.

New battle looming over artists' taxes; article. *G&M* Nov 21, 1987: pC6.

Six Palm Trees hilarious, moving family tale; theatre review. photo · *G&M* July 9, 1987: pD6.

Rogal, Stan

At the expense of repeating yourself; poem. *Arc* Spring 1987; No 18: p65.

Cargo; poem. *Poetry Can R* Fall 1987; Vol 9 No 1: p10.

Good night Prometheus; poem. *Arc* Spring 1987; No 18: p65.

Shaping; poem. *Alpha* Winter 1987; Vol 11: p30.

Strange flowers; poem. *Alpha* Winter 1987; Vol 11: p30.

[Untitled]; poetry excerpts from *In Search of the Emerald City*. *Fiddlehead* Spring 1987; No 151: p94–95.

Rogers, Linda

Anybody home; reviews of *The Last Echo* and *Wise-Ears*. *Can Lit* Winter 1987; No 115: p204–205.

Setting the hook; poem. *Can Lit* Summer-Fall 1987; No 113–114: p75.

West coast report: David Day; regional column. *Poetry Can R* Summer 1987; Vol 8 No 4: p23.

The west coast: the Spirit Quest Festival; regional column. *Poetry Can R* Fall 1987; Vol 9 No 1: p22.

Rolfe, C.D.

[Untitled]; review of *Les Rapports culturels entre le Québec et les États-Unis. British J of Can Studies* June 1987; Vol 2 No 1: p167–168.

Romney, Claude

Une oeuvre multiforme: les livres d'Yves Thériault pour adolescents; article. bibliog · *Can Child Lit* 1987; No 47: p12–22.

Rooke, Constance

Between the world and the word: John Metcalf's "The Teeth of My Father"; article. *New Q* Spring-Summer 1987; Vol 7 No 1–2: p240–246.

[Untitled]; review of *The Progress of Love. Malahat R (special issue)* March 1987; No 78: p152.

[Untitled]; review of *A Stone Watermelon. Malahat R* June 1987; No 79: p156.

[Untitled]; review of *Adele at the End of the Day. Malahat R* June 1987; No 79: p161.

[Untitled]; review of *Beyond Forget. Malahat R* Sept 1987; No 80: p130–131.

[Untitled]; review of *Beneath the Western Slopes. Malahat R* Sept 1987; No 80: p137.

[Untitled]; review of *Inspecting the Vaults. Malahat R* Dec 1987; No 81: p101.

[Untitled]; review of *The Color of Blood. Malahat R* Dec 1987; No 81: p101–102.

[Untitled]; review of *The Butterfly Chair. Malahat R* Dec 1987; No 81: p102.

[Untitled]; review of *Memory Board. Malahat R* Dec 1987; No 81: p102.

[Untitled]; review of *Heroine. Malahat R* Dec 1987; No 81: p103.

Rooke, Leon

The best good girl ever; short story. *Event* Summer 1987; Vol 16 No 2: p70–76.

The composers; short story. *Grain* Spring 1987; Vol 15 No 1: p50–56.

LR loves GL; short story. *Exile* 1987; Vol 12 No 1: p92–104.

Neighbourhood watch; short story. *Waves* Winter 1987; Vol 15 No 3: p16–23.

A story for Constance; short story. *Fiddlehead* Spring 1987; No 151: p23–25.

The sugar derby; short story. *Prism* Winter 1987; Vol 25 No 2: p30.

Those who can't cut it with Mary; short story. *Descant* Winter 1987; Vol 18 No 4: p59–61.

Roscoe, Patrick

China; short story. illus · *Can Auth & Book* Summer 1987; Vol 62 No 4: p14–16.

Poppies always fall; short story. illus · *Can Forum* Feb 1987; Vol 66 No 766: p30–35.

Rose, Anne

Daphne; poem. *Matrix* Fall 1987; No 25: p55.

Rose, Marilyn J.

[Untitled]; review of *Cocktails at the Mausoleum. U of Windsor R* Spring-Summer 1987; Vol 20 No 2: p97–101.

Rose, Phyllis

One step ahead of the zeitgeist; review of *Overhead in a Balloon. NYT Book R* March 15, 1987: p7.

Rosenberg, Jerome H.

An Atwood anatomy; review of *Margaret Atwood: A Feminist Poetics. Essays on Can Writ* Winter 1987; No 35: p88–92.

Rosenberg, Lori Ann

Lay it on the line; poem. *Room of One's Own* Sept 1987; Vol 11 No 4: p108.

Rosenblatt, Joe

The love object, 1945; short story. *Prairie Fire* Spring 1987; Vol 8 No 1: p35–41.

National debt; letter to the editor. *Books in Can* Jan-Feb 1987; Vol 16 No 1: p38.

Rosengarten, Herbert

[Untitled]; review of *The Beginnings of the Book Trade in Canada. Eng Studies in Can* June 1987; Vol 13 No 2: p220–224.

Rosmarin, Léonard

Dans la gueule du loup; review of *Gueule-de-loup. Can Child Lit* 1987; No 45: p63–64.

Ross, Catherine Sheldrick

The Livesay papers; review of *The Papers of Dorothy Livesay. Can Poet* Fall-Winter 1987; No 21: p116–117.

Whereness; review of *Resident Alien. Can Lit* Spring 1987; No 112: p164–165.

Ross, Elsie

Violence a theme of life in Chile; article. photo · *CH* July 27, 1987: pA5.

Ross, Oakland

On fiction, TV and losers; article. photo · *G&M* April 18, 1987: pC1.

"Suddenly, you wake up and you're 80"; biographical article. photo · *G&M* April 18, 1987: pC1.

Ross, Sally

An historical novel on Acadians deported to France; review of *Le Chemin des Huit-Maisons. Atlan Prov Book R* Nov-Dec 1987; Vol 14 No 4: p11.

Short stories from Caraquet; review of *Sur les pas de la mer. Atlan Prov Book R* May-June 1987; Vol 14 No 2: p9.

Ross, Veronica

White sky; short story. *New Q* Spring-Summer 1987; Vol 7 No 1–2: p77–84.

Roth, Jackie

Marital pursuits; short story. photo · *TS* July 8, 1987: pA21.

Rousseau, Pierre

[Untitled]; editorial reply. *Jeu* 1987; No 43: p181.

Rowan, Renée

Le Conseil de la santé récupère une pièce boudée par l'hôpital Louis-H. Lafontaine; article. photo · *MD* April 30, 1987: p13.

L'écriture en prison: à la foix thérapie et création; article about prison writing. photo · *MD* March 28, 1987: pD1, D8.

Le Père Gustave Lamarche s'éteint; obituary. photo · *MD* Oct 13, 1987: p3.

Roy, André

Le dragueur surréaliste; poem. *Estuaire* Autumn 1987; No 46: p21.

La surface du monde; review of *Carnage pâle*. *Estuaire* Winter 1986–87; No 43: p79–80.

[Untitled]; prose excerpts from *Le Retour*. *Estuaire* Spring 1987; No 44: p67–70.

[Untitled]; review of *Amérique intérieure*. *Estuaire* Summer 1987; No 45: p49.

[Untitled]; review of *Les Métamorphoses d'Ishtar*. *Estuaire* Autumn 1987; No 46: p85.

Roy, Bruno

Manifeste: au jeu; review of *L'Enjeu du manifeste / le manifeste en jeu*. *Moebius* Spring 1987; No 32: p133–136.

Roy, Johanne

La difficile reconnaissance des gens de lettres; article. *MD* May 23, 1987: pD2.

L'étude des lettres québécoises est obligatoire à Liège; article. *MD* April 9, 1987: p13.

Son trac le plus fou, Anne Hébert le ressent devant la page blanche; article. photo · *MD* May 1, 1987: p12.

Roy, Robert

Vrai et faux; letter to the editor. *MD* Jan 8, 1987: p8.

Royer, Jacqueline

[Untitled]; poetry excerpt from *Les Cieux grattés*. *Estuaire* Winter 1986–87; No 43: p49–50.

Royer, Jean

Le 27e prix Québec-Paris va à Jacques Boulerice; article. *MD* Feb 27, 1987: p7.

"Alliance-Québec fait la guerre avec les mots de la paix"; article. photo · *MD* March 16, 1987: p11, 14.

Les alouettes en colère. . . .; article. *MD* March 14, 1987: pD1-D2.

Antonio d'Alfonso ou "l'érotisme des mots"; review of *L'Autre rivage*. photo · *MD* June 20, 1987: pD2.

Barcelo, le jogger heureux; review of *Aaa, aâh, ha ou les amours malaisées*. photo · *MD* Jan 31, 1987: pB3.

Une bombe dans la tête; review of *Éroshima*. *MD* Oct 10, 1987: pD3.

Bonne anné, Anne Hébert!; editorial. *MD* Jan 5, 1987: p10.

Carole David et France Mongeau lauréates du prix Nelligan 1986; article. photo · *MD* March 10, 1987: p11.

Le CDA dévoile la liste des finalistes; article. photo · *MD* April 30, 1987: p13.

Le Centre culturel de Longueuil prend le nom de Jacques Ferron; article. photo · *MD* Oct 16, 1987: p15.

De l'entretien; article about interviewing. *Études fran* Winter 1987; Vol 22 No 3: p117–123.

Les derniéres feuilles de l'été; reviews. photo · *MD* Oct 3, 1987: pD3.

Dessins d'écrivains; review of *Les Écrivains s'illustrent*. *MD* March 21, 1987: pD2.

Deux nouveaux acadeémciens; article. *MD* Oct 19, 1987: p9.

Deux récits de l'intelligence et du coeur; reviews of *Chambres* and *Catégoriques un deux et trois*. *MD* Jan 3, 1987: pC4.

Écrire l'amour c'est parler de soi; article. illus · *MD* May 2, 1987: pD1-D2.

"Écrire pour se donner ce qu'on n'a pas dans la vraie vie"; article. photo · *MD* June 6, 1987: pD3.

Estuaire au carrefour des poésies; editorial · *Estuaire* Spring 1987; No 44: p5–8.

Et le Verbe s'est fait oreille; article about La Littérature de l'oreille. photo · *MD* Sept 11, 1987: p13.

Le Festival national du livre est ouvert!; article. *MD* April 28, 1987: p17.

Fondation de Guérin littérature: 25 titres en 1987; article. photo · *MD* Feb 21, 1987: pB3.

La Fondations des Forges couronne André Roy; article. photo · *MD* Sept 23, 1987: p11.

François Hébert, moraliste sans morale; reviews of *L'Homme aux maringouins* and *Le Dernier chant de l'avant-dernier dodo*. *MD* Feb 7, 1987: pB3.

François Hébert: un auteur derrière sa pipe; article. photo · *MD* Feb 14, 1987: pC1, C6.

Un grand prix littéraire Guérin; article. *MD* Feb 21, 1987: pB3.

Le grand prix Logidisque de la science-fiction et du fantastique est attribué à Esther Rochon; article. photo · *MD* April 14, 1987: p11.

Guillevic au Festival national de poésie: "Vous êtes plus francophones que les Français"; article. *MD* Oct 14, 1987: p13.

Jacques Boulerice: pour une autre enfance; reviews of *Apparence* and *Distance*. *MD* Feb 14, 1987: pC3.

Jean Éthier-Blais: "La littérature, c'est tout ce que nous avons"; article. photo · *MD* Jan 24, 1987: pB1, B4.

Jeanne-Mance Delisle: "Je cherche le tragique de l'âme québécoise"; article. photo · *MD* June 13, 1987: pD2.

Un jour de rage, Jean-Marie Poupart s'est mis dans de "beaux draps"; article. photo · *MD* June 6, 1987: pD4.

Jovette Marchessault: le roman de la réconciliation; article. photo · *MD* Oct 8, 1987: p15.

L'administration Doré ressuscite le Grand Prix littéraire de Montréal; article. photo · *MD* Sept 4, 1987: p13.

L'année littéraire 86: René, Jacques et les autres. . . .; survey article. photo · *MD* Jan 10, 1987: pB1, B5.

L'âme japonaise de Paul Ohl; article. photo · *MD* March 5, 1987: p9.

Le Loisir littéraire du Québec fête ses 25 ans; article. photo · *MD* May 2, 1987: pD2.

L'originalité et l'oralité; reviews of *Coq à deux têtes* and *Les Terres du songe*. *MD* May 30, 1987: pD3.

L'Union des écrivains maintient la sonnerie d'alarme sur la langue; article. photo · *MD* Sept 3, 1987: p13, 15.

Marco Micone propose la cohabitation; article. photo · *MD* March 17, 1987: p14.

"Le monde en un seul mot"; review of *Verbe silence*. *MD* May 30, 1987: pD5.

Naïm Kattan: "J'ai choisi Montréal pour vivre en français"; article. photo · *MD* April 25, 1987: pD5.

Ninon Larochelle mérite le prix de la nouvelle de Radio-Canada; article. *MD* Feb 20, 1987: p7.

Notes de lecture; reviews of periodicals. *MD* March 21, 1987: pC7.

Notes de lecture; reviews of periodicals. *MD* March 21, 1987: pD8.

Notes de lectures; reviews of *La Mort aurorale* and *Écoute, Sultane*. *MD* May 23, 1987: pD2.

Les ondes littéraires; list of radio and television programmes. *MD* Sept 12, 1987: pD2.

Les ondes littéraires; list of radio and television programmes. *MD* Sept 19, 1987: pD2.

Les ondes littéraires; list of radio and television programmes. *MD* Sept 26, 1987: pD2.

Les ondes littéraires; list of radio and television programs. *MD* Oct 3, 1987: pD2.

Les ondes littéraires; list of radio and television programs. *MD* Oct 10, 1987: pD2.

Les ondes littéraires; list of radio and television programs. *MD* Oct 17, 1987: pD2.

Les ondes littéraires; list of radio and television programs. *MD* Oct 24, 1987: pD2.

La passion selon Lise Harou; review of *À propos de Maude*. *MD* Jan 10, 1987: pB3.

Paul-Marie Lapointe, poète d'aujourd'hui; article. photo · *MD* April 18, 1987: pD1, D3.

Photo de famille; article. photo · *MD* Sept 28, 1987: p9.

Pierre Vadeboncoeur remporte le prix Canada-Suisse; article. photo · *MD* March 31, 1987: p17.

La poésie n'est pas une science mais une parole; reviews of *Le Tombeau d'Adélina Albert* and *Qu'en carapaces de mes propres ailes*. *MD* April 25, 1987: pD4.

La poésie québécoise en revues françaises; reviews of French periodicals. *MD* May 2, 1987: pD3.

La poésie spirituelle de Gustave Lamarche; article. photo · *MD* Oct 17, 1987: pD2.

Poésie: trois rétrospectives; reviews of poetry books. photo · *MD* Feb 9, 1987: p11.

Portrait de Piazza au coeur de la ville; review of *Blues Note*. photo · *MD* Jan 17, 1987: pB3.

Pour un portrait de Saint-Denys Garneau review of *Le Choix de Jacques Blais dans l'oeuvre de Saint-Denys Garneau*. *MD* May 23, 1987: pD2.

"Pourquoi tous les adultes ne sont-ils pas des artistes?"; article. photo · *MD* June 20, 1987: pD1, D8.

Prix du Conseil des arts; article. *MD* April 25, 1987: pD3.

Q-S congédiera Jasmin mais gardera l'émission; article. *MD* Jan 15, 1987: p6.

Quatre Saisons laisse tomber son émission littéraire; article. *MD* June 17, 1987: p13.

Le Québec de Félix Leclerc. review of *Félix Leclerc, le roi heureux*. *MD* Jan 24, 1987: pB3-B4.

"Regarder le monde et découvrir ce qui attend de na[i]tre": Fernand Ouellette et le retour de la poésie; article. photo · *MD* June 13, 1987: pD1, D8.

Renaud Longchamps: le vertige derrière la découverte; article. photo · *MD* April 4, 1987: pD3.

La Rencontre des écrivains: "une aventure majeure"; article. *MD* April 27, 1987: p11, 15.

La rentrée littéraire; preview of fall book list. photo · *MD* Sept 12, 1987: pD1, D8.

Roger Bellemare: de la musique sur des poèmes de Miron et Anne Hébert; article. photo · *MD* May 20, 1987: p12.

Le Salon du livre de l'Outaouais; article. photo · *MD* April 4, 1987: pD2.

Le sentiment de la langue; reviews of *"Quand on a une langue on peut aller à Rome"* and *Les Changeurs de signes*. *MD* Feb 28, 1987: pC3.

Suzanne Jacob: les grand boulevards intérieurs; article. photo · *MD* Jan 31, 1987: pB1.

Suzanne Lamy: elle était le double d'Ariane et un théoricienne passionnée; obituary. photo · *MD* Feb 28, 1987: pC3.

Le troisième Festival nationale de poésie; article. photo · *MD* Sept 26, 1987: pD8.

[Untitled]; review of *Aaa, aàh, ha ou les amours malaisées*. *MD* Jan 23, 1987: p7.

[Untitled]; review of *La Passion selon Galatée*. *MD* Jan 30, 1987: p7.

[Untitled]; review of *Terroristes d'amour*. *MD* March 13, 1987: p15.

Les vertus d'un premier recueil; reviews of poetry books. photo · *MD* March 21, 1987: pD3.

La vie littéraire; column. photo · *MD* Jan 3, 1987: pC2.

La vie littéraire; column. photo · *MD* Jan 10, 1987: pB2.

La vie littéraire; column. *MD* Jan 17, 1987: pB2.

La vie littéraire; column. photo · *MD* Jan 24, 1987: pB2.

La vie littéraire; column. *MD* Jan 31, 1987: pB2.

La vie littéraire; column. *MD* Feb 7, 1987: pB2.

La vie littéraire; column. *MD* Feb 14, 1987: pC2.

La vie littéraire; column. *MD* Feb 21, 1987: pB2.

La vie littéraire; column. *MD* Feb 28, 1987: pC2.

La vie littéraire; column. *MD* March 7, 1987: pB2.

La vie littéraire; column. photo · *MD* March 14, 1987: pD4.

La vie littéraire; column. photo · *MD* March 21, 1987: pD2.

La vie littéraire; column. photo · *MD* March 28, 1987: pD2.

La vie littéraire; column. *MD* April 4, 1987: pD2.

La vie littéraire; column. photo · *MD* April 11, 1987: pD2.

La vie littéraire; column. photo · *MD* April 18, 1987: pD2.

La vie littéraire; column. *MD* April 25, 1987: pD2.

La vie littéraire; column. photo · *MD* May 2, 1987: pD2.

La vie littéraire; column. *MD* May 9, 1987: pD2.

La vie littéraire; column. photo · *MD* May 16, 1987: pD2.

La vie littéraire; column. photo · *MD* May 23, 1987: pD2.

La vie littéraire; column. photo · *MD* May 30, 1987: pD2.

La vie littéraire; column. photo · *MD* June 6, 1987: pD2.

La vie littéraire; column. photo · *MD* June 13, 1987: pD2.

La vie littéraire; column. photo · *MD* June 20, 1987: pD2.

La vie littéraire; column. *MD* Sept 12, 1987: pD2.

La vie littéraire; column. photo · *MD* Sept 19, 1987: pD2.

La vie littéraire; column. photo · *MD* Sept 26, 1987: pD2.

La vie littéraire; column. *MD* Oct 3, 1987: pD2.

La vie littéraire; column. photo · *MD* Oct 10, 1987: pD2.

La vie littéraire; column. photo · *MD* Oct 17, 1987: pD2.

La vie littéraire; column. *MD* Oct 24, 1987: pD2.

La vitrine du livre; reviews. *MD* March 14, 1987: pD4.

La vitrine du livre; reviews. photo · *MD* March 21, 1987: pD2.

La vitrine du livre; reviews. photo · *MD* March 28, 1987: pD2.

La vitrine du livre; reviews. photo · *MD* April 4, 1987: pD2.

La vitrine du livre; reviews. *MD* April 11, 1987: pD2.

La vitrine du livre; reviews. photo · *MD* April 18, 1987: pD2.

La voix familière de Gérald Godin; review of *Ils ne demandaient qu'à brûler*. photo · *MD* Sept 12, 1987: pD3.

Rubinsky, Holley Ballard

On an island; short story. *Event* Summer 1987; Vol 16 No 2: p33–44.

Preacher's geese; short story. *Malahat R* Dec 1987; No 81: p5–14.

Rubio, Mary

Canadian children's literature 1983 / Bibliographie de la littérature canadienne pour la jeunesse: 1983; bibliography. *Can Child Lit* 1987; No 47: p29–56.

Mini-reviews; reviews of children's stories. *Can Child Lit* 1987; No 46: p105–109.

Mini-reviews; reviews of children's stories. *Can Child Lit* 1987; No 47: p96–99.

Rudakoff, Judith

Beyond the Fringe; reviews of plays. *Books in Can* March 1987; Vol 16 No 2: p18.

[Untitled]; reviews of plays. *Can Theatre R* Summer 1987; No 51: p86–87.

Ruebsaat, Norbert

Pontiac; short story. *Writing* Dec 1987; No 20: p46–50.

Reading Brian Fawcett; reviews of *Cambodia* and *The Secret Journal of Alexander Mackenzie*. *Event* Summer 1987; Vol 16 No 2: p118–121.

Ruelland, Jacques-G.

Un choix délibéré pour la vie; review of *Pourquoi pas dix?*. *MD* Nov 14, 1987: pD15.

Runnells, Rory

Challenging the commonplaces; introduction to play excerpt from *The King of America*. *Prairie Fire* Spring 1987; Vol 8 No 1: p56.

Ruprecht, Alvina

Effets sonores et signification dans les Belles-soeurs de Michel Tremblay; article. *Voix et images* Spring 1987; Vol 12 No 3: p439–451.

Rush, Jerry M.

Glenn Gould's idea of north; poem. *Northward J* 1987; No 42: p32.

Hollow pages; poem. *NeWest R* Dec 1987; Vol 13 No 4: p18.

Myth III; poem. *Northward J* 1987; No 42: p32.

They are instinctively wise; poem. *NeWest R* Dec 1987; Vol 13 No 4: p15.

White whale song; poem. *Northward J* 1987; No 42: p32.

Witchcraft / or Love is a burrowing; poem. *NeWest R* Dec 1987; Vol 13 No 4: p19.

Rusk, James

Writer realizes a dream with Bethune film; article. photo · *G&M* April 15, 1987: pC5.

Russell, Anne E.

[Untitled]; review of *Masques of Morality*. *Quill & Quire* Oct 1987; Vol 53 No 10: p23.

Russell, Judith

[Untitled]; reviews of *Rough Passage* and *April Raintree*. *Queen's Q* Spring 1987; Vol 94 No 1: p191–193.

Ruttan, Karen

[Untitled]; review of *Cloud Gate. Poetry Can R* Spring 1987; Vol 8 No 2–3: p40.

[Untitled]; review of *Undressing the Dark. Poetry Can R* Summer 1987; Vol 8 No 4: p37.

[Untitled]; review of *A Hinge of Spring. Poetry Can R* Fall 1987; Vol 9 No 1: p32–33.

[Untitled]; review of *Exile Home. Poetry Can R* Fall 1987; Vol 9 No 1: p35.

Ruvinsky, Joan

Beep; prose poem. *Prism* Summer 1987; Vol 25 No 4: p119–120.

[Untitled]; reviews of *In the Second Person* and *Double Standards. Rubicon* Spring 1987; No 8: p178–181.

[Untitled]; poem. *Quarry* Summer 1987; Vol 36 No 3: p25.

[Untitled]; poem. *Quarry* Summer 1987; Vol 36 No 3: p26–27.

Ruzesky, Jay

[Untitled]; review of *Malcolm Lowry: Vancouver Days. Malahat R* Dec 1987; No 81: p109–110.

Rysstad, Jean

Contiguous; short story. *U of Windsor R* Spring-Summer 1987; Vol 20 No 2: p1–6.

The sugar jigsaw; short story. *New Q* Spring-Summer 1987; Vol 7 No 1–2: p126–132.

Sabourin, Claude

Rencontre étonnante; review of *L'Ours et le kangourou. Lettres québec* Winter 1986–87; No 44: p82.

Sabourin, Jean-Guy

Narcisse se regarde dans l'eau jusqu'à y plonger. . . .; theatre review of *Le Vrai monde?. Liberté* Dec 1987; Vol 29 No 6: p144–145.

Sabourin, Marie-André

Histoire; short story. *Moebius* Winter 1987; No 31: p31–33.

Saddlemyer, Ann

On the necessity of criticising criticism; essay. abstract · *Theatre Hist in Can (special issue)* Spring 1987; Vol 8 No 1: p135–140.

Safarik, Allan

The timetable; poem. *CV 2* Spring 1987; Vol 10 No 3: p41–42.

Sagaris, Lake

Wind; poem. *Dandelion* Fall-Winter 1987; Vol 14 No 2: p25.

Saint-Jacques, Denis

Colloque Auteur(e) pour vivre; article. *Lettres québec* Autumn 1987; No 47: p10.

Des dames de fleurs; review of *Des Cerisiers en fleurs, c'est si joli!. MD* Nov 21, 1987: pD2.

Saint-Martin, Fernande

Par-delà la censure, les séductions du vrai; article. *Moebius (special issue)* Spring 1987; No 32: p97–105.

Saint-Martin, Lori

André Belleau: une voix reconnaissable entre toutes; review of *Surprendre les voix.* photo · *MD* Jan 24, 1987: pB3.

Carte postale; short story. *Moebius* Winter 1987; No 31: p109–110.

"Crois ou meurs": à quand le manifeste vidéo-clip?; review of *L'Enjeu du manifeste / le manifeste en jeu.* photo · *MD* April 18, 1987: pD2.

Des genres éclatés, près du "texte infini"; review of *Extase et déchirure.* photo · *MD* Oct 17, 1987: pD3.

Un essai original sur l'impérialisme culturel; review of *L'Amour de la carte postale. MD* May 30, 1987: pD3.

Le goût de prolonger le dialogue avec les écrivains; review of *Écrivains contemporains, entretiens 4.* photo · *MD* Nov 7, 1987: pD3.

La modernité québécoise "pure laine"; review of *À double sens. MD* May 9, 1987: pD3.

Naïm Kattan de Bagdad à Montréal; review of *Le Repos et l'oubli.* photo · *MD* June 6, 1987: pD2.

Ontarois entre deux langues; reviews of *Nouvelles de la capitale* and *L'Obomsawin. MD* Dec 12, 1987: pD4.

Portrait du Québécois au repos; review of *Les Pratiques culturelles des Québécois. MD* April 25, 1987: pD4.

Pour transformer l'essence même de la pensée; review of *Surréalisme et littérature québécoise. MD* Oct 31, 1987: pD3.

Quatres couples (fables); short story. *Liberté* Dec 1987; Vol 29 No 6: p39–42.

Suzanne Lamy, pour une morale de la critique; article. *Voix et images* Autumn 1987; Vol 13 No 1: p29–40.

Saint-Pierre, Jacques

ABC de la censure; series of connected short stories. *Moebius (special issue)* Spring 1987; No 32: p75–81.

[Untitled]; review of *Chambres. Moebius (special issue)* Spring 1987; No 32: p120–121.

[Untitled]; review of *Le Désert blanc. Moebius (special issue)* Spring 1987; No 32: p121–123.

[Untitled]; reviews of poetry books. *Moebius* Spring 1987; No 32: p128–130.

[Untitled]; review of *La Cavée. Moebius* Autumn 1987; No 34: p125–126.

Salmaniw, Steve

War and peace; excerpt from a novel in progress. *Alpha* Winter 1987; Vol 11: p15–17.

Salvail, Danielle

[Untitled]; theatre review of *It Must Be Sunday.* photo · *Jeu* 1987; No 42: p156–158.

Sanger, Peter

Finding D'Sonoqua's child: myth, truth and lies in the prose of Emily Carr; article. photo · *Antigonish R* 1987; No 69–70: p211–239.

Saouter, Catherine

Le Matou d'Yves Beauchemin: du fait littéraire à la cha[i]ne de productions-médias; article. *Voix et images* Spring 1987; Vol 12 No 3: p393–402.

Sarah, Robyn

The aging woman with braids; poem. *Poetry Can R* Spring 1987; Vol 8 No 1–2: p12.

Before snow; poem. *Queen's Q* Summer 1987; Vol 94 No 2: p286.

Detour; prose poem. *Poetry Can R* Spring 1987; Vol 8 No 1–2: p12.

Interim; poem. *Can Forum* March 1987; Vol 66 No 767: p34.

March, last quarter; poem. *Poetry Can R* Spring 1987; Vol 8 No 1–2: p12.

Nature walk; poem. *Poetry Can R* Spring 1987; Vol 8 No 1–2: p12.

Shed; poem. *Prism* Winter 1987; Vol 25 No 2: p53.

Sufficient; poem. *Prism* Winter 1987; Vol 25 No 2: p54.

Walking a dog in the rain; poem. *Poetry Can R* Spring 1987; Vol 8 No 1–2: p12.

Zero holding; poem. *Can Forum* Feb 1987; Vol 66 No 766: p35.

Sarkadi, Laurie

Pressing poetry: why Red Deer College Press is alive and well and thriving in the middle of Alberta; article. *NeWest R* Feb 1987; Vol 12 No 6: p14.

Sarkonak, Ralph

Cartographies; review of *Études françaises*. *Can Lit* Summer-Fall 1987; No 113–114: p244–245.

The text as crossroads; review of *La Québécoite*. *Can Lit* Spring 1987; No 112: p100–102.

Theory comes out of the closet; essay. *Can Lit* Spring 1987; No 112: p61–63.

Sartorello, Lori

The mundane; poem. *Antigonish R* Winter 1987; No 68: p38.

Saunders, Janet

Three absolute page-turners; reviews of *Crang Plays the Ace* and *Gallows View*. photo · *WFP* May 9, 1987: p56.

Saunders, Leslie

Jazz dream from a difficult labour; poem. *Quarry* Winter 1987; Vol 36 No 1: p27–28.

Second delivery; poem. *Quarry* Winter 1987; Vol 36 No 1: p28.

Saunders, Leslie H.

So-called fiction serves no purpose; letter to the editor. *TS* March 24, 1987: pA20.

Saunders, Margaret

For Ginger (on her 19th birthday); poem. *Can Auth & Book* Winter 1987; Vol 62 No 2: p22.

Saunders, Robert

Writers at war found wanting; review of *The Great War of Words*. *WFP* Nov 7, 1987: p54.

Saunders, Tom

Bandy Papers mix bizarre humor with just a touch of the tragic; review of *This One's on Me*. *WFP* Nov 7, 1987: p54.

Detective with a difference; review of *The Mournful Demeanor of Lieutenant Boruvka*. photo · *WFP* Sept 26, 1987: p64.

The tribulations of an author; review of *Enchantment and Sorrow*. photo · *WFP* Dec 19, 1987: p51.

Savard, Marie

Non-lieu; short story. *Moebius* Summer 1987; No 33: p77–79.

Scanlan, Larry

Guiding the way to our literary history and geography; review of *The Oxford Illustrated Literary Guide to Canada*. photo · *Quill & Quire* Dec 1987; Vol 53 No 12: p21.

Scharf, John S.

[Untitled]; letter to the editor. *G&M* Nov 30, 1987: pA6.

Schecter, Stephen

L'anarchie à Venise; essay. *Liberté* Dec 1987; Vol 29 No 6: p43–53.

Scheier, Libby

The case for creative chaos: writing and gender; essay. photo · *Poetry Can R* Fall 1987; Vol 9 No 1: p8–9.

[Untitled]; review of *The Self-Completing Tree*. *Cross Can Writ Q* 1987; Vol 9 No 3–4: p39–40.

Schelle, Susan

[Untitled]; letter to the editor. *G&M* Dec 19, 1987: pD7.

Schissel, Wendy

"Uncertain steerage"; review of *E.J. Pratt: The Truant Years*. *Ariel* Jan 1987; Vol 18 No 1: p76–78.

Schmauder, Christopher

Moonbase 2000; short story. photo · *TS* July 14, 1987: pG12.

Schmidt, Anita

Here since 1921; letter to the editor. *WFP* Nov 13, 1987: p6.

Not overpaid; letter to the editor. *WFP* Sept 19, 1987: p7.

Schmidt, Brenda M.

If at first you don't succeed; review of *Starring Quincy Rumpel*. *Can Child Lit* 1987; No 46: p81–82.

Schnurmacher, Thomas

Author Jacobson has more than the gift of the gab; column. *MG* Dec 4, 1987: pC1.

Cairo professor in Westmount synagogue as guest speaker; column. *MG* April 30, 1987: pE2.

Canada's songbird: picky she's not; column. *MG* May 8, 1987: pD1.

Canadian writers fly south for fest; column. *MG* Oct 7, 1987: pH1.

Great Montrealer Hugh MacLennan feted at Racket Club; column. *MG* March 13, 1987: pH1.

Hart broken? Manager calls it quits; column. *MG* Nov 12, 1987: pE2.

It's home-movie time – but let's just skip Debbie Does Dorion; column. *MG* Feb 10, 1987: pB6.

Liz barges down the Nile in triumph; column. *MG* April 21, 1987: pC11.

Liz says she laughed at the fat jokes; column. *MG* Oct 9, 1987: pC1.

Meatball Al guards pearly gates in adolescent farce; column. *MG* May 7, 1987: pD12.

Miami Vice's Don Johnson a Stowe-away in resort town; column. *MG* Jan 21, 1987: pF6.

Montreal misses and misters just don't have that Flare; column. photo · *MG* Jan 29, 1987: pC12.

A novel approach to presenting her work; column. *MG* May 5, 1987: pB6.

Now great-grandma gets to cry wolf, too; column. *MG* Dec 16, 1987: pF1.

Star Trek's Capt. Kirk beaming up to Montreal; column. *MG* Aug 11, 1987: pC8.

Schoenberg, Mark

[Untitled]; theatre review of *The Last Bus*. photo · *Maclean's* Feb 23, 1987; Vol 100 No 8: p55.

Scholar, Michael

[Untitled]; theatre review of *Quartet for Three Actors*. *Maclean's* Jan 26, 1987; Vol 100 No 4: p55.

Schomperlen, Diane

She wants to tell me; short story. *Quarry* Winter 1987; Vol 36 No 1: p64–72.

Schorn, Grant F.G.

Errors hurt prize-winning story; letter to the editor. *CH* Aug 8, 1987: pA6.

Schrey, E.

Le-Grau-du-Roi; poem. *Quarry* Winter 1987; Vol 36 No 1: p95–96.

Lighthouse of La Gacholle; poem. *Quarry* Winter 1987; Vol 36 No 1: p94.

Mas Le Paradis; poem. *Quarry* Winter 1987; Vol 36 No 1: p94–95.

Schroeder, Andreas

The mill; short story. *Grain* Winter 1987; Vol 15 No 4: p18–21.

Some musings on narrative in Canadian fiction; essay. *Grain* Winter 1987; Vol 15 No 4: p14–17.

Schut, Laurie

Threads of fire beads of light; poem. *Event* March 1987; Vol 16 No 1: p38–39.

Schwartz, Susan

Mitchell praises academic life; article. photo · *MG* Dec 5, 1987: pJ13.

Tip sheet: . . . .Irving Layton; column. photo · *MG* Dec 9, 1987: pE14.

Tip sheet: . . . .writers meet; column. photo · *MG* Oct 14, 1987: pC9.

Tip sheet: doctor to speak on AIDS and food industry; column. photo · *MG* April 1, 1987: pC10.

Tip sheet: educator to speak on learning-disabled children; column. *MG* March 11, 1987: pD10.

Tip sheet: experts to lead forum on drug abuse; column. *MG* Jan 14, 1987: pE3.

Tip sheet: forum will focus on AIDS, media; column. *MG* June 17, 1987: pH2.

Tip sheet: Lakeshore artists to hold spring exhibition and sale; column. *MG* April 8, 1987: pE13.

Tip sheet: Save the Children seeks funds for millions of starving children; column. *MG* April 29, 1987: pE11.

Tip sheet: storytellers will present a night for lovers, liars and lunatics; column. photo · *MG* Feb 11, 1987: pD3.

Schwartzwald, Robert

[Untitled]; review of *L'Édition littéraire au Québec de 1940 à 1960*. *Études lit* Spring-Summer 1987; Vol 20 No 1: p193–199.

Sciff-Zamaro, Roberta

The re / membering of the female power in Lady Oracle; article. *Can Lit* Spring 1987; No 112: p32–38.

Scobie, Stephen

Arachne's progress; review of *No Fixed Address*. *Brick* Winter 1987; No 29: p37–40.

Definitions of theory; poem. *Poetry Can R* Summer 1987; Vol 8 No 4: p13.

Felix Paul Greve; poem. *Prairie Fire* Winter 1987–88; Vol 8 No 4: p82.

[Untitled]; reviews of *Private Properties* and *Second Nature*. *Malahat R (special issue)* March 1987; No 78: p153–154.

[Untitled]; review of *Killing the Swan*. *Malahat R (special issue)* March 1987; No 78: p154.

[Untitled]; reviews of *The Self-Completing Tree* and *The Collected Poems*. *Malahat R (special issue)* March 1987; No 78: p154–155.

[Untitled]; reviews of *The Fabulous Disguise of Ourselves* and *The Power to Move*. *Malahat R* June 1987; No 79: p166.

[Untitled]; review of *Afterworlds*. *Malahat R* June 1987; No 79: p168.

[Untitled]; review of *The Moving Light*. *Malahat R* Sept 1987; No 80: p140.

[Untitled]; review of *How to Read Faces*. *Malahat R* Sept 1987; No 80: p140–141.

[Untitled]; reviews of poetry books. *Malahat R* Dec 1987; No 81: p104–106.

[Untitled]; review of *Instructions*. *Malahat R* Dec 1987; No 81: p106.

[Untitled]; review of *Not Noir*. *Malahat R* Dec 1987; No 81: p108.

Scott, Chris

Upper-case action and epic adventure; review of *Booby Trap*. photo · *G&M* Aug 22, 1987: pC16.

Scott, F.R.

Dancing; poem. photo · *Brick (special issue)* Summer 1987; No 30: p59.

A grain of rice; poem. *Brick (special issue)* Summer 1987; No 30: p43.

Last rites; poem. *Brick (special issue)* Summer 1987; No 30: p7–8.

Laurentian Shield; poem. *Brick (special issue)* Summer 1987; No 30: p18.

The unnamed lake; poem. *Brick (special issue)* Summer 1987; No 30: p8.

[Untitled]; autobiographical essays. *Brick (special issue)* Summer 1987; No 30: ppassim.

Scott, Jon C.

Picture-power; reviews of *Very Last First Time* and *Zoom Away*. *Can Lit* Spring 1987; No 112: p159–162.

Scott, M.L.

New Albertan fiction; reviews of *Green Eyes, Dukes and Kings* and *Frogs*. *NeWest R* Summer 1987; Vol 12 No 10: p12.

Scott, Marian Dale

[Untitled]; biographical articles. *Brick (special issue)* Summer 1987; No 30: ppassim.

Scott, Peter Dale

Flight; poem. *Brick (special issue)* Summer 1987; No 30: p64.

Scott, Susan

Albertan's time travel tale offers reassurance; review of *The Doll*. photo · *CH* Sept 27, 1987: pE6.

Authors ease teen angst in the wilds of Alberta; reviews of young adult novels. photo · *CH* April 23, 1987: pD1.

Clark's Moons reflect mythic light; review of *The Moons of Madeleine*. *CH* March 1, 1987: pC8.

Cultural collisions fascinate; review of *The Moneylenders of Shahpur*. *CH* April 12, 1987: pF7.

Fraser stirs deep fears to provide understanding; review of *My Father's House*. *CH* Oct 25, 1987: pE5.

Satisfying youth mystery also portrays way of life; review of *The Cowboy Kid*. photo · *CH* July 11, 1987: pE10.

Science fiction story probes relationships; review of *The Dream Catcher*. *CH* July 12, 1987: pE4.

Scotton, Ann

[Untitled]; biographical articles. *Brick (special issue)* Summer 1987; No 30: ppassim.

Scov-Nielsen, Kurt

Amnesty; poem. *Fiddlehead* Spring 1987; No 151: p91.

The breakfast club; poem. *Fiddlehead* Spring 1987; No 151: p92.

Ghosts; poem. *Fiddlehead* Spring 1987; No 151: p93.

Scoville, Lorna

Kinsella's losers triumph; review of *The Alligator Report*. photo · *CH* March 29, 1987: pE5.

[Untitled]; review of *After the Fact*. *CH* May 3, 1987: pE6.

Scowcroft, Ann

[Untitled]; review of *The Montreal Story Tellers*. *Rubicon* Spring 1987; No 8: p197–199.

[Untitled]; review of *Century*. *Rubicon* Fall 1987; No 9: p153–155.

Scrivener, Leslie

A career of love; article. photo · *TS* Nov 8, 1987: pD1-D2.

'Daring girl' who captured author's heart stars in book; article. biog photo · *TS* Dec 6, 1987: pD5.

Farley Mowat's writing for fun now; article. photo · *TS* Oct 18, 1987: pD1-D2.

Magazine's literary mentor leaves with mixed emotions; article. photo · *CH* July 12, 1987: pE6.

Mr. Saturday Night; biographical article. photo · *TS* July 5, 1987: pD1-D2.

On Sundays this businessman writes; article. photo · *TS* Dec 6, 1987: pD1-D2.

Rewriting paid off for contest winner; article. photo · *TS* June 28, 1987: pA16.

Storyteller relives her youth; article. photo · *TS* Dec 20, 1987: pD6.

Storyteller's credo: 'I rearrange reality'; article about Fred Hill. photo · *TS* Aug 16, 1987: pD1, D5.

Scruton, Roger

Vanished consolations; reviews of *Dvorak in Love* and *Mirákl*. *Times Lit Supp* Jan 23, 1987; No 4373: p83.

Seaman, Andrew

Thomas H. Raddall, a decade later; reviews of *The Dreamers* and *A Name for Himself*. *Atlan Prov Book R* Feb-March 1987; Vol 14 No 1: p19.

Seidner, Eva

A master's sharp eye; interview with Robertson Davies. photo · *Maclean's* Oct 19, 1987; Vol 100 No 42: p8–9, 12.

An uncensored view; interview with Josef Skvorecky. photo · *Maclean's* May 11, 1987; Vol 100 No 19: pT3-T4.

Sekulic, Christine

Christine 'truly enjoyed' this book; review of *Hey World, Here I Am!*. TS Feb 1, 1987: pA20.

Seller, Robert M.

Poignant tales of P.E.I. life give pleasure; review of *The Governor of Prince Edward Island. CH* April 5, 1987: pE5.

Selman, Jan

Three cultures, one issue; essay. photo · *Can Theatre R* Winter 1987; No 53: p11–19.

Serafino, Allan

Prairie grasses; poem. *Wascana R* Fall 1987; Vol 22 No 2: p38–39.

Serviss, Shirley A.

Confession; poem. *New Q* Winter 1987; Vol 6 No 4: p92–93.

Exorcism; poem. *CV 2* Summer 1987; Vol 10 No 4: p21.

Letter; poem. *New Q* Winter 1987; Vol 6 No 4: p91.

Sychronicity; poem. *CV 2* Summer 1987; Vol 10 No 4: p22.

Tragedy; poem. *New Q* Spring-Summer 1987; Vol 7 No 1–2: p196.

Wedding blues; poem. *CV 2* Summer 1987; Vol 10 No 4: p20.

The wicked stepmother; poem. *New Q* Spring-Summer 1987; Vol 7 No 1–2: p195.

Winterkill; poem. *New Q* Winter 1987; Vol 6 No 4: p94.

Shadbolt, Jack

Green fire; poem. *Can Lit* Summer-Fall 1987; No 113–114: p58–59.

The way in; poem. *Can Lit* Summer-Fall 1987; No 113–114: p60.

Sharkey, Shirley

Into the bosom of justice; short story. photo · *TS* Aug 18, 1987: pE15.

Shave, Kar

Some guests; poem. *Quarry* Fall 1987; Vol 36 No 4: p71.

Sunwapta Falls; poem. *Quarry* Fall 1987; Vol 36 No 4: p72.

Shaw, Joan Fern

An allergy to marigolds; short story. *Prism* Autumn 1987; Vol 26 No 1: p95–104.

Chekhov's eating habits; short story. *Quarry* Spring 1987; Vol 36 No 2: p25–31.

Delivery; poem. *Can Auth & Book* Spring 1987; Vol 62 No 3: p23.

The heart has vocal chords; poem. *Fiddlehead* Winter 1987; No 154: p46.

Meeting Alden; poem. *Fiddlehead* Winter 1987; No 154: p47.

Sink; short story. illus · *Fireweed* Winter 1987; No 24: p93–95.

Standard deviation; short story. *Room of One's Own* April 1987; Vol 11 No 3: p71–78.

Tempest; poem. *Fiddlehead* Winter 1987; No 154: p46.

That there Nietzsche; short story. *Event* March 1987; Vol 16 No 1: p12–24.

Think of the possibilities; short story. *Matrix* Spring 1987; No 24: p2–8.

Shay, Timothy

Hot cereal dream; poem. *NeWest R* Sept 1987; Vol 13 No 1: p13.

The sun and the shower; poem. *CV 2* Summer 1987; Vol 10 No 4: p23.

Sheard, Sarah

[Untitled]; letter to the editor. *Tor Life* Oct 1987; Vol 21 No 15: p12.

Sheehy, Donald G.

Bestiary (minor); poem. *Queen's Q* Winter 1987; Vol 94 No 4: p917.

Shek, B.-Z.

[Untitled]; reviews of *Itinéraire de Liverpool à Québec* and *Colloque Louis Hémon. U of Toronto Q* Fall 1987; Vol 57 No 1: p179–182.

[Untitled]; reviews of critical works. *U of Toronto Q* Fall 1987; Vol 57 No 1: p192–199.

Shelly, Nadine

Red ribbon; poem. *Grain* Winter 1987; Vol 15 No 4: p34.

Velvet; poem. *Grain* Winter 1987; Vol 15 No 4: p35.

Shepherd, Diana

Bestsellers on TV, and a sunny summer romance; column. *Quill & Quire* Sept 1987; Vol 53 No 9: p72.

Doubleday clubs leading the way with more Canadian content; article. *Quill & Quire* Nov 1987; Vol 53 No 11: p13.

Dreaming of a bright Christmas: booksellers report a strong season so far; article. illus · *Quill & Quire* Dec 1987; Vol 53 No 12: p7–8.

Looking forward to the fall list for kids; preview of fall book list. *Quill & Quire (Books for Young People)* Aug 1987; Vol 53 No 8: p3–4, 10.

Sherman, Jason

Aural dilemmas; radio review of *Sextet. Books in Can* March 1987; Vol 16 No 2: p5–7.

Blyth musical succeeds where drama fails; theatre reviews of *Girls in the Gang* and *Bush Fire*. photo · *TS* Aug 7, 1987: pE10.

Knockouts; review of *Two Voices. G&M* Sept 26, 1987: pC22.

Other voices; review article about *The Garden of Eloise Loon*. biog · *Books in Can* Jan-Feb 1987; Vol 16 No 1: p31–32.

Reclaiming the Doras; article. photo · *Can Theatre R* Summer 1987; No 51: p25–31.

The spoiled broth; review of *Coming Attractions 5*. *G&M* Nov 14, 1987: pE5.

Walls of prose; review of *Some Friends of Mine*. *G&M* Nov 14, 1987: pE11.

Sherman, Joseph

Poets' league: debt free at last; article. *Quill & Quire* July 1987; Vol 53 No 7: p43.

Sherman, Kenneth

Adam names the beast; poem. *Malahat R* Dec 1987; No 81: p65–66.

After; poem. *Malahat R* Dec 1987; No 81: p67.

Black Adam's blues; poem. *Malahat R* Dec 1987; No 81: p69.

Dark shed; poem. *Can Forum* April 1987; Vol 67 No 768: p26.

Diviner; poem. *Can Forum* April 1987; Vol 67 No 768: p27.

Goldman; poem. *Prism* Summer 1987; Vol 25 No 4: p96.

Mad Eve sings; poem. *Malahat R* Dec 1987; No 81: p68.

The new public pier; poem. *Can Forum* April 1987; Vol 67 No 768: p27.

Rainbowed hoops of affection; poem. illus · *Can Forum* April 1987; Vol 67 No 768: p26–27.

A song, experiential II; poem. *Can Forum* April 1987; Vol 67 No 768: p27.

A song, experiential; poem. *Can Forum* April 1987; Vol 67 No 768: p26–27.

Synagogue, Jackson's Point; poem. *Can Forum* April 1987; Vol 67 No 768: p26.

Shewan, Kathy S.

Emma; poem. *Antigonish R* 1987; No 69–70: p163.

Shields, Carol

Dog days; poem. *Can Forum* Jan 1987; Vol 66 No 765: p20.

Dressing up for the carnival; short story. *Malahat R* June 1987; No 79: p23–27.

Shields, E.F.

Mauberley's lies: fact and fiction in Timothy Findley's *Famous Last Words*; article. abstract · *J of Can Studies* Winter 1987–88; Vol 22 No 4: p44–59.

Shikatani, Gerry

The bend; poem. *Waves* Winter 1987; Vol 15 No 3: p52–53.

Contexte; prose poem. *Capilano R* 1987; No 44: p54.

Guadaquivir; poem. *Waves* Winter 1987; Vol 15 No 3: p54.

Metapoeic; poem. *Cross Can Writ Q* 1987; Vol 9 No 3–4: p13.

Palmerston Boulevard; poem. *Poetry Can R* Fall 1987; Vol 9 No 1: p12.

The Prado: signs, secrets and sacred objects; poem. *Malahat R* June 1987; No 79: p118–121.

Restauration; prose poem. *Capilano R* 1987; No 44: p51–52.

Strays; poem. *Poetry Can R* Fall 1987; Vol 9 No 1: p12.

Texte; poem. *Capilano R* 1987; No 44: p53.

This is about meditation; prose poem. *Capilano R* 1987; No 44: p49–50.

Umbrian spring; poem. *Malahat R* June 1987; No 79: p122–124.

Shilling, Grant

Inside the contest; essay. *Can Auth & Book* Spring 1987; Vol 62 No 3: p13–14.

The steal; poem. *Grain* Fall 1987; Vol 15 No 3: p38.

Tom Wayman's work poetry; article. *Poetry Can R* Spring 1987; Vol 8 No 2–3: p20–21.

Shingler, John

Reflecting South Africa; review of *Bloodsong*. photo · *MG* Oct 3, 1987: pJ12.

Shoemaker, Donna

New Gordon Pinsent play embodies spirit of friend; article. photo · *CH* July 27, 1987: pB8.

Shook, Karen

Work like Atwood's to endure; letter to the editor. *MG* Feb 23, 1987: pB2.

Shopsowitz, Karen

Metro high schools enter drama festival; article. *TS (Neighbours)* Feb 10, 1987: p24.

Shortell, Ann

An author's painful secrets; biographical article. photo · *Maclean's* Dec 7, 1987; Vol 100 No 49: p50.

Shreiber, Tracey

Laurence selected own funeral music; article. *WFP* Jan 8, 1987: p33.

Shreve, Sandy

Canadians driving the I-5 to Seattle while the U.S. bombed Libya; poem. *Waves* Winter 1987; Vol 15 No 3: p55.

Clouds; poem. *Poetry Can R* Summer 1987; Vol 8 No 4: p30.

Compensation; poem. *Fireweed* Fall 1987; No 25: p45.

Homage; poem. *Poetry Can R* Summer 1987; Vol 8 No 4: p30.

Laid off; poem. *Fireweed* Fall 1987; No 25: p46.

Magpies in the palm trees; poem. *Poetry Can R* Summer 1987; Vol 8 No 4: p30.

Quilting bee; poem. *Fireweed* Fall 1987; No 25: p46.

Spring fever; poem. *Fireweed* Fall 1987; No 25: p47.

Taking back the night; poem. *Poetry Can R* Summer 1987; Vol 8 No 4: p30.

Wings; poem. *Poetry Can R* Summer 1987; Vol 8 No 4: p30.

Shuell, Phyllis A.

Women no longer talk of Michelangelo; poem. *New Q* Fall 1987; Vol 7 No 3: p94–97.

Shugard, Alan

Dust bowl to never land; review of *Dustship Glory. Can Lit* Winter 1987; No 115: p196–197.

Shutiak, Laura

Blitz immerses students in theatre; article. photo · *CH* Feb 16, 1987: pE5.

Students blitz stage in weekend workshop; article. *CH* Feb 13, 1987: pF11.

Sibum, Norm

Propertius in May; poem. illus · *Antigonish R* Winter 1987; No 68: p129–131.

Sigal, Clancy

Cardinal Bem on the run; review of *The Color of Blood. NYT Book R* Sept 27, 1987: p11.

Siggins, Maggie

Moose Jaw meets Mao; article. biog photo · *G&M* March 21, 1987: pE1, E6.

Sigurdson, Norman

Bigger canvas suits Shields; review of *Swann: A Mystery.* photo · *WFP* Oct 17, 1987: p61.

Carol Shields: raising everyday lives to the level of art; review of *Swann: A Mystery.* photo · *Quill & Quire* Nov 1987; Vol 53 No 11: p21.

Comic novel falls flat; review of *The Promised Land.* photo · *WFP* May 2, 1987: p84.

Fabulist fictions fail to get passing grade; review of *Hard Confessions. WFP* Oct 31, 1987: p52.

A mixed bag of short stories; reviews of short story anthologies. *WFP* Feb 28, 1987: p54.

Perils of a double life; review of *Time in the Air. WFP* Jan 10, 1987: p66.

[Untitled]; review of *The Ice Eaters. Quill & Quire* Sept 1987; Vol 53 No 9: p79.

[Untitled]; review of *Dancing on the Shore. Quill & Quire* Sept 1987; Vol 53 No 9: p80.

[Untitled]; reviews of *Telling the Tale* and *The Parrot Who Could. Books in Can* Nov 1987; Vol 16 No 8: p25–26.

[Untitled]; review of *Corkscrew. Quill & Quire* Nov 1987; Vol 53 No 11: p24–25.

[Untitled]; review of *A Dream Like Mine. Quill & Quire* Dec 1987; Vol 53 No 12: p24–25.

[Untitled]; review of *Hardwired Angel. Quill & Quire* Dec 1987; Vol 53 No 12: p25.

Silber, C.A.

[Untitled]; review of *The Creating Word. U of Toronto Q* Fall 1987; Vol 57 No 1: p140–142.

Sileika, Antanas

Half-mad bohemian lyricism; review of *Amadou. G&M* Dec 26, 1987: pC23.

Little magic; review of *Hard Confessions. G&M* Dec 12, 1987: pE9.

Silvera, Makeda

Canada sweet, girl; short story. illus · *Fireweed* Fall 1987; No 25: p11–19.

Simaluk, Vern

Oilman's experience launched career of novelist; biographical article. *CH* May 1, 1987: pF6.

Simon, Louise

The dawn swim; poem. *Quarry* Winter 1987; Vol 36 No 1: p18.

Our hired man; poem. *New Q* Fall 1987; Vol 7 No 3: p81–82.

Probie days; poem. *Quarry* Winter 1987; Vol 36 No 1: p17.

Spring elopement; poem. *New Q* Fall 1987; Vol 7 No 3: p83.

The voice of truth in Kim Maltman's Softened Violence; review article. *Quarry* Winter 1987; Vol 36 No 1: p125–130.

Simon, Sherry

Suzanne Lamy: le féminin au risque de la critique; article. *Voix et images* Autumn 1987; Vol 13 No 1: p52–64.

Simpson, Fraser

Words from Everyman; letter to the editor. *G&M* May 2, 1987: pD7.

Sims, Peter

On looking up a word in the dictionary; poem. *Quarry* Winter 1987; Vol 36 No 1: p116–117.

Photography "in camera"; article. *Can Lit* Summer-Fall 1987; No 113–114: p145–166.

"Ravishing is writing"; poem. *Grain* Spring 1987; Vol 15 No 1: p43–44.

A small box; poem. *Quarry* Winter 1987; Vol 36 No 1: p115.

Singleton, Martin

[Untitled]; reviews of poetry books. *Cross Can Writ Q* 1987; Vol 9 No 2: p19–20.

[Untitled]; reviews of poetry books. *Cross Can Writ Q* 1987; Vol 9 No 3–4: p38–39.

Siotis, Dino

House sale; poem. *Poetry Can R* Fall 1987; Vol 9 No 1: p26.

Sirett, Neff

How the argument began; poem. *Grain* Winter 1987; Vol 15 No 4: p42.

Letters; poem. *Grain* Summer 1987; Vol 15 No 2: p15–16.

Singing lesson; poem. *Grain* Summer 1987; Vol 15 No 2: p17.

To a friend who was till he entered U of T; poem. *Grain* Summer 1987; Vol 15 No 2: p14.

Skarstedt, Sonia A.

The addict; poem. *Poetry Can R* Spring 1987; Vol 8 No 1–2: p13.

Skelton, Joan

Big bad wolf; short story. *Northward J* 1987; No 40: p43–53.

Skelton, Robin

Poetry: packing all the power into two of seven titles; reviews of poetry books. photo · *Quill & Quire* May 1987; Vol 53 No 5: p24.

[Untitled]; review of *Tiger in the Skull. Poetry Can R* Spring 1987; Vol 8 No 2–3: p42.

Skene, Reg

Actor captures depths of play's leading character; theatre review of *Salt-Water Moon. WFP* Jan 8, 1987: p33.

Actress draws powerful portraits of heroines in Laurence's work; theatre review of *The Women of Margaret Laurence. WFP* May 14, 1987: p46.

Courier's inner conflict makes terrific theatre; theatre review of *The Courier. WFP* May 7, 1987: p43.

Crafty lust: a prof[i]le of Bruce McManus. *Border Cross* Summer 1987; Vol 6 No 3: p53–57.

Curtain falls on season of mediocrity; article. photo · *WFP* May 22, 1987: p35.

Disturbing play incoherent; theatre review of *Parasols. WFP* May 1, 1987: p35.

Dogs with No Tails delivers pain, laughs; theatre review. *WFP* July 4, 1987: p40.

Exciting, refreshing City Limits tops theatre season; theatre review. *WFP* Jan 24, 1987: p22.

Festival One offers hope for new wave of creative theatre; theatre reviews. *WFP* May 11, 1987: p17.

Funny play fails to fulfil promise; theatre review of *Schedules. WFP* Jan 23, 1987: p31.

Hockey metaphor fails to make dramatic point; theatre review of *Life After Hockey. WFP* March 19, 1987: p41.

Invisible Kids suffers from poor focus; theatre review. *WFP* Feb 5, 1987: p37.

Japanese steal show at children's festival; review. *WFP* May 27, 1987: p36.

Making the prairie connection; theatre reviews. *NeWest R* Dec 1987; Vol 13 No 4: p16.

MTC shows ability with Doc production; theatre review. *WFP* Feb 6, 1987: p29.

Picture of rebellious victim of cerebral palsy gripping, raises audience awareness; theatre review of *Franklin. WFP* May 4, 1987: p29.

Play takes comic look at fear of mortality; theatre review of *Dewline. WFP* Feb 27, 1987: p33.

Race relations documentary emotion-packed experience; theatre review of *Skin. WFP* Feb 6, 1987: p29.

Shows allow older children to explore tough social issues; theatre review of *One in a Million. WFP* May 30, 1987: p25.

Stories create magic moments for audience at Festival One; theatre review of *Dragon Snapper. WFP* May 4, 1987: p29.

Theatrical satire hits target; theatre review of *Dixieland's Night of Shame. WFP* May 8, 1987: p23.

White Dogs exposes harmful legacy of rational thought; theatre review of *The White Dogs of Texas. WFP* April 28, 1987: p32.

Williams' King Of America intelligent, rich and funny; theatre review. *WFP* May 3, 1987: p15.

Skvorecky, Josef

The supernatural powers of Lieutenant Boruvka; short story. illus trans · *Can Forum* May 1987; Vol 67 No 769: p17–25.

Slade, Peter

More saturated with colour; review of *No Fixed Admission. NeWest R* Feb 1987; Vol 12 No 6: p18.

Slavens, Kerry

Natalya longing; poem. *Malahat R* Dec 1987; No 81: p81–82.

A perfect day; poem. *Malahat R* Dec 1987; No 81: p83.

Slinger, Joey

New books by old favorites just in time for gift season; humorous essay. *TS* Dec 3, 1987: pA6.

Saturday Night fiasco shakes your faith in tycoonery; humorous essay. *TS* July 7, 1987: pA6.

Words don't do Colombo justice – you can quote me; humorous essay. *TS* Dec 18, 1987: pA6.

Slopen, Beverley

Book world: a legend in journalism hits gold in life and print; column. *TS* Oct 11, 1987: pA23.

Book world: a little-known bestseller; column. *TS* Jan 11, 1987: pA16.

Book world: a 'nice little hobby' that finally paid off; column. photo · *TS* May 3, 1987: pA25.

Book world: a showcase for the book-maker's art; column. *TS* Dec 6, 1987: pC8.

Book world: a success story that started with a cow; column. *TS* March 29, 1987: pA18.

Book world: a tip of the hat to small presses; column. photo · *TS* Aug 9, 1987: pA20.

Book world: adults who love children's books gather at 'Roundtable'; column. *TS* Aug 16, 1987: pA21.

Book world: Air India bombing 'a Canadian tragedy'; column. *TS* Feb 8, 1987: pG9.

Book world: anti-Khomeini plotter's story told in new book; column. *TS* Sept 6, 1987: pA18.

Book world: championing books called 'out of print'; column. *TS* Dec 20, 1987: pE5.

Book world: Clarkson brings pool of goodwill to M&S job; column. *TS* March 15, 1987: pA22.

Book world: Coach House Press divides to conquer; column. *TS* Jan 4, 1987: pB7.

Book world: Collins (Murdoch) fine-tunes a new purchase; column. *TS* July 12, 1987: pA18.

Book world: ex-publisher finds dealing with publishers gives him a pain; column about Jack McClelland. *TS* Dec 13, 1987: pE6.

Book world: firm's growth is not merely a matter of luck; column. *TS* Oct 4, 1987: pA20.

Book world: from unhappy housewife to busy biographer; column. photo · *TS* May 24, 1987: pA18.

Book world: Great Literary Dinner Party takes off; column. photo · *TS* July 19, 1987: pA20.

Book world: Grolier moves into children's fiction; column. *TS* March 22, 1987: pA20.

Book world: Gzowski's $$$ aid welcomed; column. *TS* June 14, 1987: pA18.

Book world: 'I swear by Apollo' and CIA; column. *TS* April 12, 1987: pA20.

Book world: incest victim created a 'twin' to survive; column. photo · *TS* June 21, 1987: pA22.

Book world: inside Iran: a woman's prison-like existence; column. photo · *TS* Aug 2, 1987: pC10.

Book world: Japan likes Toronto 'letters'; column. *TS* May 17, 1987: pA16.

Book world: M&S and Penguin join in paperback Berton books; column. *TS* March 8, 1987: pA14.

Book world: Maggie Smith as Judith Hearne?; column. *TS* Jan 25, 1987: pB6.

Book world: McClelland moves to quash 'secret' biography; column. photo · *TS* Feb 12, 1987: pF1.

Book world: Mowat writing life of slain gorilla expert; column. *TS* Feb 1, 1987: pB6.

Book world: 'My year for films': Brian Moore; column. photo · *TS* Nov 8, 1987: pA18.

Book world: 'new' terrorists like their perks, author suggests; column. *TS* May 10, 1987: pA22.

Book world: Ojibwa's diary led to biography; column. *TS* Nov 29, 1987: pA20.

Book world: Owl magazine publisher wades into film field; column. *TS* Sept 20, 1987: pA20.

Book world: radical right illumined; column. *TS* Oct 18, 1987: pC8.

Book world: the Bay saga: before Vol. 3 comes Vol. 2 1 / 2; column. *TS* Nov 22, 1987: pC8.

Book world: the man who stole millions; column. *TS* April 19, 1987: pA18.

Book world: the publisher who caught 'Spy Catcher'; column. *TS* June 7, 1987: pG10.

Book world: what about Frankfurt? A hemline dilemma; column. *TS* Sept 13, 1987: pA22.

Book world: when a publicist needs a lawyer. . . .; column. *TS* Nov 15, 1987: pA22.

Book world: where the $$$ land – legally; column. *TS* March 1, 1987: pA15.

Book world: will they leave the boss' book on sale?; column. *TS* Nov 1, 1987: pH6.

Book world: winners or losers? Wait for returns; column. *TS* Feb 22, 1987: pA18.

Book world: writers sell selves to the booksellers; column. *TS* July 5, 1987: pA18.

Paperclips: 25 years of minding McClelland's business. . . .political yarns; column. photo · *Quill & Quire* April 1987; Vol 53 No 4: p12.

Paperclips: a woman's break with Catholicism. . . .calling for crime; column. *Quill & Quire* Nov 1987; Vol 53 No 11: p17.

Paperclips: booksellers take to the air. . . .noteworthy biographer for Gould; column. *Quill & Quire* Jan 1987; Vol 53 No 1: p11.

Paperclips: bush league authors. . . .much depends on Visser. . . .prosaic retirement; column. *Quill & Quire* Dec 1987; Vol 53 No 12: p20.

Paperclips: helping U.S. librarians fill their shelves. . . .the party animal; column. photo · *Quill & Quire* Feb 1987; Vol 53 No 2: p7.

Paperclips: impressive feminists. . . .vampire visionary. . . .crossing the border; column. photo · *Quill & Quire* Oct 1987; Vol 53 No 10: p15.

Paperclips: publishing on-stage. . . .P.K. Page's love song to Brazil; column. photo · *Quill & Quire* May 1987; Vol 53 No 5: p14.

Paperclips: Rivoche's robots. . . .on the cookbook beat. . . .Templeton's teddy; column. *Quill & Quire* March 1987; Vol 53 No 3: p64.

Paperclips: the Lovesick ladies. . . .a writer's parole. . . .Eden changes hands; column. *Quill & Quire* June 1987; Vol 53 No 6: p28.

Paperclips: the radical right in our midst. . . .a horse and writer; column. *Quill & Quire* Sept 1987; Vol 53 No 9: p66.

Poets! Read on; article. *TS* Dec 20, 1987: pE5.

Slosberg, Steven

[Untitled]; review of *Inspecting the Vaults*. *NYT Book R* Sept 20, 1987: p26.

Slott, Kathryn

Repression, obsession and re-emergence in Hébert's Les Fous de Bassan; article. *Amer R of Can Studies* Autumn 1987; Vol 17 No 3: p297–307.

Small, J.M.

Semi-private investigation; short story. *TS* Aug 25, 1987: pG7.

Smallbridge, John

"Somewhere meant for me"; editorial. photo · *Can Child Lit* 1987; No 48: p3–4.

Smart, Carolyn

Multiplication; poem. *Quarry* Winter 1987; Vol 36 No 1: p58–60.

Winnipeg; poem. *Quarry* Winter 1987; Vol 36 No 1: p61–63.

Smart, Patricia

Entre la maison, l'eau et le cosmos: l'écriture féminine; reviews of novels. *Voix et images* Winter 1987; No 35: p334–337.

Impasses ou issues? L'imaginaire masculin face à la femme; reviews of *Les Silences du corbeau* and *À double sens*. *Voix et images* Spring 1987; Vol 12 No 3: p555–560.

Woman as object, women as subjects, & the consequences for narrative: Hubert Aquin's Neige noire and the impasse of post-modernism; article. *Can Lit* Summer-Fall 1987; No 113–114: p168–178.

Smith, Allen

Alpine heliport; poem. *Matrix* Spring 1987; No 24: p32.

Bad break; poem. *Arc* Fall 1987; No 19: p78.

Different dimensions; poem. *Alpha* Winter 1987; Vol 11: p10.

Firebreak; poem. *Alpha* Winter 1987; Vol 11: p10.

Longevity game; poem. *Matrix* Spring 1987; No 24: p57.

Smith, Barbara

Sara's gift; children's story. *Dandelion* Fall-Winter 1987; Vol 14 No 2: p94–102.

Smith, Bobbie Jean

New shoes; short story. *Quarry* Spring 1987; Vol 36 No 2: p64–65.

Smith, Brad

[Untitled]; prose excerpt from *Rises a Moral Man*. *Northward J* 1987; No 40: p29–42.

Smith, Dan

Finding cheer between the lines; article. photo · *TS* March 21, 1987: pM5.

Smith, Dorothy Cameron

[Untitled]; poem. *Can Auth & Book* Summer 1987; Vol 62 No 4: p23.

Smith, Douglas

[Untitled]; poetry excerpts from *A Savage Prism*. *Poetry Can R* Spring 1987; Vol 8 No 2–3: p18.

[Untitled]; reviews of poetry books. *Poetry Can R* Spring 1987; Vol 8 No 2–3: p39–40.

Smith, Kay

Dream the child again; poem. *Fiddlehead* Autumn 1987; No 153: p11–14.

Old women and love; poem. *Can Lit* Spring 1987; No 112: p39.

Orchard morning; poem. *Can Lit* Spring 1987; No 112: p8.

When God is silent; poem. *Fiddlehead* Autumn 1987; No 153: p15.

Smith, Mary Ainslie

Back to the future; reviews of children's books. *Books in Can* March 1987; Vol 16 No 2: p37–39.

Living in the past; reviews of children's novels. *Books in Can* June-July 1987; Vol 16 No 5: p35–37.

Roughing it in the bush; reviews of children's books. *Books in Can* Aug-Sept 1987; Vol 16 No 6: p34–36.

Ways of escape; reviews of children's books. *Books in Can* Dec 1987; Vol 16 No 9: p11–14.

Smith, Nancy

Another night on the town; poem. *Waves* Spring 1987; Vol 15 No 4: p58–59.

Life is an abandoned broth, boiled over and burnt on the bottom; poem. illus · *Can Auth & Book* Summer 1987; Vol 62 No 4: p19.

Wives of the house; poem. *Waves* Spring 1987; Vol 15 No 4: p59.

Smith, Patricia Keeney

Elspeth Cameron and Irving Layton; reviews of *Irving Layton: A Portrait* and *Waiting for the Messiah*. *U of Toronto Q* Spring 1987; Vol 56 No 3: p467–470.

Painful scrutiny of relationships; reviews of poetry books. *TS* May 30, 1987: pM9.

Penny Kemp: creating the world she inhabits; article. photo · *Cross Can Writ Q* 1987; Vol 9 No 2: p8–9, 28–29.

Three poets dare to reject labelling; reviews of poetry books. *TS* July 4, 1987: pM4.

Smith, Russell

(I need money); poem. *Queen's Q* Winter 1987; Vol 94 No 4: p900.

Ontario; poem. *Queen's Q* Winter 1987; Vol 94 No 4: p901–903.

Smith, Steven

High density; poem. *Cross Can Writ Q* 1987; Vol 9 No 3–4: p20.

Ontario report: a rite to remember; regional column. *Poetry Can R* Spring 1987; Vol 8 No 2–3: p24.

Ontario report: advancing & retreating with Ontario Lit.; regional column. *Poetry Can R* Summer 1987; Vol 8 No 4: p22.

Smith, Winston

[Untitled]; review of *Other Voices*. *Rubicon* Fall 1987; No 9: p160–163.

Smithies, Sarah

[Untitled]; review of *Margaret in the Middle*. *TS* Jan 18, 1987: pC8.

Snow, John Vance

Poet records two years in paradise; review of *Brazilian Journal*. *CH* Aug 30, 1987: pE4.

Unpleasant, harsh novel probes social ills; review of *A Dream Like Mine*. photo · *CH* Nov 29, 1987: pE6.

Socken, Paul G.

The bible and myth in Antonine Maillet's Pélagie-la-Charrette; article. *Studies in Can Lit* 1987; Vol 12 No 2: p187–198.

Bonds of dignity; review of *Gabrielle Roy*. *Can Lit* Winter 1987; No 115: p193–194.

De se dire; review of *Les Oeuvres de création et le français au Québec*. *Can Lit* Winter 1987; No 115: p164–165.

Questionner et rêver; review of *Voix d'écrivains: entretiens*. *Can Lit* Spring 1987; No 112: p171–172.

Roy's language; review of *The Play of Language and Spectacle*. *Can Lit* Spring 1987; No 112: p194.

Söderlind, Sylvia

Views from afar; review of *Gaining Ground. Essays on Can Writ* Winter 1987; No 35: p111–116.

Soldevila, Philippe

Magie et mysticisme: comment (ne pas) expliquer l'inexplicable; essay. photo · *Jeu* 1987; No 45: p171–176.

Solecki, Sam

The immoralist; review of *Helmet of Flesh*. *Can Lit* Winter 1987; No 115: p146–148.

Solnicki, Jill Newman

The crossing; poem. *Fiddlehead* Spring 1987; No 151: p16.

A girl's best friend; poem. *Atlantis* Fall 1987; Vol 13 No 1: p153.

Surgery; poem. *Fiddlehead* Spring 1987; No 151: p16.

Walking in fog; poem. *Tor Life* Oct 1987; Vol 21 No 1[5]: p122.

Solway, David

The end of poetry; essay. *Can Lit* Winter 1987; No 115: p127–134.

Night; poem. *Malahat R* Sept 1987; No 80: p115.

Sommer, Richard

Mountain farm; poem. *Matrix* Spring 1987; No 24: p15–17.

The taste; poem. *Malahat R* June 1987; No 79: p77.

A temple of bees; poem. *Malahat R* June 1987; No 79: p78.

Time; poem. *Malahat R* June 1987; No 79: p79–80.

Sonin, Ray

The old man goes out; short story. biog photo · *TS* July 1, 1987: pA12.

Sorestad, Glen

Adilman; poem. *Queen's Q* Winter 1987; Vol 94 No 4: p917.

Along the Promenade des Anglais; poem. *Prism* Winter 1987; Vol 25 No 2: p29.

Black leather night; poem. *Ariel* April 1987; Vol 18 No 2: p44.

The man who would be a fish; poem. *Poetry Can R* Spring 1987; Vol 8 No 2–3: p63.

Sunday afternoon at De Keulse Pot, Amsterdam; poem. *Quarry* Summer 1987; Vol 36 No 3: p47–48.

Taking wing; poem. *Poetry Can R* Spring 1987; Vol 8 No 2–3: p63.

Travelling to Dieppe; poem. *Quarry* Summer 1987; Vol 36 No 3: p45–46.

The well; poem. *Poetry Can R* Spring 1987; Vol 8 No 2–3: p63.

Wood mountain nocturne; poem. *Wascana R* Spring 1987; Vol 22 No 1: p35.

Sotiriou, Popi

Journey 1982; poem. *Poetry Can R* Fall 1987; Vol 9 No 1: p26.

Souchard, Maryse

Monsieur Pitou; short story. *Prairie Fire* Autumn 1987; Vol 8 No 3: p72–75.

Souster, Raymond

Calamar; poem. *Poetry Can R* Summer 1987; Vol 8 No 4: p11.

A cold wind's blowing; poem. *Quarry* Summer 1987; Vol 36 No 3: p50.

Declaration; poem. *Capilano R* 1987; No 42: p9.

Don't cross me, cat; poem. *Quarry* Summer 1987; Vol 36 No 3: p52.

Hanlan's Point holiday; poem. *Capilano R* 1987; No 42: p4–6.

The house around the corner; poem. *Capilano R* 1987; No 42: p7.

The Humberside Special; poem. *Quarry* Summer 1987; Vol 36 No 3: p51.

Jumping the falls; poem. *Fiddlehead* Winter 1987; No 154: p40.

Making pasta together; poem. *Queen's Q* Autumn 1987; Vol 94 No 3: p658–659.

Marathon swimmer; poem. *Fiddlehead* Winter 1987; No 154: p41.

My last maple; poem. *New Q* Fall 1987; Vol 7 No 3: p79.

Pictures from a long-lost world: religious riots, Calcutta, August 1946; poem. *Quarry* Summer 1987; Vol 36 No 3: p49.

Plain fact; poem. *Capilano R* 1987; No 42: p8.

Repairing St James' Cathedral spire; poem. *Poetry Can R* Summer 1987; Vol 8 No 4: p11.

The rescue and after; poem. *Poetry Can R* Summer 1987; Vol 8 No 4: p11.

Street-corner trombone; poem. *Poetry Can R* Summer 1987; Vol 8 No 4: p11.

Tonight I feel the same bell-ringing joy; poem. *Fiddlehead* Winter 1987; No 154: p39.

Yorkville Avenue revisited; poem. *New Q* Fall 1987; Vol 7 No 3: p80.

Southam, Brenda

Incest 'split' writer; article. photo · *CH* Oct 31, 1987: pB7.

Spadoni, Carl

Riding off in all directions; review of *Leacock: A Biography*. *Essays on Can Writ* Winter 1987; No 35: p74–81.

[Untitled]; review of *Stephen Leacock: A Reappraisal*. *Queen's Q* Winter 1987; Vol 94 No 4: p1028–1030.

Sparshott, Francis

On "On Turning Tail"; essay. *Grain* Spring 1987; Vol 15 No 1: p15.

On turning tail; poem. *Grain* Spring 1987; Vol 15 No 1: p14.

Poetic form; essay. *Grain* Spring 1987; Vol 15 No 1: p11–13.

A tale from Valéry: haute école; poem. *Grain* Spring 1987; Vol 15 No 1: p13.

Speak, Dorothy

Avalon; short story. *U of Windsor R* Fall-Winter 1987; Vol 20 No 1: p55 70.

Summer sky – white ship; short story. *New Q* Spring-Summer 1987; Vol 7 No 1–2: p36–49.

Tube; short story. *Room of One's Own* April 1987; Vol 11 No 3: p55–66.

Spears, Heather

At the art therapist's; poem. *Can Lit* Summer-Fall 1987; No 113–114: p108.

Five drawings at the world poetry festival, Toronto, May 1986. *Can Lit* Summer-Fall 1987; No 113–114: p109–113.

To my body at birth; poem. *Prairie J of Can Lit* 1987; No 8: p29.

Spears, Tom

Blyth spirit makes theatre festival labor of love; article. photo · *TS* June 19, 1987: pD5.

With used scars on their sleeves; review of *Night Driving*. *TS* April 11, 1987: pM8.

Spencer, Anne

Sonnet; poem. *Can Auth & Book* Winter 1987; Vol 62 No 2: p22.

Storytellers unlimited; article. photo · *Can Auth & Book* Summer 1987; Vol 62 No 4: p6.

Spettigue, D.O.

Recent Canadian fiction; reviews of novels. *Queen's Q* Summer 1987; Vol 94 No 2: p366–375.

[Untitled]; reviews of *Robertson Davies* and *Robertson Davies, Playwright*. *Queen's Q* Autumn 1987; Vol 94 No 3: p722–724.

Spicer, Bob

Romance; poem. *Poetry Can R* Fall 1987; Vol 9 No 1: p11.

Spicer, Keith

Canada needs writers like Margaret Laurence; essay. photo · *MG* Jan 8, 1987: pB3.

Sproxton, Birk

Making Mickey; short story. *Prairie Fire* Winter 1987–88; Vol 8 No 4: p78–81.

A story like a shovel; short story. *Border Cross* Summer 1987; Vol 6 No 3: p51–52.

St. George, Elyse Yates

Spotted jackal watches; poem. *NeWest R* Sept 1987; Vol 13 No 1: p7.

White coyote; poem. *NeWest R* Sept 1987; Vol 13 No 1: p7.

St-Germain, Monique

Brèches; poetry excerpt from *L'Oeuvre au miroir*. *Estuaire* Winter 1986–87; No 43: p23–26.

St. Jacques, Elizabeth

Reflection; poem. *Can Auth & Book* Summer 1987; Vol 62 No 4: p22.

St-Pierre, Jacques

[Untitled]; reviews of poetry books. *Moebius* Winter 1987; No 31: p137–139.

[Untitled]; reviews of *Mon mari le docteur* and *Américane*. *Moebius* Winter 1987; No 31: p139–140.

[Untitled]; review of *Cette fois, Jeanne. . . ..*. *Moebius* Summer 1987; No 33: p133–135.

[Untitled]; reviews of *Journal*. *Moebius* Summer 1987; No 33: p140–142.

Stacey, Medina

Nowhere special; short story. *Fiddlehead* Autumn 1987; No 153: p37–40.

Staines, David

[Untitled]; review of *Gaining Ground*. *Eng Studies in Can* March 1987; Vol 13 No 1: p119–120.

[Untitled]; review of *Encounters and Explorations*. *Amer R of Can Studies* Spring 1987; Vol 17 No 1: p117–118.

Stallworthy, Bob

At Burley's store; poem. *Waves* Winter 1987; Vol 15 No 3: p73.

Stange, Ken

Abel on kinetic energy (variation 2); poem. *Northward J* 1987; No 43: p11.

Amos on aging (variation 2); poem. *Northward J* 1987; No 43: p4.

Amos on hanging (variation 1); poem. *Northward J* 1987; No 43: p17.

Computer literacy : computer literature; essay. illus · *Quarry* Spring 1987; Vol 36 No 2: p94–108.

Computer poetry; essay. *Northward J* 1987; No 43: p5–9.

Germaine on being in heat (variation 2); poem. *Northward J* 1987; No 43: p16.

Jane in captivity (variation 1); poem. *Northward J* 1987; No 43: p14.

Jeff on revolution (variation 1); poem. *Northward J* 1987; No 43: p19.

Sheena in picures (variation 1); poem. *Northward J* 1987; No 43: p15.

Suzanne dreaming (variation 1); poem. *Northward J* 1987; No 43: p12.

Suzanne on statistics (variation 1); poem. *Northward J* 1987; No 43: p13.

Suzanne on symmetry (variation 1); poem. *Northward J* 1987; No 43: p18.

[Untitled]; review of *Pieces of Map, Pieces of Music. Poetry Can R* Summer 1987; Vol 8 No 4: p35–36.

Ursula on dreaming (variation 2); poem. *Northward J* 1987; No 43: p10.

Stanton, Julie

Le Léon-Gérin à Louis-Edmond Hamelin; le Marie-Victorin à Pierre Deslongchamps; article. photo · *MD* Nov 10, 1987: p13.

Remise des prix d'excellence de la culture; article. photo · *MD* Oct 27, 1987: p11.

Les troupes jouent le tout pour le tout; article. photo · *MD* Dec 5, 1987: pC5.

Steele, Charles R.

Canada's new-critical anthologists; article. *Ariel* July 1987; Vol 18 No 3: p77–85.

Dancing with snowflakes: monologue with the silent author; article. *Dandelion* Spring-Summer 1987; Vol 14 No 1: p72–80.

[Untitled]; reviews of *Flavian's Fortune* and *The Story of Bobby O'Malley. Queen's Q* Winter 1987; Vol 94 No 4: p1019–1022.

Steele, Leighton

95 Seward; poem. *Antigonish R* 1987; No 69–70: p142.

Olive Street, Santa Barbara; poem. *Antigonish R* 1987; No 69–70: p143.

Stefaniuk, Walter

2 Star writers, photographer take top newspaper award; article. *TS* May 3, 1987: pA2.

Steffler, Margaret

Learning to accept change and loss; review of *The Baby Project. Can Child Lit* 1987; No 47: p90–91.

Stein, Susan Stromberg

Differing with Dudek; letter to the editor. photo · *G&M* Dec 26, 1987: pD7.

Steiner, Jr., Louis

Dioboloi; poem. *Quarry* Summer 1987; Vol 36 No 3: p16.

Outcrop; poem. *Quarry* Summer 1987; Vol 36 No 3: p16.

Steinfeld, J.J.

Death in Fiji; short story. *Alpha* Winter 1987; Vol 11: p23–28.

Stenberg, Peter

Grief & memory; reviews of poetry books. *Can Lit* Spring 1987; No 112: p169–171.

Stenson, Fred

Coffee for two, one with milk; short story. *Grain* Spring 1987; Vol 15 No 1: p84–89.

Stevens, James

Thoroughly modern children; short story. illus · *Alpha* Winter 1987; Vol 11: p5–6.

Stevens, Peter

[Untitled]; review of *Spider Blues. Queen's Q* Autumn 1987; Vol 94 No 3: p717–719.

Stevenson, Grace

Regeneration; short story. photo · *TS* July 21, 1987: pB5.

Stevenson, Richard

An auspicious debut; review of *What We Bring Home. Prairie Fire* Summer 1987; Vol 8 No 2: p60–62.

Busy Lizzie (imptiens walleriana); poem. *Arc* Spring 1987; No 18: p67.

Hindu rope (hoya compacta regalis); poem. *Arc* Spring 1987; No 18: p66.

In voice; reviews of poetry books. *Can Lit* Spring 1987; No 112: p167–169.

Urn plant (aechmea fasciata); poem. *Arc* Spring 1987; No 18: p69.

Weeping fig (ficus benjamina); poem. *Arc* Spring 1987; No 18: p68.

Stewart, Jack F.

Iconographies; reviews of *Out of the Storm* and *The End of Ice. Can Lit* Spring 1987; No 112: p166–167.

Image and mood: recent poems by Michael Bullock; article. *Can Lit* Winter 1987; No 115: p107–121.

Stewart, N.J.

Story award order should be inverted; letter to the editor. *CH* Aug 26, 1987: pA6.

Stewart, Robert

[Untitled]; review of *The Color of Blood.* illus · *MG* Sept 5, 1987: pJ1.

Stewart-Patterson, David

Ottawa copyright bill aids artists, gets tough with book, tape pirates; article. *G&M* May 28, 1987 pA1–A2.

Stich, K.P.

German contexts in Canadian literature; review of *The Old World and the New. Essays on Can Writ* Spring 1987; No 34: p185–189.

Grove's "Stella"; article. illus · *Can Lit* Summer-Fall 1987; No 113–114: p258–262.

Stockdale, John C.

What can a person do; poem. *Prairie J of Can Lit* 1987; No 8: p27.

Stockholder, Kay

Freudian farce; review of *Who's Afraid of Sigmund Freud?*. *Can Lit* Spring 1987; No 112: p162–164.

Stoicheff, Peter

[Heading Out]; review. *NeWest R* Sept 1987; Vol 13 No 1: p17.

Storey, Raymond

Foreward; introduction to *The Last Bus*. photo · *Can Theatre R* Summer 1987; No 51: p44.

The last bus; play. photo · *Can Theatre R* Summer 1987; No 51: p43–65.

Stortz, Joan Colgan

Birthday greetings; poem. *Can Auth & Book* Fall 1987; Vol 63 No 1: p17.

Stott, Jim

Story contest guidelines could have been clearer; article. *CH* July 30, 1987: pA10.

Stouck, David

Vancouver mind; reviews of *Vancouver Short Stories* and *Vancouver Fiction*. *Can Lit* Spring 1987; No 112: p157–159.

Straram, Patrick

Blues clair, Kurapel le Guanaco gaucho; essay. *Moebius* Summer 1987; No 33: p81–106.

Streiling, Richard

[Untitled]; review of *Canadian Sunset*. *Quill & Quire* Jan 1987; Vol 53 No 1: p27.

[Untitled]; review of *Dogstones*. *Quill & Quire* Feb 1987; Vol 53 No 2: p20.

[Untitled]; review of *Adele at the End of the Day*. *Quill & Quire* March 1987; Vol 53 No 3: p71.

[Untitled]; review of *Second Nature*. *Quill & Quire* March 1987; Vol 53 No 3: p75.

Strongin, Lynn

Spent; poem. *Antigonish R* Winter 1987; No 68: p12.

Struthers, Ann

Sioux City; poem. *Prairie J of Can Lit* 1987; No 8: p32.

Struthers, Betsy

When the father leaves; poem. *Can Forum* May 1987; Vol 67 No 769: p7.

Stuart, Judith

In memoriam: the Rainbow Warrior; poem. *Can Auth & Book* Spring 1987; Vol 62 No 3: p22.

So everybody's mortal; poem. *Room of One's Own* Jan 1987; Vol 11 No 2: p42–43.

Stuewe, Paul

High ideas from a split end; review of *North of Intention*. *G&M* July 11, 1987: pC15.

Many happy returns; review of *The Oxford Illustrated Literary Guide to Canada*. *Books in Can* Nov 1987; Vol 16 No 8: p12–14.

Minding their Poes and cues; review of *Invisible Fictions*. *Books in Can* Aug-Sept 1987; Vol 16 No 6: p24.

Rewriting the past; article. *Books in Can* Aug-Sept 1987; Vol 16 No 6: p13–14.

Sturmanis, Dona

The 3-Day Novel Contest; article. photo · *Can Auth & Book* Spring 1987; Vol 62 No 3: p12–13.

[Untitled]; poem. *Can Auth & Book* Winter 1987; Vol 62 No 2: p22.

[Untitled]; review of *Other Selves*. *Can Auth & Book* Winter 1987; Vol 62 No 2: p23–24.

[Untitled]; review of *Mobile Homes*. *Can Auth & Book* Spring 1987; Vol 62 No 3: p25.

Suderman, Brenda

Grief and love; review of *I Sing for My Dead in German*. *Prairie Fire* Autumn 1987; Vol 8 No 3: p115–117.

Suknaski, Andrew

Divining west; poetry excerpt from *Celestial Madness*. *Prairie Fire* Winter 1987–88; Vol 8 No 4: p50–53.

Sullivan, C.J.

No fear of castration; letter to the editor. *G&M* Nov 20, 1987: pA6.

Sullivan, Joan

Sheer 'persistence' keeps literary magazine alive; article. *G&M* Nov 23, 1987: pC9.

Sullivan, Rosemary

The black box; poem. *Malahat R* Dec 1987; No 81: p39.

A daring invention of a new character; review of *Heroine*. *G&M* Sept 19, 1987: pC19.

The dark pines of the mind: the symbol of the forest in Canadian literature; article. abstract · *Études can* 1987; No 23: p173–182.

Elegy: for Elizabeth Smart; poem. *CV 2* Summer 1987; Vol 10 No 4: p11.

Elegy; poem. *CV 2* Summer 1987; Vol 10 No 4: p9–10.

The forest and the trees; article. *Brick* Winter 1987; No 29: p43–46.

Homecoming; poem. *Malahat R* Dec 1987; No 81: p43.

Mamita; poem. *Malahat R* Dec 1987; No 81: p41.

Passe-port; poem. *Malahat R* Dec 1987; No 81: p40.

The poem fights with the buzz saw; poem. *CV 2* Summer 1987; Vol 10 No 4: p13.

Sisters of the Holy Name; poem. *CV 2* Summer 1987; Vol 10 No 4: p12.

Talca: city of thunder; poem. *Malahat R* Dec 1987; No 81: p42.

Who are the immigrant writers and what have they done?; essay. *G&M* Oct 17, 1987: pE1.

Sullivan, Thomas P.

[Untitled]; review of *The Promised Land*. *Quill & Quire* May 1987; Vol 53 No 5: p20, 22.

[Untitled]; review of *Tranter's Tree*. *Quill & Quire* May 1987; Vol 53 No 5: p22.

[Untitled]; review of *This One's on Me*. *Quill & Quire* Nov 1987; Vol 53 No 11: p25.

Summerhayes, Don

Chrome chairs recovered; poem. photo · *Malahat R* June 1987; No 79: p95–96.

Deadwood, South Dakota, spring 1977; poem. *Arc* Fall 1987; No 19: p79–80.

Eau'd to my barbers; poem. *Arc* Fall 1987; No 19: p80.

I know I am smiling; poem. *Malahat R* June 1987; No 79: p94.

Summers, Frances J.

Bibliographie de Yves Beauchemin; bibliography. *Voix et images* Spring 1987; Vol 12 No 3: p416–428.

Entrevue avec Yves Beauchemin; interview. *Voix et images* Spring 1987; Vol 12 No 3: p360–374.

Le réception critique du Matou; article. *Voix et images* Spring 1987; Vol 12 No 3: p383–392.

Surette, Leon

Full stops; review of *Economic Sex*. *Can Lit* Winter 1987; No 115: p245–246.

Surguy, Phil

Laughing on the outside; essay. *Books in Can* Dec 1987; Vol 16 No 9: p4–5.

Sutherland, Alison

[The Woman Who Is the Midnight Wind]; review. *Atlan Prov Book R* May-June 1987; Vol 14 No 2: p9.

Sutherland, Fraser

Ballads and ditties for grown-ups; reviews of poetry books. illus · *G&M* Nov 7, 1987: pC21.

The cosmic ruminant's vision; review of *The Collected Poems*. photo · *G&M* Jan 3, 1987: pE16.

From ivy-covered professors; reviews of poetry books. *G&M* Oct 17, 1987: pE9.

The impersonation of the irresistible; reviews of poetry books. *G&M* Sept 5, 1987: pC15.

Literary tricks and the larger concerns; reviews of *Delayed Mercy* and *Afterworlds*. photo · *G&M* Aug 8, 1987: pC19.

Male myths, obliterated lesbians and powerful dreams; reviews of poetry books. photo · *G&M* Feb 14, 1987: pE19.

Mapping inner and outer selves; review of *Tiger in the Skull* and *Dogstones*. *G&M* Feb 28, 1987: pE18.

The mermaid inn: flight of the Lisbon taxi; essay. photo · *G&M* Aug 15, 1987: pD6.

The pastoral myth and its observers; reviews of poetry books. *G&M* Sept 26, 1987: pC23.

A plumber of bathetic depths; reviews of *Islands* and *The Collected Poems of George Whalley*. photo · *G&M* July 18, 1987: pC15.

Poetry, science, mind and religion; reviews of poetry books. photo · *G&M* Jan 31, 1987: pE19.

Poetry and the loving Spanish tongue; reviews of poetry books. *G&M* May 30, 1987: pC21.

The reader's duties; review of *Schedules of Silence*. *G&M* June 6, 1987: pC19.

Rush job, high gloss and high-risk realism; reviews of poetry books. *G&M* March 21, 1987: pE18.

Umbrellas for a torrent of Canadian poems; reviews of poetry anthologies. *G&M* March 28, 1987: pE19.

The virtuous poet; review of *Zembla's Rocks*. *G&M* April 18, 1987: pC18.

Sutherland, Ronald

Living inspirations; review of *Enchantment and Sorrow*. photo · *G&M* Dec 26, 1987: pC23.

The mermaid inn: on Frank Scott's veranda; essay. photo · *G&M* Aug 1, 1987: pD6.

[Untitled]; biographical articles. *Brick (special issue)* Summer 1987; No 30: ppassim.

Sutherland, W. Mark

A case history; poem. *Waves* Winter 1987; Vol 15 No 3: p56.

Dream sequence; poem. *Poetry Can R* Spring 1987; Vol 8 No 1–2: p15.

Fascist confetti #2; poem. *Queen's Q* Autumn 1987; Vol 94 No 3: p602.

The history of miracles; poem. *Waves* Winter 1987; Vol 15 No 3: p57.

Sutton, Janice

Bal; short story. *Tor South Asian R* Spring 1987; Vol 5 No 3: p52–62.

Swan, Susan

Conventional wisdom; letter to the editor. *Books in Can* Oct 1987; Vol 16 No 7: p40.

Return to lotus land; review of *The Honorary Patron* *Maclean's* Oct 26, 1987; Vol 100 No 43: p52f.

Sluts; short story. *Prism* Summer 1987; Vol 25 No 4: p35–42.

Why I decided I don't want to write a bestseller; essay. *G&M* Nov 14, 1987: pE5.

Swannell, Anne

Be it ever so awful they'll publish your poem; essay. *Cross Can Writ Q* 1987; Vol 9 No 3–4: p63.

Letter to the Canada Council; essay. *Cross Can Writ Q* 1987; Vol 9 No 3–4: p35.

On nothingness and being in Boxley Wood; poem. *Poetry Can R* Spring 1987; Vol 8 No 1–2: p10.

One December; poem. *Poetry Can R* Spring 1987; Vol 8 No 1–2: p10.

Skating; poem. *New Q* Winter 1987; Vol 6 No 4: p95.

Sward, Robert

[Untitled]; review of *The Twelfth Transforming*. *Can Auth & Book* Winter 1987; Vol 62 No 2: p23.

Swede, George

Experiskinno poetry – then and now; editorial article. photo · *Cross Can Writ Q* 1987; Vol 9 No 3–4: p3–5.

Sweet, Lois

Our women artists face discrimination; column. *TS* Jan 26, 1987: pC1.

Studio D faces big job small budget; article. photo · *TS* May 4, 1987: pC1, C3.

Teens need to see play on vital issue; column. *TS* April 20, 1987: pC1.

Swenson, Sally

Snapshots of China; review of *Through the Nan Da Gate*. *Arc* Spring 1987; No 18: p70–71.

Szaffkó, Péter

The Indian in contemporary North American drama; article. *Can Drama* 1987; Vol 13 No 2: p182–186.

Szohner, Gabriel J.

Waiting for the Starwatcher; short story. *Prairie J of Can Lit* 1987; No 9: p14–23.

Szumigalski, Anne

The child as mother to the woman; prose excerpt from *Four, an Imagined and Remembered Childhood*. *Grain* Winter 1987; Vol 15 No 4: p7–8.

Think of a word; prose poem. *Prairie Fire* Winter 1987–88; Vol 8 No 4: p10–11.

[Untitled]; poem. *Prairie Fire* Winter 1987–88; Vol 8 No 4: p9.

Tard, Louis-Martin

[Untitled]; excerpt from *Il y aura toujours des printemps en Amérique*. photo · *MD* Sept 26, 1987: pD1, D8.

Tarente, Nathalie

L'entre-voyeuse; short story. *Moebius* Autumn 1987; No 34: p61–64.

Tarnapolski, Walter

[Untitled]; biographical articles. *Brick (special issue)* Summer 1987; No 30: ppassim.

Tassinari, Lamberto

Soyons francs; essay. illus · *Liberté (special issue)* 1987: p50–53.

Tata, Sam

Bombay Bohemia: party at Alberta's; poem. *Descant* Fall 1987; Vol 18 No 3: p22.

Canvas by Amrita Sher Gil: Bombay; poem. *Descant* Fall 1987; Vol 18 No 3: p23.

Colaba: blind man in the rain; poem. *Descant* Fall 1987; Vol 18 No 3: p21.

Death of a Mahatma (Mohandas Karamchand Gandhi 1869–1948); poem. *Descant* Fall 1987; Vol 18 No 3: p24.

Exhibition by Shiavax Chavda; poem. *Descant* Fall 1987; Vol 18 No 3: p30.

Foggy morning: Calcutta; poem. *Descant* Fall 1987; Vol 18 No 3: p27.

Girl singing (a painting by George Keyt); poem. *Descant* Fall 1987; Vol 18 No 3: p26.

Old ruins: Delhi; poem. *Descant* Fall 1987; Vol 18 No 3: p25.

Rajabai Tower at noon: Bombay; poem. *Descant* Fall 1987; Vol 18 No 3: p29.

Temple at Tanjore; poem. *Descant* Fall 1987; Vol 18 No 3: p19.

To a lady in an urban landscape (recollections of a Kangra painting); poem. *Descant* Fall 1987; Vol 18 No 3: p28.

Train journey before the monsoon; poem. *Descant* Fall 1987; Vol 18 No 3: p20.

Taylor, Andrew

Frost shadows; reviews of poetry books. *Can Lit* Winter 1987; No 115: p197–199.

Taylor, Bruce

Poppa; poem. *Queen's Q* Summer 1987; Vol 94 No 2: p444–445.

Taylor, Drew

Legends on the stage; article. photo · *Maclean's* Oct 19, 1987; Vol 100 No 42: p69.

Taylor, Joan

Photograph of a mother; poem. *Ariel* July 1987; Vol 18 No 3: p29.

Taylor, Joan Crate

Boarding school; poem. *Fiddlehead* Autumn 1987; No 153: p75.

I am a prophet; poem. *Fiddlehead* Autumn 1987; No 153: p76–77.

Taylor, Linda

The Rathbones' family skeletons; review of *Under the House*. *Times Lit Supp* Dec 18, 1987; No 4420: p1409.

Taylor, Scott

An end-to-end rush; review of *King Leary*. *WFP* Nov 14, 1987: p50.

Tefs, Wayne

Coughs, memory lapses, uncle's hands; short story. *Dandelion* Spring-Summer 1987; Vol 14 No 1: p57-61.

Teleky, Richard

Village of the damned; review of *Heartbreaks Along the Road*. photo · *Maclean's* Nov 2, 1987; Vol 100 No 44: p52f.

Tener, Anne E.

The glasses; short story. *Quarry* Fall 1987; Vol 36 No 4: p50-54.

Passage home; short story. *Room of One's Own* Jan 1987; Vol 11 No 2: p59-63.

Ternar, Yesim

Tedescu's visitation; short story. *Rubicon* Fall 1987; No 9: p62-71.

Tessler, Howard

[Untitled]; review of *The Bottle and the Bushman*. *Rubicon* Fall 1987; No 9: p195-196.

[Untitled]; review of *Donkey Dance*. *Rubicon* Fall 1987; No 9: p202-203.

Thacker, Robert

Conferring Munro; review of *The Art of Alice Munro. Essays on Can Writ* Spring 1987; No 34: p162-169.

Munro's progress; review of *The Progress of Love. Can Lit* Winter 1987; No 115: p239-242.

[Untitled]; review of *Prairie Women. Amer R of Can Studies* Spring 1987; Vol 17 No 1: p113-115.

Thaler, Danielle

Anne, ma soeur Anne. . . .; review of *Anne. . . .la maison aux pignons verts. Can Child Lit* 1987; No 46: p72-73.

Thatcher, Philip

Low tide at Gabriola; poem. *Event* Summer 1987; Vol 16 No 2: p62.

Théoret, France

Fiction et métissage ou écrire l'imaginaire du réel; essay. bibliog biog · *La Nouvelle barre du jour (special issue)* 1987; No 201-202: p65-78.

[Untitled]; prose excerpt from *L'Homme qui peignait Staline*. illus · *La Nouvelle barre du jour* Feb 1987; No 193: p69-79.

Thériault, Marie José

Deux livres pour partir en voyage; reviews of *Mourir comme un chat* and *Banc de Brume*. photo · *Lettres québec* Autumn 1987; No 47: p31-32.

Un livre pour tester la conscience; review of *L'Obsédante obèse*. photo · *Lettres québec* Autumn 1987; No 47: p30-31.

Tous feux éteints; review of *L'Homme de Hong Kong*. *Lettres québec* Winter 1986-87; No 44: p34-35.

Trois voyages – petit, moyen et grand – du littératage à la littérature; reviews of short story books. photo · *Lettres québec* Spring 1987; No 45: p30-32.

Les vertus de la retenue et du silence; reviews of poetry books. photo · *Lettres québec* Summer 1987; No 46: p30-32.

Thériault, Normand

De l'installation; essay. illus photo · *La Nouvelle barre du jour (special issue)* 1987; No 185: p9-61.

Thério, Adrien

400,000$; editorial. *Lettres québec* Winter 1986-87; No 44: p10-11.

Une collecion qui part de bon pied; article. *Lettres québec* Summer 1987; No 46: p77.

Des revues presque indispensables; reviews of periodicals. *Lettres québec* Autumn 1987; No 47: p63-65.

Dits et faits; column. photo · *Lettres québec* Summer 1987; No 46: p6.

Hommage à Suzanne Lamy; obituary. photo · *Lettres québec* Summer 1987; No 46: p8.

Un homme plein d'artifices; review of *Un Homme et son péché* (critical edition). photo · *Lettres québec* Spring 1987; No 45: p62-63.

Littérature québécoise d'hier et d'aujourd'hui on en parle je vous donne des addresses; editorial. *Lettres québec* Summer 1987; No 46: p10-12.

Une première dans l'histoire intellectuelle du Québec; article. *Lettres québec* Winter 1986-87; No 44: p11.

Une première traduction de L'Appel de la race; review of *The Iron Wedge*. *Lettres québec* Winter 1986-87; No 44: p85.

Présentation; introduction to prose excerpts from *Du sommet d'un arbre*. photo · *Lettres québec* Spring 1987; No 45: p8.

La recherche de l'amour; review of *Aimer*. *Lettres québec* Winter 1986-87; No 44: p79.

Sommaires; reviews. *Lettres québec* Summer 1987; No 46: p80.

La structure de la grande machine à faire des livres; review of *L'Institution littéraire*. *Lettres québec* Winter 1986-87; No 44: p84.

Tinamer ou le bon côté des choses; review of *L'Amélanchier*. *Lettres québec* Winter 1986-87; No 44: p77.

[Untitled]; introduction. photo · *Lettres québec* Autumn 1987; No 47: p55.

Théry, Chantal

La droite amoureuse rallume ses brasiers; reviews of *La Peur du Grand Amour* and *La Corrida de l'amour*. *Lettres québec* Winter 1986-87; No 44: p69-71.

Thibault, André

Les 150 ans du premier roman québécois; article. illus · *MD* Sept 12, 1987: pD3, D8.

Thibaux, Hélène

[Untitled]; review of *Au coeur de l'instant*. *Estuaire* Winter 1986–87; No 43: p76.

[Untitled]; review of *À vouloir vaincre l'absence*. *Estuaire* Winter 1986–87; No 43: p78–79.

[Untitled]; review of *Hors champ*. *Estuaire* Spring 1987; No 44: p81.

[Untitled]; review of *Lignes de nuit*. *Estuaire* Spring 1987; No 44: p81–82.

[Untitled]; reviews of *Un goût de sel* and *Effets de l'oeil*. *Estuaire* Autumn 1987; No 46: p86–87.

Thibodeau, Serge Patrice

L'éveil, et qui monte, allège à l'excès; poem. *Moebius* Autumn 1987; No 34: p111–113.

Thieme, John

Floating signs; review of *The Alley Cat*. *Can Lit* Summer-Fall 1987; No 113–114: p249–251.

Thomas, Audrey

Fool for love; review of *Necessary Secrets*. photo · *Books in Can* April 1987; Vol 16 No 3: p17–18.

[Untitled]; biographical articles. *Brick (special issue)* Summer 1987; No 30: ppassim.

Thomas, Clara

[Untitled]; review of *Sounding the Iceberg*. *U of Toronto Q* Fall 1987; Vol 57 No 1: p158–160.

Thomas, Gerald

Folktales; review of *Les Vieux m'ont conté*. *Can Lit* Winter 1987; No 115: p242–245.

Thomas, Joan

An unsuccessful satire; review of *The Dancing Chicken*. *WFP* Nov 28, 1987: p58.

Thomas, Mark

Rereading Lowry's "Lunar Caustic"; article. *Can Lit* Spring 1987; No 112: p195–197.

Thomas, Sophia

Reading Jacques Derrida, on the beach; poem. *New Q* Winter 1987; Vol 6 No 4: p96.

Thomas, Sophie

Opaque criticism; letter to the editor. *G&M* July 25, 1987: pD7.

[Untitled]; poem. *CV 2* Summer 1987; Vol 10 No 4: p19.

Thompson, Alexa

Sara[h] Jackson's book works; reviews of books by Sarah Jackson. *Atlan Prov Book R* Sept-Oct 1987; Vol 14 No 3: p15.

Thompson, Diana

To Bristol; poem. *Atlantis* Spring 1987; Vol 12 No 2: p98.

Thompson, Kent

Allowances must be made; review of *A Collection of Short Stories*. *Atlan Prov Book R* Sept-Oct 1987; Vol 14 No 3: p12.

The lively art; reviews of *Double Exposures* and *Frogs*. *Fiddlehead* Winter 1987; No 154: p87–91.

Thompson, M.A.

[Untitled]; review of *Visitations*. *Quarry* Summer 1987; Vol 36 No 3: p80–82.

Thompson, Ruth

One Yellow Rabbit great; letter to the editor. *CH* June 15, 1987: pA6.

Thorne, Barry

[Untitled]; review of *Varieties of Exile*. *Eng Studies in Can* Dec 1987; Vol 13 No 4: p480–483.

Thornhill, Jan

St. Francis and the birds; short story. *Fiddlehead* Summer 1987; No 152: p54–61.

Thornton, Russell

A door; poem. *Prism* Winter 1987; Vol 25 No 2: p17.

Double; poem. *Germination* Fall 1987; Vol 11 No 1: p46.

Echo; poem. *U of Windsor R* Fall-Winter 1987; Vol 20 No 1: p93.

Racoons; poem. *Germination* Fall 1987; Vol 11 No 1: p48.

Ravine creek in December; poem. *Prism* Winter 1987; Vol 25 No 2: p16.

Song; poem. *U of Windsor R* Fall-Winter 1987; Vol 20 No 1: p92.

You want to talk to rain; poem. *Germination* Fall 1987; Vol 11 No 1: p47.

Thorpe, Carole

There is, in you; poem. *Room of One's Own* April 1987; Vol 11 No 3: p98.

Thorpe, Douglas

What troubles troubled kids; review of *Last Chance Summer*. *Can Child Lit* 1987; No 46: p86–87.

Thorpe, Michael

Recent Atlantic poetry: a survey: 1980–1985: III New Brunswick summary; article. bibliog · *Antigonish R* Winter 1987; No 68: p133–148.

Structures of meditation; reviews of *Meditations* and *Midnight Found You Dancing*. *Fiddlehead* Spring 1987; No 151: p115–120.

Thurlow, Ann

F-words at Green Gables; article. photo · *Maclean's* July 13, 1987; Vol 100 No 28: p49.

Tiessen, Paul

Critical programmes; reviews of *Malcolm Lowry* and *Four Contemporary Novelists*. *Can Lit* Winter 1987; No 115: p157–159.

Tihanyi, Eva

Animal story; poem. *CV 2* Spring 1987; Vol 10 No 3: p44.

Excesses; reviews of poetry books. *Can Lit* Winter 1987; No 115: p200–202.

A green world; review of *Collected Poems*. *Waves* Winter 1987; Vol 15 No 3: p78–80.

Leavetaking; poem. *Room of One's Own* April 1987; Vol 11 No 3: p79.

Purgatory; poem. *Room of One's Own* April 1987; Vol 11 No 3: p80.

[Untitled]; review of *Lovhers*. *Poetry Can R* Spring 1987; Vol 8 No 2–3: p40–41.

Timmins, Michael

Missing children; poem. *Event* March 1987; Vol 16 No 1: p60.

Tivy, Patrick

Storyteller weaves gripping tales; column. illus · *CH* April 3, 1987: pC2.

Tivy on Wednesday; column. *CH* Nov 4, 1987: pB1.

Todd, Jack

Plateau is scene for fiction's famous characters; article. photo · *MG* May 23, 1987: pJ2.

Todkill, Anne

[Untitled]; review of *The Weight of Oranges*. *Quarry* Winter 1987; Vol 36 No 1: p131–133.

Toews, Marjorie

At the age of sixteen; poem. *CV 2* Summer 1987; Vol 10 No 4: p17.

Montreal; poem. *CV 2* Summer 1987; Vol 10 No 4: p18.

Tombs, George

Après la guerre; review of *After the Fact*. *MD* June 20, 1987: pD6.

Tompkins, Joanne

Yesterday's heroes; review of *The Dreamers*. *Books in Can* June-July 1987; Vol 16 No 5: p32–33.

Tostevin, Lola Lemire

Diana Hartog: poetry beyond revision; review of *Candy from Strangers*. *Brick* Winter 1987; No 29: p9–13.

Don't sit around language: an interview with Fred Wah. *Poetry Can R* Fall 1987; Vol 9 No 1: p3–5.

The pregnant pause as conceptual space (or gimme a break); essay. *Open Letter* Spring 1987; Vol 6 No 7: p74–76.

[Untitled]; poetry excerpt from *Double Standards*. *Can Forum* Jan 1987; Vol 66 No 765: p38.

Toth, Derrick

MacLennan happy with plans to stage his Barometer Rising; article. photo · *CH* Sept 26, 1987: pG1.

Totzke, Michael

Black October; article. *Tor Life* Sept 1987; Vol 21 No 13: p17.

Tougas, Colette

Mister Mystère; short story. *Estuaire* Autumn 1987; No 46: p25–27.

Tourigny, Maurice

Tamara: intrigue, champagne et amuse-gueules; article. photo · *MD* Nov 14, 1987: pC6.

Towell, Larry

Highlands; poem. *Waves* Winter 1987; Vol 15 No 3: p50–51.

Sonsonate; poem. *New Q* Fall 1987; Vol 7 No 3: p57–60.

[Untitled]; review of *Sandinista*. *Queen's Q* Autumn 1987; Vol 94 No 3: p696–698.

Townsend, Martin

Finding fantasy in a Québécois anthology; review of *Invisible Fictions*. *Quill & Quire* Aug 1987; Vol 53 No 8: p32.

[Untitled]; review of *One Out of Four*. *Quill & Quire* Feb 1987; Vol 53 No 2: p17.

[Untitled]; review of *All the Bright Company*. *Quill & Quire* June 1987; Vol 53 No 6: p31.

[Untitled]; review of *The Parrot Who Could*. *Quill & Quire* July 1987; Vol 53 No 7: p65.

[Untitled]; review of *Red Wolf, Red Wolf*. *Quill & Quire* Sept 1987; Vol 53 No 9: p79.

Trainer, Yvonne

Firewood; poem. *Fiddlehead* Winter 1987; No 154: p14.

For the record; poem. *Can Lit* Winter 1987; No 115: p27.

Know them; poem. *Fiddlehead* Winter 1987; No 154: p13.

Letters to Mary; poem. *Can Lit* Winter 1987; No 115: p6–8.

Penny; poem. *Fiddlehead* Winter 1987; No 154: p12.

Poet in the schools; poem. *Poetry Can R* Fall 1987; Vol 9 No 1: p22.

Three rocks jutting up from snow; poem. *Can Lit* Winter 1987; No 115: p64.

Tranfield, Pam

For you who tell us what to do when; poem. *Fireweed* Fall 1987; No 25: p50–51.

Take home something for the children; poem. *Fireweed* Fall 1987; No 25: p48–49.

Tranquille, Henri

Les vacances d'un chroniqueur; letter to the editor. *MD* July 27, 1987: p6.

Treadwell, Florence

Farewell; poem. *Poetry Can R* Spring 1987; Vol 8 No 1–2: p13.

Tregebov, Rhea

National Portrait Gallery, London; poem. *Can Lit* Summer-Fall 1987; No 113–114: p10.

Story and poetry: narrative strategies in recent Canadian poetry; article. *Quarry* Winter 1987; Vol 36 No 1: p118–124.

[Untitled]; review of *Fables from the Women's Quarters. Fireweed* Winter 1987; No 24: p103–106.

Trehearne, Brian

Preliminaries for a life of Standish O'Grady; biographical article. *Can Poet* Fall-Winter 1987; No 21: p81–92.

Tremblay, Odile

Quand le facteur se fait libraire. . . .; article. photo · *MD* May 16, 1987: pD1, D8.

Trichur, Rita

Late again, George and Jeff?; children's story. *TS* March 22, 1987: pH6.

Trigueiro, David

Mag's humor may have done it in; article. *CH* Dec 18, 1987: pA4.

Trudeau, Pierre

On the occasion of Frank Scott's seventieth birthday; essay. photo · *Brick (special issue)* Summer 1987; No 30: p47–48.

Trudel, Clément

L'Indien imaginaire: de Buffalo Bill à la "sagamité"; article. photo · *MD* Aug 29, 1987: pC13.

Truhlar, Richard

Sound poetry: serious play; article. illus · *Cross Can Writ Q* 1987; Vol 9 No 3–4: p16–18.

You are what you write; essay. *Poetry Can R* Fall 1987; Vol 9 No 1: p12.

Trujillo, Renato

El Maldito; short story. *Queen's Q* Winter 1987; Vol 94 No 4: p959–965.

The elixir; short story. illus · *Can Forum* Oct 1987; Vol 67 No 772: p22–27.

Truss, Jan

[Village of Idiots]; theatre review. *NeWest R* Feb 1987; Vol 12 No 6: p16.

Tucker, John

George Johnston's The Saga Of Gisli; article. *Malahat R (special issue)* March 1987; No 78: p83–91.

Tudor, Kathleen

Books in Motion / Livres en tournee; article. photo · *Atlan Prov Book R* Nov-Dec 1987; Vol 14 No 4: p8.

Turbide, Diane

Bologna score-card Part I; article. photo · *Quill & Quire* June 1987; Vol 53 No 6: p22–23.

Turcotte, Claude

Micheline Tremblay relance une entreprise au passé prestigieux; article. photo · *MD* March 2, 1987: p9.

Turcotte, Élise

Les paysages; prose excerpt from *La Collection de portraits. Estuaire* Autumn 1987; No 46: p41–42.

Turgeon, Serge

Les artistes doivent veiller au grain; essay. *MD* March 11, 1987: p11.

Turner, Barbara

In the skin of Michael Ondaatje: giving voice to a social conscience; review article about *In the Skin of a Lion.* photo · *Quill & Quire* May 1987; Vol 53 No 5: p21–22.

Turner, Doug

Dinnertime 1; poem. *NeWest R* April 1987; Vol 12 No 8: p14.

Dinnertime 2; poem. *NeWest R* April 1987; Vol 12 No 8: p14.

The kid; poem. *Antigonish R* Winter 1987; No 68: p113.

Turner, Margaret E.

Fiction, break, silence: language. Sheila Watson's The Double Hook; article. *Ariel* April 1987; Vol 18 No 2: p65–78.

Turner, Michael B.

Rip tide; poem. *Prism* Spring 1987; Vol 25 No 3: p68.

Sure sign of fish; poem. *Prism* Spring 1987; Vol 25 No 3: p67.

Sure sign of fish; poem. *Antigonish R* 1987; No 69–70: p194.

Turner, Ron

[Untitled]; review of *The Creative Circus Book. Quarry* Spring 1987; Vol 36 No 2: p113–116.

Tutunjian, Jerry

In swat, exactly; essay. illus · *Idler* Sept-Oct 1987; No 14: p44–46.

Tuzlak, Ruhi E.

[Untitled]; letter to the editor. *G&M* Jan 21, 1987: pA7.

Twigg, Alan

For batter or verse; biographical article. photo · *Books in Can* Nov 1987; Vol 16 No 8: p7–8, 10.

Interview with Josef Skvorecky. *Dandelion* Fall-Winter 1987; Vol 14 No 2: p136–142.

Interview with Sandra Birdsell. photo · *NeWest R* Nov 1987; Vol 13 No 3: p2–3.

Minding their q's and a's; review of *Speaking for Myself. Books in Can* May 1987; Vol 16 No 4: p31–32.

Tyndall, Paul

The door; poem. *Antigonish R* 1987; No 69–70: p168.

Driving westward into Val D'Or; poem. *Antigonish R* 1987; No 69–70: p168.

Portrait of the artist as a middle-aged schlemiel; review of *Our Hero in the Cradle of Confederation. Atlan Prov Book R* Sept-Oct 1987; Vol 14 No 3: p12.

Uhlig, Mark A.

From the land of the terrifically believable; article. photo · *NYT Book R* Sept 27, 1987: p13.

Uhrig, Robert J.

Buddy system; short story. photo · *TS* Aug 26, 1987: pA25.

Umezawa, Rui

Bar hopping; review of *Incubation. G&M* June 20, 1987: pC19.

Underhill, Frank

[Untitled]; biographical articles. *Brick (special issue)* Summer 1987; No 30: ppassim.

Urbas, Jeannette

Nothing would ever change; short story. *Room of One's Own* Jan 1987; Vol 11 No 2: p80–88.

A teddy bear's tale; review of *Spring Tides. Can Forum* Jan 1987; Vol 66 No 765: p39–40.

Urquhart, Jane

The celebrations of Tim Lilburn; review of *Names of God. Brick* Fall 1987; No 31: p39–40.

Urquhart, John A.

[Untitled]; reviews of *The Cutting Season* and *A Nest of Singing Birds. Prairie J of Can Lit* 1987; No 8: p50–54.

Ursell, Geoffrey

There ain't nobody here but us chickens; short story. *Grain* Summer 1987; Vol 15 No 2: p36–45.

Usmiani, Renate

Hyperrealism: Michel Tremblay and Franz Xaver Kroetz; article. *Can Drama* 1987; Vol 13 No 2: p201–209.

[Untitled]; review of *Theatre and Politics in Modern Quebec. Can Theatre R* Spring 1987; No 50: p84–85.

UU, David

Data supplies; poem. *Cross Can Writ Q* 1987; Vol 9 No 3–4: p11.

The language fetishist; poem. *Cross Can Writ Q* 1987; Vol 9 No 3–4: p11.

Vadeboncoeur, Pierre

Il inspirait la gratitude; essay. *Liberté* Feb 1987; Vol 29 No 1: p90–91.

Le présent au sens fort; essay. *Liberté (special issue)* 1987: p14–19.

Vaillancourt, Pierre-Louis

Montréal dans les années 50; review of *La Bagarre.* photo · *Lettres québec* Spring 1987; No 45: p57–59.

Vaïs, Michel

Bloc-notes; column. *Jeu* 1987; No 42: p190–191.

Bloc-notes; column. *Jeu* 1987; No 43: p179–180.

Bloc-notes; column. *Jeu* 1987; No 44: p215–218.

Bloc-notes; column. photo · *Jeu* 1987; No 45: p227–231.

De qui se moque Le Devoir?; editorial. photo · *Jeu* 1987; No 45: p7–9.

Entre le jouet de pacotille et la voûte céleste: le voyage des personnages à travers les objets; article. photo · *Jeu* 1987; No 45: p98–110.

Nudisme et fiction; letter to the editor. *MD* Aug 13, 1987: p8.

Suspense au fond du gouffre; theatre review of *Le Night Cap Bar.* photo · *Jeu* 1987; No 44: p175–177.

Vaisius, Andrew

A life rarefied; review of *The Collected Poems. Waves* Spring 1987; Vol 15 No 4: p80–83.

Society; poem. *New Q* Winter 1987; Vol 6 No 4: p97–98.

Talk; prose poem. *Prism* Summer 1987; Vol 25 No 4: p97.

[Untitled]; reviews of *Blind Painting* and *Small Horses & Intimate Beasts. Poetry Can R* Spring 1987; Vol 8 No 2–3: p59.

[Untitled]; review of *Trace. Poetry Can R* Fall 1987; Vol 9 No 1: p33.

Work works well; review of *Shop Talk. Waves* Winter 1987; Vol 15 No 3: p81–84.

Valgardson, W.D.

The man who was always running out of toilet paper; short story. photo · *Border Cross* Spring 1987; Vol 6 No 2: p43–45.

My trip to Iceland; essay. *Books in Can* Jan-Feb 1987; Vol 16 No 1: p4, 6–7.

Nordic journey; essay. *Books in Can* Nov 1987; Vol 16 No 8: p3–4.

van Herk, Aritha

Calgary: this growing graveyard; poem. illus photo · *NeWest R* Dec 1987; Vol 13 No 4: p5–11.

A Latin for thieves; short story. *Dandelion* Fall-Winter 1987; Vol 14 No 2: p103–109.

(No parrot / no crow / no parrot); essay. *Prairie Fire* Winter 1987–88; Vol 8 No 4: p12, 14–20.

The summer before Browning died; review of *The Whirlpool. Brick* Fall 1987; No 31: p15–17.

[Untitled]; review of *In the Skin of a Lion. Malahat R* Sept 1987; No 80: p134–137.

Van Luven, Lynne

[The Rich Man]; theatre review. *NeWest R* Nov 1987; Vol 13 No 3: p18.

[Untitled]; review of *New Works I. Can Theatre R* Winter 1987; No 53: p81–82.

Van Oosten, Ursula C.

Friend or foe; poem. *Can Auth & Book* Summer 1987; Vol 62 No 4: p23.

van Rjndt, Philippe

During or after, war is still hell; review of *The League of Night and Fog. TS* July 11, 1987: pM4.

Would-be world-class thrillers need plots to be complete; reviews of *Equinox* and *Fire Eyes*. photo · *Quill & Quire* April 1987; Vol 53 No 4: p28.

Van Steen, Marcus

A sense of loss; short story. photo · *TS* Aug 2, 1987: pD5.

Van Vliet, Kim

The family business; reviews of *What Feathers Are For* and *Squid Inc 86. Waves* Spring 1987; Vol 15 No 4: p88–91.

Van Wart, Alice

[Untitled]; reviews of *Vigil* and *The Whirlpool. Can Forum* Aug-Sept 1987; Vol 67 No 771: p46–48.

Van Wynsberghe, Scott

Novel needs a miracle; review of *Children of the Shroud. WFP* Oct 10, 1987: p30.

Winners have wounds, too; review of *Unknown Soldier. WFP* Oct 31, 1987: p52.

Vanasse, André

André Belleau, professeur et essayiste (1930–1986); obituary. photo · *Lettres québec* Winter 1986–87; No 44: p12.

Vander Meulen, Jim

It is not easy to have a picnic in the summer fallow; poem. *NeWest R* Sept 1987; Vol 13 No 1: p15.

[Untitled]; poem. *Grain* Fall 1987; Vol 15 No 3: p30.

Vanderhoof, Ann

Big names and lesser lights make festival shine; article. photo · *Quill & Quire* Jan 1987; Vol 53 No 1: p8–9.

PLR: writers registered and sampling under way; article. *Quill & Quire* Feb 1987; Vol 53 No 2: p14.

Vanderlip, Brian

[Untitled]; review of *A Sacrifice of Fire. Poetry Can R* Spring 1987; Vol 8 No 2–3: p43–44.

[Untitled]; reviews of poetry books. *Poetry Can R* Spring 1987; Vol 8 No 2–3: p60–61.

[Untitled]; review of *The Possibilities of Chinese Trout. Poetry Can R* Fall 1987; Vol 9 No 1: p34–35.

[Untitled]; review of *Broken Ghosts. Poetry Can R* Fall 1987; Vol 9 No 1: p38.

Vanstone, Ellen

Prize writer; article. photo · *Tor Life* March 1987; Vol 21 No 4: p10–11.

VanVeen, Debra

Love manifestation; poem. *Room of One's Own* Sept 1987; Vol 11 No 4: p71.

Perfume and horse sweat; poem. *Room of One's Own* Sept 1987; Vol 11 No 4: p72.

Vardon, John

Foreword. *New Q* Spring-Summer 1987; Vol 7 No 1–2: p149.

[Untitled]; reviews of poetry books. *Poetry Can R* Spring 1987; Vol 8 No 2–3: p53.

Vardon, John F.

[Untitled]; reviews of *The Louis Riel Organ & Piano Co.* and *The North Book. Poetry Can R* Spring 1987; Vol 8 No 2–3: p47.

Vasseur, Annie Molin

[Untitled]; poem. *Estuaire* Autumn 1987; No 46: p33–38.

Verduyn, Christl

Marian Engel's family fictions: Lunatic Villas; article. *New Q* Spring-Summer 1987; Vol 7 No 1–2: p274–283.

[Untitled]; review of *Sub / version. Amer R of Can Studies* Summer 1987; Vol 17 No 2: p259–260.

Vernon, Lorraine

2: continuing; short story. *Event* Summer 1987; Vol 16 No 2: p86–96.

Fire and ice; poem. *Queen's Q* Summer 1987; Vol 94 No 2: p355–356.

Golden age; short story. *Room of One's Own* Jan 1987; Vol 11 No 2: p89–98.

Grandchild: Theresa M.; poem. *New Q* Spring-Summer 1987; Vol 7 No 1–2: p197.

Japanese painting; prose poem. *Germination* Fall 1987; Vol 11 No 1: p44–45.

Picture frame; poem. *New Q* Spring-Summer 1987; Vol 7 No 1–2: p198.

The walking poem; prose poem. *Germination* Fall 1987; Vol 11 No 1: p42.

Whistlers; prose poem. *Germination* Fall 1987; Vol 11 No 1: p43.

Viau, Robert

L'evasion et l'education; review of *La Note de passage. Can Child Lit* 1987; No 48: p95–97.

Pierre Mathieu: le silence rompu; interview. bibliog photo · *Lettres québec* Autumn 1987; No 47: p46–48.

Une ultime vision de l'idéal; review of *L'Espagnole et la Pékinoise. Can Child Lit* 1987; No 47: p88–89.

Vice, Sue

The mystique of mezcal; article. *Can Lit* Spring 1987; No 112: p197–202.

Vigeant, Louise

(Im)pure theatre; article. photo trans · *Can Theatre R* Spring 1987; No 50: p14–19.

[Untitled]; theatre review of *Mao Tsé Toung ou soirée de musique au consulat*. photo · *Jeu* 1987; No 43: p156–159.

Vue lointaine d'un Québec pas si moderne; review of *Theatre and Politics in Modern Québec*. *Jeu* 1987; No 45: p222–223.

Viselli, Sante A.

Valeurs ludiques et valeurs fonctionelles: Le Visiteur du soir de Robert Soulières; article. *Can Child Lit* 1987; No 45: p6–13.

Visser, Carla

Historicity in historical fiction: Burning Water and The Temptations Of Big Bear; article. *Studies in Can Lit* 1987; Vol 12 No 1: p90–111.

Vogan, Rebecca

Editor's note. *Quarry* Spring 1987; Vol 36 No 2: p5–7.

Voyer, Pierre

[Untitled]; prose excerpt from *Les Enfants parfaits*. photo · *MD* Nov 21, 1987: pD1, D10.

Wachowicz, Barbara

L.M. Montgomery: at home in Poland; article. photo · *Can Child Lit* 1987; No 46: p7–35.

Wachtel, Eleanor

Different strokes; review of *The Dancing Chicken*. *Books in Can* Dec 1987; Vol 16 No 9: p19–20.

The invention of Jack Hodgins; article. photo · *Books in Can* Aug-Sept 1987; Vol 16 No 6: p6–10.

Mystery woman; biographical article. photo · *Books in Can* June-July 1987; Vol 16 No 5: p6–9.

Paulette Jiles; interview. photo · *Books in Can* Jan-Feb 1987; Vol 16 No 1: p36–38.

Waddington, Miriam

Journey to Winnipeg; poem, includes essay. *Grain* Fall 1987; Vol 15 No 3: p6–8.

Languages; poem. *Can Forum* Oct 1987; Vol 67 No 772: p21.

The last landscape; poem. *Can Forum* Oct 1987; Vol 67 No 772: p20.

Let mysteries remain; poems. *Can Forum* Oct 1987; Vol 67 No 772: p20–21.

The mermaid inn: fiction reveals many truths; essay. photo · *G&M* Nov 28, 1987: pD6.

Mysteries; poem. *Can Forum* Oct 1987; Vol 67 No 772: p20–21.

Spring night at home; poem. *Can Forum* Oct 1987; Vol 67 No 772: p21.

Wade Rose, Barbara

Lady of the house; review of *Brazilian Journal*. *Books in Can* June-July 1987; Vol 16 No 5: p29–30.

Wagner, Anton

Elsie Park Gowan: distinctively Canadian; article. abstract bibliog biog · *Theatre Hist in Can (special issue)* Spring 1987; Vol 8 No 1: p68–82.

Wagner, Vit

Africa Solo works best when related in song; theatre review. photo · *TS* Nov 13, 1987: pE26.

Artist gives surreal play haunting backdrop; column. *TS* Oct 2, 1987: pE12.

Blowing bubbles with Simone and Sartre; column. photo · *TS* Nov 6, 1987: pE4.

Curse of the shopping class; article. photo · *TS* Sept 25, 1987: pE1, E3.

Director a natural for New Canadian Kid; column. *TS* Dec 18, 1987: pD12.

Director says Lorca tragedy a timeless tale; column. photo · *TS* Oct 30, 1987: pE4.

Duo borrows big from Smothers Brothers' style; column. *TS* Nov 27, 1987: pD12.

Intensity exhausting in ugly Steel Kiss; theatre review. *TS* Oct 2, 1987: pE12.

International kids' theatre festival hopes to touch child in everyone; article. *TS* May 8, 1987: pD11.

Isaac's cast puts its 500 years to good use; column. *TS* Nov 13, 1987: pE16.

Jacob Two-Two star hits 'big time' at age 7; column. *TS* Oct 16, 1987: pD10.

Jenny without Lenny takes adoring Toronto; article about Jennifer Warnes. photo · *TS* June 15, 1987: pD1.

Lana Turner steals the show; theatre review of *The Postman Rings Once*. photo · *TS* Oct 9, 1987: pE9.

The laugh's on apartheid in one-man show; column. photo · *TS* Sept 25, 1987: pE6.

New drama paints portrait of Emily Carr; column. photo · *TS* Nov 20, 1987: pE4.

Semmelweiss role just what doctor ordered; column. photo · *TS* Dec 4, 1987: pD7.

Short plays confront man's helplessness; theatre review of *When I'm Big*. *TS* Dec 1, 1987: pH4.

Simple folk wax poetic in wordy one-act plays; theatre review of *Straight Ahead / Blind Dancers*. photo · *TS* Nov 27, 1987: pD12.

Two one-person shows long on self-indulgence; theatre review of *Hellbound Train*. *TS* Nov 11, 1987: pH5.

Warnes goes solo with Cohen songs; article about Jennifer Warnes. photo · *TS* June 12, 1987: pE13.

Wah, Fred

Mht 64; poem. *Open Letter (special issue)* Fall 1987; Vol 6 No 9: p55.

Mht 65; poem. *Open Letter (special issue)* Fall 1987; Vol 6 No 9: p56.

Mht 66; poem. *Open Letter (special issue)* Fall 1987; Vol 6 No 9: p57.

Mht 68; poem. *Open Letter (special issue)* Fall 1987; Vol 6 No 9: p58.

Music at the heart of thinking #35; poem. *Poetry Can R* Fall 1987; Vol 9 No 1: p4.

Music at the heart of thinking #38; poem. *Poetry Can R* Fall 1987; Vol 9 No 1: p4.

Music at the heart of thinking #70; poem. *Prairie Fire* Winter 1987–88; Vol 8 No 4: p43.

Music at the heart of thinking #71; poem. *Prairie Fire* Winter 1987–88; Vol 8 No 4: p43.

Music at the heart of thinking #72; poem. *Prairie Fire* Winter 1987–88; Vol 8 No 4: p44.

Music at the heart of thinking #73; poem. *Prairie Fire* Winter 1987–88; Vol 8 No 4: p44.

Music at the heart of thinking #74; poem. *Prairie Fire* Winter 1987–88; Vol 8 No 4: p45.

Music at the heart of thinking no. 19; poem. *Cross Can Writ Q* 1987; Vol 9 No 3–4: p11.

Music at the heart of thinking; prose poem. *Brick* Winter 1987; No 29: p48–49.

Oranges and onions; reviews of *White of the Lesser Angels* and *The Abbotsford Guide to India*. *Books in Can* March 1987; Vol 16 No 2: p32, 34.

Wakulich, Bob

[Untitled]; review of *The Unsettling of the West*. *CH* May 31, 1987: pF5.

Walker, Morley

At least it's easy to read; review of *Caprice*. *WFP* May 16, 1987: p70.

Festival eyes Brandon move; article. photo · *WFP* April 23, 1987: p43.

Male director adds richness to short-story filming, author says; article. photo · *WFP* March 19, 1987: p42.

Pioneer lady on stage; article. photo · *WFP* April 30, 1987: p26.

Playwright's opening night began with car that bombed; article. photo · *WFP* March 29, 1987: p14.

South African stories convey clear moral vision; review of *Bloodsong*. *WFP* Sept 26, 1987: p64.

Tale of growing up is a true standout; review of *The Woman Upstairs*. *WFP* July 11, 1987: p57.

Totally impenetrable prose; review of *Private and Fictional Words*. *WFP* Oct 17, 1987: p61.

Tough, taut short stories; review of *Night Driving*. *WFP* May 2, 1987: p84.

Winner is a real stinker; review of *Hardwired Angel*. *WFP* Sept 5, 1987: p58.

Wallace, Bob

Competition; editorial. *Can Theatre R* Summer 1987; No 51: p3.

Wallace, Bronwen

Gifts; poem. *Event* March 1987; Vol 16 No 1: p25–27.

Houses; poem. *Quarry* Winter 1987; Vol 36 No 1: p40–41.

Idyll; poem. *Malahat R* June 1987; No 79: p31–34.

Koko; poem. *Malahat R* June 1987; No 79: p28–30.

Lifelines; poem. *Malahat R* June 1987; No 79: p39–42.

Neighbours; poem. *Quarry* Winter 1987; Vol 36 No 1: p8–11.

Ordinary morning; poem. *Malahat R* June 1987; No 79: p35–38.

Seeing is believing; poem. *Quarry* Winter 1987; Vol 36 No 1: p73–76.

Stunts; poem. *Event* March 1987; Vol 16 No 1: p28–29.

[Untitled]; review of *Second Nature*. *Poetry Can R* Spring 1987; Vol 8 No 2–3: p37–38.

Wallace, Jo-Ann

The language of fantasy; reviews of *The Emperor's Panda* and *Amanda Greenleaf Visits a Distant Star*. *Can Child Lit* 1987; No 47: p73–74.

Waller-Vintar, Jacquelyn

April 11, 1963; short story. photo · *TS* July 19, 1987: pD5.

Walsh, Ann L.

Still waters; poem. *Quarry* Fall 1987; Vol 36 No 4: p65–68.

Walters, Shanda

That first doubt; poem. *NeWest R* Sept 1987; Vol 13 No 1: p8.

Walton, Mike

Crang: super-mouth sleuth; review of *Crang Plays the Ace*. *TS* April 12, 1987: pA21.

'Female ferrets and crime-busting babes'; reviews of paperback books. *TS* Feb 8, 1987: pG9.

It's fiction, but it's unmistakably 'King'; review of *King Leary*. photo · *TS* Oct 18, 1987: pC8.

A solid first effort from a Toronto cop; review of *The Glorious East Wind*. photo · *TS* Dec 26, 1987: pK7.

Ward, Sheila

Canadian-set mysteries; reviews of children's novels by Eric Wilson. *Can Child Lit* 1987; No 48: p91–93.

Wardle, Vivienne

Ella Cinderella; short story. photo · *TS* July 25, 1987: pM11.

Ware, Beverley

Play about equality of the sexes impressing Metro area children; article. *TS (Neighbors)* Aug 18, 1987: p20.

Play discourages children from sexual stereotyping; article. photo · *TS (Neighbors)* Aug 11, 1987: p6.

Ware, Martin

Newfoundland and Labrador: TickleAce poised; regional column. *Poetry Can R* Summer 1987; Vol 8 No 4: p12.

Warland, Betsy

[Untitled]; poetry excerpt from *Serpent (W)rite*. *Cross Can Writ Q* 1987; Vol 9 No 3–4: p5.

Warnick, Paul

Contest winner makes waves with short story called Goldfish; article. *TS* Aug 2, 1987: pA2.

Judges getting to work on short story contest; article. *TS* March 8, 1987: pA2.

Warren, Dianne

The winter road; short story. *Grain* Summer 1987; Vol 15 No 2: p26–34.

Warren, Ina

Genies: daring to be different; article. photo · *MG* March 17, 1987: pC10.

Warren, Louise

Comme deux femmes peintres; poem sequence. illus · *La Nouvelle barre du jour* 1987; No 199: p9–70.

Warrior, Emma Lee

Compatriots; short story. *Can Fic Mag (special issue)* 1987; No 60: p129–137.

Warsh, Sylvia Maultash

Lost in Banff, Alberta; poem. *Waves* Winter 1987; Vol 15 No 3: p60.

Victorian sensibility; poem. *Can Forum* Nov 1987; Vol 67 No 773: p39.

Wasserman, Jerry

Büchner in Canada: Woyzeck and the development of English-Canadian theatre; article. abstract photo · *Theatre Hist in Can* Fall 1987; Vol 8 No 2: p181–192.

Drama; survey review article. *U of Toronto Q* Fall 1987; Vol 57 No 1: p62–74.

Waters, Paul

Hong Kong is a jungle in Toronto cop's thriller; review of *The Glorious East Wind. MG* Oct 31, 1987: pJ14.

Killer stalks wet streets of Vancouver; review of *The Goldfish Bowl. MG* Dec 24, 1987: pL9.

Watling, Doug

[Untitled]; reviews of *Psalms from the Suburbs* and *Sympathetic Magic. Poetry Can R* Spring 1987; Vol 8 No 2–3: p51.

Watson, Dana

[Untitled]; review of *Mrs. Dunphy's Dog. CH* Dec 6, 1987: pD9.

Watson, Diane

New images for old favourites; review of *The Cremation of Sam McGee. Can Child Lit* 1987; No 48: p87–90.

Watson, Kathy

Helped on way; letter to the editor. photo · *WFP* Nov 29, 1987: p6.

Watt, Frank W.

Humane vision; review of *Another Country. Can Lit* Winter 1987; No 115: p202–203.

Watts, Charles

The Hungarian's place; review of *10 Poems. Brick* Winter 1987; No 29: p55–60.

Poem: May rain; poem. *Writing* Jan 1987; No 17: p18–21.

Wayman, Tom

It's not you, it's your machine; poem. *New Q* Fall 1987; Vol 7 No 3: p87–89.

Kootenay green (12% alcohol by volume); poem. *Fiddlehead* Autumn 1987; No 153: p16.

The poet Milton Acorn crosses into the republic of Heaven; poem. *Malahat R* Sept 1987; No 80: p125–129.

There is a love with a wound; poem. *Fiddlehead* Autumn 1987; No 153: p17.

The tunnel; poem. *Fiddlehead* Autumn 1987; No 153: p19.

Unemployed; poem. *Event* Summer 1987; Vol 16 No 2: p107–109.

Vancouver winter; poem. *New Q* Fall 1987; Vol 7 No 3: p86.

What the cat sees; poem. *Fiddlehead* Autumn 1987; No 153: p18.

Why part-time staff do not receive prorated benefits; poem. *Poetry Can R* Spring 1987; Vol 8 No 2–3: p20.

Weatherbie, Leo

The real world; poem. *Alpha* Winter 1987; Vol 11: p8.

Weaver, Robert

[Untitled]; biographical articles. *Brick (special issue)* Summer 1987; No 30: ppassim.

Webb, Jane

CanLit in the kitchen and food to keep you fit; review of *The CanLit Foodbook. Quill & Quire* Nov 1987; Vol 53 No 11: p24.

Webb, Phyllis

"Attend"; poem. *Grain* Winter 1987; Vol 15 No 4: p12–13.

Ghazal-maker; review of *Sea Run. Can Lit* Spring 1987; No 112: p156–157.

Gwendolyn MacEwen 1941–1987; poem. *Malahat R* Dec 1987; No 81: p[n.p.].

Unearned numinosity; essay. *Grain* Winter 1987; Vol 15 No 4: p9–11.

[Untitled]; biographical articles. *Brick (special issue)* Summer 1987; No 30: ppassim.

Weekes, Florence M.

Bookmark; poem. *Can Auth & Book* Summer 1987; Vol 62 No 4: p22.

Weeks, Ramona

Friend's diary; poem. *Queen's Q* Spring 1987; Vol 94 No 1: p33.

Wegner, Diana

Poetry and solidarity – uneasy bedfellows?; review of *The Face of Jack Munro*. *Event* Summer 1987; Vol 16 No 2: p110–115.

Weiner, Chris

Angry librarians set to bolt doors over anti-porn bill; article. photo · *TS* Dec 8, 1987: pA6.

Weinmayr, Gen

[Untitled]; review of *The Wheels on the Bus*. *CH* Dec 6, 1987: pD9.

Weintraub, William

Brazil dreaming; review of *Brazilian Journal*. illus · *MG* July 25, 1987: pJ7.

Weinzweig, Helen

Desire; excerpt from a novel in progress. illus · *Books in Can* Jan-Feb 1987; Vol 16 No 1: p12–13.

Weis, Lyle

Bipolar paths of desire: D.C. Scott's poetic and narrative structures; article. *Studies in Can Lit* 1987; Vol 12 No 1: p35–53.

A touching, but unsentimental story; review of *Plan B Is Total Panic*. *Can Child Lit* 1987; No 45: p72–73.

Weiss, Allan

In the mode; reviews of short story collections. *Books in Can* April 1987; Vol 16 No 3: p30–31.

Sins of omission; review of *The Oxford Book of Canadian Short Stories in English*. *Books in Can* Jan-Feb 1987; Vol 16 No 1: p21–22.

Travelling light; review of *Night Driving*. *Books in Can* April 1987; Vol 16 No 3: p36–37.

[Untitled]; review of *Unknown Soldier*. *Books in Can* Aug-Sept 1987; Vol 16 No 6: p26.

Weiss, Jonathan M.

[Untitled]; review of *Theatre and Politics in Modern Quebec*. *Amer R of Can Studies* Autumn 1987; Vol 17 No 3: p358–359.

Weiss, Peter Eliot

Give my regards to Hell's Kitchen; essay. photo · *Can Theatre R* Fall 1987; No 52: p89–91.

Welch, Liliane

Anaesthetist: drifting in Elysium; poem. *Poetry Can R* Spring 1987; Vol 8 No 1–2: p9.

Anaesthetist: fording the dark; poem. *Poetry Can R* Spring 1987; Vol 8 No 1–2: p9.

Forging; poem. *Poetry Can R* Spring 1987; Vol 8 No 1–2: p9.

Hands; poem. *Poetry Can R* Spring 1987; Vol 8 No 1–2: p8.

My grandfather: he raged through Venice; poem. *New Q* Winter 1987; Vol 6 No 4: p99–100.

My grandfather: the walls of Troy; poem. *New Q* Winter 1987; Vol 6 No 4: p101.

My grandfather: to Carthage he came in love with loving; poem. *New Q* Winter 1987; Vol 6 No 4: p102–103.

Novels / poems; poem. *Queen's Q* Autumn 1987; Vol 94 No 3: p590.

Poetry as cheirography; essay. illus · *Poetry Can R* Spring 1987; Vol 8 No 1–2: p8–9.

Wellwood, Vida

Fred & Freda have an energy crisis; short story. photo · *TS* July 23, 1987: pB28.

Welsh-Vickar, Gillian

Prairie Pens – bright talent in small places; article. photo · *Can Auth & Book* Winter 1987; Vol 62 No 2: p7.

Susan Bowden: history is people; article. photo · *Can Auth & Book* Summer 1987; Vol 62 No 4: p9.

Wesley, Valerie Wilson

[Untitled]; review of *Nine Men Who Laughed*. *NYT Book R* Aug 23, 1987: p16–17.

Wesseler, Marlis

The wall; short story. *Grain* Summer 1987; Vol 15 No 2: p62–66.

West, David A.

[Untitled]; letter to the editor. *G&M* Nov 21, 1987: pD7.

West, Paul

Steeped in lechery; review of *Deaf to the City*. illus · *NYT Book R* Sept 20, 1987: p12–13.

Wevill, David

Figure of eight; poem. *Exile* 1987; Vol 12 No 1: p63–76.

Inhabitant; poem. *Exile* 1987; Vol 12 No 1: p59.

Making plans; poem. *Exile* 1987; Vol 12 No 1: p57.

Patterns leaves make; poem. *Exile* 1987; Vol 12 No 1: p58.

Premonition; poem. *Exile* 1987; Vol 12 No 1: p62.

Soleá; poem. *Exile* 1987; Vol 12 No 1: p60–61.

Whalen, Terry

Lorne Pierce's 1927 interview with Charles G.D. Roberts (as reported by Margaret Lawrence); introduction. *Can Poet* Fall-Winter 1987; No 21: p59–62.

Wharton, Calvin

Bend; poem. *Matrix* Fall 1987; No 25: p28.

Inside the Kootenay School of Writing; article. photo · *Cross Can Writ Q* 1987; Vol 9 No 1: p8–9, 29.

The KSW student view; article. *Cross Can Writ Q* 1987; Vol 9 No 1: p9.

Wheatley, Patience

The conquest of Mexico – Montreal 1980; poem. *Quarry* Winter 1987; Vol 36 No 1: p91–92.

June 1943: recruit; poem. *Poetry Can R* Fall 1987; Vol 9 No 1: p5.

Mica mine; poem. *Germination* Fall 1987; Vol 11 No 1: p52.

Purpose; poem. *Poetry Can R* Fall 1987; Vol 9 No 1: p5.

Summer 1944: butchers; poem. *Poetry Can R* Fall 1987; Vol 9 No 1: p5.

[Untitled]; poetry excerpt from Snaps of the Trip. *Quarry* Winter 1987; Vol 36 No 1: p92–93.

Whipple, George

[Untitled]; reviews of poetry books. *Poetry Can R* Spring 1987; Vol 8 No 2–3: p53.

White, Carol

Saving the pieces; short story. photo · *TS* Aug 16, 1987: pD5.

White, Gail

What the children still believe; poem. *Room of One's Own* April 1987; Vol 11 No 3: p50–51.

White, Roger

Author! Author!; poem. *Can Auth & Book* Spring 1987; Vol 62 No 3: p23.

White, Stephen

Poets' club offers sympathetic ears; article. *TS (Neighbours)* March 24, 1987: p25.

Whitehead, Gary

I can fix anything; short story. *Prism* Summer 1987; Vol 25 No 4: p77–87.

Whitelaw, Marjory

Early Canadian publishing; review of *The Beginnings of the Book Trade in Canada*. *Atlan Prov Book R* Feb-March 1987; Vol 14 No 1: p16.

Whiteman, Bruce

But where is the poetry?; reviews of *Road Dances* and *Counterpane*. *Essays on Can Writ* Spring 1987; No 34: p48–49.

Camargue journal; essay. illus photo · *Brick* Fall 1987; No 31: p43–46.

En avoir fini avec le corps seul; prose poem. illus · *Brick* Fall 1987; No 31: p47.

Seeker & finder; reviews of *Canada Gees Mate for Life* and *Rootless Tree*. *Can Lit* Winter 1987; No 115: p148–150.

The tradition: "Her long duty cut short": on Anne Wilkinson; column. *Poetry Can R* Fall 1987; Vol 9 No 1: p10.

The tradition: John Sutherland, 1919–1956; column. *Poetry Can R* Summer 1987; Vol 8 No 4: p10.

The tradition: Patrick Anderson; column. *Poetry Can R* Spring 1987; Vol 8 No 1–2: p10.

[Untitled]; reviews of poetry books. *Cross Can Writ Q* 1987; Vol 9 No 2: p21–22, 26.

[Untitled]; review of *Seed Catalogue*. *Poetry Can R* Summer 1987; Vol 8 No 4: p34–35.

[Untitled]; review of *North of Intention*. *Books in Can* Oct 1987; Vol 16 No 7: p21.

[Untitled]; review of *The Northern Red Oak*. *Books in Can* Oct 1987; Vol 16 No 7: p26.

Victims of a bleak universe; reviews of poetry books. *Books in Can* Jan-Feb 1987; Vol 16 No 1: p22–23.

A view from outside; review of *Gaining Ground*. *Prairie Fire* Winter 1987–88; Vol 8 No 4: p99–100.

Whitfield, Agnès

La fiction de nos devanciers; reviews of *Le Roman québécois de 1944 à 1965* and *Un Roman du regard*. photo · *Lettres québec* Winter 1986–87; No 44: p56–58.

Le jeu du manifeste littéraire; review of *L'Enjeu du manifeste / Le manifeste en jeu*. *Lettres québec* Autumn 1987; No 47: p51–52.

La modernité: des formes qui (s')inquiètent; reviews of critical works. photo · *Lettres québec* Summer 1987; No 46: p56–58.

Nouvelles frontières thériques; review of *Pragmatique de la poésie québécoise*. *Lettres québec* Spring 1987; No 45: p53–54.

[Untitled]; review of *Hertel, l'homme et l'oeuvre*. *Queen's Q* Autumn 1987; Vol 94 No 3: p687–688.

Whitney, Paulette Faith

The bills you sent; poem. *Room of One's Own* Jan 1987; Vol 11 No 2: p68–69.

Whittall, James

The decorative vase (three perspectives); poem. *Can Forum* Jan 1987; Vol 66 No 765: p8.

Wickers, Brian

Mote; poem. *Prism* Spring 1987; Vol 25 No 3: p36.

Wiebe, Armin

A great book; review of *Flicker and Hawk*. *Prairie Fire* Autumn 1987; Vol 8 No 3: p102–107.

Wien, Carol Anne

A stocking stuffer anthology; review of *Seaweed in Your Stocking*. *Can Child Lit* 1987; No 47: p92–93.

Wigston, Nancy

An acute eye trained on a nasty subject; review of *My Father's House*. photo · *G&M* Sept 12, 1987: pC17.

Edward Phillips; interview. photo · *Books in Can* April 1987; Vol 16 No 3: p39–40.

Lois Braun; interview. photo · *Books in Can* Aug-Sept 1987; Vol 16 No 6: p36–38.

Rohinton Mistry; interview. photo · *Books in Can* June-July 1987; Vol 16 No 5: p38–39.

The vision of the self-exiled; review of *Tales from Firozsha Baag.* photo · *G&M* May 2, 1987: pC17.

Wilkins, Charles

Bernice Thurman Hunter: a world of wonder from her own past; article. photo · *Quill & Quire (Books for Young People)* Oct 1987; Vol 53 No 10: p12.

Williams, Alan

Excerpts from The King Of America. *Prairie Fire* Spring 1987; Vol 8 No 1: p57–59.

Williams, Barbara

Australia: of festivals and fringes; column. *Poetry Can R* Summer 1987; Vol 8 No 4: p28.

Williams, Deloris

Forcément de l'amour; reviews of *Forcément dans la tête* and *De ce nom de l'amour. Can Lit* Summer-Fall 1987; No 113–114: p233–235.

Williams, Penny

Universe probed from the shore; review of *Dancing on the Shore. CH* Oct 18, 1987: pC7.

Williamson, David

Crime novels provide a study in contrasts; reviews of *Doubtful Motives* and *A Body Surrounded by Water.* photo · *WFP* Aug 1, 1987: p50.

Delving into artistic mystery; review of *Five New Facts About Giorgione.* photo · *WFP* Dec 19, 1987: p50.

Fiction debut is impressive; review of *A Stone Watermelon.* photo · *WFP* Feb 7, 1987: p59.

Fine books for in-betweens; reviews of young adult books. *WFP* Dec 5, 1987: p57.

Fine writing saves novel; review of *Tranter's Tree. WFP* July 11, 1987: p57.

Hodgins loses sense of humor; review of *The Honorary Patron.* photo · *WFP* Oct 24, 1987: p54.

Michael Ondaatje turns in a memorable performance; review of *In the Skin of a Lion.* photo · *WFP* Aug 29, 1987: p52.

Novel doesn't make it; review of *Remembering Summer. WFP* July 25, 1987: p33.

Novel's reach exceeds its grasp; review of *Between Men.* photo · *WFP* Sept 26, 1987: p64.

One-word titles hot among book choices; reviews. *WFP* Dec 10, 1987: p11A.

Overpowering ambiguity; review of *After the Fact. WFP* April 11, 1987: p60.

Overworked motif is just new kind of exploitation; review of *Contact Prints. WFP* June 27, 1987: p58.

Ray Smith's stories are prodding and perplexing; review of *Century. WFP* March 21, 1987: p58.

A search for the perfect pairing; review of *Adele at the End of the Day.* photo · *WFP* April 25, 1987: p54.

Shadow of violence seems out of place in deft, lightly comic novel; review of *Getting Married in Buffalo Jump. WFP* Sept 5, 1987: p58.

Tributes to two writers; review of *The Alligator Report. WFP* March 7, 1987: p70.

Under a prairie muse: ten years of Manitoba fiction; survey article. *Prairie Fire* Autumn 1987; Vol 8 No 3: p79–85.

Who is muddled?; letter to the editor. *WFP* Sept 29, 1987: p6.

Writer-in-residence is worthwhile project; letter to the editor. *WFP* Sept 19, 1987: p7.

Writing for fun and profit; review of *Red Wolf, Red Wolf.* photo · *WFP* Sept 19, 1987: p64.

Williamson, Janice

Of women and fish; poem. *CV 2* Spring 1987; Vol 10 No 3: p18–19.

Sounding the difference: an interview with Smaro Kamboureli and Lola Tostevin. illus · *Can Forum* Jan 1987; Vol 66 No 765: p33–38.

Willis, David

[Untitled]; review of *The Lucky Ones. Queen's Q* Summer 1987; Vol 94 No 2: p482–483.

Willis, Gary

Speaking the silence: Joy Kogawa's Obasan; article. *Studies in Can Lit* 1987; Vol 12 No 2: p239–250.

Willmot, Rod

Five haiku; poem sequence. *Can Lit* Summer-Fall 1987; No 113–114: p127.

Willmott, Brooke

[Untitled]; review of *The Incredible Journey. TS* March 15, 1987: pH6.

Wilson, Alan R.

From counting to 100; poem. *Can Lit* Winter 1987; No 115: p78–80.

[Untitled]; poetry excerpt from *Counting to 100. Antigonish R* 1987; No 69–70: p190–193.

Wilson, Ann

A jury of her peers; article about the Canada Council. photo · *Can Theatre R* Summer 1987; No 51: p4–8.

Wilson, Deborah

Death in High Park inspiration for play; article. photo · *G&M* Oct 17, 1987: pA13.

Wilson, Jack Lowther

Abstract; poem. *Queen's Q* Spring 1987; Vol 94 No 1: p80.

Wilson, Keith

Peacetime; reviews of *Spectral Evidence* and *Fish-Hooks. Can Lit* Spring 1987; No 112: p154–156.

Wilson, Valerie J.

Poet laureates, yes perversion poetry, no; letter to the editor. *TS* July 31, 1987: pA20.

Wimhurst, David

CIA gambits aren't what they used to be; review of *Equinox*. *MG* May 16, 1987: pJ8.

Wind, Chris

Chryseis and Briseis; poem. *Antigonish R* 1987; No 69–70: p38.

Encounter; short story. *Alpha* Winter 1987; Vol 11: p36–38.

Persephone; poem. *Atlantis* Fall 1987; Vol 13 No 1: p12.

Rondo; poem. *Ariel* April 1987; Vol 18 No 2: p79.

Windeler, Janet

[Untitled]; reviews. *Cross Can Writ Q* 1987; Vol 9 No 2: p25–26.

[Untitled]; reviews of *Heading Out* and *Relations: Family Portraits*. *Cross Can Writ Q* 1987; Vol 9 No 3–4: p42–43.

Windley, Carol

Los Alamos: summer, 1945; poem. *Prism* Summer 1987; Vol 25 No 4: p126–127.

Winks, Robin W.

"Whodunit?" Canadian society as reflected in its detective fiction; article. bibliog · *Amer R of Can Studies* Winter 1987–88; Vol 17 No 4: p373–381.

Winslow, Carie

Yearnings; poem. *Atlantis* Spring 1987; Vol 12 No 2: p81.

Winston, Iris

[Untitled]; review of *Necessary Secrets*. *CH* May 31, 1987: pF5.

Winter, K.A.

The jolly trolley; short story. *Fiddlehead* Autumn 1987; No 153: p53–56.

Winter, Michael

I, foreign I; prose poem. *Capilano R* 1987; No 44: p75–76.

Wintrob, Suzanne

Poets, 66–88, publish their own book; article. *TS (Neighbours)* March 10, 1987: p18.

Wirsig, Kirk

An apology to pigs and fishes; poem. *Fiddlehead* Summer 1987; No 152: p45.

Carol is the body bow; poem. *Fiddlehead* Summer 1987; No 152: p43.

I remember; poem. *Antigonish R* 1987; No 69–70: p54.

Lilly teases licitly; poem. *Fiddlehead* Summer 1987; No 152: p43.

Naomi, could you be the milk maid come?; poem. *Fiddlehead* Summer 1987; No 152: p42.

When the dogs come home; poem. *Fiddlehead* Summer 1987; No 152: p44.

Wiseman, Christopher

Beneath the visiting moon; prose poem. *Prairie Fire* Summer 1987; Vol 8 No 2: p12.

Confident voices heard through poetry collections; reviews of poetry books. *CH* Feb 8, 1987: pE5.

School photograph; poem. *Wascana R* Spring 1987; Vol 22 No 1: p18–19.

State of the art; poem. *Wascana R* Spring 1987; Vol 22 No 1: p20–21.

Still fighting, almost down; poem. *Prairie Fire* Summer 1987; Vol 8 No 2: p11–12.

Thistledown presents prairie poets in full bloom; reviews of poetry books. *CH* May 24, 1987: pE6.

Wishinsky, Frieda

A fun bunch of books to read and look at; reviews of *Big Sarah's Little Boots* and *Ringtail*. *Quill & Quire (Books for Young People)* Aug 1987; Vol 53 No 8: p3.

Taking the Degrassi kids from screen to page; reviews of *Casey Draws the Line* and *Griff Gets a Hand*. photo · *Quill & Quire (Books for Young People)* June 1987; Vol 53 No 6: p3.

[Untitled]; review of *Moira's Birthday*. *Quill & Quire (Books for Young People)* Dec 1987; Vol 53 No 12: p6, 8.

Wittmann, Horst

Kanada made me; article. *Books in Can* Oct 1987; Vol 16 No 7: p3–4.

Wong, Jan

A yen for Anne: Japanese fans of Green Gables heroine give PEI economy a lift; article. photo · *G&M* Aug 15, 1987: pD2.

Wood, Chris

The agitprop players; article. photo · *Maclean's* June 8, 1987; Vol 100 No 23: p55.

Wood, Tom

Playwright recalls double-bill dementia; essay. photo · *TS* Jan 23, 1987: pD3.

Woodbury, Mary

A poet is not born in the maternity wing; short story. *New Q* Spring-Summer 1987; Vol 7 No 1–2: p113–125.

Woodcock, George

The leopard's spots; article. *Tor South Asian R* Spring 1987; Vol 5 No 3: p41–51.

Patronage Canadian style; essay. photo · *Cross Can Writ Q* 1987; Vol 9 No 3–4: p32–33, 57–58.

Relations & families; review of *Time of Their Lives*. *Can Lit* Summer-Fall 1987; No 113–114: p235–239.

The sweet taste of digression; review of *Nadine*. *Event* March 1987; Vol 16 No 1: p95–97.

The triumphant exile; review of *Another Country. Essays on Can Writ* Winter 1987; No 35: p82–87.

[Untitled]; review of *Autobiography of Oliver Goldsmith. Can Lit* Spring 1987; No 112: p224–225.

[Untitled]; review of *Virgin Science. Poetry Can R* Spring 1987; Vol 8 No 2–3: p38.

[Untitled]; review of *Poems. Poetry Can R* Spring 1987; Vol 8 No 2–3: p56–57.

[Untitled]; review of *Dogstones. Poetry Can R* Summer 1987; Vol 8 No 4: p37–38.

[Untitled]; review of *The Iron Wedge. Can Lit* Winter 1987; No 115: p290.

Woodgold, Rolf

Atwood's questions; letter to the editor. *G&M* Nov 17, 1987: pA6.

Woods, Elizabeth

The offering; poem. *Fiddlehead* Winter 1987; No 154: p48.

[Untitled]; review of *Vancouver Poetry. Malahat R (special issue)* March 1987; No 78: p158–159.

[Untitled]; reviews of poetry books. *Poetry Can R* Spring 1987; Vol 8 No 2–3: p49.

[Untitled]; review of *Changes of State. Malahat R* June 1987; No 79: p166–168.

[Untitled]; essay. *Cross Can Writ Q* 1987; Vol 9 No 3–4: p23.

[Untitled]; review of *How to Read Faces. Poetry Can R* Fall 1987; Vol 9 No 1: p37.

Woods, Thomas S.

Fine writing about a tale worth telling; review of *Tuppence Ha'penny Is a Nickel. G&M* Sept 12, 1987: pC19.

A novel a poet can write; review of *Adele at the End of the Day. G&M* May 30, 1987: pC19.

Sharing touching reveries; review of *Visitations. G&M* July 11, 1987: pC14.

Squandered craft; review of *Steven le Herault. G&M* Sept 19, 1987: pC17.

Woodward, Calvin

Robertson Davies honored by U.S. arts club; article. photo · *G&M* Feb 26, 1987: pC5.

Wreggitt, Andrew

The lawn bowlers; poem. *Waves* Spring 1987; Vol 15 No 4: p45–46.

Twelve of my own; poem. *Waves* Spring 1987; Vol 15 No 4: p44–45.

[Untitled]; review of *The Night the Dog Smiled. Event* March 1987; Vol 16 No 1: p107–108.

Wit and humor mark poetry; reviews of *Second Nature* and *Private Properties. CH* Jan 11, 1987: pF4.

Wright, Eric

Crime in the Crimea. . . .where glasnost and mystery meet; essay. photo · *Quill & Quire* Sept 1987; Vol 53 No 9: p75.

A deeper sense of outrage, an afternoon with Mordecai Richler; interview. *Descant (special issue)* Spring-Summer 1987; Vol 18 No 1–2: p168–173.

Wright, Jane Barker

Watercolour workshop; short story. *Grain* Fall 1987; Vol 15 No 3: p48–51.

Wynand, Derk

Animal kingdom; poem. *Malahat R* June 1987; No 79: p12.

A deal we could live with; poem. *Malahat R* Dec 1987; No 81: p56–57.

Earthquake; poem. *Malahat R* June 1987; No 79: p5–6.

Engagement; poem. *Dandelion* Spring-Summer 1987; Vol 14 No 1: p20.

Failing words; poem. *Malahat R* June 1987; No 79: p8.

Imprecise moment; poem. *Dandelion* Spring-Summer 1987; Vol 14 No 1: p21.

In December; poem. *Can Lit* Winter 1987; No 115: p126.

In Estoril, and not only there; poem. *Dandelion* Spring-Summer 1987; Vol 14 No 1: p19.

In the gardens at Queluz; poem. *Malahat R* June 1987; No 79: p7.

Old town; poem. *Malahat R* June 1987; No 79: p9–10.

One arsonist, two firemen; poem. *Malahat R* June 1987; No 79: p14–15.

One version of love; poem. *Malahat R* Dec 1987; No 81: p60–61.

Railing through Europe; poem. *Fiddlehead* Winter 1987; No 154: p62–63.

Safe in a country not at war; poem. *New Q* Fall 1987; Vol 7 No 3: p74–75.

Seascape with donkey; poem. *Malahat R* Dec 1987; No 81: p62–63.

Some lines in the morning; poem. *Malahat R* June 1987; No 79: p13.

Stormy night; poem. *Malahat R* Dec 1987; No 81: p58–59.

Vital distractions; poem. *Can Lit* Winter 1987; No 115: p47.

When I grew up; poem. *Malahat R* June 1987; No 79: p16.

Widow; poem. *Malahat R* June 1987; No 79: p11.

Wynne-Jones, Tim

Calls to the wild; reviews of young adult novels. *G&M* May 2, 1987: pC19.

A cat's brilliant new escapade; review of *Can You Catch Josephine?. G&M* Sept 19, 1987: pC19.

A checked list of the very best; reviews of children's books. *G&M* Dec 12, 1987: pE1,E4.

Dreams of magical change; review of *Morgan the Magnificent. G&M* Dec 19, 1987: pC26.

Escape from reality; review of *There's a Dragon in My Closet. G&M* April 18, 1987: pC18.

An eye for Thresholds; essay. photo · *Can Child Lit* 1987; No 48: p42–54.

Familiarity and TV's stranglehold on life; reviews of children's books. *G&M* Nov 14, 1987: pE4.

Fiction just loaded with personality; reviews of children's novels. photo · *G&M* Nov 28, 1987: pC22.

Hard perspectives on traumatic family break-ups; review of *The Doll*. *G&M* Oct 3, 1987: pC22.

How suspense dies when it is misused; reviews of young adult novels. *G&M* Aug 8, 1987: pC19.

Light words and humor about unions; reviews. *G&M* Oct 17, 1987: pE11.

Lite-lit for children has arrived; reviews of children's books. *G&M* March 7, 1987: pE19.

London writer awarded children's book prize; article. photo · *G&M* March 20, 1987: pD5.

The magic of myth and love of legend; reviews of children's books. *G&M* July 25, 1987: pC17.

Much more than a love story; reviews of *Salmonberry Wine* and *A Handful of Time*. *G&M* June 27, 1987: pE20.

Rare joy and simple truth; reviews of *Tales of a Gambling Grandma* and *Love You Forever*. *G&M* Jan 24, 1987: pE19.

Satisfying prizes; column. *G&M* May 16, 1987: pC19.

Three noble stories; review of *Rainy Day Magic*. *G&M* May 30, 1987: pC21.

Triumphant return; reviews of *Jacob Two-Two and the Dinosaur* and *Pop Bottles*. *G&M* June 13, 1987: pC19.

Western publisher produces winners only; reviews of *Last Chance Summer* and *The Empty Chair*. *G&M* Feb 21, 1987: pE19.

Wit, enjoyment and urgency; reviews of children's poetry books. *G&M* Feb 7, 1987: pE19.

Yacowar, Maurice

In character; review of *The Blue Notebook*. *Can Lit* Spring 1987; No 112: p148–149.

Yanacopoulo, Andrée

Suzanne Lamy. D'un texte l'autre; introduction. *Voix et images* Autumn 1987; Vol 13 No 1: p8.

Yanofsky, Joel

Confusion as high art; review of *Italia Perversa*. photo · *MG* Aug 8, 1987: pJ2.

F.R. Scott: his life was his finest hour; review of *The Politics of the Imagination*. photo · *MG* Nov 14, 1987: pJ9.

Kafka, Addams family creep into these tales of the macabre; review of *Inspecting the Vaults*. photo · *MG* Feb 7, 1987: pB7.

King Leary: his ego is as big as a rink, and his heart hard as a puck; review. *MG* Oct 24, 1987: pJ13.

Poetic successes; reviews of *The Difficulty of Living on Other Planets* and *Fortunate Exile*. illus · *MG* Dec 19, 1987: pJ11.

The price of progress; review of *The Woman Who Is the Midnight Wind*. *Books in Can* June-July 1987; Vol 16 No 5: p18–19.

Three-day wonder; essay. *Books in Can* Nov 1987; Vol 16 No 8: p5–6.

[Untitled]; review of *Big Plans*. *Books in Can* Aug-Sept 1987; Vol 16 No 6: p25.

'You can't have too much romance'; essay. illus · *MG* May 2, 1987: pH11.

Yardley, M. Jeanne

The maple leaf as maple leaf: facing the failure of the search for emblems in Canadian literature; article. *Studies in Can Lit* 1987; Vol 12 No 2: p251–263.

Yergeau, Robert

Brault ou la mémoire du poème; review of *Poèmes 1*. photo · *Lettres québec* Spring 1987; No 45: p40–41.

Désert, attente, silence; reviews of poetry books. photo · *Lettres québec* Autumn 1987; No 47: p44–45.

Il y a des poèmes que nous habitons tous; reviews of poetry books. *Lettres québec* Winter 1986–87; No 44: p36–37.

L'amour la mort; reviews of poetry books. photo · *Lettres québec* Summer 1987; No 46: p37–38.

Poésie; survey review article. *U of Toronto Q* Fall 1987; Vol 57 No 1: p50–62.

Songe, révolte et manifeste; reviews of poetry books. photo · *Lettres québec* Spring 1987; No 45: p38–39.

Yoon, Jean

Because I'm sexual now; short story. illus · *Fireweed* Winter 1987; No 24: p8–11.

York, Lorraine M.

Apple-pie beds and water bombs; review of *The Daring Game*. *Can Child Lit* 1987; No 46: p79–81.

"Citizens-in-language"; reviews of *The Louis Riel Organ & Piano Co.* and *Waiting for Saskatchewan*. *Essays on Can Writ* Winter 1987; No 35: p171–177.

"Gulfs" and "connections": the fiction of Alice Munro; article. *Essays on Can Writ* Winter 1987; No 35: p135–146.

Joyless in Jubilee?; review of *Alice Munro*. *Essays on Can Writ* Spring 1987; No 34: p157–161.

The rival bards; article. *Can Lit* Spring 1987; No 112: p211–216.

York, Thomas

Death and dying dogs old soldier; review of *Unknown Soldier*. *CH* Oct 25, 1987: pE5.

Dense, mystic tale requires much of reader; review of *Selakhi*. *CH* Dec 27, 1987: pE6.

Lowry's B.C. connection examined; review of *Malcolm Lowry: Vancouver Days*. *CH* June 28, 1987: pF8.

Young, Alan R.

Atlantic heritage; review of *The Atlantic Anthology, Volume Two*. *Can Lit* Spring 1987; No 112: p148.

New Brunswick letters; review of *The Bicentennial Lectures on New Brunswick Literature*. *Can Lit* Spring 1987; No 112: p146–148.

Passions and ironies; review of *A Model Lover. Fiddlehead* Summer 1987; No 152: p98–100.

Young, John A.

Board fought banning; letter to the editor. photo · *G&M* Dec 19, 1987: pD7.

Young, Kathryn

Writers get their cheques; article. *G&M* March 18, 1987: pC3.

Young, Pamela

A bookman bids farewell; article about Jack McClelland. photo · *Maclean's* March 2, 1987; Vol 100 No 9: p50.

Joys for young readers; reviews of children's books. *Maclean's* Dec 7, 1987; Vol 100 No 49: p54, 56.

Young, Patricia

Bath water; poem. *Event* Summer 1987; Vol 16 No 2: p7.

Daylight savings; poem. *CV 2* Spring 1987; Vol 10 No 3: p20.

Dinner conversation; poem. illus · *Antigonish R* Winter 1987; No 68: p90–91.

Fire; poem. *NeWest R* Summer 1987; Vol 12 No 10: p14.

Goose-girl; poem. *CV 2* Spring 1987; Vol 10 No 3: p21–22.

Ill in Venice; poem. *Room of One's Own* April 1987; Vol 11 No 3: p26.

Indian summer; poem. *Event* Summer 1987; Vol 16 No 2: p10.

No hands; poem. *Event* Summer 1987; Vol 16 No 2: p9.

No one is listening; poem. *Can Forum* June-July 1987; Vol 67 No 770: p49.

Sex is; poem. *Event* Summer 1987; Vol 16 No 2: p8–9.

Young, Scott

'Cocoon-like' Canlit hard on authors; letter to the editor. *TS* Dec 20, 1987: pB2.

Young, Terence

On this plane my wife and I are still dancing; short story. *Malahat R* June 1987; No 79: p149–154.

Zachariah, Mathew

Crusz; review of *Singing Against the Wind. Can Lit* Spring 1987; No 112: p188–189.

Zacharin, Noah

For people; review of *Seventy-One Poems for People. Can Lit* Spring 1987; No 112: p145–146.

Zapparoli, David

Saturday Night does its job well; letter to the editor. *TS* July 20, 1987: pA16.

Zekas, Rita

My Cousin's director brings you tears next; article. photo · *TS* Oct 18, 1987: pG6.

Tennant gets top award for costume and design; article. *TS* Oct 14, 1987: pE1.

Veterans give proteges a $5,000 career boost; article. photo · *TS* May 7, 1987: pD1.

Zerbisias, Antonia

Herrndorf is the sum of his arts; article about Peter Herrndorf. photo · *TS* Oct 10, 1987: pH1,H3.

Zichy, Francis

The narrator, the reader, and Mariposa: the cost of preserving the status quo in Sunshine Sketches Of A Little Town; article. abstract · *J of Can Studies* Spring 1987; Vol 22 No 1: p51–65.

Zieroth, Dale

Afternoon and evening; poem. *Can Lit* Winter 1987; No 115: p124.

Aphasia; poem. *Can Lit* Winter 1987; No 115: p122.

Margaret Laurence 1926–1987; obituary. *Event* March 1987; Vol 16 No 1: p7.

November sun; poem. *Can Lit* Winter 1987; No 115: p105–106.

Pictures from home. . . .; editorial. *Event* Summer 1987; Vol 16 No 2: p5–6.

Zimmerman, Kate

Atmospheric nature is strength of play; theatre review of *Fall of the House of Krebbs*. photo · *CH* Oct 2, 1987: pE10.

Audience relishes stale farce; theatre review of *The Hand That Cradles the Rock*. *CH* May 3, 1987: pE2.

Author skewers films' popularity in new ATP play; article. photo · *CH* Sept 11, 1987: pF1.

Black comedy lacks direction; theatre review of *Joe Egg*. photo · *CH* Feb 22, 1987: pE5.

Calgary troupes draw fair share of plaudits at Fringe; article. *CH* Aug 21, 1987: pC1.

Dinner farce lacking consistency; theatre review of *Sinners*. *CH* Sept 6, 1987: pE6.

Events inspired new play; article. *CH* Sept 25, 1987: pF3.

Fine acting, solid directing outweigh set's shortcomings; theatre review of *Confusions*. *CH* Jan 26, 1987: pB6.

Friends blend skills into theatre piece; article. *CH* Nov 22, 1987: pA15.

Fringe a fertile theatrical breeding ground; article. *CH* Aug 25, 1987: pD8.

Fringe fun for families; article. *CH* Aug 18, 1987: pD5.

Johnstone's Beast rants, bewilders; theatre review of *The Beast with Five Fingers*. *CH* May 24, 1987: pE5.

Kids play key role in Storybook tale; theatre review of *Stick with Molasses*. photo · *CH* Feb 2, 1987: pB6.

Local troupes catch the spirit; article. *CH* Aug 14, 1987: pD1.

Mill life provided fuel for persona; article. photo · *CH* Nov 2, 1987: pB6.

Misery of unemployment hits home in poetic play; theatre review of *Rembrandt Brown*. *CH* April 25, 1987: pD3.

Musical comedy written as a true labor of love; article. photo · *CH* Dec 4, 1987: pE2.

Musical's lyrics at odds with uncomplicated story; theatre review of *Numbers. CH* Nov 29, 1987: pE3.

Off-the-wall play hit with audience; theatre review of *Geeks in Love. CH* March 1, 1987: pC5.

Once upon a time....; article. photo · *CH* May 31, 1987: pF1.

Other cultures featured in tales for youths; reviews of *The Unmasking of 'Ksan* and *Naomi's Road. CH* July 19, 1987: pE4.

Patience is a trademark of Fringe patrons; article. photo · *CH* Aug 17, 1987: pD7.

Play open to public but locale is secret; article. *CH* Jan 30, 1987: pC10.

Playwright finds unlikable cast proving popular; article. *CH* Sept 4, 1987: pE1.

Playwright probes kids' fear of summer camp; article. photo · *CH* April 24, 1987: pD1.

Polygons to cavort on stage; article. photo · *CH* Nov 26, 1987: pC1.

Porn purveyors assailed in play; theatre review of *Intimate Invasion. CH* Nov 15, 1987: pF2.

Quest Theatre's fare suited to younger audiences; theatre review of *One in a Million. CH* June 5, 1987: pC2.

Rabbit writers team up to parody anti-Semitism; article. photo · *CH* May 28, 1987: pC15.

Rabbit's experiment titillates; article. photo · *CH* Feb 9, 1987: pE6.

Savory characters spice clever play; theatre review of *How the Other Half Loves. CH* March 15, 1987: pE2.

Schools' forced funding cutbacks can't quell Quest; article. photo · *CH* Oct 22, 1987: pD1.

Stage thriller condensed for Lunchbox crowds; article. *CH* Oct 30, 1987: pE8.

Tale of economic woe became family affair; article. *CH* April 23, 1987: pD3.

Theatrical talent unites to help fledgling troupe; article. *CH* Nov 13, 1987: pE10.

Timid pussyfooting defuses play's satirical intent; theatre review of *Ilsa, Queen of the Nazi Love Camp. CH* May 30, 1987: pF5.

Tricks can't save flimsy play; theatre review of *It's Magic. CH* June 13, 1987: pF2.

Troupe's first venture brave but flat; theatre review of *The Worlds of William Korth.* photo · *CH* April 16, 1987: pE5.

Weather takes toll on Fringe audiences; article. *CH* Aug 19, 1987: pD2.

Ziolkowski, Carmen

Room number 100; poem. *Can Auth & Book* Summer 1987; Vol 62 No 4: p23.

Zonailo, Carolyn

Of gardens; short story. *New Q* Winter 1987; Vol 6 No 4: p11–14.

Writers on their work: the idea of poetry as the visible rainbow; essay. photo · *Poetry Can R* Fall 1987; Vol 9 No 1: p6.

Zuck, Robyn

An index to Descant 1–50. *Descant* Fall 1987; Vol 18 No 3: p99–181.

Zwicky, Jan

High summer; poem. *Ariel* July 1987; Vol 18 No 3: p47.

March Nineteenth; poem. *Ariel* July 1987; Vol 18 No 3: p48.

Zydek, Fredrick

Bobcat; poem. *Wascana R* Spring 1987; Vol 22 No 1: p79–80.

Salmon spree; poem. *Wascana R* Spring 1987; Vol 22 No 1: p81.

Zyvatkauskas, Betty

Excursions; column. illus · *G&M (Toronto Magazine)* Oct 1987; Vol 2 No 7: p31.

Summer theatre takes on a new twist; article. photo · *G&M* July 11, 1987: pE7.

Subject Index: *Guide to Critical Coverage of Canadian Writers, Books and Themes*

10 POEMS/Poems by Norm Sibum

The Hungarian's place; review of *10 Poems*. Charles Watts. *Brick* Winter 1987; No 29: p55–60.

THE 101 MIRACLES OF HOPE CHANCE/Play by Allan Stratton

TV evangelism thriller merits rerun on radio; theatre review of *The 101 Miracles of Hope Chance*. Stephen Godfrey. *G&M* Dec 7, 1987: pD9.

Evangelical lampoon offers lightweight fun; theatre review of *The 101 Miracles of Hope Chance*. Randal McIlroy. *WFP* Nov 20, 1987: p35.

1812: BROCK WANTS YOU/Play by Michael Brown

War play pokes fun at military, politicians; article. Sean Collins. photo · *TS (Neighbours)* May 5, 1987: p24.

1837: THE FARMERS' REVOLT/Play by Rick Salutin and Theatre Passe Muraille collective

Play retells story of 1837 rebellion; article. Lynne Ainsworth. photo · *TS (Neighbours)* June 30, 1987: p19.

Farmer's Rebellion stands test of time; theatre review of *1837: The Farmers' Revolt*. Ray Conlogue. *G&M* Dec 8, 1987: pD7.

1837 revolt hits centre stage; article. Robert Davis. photo · *TS (Neighbors)* Aug 11, 1987: p16.

Summer theatre takes on a new twist; article. Betty Zyvatkauskas. photo · *G&M* July 11, 1987: pE7.

A CREVE LES YEUX, A CREVE LE COEUR/INTIMATE INVASION — A CONCERNED LOOK AT PORNOGRAPHY/Play by Théâtre Parminou collective

Play examines porn issues; theatre review of *Intimate Invasion*. Brian Brennan. *CH* Nov 6, 1987: pE8.

Actors explore effects of porn; article. Brad Oswald. photo · *WFP* Sept 9, 1987: p36.

Porn purveyors assailed in play; theatre review of *Intimate Invasion*. Kate Zimmerman. *CH* Nov 15, 1987: pF2.

À DOUBLE SENS. CHANGES SUR QUELQUES PRATIQUES MODERNES/Critical work by Hugues Corriveau and Normand de Bellefeuille

La vitrine du livre; reviews of *À double sens* and *Le Fils d'Ariane*. Guy Ferland. *MD* Feb 14, 1987: pC2.

Qui a peur de l'intellectuel in 1987?; reviews. Pierre Milot. *Voix et images* Spring 1987; Vol 12 No 3: p530–534. [CANADIAN LITERARY PERIODICALS]

La modernité québécoise "pure laine"; review of *À double sens*. Lori Saint-Martin. *MD* May 9, 1987: pD3.

Impasses ou issues? L'imaginaire masculin face à la femme; reviews of *Les Silences du corbeau* and *À double sens*. Patricia Smart. *Voix et images* Spring 1987; Vol 12 No 3: p555–560.

La modernité: des formes qui (s')inquiètent; reviews of critical works. Whitfield. photo · *Lettres québec* Summer 1987; No 46: p56–58.

À LA FAÇON D'UN CHARPENTIER/Poems and prose by Paul Savoie

The poet builds; review of *À la façon d'un charpentier*. Alexandre Amprimoz. *Prairie Fire* Autumn 1987; Vol 8 No 3: p118–119.

À LA RECHERCHE DE M./Play by Jacques Bélanger and Marie-Hélène Letendre

[Untitled]; theatre review of *À la recherche de M.*. Diane Pavlovic. photo · *Jeu* 1987; No 42: p167–168.

À PROPOS DE MAUDE/Novel by Lise Harou

La passion selon Lise Harou; review of *À propos de Maude*. Jean Royer. *MD* Jan 10, 1987: pB3.

À VOULOIR VAINCRE L'ABSENSE/Poems by Julie Stanton

[Untitled]; review of *À vouloir vaincre l'absence*. Hélène Thibaux. *Estuaire* Winter 1986–87; No 43: p78–79.

A.M. KLEIN: LITERARY ESSAYS AND REVIEWS/Prose by A.M. Klein

Esoteric callings; review of *A.M. Klein: Literary Essays and Reviews*. Sharon Drache. *G&M* May 16, 1987: pC19.

AAA, AÂH, HA OU LES AMOURS MALAISÉES/Novels by François Barcelo

La vitrine du livre; review of *Aaa, aâh, ha ou les amours malaisés*. Guy Ferland. *MD* Jan 3, 1987: pC2.

À l'impossible certains sont tenus; reviews of *Benito* and *Aaa, Aâh, Ha ou les amours malaisées*. Pierre Hébert. *Voix et images* Autumn 1987; Vol 13 No 1: p192–194.

Aaa! Aâh! Ha! que de belles catastrophes narratives!; reviews. Michel Lord. photo · *Lettres québec* Spring 1987; No 45: p32–35.

[Untitled]; review of *Aaa, aâh, ha ou les amours malaisées*. Jean Royer. *MD* Jan 23, 1987: p7.

Barcelo, le jogger heureux; review of *Aaa, aâh, ha ou les amours malaisées*. Jean Royer. photo · *MD* Jan 31, 1987: pB3.

THE ABBOTSFORD GUIDE TO INDIA/Poems by Frank Davey

B.C. international — in search of new subjects and forms; reviews. Gillian Harding-Russell. *Event* Summer 1987; Vol 16 No 2: p125–127.

[Untitled]; reviews of poetry books. Stephen Scobie. *Malahat R* Dec 1987; No 81: p104–106.

Oranges and onions; reviews of *White of the Lesser Angels* and *The Abbotsford Guide to India*. Fred Wah. *Books in Can* March 1987; Vol 16 No 2: p32,34.

ABERCROMBIE, NORA

Wacky novel competition hits bottom with a thud; review of *Hardwired Angel*. William French. *G&M* Aug 25, 1987: pD7.

Edmonton winners in Pulp contest; article. Charles Mandel. *Quill & Quire* Jan 1987; Vol 53 No 1: p18. [AWARDS, LITERARY]

[Untitled]; review of *Hardwired Angel*. Norman Sigurdson. *Quill & Quire* Dec 1987; Vol 53 No 12: p25.

Winner is a real stinker; review of *Hardwired Angel*. Morley Walker. *WFP* Sept 5, 1987: p58.

ABLEY, MARK

Hidden in prairies are little oddities, large truths; review of *Beyond Forget*. Lucinda Chodan. photo · *MG* Jan 31, 1987: pB8.

Young man goes west, again; review of *Beyond Forget*. Gwen Dambrofsky. photo · *TS* Feb 14, 1987: M4.

Lost horizons; review of *Beyond Forget*. Douglas Glover. *Books in Can* Jan-Feb 1987; Vol 16 No 1: p20.

A love for the land in the west that once was; review of *Beyond Forget*. Don Kerr. photo · *Quill & Quire* Jan 1987; Vol 53 No 1: p31.

[Untitled]; review of *Beyond Forget*. Andrew H. Malcolm. *NYT Book R* July 5, 1987: p15.

[Untitled]; review of *Beyond Forget*. George Melnyk. photo · *NeWest R* Nov 1987; Vol 13 No 3: p14.

[Untitled]; review of *Beyond Forget*. Peter Millard. photo · *NeWest R* Nov 1987; Vol 13 No 3: p15.

[Untitled]; review of *Beyond Forget*. Constance Rooke. *Malahat R* Sept 1987; No 80: p130–131.

ABOVE THE TILTED EARTH/Poems by Dorothy Corbett Gentleman

Small press reviews; reviews of poetry books. Shaunt Basmajian. *Cross Can Writ Q* 1987; Vol 9 No 1: p25.

[Untitled]; reviews of *The Proper Lover* and *Above the Tilted Earth*. Barbara Carey. *Poetry Can R* Summer 1987; Vol 8 No 4: p34.

ABRA/Novel by Joan Barfoot

New in paper; reviews of novels. *TS* Aug 30, 1987: pA18.
[FIRST NOVELS: BOOK REVIEWS]

ACADIAN POETRY NOW/POÉSIE ACADIENNE CONTEMPORAINE/Anthology

[Untitled]; review of *Acadian Poetry Now/Poésie acadienne contemporaine*. Tom Marshall. *Poetry Can R* Spring 1987; Vol 8 No 2–3: p48–49.
[ANTHOLOGIES: BOOK REVIEWS]

ACKERMAN, MARIANNE

La vie littéraire; column. Jean Royer. *MD* Feb 14, 1987: pC2.
[AWARDS, LITERARY; CANADIAN LITERARY PERIODICALS; COMPETITIONS, LITERARY; FICTION READINGS; POETRY READINGS; RADIO AND CANADIAN LITERATURE]

ACORN, MILTON

Wakes for Acorn; article. *TS* March 1, 1987: pC4.
[POETRY READINGS]

Acorn Award; notice. *Quill & Quire* Jan 1987; Vol 53 No 1: p18.
[AWARDS, LITERARY]

[Untitled]; letter about Milton Acorn. *Brick (special issue)* Summer 1987; No 30: p58.

Friends bring poet back to life at wake; article. John Allemang. photo · *G&M* March 23, 1987: pC12.

Milton Acorn (1923–1986); obituary. George Bowering. *Can Lit* Spring 1987; No 112: p216–218.

Passion without precision; review of *The Uncollected Acorn*. George Elliott Clarke. *Atlan Prov Book R* May-June 1987; Vol 14 No 2: p11

Milton Acorn: in memoriam; obituary. James Deahl. photo · *Poetry Can R* Spring 1987; Vol 8 No 1–2: p6.

Standing up for himself; reviews of *The Uncollected Acorn* and *Whiskey Jack*. Paul Denham. *Books in Can* June-July 1987; Vol 16 No 5: p30,32.

Spleen may write the poem, but Layton's heart will speak tomorrow; reviews of poetry books. Trevor Ferguson. *MG* Sept 26, 1987: J11.

Acorn: swept up in imagery; review of *Whiskey Jack*. Maggie Helwig. photo · *TS* Feb 8, 1987: pG8.

[Untitled]; reviews of *The Uncollected Acorn* and *A Stand of Jackpine*. David Leahy. *Rubicon* Fall 1987; No 9: p167–168.

Into the depths of Milton Acorn's passion; review of *Milton Acorn: The Uncollected Acorn*. Colin Lowndes. photo · *G&M* March 21, 1987: pE18.

Acorn's poems pro-life; review of *The Uncollected Acorn*. Lesley McAllister. *TS* June 13, 1987: M4.

The idea of a poem: an interview with Milton Acorn. Jon Pearce. *Can Poet* Fall-Winter 1987; No 21: p93–102.

The Milton Acorn Memorial People's Poetry Award; article. Ted Plantos. illus · *Poetry Can R* Summer 1987; Vol 8 No 4: p17.
[AWARDS, LITERARY]

In spite of alienation, Acorn did go home again; essay. Erika Ritter. photo · *TS* Sept 12, 1987: M2.

Poetry: packing all the power into two of seven titles; reviews of poetry books. Robin Skelton. photo · *Quill & Quire* May 1987; Vol 53 No 5: p24.

Rush job, high gloss and high-risk realism; reviews of poetry books. Fraser Sutherland. *G&M* March 21, 1987: pE18.

ADAM, IAN

Red Deer Press series champions western writers; reviews of poetry books. Murdoch Burnett. *CH* Dec 13, 1987: pC11.

ADAMS, JOHN COLDWELL

[Untitled]; article. *G&M* Feb 28, 1987: pE3.

Blind men and elephants; essay. John Coldwell Adams. illus · *Can Auth & Book* Spring 1987; Vol 62 No 3: p7–8.
[BOOK REVIEWING]

[Untitled]; review of *Sir Charles God Damn*. Christopher Armitage. *Amer R of Can Studies* Winter 1987–88; Vol 17 No 4: P439–440.

Torn between love and loyalty; reviews of *Sir Charles God Damn* and Sir Charles G.D. Roberts: A Biography. David McFadden. photo · *Brick* Fall 1987; No 31: p55–59.

[Untitled]; reviews of *The Collected Poems of Sir Charles G.D. Roberts* and *Sir Charles God Damn*. Mary McGillivray. *Queen's Q* Winter 1987; Vol 94 No 4: p1039–1042.

ADAMSON, ARTHUR

Artist colony; article. Kevin Prokosh. *WFP* Aug 4, 1987: p27.

ADDOLORATA/Play by Marco Micone

Masques, personnages et personnes; reviews of plays. André-G. Bourassa. photo · *Lettres québec* Summer 1987; No 46: p51–52.

La vitrine du livre; reviews. Jean Royer. *MD* April 11, 1987: pD2.
[CANADIAN LITERARY PERIODICALS]

ADELE AT THE END OF THE DAY/Novel by Tom Marshall

[Untitled]; reviews of novels. Beverley Daurio. *Cross Can Writ Q* 1987; Vol 9 No 3–4: p45–46.

Love and sin in Rosedale; review of *Adele at the End of the Day*. Elaine Kahn. *TS* April 19, 1987: pA18.

Vivid imagination drives novel's slender plot line; review of *Adele at the End of the Day*. P. Scott Lawrence. photo · *MG* April 11, 1987: pG5.

Daring novel rewarding read; review of *Adele at the End of the Day*. Kenneth McGoogan. *CH* April 26, 1987: pE5.

Mother and son; review of *Adele at the End of the Day*. Kenneth McGoogan. *Books in Can* April 1987; Vol 16 No 3: p20.

[Untitled]; review of *Adele at the End of the Day*. Constance Rooke. *Malahat R* June 1987; No 79: p161.

[Untitled]; review of *Adele at the End of the Day*. Richard Streiling. *Quill & Quire* March 1987; Vol 53 No 3: p71.

A search for the perfect pairing; review of *Adele at the End of the Day*. David Williamson. photo · *WFP* April 25, 1987: p54.

A novel a poet can write; review of *Adele at the End of the Day*. Thomas S. Woods. *G&M* May 30, 1987: pC19.

ADILMAN, MONA ELAINE

Small press reviews; reviews of poetry books. Shaunt Basmajian. *Cross Can Writ Q* 1987; Vol 9 No 1: p25.

[Untitled]; reviews of poetry books. Anne Cimon. *Poetry Can R* Spring 1987; Vol 8 No 2–3: p62.

ADULT ENTERTAINMENT/Short stories by John Metcalf

[Untitled]; review of *Adult Entertainment*. Scot Bishop. *Rubicon* Fall 1987; No 9: p196–197.

[Untitled]; reviews of short story collections. Pauline Carey. *Cross Can Writ Q* 1987; Vol 9 No 3–4: p46–47.

[Untitled]; review of *Adult Entertainment*. Oliver Gorse. *Idler* March-April 1987; No 12: p60.

[Untitled]; review of *Adult Entertainment*. Mary Millar. *Queen's Q* Winter 1987; Vol 94 No 4: p1024–1026.

ADVICE TO MY FRIENDS/Poems by Robert Kroetsch

Trope as topos in the poetry of Robert Kroetsch; review article about *Advice to My Friends*. E.F. Dyck. *Prairie Fire* Winter 1987–88; Vol 8 No 4: p86,88–93.

Discourse of the other; review of *Advice to My Friends*. Paul Hjartarson. *Can Lit* Winter 1987; No 115: p135–138

AFRAID OF THE DARK/Children's story by Barry Dickson

Thrills and chills: hints for Hallowe'en reading; reviews of children's books. Joan McGrath. illus · *Quill & Quire (Books for Young People)* Oct 1987; Vol 53 No 10: p8.
[ANTHOLOGIES: BOOK REVIEWS]

AFRICA SOLO/Play by Djanet Sears

Gonna take a sentimental journey; theatre review of *Africa Solo*. Ray Conlogue. photo · *G&M* Nov 18, 1987: pC7.

Blowing bubbles with Simone and Sartre; column. Vit Wagner. photo · *TS* Nov 6, 1987: pE4.
[TRANSLATIONS OF CANADIAN LITERATURE]

Africa Solo works best when related in song; theatre review. Vit Wagner. photo · *TS* Nov 13, 1987: pE26.

THE AFRICAN ROSCIUS/Play by Robin Breon

More history lesson than drama; theatre review of *The African Roscius*. Liam Lacey. photo · *G&M* July 15, 1987: pC6.

AFTER SIX DAYS/Novel by Keith Harrison

A question of taste; reviews of *After Six Days* and *Mario*. Noreen Golfman. *Can Lit* Spring 1987; No 112: p104–107.

AFTER THE FACT/Novel by Hélène Holden

Airing Canlit chestnuts; review of *After the Fact*. Elizabeth Brady. *Fiddlehead* Autumn 1987; No 153: p103–106.

A rich, feminist novel from Quebec; reviews of *A Forest for Zoe* and *After the Fact*. Geoff Hancock. *TS* Feb 15, 1987: pA19.

[Untitled]; review of *After the Fact*. Lorna Scoville. *CH* May 3, 1987: pE6.

Après la guerre; review of *After the Fact*. George Tombs. *MD* June 20, 1987: pD6.

Overpowering ambiguity; review of *After the Fact*. David Williamson. *WFP* April 11, 1987: p60.

AFTER THE REVOLUTION/Poems by John Weier

Chapbooks range from good to silly; reviews of poetry books. Robert Quickenden. *WFP* Jan 31, 1987: p55.

AFTERNOON STARLIGHT/Poems by Charles Noble

Quilted patch; reviews of poetry books. Uma Parameswaran. Teresa Mallam. *Can Lit* Spring 1987; No 112: p176–179.

Witty plenitude; review of *Afternoon Starlight*. Douglas Reimer. *Prairie Fire* Spring 1987; Vol 8 No 1: p91–93.

AFTERNOON TEA/Short stories by Brad Robinson

[Untitled]; review of *Afternoon Tea*. Shelagh Garland. *Books in Can* May 1987; Vol 16 No 4: p20.

Poor George and Jessie, poor reader; review of *Afternoon Tea*. Maggie Helwig. *TS* Feb 28, 1987: M6.

Excellent illusions, cloying clichés in short-story collections; reviews of *Afternoon Tea* and *Inspecting the Vaults*. Brent Ledger. photo · *Quill & Quire* March 1987; Vol 53 No 3: p72.

Book world: a little-known bestseller; column. Beverley Slopen. *TS* Jan 11, 1987: pA16.

AFTERWORLDS/Poems by Gwendolyn MacEwen

MacEwen and McKay; reviews of *Afterworlds* and *Sanding Down This Rocking Chair on a Windy Night*. Barry Dempster. *Poetry Can R* Fall 1987; Vol 9 No 1: p29-30.

So you think poetry no longer exists for readers?; reviews of *Afterworlds* and *Sanding Down This Rocking Chair on a Windy Night*. Judith Fitzgerald. photo · *TS* May 3, 1987: pA24.

Anarchy and afterthoughts; review of *Afterworlds*. Susan Glickman. *Books in Can* June-July 1987; Vol 16 No 5: p26.

[Untitled]; reviews of *Afterworlds* and *Sanding Down This Rocking Chair on a Windy Night*. Barbara Powell. *Wascana R* Fall 1987; Vol 22 No 2: p88-91.

[Untitled]; review of *Afterworlds*. Stephen Scobie. *Malahat R* June 1987; No 79: p168.

Poetry: packing all the power into two of seven titles; reviews of poetry books. Robin Skelton. photo · *Quill & Quire* May 1987; Vol 53 No 5: p24.

Literary tricks and the larger concerns; reviews of *Delayed Mercy* and *Afterworlds*. Fraser Sutherland. photo · *G&M* Aug 8, 1987: pC19.

AGENTS, LITERARY

Making the rights move: why publishers are paying so much more; article. Hamish Cameron. photo · *Quill & Quire* March 1987; Vol 53 No 3: p8,10.
[AUTHORS, CANADIAN; PUBLISHING AND PUBLISHERS IN CANADA]

Nelligan n'tait pas fou, il acceptait seulement de passer pour ce fou qui s'appelait Nelligan. review of *Nelligan n'était pas fou!*. Réjean Robidoux. *Lettres québec* Winter 1986-87; No 44: p74-76.

Book world: adults who love children's books gather at 'Roundtable'; column. Beverley Slopen. *TS* Aug 16, 1987: pA21.
[WRITERS' ORGANIZATIONS]

Book world: ex-publisher finds dealing with publishers gives him a pain; column about Jack McClelland. Beverley Slopen. *TS* Dec 13, 1987: pE6.

AGONIE/DEATH-WATCH/Novel by Jacques Brault

Lament for a nation; review of *Death-Watch*. Marianne Ackerman. *Maclean's* Oct 19, 1987; Vol 100 No 42: p60a.
[FIRST NOVELS: BOOK REVIEWS]

Two novels offer pain — and incidental pleasures; reviews of *Death-Watch* and *Five Facts about Giorgione*. Ken Adachi. *TS* Aug 30, 1987: pA19.

La poésie dans la prose, ou le clochard illuminé; article. André Brochu. illus · *Voix et images* Winter 1987; No 35: p212-220.

AH, L'AMOUR L'AMOUR/Novel by Noël Audet

Dans les poches; reviews of paperback books. Guy Ferland. *MD* Oct 31, 1987: pD6.

AIMER: 10 NOUVELLES PAR 10 AUTEURS QUÉBÉCOIS/Short story anthology

Des contes et des nouvelles pour rêver; reviews of short story books. Dominique Garand. *Voix et images* Spring 1987; Vol 12 No 3: p551-555.
[ANTHOLOGIES: BOOK REVIEWS]

La recherche de l'amour. review of *Aimer*. Adrien Thério. *Lettres québec* Winter 1986-87; No 44: p79.
[ANTHOLOGIES: BOOK REVIEWS]

AITKEN, JOHAN LYALL

[Untitled]; review of *Masques of Morality*. Tracy Shepherd Matheson. *Books in Can* Oct 1987; Vol 16 No 7: p21.

[Untitled]; review of *Masques of Morality*. Anne E. Russell. *Quill & Quire* Oct 1987; Vol 53 No 10: p23.

AKENSON, DON

The made who made Ontario Orange; review of *The Orangeman*. Richard Campbell. photo · *TS* Feb 8, 1987: pG8.

Literary 'docudrama' captures the essence; review of *The Orangeman*. Roger Hall. photo · *G&M* Feb 14, 1987: pE19.

[Untitled]; review of *The Orangeman*. Peter D. James. *Quill & Quire* Feb 1987; Vol 53 No 2: p17.

[Untitled]; review of *The Orangeman*. Royce MacGillivray. *Books in Can* Jan-Feb 1987; Vol 16 No 1: p27.

So-called fiction serves no purpose; letter to the editor. Leslie H. Saunders. *TS* March 24, 1987: pA20.

ALARIE, DONALD

La vie littéraire; column. Marc Morin. *MD* Nov 14, 1987: pD14.
[AWARDS, LITERARY; CHILDREN'S LITERATURE; POETRY READINGS]

La vitrine du livre; reviews. Jean Royer. *MD* March 14, 1987: pD4.
[CANADIAN LITERARY PERIODICALS]

ALBANESE, VINCENZO

Montreal poets inspired by travel in hot countries; reviews of poetry books. Barbara Black. *MG* March 28, 1987: pE9.

Slight drag but Cormorant takes off; reviews of *Slow Mist* and *Exile Home/Exilio En la Patria*. Keith Garebian. photo · *TS* March 28, 1987: M4.

ALBERT, LYLE VICTOR

Architecture offers author comic design; article. Martin Morrow. photo · *CH* Dec 31, 1987: pD1.

ALBERTA BOUND: THIRTY STORIES BY ALBERTA WRITERS/Anthology

Today's assignment: short fiction that's worth a long look; reviews of short story books. Douglas Hill. *G&M* March 14, 1987: pE19.
[ANTHOLOGIES: BOOK REVIEWS]

[Untitled]; review of *Alberta Bound*. Brent Ledger. *Quill & Quire* April 1987; Vol 53 No 4: p27–28.
[ANTHOLOGIES: BOOK REVIEWS]

[Untitled]; review of *Alberta Bound*. Michael Mirolla. *Dandelion* Fall-Winter 1987; Vol 14 No 2: p143–145.
[ANTHOLOGIES: BOOK REVIEWS]

Lively collection; review of *Alberta Bound*. John Parr. *TS* June 7, 1987: pG11.
[ANTHOLOGIES: BOOK REVIEWS]

ALBERTINE, EN CINQ TEMPS/ALBERTINE, IN FIVE TIMES/Play by Michel Tremblay

[Untitled]; review of *Albertine, in Five Times*. Carolellen Norskey. *Quill & Quire* June 1987; Vol 53 No 6: p31.

THE ALCHEMY OF CLOUDS/Poems by Mark Frutkin

Recent poetry; reviews of poetry books. Terrence Craig. *Atlan Prov Book R* Feb-March 1987; Vol 14 No 1: p18.

Four poets; reviews of poetry books. Randall Maggs. *Can Lit* Winter 1987; No 115: p280–284.

ALDERSON, SUE ANN

Snoring, smuggling, and snuggling; reviews of children's stories. Susan Perren. *Quill & Quire (Books for Young People)* Dec 1987; Vol 53 No 12: p8.

ALERTE CE SOIR À 22 HEURES/Children's novel by Madeleine Gaudreault-Labrecque

Simplicité et dynamisme; review of *Alerte ce soir à 22 heures*. Kenneth W. Meadwell. *Can Child Lit* 1987; No 45: p70–71.

ALFORD, EDNA

[Untitled]; review of *The Garden of Eloise Loon*. Audrey Andrews. *Dandelion* Spring-Summer 1987; Vol 14 No 1: p89–91.

Other voices; review article about *The Garden of Eloise Loon*. Jason Sherman. biog · *Books in Can* Jan-Feb 1987; Vol 16 No 1: p31–32.

ALIBI: A NOVEL/Novel by Robert Kroetsch

A deconstructive narratology; reading Robert Kroetsch's *Alibi*; article. Susan Rudy Dorscht. *Open Letter* Summer 1987; Vol 6 No 8: p78–83.
[METAFICTION; STRUCTURALIST WRITING AND CRITICISM]

The alibis of Kroetsch and Butler; introduction to Alibi Drawings. Terrence Heath. *Border Cross* Summer 1987; Vol 6 No 3: p31–32.

ALICE MUNRO/Critical work by B. Pfaus

Joyless in Jubilee?; review of *Alice Munro*. Lorraine M. York. *Essays on Can Writ* Spring 1987; No 34: p157–161.

ALICE SPRINGS/Poems by Beth Learn

[Untitled]; reviews of poetry books. Anne Burke. *Poetry Can R* Summer 1987; Vol 8 No 4: p38.

ALL OTHER DESTINATIONS ARE CANCELLED/Play by Colleen Murphy

Destinations strays off course despite strong cast, director; theatre review of *All Other Destinations Are Cancelled*. Ray Conlogue. photo · *G&M* Feb 25, 1987: pC10.

New Canadian drama needs leaner approach; theatre review of *All Other Destinations Are Cancelled*. Robert Crew. photo · *TS* Feb 25, 1987: pF3.

Editor's notebook; editorial. John Flood. *Northward J* 1987; No 42: p2.

ALL THE BRIGHT COMPANY: RADIO DRAMA PRODUCED BY ANDREW ALLAN/Anthology of radio plays

[Untitled]; review of *All the Bright Company*. L.W. Conolly. *Can Drama* 1987; Vol 13 No 2: p231–233.
[ANTHOLOGIES: BOOK REVIEWS]

A megalomania for radio drama; reviews of *All the Bright Company* and *Image in the Mind*. Bronwyn Drainie. photo · *G&M* Nov 28, 1987: pC19.
[ANTHOLOGIES: BOOK REVIEWS]

College guide leaves no term unstoned; review of *All the Bright Company*. Lew Gloin. *TS* Sept 13, 1987: pA22.
[ANTHOLOGIES: BOOK REVIEWS]

Recalling the best of CBC radio drama; article. Ian Mayer. *G&M* Nov 14, 1987: pC20.
[RADIO AND CANADIAN LITERATURE]

[Untitled]; review of *All the Bright Company*. Martin Townsend. *Quill & Quire* June 1987; Vol 53 No 6: p31.
[ANTHOLOGIES: BOOK REVIEWS]

ALL THE POLARITIES: COMPARATIVE STUDIES IN CONTEMPORARY CANADIAN NOVELS IN FRENCH AND ENGLISH/Critical work by Philip Stratford

[Untitled]; reviews of *Blind Painting* and *All the Polarities*. Estelle Dansereau. *Quarry* Summer 1987; Vol 36 No 3: p82–86.

[Untitled]; reviews of critical works. Don Gutteridge. *Queen's Q* Summer 1987; Vol 94 No 2: p464–467.

On both hands; review of *All the Polarities*. Patricia Merivale. *Can Lit* Summer-Fall 1987; No 113–114: p207–212.

ALL THE WAY HOME/Novel by Gabrielle Poulin

[Untitled]; review of *All the Way Home*. Peter S. Noble. *British J of Can Studies* June 1987; Vol 2 No 1: p182–183.

ALL THE WAY HOME/Novel by Max Braithewaite

[Untitled]; review of *All the Way Home*. Hallvard Dahlie. *Queen's Q* Summer 1987; Vol 94 No 2: p480–482.

Parody & legacy; reviews. Lorna Irvine. *Can Lit* Winter 1987; No 115: p264–267.
[FIRST NOVELS: BOOK REVIEWS]

ALLAIRE, GEORGES

Un choix délibéré pour la vie; review of *Pourquoi pas dix?*. Jacques-G. Ruelland. *MD* Nov 14, 1987: pD15.

ALLAN, TED

'Squowse' sparkles for kids; theatre review of *Willie the Squowse*. Ray Conlogue. photo · *G&M* Dec 11, 1987: pD6.
[DRAMATIC ADAPTATIONS OF CANADIAN LITERATURE]

Authors talk about books as movies; article. Peter Goddard. *TS* Oct 20, 1987: H4.
[FESTIVALS, LITERARY]

Award-winning children's story lights up stage; article. Christopher Hume. photo · *TS* Dec 3, 1987: pB5.

Delightfully tiny Willie makes a big impression; theatre review of *Willie the Squowse*. Christopher Hume. photo · *TS* Dec 11, 1987: pD14.
[DRAMATIC ADAPTATIONS OF CANADIAN LITERATURE]

Writer realizes a dream with Bethune film; article. James Rusk. photo · *G&M* April 15, 1987: pC5.

Rewriting the past; article. Paul Stuewe. *Books in Can* Aug-Sept 1987; Vol 16 No 6: p13–14.

ALLEN, CHARLOTTE VALE

Summer reading for quiet times; review of *Illusions*. Lew Gloin. photo · *TS* Aug 9, 1987: pA21.

[Untitled]; review of *Illusions*. Ann Jansen. *Quill & Quire* June 1987; Vol 53 No 6: p32.

Escapes into feminine victimization; review of *Illusions*. Ruth Manson. *G&M* July 25, 1987: pC16.

ALLEN, ROBERT

Montreal poets inspired by travel in hot countries; reviews of poetry books. Barbara Black. *MG* March 28, 1987: pE9.

Poets in search of praise; reviews of *One Night at the Indigo Hotel* and *The Bones of Their Occasion*. Keith Garebian. *TS* May 16, 1987: M4

An interview with Robert Allen. Philip Lanthier. biog bibliog photo · *Matrix* Fall 1987; No 25: p34–49.

A note on The Hawryliw Process; article. Philip Lanthier. *Matrix* Fall 1987; No 25: p39–40.

THE ALLEY CAT

See LE MATOU/THE ALLEY CAT/Novel by Yves Beauchemin

THE ALLIGATOR REPORT/Short stories by W.P. Kinsella

[Untitled]; reviews of short story collections. Pauline Carey. *Cross Can Writ Q* 1987; Vol 9 No 3–4: p46–47.

[Untitled]; review of *The Alligator Report*. Cary Fagan. *Books in Can* April 1987; Vol 16 No 3: p24.

Gators, jugglers and the gerbil that ate L.A.; review of *The Alligator Report*. William French. illus · *G&M* Feb 19, 1987: pC1.

[Untitled]; review of *The Alligator Report*. Alice Gur-Arie. *Quill & Quire* May 1987; Vol 53 No 5: p20.

Kinsella's losers triumph; review of *The Alligator Report*. Lorna Scoville. photo · *CH* March 29, 1987: pE5.

Tributes to two writers; review of *The Alligator Report*. David Williamson. *WFP* March 7, 1987: p70.

ALLISON, GAY

Women are the root of all change; reviews of *The Unravelling* and *The Merzbook*. Lesley McAllister. photo · *TS* Nov 14, 1987: M4.

ALMON, BERT

Something in common; reviews of poetry books. Cary Fagan. *Prairie Fire* Spring 1987; Vol 8 No 1: p83–87.

[Untitled]; review of *Deep North*. Sparling Mills. *Poetry Can R* Spring 1987; Vol 8 No 2–3: p59–60.

Quilted patch; reviews of poetry books. Uma Parameswaran. Teresa Mallam. *Can Lit* Spring 1987; No 112: p176–179.

ALMOST JAPANESE/Novel by Sarah Sheard

Disappearing into Japan; review of *Almost Japanese*. Kathy Jones. *NYT Book R* Aug 16, 1987: p23.
[FIRST NOVELS: BOOK REVIEWS]

ALONZO, ANNE-MARIE

Dits et faits; column. photo · *Lettres québec* Spring 1987; No 45: p6–7.
[AWARDS, LITERARY; PUBLISHING AND PUBLISHERS IN CANADA; TRANSLATIONS OF CANADIAN LITERATURE; WRITERS' ORGANIZATIONS]

Maniaques depressifs; reviews of poetry books. Mark Benson. *Can Lit* Spring 1987; No 112: p138–141.

La vitrine du livre; reviews. Guy Ferland. *MD* May 23, 1987: pD4.

La tentation du romanesque; reviews of poetry books. Richard Giguère. photo · *Lettres québec* Autumn 1987; No 47: p37–39.

Notes de lectures; reviews of *La Mort aurorale* and *Écoute, Sultane*. Jean Royer. *MD* May 23, 1987: pD2.

THE ALTERNATE GUIDE/Poems by Monty Reid

A choice of codes; reviews of poetry books. Thomas Gerry. illus · *NeWest R* Nov 1987; Vol 13 No 3: p16–17.

Kinetic space; reviews of poetry books. Robert James Merrett. *Can Lit* Summer-Fall 1987; No 113–114: p241–243.

A MAZING SPACE: WRITING CANADIAN WOMEN WRITING/Critical essays collection

Kicking against the pricks; review of *A Mazing Space*. Sylvia M. Brown. *Books in Can* Dec 1987; Vol 16 No 9: p36–37.

La vitrine du livre; reviews. Guy Ferland. *MD* Sept 19, 1987: pD4.

A wealth of provocative and inspiring literary criticism; reviews. Douglas Hill. *G&M* Sept 5, 1987: pC13.
[ANTHOLOGIES: BOOK REVIEWS]

AMÉRICANE/Novel by Renaud Longchamps

Une Amérique d'arrière-cour; review of *Américane*. Jacques Michon. *MD* Oct 17, 1987: pD3–D4.

[Untitled]; reviews of *Mon mari le docteur* and *Américane*. Jacques St-Pierre. *Moebius* Winter 1987; No 31: p139–140.

AMÉRIQUE INTÉRIEURE/Poems by Alain Blanchet

[Untitled]; review of *Amérique intérieure*. André Roy. *Estuaire* Summer 1987; No 45: p49.

[Untitled]; reviews of poetry books. Jacques St-Pierre. *Moebius* Winter 1987; No 31: p137–139.

AMADOU/Novel by Louise Maheux-Forcier

Half-mad bohemian lyricism; review of *Amadou*. Anatanas Sileika. *G&M* Dec 26, 1987: pC23.

AMANDA GREENLEAF VISITS A DISTANT STAR/ Children's novel by Ed Kavanagh

The language of fantasy; reviews of *The Emperor's Panda* and *Amanda Greenleaf Visits a Distant Star*. Jo-Ann Wallace. *Can Child Lit* 1987; No 47: p73–74.

AMBRE GRIS/Poems by Michel Lemaire

De Bellefeuille, Nepveu, Lemaire, Royer; reviews of poetry books. Jean-Pierre Issenhuth. *Liberté* Aug 1987; Vol 29 No 4: p78–87.

AMOROSA/Novel by Monique Larouche-Thibault

Conservatisme; reviews of novels. Neil B. Bishop. *Can Lit* Winter 1987; No 115: p169–172.

AMPRIMOZ, ALEXANDRE

Chronique: reflets et signes; review of *Bouquet de signes*. Marguerite Andersen. *Poetry Can R* Summer 1987; Vol 8 No 4: p23.

Fabulist fictions fail to get passing grade; review of *Hard Confessions*. Norman Sigurdson. *WFP* Oct 31, 1987: p52.

Little magic; review of *Hard Confessions*. Antanas Sileika. *G&M* Dec 12, 1987: pE9.

AND I'M NEVER COMING BACK/Children's story by Jacqueline Dumas

One miss, one hit; reviews of *And I'm Never Coming Back* and *Madam Piccolo and the Craziest Pickle Party Ever*. Sylvia Markle-Craine. *Can Child Lit* 1987; No 48: p100–102.

AND WHEN I WAKE/Play by James W. Nichol

Murder mystery hatched in eerie isolated farmhouse; article. Brian Brennan. *CH* March 13, 1987: pC1.

Hackneyed pot-boiler contains few surprises; theatre review of *And When I Wake*. Brian Brennan. photo · *CH* March 15, 1987: pE2.

TC performance gave entertainment; letter to the editor. D.A. Brink. *CH* April 7, 1987: pA6.

ANDERSON, MARY

[Untitled]; reviews of poetry books. Anne Burke. *Poetry Can R* Summer 1987; Vol 8 No 4: p38.

ANDERSON, PATRICK

The tradition: Patrick Anderson; column. Bruce Whiteman. *Poetry Can R* Spring 1987; Vol 8 No 1–2: p10.

ANDRÈS, BERNARD-J.

Le théâtre qu'on joue; theatre reviews. André Dionne. illus photo · *Lettres québec* Spring 1987; No 45: p47–48.

[Untitled]; theatre review of *Rien voir*. Diane Pavlovic. *Jeu* 1987; No 42: p170.

ANDREWS, JAN

The Canadian north; review of *Very Last First Time*. Mary Ellen Binder. *Can Child Lit* 1987; No 45: p82–86.

Picture-power; reviews of *Very Last First Time* and *Zoom Away*. Jon C. Scott. *Can Lit* Spring 1987; No 112: p159–162.

ANFOUSSE, GINETTE

Poet-politician wins literary prize; article. *G&M* Nov 20, 1987: pD11.
[AWARDS, LITERARY]

Le retour de Jiji et Pichou; review of *Je boude*. Sandra Beckett. *Can Child Lit* 1987; No 47: p77–78.

Anne Hébert, Wilfrid Lemoyne, Ginette Anfousse reoivent les premiers prix Fleury-Mesplet; article. Paul Cauchon. photo · *MD* Nov 20, 1987: p13–14.
[AWARDS, LITERARY]

Ginette Anfousse: il fallait une nouvelle héroïne et Rosalie est née; article. Dominique Demers. photo · *MD* April 11, 1987: pD1.

Les malheurs de Rosalie ou l'éloge de l'enfance; reviews of children's books. Dominique Demers. *MD* May 2, 1987: pD3.

Littérature jeunesse; reviews of children's books. Dominique Demers. *MD* Nov 21, 1987: pD6.

Baby of the family gets respect raising flock of Canada geese; reviews of children's books. Janice Kennedy. *MG* Oct 3, 1987: J13.

Un sapristi de bon livre; review of [I]Les Catastrophes de Rosalie. Claire-Lise Malarte. *Can Child Lit* 1987; No 48: p102–104.

ANGÉLINE DE MONTBRUN/Novel by Laure Conan

Laure Conan and Madame de La Fayette: rewriting the female plot; article. Mary Jean Green. *Essays on Can Writ* Spring 1987; No 34: p50–63.
[FEMINIST WRITING AND CRITICISM; WOMEN WRITERS]

THE ANGER IN ERNEST AND ERNESTINE/Play by Robert Morgan et al

Ernest and Ernestine are funny and familiar; theatre review of *The Anger of Ernest and Ernestine*. Liam Lacey. photo · *G&M* May 28, 1987: pD6.

Well-wrought Anger comedy marred only by false-note finale; theatre review of *The Anger in Ernest and Ernestine*. Henry Mietkiewicz. photo · *TS* May 29, 1987: pE12.

ANGERS, FÉLICIT

See **CONAN, LAURE (pseud.)**

ANGERS, FRANÇOIS-RÉAL

Tout texte fondateur en cache un autre!; reviews of *Les Révélations du crime* and *L'Influence d'un livre*. Patrick Imbert. *Lettres québec* Autumn 1987; No 47: p58–60.

ANI CROCHE/Children's novel by Bertrand Gauthier

Plus adulte que les adultes; review of *Ani Croche*. Marie Naudin. *Can Child Lit* 1987; No 45: p61–62.

ANIMAL STORIES

[Untitled]; reviews of poetry books. Shaunt Basmajian. *Cross Can Writ Q* 1987; Vol 9 No 3–4: p44,49.
[ANTHOLOGIES: BOOK REVIEWS]

"The old kinship of earth": science, man and nature in the animal stories of Charles G.D. Roberts; article. Thomas R. Dunlap. abstract · *J of Can Studies* Spring 1987; Vol 22 No 1: p104–120.

THE ANIMALS WITHIN/Poems by David Day

Crimes of the heart; reviews of *Gothic* and *The Animals Within*. Al Purdy. *Books in Can* April 1987; Vol 16 No 3: p32,34.

ANNE HÉBERT: ARCHITEXTURE ROMANESQUE/ Critical work by Janet M. Paterson

[Untitled]; review of *Anne Hébert: architexture romanesque*. Mary Jean Green. *Amer R of Can Studies* Spring 1987; Vol 17 No 1: p115–116.

[Untitled]; review of *Anne Hébert: architexture romanesque*. Jean Marmier. *Études can* June 1987; No 22: p133–134.

THE ANNE OF GREEN GABLES STORYBOOK/Novel adaptation by Fiona McHugh

Gammer Gurton leaps from early English stage into the 20th century; reviews of children's books. Janice Kennedy. *MG* Nov 21, 1987: J13.

Literary lions linger in libraries; reviews of children's books. Joan McGrath. *TS* Dec 20, 1987: pE5.

A quality spin-off; review of *The Anne of Green Gables Storybook*. Linda Pearse. *Atlan Prov Book R* Nov-Dec 1987; Vol 14 No 4: p4.

ANNE OF GREEN GABLES/ANNE...LA MAISON AUX PIGNONS VERTS/Novel by Lucy Maud Montgomery

Disney to show Anne sequel seven months before Canada; article. *WFP* Feb 14, 1987: p23.
[TELEVISION AND CANADIAN LITERATURE]

U.S. to see Anne sequel first; article. *CH* Feb 15, 1987: pE3.
[TELEVISION AND CANADIAN LITERATURE]

CBS wins 5 Peabody awards; article. *G&M* April 28, 1987: pC9.
[TELEVISION AND CANADIAN LITERATURE]

Anne pockets Peabody award; article. *TS* April 26, 1987: pC7.
[TELEVISION AND CANADIAN LITERATURE]

'Green Gables' wins award; article. *MG* April 28, 1987: pA14.

U.S. critics rave over Anne of Green Gables sequel; article. photo · *MG* May 26, 1987: pD10.
[INTERNATIONAL REVIEWS OF CANADIAN LITERATURE; TELEVISION AND CANADIAN LITERATURE]

Green Gables sequel a winner; article. *MG* Oct 7, 1987: H1.
[TELEVISION AND CANADIAN LITERATURE]

Anne a U.S. favorite; article. *WFP* Oct 7, 1987: p41.
[TELEVISION AND CANADIAN LITERATURE]

Anne of Green Gables — the Sequel; television review. Jim Bawden. photo · *TS* Dec 5, 1987: pF1,F12.
[TELEVISION AND CANADIAN LITERATURE]

Anne II: Canadians' love affair resumes; article. Mike Boone. photo · *MG* Dec 4, 1987: pC1.
[TELEVISION AND CANADIAN LITERATURE]

Brilliantly crafted Green Gables sequel Follows naturally; television review. Mike Boone. *MG* Dec 4, 1987: pC8.
[TELEVISION AND CANADIAN LITERATURE]

Anne to be adapted for ballet; article. Donald Campbell. *WFP* Nov 26, 1987: p83.

Dans les poches; reviews. Guy Ferland. *MD* Sept 26, 1987: pD6.

Anne's secret quality keeps her coming back; column. Robert Fulford. *TS* Dec 5, 1987: pF1.
[TELEVISION AND CANADIAN LITERATURE]

Anne of Green Gables in translation; review of *Anne...la Maison aux pignons verts*. Martine Jacquot. *Atlan Prov Book R* Feb-March 1987; Vol 14 No 1: p13.

Anne of Green Gables grows up; article. Brian D. Johnson. Barbara MacAndrew. photo · *Maclean's* Dec 7, 1987; Vol 100 No 49: p46–48,50.
[TELEVISION AND CANADIAN LITERATURE]

Anne's back home, safe and sound; theatre review of *Anne of Green Gables*. Deirdre Kelly. photo · *G&M* June 29, 1987: pC9.
[DRAMATIC ADAPTATIONS OF CANADIAN LITERATURE]

Gammer Gurton leaps from early English stage into the 20th century; reviews of children's books. Janice Kennedy. *MG* Nov 21, 1987: J13.

[Untitled]; review of *Anne...La Maison aux pignons verts*. Eva-Marie Kröler. *Can Lit* Winter 1987; No 115: p290.

Group brings back Anne of Green Gables; article. Muriel Leeper. *TS (Neighbours)* April 7, 1987: p21.
[DRAMATIC ADAPTATIONS OF CANADIAN LITERATURE]

Anne of Green Gables opens with lively spirit; theatre review. Muriel Leeper. *TS (Neighbours)* April 28, 1987: p14.
[DRAMATIC ADAPTATIONS OF CANADIAN LITERATURE]

Literary lions linger in libraries; reviews of children's books. Joan McGrath. *TS* Dec 20, 1987: pE5.

Anne of Green Gables bland as porridge; theatre review. Randal McIlroy. *WFP* Dec 20, 1987: p20.
[DRAMATIC ADAPTATIONS OF CANADIAN LITERATURE]

A quality spin-off; review of *The Anne of Green Gables Storybook*. Linda Pearse. *Atlan Prov Book R* Nov-Dec 1987; Vol 14 No 4: p4.

Asimov robotics . . . orchestral overtures . . . marvellous Munsch; reviews of tape versions of children's books. Richard Perry. photo · *Quill & Quire (Books for Young People)* Aug 1987; Vol 53 No 8: p10.
[AUDIO-VISUALS AND CANADIAN LITERATURE]

Book world: will they leave the boss' book on sale?; column. Beverley Slopen. *TS* Nov 1, 1987: H6.
[TRANSLATIONS OF CANADIAN LITERATURE]

Anne, ma soeur Anne . . . ; review of *Anne . . . la maison aux pignons verts.* Danielle Thaler. *Can Child Lit* 1987; No 46: p72–73

F-words at Green Gables; article. Ann Thurlow. photo · *Maclean's* July 13, 1987; Vol 100 No 28: p49.
[DRAMATIC ADAPTATIONS OF CANADIAN LITERATURE; FESTIVALS, DRAMA]

ANNOTATIONS, SHORT REVIEWS, BOOK LISTS

Zeitschriftenschau; annotated list of periodicals. *Zeitschrift Kanada-Studien* 1987; Vol 7 No 1: p277–281.

Notable books of the year; survey article. *NYT Book R* Dec 6, 1987: p54,56,60,62,66,70,72.

New books; list of recent publications. *J of Can Studies* Winter 1987–88; Vol 22 No 4: p168–170.

Choice of 1987: fiction out front in 10 of the 'best'; reviews. Ken Adachi. photo · *TS* Dec 5, 1987: M6.

Too much of a good thing is wonderful; reviews of children's books. Sid Adilman. illus · *TS* Dec 5, 1987: M4.

Getting ready for the Calgary Olympics; reviews of children's books. Sid Adilman. *TS* Dec 5, 1987: M10.

L'interrogation totale de la mort; reviews of poetry books. André Brochu. *Voix et images* Autumn 1987; Vol 13 No 1: p165–174.
[CANADIAN LITERARY PERIODICALS]

Listings; annotations. Ann Cotterell. *British J of Can Studies* June 1987; Vol 2 No 1: p191–193.

Experts recommend books for children; column. Joan Craven. *CH (Neighbors)* Aug 26, 1987: pA4.

Perfect time to buy child a favorite book; column. Joan Craven. *CH (Neighbors)* Nov 25, 1987: pA12.

Notable paperbacks; checklist. George Johnson. Patricia T. O'Conner. *NYT Book R* Dec 6, 1987: p90–93.

Getting a head start on Christmas; reviews of children's books. Janice Kennedy. *MG* Dec 12, 1987: I12.

Current Canadian studies; column. Victor A. Konrad. *Amer R of Can Studies* Autumn 1987; Vol 17 No 3: p360–366.
[CANADIAN LITERARY PERIODICALS]

Current Canadian studies; column. Victor A. Konrad. *Amer R of Can Studies* Winter 1987–88; Vol 17 No 4: p464–469.

Revue des revues; annotated list of periodicals. Jean-Michel Lacroix. *Études can* June 1987; No 22: p141–175.

Parutions récentes; list of recent publications. Pierre Lavoie. *Jeu* 1987; No 44: p219–221.

L'effet science-fiction tous azimuts: la SF québécoise en 1986–1987; reviews of science fiction books and periodicals. Michel Lord. *Voix et images* Autumn 1987; Vol 13 No 1: p180–189.
[ANTHOLOGIES: BOOK REVIEWS; CANADIAN LITERARY PERIODICALS; FIRST NOVELS: BOOK REVIEWS]

Poetry to stuff into a stocking; reviews of poetry books. Mark Lowey. photo · *CH* Dec 13, 1987: pC8.

Ingenuity needed to encourage kids to read; article. Sharon E. McKay. *TS (Neighbors)* Dec 8, 1987: p21.

Of fantasies and those magical visits; reviews of science fiction and fantasy books. Henry Mietkiewicz. *TS* Dec 5, 1987: M19.

Les derniéres feuilles de l'été; reviews. Jean Royer. photo · *MD* Oct 3, 1987: pD3.

Ways of escape; reviews of children's books. Mary Ainslie Smith. *Books in Can* Dec 1987; Vol 16 No 9: p11–14.

A checked list of the very best; reviews of children's books. Tim Wynne-Jones. *G&M* Dec 12, 1987: pE1.E4.

Joys for young readers; reviews of children's books. Pamela Young. *Maclean's* Dec 7, 1987; Vol 100 No 49: p54,56.

ANOTHER COUNTRY: WRITINGS BY AND ABOUT HENRY KREISEL/Compilation

[Untitled]; reviews of *Robert Kroetsch* and *Another Country.* Russell Brown. *U of Toronto Q* Fall 1987; Vol 57 No 1: p161–166.

[Untitled]; review of *Another Country.* Peter Halewood. *Rubicon* Spring 1987; No 8: p218–219.

[Untitled]; review of *Another Country.* F.L. Radford. *World Lit in Eng* Spring 1987; Vol 27 No 1: p60–62.

Humane vision; review of *Another Country.* Frank W. Watt. *Can Lit* Winter 1987; No 115: p202–203.

The triumphant exile; review of *Another Country.* George Woodcock. *Essays on Can Writ* Winter 1987; No 35: p82–87.

ANOTHER MORNING/Play by Steve Petch

Typical folks tell powerful internment story; theatre review of *Another Morning.* Stephen Godfrey. photo · *G&M* April 24, 1987: pC5.

ANOTHER SEASON'S PROMISE/Play by Anne Chislett and Keith Roulston

[Another Season's Promise]; theatre review. Susan Minsos. *NeWest R* Dec 1987; Vol 13 No 4: p17.

ANTHOLOGIES: BOOK REVIEWS

[Untitled]; review of *The Atlantic Anthology, Volume Two: Poetry. Quarry* Winter 1987; Vol 36 No 1: p135–137.

Sommaires; reviews. *Lettres québec* Winter 1986–87; No 44: p87.

Quebec nurses its surrealists; review of *Intimate Strangers.* Ken Adachi. photo · *TS* June 13, 1987: M4.

[Untitled]; review of *Wordseed.* Rod Anderson. *Poetry Can R* Spring 1987; Vol 8 No 2–3: p50.

SF for survival; review of *Tesseracts*. Douglas Barbour. *Can Lit* Spring 1987; No 112: p141–143

[Untitled]; review of *Relations*. Ellie Barton. *Quarry* Fall 1987; Vol 36 No 4: p86–87.

[Untitled]; reviews of *Squid Inc. 86* and *The Buda Books Poetry Series*. Shaunt Basmajian. *Cross Can Writ Q* 1987; Vol 9 No 3–4: p43.

Choisir la poésie: une tentative mitigée; review of *Choisir la poésie*. Caroline Bayard. *Lettres québec* Spring 1987; No 45: p42–43.

The review review; review of *The Anthology Anthology*. Donna Bennett. *Essays on Can Writ* Spring 1987; No 34: p119–126.

South African journalist finds a tragic answer to question of apartheid; reviews of *Intimate Strangers* and *After the Fact*. Barbara Black. *MG* Feb 7, 1987: pB9.

Au rayon de la nouvelle: l'écriture sur commande; reviews of *Qui a peur de? . . .* and *L'Aventure, la mésaventure*. Jean-Roch Boivin. photo · *MD* Dec 24, 1987: pC11.

Stories painful and fresh; review of *The Old Dance*. Patricia Bradbury. *Quill & Quire* Jan 1987; Vol 53 No 1: p28.

Age and the masters of short fiction; review of *Night Light*. Pauline Carey. *G&M* Jan 10, 1987: pE14.

In the name of the Mother; review of *SP/ELLES*. Barbara Carey. *Books in Can* Jan-Feb 1987; Vol 16 No 1: p20–21.

[Untitled]; review of *Night Light*. Barbara Carey. *Quill & Quire* Jan 1987; Vol 53 No 1: p26–27.

[Untitled]; reviews. Anne Cimon. *Cross Can Writ Q* 1987; Vol 9 No 3–4: p47–48.

Embracing the wilderness; reviews of *The Oxford Book of Canadian Short Stories in English* and *Bluebeard's Egg*. John Clute. *Times Lit Supp* June 12, 1987; No 4393: p626.

De l'ouest, des nouvelles et de l'histoire; reviews of short story books. Paulette Collet. photo · *Lettres québec* Summer 1987; No 46: p68–70.

[Untitled]; review of *Five from the Fringe*. L.W. Conolly. *World Lit in Eng* Spring 1987; Vol 27 No 1: p56–58.

[Untitled]; review of *All the Bright Company*. L.W. Conolly. *Can Drama* 1987; Vol 13 No 2: p231–233.

Une anthologie d'auteurs canadiens traduits en allemand; review of *Erkundungen, 26 kanadische Erzähler*. Diane-Monique Daviau. *Lettres québec* Summer 1987; No 46: p72–73.

Van lit; reviews of *Vancouver: Soul of a City* and *Vancouver Poetry*. Margaret Doyle. *Can Lit* Winter 1987; No 115: p188–190.

[Untitled]; review of *Wordseed*. Margaret Drage. *Cross Can Writ Q* 1987; Vol 9 No 2: p22.

A megalomania for radio drama; reviews of *All the Bright Company* and *Image in the Mind*. Bronwyn Drainie. photo · *G&M* Nov 28, 1987: pC19.

[Untitled]; review of *The Old Dance*. Mark Duncan. *Border Cross* Spring 1987; Vol 6 No 2: p29–30.

[Untitled]; review of *SP/ELLES*. Paul Dutton. *Quill & Quire* Feb 1987; Vol 53 No 2: p20.

Looking beyond the landscape; review of *Heading Out*. E.F. Dyck. *Books in Can* April 1987; Vol 16 No 3: p34.

Blewointment: rites of passage; review of *The Last Blewointment Anthology: Volume One*. Len Early. *Essays on Can Writ* Winter 1987; No 35: p178–181.

Disappearing solitudes; review of *Invisible Fictions*. Michael Estok. *Atlan Prov Book R* Sept-Oct 1987; Vol 14 No 3: p12.

To make a short story long; review of *On Middle Ground*. Cary Fagan. *Books in Can* Aug-Sept 1987; Vol 16 No 6: p19–20.

Quebec fiction writers dwell in realm of dreams, madness, surrealism; review of *Invisible Fictions*. Trevor Ferguson. *MG* July 18, 1987: J9.

La vitrine du livre; reviews of *Poètes québécois contemporains* and *Comparaison et raison*. Guy Ferland. *MD* Oct 10, 1987: pD4.

La vitrine du livre; reviews. Guy Ferland. *MD* Nov 14, 1987: pD16.

La vitrine du livre; reviews of *Le Québec en poésie* and *L'Aventure, la mésaventure*. Guy Ferland. *MD* Nov 28, 1987: pD11.

Destinations; reviews of *Essential Words* and *Voix-Off*. Marya Fiamengo. *Can Lit* Spring 1987; No 112: p112–114.

Skin deep; review of *Other Voices*. Ray Filip. *Books in Can* Oct 1987; Vol 16 No 7: p28–29.

Food for thought and literature; review of *The CanLit Foodbook*. William French. *G&M* Nov 14, 1987: pE3.

High performance; review of *87: Best Canadian Stories*. William French. *G&M* Dec 19, 1987: pC21.

Du réel à l'imaginaire; review of *Planéria*. René Gagné. *Can Child Lit* 1987; No 47: p94–95.

Des regards qui s'attardent; review of *Plages*. Chantal Gamache. *MD* April 4, 1987: pD3.

"Un bless qui se sauve"; review of *Le Pouvoir des mots, les maux du pouvoir*. Chantal Gamache. *Lettres québec* Winter 1986–87; No 44: p83.

Des contes et des nouvelles pour rêver; reviews of short story books. Dominique Garand. *Voix et images* Spring 1987; Vol 12 No 3: p551–555.

Gender aside, a strong collection of stories by Canadian women; review of *More Stories by Canadian Women*. Keith Garebian. *TS* Oct 31, 1987: M11.

Native dramas; review of *The Land Called Morning*. Thomas Gerry. *Can Child Lit* 1987; No 46: p97–98.

College guide leaves no term unstoned; review of *All the Bright Company*. Lew Gloin. *TS* Sept 13, 1987: pA22.

From Ahmadabad to Tennessee; reviews of *86: Best Canadian Stories* and *Coming Attractions 4*. Wayne Grady. *Books in Can* March 1987; Vol 16 No 2: p29–30.

Collection highlights neglected genre; review of *On Middle Ground*. G.P. Greenwood. *CH* Oct 4, 1987: pE6.

Cultural heritage; review of *Pieces of the Jigsaw Puzzle*. Regine Haensel. *Prairie Fire* Autumn 1987; Vol 8 No 3: p120–122.

[Untitled]; review of *Coming Attractions 5*. Janet Hamilton. *Quill & Quire* Dec 1987; Vol 53 No 12: p22.

Canada's short fiction shortchanged here; reviews of *87: Best Canadian Stories* and *Coming Attractions 5*. Geoff Hancock. *TS* Dec 27, 1987: pE19.

[Untitled]; review of *Vancouver Poetry*. Glenn Hayes. *Poetry Can R* Fall 1987; Vol 9 No 1: p36–37.

Today's assignment: short fiction that's worth a long look; reviews of short story books. Douglas Hill. *G&M* March 14, 1987: pE19.

A wealth of provocative and inspiring literary criticism; reviews. Douglas Hill. *G&M* Sept 5, 1987: pC13.

Relevant writing; reviews of *Private and Fictional Words* and *More Stories by Canadian Women*. Ann Holloway. *G&M* Nov 28, 1987: pC22.

Flaws, good work mark collections; reviews of *The Sliding-back Hills* and *Heading Out*. Mark Jarman. *CH* April 26, 1987: pE5.

A delightful anthology; review of *Prairie Jungle*. Ronnie Kennedy. *Can Child Lit* 1987; No 45: p57–58.

Strength from Quebec; review of *Intimate Strangers*. H.J. Kirchhoff. photo · *G&M* Jan 31, 1987: pE18.

Experiments and flat yarns; review of *Pure Fiction*. H.J. Kirchhoff. *G&M* Jan 17, 1987: pE18.

Varied and valuable; review of *Pure Fiction*. Hilda Kirkwood. *Waves* Spring 1987; Vol 15 No 4: p76–77.

[Untitled]; review of *Intimate Strangers*. Brent Ledger. *Quill & Quire* Feb 1987; Vol 53 No 2: p17.

[Untitled]; review of *Alberta Bound*. Brent Ledger. *Quill & Quire* April 1987; Vol 53 No 4: p27–28.

Story anthologies: the tried, the true, and the best of the new; reviews of short story anthologies. Brent Ledger. photo · *Quill & Quire* Jan 1987; Vol 53 No 1: p29.

L'effet science-fiction tous azimuts: la SF québécoise en 1986–1987; reviews of science fiction books and periodicals. Michel Lord. *Voix et images* Autumn 1987; Vol 13 No 1: p180–189.
[ANNOTATIONS, SHORT REVIEWS, BOOK LISTS; CANADIAN LITERARY PERIODICALS; FIRST NOVELS: BOOK REVIEWS]

Entre la réussite et l'échec; reviews of science fiction books. Michel Lord. photo · *Lettres québec* Autumn 1987; No 47: p33–34.
[FIRST NOVELS: BOOK REVIEWS]

The allure of Alberta in history and contemporary life; review of *The Best of Alberta*. Charles Mandel. photo · *Quill & Quire* Dec 1987; Vol 53 No 12: p27.

A change of climate; review of *A Shapely Fire*. Alberto Manguel. *Books in Can* Nov 1987; Vol 16 No 8: p33–34.

Best picks of feminism; review of *Fireworks*. Ruth Manson. *G&M* May 2, 1987: pC18.

Anthology samples Prairie writing; review of *The Old Dance*. Dave Margoshes. *CH* Feb 22, 1987: pE6.

A different kind of Quebec; review of *Invisible Fictions*. Dave Margoshes. *G&M* July 18, 1987: pC15.

[Untitled]; review of *Dancing Visions*. Allan Markin. *Poetry Can R* Spring 1987; Vol 8 No 2–3: p60.

[Untitled]; review of *Acadian Poetry Now/Poésie acadienne contemporaine*. Tom Marshall. *Poetry Can R* Spring 1987; Vol 8 No 2–3: p48–49.

Thrills and chills: hints for Hallowe'en reading; reviews of children's books. Joan McGrath. illus · *Quill & Quire (Books for Young People)* Oct 1987; Vol 53 No 10: p8.

Quebec's literary lights shed old traditions; review of *Intimate Strangers*. Michael Mirolla. *CH* March 8, 1987: pE5.

[Untitled]; review of *Alberta Bound*. Michael Mirolla. *Dandelion* Fall-Winter 1987; Vol 14 No 2: p143–145.

Stories by Quebec writers cover magical terrain; review of *Invisible Fictions*. Michael Mirolla. *CH* Oct 25, 1987: pE5.

Making connections; review of *More Stories by Canadian Women*. W.H. New. *Books in Can* Oct 1987; Vol 16 No 7: p31–32.

Dramatic fringe; reviews of *Five from the Fringe* and *Politics and the Playwright: George Ryga*. James Noonan. *Can Lit* Winter 1987; No 115: p235–238.

[Untitled]; review of *On Middle Ground*. Carolellen Norskey. *Quill & Quire* Sept 1987; Vol 53 No 9: p78.

Children of the world; review of *Intimate Strangers*. I.M. Owen. *Books in Can* Jan-Feb 1987; Vol 16 No 1: p17–18.

[Untitled]; review of *Sextet*. Malcolm Page. *Theatre Hist in Can (special issue)* Spring 1987; Vol 8 No 1: p129–133.

[Untitled]; reviews. Andrew Parkin. *Poetry Can R* Summer 1987; Vol 8 No 4: p36–37.
[CANADIAN LITERARY PERIODICALS]

[Untitled]; reviews of poetry books. Andrew Parkin. *Poetry Can R* Fall 1987; Vol 9 No 1: p37.

Lively collection; review of *Alberta Bound*. John Parr. *TS* June 7, 1987: pG11.

[Five from the Fringe]; review. Don Perkins. *NeWest R* April 1987; Vol 12 No 8: p18.

Fiction for children: history and mystery; reviews of *Rats in the Sloop* and *Shivers in Your Nightshirt*. Dorothy Perkyns. *Atlan Prov Book R* Feb-March 1987; Vol 14 No 1: p14.

The Wife of Bath today — games of love; review of *The Old Dance*. Alex Pett. *Event* March 1987; Vol 16 No 1: p100–102.

Short fiction is thriving; review of *86: Best Canadian Stories*. Jamie Portman. *CH* Jan 18, 1987: pE4.

[Untitled]; reviews. Lisbie Rae. *Can Drama* 1987; Vol 13 No 2: p229–231.

Beyond the Fringe; reviews of plays. Judith Rudakoff. *Books in Can* March 1987; Vol 16 No 2: p18.

The spoiled broth; review of *Coming Attractions 5*. Jason Sherman. *G&M* Nov 14, 1987: pE5.

A mixed bag of short stories; reviews of short story anthologies. Norman Sigurdson. *WFP* Feb 28, 1987: p54.

[Untitled]; review of *Other Voices*. Winston Smith. *Rubicon* Fall 1987; No 9: p160–163.

[Untitled]; reviews of poetry books. Douglas Smith. *Poetry Can R* Spring 1987; Vol 8 No 2–3: p39–40.

[Heading Out]; review. Peter Stoicheff. *NeWest R* Sept 1987; Vol 13 No 1: p17.

Vancouver mind; reviews of *Vancouver Short Stories* and *Vancouver Fiction*. David Stouck. *Can Lit* Spring 1987; No 112: p157–159.

Minding their Poes and cues; review of *Invisible Fictions*. Paul Stuewe. *Books in Can* Aug-Sept 1987; Vol 16 No 6: p24.

Male myths, obliterated lesbians and powerful dreams; reviews of poetry books. Fraser Sutherland. photo · *G&M* Feb 14, 1987: pE19.

Umbrellas for a torrent of Canadian poems; reviews of poetry anthologies. Fraser Sutherland. *G&M* March 28, 1987: pE19.

Poetry and the loving Spanish tongue; reviews of poetry books. Fraser Sutherland. *G&M* May 30, 1987: pC21.

Trois voyages — petit, moyen et grand — du littératage à la littérature; reviews of short story books. Marie José Thériault. photo · *Lettres québec* Spring 1987; No 45: p30–32.

La recherche de l'amour. review of *Aimer*. Adrien Thério. *Lettres québec* Winter 1986–87; No 44: p79.

[Untitled]; review of *All the Bright Company*. Martin Townsend. *Quill & Quire* June 1987; Vol 53 No 6: p31.

Finding fantasy in a Québécois anthology; review of *Invisible Fictions*. Martin Townsend. *Quill & Quire* Aug 1987; Vol 53 No 8: p32.

[Untitled]; review of *The Creative Circus Book*. Ron Turner. *Quarry* Spring 1987; Vol 36 No 2: p113–116.

Work works well; review of *Shop Talk*. Andrew Vaisius. *Waves* Winter 1987; Vol 15 No 3: p81–84.

[Untitled]; review of *Trace*. Andrew Vaisius. *Poetry Can R* Fall 1987; Vol 9 No 1: p33.

[Untitled]; review of *New Works I*. Lynne van Luven. *Can Theatre R* Winter 1987; No 53: p81–82.

The family business; reviews of *What Feathers Are For* and *Squid Inc 86*. Kim Van Vliet. *Waves* Spring 1987; Vol 15 No 4: p88–91.

Sins of omission; review of *The Oxford Book of Canadian Short Stories in English*. Allan Weiss. *Books in Can* Jan-Feb 1987; Vol 16 No 1: p21–22.

[Untitled]; review of *The Northern Red Oak*. Bruce Whiteman. *Books in Can* Oct 1987; Vol 16 No 7: p26.

A stocking stuffer anthology; review of *Seaweed in Your Stocking*. Carol Anne Wien. *Can Child Lit* 1987; No 47: p92–93.

[Untitled]; reviews of *Heading Out* and *Relations: Family Portraits*. Janet Windeler. *Cross Can Writ Q* 1987; Vol 9 No 3–4: p42–43.

[Untitled]; review of *Vancouver Poetry*. Elizabeth Woods. *Malahat R (special issue)* March 1987; No 78: p158–159.

Atlantic heritage; review of *The Atlantic Anthology, Volume Two*. Alan R. Young. *Can Lit* Spring 1987; No 112: p148.

THE ANTHOLOGY ANTHOLOGY/Anthology of radio broadcasts

The review review; review of *The Anthology Anthology*. Donna Bennett. *Essays on Can Writ* Spring 1987; No 34: p119–126.
[ANTHOLOGIES: BOOK REVIEWS]

ANYONE CAN SEE I LOVE YOU/Poems by Marilyn Bowering

[Untitled]; review of *Anyone Can See I Love You*. Phil Hall. *Books in Can* Aug-Sept 1987; Vol 16 No 6: p27–28.

[Untitled]; reviews of poetry books. Stephen Scobie. *Malahat R* Dec 1987; No 81: p104–106.

The impersonation of the irresistible; reviews of poetry books. Fraser Sutherland. *G&M* Sept 5, 1987: pC15.

ANYTIME STORIES/Children's stories by Leo Sawicki

Native heritage is displayed in three timely books; reviews of children's books. Janice Kennedy. *MG* April 4, 1987: H11.

THE APOCALYPSE

Apocalyptic imaginations: notes on Atwood's The Handmaid's Tale and Findley's Not Wanted on the Voyage; article. W.J. Keith. *Essays on Can Writ* Winter 1987; No 35: p123–134.
[BIBLICAL MYTHS AND MYTHOLOGY; GOD IN LITERATURE; SATIRIC WRITING]

APPARENCE/Poems by Jacques Boulerice

Des échappées de lumière . . . ; review of *Apparence*. Jean-François Dowd. *MD* April 28, 1987: p17.

Jacques Boulerice: pour une autre enfance; reviews of *Apparence* and *Distance*. Jean Royer. *MD* Feb 14, 1987: pC3.

APPIGNANESI, RICHARD

Confusion as high art; review of *Italia Perversa*. Joel Yanofsky. photo · *MG* Aug 8, 1987: J2.

THE APPRENTICESHIP OF DUDDY KRAVITZ/Novel by Mordecai Richler

Duddy revised; article. *WFP* April 23, 1987: p44.
[DRAMATIC ADAPTATIONS OF CANADIAN LITERATURE]

A revised Duddy to open in U.S.; article. *G&M* April 23, 1987: pC3.
[DRAMATIC ADAPTATIONS OF CANADIAN LITERATURE]

Mixed reviews for Duddy as musical breathes anew; article. photo · *G&M* Sept 30, 1987: pC7.
[DRAMATIC ADAPTATIONS OF CANADIAN LITERATURE; INTERNATIONAL REVIEWS OF CANADIAN LITERATURE]

Philadelphia gives resurrection of Richler's Duddy Kravitz mixed reviews; article. *WFP* Oct 2, 1987: p24.
[DRAMATIC ADAPTATIONS OF CANADIAN LITERATURE; INTERNATIONAL REVIEWS OF CANADIAN LITERATURE]

People; column. Marsha Boulton. *Maclean's* Aug 10, 1987; Vol 100 No 32: p43.
[DRAMATIC ADAPTATIONS OF CANADIAN LITERATURE]

Theatre notes; column. Brian Brennan. *CH* May 11, 1987: pC6.
[DRAMATIC ADAPTATIONS OF CANADIAN LITERATURE; WRITERS' WORKSHOPS]

The Philadelphia experiment: a disaster in Canada, Duddy tries again in U.S.; article. Lucinda Chodan. photo · *MG* Sept 29, 1987: pB5.
[DRAMATIC ADAPTATIONS OF CANADIAN LITERATURE]

Tammy saw cats on wings; column. Doreen Martens. *WFP* Aug 12, 1987: p21.
[DRAMATIC ADAPTATIONS OF CANADIAN LITERATURE]

Miami Vice's Don Johnson a Stowe-away in resort town; column. Thomas Schnurmacher. *MG* Jan 21, 1987: pF6.
[DRAMATIC ADAPTATIONS OF CANADIAN LITERATURE]

Star Trek's Capt. Kirk beaming up to Montreal; column. Thomas Schnurmacher. *MG* Aug 11, 1987: pC8.
[DRAMATIC ADAPTATIONS OF CANADIAN LITERATURE]

APRÈS L'ÉDEN/Short stories by Marcel Godin

Des contes et des nouvelles pour rêver; reviews of short story books. Dominique Garand. *Voix et images* Spring 1987; Vol 12 No 3: p551–555.
[ANTHOLOGIES: BOOK REVIEWS]

Trois voyages — petit, moyen et grand — du littératage à la littérature; reviews of short story books. Marie José Thériault. photo · *Lettres québec* Spring 1987; No 45: p30–32.
[ANTHOLOGIES: BOOK REVIEWS]

APRIL RAINTREE/Novel by Beatrice Culleton

[Untitled]; reviews of *Rough Passage* and *April Raintree*. Judith Russell. *Queen's Q* Spring 1987; Vol 94 No 1: p191–193.

APRIL, JEAN-PIERRE

Aaa! Aâh! Ha! que de belles catastrophes narratives!; reviews. Michel Lord. photo · *Lettres québec* Spring 1987; No 45: p32–35.

AQUIN, HUBERT

Hubert Aquin: un héros extérieur à nous mêmes; column. Jean Êthier-Blais. photo · *MD* March 14, 1987: pD5.

Prochain épisode: notes de re-cherche; article. Alexandre Amprimoz. *Studies in Can Lit* 1987; Vol 12 No 1: p129–145.

Current Canadian studies; column. Victor A. Konrad. *Amer R of Can Studies* Autumn 1987; Vol 17 No 3: p360–366.
[ANNOTATIONS, SHORT REVIEWS, CANADIAN LITERARY PERIODICALS]

[Untitled]; review of *Hubert Aquin ou la quête interrompue*. Janet M. Paterson. *U of Toronto Q* Fall 1987; Vol 57 No 1: p182–183.

Woman as object, women as subjects, & the consequences for narrative: Hubert Aquin's Neige noire and the impasse of post-modernism; article. Patricia Smart. *Can Lit* Summer-Fall 1987; No 113–114: p168–178.
[FEMINIST WRITING AND CRITICISM; POSTMODERNIST WRITING AND CRITICISM]

AN ARBITRARY DICTIONARY/Poems by John Pass

Something in common; reviews of poetry books. Cary Fagan. *Prairie Fire* Spring 1987; Vol 8 No 1: p83–87.

ARCADE/Periodical

La vitrine du livre; reviews. Jean Royer. photo · *MD* March 28, 1987: pD2.
[CANADIAN LITERARY PERIODICALS]

ARCHAMBAULT, GILLES

Le malin plaisir de déplaire; review of *L'Obsèdante obèse*. Réjean Beaudoin. *Liberté* Oct 1987; Vol 29 No 5: p161–162.

Gilles Archambault et l'art de la sourdine; review of *L'Obsèdante obèse et autres agressions*. Jean-Roch Boivin. photo · *MD* June 20, 1987: pD3.

Introspection; review of *Standing Flight*. Pauline Carey. *G&M* Jan 31, 1987: pE18.

[Untitled]; reviews of *Standing Flight* and *The Legacy*. Cary Fagan. *Cross Can Writ Q* 1987; Vol 9 No 2: p24–25.

La vitrine du livre; reviews. Guy Ferland. *MD* May 23, 1987: pD4.

Two Quebec novels in translation; reviews of *Standing Flight* and *The Legacy*. Theresia Quigley. *Fiddlehead* Summer 1987; No 152: p95–98.

Recent Canadian fiction; reviews of novels. D.O. Spettigue. *Queen's Q* Summer 1987; Vol 94 No 2: p366–375.
[FIRST NOVELS: BOOK REVIEWS]

Un livre pour tester la conscience; review of *L'Obsèdante obèse*. Marie José Thériault. photo · *Lettres québec* Autumn 1987; No 47: p30–31.

ARCHIBALD LAMPMAN/Critical work by L.R. Early

[Untitled]; reviews of *Archibald Lampman* and *John Metcalf*. Dennis Duffy. *Eng Studies in Can* Sept 1987; Vol 13 No 3: p355–357.

Poet-confessor; review of *Archibald Lampman*. John Ower. *Can Lit* Winter 1987; No 115: p167–169.

ARGUIN, MAURICE

La fiction de nos devanciers; reviews of *Le Roman québécois de 1944 1965* and *Un Roman du regard*. Agnès Whitfield. photo · *Lettres québec* Winter 1986–87; No 44: p56–58.

ARIA/Play by Tomson Highway

Uneven but energetic look at life as a native woman; theatre review of *Aria*. Ray Conlogue. *G&M* March 12, 1987: pC7.

Like a chameleon Kliest breathes life into Aria's women; theatre review of *Aria*. Robert Crew. photo · *TS* March 6, 1987: pD11.

ARMA VIRUMQUE CANO/Poems by Wayne Ray

[Untitled]; reviews of poetry books. Elizabeth Woods. *Poetry Can R* Spring 1987; Vol 8 No 2–3: p49.

AN ARMADILLO IS NOT A PILLOW/Children's poems by Lois Simmie

Sam McGee leads the way in showing the potential of poetry; reviews of children's poetry books. Janice Kennedy. *MG* March 7, 1987: H10.

Two sensitive poets; reviews of *Some Talk Magic* and *An Armadillo Is Not a Pillow*. Sylvia Middlebro'. Tom Middlebro'. *Can Child Lit* 1987; No 46: p99–100.

Funny books are a joy to find; reviews of *An Armadillo Is Not a Pillow* and *Tales of a Gambling Grandma*. Helen Norrie. *WFP* Feb 14, 1987: p60.

Wit, enjoyment and urgency; reviews of children's poetry books. Tim Wynne-Jones. *G&M* Feb 7, 1987: pE19.

ARMSTRONG, JEANNETTE C.

Intense tale; review of *Slash*. M.T. Kelly. *G&M* June 6, 1987: pC19.

ARNASON, DAVID

Nouvelles du centre; article. Michel Fabre. *Afram* June 1987; No 25: p1–2

Washing Machine give hilarious twist to technophobia tale; television review. Doreen Martens. photo · *WFP* March 21, 1987: p25.
[TELEVISION AND CANADIAN LITERATURE]

Poets exhibit vast differences; reviews of *Flicker and Hawk* and *Skrag*. Robert Quickenden. *WFP* May 16, 1987: p70.

Local playwright wins literary tripleheader; article. Barbara Robson. photo · *WFP* Feb 25, 1987: p34.

Play takes comic look at fear of mortality; theatre review of *Dewline*. Reg Skene. *WFP* Feb 27, 1987: p33.

From ivy-covered professors; reviews of poetry books. Fraser Sutherland. *G&M* Oct 17, 1987: pE9.

ARNETT, TOM

Tom Arnett: portrait of a pro; biographical article. Heather Kirk. photo · *Cross Can Writ Q* 1987; Vol 9 No 2: p14–15,30.

ARRIVALS: CANADIAN POETRY IN THE EIGHTIES/ Poetry anthology

Umbrellas for a torrent of Canadian poems; reviews of poetry anthologies. Fraser Sutherland. *G&M* March 28, 1987: pE19.
[ANTHOLOGIES: BOOK REVIEWS]

ARRIVING AT NIGHT/Poems by Christopher Levenson

[Untitled]; review of *Arriving at Night*. Philip Kokotailo. *U of Windsor R* Spring-Summer 1987; Vol 20 No 2: p90–92.

[Untitled]; reviews of poetry books. Stephen Morrissey. *Poetry Can R* Fall 1987; Vol 9 No 1: p32.

ART DEAD: THE PREMATURE DEATH OF ART IN OUR TIME (A REVIEW)/Play by Daniel Libman

Flashes of gold among the dross at Fringe festival; theatre reviews. Liam Lacey. *G&M* Aug 19, 1987: pC5.
[FESTIVALS, DRAMA]

THE ART OF ALICE MUNRO: SAYING THE UNSAY-ABLE/Critical essays collection

[Untitled]; reviews of *Probable Fictions* and *The Art of Alice Munro*. Winnifred M. Bogaards. *Eng Studies in Can* March 1987; Vol 13 No 1: p115–119.

Conferring Munro; review of *The Art of Alice Munro*. Robert Thacker. *Essays on Can Writ* Spring 1987; No 34: p162–169.

THE ART OF DARKNESS/Poems by David McFadden

The dying generations; reviews of poetry books. Dermot McCarthy. *Essays on Can Writ* Spring 1987; No 34: p24–32.

ARTHUR DE BUSSIÈRES, POÈTE, ET L'ÉCOLE LITTÉ-RAIRE DE MONTRÉAL/Critical work by Wilfrid Paquin

[Untitled]; review of *Arthur de Bussières, poète, et l'École litté-raire de Montréal*. David M. Hayne. *U of Toronto Q* Fall 1987; Vol 57 No 1: p178–179.

ARTICHOKE/Play by Joanna McClelland Glass

Piggery kicks off '87 seasons with warm and witty winner; theatre review of *Artichoke*. Marianne Ackerman. *MG* June 29, 1987: pD9.

[Untitled]; theatre review of *Artichoke*. Marianne Ackerman. *MG* July 3, 1987: pC10.

Credit Valley's Artichoke has lots of heart; theatre review. Lynn Moore. photo · *TS (Neighbours)* Feb 24, 1987: p16.

ARTIST FIGURE

George, Leda, and a poured concrete balcony: a study of three aspects of the evolution of Lady Oracle; article. Carol L. Beran. *Can Lit* Spring 1987; No 112: p18–28.

The descent into hell of Jacques Laruelle: chapter I of Under The Volcano; article. David Falk. *Can Lit* Spring 1987; No 112: p72–83.
[CONFESSIONAL WRITING]

Shape shifters: Canadian women novelists challenge tradi-tion; article. Linda Hutcheon. illus · *Can Forum* Jan 1987; Vol 66 No 765: p26–32.
[FEMINIST WRITING AND CRITICISM; STRUCTURALIST WRITING AND CRITICISM; WOMEN WRITERS]

Sailing the oceans of the world; article. Lorna Irvine. *New Q* Spring-Summer 1987; Vol 7 No 1–2: p284–293.
[FEMINIST WRITING AND CRITICISM; WOMEN IN LITERATURE]

The writer-as-a-young-woman and her family: Montgom-ery's Emily; article. Judith Miller. *New Q* Spring-Summer 1987; Vol 7 No 1–2: p301–319.
[THE FAMILY IN CANADIAN LITERATURE; WOMEN IN LITERATURE]

The Bell Jar and Mrs. Blood: portraits of the artist as divided woman; article. Elizabeth Potvin. abstract · *Atlantis* Fall 1987; Vol 13 No 1: p38–46.
[FEMINIST WRITING AND CRITICISM; WOMEN IN LITERATURE]

Between the world and the word: John Metcalf's "The Teeth of My Father"; article. Constance Rooke. *New Q* Spring-Sum-mer 1987; Vol 7 No 1–2: p240–246.
[THE FAMILY IN CANADIAN LITERATURE; METAFICTION]

AS BIRDS BRING FORTH THE SUN/Short stories by Alistair MacLeod

[Untitled]; reviews of short story collections. David Helwig. *Queen's Q* Winter 1987; Vol 94 No 4: p1022–1024.

ASHBOURN/Poems by John Reibetanz

[Untitled]; review of *Ashbourn*. Thomas Dilworth. *U of Wind-sor R* Spring-Summer 1987; Vol 20 No 2: p88–90.

[Untitled]; review of *Ashbourn*. Jeffery Donaldson. *Rubicon* Fall 1987; No 9: p169–170.

[Untitled]; review of *Ashbourn*. Gideon Forman. *Books in Can* June-July 1987; Vol 16 No 5: p24

ASHES, ASHES, ALL FALL DOWN/Novel by Zdena Sali-vavora

Small regional presses as saviors of cultural information; reviews of fictional works. Douglas Hill. *G&M* Oct 10, 1987: pC21.
[FIRST NOVELS: BOOK REVIEWS]

ASKA, WARABÉ

Mini-reviews; reviews of children's books. Margaret Paré. *Can Child Lit* 1987; No 45: p93–96.

ASTRALES JACHÈRES/Poems by Daniel Dargis

[Untitled]; review of *Astrales jachères*. Hugues Corriveau. *Estuaire* Summer 1987; No 45: p51–52.

AT THE EDGE OF CLEAR CARVING/Poems by Heather Lee Crosby

[Untitled]; reviews of poetry books. Shaunt Basmajian. *Cross Can Writ Q* 1987; Vol 9 No 3–4: p44,49.
[ANTHOLOGIES: BOOK REVIEWS]

ATHERTON, FRANCIS X.

Lively story of immigrants needs a sequel; review of *Tuppence Ha'penny Is a Nickel*. Joan McGrath. *TS* Aug 30, 1987: pA19.

Fine writing about a tale worth telling; review of *Tuppence Ha'penny Is a Nickel*. Thomas S. Woods. *G&M* Sept 12, 1987: pC19.

THE ATLANTIC ANTHOLOGY/Anthology

[Untitled]; review of *The Atlantic Anthology, Volume Two: Poetry*. *Quarry* Winter 1987; Vol 36 No 1: p135–137.
[ANTHOLOGIES: BOOK REVIEWS]

[Untitled]; review of *The Atlantic Anthology*. John Ferns. *British J of Can Studies* June 1987; Vol 2 No 1: p184–185.
[ANTHOLOGIES: BOOK REVIEWS]

Atlantic heritage; review of *The Atlantic Anthology, Volume Two*. Alan R. Young. *Can Lit* Spring 1987; No 112: p148.
[ANTHOLOGIES: BOOK REVIEWS]

ATLANTIC PROVINCES DRAMA

Atlantic theatre: a review article. Richard Paul Knowles. *J of Can Studies* Spring 1987; Vol 22 No 1: p135–140.

ATLANTIC PROVINCES LITERATURE: BIBLIOGRAPHY

Atlantic soundings: a checklist of recent literary publications of Atlantic Canada. *Fiddlehead* Spring 1987; No 151: p97–106.

ATLANTIC PROVINCES WRITING AND WRITERS

Personal fallacy be damned!; column. Harry Bruce. *Atlan Insight* Dec 1987; Vol 9 No 12: p16.

The price of rights: the role of the literary agent; article. Hamish Cameron. photo · *Quill & Quire* April 1987; Vol 53 No 4: p4–5.

Recent Atlantic poetry: a survey: 1980–1985: III New Brunswick summary; article. Michael Thorpe. bibliog · *Antigonish R* Winter 1987; No 68: p133–148.

ATTERRISSAGE FORCÉ/Children's novel by Joceline Sanschagrin

Les malheurs de Rosalie ou l'éloge de l'enfance; reviews of children's books. Dominique Demers. *MD* May 2, 1987: pD3.

ATWOOD, MARGARET

Atwood novel nominated for prize; article. *G&M* Feb 25, 1987: pC7.

Atwood novel up for Paris prize; article. *TS* Feb 25, 1987: pF1.
[AWARDS, LITERARY]

Atwood among Ms. women of the year; article. photo · *WFP* Jan 14, 1987: p41.

Prix Hemingway: Margaret Atwood en nomination; article. *MD* Feb 24, 1987: p7.
[AWARDS, LITERARY]

Atwood novel cited for honor; article. *CH* Feb 26, 1987: pF13.
[AWARDS, LITERARY]

With pen in hand and p.c. in closet; article. illus · *G&M (Toronto Magazine)* Jan 1987; Vol 1 No 10: p9.

Atwood serving up food book; article. *WFP* April 16, 1987: p39.

Atwood blasts park 'ransom'; article. *CH* June 21, 1987: pC7.

Ritz literary prize goes to U.S. author; article. *G&M* April 7, 1987: pC7.
[AWARDS, LITERARY]

L'Américain Peter Taylor remporte le prix littéraire Ritz-Hemingway; article. *MD* April 7, 1987: p12.
[AWARDS, LITERARY]

American beats Atwood for Hemingway prize; article. *TS* April 7, 1987: pB1.
[AWARDS, LITERARY]

Margaret Atwood loses Commonwealth prize; article. *TS* Dec 2, 1987: pB1.
[AWARDS, LITERARY]

Jamaican writer upsets Atwood to capture prize; article. *MG* Dec 2, 1987: H2.
[AWARDS, LITERARY]

Let the voters decide on deal for free trade Atwood urges; article. *TS* Nov 4, 1987: pA4.
[CULTURAL IDENTITY]

Atwood suffers upset; article. *WFP* Dec 2, 1987: p49.
[AWARDS, LITERARY]

Free-trade assurances fail to set Atwood's mind at ease; article. *CH* Nov 5, 1987: pF7.
[CULTURAL IDENTITY]

Atwood serves up anthology; article. *CH* Dec 2, 1987: pC4.

Margaret Atwood's new anthology food for thought; column. Ken Adachi. photo · *TS* April 13, 1987: pB1.

Atwood anthology ranges from tart to tangy; article. Julian Armstrong. illus · *MG* Nov 11, 1987: pE2.

Fine script moves Heaven On Earth right to heart; television review. Jim Bawden. photo · *TS* Feb 28, 1987: pF1

Atwood at the cottage; column. Jim Bawden. *TS* April 2, 1987: pG2.

[TELEVISION AND CANADIAN LITERATURE]

Atwood offers rich Canadian perspective; letter to the editor. Blair Bell. *Fin Post* Nov 30, 1987: p15.

George, Leda, and a poured concrete balcony: a study of three aspects of the evolution of Lady Oracle; article. Carol L. Beran. *Can Lit* Spring 1987; No 112: p18–28.

[ARTIST FIGURE]

Heaven On Earth: TV drama at its best; television review. Mike Boone. *MG* Feb 27, 1987: pC7.

A Swiftian sermon; review of *The Handmaid's Tale*. Ildikó de Papp Carrington. *Essays on Can Writ* Spring 1987; No 34: p127–132.

Embracing the wilderness; reviews of *The Oxford Book of Canadian Short Stories in English* and *Bluebeard's Egg*. John Clute. *Times Lit Supp* June 12, 1987; No 4393: p626.

[ANTHOLOGIES: BOOK REVIEWS]

People; column. Yvonne Cox. *Maclean's* Nov 16, 1987; Vol 100 No 46: p64.

Troupe's translation of Atwood promises more than it delivers; review of dance based on *Murder in the Dark*. Michael Crabb. *TS* June 7, 1987: pG2.

[Untitled]; review of *Autobiographical and Biographical Writing in the Commonwealth*. Héliane Daziron. *Afram* Jan 1987; No 24: p75.

Library doors closed as porn bill ridiculed; article. Donn Downey. photo · *G&M* Dec 11, 1987: pD18.

[CENSORSHIP]

Bright lights of the city; article. Harriet Eisenkraft and Ned Boone. photo · *Tor Life* May 1987; Vol 21 No 7: p54–58,78, 80–81,83.

[Untitled]; review of *The Handmaid's Tale*. Michel Fabre. *Études can* June 1987; No 22: p136–138.

[Untitled]; review of *The Handmaid's Tale*. Michel Fabre. *Afram* Jan 1987; No 24: p54–56.

New award celebrates Commonwealth writers; column. William French. photo · *G&M* Nov 17, 1987: pD7.

[AWARDS, LITERARY; WRITERS-IN-RESIDENCE]

[Untitled]; letter to the editor. Dan Gawthrop. *G&M* Nov 21, 1987: pD7.

Telling it over again: Atwood's art of parody; article. Barbara Godard. *Can Poet* Fall-Winter 1987; No 21: p1–30.

[FEMINIST WRITING AND CRITICISM; MYTHS AND LEGENDS IN CANADIAN LITERATURE; STRUCTURALIST WRITING AND CRITICISM]

Of headlines, AIDS causes, Lindbergh, and Atwood; article. Rod Goodman. *TS* May 2, 1987: pB2.

Atwood displays talent for fiction; letter to the editor. Patrick Gough. *G&M* Nov 21, 1987: pD7.

On Atwood; essay. David Halliday. *Waves* Spring 1987; Vol 15 No 4: p51–54.

Film stars stage celebrity bashes; column. Dave Haynes. *WFP* June 19, 1987: p21.

[INTERNATIONAL REVIEWS OF CANADIAN LITERATURE]

The religious roots of the feminine identity issue: Margaret Laurence's The Stone Angel and Margaret Atwood's Surfacing; article. Evelyn J. Hinz. abstract · *J of Can Studies* Spring 1987; Vol 22 No 1: p17–31.

[BIBLICAL MYTHS AND MYTHOLOGY; FEMINIST WRITING AND CRITICISM; GOD IN LITERATURE]

[Untitled]; letter to the editor. A. Trevor Hodge. *G&M* Nov 21, 1987: pD7.

Atwood urges stop to plans for road in wilderness area; article. David Israelson. *TS* Feb 17, 1987: pC14.

Atwood, Newman taped for Yule; article. Frank Jones. photo · *TS* Nov 21, 1987: M6.

[AUDIO-VISUALS AND CANADIAN LITERATURE]

Apocalyptic imaginations: notes on Atwood's The Handmaid's Tale and Findley's Not Wanted on the Voyage; article. W.J. Keith. *Essays on Can Writ* Winter 1987; No 35: p123–134.

[THE APOCALYPSE; BIBLICAL MYTHS AND MYTHOLOGY; GOD IN LITERATURE; SATIRIC WRITING]

Margaret Atwood's The Handmaid's Tale and the dystopian tradition; article. Amin Malak. *Can Lit* Spring 1987; No 112: p9–16.

[UTOPIA/DYSTOPIA]

CanLit's queen gets one cold shoulder from U.S.; article. Richard Marin. illus · *MG* Jan 31, 1987: pB7.

[INTERNATIONAL REVIEWS OF CANADIAN LITERATURE]

[Untitled]; review of *Selected Poems II*. Tom Marshall. *Poetry Can R* Spring 1987; Vol 8 No 2–3: p40.

[Untitled]; letter to the editor. Don McCutchan. *G&M* Nov 20, 1987: pA6.

Author deserves a fair hearing; letter to the editor. Alec McEwen. photo · *Fin Post* Nov 23, 1987: p19.

Poets help celebrate Dandelion; column. Kenneth McGoogan. *CH* June 28, 1987: pF8.

[AWARDS, LITERARY; CANADIAN LITERARY PERIODICALS; POETRY READINGS; WRITERS' ORGANIZATIONS]

Recipes, poetry, prose a tasty concoction; article. Diane Menzies. photo · *TS* Dec 2, 1987: pC1,C9.

Foodbook combines recipes, dash of prose; article. Diane Menzies. photo · *WFP* Nov 18, 1987: p38.

Writer from Jamaica wins literary award; article. Karen Morch. *G&M* Dec 2, 1987: pC6.

[AWARDS, LITERARY]

Atwood not disappointed at losing Commonwealth Prize; article. Karen Morch. photo · *CH* Dec 3, 1987: pF3.

[AWARDS, LITERARY]

[Untitled]; review of *La Servante écarlate*. Marc Morin. *MD* Nov 28, 1987: pD8.

Otherworlds; editorial. W.H. New. *Can Lit* Winter 1987; No 115: p3–6

Food and power: Homer, Carroll, Atwood and others; article. Mervyn Nicholson. *Mosaic* Summer 1987; Vol 20 No 3: p37–55.

[MYTHS AND LEGENDS IN CANADIAN LITERATURE]

New & noteworthy; review of *The Handmaid's Tale*. Patricia T. O'Connor. photo · *NYT Book R* Feb 8, 1987: p38.

Atwood keeps high profile among Québécois readers; article. Francine Pelletier. photo · *MG* May 26, 1987: pD9.

Innovation and athletic interpretation mingle in Dutch treatment of Atwood; review of dance based on *Murder in the Dark*. Lisa Rochon. *G&M* June 8, 1987: pC10.

An Atwood anatomy; review of *Margaret Atwood: A Feminist Poetics*. Jerome H. Rosenberg. *Essays on Can Writ* Winter 1987; No 35: p88–92.

"Pourquoi tous les adultes ne sont-ils pas des artistes?"; article. Jean Royer. photo · *MD* June 20, 1987: pD1,D8.

[Untitled]; letter to the editor. John S. Scharf. *G&M* Nov 30, 1987: pA6.

The re/membering of the female power in Lady Oracle; article. Roberta Sciff-Zamaro. *Can Lit* Spring 1987; No 112: p32–38.
[FEMINIST WRITING AND CRITICISM; MYTHS AND LEGENDS IN CANADIAN LITERATURE]

Work like Atwood's to endure; letter to the editor. Karen Shook. *MG* Feb 23, 1987: pB2.

Book world: Clarkson brings pool of goodwill to M&S job; column. Beverley Slopen. *TS* March 15, 1987: pA22.
[AWARDS, LITERARY; PUBLISHING AND PUBLISHERS IN CANADA]

No fear of castration; letter to the editor. C.J. Sullivan. *G&M* Nov 20, 1987: pA6.

Prize writer; article. Ellen Vanstone. photo · *Tor Life* March 1987; Vol 21 No 4: p10–11.
[AWARDS, LITERARY]

[Untitled]; letter to the editor. David A. West. *G&M* Nov 21, 1987: pD7.

Victims of a bleak universe; reviews of poetry books. Bruce Whiteman. *Books in Can* Jan-Feb 1987; Vol 16 No 1: p22–23.

Atwood's questions; letter to the editor. Rolf Woodgold. *G&M* Nov 17, 1987: pA6.

Veterans give proteges a $5,000 career boost; article. Reta Zekas. photo · *TS* May 7, 1987: pD1.
[AWARDS, LITERARY]

AU COEUR DE L'INSTANT/Poems by Célyne Fortin

[Untitled]; review of *Au coeur de l'instant*. Hélène Thibaux. *Estuaire* Winter 1986–87; No 43: p76.

AU MILIEU, LA MONTAGNE/Novel by Roger Viau

Radiographie urbaine; review of *Au milieu, la montagne*. Jean-François Chassay. photo · *MD* Oct 24, 1987: pD3.

Dans les poches; reviews. Guy Ferland. *MD* Sept 26, 1987: pD6.

Le prolétariat montréalais cras; review of *Au milieu la montagne*. Patrick Imbert. photo · *Lettres québec* Winter 1986–87; No 44: p63–64.

AU PAYS DES GOUTTES/Children's story by Madeleine Gagnon

Rêverie sur l'eau; review of *Au pays des gouttes*. Jurate Kaminskas. *Can Child Lit* 1987; No 47: p75–76.

AU SEPTIÈME CIEL/Play by Jean Daigle

Theatre encore; reviews of *L'Ours et le kangourou* and *Au septième ciel*. Carrol F. Coates. *Can Lit* Winter 1987; No 115: p255–257.

AU TEMPS DE LA PRAIRIE/Play by Marcien Ferland

Riel play aims to right wrongs; article. Kevin Prokosh. photo · *WFP* March 5, 1987: p36.

AUBERT, ROSEMARY

Nurturing a romantic spirit; article. Virginia Corner. illus photo · *TS* July 6, 1987: pC1.

AUBRY, SUZANNE

Masques, personnages et personnes; reviews of plays. André-G. Bourassa. photo · *Lettres québec* Summer 1987; No 46: p51–52.

Night of Little Knives aims its barbs at cults; theatre review of *La Nuit des p'tits couteaux*. Matthew Fraser. photo · *G&M* Jan 19, 1987: pC9.

Aubry play superb theatre; theatre review of *La Nuit des p'tits couteaux*. Wayne Grigsby. *MG* Jan 16, 1987: pD2.

AUDE

Deux livres pour partir en voyage; reviews of *Mourir comme un chat* and *Banc de Brume*. Marie José Thériault. photo · *Lettres québec* Autumn 1987; No 47: p31–32.

AUDET, NOEL

Dans les poches; reviews of paperback books. Guy Ferland. *MD* Oct 31, 1987: pD6.

AUDIO-VISUALS AND CANADIAN LITERATURE

Film tribute to Margaret Laurence; article. *TS* Jan 13, 1987: pB1.

Billboard: Christian women's club plans lunch program; column. *WFP* March 8, 1987: p12.

Films to be shown at Laurence tribute; article. *G&M* Jan 20, 1987: pD9.

Book Bits expanding; article. *Quill & Quire* June 1987; Vol 53 No 6: p24.

Free premiere set for Firewords; article. *TS* April 12, 1987: pC6.

Poésie québécoise sur cassettes; article. photo · *MD* Oct 27, 1987: p13.

Saturday Night film dispiriting; column. Ken Adachi. photo · *TS* Sept 7, 1987: pB2.
[CANADIAN LITERARY PERIODICALS]

Books offer children world of adventure; reviews. Joan Craven. *CH (Neighbors)* April 1, 1987: pA7.

La poésie québécoise dénaturée dans la capitale française; essay. Jean-François Doré. *MD* Dec 5, 1987: pC2.
[FRANCE-CANADA LITERARY RELATIONS]

Une littérature qui flatte l'oreille; article. Jean-François Doré. *MD* Dec 10, 1987: p13.

Fiction, women writers preferred by readers, survey finds; column. William French. photo · *G&M* April 28, 1987: pC5.
[AUTHORS, CANADIAN]

Poetry videos trying to tap youth market; column. Peter Goddard. photo · *TS* Jan 21, 1987: pD3.

The ears have it: audio cassettes selling soundly in stores; article. Gord Graham. photo · *Quill & Quire* April 1987; Vol 53 No 4: p6,8.

A fox shows off its cunning; review of tape version of *The Red Fox*. Frank Jones. *TS* Sept 26, 1987: M4.

Atwood, Newman taped for Yule; article. Frank Jones. photo · *TS* Nov 21, 1987: M6.

Second début; article. Françoise Lafleur. photo · *MD* Nov 14, 1987: pD11.

À l'écoute de la poésie d'ici; article. Françoise Lafleur. *MD* Dec 19, 1987: pD10.

Les arts de la scène à l'heure de l'expérimentation vidéographique; article. Christian Langlois and Diane Pavlovic. photo · *Jeu* 1987; No 44: p126–132.

De bien belles rencontres chez Hermès; article. Marie Laurier. photo · *MD* Dec 31, 1987: pC9–C10.
[AUTHORS, CANADIAN; BOOK TRADE IN CANADA]

Scarborough publisher banking on audio books; article. Alex Law. photo · *TS (Neighbors)* Sept 22, 1987: p6.

Culture director's tribute to author captured sentiment; column. Kenneth McGoogan. photo · *CH* Jan 27, 1987: pB6.
[POETRY READINGS]

Firm has an ear for kids' books; article. Kenneth McGoogan. *CH* Feb 17, 1987: pC7.
[CHILDREN'S LITERATURE]

Winkler catches Layton on film; article. Paul McKie. photo · *WFP* Feb 27, 1987: p33.

Le réel théâtral et le réel médiatique; essay. Serge Ouaknine. photo · *Jeu* 1987; No 44: p94–111.

La scène peuplée d'écrans; introduction. Diane Pavlovic. photo · *Jeu* 1987; No 44: p91–92

L'être et le paraître: une question du XVIIe siècle posée aujourd'hui; article. Diane Pavlovic. photo · *Jeu* 1987; No 44: p154–168.
[POSTMODERNIST WRITING AND CRITICISM]

Pair of thrillers . . . giving the Devil his due . . . sci-fi fare; review of tape version of *The Red Fox*. Richard Perry. photo · *Quill & Quire* Aug 1987; Vol 53 No 8: p38.

Asimov robotics . . . orchestral overtures . . . marvellous Munsch; reviews of tape versions of children's books. Richard Perry. photo · *Quill & Quire (Books for Young People)* Aug 1987; Vol 53 No 8: p10.

Revolting teddies . . . time-travelling tot . . . rhymes macabre; reviews of tape versions of *The Olden Days Coat* and *Auntie's Knitting a Baby*. Richard Perry. photo · *Quill & Quire (Books for Young People)* Oct 1987; Vol 53 No 10: p14

Et le Verbe s'est fait oreille; article about La Littérature de l'oreille. Jean Royer. photo · *MD* Sept 11, 1987: p13.

La vie littéraire; column. Jean Royer. photo · *MD* Sept 26, 1987: pD2.
[CONFERENCES, LITERARY; INTERNATIONAL WRITERS' ORGANIZATIONS; PUBLISHING AND PUBLISHERS IN CANADA; WRITERS' ORGANIZATION]

Book world: anti-Khomeini plotter's story told in new book; column. Beverley Slopen. *TS* Sept 6, 1987: pA18.
[AUTHORS, CANADIAN; CANADIAN LITERARY PERIODICALS]

AUGUST NIGHTS/Short stories by Hugh Hood

[Untitled]; review of *August Nights*. Thomas Gerry. *Rubicon* Spring 1987; No 8: p208–210.

[Untitled]; reviews of *August Nights* and *Jokes for the Apocalypse*. Lesley McAllister. *Cross Can Writ Q* 1987; Vol 9 No 2: p24.

AUNTIE'S KNITTING A BABY/Children's poems by Lois Simmie

Revolting teddies . . . time-travelling tot . . . rhymes macabre; reviews of tape versions of *The Olden Days Coat* and *Auntie's Knitting a Baby*. Richard Perry. photo · *Quill & Quire (Books for Young People)* Oct 1987; Vol 53 No 10: p14

AUSTRALIA-CANADA LITERARY RELATIONS

Australian receives $3,000 literary prize; article. *G&M* April 14, 1987: pC7.
[AWARDS, LITERARY]

Prix du Conseil des arts; article. Jean Royer. *MD* April 25, 1987: pD3.
[AWARDS, LITERARY]

AUTHORS, CANADIAN

Authors seek stories about military, politics, literature; article. *TS* Feb 13, 1987: pD21.

New faces; survey article. photo · *TS* March 7, 1987: K1-K4.

Writer's writers; article. photo · *Books in Can* Jan-Feb 1987; Vol 16 No 1: p8–11.

Party with a writer; article. *WFP* May 2, 1987: p31.

Advice and dissent; article. illus · *Books in Can* May 1987; Vol 16 No 4: p12–14.

Levesque dines with Trudeau to aid CanLit; article. *TS* Sept 20, 1987: pG8.

Ottawa needs poetic justice; editorial. *MG* Sept 10, 1987: pB2.

Old foes together for dinner; article. photo · *MG* Sept 18, 1987: pC1.

Deux nouveaux guides au service des artistes; article. *MD* July 8, 1987: p15.

La Société des écrivains proteste contre la nomination d'un troisième poète lauréat anglophone à Ottawa; article. *MD* Sept 9, 1987: p14.
[WRITERS' ORGANIZATIONS]

Literary dinners put baseball on hold; article. *WFP* Aug 28, 1987: p31.

Political enemies to dine for literature; article. *CH* Sept 19, 1987: pD6.

CBA '87: business plans, business tax, business books, and a 35th birthday bash; schedule of events. photo · *Quill & Quire* July 1987; Vol 53 No 7: p26.
[BOOK TRADE IN CANADA]

Literary dinner a national affair; article. *Quill & Quire* Sept 1987; Vol 53 No 9: p70.

Trudeau, Levesque celebrate Canlit; article. *G&M* Sept 19, 1987: pC10.

Writers to read at fund-raiser; article. *TS* Oct 26, 1987: pD6.

Pierre and René trade 'punches'; article. *MG* Oct 31, 1987: pA3.

Bookstyles of the famous; article. *MG* Dec 5, 1987: J2.

Le droit d'auteur en feuillets; article. *MD* Oct 3, 1987: pD2.
[COPYRIGHT]

Artists blast officials over tax reform; article. *WFP* Oct 2, 1987: p21.
[WRITERS' ORGANIZATIONS]

Literary Dinner cancelled; article. *CH* Oct 20, 1987: pC11.

M & S speaks out against free trade; article. *G&M* Nov 6, 1987: pD4.

Making a list and checking it twice: Q&Q asks people in the children's book world what they're giving their young friends for Christmas; article. photo · *Quill & Quire (Books for Young People)* Dec 1987; Vol 53 No 12: p11.

Literary feasts raise cash; article. *Fin Post* Oct 26, 1987: p21.

Authors, booksellers angry over sale plan; article. Ken Adachi. *TS* Feb 12, 1987: pF4.
[BOOK TRADE IN CANADA]

Frye in good position to take Governor-General's prize; column. Ken Adachi. photo · *TS* April 30, 1987: H1.
[GOVERNOR GENERAL'S AWARDS]

Everything's coming up roses for busy Canadian publishers; article. Ken Adachi. photo · *TS* Sept 22, 1987: pC2.
[PUBLISHING AND PUBLISHERS IN CANADA]

Authors ham it up on TV special; column. Ken Adachi. photo · *TS* Oct 12, 1987: pB5.
[TELEVISION AND CANADIAN LITERATURE]

Writers in prison benefit from gala; column. Ken Adachi. photo · *TS* Nov 9, 1987: pC1.

Year in books had a familiar ring; survey article. Ken Adachi. photo · *TS* Dec 27, 1987: pE19.

Authors outraged by fire sale prices; article. John Allemang. *G&M* Feb 13, 1987: pC11.
[BOOK TRADE IN CANADA]

No lack of food for thought; article. John Allemang. photo · *G&M* Oct 29, 1987: pD3.

Literary language turns inflammatory at glossy benefit dinner; article. Nick Auf der Maur. *MG* Nov 9, 1987: pA2.

Recipes to dispel bad taste of food in Canadian fiction; article. Elizabeth Baird. *TS* Nov 25, 1987: pC6.

Writers for dinner; article. Julia Bennett. photo · *Maclean's* Dec 7, 1987; Vol 100 No 49: S1.

Sex Tips to open Lunchbox season; article. Brian Brennan. *CH* Aug 8, 1987: pF2.

Making the rights move: why publishers are paying so much more; article. Hamish Cameron. photo · *Quill & Quire* March 1987; Vol 53 No 3: p8,10.
[AGENTS, LITERARY; PUBLISHING AND PUBLISHERS IN CANADA]

CBA '87; article. Hamish Cameron. photo · *Quill & Quire* Sept 1987; Vol 53 No 9: p6,10,12.
[BOOK TRADE IN CANADA]

Arts crowd feels chill: cultural community lines up against pact; article. Donald Campbell. *WFP* Dec 19, 1987: p44.
[CULTURAL IDENTITY]

London dinner honors authors from Canada; column. Zena Cherry. *G&M* Jan 22, 1987: pA17.

'Great literary dinner' attracts 17 authors; column. Zena Cherry. *G&M* Oct 29, 1987: pA20.

Hostess fumes over no-shows; article about the Great Literary Dinner Party. Rod Currie. photo · *G&M* Aug 28, 1987: pD10.

Literary celebrities featured on menu; article. Rosie DiManno. *TS* Sept 25, 1987: pE28.

Poetic licence: yes, you can discuss literature and bend an elbow here; essay. Judith Fitzgerald. illus · *TS* Aug 9, 1987: pA21.

[Untitled]; letter to the editor. Kathleen Flaherty. *TS* Nov 27, 1987: pD11.

Short stories dwell on death and dying; letter to the editor. Alexander Forint. *TS* July 14, 1987: pA12.

Canadian authors spend spare time reading each other; article. William French. photo · *G&M* Feb 17, 1987: pC7.

Fiction, women writers preferred by readers, survey finds; column. William French. photo · *G&M* April 28, 1987: pC5.
[AUDIO-VISUALS AND CANADIAN LITERATURE]

U.S. school bans use of Farley Mowat book; column. William French. *G&M* May 12, 1987: pC7.
[CENSORSHIP]

Promotion ordeal inspires Berton to do even more; column. William French. *G&M* Sept 15, 1987: pA21.
[WRITERS' ORGANIZATIONS]

Day the book world changed forever; column. Robert Fulford. *TS* Aug 1, 1987: M7.

[Untitled]; letter to the editor. Susan Halpin. *TS* Nov 27, 1987: pD11.

Writers rank high in Chinese society; article. Dorris Heffron. photo · *Quill & Quire* Nov 1987; Vol 53 No 11: p11.
[CHINA-CANADA LITERARY RELATIONS]

'Great Literary Dinner Party' proceeds start trickling out to deserving writers; article. Heather Hill. *MG* May 30, 1987: J8.

Celebs help publishing house launch fall season; article. Heather Hill. *MG* Aug 28, 1987: pC1.
[PUBLISHING AND PUBLISHERS IN CANADA]

Scarborough authors to sign books; article. Paul Irish. *TS (Neighbours)* April 21, 1987: p13.

Writers revive censorship-pornography debate; article. Liam Lacey. photo · *G&M* June 1, 1987: pC9.
[CENSORSHIP; WOMEN WRITERS; WRITERS' ORGANIZATIONS]

De bien belles rencontres chez Hermès; article. Marie Laurier. photo · *MD* Dec 31, 1987: pC9–C10.
[AUDIO-VISUALS AND CANADIAN LITERATURE; BOOK TRADE IN CANADA]

It's tougher in French, too; article. Katherine Macklem. photo · *MG* Sept 28, 1987: pB9.
[WOMEN WRITERS]

Authors' earnings: account books talk; article. Katherine Macklem. *MG* Sept 28, 1987: pB9.
[WOMEN WRITERS]

The secret sharer; article. Alberto Manguel. illus · *Sat Night* July 1987; Vol 102 No 7: p39–41.
[PUBLISHERS AND PUBLISHING IN CANADA]

Youth writers flourish in Alberta; article. Kenneth McGoogan. photo · *CH* Feb 21, 1987: pG1.
[CHILDREN'S LITERATURE]

Literary extravaganza goes national; column. Kenneth McGoogan. *CH* April 5, 1987: pE5.
[FILM ADAPTATIONS OF CANADIAN LITERATURE; WRITERS' ORGANIZATIONS; WRITERS' WORKSHOPS]

Big day for literary fund-raisers; column. Kenneth McGoogan. *CH* Oct 18, 1987: pC7.

Writers praise Robert Fulford; article. Henry Mietkiewicz. photo · *TS* June 26, 1987: pE25.

Why has the wheel been reinvented so often? I forget; column. Mavor Moore. *G&M* July 11, 1987: pC1.

Arts enrich lives as well as pockets; column. Mavor Moore. *G&M* Aug 15, 1987: pC3.
[WRITERS' ORGANIZATIONS]

Summer-stock circuit rises to new heights in southern Ontario; article. Jamie Portman. photo · *CH* July 7, 1987: pC8.

Young bards suffer image problem; article. Kevin Prokosh. photo · *WFP* Sept 5, 1987: p29–30.

New battle looming over artists' taxes; article. Lisa Rochon. *G&M* Nov 21, 1987: pC6.

L'écriture en prison: à la foix thérapie et création; article about prison writing. Renée Rowan. photo · *MD* March 28, 1987: pD1,D8.

La difficile reconnaissance des gens de lettres; article. Johanne Roy. *MD* May 23, 1987: pD2.
[AWARDS, LITERARY; WRITERS' ORGANIZATIONS]

La vie littéraire; column. Jean Royer. photo · *MD* June 20, 1987: pD2.
[POETRY READINGS; RADIO AND CANADIAN LITERATURE; TELEVISION AND CANADIAN LITERATURE]

Photo de famille; article. Jean Royer. photo · *MD* Sept 28, 1987: p9.
[CANADIAN LITERARY PERIODICALS]

Doubleday clubs leading the way with more Canadian content; article. Diana Shepherd. *Quill & Quire* Nov 1987; Vol 53 No 11: p13.

Book world: Maggie Smith as Judith Hearne?; column. Beverley Slopen. *TS* Jan 25, 1987: pB6.
[FILM ADAPTATIONS OF CANADIAN LITERATURE]

Paperclips: helping U.S. librarians fill their shelves . . . the party animal; column. Beverley Slopen. photo · *Quill & Quire* Feb 1987; Vol 53 No 2: p7.
[PUBLISHING AND PUBLISHERS IN CANADA]

Book world: 'new' terrorists like their perks, author suggests; column. Beverley Slopen. *TS* May 10, 1987: pA22.

Book world: anti-Khomeini plotter's story told in new book; column. Beverley Slopen. *TS* Sept 6, 1987: pA18.
[AUDIO-VISUALS AND CANADIAN LITERATURE; CANADIAN LITERARY PERIODICALS]

Book world: Great Literary Dinner Party takes off; column. Beverley Slopen. photo · *TS* July 19, 1987: pA20.

Book world: a legend in journalism hits gold in life and print; column. Beverley Slopen. *TS* Oct 11, 1987: pA23.

Finding cheer between the lines; article. Dan Smith. photo · *TS* March 21, 1987: M5.

Five drawings at the world poetry festival, Toronto, May 1986. Heather Spears. *Can Lit* Summer-Fall 1987; No 113–114: p109–113.

Dits et faits; column. Adrien Thério. photo · *Lettres québec* Summer 1987; No 46: p6.
[CANADIAN LITERARY PUBLISHING; CONFERENCES, LITERARY; GOVERNMENT GRANTS FOR WRITERS/PUBLISHERS; LIBRARY SERVICES AND CANADIAN LITERATURE]

One-word titles hot among book choices; reviews. David Williamson. *WFP* Dec 10, 1987: p11A

AUTOBIOGRAPHICAL WRITING

See also **CONFESSIONAL WRITING**

Du sommet d'un arbre ou le regard en plongée et en quatre temps; article. Renald Bérubé. *Voix et images* Spring 1987; Vol 12 No 3: p404–415.

In the eye of abjection: Marie Cardinal's The Words to Say It; article. Patricia Elliot. *Mosaic* Fall 1987; Vol 20 No 4: p71–81.

La question des journaux intimes; article. Lise Gauvin. *Études fran* Winter 1987; Vol 22 No 3: p101–115.
[RADIO AND CANADIAN LITERATURE]

Jalons pour une narratologie du journal intime: le statut du récit dans le Journal d'Henriette Dessaulles; article. Pierre Hébert. *Voix et images* Autumn 1987; Vol 13 No 1: p140–156.
[STRUCTURALIST WRITING AND CRITICISM]

Canadian servicemen's memoirs of the Second World War; article. Michael A. Mason. *Mosaic* Fall 1987; Vol 20 No 4: p11–22.
[WAR IN CANADIAN LITERATURE]

AUTOBIOGRAPHIES/Journals by Elizabeth Smart

[Untitled]; review of *Autobiographies*. Patricia Bradbury. *Quill & Quire* Nov 1987; Vol 53 No 11: p27.

AUTOBIOGRAPHY OF OLIVER GOLDSMITH: A CHAPTER IN CANADA'S LITERARY HISTORY/Journals by Oliver Goldsmith

[Untitled]; review of *Autobiography of Oliver Goldsmith*. Maurice Lebel. *Études can* June 1987; No 22: p134–136.

[Untitled]; review of *Autobiography of Oliver Goldsmith*. George Woodcock. *Can Lit* Spring 1987; No 112: p224–225.

AVANT QU'LES AUTRES LE FASSENT/Play by Claude Dorge et al

Franco-Manitoban satire translates sense of deja vu; theatre review of *Avant qu'les autres le fassent*. Philip Clark. *WFP* Oct 17, 1987: p34.

Entertaining; letter to the editor. Richard McCarthy. *WFP* Nov 7, 1987: p7.

Cercle tries for last laugh first; article. Brad Oswald. photo · *WFP* Oct 16, 1987: p33.

AVANT-GARDE WRITING

See POSTMODERNIST WRITING AND CRITICISM

AVEC PLUS OU MOINS DE RIRE/Short stories by Maurice Constantin-Weyer

De l'ouest, des nouvelles et de l'histoire; reviews of short story books. Paulette Collet. photo · *Lettres québec* Summer 1987; No 46: p68–70.
[ANTHOLOGIES: BOOK REVIEWS]

AWARDS, LITERARY

See also GOVERNOR GENERAL'S AWARDS

Calgary playwright honored; article. *G&M* Jan 30, 1987: pD5.

Robertson Davies wins medal of honor; article. *G&M* Feb 11, 1987: pC7.

Atwood novel nominated for prize; article. *G&M* Feb 25, 1987: pC7.

Short list announced for first novel award; article. *G&M* March 12, 1987: pC1.

Nova Scotia writer wins CBC short story contest; article. *TS* Jan 14, 1987: pF2.

Eight playwrights compete for Chalmers Awards; article. *TS* Jan 19, 1987: pD1.

Novelist Hugh MacLennan honored by Princeton University; article. *TS* Jan 21, 1987: pD3.

New York arts club to honor Robertson Davies; article. *TS* Feb 11, 1987: pF1.

Atwood novel up for Paris prize; article. *TS* Feb 25, 1987: pF1.

New York arts club lauds genius of Davies; article. *TS* Feb 26, 1987: pB3.

Five titles short-listed in first novel contest; article. *TS* March 11, 1987: pE1.

London writer wins international award; article. *TS* March 20, 1987: pD21.

Novelist MacLennan winner of prestigious award from Princeton; article. photo · *MG* Jan 20, 1987: pD10.

Keefer wins short story award for the second consecutive year; article. *WFP* Jan 14, 1987: p42.

Author wins medal; article. *WFP* Jan 21, 1987: p32.

Playwright Murrell wins Chalmers award; article. *WFP* Jan 31, 1987: p26.

Davies joins illustrious literary company; article. *WFP* Feb 25, 1987: p36.

Prix Hemingway: Margaret Atwood en nomination; article. *MD* Feb 24, 1987: p7.

Marie-Claire Blais et Yves Berger parmi les finalistes du prix Prince-Rainier-III; article. photo · *MD* March 7, 1987: pB3.

Winning play named; article. *CH* Jan 28, 1987: pD2.

Murrell play wins '86 Chalmers; article. *CH* Jan 30, 1987: pC9.

Calgary playwright nets $1,000 for script; article. *CH* Feb 11, 1987: pF7.

Davies honored; article. *CH* Feb 26, 1987: pF11.

Atwood novel cited for honor; article. *CH* Feb 26, 1987: pF13.

Ontario writer wins children's book award; article. *CH* March 21, 1987: pA20.

Keefer collects literary prize; article. *G&M* Jan 14, 1987: pC7.

Princeton honors Hugh MacLennan; article. *G&M* Jan 21, 1987: pC7.

Editorial: the George Wicken Prize. *Essays on Can Writ* Spring 1987; No 34: p1.
[COMPETITIONS, LITERARY]

CBC radio winners; article. *Quill & Quire* March 1987; Vol 53 No 3: p61.

Windsor writer wins $3,000 in first-novel contest; article. *WFP* April 4, 1987: p28.

Medal finalists picked; article. *WFP* April 8, 1987: p37.

Kinsella wins Leacock medal; article. *WFP* April 25, 1987: p27.

U.S.-born writer wins book award; article. *WFP* April 29, 1987: p41.

Trio named to receive awards from Canadian authors' group; article. photo · *WFP* May 14, 1987: p46.

No winner for Seal; article. *WFP* May 16, 1987: p26.

Winnipegger wins; article. *WFP* May 21, 1987: p48.

Buried On Sunday wins Ellis award; article. *WFP* May 27, 1987: p36.

Two Manitoba authors win awards; article. *WFP* May 30, 1987.

Highway play due in city; article. *WFP* June 26, 1987: p35.

Murrell lauded; article. *CH* May 14, 1987: pC12.

No winner for Seal first novel award; article. *CH* May 17, 1987: pE3.

Town and country; article. photo · *Books in Can* April 1987; Vol 16 No 3: p6–8.
[FIRST NOVELS]

National Arts Club honours Davies; article. *Quill & Quire* April 1987; Vol 53 No 4: p20.

Finalists for 1987 Toronto Book Awards; article. *Quill & Quire* April 1987; Vol 53 No 4: p20.

WHS/BiC award; article. photo · *Quill & Quire* May 1987; Vol 53 No 5: p12.

Egoff prize established; article. *Quill & Quire* June 1987; Vol 53 No 6: p14.

Lunn, Gay, Reid, Poulin garner kids' book awards; article. *Quill & Quire (Books for Young People)* June 1987; Vol 53 No 6: p4.

Kinsella wins Leacock award; article. *Quill & Quire* June 1987; Vol 53 No 6: p24.

Authors honour their best; article. *Quill & Quire* June 1987; Vol 53 No 6: p24.

The people honour Faiers; article. *Quill & Quire* June 1987; Vol 53 No 6: p24.

Crime winners no mystery; article. *Quill & Quire* June 1987; Vol 53 No 6: p26.

Winners of the Floyd S. Chalmers Canadian Play Award/ Winners of the Chalmers Canadian Children's Play Awards. *Can Theatre R* Summer 1987; No 51: p24.

Council award goes to Lunn; article. *G&M* April 30, 1987: pC1.

Three writers at The Globe win awards; article. *G&M* May 4, 1987: pA11.

Sullivan honored for poetry book; article. *G&M* May 9, 1987: pC4.

Lawrence captures $3,000 literary prize; article. *G&M* April 3, 1987: pD9.

Leacock finalists vie for $3,500 awards; article. *G&M* April 7, 1987: pC7.

Ritz literary prize goes to U.S. author; article. *G&M* April 7, 1987: pC7.

Australian receives $3,000 literary prize; article. *G&M* April 14, 1987: pC7.
[AUSTRALIA-CANADA LITERARY RELATIONS]

Kinsella collects the Leacock medal; article. *G&M* April 24, 1987: pC5.

'My year for awards'; article. *G&M* April 25, 1987: pC5.

Hopes and Dreams translate into award; article. *G&M* May 18, 1987: pD9.
[TRANSLATIONS OF CANADIAN LITERATURE]

Guild honors Pollock, van Herk; article. *G&M* May 13, 1987: pC5.

Authors association honors Purdy, Murrell and Foster; article. photo · *G&M* May 14, 1987: pC3.

[Untitled]; article. *G&M* May 16, 1987: pC11.

Crime pays for Arthur winners; article. *G&M* May 23, 1987: pC14.

Council hands out translation prizes; article. *G&M* June 2, 1987: pC7.
[TRANSLATIONS OF CANADIAN LITERATURE]

Booksellers honor Globe editor; article. *G&M* June 30, 1987: pD7.

Tundra publisher wins Orpen award; article. *G&M* June 20, 1987: pC11.
[PUBLISHING AND PUBLISHERS IN CANADA]

Un prix Logidisque pour la sf et le fantastique; article. *MD* April 7, 1987: p11.
[SCIENCE FICTION]

L'Américain Peter Taylor remporte le prix littéraire Ritz-Hemingway; article. *MD* April 7, 1987: p12.

Le Conseil des arts du Canada attribue ses prix de littérature-jeunesse; article. *MD* April 28, 1987: p14.

Jean Éthier-Blais remporte le prix France-Québec 1987; article. *MD* June 12, 1987: p3.

Dits et faits; column. photo · *Lettres québec* Spring 1987; No 45: p6–7.
[PUBLISHING AND PUBLISHERS IN CANADA; TRANSLATIONS OF CANADIAN LITERATURE; WRITERS' ORGANIZATIONS]

Karen Lawrence wins first-novel competition; article. photo · *TS* April 3, 1987: pD22.

American beats Atwood for Hemingway prize; article. *TS* April 7, 1987: pB1.

Authors association boosts children's stories; article. *TS* April 15, 1987: pD1.
[WRITERS' ORGANIZATIONS]

B.C.'s Kinsella wins Leacock humor award; article. *TS* April 24, 1987: pE22.

Literary winners announced; article. *TS* May 13, 1987: pB4.

No 1987 winner for $50,000 award; article. *TS* May 17, 1987: pA16.

Ontario writer wins Canada Council prize; article. *TS* April 28, 1987: pG4.

Crime writers name candidates for awards; article. *TS* May 19, 1987: H1.

Short story contest winners announced next Sunday; article. *TS* June 21, 1987: pA2.

Life of Helen Alone wins novel prize; article. *MG* April 3, 1987: pC2.

Gazette feature writer wins national award; article. *MG* May 4, 1987: pA2.

Hopes and Dreams wins Glassco prize; article. *MG* May 11, 1987: pB4.

Canadian Authors Association leaves fiction prize unawarded; article. photo · *MG* May 15, 1987: pD8.

The Mikado nominated for 7 Dora Mavor Moore awards; article. *MG* May 28, 1987: pC5.

Awards for children's literature in Canada/Prix de littérature jeunesse au Canada; list of awards. *Can Child Lit* 1987; No 47: P4.

Round table: responses, notes and queries; column. *Can Child Lit* 1987; No 47: p102–103.
[LIBRARY SERVICES AND CANADIAN LITERATURE; WRITERS' ORGANIZATIONS]

Prix et distinctions; list of award winners. photo · *Lettres québec* Summer 1987; No 46: p7.

Editor French wins president's award; article. *MG* July 2, 1987: pE4.

Un autre prix littéraire pour la francophonie; article. *MD* Sept 5, 1987: pC7.

Reviewer was right; article. *WFP* July 3, 1987: p17.

Toronto artists win recognition; article. *WFP* Sept 23, 1987: p46.

Brooker wins TC award; article. *CH* July 7, 1987: pC6.

Munsch, Reimer win Metcalf awards; article. *Quill & Quire* July 1987; Vol 53 No 7: p53.

No Seal first-novel winner; article. *Quill & Quire* July 1987; Vol 53 No 7: p53.

Writers Guild of Alberta awards; article. *Quill & Quire* July 1987; Vol 53 No 7: p54.

Awards; article. *Quill & Quire* Aug 1987; Vol 53 No 8: p24.

$10,000 writing award established; article. *Quill & Quire* Aug 1987; Vol 53 No 8: p24.

Apt appraisal; article. *Quill & Quire* Aug 1987; Vol 53 No 8: p27.

Awards; article. *Quill & Quire* Sept 1987; Vol 53 No 9: p71.

Brooker wins playwright award; article. *G&M* July 1, 1987: pC6.

Calgary poet takes $1,000 award; article. *G&M* July 20, 1987: pC9.

Frye, Wieland are among arts awards winners; article. photo · *G&M* Sept 23, 1987: pC7.

Murdoch ahead in Booker race; article. photo · *G&M* Sept 25, 1987: pD11.

Cross-Canada Writers' Quarterly 1987 annual writing competition; list of award winners. *Cross Can Writ Q* 1987; Vol 9 No 3–4: p60.

Dits et faits; column. *Lettres québec* Autumn 1987; No 47: p6.
[COMPETITIONS, LITERARY; CONFERENCES, LITERARY; WRITERS' ORGANIZATIONS]

Acorn Award; notice. *Quill & Quire* Jan 1987; Vol 53 No 1: p18.

PMC awards; article. *Quill & Quire* Jan 1987; Vol 53 No 1: p20.

Winners chosen in writing competition; article. *Quill & Quire* Jan 1987; Vol 53 No 1: p20.

Penelope Lively wins Booker prize; article. *TS* Oct 30, 1987: pE22.

Margaret Atwood loses Commonwealth prize; article. *TS* Dec 2, 1987: pB1.

British author beats out Brian Moore for Booker; article. *MG* Oct 30, 1987: pC9.

Poet, theatre great among winners of Prix du Québec; article. *MG* Nov 10, 1987: pB4.

Periodical marketers pick Chrétien memoir as top book; article. *MG* Nov 18, 1987: pD1.

A world of books in Quebec; survey article. illus photo · *MG* Nov 21, 1987: J11.
[CANADIAN LITERARY PUBLISHING; QUEBEC LITERATURE (FRENCH LANGUAGE): HISTORY AND CRITICISM]

Jamaican writer upsets Atwood to capture prize; article. *MG* Dec 2, 1987: H2.

Prix; list of award winners. photo · *Lettres québec* Winter 1986–87; No 44: p7.

Penelope Lively décroche le Booker Prize; article. *MD* Oct 30, 1987: p14.

Cinq finalistes au Grand Prix du livre; article. *MD* Nov 13, 1987: p14.

Premier lauréat après cinq années d'absence; article. *MD* Nov 14, 1987: pD9.

Le Renaudot à René-Jean Clot; article. *MD* Nov 16, 1987: p9.

La palme à Ollivier et à Ouellette; article. photo · *MD* Nov 18, 1987: p11.

Week-end; column. *MD* Nov 21, 1987: pA10.
[WRITERS' ORGANIZATIONS]

Louise de Gonzague Pelletier à Place aux poètes; article. *MD* Dec 2, 1987: p14.
[POETRY READINGS]

Marketers name top paperbacks; article. *TS* Nov 17, 1987: pF4.

Findley takes prize; article. *WFP* Nov 18, 1987: p50.

Ross captures top award of $200 in non-fiction writing contest; article. *WFP* Nov 26, 1987: p79.

Atwood suffers upset; article. *WFP* Dec 2, 1987: p49.

Lively wins Booker Prize; article. *CH* Oct 31, 1987: H4.

The Telling of Lies top of paperbacks; article. *CH* Nov 17, 1987: pE8.

Round table: responses, notes and queries; column. *Can Child Lit* 1987; No 45: p98–99.
[CONFERENCES, LITERARY]

Moore moves ahead in race for Booker; article. *G&M* Oct 27, 1987: pD7.

[Untitled]; article. *G&M* Oct 31, 1987.

First novel wins award; article. *G&M* Nov 9, 1987: pD11.

Poet-politician wins literary prize; article. *G&M* Nov 20, 1987: pD11.

Prix du Public goes to Cousture; article. *G&M* Nov 25, 1987: pC5.

B.C. Book Prizes short-list release; article. *Quill & Quire* Oct 1987; Vol 53 No 10: p12–13.

Books nominated for U.S. award; article. *Quill & Quire (Books for Young People)* Oct 1987; Vol 53 No 10: p8.

TO Arts Awards; article. *Quill & Quire* Dec 1987; Vol 53 No 12: p14.

Off-stage drama in awards; article. Marianne Ackerman. *MG* May 4, 1987: pB9.
[FESTIVALS, DRAMA]

L'Actualite picks up six magazine awards; article. Ken Adachi. *TS* May 22, 1987: pE21.
[CANADIAN LITERARY PERIODICALS]

Latecomer to fiction-writing a talent to watch; column. Ken Adachi. photo · *TS* Oct 19, 1987: pC5.
[FESTIVALS, LITERARY]

Arts awards lack flash and glamour; column. Sid Adilman. *TS* Oct 17, 1987: H2.

Last-minute readers and party-bound writers; article. John Allemang. photo · *G&M* Oct 21, 1987: pC9.
[FESTIVALS, LITERARY]

The official truth; letter to the editor. Joan Barfoot. *Books in Can* Aug-Sept 1987; Vol 16 No 6: p39.

Nouvel élan; letter to the editor. Ferdinand Biondi. *MD* Sept 18, 1987: p10.

Le Duvernay à Gérald Godin, le Victor-Morin à André Brassard; article. Sylvain Blanchard. *MD* Oct 9, 1987: p13–14.

Le prix David va à Fernand Ouellette; article. Sylvain Blanchard. photo · *MD* Nov 5, 1987: p15.

Broadway's grip on theatre deceiving; column. Brian Brennan. *CH* Aug 6, 1987: pC2.

Author spent prize money early; article. Donald Campbell. photo · *WFP* June 24, 1987: p27.

Anne Hébert, Wilfrid Lemoyne, Ginette Anfousse reçoivent les premiers prix Fleury-Mesplet; article. Paul Cauchon. photo · *MD* Nov 20, 1987: p13–14.

Arlette Cousture obtient le Prix du public; article. Paul Cauchon. photo · *MD* Nov 24, 1987: p11.

Leacock celebration honors medal winner; column. Zena Cherry. *G&M* May 26, 1987: pD12.

Mikado, B-Movie big Dora winners; article. Ray Conlogue. photo · *G&M* June 23, 1987: pD8.

People; column. Yvonne Cox. photo · *Maclean's* Jan 26, 1987; Vol 100 No 4: p48.

People; column. Yvonne Cox. photo · *Maclean's* Feb 2, 1987; Vol 100 No 5: p32.

People; column. Yvonne Cox. *Maclean's* May 18, 1987; Vol 100 No 20: p36.

Murrell wins top theatre award; article. Robert Crew. photo · *TS* Jan 30, 1987: pD21.

The Mikado hits a high note with seven Dora Awards; article. Robert Crew. photo · *TS* June 23, 1987: pE3.

Neville to extend stay at Stratford for a year; column. Robert Crew. *TS* June 24, 1987: pF1.

Francine d'Amour, prix Guérin; article. Angèle Dagenais. photo · *MD* Nov 5, 1987: p13.

Sylvain Trudel remporte le Prix Molson; article. Angèle Dagenais. photo · *MD* Nov 11, 1987: p11.

Le Salon du livre de Québec: c'est parti!; article. Hélène de Billy. photo · *MD* April 29, 1987: p13.
[CONFERENCES, LITERARY]

Lepage play romps away with festival Grand Prize; article. Pat Donnelly. *MG* June 8, 1987: pD7.

Kingston editor retains theatre critics' award; article. Pat Donnelly. *MG* Oct 5, 1987: pB15.

Getting on a literary roulette wheel; reviews of fictional works. Trevor Ferguson. *MG* Nov 14, 1987: J11.
[FIRST NOVELS: BOOK REVIEWS]

Hyde is named Author of the Year; article. Matthew Fraser. photo · *G&M* Nov 17, 1987: pD7.

Change is in the wind; column. William French. photo · *G&M* May 19, 1987: pC9.

New award celebrates Commonwealth writers; column. William French. photo · *G&M* Nov 17, 1987: pD7.
[WRITERS-IN-RESIDENCE]

Making short work of an award winner; column. William French. *G&M* Dec 8, 1987: pD5.
[GOVERNOR GENERAL'S AWARDS]

Win some, lose some; letter to the editor. Terence M. Green. *Books in Can* Aug-Sept 1987; Vol 16 No 6: p40.

Literary prizes exclude minorities; letter to the editor. Gwen Hauser. *TS* May 22, 1987: pA18.

N.Y. honor for Robertson Davies; article. Heather Hill. *MG* Feb 11, 1987: pB5.

Book fair to expand, offers new prizes; article. Heather Hill. photo · *MG* Sept 4, 1987: pC2.
[CONFERENCES, LITERARY]

French literary prize falls because of budget cuts; article. Heather Hill. *MG* Sept 9, 1987: H1.

... Lest ye be judged; article. Nigel Hunt. photo · *Can Theatre R* Summer 1987; No 51: p17–23.

Win some, lose some more; letter to the editor. Jack Jensen. *Books in Can* Nov 1987; Vol 16 No 8: p40.

CAA opposes pornography bill; article. Fred Kerner. *Quill & Quire* Aug 1987; Vol 53 No 8: p24.
[CENSORSHIP; WRITERS' ORGANIZATIONS]

From the Frye pen into the foyer; article. Martin Knelman. photo · *Tor Life* Aug 1987; Vol 21 No 11: p10.

Le grand prix va à Robert Lepage; article. Robert Lévesque. photo · *MD* June 8, 1987: p1,8.

Robert Lepage, de Nyon en Avignon; article. Robert Lévesque. photo · *MD* Aug 6, 1987: p11.

Limoges, principale vitrine du théâtre québécois en Europe; column. Robert Lévesque. photo · *MD* Sept 29, 1987: p13.
[CANADIAN LITERARY PERIODICALS; FESTIVALS, DRAMA]

Prix et distinctions; list of award winners. Gaétan Lévesque. photo · *Lettres québec* Autumn 1987; No 47: p7.
[GOVERNOR GENERAL'S AWARDS]

Le théâtre du Rire joue gagnant; column. Robert Lévesque. *MD* Oct 13, 1987: p11.

The Mikado paces Dora nominees; article. Liam Lacey. *G&M* May 27, 1987: pC8.

L'Académie canadienne française accueille Félix; article. Marie Laurier. photo · *MD* Dec 24, 1987: pA7.

Pickering crime writer hopes to steal award; article. Alex Law. photo · *TS (Neighbours)* May 19, 1987: p17.

Definite Jessie material; article. Mark Leiren-Young. photo · *Can Theatre R* Summer 1987; No 51: p32–35.

Entrances and exits; column. Mark Leiren-Young. photo · *Can Theatre R* Fall 1987; No 52: p91–94.

[Untitled]; letter to the editor. Paul Leonard. *Can Theatre R* Winter 1987; No 53: p4.

Congratulations!; notice. Bernice Lever. *Waves* Winter 1987; Vol 15 No 3: p89.

The Milton Acorn People's Award; notice. Bernice Lever. *Waves* Winter 1987; Vol 15 No 3: p89.

Edmonton winners in Pulp contest; article. Charles Mandel. *Quill & Quire* Jan 1987; Vol 53 No 1: p18.

Laurels in literature; article. Alberto Manguel. *Maclean's* Nov 2, 1987; Vol 100 No 44: p52a-52b.

Dandelion uncovers new voice; column. Kenneth McGoogan. photo · *CH* Feb 1, 1987: pC8.
[CANADIAN LITERARY PERIODICALS; POETRY READINGS]

Festival winds bring W.O. home; column. Kenneth McGoogan. *CH* March 1, 1987: pC8.
[CONFERENCES, LITERARY; FESTIVALS, LITERARY]

Writers plan on doing it with style; column. Kenneth McGoogan. *CH* March 22, 1987: pF5.
[COMPETITIONS, LITERARY; FESTIVALS, LITERARY]

U of A alumna wins novel contest; column. Kenneth McGoogan. *CH* April 2, 1987: pD14.
[FESTIVALS, LITERARY; POETRY READINGS]

Calgary writers take top honors; column. Kenneth McGoogan. *CH* April 9, 1987: pE7.
[GOVERNMENT GRANTS TO WRITERS/PUBLISHERS]

Manitoban attracts nationwide attention; column. Kenneth McGoogan. photo · *CH* April 12, 1987: pF7.

Calgary writers clean up; article. Kenneth McGoogan. photo · *CH* May 10, 1987: pE2.

Short-story prize doubled for winner; column. Kenneth McGoogan. *CH* May 24, 1987: pE6.
[COMPETITIONS, LITERARY]

Writers, publishers, libraries rejoice; column. Kenneth McGoogan. *CH* June 14, 1987: pE6.
[GOVERNMENT GRANTS FOR WRITERS/PUBLISHERS]

Editor's ethnic tale wins short-story event; article. Kenneth McGoogan. *CH* June 27, 1987: pA8.

Poets help celebrate Dandelion; column. Kenneth McGoogan. *CH* June 28, 1987: pF8.
[CANADIAN LITERARY PERIODICALS; POETRY READINGS; WRITERS' ORGANIZATIONS]

McDonald scores with Canada's booksellers; article. Kenneth McGoogan. *CH* June 30, 1987: pE1.

Literary world loses a champion; column. Kenneth McGoogan. *CH* July 12, 1987: pE4.
[CONFERENCES, LITERARY; PUBLISHING AND PUBLISHERS IN CANADA; SCIENCE FICTION; WRITERS' WORKSHOPS]

J.P. Donleavy here in '88; column. Kenneth McGoogan. *CH* July 26, 1987: pE5.
[CANADIAN LITERARY PERIODICALS; CANADIAN LITERARY PUBLISHING; FESTIVALS, LITERARY]

Calgary poets dominate nationwide competition; article. Kenneth McGoogan. *CH* July 30, 1987: pC2.

Festival attracts kids' writers; column. Kenneth McGoogan. *CH* Sept 20, 1987: pE6.
[CHILDREN'S LITERATURE; FESTIVALS, LITERARY]

Vancouver man wins pulp prize; article. Kenneth McGoogan. *CH* Nov 11, 1987: pA18.

Dora Awards still waiting for stardom; column. Henry Mietkiewicz. photo · *TS* June 20, 1987: J6.

Writer from Jamaica wins literary award; article. Karen Morch. *G&M* Dec 2, 1987: pC6.

Atwood not disappointed at losing Commonwealth Prize; article. Karen Morch. photo · *CH* Dec 3, 1987: pF3.

La vie littéraire; column. Marc Morin. *MD* Nov 14, 1987: pD14.
[CHILDREN'S LITERATURE; POETRY READINGS]

La vie littéraire; column. Marc Morin. photo · *MD* Dec 19, 1987: pD2.
[FICTION READINGS; POETRY READINGS]

How my novel of manners won the prize for crime; essay. Edward Phillips. illus · *MG* June 27, 1987: I3.

Sue just knew she was going to win — and she did; article. John Picton. photo · *TS* June 28, 1987: pA17.

The Milton Acorn Memorial People's Poetry Award; article. Ted Plantos. illus · *Poetry Can R* Summer 1987; Vol 8 No 4: p17.

Toronto honors the best with annual arts awards; article. Greg Quill. photo · *TS* Sept 23, 1987: pF1.

La difficile reconnaissance des gens de lettres; article. Johanne Roy. *MD* May 23, 1987: pD2.
[AUTHORS, CANADIAN; WRITERS' ORGANIZATIONS]

La vie littéraire; column. Jean Royer. photo · *MD* Jan 10, 1987: pB2.
[POETRY READINGS; RADIO AND CANADIAN LITERATURE; TELEVISION AND CANADIAN LITERATURE; WRITERS' WORKSHOPS]

La vie littéraire; column. Jean Royer. *MD* Jan 17, 1987: pB2.
[CONFERENCES, LITERARY; RADIO AND CANADIAN LITERATURE; TELEVISION AND CANADIAN LITERATURE]

La vie littéraire; column. Jean Royer. photo · *MD* Jan 24, 1987: pB2.
[POETRY READINGS; PUBLISHING AND PUBLISHERS IN CANADA; RADIO AND CANADIAN LITERATURE; WRITERS' WORKSHOPS]

La vie littéraire; column. Jean Royer. *MD* Feb 14, 1987: pC2.
[CANADIAN LITERARY PERIODICALS; COMPETITIONS, LITERARY; FICTION READINGS; POETRY READINGS; RADIO AND CANADIAN LITERATURE]

Ninon Larochelle mérite le prix de la nouvelle de Radio-Canada; article. Jean Royer. *MD* Feb 20, 1987: p7.

Un grand prix littéraire Guérin; article. Jean Royer. *MD* Feb 21, 1987: pB3.
[COMPETITIONS, LITERARY]

Le 27e prix Québec-Paris va à Jacques Boulerice; article. Jean Royer. *MD* Feb 27, 1987: p7.

La vie littéraire; column. Jean Royer. *MD* Feb 28, 1987: pC2.
[CANADIAN LITERARY PERIODICALS; CANADIAN LITERARY PUBLISHING; CONFERENCES, LITERARY; RADIO AND CANADIAN LITERATURE]

La vie littéraire; column. Jean Royer. *MD* March 7, 1987: pB2.
[CANADIAN LITERARY PUBLISHING; POETRY READINGS; RADIO AND CANADIAN LITERATURE; TELEVISION AND CANADIAN LITERATURE; WRITERS' ORGANIZATIONS]

La vie littéraire; column. Jean Royer. photo · *MD* March 14, 1987: pD4.
[POETRY READINGS; RADIO AND CANADIAN LITERATURE; TELEVISION AND CANADIAN LITERATURE]

La vie littéraire; column. Jean Royer. photo · *MD* March 21, 1987: pD2.
[CANADIAN LITERARY PUBLISHING; COMPETITIONS, LITERARY; POETRY READINGS; RADIO AND CANADIAN LITERATURE; TELEVISION AND CANADIAN LITERATURE]

Pierre Vadeboncoeur remporte le prix Canada-Suisse; article. Jean Royer. photo · *MD* March 31, 1987: p17.

La vie littéraire; column. Jean Royer. photo · *MD* April 11, 1987: pD2.
[FILM ADAPTATIONS OF CANADIAN LITERATURE; POETRY READINGS; RADIO AND CANADIAN LITERATURE; TELEVISION AND CANADIAN LITERATURE]

Le grand prix Logidisque de la science-fiction et du fantastique est attribué à Esther Rochon; article. Jean Royer. photo · *MD* April 14, 1987: p11.
[SCIENCE FICTION]

La vie littéraire; column. Jean Royer. *MD* April 25, 1987: pD2.
[CONFERENCES, LITERARY; FESTIVALS, LITERARY; FICTION READINGS; POETRY READINGS; RADIO AND CANADIAN LITERATURE; TELEVISION AND CANADIAN LITERATURE]

Prix du Conseil des arts; article. Jean Royer. *MD* April 25, 1987: pD3.
[AUSTRALIA-CANADA LITERARY RELATIONS]

La vie littéraire; column. Jean Royer. photo · *MD* May 2, 1987: pD2.
[INTERNATIONAL REVIEWS OF CANADIAN LITERATURE; RADIO AND CANADIAN LITERATURE; TELEVISION AND CANADIAN LITERATURE; WRITERS' ORGANIZATIONS]

La vie littéraire; column. Jean Royer. photo · *MD* May 16, 1987: pD2.
[CONFERENCES, LITERARY; PUBLISHING AND PUBLISHERS IN CANADA; RADIO AND CANADIAN LITERATURE; TELEVISION AND CANADIAN LITERATURE]

La vie littéraire; column. Jean Royer. photo · *MD* May 30, 1987: pD2.
[CANADIAN LITERARY PUBLISHING; COMPETITIONS, LITERARY; FESTIVALS, LITERARY; RADIO AND CANADIAN LITERATURE; TELEVISION AND CANADIAN LITERATURE]

La vie littéraire; column. Jean Royer. photo · *MD* June 13, 1987: pD2.
[COMPETITIONS, LITERARY; POETRY READINGS; RADIO AND CANADIAN LITERATURE; TELEVISION AND CANADIAN LITERATURE; WRITERS' ORGANIZATIONS]

L'administration Doré ressuscite le Grand Prix littéraire de Montréal; article. Jean Royer. photo · *MD* Sept 4, 1987: p13.

La vie littéraire; column. Jean Royer. *MD* Sept 12, 1987: pD2.
[CONFERENCES, LITERARY; POETRY PERFORMANCE; POETRY READINGS]

La vie littéraire; column. Jean Royer. photo · *MD* Sept 19, 1987: pD2.
[CONFERENCES, LITERARY; FICTION READINGS; POETRY READINGS; PUBLISHING AND PUBLISHERS IN CANADA]

La Fondations des Forges couronne André Roy; article. Jean Royer. photo · *MD* Sept 23, 1987: p11.

La vie littéraire; column. Jean Royer. *MD* Oct 3, 1987: pD2.
[CANADIAN LITERARY PUBLISHING; POETRY READINGS; WRITERS' WORKSHOPS]

Deux nouveaux académéciens; article. Jean Royer. *MD* Oct 19, 1987: p9.

Rewriting paid off for contest winner; article. Leslie Scrivener. photo · *TS* June 28, 1987: pA16.

Reclaiming the Doras; article. Jason Sherman. photo · *Can Theatre R* Summer 1987; No 51: p25-31.

Book world: Clarkson brings pool of goodwill to M&S job; column. Beverley Slopen. *TS* March 15, 1987: pA22.
[PUBLISHING AND PUBLISHERS IN CANADA]

Book world: writers sell selves to the booksellers; column. Beverley Slopen. *TS* July 5, 1987: pA18.

Remise des prix d'excellence de la culture; article. Julie Stanton. photo · *MD* Oct 27, 1987: p11.

Le Léon-Gérin à Louis-Edmond Hamelin; le Marie-Victorin à Pierre Deslongchamps; article. Julie Stanton. photo · *MD* Nov 10, 1987: p13.

2 Star writers, photographer take top newspaper award; article. Walter Stefaniuk. *TS* May 3, 1987: pA2.

Story award order should be inverted; letter to the editor. N.J. Stewart. *CH* Aug 26, 1987: pA6.

400,000$; editorial. Adrien Thério. *Lettres québec* Winter 1986-87; No 44: p10-11.
[FRANCE-CANADA LITERARY RELATIONS]

Une première dans l'histoire intellectuelle du Québec; article. Adrien Thério. *Lettres québec* Winter 1986-87; No 44: p11.

De qui se moque Le Devoir?; editorial. Michel Vaïs. photo · *Jeu* 1987; No 45: p7-9.
[CANADIAN LITERARY PERIODICALS; WRITERS' ORGANIZATIONS]

Bloc-notes; column. Michel Vaïs. photo · *Jeu* 1987; No 45: p227-231.
[GOVERNMENT GRANTS FOR WRITERS/PUBLISHERS; WRITERS' ORGANIZATIONS]

Prize writer; article. Ellen Vanstone. photo · *Tor Life* March 1987; Vol 21 No 4: p10-11.

Competition; editorial. Bob Wallace. *Can Theatre R* Summer 1987; No 51: p3.

Robertson Davies honored by U.S. arts club; article. Calvin Woodward. photo · *G&M* Feb 26, 1987: pC5.

London writer awarded children's book prize; article. Tim Wynne-Jones. photo · *G&M* March 20, 1987: pD5.

Triumphant return; reviews of *Jacob Two-Two and the Dinosaur* and *Pop Bottles*. Tim Wynne-Jones. *G&M* June 13, 1987: pC19.

Satisfying prizes; column. Tim Wynne-Jones. *G&M* May 16, 1987: pC19.

Veterans give proteges a $5,000 career boost; article. Reta Zekas. photo · *TS* May 7, 1987: pD1.

Tennant gets top award for costume and design; article. Rita Zekas. *TS* Oct 14, 1987: pE1.

Herrndorf is the sum of his arts; article about Peter Herrndorf. Antonia Zerbisias. photo · *TS* Oct 10, 1987: H1,H3.

BÉLISLE, MARIE

[Untitled]; review of *Nous passions*. Antonio D'Alfonso. *Estuaire* Summer 1987; No 45: p49.

B-MOVIE, THE PLAY/Play by Tom Wood

B-Movie wins laughs with gags, old lines; theatre review of *B-Movie, the Play*. Brian Brennan. *CH* Sept 19, 1987: pD6.

Story of hit play's fade-out reads like a B-Movie script; article. Ray Conlogue. photo · *G&M* April 16, 1987: pD1.

B-Movie's devilish wit proves nothing succeeds like excess; theatre review of *B-Movie, The Play*. Robert Crew. photo · *TS* Jan 23, 1987: pD18.

B-Movie the play gets flood of offers; column. Robert Crew. photo · *TS* Feb 11, 1987: pF1.

Funny theatre piece says life imitates movie life; article. Rod Currie. *CH* Jan 24, 1987: pA11.

B-Movie could extend run but 'that would be suicide'; article. Mira Friedlander. photo · *TS* March 13, 1987: pC11

B-Movie features Grade-A laughs; theatre review. Liam Lacey. photo · *G&M* Jan 22, 1987: pC3.

Playwright recalls double-bill dementia; essay. Tom Wood. photo · *TS* Jan 23, 1987: pD3.

Author skewers films' popularity in new ATP play; article. Kate Zimmerman. photo · *CH* Sept 11, 1987: pF1.

BA HA HA/Play by Lyle Victor Albert

Architecture offers author comic design; article. Martin Morrow. photo · *CH* Dec 31, 1987: pD1.

BABA JACQUES DASS AND TURMOIL AT CÔTE DES NEIGES CEMETERY/Play by Rana Bose

A rare glimpse at our multiculturalism; theatre review of *Baba Jacques Dass and Turmoil at Côte des Neiges Cemetery*. Pat Donnelly. *MG* Oct 17, 1987: pD9.

BABBY, ELLEN REISMAN

Roy's language; review of *The Play of Language and Spectacle*. Paul G. Socken. *Can Lit* Spring 1987; No 112: p194.

THE BABY PROJECT/Children's novel by Sarah Ellis

Tales for teenagers feature strong, viable family units; reviews of *The Baby Project* and *Payment in Death*. Jane Kent. *CH* April 12, 1987: pF7.

Learning to accept change and loss; review of *The Baby Project*. Margaret Steffler. *Can Child Lit* 1987; No 47: p90–91.

BACHELOR-MAN/Play by Winston Kam

Play's premise unfulfilled; theatre review of *Bachelor-Man*. Robert Crew. *TS* Nov 13, 1987: pE26.

[Untitled]; letter to the editor. Scott Fairweather. *TS* Dec 4, 1987: pD10.

Bachelor uses intriguing techniques; theatre review of *Bachelor-Man*. Liam Lacey. photo · *G&M* Nov 14, 1987: pC8.

Blowing bubbles with Simone and Sartre; column. Vit Wagner. photo · *TS* Nov 6, 1987: pE4.
[TRANSLATIONS OF CANADIAN LITERATURE]

BACK ON TUESDAY/Novel by David Gilmour

Juicy real-life crime tales heat up fall book lists; column. Sid Adilman. *TS* Oct 3, 1987: J1.
[FILM ADAPTATIONS OF CANADIAN LITERATURE]

Shallow griefs; review of *Back on Tuesday*. Diana Brydon. *Can Lit* Winter 1987; No 115: p194–195.
[FIRST NOVELS: BOOK REVIEW]

[Untitled]; reviews. Beverley Daurio. *Cross Can Writ Q* 1987; Vol 9 No 2: p23.
[FIRST NOVELS: BOOK REVIEWS]

BACKING INTO HEAVEN/Poems by Steve Noyes

[Untitled]; reviews of poetry books. Anne Archer. *Queen's Q* Winter 1987; Vol 94 No 4: p1042–1043.

Tellings; reviews of poetry books. Susan Rudy Dorscht. *Can Lit* Winter 1987; No 115: p257–260.

[Untitled]; reviews of poetry books. Stephen Morrissey. *Poetry Can R* Spring 1987; Vol 8 No 2–3: p49.

First books from five regional presses; reviews of poetry books. Colin Morton. *Arc* Spring 1987; No 18: p52–59.

BACKYARD BEGUINE/Play by David King

A madcap journey out to the Backyard; theatre review of *Backyard Beguine*, includes profile. Stephen Godfrey. photo · *G&M* April 8, 1987: pC7.

BAG LADY/Poems by Sarah Jackson

Sara[h] Jackson's book works; reviews of books by Sarah Jackson. Alexa Thompson. *Atlan Prov Book R* Sept-Oct 1987; Vol 14 No 3: p15.

LA BAGARRE/Novel by Gérard Bessette

Montréal dans les années 50; review of *La Bagarre*. Pierre-Louis Vaillancourt. photo · *Lettres québec* Spring 1987; No 45: p57–59.

BAGDAD/Novel by Ian Dennis

Parody & legacy; reviews. Lorna Irvine. *Can Lit* Winter 1987; No 115: p264–267.
[FIRST NOVELS: BOOK REVIEWS]

Recent Canadian fiction; reviews of novels. D.O. Spettigue. *Queen's Q* Summer 1987; Vol 94 No 2: p366–375.
[FIRST NOVELS: BOOK REVIEWS]

BAIGENT, BERYL

[Untitled]; reviews of poetry books. Anita Hurwitz. *Poetry Can R* Spring 1987; Vol 8 No 2–3: p50–51.

BAILEY, D.F.

Urban scrawl; reviews of first novels. Janice Kulyk Keefer. *Books in Can* Aug-Sept 1987; Vol 16 No 6: p33–34.
[FIRST NOVELS: BOOK REVIEWS]

Explosive debut made by writer; review of *Fire Eyes*. Michael Mirolla. photo · *CH* Sept 13, 1987: pE5.
[FIRST NOVELS: BOOK REVIEWS]

Not meant to be a thriller; letter to the editor. Bella Pomer. *Quill & Quire* June 1987; Vol 53 No 6: p4

Would-be world-class thrillers need plots to be complete; reviews of *Equinox* and *Fire Eyes*. Philippe van Rjndt. photo · *Quill & Quire* April 1987; Vol 53 No 4: p28.

BAILEY, DON

Local film stretched to eight-part TV series; article. *WFP* Jan 17, 1987: p21.
[TELEVISION AND CANADIAN LITERATURE]

Author's crimes behind him, but emotional ghosts remain; article. Donald Campbell. *WFP* Dec 26, 1987: p20.

Examining the blight of solitude; review of *Bring Me Your Passion*. Keith Garebian. *TS* Dec 27, 1987: pE19.

All Sales Final subtle family drama focusing on lost romance, death; column. Paul McKie. photo · *WFP* Oct 17, 1987: p30.
[TELEVISION AND CANADIAN LITERATURE]

BAILLIE, ROBERT

[Untitled]; review of *Les Voyants*. Sylvie-L. Bergeron. *Moebius* Summer 1987; No 33: p137–139.

BAIN PUBLIC/Play by Théâtre Petit à Petit collective

[Untitled]; theatre review of *Bain public*. Pierre Lavoie. photo · *Jeu* 1987; No 42: p168–169.

BAKER, STEVEN

Wanted! One detective show; theatre review of *Wanted!*. Robert Davis. photo · *TS (Neighbours)* May 26, 1987: p19.

BALCARCE, ALBERTO

[Untitled]; review of *A Long Night of Death*. Barbara Carey. *Books in Can* Jan-Feb 1987; Vol 16 No 1: p25.
[FIRST NOVELS: BOOK REVIEWS]

Latin terror; review of *A Long Night of Death*. Pauline Carey. *G&M* Aug 22, 1987: pC14.
[FIRST NOVELS: BOOK REVIEWS]

Under dark cover of stark militarism; review of *A Long Night of Death*. Lesley McAllister. *TS* April 25, 1987: M7.
[FIRST NOVELS: BOOK REVIEWS]

[Untitled]; review of *A Long Night of Death*. Rachel Rafelman. *Quill & Quire* Feb 1987; Vol 53 No 2: p17.
[FIRST NOVELS: BOOK REVIEWS]

BALLANTINE, BILL

Bat Masterson deals with words and how they can shape identity; theatre review of *Bat Masterson's Last Regular Job*. Ray Conlogue. photo · *G&M* Oct 10, 1987: pC6.

Space crunch may kill Solar Stage; column. Robert Crew. *TS* Aug 9, 1987: pC3.

Bat Masterson keeps on and on; theatre review of *Bat Masterson's Last Regular Job*. Robert Crew. photo · *TS* Oct 11, 1987: pC3.

Artist gives surreal play haunting backdrop; column. Vit Wagner. *TS* Oct 2, 1987: pE12.

BALTENSPERGER, PETER

[Untitled]; reviews of poetry books. Shaunt Basmajian. *Cross Can Writ Q* 1987; Vol 9 No 3-4: p44,49.
[ANTHOLOGIES: BOOK REVIEWS]

BANC DE BRUME OU LES AVENTURES DE LA PETITE FILLE QUE L'ON CROYAIT PARTIE AVEC L'EAU DE BAIN/Short stories by Aude

Deux livres pour partir en voyage; reviews of *Mourir comme un chat* and *Banc de Brume*. Marie José Thériault. photo · *Lettres québec* Autumn 1987; No 47: p31–32.

BANNERJI, HIMANI

Hard time, maximum time; reviews of *The Only Minority Is the Bourgeoisie* and *Doing Time*. Marlene Philip. *Tor South Asian R* Spring 1987; Vol 5 No 3: p28–34.

BARBOUR, DOUGLAS

Trimly clipped and barboured; reviews of *Visible Visions* and *The Harbingers*. Louis K. MacKendrick. *Essays on Can Writ* Spring 1987; No 34: p39–43.

BARCELO, FRANÇOIS

La vitrine du livre; review of *Aaa, aâh, ha ou les amours malaisés*. Guy Ferland. *MD* Jan 3, 1987: pC2.

À l'impossible certains sont tenus; reviews of *Benito* and *Aaa, Aâh, Ha ou les amours malaisées*. Pierre Hébert. *Voix et images* Autumn 1987; Vol 13 No 1: p192–194.

Aaa! Aâh! Ha! que de belles catastrophes narratives!; reviews. Michel Lord. photo · *Lettres québec* Spring 1987; No 45: p32–35.

[Untitled]; review of *Aaa, aàh, ha ou les amours malaisées*. Jean Royer. *MD* Jan 23, 1987: p7.

La vie littéraire; column. Jean Royer. *MD* Jan 31, 1987: pB2.
[CANADIAN LITERARY PERIODICALS; COMPETITIONS, LITERARY; RADIO AND CANADIAN LITERATURE; TELEVISION AND CANADIAN LITERATURE]

Barcelo, le jogger heureux; review of *Aaa, aâh, ha ou les amours malaisées*. Jean Royer. photo · *MD* Jan 31, 1987: pB3.

BARCLAY, BYRNA

Anybody home; reviews of *The Last Echo* and *Wise-Ears*. Linda Rogers. *Can Lit* Winter 1987; No 115: p204–205.

BARCUS, W.D.

World of wonders; reviews of first novels. Janice Kulyk Keefer. *Books in Can* May 1987; Vol 16 No 4: p37–38.
[FIRST NOVELS: BOOK REVIEWS]

BARFOOT, JOAN

New in paper; reviews of novels. *TS* Aug 30, 1987: pA18.
[FIRST NOVELS: BOOK REVIEWS]

[Untitled]; review of *Dancing in the Dark*. Maryann Ayim. *Atlantis* Fall 1987; Vol 13 No 1: p189–191.

Ours as daughters; reviews of *Duet for Three* and *Flitterin' Judas*. Nancy Bailey. *Can Lit* Spring 1987; No 112: p143–145.

Dancing In The Dark: what happens when a homemaker cracks; film review. Bruce Bailey. photo · *MG* Jan 17, 1987: pD4.
[FILM ADAPTATIONS OF CANADIAN LITERATURE]

Burgess touch refreshes yet another Roman tale; reviews of *Dancing in the Dark* and *John and the Missus*. Barbara Black. *MG* April 11, 1987: pG7.

The official truth; letter to the editor. Mary Ellen Csamer. *Books in Can* June-July 1987; Vol 16 No 5: p40.

A magnificent greed; review of *Duet for Three*. Robb Forman Dew. *NYT Book R* April 5, 1987: p19.

A marriage of fact and fiction; article. Liam Lacey. photo · *G&M* Jan 19, 1987: pC9.

Get new year off to good start with Dancing In The Dark; film review. Paul McKie. photo · *WFP* Jan 4, 1987: p14.
[FILM ADAPTATIONS OF CANADIAN LITERATURE]

BARKHOUSE, JOYCE

Halifax writer gives life to people forgotten in Canadian history books; article. *WFP* Dec 31, 1987: p29.

Shadows of a dream; review of *A Forest for Zoe*. Brent Ledger. *Books in Can* June-July 1987; Vol 16 No 5: p17-18.

Thomas H. Raddall, a decade later; reviews of *The Dreamers* and *A Name for Himself*. Andrew Seaman. *Atlan Prov Book R* Feb-March 1987; Vol 14 No 1: p19.

BARNAO, JACK
See WOOD, TED

BARNES, LILLY

Zig-zag management; reviews of *Nadine* and *A Hero Travels Light*. Anthony S. Brennan. *Fiddlehead* Winter 1987; No 154: p91-95.

Cruel events; review of *A Hero Travels Light*. Pauline Carey. *G&M* Jan 24, 1987: pE18.

[Untitled]; review of *A Hero Travels Light*. Candace Carman. *Books in Can* Jan-Feb 1987; Vol 16 No 1: p25.

Childhood endured across frontiers; review of *A Hero Travels Light*. Maggie Helwig. *TS* Feb 21, 1987: M6.

BARNIEH, ZINA

Playwright probes kids' fear of summer camp; article. Kate Zimmerman. photo · *CH* April 24, 1987: pD1.

BAROMETER RISING/Novel by Hugh MacLennan

Barometer's rising the curtain in Halifax; article. *TS* Sept 26, 1987: pG10.

Neptune Theatre's Barometer Rising too faithful to book; theatre review. Matthew Fraser. *G&M* Nov 9, 1987: pD9.
[DRAMATIC ADAPTATIONS OF CANADIAN LITERATURE]

Death on the waterfront; theatre review of *Barometer Rising*, includes profile. Stephen Pedersen. photo · *Maclean's* Nov 23, 1987; Vol 100 No 47: p57.
[DRAMATIC ADAPTATIONS OF CANADIAN LITERATURE]

Halifax blast commemorated in effective stage production; theatre review of *Barometer Rising*. Jamie Portman. *CH* Nov 12, 1987: pD2.
[DRAMATIC ADAPTATIONS OF CANADIAN LITERATURE]

A sound beyond hearing; article. Tom Regan. photo · *Atlan Insight* Dec 1987; Vol 9 No 12: p19-21.
[DRAMATIC ADAPTATIONS OF CANADIAN LITERATURE]

MacLennan happy with plans to stage his Barometer Rising; article. Derrick Toth. photo · *CH* Sept 26, 1987: pG1.
[DRAMATIC ADAPTATIONS OF CANADIAN LITERATURE]

BASE, RON

Atlantis in The Twilight Zone; column. Sid Adilman. *TS* Oct 20, 1987: H1.

Matinee Idol winner a model mother of 2; article. Christopher Hume. photo · *TS* June 19, 1987: pD23.

BASEBALL CRAZY/Young adult novel by Martyn Godfrey

Fine books for in-betweens; reviews of young adult books. David Williamson. *WFP* Dec 5, 1987: p57.

BASMAJIAN, SHAUNT

[Untitled]; review of *Poets Who Don't Dance*. Rod Anderson. *Poetry Can R* Spring 1987; Vol 8 No 2-3: p58.

Grief & memory; reviews of poetry books. Peter Stenberg. *Can Lit* Spring 1987; No 112: p169-171.

BAT MASTERSON'S LAST REGULAR JOB/Play by Bill Ballantine

Bat Masterson deals with words and how they can shape identity; theatre review of *Bat Masterson's Last Regular Job*. Ray Conlogue. photo · *G&M* Oct 10, 1987: pC6

Space crunch may kill Solar Stage; column. Robert Crew. *TS* Aug 9, 1987: pC3.

Bat Masterson keeps on and on; theatre review of *Bat Masterson's Last Regular Job*. Robert Crew. photo · *TS* Oct 11, 1987: pC3.

Artist gives surreal play haunting backdrop; column. Vit Wagner. *TS* Oct 2, 1987: pE12.

BATCHELOR, RHONDA

[Untitled]; review of *Bearings*. *Queen's Q* Spring 1987; Vol 94 No 1: p251-252.

BATES, CATHERINE

Quilted patch; reviews of poetry books. Uma Parameswaran. Teresa Mallam. *Can Lit* Spring 1987; No 112: p176-179.

Tip sheet: . . . writers meet; column. Susan Schwartz. photo · *MG* Oct 14, 1987: pC9.
[WRITERS' ORGANIZATIONS]

But where is the poetry?; reviews of *Road Dances* and *Counterpane*. Bruce Whiteman. *Essays on Can Writ* Spring 1987; No 34: p48-49.

BATTEN, JACK

Murder & mayhem: Spenser's clones; review of *Crang Plays the Ace*. Margaret Cannon. photo · *G&M* April 25, 1987: pC19.
[FIRST NOVELS: BOOK REVIEWS]

Nearly 30 years and still promising; column. Robert Fulford. *TS* May 2, 1987: M5.

More in anger than in sorrow; letter to the editor. Marjorie Harris. *Quill & Quire* April 1987; Vol 53 No 4: p3.

Grime and punishment; review of *Crang Plays the Ace*. Douglas Malcolm. *Books in Can* April 1987; Vol 16 No 3: p35.
[FIRST NOVELS: BOOK REVIEWS]

First novels set to different literary keys; reviews of *Crang Plays the Ace* and *Gallows View*. James Mennie. photo · *MG* April 11, 1987: pG6.
[FIRST NOVELS: BOOK REVIEWS]

Mysteries to feed the mind with varying tastes; reviews of *Crang Plays the Ace* and *To an Easy Grave*. John North. photo · *Quill & Quire* March 1987; Vol 53 No 3: p74.
[FIRST NOVELS: BOOK REVIEWS]

Three absolute page-turners; reviews of *Crang Plays the Ace* and *Gallows View*. Janet Saunders. photo · *WFP* May 9, 1987: p56.
[FIRST NOVELS: BOOK REVIEWS]

Crang: super-mouth sleuth; review of *Crang Plays the Ace*. Mike Walton. *TS* April 12, 1987: pA21.
[FIRST NOVELS: BOOK REVIEWS]

BATTLER, LESLEY

Getting on a literary roulette wheel; reviews of fictional works. Trevor Ferguson. *MG* Nov 14, 1987: J11.
[FIRST NOVELS: BOOK REVIEWS]

BAUER, NANCY

Anybody home; reviews of *The Last Echo* and *Wise-Ears*. Linda Rogers. *Can Lit* Winter 1987; No 115: p204–205.

Recent Canadian fiction; reviews of novels. D.O. Spettigue. *Queen's Q* Summer 1987; Vol 94 No 2: p366–375.
[FIRST NOVELS: BOOK REVIEWS]

BEARINGS/Poems by Rhonda Batchelor

[Untitled]; review of *Bearings*. *Queen's Q* Spring 1987; Vol 94 No 1: p251–252.

THE BEAST WITH FIVE FINGERS/Play by Keith Johnstone

Playwright reaps laughs from reality; article. Elliott Gould. photo · *CH* May 22, 1987: pF1.

Johnstone's Beast rants, bewilders; theatre review of *The Beast with Five Fingers*. Kate Zimmerman. *CH* May 24, 1987: pE5.

BEAUCAIRE, SUZANNE

Pourquoi a-t-on peur de Maude?; theatre review of *"JAM-MÉE, les nerfs! les nerfs!"*. Patricia Badoux. photo · *MD* May 7, 1987: p13.

Le Conseil de la santé récupère une pièce boudée par l'hôpital Louis-H. Lafontaine; article. Renée Rowan. photo · *MD* April 30, 1987: p13.

BEAUCHAMP, HÉLÈNE

[Untitled]; review of *Le Théâtre pour enfants au Québec: 1950–1980*. Gilbert David. *Jeu* 1987; No 42: p176–179.

Une analyse éclairante du théâtre pour enfants; review of *Le Théâtre pour enfants au Québec*. Elvine Gignac-Pharand. *Can Child Lit* 1987; No 46: p95–96.

BEAUCHEMIN, YVES

Dits et faits; column. photo · *Lettres québec* Spring 1987; No 45: p6–7.
[AWARDS, LITERARY; PUBLISHING AND PUBLISHERS IN CANADA; TRANSLATIONS OF CANADIAN LITERATURE; WRITERS' ORGANIZATIONS]

[Untitled]; review of *The Alley Cat*. *Queen's Q* Spring 1987; Vol 94 No 1: p252.

Vivre de sa plume au Québec: interview de Lettres québécoises avec Yves Beauchemin romancier; interview. photo · *Lettres québec* Winter 1986–87; No 44: p13–14.

Les Gens du livre ont 25 ans; article. *MD* Nov 7, 1987: pD3

Le Matou author used radio journalism for artistic ends; review of *Du sommet d'un arbre*. Benoit Aubin. photo · *MG* Jan 3, 1987: pB7.

Du sommet d'un arbre ou le regard en plongée et en quatre temps; article. Renald Bérubé. *Voix et images* Spring 1987; Vol 12 No 3: p404–415.
[AUTOBIOGRAPHICAL WRITING]

L'inscription du littéraire dans Le Matou d'Yves Beauchemin; article. Micheline Beauregard. abstract · *Études lit* Spring-Summer 1987; Vol 20 No 1: p131–147.
[METAFICTION]

The Yankee devils!; review of *The Alley Cat*. Bob Coleman. *NYT Book R* Jan 11, 1987: p14.

[Untitled]; review of *The Alley Cat*. Charles Foran. *Rubicon* Spring 1987; No 8: p176–178.

En toute simplicité; review of *Voix et images*. Chantal Gamache. photo · *MD* Nov 7, 1987: pD3.
[CANADIAN LITERARY PERIODICALS]

Current Canadian studies; column. Victor A. Konrad. *Amer R of Can Studies* Autumn 1987; Vol 17 No 3: p360–366.
[ANNOTATIONS, SHORT REVIEWS, ; CANADIAN LITERARY PERIODICALS]

Voix et images 36; review. Gaëtan Lévesque. *Lettres québec* Autumn 1987; No 47: p66.
[CANADIAN LITERARY PERIODICALS]

Yves Beauchemin, en toute simplicité: présentation; editorial. Yves Lacroix. *Voix et images* Spring 1987; Vol 12 No 3: p358.

Entrevue avec Yves Beauchemin; interview. Yves Lacroix. *Voix et images* Spring 1987; Vol 12 No 3: p376–382.

Beauchemin's The Alley Cat as modern myth; article. Constantina Mitchell. *Amer R of Can Studies* Winter 1987–88; Vol 17 No 4: p409–418.
[MYTHS AND LEGENDS IN CANADIAN LITERATURE; POLITICAL WRITING]

"Alliance-Québec fait la guerre avec les mots de la paix"; article. Jean Royer. photo · *MD* March 16, 1987: p11,14.
[CULTURAL IDENTITY; WRITERS' ORGANIZATIONS]

Le Matou d'Yves Beauchemin: du fait littéraire à la chaîne de productions-médias; article. Catherine Saouter. *Voix et images* Spring 1987; Vol 12 No 3: p393–402.
[FILM ADAPTATIONS OF CANADIAN LITERATURE; TELEVISION AND CANADIAN LITERATURE]

Entrevue avec Yves Beauchemin; interview. Frances J. Summers. *Voix et images* Spring 1987; Vol 12 No 3: p360–374.

Le réception critique du Matou; article. Frances J. Summers. *Voix et images* Spring 1987; Vol 12 No 3: p383–392.
[INTERNATIONAL REVIEWS OF CANADIAN LITERATURE]

Bibliographie de Yves Beauchemin; bibliography. Frances J. Summers. *Voix et images* Spring 1987; Vol 12 No 3: p416–428.
[CANADIAN LITERATURE: BIBLIOGRAPHY]

Présentation; introduction to prose excerpts from *Du sommet d'un arbre*. Adrien Thério. photo · *Lettres québec* Spring 1987; No 45: p8.

Floating signs; review of *The Alley Cat*. John Thieme. *Can Lit* Summer-Fall 1987; No 113–114: p249–251.

BEAUCHESNE, YVES

Littérature jeunesse; reviews of children's books. Dominique Demers. *MD* Nov 21, 1987: pD6.

Pour les adolescents: quatre mains et deux solitudes; reviews of young adult novels. Dominique Demers. photo · *MD* Dec 19, 1987: pD6–D7.

BEAUDET, MARIE-ANDRÉE

La modernité: des formes qui (s')inquiètent; reviews of critical works. Whitfield. photo · *Lettres québec* Summer 1987; No 46: p56–58.

BEAUDIN, LOUISE

Mini-comptes rendus; review of *L'Arbre mort*. François Paré. *Can Child Lit* 1987; No 45: p96–97.

BEAULIEU, CHRISTIAN

Un jeune couple de Québécois en quête du "ginseng de l'âme"; review of *Nichan*. Jean-Roch Boivin. photo · *MD* Sept 12, 1987: pD2.
[FIRST NOVELS: BOOK REVIEWS]

BEAULIEU, GERMAINE

[Untitled]; review of *Textures en textes*. Anne-Marie Alonzo. *Estuaire* Spring 1987; No 44: p79.

La vitrine du livre; reviews. Guy Ferland. *MD* Aug 29, 1987: pC12.

[Untitled]; reviews of poetry books. Jacques St-Pierre. *Moebius* Winter 1987; No 31: p137–139.

BEAULIEU, VICTORY-LÉVY

Entretien-fiction avec Victor-Lévy Beaulieu; fictional essay. Gaëtan Anderson. photo · *Moebius* Winter 1987; No 31: p5–21.

Le livre d'Abel; review of *Steven le Hérault*. Neil B. Bishop. *Can Lit* Spring 1987; No 112: p126–128.

[Untitled]; notice. Paul Cauchon. photo · *MD* Oct 9, 1987: p15.
[TELEVISION AND CANADIAN LITERATURE]

La Bibliothèque Nationale fait sensation au Salon du livre; article. Paul Cauchon. photo · *MD* Nov 21, 1987: pA7.
[CONFERENCES, LITERARY]

To be continued; review of *Steven, le hérault*. Wayne Grady. *Books in Can* June-July 1987; Vol 16 No 5: p20.

[Untitled]; review of *Steven, Le Herault*. John Gregory. *Quill & Quire* April 1987; Vol 53 No 4: p28.

Un beau roman; review of *L'Héritage*. Alice Parizeau. photo · *MD* Dec 12, 1987: pD5.

Squandered craft; review of *Steven le Herault*. Thomas S. Woods. *G&M* Sept 19, 1987: pC17.

BEAUSOLEIL, CLAUDE

La culture de la confusion; reviews of *Extase et déchirure* and *L'Amour de la carte postale*. Réjean Beaudoin. *Liberté* Dec 1987; Vol 29 No 6: p107–113.

La fiction du réel / le réel de la fiction; reviews of poetry books. André Brochu. *Voix et images* Winter 1987; No 35: p322–330.

La vie littéraire; column. Marc Morin. *MD* Dec 5, 1987: pD2.
[CANADIAN LITERARY PUBLISHING; CONFERENCES, LITERARY; POETRY READINGS; WRITERS' ORGANIZATIONS]

Des genres éclatés, près du "texte infini"; review of *Extase et déchirure*. Lori Saint-Martin. photo · *MD* Oct 17, 1987: pD3.

Il y a des poèmes que nous habitons tous; reviews of poetry books. Robert Yergeau. *Lettres québec* Winter 1986–87; No 44: p36–37.

BEAUTIFUL CITY/Play by George F. Walker

[Untitled]; theatre review of *Beautiful City*. John Bemrose. photo · *Maclean's* Oct 19, 1987; Vol 100 No 42: p70.

Flaws show in Beautiful City; theatre review. Ray Conlogue. photo · *G&M* Oct 1, 1987: pD5.

Play's real anger diluted: potential George Walker firecracker fizzles into sentimentality; theatre review of *Beautiful City*. Robert Crew. photo · *TS* Oct 1, 1987: pE1.

BEAUX DRAPS/Novel by Jean-Marie Poupart

Le suicide comme métaphore; review of *Beaux draps*. Jean-Roch Boivin. *MD* May 30, 1987: pD3.

La vitrine du livre; review of *Beaux draps*. Guy Ferland. *MD* May 16, 1987: pD4.

BECOMING LIGHT/Poems by Robyn Sarah

[Untitled]; review of *Becoming Light*. Marc Côté. *Books in Can* Dec 1987; Vol 16 No 9: p31.

BEDARD, MICHAEL

Fiction just loaded with personality; reviews of children's novels. Tim Wynne-Jones. photo · *G&M* Nov 28, 1987: pC22.
[FIRST NOVELS: BOOK REVIEWS]

THE BEEKEEPER'S DAUGHTER/Poems by Bruce Hunter

[Untitled]; reviews of *The Beekeeper's Daughter* and *Midnight Found You Dancing*. Robert Hilles. *Poetry Can R* Spring 1987; Vol 8 No 2–3: p41.

The space of images; reviews of poetry books. Lavinia Inbar. *Can Lit* Summer-Fall 1987; No 113–114: p245–247.

LE BEFFROI/Periodical

La revue des revues; reviews of periodicals. Guy Ferland. *MD* Sept 19, 1987: pD6.
[CANADIAN LITERARY PERIODICALS]

Trois premiers numéros: Le Beffroi, Filigrane, Kérosène; reviews. Robert Melançon. *Liberté* April 1987; Vol 29 No 2: p125–128.
[CANADIAN LITERARY PERIODICALS]

La littérature est inactuelle; reviews of *La Nouvelle barre du jour* and *Le Beffroi*. Robert Melançon. *Liberté* Aug 1987; Vol 29 No 4: p102–108.

Ding et Dong; reviews of periodicals. Robert Melançon. *Liberté* Dec 1987; Vol 29 No 6: p122–129.
[CANADIAN LITERARY PERIODICALS]

Philosophie et littérature en revue(s): genres et styles mêlés; reviews of *Le Beffroi* and *Sédiments*. Ginette Michaud. *Liberté* April 1987; Vol 29 No 2: p129–133.
[CANADIAN LITERARY PERIODICALS]

La vitrine du livre; reviews. Jean Royer. photo · *MD* March 21, 1987: pD2.
[CANADIAN LITERARY PERIODICALS]

La vitrine du livre; reviews. Jean Royer. photo · *MD* April 18, 1987: pD2.
[CANADIAN LITERARY PERIODICALS]

Sommaires; reviews. Adrien Thério. *Lettres québec* Summer 1987; No 46: p80.

BEGAMUDRÉ, VEN

World of wonders; reviews of first novels. Janice Kulyk Keefer. *Books in Can* May 1987; Vol 16 No 4: p37–38.
[FIRST NOVELS: BOOK REVIEWS]

[Untitled]; review of *Sacrifices*. Daniel McBride. *Tor South Asian R* Summer 1987; Vol 6 No 1: p83–85.

THE BEGINNING OF THE SKY/Poems by Anne Burke

[Untitled]; reviews of poetry books. Elizabeth Woods. *Poetry Can R* Spring 1987; Vol 8 No 2–3: p49.

THE BEGINNINGS OF THE BOOK TRADE IN CANADA/Critical work by George L. Parker

[Untitled]; review of *The Beginnings of the Book Trade in Canada*. Herbert Rosengarten. *Eng Studies in Can* June 1987; Vol 13 No 2: p220–224

Early Canadian publishing; review of *The Beginnings of the Book Trade in Canada*. Marjory Whitelaw. *Atlan Prov Book R* Feb-March 1987; Vol 14 No 1: p16.

BEHIND THE ORCHESTRA/Poems by Renato Trujillo

[Untitled]; review of *Behind the Orchestra*. Raymond Filip. *Books in Can* Nov 1987; Vol 16 No 8: p26.

BEHRENS, PETER

[Untitled]; review of *Night Driving*. *Quill & Quire* March 1987; Vol 53 No 3: p71–72.

Life slices; review of *Night Driving*. Laszlo Buhasz. *G&M* June 6, 1987: pC19.

These 'night drivers' travel stark roads that enjoy neither beginning nor an end; review of *Night Driving*. Michael Carin. photo · *MG* April 25, 1987: H12.

Interesting stories reach into dark depths; review of *Night Driving*. Mark Jarman. *CH* May 31, 1987: pF5.

Book world: a 'nice little hobby' that finally paid off; column. Beverley Slopen. photo · *TS* May 3, 1987: pA25.

With used scars on their sleeves; review of *Night Driving*. Tom Spears. *TS* April 11, 1987: M8.

Tough, taut short stories; review of *Night Driving*. Morley Walker. *WFP* May 2, 1987: p84.

Travelling light; review of *Night Driving*. Allan Weiss. *Books in Can* April 1987; Vol 16 No 3: p36–37.

BEING AT HOME WITH CLAUDE/Play by René Daniel Dubois

Dubois: Toronto's playwright-of-the-hour; theatre reviews. Marianne Ackerman. photo · *MG* May 5, 1987: pB6.

Deux pièces en forme d'interrogatoire; reviews of *Being at Home with Claude* and *Fragments d'une lettre d'adieu lus par des géologues*. André-G. Bourassa. photo · *Lettres québec* Spring 1987; No 45: p50–51.

Tragic truth in Being at Home; theatre review of *Being at Home with Claude*. Ray Conlogue. photo · *G&M* April 8, 1987: pC8.

Young Quebec writer pens remarkable play; theatre review of *Being at Home with Claude*. Robert Crew. photo · *TS* April 8, 1987: pD3.

Les jeunes loups; reviews. Lucie Robert. *Voix et images* Spring 1987; Vol 12 No 3: p561–564.
[CANADIAN LITERARY PERIODICALS]

BEISSEL, HENRY

Drama of failed pole trek unfulfilled; reviews of *Flight of the Falcon* and *Poems New and Selected*. Keith Garebian. *TS* Oct 31, 1987: M5.

From ivy-covered professors; reviews of poetry books. Fraser Sutherland. *G&M* Oct 17, 1987: pE9.

BÉLANGER, JACQUES

[Untitled]; theatre review of *À la recherche de M.*. Diane Pavlovic. photo · *Jeu* 1987; No 42: p167–168.

BELGIUM-CANADA LITERARY RELATIONS

Le Québec à Liège; article. Jacques Dubois. *Voix et images* Spring 1987; Vol 12 No 3: p566–567.
[BELGIUM-CANADA LITERARY RELATIONS; CONFERENCES, LITERARY]

L'étude des lettres québécoises est obligatoire à Liège; article. Johanne Roy. *MD* April 9, 1987: p13.
[CANADIAN LITERATURE: STUDY AND TEACHING]

BELL, CAROLINE

Snoring, smuggling, and snuggling; reviews of children's stories. Susan Perren. *Quill & Quire (Books for Young People)* Dec 1987; Vol 53 No 12: p8.

BELL, WILLIAM

A little help on the dull days; reviews of children's books. Joan McGrath. *TS* Aug 2, 1987: pC11.

UNE BELLE JOURNÉE D'AVANCE/Novel by Robert Lalonde

Conservatisme; reviews of novels. Neil B. Bishop. *Can Lit* Winter 1987; No 115: p169–172.

BELLEAU, ANDRÉ

J'ai surpris la voix d'un érudit aimable; column. Jean Éthier-Blais. *MD* April 18, 1987: pD8.

"J'aime mieux vivre que me définir"; article. Marc Angenot. *Liberté* Feb 1987; Vol 29 No 1: p46–50.

Au revoir et samedi matin . . . ; essay. Jacques Belleau. *Liberté* Feb 1987; Vol 29 No 1: p58–60.

Une conversation dans le noir; essay. Jacques Brault. *Liberté* Feb 1987; Vol 29 No 1: p61–62.

Votre leon d'humanité; essay. Annie Brisset. *Liberté* April 1987; Vol 29 No 2: p106–107.

Portrait boug d'André B. (extraits de journal); journal excerpts. André Carpentier. *Liberté* Feb 1987; Vol 29 No 1: p63–65.

André Belleau, lecteur de Rabelais; article. Diane Desrosiers-Bonin. *Liberté* Feb 1987; Vol 29 No 1: p51–53.

Le fragment de Nadine; essay. Jacques Folch-Ribas. *Liberté* Feb 1987; Vol 29 No 1: p66–67.

A la mémoire d'André Belleau; essay. Madeleine Gagnon. *Liberté* Feb 1987; Vol 29 No 1: p68–69.

André Belleau et le Cercle Bakhtin; article. Chantal Gamache. *Liberté* Feb 1987; Vol 29 No 1: p54–57.

La peine capitale; essay. Jacques Godbout. *Liberté* Feb 1987; Vol 29 No 1: p70–74.

Présentation; editorial. François Hébert. *Liberté* Feb 1987; Vol 29 No 1: p2.

Célébration de la difference; essay. Naïm Kattan. *Liberté* Feb 1987; Vol 29 No 1: p75–76

Avec André Belleau et Bakhtine en Sardaigne; essay. Wladimir Krysinski. *Liberté* April 1987; Vol 29 No 2: p108–110.

Sur un concept de Bakhtine; essay. Ren Lapierre. *Liberté* Feb 1987; Vol 29 No 1: p77–78.

André Belleau: entretien autobiographique; interview. Wilfrid Lemoine. *Liberté* Feb 1987; Vol 29 No 1: p4–27.

L'étonnement Belleau; essay. Wilfrid Lemoine. *Liberté* Feb 1987; Vol 29 No 1: p79–81.

André Belleau; obituary. Laurent Mailhot. *Études fran* Winter 1987; Vol 22 No 3: p3–5.

Pour mémoire; article. Gilles Marcotte. *Liberté* Feb 1987; Vol 29 No 1: p39–45.

Belleau; review of *Surprendre les voix*. Robert Melançon. *Liberté* April 1987; Vol 29 No 2: p137–139.

Ph.D., écrivain; article. Robert Melançon. *Liberté* Feb 1987; Vol 29 No 1: p32–3.

André Belleau (1930–1986); essay. Fernand Ouellette. *Liberté* Feb 1987; Vol 29 No 1: p28–31.

La nuit transfigure; essay. Michel Pierssens. *Liberté* Feb 1987; Vol 29 No 1: p82–84.

Un collaborateur clair; essay. Jean-Guy Pilon. *Liberté* Feb 1987; Vol 29 No 1: p85.

Le destinataire privilège; essay. François Ricard. *Liberté* Feb 1987; Vol 29 No 1: p86–87.

La conscience comme trame de vie; essay. Suzanne Robert. *Liberté* Feb 1987; Vol 29 No 1: p88–89.

André Belleau: une voix reconnaissable entre toutes; review of *Surprendre les voix*. Lori Saint-Martin. photo · *MD* Jan 24, 1987: pB3.

Il inspirait la gratitude; essay. Pierre Vadeboncoeur. *Liberté* Feb 1987; Vol 29 No 1: p90–91.

André Belleau, professeur et essayiste (1930–1986); obituary. André Vanasse. photo · *Lettres québec* Winter 1986–87; No 44: p12.

BELLEFEUILLE, ROBERT

Théâtre au masculin; reviews of plays. Jane Moss. *Can Lit* Spring 1987; No 112: p180–183.

LES BELLES-SOEURS/Play by Michel Tremblay

Effets sonores et signification dans les Belles-soeurs de Michel Tremblay; article. Alvina Ruprecht. *Voix et images* Spring 1987; Vol 12 No 3: p439–451.
[STRUCTURALIST WRITING AND CRITICISM]

BELLINGHAM, BRENDA

Romance and rebellion in young adult fiction; reviews of *Nobody Asked Me* and *Storm Child*. Sarah Ellis. *Can Child Lit* 1987; No 46: p87–89.

BEN'S SNOW SONG: A WINTER PICNIC/Children's story by Hazel J. Hutchins

Snoring, smuggling, and snuggling; reviews of children's stories. Susan Perren. *Quill & Quire (Books for Young People)* Dec 1987; Vol 53 No 12: p8.

BENEATH THE WESTERN SLOPES/Short stories by Patrick Roscoe

Stories of the medieval in the present day; reviews of *Beneath the Western Slopes* and *Medieval Hour in the Author's Mind*. Clark Blaise. *Quill & Quire* June 1987; Vol 53 No 6: p34.

New author weaves poetic stories into magical fantasy; review of *Beneath the Western Slopes*. Cecelia Frey. *CH* Sept 20, 1987: pE6.

Writer leads us on his Mexican magical mystery tour; review of *Beneath the Western Slopes*. P. Scott Lawrence. photo · *MG* July 18, 1987: J8.

Reader left with agreeable sense of déjà vu; reviews of *Beneath the Western Slopes* and *The Woman Upstairs*. Hugh McKellar. *TS* Aug 9, 1987: pA21.

[Untitled]; review of *Beneath the Western Slopes*. Constance Rooke. *Malahat R* Sept 1987; No 80: p137.

BENITO/Novel by François Gravel

Benito, vierge et rêveur de profession; review of *Benito*. Réjean Beaudoin. *Liberté* Oct 1987; Vol 29 No 5: p163.

Benito ou la confirmation d'un talent de romancier; review of *Benito*. Yvon Bernier. photo · *Lettres québec* Autumn 1987; No 47: p24–25.

L'histoire d'un homme qui voulait la paix; review of *Benito*. Jean-Roch Boivin. photo · *MD* May 16, 1987: pD3.

À l'impossible certains sont tenus; reviews of *Benito* and *Aaa, Aâh, Ha ou les amours malaisées*. Pierre Hébert. *Voix et images* Autumn 1987; Vol 13 No 1: p192–194.

BENSON, EUGENE

[Untitled]; review of *English-Canadian Theatre*. Rota Herzberg Lister. *Can Drama* 1987; Vol 13 No 2: p227–228.

A cogent view of Canadian theatre; review of *English-Canadian Theatre*. Margaret Penman. photo · *TS* Dec 27, 1987: pE18.

BERESFORD-HOWE, CONSTANCE

Canadian author to give reading; article. *TS (Neighbours)* April 21, 1987: p8.
[FICTION READINGS]

From mind to mind; reviews of *Night Studies* and *Wishbones*. H.W. Connor. *Can Lit* Spring 1987; No 112: p118–120.
[FIRST NOVELS: BOOK REVIEWS]

BERGER, YVES

Amérique, utopie; review of *Les Matins du Nouveau Monde*. Jacques Folch-Ribas. *Liberté* June 1987; Vol 29 No 3: p106–107.

BERGERON, BERTRAND

La vie littéraire; column. Marc Morin. *MD* Nov 14, 1987: pD14.
[AWARDS, LITERARY; CHILDREN'S LITERATURE; POETRY READINGS]

BERSIANIK, LOUKY

Free premiere set for Fireworks; article. *TS* April 12, 1987: pC6.
[AUDIO-VISUALS AND CANADIAN LITERATURE]

BERTIL, E. [pseud.]

Imperfect conquests; reviews of *The Manor House of De Villeray* and *Le Tour du Québec par deux enfants*. Anthony Raspa. *Can Lit* Winter 1987; No 115: p172–174.
[CANADIAN LITERARY PERIODICALS]

BERTIN, JACQUES

[Untitled]; review of *Felix Leclerc, le roi heureux*. Nicole Décarie. *Moebius* Spring 1987; No 32: p125–127.

Mais Félix a préféré rester dans son ile . . . ; article. Gilles Lesage. photo · *MD* Jan 28, 1987: p1,10.

Le Québec de Félix Leclerc; review of *Félix Leclerc, le roi heureux*. Jean Royer. *MD* Jan 24, 1987: pB3–B4.

BESSETTE, GRARD

Dans les poches; reviews. Guy Ferland. *MD* Sept 26, 1987: pD6.

La vitrine du livre; reviews. Guy Ferland. *MD* Nov 14, 1987: pD16.
[ANTHOLOGIES: BOOK REVIEWS]

L'Académie canadienne française accueille Félix; article. Marie Laurier. photo · *MD* Dec 24, 1987: pA7.
[AWARDS, LITERARY]

Bar hopping; review of *Incubation*. Rui Umezawa. *G&M* June 20, 1987: pC19.

Montréal dans les années 50; review of *La Bagarre*. Pierre-Louis Vaillancourt. photo · *Lettres québec* Spring 1987; No 45: p57–59.

BEST CANADIAN STORIES/Anthology series

High performance; review of *87: Best Canadian Stories*. William French. *G&M* Dec 19, 1987: pC21.
[ANTHOLOGIES: BOOK REVIEWS]

From Ahmadabad to Tennessee; reviews of *86: Best Canadian Stories* and *Coming Attractions 4*. Wayne Grady. *Books in Can* March 1987; Vol 16 No 2: p29–30.

Canada's short fiction shortchanged here; reviews of *87: Best Canadian Stories* and *Coming Attractions 5*. Geoff Hancock. *TS* Dec 27, 1987: pE19.
[ANTHOLOGIES: BOOK REVIEWS]

Story anthologies: the tried, the true, and the best of the new; reviews of short story anthologies. Brent Ledger. photo · *Quill & Quire* Jan 1987; Vol 53 No 1: p29.
[ANTHOLOGIES: BOOK REVIEWS]

Stories vivid, unpleasant—and memorable; reviews of short story books. John Mills. *Fiddlehead* Autumn 1987; No 153: p91–95.

Short fiction is thriving; review of *86: Best Canadian Stories*. Jamie Portman. *CH* Jan 18, 1987: pE4.
[ANTHOLOGIES: BOOK REVIEWS]

THE BEST OF ALBERTA/Anthology

The allure of Alberta in history and contemporary life; review of *The Best of Alberta*. Charles Mandel. photo · *Quill & Quire* Dec 1987; Vol 53 No 12: p27.
[ANTHOLOGIES: BOOK REVIEWS]

Tivy on Wednesday; column. Patrick Tivy. *CH* Nov 4, 1987: pB1.

BETTS, JIM

Dubois: Toronto's playwright-of-the-hour; theatre reviews. Marianne Ackerman. photo · *MG* May 5, 1987: pB6.

The Fabulous Kelley fails to fulfil promise; theatre review. Robert Crew. *TS* April 30, 1987: H3.

Last Voyage appeals to all; theatre review of *The Last Voyage of the Devil's Wheel*. Pat Donnelly. photo · *MG* Dec 16, 1987: pF3.

Star-spangled shows high-stepping to T.O.; article. Henry Mietkiewicz. photo · *TS* June 26, 1987: pE1,E3.

BETWEEN MEN/Novel by Katherine Govier

[Untitled]; review of *Between Men*. *Can Forum* Nov 1987; Vol 67 No 773: p38.

The fight for love and truth hampered by riddle of past; reviews of *Between Men* and *Getting Married in Buffalo Jump*. Ken Adachi. photo · *TS* Oct 17, 1987: M4.

Frontier women: two tales in search of the perfect marriage; reviews of *Between Men* and *Getting Married in Buffalo Jump*. Ruby Andrew. photo · *Quill & Quire* Sept 1987; Vol 53 No 9: p76.

Unlikely characters populate realistic Calgary urbanscape; review of *Between Men*. Lucinda Chodan. photo · *MG* Oct 24, 1987: J13.

Mawkish history; review of *Between Men*. William French. *G&M* Sept 26, 1987: pC21.

Heart of the city; review of *Between Men*. Kenneth McGoogan. *Books in Can* Aug-Sept 1987; Vol 16 No 6: p18-19.

Book puts Calgary on literary map; review of *Between Men*. Kenneth McGoogan. photo · *CH* Sept 5, 1987: H7.

A mating of east and west; review of *Between Men*. Mary W. Riskin. *Maclean's* Oct 12, 1987; Vol 100 No 41: p56h

Novel's reach exceeds its grasp; review of *Between Men*. David Williamson. photo · *WFP* Sept 26, 1987: p64.

BEYOND FORGET: REDISCOVERING THE PRAIRIES/ Essays by Mark Abley

Hidden in prairies are little oddities, large truths; review of *Beyond Forget*. Lucinda Chodan. photo · *MG* Jan 31, 1987: pB8.

Young man goes west, again; review of *Beyond Forget*. Gwen Dambrofsky. photo · *TS* Feb 14, 1987: M4.

Lost horizons; review of *Beyond Forget*. Douglas Glover. *Books in Can* Jan-Feb 1987; Vol 16 No 1: p20.

A love for the land in the west that once was; review of *Beyond Forget*. Don Kerr. photo · *Quill & Quire* Jan 1987; Vol 53 No 1: p31.

[Untitled]; review of *Beyond Forget*. Andrew H. Malcolm. *NYT Book R* July 5, 1987: p15.

[Untitled]; review of *Beyond Forget*. George Melnyk. photo · *NeWest R* Nov 1987; Vol 13 No 3: p14.

[Untitled]; review of *Beyond Forget*. Peter Millard. photo · *NeWest R* Nov 1987; Vol 13 No 3: p15.

[Untitled]; review of *Beyond Forget*. Constance Rooke. *Malahat R* Sept 1987; No 80: p130-131.

BEYOND THE BLUE MOUNTAINS: AN AUTOBIOG- RAPHY/Autobiography by George Woodcock

George Woodcock's glassy prose banishes pain, passion; review of *Beyond the Blue Mountains*. Mark Abley. photo · *MG* Dec 31, 1987: pB7.

There are times when you must go home again; review of *Beyond the Blue Mountains*. Ken Adachi. photo · *TS* Nov 28, 1987: M4.

The driven writer; review of *Beyond the Blue Mountains*. William French. *G&M* Nov 21, 1987: pC21.

BEYOND: POEMS BOOK NINE/Poems by J. Alvin Speers

[Untitled]; reviews of poetry books. Anne Burke. *Poetry Can R* Summer 1987; Vol 8 No 4: p38.

BHAGGIYADATTA, KRISANTHA SRI

Hard time, maximum time; reviews of *The Only Minority Is the Bourgeoisie* and *Doing Time*. Marlene Philip. *Tor South Asian R* Spring 1987; Vol 5 No 3: p28-34.

BHATIA, JUNE

The romance of the Far East; review of *The Moneylenders of Shahpur*. James P. Carley. *G&M* July 25, 1987: pC15.

Edmonton author's a hit in England; article. Kathy English. photo · *TS* March 8, 1987: pD5.

Cultural collisions fascinate; review of *The Moneylenders of Shahpur*. Susan Scott. *CH* April 12, 1987: pF7.

Book world: a little-known bestseller; column. Beverley Slopen. *TS* Jan 11, 1987: pA16.

BIANCHI, JOHN

Baby of the family gets respect raising flock of Canada geese; reviews of children's books. Janice Kennedy. *MG* Oct 3, 1987: J13.

Mini-reviews; reviews of children's books. Margaret Paré. *Can Child Lit* 1987; No 45: p93-96.

Familiarity and TV's stranglehold on life; reviews of children's books. Tim Wynne-Jones. *G&M* Nov 14, 1987: pE4.
[FESTIVALS, LITERARY]

BIBLICAL MYTHS AND MYTHOLOGY

The religious roots of the feminine identity issue: Margaret Laurence's The Stone Angel and Margaret Atwood's Surfacing; article. Evelyn J. Hinz. abstract · *J of Can Studies* Spring 1987; Vol 22 No 1: p17-31.
[FEMINIST WRITING AND CRITICISM; GOD IN LITERATURE]

Apocalyptic imaginations: notes on Atwood's The Handmaid's Tale and Findley's Not Wanted on the Voyage; article. W.J. Keith. *Essays on Can Writ* Winter 1987; No 35: p123-134.
[THE APOCALYPSE; GOD IN LITERATURE; SATIRIC WRITING]

Religion, place, & self in early twentieth-century Canada: Robert Norwood's poetry; article. Alex Kizuk. *Can Lit* Winter 1987; No 115: p66-77.
[RELIGIOUS THEMES]

Image juxtaposition in A Jest Of God; article. B.A. Legendre. *Studies in Can Lit* 1987; Vol 12 No 1: p53-68.

The bible and myth in Antonine Maillet's Pélagie-la-Charrette; article. Paul G. Socken. *Studies in Can Lit* 1987; Vol 12 No 2: p187-198.
[VIOLENCE IN CANADIAN LITERATURE]

BIBLIOGRAPHIE ANALYTIQUE D'YVES THÉRIAULT, 1940–1984/Annotated bibliography by Denis Carrier

Une bibliographie indispensable; review of *Bibliographie analytique d'Yves Thériault, 1940–1984*. Anthony Purdy. *Can Child Lit* 1987; No 45: p54-55.

THE BICENTENNIAL LECTURES ON NEW BRUNS- WICK LITERATURE/Critical essays

New Brunswick letters; review of *The Bicentennial Lectures on New Brunswick Literature*. Alan R. Young. *Can Lit* Spring 1987; No 112: p146-148.

BIG PLANS/Short stories by Paul de Barros

Today's assignment: short fiction that's worth a long look; reviews of short story books. Douglas Hill. *G&M* March 14, 1987: pE19.
[ANTHOLOGIES: BOOK REVIEWS]

[Untitled]; review of *Big Plans*. Joel Yanofsky. *Books in Can* Aug-Sept 1987; Vol 16 No 6: p25.

BIG SARAH'S LITTLE BOOTS/Children's story by Paulette Bourgeois

Book captures emotional moment for child; reviews of *Big Sarah's Little Boots* and *A Difficult Day*. Joan Craven. *CH (Neighbors)* Oct 28, 1987: pA18.

Baby of the family gets respect raising flock of Canada geese; reviews of children's books. Janice Kennedy. *MG* Oct 3, 1987: J13.

[Untitled]; review of *Big Sarah's Little Boots*. Rosemary Kennedy. *CH* Dec 6, 1987: pD9

A title that will grab teenagers; reviews of children's books. Joan McGrath. *TS* Oct 25, 1987: pA18.

A fun bunch of books to read and look at; reviews of *Big Sarah's Little Boots* and *Ringtail*. Frieda Wishinsky. *Quill & Quire (Books for Young People)* Aug 1987; Vol 53 No 8: p3.

BIGRAS, JULIEN

Des contes pour guérir; article. Dominique Demers. photo · *MD* May 30, 1987: pD6.

BILICO/Play by Marco Micone

Le théâtre qu'on joue; theatre reviews. André Dionne. illus photo · *Lettres québec* Spring 1987; No 45: p47–48.

[Untitled]; theatre review of *Bilico*. Diane Pavlovic. photo · *Jeu* 1987; No 42: p149–151.

BILLINGS, ROBERT

Noted poet buried; article. *WFP* June 30, 1987: p37.

Critic brought writers to public's attention; obituary. *G&M* June 30, 1987: pD16.

Funeral held for poet Billings; article. *MG* June 30, 1987: pC9.

[Untitled]; essay. Roo Borson. *Poetry Can R* Summer 1987; Vol 8 No 4: p15.

Editorial. Beverley Daurio. *Poetry Can R* Spring 1987; Vol 8 No 1–2: p2.

[Untitled]; essay. Barry Dempster. *Poetry Can R* Summer 1987; Vol 8 No 4: p15.

[Untitled]; essay. Mary di Michele. *Poetry Can R* Summer 1987; Vol 8 No 4: p14.

Dreaming for our children; column. Mary di Michele. *Poetry Can R* Fall 1987; Vol 9 No 1: p19.

[Untitled]; essay. David Donnell. *Poetry Can R* Summer 1987; Vol 8 No 4: p15.

[Untitled]; reviews of *The Revels* and *Northern Poems: Where the Heart Catches Its Breath*. Gary Draper. *Poetry Can R* Spring 1987; Vol 8 No 2–3: p37.

[Untitled]; essay. Greg Gatenby. *Poetry Can R* Summer 1987; Vol 8 No 4: p15.

[Untitled]; essay. Maria Jacobs. *Poetry Can R* Summer 1987; Vol 8 No 4: p14.

[Untitled]; essay. Kim Maltman. *Poetry Can R* Summer 1987; Vol 8 No 4: p14.

Robert Billings, 38, poet, critic, teacher; obituary. Alexandra Radkewycz. photo · *TS* June 29, 1987: pA23.

[Untitled]; reviews of poetry books. Martin Singleton. *Cross Can Writ Q* 1987; Vol 9 No 2: p19–20.

BILLY AND THE BUBBLESHIP/MAD QUEEN OF MORDRA/Children's novel by Elwy Yost

Tales that will tempt tots of all ages; review of *Mad Queen of Mordra*. Joan McGrath. *TS* Sept 19, 1987: M6.

BILLY BISHOP GOES TO WAR/Play by John Gray

Language and structure in Billy Bishop Goes To War; article. Jean MacIntyre. *Can Drama* 1987; Vol 13 No 1: p50–59.

BILSON, GEOFFREY

[Untitled]; letter to the editor. Geoffrey Bilson. *Can Child Lit* 1987; No 45: p98.

BINNS, RONALD

[Untitled]; reviews of critical works. Ronald B. Hatch. *Eng Studies in Can* March 1987; Vol 13 No 1: p107–115.

Critical programmes; reviews of *Malcolm Lowry* and *Four Contemporary Novelists*. Paul Tiessen. *Can Lit* Winter 1987; No 115: p157–159.

BIRDSELL, SANDRA

Birdsell early pick; article. *WFP* Feb 13, 1987: p27.
[TRANSLATIONS OF CANADIAN LITERATURE]

Birdsell drama wrapped; article. *WFP* Sept 25, 1987: p29.
[TELEVISION AND CANADIAN LITERATURE]

Birdsell says she's touched by her own film; article. Donald Campbell. photo · *WFP* Oct 30, 1987: p29.
[FILM ADAPTATIONS OF CANADIAN LITERATURE]

A new horizon; biographical article. Stephen Godfrey. photo · *G&M* May 16, 1987: pC1.

The Lafreniere family of Agassiz; reviews of *Night Travellers* and *Ladies of the House*. J.K. Johnstone. illus · *NeWest R* April 1987; Vol 12 No 8: p12.

"The missing story"; introduction to play excerpt from *The Revival*. Kim McCaw;. *Prairie Fire* Spring 1987; Vol 8 No 1: p42–43.

Niagara Falls boring television; television review. Paul McKie. photo · *WFP* Nov 9, 1987: p22.
[TELEVISION AND CANADIAN LITERATURE]

Novelist, poet Kroetsch receives top payment under library fee plan; article. Barbara Robson. *WFP* April 22, 1987: p38.
[GOVERNMENT GRANTS FOR WRITERS/PUBLISHERS; LIBRARY SERVICES AND CANADIAN LITERATURE]

Interview with Sandra Birdsell. Alan Twigg. photo · *NeWest R* Nov 1987; Vol 13 No 3: p2–3.

Male director adds richness to short-story filming, author says; article. Morley Walker. photo · *WFP* March 19, 1987: p42.
[TELEVISION AND CANADIAN LITERATURE]

BIRNEY, EARLE

Poet Earle Birney in critical condition after cardiac arrest; article. *G&M* March 20, 1987: pA14.

Honored poet Earle Birney critically ill; article. *TS* March 20, 1987: pA6.

Poet ill; article. *MG* March 21, 1987: pA5.

Poet's health failing; article. *WFP* March 21, 1987: p29.

Poet Birney stable; article. *WFP* March 23, 1987: p17.

Birney's condition slightly improved; article. *WFP* March 25, 1987: p44.

Birney rallies slightly; article. *CH* March 25, 1987: pC9.

Passages; column. *Maclean's* March 30, 1987; Vol 100 No 13: p4.

Poet Earle Birney improves in hospital; article. *TS* April 14, 1987: pD3.

Earle Birney stable after heart attack; article. *MG* April 7, 1987: pA10.

From the hazel bough of Yeats: Birney's masterpiece; article. David Latham. *Can Poet* Fall-Winter 1987; No 21: p52–58.

BIRO, FREDERICK

[Untitled]; review of *The Perfect Circus*. Joan McGrath. *Quill & Quire* March 1987; Vol 53 No 3: p72–73.

THE BISHOP/Novel by David Helwig

Sainty, beloved bishop relives past as he lies dying; review of *The Bishop*. Barbara Black. *MG* Sept 19, 1987: J8.

Maple Leaf memories in print; reviews of *The Bishop* and *The Glassy Sea*. Lew Gloin. *TS* July 12, 1987: pA18.

A humanistic vision of the lives of churchmen and women; reviews of *The Glassy Sea* and *The Bishop*. Douglas Hill. *G&M* Sept 12, 1987: pC17.

Death with the proper shaman; review of *The Bishop*. John Leggett. *NYT Book R* Jan 11, 1987: p23.

BISSETT, BILL

[Untitled]; reviews of *Canada Gees Mate for Life* and *Zygal*. Phil Hall. *Poetry Can R* Fall 1987; Vol 9 No 1: p34.

Seeker & finder; reviews of *Canada Gees Mate for Life* and *Rootless Tree*. Bruce Whiteman. *Can Lit* Winter 1987; No 115: p148–150.

BISSOONDATH, NEIL

New faces; survey article. photo · *TS* March 7, 1987: K1-K4.
[AUTHORS, CANADIAN]

BITING NAILS/Play by Gail Robinson

Melody Farm feels like two plays trying to be one; theatre reviews of *Melody Farm* and *Biting Nails*. Stephen Godfrey. photo · *G&M* Feb 18, 1987: pC7.

THE BLACK BONSPIEL OF WULLIE MacCRIMMON/ Play by W.O. Mitchell

Black Bonspiel presents a devil of a problem; theatre review of *The Black Bonspiel of Wullie MacCrimmon*. Ray Conlogue. photo · *G&M* April 18, 1987: pC7.

BLACK ROBE/Novel by Brian Moore

Quebec director thrills 'n' chills; article about Yves Simoneau. photo · *TS* Feb 7, 1987: pG9.
[FILM ADAPTATIONS OF CANADIAN LITERATURE]

[Untitled]; review of *Black Robe*. *Fin Post (Moneywise Magazine)* April 1987: p10.

Devil, angel: Alliance has it covered; column. Sid Adilman. *TS* May 16, 1987: pG3.
[FILM ADAPTATIONS OF CANADIAN LITERATURE]

Brian Moore's Jesuit priest travels into heart of darkness; reviews of novels. Barbara Black. *MG* March 7, 1987: H11.

Sorceries; review of *Black Robe*. Kerry McSweeney. *Essays on Can Writ* Spring 1987; No 34: p111–118.

Book world: Maggie Smith as Judith Hearne?; column. Beverley Slopen. *TS* Jan 25, 1987: pB6.
[AUTHORS, CANADIAN; FILM ADAPTATIONS OF CANADIAN LITERATURE]

BLACK SWAN/Short stories by Gertrude Story

[Untitled]; review of *Black Swan*. Weyman Chan. *Dandelion* Spring-Summer 1987; Vol 14 No 1: p87–89.

[Untitled]; review of *Black Swan*. Gideon Forman. *Books in Can* May 1987; Vol 16 No 4: p20–21.

A true voice; review of *Black Swan*. Hilda Kirkwood. *Waves* Spring 1987; Vol 15 No 4: p74–76.

[Untitled]; review of *Black Swan*. Mary S. Ladky. *Rubicon* Fall 1987; No 9: p200–201.

Enduring a thankless existence with father; reviews of *Black Swan* and *Small Regrets*. Hugh McKellar. *TS* Jan 31, 1987: M4.

Stories vivid, unpleasant—and memorable; reviews of short story books. John Mills. *Fiddlehead* Autumn 1987; No 153: p91–95.

BLACK, AYANNA

Each to her own rhythm; reviews of poetry books. Lesley McAllister. *TS* July 25, 1987: M5.

BLAINE'S WAY/Young adult novel by Monica Hughes

There and back again; review of *Blaine's Way*. Mary Pritchard. *Can Child Lit* 1987; No 46: p66–67.

BLAIS, MARIE-CLAIRE

Marie-Claire Blais et Yves Berger parmi les finalistes du prix Prince-Rainier-III; article. photo · *MD* March 7, 1987: pB3.
[AWARDS, LITERARY]

L'art pictural dans les derniers romans de Marie-Claire Blais; article. Marie Couillard. *Can Lit* Summer-Fall 1987; No 113–114: p268–272.

Dans les poches; reviews of paperback books. Guy Ferland. *MD* Oct 31, 1987: pD6.

Lire et relire Marie-Claire Blais; review of *L'Oeuvre romanesque de Marie-Claire Blais*. Chantal Gamache. *Lettres québec* Spring 1987; No 45: p52.

[Untitled]; review of *L'Oeuvre romanesque de Marie-Claire Blais*. Annette Hayward. *U of Toronto Q* Fall 1987; Vol 57 No 1: p183–184.

Une belle et dense histoire difficile à porter à l'écran; article. Francine Laurendeau. photo · *MD* Oct 24, 1987: pC1,C12.
[FILM ADAPTATIONS OF CANADIAN LITERATURE]

La forêt dans l'oeuvre imaginaire de Marie-Claire Blais; article. Irène Oore. abstract · *Études can* 1987; No 23: p93–108.
[NATURE IN CANADIAN LITERATURE]

La vitrine du livre; reviews. Jean Royer. photo · *MD* March 28, 1987: pD2.
[CANADIAN LITERARY PERIODICALS]

Steeped in lechery; review of *Deaf to the City*. Paul West. illus · *NYT Book R* Sept 20, 1987: p12–13.

BLAISE, CLARK

Fear cancels tour; article. *WFP* May 29, 1987: p31.

[Untitled]; review of *Resident Alien*. *Queen's Q* Spring 1987; Vol 94 No 1: p254.

Whereness; review of *Resident Alien*. Catherine Sheldrick Ross. *Can Lit* Spring 1987; No 112: p164–165.

Photography "in camera"; article. Peter Sims. *Can Lit* Summer-Fall 1987; No 113–114: p145–166.

Book world: Air India bombing 'a Canadian tragedy'; column. Beverley Slopen. *TS* Feb 8, 1987: pG9.

BLAKESLEE, MARY

[Untitled]; reviews of *Edythe With a Y* and *It Isn't Easy Being Ms. Teeny Wonderful*. Patty Lawlor. *Quill & Quire (Books for Young People)* April 1987; Vol 53 No 4: p8.

[Untitled]; review of *Outta Sight*. Patty Lawlor. *Quill & Quire (Books for Young People)* Aug 1987; Vol 53 No 8: p7.

Family ties and mysteries; reviews of children's novels. Joan McGrath. *Quill & Quire (Books for Young People)* Dec 1987; Vol 53 No 12: p10.

BLANCHET, ALAIN

[Untitled]; review of *Amérique intérieure*. André Roy. *Estuaire* Summer 1987; No 45: p49.

[Untitled]; reviews of poetry books. Jacques St-Pierre. *Moebius* Winter 1987; No 31: p137–139.

BLEUS DE MINE/Poems by Anne-Marie Alonzo

Maniaques depressifs; reviews of poetry books. Mark Benson. *Can Lit* Spring 1987; No 112: p138–141.

BLICKER, SEYMOUR

Up Your Alley is a jangle of conflicting styles; theatre review. Ray Conlogue. photo · *G&M* Jan 15, 1987: pD4.
[DRAMATIC ADAPTATIONS OF CANADIAN LITERATURE]

Curtain rises on new play, new theatre; theatre review of *Up Your Alley*. Wayne Grigsby. *MG* Jan 12, 1987: pB5.

BLIND PAINTING

See PEINTURE AVEUGLE/BLIND PAINTING/Poems by Robert Melançon

BLIND ZONE/Poems by Steven Smith

[Untitled]; reviews of *Blind Zone* and *Wenkchemna*. Dennis Duffy. *Poetry Can R* Spring 1987; Vol 8 No 2–3: p45.

Excesses; reviews of poetry books. Eva Tihanyi. *Can Lit* Winter 1987; No 115: p200–202.

BLIZZARD SUR QUÉBEC/Novel by Alice Parizeau

Blizzard . . . : un sommet dans l'art d'Alice Parizeau; review of *Blizzard sur Québec*. Jean Éthier-Blais. *MD* Dec 5, 1987: pD10.

Un roman à la gloire de l'Hydro-Québec; review of *Blizzard sur Québec*. Jean-Roch Boivin. *MD* Nov 21, 1987: pD3.

BLODGETT, E.D.

A sophisticated, compelling dialogue; review of *Configuration*. Estelle Dansereau. *Essays on Can Writ* Spring 1987; No 34: p174–179.

LA BLONDE D'YVON/Novel by Alain Poissant

Auprès de ma blonde, qu'il fait bon, fait bon . . . ; review of *La Blonde d'Yvon*. Jean-Roch Boivin. *MD* Oct 17, 1987: pD3.

BLONDEAU, DOMINIQUE

Aujourd'hui; column. *MD* April 7, 1987: p10.
[FICTION READINGS]

Cette fleur qui veut occuper tout la place; review of *La Poursuite*. Jean Éthier-Blais. *MD* May 23, 1987: pD8.

Être adolescent, aujourd'hui; review of *La Poursuite*. Pierre Hébert. photo · *Lettres québec* Spring 1987; No 45: p28–29.

[Untitled]; review of *La Poursuite*. Hélène Rioux. *Moebius* Winter 1987; No 31: p135–137.

BLOOD RELATIONS/Play by Sharon Pollock

Blood Relations script at fault; theatre review. Robert Davis. photo · *TS (Neighbours)* April 7, 1987: p16.

Lizzie Borden story staged in Pickering; article. Paul Irish. *TS (Neighbours)* March 24, 1987: p14.

Production of Blood Relations offers electric performances; theatre review. Alex Law. photo · *TS (Neighbours)* April 7, 1987: p16.

BLOODSONG AND OTHER STORIES OF SOUTH AFRICA/Short stories by Ernst Havemann

[Untitled]; review of *Bloodsong*. Michael Bloom. *NYT Book R* Aug 23, 1987: p16.

Crossing the bar; review of *Bloodsong*. John Goddard. *Books in Can* Dec 1987; Vol 16 No 9: p33,35.

Moving tales of homelands left behind; reviews of *Bloodsong* and *Tales from Firozsha Baag*. Janet Hamilton. photo · *Quill & Quire* June 1987; Vol 53 No 6: p32.

Inside South Africa, fictionally; article, includes review of *Bloodsong*. Ross Klatte. photo · *CH* July 26, 1987: pE5.

Reflecting South Africa; review of *Bloodsong*. John Shingler. photo · *MG* Oct 3, 1987: J12.

South African stories convey clear moral vision; review of *Bloodsong*. Morley Walker. *WFP* Sept 26, 1987: p64.

BLOODY JACK/Long poem by Dennis Cooley

Stealing the text: George Bowering's Kerrisdale Elegies and Dennis Cooley's Bloody Jack; article. Smaro Kamboureli. *Can Lit* Winter 1987; No 115: p9–23.
[CANADIAN LONG POEM; STRUCTURALIST WRITING AND CRITICISM]

BLUE BUFFALO/Periodical

Mainstreet Calgary; column. *CH (Neighbors)* July 22, 1987: pA6.
[CANADIAN LITERARY PERIODICALS]

J.P. Donleavy here in '88; column. Kenneth McGoogan. *CH* July 26, 1987: pE5.
[AWARDS, LITERARY; CANADIAN LITERARY PERIODICALS; CANADIAN LITERARY PUBLISHING; FESTIVALS, LITERARY]

BLUE HANDS/Play by Jesse Glenn Bodyan

Beyond the Fringe; reviews of plays. Judith Rudakoff. *Books in Can* March 1987; Vol 16 No 2: p18.

THE BLUE HOUSE/Novel by Lesley McAllister

TV's generation suffers detachment; reviews of *The Blue House* and *Not Noir*. Colline Caulder. *TS* Nov 28, 1987: M5.

Book was fiction and piece fictitious too; letter to the editor. Beverley Daurio. *TS* Dec 27, 1987: pB2.

Small regional presses as saviors of cultural information; reviews of fictional works. Douglas Hill. *G&M* Oct 10, 1987: pC21.
[FIRST NOVELS: BOOK REVIEWS]

THE BLUE NOTEBOOK: REPORTS ON CANADIAN CULTURE/Critical essays by Doug Fetherling

[Untitled]; review of *The Blue Notebook*. *Queen's Q* Summer 1987; Vol 94 No 2: p461–464.

[Untitled]; review of *The Blue Notebook*. Lynette Hunter. *British J of Can Studies* June 1987; Vol 2 No 1: p188–189.

In character; review of *The Blue Notebook*. Maurice Yacowar. *Can Lit* Spring 1987; No 112: p148–149.

THE BLUE ONTARIO HEMINGWAY BOAT RACE/Short stories by David Donnell

Settling with style; review of *The Blue Ontario Hemingway Boat Race*. Patrick Coleman. *Essays on Can Writ* Winter 1987; No 35: p152–155.

BLUE RIDERS/Poems by Laurence Hutchman

Domanski, Harris, Hutchman; reviews of poetry books. Barry Dempster. *Poetry Can R* Summer 1987; Vol 8 No 4: p31.

[Untitled]; review of *Blue Riders*. Gerald Doerksen. *Rubicon* Spring 1987; No 8: p222–223.

In voice; reviews of poetry books. Richard Stevenson. *Can Lit* Spring 1987; No 112: p167–169.

BLUEBEARD'S EGG/Short stories by Margaret Atwood

Embracing the wilderness; reviews of *The Oxford Book of Canadian Short Stories in English* and *Bluebeard's Egg*. John Clute. *Times Lit Supp* June 12, 1987; No 4393: p626.
[ANTHOLOGIES: BOOK REVIEWS]

Film stars stage celebrity bashes; column. Dave Haynes. *WFP* June 19, 1987: p21.
[INTERNATIONAL REVIEWS OF CANADIAN LITERATURE]

New & noteworthy; review of *Bluebeard's Egg*. George Johnson. *NYT Book R* Nov 22, 1987: p50.

BLUES NOTE/Short stories by François Piazza

Portrait de Piazza au coeur de la ville; review of *Blues Note*. Jean Royer. photo · *MD* Jan 17, 1987: pB3.

A BODY SURROUNDED BY WATER/Novel by Eric Wright

Inspector Salter of Green Gables; review of *A Body Surrounded by Water*. Ken Adachi. *TS* July 12, 1987: pA19

[Untitled]; review of *A Body Surrounded by Water*. Ruby Andrew. *Quill & Quire* Oct 1987; Vol 53 No 10: p22–23.

[Untitled]; reviews of *Doubtful Motives* and *A Body Surrounded by Water*. Paul Cabray. *MG* Aug 15, 1987: L2.

Murder & mayhem: the English style of the whodunits; reviews of *A Body Surrounded by Water* and *Doubtful Motives*. Margaret Cannon. photo · *G&M* July 18, 1987: pC17.

[Untitled]; review of *A Body Surrounded by Water*. Douglas Malcolm. *Books in Can* Aug-Sept 1987; Vol 16 No 6: p25.

From P.E.I. to Big Apple; review of *A Body Surrounded by Water*. Kenneth McGoogan. *CH* Aug 2, 1987: pC8.

Crime novels provide a study in contrasts; reviews of *Doubtful Motives* and *A Body Surrounded by Water*. David Williamson. photo · *WFP* Aug 1, 1987: p50.

BODYAN, JESSE GLENN

Beyond the Fringe; reviews of plays. Judith Rudakoff. *Books in Can* March 1987; Vol 16 No 2: p18.

BOISVERT, FRANCE

Les bienfaits de la bombe; review of *Les Samourailles*. Jean-François Chassay. *MD* Dec 5, 1987: pD4.
[FIRST NOVELS: BOOK REVIEWS]

BOISVERT, YVES

La vie littéraire; column. Marc Morin. photo · *MD* Nov 28, 1987: pD12.
[CANADIAN LITERARY PERIODICALS]

La vie littéraire; column. Marc Morin. *MD* Dec 5, 1987: pD2.
[CANADIAN LITERARY PUBLISHING; CONFERENCES, LITERARY; POETRY READINGS; WRITERS' ORGANIZATIONS]

La vie littéraire; column. Jean Royer. photo · *MD* April 18, 1987: pD2.
[INTERNATIONAL WRITERS' ORGANIZATIONS; RADIO AND CANADIAN LITERATURE; TELEVISION AND CANADIAN LITERATURE]

BOLT, DAVID

Lacrosse road trips inspired Bolt's play; article. Bob Blakey. photo · *CH* Jan 24, 1987: pA11.

Play lacks clear plot; theatre review of *Winning*. Brian Brennan. photo · *CH* Jan 26, 1987: pB6.

Three Toronto plays premiere at Calgary fest; article, includes theatre reviews. Robert Crew. photo · *TS* Feb 10, 1987: pB4.
[FESTIVALS, DRAMA]

New-play festival deserves a curtain call; theatre reviews. Stephen Godfrey. photo · *G&M* Feb 10, 1987: pC5.
[FESTIVALS, DRAMA]

BONENFANT, RÉJEAN

Les noeuds sacrés de l'âme, de la terre et du sang; reviews of novels. Réjean Beaudoin. *Liberté* Oct 1987; Vol 29 No 5: p106–114.

Un roman biparental lourd de bonnes intentions; review of *Les Trains d'exils*. Jean-Roch Boivin. *MD* July 25, 1987: pC7.

THE BONES OF THEIR OCCASION/Poems by Jerry Rush

[The Bones of Their Occasion]; review. Robert Currie. photo · *NeWest R* Dec 1987; Vol 13 No 4: p15.

Poets in search of praise; reviews of *One Night at the Indigo Hotel* and *The Bones of Their Occasion*. Keith Garebian. *TS* May 16, 1987: M4.

BONHEUR D'OCCASION/THE TIN FLUTE/Novel by Gabrielle Roy

Restaurant dining room evokes early Quebec era; article. Annabelle King. *MG* Nov 28, 1987: I5.

BONJOUR L'ARBRE/Children's story by Cécile Gagnon

Quand un ours polaire dérive vers le sud; reviews of children's stories by Cécile Gagnon. Solange Boudreau. *Can Child Lit* 1987; No 47: p62–63.

BONJOUR, LÀ, BONJOUR/Play by Michel Tremblay

Stylish direction freshens Bonjour; theatre review of *Bonjour, là, bonjour*. Pat Donnelly. photo · *MG* Nov 25, 1987: H4.

[Untitled]; theatre reviews. Pat Donnelly. *MG* Nov 27, 1987: pC7.

[Untitled]; theatre reviews. Pat Donnelly. *MG* Dec 4, 1987: pC6.

Une apocalypse du désassorti; theatre review of *Bonjour, là, bonjour*. Robert Lévesque. photo · *MD* Nov 24, 1987: p11.

[Untitled]; theatre reviews. Robert Lévesque. *MD* Dec 4, 1987: p15.

BOOBY TRAP/Novel by William Stevenson

Was this book written with Ollie in mind?; review of *Booby Trap*. Max Crittenden. *TS* July 19, 1987: pA20.

[Untitled]; review of *Booby Trap*. John North. *Quill & Quire* July 1987; Vol 53 No 7: p65.

Upper-case action and epic adventure; review of *Booby Trap*. Chris Scott. photo · *G&M* Aug 22, 1987: pC16.

A BOOK DRAGON/Children's novel by Donn Kushner

Renaissance man Donn Kushner a delightful challenge for children; article. Bernie Goedhart. photo · *Quill & Quire (Books for Young People)* Dec 1987; Vol 53 No 12: p1,3.

Gammer Gurton leaps from early English stage into the 20th century; reviews of children's books. Janice Kennedy. *MG* Nov 21, 1987: J13.

A dragon stands on guard; review of *A Book Dragon*. Joan McGrath. *TS* Dec 20, 1987: pE5.

THE BOOK OF FEARS/Short stories by Susan Kerslake

Rare/fear; reviews of *Green Eyes, Dukes & Kings* and *The Book of Fears*. Thomas Gerry. *Can Lit* Spring 1987; No 112: p107–108.

BOOK REVIEWING

Blind men and elephants; essay. John Coldwell Adams. illus · *Can Auth & Book* Spring 1987; Vol 62 No 3: p7–8.

Trouble with reviews — is reviewers, writer says; essay. Katherine Govier. photo · *TS* Dec 6, 1987: pC9.

Book reviewing is operating in a closed shop; essay. Katherine Govier. photo · *CH* Dec 9, 1987: pF1–F2.

Literary heist; article. Wayne Grady. illus · *Sat Night* Nov 1987; Vol 102 No 11: p61–64.

Censors, reviews hot topics at Writers Union AGM; article. Christina Hartling. photo · *Quill & Quire* Aug 1987; Vol 53 No 8: p22–23.
[CENSORSHIP; WRITERS' ORGANIZATIONS]

No conflict of interest in Globe book review; letter to the editor. Jack Kapica. *TS* Dec 21, 1987: pA14.

Book review editors take the hot seat at writers' conference; article. Liam Lacey. photo · *G&M* May 30, 1987: pC5.
[CONFERENCES, LITERARY; WRITERS' ORGANIZATIONS]

Metcalf chairs debate; column. Kenneth McGoogan. *CH* March 8, 1987: pE5.

Writers' union condemns censorship bill; article. Kenneth McGoogan. photo · *CH* June 2, 1987: pF6.
[CENSORSHIP; WRITERS' ORGANIZATIONS]

'Cocoon-like' Canlit hard on authors; letter to the editor. Scott Young. *TS* Dec 20, 1987: pB2.

BOOK TRADE IN CANADA

CBA '87: business plans, business tax, business books, and a 35th birthday bash; schedule of events. photo · *Quill & Quire* July 1987; Vol 53 No 7: p26.
[AUTHORS, CANADIAN]

Book store aims to please the theatre and movie crowd; article. Marianne Ackerman. *MG* Feb 17, 1987: pE8.
[CANADIAN LITERARY PERIODICALS]

Authors, booksellers angry over sale plan; article. Ken Adachi. *TS* Feb 12, 1987: pF4.
[AUTHORS, CANADIAN]

Authors outraged by fire sale prices; article. John Allemang. *G&M* Feb 13, 1987: pC11.
[AUTHORS, CANADIAN]

Books in motion; article. Peggy Amirault. *Quill & Quire* Aug 1987; Vol 53 No 8: p24.

What you see is what you buy: new directions in mass-market promotion; article. Laurie Bildfell. *Quill & Quire* Dec 1987; Vol 53 No 12: p4,6.

CBA '87; article. Hamish Cameron. photo · *Quill & Quire* Sept 1987; Vol 53 No 9: p6,10,12.
[AUTHORS, CANADIAN]

Gloves off as book industry assails feds; article. Hamish Cameron. photo · *Quill & Quire* Jan 1987; Vol 53 No 1: p12.

Buoyant mood at booksellers' annual meeting; column. William French. *G&M* June 30, 1987: pD7.
[CENSORSHIP]

Noël, période bénie pour les libraires; article. France Lafuste. photo · *MD* Nov 28, 1987: pD1.

De bien belles rencontres chez Hermès; article. Marie Laurier. photo · *MD* Dec 31, 1987: pC9–C10.
[AUDIO-VISUALS AND CANADIAN LITERATURE; AUTHORS, CANADIAN]

Readers, writers of tomorrow; column. Joan McGrath. *TS* July 5, 1987: pA18.

Le phénomène des best-sellers au Québec; article. Marc Morin. photo · *MD* Nov 21, 1987: pD1,D12.

Dreaming of a bright Christmas: booksellers report a strong season so far; article. Diana Shepherd. illus · *Quill & Quire* Dec 1987; Vol 53 No 12: p7–8.

Books in Motion / Livres en tournee; article. Kathleen Tudor. photo · *Atlan Prov Book R* Nov-Dec 1987; Vol 14 No 4: p8.

BOOKER, JEAN

Family ties and mysteries; reviews of children's novels. Joan McGrath. *Quill & Quire (Books for Young People)* Dec 1987; Vol 53 No 12: p10.

BOOKS IN CANADA/Periodical

Banff Centre lands novelist; column. Kenneth McGoogan. *CH* Feb 22, 1987: pE6.
[CANADIAN LITERARY PERIODICALS; PUBLISHING AND PUBLISHERS IN CANADA; WRITERS' WORKSHOPS]

BOOTH, ALLEN

Short plays confront man's helplessness; theatre review of *When I'm Big*. Vit Wagner. *TS* Dec 1, 1987: H4

Duo borrows big from Smothers Brothers' style; column. Vit Wagner. *TS* Nov 27, 1987: pD12.

BORDEN, WALTER

Tightrope Time a poetic one-man show that spans black history of Nova Scotia; theatre review. Pat Donnelly. photo · *MG* Sept 10, 1987: pC14.

[Untitled]; theatre reviews. Pat Donnelly. *MG* Sept 11, 1987: pC8.

Walter Borden en 12 temps . . . ; theatre review of *Tightrope Time*. Marc Morin. *MD* Sept 15, 1987: p11.

BORDER CROSSINGS/Poems by Richard Woollatt

Twice-dead magazine wins honor; article. photo · *WFP* Aug 27, 1987: p42.

Small press reviews; reviews of poetry books. Shaunt Basmajian. *Cross Can Writ Q* 1987; Vol 9 No 1: p25.

[Untitled]; reviews of poetry books. George Whipple. *Poetry Can R* Spring 1987; Vol 8 No 2–3: p53.

BORDERLINE/Novel by Janette Turner Hospital

Brian Moore's Jesuit priest travels into heart of darkness; reviews of novels. Barbara Black. *MG* March 7, 1987: H11.

New & noteworthy; review of *Borderline*. Patricia T. O'Connor. *NYT Book R* May 10, 1987: p34.

BORDERTOWN CAFE/Play by Kelly Rebar

Domestic drama that hits home; article, includes theatre reviews. John Bemrose. photo · *Maclean's* Aug 17, 1987; Vol 100 No 33: p49.
[FESTIVALS, DRAMA]

Dilemma in Bordertown; theatre review of *Bordertown Cafe*. Ray Conlogue. photo · *G&M* July 4, 1987: pC9.

Blyth's Cafe dishes up cliches; theatre review of *Bordertown Cafe*. Robert Crew. *TS* June 26, 1987: pE4.

Play lacks strong shape; theatre review of *Bordertown Cafe*. Randal McIlroy. *WFP* Oct 2, 1987: p19.

Border play proves timely; article. Brad Oswald. photo · *WFP* Sept 30, 1987: p41.

Alberta play bombs at Blyth festival; theatre review of *Bordertown Cafe*. Jamie Portman. *CH* July 2, 1987: pF1.

Making the prairie connection; theatre reviews. Reg Skene. *NeWest R* Dec 1987; Vol 13 No 4: p16.

BORROWED BEAUTY/Poems by Maxine Tynes

Maxine Tynes' first book of poems; review of *Borrowed Beauty*. Joanne Light. photo · *Atlan Prov Book R* Sept-Oct 1987; Vol 14 No 3: p14.

BORSON, ROO

An interview with Roo Borson. David Manicom. biog photo · *Rubicon* Spring 1987; No 8: p53–85.

Kinetic space; reviews of poetry books. Robert James Merrett. *Can Lit* Summer-Fall 1987; No 113–114: p241–243.

BOSE, RANA

A rare glimpse at our multiculturalism; theatre review of *Baba Jacques Dass and Turmoil at Côte des Neiges Cemetery*. Pat Donnelly. *MG* Oct 17, 1987: pD9.

BOSS OF THE NAMKO DRIVE/Young adult novel by Paul St. Pierre

Growing up in the saddle; review of *Boss of the Namko Drive*. Chris Ferns. *Can Child Lit* 1987; No 47: p81–82.

THE BOTTLE AND THE BUSHMAN: POEMS OF THE PRODIGAL SON/Poems by Mohamud S. Togane

[Untitled]; reviews of poetry books. Anne Archer. *Queen's Q* Winter 1987; Vol 94 No 4: p1042–1043.

A Somali voice in cold Canada; review of *The Bottle and the Bushman*. Harold Barratt. *Fiddlehead* Summer 1987; No 152: p89–91.

[Untitled]; review of *The Bottle and the Bushman*. Jacqueline Damato. *Can Auth & Book* Winter 1987; Vol 62 No 2: p24.

[Untitled]; reviews of poetry books. Stephen Morrissey. *Poetry Can R* Spring 1987; Vol 8 No 2–3: p49.

[Untitled]; review of *The Bottle and the Bushman*. Howard Tessler. *Rubicon* Fall 1987; No 9: p195–196.

BOTTLED ROSES/Short stories by Darlene Madott

[Untitled]; review of *Bottled Roses*. *Queen's Q* Spring 1987; Vol 94 No 1: p253.

Memory & words; reviews of *Fables of Brunswick Avenue* and *Bottled Roses*. Michael Helm. *Can Lit* Spring 1987; No 112: p92–95.

BOUCHARD, CAMILLE

Faiblesses d'un roman ambitieux; review of *Les Griffes de l'empire*. Alexandre Amprimoz. *Can Child Lit* 1987; No 47: p86–87.

BOUCHARD, CLAUDE

Présentation; introduction. René Lapierre. *Liberté* Aug 1987; Vol 29 No 4: p4–5.

BOUCHARD, LOUISE-ANNE

Léonce, Léonil . . . et Sept fois Jeanne; reviews of *Cette fois, Jeanne . . .* and *La Double vie de Léonce et Léonil*. Louise Milot. photo · *Lettres québec* Autumn 1987; No 47: p17–18.
[FIRST NOVELS: BOOK REVIEWS]

Une fille bien de son siècle; review of *Cette fois, Jeanne . . . .* Madeleine Ouellette-Michalska. *MD* Sept 5, 1987: pC9.
[FIRST NOVELS: BOOK REVIEWS]

[Untitled]; review of *Cette fois, Jeanne . . . .* Jacques St-Pierre. *Moebius* Summer 1987; No 33: p133–135.
[FIRST NOVELS: BOOK REVIEWS]

BOUCHARD, MICHEL-MARC

Homosexual passion, religious theatre crux of Les Feluettes; theatre review. Pat Donnelly. *MG* Sept 12, 1987: pD13.

[Untitled]; theatre reviews of *Tête à tête* and *Les Feluettes*. Pat Donnelly. *MG* Sept 18, 1987: pC8.

A work of power, imagination; article. Matthew Fraser. photo · *G&M* Nov 30, 1987: pC9.

Michel-Marc Bouchard: Roberval, 1912, j'avais 19 ans . . . ; article. Robert Lévesque. photo · *MD* Sept 12, 1987: pC1–C2.

Bouchard et les feux de Roberval; theatre review of *Les Feluettes*. Robert Lévesque. photo · *MD* Sept 25, 1987: p13.

Limoges, principale vitrine du théâtre québécois en Europe; column. Robert Lévesque. photo · *MD* Sept 29, 1987: p13.
[AWARDS, LITERARY; CANADIAN LITERARY PERIODICALS; FESTIVALS, DRAMA]

Les Feluettes seront en France en 1988; article. Robert Lévesque. photo · *MD* Nov 5, 1987: p13.
[FRANCE-CANADA LITERARY RELATIONS]

[Untitled]; theatre review of *Les Feluettes*. Robert Lévesque. *MD* Nov 27, 1987: p15.

[Untitled]; theatre reviews. Robert Lévesque. *MD* Dec 4, 1987: p15.

BOUCHER, DENISE

De l'Italie, de l'art et de la civilisation; review of *Lettres d'Italie*. Jean-Roch Boivin. photo · *MD* Sept 19, 1987: pD3.

La guerre de religion de Denise Boucher; column. Robert Lévesque. photo · *MD* Jan 13, 1987: p6.
[DRAMATIC READINGS]

BOUCHER, JEAN-PIERRE

Dits et faits; column. Adrien Thério. photo · *Lettres québec* Summer 1987; No 46: p6.
[AUTHORS, CANADIAN; CANADIAN LITERARY PUBLISHING; CONFERENCES, LITERARY; GOVERNMENT GRANTS FOR WRITERS/PUBLISHERS; LIBRARY SERVICES AND CANADIAN LITERATURE]

BOULERICE, JACQUES

Prix et distinctions; list of award winners. photo · *Lettres québec* Summer 1987; No 46: p7.
[AWARDS, LITERARY]

Des échappées de lumière . . . ; review of *Apparence*. Jean-François Dowd. *MD* April 28, 1987: p17.

Jacques Boulerice: pour une autre enfance; reviews of *Apparence* and *Distance*. Jean Royer. *MD* Feb 14, 1987: pC3.

Le 27e prix Québec-Paris va à Jacques Boulerice; article. Jean Royer. *MD* Feb 27, 1987: p7.
[AWARDS, LITERARY]

La vie littéraire; column. Jean Royer. photo · *MD* March 21, 1987: pD2.
[AWARDS, LITERARY; CANADIAN LITERARY PUBLISHING; COMPETITIONS, LITERARY; POETRY READINGS; RADIO AND CANADIAN LITERATURE; TELEVISION AND CANADIAN LITERATURE]

BOUQUET DE SIGNES/Poems by Alexandre Amprimoz

Chronique: reflets et signes; review of *Bouquet de signes*. Marguerite Andersen. *Poetry Can R* Summer 1987; Vol 8 No 4: p23.

BOURAOUI, HÉDI

Chronique: Bouraoui, Cahiers blues; reviews of *Reflet pluriel* and French periodical featuring French-Canadian literature. Marguerite Andersen. *Poetry Can R* Fall 1987; Vol 9 No 1: p16.

BOURASSA, ANDRÉ-G.

Pour transformer l'essence même de la pensée; review of *Surréalisme et littérature québécoise*. Lori Saint-Martin. *MD* Oct 31, 1987: pD3.

BOURBON STREET POETRY WORKSHOP: ECPHORE INSTALATION PIECE/Poetry anthology

[Untitled]; reviews of poetry books. Andrew Parkin. *Poetry Can R* Fall 1987; Vol 9 No 1: p37.
[ANTHOLOGIES: BOOK REVIEWS]

BOURGEOIS, PAULETTE

Book captures emotional moment for child; reviews of *Big Sarah's Little Boots* and *A Difficult Day*. Joan Craven. *CH (Neighbors)* Oct 28, 1987: pA18.

Baby of the family gets respect raising flock of Canada geese; reviews of children's books. Janice Kennedy. *MG* Oct 3, 1987: J13.

[Untitled]; review of *Big Sarah's Little Boots*. Rosemary Kennedy. *CH* Dec 6, 1987: pD9.

A title that will grab teenagers; reviews of children's books. Joan McGrath. *TS* Oct 25, 1987: pA18.

A fun bunch of books to read and look at; reviews of *Big Sarah's Little Boots* and *Ringtail*. Frieda Wishinsky. *Quill & Quire (Books for Young People)* Aug 1987; Vol 53 No 8: p3.

BOWDEN, SUSAN

Bowden to sign books; article. *WFP* Nov 28, 1987: p6.

Susan Bowden: history is people; article. Gillian Welsh-Vickar. photo · *Can Auth & Book* Summer 1987; Vol 62 No 4: p9.

BOWERING, GEORGE

Angel with a lariat; review of *Caprice*, includes profile. John Bemrose. photo · *Maclean's* June 29, 1987; Vol 100 No 26: p49–50

[Untitled]; review of *Delayed Mercy*. Mary di Michele. *Books in Can* June-July 1987; Vol 16 No 5: p23–24.

Zane Grey heroine turns Western novel upside down; review of *Caprice*. Trevor Ferguson. *MG* May 9, 1987: I9.

Bowering's capricious Western; review of *Caprice*. Maggie Helwig. *TS* May 17, 1987: pA17.

Stealing the text: George Bowering's Kerrisdale Elegies and Dennis Cooley's Bloody Jack; article. Smaro Kamboureli. *Can Lit* Winter 1987; No 115: p9–23.
[CANADIAN LONG POEM; STRUCTURALIST WRITING AND CRITICISM]

Trieste and George Bowering's Burning Water; article. Eva-Marie Kröller. *Open Letter* Summer 1987; Vol 6 No 8: p44–54.
[MYTHS AND LEGENDS IN CANADIAN LITERATURE]

Imagining history: the romantic background of George Bowering's Burning Water; article. Edward Lobb. *Studies in Can Lit* 1987; Vol 12 No 1: p112–128.
[HISTORICAL FICTION]

Horsing around; review of *Caprice*. Charles Mandel. *G&M* May 23, 1987: pC23.

Smart-aleck of Can-Lit scores again; review of *Caprice*. Kenneth McGoogan. photo · *CH* May 17, 1987: pE5.

As for me and my horse; review of *Caprice*. Kenneth McGoogan. *Books in Can* June-July 1987; Vol 16 No 5: p15–16.

Triptych; editorial article. Laurie Ricou. *Can Lit* Summer-Fall 1987; No 113–114: p4–6.

Bowering's western: woolly post-modernist chic; review of *Caprice*. Paul Roberts. photo · *Quill & Quire* May 1987; Vol 53 No 5: p19.

Three poets dare to reject labelling; reviews of poetry books. Patricia Smith. *TS* July 4, 1987: M4.

Literary tricks and the larger concerns; reviews of *Delayed Mercy* and *Afterworlds*. Fraser Sutherland. photo · *G&M* Aug 8, 1987: pC19.

For batter or verse; biographical article. Alan Twigg. photo · *Books in Can* Nov 1987; Vol 16 No 8: p7–8,10.

Historicity in historical fiction: Burning Water and The Temptations Of Big Bear; article. Carla Visser. *Studies in Can Lit* 1987; Vol 12 No 1: p90–111.
[HISTORICAL FICTION]

At least it's easy to read; review of *Caprice*. Morley Walker. *WFP* May 16, 1987: p70.

For people; review of *Seventy-One Poems for People*. Noah Zacharin. *Can Lit* Spring 1987; No 112: p145–146.

BOWERING, MARILYN

[Untitled]; review of *Anyone Can See I Love You*. Phil Hall. *Books in Can* Aug-Sept 1987; Vol 16 No 6: p27–28.

[Untitled]; reviews of poetry books. Stephen Scobie. *Malahat R* Dec 1987; No 81: p104–106.

The impersonation of the irresistible; reviews of poetry books. Fraser Sutherland. *G&M* Sept 5, 1987: pC15.

BOWERS, RICK

People and P.E.I.; review of *The Governor of Prince Edward Island*. Frank J. Ledwell. *Atlan Prov Book R* Feb-March 1987; Vol 14 No 1: p9.

Poignant tales of P.E.I. life give pleasure; review of *The Governor of Prince Edward Island*. Robert M. Seller. *CH* April 5, 1987: pE5.

BOYD, PAMELA

[Untitled]; reviews. Lisbie Rae. *Can Drama* 1987; Vol 13 No 2: p229–231.
[ANTHOLOGIES: BOOK REVIEWS]

BOYLE, HARRY J.

Book world: from unhappy housewife to busy biographer; column. Beverley Slopen. photo · *TS* May 24, 1987: pA18.

BRÉBEUF AND HIS BRETHREN/Long poem by E.J. Pratt

Fort and forest: instability in the symbolic code of E.J. Pratt's Brebeuf and His Brethren; article. Frank Davey. abstract · *Études can* 1987; No 23: p183–194.
[RELIGIOUS THEMES]

BRADFORD, KARLEEN

History comes alive; review of *The Nine Days Queen*. Marjory Body. *Can Child Lit* 1987; No 48: p85–86.

BRADLEY, DANIEL F.

[Untitled]; reviews of poetry books. Shaunt Basmajian. *Cross Can Writ Q* 1987; Vol 9 No 3–4: p44,49.
[ANTHOLOGIES: BOOK REVIEWS]

BRAITHWAITE, MAX

[Untitled]; review of *All the Way Home*. Hallvard Dahlie. *Queen's Q* Summer 1987; Vol 94 No 2: p480–482.

Parody & legacy; reviews. Lorna Irvine. *Can Lit* Winter 1987; No 115: p264–267.
[FIRST NOVELS: BOOK REVIEWS]

BRANDEN, VICTORIA

Ours as daughters; reviews of *Duet for Three* and *Flitterin' Judas*. Nancy Bailey. *Can Lit* Spring 1987; No 112: p143–145.

BRANDIS, MARIANNE

Even parents are people; review of *The Quarter-Pie Window*. William Blackburn. *Can Child Lit* 1987; No 46: p76–77

Underwing; reviews of *In the Shadow of the Vulture* and *The Quarter-Pie Window*. Ronald B. Hatch. *Can Lit* Spring 1987; No 112: p95–97.

BRANDT, DI

Books break cultural silence, look at fumbled conversation; article. Donald Campbell. photo · *WFP* Dec 7, 1987: p16.

Artist colony; article. Kevin Prokosh. *WFP* Aug 4, 1987: p27.

BRAULT, JACQUES

Dits et faits; column. photo · *Lettres québec* Spring 1987; No 45: p6–7.
[AWARDS, LITERARY; PUBLISHING AND PUBLISHERS IN CANADA; TRANSLATIONS OF CANADIAN LITERATURE; WRITERS' ORGANIZATIONS]

Two novels offer pain — and incidental pleasures; reviews of *Death-Watch* and *Five Facts about Giorgione*. Ken Adachi. *TS* Aug 30, 1987: pA19.

Jacques Brault: le quotidien transfiguré; introduction. André Brochu. illus · *Voix et images* Winter 1987; No 35: p187.

La poésie dans la prose, ou le clochard illuminé; article. André Brochu. illus · *Voix et images* Winter 1987; No 35: p212–220.

Témoinage: la leon des choses; article. Jean-Claude Brochu. illus · *Voix et images* Winter 1987; No 35: p250–254.

Bibliographie de Jacques Brault; bibliography. Roger Chamberland. *Voix et images* Winter 1987; No 35: p256–264.

[Untitled]; review of *Poèmes 1*. Jean Chapdelaine Gagnon. *Estuaire* Spring 1987; No 44: p79–80.

L'intérêt de Voix & images pour les aventures culturelles de notre société; review. Chantal Gamache. *MD* April 25, 1987: pD3.
[CANADIAN LITERARY PERIODICALS]

Brault, Fischer, Liscano; review of *Poèmes 1*. Jean-Pierre Issenhuth. *Liberté* June 1987; Vol 29 No 3: p74–79.

Jacques Brault essayiste; article. Michel Lemaire. *Voix et images* Winter 1987; No 35: p222–238.

Poésie de novembre; article. Gilles Marcotte. illus · *Voix et images* Winter 1987; No 35: p239–249.

De la poésie et de quelques circonstances: entretien avec Jacques Brault; interview. Robert Melançon. illus · *Voix et images* Winter 1987; No 35: p188–211.

Poésie: trois rétrospectives; reviews of poetry books. Jean Royer. photo · *MD* Feb 9, 1987: p11.

Brault ou la mémoire du poème; review of *Poèmes 1*. Robert Yergeau. photo · *Lettres québec* Spring 1987; No 45: p40–41.

BRAUN, LOIS

Mainstreet Calgary; column. *CH (Neighbors)* March 26, 1987: pA4.
[FICTION READINGS]

[Untitled]; review of *A Stone Watermelon*. Ruby Andrew. *Quill & Quire* April 1987; Vol 53 No 4: p28–29.

[Untitled]; review of *A Stone Watermelon*. Howard Curle. *Border Cross* Summer 1987; Vol 6 No 3: p21.

Prairie writer displays poise and assurance in book of short stories; review of *A Stone Watermelon*. William French. photo · *G&M* March 5, 1987: pD1.

Victims left poised, petrified; review of *A Stone Watermelon*. Cecelia Frey. *CH* April 12, 1987: pF7.

[Untitled]; review of *A Stone Watermelon*. Isabel Huggan. *Books in Can* April 1987; Vol 16 No 3: p25.

Manitoban attracts nationwide attention; column. Kenneth McGoogan. photo · *CH* April 12, 1987: pF7.
[AWARDS, LITERARY]

Engaging stories by newcomer; review of *A Stone Watermelon*. John Parr. *TS* March 29, 1987: pA19.

Award nomination 'petrifies' Prairie storyteller; article. Barbara Robson. photo · *WFP* May 23, 1987: p21–22.
[GOVERNOR GENERAL'S AWARDS]

[Untitled]; review of *A Stone Watermelon*. Constance Rooke. *Malahat R* June 1987; No 79: p156.

Lois Braun; interview. Nancy Wigston. photo · *Books in Can* Aug-Sept 1987; Vol 16 No 6: p36–38.

Fiction debut is impressive; review of *A Stone Watermelon*. David Williamson. photo · *WFP* Feb 7, 1987: p59.

THE BRAVE NEVER WRITE POETRY/Poems by Jones

In voice; reviews of poetry books. Richard Stevenson. *Can Lit* Spring 1987; No 112: p167–169.

BRAZILIAN JOURNAL/Journal by P.K. Page

Page on places and things pure pleasure; review of *Brazilian Journal*. Ken Adachi. photo · *TS* June 27, 1987: M4.

[Untitled]; review of *Brazilian Journal*. Ruby Andrew. *Quill & Quire* May 1987; Vol 53 No 5: p22,24.

The ambassador's wife; review of *Brazilian Journal*. John Bemrose. illus · *Maclean's* Aug 10, 1987; Vol 100 No 32: p51.

[Untitled]; review of *Brazilian Journal*. Adelle Castelo. *Idler* Sept-Oct 1987; No 14: p49.

Tropical dreaming; review of *Brazilian Journal*. William French. *G&M* June 27, 1987: pE17.

The poet in the pink palace; review article about *Brazilian Journal*. George Galt. photo · *Sat Night* Sept 1987; Vol 102 No 9: p61–63.

[Untitled]; review of *Brazilian Journal*. M.K. Louis. *Malahat R* June 1987; No 79: p162–164.

Paperclips: publishing on-stage . . . P.K. Page's love song to Brazil; column. Beverley Slopen. photo · *Quill & Quire* May 1987; Vol 53 No 5: p14.

Poet records two years in paradise; review of *Brazilian Journal*. John Vance Snow. *CH* Aug 30, 1987: pE4

Lady of the house; review of *Brazilian Journal*. Barbara Wade Rose. *Books in Can* June-July 1987; Vol 16 No 5: p29–30.

Brazil dreaming; review of *Brazilian Journal*. William Weintraub. illus · *MG* July 25, 1987: J7.

BREAKING TRAIL/Poems by Phyllis Larkin

[Untitled]; reviews of poetry books. George Whipple. *Poetry Can R* Spring 1987; Vol 8 No 2–3: p53.

BREAKOUT/Play by Masani (Charmaine) Montague

Breakout's only strength is in its message; theatre review. Alex Law. photo · *TS (Neighbours)* March 31, 1987: p18.

BREON, ROBIN

More history lesson than drama; theatre review of *The African Roscius*. Liam Lacey. photo · *G&M* July 15, 1987: pC6.

BREWSTER, ELIZABETH

No need to explain; review of *Visitations*. Anne Denoon. *Books in Can* Aug-Sept 1987; Vol 16 No 6: p21,24.

[Untitled]; review of *Visitations*. M.A. Thompson. *Quarry* Summer 1987; Vol 36 No 3: p80–82.

Sharing touching reveries; review of *Visitations*. Thomas S. Woods. *G&M* July 11, 1987: pC14.

BRICK/Periodical

Feminist quarterly honors Laurence; column. Ken Adachi. *TS* Nov 16, 1987: pC5.
[CANADIAN LITERARY PERIODICALS; FICTION READINGS]

Spleen may write the poem, but Layton's heart will speak tomorrow; reviews of poetry books. Trevor Ferguson. *MG* Sept 26, 1987: J11.

BRIDES IN SPACE/Play by Peggy Thompson

Brides in Space launched on a mission impossible; theatre review of *Brides in Space*. Stephen Godfrey. photo · *G&M* Jan 15, 1987: pD1.

THE BRIDGE OUT OF TOWN/Short stories by Jack Mac-Donald

[Untitled]; reviews of *The Bridge Out of Town* and *A Model Lover*. Clifford G. Holland. *Queen's Q* Summer 1987; Vol 94 No 2: p472–474.

[Untitled]; review of *The Bridge Out of Town*. Ruth Manson. *Quill & Quire* March 1987; Vol 53 No 3: p71.

BRING ME YOUR PASSION/Short stories by Don Bailey

Examining the blight of solitude; review of *Bring Me Your Passion*. Keith Garebian. *TS* Dec 27, 1987: pE19.

BRINGHURST, ROBERT

[Untitled]; review of *Pieces of Map, Pieces of Music*. Ron Clark. *Wascana R* Spring 1987; Vol 22 No 1: p92–95.

Breathing in tune and time; review of *Pieces of Map, Pieces of Music*. Gwladys V. Downes. *Event* Summer 1987; Vol 16 No 2: p115–118.

Making draft horses out of the gods: an interview with Robert Bringhurst. Kritjana Gunnars. photo · *Prairie Fire* Spring 1987; Vol 8 No 1: p4–15.

[Untitled]; reviews of poetry books. Tom Marshall. *Cross Can Writ Q* 1987; Vol 9 No 1: p24–25.

[Untitled]; review of *Pieces of Map, Pieces of Music*. Peter O'Brien. *Rubicon* Fall 1987; No 9: p203–204.

[Untitled]; review of *Pieces of Map, Pieces of Music*. Ken Stange. *Poetry Can R* Summer 1987; Vol 8 No 4: p35–36.

Poetry, science, mind and religion; reviews of poetry books. Fraser Sutherland. photo · *G&M* Jan 31, 1987: pE19.

BRISSET, ANNIE

Kingston editor retains theatre critics' award; article. Pat Donnelly. *MG* Oct 5, 1987: pB15.
[AWARDS, LITERARY]

Le théâtre du Rire joue gagnant; column. Robert Lévesque. *MD* Oct 13, 1987: p11.
[AWARDS, LITERARY]

BRITISH COLUMBIA WRITING AND WRITERS

West coast recollections; article. Judith Copithorne. *Cross Can Writ Q* 1987; Vol 9 No 3–4: p10.
[POSTMODERNIST WRITING AND CRITICISM]

The mermaid inn: the silent voices of the past; essay. Charles Lillard. photo · *G&M* Sept 12, 1987: pD6.

La forêt chez les écrivains anglophones; article. Danièle Pitavy. abstract · *Études can* 1987; No 23: p147–157.
[CANADIAN IMAGINATION; COLONIAL LITERATURE; NATURE IN CANADIAN LITERATURE]

BROCHMANN, ELIZABETH

Romance and rebellion in young adult fiction; reviews of *Nobody Asked Me* and *Storm Child*. Sarah Ellis. *Can Child Lit* 1987; No 46: p87–89.

BRODEUR, HELENE

Une voix ontarienne; review of *Chroniques du Nouvel-Ontario*. Mark Benson. *Can Lit* Winter 1987; No 115: p251–253.

La forêt dans le roman "ontarois"; article. Yolande Grisé. abstract · *Études can* 1987; No 23: p109–122.
[MYTHS AND LEGENDS IN CANADIAN LITERATURE; NATURE IN CANADIAN LITERATURE]

BROKEN ENGLISH/Novel by David Thompson

Three new faces deserving discovery; reviews of crime novels. Margaret Cannon. photo · *G&M* Oct 17, 1987: pE4.

Plotting against the royals; reviews of *Broken English* and *Merlin's Web*. Brian Kappler. *MG* Nov 7, 1987: K13.

Local heroes; reviews of first novels. Janice Kulyk Keefer. *Books in Can* Nov 1987; Vol 16 No 8: p35,37.
[FIRST NOVELS: BOOK REVIEWS]

[Untitled]; review of *Broken English*. John North. *Quill & Quire* Nov 1987; Vol 53 No 11: p24.
[FIRST NOVELS: BOOK REVIEWS]

BROKEN GHOSTS/Poems by Roger Moore

Recent poetry; reviews of poetry books. Terrence Craig. *Atlan Prov Book R* Feb-March 1987; Vol 14 No 1: p18.

[Untitled]; review of *Broken Ghosts*. Brian Vanderlip. *Poetry Can R* Fall 1987; Vol 9 No 1: p38.

BROOKER, BLAKE

Brooker wins TC award; article. *CH* July 7, 1987: pC6.
[AWARDS, LITERARY]

Brooker wins playwright award; article. *G&M* July 1, 1987: pC6.
[AWARDS, LITERARY]

One Yellow Rabbit great; letter to the editor. Ruth Thompson. *CH* June 15, 1987: pA6.

Tale of economic woe became family affair; article. Kate Zimmerman. *CH* April 23, 1987: pD3.

Misery of unemployment hits home in poetic play; theatre review of *Rembrandt Brown*. Kate Zimmerman. *CH* April 25, 1987: pD3.

Rabbit writers team up to parody anti-Semitism; article. Kate Zimmerman. photo · *CH* May 28, 1987: pC15.

Timid pussyfooting defuses play's satirical intent; theatre review of *Ilsa, Queen of the Nazi Love Camp*. Kate Zimmerman. *CH* May 30, 1987: pF5.

Friends blend skills into theatre piece; article. Kate Zimmerman. *CH* Nov 22, 1987: pA15.

BROOKS, JACK

[Untitled]; reviews of poetry books. Anne Cimon. *Poetry Can R* Spring 1987; Vol 8 No 2–3: p62.

BROSSARD, JACQUES

L'inquiétante étrangeté des récits de Jacques Brossard; review of *Le Sang du souvenir*. Jacques Michon. *MD* Sept 5, 1987: pC7.

BROSSARD, NICOLE

Free premiere set for Firewords; article. *TS* April 12, 1987: pC6.
[AUDIO-VISUALS AND CANADIAN LITERATURE]

Aujourd'hui; column. *MD* Oct 27, 1987: p10.

La vitrine du livre; reviews. Guy Ferland. *MD* Nov 21, 1987: pD4.

La question des journaux intimes; article. Lise Gauvin. *Études fran* Winter 1987; Vol 22 No 3: p101–115.
[AUTOBIOGRAPHICAL WRITING; RADIO AND CANADIAN LITERATURE]

[Untitled]; review of *Féminins singuliers*. Anne-Marie Picard. *U of Toronto Q* Fall 1987; Vol 57 No 1: p200–201.

[Untitled]; review of *Lovhers*. Eva Tihanyi. *Poetry Can R* Spring 1987; Vol 8 No 2–3: p40–41.

BROUILLET, CHRYSTINE

Christine comme un poison dans l'eau; article. Hélène de Billy. *MD* April 30, 1987: p13.
[CONFERENCES, LITERARY]

La vitrine du livre; reviews. Guy Ferland. *MD* May 9, 1987: pD4.

[Untitled]; review of *Le Poison dans l'eau*. Alberto Manguel. *Books in Can* Nov 1987; Vol 16 No 8: p24–25.

Comme il vous plaira; review of *Le Complot*. Irène Oore. *Can Child Lit* 1987; No 46: p90–92.

BROWN, KENNETH

Red Deer College Arts Centre: life after hockey?; article. Carolyn Dearden. photo · *NeWest R* Feb 1987; Vol 12 No 6: p15–16.

The great Canadian dream; article. Kevin Prokosh. photo · *WFP* March 18, 1987: p35.

Hockey metaphor fails to make dramatic point; theatre review of *Life After Hockey*. Reg Skene. *WFP* March 19, 1987: p41.

BROWN, MICHAEL

War play pokes fun at military, politicians; article. Sean Collins. photo · *TS (Neighbours)* May 5, 1987: p24.

BROWN, PAUL CAMERON

[Untitled]; reviews of *Psalms from the Suburbs* and *Sympathetic Magic*. Doug Watling. *Poetry Can R* Spring 1987; Vol 8 No 2–3: p51.

BRULOTTE, GAÉTAN

L'étrangeté du quotidien; review of *Le Surveillant*. Réjean Beaudoin. *Liberté* June 1987; Vol 29 No 3: p104–105

La vie littéraire; column. Marc Morin. photo · *MD* Dec 19, 1987: pD2.
[AWARDS, LITERARY; FICTION READINGS; POETRY READINGS]

BRUNEAU, ANDRÉ

La reconstitution de tableaux d'époque; review of *Du soufre dans les lampions*. Madeleine Ouellette-Michalska. photo · *MD* April 25, 1987: pD3.

BRUNEAU, ROCHELLE

Drama fest heads for grand finale; theatre reviews of *Jack of Hearts* and *Collideoscope*. Marianne Ackerman. photo · *MG* May 1, 1987: pD3.
[FESTIVALS, DRAMA]

The effort is there but results disappoint; theatre review of *Jack of Hearts*. Pat Donnelly. *MG* July 18, 1987: pD8.

BUCKLER, ERNEST

Ernest Buckler's holy family; article. Leona M. Deorksen. *New Q* Spring-Summer 1987; Vol 7 No 1–2: p232–239.
[THE FAMILY IN CANADIAN LITERATURE]

THE BUDA BOOKS POETRY SERIES: MONTREAL ANTHOLOGY/Poetry anthology

[Untitled]; reviews of *Squid Inc. 86* and *The Buda Books Poetry Series*. Shaunt Basmajian. *Cross Can Writ Q* 1987; Vol 9 No 3–4: p43.

[Untitled]; reviews of poetry books. Douglas Smith. *Poetry Can R* Spring 1987; Vol 8 No 2–3: p39–40.
[ANTHOLOGIES: BOOK REVIEWS]

BUELL, JOHN

This famous Montreal writer keeps a low profile; article. Barbara Black. photo · *MG* May 16, 1987: J7.

BUFFIE, MARGARET

City writer to lecture; article. *WFP* Nov 14, 1987: p20.

Billboard: cooking with tofu to be demonstrated; column. *WFP* Nov 17, 1987: p33.

Past and present merge in painful, haunting tales; reviews of *False Face* and *Who Is Frances Rain?*. Peter Carver. photo · *Quill & Quire (Books for Young People)* Oct 1987; Vol 53 No 10: p10.
[FIRST NOVELS: BOOK REVIEWS]

Chit chat; column. Maria Casas. *Quill & Quire (Books for Young People)* Oct 1987; Vol 53 No 10: p8.

Literary lions linger in libraries; reviews of children's books. Joan McGrath. *TS* Dec 20, 1987: pE5.

A mystery in Manitoba; review of *Who Is Frances Rain?*. Helen Norrie. *WFP* Dec 5, 1987: p57.
[FIRST NOVELS: BOOK REVIEWS]

BUITENHUIS, PETER

[Untitled]; review of *The Great War of Words*. Martin Dowding. *Quill & Quire* Nov 1987; Vol 53 No 11: p25.

Propagandists had huge impact; article. John Ferri. *TS* Nov 8, 1987: pA16.

First World War propaganda undermined truth about second; article. John Ferri. photo · *CH* Nov 11, 1987: pA5.

Fighting words; review of *The Great War of Words*. David Glassco. *Can Forum* Nov 1987; Vol 67 No 773: p36–37.

Writers of the 'foul literature of glory'; review of *The Great War of Words*. Sandra Martin. *G&M* Oct 24, 1987: pC19.

Hyping the good fight; review of *The Great War of Words*. Desmond Morton. *Books in Can* Nov 1987; Vol 16 No 8: p14–15.

Writers at war found wanting; review of *The Great War of Words*. Robert Saunders. *WFP* Nov 7, 1987: p54.

BULGER, LAURA

Relating the newcomers' pain; article. Sarah Jane Growe. photo · *TS* Jan 8, 1987: pD1,D4.

Roots, new country put author, lecturer on tug-of-war path; article. Phil Johnson. photo · *TS (Neighbours)* Feb 3, 1987: p14.

BULLOCK, MICHAEL

Image and mood: recent poems by Michael Bullock; article. Jack F. Stewart. *Can Lit* Winter 1987; No 115: p107–121.
[MYTHS AND LEGENDS IN CANADIAN LITERATURE; SURREALISM]

THE BUMPER BOOK/Critical essays

[Untitled]; review of *The Bumper Book*. A.R. Kizuk. *U of Toronto Q* Fall 1987; Vol 57 No 1: p150–151.

[Untitled]; review of *The Bumper Book*. Brent Ledger. *Quill & Quire* March 1987; Vol 53 No 3: p73–74.

Beyond the merely competent; reviews of critical works. Larry McDonald. *Atlan Prov Book R* Sept-Oct 1987; Vol 14 No 3: p11.
[CANADIAN LITERARY PERIODICALS]

Metcalf chairs debate; column. Kenneth McGoogan. *CH* March 8, 1987: pE5.
[BOOK REVIEWING]

THE BUNGALO BOYS: LAST OF THE TREE RANCHERS/Children's story by John Bianchi

Mini-reviews; reviews of children's books. Margaret Paré. *Can Child Lit* 1987; No 45: p93–96

BURDMAN, RALPH

Marriage of true minds; theatre review of *Tête à tête*. John Bemrose. photo · *Maclean's* Sept 21, 1987; Vol 100 No 38: p50.

The state of theatre: avant-garde advances bewilder actors, critics; article. Brian Brennan. photo · *CH* Oct 18, 1987: pC4.
[POSTMODERNIST WRITING AND CRITICISM]

Tete-a-Tete worthwhile for its wit and elegance; theatre review. Ray Conlogue. photo · *G&M* Nov 13, 1987: pD13.

Play dares to add levity to legacy; theatre review of *Tête à tête*. Robert Crew. photo · *TS* Nov 15, 1987: pC2.

From English to French to English; article. Pat Donnelly. photo · *MG* Sept 5, 1987: pC6.

Lightweight Tête-à-Tête an evening of intimacy; theatre review. Pat Donnelly. *MG* Sept 10, 1987: pC14.

[Untitled]; theatre reviews. Pat Donnelly. *MG* Sept 11, 1987: pC8.

[Untitled]; theatre reviews of *Tête à tête* and *Les Feluettes*. Pat Donnelly. *MG* Sept 18, 1987: pC8.

[Untitled]; theatre review of *Tête à tête*. Solange Lévesque. photo · *Jeu* 1987; No 43: p167–168.

[Untitled]; theatre reviews of *Oublier* and *Tête à tête*. Robert Lévesque. *MD* Nov 6, 1987: p15.

Une centième au Café de la Place; article. Robert Lévesque. photo · *MD* Dec 3, 1987: p13.

[Untitled]; theatre reviews. Gina Mallet. *G&M (Toronto Magazine)* Nov 1987; Vol 2 No 8: p29.

Blowing bubbles with Simone and Sartre; column. Vit Wagner. photo · *TS* Nov 6, 1987: pE4.
[TRANSLATIONS OF CANADIAN LITERATURE]

BUREAU, GINETTE

À surveiller; column. *MD* Nov 23, 1987: p8.

BURKE, ANNE

[Untitled]; reviews of poetry books. Elizabeth Woods. *Poetry Can R* Spring 1987; Vol 8 No 2–3: p49.

BURKMAN, KAY

In voice; reviews of poetry books. Richard Stevenson. *Can Lit* Spring 1987; No 112: p167–169.

BURNETT, MURDOCH

Here's looking at you: Murdoch Burnett; column. photo · *CH (Sunday Magazine)* Jan 11, 1987: p2.

Mainstreet Calgary; column. *CH (Neighbors)* Dec 2, 1987: pA11,A14–A15.
[POETRY READINGS]

Mainstreet Calgary; column. *CH (Neighbors)* Dec 9, 1987: pA17–A18.
[COMPETITIONS, LITERARY; POETRY READINGS]

Fresh jazz flowing in clubs; article. James Muretich. photo · *CH* June 25, 1987: pD1.

BURNETT, VIRGIL

The human comedy; review of *Farewell Tour*. Brian Fawcett. *Books in Can* April 1987; Vol 16 No 3: p18.

Collection charms despite certain bias; review of *Farewell Tour*. Maggie Helwig. *TS* May 9, 1987: M10.

Today's assignment: short fiction that's worth a long look; reviews of short story books. Douglas Hill. *G&M* March 14, 1987: pE19.
[ANTHOLOGIES: BOOK REVIEWS]

[Untitled]; review of *Farewell Tour*. David Homel. *Quill & Quire* April 1987; Vol 53 No 4: p28.

BURNFORD, SHEILA

[Untitled]; review of *The Incredible Journey*. Brooke Willmott. *TS* March 15, 1987: H6.

BURNING CHROME/Short stories by William Gibson

Future and past histories: repeating winning formulae simply not on the cards; review of *Burning Chrome*. Douglas Barbour. *TS* March 7, 1987: M4.

BURNING WATER/Novel by George Bowering

Trieste and George Bowering's Burning Water; article. Eva-Marie Kröler. *Open Letter* Summer 1987; Vol 6 No 8: p44–54.
[MYTHS AND LEGENDS IN CANADIAN LITERATURE]

BURNS, MARY

[Untitled]; review of *Suburbs of the Arctic Circle*. Theresa Hurley. *Quarry* Spring 1987; Vol 36 No 2: p111–113.

Circle games; reviews of fictional works. Barbara Leckie. *Can Lit* Winter 1987; No 115: p278–280.

Everything by thought waves; reviews of short story collections. Patricia Matson. *Event* March 1987; Vol 16 No 1: p97–100.

BURRS, MICK

Interview with Mick Burrs. Doris Hillis. bibliog biog photo · *Prairie J of Can Lit* 1987; No 8: p5–19.

BUSH FIRE/Play by Laurie Fyffe

Domestic drama that hits home; article, includes theatre reviews. John Bemrose. photo · *Maclean's* Aug 17, 1987; Vol 100 No 33: p49.
[FESTIVALS, DRAMA]

Blyth musical succeeds where drama fails; theatre reviews of *Girls in the Gang* and *Bush Fire*. Jason Sherman. photo · *TS* Aug 7, 1987: pE10.

BUSS, HELEN M.

Matrimony; review of *Mother and Daughter Relationships in the Manawaka Works of Margaret Laurence*. Connie Bellamy. *Essays on Can Writ* Winter 1987; No 35: p93–99.

BUSSIERES, SIMONE

Échos des rêveries enfantines; review of *Dans mon petit violon*. Line Paré. *Can Child Lit* 1987; No 46: p101–102.

BUTALA, SHARON

[Untitled]; reviews of *Noman's Land* and *Queen of the Headaches*. Anne Cimon. *Cross Can Writ Q* 1987; Vol 9 No 1: p20–21.

Interview with Sharon Butala. Doris Hillis. *Wascana R* Spring 1987; Vol 22 No 1: p37–53.

Matter-of-fact visions; reviews of *Learning by Heart* and *Queen of the Headaches*. Hilda Kirkwood. *Can Forum* Jan 1987; Vol 66 No 765: p39.

The essence of the prairies; review of *Queen of the Headaches*. Margaret Owen. *Prairie Fire* Summer 1987; Vol 8 No 2: p63–65.

BUTLER, AUDREY

Some good moments in Cradle Pin despite awkward direction; theatre review. Ray Conlogue. photo · *G&M* Sept 17, 1987: pD5.

Wrestling tale grip quite easy to slip; theatre review of *Cradle Pin*. Robert Crew. photo · *TS* Sept 18, 1987: pD16.

THE BUTTERFLY CHAIR/Novel by Marion Quednau

Risk-taking writer off to a good start; review of *The Butterfly Chair*. Ken Adachi. *TS* Nov 22, 1987: pC9.
[FIRST NOVELS: BOOK REVIEWS]

A brutal inheritance; review of *The Butterfly Chair*. Celina Bell. *Maclean's* Dec 7, 1987; Vol 100 No 49: T8.
[FIRST NOVELS: BOOK REVIEWS]

Novel about family tragedy a powerful debut; review of *The Butterfly Chair*. William French. illus · *G&M* Dec 3, 1987: pA25.
[FIRST NOVELS: BOOK REVIEWS]

[Untitled]; review of *The Butterfly Chair*. Joan McGrath. *Quill & Quire* Sept 1987; Vol 53 No 9: p78–79.
[FIRST NOVELS: BOOK REVIEWS]

[Untitled]; review of *The Butterfly Chair*. Constance Rooke. *Malahat R* Dec 1987; No 81: p102.
[FIRST NOVELS: BOOK REVIEWS]

BUTTERSCOTCH DREAMS/Children's poems by Sonja Dunn

A trio of poets to tickle a child's fancy; reviews of children's poetry books. Adele Ashby. *Quill & Quire (Books for Young People)* June 1987; Vol 53 No 6: p10.

BUTTON, MARSHALL

Mill life provided fuel for persona; article. Kate Zimmerman. photo · *CH* Nov 2, 1987: pB6.

BY CANOE & MOCCASIN/Children's stories by Basil H. Johnston

The magic of myth and love of legend; reviews of children's books. Tim Wynne-Jones. *G&M* July 25, 1987: pC17.

BY HOOK OR BY CROOK/Children's poems by Meguido Zola

Youngsters get choice of beautiful books; reviews. Helen Norrie. *WFP* Dec 5, 1987: p57.

C'EST ENCORE LE SOLITAIRE QUI PARLE/Poems by André Roy

André Roy ou l'invention d'un littéral métaphysique; introduction. Marie-Andrée Beaudet. *Estuaire* Spring 1987; No 44: p63–66.

Les mots retrouvent tous leurs pouvoirs; review of *C'est encore le solitaire qui parle*. Gérald Gaudet. photo · *MD* Sept 5, 1987: pC9.

C'ÉTAIT AVANT LA GUERRE À L'ANSE À GILLES/Play by Marie Laberge

Idéologie féministe dans Le Temps sauvage et C'était avant la guerre l'Anse Gilles; article. Monique Genuist. abstract · *Theatre Hist in Can (special issue)* Spring 1987; Vol 8 No 1: p49–58.
[FEMINIST DRAMA]

CÔTÉ, DENIS

Les clichés du futur; review of *Les Géants de Blizzard*. Chantal de Grandpré. *Can Child Lit* 1987; No 46: p68–70.

CACCIA, FULVIO

Transculture; reviews of poetry books. Viviana Comensoli. *Can Lit* Spring 1987; No 112: p120–123.

CAGE/Novel by George McWhirter

Brave novel needs power of a narrative; review of *Cage*. Ken Adachi. *TS* June 21, 1987: pA23.

[Untitled]; review of *Cage*. Shelagh Garland. *Books in Can* Oct 1987; Vol 16 No 7: p24.

[Untitled]; review of *Cage*. Gail Greenwood. *CH* Sept 27, 1987: pE6.

A gringo's view of Mexico; review of *Cage*. T.F. Rigelhof. *G&M* July 18, 1987: pC17

CAHIERS D'ANATOMIE (COMPLICITS)/Poems by Michel Savard

Maniaques depressifs; reviews of poetry books. Mark Benson. *Can Lit* Spring 1987; No 112: p138–141.

THE CAKE THAT MACK ATE/Children's story by Rose Robart

Mini-reviews; reviews of children's stories. Mary Rubio. *Can Child Lit* 1987; No 46: p105–109.

CALL, FRANK OLIVER

One man's access to prophecy: the sonnet series of Frank Oliver Call; article. R. Alex Kizuk. *Can Poet* Fall-Winter 1987; No 21: p31–41.

CALLAGHAN, BARRY

Treasured memoir; letter to the editor. George W. Bancroft. *Tor Life* July 1987; Vol 21 No 10: p8.

Vandals' $150,000 rampage trashes home; article. Dale Brazao. photo · *TS* Oct 13, 1987: pA2.

[Untitled]; editorial. Marq de Villiers. *Tor Life* June 1987; Vol 21 No 9: p6.

Bright lights of the city; article. Harriet Eisenkraft. Ned Boone. photo · *Tor Life* May 1987; Vol 21 No 7 : p54–58, 78, 80–81, 83.

Home of Toronto writer ransacked; article. Robert MacLeod. photo · *G&M* Oct 14, 1987: pA15.

On the carpet: a memoir of Layton and Callaghan; column. David O'Rourke. photo · *Poetry Can R* Fall 1987; Vol 9 No 1: p14–15.

Paperclips: the radical right in our midst . . . a horse and writer; column. Beverley Slopen. *Quill & Quire* Sept 1987; Vol 53 No 9: p66.

CALLAGHAN, MORLEY

It's good to see and hear feisty Callaghan; television review of *Morley Callaghan: First Person Singular*. Ken Adachi. photo · *TS* March 24, 1987: pC6.
[TELEVISION AND CANADIAN LITERATURE]

Childhood experiences in The Loved and the Lost; article. Donald R. Bartlett. *New Q* Spring-Summer 1987; Vol 7 No 1–2: p294–300.
[THE FAMILY IN CANADIAN LITERATURE]

Portraits of patriarchs; television review of *First Person Singular*. John Bemrose. photo · *Maclean's* March 30, 1987; Vol 100 No 13: p63.

[They Shall Inherit the Earth]; review. Dorothy Livesay. *Brick* Winter 1987; No 29: p47–48.

Morley Callaghan, past & present; television review of *Morley Callaghan: First Person Singular*. Gina Mallet. photo · *Chatelaine* April 1987; Vol 60 No 4: p22.
[TELEVISION AND CANADIAN LITERATURE]

Choreographer's dance fantasy pieces dramatic, sensuous; column. Doreen Martens. *WFP* March 23, 1987: p17.
[TELEVISION AND CANADIAN LITERATURE]

CAMBODIA: A BOOK FOR PEOPLE WHO FIND TELEVISION TOO SLOW/Novel by Brian Fawcett

B.C. writer deliberately jars Jell-O minds; article. Ken Adachi. biog photo · *TS* March 7, 1987: M4.

Portrait of a society whose vision is shaped by television; review of *Cambodia*. Mary Ambrose. *G&M* July 25, 1987: pC15.

Cambodia: whose idea is this?; review article about *Cambodia*. Jeff Berg. *West Coast R* Spring 1987; Vol 21 No 4: p73–77.

[Untitled]; review of *Cambodia*. Clint Burnham. *Malahat R* June 1987; No 79: p156–157.

A prose experiment; review of *Cambodia: A Book for People Who Find Television Too Slow*. Dennis Corcoran. *TS* Feb 15, 1987: pA18.

[Untitled]; reviews of novels. Beverley Daurio. *Cross Can Writ Q* 1987; Vol 9 No 3–4: p45–46.

Down the tube; review of *Cambodia*. Mary di Michele. *Books in Can* Jan-Feb 1987; Vol 16 No 1: p23.

Probing horror with footnotes; review of *Cambodia*. Seymour Hamilton. *CH* May 17, 1987: pE5.

[Untitled]; review of *Cambodia*. Geoff Heinricks. *Quill & Quire* June 1987; Vol 53 No 6: p31–32.

Moving pictures; review of *Cambodia*. Maggie Helwig. illus · *Can Forum* Aug-Sept 1987; Vol 67 No 771: p39–41.

Today's assignment: short fiction that's worth a long look; reviews of short story books. Douglas Hill. *G&M* March 14, 1987: pE19.
[ANTHOLOGIES: BOOK REVIEWS]

Reading Brian Fawcett; reviews of *Cambodia* and *The Secret Journal of Alexander Mackenzie*. Norbert Ruebsaat. *Event* Summer 1987; Vol 16 No 2: p118–121.

CAMERON, ANNE

Problem of perception distorts debate on pornography bills; column. June Callwood. *G&M* July 1, 1987: pA2.
[CENSORSHIP]

[Untitled]; review of *Dzelarhons*. Adelle Castelo. *Quill & Quire* March 1987; Vol 53 No 3: p73.

[Untitled]; review of *Dzelarhons*. Frances Duncan. *Room of One's Own* Sept 1987; Vol 11 No 4: p112–115.

Customs detains book recounting Indian legends; article. Stephen Godfrey. *G&M* June 22, 1987: pC9.
[CENSORSHIP]

Fine short stories examine contemporary domestic life; reviews of *Dzelarhons* and *Afternoon Tea*. Douglas Hill. *G&M* Jan 24, 1987: pE17.

A lesson from myths: live in harmony; review of *Dzelarhons*. Catherine Macleod. *TS* April 5, 1987: pA22.

[Untitled]; reviews of *Orca's Song* and *Raven Returns the Water*. Eva Martin. *Quill & Quire (Books for Young People)* Oct 1987; Vol 53 No 10: p23

[Untitled]; review of *Dzelarhons*. Sherie Posesorski. *Books in Can* June-July 1987; Vol 16 No 5: p22.

CAMERON, BARRY

[Untitled]; reviews of *Archibald Lampman* and *John Metcalf*. Dennis Duffy. *Eng Studies in Can* Sept 1987; Vol 13 No 3: p355–357.

CAMERON, ELSPETH

In ordinary life we don't assume we know anyone; article. Ken Adachi. *TS* Sept 19, 1987: M5.
[CANADIAN LITERATURE: BIOGRAPHY]

Lazarovitch to Layton; review of *Irving Layton: A Portrait*. Ben Jones. *Can Lit* Winter 1987; No 115: p160–162.

Elspeth Cameron and Irving Layton; reviews of *Irving Layton: A Portrait* and *Waiting for the Messiah*. Patricia Keeney Smith. *U of Toronto Q* Spring 1987; Vol 56 No 3: p467–470.

LE CAMION

See **MATTHEW AND THE MIDNIGHT TOW TRUCK/ Children's story by Allen Morgan**

CAMPBELL, ANNE

[Untitled]; reviews of *Through the Nan Da Gate* and *Death Is an Anxious Mother*. Nancy Batty. *Dandelion* Spring-Summer 1987; Vol 14 No 1: p84–87.

Still lifes; reviews of poetry books. Laurence Hutchman. *Can Lit* Winter 1987; No 115: p263–264.

[Untitled]; reviews of poetry books. Sheila Martindale. *Cross Can Writ Q* 1987; Vol 9 No 2: p20–21.

CAMPBELL, HAZEL D.

Putrefying sore; reviews of fictional works. Kathryn Chittick. *Can Lit* Spring 1987; No 112: p128–129.

CAMPBELL, K.C.

Tricks can't save flimsy play; theatre review of *It's Magic*. Kate Zimmerman. *CH* June 13, 1987: pF2.

CAMPBELL, WILFRED

Priest became Canada's 'Poet Laureate'; biographical article. Donald Jones. photo · *TS* Dec 26, 1987: K3.

CAN YOU CATCH JOSEPHINE?

See **PEUT-TU ATTRAPER JOSEPHINE?/CAN YOU CATCH JOSEPHINE?/Children's story by Stéphane Poulin**

CAN YOU PROMISE ME SPRING?/Young adult novel by Alison Lohans Pirot

Living to tell the tale: survival guides for adolescent readers; reviews of *Can You Promise Me Spring?* and *We're Friends, Aren't We?*. Joanne Buckley. *Can Child Lit* 1987; No 46: p78–79.

[Untitled]; review of *Can You Promise Me Spring?*. Betty Dyck. *Can Auth & Book* Spring 1987; Vol 62 No 3: p25.

CANAC-MARQUIS, NORMAND

Syndrome obscure yet polished; theatre review of *Le Syndrome de Cézanne*. Pat Donnelly. *MG* March 5, 1987: pD13.

Kingston editor retains theatre critics' award; article. Pat Donnelly. *MG* Oct 5, 1987: pB15.
[AWARDS, LITERARY]

Le théâtre du Rire joue gagnant; column. Robert Lévesque. *MD* Oct 13, 1987: p11.
[AWARDS, LITERARY]

Mécanique violente et masques aimables; theatre review of *Le Syndrome de Cézanne*. Paul Lefebvre. photo · *MD* Feb 23, 1987: p10.

[Untitled]; theatre review of *Le Syndrome de Cézanne*. Paul Lefebvre. *MD* Feb 27, 1987: p7.

CANADA GEES MATE FOR LIFE/Poems by bill bissett

[Untitled]; reviews of *Canada Gees Mate for Life* and *Zygal*. Phil Hall. *Poetry Can R* Fall 1987; Vol 9 No 1: p34.

Seeker & finder; reviews of *Canada Gees Mate for Life* and *Rootless Tree*. Bruce Whiteman. *Can Lit* Winter 1987; No 115: p148–150.

CANADIAN AUTHOR & BOOKMAN/Periodical

The view from here; editorial. Anne Osborne. *Can Auth & Book* Summer 1987; Vol 62 No 4: p2.
[CANADIAN LITERARY PERIODICALS]

CANADIAN CHILDREN'S ANNUAL/Periodical

Christmas books offer fun learning to curious children; review of *Canadian Children's Annual*. *TS* Dec 6, 1987: pE6.

CANADIAN CRUSOES: A TALE OF THE RICE LAKE PLAINS/Novel by Catharine Parr Traill

Canada the way it used to be; review of *Canadian Crusoes*. M.T. Kelly. *G&M* Jan 10, 1987: pE17.

[Untitled]; review of *Canadian Crusoes*. Michael Peterman. *U of Toronto Q* Fall 1987; Vol 57 No 1: p160–161.

CANADIAN DRAMA: HISTORY AND CRITICISM

The very best of company: perceptions of a Canadian attitude towards war and nationalism in three contemporary plays; article. John S. Bolin. *Amer R of Can Studies* Autumn 1987; Vol 17 No 3: p309–322.
[CULTURAL IDENTITY]

From profound and provocative to simplistic and obscure; article. Ray Conlogue. photo · *G&M* Dec 26, 1987: pC3.

Here are the highlights of biggest stage season; column. Robert Crew. photo · *TS* Sept 25, 1987: pE3,E6

Conversing with spirits of the dead; survey article. Robert Crew. photo · *TS* Dec 26, 1987: pE3.

The ideological formation of political theatre in Canada; article. Alan Filewod. abstract · *Theatre Hist in Can* Fall 1987; Vol 8 No 2: p254–263.
[COLONIALISM; POLITICAL WRITING]

Leaping in triumph across cultural frontiers; article. Matthew Fraser. photo · *G&M* Dec 26, 1987: pC10.

Enter stage centre: can Toronto build a national theatre?; article. Keith Garebian. *Can Forum* Aug-Sept 1987; Vol 67 No 771: p24–29.

Büchner in Canada: Woyzeck and the development of English-Canadian theatre; article. Jerry Wasserman. abstract photo · *Theatre Hist in Can* Fall 1987; Vol 8 No 2: p181–192.
[POLITICAL WRITING]

Drama; survey review article. Jerry Wasserman. *U of Toronto Q* Fall 1987; Vol 57 No 1: p62–74.

CANADIAN FICTION: HISTORY AND CRITICISM

Fiction; survey review article. Michael F.N. Dixon. *U of Toronto Q* Fall 1987; Vol 57 No 1: p1–7.

Fiction; survey review article. Mark Levene. *U of Toronto Q* Fall 1987; Vol 57 No 1: p7–21.

CANADIAN FORUM/Periodical

Expansion blamed for red ink at CBC's sales division; column. Sid Adilman. *TS* Nov 2, 1987: pC4.
[CANADIAN LITERARY PERIODICALS]

Remembering the beginning: Barker Fairley on the origins of the Forum; interview. Hilda Kirkwood. illus · *Can Forum* Jan 1987; Vol 66 No 765: p6–8.
[CANADIAN LITERARY PERIODICALS]

CANADIAN IDENTITY

See **CULTURAL IDENTITY**

CANADIAN IMAGINATION

Du jardin à la forêt; essay. Naim Kattan. abstract · *Études can* 1987; No 23: p65–70.

La forêt chez les écrivains anglophones; article. Danièle Pitavy. abstract · *Études can* 1987; No 23: p147–157.
[BRITISH COLUMBIA WRITING AND WRITERS; COLONIAL LITERATURE; NATURE IN CANADIAN LITERATURE]

CANADIAN LANDSCAPE

Fluid landscape/static land: the traveller's vision; article. Richard C. Davis. *Essays on Can Writ* Spring 1987; No 34: p140–156.

The forest and the trees; article. Rosemary Sullivan. *Brick* Winter 1987; No 29: p43–46.
[NATURE IN CANADIAN LITERATURE]

CANADIAN LITERARY LANDMARKS

Laurence's girlhood home an arts centre; article. biog photo · *MG* Jan 7, 1987: pE5.

Laurence memorial opened; article. *WFP* June 24, 1987: p26.

Rainbow brings smile; article. *WFP* June 26, 1987: p42.

What's happening: Stephansson's home site of crafts fair; column. photo · *CH* June 12, 1987: pF6–F7.

Les trois Marias; article. *MD* April 16, 1987: p15.

Laurence home made historical site; article. *MG* June 26, 1987: pC2.

Home of soldier-poet is memorial; article. biog · *TS* Oct 24, 1987: pE38.

Le Musée Louis-Hémon voile "l'hymen" de Maria Chapdelaine; article. *MD* Nov 28, 1987: pA7.

Laurence service; letter to the editor. Brian Curtis. photo · *WFP* Jan 26, 1987: p6.

The best part of going out; editorial. Paul Denham. *NeWest R* Oct 1987; Vol 13 No 2: p1.

Poetry sweatshops add a new twist to Olympic tradition; column. William French. *G&M* March 3, 1987: pC7.
[COMPETITIONS, LITERARY; FESTIVALS, LITERARY; POETRY READINGS]

Neepawa forgives its most famous citizen; article. Dan Lett. photo · *TS* Oct 18, 1987: pD5.

Plateau is scene for fiction's famous characters; article. Jack Todd. photo · *MG* May 23, 1987: J2.

CANADIAN LITERARY PERIODICALS

Saturday Night: 100 ans et des plumes; article. *MD* Jan 7, 1987: p8.

Quelle culture politique existe au Québec? Une conférence-débat du magazine Vice versa; article. *MD* Feb 25, 1987: p9.

Five years of TSAR; editorial. *Tor South Asian R* Spring 1987; Vol 5 No 3: p1–2.

Black buys Saturday Night magazine; article. photo · *WFP* June 19, 1987: p24.

Fulford bails out as editor in Saturday Night takeover; article. photo · *WFP* June 25, 1987: p19.

Black buys Saturday Night; article. *CH* June 19, 1987: pF2.

Robert Fulford quits Saturday Night post; article. *CH* June 25, 1987: pD1.

Editorial. *Fireweed* Winter 1987; No 24: p5–7.

Markets & events; column. *Cross Can Writ Q* 1987; Vol 9 No 2: p31–32.
[WRITERS' WORKSHOPS]

Saturday Night's editor Fulford quits; article. *MG* June 25, 1987: pE1.

Index to volume 19/4 — volume 21/4. *West Coast R* Spring 1987; Vol 21 No 4: p83–88.

New owner running into problems trying to get staff for Saturday Night; article. *TS* July 5, 1987: pA12.

Black completes deal to buy Saturday Night; article. *TS* July 9, 1987: pA3.

Tempus fugit, but not in poetry; article. *TS* Aug 23, 1987: pA20.

Poetry magazine holds rummage sale; article. *TS* Sept 30, 1987: pD1.

Black takes over Saturday Night; article. *MG* July 9, 1987: pD7.

Conrad Black met enfin la main sur Saturday Night; article. *MD* July 9, 1987: p9.

Magazine's new editor to earn 'unprecedented' salary; article. *WFP* July 7, 1987: p28.

Magazine purchase completed; article. *WFP* July 9, 1987: p15.

Fraser new editor; article. *WFP* July 17, 1987: p34.

Saturday Night shakeup unlikely, new editor says; article. *WFP* July 18, 1987: p31.

Twice-dead magazine wins honor; article. photo · *WFP* Aug 27, 1987: p42.

Six-figure salary rumored for Saturday Night's new editor; article. *CH* July 7, 1987: pC6.

Black closes Saturday Night deal; article. photo · *CH* July 9, 1987: pF2.

Fraser accepts post at Saturday Night; article. *CH* July 17, 1987: pF10.

Mainstreet Calgary; column. *CH (Neighbors)* July 22, 1987: pA6.

Saturday Night deal goes through; article. *G&M* July 9, 1987: pD5.

Saturday Night's Macfarlane leaves 'with great regret'; article. *G&M* July 10, 1987: pD5.

"Question de poésie": un colloque de la revue Estuaire le 20 novembre au salon du livre; article. *MD* Nov 16, 1987: p9.
[CONFERENCES, LITERARY]

Moebius ou l'ironie du repli; editorial. *Moebius* Winter 1987; No 31: p1–2

Letters from the editors; letters to the editor. *Prairie J of Can Lit* 1987; No 8: p20–27
[CANADIAN LITERARY PUBLISHING]

Book store aims to please the theatre and movie crowd; article. Marianne Ackerman. *MG* Feb 17, 1987: pE8.
[BOOK TRADE IN CANADA]

L'Actualite picks up six magazine awards; article. Ken Adachi. *TS* May 22, 1987: pE21.
[AWARDS, LITERARY]

But will Black respect Saturday Night on Sunday morning?; column. Ken Adachi. *TS* June 19, 1987: pD23.

Saturday Night film dispiriting; column. Ken Adachi. photo · *TS* Sept 7, 1987: pB2.
[AUDIO-VISUALS AND CANADIAN LITERATURE]

Take a look at a 'little' magazine; review of *Descant*. Ken Adachi. *TS* July 19, 1987: pA21.

Magazine to have face lift; column. Ken Adachi. photo · *TS* Dec 15, 1987: pG4.

Feminist quarterly honors Laurence; column. Ken Adachi. *TS* Nov 16, 1987: pC5.
[FICTION READINGS]

Radio's Scales of Justice seen as possible CTV series; column. Sid Adilman. *TS* Dec 30, 1987: pB1.

Expansion blamed for red ink at CBC's sales division; column. Sid Adilman. *TS* Nov 2, 1987: pC4.

D'où vient Voix et images?; article. Jacques Allard. *Voix et images* Winter 1987; No 35: p294–303.

De Voix et images du pays à Voix et images: 20 ans déjà; editorial. Bernard-J. Andrès. *Voix et images* Autumn 1987; Vol 13 No 1: p5–6.

Littérature et recherche universitaire: la question des revues; introduction. Bernard Andrès. *Voix et images* Winter 1987; No 35: p266.
[CONFERENCES, LITERARY]

La littérature québécoise à Voix et images: créneau ou ghetto?; article. Bernard Andrès. *Voix et images* Winter 1987; No 35: p303–312.

Little literary magazine packs loads of pleasure; article. Nick Auf der Maur. *MG* June 19, 1987: pA2.

A fitting homage; review of *Études littéraire* (special issue). Ellen Reisman Babby. *Essays on Can Writ* Spring 1987; No 34: p190–195.

Saturday Night editor envisions moe changes; article. Ian Bailey. photo · *WFP* Dec 21, 1987: p35.

Saturday Night's new editor champing at bit; article. Ian Bailey. photo · *CH* Dec 22, 1987: pD8.

Telling tales on Saturday Night; column. George Bain. *Maclean's* July 27, 1987; Vol 100 No 30: p44.

Le récit à la NBJ; review of *La Nouvelle barre du jour*. Caroline Bayard. *Lettres québec* Summer 1987; No 46: p34–35.

[Untitled]; review of *(f.)Lip*. Maggie Berg. *Rubicon* Fall 1987; No 9: p194–195.

Saturday Night intriguing tale of intrigue; letter to the editor. Pierre Berton. *TS* July 8, 1987: pA18.

Analyse spectrale d'Études françaises; article. Bernard Beugnot. *Voix et images* Winter 1987; No 35: p278–284.

Littérature sur mesure: de la nouvelle à la page; review of *XYZ*. Jean-Roch Boivin. *MD* Oct 10, 1987: pD2–D3.

Saturday Night branches out in search of publishing profits; article. Pat Brennan. photo · *TS* Jan 6, 1987: pE1.

L'interrogation totale de la mort; reviews of poetry books. André Brochu. *Voix et images* Autumn 1987; Vol 13 No 1: p165–174.
[ANNOTATIONS, SHORT REVIEWS, BOOK LISTS]

Editorial. Jane Casey. *CV* 2 Spring 1987; Vol 10 No 3: p6–7.

[Untitled]; review of *La Nouvelle barre du jour* (special issue). Ginette Castro. *Études can* June 1987; No 22: p131.

Payment to writers; letter to the editor. R.S. Craggs. *Can Auth & Book* Spring 1987; Vol 62 No 3: p2.

Saturday Night observes 100th birthday; article. Rod Currie. *WFP* Jan 6, 1987: p26.

Saturday Night's first century; editorial. Christopher Dafoe. *WFP* Jan 18, 1987: p6.

Qui de neuf du côté universitaire?; reviews of periodicals. Carole David. *MD* Jan 17, 1987: pB5,B7.

La nouvelle, le clip de l'écriture; review of *XYZ*. Carole David. *MD* March 7, 1987: pB2.

Les revues se font voir pour être lues; article. Carole David. *MD* March 14, 1987: pD3.

Moebius ou les vertus paradoxales de l'athéisme; column. Carole David. photo · *MD* April 11, 1987: pD3.

Un numéro d'Études françaises explore les rapports de la littérature et des médias; review. Carole David. *MD* May 9, 1987: pD2.

Spleen may write the poem, but Layton's heart will speak tomorrow; reviews of poetry books. Trevor Ferguson. *MG* Sept 26, 1987: J11.

La vitrine du livre; reviews. Guy Ferland. *MD* March 7, 1987: pB2.

La vitrine du livre; reviews. Guy Ferland. *MD* June 6, 1987: pD4.

La vitrine du livre; reviews. Guy Ferland. *MD* June 20, 1987: pD4.

La vitrine du livre; reviews of *Trois* and *Vice Versa*. Guy Ferland. *MD* July 4, 1987: pC6.

La vitrine du livre; reviews of *Le Jeu illocutoire* and *XYZ*. Guy Ferland. *MD* Aug 1, 1987: pC6.

La vitrine du livre; reviews of periodicals. Guy Ferland. *MD* Sept 5, 1987: pC8.

La revue des revues; reviews of periodicals. Guy Ferland. *MD* Sept 19, 1987: pD6.

La revue des revues; reviews of periodicals. Guy Ferland. *MD* Oct 17, 1987: pD6

La revue des revues; reviews of periodicals. Guy Ferland. *MD* Dec 5, 1987: pD6.

The end of Fulford's era; article. Doug Fetherling. *Maclean's* July 6, 1987; Vol 100 No 27: p53.

Editor's notebook; editorial. John Flood. *Northward J* 1987; No 41: p2.

Saturday Night changes will take time to implement; column. William French. photo · *G&M* Dec 15, 1987: pD5.

Old heck; column. Robert Fulford. illus · *Sat Night* Nov 1987; Vol 102 No 11: p7–8,10–11.

Les voix des Amériques; review of *Voix et images* (special issue). Chantal Gamache. *MD* March 21, 1987: pD2.

L'intérêt de Voix & images pour les aventures culturelles de notre société; review. Chantal Gamache. *MD* April 25, 1987: pD3.

En toute simplicité; review of *Voix et images*. Chantal Gamache. photo · *MD* Nov 7, 1987: pD3.

Saturday Night celebrates sobriety; article. Peter Goddard. photo · *TS* Jan 6, 1987: pD4.

Conrad Black deal to buy Saturday Night said up in air; article. Richard Gwyn. *TS* July 3, 1987: pA1,A4.

What's Black and White and may or may not be read all over?; article. David Hayes. photo · *Tor Life* Dec 1987; Vol 21 No 18: p54–60,108,110–111.

Pretentieux? Idéalistes? Elitistes?; article. François Hébert. *Liberté* Feb 1987; Vol 29 No 1: p159–160.

Reconnaissance à André Roy; review of *Vagabondages*. Jean-Pierre Issenhuth. *Liberté* Oct 1987; Vol 29 No 5: p162–163.

Pages for the powerful; article. Brian D. Johnson. photo · *Maclean's* Jan 19, 1987; Vol 100 No 3: p62.

Keeping tabs on the poetry explosion; review of *Canadian Poetry Chronicle (1984)*. W.J. Keith. *Essays on Can Writ* Winter 1987; No 35: p100–104.

Conrad Black purchases Saturday Night magazine; article. Kenneth Kidd. *TS* June 19, 1987: pF1.

Remembering the beginning: Barker Fairley on the origins of the Forum; interview. Hilda Kirkwood. illus · *Can Forum* Jan 1987; Vol 66 No 765: p6–8.

John Fraser: child star; article. Martin Knelman. photo · *Tor Life* Dec 1987; Vol 21 No 18: p12.

Current Canadian studies; column. Victor A. Konrad. *Amer R of Can Studies* Autumn 1987; Vol 17 No 3: p360–366.
[ANNOTATIONS, SHORT REVIEWS]

Limoges, principale vitrine du théâtre québécois en Europe; column. Robert Lévesque. photo · *MD* Sept 29, 1987: p13.
[AWARDS, LITERARY; FESTIVALS, DRAMA]

Voix et images 36; review. Gaëtan Lévesque. *Lettres québec* Autumn 1987; No 47: p66.

Robert Fulford resigns as editor of Saturday Night; article. Liam Lacey. photo · *G&M* June 25, 1987: pD1.

Saturday Night sale unsure, search for editor continues; article. Liam Lacey. *G&M* July 4, 1987: pC4.

L'édition ontaroise: un monde à découvrir; article. Françoise Lafleur. *MD* Nov 19, 1987: p13.
[PUBLISHING AND PUBLISHERS IN CANADA]

De l'érudition: l'esprit et la lettre; reviews of periodicals. Suzanne Lamy. *Voix et images* Winter 1987; No 35: p342–346.

Could be disaster story for children's magazine; article. Renate Lerch. *Fin Post* Oct 5, 1987: p3.

Editor's note. Bernice Lever. *Waves* Spring 1987; Vol 15 No 4: p94.

L'effet science-fiction tous azimuts: la SF québécoise en 1986–1987; reviews of science fiction books and periodicals. Michel Lord. *Voix et images* Autumn 1987; Vol 13 No 1: p180–189.
[ANNOTATIONS, SHORT REVIEWS, BOOK LISTS; ANTHOLOGIES: BOOK REVIEWS; FIRST NOVELS: BOOK REVIEWS]

Études françaises, vingt ans après; article. Laurent Mailhot. *Voix et images* Winter 1987; No 35: p284–287.

Sale of magazine stalled over debt; article. Jonathan Manthorpe. *CH* July 4, 1987: pC6.

Splash of grey heralds Saturday Night centenary; article. John Bentley Mays. photo · *G&M* Jan 5, 1987: pC9.

Fraser to be editor of Saturday Night; article. John Bentley Mays. photo · *G&M* July 17, 1987: pD11.

Beyond the merely competent; reviews of critical works. Larry McDonald. *Atlan Prov Book R* Sept-Oct 1987; Vol 14 No 3: p11.

[Untitled]; review of *Études littéraires*. Barbara McEwen. *Theatre Hist in Can* Fall 1987; Vol 8 No 2: p234–237.

Literary giants got rotten reviews; column. Kenneth McGoogan. *CH* Jan 18, 1987: pE4.
[POETRY READINGS]

100-year-old magazine filled with literary gems; column. Kenneth McGoogan. *CH* Jan 25, 1987: pE4.

Dandelion uncovers new voice; column. Kenneth McGoogan. photo · *CH* Feb 1, 1987: pC8.
[AWARDS, LITERARY; POETRY READINGS]

Banff Centre lands novelist; column. Kenneth McGoogan. *CH* Feb 22, 1987: pE6.
[PUBLISHING AND PUBLISHERS IN CANADA; WRITERS' WORKSHOPS]

Poets help celebrate Dandelion; column. Kenneth McGoogan. *CH* June 28, 1987: pF8.
[AWARDS, LITERARY; POETRY READINGS; WRITERS' ORGANIZATIONS]

J.P. Donleavy here in '88; column. Kenneth McGoogan. *CH* July 26, 1987: pE5.
[AWARDS, LITERARY; CANADIAN LITERARY PUBLISHING; FESTIVALS, LITERARY]

Trois premiers numéros: Le Beffroi, Filigrane, Kérosène; reviews. Robert Melançon. *Liberté* April 1987; Vol 29 No 2: p125–128.

Devenez mécène, abonnez-vous!; reviews of periodicals. Robert Melançon. *Liberté* June 1987; Vol 29 No 3: p80–87.

La littérature est inactuelle; reviews of *La Nouvelle barre du jour* and *Le Beffroi*. Robert Melançon. *Liberté* Aug 1987; Vol 29 No 4: p102–108.

Ding et Dong; reviews of periodicals. Robert Melançon. *Liberté* Dec 1987; Vol 29 No 6: p122–129.

Philosophie et littérature en revue(s): genres et styles mêlés; reviews of *Le Beffroi* and *Sédiments*. Ginette Michaud. *Liberté* April 1987; Vol 29 No 2: p129–133.

Fulford leaves his Saturday Night post; article. Henry Mietkiewicz. photo · *TS* June 25, 1987: pA2.

Publisher to cut Sauve anecdote in book of gossip; column. Henry Mietkiewicz. *TS* July 10, 1987: pE23.

John Fraser new Saturday Night editor; column. Henry Mietkiewicz. *TS* July 17, 1987: pE23.

Qui a peur de l'intellectuel in 1987?; reviews. Pierre Milot. *Voix et images* Spring 1987; Vol 12 No 3: p530–534.

Études littéraires est-elle indispensable?; essay. Louise Milot. *Voix et images* Winter 1987; No 35: p267–271.

Poulin; review of *Études françaises (special issue)*. Anne Marie Miraglia. *Can Lit* Spring 1987; No 112: p152–154.

Pauvre choix; letter to the editor. Roger Moisan. *MD* Feb 7, 1987: pA18.

La vie littéraire; column. Marc Morin. photo · *MD* Nov 28, 1987: pD12.

The view from here; editorial. Anne Osborne. *Can Auth & Book* Summer 1987; Vol 62 No 4: p2.

Constantes et ruptures en recherche littéraire: le cas d'Études littéraires; article. Jean-Marcel Paquette. *Voix et images* Winter 1987; No 35: p271–277.

[Untitled]; reviews. Andrew Parkin. *Poetry Can R* Summer 1987; Vol 8 No 4: p36–37.
[ANTHOLOGIES: BOOK REVIEWS]

Constitution d'une avant-garde littéraire; article. Jacques Pelletier. abstract · *Études lit* Spring-Summer 1987; Vol 20 No 1: p111–130.
[POLITICAL WRITING; POSTMODERNIST WRITING AND CRITICISM; QUEBEC LITERATURE (FRENCH LANGUAGE): HISTORY AND CRITICISM]

L'air du temps; review of *Sédiments 1986*. Jacques Pelletier. *Voix et images* Spring 1987; Vol 12 No 3: p524–527.

Atlantic alternatives in theatre; review of *Canadian Theatre Review*. Richard Perkyns. *Atlan Prov Book R* Feb-March 1987; Vol 14 No 1: p11.

The literary editor: unsung cultural hero; editorial. Ted Plantos. *Cross Can Writ Q* 1987; Vol 9 No 1: p2.

Imperfect conquests; reviews of *The Manor House of De Villeray* and *Le Tour du Québec par deux enfants*. Anthony Raspa. *Can Lit* Winter 1987; No 115: p172–174.

Les jeunes loups; reviews. Lucie Robert. *Voix et images* Spring 1987; Vol 12 No 3: p561–564.

La vie littéraire; column. Jean Royer. *MD* Jan 31, 1987: pB2.
[COMPETITIONS, LITERARY; RADIO AND CANADIAN LITERATURE; TELEVISION AND CANADIAN LITERATURE]

La vie littéraire; column. Jean Royer. *MD* Feb 14, 1987: pC2.
[AWARDS, LITERARY; COMPETITIONS, LITERARY; FICTION READINGS; POETRY READINGS; RADIO AND CANADIAN LITERATURE]

La vie littéraire; column. Jean Royer. *MD* Feb 28, 1987: pC2.
[AWARDS, LITERARY; CANADIAN LITERARY PUBLISHING; CONFERENCES, LITERARY; RADIO AND CANADIAN LITERATURE]

Le sentiment de la langue; reviews of *"Quand on a une langue on peut aller à Rome"* and *Les Changeurs de signes.* Jean Royer. *MD* Feb 28, 1987: pC3.

La vitrine du livre; reviews. Jean Royer. *MD* March 14, 1987: pD4.

Notes de lecture; reviews of periodicals. Jean Royer. *MD* March 21, 1987: pC7.

La vitrine du livre; reviews. Jean Royer. photo · *MD* March 21, 1987: pD2.

Notes de lecture; reviews of periodicals. Jean Royer. *MD* March 21, 1987: pD8.

La vitrine du livre; reviews. Jean Royer. photo · *MD* March 28, 1987: pD2.

La vitrine du livre; reviews. Jean Royer. photo · *MD* April 4, 1987: pD2.

La vitrine du livre; reviews. Jean Royer. *MD* April 11, 1987: pD2.

La vitrine du livre; reviews. Jean Royer. photo · *MD* April 18, 1987: pD2.

Estuaire au carrefour des poésies; editorial Jean Royer. *Estuaire* Spring 1987; No 44: p5–8.

Photo de famille; article. Jean Royer. photo · *MD* Sept 28, 1987: p9.
[AUTHORS, CANADIAN]

La vie littéraire; column. Jean Royer. photo · *MD* Oct 17, 1987: pD2.
[COMPETITIONS, LITERARY; CONFERENCES, LITERARY; FICTION READINGS; WRITERS' ORGANIZATIONS]

Cartographies; review of *Études françaises.* Ralph Sarkonak. *Can Lit* Summer-Fall 1987; No 113–114: p244–245.

Mr. Saturday Night; biographical article. Leslie Scrivener. photo · *TS* July 5, 1987: pD1–D2.

Magazine's literary mentor leaves with mixed emotions; article. Leslie Scrivener. photo · *CH* July 12, 1987: pE6.

Saturday Night fiasco shakes your faith in tycoonery; humorous essay. Joey Slinger. *TS* July 7, 1987: pA6.

Book world: anti-Khomeini plotter's story told in new book; column. Beverley Slopen. *TS* Sept 6, 1987: pA18.
[AUDIO-VISUALS AND CANADIAN LITERATURE; AUTHORS, CANADIAN]

Book world: the Bay saga: before Vol. 3 comes Vol. 2 1/2; column. Beverley Slopen. *TS* Nov 22, 1987: pC8.

Sheer 'persistence' keeps literary magazine alive; article. Joan Sullivan. *G&M* Nov 23, 1987: pC9.

Experiskinno poetry — then and now; editorial article. George Swede. photo · *Cross Can Writ Q* 1987; Vol 9 No 3–4: p3–5.
[CANADIAN LITERARY PUBLISHING; POSTMODERNIST WRITING AND CRITICISM]

Hommage à Suzanne Lamy; obituary. Adrien Thério. photo · *Lettres québec* Summer 1987; No 46: p8.

Littérature québécoise d'hier et d'aujourd'hui on en parle je vous donne des addresses; editorial. Adrien Thério. *Lettres québec* Summer 1987; No 46: p10–12.
[FRANCE-CANADA LITERARY RELATIONS]

Sommaires; reviews. Adrien Thério. *Lettres québec* Summer 1987; No 46: p80.

Des revues presque indispensables; reviews of periodicals. Adrien Thério. *Lettres québec* Autumn 1987; No 47: p63–65.

Black October; article. Michael Totzke. *Tor Life* Sept 1987; Vol 21 No 13: p17.

Mag's humor may have done it in; article. David Trigueiro. *CH* Dec 18, 1987: pA4.

De qui se moque Le Devoir?; editorial. Michel Vaïs. photo · *Jeu* 1987; No 45: p7–9.
[AWARDS, LITERARY; WRITERS' ORGANIZATIONS]

Newfoundland and Labrador: TickleAce poised; regional column. Martin Ware. *Poetry Can R* Summer 1987; Vol 8 No 4: p12.

The tradition: John Sutherland, 1919–1956; column. Bruce Whiteman. *Poetry Can R* Summer 1987; Vol 8 No 4: p10.

Saturday Night does its job well; letter to the editor. David Zapparoli. *TS* July 20, 1987: pA16.

An index to Descant 1–50. Robyn Zuck. *Descant* Fall 1987; Vol 18 No 3: p99–181.

CANADIAN LITERARY PUBLISHING

Hat trick; article. *WFP* May 1, 1987: p33.
[GOVERNOR GENERAL'S AWARDS]

Les cinquante ans de Fides; interview with Micheline Tremblay. photo · *Lettres québec* Summer 1987; No 46: p15–17.

Anansi press suspending operations; article. *TS* Dec 10, 1987: pB3.

A world of books in Quebec; survey article. illus photo · *MG* Nov 21, 1987: J11.
[AWARDS, LITERARY; QUEBEC LITERATURE (FRENCH LANGUAGE): HISTORY AND CRITICISM]

Le Norot: 15 ans; article. photo · *Lettres québec* Winter 1986–87; No 44: p7.

House of Anansi to take year off; article. *G&M* Dec 11, 1987: pD5.

Letters from the editors; letters to the editor. *Prairie J of Can Lit* 1987; No 8: p20–27.
[CANADIAN LITERARY PERIODICALS]

Thunder Creek Publishing Co-op; article. Anne Burke. *Cross Can Writ Q* 1987; Vol 9 No 2: p32.

The small press; editorial. Anne Burke. *Prairie J of Can Lit* 1987; No 8: p4.

Dix années de littérature pour jeunes Québécois; article. Dominique Demers. photo · *MD* Nov 14, 1987: pD10.
[CHILDREN'S LITERATURE]

Montreal's Eden Press has impressive spring book list; article. Heather Hill. photo · *MG* March 13, 1987: pG7.

The effect of the international children's book industry on Canadian publishing endeavours for children and young people; article. Ronald A. Jobe. *Can Child Lit* 1987; No 47: p7–11.
[CHILDREN'S LITERATURE; CONFERENCES, LITERARY; EUROPE-CANADA LITERARY RELATIONS]

Going to the fair? Take along a page of your best writing; article. H.J. Kirchhoff. illus · *G&M* May 1, 1987: pC8.
[CONFERENCES, LITERARY]

Une fournée de nouveaux micro-livres chez Stanké; article. Marie Laurier. photo · *MD* Sept 26, 1987: pD3.

Le Seuil diffusera des auteurs du Boréal; article. Marie Laurier. photo · *MD* Oct 1, 1987: p13.
[FRANCE-CANADA LITERARY RELATIONS]

Prendre possession de nos biens; article about La Bibliothèque du Nouveau Monde. Yvan G. Lepage. photo · *Lettres québec* Spring 1987; No 45: p60–61.

The restoration of CanLit; article, includes review. Marion McCormick. photo · *MG* March 7, 1987: H10.
[CANADIAN LITERATURE: BIBLIOGRAPHY]

Ragweed still adding up cost of fire; article. Lori McDougall. *Quill & Quire* Sept 1987; Vol 53 No 9: p71.

Poets propelled by Thistledown; article. Kenneth McGoogan. *CH* April 12, 1987: pF2.

J.P. Donleavy here in '88; column. Kenneth McGoogan. *CH* July 26, 1987: pE5.
[AWARDS, LITERARY; CANADIAN LITERARY PERIODICALS; FESTIVALS, LITERARY]

Red Deer Press lauches series; column. Kenneth McGoogan. photo · *CH* Nov 22, 1987: pA16.

La vie littéraire; column. Marc Morin. *MD* Dec 5, 1987: pD2.
[CONFERENCES, LITERARY; POETRY READINGS; WRITERS' ORGANIZATIONS]

[Untitled]; letter to the editor. Robbie Newton. *NeWest R* Summer 1987; Vol 12 No 10: p1.

La vie littéraire; column. Jean Royer. *MD* Feb 21, 1987: pB2.
[COMPETITIONS, LITERARY; POETRY READINGS; TELEVISION AND CANADIAN LITERATURE; WRITERS' ORGANIZATIONS]

Fondation de Guérin littérature: 25 titres en 1987; article. Jean Royer. photo · *MD* Feb 21, 1987: pB3.

La vie littéraire; column. Jean Royer. *MD* Feb 28, 1987: pC2.
[AWARDS, LITERARY; CANADIAN LITERARY PERIODICALS; CONFERENCES, LITERARY; RADIO AND CANADIAN LITERATURE]

La vie littéraire; column. Jean Royer. *MD* March 7, 1987: pB2.
[AWARDS, LITERARY; POETRY READINGS; RADIO AND CANADIAN LITERATURE; TELEVISION AND CANADIAN LITERATURE; WRITERS' ORGANIZATIONS]

La vie littéraire; column. Jean Royer. photo · *MD* March 21, 1987: pD2.
[AWARDS, LITERARY; COMPETITIONS, LITERARY; POETRY READINGS; RADIO AND CANADIAN LITERATURE; TELEVISION AND CANADIAN LITERATURE]

La vie littéraire; column. Jean Royer. photo · *MD* May 30, 1987: pD2.
[AWARDS, LITERARY; COMPETITIONS, LITERARY; FESTIVALS, LITERARY; RADIO AND CANADIAN LITERATURE; TELEVISION AND CANADIAN LITERATURE]

La vie littéraire; column. Jean Royer. *MD* Oct 3, 1987: pD2.
[AWARDS, LITERARY; POETRY READINGS; WRITERS' WORKSHOPS]

La vie littéraire; column. Jean Royer. photo · *MD* Oct 10, 1987: pD2.
[FESTIVALS, LITERARY; FRANCE-CANADA LITERARY RELATIONS]

Pressing poetry: why Red Deer College Press is alive and well and thriving in the middle of Alberta; article. Laurie Sarkadi. *NeWest R* Feb 1987; Vol 12 No 6: p14.

Hart broken? Manager calls it quits; column. Thomas Schnurmacher. *MG* Nov 12, 1987: pE2.

Book world: Coach House Press divides to conquer; column. Beverley Slopen. *TS* Jan 4, 1987: pB7.

Book world: a success story that started with a cow; column. Beverley Slopen. *TS* March 29, 1987: pA18.

Book world: Gzowski's $$$ aid welcomed; column. Beverley Slopen. *TS* June 14, 1987: pA18.

Book world: a tip of the hat to small presses; column. Beverley Slopen. photo · *TS* Aug 9, 1987: pA20.

Experiskinno poetry — then and now; editorial article. George Swede. photo · *Cross Can Writ Q* 1987; Vol 9 No 3–4: p3–5.
[CANADIAN LITERARY PERIODICALS; POSTMODERNIST WRITING AND CRITICISM]

Dits et faits; column. Adrien Thério. photo · *Lettres québec* Summer 1987; No 46: p6.
[AUTHORS, CANADIAN; CONFERENCES, LITERARY; GOVERNMENT GRANTS FOR WRITERS/PUBLISHERS; LIBRARY SERVICES AND CANADIAN LITERATURE]

CANADIAN LITERATURE (19TH CENTURY): HISTORY AND CRITICISM

L'autonomisation de la "littérature nationale" au XIXe siècle; article. Maurice Lemire. abstract · *Études lit* Spring-Summer 1987; Vol 20 No 1: p75–98.
[COLONIALISM; CULTURAL IDENTITY; FRANCE-CANADA LITERARY RELATIONS; RELIGIOUS THEMES]

CANADIAN LITERATURE (20TH CENTURY): HISTORY AND CRITICISM

"All we North Americans": literary culture and the continentalist ideal, 1919–1939; article. Graham Carr. *Amer R of Can Studies* Summer 1987; Vol 17 No 2: p145–157.
[COLONIALISM; CULTURAL IDENTITY; UNITED STATES-CANADA LITERARY RELATIONS]

CANADIAN LITERATURE IN ENGLISH/Critical work by W.J. Keith

[Untitled]; review of *Canadian Literature in English*. L.W. Conolly. *Theatre Hist in Can* Fall 1987; Vol 8 No 2: p247–249.

[Untitled]; review of *Canadian Literature in English*. John Orange. *U of Windsor R* Spring-Summer 1987; Vol 20 No 2: p92–94.

CANADIAN LITERATURE: BIBLIOGRAPHY

A selected bibliography of Franco-Manitoban writing. *Prairie Fire* Autumn 1987; Vol 8 No 3: p123–124.

Ten years of Manitoba fiction in English: a selected bibliography. *Prairie Fire* Autumn 1987; Vol 8 No 3: p124–125.

[Untitled]; bibliography. Moshie Dahms. *J of Common Lit* 1987; Vol 22 No 2: p43–60.

Tableau chronologique des interventions à portée manifestaires qui ont marqué l'évolution du féminisme au Québec; bibliography. Jeanne Demers. Line McMurray. *La Nouvelle barre du jour (special issue)* 1987; No 194: p21–94.

The restoration of CanLit; article, includes review. Marion McCormick. photo · *MG* March 7, 1987: H10.
[CANADIAN LITERARY PUBLISHING]

Théâtrographie illustrée; list of plays. Diane Pavlovic. photo · *Jeu* 1987; No 44: p169–174.

Bibliographie de Yves Beauchemin; bibliography. Frances J. Summers. *Voix et images* Spring 1987; Vol 12 No 3: p416–428.

CANADIAN LITERATURE: BIOGRAPHY

In ordinary life we don't assume we know anyone; article. Ken Adachi. *TS* Sept 19, 1987: M5.

Dated lives: English-Canadian literary biography; article. Graham Carr. *Essays on Can Writ* Winter 1987; No 35: p57–73.

CANADIAN LITERATURE: HISTORY AND CRITICISM

Introduction; survey article. W.H. New. *J of Common Lit* 1987; Vol 22 No 2: p30–43.

CANADIAN LITERATURE: STUDY AND TEACHING

De quoi mourir en beauté?; article. André Brochu. *Études fran* Autumn-Winter 1987; Vol 23 No 1–2: p119–129.

Rapport du jury de composition française; essay, includes introduction. Georges-A. Courchesne. *Études lit* Spring-Summer 1987; Vol 20 No 1: p174–183.

Déclin de l'enseignement de notre littérature; article. André Désiront. illus · *MD (Livre d'ici)* Sept 12, 1987: p16–17.

St. Agnes' Eve; or, criticism becomes part of literature; fictional essay. Martin Kevan. *Essays on Can Writ* Winter 1987; No 35: p37–56.

Le complexe de Quichotte; article. Pierre Lavoie. illus photo · *Jeu* 1987; No 44: p8–13.

Thematic criticism, literary nationalism, and the critic's new clothes; article. T.D. MacLulich. *Essays on Can Writ* Winter 1987; No 35: p17–36.
[CULTURAL IDENTITY; STRUCTURALIST WRITING AND CRITICISM]

Présentation; editorial. Clément Moisan. Denis Saint-Jacques. *Études lit* Spring-Summer 1987; Vol 20 No 1: p9–16.
[CANADIAN LITERATURE: STUDY AND TEACHING; POSTMODERNIST WRITING AND CRITICISM; STRUCTURALIST WRITING AND CRITICISM]

L'étude des lettres québécoises est obligatoire à Liège; article. Johanne Roy. *MD* April 9, 1987: p13.
[BELGIUM-CANADA LITERARY RELATIONS]

The maple leaf as maple leaf: facing the failure of the search for emblems in Canadian literature; article. M. Jeanne Yardley. *Studies in Can Lit* 1987; Vol 12 No 2: p251–263.

CANADIAN LONG POEM

Stealing the text: George Bowering's Kerrisdale Elegies and Dennis Cooley's Bloody Jack; article. Smaro Kamboureli. *Can Lit* Winter 1987; No 115: p9–23.
[STRUCTURALIST WRITING AND CRITICISM]

CANADIAN POETRY CHRONICLE/Periodical

Keeping tabs on the poetry explosion; review of *Canadian Poetry Chronicle (1984)*. W.J. Keith. *Essays on Can Writ* Winter 1987; No 35: p100–104.
[CANADIAN LITERARY PERIODICALS]

CANADIAN POETRY: HISTORY AND CRITICISM

Poetry; survey review article. Ronald B. Hatch. *U of Toronto Q* Fall 1987; Vol 57 No 1: p33–50

Of poets and hackers: notes on Canadian post-modern poets; article. Don Precosky. *Studies in Can Lit* 1987; Vol 12 No 1: p146–155.
[POSTMODERNIST WRITING AND CRITICISM]

Canada's new-critical anthologists; article. Charles R. Steele. *Ariel* July 1987; Vol 18 No 3: p77–85.

Story and poetry: narrative strategies in recent Canadian poetry; article. Rhea Tregebov. *Quarry* Winter 1987; Vol 36 No 1: p118–124.

CANADIAN SHORT STORY: HISTORY AND CRITICISM

Wanted: dead or alive; editorial. Beatrice Fines. *Can Auth & Book* Winter 1987; Vol 62 No 2: ii

Brevity, soul and wit; article. Alberto Manguel. photo · *Maclean's* Sept 21, 1987; Vol 100 No 38: p53–54.
[PUBLISHING AND PUBLISHERS IN CANADA]

CANADIAN SUNSET/Novel by David McFadden

Canadian Quixote flogs death; review of *Canadian Sunset*. Audrey Andrews. *CH* April 18, 1987: pE5.

Is this the ultimate CanLit novel?; review of *Canadian Sunset*. Pauline Carey. *G&M* Feb 28, 1987: pE20.

Believing is seeing; review of *Canadian Sunset*. Mark Czarnecki. *Books in Can* Jan-Feb 1987; Vol 16 No 1: p19–20.

[Untitled]; reviews of novels. Beverley Daurio. *Cross Can Writ Q* 1987; Vol 9 No 3–4: p45–46.

[Untitled]; review of *Canadian Sunset*. Richard Streiling. *Quill & Quire* Jan 1987; Vol 53 No 1: p27.

CANADIAN THEATRE REVIEW/Periodical

Atlantic alternatives in theatre; review of *Canadian Theatre Review*. Richard Perkyns. *Atlan Prov Book R* Feb-March 1987; Vol 14 No 1: p11.

[CANADIAN LITERARY PERIODICALS]

CANADIAN WRITERS AND THEIR WORKS: ESSAYS ON FORM, CONTEXT AND DEVELOPMENT/Series of critical works

Introductory; review of *Canadian Writers and Their Works*. Barbara Pell. *Can Lit* Spring 1987; No 112: p179–180.

CANADIAN WRITERS AT WORK: INTERVIEWS WITH GEOFF HANCOCK/Interview compilation

10 Canadian writers talk shop; review of *Canadian Writers at Work*. Ken Adachi. *TS* Dec 13, 1987: pE7.

CANADIAN WRITERS SINCE 1960 (FIRST SERIES)/Biographical guide

It's CanLit's turn on literary assembly line; review of *Canadian Writers Since 1960 (First Series)*. William French. *G&M* Jan 20, 1987: pD9.

A CANDLE FOR CHRISTMAS/Children's story by Jean Speare

[Untitled]; review of *A Candle for Christmas*. Rosemary L. Bray. *NYT Book R* Dec 6, 1987: p81.

Mini-reviews; reviews of children's stories. Mary Rubio. *Can Child Lit* 1987; No 46: p105–109.

CANDY FROM STRANGERS/Poems by Diana Hartog

[Untitled]; review of *Candy from Strangers*. Susan Glickman. *Poetry Can R* Spring 1987; Vol 8 No 2–3: p42–43.

Western Canadian poets display talents in new volume; reviews of poetry books. G.P. Greenwood. *CH* July 5, 1987: pF7.

[Untitled]; reviews of *Candy from Strangers* and *Second Nature*. Roberta Morris. *Cross Can Writ Q* 1987; Vol 9 No 3–4: p42.

Male myths, obliterated lesbians and powerful dreams; reviews of poetry books. Fraser Sutherland. photo · *G&M* Feb 14, 1987: pE19.

Diana Hartog: poetry beyond revision; review of *Candy from Strangers*. Lola Lemire Tostevin. *Brick* Winter 1987; No 29: p9–13.

CANHAM, MARSHA

'Romance' writer's research earns her awards; article. photo · *TS (Neighbours)* March 31, 1987: p12.

THE CANLIT FOOD BOOK/Compilation

Atwood serves up anthology; article. *CH* Dec 2, 1987: pC4.

Margaret Atwood's new anthology food for thought; column. Ken Adachi. photo · *TS* April 13, 1987: pB1.

Atwood anthology ranges from tart to tangy; article. Julian Armstrong. illus · *MG* Nov 11, 1987: pE2.

Recipes to dispel bad taste of food in Canadian fiction; article. Elizabeth Baird. *TS* Nov 25, 1987: pC6.

[AUTHORS, CANADIAN]

[Untitled]; review of *Margaret Atwood's CanLit Foodbook*. Timothy Chamberlain. *Books in Can* Dec 1987; Vol 16 No 9: p27.

People; column. Yvonne Cox. *Maclean's* Nov 16, 1987; Vol 100 No 46: p64.

Food for thought and literature; review of *The CanLit Foodbook*. William French. *G&M* Nov 14, 1987: pE3.

A literary smorgasbord; review of *The CanLit Foodbook*. Alberto Manguel. photo · *Maclean's* Nov 23, 1987; Vol 100 No 47: p54b

Recipes, poetry, prose a tasty concoction; article. Diane Menzies. photo · *TS* Dec 2, 1987: pC1,C9.

Foodbook combines recipes, dash of prose; article. Diane Menzies. photo · *WFP* Nov 18, 1987: p38.

It's more which than what; review of *The CanLit Foodbook*. Erika Ritter. *TS* Dec 5, 1987: M14.

Writing a book the perfect gift; review of *The CanLit Foodbook*. Erika Ritter. *CH* Dec 6, 1987: pB1.

CanLit in the kitchen and food to keep you fit; review of *The CanLit Foodbook*. Jane Webb. *Quill & Quire* Nov 1987; Vol 53 No 11: p24

CANTIN, REYNALD

Littérature jeunesse; reviews of children's books. Dominique Demers. *MD* Nov 21, 1987: pD6.

CAPRICE/Novel by George Bowering

Angel with a lariat; review of *Caprice*, includes profile. John Bemrose. photo · *Maclean's* June 29, 1987; Vol 100 No 26: p49–50.

Zane Grey heroine turns Western novel upside down; review of *Caprice*. Trevor Ferguson. *MG* May 9, 1987: I9.

Bowering's capricious Western; review of *Caprice*. Maggie Helwig. *TS* May 17, 1987: pA17.

Horsing around; review of *Caprice*. Charles Mandel. *G&M* May 23, 1987: pC23.

Smart-aleck of Can-Lit scores again; review of *Caprice*. Kenneth McGoogan. photo · *CH* May 17, 1987: pE5.

As for me and my horse; review of *Caprice*. Kenneth McGoogan. *Books in Can* June-July 1987; Vol 16 No 5: p15–16.

Bowering's western: woolly post-modernist chic; review of *Caprice*. Paul Roberts. photo · *Quill & Quire* May 1987; Vol 53 No 5: p19.

At least it's easy to read; review of *Caprice*. Morley Walker. *WFP* May 16, 1987: p70.

CARBON 14 THEATRE COLLECTIVE

[Untitled]; theatre review of *Opium*. Danièle Le Blanc. photo · *Jeu* 1987; No 43: p155–156.

Lorne Brass: enfant de la télé; essay. Lorne Brass. photo · *Jeu* 1987; No 44: p124–125.

Evocative, but laced with ennui; theatre review of *Opium*. Ray Conlogue. photo · *G&M* Jan 14, 1987: pC7.

Carbone 14 does it again; theatre review of *Opium*. Wayne Grigsby. *MG* Jan 12, 1987: pB8.

[Untitled]; theatre reviews of *Fire* and *Opium*. Wayne Grigsby. *MG* Jan 16, 1987: pD10.

Büchner, Marivaux, Shephard, Gélinas: un mois théâtral chargé; column. Robert Lévesque. photo · *MD* Jan 6, 1987: p4.

Les pièges de l'esthétique; theatre review of *Opium*. Robert Lévesque. photo · *MD* Jan 16, 1987: p7.

Gilles Maheu: corps à corps; article. Diane Pavlovic. photo trans · *Can Theatre R* Fall 1987; No 52: p22–29.

CARDINAL, MARIE

Le Renaudot à René-Jean Clot; article. *MD* Nov 16, 1987: p9.
[AWARDS, LITERARY]

Experimental theatre: only some works; theatre review of *Nouvelles pour le théâtre*. Marianne Ackerman. *MG* Feb 5, 1987: pE6.

De la drogue, de la passion de l'absolu et de l'amour dont toujours tout reste à dire; review of *Les Grands désordres*. Jean-Roch Boivin. photo · *MD* Oct 24, 1987: pD5.

Marie Cardinal: la drogue comme révélateur; article. Paul Cauchon. photo · *MD* Nov 14, 1987: pD13,D19.

In the eye of abjection: Marie Cardinal's The Words to Say It; article. Patricia Elliot. *Mosaic* Fall 1987; Vol 20 No 4: p71–81.
[AUTOBIOGRAPHICAL WRITING]

"Nouvelles pour le théâtre"; column. Robert Lévesque. *MD* Jan 27, 1987: p5.

CARDUCCI, LISA

À surveiller; column. *MD* Oct 6, 1987: p10.

CAREFOOT, ERNIE

Jacob Two-Two star hits 'big time' at age 7; column. Vit Wagner. *TS* Oct 16, 1987: pD10.

CAREY, BARBARA

Between the sexes; reviews of poetry books. Mary di Michele. *Books in Can* March 1987; Vol 16 No 2: p31–32.

Seasons, time and memory; reviews of poetry books. Lesley McAllister. *TS* March 21, 1987: M5.

[Untitled]; review of *Undressing the Dark*. Karen Ruttan. *Poetry Can R* Summer 1987; Vol 8 No 4: p37.

[Untitled]; reviews of poetry books. Martin Singleton. *Cross Can Writ Q* 1987; Vol 9 No 3–4: p38–39.

CARMAN, BLISS

Confederation poets; reviews. Ronald B. Hatch. *Can Lit* Winter 1987; No 115: p223–225.

CARNAGE PÂLE/Poems by Marc Villard

La surface du monde; review of *Carnage pâle*. André Roy. *Estuaire* Winter 1986–87; No 43: p79–80.

CARNEVALI, IDA

Temptonga doesn't let audience in on the plot; theatre review. Henry Mietkiewicz. photo · *TS* April 10, 1987: pD12.

CARNIVAL/Children's novel by Mary Blakeslee

Family ties and mysteries; reviews of children's novels. Joan McGrath. *Quill & Quire (Books for Young People)* Dec 1987; Vol 53 No 12: p10.

CARNIVALIZATION

Robertson Davies' dialogic imagination; article. Barbara Godard. *Essays on Can Writ* Spring 1987; No 34: p64–80.
[STRUCTURALIST WRITING AND CRITICISM]

Pélagie-la-Charrette and the carnivalesque; article. Robin Howells. *British J of Can Studies* June 1987; Vol 2 No 1: p48–60.

Carnivalesque and parody in Le Jardin des délices; article. John Lennox. *Can Lit* Spring 1987; No 112: p48–58.

CARON, LOUIS

La forêt dans l'oeuvre de Louis Caron: une puissance libératrice; article. Georges L. Bérubé. abstract · *Études can* 1987; No 23: p123–133.
[HISTORICAL THEMES; NATURE IN CANADIAN LITERATURE]

La vie littéraire; column. Marc Morin. photo · *MD* Nov 28, 1987: pD12.
[CANADIAN LITERARY PERIODICALS]

[Untitled]; reviews of novels. Alice Parizeau. *MD* Nov 28, 1987: pD9.

La vie littéraire; column. Jean Royer. photo · *MD* Jan 24, 1987: pB2.
[AWARDS, LITERARY; POETRY READINGS; PUBLISHING AND PUBLISHERS IN CANADA; RADIO AND CANADIAN LITERATURE; WRITERS' WORKSHOPS]

CARON, ROGER

Wardens invite author back to jail; article. photo · *TS* March 28, 1987: pG9.

Cons and prose; biographical article. John Goddard. photo · *Books in Can* May 1987; Vol 16 No 4: p8–11.

THE CARPENTER OF DREAMS/Poems by W.D. Valgardson

Narrative tendencies; reviews of poetry books. Phil Hall. *Waves* Winter 1987; Vol 15 No 3: p84–88.

[Untitled]; review of *The Carpenter of Dreams*. Ann Knight. *Poetry Can R* Spring 1987; Vol 8 No 2–3: p44.

CARPENTER, DAVID

[Untitled]; reviews of *August Nights* and *Jokes for the Apocalypse*. Lesley McAllister. *Cross Can Writ Q* 1987; Vol 9 No 2: p24.

CARR, EMILY

La forêt dans l'oeuvre littéraire et picturale d'Emily Carr; article. Jean-Marcel Duciaume. abstract biog · *Études can* 1987; No 23: p135–145.
[NATIVE CANADIANS IN LITERATURE; NATURE IN CANADIAN LITERATURE]

La forêt chez les écrivains anglophones; article. Danièle Pitavy. abstract · *Études can* 1987; No 23: p147–157.
[BRITISH COLUMBIA WRITING AND WRITERS; CANADIAN IMAGINATION; COLONIAL LITERATURE; NATURE IN CANADIAN LITERATURE]

Finding D'Sonoqua's child: myth, truth and lies in the prose of Emily Carr; article. Peter Sanger. photo · *Antigonish R* 1987; No 69–70: p211–239.

CARRIER, DENIS

Une bibliographie indispensable; review of *Bibliographie analytique d'Yves Thériault, 1940–1984*. Anthony Purdy. *Can Child Lit* 1987; No 45: p54–55.

CARRIER, ROCH

Heartbreak road; review article about *Heartbreaks Along the Road*. Mark Abley. illus · *Sat Night* Oct 1987; Vol 102 No 10: p59–62.

Quebec native son sums up his feelings on la belle province; review of *Heartbreaks Along the Road*. Ken Adachi. photo · *TS* Oct 24, 1987: M4.

L'esthétique de "Jolis deuils"; article. Cécile Cloutier. *Can Lit* Spring 1987; No 112: p40–47.

Theatre encore; reviews of *L'Ours et le kangourou* and *Au septième ciel*. Carrol F. Coates. *Can Lit* Winter 1987; No 115: p255–257.

The road to evil; review of *Heartbreaks Along the Road*. William French. *G&M* Oct 17, 1987: pE3.

Hockey sweaters and picture books: matching the external image with the inner content; review of *The Hockey Sweater*. Marie-Louise Gay. *Can Child Lit* 1987; No 45: p90–91.

French book fair aims for more anglophones; article. Heather Hill. *MG* Nov 6, 1987: pC1.
[CONFERENCES, LITERARY]

[Untitled]; article. Patricia Hluchy and Bruce Wallace. *Maclean's* Nov 2, 1987; Vol 100 No 44: p52f

These roads lead to Roch; review of *Heartbreaks Along the Road*. P. Scott Lawrence. photo · *MG* Dec 19, 1987: J12.

Dead end; review of *Heartbreaks Along the Road*. Brent Ledger. *Books in Can* Dec 1987; Vol 16 No 9: p21–22.

Carnivalesque and parody in Le Jardin des délices; article. John Lennox. *Can Lit* Spring 1987; No 112: p48–58.
[CARNIVALIZATION]

Rencontre tonnante; review of *L'Ours et le kangourou*. Claude Sabourin. *Lettres québec* Winter 1986–87; No 44: p82.

Village of the damned; review of *Heartbreaks Along the Road*. Richard Teleky. photo · *Maclean's* Nov 2, 1987; Vol 100 No 44: p52f.

CARTIER, GEORGES

Un polar polyphonique à la recherche du temps perdu; review of *Notre-Dame du colportage*. Jean-Roch Boivin. *MD* Dec 5, 1987: pD3.

CARYOPSE OU LE MONDE ENTIER/Play by Laurence Tardif

Poetic, spell-binding Caryopse is theatre for thinking person; theatre review of *Caryopse ou le monde entier*. Pat Donnelly. *MG* Oct 30, 1987: pC2.

CASEY DRAWS THE LINE AND OTHER STORIES/ Children's stories by Kit Hood et al

Taking the Degrassi kids from screen to page; reviews of *Casey Draws the Line* and *Griff Gets a Hand*. Frieda Wishinsky. photo · *Quill & Quire (Books for Young People)* June 1987; Vol 53 No 6: p3.

CASHMAN, CHERYL

Cashman trades size for liveliness; article. Lynn Blanchard. photo · *G&M* Dec 14, 1987: pC12.

LES CATASTROPHES DE ROSALIE/Children's novel by Ginette Anfousse

Les malheurs de Rosalie ou l'éloge de l'enfance; reviews of children's books. Dominique Demers. *MD* May 2, 1987: pD3.

Un sapristi de bon livre; review of *Les Catastrophes de Rosalie*. Claire-Lise Malarte. *Can Child Lit* 1987; No 48: p102–104.

CATÉGORIQUES UN DEUX ET TROIS/Poems by Normand de Bellefeuille

[Untitled]; reviews of *Lascaux* and *Catégoriques un deux trois*. Richard Boutin. *Estuaire* Summer 1987; No 45: p52–54.

De Bellefeuille, Nepveu, Lemaire, Royer; reviews of poetry books. Jean-Pierre Issenhuth. *Liberté* Aug 1987; Vol 29 No 4: p78–87.

La répétition de l'intime; reviews of poetry books. André Marquis. photo · *Lettres québec* Spring 1987; No 45: p44–46.

Deux récits de l'intelligence et du coeur; reviews of *Chambres* and *Catégoriques un deux et trois*. Jean Royer. *MD* Jan 3, 1987: pC4.

THE CAVE OF SNORES/Children's story by Dennis Haseley

Snoring, smuggling, and snuggling; reviews of children's stories. Susan Perren. *Quill & Quire (Books for Young People)* Dec 1987; Vol 53 No 12: p8.

LA CAVE/Novel by Guy Cloutier

Une rêverie à deux voix; review of *La Cavée*. Jacques Michon. photo · *MD* June 20, 1987: pD3.

[Untitled]; review of *La Cavée*. Jacques Saint-Pierre. *Moebius* Autumn 1987; No 34: p125–126.

CAVENDISII, NICOLA

Canadians on Broadway; article. Brian Brennan. photo · *CH* April 4, 1987: pB4.

CE QUI RESTE DU DÉSIR/Play by Claude Poissant

Director, cast work wonders; theatre review of *Ce qui reste du désir*. Marianne Ackerman. photo · *MG* March 18, 1987: pD3.

Le théâtre qu'on joue; theatre reviews. André Dionne. photo · *Lettres québec* Summer 1987; No 46: p47–48.

Heureusement pour le théâtre, l'argent n'a pas d'odeur; article. Paul Lefebvre. photo · *MD* March 14, 1987: pC3.

CEDERBERG, FRED

Cheap thrills; reviews of *The Last Hunter* and *Gallows View*. Janice Kulyk Keefer. *Books in Can* June-July 1987; Vol 16 No 5: p37–38.
[FIRST NOVELS: BOOK REVIEWS]

CENSORSHIP

International writers' organization concerned with Canada's porn laws; article. *WFP* May 16, 1987: p56.
[INTERNATIONAL WRITERS' ORGANIZATIONS]

Foreword; editorial. *Malahat R (special issue)* March 1987; No 78: p1–4.

Outcome of Bell Jar libel suit closely monitored by publishers; column. Ken Adachi. *TS* Jan 26, 1987: pD4.

The Mermaid Inn: the return of the asterisk; essay. Margaret Atwood. photo · *G&M* June 27, 1987: pD6.

Les métamorphoses masquées de la censure; essay. Pierre Bertrand. *Moebius (special issue)* Spring 1987; No 32: p87–95.

Librarians have cause for porn bill concern; essay. A. Alan Borovoy. photo · *TS* Nov 21, 1987: pA2.

Librarians fear 'censorship' in new porn law; article. Louise Brown. photo · *TS* Nov 16, 1987: pA1,A8.

Problem of perception distorts debate on pornography bills; column. June Callwood. *G&M* July 1, 1987: pA2.

The legacy of Margaret Laurence; article. Michael Cardy. *Can Auth & Book* Summer 1987; Vol 62 No 4: p3.

Theatre people censure censorship; column. Robert Crew. photo · *TS* Dec 19, 1987: K2.

Library doors closed as porn bill ridiculed; article. Donn Downey. photo · *G&M* Dec 11, 1987: pD18.

Writing: the pain & the pleasure; essay. Timothy Findley. illus · *TS* March 21, 1987: M1,M5.
[INTERNATIONAL WRITERS' ORGANIZATIONS]

U.S. school bans use of Farley Mowat book; column. William French. *G&M* May 12, 1987: pC7.
[AUTHORS, CANADIAN]

Buoyant mood at booksellers' annual meeting; column. William French. *G&M* June 30, 1987: pD7.
[BOOK TRADE IN CANADA]

Personal recollections of controversy that made Margaret Laurence weep; article. John Goddard. photo · *MG* Jan 10, 1987: pB8.

Customs detains book recounting Indian legends; article. Stephen Godfrey. *G&M* June 22, 1987: pC9.

The Mermaid Inn: whither pornography?; essay. Warren Graves. photo · *G&M* June 13, 1987: pD6.

Censors, reviews hot topics at Writers Union AGM; article. Christina Hartling. photo · *Quill & Quire* Aug 1987; Vol 53 No 8: p22–23.
[BOOK REVIEWING; WRITERS' ORGANIZATIONS]

CAA opposes pornography bill; article. Fred Kerner. *Quill & Quire* Aug 1987; Vol 53 No 8: p24.
[AWARDS, LITERARY; WRITERS' ORGANIZATIONS]

Deneau Publishers seeks reorganization; column. H.J. Kirchhoff. *G&M* Dec 29, 1987: pC8.
[PUBLISHING AND PUBLISHERS IN CANADA; WRITERS' ORGANIZATIONS]

Writers revive censorship-pornography debate; article. Liam Lacey. photo · *G&M* June 1, 1987: pC9.
[AUTHORS, CANADIAN; WOMEN WRITERS; WRITERS' ORGANIZATIONS]

Book industry groups protest anti-porn bill; article. Liam Lacey. *G&M* Sept 17, 1987: pD6.

La censure éditoriale: quelques repères; article. Claude Lebuis. *Moebius (special issue)* Spring 1987; No 32: p23–31.

Le projet de loi C-54 sur la pornographie: une menace potentielle pour les arts; essay. Pierre MacDuff. photo · *Jeu* 1987; No 45. *WFP* May 16, 1987: p56.
[INTERNATIONAL WRITERS' ORGANIZATIONS]

Seized books spark assistance; article. Charles Mandel. *Quill & Quire* April 1987; Vol 53 No 4: p15–16.

Writers' union condemns censorship bill; article. Kenneth McGoogan. photo · *CH* June 2, 1987: pF6.
[BOOK REVIEWING; WRITERS' ORGANIZATIONS]

Alberta writers to fight 'censorship' bill; column. Kenneth McGoogan. *CH* Nov 29, 1987: pE6.
[COMPETITIONS, LITERARY; FESTIVALS, LITERARY; WRITERS' ORGANIZATIONS]

C-54, what are you? Proposed censorship legislation is loony; essay. Judith Merril. photo · *Quill & Quire* Dec 1987; Vol 53 No 12: p16–17.

Porn bill will fling us back to 19th century; letter to the editor. Hope Morritt. *TS* May 26, 1987: pA20.

Par-delà la censure, les séductions du vrai; article. Fernande Saint-Martin. *Moebius (special issue)* Spring 1987; No 32: p97–105.
[STRUCTURALIST WRITING AND CRITICISM]

Book world: Gzowski's $$$ aid welcomed; column. Beverley Slopen. *TS* June 14, 1987: pA18.

Canada needs writers like Margaret Laurence; essay. Keith Spicer. photo · *MG* Jan 8, 1987: pB3.

Angry librarians set to bolt doors over anti-porn bill; article. Chris Weiner. photo · *TS* Dec 8, 1987: pA6.

Board fought banning; letter to the editor. John A. Young. photo · *G&M* Dec 19, 1987: pD7.

THE CENTAUR'S MOUNTAIN/Poems by Philip Resnick

[Untitled]; review of *The Centaur's Mountain*. Corrado Federici. *Poetry Can R* Summer 1987; Vol 8 No 4: p33.

CENTURY/Short stories by Ray Smith

Somewhere in time; review of *Century*. Barry Dempster. illus · *Can Forum* Aug-Sept 1987; Vol 67 No 771: p45–46.

[Untitled]; reviews of short story collections. David Helwig. *Queen's Q* Winter 1987; Vol 94 No 4: p1022–1024.

Author reveal's book's skeleton; review of *Century*. Michael Mirolla. *CH* Jan 4, 1987: pE4.

Ray Smith's world; reviews of *Century* and *The Montreal Story Tellers*. T.F. Rigelhof. *Atlan Prov Book R* Feb-March 1987; Vol 14 No 1: p17.

[Untitled]; review of *Century*. Ann Scowcroft. *Rubicon* Fall 1987; No 9: p153–155.

Ray Smith's stories are prodding and perplexing; review of *Century*. David Williamson. *WFP* March 21, 1987: p58.

CERVANTÈS, FRANÇOIS

Music, theatre union needs fine tuning; theatre reviews of *Le Dernier quatuor d'un homme sourd* and *La Goutte*. Pat Donnelly. *MG* Nov 18, 1987: pD3.

Quatre personnages en quête d'une pièce; theatre review of *Le Dernier quatuor d'un homme sourd*. Robert Lévesque. photo · *MD* Nov 20, 1987: p13.

CES TIREMENTS DU REGARD/Poems by Luc Lecompte

Des livres ou des poètes?; reviews of *La Chevelure de Bérénice* and *Ces étirements du regard*. André Marquis. photo · *Lettres québec* Summer 1987; No 46: p35–36.

[Untitled]; reviews of poetry books. Jacques Saint-Pierre. *Moebius* Spring 1987; No 32: p128–130.

CETTE FOIS, JEANNE . . . /Novel by Louise-Anne Bouchard

Léonce, Léonil . . . et Sept fois Jeanne; reviews of *Cette fois, Jeanne . . .* and *La Double vie de Léonce et Léonil*. Louise Milot. photo · *Lettres québec* Autumn 1987; No 47: p17–18.
[FIRST NOVELS: BOOK REVIEWS]

Une fille bien de son siècle; review of *Cette fois, Jeanne . . . .* Madeleine Ouellette-Michalska. *MD* Sept 5, 1987: pC9.
[FIRST NOVELS: BOOK REVIEWS]

[Untitled]; review of *Cette fois, Jeanne . . . .* Jacques St-Pierre. *Moebius* Summer 1987; No 33: p133–135.
[FIRST NOVELS: BOOK REVIEWS]

CHAKYAK/Play by Ernie Carefoot

Jacob Two-Two star hits 'big time' at age 7; column. Vit Wagner. *TS* Oct 16, 1987: pD10.

CHAMBERLAND, PAUL

Une mystique du désir; review of *Marcher dans Outremont ou ailleurs*. Jean-Roch Boivin. photo · *MD* June 13, 1987: pD3.

La vitrine du livre; reviews. Guy Ferland. *MD* May 23, 1987: pD4.

Entretien; interview with Paul Chamberland. Dominique Garand. *Moebius* Summer 1987; No 33: p5–24.

CHAMBERLAND, ROGER

La modernité: des formes qui s'inquiètent; reviews of critical works. Whitfield. photo · *Lettres québec* Summer 1987; No 46: p56–58.

LA CHAMBRE DES MIRACLES/Poems by François Charron

[Untitled]; reviews of *Le Fait de vivre ou d'avoir vécu* and *La Chambre des miracles*. Hélène Dorion. *Estuaire* Summer 1987; No 45: p50–51.

François Charron: "la précieuse leon de la tendresse"; review of *La Chambre des miracles*. Gérald Gaudet. photo · *MD* May 16, 1987: pD2.

CHAMBRES/Poems by Louise Dupré

[Untitled]; review of *Chambres*. Anne-Marie Alonzo. *Estuaire* Winter 1986–87; No 43: p75–76.

La répétition de l'intime; reviews of poetry books. André Marquis. photo · *Lettres québec* Spring 1987; No 45: p44–46.

Deux récits de l'intelligence et du coeur; reviews of *Chambres* and *Catégoriques un deux et trois*. Jean Royer. *MD* Jan 3, 1987: pC4.

[Untitled]; review of *Chambres*. Jacques Saint-Pierre. *Moebius (special issue)* Spring 1987; No 32: p120–121.

CHAMP/Poems by Kay Burkman

In voice; reviews of poetry books. Richard Stevenson. *Can Lit* Spring 1987; No 112: p167–169.

CHAN, WEYMAN

Author's heritage provides fuel for stories; article. Cristine Bye. photo · *CH (Sunday Magazine)* July 19, 1987: p9.

Winning story first-class work; letter to the editor. Bruce D. Holt. *CH* Aug 15, 1987: pA6.

Errors hurt prize-winning story; letter to the editor. Grant F.G. Schorn. *CH* Aug 8, 1987: pA6.

CHANGES OF STATE/Poems by Gary Geddes

[Untitled]; review of *Changes of State*. Robert Gibbs. *Poetry Can R* Fall 1987; Vol 9 No 1: p33–34.

Narrative tendencies; reviews of poetry books. Phil Hall. *Waves* Winter 1987; Vol 15 No 3: p84–88.

[Untitled]; review of *Changes of State*. Laurence Hutchman. *Rubicon* Spring 1987; No 8: p190–193.

Tiger poems; reviews of poetry books. M. Travis Lane. *Fiddlehead* Autumn 1987; No 153: p88–91.

[Untitled]; review of *Changes of State*. Louise Longo. *Books in Can* Jan-Feb 1987; Vol 16 No 1: p27–28.

[Untitled]; reviews of poetry books. Bruce Whiteman. *Cross Can Writ Q* 1987; Vol 9 No 2: p21–22,26.

[Untitled]; review of *Changes of State*. Elizabeth Woods. *Malahat R* June 1987; No 79: p166–168.

LES CHANGEURS DE SIGNES/Prose poems by Michael Delisle

[Untitled]; reviews of *Les Mémoires artificielles* and *Les Changeurs de signes*. Jacques Paquin. *Estuaire* Autumn 1987; No 46: p83–84.

Le sentiment de la langue; reviews of *"Quand on a une langue on peut aller à Rome"* and *Les Changeurs de signes*. Jean Royer. *MD* Feb 28, 1987: pC3.
[CANADIAN LITERARY PERIODICALS]

CHARLEBOIS, JEAN

La fiction du réel/le réel de la fiction; reviews of poetry books. André Brochu. *Voix et images* Winter 1987; No 35: p322–330.

CHARPENTIER, RÉJANE

Coeur à coeur en plein coeur du parc Lafontaine; theatre review. Angèle Dagenais. photo · *MD* Sept 25, 1987: p14.

Imaginative kids' plays hit the spot; theatre reviews of *The Knocks* and *Coeur à coeur*. Pat Donnelly. *MG* April 9, 1987: pE8.

Funny British play praises non-conformity; theatre reviews of *Comment devenir parfait en trois jours* and *Coeur à coeur*. Christopher Hume. *TS* May 14, 1987: pF7.

CHARRON, CLAUDE

Un roman bâclé qui fera fureur dans les supermarchés; review of *Probablement l'Espagne*. Jean-Roch Boivin. *MD* Nov 14, 1987: pD15.
[FIRST NOVELS: BOOK REVIEWS]

[Untitled]; review of *Probablement l'Espagne*. Pierre Gobeil. *Moebius* Autumn 1987; No 34: p123–125.

Claude Charron, complice de la liberté; article. Isabelle Paré. photo · *MD* Nov 14, 1987: pD13

CHARRON, FRANÇOIS

La démarche de François Charron; review of *Le Fait de vivre ou d'avoir vu*. Caroline Bayard. *Lettres québec* Winter 1986–87; No 44: p48–49.

La fiction du réel/le réel de la fiction; reviews of poetry books. André Brochu. *Voix et images* Winter 1987; No 35: p322–330.

[Untitled]; reviews of *Le Fait de vivre ou d'avoir vécu* and *La Chambre des miracles*. Hélène Dorion. *Estuaire* Summer 1987; No 45: p50–51.

François Charron: "la précieuse leon de la tendresse"; review of *La Chambre des miracles*. Gérald Gaudet. photo · *MD* May 16, 1987: pD2.

Vivre de sa plume au Québec; interview with François Charron. Gérald Gaudet. photo · *Lettres québec* Automn 1987; No 47: p11–13.

Constitution d'une avant-garde littéraire; article. Jacques Pelletier. abstract · *Études lit* Spring-Summer 1987; Vol 20 No 1: p111–130.
[CANADIAN LITERARY PERIODICALS; POLITICAL WRITING; POST-MODERNIST WRITING AND CRITICISM; QUEBEC LITERATURE (FRENCH LANGUAGE): HISTORY AND CRITICISM]

La vie littéraire; column. Jean Royer. photo · *MD* Jan 24, 1987: pB2.
[AWARDS, LITERARY; POETRY READINGS; PUBLISHING AND PUBLISHERS IN CANADA; RADIO AND CANADIAN LITERATURE; WRITERS' WORKSHOPS]

CHATILLON, PIERRE

La vie littéraire; column. Jean Royer. photo · *MD* April 11, 1987: pD2.
[AWARDS, LITERARY; FILM ADAPTATIONS OF CANADIAN LITERATURE; POETRY READINGS; RADIO AND CANADIAN LITERATURE; TELEVISION AND CANADIAN LITERATURE]

CHAURETTE, NORMAND

Deux pièces en forme d'interrogatoire; reviews of *Being at Home with Claude* and *Fragments d'une lettre d'adieu lus par des géologues*. André-G. Bourassa. photo · *Lettres québec* Spring 1987; No 45: p50–51.

Des dramaturges ayant en commun l'usage du français; theatre review of *Fragments d'une lettre d'adieu lus par des géologues*. Robert Lévesque. *MD* Sept 9, 1987: p13.

Des estivants sans été; theatre review of *La Société de Métis*. Robert Lévesque. *MD* Sept 29, 1987: p13.

Les jeunes loups; reviews. Lucie Robert. *Voix et images* Spring 1987; Vol 12 No 3: p561–564.
[CANADIAN LITERARY PERIODICALS]

LE CHEMIN BRULÉ/Poems by Jean Royer

[Untitled]; review of *Le Chemin brulé*. Antonio D'Alfonso. *Estuaire* Winter 1986–87; No 43: p77–78.

Il y a des poèmes que nous habitons tous; reviews of poetry books. Robert Yergeau. *Lettres québec* Winter 1986–87; No 44: p36–37.

LE CHEMIN DES HUIT-MAISONS/Novel by Jeanne Ducluzeau

An historical novel on Acadians deported to France; review of *Le Chemin des Huit-Maisons*. Sally Ross. *Atlan Prov Book R* Nov-Dec 1987; Vol 14 No 4: p11.

CHERNIAK, LEAH

Talented comediennes energetic and funny; theatre review of *Fertility*. Robert Crew. *TS* March 6, 1987: pD21.

The Mikado hits a high note with seven Dora Awards; article. Robert Crew. photo · *TS* June 23, 1987: pE3.
[AWARDS, LITERARY]

Neville to extend stay at Stratford for a year; column. Robert Crew. *TS* June 24, 1987: pF1.
[AWARDS, LITERARY]

Ernest and Ernestine are funny and familiar; theatre review of *The Anger of Ernest and Ernestine*. Liam Lacey. photo · *G&M* May 28, 1987: pD6.

Well-wrought Anger comedy marred only by false-note finale; theatre review of *The Anger in Ernest and Ernestine*. Henry Mietkiewicz. photo · *TS* May 29, 1987: pE12.

CHERRY, FRANCES

Mini-comptes rendus; reviews of *Legs et Bizou/Legs and Bizou* and *Une Journée de Sophie Lachance*. Claudine Lesage. *Can Child Lit* 1987; No 46: p110.

CHEVALIER, DIANE

A plea to understand adults; theatre review of *Coup de Fil*. Pat Donnelly. *MG* Feb 10, 1987: pB7.

L'envers de l'abandon; theatre review of *Coup de fil*. Paul Lefebvre. photo · *Jeu* 1987; No 44: p192–193.

LA CHEVELURE DE BÉRÉNICE/Poems by Pierre Trottier

Des livres ou des poètes?; reviews of *La Chevelure de Bérénice* and *Ces étirements du regard*. André Marquis. photo · *Lettres québec* Summer 1987; No 46: p35–36.

[Untitled]; reviews of poetry books. Jacques Saint-Pierre. *Moebius* Spring 1987; No 32: p128–130.

UN CHIEN, UN VÉLO ET DES PIZZAS/Children's novel by Cécile Gagnon

L'embarras du choix; review of *Un Chien, un vélo et des pizzas*. Dominique Demers. *MD* Nov 28, 1987: pD6.

CHILDREN'S DRAMA

Les trois saisons de la Maison Théâtre: bilan critique de la programmation de la Maison québécoise du Théâtre pour article. Hélène Beauchamp. photo · *Can Child Lit* 1987; No 48: p77–84.

Taking the "kiddie stuff" seriously: the 1987 Edmonton International Children's Festival; article. Moira Day. photo · *NeWest R* Oct 1987; Vol 13 No 2: p6–8.
[FESTIVALS, DRAMA]

Child's play? Far from it; article. Pat Donnelly. photo · *MG* July 31, 1987: pC1.
[FESTIVALS, DRAMA]

Theatre for young people on the upswing in Montreal; article. Pat Donnelly. photo · *MG* Oct 23, 1987: pC3

STARR: teaching responsible sex; article. Deborah Foster. photo · *Can Theatre R* Winter 1987; No 53: p76–78.

Inside the giant: Fringe for kids; article. Katherine IKoller. photo · *NeWest R* Oct 1987; Vol 13 No 2: p11.
[FESTIVALS, DRAMA]

Théâtre et adolescence; article. Paul Lefebvre. photo · *MD* March 7, 1987: pB1,B7.

Le bénévolat au théâtre: un concours oblig: entretien avec Madeleine Rivest, de la Maison Théâtre; interview. Michel Peterson and Lorraine Camerlain. photo · *Jeu* 1987; No 42: p135–139.

Les troupes jouent le tout pour le tout; article. Julie Stanton. photo · *MD* Dec 5, 1987: pC5.

Poetry part of festival; article. *G&M* July 14, 1987: pC7.
[FESTIVALS, LITERARY]

Frankfurt follow-up; article. *Quill & Quire* Jan 1987; Vol 53 No 1: p18.
[EUROPE-CANADA LITERARY RELATIONS]

Kid-lit fest on at ROM; article. *TS* Nov 13, 1987: pE18.
[FESTIVALS, DRAMA]

Alligator Pie leads way to healthy kid-lit market; article. *WFP* Nov 9, 1987: p24.

Science slant for annual festival; article. *Quill & Quire (Books for Young People)* Oct 1987; Vol 53 No 10: p8.
[FESTIVALS, LITERARY]

Chit chat; column. Maria Casas. *Quill & Quire (Books for Young People)* April 1987; Vol 53 No 4: p3.
[CHINA-CANADA LITERARY RELATIONS; WRITERS-IN-RESIDENCE]

Every old person is Somebody: the image of aging in Canadian children's literature; article. Patricia de Vries. *Can Child Lit* 1987; No 46: p37–44.

La vague-jeunesse sera choyée; article. Dominique Demers. photo · *MD* Nov 14, 1987: pD10.
[CONFERENCES, LITERARY]

Dix années de littérature pour jeunes Québécois; article. Dominique Demers. photo · *MD* Nov 14, 1987: pD10.
[CANADIAN LITERARY PUBLISHING]

Un grand voyage . . . ; essay. Dominique Demers. *MD* Nov 28, 1987: pD6.

Chouette: des livres, des jeux, des jouets; article. Dominique Demers. photo · *MD* Dec 5, 1987: pD6.
[PUBLISHING AND PUBLISHERS IN CANADA]

Female images in some (mostly Canadian) children's books; article. Frances Duncan. *Room of One's Own* Sept 1987; Vol 11 No 4: p11–24.
[WOMEN IN LITERATURE]

Promenade au Salon du livre; article. Guy Ferland. *MD* Nov 24, 1987: p13.
[FRANCE-CANADA LITERARY RELATIONS]

Tundra turns 20; article. Heather Hill. photo · *MG* May 2, 1987: H13.
[PUBLISHING AND PUBLISHERS IN CANADA]

The good fight; article about May Cutler. David Homel. photo · *Books in Can* Dec 1987; Vol 16 No 9: p8–10.
[PUBLISHING AND PUBLISHERS IN CANADA]

Drawing power; article. Christopher Hume. illus photo · *TS* Nov 1, 1987: pC1,C5.

Canadian books for kids gain fame; article. Manfred Jager. photo · *WFP* Oct 20, 1987: p33.

The effect of the international children's book industry on Canadian publishing endeavours for children and young people; article. Ronald A. Jobe. *Can Child Lit* 1987; No 47: p7–11.
[CANADIAN LITERARY PUBLISHING; CONFERENCES, LITERARY; EUROPE-CANADA LITERARY RELATIONS]

Nation-wide book festival opens this weekend; article. Janice Kennedy. *MG* Nov 14, 1987: pD1.
[FESTIVALS, LITERARY]

Une fête autour d'un conte; article. Françoise Lafleur. photo · *MD* Dec 16, 1987: p11.
[FESTIVALS, LITERARY]

Firm has an ear for kids' books; article. Kenneth McGoogan. *CH* Feb 17, 1987: pC7.
[AUDIO-VISUALS AND CANADIAN LITERATURE]

Youth writers flourish in Alberta; article. Kenneth McGoogan. photo · *CH* Feb 21, 1987: pG1.
[AUTHORS, CANADIAN]

Festival attracts kids' writers; column. Kenneth McGoogan. *CH* Sept 20, 1987: pE6.
[AWARDS, LITERARY; FESTIVALS, LITERARY]

La vie littéraire; column. Marc Morin. *MD* Nov 14, 1987: pD14.
[AWARDS, LITERARY; POETRY READINGS]

La vie littéraire; column. Marc Morin. *MD* Nov 21, 1987: pD2.
[COMPETITIONS, LITERARY; POETRY READINGS]

Looking forward to the fall list for kids; preview of fall book list. Diana Shepherd. *Quill & Quire (Books for Young People)* Aug 1987; Vol 53 No 8: p3–4,10.

Book world: Grolier moves into children's fiction; column. Beverley Slopen. *TS* March 22, 1987: pA20.
[PUBLISHING AND PUBLISHERS IN CANADA]

Book world: Owl magazine publisher wades into film field; column. Beverley Slopen. *TS* Sept 20, 1987: pA20.
[FILM ADAPTATIONS OF CANADIAN LITERATURE; PUBLISHING AND PUBLISHERS IN CANADA]

Book world: 'My year for films': Brian Moore; column. Beverley Slopen. photo · *TS* Nov 8, 1987: pA18.
[FILM ADAPTATIONS OF CANADIAN LITERATURE; PUBLISHING AND PUBLISHERS IN CANADA]

Bologna score-card Part I; article. Diane Turbide. photo · *Quill & Quire* June 1987; Vol 53 No 6: p22–23.
[CONFERENCES, LITERARY]

An eye for Thresholds; essay. Tim Wynne-Jones. photo · *Can Child Lit* 1987; No 48: p42–54.

CHILDREN'S LITERATURE: BIBLIOGRAPHY

New publications; article. *Quill & Quire* Nov 1987; Vol 53 No 11: p19.

Translations of children's books in Canada; article. André Gagnon. bibliog · *Can Child Lit* 1987; No 45: p14–53.
[TRANSLATIONS OF CANADIAN LITERATURE]

Canadian children's literature 1983 / Bibliographie de la littérature canadienne pour la jeunesse: 1983; bibliography. Mary Rubio and Ramona Montagnes. *Can Child Lit* 1987; No 47: p29–56.

CHILDREN'S LITERATURE: STUDY AND TEACHING

Annick launches classroom kits; article. Lori McDougall. *Quill & Quire (Books for Young People)* Oct 1987; Vol 53 No 10: p23–24.

CHILDREN OF ABEL/Poems by Seymour Mayne

[Untitled]; review of *Children of Abel*. Barbara Carey. *Books in Can* March 1987; Vol 16 No 2: p27.

[Untitled]; review of *Children of Abel*. Harold Jack Heft. *Rubicon* Fall 1987; No 9: p176–177.

[Untitled]; reviews of poetry books. Stephen Morrissey. *Poetry Can R* Fall 1987; Vol 9 No 1: p32.

"Give me melancholy or give me death"; reviews of *Children of Abel* and *The Moving Light*. Harry Prest. *U of Windsor R* Fall-Winter 1987; Vol 20 No 1: p95–98.

CHILDREN OF BYZANTIUM/Novel by Katherine Vlassie

Getting on a literary roulette wheel; reviews of fictional works. Trevor Ferguson. *MG* Nov 14, 1987: J11.
[FIRST NOVELS: BOOK REVIEWS]

Heart of darkness; reviews of first novels. Janice Kulyk Keefer. *Books in Can* Dec 1987; Vol 16 No 9: p37–39.
[FIRST NOVELS: BOOK REVIEWS]

CHILDREN OF THE SHROUD/Novel by Garfield Reeves-Stevens

[Untitled]; review of *Children of the Shroud*. John North. *Quill & Quire* Sept 1987; Vol 53 No 9: p79.

Novel needs a miracle; review of *Children of the Shroud*. Scott Van Wynsberghe. *WFP* Oct 10, 1987: p30.

CHINA-CANADA LITERARY RELATIONS

Trade mission to China in May; article. *Quill & Quire* April 1987; Vol 53 No 4: p17–18.

Opening the book on China: contacts before contracts on the Far Eastern front; article. Hamish Cameron. photo · *Quill & Quire* Nov 1987; Vol 53 No 11: p10–11.

CBPC mission looking to long-term China trade; article. Hamish Cameron. photo · *Quill & Quire* Nov 1987; Vol 53 No 11: p11.

Chit chat; column. Maria Casas. *Quill & Quire (Books for Young People)* April 1987; Vol 53 No 4: p3.
[CHILDREN'S LITERATURE; WRITERS-IN-RESIDENCE]

Writers rank high in Chinese society; article. Dorris Heffron. photo · *Quill & Quire* Nov 1987; Vol 53 No 11: p11.
[AUTHORS, CANADIAN]

Moose Jaw meets Mao; article. Maggie Siggins. biog photo · *G&M* March 21, 1987: pE1,E6.

CHINA: SHOCKWAVES/Poems by Nancy-Gay Rotstein

[Untitled]; review of *China Shockwaves*. Barbara Carey. *Books in Can* June-July 1987; Vol 16 No 5: p23.

Poet tries to capture true cadence of China; article. Eric Dawson. photo · *CH* Dec 10, 1987: pF5.

Poets view China, Dada; reviews of *China: Shockwaves* and *The Merzbook*. Robert Quickenden. *WFP* Dec 5, 1987: p56

CHISLETT, ANNE

[Another Season's Promise]; theatre review. Susan Minsos. *NeWest R* Dec 1987; Vol 13 No 4: p17.

CHISLETT, GAIL

Mini-reviews; reviews of children's books. Margaret Paré. *Can Child Lit* 1987; No 45: p93–96.

CHOISIR LA POÉSIE/Poetry anthology

Choisir la poésie: une tentative mitigée; review of *Choisir la poésie*. Caroline Bayard. *Lettres québec* Spring 1987; No 45: p42–43.
[ANTHOLOGIES: BOOK REVIEWS]

LE CHOIX DE JACQUES BLAIS DANS L'OEUVRE DE SAINT-DENYS GARNEAU/Poems by Hector de Saint-Denys Garneau

Pour un portrait de Saint-Denys Garneau; review of *Le Choix de Jacques Blais dans l'oeuvre de Saint-Denys Garneau*. Jean Royer. *MD* May 23, 1987: pD2.

LE CHOIX DE JEAN PANNETON DANS L'OEUVRE DE RINGUET/Compilation

Si Ringuet n'avait pas regardé l'atlas; review of *Le Choix de Jean Panneton dans l'oeuvre de Ringuet*. Madeleine Ouellette-Michalska. photo · *MD* Sept 19, 1987: pD3.

LE CHOIX DE MARCEL DUBÉ DANS L'OEUVRE DE MARCEL DUBÉ/Play excerpts by Marcel Dubé

La vitrine du livre; reviews. Jean Royer. photo · *MD* March 21, 1987: pD2.
[CANADIAN LITERARY PERIODICALS]

Sommaires; reviews. Adrien Thério. *Lettres québec* Summer 1987; No 46: p80.

LE CHOIX DE MARIE JOSÉ THÉRIAULT DANS L'OEUVRE D'YVES THÉRIAULT/Short stories by Yves Thériault

Sommaires; reviews. Adrien Thério. *Lettres québec* Summer 1987; No 46: p80.

CHOYCE, LESLEY

Muscular idea; review of *The Dream Auditor*. Laszlo J. Buhasz. *G&M* May 9, 1987: pC21.

Rough gems; review of *The Dream Auditor*. Laszlo J. Buhasz. *G&M* June 20, 1987: pC19.

A note on political poems; editorial. Allan Cooper. *Germination* Fall 1987; Vol 11 No 1: p25.
[POLITICAL WRITING]

[Untitled]; review of *The Dream Auditor*. Cary Fagan. *Books in Can* June-July 1987; Vol 16 No 5: p22.

The space of images; reviews of poetry books. Lavinia Inbar. *Can Lit* Summer-Fall 1987; No 113-114: p245-247.

[Untitled]; review of *The Top of the Heart*. Sparling Mills. *Poetry Can R* Spring 1987; Vol 8 No 2-3: p41-42.

Iconographies; reviews of *Out of the Storm* and *The End of Ice*. Jack F. Stewart. *Can Lit* Spring 1987; No 112: p166-167.

CHRONIQUES DU NOUVEL-ONTARIO/Novel trilogy by Hélène Brodeur

Une voix ontarienne; review of *Chroniques du Nouvel-Ontario*. Mark Benson. *Can Lit* Winter 1987; No 115: p251-253.

La forêt dans le roman "ontarois"; article. Yolande Grisé. abstract · *Études can* 1987; No 23: p109-122.
[MYTHS AND LEGENDS IN CANADIAN LITERATURE; NATURE IN CANADIAN LITERATURE]

CIMENT, JILL

The absurd majesty of desires; review of *Small Claims*. Sherie Posesorski. *G&M* Jan 31, 1987: pE20.

A CITY CALLED JULY/Novel by Howard Engel

New in paper; review of *A City Called July*. *TS* Aug 16, 1987: pA18.

Criminal proceedings; review of *A City Called July*. T.J. Binyon. *Times Lit Supp* July 17, 1987; No 4398: p778.

Crime; review of *A City Called July*. Newgate Callendar. *NYT Book R* March 8, 1987: p29.

Comic solutions; review of *A City Called July*. Roderick W. Harvey. *Can Lit* Winter 1987; No 115: p214-216.

Paperback PIs battle crime; review of *A City Called July*. Kenneth McGoogan. photo · *CH* Sept 6, 1987: pE7.

CITY LIMITS/Play by Martin Fishman

Canadian playwrights give urban life short shrift, says one writer who didn't; article. Kevin Prokosh. *WFP* Jan 22, 1987: p35.

Exciting, refreshing City Limits tops theatre season; theatre review. Reg Skene. *WFP* Jan 24, 1987: p22.

CLAING, ROBERT

Experimental theatre: only some works; theatre review of *Nouvelles pour le théâtre*. Marianne Ackerman. *MG* Feb 5, 1987: pE6.

Le théâtre qu'on joue; theatre reviews. André Dionne. photo · *Lettres québec* Winter 1986-87; No 44: p53-54.

"Nouvelles pour le théâtre"; column. Robert Lévesque. *MD* Jan 27, 1987: p5.

CLARA/Novel by Jacqueline Déry Mochon

Hésitation; review of *Clara*. Frédéric Charbonneau. *Lettres québec* Autumn 1987; No 47: p70.

CLARK, JOAN

Clark's Moons reflect mythic light; review of *The Moons of Madeleine*. Susan Scott. *CH* March 1, 1987: pC8

Back to the future; reviews of children's books. Mary Ainsley Smith. *Books in Can* March 1987; Vol 16 No 2: p37-39.

CLARK, MARK

Surprising weight from the newcomers; reviews of *The Glorious East Wind* and *Ripper*. Margaret Cannon. *G&M* Nov 7, 1987: pC23.
[FIRST NOVELS: BOOK REVIEWS]

Jack the Ripper is wealthy MD in thriller with social conscience; review of *Ripper*. Peggy Curran. *MG* Nov 7, 1987: K13.

CLARKE, AUSTIN

[Untitled]; review of *Nine Men Who Laughed*. Valerie Wilson Wesley. *NYT Book R* Aug 23, 1987: p16-17.

CLARKE, GEORGE ELLIOTT

The poems of George Elliott Clarke; introduction. Allan Cooper. *Germination* Fall 1987; Vol 11 No 1: p7-8.

CLARKE, MARGARET

Theatre company faces stiff test; article. Brad Oswald. photo · *WFP* Sept 23, 1987: p44.

[Untitled]; reviews of *The Cutting Season* and *A Nest of Singing Birds*. John A. Urquhart. *Prairie J of Can Lit* 1987; No 8: p50-54.
[FIRST NOVELS: BOOK REVIEWS]

CLAUDAIS, MARCELYNE

Des dames de fleurs; review of *Des Cerisiers en fleurs, c'est si joli!*. Denis Saint-Jacques. *MD* Nov 21, 1987: pD2.

CLAUDE GAUVREAU: LA LIBRATION DU REGARD/ Critical work by Roger Chamberland

La modernité: des formes qui s'inquiètent; reviews of critical works. Whitfield. photo · *Lettres québec* Summer 1987; No 46: p56–58.

CLEAVER, ELIZABETH

Meaningful nonsense; reviews of children's books. Adrienne Kertzer. *Can Lit* Winter 1987; No 115: p165–167.

CLONE PATROL/Children's novel by G.P. Jordan

Pulp science fiction: slick adventures in a moral void; reviews of *Clone Patrol* and *Satellite Skyjack*. Eva Martin. *Quill & Quire (Books for Young People)* June 1987; Vol 53 No 6: p8.

CLOUD GATE/Poems by Claudia E. Lapp

[Untitled]; review of *Cloud Gate*. Anne Cimon. *Rubicon* Spring 1987; No 8: p221–222.

[Untitled]; review of *Cloud Gate*. Karen Ruttan. *Poetry Can R* Spring 1987; Vol 8 No 2–3: p40.

CLOUDS FLYING BEFORE THE EYE/Poems by Harry Thurston

Landscapes & eyes; reviews of poetry books. Karl Jirgens. *Can Lit* Spring 1987; No 112: p192–193.

CLOUTIER, CÉCILE

Munro short story collection wins award; article. *WFP* May 29, 1987: p34.
[GOVERNOR GENERAL'S AWARDS]

Le prix du Gouverneur général à Yvon Rivard; article. *MD* May 28, 1987: p2.
[GOVERNOR GENERAL'S AWARDS]

Governor General's Award to Munro amid poetry protest; article. photo · *MG* May 28, 1987: pC1.
[GOVERNOR GENERAL'S AWARDS]

Governor General's award winners; article. *Quill & Quire* July 1987; Vol 53 No 7: p53–54.
[GOVERNOR GENERAL'S AWARDS]

Frye finally wins elusive award for best non-fiction book of '86; article. Ken Adachi. photo · *TS* May 28, 1987: H1.
[GOVERNOR GENERAL'S AWARDS]

Yvon Rivard et Northrop Frye parmi les lauréats des prix du gouverneur général; article. Robert Lévesque. photo · *MD* May 28, 1987: p13.
[GOVERNOR GENERAL'S AWARDS]

Prix et distinctions; list of award winners. Gaétan Lévesque. photo · *Lettres québec* Autumn 1987; No 47: p7.
[AWARDS, LITERARY; GOVERNOR GENERAL'S AWARDS]

26 ans d'criture, deux trajectoires opposes; reviews of *L'écouté* and *SoirS sans AtouT*. André Marquis. photo · *Lettres québec* Winter 1986–87; No 44: p42–43.

Munro wins third Governor General's Award; article. Jamie Portman. photo · *CH* May 28, 1987: pC9.
[GOVERNOR GENERAL'S AWARDS]

[Untitled]; review of *L'Écouté*. Bernard Pozier. *Estuaire* Winter 1986–87; No 43: p75.

Munro wins top literary prize; article. Lisa Rochon. photo · *G&M* May 28, 1987: pD1.
[GOVERNOR GENERAL'S AWARDS]

Poésie: trois rétrospectives; reviews of poetry books. Jean Royer. photo · *MD* Feb 9, 1987: p11.

La vie littéraire; column. Jean Royer. photo · *MD* June 6, 1987: pD2.
[GOVERNOR GENERAL'S AWARDS; INTERNATIONAL REVIEWS OF CANADIAN LITERATURE; RADIO AND CANADIAN LITERATURE; TELEVISION AND CANADIAN LITERATURE]

CLOUTIER, GUY

Une rêverie à deux voix; review of *La Cavée*. Jacques Michon. photo · *MD* June 20, 1987: pD3.

[Untitled]; review of *La Cavée*. Jacques Saint-Pierre. *Moebius* Autumn 1987; No 34: p125–126.

CLOUTIER, LOUISE

Letinsky Cafe dishes out fantasy play focusing on ghost of Marilyn Monroe; theatre review. Philip Clark. *WFP* Feb 7, 1987: p23.

COCAINE — THE BOARD GAME/Play by Tamahnous Theatre collective

Cocaine use to be probed in B.C. play; article. *WFP* July 26, 1987: p16.

COCKTAILS AT THE MAUSOLEUM/Poems by Susan Musgrave

Voice of one's own; review of *Cocktails at the Mausoleum*. Richard Bevis. *Can Lit* Winter 1987; No 115: p186–188.

[Untitled]; review of *Cocktails at the Mausoleum*. Marilyn J. Rose. *U of Windsor R* Spring-Summer 1987; Vol 20 No 2: p97–101.

COE, RICHARD N.

Teacher battles doublespeak; article. photo · *WFP* Feb 22, 1987: p11.

COEUR À COEUR/HEART TO HEART/Children's play by Rejean Charpentier

Coeur à coeur en plein coeur du parc Lafontaine; theatre review. Angèle Dagenais. photo · *MD* Sept 25, 1987: p14.

Imaginative kids' plays hit the spot; theatre reviews of *The Knocks* and *Coeur à coeur*. Pat Donnelly. *MG* April 9, 1987: pE8.

Funny British play praises non-conformity; theatre reviews of *Comment devenir parfait en trois jours* and *Coeur à coeur*. Christopher Hume. *TS* May 14, 1987: pF7.

LE COEUR DÉCOUVERT: ROMAN D'AMOURS/Novel by Michel Tremblay

"Ce morceau de chair inexpliqué qu'il faut bien appeler le coeur...''; review of *La Coeur découverte*. Yvon Bernier. photo · *Lettres québec* Spring 1987; No 45: p26–27.

[Untitled]; review of *Le Coeur découvert*. Michel Gosselin. *Moebius* Winter 1987; No 31: p141–142.

Out of this world; review of *Le Coeur découvert*. Alberto Manguel. *Books in Can* April 1987; Vol 16 No 3: p31–32.

Couples; reviews of novels. Jacques Michon. *Voix et images* Autumn 1987; Vol 13 No 1: p189–192.

COGHILL, JOY

Emily Carr play; letter to the editor. William Angus. *G&M* Sept 29, 1987: pA6.

Play born out of obsession; article. Stephen Godfrey. photo · *G&M* Sept 12, 1987: pC9.

Another playwright foiled by Emily Carr; theatre review of *Song of This Place*. Stephen Godfrey. photo · *G&M* Sept 18, 1987: pD11.

COGSWELL, FRED

[Untitled]; review of *Meditations*. Glenn Hayes. *Poetry Can R* Spring 1987; Vol 8 No 2–3: p58–59.

Structures of meditation; reviews of *Meditations* and *Midnight Found You Dancing*. Michael Thorpe. *Fiddlehead* Spring 1987; No 151: p115–120.

New Brunswick letters; review of *The Bicentennial Lectures on New Brunswick Literature*. Alan R. Young. *Can Lit* Spring 1987; No 112: p146–148.

COHEN, LEONARD

People; column. Yvonne Cox. *Maclean's* Jan 12, 1987; Vol 100 No 2: p29.

People; column. Yvonne Cox. *Maclean's* Dec 21, 1987; Vol 100 No 51: p30.

Jennifer Warnes brings home the songs of Leonard Cohen; article. John Griffin. photo · *MG* June 11, 1987: pG1.

Cohen's spirit everywhere during tribute by Warnes; article about Jennifer Warnes. John Griffin. *MG* June 19, 1987: pC1.

Warnes warm to Cohen's material; column. Deirdre Kelly. *G&M* May 30, 1987: pC18.
[FESTIVALS, LITERARY]

Montreal misses and misters just don't have that Flare; column. Thomas Schnurmacher. photo · *MG* Jan 29, 1987: pC12.

Canada's songbird: picky she's not; column. Thomas Schnurmacher. *MG* May 8, 1987: pD1.

Book world: Owl magazine publisher wades into film field; column. Beverley Slopen. *TS* Sept 20, 1987: pA20.
[CHILDREN'S LITERATURE; FILM ADAPTATIONS OF CANADIAN LITERATURE; PUBLISHING AND PUBLISHERS IN CANADA]

Warnes goes solo with Cohen songs; article about Jennifer Warnes. Vit Wagner. photo · *TS* June 12, 1987: pE13.

Jenny without Lenny takes adoring Toronto; article about Jennifer Warnes. Vit Wagner. photo · *TS* June 15, 1987: pD1.

COHEN, MATT

New in paper; reviews of novels. *TS* Aug 30, 1987: pA18.
[FIRST NOVELS: BOOK REVIEWS]

Zig-zag management; reviews of *Nadine* and *A Hero Travels Light*. Anthony S. Brennan. *Fiddlehead* Winter 1987; No 154: p91–95.

The wonders and pleasures of fictional empire-building; reviews of novels by Matt Cohen. Douglas Hill. photo · *G&M* Jan 3, 1987: pE15.

[Untitled]; review of *Nadine*. Karen Rile. *NYT Book R* Aug 9, 1987: p20

Recent Canadian fiction; reviews of novels. D.O. Spettigue. *Queen's Q* Summer 1987; Vol 94 No 2: p366–375.
[FIRST NOVELS: BOOK REVIEWS]

The sweet taste of digression; review of *Nadine*. George Woodcock. *Event* March 1987; Vol 16 No 1: p95–97.

LA COHORTE FICTIVE/Novel by Monique Larue

La vitrine du livre; reviews. Guy Ferland. *MD* March 7, 1987: pB2.
[CANADIAN LITERARY PERIODICALS]

COITEUX, LOUISE

Forcément de l'amour; reviews of *Forcément dans la tête* and *De ce nom de l'amour*. Deloris Williams. *Can Lit* Summer-Fall 1987; No 113–114: p233–235.

COL LA GE/Poems by Daniel F. Bradley

[Untitled]; reviews of poetry books. Shaunt Basmajian. *Cross Can Writ Q* 1987; Vol 9 No 3–4: p44,49.
[ANTHOLOGIES: BOOK REVIEWS]

COLEMAN, VICTOR

[Untitled]; review of *From the Dark Wood*. Beverley Daurio. *Poetry Can R* Spring 1987; Vol 8 No 2–3: p47.

COLES, DON

[Untitled]; review of *Landslides*. Stephen Brockwell. *Rubicon* Fall 1987; No 9: p182–184.

Meddling with time; review of *Landslides*. Rita Donovan. *Fiddlehead* Summer 1987; No 152: p100–104.

"All in war with time": the poetry of Don Coles; article. Susan Glickman. *Essays on Can Writ* Winter 1987; No 35: p156–170.

Confident voices heard through poetry collections; reviews of poetry books. Christopher Wiseman. *CH* Feb 8, 1987: pE5.

THE COLLECTED POEMS OF GEORGE WHALLEY/ Poems by George Whalley

You ask me what I'm thinking; reviews of poetry books. M. Travis Lane. *Fiddlehead* Winter 1987; No 154: p95–104.

[Untitled]; review of *The Collected Poems of George Whalley*. David Lewis. *Queen's Q* Winter 1987; Vol 94 No 4: p1045–1047.

Three poets dare to reject labelling; reviews of poetry books. Patricia Smith. *TS* July 4, 1987: M4.

A plumber of bathetic depths; reviews of *Islands* and *The Collected Poems of George Whalley*. Fraser Sutherland. photo · *G&M* July 18, 1987: pC15.

THE COLLECTED POEMS OF SIR CHARLES G.D. ROBERTS/Poems by Sir Charles G.D. Roberts

A New Brunswick Roberts; review of *The Collected Poems of Sir Charles G.D. Roberts*. D.M.R. Bentley. *Can Lit* Spring 1987; No 112: p133–136.

[Untitled]; reviews of *The Collected Poems of Sir Charles G.D. Roberts* and *Sir Charles God Damn*. Mary McGillivray. *Queen's Q* Winter 1987; Vol 94 No 4: p1039–1042.

THE COLLECTED POEMS/Poems by Al Purdy

[Untitled]; review of *The Collected Poem*. Bert Almon. *Poetry Can R* Summer 1987; Vol 8 No 4: p32.

Giant steps; review of *Collected Poems*. George Galt. *Books in Can* Jan-Feb 1987; Vol 16 No 1: p16–17.

[Untitled]; reviews of poetry books. Bruce Hunter. *Cross Can Writ Q* 1987; Vol 9 No 3–4: p40–42.

[Untitled]; review of *The Collected Poems*. Laurence Hutchman. *Rubicon* Fall 1987; No 9: p179–182.

St. Al and the heavenly bodies; review of *The Collected Poems*. D.G. Jones. *Brick* Winter 1987; No 29: p14–20.

[Untitled]; review of *The Collected Poems*. Tom Marshall. *Queen's Q* Summer 1987; Vol 94 No 2: p475–477.

[Untitled]; reviews of *The Self-Completing Tree* and *The Collected Poems*. Stephen Scobie. *Malahat R (special issue)* March 1987; No 78: p154–155.

Poetry: packing all the power into two of seven titles; reviews of poetry books. Robin Skelton. photo · *Quill & Quire* May 1987; Vol 53 No 5: p24.

The cosmic ruminant's vision; review of *The Collected Poems*. Fraser Sutherland. photo · *G&M* Jan 3, 1987: pE16.

A life rarefied; review of *The Collected Poems*. Andrew Vaisius. *Waves* Spring 1987; Vol 15 No 4: p80–83.

COLLECTED POEMS/Poems by Miriam Waddington

Tiger poems; reviews of poetry books. M. Travis Lane. *Fiddlehead* Autumn 1987; No 153: p88–91.

[Untitled]; review of *Collected Poems*. Tom Marshall. *Queen's Q* Summer 1987; Vol 94 No 2: p474–475.

A green world; review of *Collected Poems*. Eva Tihanyi. *Waves* Winter 1987; Vol 15 No 3: p78–80.

A COLLECTION OF SHORT STORIES/Short stories by Percy Janes

Allowances must be made; review of *A Collection of Short Stories*. Kent Thompson. *Atlan Prov Book R* Sept-Oct 1987; Vol 14 No 3: p12.

A COLLECTION OF STORIES/Short stories by Otto Tucker

Humour from the heart; review of *A Collection of Stories*. Tom Dawe. *Atlan Prov Book R* Sept-Oct 1987; Vol 14 No 3: p13.

COLLEY, PETER

The Piggery scores a direct hit with scary-funny Canadian play; theatre review of *I'll Be Back Before Midnight*. Pat Donnelly. *MG* July 21, 1987: pD2.

[Untitled]; theatre review of *I'll Be Back Before Midnight*. Pat Donnelly. *MG* July 24, 1987: pC10.

Tried-and-true still packs punch in stage thriller; theatre review of *The Mark of Cain*. Martin Morrow. photo · *CH* Nov 3, 1987: pF11

Stage thriller condensed for Lunchbox crowds; article. Kate Zimmerman. *CH* Oct 30, 1987: pE8.

COLLIDEOSCOPE/Play by Guy Rodgers

Drama fest heads for grand finale; theatre reviews of *Jack of Hearts* and *Collideoscope*. Marianne Ackerman. photo · *MG* May 1, 1987: pD3.
[FESTIVALS, DRAMA]

COLLIER, DIANA G.

For the sake of Clarity; letter to the editor. Annette Gordon. *Books in Can* Nov 1987; Vol 16 No 8: p40.
[FIRST NOVELS]

Urban scrawl; reviews of first novels. Janice Kulyk Keefer. *Books in Can* Aug-Sept 1987; Vol 16 No 6: p33–34.
[FIRST NOVELS: BOOK REVIEWS]

COLLOQUE LOUIS HÉMON. QUIMPER/Conference report

[Untitled]; reviews of *Itinéraire de Liverpool à Québec* and *Colloque Louis Hémon*. B.-Z. Shek. *U of Toronto Q* Fall 1987; Vol 57 No 1: p179–182.

COLLURA, MARY-ELLEN LANG

Littérature jeunesse; reviews of children's books. Domique Demers. *MD* Oct 10, 1987: pD6.

COLOMBO, JOHN ROBERT

Random musings of a middle-aged middle-class male; reviews of poetry books. Lesley McAllister. *TS* Oct 10, 1987: M4.

Words don't do Colombo justice — you can quote me; humorous essay. Joey Slinger. *TS* Dec 18, 1987: pA6.

Book world: a little-known bestseller; column. Beverley Slopen. *TS* Jan 11, 1987: pA16.

Ballads and ditties for grown-ups; reviews of poetry books. Fraser Sutherland. illus · *G&M* Nov 7, 1987: pC21.

COLONIAL LITERATURE

Faire de la terre ou faire la guerre? L'intertexte napoléonien dans le roman de défrichement québécois; article. Robert Major. abstract · *Études can* 1987; No 23: p71–86.

La forêt chez les écrivains anglophones; article. Danièle Pitavy. abstract · *Études can* 1987; No 23: p147–157.
[BRITISH COLUMBIA WRITING AND WRITERS; CANADIAN IMAGINATION; NATURE IN CANADIAN LITERATURE]

COLONIALISM

"O brave new world": colonialism in Hunter Duvar's De Roberval; article. Mark Blagrave. *Can Drama* 1987; Vol 13 No 2: p175–181.

[NATIVE CANADIANS IN LITERATURE]

Canadian (tw)ink: surviving the white-outs; article. Gary Boire. *Essays on Can Writ* Winter 1987; No 35: p1–16.

[HISTORICAL THEMES; MODERNIST WRITING AND CRITICISM; NATIVE CANADIANS IN LITERATURE]

"All we North Americans": literary culture and the continentalist ideal, 1919–1939; article. Graham Carr. *Amer R of Can Studies* Summer 1987; Vol 17 No 2: p145–157.

[CANADIAN LITERATURE (20TH CENTURY): HISTORY AND CRITICISM; CULTURAL IDENTITY; UNITED STATES-CANADA LITERARY RELATIONS]

The ideological formation of political theatre in Canada; article. Alan Filewod. abstract · *Theatre Hist in Can* Fall 1987; Vol 8 No 2: p254–263.

[CANADIAN DRAMA: HISTORY AND CRITICISM; POLITICAL WRITING]

L'autonomisation de la "littérature nationale" au XIXe siècle; article. Maurice Lemire. abstract · *Études lit* Spring-Summer 1987; Vol 20 No 1: p75–98.

[CANADIAN LITERATURE (19TH CENTURY): HISTORY AND CRITICISM, CULTURAL IDENTITY; FRANCE-CANADA LITERARY RELATIONS; RELIGIOUS THEMES]

THE COLOR OF BLOOD/LE COULEUR DU SANG/Novel by Brian Moore

[Untitled]; review of *The Color of Blood*. *New Yorker* Oct 19, 1987; Vol 63 No 35: p120.

Something gravely missing in Brian Moore's last novel; review of *The Color of Blood*. Ken Adachi. photo · *TS* Sept 5, 1987: M4.

Polish nightmares; review of *The Color of Blood*. Neal Ascherson. illus · *New York R of Books* Dec 17, 1987; Vol 34 No 20: p44,46,48.

A clash of crimsons; review of *The Color of Blood*. John Bemrose. *Maclean's* Oct 19, 1987; Vol 100 No 42: p6of

Moore shatters illusion in the search for spiritual survival; review of *The Color of Blood*. Patricia Bradbury. photo · *Quill & Quire* Aug 1987; Vol 53 No 8: p29.

Le primat et le patriote; review of *La Couleur du sang*. Paul-André Comeau. *MD* Dec 12, 1987: pD8.

Under the red robe; review of *The Color of Blood*. Anne-Marie Conway. *Times Lit Supp* Oct 2, 1987; No 4409: p1073.

Moore didn't finish his suspense novel; review of *The Color of Blood*. Catherine Ford. *CH* Sept 5, 1987: H7.

The holy murder; review of *The Color of Blood*. William French. *G&M* Sept 5, 1987: pC13.

For God's sake; review of *The Color of Blood*. Douglas Glover. *Books in Can* Oct 1987; Vol 16 No 7: p18.

Moore's latest disappointing; review of *The Color of Blood*. Tom Oleson. photo · *WFP* Sept 5, 1987: p58.

[Untitled]; review of *The Color of Blood*. Constance Rooke. *Malahat R* Dec 1987; No 81: p101–102.

Cardinal Bem on the run; review of *The Color of Blood*. Clancy Sigal. *NYT Book R* Sept 27, 1987: p11.

[Untitled]; review of *The Color of Blood*. Robert Stewart. illus · *MG* Sept 5, 1987: J1

THE COLOURS OF WAR/Novel by Matt Cohen

The wonders and pleasures of fictional empire-building; reviews of novels by Matt Cohen. Douglas Hill. photo · *G&M* Jan 3, 1987: pE15.

COME INTO MY ROOM/Children's poems by Goldie Olszynko Gryn

[Untitled]; reviews of *Come into My Room* and *Hey World, Here I Am!*. Adele Ashby. *Quill & Quire (Books for Young People)* April 1987; Vol 53 No 4: p5.

Sam McGee leads the way in showing the potential of poetry; reviews of children's poetry books. Janice Kennedy. *MG* March 7, 1987: H10.

COMING ATTRACTIONS/Short story anthology series

From Ahmadabad to Tennessee; reviews of *86: Best Canadian Stories* and *Coming Attractions 4*. Wayne Grady. *Books in Can* March 1987; Vol 16 No 2: p29–30.

[ANTHOLOGIES: BOOK REVIEWS]

[Untitled]; review of *Coming Attractions 5*. Janet Hamilton. *Quill & Quire* Dec 1987; Vol 53 No 12: p22.

[ANTHOLOGIES: BOOK REVIEWS]

Canada's short fiction shortchanged here; reviews of *87: Best Canadian Stories* and *Coming Attractions 5*. Geoff Hancock. *TS* Dec 27, 1987: pE19.

[ANTHOLOGIES: BOOK REVIEWS]

Story anthologies: the tried, the true, and the best of the new; reviews of short story anthologies. Brent Ledger. photo · *Quill & Quire* Jan 1987; Vol 53 No 1: p29.

[ANTHOLOGIES: BOOK REVIEWS]

The spoiled broth; review of *Coming Attractions 5*. Jason Sherman. *G&M* Nov 14, 1987: pE5.

[ANTHOLOGIES: BOOK REVIEWS]

A mixed bag of short stories; reviews of short story anthologies. Norman Sigurdson. *WFP* Feb 28, 1987: p54.

[ANTHOLOGIES: BOOK REVIEWS]

COMME UN LEXIQUE DES ABÎMES/Poems by Gilbert Langevin

La fiction du réel/le réel de la fiction; reviews of poetry books. André Brochu. *Voix et images* Winter 1987; No 35: p322–330.

Songe, révolte et manifeste; reviews of poetry books. Robert Yergeau. photo · *Lettres québec* Spring 1987; No 45: p38–39.

COMPARAISON ET RAISON: ESSAIS SUR L'HISTOIRE ET L'INSTITUTION DES LITTÉRATURES CANADIENNE ET QUÉBÉCOISE/Critical essays by Clément Moisan

La vitrine du livre; reviews of *Poètes québécois contemporains* and *Comparaison et raison*. Guy Ferland. *MD* Oct 10, 1987: pD4.

[ANTHOLOGIES: BOOK REVIEWS]

COMPENDIUM/Poems by Carolyn Zonailo

[Untitled]; reviews of poetry books. Lavinia Inbar. illus · *Poetry Can R* Spring 1987; Vol 8 No 2–3: p51–53.

COMPETITIONS, LITERARY

Magazine sponsors writing contest; article. *G&M* Feb 14, 1987: pE13.

Prize worth $8,600 for top short story; article. illus · *TS* Jan 11, 1987: pA2.

Manuscripts accepted; article. *WFP* Jan 22, 1987: p36.

Billboard: Women's Institute topic is tax; column. *WFP* Jan 28, 1987: p30.

Invitation to writers; article. *WFP* Feb 27, 1987: p34.

Billboard: Red Cross seeks return of unused canes, crutches; column. *WFP* March 9, 1987: p21.
[POETRY READINGS]

Candidatures pour les Prix du Québec 1987; article. *MD* March 7, 1987: pB5.

Editorial: the George Wicken Prize. *Essays on Can Writ* Spring 1987; No 34: p1.
[AWARDS, LITERARY]

Chap-book award; article. *Quill & Quire* Feb 1987; Vol 53 No 2: p11.

Competitions; notice. *Quill & Quire* March 1987; Vol 53 No 3: p61.

Billboard: CUSO holds information meet; column. *WFP* June 23, 1987: p27.

Competitions; article. *Quill & Quire* April 1987; Vol 53 No 4: p20.

From Ahmadabad to Tennessee: reviews of *86: Best Canadian Stories* and *Coming Attractions 4*. Wayne Grady. *Books in Can* March 1987; Vol 16 No 2: p29–30.
[ANTHOLOGIES: BOOK REVIEWS]

[Untitled]; review of *Coming Attractions 5*. Janet Hamilton. *Quill & Quire* Dec 1987; Vol 53 No 12: p22.
[ANTHOLOGIES: BOOK REVIEWS]

Canada's short fiction shortchanged here; reviews of *87: Best Canadian Stories* and *Coming Attractions 5*. Geoff Hancock. *TS* Dec 27, 1987: pE19.
[ANTHOLOGIES: BOOK REVIEWS]

Poets to speak with rhyme and rhythm; article. *TS (Neighbours)* June 16, 1987: p24.

La période de mise en candidature est en cours pour les Prix du Québec; article. *MD* April 8, 1987: p17.

Proposition de candidatures pour les Prix du Québec 1987; article. *MD* April 28, 1987: p14.

Radio literary contest now accepting submissions; article. *TS* May 27, 1987: pE1.

Books on Ontario society eligible for $10,000 award; article. *TS* June 18, 1987: pE1.

Contests; column. *Can Auth & Book* Summer 1987; Vol 62 No 4: p28.

Tip sheet: young playwrights can enter second annual competition; column. *MG* Sept 29, 1987: pE7.

Poètes, vos patins; article about the Poetry Sweatshop. photo · *MD* July 21, 1987: p9.

Poetry shop returns; article. *WFP* Sept 15, 1987: p30.

Showcase for talent; article. *WFP* Sept 23, 1987: p47.

Billboard: Jon Sigurdson holds fall tea today; column. *WFP* Sept 26, 1987: p43.
[FICTION READINGS; WRITERS' ORGANIZATIONS]

Experience speaks in writing contest; article. *CH* Sept 25, 1987: pF7.

Poetry by Dutch Immigrants sought; notice. *Arc* Fall 1987; No 19: p84.

Call for entries; article. *Quill & Quire* July 1987; Vol 53 No7: p55.

Dits et faits; column. *Lettres québec* Autumn 1987; No 47: p6.
[AWARDS, LITERARY; CONFERENCES, LITERARY; WRITERS' ORGANIZATIONS]

Un concours littéraire pour les aînés; article. *MD* Oct 10, 1987: pD3.

Nov. 1 deadline set in competition for poets, non-fiction writers; article. *WFP* Oct 2, 1987: p23.

Deadline for poets; article. *WFP (Weekly)* Oct 11, 1987: p15.

Contests; article. *Quill & Quire* Oct 1987; Vol 53 No 10: p13.

Contest; article. *Quill & Quire* Nov 1987; Vol 53 No 11: p16.

Contests; article. *Quill & Quire* Dec 1987; Vol 53 No 12: p15.

Mainstreet Calgary; column. *CH (Neighbors)* Dec 9, 1987: pA17–A18.
[POETRY READINGS]

Book awards deadline near; article. *CH* Dec 12, 1987: H5.

Sweatshops give budding poets shot at Olympic gold; article. Bob Blakey. *CH* Aug 18, 1987: pD7.

Versifiers rhyme for gold at first poetry Olympics; article. Bill Brownstein. *MG* July 21, 1987: pD1.

This poetic winner could rhyme on a dime anytime; column. Bill Brownstein. *MG* July 25, 1987: pD12.

Toronto team wants poetry back in Olympic Games lineup; article. Don Campbell. photo · *WFP* July 25, 1987: p46.

Poetry sweatshops add a new twist to Olympic tradition; column. William French. *G&M* March 3, 1987: pC7.
[CANADIAN LITERARY LANDMARKS; FESTIVALS, LITERARY; POETRY READINGS]

The grisly trade in animals; column. William French. *G&M* Sept 29, 1987: pD5.

No claims to priority; letter to the editor, includes poem. Jim Gibson. *CH* Sept 9, 1987: pA6.

The poetry sweatshop; article. Liane Heller. photo · *Cross Can Writ Q* 1987; Vol 9 No 1: p5–6,28.
[POETRY READINGS]

Writers are serious; letter to the editor. Clive Jolly. *CH* Sept 9, 1987: pA6.

A whole lotta scribblin' goin' on; article about Poetry Sweatshop. Urjo Kareda. photo · *G&M (Toronto Magazine)* March 1987; Vol 1 No 12: p12–13.
[POETRY READINGS]

Le Café de la Place se bilinguise; article. Robert Lévesque. photo · *MD* May 22, 1987: p15.

Chap-book award; notice. Bernice Lever. *Waves* Winter 1987; Vol 15 No 3: p89.

Poetry Sweatshop moves west; article. Charles Mandel. photo · *Quill & Quire* Oct 1987; Vol 53 No 10: p10.

Sweatshop atmosphere wrong place to encourage real poetry; letter to the editor. Sid Marty. photo · *CH* Aug 30, 1987: pB4.

Putting pen to paper could reap $1,000; article. Kenneth McGoogan. *CH* Feb 4, 1987: pF1.

Writers plan on doing it with style; column. Kenneth McGoogan. *CH* March 22, 1987: pF5.
[AWARDS, LITERARY; FESTIVALS, LITERARY]

Short-story prize doubled for winner; column. Kenneth McGoogan. *CH* May 24, 1987: pE6.
[AWARDS, LITERARY]

Novel tourney nears; article. Kenneth McGoogan. illus · *CH* Aug 28, 1987: pC1.

Alberta writers to fight 'censorship' bill; column. Kenneth McGoogan. *CH* Nov 29, 1987: pE6.
[CENSORSHIP; FESTIVALS, LITERARY; WRITERS' ORGANIZATIONS]

La vie littéraire; column. Marc Morin. *MD* Oct 31, 1987: pD2.
[POETRY READINGS; WRITERS' ORGANIZATIONS]

La vie littéraire; column. Marc Morin. *MD* Nov 21, 1987: pD2.
[CHILDREN'S LITERATURE; POETRY READINGS]

La vie littéraire; column. Marc Morin. *MD* Dec 24, 1987: pC10.
[CONFERENCES, LITERARY; POETRY READINGS]

Poets train for Winter Olympics in Calgary; article. Greg Quill. *TS* May 13, 1987: pB5.

La vie littéraire; column. Jean Royer. *MD* Jan 31, 1987: pB2.
[CANADIAN LITERARY PERIODICALS; RADIO AND CANADIAN LITERATURE; TELEVISION AND CANADIAN LITERATURE]

La vie littéraire; column. Jean Royer. *MD* Feb 7, 1987: pB2.
[CONFERENCES, LITERARY; POETRY READINGS; PUBLISHING AND PUBLISHERS IN CANADA; TELEVISION AND CANADIAN LITERATURE; WRITERS' WORKSHOPS]

La vie littéraire; column. Jean Royer. *MD* Feb 14, 1987: pC2.
[AWARDS, LITERARY; CANADIAN LITERARY PERIODICALS; FICTION READINGS; POETRY READINGS; RADIO AND CANADIAN LITERATURE]

La vie littéraire; column. Jean Royer. *MD* Feb 21, 1987: pB2.
[CANADIAN LITERARY PUBLISHING; POETRY READINGS; TELEVISION AND CANADIAN LITERATURE; WRITERS' ORGANIZATIONS]

Un grand prix littéraire Guérin; article. Jean Royer. *MD* Feb 21, 1987: pB3.
[AWARDS, LITERARY]

La vie littéraire; column. Jean Royer. photo · *MD* March 21, 1987: pD2.
[AWARDS, LITERARY; CANADIAN LITERARY PUBLISHING; POETRY READINGS; RADIO AND CANADIAN LITERATURE; TELEVISION AND CANADIAN LITERATURE]

La vie littéraire; column. Jean Royer. photo · *MD* May 30, 1987: pD2.
[AWARDS, LITERARY; CANADIAN LITERARY PUBLISHING; FESTIVALS, LITERARY; RADIO AND CANADIAN LITERATURE; TELEVISION AND CANADIAN LITERATURE]

La vie littéraire; column. Jean Royer. photo · *MD* June 13, 1987: pD2.
[AWARDS, LITERARY; POETRY READINGS; RADIO AND CANADIAN LITERATURE; TELEVISION AND CANADIAN LITERATURE; WRITERS' ORGANIZATIONS]

La vie littéraire; column. Jean Royer. photo · *MD* Oct 17, 1987: pD2.
[CANADIAN LITERARY PERIODICALS; CONFERENCES, LITERARY; FICTION READINGS; WRITERS' ORGANIZATIONS]

Inside the contest; essay. Grant Shilling. *Can Auth & Book* Spring 1987; Vol 62 No 3: p13–14.

Book world: a showcase for the book-maker's art; column. Beverley Slopen. *TS* Dec 6, 1987: pC8.

Poets! Read on; article. Beverley Slopen. *TS* Dec 20, 1987: pE5.

Paperclips: a woman's break with Catholicism . . . calling for crime; column. Beverley Slopen. *Quill & Quire* Nov 1987; Vol 53 No 11: p17.

The 3–Day Novel Contest; article. Dona Sturmanis. photo · *Can Auth & Book* Spring 1987; Vol 62 No 3: p12–13.

Bloc-notes; column. Michel Vaïs. *Jeu* 1987; No 44: p215–218.
[CONFERENCES, LITERARY; GOVERNOR GENERAL'S AWARDS; RADIO AND CANADIAN LITERATURE]

Judges getting to work on short story contest; article. Paul Warnick. *TS* March 8, 1987: pA2.

Three-day wonder; essay. Joel Yanofsky. *Books in Can* Nov 1987; Vol 16 No 8: p5–6.

LE COMPLOT/Young adult novel by Chrystine Brouillet

Comme il vous plaira; review of *Le Complot*. Irène Oore. *Can Child Lit* 1987; No 46: p90–92.

CONAN, LAURE (pseud.)

Laure Conan and Madame de La Fayette: rewriting the female plot; article. Mary Jean Green. *Essays on Can Writ* Spring 1987; No 34: p50–63.
[FEMINIST WRITING AND CRITICISM; WOMEN WRITERS]

CONCRETE POETRY

Defying linear deification — contemporary Toronto visual poetry; article. J.W. Curry. illus · *Cross Can Writ Q* 1987; Vol 9 No 3–4: p6–8.
[ONTARIO WRITING AND WRITERS; POSTMODERNIST WRITING AND CRITICISM]

CONE, TOM

The play's the thing, despite thieves, greed and flops; article. Stephen Godfrey. photo · *G&M* Aug 8, 1987: pC1.

CONFABULATIONS: POEMS FOR MALCOLM LOWRY/Poems by Sharon Thesen

Lowry's mouths; review of *Confabulations*. Ronald Binns. *Can Lit* Spring 1987; No 112: p85–87.

Confabulation; review of *Confabulations*. Sherrill Grace. illus · *Essays on Can Writ* Spring 1987; No 34: p18–23.

CONFEDERATION POETRY AND POETS

Taking to the woods: of myths, metaphors and poets; article. Barbara Godard. abstract · *Études can* 1987; No 23: p159–171.
[CULTURAL IDENTITY; WILDERNESS WRITING]

LA CONFÉRENCE INACHEVÉE, LE PAS DE GAMELIN ET AUTRES RÉCITS/Short stories by Jacques Ferron

Par-delà la mort, le docteur Ferron continue de soigner nos âmes; review of *La Conférence inachevée*. Jean-Roch Boivin. photo · *MD* June 27, 1987: pC8.

La vitrine du livre; reviews. Guy Ferland. *MD* June 6, 1987: pD4.
[CANADIAN LITERARY PERIODICALS]

Le testament d'un artiste; review of *La Conférence inachevée*. Yolande Grisé. photo · *Lettres québec* Autumn 1987; No 47: p35–36.

CONFERENCE REPORTS: REVIEWS AND ARTICLES

In principio; reviews. Laurel Boone. *Can Lit* Winter 1987; No 115: p209–211.

[Untitled]; review of *In the Feminine*. Janice Kulyk Keefer. *U of Toronto Q* Fall 1987; Vol 57 No 1: p201–203.

Body & language; review of *In the Feminine*. Thelma McCormack. *Can Lit* Winter 1987; No 115: p142–144.

[Untitled]; review of *A Public and Private Voice*. Margaret Gail Osachoff. *U of Windsor R* Spring-Summer 1987; Vol 20 No 2: p94–97.

[Untitled]; reviews of *Itinéraire de Liverpool à Québec* and *Colloque Louis Hémon*. B.-Z. Shek. *U of Toronto Q* Fall 1987; Vol 57 No 1: p179–182.

De se dire; review of *Les Oeuvres de création et le français au Québec*. Paul G. Socken. *Can Lit* Winter 1987; No 115: p164–165.

[Untitled]; review of *Stephen Leacock: A Reappraisal*. Carl Spadoni. *Queen's Q* Winter 1987; Vol 94 No 4: p1028–1030.

La structure de la grande machine faire des livres; review of *L'Institution littéraire*. Adrien Thério. *Lettres québec* Winter 1986–87; No 44: p84.

CONFERENCES, LITERARY

Memorial conference; article. *WFP* Feb 13, 1987: p29.

Canadian Studies news and notes; column. *J of Can Studies* Spring 1987; Vol 22 No 1: p161–163.
[WRITERS' WORKSHOPS]

Canadian studies news and notes; column. *J of Can Studies* Summer 1987; Vol 22 No 2: p210–211.

Latin American, Canadian writers to meet; article. *G&M* April 11, 1987: pE11.

Question de poésie: le 1er colloque d'Éstuaire; notice. *Estuaire* Spring 1987; No 44: p87.

Conference on the short story; notice. *Afram* June 1987; No 25: p7.

Dits et faits; column. *Lettres québec* Autumn 1987; No 47: p6.
[AWARDS, LITERARY; COMPETITIONS, LITERARY; WRITERS' ORGANIZATIONS]

Les écrivains souhaitent une meilleure "couverture" des médias; article. *MD* Nov 14, 1987: pD15.
[RADIO AND CANADIAN LITERATURE; TELEVISION AND CANADIAN LITERATURE]

"Question de poésie": un colloque de la revue Estuaire le 20 novembre au salon du livre; article. *MD* Nov 16, 1987: p9.
[CANADIAN LITERARY PERIODICALS]

La fête du livre débute ce soir; article, includes schedule of events. *MD* Nov 19, 1987: p13.

Aujourd'hui au salon du livre; schedule of events. *MD* Nov 20, 1987: p13.

Round table: responses, notes and queries; column. *Can Child Lit* 1987; No 45: p98–99.
[AWARDS, LITERARY]

Editorial note; editorial. *Can Child Lit* 1987; No 48: p2.

English theatre in spotlight; article. Marianne Ackerman. *MG* May 2, 1987: H1.

Littérature et recherche universitaire: la question des revues; introduction. Bernard Andrès. *Voix et images* Winter 1987; No 35: p266.
[CANADIAN LITERARY PERIODICALS]

(French) fun at the fair; article. Barbara Black. *MG* Nov 28, 1987: J11.

Export sales depend on Frankfurt presence; article. Hamish Cameron. photo · *Quill & Quire* Dec 1987; Vol 53 No 12: p10.
[EUROPE-CANADA LITERARY RELATIONS]

Le Salon du livre se veut montréalais; article. Paul Cauchon. photo · *MD* Nov 6, 1987: p13.

Godin, lauréat de la ville de Montréal; article. Paul Cauchon. photo · *MD* Nov 20, 1987: p12.

La Bibliothèque Nationale fait sensation au Salon du livre; article. Paul Cauchon. photo · *MD* Nov 21, 1987: pA7.

On se marche sur les pieds au Salon; article. Paul Cauchon. photo · *MD* Nov 23, 1987: p1,8.

Même Proust y trouve son compte; article. Paul Cauchon. photo · *MD* Nov 24, 1987: p11.

Le Salon du livre le plus populaire depuis dix ans; article. Paul Cauchon. photo · *MD* Nov 25, 1987: p11.

Le 16e Salon du livre de Québec: la francophonie est au rendez-vous; article. Hélène de Billy. photo · *MD* April 25, 1987: pD1,D6.

À l'affiche du Salon du livre de Québec; article. Hélène de Billy. photo · *MD* April 27, 1987: p11–12

Le Salon du livre de Québec: c'est parti!; article. Hélène de Billy. photo · *MD* April 29, 1987: p13.
[AWARDS, LITERARY]

Christine comme un poison dans l'eau; article. Hélène de Billy. *MD* April 30, 1987: p13.

Mais Anne Hébert était là; article. Hélène de Billy. *MD* May 4, 1987: p9–10.

La vague-jeunesse sera choyée; article. Dominique Demers. photo · *MD* Nov 14, 1987: pD10.
[CHILDREN'S LITERATURE]

Le Québec à Liège; article. Jacques Dubois. *Voix et images* Spring 1987; Vol 12 No 3: p566–567.
[BELGIUM-CANADA LITERARY RELATIONS]

Colloque de l'Académie Québec/Francophonie; article. Jean-Pierre Duquette. *Lettres québec* Spring 1987; No 45: p69.

Canada's a hit with this group; article. Michael Farber. *MG* Oct 9, 1987: pA3.
[UNITED STATES-CANADA LITERARY RELATIONS]

La règne du genre mort; article. Guy Ferland. *MD* Oct 26, 1987: p11.

Six days of praise for the printed page; article about the Salon du livre de Montréal. Matthew Fraser. photo · *G&M* Nov 7, 1987: pC13.

L'industrie du livre y trouve son compte; article. Jean Chapdelaine Gagnon. *MD* Nov 14, 1987: pD8.

Pour tous les goûts; article, include schedule of events. Françoise Genest. photo · *MD* Nov 14, 1987: pD6–D7.

Sept autres Salons dont on néglige souvent l'impact; article. Françoise Genest. *MD* Nov 14, 1987: pD8.

À la mecque du livre, des bibliophiles et des femmes; article. Françoise Genest. *MD* Nov 14, 1987: pD8.

UBC plans Lowry symposium; article. Stephen Godfrey. *G&M* April 30, 1987: pC1.

Writing Saskatchewan — a literary symposium; article. Dennis Gruending. photo · *NeWest R* Nov 1987; Vol 13 No 3: p9–11.
[PRAIRIE WRITING AND WRITERS]

Book fair to expand, offers new prizes; article. Heather Hill. photo · *MG* Sept 4, 1987: pC2.
[AWARDS, LITERARY]

French book fair aims for more anglophones; article. Heather Hill. *MG* Nov 6, 1987: pC1.

New lines, Lévesque make for lively Salon du Livre; article. David Homel. photo · *Quill & Quire* Jan 1987; Vol 53 No 1: p14–15.

Manitoba writers gather for literary conference; article. Manfred Jager. *WFP* Oct 22, 1987: p46.
[WRITERS' ORGANIZATIONS]

The effect of the international children's book industry on Canadian publishing endeavours for children and young people; article. Ronald A. Jobe. *Can Child Lit* 1987; No 47: p7–11.
[CANADIAN LITERARY PUBLISHING; CHILDREN'S LITERATURE; EUROPE-CANADA LITERARY RELATIONS]

Native heritage is displayed in three timely books; reviews of children's books. Janice Kennedy. *MG* April 4, 1987: H11.

Going to the fair? Take along a page of your best writing; article. H.J. Kirchhoff. illus · *G&M* May 1, 1987: pC8.
[CANADIAN LITERARY PUBLISHING]

Robert Lepage, globe-trotter; column. Robert Lévesque. photo · *MD* Oct 20, 1987: p13,15.

Book review editors take the hot seat at writers' conference; article. Liam Lacey. photo · *G&M* May 30, 1987: pC5.
[BOOK REVIEWING; WRITERS' ORGANIZATIONS]

Le Salon fait la fête et se donne un objectif: conquérir les jeunes; article. France Lafuste. *MD* Nov 14, 1987: pD3.

Une immense "auberge espagnole" prête à accueillir ses 80,000 visiteurs; article. Marie Laurier. photo · *MD* Oct 31, 1987: pD1,D8.

Book beat's busy next week; article. Kenneth McGoogan. *CH* Feb 4, 1987: pF4.
[POETRY READINGS]

Festival winds bring W.O. home; column. Kenneth McGoogan. *CH* March 1, 1987: pC8.
[AWARDS, LITERARY; FESTIVALS, LITERARY]

Writers' event grows on young people; column. Kenneth McGoogan. *CH* March 29, 1987: pE5.
[WRITERS' WORKSHOPS]

Experts offered the write advice; article. Kenneth McGoogan. photo · *CH* April 6, 1987: pD6.

First novel turned into TV movie; column. Kenneth McGoogan. *CH* May 3, 1987: pE6.
[TELEVISION AND CANADIAN LITERATURE]

Calgary project makes kids published writers; article. Kenneth McGoogan. *Quill & Quire (Books for Young People)* June 1987; Vol 53 No 6: p4.

Literary world loses a champion; column. Kenneth McGoogan. *CH* July 12, 1987: pE4.
[AWARDS, LITERARY; PUBLISHING AND PUBLISHERS IN CANADA; SCIENCE FICTION; WRITERS' WORKSHOPS]

For the record; letter to the editor. C.D. Minni. *Books in Can* Jan-Feb 1987; Vol 16 No 1: p38.
[ITALIAN-CANADIAN WRITING AND WRITERS]

La vie littéraire; column. Marc Morin. *MD* Dec 5, 1987: pD2.
[CANADIAN LITERARY PUBLISHING; POETRY READINGS; WRITERS' ORGANIZATIONS]

La vie littéraire; column. Marc Morin. *MD* Dec 24, 1987: pC10.
[COMPETITIONS, LITERARY; POETRY READINGS]

L'avenir du français au Québec; article. Dominique Parent. *Lettres québec* Summer 1987; No 46: p9.
[WRITERS' ORGANIZATIONS]

Quebec publishers meet English Canada at Frankfurt; article. Jeanne Poulin. *Quill & Quire* Dec 1987; Vol 53 No 12: p11.
[EUROPE-CANADA LITERARY RELATIONS]

Au sommet, l'univers littéraire francophone; article. Bernard Racine. *MD* Aug 15, 1987: pC2.

Son trac le plus fou, Anne Hébert le ressent devant la page blanche; article. Johanne Roy. photo · *MD* May 1, 1987: p12.

La vie littéraire; column. Jean Royer. *MD* Jan 17, 1987: pB2.
[AWARDS, LITERARY; RADIO AND CANADIAN LITERATURE; TELEVISION AND CANADIAN LITERATURE]

La vie littéraire; column. Jean Royer. *MD* Feb 7, 1987: pB2.
[COMPETITIONS, LITERARY; POETRY READINGS; PUBLISHING AND PUBLISHERS IN CANADA; TELEVISION AND CANADIAN LITERATURE; WRITERS' WORKSHOPS]

La vie littéraire; column. Jean Royer. *MD* Feb 28, 1987: pC2.
[AWARDS, LITERARY; CANADIAN LITERARY PERIODICALS; CANADIAN LITERARY PUBLISHING; RADIO AND CANADIAN LITERATURE]

La vie littéraire; column. Jean Royer. photo · *MD* March 28, 1987: pD2.
[FESTIVALS, LITERARY; GOVERNMENT GRANTS FOR WRITERS/PUBLISHERS; RADIO AND CANADIAN LITERATURE; TELEVISION AND CANADIAN LITERATURE]

Le Salon du livre de l'Outaouais; article. Jean Royer. photo · *MD* April 4, 1987: pD2.

La vie littéraire; column. Jean Royer. *MD* April 25, 1987: pD2.
[AWARDS, LITERARY; FESTIVALS, LITERARY; FICTION READINGS; POETRY READINGS; RADIO AND CANADIAN LITERATURE; TELEVISION AND CANADIAN LITERATURE

La Rencontre des écrivains: "une aventure majeure"; article. Jean Royer. *MD* April 27, 1987: p11,15.

Écrire l'amour c'est parler de soi; article. Jean Royer. illus · *MD* May 2, 1987: pD1–D2.

La vie littéraire; column. Jean Royer. *MD* May 9, 1987: pD2.
[POETRY READINGS; RADIO AND CANADIAN LITERATURE; TELEVISION AND CANADIAN LITERATURE]

La vie littéraire; column. Jean Royer. photo · *MD* May 16, 1987: pD2.
[AWARDS, LITERARY; PUBLISHING AND PUBLISHERS IN CANADA; RADIO AND CANADIAN LITERATURE; TELEVISION AND CANADIAN LITERATURE]

La vie littéraire; column. Jean Royer. *MD* Sept 12, 1987: pD2.
[AWARDS, LITERARY; POETRY PERFORMANCE; POETRY READINGS]

La vie littéraire; column. Jean Royer. photo · *MD* Sept 19, 1987: pD2.
[AWARDS, LITERARY; FICTION READINGS; POETRY READINGS; PUBLISHING AND PUBLISHERS IN CANADA]

La vie littéraire; column. Jean Royer. photo · *MD* Sept 26, 1987: pD2.
[AUDIO-VISUALS AND CANADIAN LITERATURE; INTERNATIONAL WRITERS' ORGANIZATIONS; PUBLISHING AND PUBLISHERS IN CANADA; WRITERS' ORGANIZATION]

La vie littéraire; column. Jean Royer. photo · *MD* Oct 17, 1987: pD2.
[CANADIAN LITERARY PERIODICALS; COMPETITIONS, LITERARY; FICTION READINGS; WRITERS' ORGANIZATIONS]

La vie littéraire; column. Jean Royer. *MD* Oct 24, 1987: pD2.
[FICTION READINGS; POETRY READINGS; WRITERS' ORGANIZATIONS]

Colloque Auteur(e) pour vivre; article. Denis Saint-Jacques. *Lettres québec* Autumn 1987; No 47: p10.

Tip sheet: Lakeshore artists to hold spring exhibition and sale; column. Susan Schwartz. *MG* April 8, 1987: pE13.

Tip sheet: Save the Children seeks funds for millions of starving children; column. Susan Schwartz. *MG* April 29, 1987: pE11.

"Somewhere meant for me"; editorial. John Smallbridge. photo · *Can Child Lit* 1987; No 48: p3–4.

Dits et faits; column. Adrien Thério. photo · *Lettres québec* Summer 1987; No 46: p6.
[AUTHORS, CANADIAN; CANADIAN LITERARY PUBLISHING; GOVERNMENT GRANTS FOR WRITERS/PUBLISHERS; LIBRARY SERVICES AND CANADIAN LITERATURE]

Bologna score-card Part I; article. Diane Turbide. photo · *Quill & Quire* June 1987; Vol 53 No 6: p22–23.
[CHILDREN'S LITERATURE]

Bloc-notes; column. Michel Vaïs. *Jeu* 1987; No 43: p179–180.

Bloc-notes; column. Michel Vaïs. *Jeu* 1987; No 44: p215–218.
[COMPETITIONS, LITERARY; GOVERNOR GENERAL'S AWARDS; RADIO AND CANADIAN LITERATURE]

Nordic journey; essay. W.D. Valgardson. *Books in Can* Nov 1987; Vol 16 No 8: p3–4.
[EUROPE-CANADA LITERARY RELATIONS]

Crime in the Crimea . . . where glasnost and mystery meet; essay. Eric Wright. photo · *Quill & Quire* Sept 1987; Vol 53 No 9: p75.
[INTERNATIONAL WRITERS' ORGANIZATIONS]

CONFESSIONAL WRITING

The descent into hell of Jacques Laruelle: chapter I of Under The Volcano; article. David Falk. *Can Lit* Spring 1987; No 112: p72–83.
[ARTIST FIGURE]

CONFIGURATION: ESSAYS ON THE CANADIAN LITERATURES/Critical work by E.D. Blodgett

A sophisticated, compelling dialogue; review of *Configuration*. Estelle Dansereau. *Essays on Can Writ* Spring 1987; No 34: p174–179.

CONLOGUE, RAY

Three writers at The Globe win awards; article. *G&M* May 4, 1987: pA11.
[AWARDS, LITERARY]

Gazette feature writer wins national award; article. *MG* May 4, 1987: pA2.
[AWARDS, LITERARY]

2 Star writers, photographer take top newspaper award; article. Walter Stefaniuk. *TS* May 3, 1987: pA2.
[AWARDS, LITERARY]

CONN, JAN

Montreal poets inspired by travel in hot countries; reviews of poetry books. Barbara Black. *MG* March 28, 1987: pE9.

[Untitled]; review of *The Fabulous Disguise of Ourselves*. Charlotte Hussey. *Rubicon* Fall 1987; No 9: p163–164.

You ask me what I'm thinking; reviews of poetry books. M. Travis Lane. *Fiddlehead* Winter 1987; No 154: p95–104.

[Untitled]; reviews of *The Fabulous Disguise of Ourselves* and *The Power to Move*. Stephen Scobie. *Malahat R* June 1987; No 79: p166.

CONNELLY, KAREN

Award-winning writer marches to own beat; article. Eva Ferguson. photo · *CH* Nov 22, 1987: pG8.

CONOLLY, L.W.

[Untitled]; review of *English-Canadian Theatre*. Rota Herzberg Lister. *Can Drama* 1987; Vol 13 No 2: p227–228.

A cogent view of Canadian theatre; review of *English-Canadian Theatre*. Margaret Penman. photo · *TS* Dec 27, 1987: pE18.

CONSTANTIN-WEYER, MAURICE

De l'ouest, des nouvelles et de l'histoire; reviews of short story books. Paulette Collet. photo · *Lettres québec* Summer 1987; No 46: p68–70.
[ANTHOLOGIES: BOOK REVIEWS]

LA CONSTELLATION DU CYGNE/Novel by Yolande Villemaire

Du privé au politique: la Constellation du Cygne de Yolande Villemaire; article. Suzanne Lamy. *Voix et images* Autumn 1987; Vol 13 No 1: p18–28.

CONTACT PRINTS/Novel by Philip Kreiner

Comic novel about the North is as sharp as frostbite; review of *Contact Prints*. Barbara Black. *MG* June 13, 1987: J8.

Dissension in the backyard of Canada's frozen near north; review of *Contact Prints*. Geoff Hancock. photo · *TS* May 3, 1987: pA24.

A gritty tale of a teacher's turmoil among the Cree; review of *Contact Prints*. Philip Kreiner. photo · *G&M* April 9, 1987: pC1.

[Untitled]; review of *Contact Prints*. Brent Ledger. *Quill & Quire* May 1987; Vol 53 No 5: p20.

Through a lens darkly; review of *Contact Prints*. Douglas Malcolm. *Books in Can* May 1987; Vol 16 No 4: p28.

Overworked motif is just new kind of exploitation; review of *Contact Prints*. David Williamson. *WFP* June 27, 1987: p58.

CONTEMPORARY VERSE 2/Periodical

Editorial. Jane Casey. *CV 2* Spring 1987; Vol 10 No 3: p6–7.
[CANADIAN LITERARY PERIODICALS]

CONTES DU PAYS DE L'ORIGNAL/Children's stories by Jean Ferguson

Mini-comptes rendus; review of *Contes du pays de l'orignal*. François Paré. *Can Child Lit* 1987; No 47: p100–101

LES CONTES DU SOMMET BLEU/THE DRAGON AND OTHER LAURENTIAN TALES/Children's stories by Claude Jasmin

Activity books kids will enjoy; reviews of *Dragon Sandwiches* and *The Dragon and Other Laurentian Tales*. *TS* Dec 20, 1987: pE8.

School's out, and books are in; reviews of children's books. Janice Kennedy. *MG* July 4, 1987: J9.

Traditional tales made new again with super illustrations; reviews of *The Dragon* and *The Lucky Old Woman*. Eva Martin. *Quill & Quire (Books for Young People)* Aug 1987; Vol 53 No 8: p7.

CONTES GOUTTES OU LE PAYS D'UN REFLET/Journal by Plume Latraverse

Une vie de Patachon bien sympathique; reviews of *D'ailleurs et d'ici* and *Contes gouttes ou le pays d'un reflet*. Yolande Grisé. photo · *Lettres québec* Summer 1987; No 46: p59–60.

CONTRASTS: COMPARATIVE ESSAYS ON ITALIAN CANADIAN WRITING/Critical essays collection

Italian-made; review of *Contrasts*. Giovanni Bonanno. *Can Lit* Winter 1987; No 115: p178–182.

[Untitled]; review of *Contrasts*. Lucienne Kroha. *Queen's Q* Spring 1987; Vol 94 No 1: p206–208.

Italian-Canadian voices; review of *Contrasts*. Kenneth W. Meadwell. *Prairie Fire* Summer 1987; Vol 8 No 2: p72–74.

LA CONVENTION/Novella by Suzanne Lamy

La voix minimale; article. Jacques Brault. *Voix et images* Autumn 1987; Vol 13 No 1: p66–69.

Avatars d'un pacte amoureux; article. Alain Piette. *Voix et images* Autumn 1987; Vol 13 No 1: p46–51.

COOK, DAVID

Landscape with politicians; review of *Northrop Frye: A Vision of the New World*. William T. Booth. *Essays on Can Writ* Winter 1987; No 35: p117–122.

[Untitled]; review of *Northrop Frye: A Vision of the New World*. Michael Hurley. *Queen's Q* Spring 1987; Vol 94 No 1: p219–222.

[Untitled]; review of *Northrop Frye: A Vision of the New World*. Mark Kingwell. *Rubicon* Spring 1987; No 8: p193–195.

[Untitled]; review of *Northrop Frye: A Vision of the New World*. Lauriat Lane, Jr. *Eng Studies in Can* Sept 1987; Vol 13 No 3: p349–352.

COOKE, RONALD

Writer won't let blindness slow him down; article. Jay Bryan. photo · *MG* July 2, 1987: pC1.
[PUBLISHING AND PUBLISHERS IN CANADA]

COOLEY, DENNIS

Red Deer Press series champions western writers; reviews of poetry books. Murdoch Burnett. *CH* Dec 13, 1987: pC11.

Stealing the text: George Bowering's Kerrisdale Elegies and Dennis Cooley's Bloody Jack; article. Smaro Kamboureli. *Can Lit* Winter 1987; No 115: p9–23.
[CANADIAN LONG POEM; STRUCTURALIST WRITING AND CRITICISM]

COOPER, ALLAN

[Untitled]; review of *Poems Released on a Nuclear Wind*. Barbara Carey. *Books in Can* Dec 1987; Vol 16 No 9: p30–31.

COOPER, BEVERLEY

Theatre Direct probes urban kids' reality; theatre reviews of *The Snake Lady* and *Thin Ice*. Ray Conlogue. *G&M* April 29, 1987: pC7.

The Mikado hits a high note with seven Dora Awards; article. Robert Crew. photo · *TS* June 23, 1987: pE3.
[AWARDS, LITERARY]

Teens need to see play on vital issue; column. Lois Sweet. *TS* April 20, 1987: pC1.

COOPER, STEPHEN

Murder for Sale turns mystery into song and dance; theatre review. Pat Donnelly. *MG* June 6, 1987: H10.

COPPENS, PATRICK

Comme un vent; reviews of poetry books. James P. Gilroy. *Can Lit* Winter 1987; No 115: p260–261.

Jacques Boulerice: pour une autre enfance; reviews of *Apparence* and *Distance*. Jean Royer. *MD* Feb 14, 1987: pC3.

COPYRIGHT

Proposed copyright law means cash for creators; article. photo · *WFP* May 28, 1987: p22.

Copyright revisions tabled today; article. *TS* May 27, 1987: pE3.

Copyright bill targets record, video, computer pirates; article. *MG* May 28, 1987: pB1.

Feds table new copyright revisions; article. *Quill & Quire* July 1987; Vol 53 No 7: p50,52.

Copyright bill goes too far critics charge; article. *MG* Oct 28, 1987: pB1.

Le droit d'auteur en feuillets; article. *MD* Oct 3, 1987: pD2.
[AUTHORS, CANADIAN]

Quick action urged on copyright bill despite appeals; article. *WFP* Nov 24, 1987: p21.

Copyright law would fine pirates $1 million; article. Martin Cohn. *TS* May 28, 1987: pA1,A4.

Pour en finir une fois pour toutes avec la réforme; article. Angèle Dagenais. *MD* Oct 16, 1987: p13–14.

Copyright worries; letter to the editor. Michael Fay. *G&M* Oct 19, 1987: pA6

Flora MacDonald has librarians in a huff; article. Carol Goar. photo · *TS* Dec 3, 1987: pA27.

Ottawa struggles to ensure authors get their due; article. Carol Goar. illus · *MG* Dec 4, 1987: pB3.
[GOVERNMENT GRANTS FOR WRITERS/PUBLISHERS; LIBRARY SERVICES AND CANADIAN LITERATURE]

Abuse of copyright; letter to the editor. Richard Lemm. *G&M* Dec 1, 1987: pA6.
[LIBRARY SERVICES AND CANADIAN LITERATURE]

Copyright groups no threat to free flow of information; letter to the editor. Douglas Lintula. *G&M* Oct 21, 1987: pA7.

Copyright Act opponents called 'irresponsible'; article. Greg Quill. *TS* Dec 29, 1987: pE1,E5.

Ottawa copyright bill aids artists, gets tough with book, tape pirates; article. David Stewart-Patterson. *G&M* May 28, 1987: pA1–A2.

COQ À DEUX TÊTES/Poems by Paul Chanel Malenfant

[Untitled]; reviews of *Les Noms du père* and *Coq à deux têtes*. Jean Chapdelaine Gagnon. *Estuaire* Autumn 1987; No 46: p85–86.

L'originalité et l'oralité; reviews of *Coq à deux têtes* and *Les Terres du songe*. Jean Royer. *MD* May 30, 1987: pD3.

CORBEIL, LOUIS-PHILIPPE

A spokesman for his time; review of *Journal de bord du gamin des ténèbres*. Guy Gauthier. *Prairie Fire* Autumn 1987; Vol 8 No 3: p113–115.

CORKSCREW/Novel by Ted Wood

[Untitled]; review of *Corkscrew*. Norman Sigurdson. *Quill & Quire* Nov 1987; Vol 53 No 11: p24–25.

LE CORPS DE L'INFINI: POÈMES 1968–1985/Poems by Jean-Marc Frechette

Chronique: soliloques; reviews of poetry books. Marguerite Andersen. *Poetry Can R* Spring 1987; Vol 8 No 2–3: p23–24.

La fiction du réel/le réel de la fiction; reviews of poetry books. André Brochu. *Voix et images* Winter 1987; No 35: p322–330.

Songe, révolte et manifeste; reviews of poetry books. Robert Yergeau. photo · *Lettres québec* Spring 1987; No 45: p38–39.

CORRECT IN THIS CULTURE/Poems by Victor Jerret Enns

[Untitled]; review of *Correct in This Culture*. Leslie Nutting. *Poetry Can R* Fall 1987; Vol 9 No 1: p38.

LA CORRIDA DE L'AMOUR: LE ROMAN HARLEQUIN/ Critical essays collection

[Untitled]; review of *La Corrida de l'amour*. Caroline Barrett. *Voix et images* Winter 1987; No 35: p348–349.

[Untitled]; letter to the editor. Andrée Gagnon. *Lettres québec* Spring 1987; No 45: p7.
[ROMANTIC FICTION]

La droite amoureuse rallume ses brasiers; reviews of *La Peur du Grand Amour* and *La Corrida de l'amour*. Chantal Thry. *Lettres québec* Winter 1986–87; No 44: p69–71.

CORRIVEAU, HUGUES

La vitrine du livre; reviews of *À double sens* and *Le Fils d'Ariane*. Guy Ferland. *MD* Feb 14, 1987: pC2.

Qui a peur de l'intellectuel in 1987?; reviews. Pierre Milot. *Voix et images* Spring 1987; Vol 12 No 3: p530–534.
[CANADIAN LITERARY PERIODICALS]

La modernité québécoise "pure laine"; review of *À double sens*. Lori Saint-Martin. *MD* May 9, 1987: pD3.

Impasses ou issues? L'imaginaire masculin face à la femme; reviews of *Les Silences du corbeau* and *À double sens*. Patricia Smart. *Voix et images* Spring 1987; Vol 12 No 3: p555–560.

La modernité: des formes qui s'inquiètent; reviews of critical works. Whitfield. photo · *Lettres québec* Summer 1987; No 46: p56–58.

Forcément de l'amour; reviews of *Forcément dans la tête* and *De ce nom de l'amour*. Deloris Williams. *Can Lit* Summer-Fall 1987; No 113–114: p233–235.

CORRIVEAU, MONIQUE

Structure sociale, stratégie textuelle: l'univers narratif de Monique Corriveau; article. Lynn Kettler Penrod. *Can Child Lit* 1987; No 46: p45–59.

COTNOIR, LOUISE

[Untitled]; review of *L'Audace des mains*. Louise Blouin. *Estuaire* Autumn 1987; No 46: p83.

COTNOIR/Novel by Jacques Ferron

"Les nouvelles de cousin Emmanuel": varieties of salvation and imagination in Ferron's Cotnoir; article. Brian Bartlett. *Studies in Can Lit* 1987; Vol 12 No 2: p177–186.

LE COULEUR DU SANG

See **THE COLOR OF BLOOD/LE COULEUR DU SANG/ Novel by Brian Moore**

COUNTERPANE/Poems by Catherine Bates

Quilted patch; reviews of poetry books. Uma Parameswaran. Teresa Mallam. *Can Lit* Spring 1987; No 112: p176–179.

But where is the poetry?; reviews of *Road Dances* and *Counterpane*. Bruce Whiteman. *Essays on Can Writ* Spring 1987; No 34: p48–49.

COUNTERPOINT/Novel by Marie Moser

Getting on a literary roulette wheel; reviews of fictional works. Trevor Ferguson. *MG* Nov 14, 1987: J11.
[FIRST NOVELS: BOOK REVIEWS]

Unkind but true: little skill in first novel; review of *Counterpoint*. Maggie Helwig. *TS* June 20, 1987: M7.
[FIRST NOVELS: BOOK REVIEWS]

Ancestors inspire novelist; column. Kenneth McGoogan. biog photo · *CH* May 31, 1987: pF5.

[Untitled]; review of *Counterpoint*. Carolellen Norskey. *Quill & Quire* Aug 1987; Vol 53 No 8: p30.
[FIRST NOVELS: BOOK REVIEWS]

COUNTRIE PLEASURES/Poems by Steve Noyes

[Untitled]; reviews of poetry books. Anne Burke. *Poetry Can R* Summer 1987; Vol 8 No 4: p38.

COUP DE FIL/Children's play by Diane Chevalier

A plea to understand adults; theatre review of *Coup de Fil*. Pat Donnelly. *MG* Feb 10, 1987: pB7.

L'envers de l'abandon; theatre review of *Coup de fil*. Paul Lefebvre. photo · *Jeu* 1987; No 44: p192–193.

COUP DE SOLEIL/Play by Jacques Pelletier

Coup De Soleil isn't great theatre, but it's a nice winter break; theatre review. Pat Donnelly. *MG* Jan 23, 1987: pC5.

LE COUPEUR DE TÊTES/Novel by Nadine McKenzie

Discours-fleuve; reviews of *Le Coupeur de têtes* and *Les Deux soeurs*. Marguerite Andersen. *Can Lit* Winter 1987; No 115: p182–184.

Straining credulity; review of *Le Coupeur de têtes*. Ann Carson. *Prairie Fire* Summer 1987; Vol 8 No 2: p75–76.

COURAGE IN THE STORM/Children's novel by Thomas H. Raddall

Title tattle; column. Martin Dowding. *Quill & Quire (Books for Young People)* Dec 1987; Vol 53 No 12: p3.
[FILM ADAPTATIONS OF CANADIAN LITERATURE; TELEVISION AND CANADIAN LITERATURE]

Three stories for children; reviews of children's books. Veronica Leonard. *Atlan Prov Book R* Nov-Dec 1987; Vol 14 No 4: p1.

Youngsters get choice of beautiful books; reviews. Helen Norrie. *WFP* Dec 5, 1987: p57.

Ways of escape; reviews of children's books. Mary Ainslie Smith. *Books in Can* Dec 1987; Vol 16 No 9: p11–14.

THE COURIER/Play by Vern Thiessen

Festival One plays singularly successful; theatre reviews. Stephen Godfrey. photo · *G&M* May 8, 1987: pF9.
[FESTIVALS, DRAMA]

Courier's inner conflict makes terrific theatre; theatre review of *The Courier*. Reg Skene. *WFP* May 7, 1987: p43.

COUSTURE, ARLETTE

Aujourd'hui; column. *MD* April 8, 1987: p12.

Prix du Public goes to Cousture; article. *G&M* Nov 25, 1987: pC5.
[AWARDS, LITERARY]

À Saint-Tite, la saga d'un patrimoine secret et sacré; column. Jean Éthier-Blais. photo · *MD* May 2, 1987: pD8.

Arlette Cousture obtient le Prix du public; article. Paul Cauchon. photo · *MD* Nov 24, 1987: p11.
[AWARDS, LITERARY]

Les étudiants du secondaire préfèrent Les Filles de Caleb; article. Angèle Dagenais. *MD* Nov 4, 1987: p14.

Ce qui arrive, quant on écrit pour communiquer; review of *Le Cri de l'oie blanche*. Pierre Hébert. photo · *Lettres québec* Summer 1987; No 46: p24–25.

Arlette Cousture, arrière-petite-fille de Caleb et vedette malgré elle; article. Marie Laurier. photo · *MD* Sept 12, 1987: pD1.

Caleb's juggernaut; article. Francine Pelletier. photo · *MG* Oct 31, 1987: J11.

COVERT, CHRISTOPHER

Play is sheer magic; theatre review of *The Unicorn Moon*. Muriel Leeper. *TS (Neighbors)* Nov 17, 1987: p14.

Unicorns and princesses hit Scarborough stage; article. Muriel Leeper. photo · *TS (Neighbors)* Oct 27, 1987: p10.

THE COWBOY KID/Children's novel by David A. Poulsen

Satisfying youth mystery also portrays way of life; review of *The Cowboy Kid*. Susan Scott. photo · *CH* July 11, 1987: pE10.

COWBOYS DON'T CRY/Young adult novel by Marilyn Halvorson

Domingo gave opera company a $40,000 break; column. Sid Adilman. *TS* March 13, 1987: pC19.

Cowboys don't cry . . . except on a movie set; article. Eric Dawson. photo · *TS* Aug 26, 1987: pD1.
[FILM ADAPTATIONS OF CANADIAN LITERATURE]

Rewrites upset author; article. Eric Dawson. *CH* Aug 27, 1987: pC2.
[FILM ADAPTATIONS OF CANADIAN LITERATURE]

Olympic festival to open with Wheeler film; article. H.J. Kirchhoff. photo · *G&M* Dec 8, 1987: pD5.
[FILM ADAPTATIONS OF CANADIAN LITERATURE]

Roll 'em, cowboys; article. Liam Lacey. photo · *G&M* Aug 29, 1987: pC1.C3.
[FILM ADAPTATIONS OF CANADIAN LITERATURE]

COX, LARRY

Mr. Jelly Roll falls short of its goal; theatre review. photo · *TS* May 1, 1987: pD24.

COX, SUSAN

Valentine Browne launching 'world tour'; column. Robert Crew. photo · *TS* Oct 15, 1987: pE1.

LA CRÉATION DE GÉRARD BESSETTE/Critical work by Réjean Robidoux

La vitrine du livre; reviews. Guy Ferland. *MD* Nov 14, 1987: pD16.
[ANTHOLOGIES: BOOK REVIEWS]

CRAC!/Children's story by Ghislaine Paquin-Back

Un livre tendre; review of *Crac!*. Ghislaine Monoré-Johnson. *Can Child Lit* 1987; No 48: p97–98.

CRADLE PIN/Play by Audrey Butler

Some good moments in Cradle Pin despite awkward direction; theatre review. Ray Conlogue. photo · *G&M* Sept 17, 1987: pD5.

Wrestling tale grip quite easy to slip; theatre review of *Cradle Pin*. Robert Crew. photo · *TS* Sept 18, 1987: pD16.

CRAIG, DAVID S.

Italian troupe offers a touch of class; theatre review of *Together/Ensemble*. Robert Crew. *TS* May 13, 1987: pB3.
[FESTIVALS, DRAMA]

CRAIG, TERRENCE

Fiction and racial attitudes; review of *Racial Attitudes in English-Canadian Fiction, 1905–1980*. Margaret Harry. *Atlan Prov Book R* Nov-Dec 1987; Vol 14 No 4: p10.

CRANG PLAYS THE ACE/Novel by Jack Batten

Murder & mayhem: Spenser's clones; review of *Crang Plays the Ace*. Margaret Cannon. photo · *G&M* April 25, 1987: pC19.
[FIRST NOVELS: BOOK REVIEWS]

Nearly 30 years and still promising; column. Robert Fulford. *TS* May 2, 1987: M5.

Grime and punishment; review of *Crang Plays the Ace*. Douglas Malcolm. *Books in Can* April 1987; Vol 16 No 3: p35.
[FIRST NOVELS: BOOK REVIEWS]

First novels set to different literary keys; reviews of *Crang Plays the Ace* and *Gallows View*. James Mennie. photo · *MG* April 11, 1987: pG6.
[FIRST NOVELS: BOOK REVIEWS]

Mysteries to feed the mind with varying tastes; reviews of *Crang Plays the Ace* and *To an Easy Grave*. John North. photo · *Quill & Quire* March 1987; Vol 53 No 3: p74.
[FIRST NOVELS: BOOK REVIEWS]

Three absolute page-turners; reviews of *Crang Plays the Ace* and *Gallows View*. Janet Saunders. photo · *WFP* May 9, 1987: p56.
[FIRST NOVELS: BOOK REVIEWS]

Crang: super-mouth sleuth; review of *Crang Plays the Ace*. Mike Walton. *TS* April 12, 1987: pA21.
[FIRST NOVELS: BOOK REVIEWS]

THE CREATING WORD

In principio; reviews. Laurel Boone. *Can Lit* Winter 1987; No 115: p209–211.
[CONFERENCE REPORTS: REVIEWS AND ARTICLES]

[Untitled]; review of *The Creating Word*. C.A. Silber. *U of Toronto Q* Fall 1987; Vol 57 No 1: p140–142.

THE CREATIVE CIRCUS BOOK/Poetry anthology

[Untitled]; review of *The Creative Circus Book*. Ron Turner. *Quarry* Spring 1987; Vol 36 No 2: p113–116.
[ANTHOLOGIES: BOOK REVIEWS]

CREIGHTON-KELLY, CHRIS

Three new political plays; theatre reviews. Malcolm Page. *Can Drama* 1987; Vol 13 No 2: p224–226.

THE CREMATION OF SAM McGEE/Poem by Robert W. Service

Sam McGee leads the way in showing the potential of poetry; reviews of children's poetry books. Janice Kennedy. *MG* March 7, 1987: H10.

Cool tale captures mystique of North; review of *The Cremation of Sam McGee*; Maggie D. McClelland. *CH* Feb 25, 1987: pE1.

New images for old favourites; review of *The Cremation of Sam McGee*. Diane Watson. *Can Child Lit* 1987; No 48: p87–90.

CREVER L'ÉCRAN. LE CINÉMA À TRAVERS DIX NOU-VELLES/Short story anthology

Trois voyages — petit, moyen et grand — du littératage à la littérature; reviews of short story books. Marie José Thériault. photo · *Lettres québec* Spring 1987; No 45: p30–32.
[ANTHOLOGIES: BOOK REVIEWS]

CRICHTON, TOM

Flashes of gold among the dross at Fringe festival; theatre reviews. Liam Lacey. *G&M* Aug 19, 1987: pC5.
[FESTIVALS, DRAMA]

LE CRIME D'OVIDE PLOUFFE/Novel by Roger Lemelin

[Untitled]; reviews of novels. Alice Parizeau. *MD* Nov 28, 1987: pD9.

CRIME FICTION

Valeurs ludiques et valeurs fonctionelles: Le Visiteur du soir de Robert Soulières; article. Alexandre Amprimoz and Sante A. Viselli. *Can Child Lit* 1987; No 45: p6–13.
[STRUCTURALIST WRITING AND CRITICISM]

A new wave of sleuths; article. Jack Batten. photo · *Maclean's* Nov 23, 1987; Vol 100 No 47: T10-T11.

Canadian crime fiction emerges from the shadows; article. Kenneth McGoogan. illus · *CH* April 13, 1987: pF1.

"Whodunit?" Canadian society as reflected in its detective fiction; article. Robin W. Winks. bibliog · *Amer R of Can Studies* Winter 1987–88; Vol 17 No 4: p373–381.

CRIMINALS IN LOVE/L'AMOUR EN DÉROUTE/Play by George F. Walker

French version of Walker play riddled with extra problems; theatre review of *L'Amour en deroute*. Ray Conlogue. photo · *G&M* Nov 16, 1987: pD12.

Magic of popular play is lost in translation; theatre review of *L'Amour en deRoute*. Margaret Penman. *TS* Nov 16, 1987: pB6.

Blowing bubbles with Simone and Sartre; column. Vit Wagner. photo · *TS* Nov 6, 1987: pE4.
[TRANSLATIONS OF CANADIAN LITERATURE]

CROOK, MARION

[Untitled]; review of *Hidden Gold Mystery*. Peter Carver. *Quill & Quire (Books for Young People)* June 1987; Vol 53 No 6: p10.

Tales for teenagers feature strong, viable family units; reviews of *The Baby Project* and *Payment in Death*. Jane Kent. *CH* April 12, 1987: pF7.

Freeman and Crook offer adventure and mystery in serial form; reviews of *Danger on the Tracks* and *Payment in Death*. Joan McGrath. photo · *Quill & Quire (Books for Young People)* April 1987; Vol 53 No 4: p9.

How suspense dies when it is misused; reviews of young adult novels. Tim Wynne-Jones. *G&M* Aug 8, 1987: pC19.

CROSBY, HEATHER LEE

[Untitled]; reviews of poetry books. Shaunt Basmajian. *Cross Can Writ Q* 1987; Vol 9 No 3–4: p44,49.
[ANTHOLOGIES: BOOK REVIEWS]

CROZIER, LORNA

The poet's double gift; review of *The Garden Going On without Us*. Catherine Hunter. *Prairie Fire* Spring 1987; Vol 8 No 1: p78–82.

Understanding zero; review of *The Garden Going On without Us*. Frances W. Kaye. *Can Lit* Winter 1987; No 115: p138–139.

CRUSZ, RIENZI

[Untitled]; review of *A Time for Loving*. Paul Denham. *Books in Can* June-July 1987; Vol 16 No 5: p24–25.

[Untitled]; reviews of *Singing Against the Wind* and *A Time for Loving*. Francis Mansbridge. *Poetry Can R* Fall 1987; Vol 9 No 1: p30.

Crusz; review of *Singing Against the Wind*. Mathew Zachariah. *Can Lit* Spring 1987; No 112: p188–189.

CRY TO THE NIGHT WIND/Children's novel by T.H. Smith

Pacific coast adventure; review of *Cry to the Night Wind*. Dave Jenkinson. *Can Child Lit* 1987; No 47: p67–68.

CUEVAS, ERNESTO R.

Walls of prose; review of *Some Friends of Mine*. Jason Sherman. *G&M* Nov 14, 1987: pE11.

CULLETON, BEATRICE

Pemmican founder to leave; article. *WFP* Oct 30, 1987: p29.

Course helps teenagers hone writing skills; article. Dan Lett. photo · *WFP* July 22, 1987: p32.
[WRITING WORKSHOPS]

[Untitled]; reviews of *Rough Passage* and *April Raintree*. Judith Russell. *Queen's Q* Spring 1987; Vol 94 No 1: p191–193.

CULTURAL IDENTITY

Let the voters decide on deal for free trade Atwood urges; article. *TS* Nov 4, 1987: pA4.

Free-trade assurances fail to set Atwood's mind at ease; article. *CH* Nov 5, 1987: pF7.

Free trade deal won't threaten culture: Richler; article. *G&M* Nov 19, 1987: pA28.

Atwood: let's not rush into free trade; essay. Margaret Atwood. *TS* Nov 5, 1987: pA30.

On the margin: looking for a literary identity; article. Donna Bennett. illus · *Can Forum* April 1987; Vol 67 No 768: p17–25.
[FEMINIST WRITING AND CRITICISM]

The very best of company: perceptions of a Canadian attitude towards war and nationalism in three contemporary plays; article. John S. Bolin. *Amer R of Can Studies* Autumn 1987; Vol 17 No 3: p309–322.
[CANADIAN DRAMA: HISTORY AND CRITICISM]

Arts crowd feels chill: cultural community lines up against pact; article. Donald Campbell. *WFP* Dec 19, 1987: p44.
[AUTHORS, CANADIAN]

"All we North Americans": literary culture and the continentalist ideal, 1919–1939; article. Graham Carr. *Amer R of Can Studies* Summer 1987; Vol 17 No 2: p145–157.
[CANADIAN LITERATURE (20TH CENTURY): HISTORY AND CRITICISM; COLONIALISM; UNITED STATES-CANADA LITERARY RELATIONS]

How to sell free trade? Bash Ontario, Richler says; article. Martin Cohn. photo · *TS* Nov 19, 1987: pA1,A8.

"Tout ici doit être reconquis"; essay. Marcel Dubé. *MD* March 2, 1987: p11.

Taking to the woods: of myths, metaphors and poets; article. Barbara Godard. abstract · *Études can* 1987; No 23: p159–171.
[CONFEDERATION POETRY AND POETS; WILDERNESS WRITING]

Le privilège exigeant d'être Québécois; essay. Michael Goldbloom. photo · *MD* March 19, 1987: p11.

Threat or inspiration?; essay. William Johnson. photo · *MG* Nov 14, 1987: pB3.

L'autonomisation de la "littérature nationale" au XIXe siècle; article. Maurice Lemire. abstract · *Études lit* Spring-Summer 1987; Vol 20 No 1: p75–98.
[CANADIAN LITERATURE (19TH CENTURY): HISTORY AND CRITICISM; COLONIALISM; FRANCE-CANADA LITERARY RELATIONS; RELIGIOUS THEMES]

The other side of the coin; editorial. Christopher Levenson. *Arc* Spring 1987; No 18: p4–7.
[GOVERNMENT GRANTS FOR WRITERS/PUBLISHERS]

Thematic criticism, literary nationalism, and the critic's new clothes; article. T.D. MacLulich. *Essays on Can Writ* Winter 1987; No 35: p17–36.
[CANADIAN LITERARY: STUDY AND TEACHING; STRUCTURALIST WRITING AND CRITICISM]

Author calls free-trade deal a disaster; article. Linda Matchan. photo · *CH* Oct 11, 1987: pE7.

Free trade imperils identity; column. Kenneth McGoogan. *CH* Dec 13, 1987: pC9.

Writer fears free trade will kill her career; article. Linda Mitcham. photo · *WFP* Oct 9, 1987: p36.

Richler toasts any deal that puts it to Ontario; article. Juliet O'Neill. photo · *CH* Nov 19, 1987: pA18.

Grove's "Nationhood" and the European immigrant; article. Enoch Padolsky. abstract · *J of Can Studies* Spring 1987; Vol 22 No 1: p32–50.
[IMMIGRANTS IN CANADIAN LITERATURE]

The mermaid inn: permanently Canadian; essay. Al Purdy. photo · *G&M* Nov 14, 1987: pD6.

La vie littéraire; column. Jean Royer. photo · *MD* Jan 3, 1987: pC2.
[TELEVISION AND CANADIAN LITERATURE; WRITERS' ORGANIZATIONS]

Les alouettes en colère . . . ; article. Jean Royer. *MD* March 14, 1987: pD1–D2.

"Alliance-Québec fait la guerre avec les mots de la paix"; article. Jean Royer. photo · *MD* March 16, 1987: p11,14.
[WRITERS' ORGANIZATIONS]

Marco Micone propose la cohabitation; article. Jean Royer. photo · *MD* March 17, 1987: p14.

La vie littéraire; column. Jean Royer. photo · *MD* May 23, 1987: pD2.
[RADIO AND CANADIAN LITERATURE; TELEVISION AND CANADIAN LITERATURE; WRITERS' ORGANIZATIONS]

Les artistes doivent veiller au grain; essay. Serge Turgeon. *MD* March 11, 1987: p11.
[WRITERS' ORGANIZATIONS]

Fiction, break, silence: language. Sheila Watson's The Double Hook; article. Margaret E. Turner. *Ariel* April 1987; Vol 18 No 2: p65–78.

CULTURE SHOCK/Play by Chris Lorne Elliott

Culture Shock: not enough substance for two-act play; theatre review. Bill Brownstein. *MG* July 13, 1987: pB9.

CURRAN, COLLEEN

Domestic drama that hits home; article, includes theatre reviews. John Bemrose. photo · *Maclean's* Aug 17, 1987; Vol 100 No 33: p49.
[FESTIVALS, DRAMA]

Cabarets, readings, workshops have Stratford in full swing; theatre review of *Miss Balmoral of the Bayview*. Robert Crew. photo · *TS* July 19, 1987: pC2

CURRIE, ROBERT

[Untitled]; reviews of poetry books. Anne Archer. *Queen's Q* Winter 1987; Vol 94 No 4: p1042–1043.

Tellings; reviews of poetry books. Susan Rudy Dorscht. *Can Lit* Winter 1987; No 115: p257–260.

[Untitled]; reviews of poetry books. Tom Marshall. *Cross Can Writ Q* 1987; Vol 9 No 1: p24–25.

CURRY, JIM

Lost innocents; reviews of *Nothing So Natural* and *Flavian's Fortune*. Peter Hinchcliffe. *Can Lit* Spring 1987; No 112: p90–91.

CURWOOD, JAMES OLIVER

Book world: Mowat writing life of slain gorilla expert; column. Beverley Slopen. *TS* Feb 1, 1987: pB6.

THE CUTTING SEASON/Novel by Margaret Clarke

[Untitled]; reviews of *The Cutting Season* and *A Nest of Singing Birds*. John A. Urquhart. *Prairie J of Can Lit* 1987; No 8: p50–54.
[FIRST NOVELS: BOOK REVIEWS]

LE CYCLE/Novel by Gérard Bessette

Dans les poches; reviews. Guy Ferland. *MD* Sept 26, 1987: pD6.

D'AILLEURS ET D'ICI/Autobiography by Raymond Lévesque

Une vie de Patachon bien sympathique; reviews of *D'ailleurs et d'ici* and *Contes gouttes ou le pays d'un reflet*. Yolande Grisé. photo · *Lettres québec* Summer 1987; No 46: p59–60.

La vitrine du livre; reviews. Jean Royer. photo · *MD* March 21, 1987: pD2.
[CANADIAN LITERARY PERIODICALS]

D'ALFONSO, ANTONIO

Un Italien au Québec: cet autre rivage jamais atteint; column. Jean Éthier-Blais. *MD* Oct 24, 1987: pD8.

[Untitled]; review of *The Other Shore*. Corrado Federici. *Poetry Can R* Spring 1987; Vol 8 No 2–3: p45–46.

Roman heartbeat; reviews of *The Other Shore* and *Moving Landscape*. Louise McKinney. *Can Lit* Winter 1987; No 115: p232–234.

[Untitled]; review of *The Other Shore*. Steve Noyes. *Rubicon* Spring 1987; No 8: p219.

Antonio d'Alfonso ou "l'érotisme des mots"; review of *L'Autre rivage*. Jean Royer. photo · *MD* June 20, 1987: pD2.

[Untitled]; reviews. Janet Windeler. *Cross Can Writ Q* 1987; Vol 9 No 2: p25–26.
[FIRST NOVELS: BOOK REVIEWS]

D'AMOUR, FRANCINE

First novel wins award; article. *G&M* Nov 9, 1987: pD11.
[AWARDS, LITERARY]

Une famille dévorée par l'ennui et le néant de vie inutiles; review of *Les Dimanches sont mortels*. Jean Éthier-Blais. *MD* Nov 21, 1987: pD12.
[FIRST NOVELS: BOOK REVIEWS]

Francine d'Amour, prix Guérin; article. Angèle Dagenais. photo · *MD* Nov 5, 1987: p13.
[AWARDS, LITERARY]

Francine d'Amour ou le plaisir d'écrire à l'état pur; article. France Lafuste. photo · *MD* Dec 5, 1987: pD1.

D'ASTOUS, CLAUDE

Entre la réussite et l'échec; reviews of science fiction books. Michel Lord. photo · *Lettres québec* Autumn 1987; No 47: p33–34.
[ANTHOLOGIES: BOOK REVIEWS; FIRST NOVELS: BOOK REVIEWS]

LE DÉSERT MAINTENANT/Poems by Yves Préfontaine

Désert, attente, silence; reviews of poetry books. Robert Yergeau. photo · *Lettres québec* Autumn 1987; No 47: p44–45.

LE DÉSERT MAUVE/Novel by Nicole Brossard

La vitrine du livre; reviews. Guy Ferland. *MD* Nov 21, 1987: pD4.

LA DÉTRESSE ET L'ENCHANTEMENT/ENCHANTMENT AND SORROW/Autobiography by Gabrielle Roy

Gabrielle Roy travelled from an impoverished household in Manitoba . . . ; review of *Enchantment and Sorrow*. Marianne Ackerman. illus · *MG* Nov 28, 1987: J9.

A lesson in how to look at life and virtues of love and courage; review of *Enchantment and Sorrow*. Ken Adachi. photo · *TS* Nov 14, 1987: M4.

Gabrielle Roy: a compelling glimpse of an enchanting life; review of *Enchantment and Sorrow*. Ruby Andrew. photo · *Quill & Quire* Dec 1987; Vol 53 No 12: p23.

Roy's candid memoirs recall joy and sorrow; review of *Enchantment and Sorrow*. Audrey Andrews. photo · *CH* Dec 20, 1987: pE6.

[Untitled]; review of *La Détresse et l'enchantement*. Jean-V. Dufresne. *MD* Nov 28, 1987: pD8.

Echoes of a tin flute; review of *Enchantment and Sorrow*. Anne Holloway. *Maclean's* Nov 23, 1987; Vol 100 No 47: p54d, 54f

Entering infinity; review of *Enchantment and Sorrow*. I.M. Owen. *Books in Can* Dec 1987; Vol 16 No 9: p17–18.

The tribulations of an author; review of *Enchantment and Sorrow*. Tom Saunders. photo · *WFP* Dec 19, 1987: p51

Book world: a tip of the hat to small presses; column. Beverley Slopen. photo · *TS* Aug 9, 1987: pA20.
[CANADIAN LITERARY PUBLISHING]

Living inspirations; review of *Enchantment and Sorrow*. Ronald Sutherland. photo · *G&M* Dec 26, 1987: pC23.

DA SILVA, JOEL

Du théâtre comme dans un moulin; article. Angèle Dagenais. photo · *MD* Nov 11, 1987: p11.

Music, theatre union needs fine tuning; theatre reviews of *Le Dernier quatuor d'un homme sourd* and *La Goutte*. Pat Donnelly. *MG* Nov 18, 1987: pD3.

DAHLIE, HALLVARD

[Untitled]; reviews of *Varieties of Exile* and *Prairie Women*. Peter Buitenhuis. *Queen's Q* Summer 1987; Vol 94 No 2: p467–470.

Languages of exile; review of *Varieties of Exile*. David Dowling. *Can Lit* Winter 1987; No 115: p216–218.

[Untitled]; review of *Varieties of Exile*. August J. Fry. *British J of Can Studies* June 1987; Vol 2 No 1: p180–181.

[Untitled]; review of *Varieties of Exile*. D.B. Jewison. *U of Toronto Q* Fall 1987; Vol 57 No 1: p151–154.

Literary 'exiles' came to Canada from choice, not need; review of *Varieties of Exile*. Marion McCormick. *MG* Jan 3, 1987: pB8.

[Untitled]; review of *Varieties of Exile*. Barry Thorne. *Eng Studies in Can* Dec 1987; Vol 13 No 4: p480–483.

DAIGLE, JEAN

Theatre encore; reviews of *L'Ours et le kangourou* and *Au septième ciel*. Carrol F. Coates. *Can Lit* Winter 1987; No 115: p255–257.

THE DAILY NEWS/Play by Rising Tide Theatre collective

Collective concern; theatre reviews of *The Daily News* and *The Fishwharf and Steamboat Men*. Terry Goldie. photo · *Can Theatre R* Spring 1987; No 50: p81–83.

DALES, KIM

Freud, Dora and Ibsen; theatre review of *Dora: A Case of Hysteria*. Mary Blackstone. photo · *NeWest R* Summer 1987; Vol 12 No 10: p17.

DALLAIRE, MICHEL

Cycles; reviews of *L'Oeil interrompu* and *Poison*. Mark Benson. *Can Lit* Spring 1987; No 112: p136–138.

DALP, JEAN-MARC

Théâtre au masculin; reviews of plays. Jane Moss. *Can Lit* Spring 1987; No 112: p180–183.

DAMAGED GOODS/Novel by Bonnie R. Wurst

Montreal needle trade is setting for comic tale about working girl; review of *Damaged Goods*, includes profile. Barbara Black. photo · *MG* July 18, 1987: J9.
[FIRST NOVELS: BOOK REVIEWS]

DANCE OF THE PARTICLES/Poems by Tom Marshall

Getting physical; reviews of *Dance of the Particles* and *Playing with Fire*. Paul Denham. *Essays on Can Writ* Spring 1987; No 34: P44–47.

DANCE WITH DESIRE/Poems by Irving Layton

[Untitled]; letter to the editor. Anne Cimon. *Books in Can* Jan-Feb 1987; Vol 16 No 1: p38.

[Untitled]; review of *Dance with Desire*. Harold Heft. *Rubicon* Spring 1987; No 8: p184–185.

[Untitled]; review of *Dance with Desire*. Liane Heller. *Cross Can Writ Q* 1987; Vol 9 No 1: p22–23.

O dear!; letter to the editor. Marion Johnson. *Books in Can* Jan-Feb 1987; Vol 16 No 1: p38.

THE DANCING CHICKEN/Novel by Susan Musgrave

Dancing Chicken more of a turkey, reviewer finds; review. Ken Adachi. *TS* Nov 8, 1987: pA19.

Marriage and violence Western-Canadian style; reviews of *Getting Married in Buffalo Jump* and *The Dancing Chicken*. William French. photo · *G&M* Nov 19, 1987: pA25.

Musgrave makes it with love, sex, death; review of *The Dancing Chicken*. Janet Hamilton. photo · *Quill & Quire* Oct 1987; Vol 53 No 10: p22.

An unsuccessful satire; review of *The Dancing Chicken*. Joan Thomas. *WFP* Nov 28, 1987: p58.

Different strokes; review of *The Dancing Chicken*. Eleanor Wachtel. *Books in Can* Dec 1987; Vol 16 No 9: p19–20.

DANCING IN THE DARK/Novel by Joan Barfoot

[Untitled]; review of *Dancing in the Dark*. Maryann Ayim. *Atlantis* Fall 1987; Vol 13 No 1: p189–191.

Dancing In The Dark: what happens when a homemaker cracks; film review. Bruce Bailey. photo · *MG* Jan 17, 1987: pD4.
[FILM ADAPTATIONS OF CANADIAN LITERATURE]

Burgess touch refreshes yet another Roman tale; reviews of *Dancing in the Dark* and *John and the Missus*. Barbara Black. *MG* April 11, 1987: pG7.

Get new year off to good start with Dancing In The Dark; film review. Paul McKie. photo · *WFP* Jan 4, 1987: p14.
[FILM ADAPTATIONS OF CANADIAN LITERATURE]

DANCING ON THE SHORE: A CELEBRATION OF LIFE AT ANNAPOLIS BASIN/Prose by Harold Horwood

A reminder 'of the covenant that binds man to moth and star'; review of *Dancing on the Shore*. William French. *G&M* Sept 17, 1987: pD1.

God's little acreage; review of *Dancing on the Shore*. Janice Kulyk Keefer. *Books in Can* Dec 1987; Vol 16 No 9: p23–24

[Untitled]; review of *Dancing on the Shore*. Norman Sigurdson. *Quill & Quire* Sept 1987; Vol 53 No 9: p80.

Universe probed from the shore; review of *Dancing on the Shore*. Penny Williams. *CH* Oct 18, 1987: pC7.

DANCING VISIONS/Poetry anthology

[Untitled]; review of *Dancing Visions*. Allan Markin. *Poetry Can R* Spring 1987; Vol 8 No 2–3: p60.
[ANTHOLOGIES: BOOK REVIEWS]

DANDELION/Periodical

Literary giants got rotten reviews; column. Kenneth McGoogan. *CH* Jan 18, 1987: pE4.
[CANADIAN LITERARY PERIODICALS; POETRY READINGS]

Dandelion uncovers new voice; column. Kenneth McGoogan. photo · *CH* Feb 1, 1987: pC8.
[AWARDS, LITERARY; CANADIAN LITERARY PERIODICALS; POETRY READINGS]

Poets help celebrate Dandelion; column. Kenneth McGoogan. *CH* June 28, 1987: pF8.
[AWARDS, LITERARY; CANADIAN LITERARY PERIODICALS; POETRY READINGS; WRITERS' ORGANIZATIONS]

DANDURAND, ANNE

La vitrine du livre; reviews of fictional works. Guy Ferland. *MD* Dec 5, 1987: pD4.

DANGER ON THE RIVER/Young adult novel by J. Robert Janes

How I spent my summer mystery; reviews of young adult novels by J. Robert Janes. James Gellert. *Can Child Lit* 1987; No 48: p93–95.

DANGER ON THE TRACKS/Children's novel by Bill Freeman

School's out, and books are in; reviews of children's books. Janice Kennedy. *MG* July 4, 1987: J9.

Freeman and Crook offer adventure and mystery in serial form; reviews of *Danger on the Tracks* and *Payment in Death*. Joan McGrath. photo · *Quill & Quire (Books for Young People)* April 1987; Vol 53 No 4: p9.

A little help on the dull days; reviews of children's books. Joan McGrath. *TS* Aug 2, 1987: pC11.

Living in the past; reviews of children's novels. Mary Ainslie Smith. *Books in Can* June-July 1987; Vol 16 No 5: p35–37.

DANIEL, LORNE

Western Canadian poets display talents in new volume; reviews of poetry books. G.P. Greenwood. *CH* July 5, 1987: pF7.

[Untitled]; reviews of poetry books. Anita Hurwitz. *Poetry Can R* Spring 1987; Vol 8 No 2–3: p38–39.

DANS L'APRÈS-MIDI CARDIAQUE/Poems by Patrice Desbiens

Maniaques depressifs; reviews of poetry books. Mark Benson. *Can Lit* Spring 1987; No 112: p138–141.

DANS L'ATTENTE D'UNE AUBE/Poems by Jean Chapdelaine Gagnon

Jean Chapdelaine Gagnon: dans l'apprentissage des langues; review of *Dans l'attente d'une aube*. Gérald Gaudet. *MD* Oct 3, 1987: pD3.

Désert, attente, silence; reviews of poetry books. Robert Yergeau. photo · *Lettres québec* Autumn 1987; No 47: p44–45.

DANS LA DISTANCE DES LIENS/Poems by Côme Lachapelle

Désert, attente, silence; reviews of poetry books. Robert Yergeau. photo · *Lettres québec* Autumn 1987; No 47: p44–45.

DANS LA TERRE PROMISE/Novel by Jean Fron and Jules Lamy

De l'ouest, des nouvelles et de l'histoire; reviews of short story books. Paulette Collet. photo · *Lettres québec* Summer 1987; No 46: p68–70.
[ANTHOLOGIES: BOOK REVIEWS]

DANS MON PETIT VIOLON, COMPTINES ET FANTAISIES/Children's poems by Simone Bussieres

Échos des rêveries enfantines; review of *Dans mon petit violon*. Line Paré. *Can Child Lit* 1987; No 46: p101–102.

LA DANSE DE L'AMANTE/Novel by Madeleine Ouellette-Michalska

La vitrine du livre; reviews. Guy Ferland. *MD* May 2, 1987: pD4.

DANZIGER, PAULA

Uncertain futures; review of *This Place Has No Atmosphere*. Anthony Horowitz. *Times Lit Supp* Oct 30, 1987; No 4413: p1205.

DAOUST, JEAN-PAUL

À surveiller; column. *MD* Nov 10, 1987: p12.

DAOUST, NORMAND

Le théâtre qu'on joue; theatre reviews. André Dionne. photo · *Lettres québec* Winter 1986–87; No 44: p53–54.

[Untitled]; theatre review of *Le Petit univers de R.P.*. Claude Poissant. photo · *Jeu* 1987; No 42: p148–149.

DARGIS, DANIEL

[Untitled]; review of *Astrales jachères*. Hugues Corriveau. *Estuaire* Summer 1987; No 45: p51–52.

THE DARING GAME/Young adult novel by Kit Pearson

Apple-pie beds and water bombs; review of *The Daring Game*. Lorraine M. York. *Can Child Lit* 1987; No 46: p79–81

DARK GALAXIES/Poems by Susan McMaster

[Untitled]; reviews of poetry books. Shaunt Basmajian. *Cross Can Writ Q* 1987; Vol 9 No 2: p22.

[Untitled]; review of *Dark Galaxies*. Anne Burke. *Poetry Can R* Spring 1987; Vol 8 No 2–3: p51.

Poetry's eye; review of *Dark Galaxies*. Margaret Dyment. *Arc* Spring 1987; No 18: p18–22.

Seasons, time and memory; reviews of poetry books. Lesley McAllister. *TS* March 21, 1987: M5.

A DARKER MAGIC/Children's novel by Michael Bedard

Fiction just loaded with personality; reviews of children's novels. Tim Wynne-Jones. photo · *G&M* Nov 28, 1987: pC22.
[FIRST NOVELS: BOOK REVIEWS]

THE DARKEST ROAD/Novel by Guy Gavriel Kay

[Untitled]; review of *The Darkest Road*. Douglas Barbour. *Malahat R* June 1987; No 79: p160–161.

Voyages of the mind; article, includes review of *The Darkest Road*. Peter Giffen. photo · *Maclean's* March 23, 1987; Vol 100 No 12: p66–67.
[FANTASY; SCIENCE FICTION]

Tapestry times three; review of *The Darkest Road*. P. Scott Lawrence. photo · *MG* March 7, 1987: H11.

[Untitled]; review of *The Darkest Road*. Alberto Manguel. *Tor Life* March 1987; Vol 21 No 4: p93,95.

'Brightly woven' the right words; review of *The Darkest Road*. Henry Mietkiewicz. *TS* April 5, 1987: pA22.

Flaws mar a major fantasy; review of *The Darkest Road*. Tom Oleson. photo · *WFP* June 13, 1987: p58.

DARKNESS ON THE EDGE OF TOWN/Play by Eugene Stickland

Darkness casts a powerful spell; theatre review of *Darkness on the Edge of Town*. H.J. Kirchhoff. photo · *G&M* May 15, 1987: pD8.

Disciplined acting shines in play etched in despair; theatre review of *Darkness on the Edge of Town*. Henry Mietkiewicz. *TS* May 12, 1987: pF4.

Prairie spaces in the big city: western theatre in Toronto; theatre reviews. Margaret Gail Osachoff. *NeWest R* Oct 1987; Vol 13 No 2: p18–19.

DAVELUY, PAULE

Anne Hébert, Wilfrid Lemoyne, Ginette Anfousse reoivent les premiers prix Fleury-Mesplet; article. Paul Cauchon. photo · *MD* Nov 20, 1987: p13–14.
[AWARDS, LITERARY]

DAVEY, FRANK

B.C. international — in search of new subjects and forms; reviews. Gillian Harding-Russell. *Event* Summer 1987; Vol 16 No 2: p125–127.

Parlour pump organs and prairie cafes; reviews of *Waiting for Saskatchewan* and *The Louis Riel Organ & Piano Company*. Phillip Lanthier. *NeWest R* April 1987; Vol 12 No 8: p13,15.

An Atwood anatomy; review of *Margaret Atwood: A Feminist Poetics*. Jerome H. Rosenberg. *Essays on Can Writ* Winter 1987; No 35: p88–92.

[Untitled]; reviews of poetry books. Stephen Scobie. *Malahat R* Dec 1987; No 81: p104–106.

[Untitled]; reviews of *The Louis Riel Organ & Piano Co.* and *The North Book*. John F. Vardon. *Poetry Can R* Spring 1987; Vol 8 No 2–3: p47.

Oranges and onions; reviews of *White of the Lesser Angels* and *The Abbotsford Guide to India*. Fred Wah. *Books in Can* March 1987; Vol 16 No 2: p32,34.

"Citizens-in-language"; reviews of *The Louis Riel Organ & Piano Co.* and *Waiting for Saskatchewan*. Lorraine York. *Essays on Can Writ* Winter 1987; No 35: p171–177.

DAVIAU, DIANE-MONIQUE

Les lectures Skol: pour les dix ans de l'Union des écrivains; article. *MD* Oct 10, 1987: pD8.
[FICTION READINGS; WRITERS' ORGANIZATIONS]

La vie littéraire; column. Jean Royer. photo · *MD* Oct 17, 1987: pD2.
[CANADIAN LITERARY PERIODICALS; COMPETITIONS, LITERARY; CONFERENCES, LITERARY; FICTION READINGS; WRITERS' ORGANIZATIONS]

DAVID, CAROLE

Montreal women split poetry prize; article. *MG* March 10, 1987: pD9.
[AWARDS, LITERARY]

Prix et distinctions; list of award winners. photo · *Lettres québec* Summer 1987; No 46: p7.
[AWARDS, LITERARY]

[Untitled]; review of *Terroristes d'amour*. Jean-Paul Dst. *Estuaire* Spring 1987; No 44: p80.

Carole David et France Mongeau lauréates du prix Nelligan 1986; article. Jean Royer. photo · *MD* March 10, 1987: p11.
[AWARDS, LITERARY]

[Untitled]; review of *Terroristes d'amour*. Jean Royer. *MD* March 13, 1987: p15.

La vie littéraire; column. Jean Royer. photo · *MD* March 14, 1987: pD4.
[AWARDS, LITERARY; POETRY READINGS; RADIO AND CANADIAN LITERATURE; TELEVISION AND CANADIAN LITERATURE]

DAVIES, ROBERTSON

Robertson Davies wins medal of honor; article. *G&M* Feb 11, 1987: pC7

New York arts club to honor Robertson Davies; article. *TS* Feb 11, 1987: pF1.
[AWARDS, LITERARY]

New York arts club lauds genius of Davies; article. *TS* Feb 26, 1987: pB3.
[AWARDS, LITERARY]

Davies joins illustrious literary company; article. *WFP* Feb 25, 1987: p36.
[AWARDS, LITERARY]

Davies suggests boring contest; column. photo · *WFP* March 7, 1987: p37.

Davies honored; article. *CH* Feb 26, 1987: pF11.
[AWARDS, LITERARY]

Novel slated for TV; article. *WFP* April 9, 1987: p45.
[TELEVISION AND CANADIAN LITERATURE]

Robertson Davies novel to become TV mini-series; article. *CH* April 9, 1987: pE2.
[TELEVISION AND CANADIAN LITERATURE]

National Arts Club honours Davies; article. *Quill & Quire* April 1987; Vol 53 No 4: p20.
[AWARDS, LITERARY]

Davies' hit novel to be TV mini-series; article. photo · *TS* April 8, 1987: pD1.
[TELEVISION AND CANADIAN LITERATURE]

[Untitled]; review of *Robertson Davies, Playwright*. Diane Bessai. *Ariel* April 1987; Vol 18 No 2: p101–104.

Nobel sentiments; article. Anthony Burgess. illus · *Sat Night* Dec 1987; Vol 102 No 12: p15–16.

People; column. Yvonne Cox. photo · *Maclean's* Feb 2, 1987; Vol 100 No 5: p32.
[AWARDS, LITERARY]

Mini-series bred from Davies' novel; article. John Haslett Cuff. photo · *G&M* April 8, 1987: pC7.
[TELEVISION AND CANADIAN LITERATURE]

Early espièglerie; review of *The Papers of Samuel Marchbanks*. Richard Deveson. *Times Lit Supp* Oct 16, 1987; No 4411: p1137.

Musical morality tales with a touch of magic; article. Robert Everett-Green. *G&M* May 12, 1987: pC10.
[FICTION READINGS]

[Untitled]; review of *Robertson Davies*. John H. Ferres. *Amer R of Can Studies* Winter 1987–88; Vol 17 No 4: p450–452.

[Untitled]; review of *Robertson Davies, Playwright*. S.F. Gallagher. *Eng Studies in Can* June 1987; Vol 13 No 2: p234–237.

Rob had presence as student in the '20s; biographical article. George Gamester. *TS* Oct 15, 1987: pA2.

Thanks to Robertson Davies; article. Lew Gloin. *TS* May 10, 1987: pA22.

Robertson Davies' dialogic imagination; article. Barbara Godard. *Essays on Can Writ* Spring 1987; No 34: p64–80.
[CARNIVALIZATION; STRUCTURALIST WRITING AND CRITICISM]

N.Y. honor for Robertson Davies; article. Heather Hill. *MG* Feb 11, 1987: pB5.
[AWARDS, LITERARY]

[Untitled]; letter to the editor. Bruce D. Holt. *G&M* April 22, 1987: pA7.

Magpie mind; review of *The Papers of Samuel Marchbanks*. Nicholas Hudson. *Can Lit* Spring 1987; No 112: p88–90.

[Untitled]; review of *What's Bred in the Bone*. Margaret Keith. *Northward J* 1987; No 43: p43–46.

Davies conjures a musical ghost for children; article about *The Harper of the Stones*. William Littler. photo · *TS* May 9, 1987: J12.
[FICTION READINGS]

Applebaum spooks score for Davies' ghost story; review of *The Harper of the Stones*. William Littler. *TS* May 12, 1987: pF4.

Dialectic, morality, and the Deptford trilogy; article. Marco P. LoVerso. *Studies in Can Lit* 1987; Vol 12 No 1: p69–89.

Northern magus; letter to the editor. Ellen Bick Meier. *Books in Can* June-July 1987; Vol 16 No 5: p40.

Robertson Davies shows he's a sexist; letter to the editor. Hope Morritt. *TS* Oct 15, 1987: pA24.

The Rebel Angels: Robertson Davies and the novel of ideas; article. James Mulvihill. *Eng Studies in Can* June 1987; Vol 13 No 2: p182–194.

Bad form in the grammar war; letter to the editor. Thomas M. Paikeday. *G&M* April 22, 1987: pA7.

[Untitled]; review of *Robertson Davies, Playwright*. Michael Peterman. *Theatre Hist in Can* Fall 1987; Vol 8 No 2: p249–252.

A master's sharp eye; interview with Robertson Davies. Eva Seidner. photo · *Maclean's* Oct 19, 1987; Vol 100 No 42: p8–9,12.

Words from Everyman; letter to the editor. Fraser Simpson. *G&M* May 2, 1987: pD7.

Book world: McClelland moves to quash 'secret' biography; column. Beverley Slopen. photo · *TS* Feb 12, 1987: pF1.
[PUBLISHING AND PUBLISHERS IN CANADA]

[Untitled]; reviews of *Robertson Davies* and *Robertson Davies, Playwright*. D.O. Spettigue. *Queen's Q* Autumn 1987; Vol 94 No 3: p722–724.

Robertson Davies honored by U.S. arts club; article. Calvin Woodward. photo · *G&M* Feb 26, 1987: pC5.
[AWARDS, LITERARY]

Veterans give proteges a $5,000 career boost; article. Reta Zekas. photo · *TS* May 7, 1987: pD1.
[AWARDS, LITERARY]

A DAY AT THE BEACH/Play by John Palmer

Palmer play shows surprising sweetness; theatre review of *A Day at the Beach*. Ray Conlogue. photo · *G&M* Dec 12, 1987: pC8.

A Day at the Beach still has a way to go; theatre review. Robert Crew. *TS* Dec 7, 1987: pC4.

DAY, DAVID

Crimes of the heart; reviews of *Gothic* and *The Animals Within*. Al Purdy. *Books in Can* April 1987; Vol 16 No 3: p32,34.

Poetry of love at its purest; reviews of poetry books. Paul Roberts. *TS* Aug 15, 1987: M10.

West coast report: David Day; regional column. Linda Rogers. *Poetry Can R* Summer 1987; Vol 8 No 4: p23.

The language of fantasy; reviews of *The Emperor's Panda* and *Amanda Greenleaf Visits a Distant Star*. Jo-Ann Wallace. *Can Child Lit* 1987; No 47: p73–74.

DAY, SHIRLEY

[Untitled]; review of *Monica's Mother Said No!*. Adele Ashby. *Quill & Quire (Books for Young People)* Dec 1987; Vol 53 No 12: p9.

Mini-reviews; reviews of children's stories. Mary Rubio. *Can Child Lit* 1987; No 47: p96–99.

DE BARROS, PAUL

Today's assignment: short fiction that's worth a long look; reviews of short story books. Douglas Hill. *G&M* March 14, 1987: pE19.
[ANTHOLOGIES: BOOK REVIEWS]

[Untitled]; review of *Big Plans*. Joel Yanofsky. *Books in Can* Aug-Sept 1987; Vol 16 No 6: p25.

DE BELLEFEUILLE, NORMAND

Le récit à la NBJ; review of *La Nouvelle barre du jour*. Caroline Bayard. *Lettres québec* Summer 1987; No 46: p34–35.

[Untitled]; reviews of *Lascaux* and *Catégoriques un deux trois*. Richard Boutin. *Estuaire* Summer 1987; No 45: p52–54.

La vitrine du livre; reviews of *À double sens* and *Le Fils d'Ariane*. Guy Ferland. *MD* Feb 14, 1987: pC2.

La vitrine du livre; reviews of *Hommes* and *Heureusement, ici il y a la guerre*. Guy Ferland. *MD* Oct 17, 1987: pD4.

De Bellefeuille, Nepveu, Lemaire, Royer; reviews of poetry books. Jean-Pierre Issenhuth. *Liberté* Aug 1987; Vol 29 No 4: p78–87.

La répétition de l'intime; reviews of poetry books. André Marquis. photo · *Lettres québec* Spring 1987; No 45: p44–46.

Qui a peur de l'intellectuel in 1987?; reviews. Pierre Milot. *Voix et images* Spring 1987; Vol 12 No 3: p530–534.
[CANADIAN LITERARY PERIODICALS]

Deux récits de l'intelligence et du coeur; reviews of *Chambres* and *Catégoriques un deux et trois*. Jean Royer. *MD* Jan 3, 1987: pC4.

Le sentiment de la langue; reviews of *"Quand on a une langue on peut aller à Rome"* and *Les Changeurs de signes*. Jean Royer. *MD* Feb 28, 1987: pC3.
[CANADIAN LITERARY PERIODICALS]

La vie littéraire; column. Jean Royer. photo · *MD* May 16, 1987: pD2.
[AWARDS, LITERARY; CONFERENCES, LITERARY; PUBLISHING AND PUBLISHERS IN CANADA; RADIO AND CANADIAN LITERATURE; TELEVISION AND CANADIAN LITERATURE]

La modernité québécoise "pure laine"; review of *À double sens*. Lori Saint-Martin. *MD* May 9, 1987: pD3.

Impasses ou issues? L'imaginaire masculin face à la femme; reviews of *Les Silences du corbeau* and *À double sens*. Patricia Smart. *Voix et images* Spring 1987; Vol 12 No 3: p555–560.

La modernité: des formes qui (s')inquiètent; reviews of critical works. Agnès Whitfield. photo · *Lettres québec* Summer 1987; No 46: p56–58.

DE BUSSIÈRES, ARTHUR

[Untitled]; review of *Arthur de Bussières, poète, et l'École littéraire de Montréal*. David M. Hayne. *U of Toronto Q* Fall 1987; Vol 57 No 1: p178–179.

DE CE NOM DE L'AMOUR/Poems by Danielle Fournier and Louise Coiteux

Forcément de l'amour; reviews of *Forcément dans la tête* and *De ce nom de l'amour*. Deloris Williams. *Can Lit* Summer-Fall 1987; No 113–114: p233–235.

DE GASPÉ, PHILIPPE-AUBERT

Tout texte fondateur en cache un autre!; reviews of *Les Révélations du crime* and *L'Influence d'un livre*. Patrick Imbert. *Lettres québec* Autumn 1987; No 47: p58–60.

La vie littéraire; column. Marc Morin. *MD* Dec 12, 1987: pD2.
[GOVERNOR GENERAL'S AWARDS; POETRY READINGS]

Les 150 ans du premier roman québécois; article. André Thibault. illus · *MD* Sept 12, 1987: pD3, D8.

DE GONZAGUE PELLETIER, LOUISE

Louise de Gonzague Pelletier à Place aux poètes; article. *MD* Dec 2, 1987: p14.
[AWARDS, LITERARY; POETRY READINGS]

DE GOUMOIS, MAURICE

La forêt dans le roman "ontarois"; article. Yolande Grisé. abstract · *Études can* 1987; No 23: p109–122.
[MYTHS AND LEGENDS IN CANADIAN LITERATURE; NATURE IN CANADIAN LITERATURE]

DE GROSBOIS, PAUL

Un beau roman historique; review of *Les Initiés de la Pointe-aux-Cageux.* Dennis Essar. *Can Child Lit* 1987; No 48: p98–100.

DE HARTOG, JAN

Comedy enjoyable despite bad acoustics, set changes; theatre review of *The Fourposter.* Alex Law. *TS (Neighbours)* March 10, 1987: p14.

DE L'AMOUR DANS LA FERRAILLE/HEARTBREAKS ALONG THE ROAD/Novel by Roch Carrier

Heartbreak road; review article about *Heartbreaks Along the Road.* Mark Abley. illus · *Sat Night* Oct 1987; Vol 102 No 10: p59–62.

Quebec native son sums up his feelings on la belle province; review of *Heartbreaks Along the Road.* Ken Adachi. photo · *TS* Oct 24, 1987: M4.

The road to evil; review of *Heartbreaks Along the Road.* William French. *G&M* Oct 17, 1987: pE3.

These roads lead to Roch; review of *Heartbreaks Along the Road.* P. Scott Lawrence. photo · *MG* Dec 19, 1987: J12.

Dead end; review of *Heartbreaks Along the Road.* Brent Ledger. *Books in Can* Dec 1987; Vol 16 No 9: p21–22.

Village of the damned; review of *Heartbreaks Along the Road.* Richard Teleky. photo · *Maclean's* Nov 2, 1987; Vol 100 No 44: p52f

DE LA ROCHE, MAZO

The fairy-tale elements in the early work of Mazo de la Roche; article. Heather Kirk. *Wascana R* Spring 1987; Vol 22 No 1: p3–17.
[FAIRY TALES]

DE LAMIRANDE, CLAIRE

Aujourd'hui; column. *MD* Feb 10, 1987: p10.
[ETHNIC-CANADIAN WRITING; WRITERS' WORKSHOPS]

DE MILLE, JAMES

James de Mille's strange manuscript; review of *A Strange Manuscript Found in a Copper Cylinder.* Janice Kulyk Keefer. *Atlan Prov Book R* May–June 1987; Vol 14 No 2: p12.

The restoration of CanLit; article, includes review. Marion McCormick. photo · *MG* March 7, 1987: H10.
[CANADIAN LITERARY PUBLISHING; CANADIAN LITERATURE: BIBLIOGRAPHY]

Copper-plating a strange fantasy; review of *A Strange Manuscript Found in a Copper Cylinder.* Paul Roberts. *TS* July 4, 1987: M10.

DE ROBERVAL/Play by Hunter Duvar

"O brave new world": colonialism in Hunter Duvar's De Roberval; article. Mark Blagrave. *Can Drama* 1987; Vol 13 No 2: p175–181.
[COLONIALISM; NATIVE CANADIANS IN LITERATURE]

DÉ, CLAIRE

Vivre de sa plume au Québec: une entrevue avec Claire Dé; interview. photo · *Lettres québec* Summer 1987; No 46: p13–14.

La vie littéraire; column. Jean Royer. photo · *MD* May 30, 1987: pD2.
[AWARDS, LITERARY; CANADIAN LITERARY PUBLISHING; COMPETITIONS, LITERARY; FESTIVALS, LITERARY; RADIO AND CANADIAN LITERATURE; TELEVISION AND CANADIAN LITERATURE]

DEAF TO THE CITY

See LE SOURD DANS LA VILLE/DEAF TO THE CITY/Novel by Anne Hébert

DEAHL, JAMES

[Untitled]; reviews of *The Uncollected Acorn* and *A Stand of Jackpine.* David Leahy. *Rubicon* Fall 1987; No 9: p167–168.

DEAR BRUCE SPRINGSTEEN/Young adult novel by Kevin Major

Major's realistic epistles to Springsteen; review of *Dear Bruce Springsteen.* Peter Carver. photo · *Quill & Quire (Books for Young People)* Aug 1987; Vol 53 No 8: p4.

Dear Bruce Springsteen one author's fan letter; article. Rosie DiManno. *TS* Oct 2, 1987: pE23.

Baby of the family gets respect raising flock of Canada geese; reviews of children's books. Janice Kennedy. *MG* Oct 3, 1987: J13.

Novels deal with family breakup; reviews of *The Doll* and *Dear Bruce Springsteen.* Helen Norrie. *WFP* Dec 5, 1987: p57.

Fiction just loaded with personality; reviews of children's novels. Tim Wynne-Jones. photo · *G&M* Nov 28, 1987: pC22.
[FIRST NOVELS: BOOK REVIEWS]

DEAR DR. CANTEEN/Poems by Greg Evason

[Untitled]; reviews of poetry books. Shaunt Basmajian. *Cross Can Writ Q* 1987; Vol 9 No 3–4: p44, 49.
[ANTHOLOGIES: BOOK REVIEWS]

DEATH IS AN ANXIOUS MOTHER/Poems by Anne Campbell

[Untitled]; reviews of *Through the Nan Da Gate* and *Death Is an Anxious Mother.* Nancy Batty. *Dandelion* Spring-Summer 1987; Vol 14 No 1: p84–87

Still lifes; reviews of poetry books. Laurence Hutchman. *Can Lit* Winter 1987; No 115: p263–264.

[Untitled]; reviews of poetry books. Sheila Martindale. *Cross Can Writ Q* 1987; Vol 9 No 2: p20–21.

DEATH RIDE/Young adult novel by Paul Kropp

Lite-lit for children has arrived; reviews of children's books. Tim Wynne-Jones. *G&M* March 7, 1987: pE19.

DECTER, ANN

[Untitled]; reviews of *Katie's Alligator Goes to Daycare* and *Tom Doesn't Visit Us Any More*. Adele Ashby. *Quill & Quire (Books for Young People)* Dec 1987; Vol 53 No 12: p8–9.

THE DEEP END/Novel by Joy Fielding

Past formula; review of *The Deep End*. Margaret Jensen. *Can Lit* Winter 1987; No 115: p176–178.

DEEP NORTH/Poems by Bert Almon

Something in common; reviews of poetry books. Cary Fagan. *Prairie Fire* Spring 1987; Vol 8 No 1: p83–87.

[Untitled]; review of *Deep North*. Sparling Mills. *Poetry Can R* Spring 1987; Vol 8 No 2–3: p59–60.

Quilted patch; reviews of poetry books. Uma Parameswaran and Teresa Mallam. *Can Lit* Spring 1987; No 112: p176–179.

THE DEEPENING OF THE COLOURS/Poems by Gail Fox

[Untitled]; review of *The Deepening of the Colours*. Mary di Michele. *Books in Can* May 1987; Vol 16 No 4: p23.

[Untitled]; reviews of *Stoning the Moon* and *The Deepening of the Colours*. Susan Huntley Elderkin. *Quarry* Summer 1987; Vol 36 No 3: p76–79.

Painful scrutiny of relationships; reviews of poetry books. Patricia Keeney Smith. *TS* May 30, 1987: M9.

DELAHAYE, GUY

Guy Delahaye, un gamin mélancolique, sourire aux lèvres; column. Jean Éthier-Blais. *MD* Sept 12, 1987: pD8.

La vitrine du livre; review of *Guy Delahaye et la modernité littéraire*. Guy Ferland. *MD* July 25, 1987: pC6.

Le "médecin de Nelligan"; review of *Guy Delahaye et la modernité littéraire*. Marcel Fournier. *MD* Aug 29, 1987: pC14.

DELAYED MERCY AND OTHER POEMS/Poems by George Bowering

[Untitled]; review of *Delayed Mercy*. Mary di Michele. *Books in Can* June-July 1987; Vol 16 No 5: p23–24.

Three poets dare to reject labelling; reviews of poetry books. Patricia Smith. *TS* July 4, 1987: M4.

Literary tricks and the larger concerns; reviews of *Delayed Mercy* and *Afterworlds*. Fraser Sutherland. photo · *G&M* Aug 8, 1987: pC19.

DELISLE, JEANNE-MANCE

Masques, personnages et personnes; reviews of plays. André-G. Bourassa. photo · *Lettres québec* Summer 1987; No 46: p51–52.

La vitrine du livre; reviews. Guy Ferland. *MD* May 9, 1987: pD4.

Des personnages et un langage qui se déchirent; review of *Un Oiseau vivant dans la gueule*. Chantal Gamache. photo · *MD* Oct 24, 1987: pD3.

'Oiseau' feeds on violent love — 'Neruda' long 2-hour stretch; theatre reviews of *Un Oiseau vivant dans la gueule* and *Off Off Off*. Francine Pelletier. *MG* June 3, 1987: pB4.

Jeanne-Mance Delisle: "Je cherche le tragique de l'âme québécoise"; article. Jean Royer. photo · *MD* June 13, 1987: pD2.

DELISLE, MICHAEL

[Untitled]; reviews of *Les Mémoires artificielles* and *Les Changeurs de signes*. Jacques Paquin. *Estuaire* Autumn 1987; No 46: p83–84.

Le sentiment de la langue; reviews of *"Quand on a une langue on peut aller à Rome"* and *Les Changeurs de signes*. Jean Royer. *MD* Feb 28, 1987: pC3.
[CANADIAN LITERARY PERIODICALS]

DEMERS, JEANNE

Manifeste: au jeu; review of *L'Enjeu du manifeste/le manifeste en jeu*. Bruno Roy. *Moebius* Spring 1987; No 32: p133–136.

"Crois ou meurs": à quand le manifeste vidéo-clip?; review of *L'Enjeu du manifeste/le manifeste en jeu*. Lori Saint-Martin. photo · *MD* April 18, 1987: pD2.

Le jeu du manifeste littéraire; review of *L'Enjeu du manifeste/Le manifeste en jeu*. Agnès Whitfield. *Lettres québec* Autumn 1987; No 47: p51–52.

DENNIS, IAN

Parody & legacy; reviews. Lorna Irvine. *Can Lit* Winter 1987; No 115: p264–267.
[FIRST NOVELS: BOOK REVIEWS]

Recent Canadian fiction; reviews of novels. D.O. Spettigue. *Queen's Q* Summer 1987; Vol 94 No 2: p366–375.
[FIRST NOVELS: BOOK REVIEWS]

DEPUIS L'AMOUR/Poems by Jean Royer

Ouellette et Royer: depuis la mort jusqu'à l'amour . . . ; reviews of *Les Heures* and *Depuis l'amour*. Jean Éthier-Blais. *MD* June 27, 1987: pC9.

[Untitled]; review of *Depuis l'amour*. Jean Chapdelaine Gagnon. *Estuaire* Summer 1987; No 45: p57–58.

De Bellefeuille, Nepveu, Lemaire, Royer; reviews of poetry books. Jean-Pierre Issenhuth. *Liberté* Aug 1987; Vol 29 No 4: p78–87.

L'amour la mort; reviews of poetry books. Robert Yergeau. photo · *Lettres québec* Summer 1987; No 46: p37–38.

DÉRIVES/Periodical

La vitrine du livre; reviews of periodicals. Guy Ferland. *MD* Sept 5, 1987: pC8.
[CANADIAN LITERARY PERIODICALS]

Ding et Dong; reviews of periodicals. Robert Melançon. *Liberté* Dec 1987; Vol 29 No 6: p122–129.
[CANADIAN LITERARY PERIODICALS]

LE DERNIER CHANT DE L'AVANT-DERNIER DODO/ Short stories by François Hébert

François Hébert, moraliste sans morale; reviews of *L'Homme aux maringouins* and *Le Dernier chant de l'avant-dernier dodo*. Jean Royer. *MD* Feb 7, 1987: pB3.

LE DERNIER QUATUOR D'UN HOMME SOURD/Play by Franine Ruel and François Cervantès

Music, theatre union needs fine tuning; theatre reviews of *Le Dernier quatuor d'un homme sourd* and *La Goutte*. Pat Donnelly. *MG* Nov 18, 1987: pD3.

Quatre personnages en quête d'une pièce; theatre review of *Le Dernier quatuor d'un homme sourd*. Robert Lévesque. photo · *MD* Nov 20, 1987: p13.

DERRIÈRE LE SILENCE/Poems by François Desnoyers

Comme un vent; reviews of poetry books. James P. Gilroy. *Can Lit* Winter 1987; No 115: p260–261.

DÉRY, FRANCINE

La vie littéraire; column. Jean Royer. photo · *MD* April 11, 1987: pD2.
[AWARDS, LITERARY; FILM ADAPTATIONS OF CANADIAN LITERATURE; POETRY READINGS; RADIO AND CANADIAN LITERATURE; TELEVISION AND CANADIAN LITERATURE]

DES CAILLOUX BLANCS POUR LES FORÊTS OBSCURES/Novel by Jovette Marchessault

"Donner naissance à des choses grandes et imparfaites"; review of *Des Cailloux blancs pour les forêts obscures*. Jean-Roch Boivin. photo · *MD* Oct 31, 1987: pD3.

La vitrine du livre; reviews. Guy Ferland. *MD* Sept 19, 1987: pD4.

Jovette Marchessault: le roman de la réconciliation; article. Jean Royer. photo · *MD* Oct 8, 1987: p15.

DES CERISIERS EN FLEURS, C'EST SI JOLI!/Novel by Marcelyne Claudais

Des dames de fleurs; review of *Des Cerisiers en fleurs, c'est si joli!*. Denis Saint-Jacques. *MD* Nov 21, 1987: pD2.

DES FLEURS POUR HARLEQUIN/Poems by Jean Forest

Comme un vent; reviews of poetry books. James P. Gilroy. *Can Lit* Winter 1987; No 115: p260–261.

DES NOUVELLES D'EDOUARD/Novel by Michel Tremblay

Des Nouvelles d'Edouard: Michel Tremblay's fugal composition; article. Ellen Reisman Babby. *Amer R of Can Studies* Winter 1987–88; Vol 17 No 4: p383–394.

DESAUTELS, DENISE

La fiction du réel/le réel de la fiction; reviews of poetry books. André Brochu. *Voix et images* Winter 1987; No 35: p322–330.

DESBIENS, PATRICE

Maniaques depressifs; reviews of poetry books. Mark Benson. *Can Lit* Spring 1987; No 112: p138–141.

DESCANT/Periodical

Take a look at a 'little' magazine; review of *Descant*. Ken Adachi. *TS* July 19, 1987: pA21.
[CANADIAN LITERARY PERIODICALS]

An index to Descant 1–50. Robyn Zuck. *Descant* Fall 1987; Vol 18 No 3: p99–181.
[CANADIAN LITERARY PERIODICALS]

DESCHÊNES, CAMILLE

Le Temps d'une paix est transposé au théâtre; article. *MD* Aug 1, 1987: pC3.

DESCHÊNES, CLAUDE

Le Temps d'une paix est transposé au théâtre; article. *MD* Aug 1, 1987: pC3.

LE DÉSERT BLANC/Short stories by Jean Éthier-Blais

[Untitled]; review of *Le Désert blanc*. Jacques Saint-Pierre. *Moebius (special issue)* Spring 1987; No 32: p121–123.

Trois voyages — petit, moyen et grand — du littératage à la littérature; reviews of short story books. Marie José Thériault. photo · *Lettres québec* Spring 1987; No 45: p30–32.
[ANTHOLOGIES: BOOK REVIEWS]

DESGENT, JEAN-MARC

La vitrine du livre; reviews. Jean Royer. photo · *MD* April 18, 1987: pD2.
[CANADIAN LITERARY PERIODICALS]

DESJARDINS, LOUISE

Maniaques depressifs; reviews of poetry books. Mark Benson. *Can Lit* Spring 1987; No 112: p138–141.

DESNOYERS, François

Comme un vent; reviews of poetry books. James P. Gilroy. *Can Lit* Winter 1987; No 115: p260–261.

DESPRÉS, ROSE

[Untitled]; review of *Sir Charles God Damn*. Christopher Armitage. *Amer R of Can Studies* Winter 1987–88; Vol 17 No 4: p439–440.

La relève poétique en Acadie?; review of *Requiem en saule pleureur*. Caroline Bayard. *Lettres québec* Spring 1987; No 45: p43.

DESROCHERS, CLÉMENCE

Cause toujours ma Clémence . . . ; article. Paul Cauchon. photo · *MD* April 10, 1987: p13.
[TELEVISION AND CANADIAN LITERATURE]

La vie littéraire; column. Jean Royer. photo · *MD* April 11, 1987: pD2.
[AWARDS, LITERARY; FILM ADAPTATIONS OF CANADIAN LITERATURE; POETRY READINGS; RADIO AND CANADIAN LITERATURE; TELEVISION AND CANADIAN LITERATURE]

Quatre Saisons laisse tomber son émission littéraire; article. Jean Royer. *MD* June 17, 1987: p13.
[TELEVISION AND CANADIAN LITERATURE]

DESROSIERS, SYLVIE

Les malheurs de Rosalie ou l'éloge de l'enfance; reviews of children's books. Dominique Demers. *MD* May 2, 1987: pD3.

DESRUISSEAUX, PIERRE

Il y a des poèmes que nous habitons tous; reviews of poetry books. Robert Yergeau. *Lettres québec* Winter 1986–87; No 44: p36–37.

DESSAULLES, HENRIETTE

Jalons pour une narratologie du journal intime: le statut du récit dans le Journal d'Henriette Dessaulles; article. Pierre Hébert. *Voix et images* Autumn 1987; Vol 13 No 1: p140–156. [AUTOBIOGRAPHICAL WRITING; STRUCTURALIST WRITING AND CRITICISM]

Light words and humor about unions; reviews. Tim Wynne-Jones. *G&M* Oct 17, 1987: pE11.

DETAINING MR. TROTSKY/Play by Robert Fothergill

[Untitled]; review of *Detaining Mr. Trotsky*. John Bemrose. *Maclean's* Nov 9, 1987; Vol 100 No 45: p70.

Making saint of Trotsky pays off for play; theatre review of *Detaining Mr. Trotsky*. Ray Conlogue. photo · *G&M* Oct 23, 1987: pD13.

Taut Trotsky play an intelligent debut; theatre review of *Detaining Mr. Trotsky*. Robert Crew. *TS* Oct 22, 1987: pB1.

Trotsky 'tough act to follow' for playwright; article. Liam Lacey. photo · *G&M* Nov 12, 1987: pA31.

Jacob Two-Two star hits 'big time' at age 7; column. Vit Wagner. *TS* Oct 16, 1987: pD10.

DEUTSCHES SCHRIFTUM IN KANADA 1835–1984; THEATER, POESIE, SATIRE, PROSA. ZUR REIHE DEUTSCHKANADISCHE SCHRIFTEN/Anthology series

[Untitled]; review of *Deutsches schriftum in Kanada 1835–1984*. Konrad Haderlein. *Zeitschrift Kanada-Studien* 1987; Vol 7 No 1: p255–263.

DEUX AMANTS AU REVOLVER/Poems by Jean-Marc Desgent

La vitrine du livre; reviews. Jean Royer. photo · *MD* April 18, 1987: pD2. [CANADIAN LITERARY PERIODICALS]

LES DEUX SOEURS/Short stories by Gilles Valais

Discours-fleuve; reviews of *Le Coupeur de têtes* and *Les Deux soeurs*. Marguerite Andersen. *Can Lit* Winter 1987; No 115: p182–184.

DEVERELL, REX

[Untitled]; theatre review of *Quartet for Three Actors*. Michael Scholar. *Maclean's* Jan 26, 1987; Vol 100 No 4: p55.

DEVERELL, WILLIAM

Novelist-lawyer's current case odder than fiction; article. *WFP* Jan 3, 1987: p10.

Author uses brainwashing scandal for 'juicy thriller' filmed in Montreal; article. photo · *WFP* Oct 9, 1987: p34.

Deverell writes about CIA experiments; article. *G&M* Oct 8, 1987: pD5.

THE DEVIL IS INNOCENT/Novel by H. Gordon Green

[Untitled]; review of *The Devil Is Innocent*. David A. Reid. *Quill & Quire* Jan 1987; Vol 53 No 1: p27.

THE DEVIL IS LOOSE!/Novel by Antonine Maillet

Stuffed with legends; review of *The Devil Is Loose!*. Roberta Buchanan. *Can Lit* Winter 1987; No 115: p213–214.

DEWDNEY, CHRISTOPHER

Speculations: cosmology and language: the new priests and the old; article. Mary di Michele. *Poetry Can R* Spring 1987; Vol 8 No 2–3: p25.

"Footprints in the snow which stop"; review of *The Immaculate Perception*. Gillian Harding-Russell. *Event* March 1987; Vol 16 No 1: p105–106.

Manifold destiny: metaphysics in the poetry of Christopher Dewdney; article. Alistair Highet. *Essays on Can Writ* Spring 1987; No 34: p2–17.

[Untitled]; review of *The Immaculate Perception*. Louise Longo. *Quill & Quire* March 1987; Vol 53 No 3: p75.

[Untitled]; review of *The Immaculate Perception*. Peter O'Brien. *Rubicon* Fall 1987; No 9: p187–190.

Painful scrutiny of relationships; reviews of poetry books. Patricia Keeney Smith. *TS* May 30, 1987: M9.

Poetry, science, mind and religion; reviews of poetry books. Fraser Sutherland. photo · *G&M* Jan 31, 1987: pE19.

DEWLINE/Play by David Arnason

Play takes comic look at fear of mortality; theatre review of *Dewline*. Reg Skene. *WFP* Feb 27, 1987: p33.

DI CICCO, PIER GIORGIO

Speculations: cosmology and language: the new priests and the old; article. Mary di Michele. *Poetry Can R* Spring 1987; Vol 8 No 2–3: p25.

[Untitled]; review of *Virgin Science*. Brian Fawcett. *Books in Can* Jan-Feb 1987; Vol 16 No 1: p28.

Poetry, science, mind and religion; reviews of poetry books. Fraser Sutherland. photo · *G&M* Jan 31, 1987: pE19.

Excesses; reviews of poetry books. Eva Tihanyi. *Can Lit* Winter 1987; No 115: p200–202.

[Untitled]; review of *Virgin Science*. George Woodcock. *Poetry Can R* Spring 1987; Vol 8 No 2–3: p38.

DI MICHELE, MARY

Di Michele in residence in Regina; article. *Quill & Quire* Oct 1987; Vol 53 No 10: p20. [WRITERS-IN-RESIDENCE]

Fine lines & fractures; review of *Immune to Gravity*. Ron Miles. *Can Lit* Spring 1987; No 112: p183–185.

A DIALOGUE WITH MASKS/Novel by Mary Melfi

[Untitled]; review of *A Dialogue with Masks*. Charlotte Hussey. *Rubicon* Spring 1987; No 8: p205–208.

DIAMOND, DAVID

Aboriginal issue takes centre stage; theatre review of *No' Xya'*. Stephen Godfrey. photo · *G&M* Nov 7, 1987: pC3.

Three new political plays; theatre reviews. Malcolm Page. *Can Drama* 1987; Vol 13 No 2: p224–226.

DIARY OF DESIRE/Poems by Judith Fitzgerald

Proof that poetry is not dead; review of *Diary of Desire*. Colline Caulder. *TS* Oct 25, 1987: pA18.

DICKSON, BARRY

Thrills and chills: hints for Hallowe'en reading; reviews of children's books. Joan McGrath. illus · *Quill & Quire (Books for Young People)* Oct 1987; Vol 53 No 10: p8.
[ANTHOLOGIES: BOOK REVIEWS]

DICKSON, H. LOVAT

Grey Owl biographer Lovat Dickson dies; obituary. photo · *MG* Jan 6, 1987: pB13.

Lovat Dickson dies; obituary. *WFP* Jan 5, 1987: p15.

Writer chronicled story of Grey Owl; obituary. *CH* Jan 6, 1987: pD6.

Literary biography of Grey Owl, Wells, was editor, publisher; obituary. photo · *G&M* Jan 5, 1987: pC12.

DICTIONNAIRE DE MOI-MÊME/Essay by Jean thier-Blais

Dans les poches; reviews of *Dictionnaire de moi-même* and *Mon cheval pour un royaume*. Guy Ferland. *MD* May 30, 1987: pD2.

DICTIONNAIRE DES OEUVRES LITTÉRAIRES DU QUÉBEC/Critical survey

[Untitled]; review of *Dictionnaire des oeuvres littéraires du Québec*. W.H. New. *Can Lit* Spring 1987; No 112: p223–224.

DIFFERENT DRAGONS/Children's novel by Jean Little

Dog in the attic; review of *Different Dragons*. Peter Blake. *Times Lit Supp* May 15, 1987; No 4389: p529.

Wars with internal dragons; reviews of *Lost and Found* and *Different Dragons*. Frances Frazer. *Can Child Lit* 1987; No 45: p91–93.

A DIFFICULT DAY/Children's story by Eugenie Fernandes

Book captures emotional moment for child; reviews of *Big Sarah's Little Boots* and *A Difficult Day*. Joan Craven. *CH (Neighbors)* Oct 28, 1987: pA18.

Morgan, May, Melinda: new heroines offer humour and fantasy; reviews of children's books. Bernie Goedhart. *Quill & Quire (Books for Young People)* Oct 1987; Vol 53 No 10: p24.

The jolly fireplace's darker side; reviews of children's books. Joan McGrath. *TS* Nov 22, 1987: pC8.

THE DIFFICULTY OF LIVING ON OTHER PLANETS/Poems by Dennis Lee

A garden of adult verse; review of *The Difficulty of Living on Other Planets*. John Bemrose. *Maclean's* Nov 16, 1987; Vol 100 No 46: p64b

Lee's whimsy cuts into heavy issues; article. Rosie DiManno. photo · *TS* Nov 1, 1987: pC2.

Playful poetry for adults, 'what a subversive idea'; article. Deirdre Kelly. photo · *G&M* Nov 3, 1987: pD8.

Lee cooks up Alligator Pie for adults; review of *The Difficulty of Living on Other Planets*. Kenneth McGoogan. *CH* Nov 8, 1987: pE6.

Ballads and ditties for grown-ups; reviews of poetry books. Fraser Sutherland. illus · *G&M* Nov 7, 1987: pC21.

Poetic successes; reviews of *The Difficulty of Living on Other Planets* and *Fortunate Exile*. Joel Yanofsky. illus · *MG* Dec 19, 1987: J11.

LES DIMANCHES SONT MORTELS/Novel by Francine d'Amour

Une famille dévorée par l'ennui et le néant de vie inutiles; review of *Les Dimanches sont mortels*. Jean Éthier-Blais. *MD* Nov 21, 1987: pD12.
[FIRST NOVELS: BOOK REVIEWS]

DINOSAUR/Children's play by Rick McNair

What's happening; notice. illus · *CH* April 10, 1987: pE7

DIRECTIVES OF AUTUMN/Poems by Ralph Gustafson

The dying generations; reviews of poetry books. Dermot McCarthy. *Essays on Can Writ* Spring 1987; No 34: p24–32.

LA DISCORDE AUX CENT VOIX/Novel by mile Ollivier

Une épopée des Caraïbes; review of *La Discorde aux cent voix*. Noël Audet. *Lettres québec* Spring 1987; No 45: p24–26.

THE DISINHERITED/Novel by Matt Cohen

The wonders and pleasures of fictional empire-building; reviews of novels by Matt Cohen. Douglas Hill. photo · *G&M* Jan 3, 1987: pE15.

DISLOCATIONS/Short stories by Janette Turner Hospital

[Untitled]; reviews of fictional works. Beverley Daurio. *Cross Can Writ Q* 1987; Vol 9 No 1: p18–19.

[Untitled]; review of *Dislocations*. Martha Ann Mueller. *Queen's Q* Autumn 1987; Vol 94 No 3: p692–694.

[Untitled]; review of *Dislocations*. Katrina Preece. *Malahat R (special issue)* March 1987; No 78: p151–152.

THE DISPOSABLES/Novel by Andrew J. Patterson

Film's end; review of *The Disposables*. John Hamilton. *G&M* June 13, 1987: pC20.
[FIRST NOVELS: BOOK REVIEWS]

DISTANCE/Poems by Patrick Coppens

Jacques Boulerice: pour une autre enfance; reviews of *Apparence* and *Distance*. Jean Royer. *MD* Feb 14, 1987: pC3.

DISTANCES/Poems by Robin Skelton

[Untitled]; review of *Distances*. Luella Kerr. *Poetry Can R* Fall 1987; Vol 9 No 1: p35–36.

THE DIVINERS/Novel by Margaret Laurence

CBC variety keeps smiling despite budget cuts; column. Sid Adilman. *TS* Feb 26, 1987: pB1.
[FILM ADAPTATIONS OF CANADIAN LITERATURE]

DIXIELAND'S NIGHT OF SHAME/Play by Alan Williams

Daredevil dramatist slips out of focus; theatre review of *Dixieland's Night of Shame*. Stephen Godfrey. photo · *G&M* May 9, 1987: pC5.

Inspired comic shares sharp observations; theatre review of *Dixieland's Night of Shame*. Henry Mietkiewicz. photo · *TS* June 2, 1987: pG3.

Theatrical satire hits target; theatre review of *Dixieland's Night of Shame*. Reg Skene. *WFP* May 8, 1987: p23.

DJWA, SANDRA

Portrait of an extraordinary man: a vibrant and influential presence in our intellectual and political life; review of *The Politics of the Imagination*. Ken Adachi. photo · *TS* Nov 21, 1987: M4.

The monument; review of *The Politics of the Imagination*. Louis Dudek. illus · *G&M* Nov 21, 1987: pC23.

F.R. Scott: just portrayal of a poetic humanist; review of *The Politics of the Imagination*. Doug Fetherling. photo · *Quill & Quire* Sept 1987; Vol 53 No 9: p80.

A very public life; review of *The Politics of the Imagination*. John Hutcheson. *Can Forum* Oct 1987; Vol 67 No 772: p40–41.

Evolution of an intellectual; review of *The Politics of the Imagination*. Allen Mills. photo · *WFP* Nov 14, 1987: p50.

F.R. Scott: his life was his finest hour; review of *The Politics of the Imagination*. Joel Yanofsky. photo · *MG* Nov 14, 1987: J9.

DO YOUR EARS HANG LOW?/Children's play by Zina Barnieh

Playwright probes kids' fear of summer camp; article. Kate Zimmerman. photo · *CH* April 24, 1987: pD1.

DOC/Play by Sharon Pollock

Remembrance of things past; review of *Doc*. Marc Côté. *Books in Can* March 1987; Vol 16 No 2: p1718.

[Untitled]; review of *Doc*. Cindy Cowan. *Can Theatre R* Fall 1987; No 52: p95–96.

Sharon Pollock: personal frictions; review of *Doc*. Richard Paul Knowles. *Atlan Prov Book R* Feb-March 1987; Vol 14 No 1: p19.

[Untitled]; review of *Doc*. Randee Loucks. *Dandelion* Fall-Winter 1987; Vol 14 No 2: p147–150.

MTC shows ability with Doc production; theatre review. Reg Skene. *WFP* Feb 6, 1987: p29.

LE DODO

See MORTIMER/Children's story by Robert Munsch

DOERKSEN, NAN

Fiction for children: history and mystery; reviews of *Rats in the Sloop* and *Shivers in Your Nightshirt*. Dorothy Perkyns. *Atlan Prov Book R* Feb-March 1987; Vol 14 No 1: p14.
[ANTHOLOGIES: BOOK REVIEWS]

DOG DAY/Play by National Theatre School collective

NTS's Dog Day a hazard in more ways than one; theatre review. Pat Donnelly. *MG* Dec 19, 1987: pE6.

THE DOG WHO WOULDN'T BE/Children's novel by Farley Mowat

Book about a funny dog; review of *The Dog Who Wouldn't Be*. Marla Maudsley. *TS* March 1, 1987: pA17.

DOGS WITH NO TAILS/Play by Bruce McManus

Dogs with No Tails delivers pain, laughs; theatre review. Reg Skene. *WFP* July 4, 1987: p40.

DOGSTONES: SELECTED AND NEW POEMS/Poems by Anne Szumigalski

[Untitled]; review of *Dogstones*. Richard Streiling. *Quill & Quire* Feb 1987; Vol 53 No 2: p20.

Mapping inner and outer selves; review of *Tiger in the Skull* and *Dogstones*. Fraser Sutherland. *G&M* Feb 28, 1987: pE18.

Victims of a bleak universe; reviews of poetry books. Bruce Whiteman. *Books in Can* Jan-Feb 1987; Vol 16 No 1: p22–23.

[Untitled]; review of *Dogstones*. George Woodcock. *Poetry Can R* Summer 1987; Vol 8 No 4: p37–38.

DOING TIME/Poems by Himani Bannerji

Hard time, maximum time; reviews of *The Only Minority Is the Bourgeoisie* and *Doing Time*. Marlene Philip. *Tor South Asian R* Spring 1987; Vol 5 No 3: p28–34.

THE DOLL/Children's novel by Cora Taylor

Big responsibilities theme of tall tale and growing-up story; reviews of *The Doll* and *Jacob's Little Giant*. Joan McGrath. photo · *Quill & Quire (Books for Young People)* Aug 1987; Vol 53 No 8: p11.

Novels deal with family breakup; reviews of *The Doll* and *Dear Bruce Springsteen*. Helen Norrie. *WFP* Dec 5, 1987: p57.

Albertan's time travel tale offers reassurance; review of *The Doll*. Susan Scott. photo · *CH* Sept 27, 1987: pE6.

Hard perspectives on traumatic family break-ups; review of *The Doll*. Tim Wynne-Jones. *G&M* Oct 3, 1987: pC22.

DOMANSKI, DON

Recent poetry; reviews of poetry books. Terrence Craig. *Atlan Prov Book R* Feb-March 1987; Vol 14 No 1: p18.

Domanski, Harris, Hutchman; reviews of poetry books. Barry Dempster. *Poetry Can R* Summer 1987; Vol 8 No 4: p31.

[Untitled]; review of *Hammerstroke*. Louise Longo. *Quill & Quire* March 1987; Vol 53 No 3: p74–75.

Rush job, high gloss and high-risk realism; reviews of poetry books. Fraser Sutherland. *G&M* March 21, 1987: pE18.

DON'T BLAME THE BEDOUINS

See NE BLÂMEZ JAMAIS LES BEDOUINS/DON'T BLAME THE BEDOUINS/Play by René-Daniel Dubois

DON'T CARE HIGH/Young adult novel by Gordon Korman

Gordon Korman: entertaining as ever; review of *Don't Care High*. Sonja Dunn. *Can Child Lit* 1987; No 46: p83.

DON'T EAT SPIDERS/Children's poems by Robert Heidbreder

Meaningful nonsense; reviews of children's books. Adrienne Kertzer. *Can Lit* Winter 1987; No 115: p165–167.

LE DON/Young adult novel by David Schinkel and Yves Beauchesne

Pour les adolescents: quatre mains et deux solitudes; reviews of young adult novels. Dominique Demers. photo · *MD* Dec 19, 1987: pD6–D7.

DONKEY DANCE & OTHER POEMS/Poems by Neil Henden

[Untitled]; reviews of poetry books. James McElroy. *Poetry Can R* Fall 1987; Vol 9 No 1: p36.

[Untitled]; review of *Donkey Dance*. Howard Tessler. *Rubicon* Fall 1987; No 9: p202–203.

DONNELL, DAVID

Awards; article. *Quill & Quire* Sept 1987; Vol 53 No 9: p71.
[AWARDS, LITERARY]

Settling with style; review of *The Blue Ontario Hemingway Boat Race*. Patrick Coleman. *Essays on Can Writ* Winter 1987; No 35: p152–155.

[Untitled]; review of *The Natural History of Water*. Gerald Hill. *Poetry Can R* Spring 1987; Vol 8 No 2–3: p45.

A design-conscious guy; reviews of *Settlements* and *The Natural History of Water*. Jan Horner. *CV 2* Spring 1987; Vol 10 No 3: p61–66.

[Untitled]; reviews of poetry books. Tom Marshall. *Cross Can Writ Q* 1987; Vol 9 No 1: p24–25.

DORA: A CASE OF HYSTERIA/Play by Kim Dales

Freud, Dora and Ibsen; theatre review of *Dora: A Case of Hysteria*. Mary Blackstone. photo · *NeWest R* Summer 1987; Vol 12 No 10: p17.

DORGE, CLAUDE

French play tackles social problems; theatre review of *Les Tremblay 2*. Philip Clark. *WFP* April 4, 1987: p23.

Franco-Manitoban satire translates sense of deja vu; theatre review of *Avant qu'les autres le fassent*. Philip Clark. *WFP* Oct 17, 1987: p34.

Entertaining; letter to the editor. Richard McCarthy. *WFP* Nov 7, 1987: p7.

Cercle tries for last laugh first; article. Brad Oswald. photo · *WFP* Oct 16, 1987: p33.

DORION, HÉLÈNE

[Untitled]; review of *Hors champ*. Hélène Thibaux. *Estuaire* Spring 1987; No 44: p81.

DOROTHY LIVESAY/Critical work by Lee Briscoe Thompson

[Untitled]; review of *Dorothy Livesay*. Lorna Irvine. *Amer R of Can Studies* Winter 1987–88; Vol 17 No 4: p452–453.

Quilting — a spiral of experience; review of *Dorothy Livesay*. R. Alex Kizuk. *Can Poet* Fall-Winter 1987; No 21: p110–115.

DORSEY, CANDAS JANE

Wacky novel competition hits bottom with a thud; review of *Hardwired Angel*. William French. *G&M* Aug 25, 1987: pD7.

Edmonton winners in Pulp contest; article. Charles Mandel. *Quill & Quire* Jan 1987; Vol 53 No 1: p18.
[AWARDS, LITERARY]

[Untitled]; review of *Hardwired Angel*. Norman Sigurdson. *Quill & Quire* Dec 1987; Vol 53 No 12: p25.

Winner is a real stinker; review of *Hardwired Angel*. Morley Walker. *WFP* Sept 5, 1987: p58.

DORSINVILLE, MAX

La vue comparatiste; review of *Le Pays natal*. C. Bouygues. *Can Lit* Winter 1987; No 115: p211–213.

DOSSIERS DE PRESSE SUR LES ÉCRIVAINS QUÉBÉCOIS/Reference guide

Dossiers de presse sur les écrivains québécois: un instrument de recherche unique pour les bibliothèques et les chercheurs; article. Claude Pelletier. *Lettres québec* Summer 1987; No 46: p74–76.

DOUBLE EXPOSURES/Short stories by Diane Schoemperlen

The lively art; reviews of *Double Exposures* and *Frogs*. Kent Thompson. *Fiddlehead* Winter 1987; No 154: p87–91.

THE DOUBLE HOOK/Novel by Sheila Watson

Miracle, mystery, and authority: rereading The Double Hook; article. Glen Deer. *Open Letter* Summer 1987; Vol 6 No 8: p25–43.
[THE FAMILY IN CANADIAN LITERATURE; MYTHS AND LEGENDS IN CANADIAN LITERATURE]

Fiction, break, silence: language. Sheila Watson's The Double Hook; article. Margaret E. Turner. *Ariel* April 1987; Vol 18 No 2: p65–78.
[CULTURAL IDENTITY]

DOUBLE STANDARDS/Poems by Lola Lemire Tostevin

[Untitled]; review of *Double Standards*. Jane Munro. *Poetry Can R* Spring 1987; Vol 8 No 2–3: p44.

[Untitled]; reviews of *In the Second Person* and *Double Standards*. Joan Ruvinsky. *Rubicon* Spring 1987; No 8: p178–181.

LE DOUBLE VIE DE LONCE ET LONIL/Novel by France Ducasse

Léonce, Léonil . . . et Sept fois Jeanne; reviews of *Cette fois, Jeanne . . .* and *La Double vie de Léonce et Léonil*. Louise Milot. photo · *Lettres québec* Autumn 1987; No 47: p17–18.
[FIRST NOVELS: BOOK REVIEWS]

France Ducasse: l'â d'or de l'enfance; review of *La Double vie de Léonce et Lénoil*. Madeleine Ouellette-Michalska. photo · *MD* May 9, 1987: pD3.

DOUBTFUL MOTIVES/Novel by Maurice Gagnon

[Untitled]; reviews of *Doubtful Motives* and *A Body Surrounded by Water*. Paul Cabray. *MG* Aug 15, 1987: L2.

Murder & mayhem: the English style of the whodunits; reviews of *A Body Surrounded by Water* and *Doubtful Motives*. Margaret Cannon. photo · *G&M* July 18, 1987: pC17.

[Untitled]; reviews of *Doubtful Motives* and *Fieldwork*. Carolellen Norskey. *Quill & Quire* Sept 1987; Vol 53 No 9: p79.
[FIRST NOVELS: BOOK REVIEWS]

Crime novels provide a study in contrasts; reviews of *Doubtful Motives* and *A Body Surrounded by Water*. David Williamson. photo · *WFP* Aug 1, 1987: p50.

DOUCET, PAUL

Bloc-notes; column. Michel Vaïs. photo · *Jeu* 1987; No 45: p227–231.
[AWARDS, LITERARY; GOVERNMENT GRANTS FOR WRITERS/PUBLISHERS; WRITERS' ORGANIZATIONS]

DOUGLAS, GILEAN

Still lifes; reviews of poetry books. Laurence Hutchman. *Can Lit* Winter 1987; No 115: p263–264.

DOWNFALL PEOPLE/Novel by Jo Anne Williams Bennett

[Untitled]; review of *Downfall People*. Frank Manley. *Books in Can* Jan-Feb 1987; Vol 16 No 1: p24–25.
[FIRST NOVELS: BOOK REVIEWS]

DOYLE, BRIAN

Chit chat; column. Maria Casas. *Quill & Quire (Books for Young People)* Oct 1987; Vol 53 No 10: p8.

DOYON, LOUISE

Prix et distinctions; list of award winners. photo · *Lettres québec* Summer 1987; No 46: p7.
[AWARDS, LITERARY]

Les Héritiers (prix Robert Cliche) et L'Écrit-vent; reviews. Noël Audet. photo · *Lettres québec* Autumn 1987; No 47: p19–21.
[FIRST NOVELS: BOOK REVIEWS]

Le Salon du livre de Québec: c'est parti!; article. Hélène de Billy. photo · *MD* April 29, 1987: p13.
[AWARDS, LITERARY; CONFERENCES, LITERARY]

DRAGON SANDWICHES/Children's story by Gwendolyn MacEwen and Maureen Paxton

Activity books kids will enjoy; reviews of *Dragon Sandwiches* and *The Dragon and Other Laurentian Tales*. *TS* Dec 20, 1987: pE8.

Familiarity and TV's stranglehold on life; reviews of children's books. Tim Wynne-Jones. *G&M* Nov 14, 1987: pE4.
[FESTIVALS, LITERARY]

DRAGON SNAPPER/Play by Vivian Palin

Festival One plays singularly successful; theatre reviews. Stephen Godfrey. photo · *G&M* May 8, 1987: pF9.
[FESTIVALS, DRAMA]

Stories create magic moments for audience at Festival One; theatre review of *Dragon Snapper*. Reg Skene. *WFP* May 4, 1987: p29.

Pioneer lady on stage; article. Morley Walker. photo · *WFP* April 30, 1987: p26.

DRAMATIC ADAPTATIONS OF CANADIAN LITERATURE

Duddy revised; article. *WFP* April 23, 1987: p44.

A revised Duddy to open in U.S.; article. *G&M* April 23, 1987: pC3.

Barometer's rising the curtain in Halifax; article. *TS* Sept 26, 1987: pG10.

Mixed reviews for Duddy as musical breathes anew; article. photo · *G&M* Sept 30, 1987: pC7.
[INTERNATIONAL REVIEWS OF CANADIAN LITERATURE]

Philadelphia gives resurrection of Richler's Duddy Kravitz mixed reviews; article. *WFP* Oct 2, 1987: p24.
[INTERNATIONAL REVIEWS OF CANADIAN LITERATURE]

People; column. Marsha Boulton. *Maclean's* Aug 10, 1987; Vol 100 No 32: p43.

Theatre notes; column. Brian Brennan. *CH* May 11, 1987: pC6.
[WRITERS' WORKSHOPS]

Season's greetings: companies take cues from holidays past; article. Brian Brennan. photo · *CH* Nov 22, 1987: pA11.

La Sagouine: home to stay; article. Sue Calhoun. photo · *Atlan Insight* April 1987; Vol 9 No 4: p19–21.

The Philadelphia experiment: a disaster in Canada, Duddy tries again in U.S.; article. Lucinda Chodan. photo · *MG* Sept 29, 1987: pB5.

Up Your Alley is a jangle of conflicting styles; theatre review. Ray Conlogue. photo · *G&M* Jan 15, 1987: pD4.

Jacob Two-Two meets The Fang in zippy musical; theatre review. Ray Conlogue. photo · *G&M* Oct 26, 1987: pC11.

'Squowse' sparkles for kids; theatre review of *Willie the Squowse*. Ray Conlogue. photo · *G&M* Dec 11, 1987: pD6.

Neptune Theatre's Barometer Rising too faithful to book; theatre review. Matthew Fraser. *G&M* Nov 9, 1987: pD9.

Child subversion reigns in delightful play; theatre review of *Jacob Two-Two Meets the Hooded Fang*. Neil Harris. *WFP* Nov 13, 1987: p37.

Fast-paced kids' tale is simply irresistible; theatre review of *Jacob Two-Two Meets the Hooded Fang*. Christopher Hume. photo · *TS* Oct 23, 1987: pE8.

Delightfully tiny Willie makes a big impression; theatre review of *Willie the Squowse*. Christopher Hume. photo · *TS* Dec 11, 1987: pD14.

Anne's back home, safe and sound; theatre review of *Anne of Green Gables*. Deirdre Kelly. photo · *G&M* June 29, 1987: pC9.

Group brings back Anne of Green Gables; article. Muriel Leeper. *TS (Neighbours)* April 7, 1987: p21.

Anne of Green Gables opens with lively spirit; theatre review. Muriel Leeper. *TS (Neighbours)* April 28, 1987: p14.

Tammy saw cats on wings; column. Doreen Martens. *WFP* Aug 12, 1987: p21.

Anne of Green Gables bland as porridge; theatre review. Randal McIlroy. *WFP* Dec 20, 1987: p20.

Children's play provides dizzy gaiety, excitement; theatre review of *Snowsuits, Birthdays, & Giants!*. Randal McIlroy. *WFP* Dec 20, 1987: p21.

New troupe's motto: laugh with Leacock; article about the Leacock Players. Brad Oswald. *WFP* Sept 1, 1987: p26.

Child power injects fun into play; article. Brad Oswald. photo · *WFP* Nov 13, 1987: p37.

Children's play not child's play; article. Brad Oswald. *WFP* Dec 16, 1987: p38.

Death on the waterfront; theatre review of *Barometer Rising*, includes profile. Stephen Pedersen. photo · *Maclean's* Nov 23, 1987; Vol 100 No 47: p57.

Halifax blast commemorated in effective stage production; theatre review of *Barometer Rising*. Jamie Portman. *CH* Nov 12, 1987: pD2.

A sound beyond hearing; article. Tom Regan. photo · *Atlan Insight* Dec 1987; Vol 9 No 12: p19–21.

Miami Vice's Don Johnson a Stowe-away in resort town; column. Thomas Schnurmacher. *MG* Jan 21, 1987: pF6.

Star Trek's Capt. Kirk beaming up to Montreal; column. Thomas Schnurmacher. *MG* Aug 11, 1987: pC8.

Actress draws powerful portraits of heroines in Laurence's work; theatre review of *The Women of Margaret Laurence*. Reg Skene. *WFP* May 14, 1987: p46.

F-words at Green Gables; article. Ann Thurlow. photo · *Maclean's* July 13, 1987; Vol 100 No 28: p49.
[FESTIVALS, DRAMA]

MacLennan happy with plans to stage his Barometer Rising; article. Derrick Toth. photo · *CH* Sept 26, 1987: pG1.

L.M. Montgomery: at home in Poland; article. Barbara Wachowicz. photo · *Can Child Lit* 1987; No 46: p7–35.
[EUROPE-CANADA LITERARY RELATIONS; TRANSLATIONS OF CANADIAN LITERATURE]

DRAMATIC READINGS

Festival on for young playwrights; article. *MG* Jan 14, 1987: pB5.
[FESTIVALS, DRAMA]

Billboard: U of M holds seminar on role of stress, immune system in voles; column. *WFP* Jan 20, 1987: p28.

Billboard: McGonigal dinner set for Feb. 19; column. *WFP* Feb 3, 1987: p30.

Billboard: fitness program for all ages; column. *WFP* Feb 24, 1987: p52.

Plays get readings; article. *WFP* April 3, 1987: p30.

Ravel reading is pay-what-you-can; article. *TS* April 26, 1987: pC7.

Playwrights gather; article. *WFP* Sept 4, 1987: p17.
[WRITERS' ORGANIZATIONS]

Playwright group marks 25th year; article. *MG* Nov 16, 1987: pC9.
[WRITERS' ORGANIZATIONS]

Rotary Club stages art show; column. *WFP* Oct 31, 1987: p33.

Billboard: women's group holding dessert party; column. *WFP* Nov 29, 1987: p18.

Premieres spice Tarragon season; column. Ray Conlogue. photo · *G&M* April 23, 1987: pC1.

Reed remembered for 'wonderful' work; column. Ray Conlogue. *G&M* Sept 22, 1987: pD7.

PUC stops here for cabaret night; article. Robert Crew. *TS* April 24, 1987: pE12.
[FESTIVALS, DRAMA]

Linda Griffiths gives NTS reading tonight; article. Pat Donnelly. photo · *MG* Nov 2, 1987: pB13.

La guerre de religion de Denise Boucher; column. Robert Lévesque. photo · *MD* Jan 13, 1987: p6.

Suspense à la Quinzaine de Québec; column. Robert Lévesque. *MD* Sept 22, 1987: p11.

Liz says she laughed at the fat jokes; column. Thomas Schnurmacher. *MG* Oct 9, 1987: pC1.

Tip sheet: experts to lead forum on drug abuse; column. Susan Schwartz. *MG* Jan 14, 1987: pE3.

Isaac's cast puts its 500 years to good use; column. Vit Wagner. *TS* Nov 13, 1987: pE16.
[FEMINIST DRAMA; FESTIVALS, DRAMA; WOMEN WRITERS]

Theatrical talent unites to help fledgling troupe; article. Kate Zimmerman. *CH* Nov 13, 1987: pE10.

DRAPEAU, RENÉE-BERTHE

[Untitled]; review of *Féminins singuliers*. Anne-Marie Picard. *U of Toronto Q* Fall 1987; Vol 57 No 1: p200–201.

THE DREAM AUDITOR/Short stories by Lesley Choyce

Muscular idea; review of *The Dream Auditor*. Laszlo J. Buhasz. *G&M* May 9, 1987: pC21.

Rough gems; review of *The Dream Auditor*. Laszlo J. Buhasz. *G&M* June 20, 1987: pC19.

[Untitled]; review of *The Dream Auditor*. Cary Fagan. *Books in Can* June-July 1987; Vol 16 No 5: p22.

THE DREAM CATCHER/Young adult novel by Monica Hughes

[Untitled]; review of *The Dream Catcher*. Callie Israel. *Quill & Quire (Books for Young People)* June 1987; Vol 53 No 6: p4,6.

Science fiction story probes relationships; review of *The Dream Catcher*. Susan Scott. *CH* July 12, 1987: pE4.

A DREAM LIKE MINE/Novel by M.T. Kelly

Revenge of the native; review of *A Dream Like Mine*. John Bemrose. photo · *Maclean's* Nov 9, 1987; Vol 100 No 45: p64g

Kelly's taut, grim narrative; review of *A Dream Like Mine*. Judith Fitzgerald. *TS* Nov 22, 1987: pC9.

The impossible dream; review of *A Dream Like Mine*. Terry Goldie. *Books in Can* Nov 1987; Vol 16 No 8: p30–31.

Reporter trips over angles of 'light' Indian story; review of *A Dream Like Mine*. Marion McCormick. *MG* Nov 21, 1987: J12.

The real story behind the story; review of *A Dream Like Mine*. T.F. Rigelhof. photo · *G&M* Oct 24, 1987: pC19.

[Untitled]; review of *A Dream Like Mine*. Norman Sigurdson. *Quill & Quire* Dec 1987; Vol 53 No 12: p24–25.

Unpleasant, harsh novel probes social ills; review of *A Dream Like Mine*. John Vance Snow. photo · *CH* Nov 29, 1987: pE6.

THE DREAMERS/Short stories by Thomas H. Raddall

Thomas H. Raddall, a decade later; reviews of *The Dreamers* and *A Name for Himself*. Andrew Seaman. *Atlan Prov Book R* Feb-March 1987; Vol 14 No 1: p19.

Yesterday's heroes; review of *The Dreamers*. Joanne Tompkins. *Books in Can* June-July 1987; Vol 16 No 5: p32–33.

DREAMS OF AN UNSEEN PLANET/Novel by Teresa Plowright

Chilling view; review of *Dreams of an Unseen Planet*. H.J. Kirchhoff. *G&M* June 13, 1987: pC20.
[FIRST NOVELS: BOOK REVIEWS]

Me, myself, and I; reviews of first novels. Janice Kulyk Keefer. *Books in Can* Oct 1987; Vol 16 No 7: p35–36,38.
[FIRST NOVELS: BOOK REVIEWS]

Hostile Earth Mother insidiously subdues human colony; review of *Dreams of an Unseen Planet*. Michael Mirolla. photo · *MG* April 4, 1987: H10.
[FIRST NOVELS: BOOK REVIEWS]

DREAMS OF SPEECH AND VIOLENCE: THE ART OF THE SHORT STORY IN CANADA AND NEW ZEALAND/Critical work by W.H. New

[Untitled]; review of *Dreams of Speech and Violence*. James Acheson. *Amer R of Can Studies* Autumn 1987; Vol 17 No 3: p352–353.

[Untitled]; review of *Dreams of Speech and Violence*. Keith Garebian. *Quill & Quire* June 1987; Vol 53 No 6: p35.

[Untitled]; review of *Dreams of Speech and Violence*. Patricia Morley. *Books in Can* Aug-Sept 1987; Vol 16 No 6: p25.

DRIVING OFFENSIVELY/Poems by Richard Stevenson

First books from five regional presses; reviews of poetry books. Colin Morton. *Arc* Spring 1987; No 18: p52–59.

DROLET, STÉPHANE

La vitrine du livre; review of *Sprotch et le tuyau manquant*. Guy Ferland. *MD* July 18, 1987: pC6.

DROUIN, DOMINIQUE

Une histoire de jeunesse; review of *Tableau de jeunesse*. Chantal Gamache. *MD* May 23, 1987: pD3.
[FIRST NOVELS: BOOK REVIEWS]

La vitrine du livre; reviews. Jean Royer. *MD* March 14, 1987: pD4.
[CANADIAN LITERARY PERIODICALS]

DU FOND REDOUT/Poems by Robert Giroux

La répétition de l'intime; reviews of poetry books. André Marquis. photo · *Lettres québec* Spring 1987; No 45: p44–46.

DU SOMMET D'UN ARBRE/Journal by Yves Beauchemin

Le Matou author used radio journalism for artistic ends; review of *Du sommet d'un arbre*. Benoit Aubin. photo · *MG* Jan 3, 1987: pB7.

Du sommet d'un arbre ou le regard en plongée et en quatre temps; article. Renald Bérubé. *Voix et images* Spring 1987; Vol 12 No 3: p404–415.
[AUTOBIOGRAPHICAL WRITING]

Présentation; introduction to prose excerpts from *Du sommet d'un arbre*. Adrien Thério. photo · *Lettres québec* Spring 1987; No 45: p8.

DU SOUFRE DANS LES LAMPIONS/Novel by André Bruneau

La reconstitution de tableaux d'époque; review of *Du soufre dans les lampions*. Madeleine Ouellette-Michalska. photo · *MD* April 25, 1987: pD3.

DUBÉ, MARCEL

Prix et distinctions; list of award winners. photo · *Lettres québec* Summer 1987; No 46: p7.
[AWARDS, LITERARY]

Stage version of early Radio-Canada drama works well; theatre review of *Florence*. Marianne Ackerman. *MG* April 1, 1987: pD8.

Le théâtre qu'on joue; theatre reviews. André Dionne. photo · *Lettres québec* Summer 1987; No 46: p47–48.

Marcel Dubé: la tragédie de l'homme blessé; interview, includes introduction. Gérald Gaudet. photo · *Lettres québec* Summer 1987; No 46: p41–46.

Prix et distinctions; list of award winners. Gaétan Lévesque. photo · *Lettres québec* Autumn 1987; No 47: p7.
[AWARDS, LITERARY; GOVERNOR GENERAL'S AWARDS]

La vie littéraire; column. Jean Royer. *MD* Feb 14, 1987: pC2.
[AWARDS, LITERARY; CANADIAN LITERARY PERIODICALS; COMPETITIONS, LITERARY; FICTION READINGS; POETRY READINGS; RADIO AND CANADIAN LITERATURE]

La vitrine du livre; reviews. Jean Royer. photo · *MD* March 21, 1987: pD2.
[CANADIAN LITERARY PERIODICALS]

La vie littéraire; column. Jean Royer. photo · *MD* June 13, 1987: pD2.
[AWARDS, LITERARY; COMPETITIONS, LITERARY; POETRY READINGS; RADIO AND CANADIAN LITERATURE; TELEVISION AND CANADIAN LITERATURE; WRITERS' ORGANIZATIONS]

La vie littéraire; column. Jean Royer. *MD* Oct 3, 1987: pD2.
[AWARDS, LITERARY; CANADIAN LITERARY PUBLISHING; POETRY READINGS; WRITERS' WORKSHOPS]

Deux nouveaux académéciens; article. Jean Royer. *MD* Oct 19, 1987: p9.
[AWARDS, LITERARY]

Sommaires; reviews. Adrien Thério. *Lettres québec* Summer 1987; No 46: p80.

DUBÉ, YVES

Dits et faits; column. photo · *Lettres québec* Spring 1987; No 45: p6–7.
[AWARDS, LITERARY; PUBLISHING AND PUBLISHERS IN CANADA; TRANSLATIONS OF CANADIAN LITERATURE; WRITERS' ORGANIZATIONS]

Opéra-fête: the power of the image; article. Solange Lévesque. photo trans · *Can Theatre R* Spring 1987; No 50: p20–25.

Dits et faits; column. Adrien Thério. photo · *Lettres québec* Summer 1987; No 46: p6.
[AUTHORS, CANADIAN; CANADIAN LITERARY PUBLISHING; CONFERENCES, LITERARY; GOVERNMENT GRANTS FOR WRITERS/PUBLISHERS; LIBRARY SERVICES AND CANADIAN LITERATURE]

DUBOIS, MICHELLE

La vie littéraire; column. Jean Royer. *MD* Jan 17, 1987: pB2.
[AWARDS, LITERARY; CONFERENCES, LITERARY; RADIO AND CANADIAN LITERATURE; TELEVISION AND CANADIAN LITERATURE]

DUBOIS, RENÉ-DANIEL

Playwright has big week ahead; article. *WFP* April 8, 1987: p35.

Dubois play heads for New York fest; article. *MG* Sept 10, 1987: pC13.

At centre stage with a message; article. photo · *Maclean's* Dec 28, 1987; Vol 100 No 52: p29.

Three openings in a week for busy young playwright; article. Marianne Ackerman. photo · *MG* April 4, 1987: pG1.

Le Printemps cool flash but no sizzle; theatre review of *Le Printemps, monsieur Deslauriers*. Marianne Ackerman. photo · *MG* April 14, 1987: pB8.

Dubois: Toronto's playwright-of-the-hour; theatre reviews. Marianne Ackerman. photo · *MG* May 5, 1987: pB6.

René-Daniel Dubois: the generous word; article. Hélène Beauchamp. Thierry Hentsch. photo trans · *Can Theatre R* Spring 1987; No 50: p29–36.

Drama's daring new voice; theatre review of *Pericles Prince of Tyre* by William Shakespeare. John Bemrose. photo · *Maclean's* April 27, 1987; Vol 100 No 17: p61.

Deux pièces en forme d'interrogatoire; reviews of *Being at Home with Claude* and *Fragments d'une lettre d'adieu lus par des géologues*. André-G. Bourassa. photo · *Lettres québec* Spring 1987; No 45: p50–51.

Tragic truth in Being at Home; theatre review of *Being at Home with Claude*. Ray Conlogue. photo · *G&M* April 8, 1987: pC8

Mystifying show looks at nature of art, magic; theatre review of *Pericles Prince of Tyre* by William Shakespeare. Ray Conlogue. photo · *G&M* April 10, 1987: pC6.

'Titanic encounter' typifies rising star's style; theatre review of *Le Printemps, monsieur Deslauriers*. Ray Conlogue. photo · *G&M* April 16, 1987: pD3.

Get set for double shot of Dubois; article. Robert Crew. photo · *TS* April 4, 1987: pF1,F8.

Young Quebec writer pens remarkable play; theatre review of *Being at Home with Claude*. Robert Crew. photo · *TS* April 8, 1987: pD3.

Dubois' Pericles not perfect but impressive nonetheless; theatre review of *Pericles Prince of Tyre* by William Shakespeare. Robert Crew. photo · *TS* April 10, 1987: pD20.

Le théâtre qu'on joue; theatre reviews of *Le Printemps, monsieur Deslauriers* and *Le Vrai monde?*. André Dionne. photo · *Lettres québec* Autumn 1987; No 47: p49–50.

Grandeur et misère: le retour du père sur la scène québécoise; article. Carole Fréchette. photo · *Jeu* 1987; No 45: p17–35.
[QUEBEC DRAMA (FRENCH LANGUAGE): HISTORY AND CRITICISM]

[Untitled]; article. John Goddard. *Maclean's* April 27, 1987; Vol 100 No 17: p61.

Dubois' Bedouins run riot through prairie theatre; theatre review of *Don't Blame the Bedouins*. Stephen Godfrey. photo · *G&M* Dec 3, 1987: pA25.

Moisson d'avril; column. Robert Lévesque. photo · *MD* March 31, 1987: p17.

Dubois chez Duceppe: les années de plomb de l'après-référendum; article. Robert Lévesque. photo · *MD* April 25, 1987: pC1,C10.

Un printemps clair-obscur; theatre review of *Le Printemps, monsieur Deslauriers*. Solange Lévesque. photo · *Jeu* 1987; No 44: p180–182.

Du côté du rococo . . . ; theatre review of *Le Troisième fils du professeur Yourolov*. Robert Lévesque. *MD* Sept 23, 1987: p11.

[Untitled]; theatre review of *Le Troisième fils du professeur Yourolov*. Robert Lévesque. *MD* Oct 2, 1987: p15.

La Russie de Basile, le Québec de Dubois; review of *Le Printemps, monsieur Deslauriers*. Robert Lévesque. photo · *MD* Oct 10, 1987: pD6.

Robert Lepage, globe-trotter; column. Robert Lévesque. photo · *MD* Oct 20, 1987: p13,15.
[CONFERENCES, LITERARY]

Bedouins voluminous toy chest filled with witty, wordy delight; theatre review of *Don't Blame the Bedouins*. Randal McIlroy. *WFP* Nov 13, 1987: p35.

Dubois' dramatic debut; article. Louise McKinney. *Tor Life* April 1987; Vol 21 No 5: p18.

Les jeunes loups; reviews. Lucie Robert. *Voix et images* Spring 1987; Vol 12 No 3: p561–564.
[CANADIAN LITERARY PERIODICALS]

DUCASSE, FRANCE

Léonce, Léonil . . . et Sept fois Jeanne; reviews of *Cette fois, Jeanne . . .* and *La Double vie de Léonce et Léonil*. Louise Milot. photo · *Lettres québec* Autumn 1987; No 47: p17–18.
[FIRST NOVELS: BOOK REVIEWS]

France Ducasse: l'â d'or de l'enfance; review of *La Double vie de Léonce et Lénoil*. Madeleine Ouellette-Michalska. photo · *MD* May 9, 1987: pD3.

DUCHARME, RÉJEAN

Chagall, Plante et Mercier . . . ; essay. Rolande Allard-Lacerte. *MD* Dec 21, 1987: p6.

[Untitled]; review of *Ha! Ha!*. Marc Côté. *Books in Can* March 1987; Vol 16 No 2: p25.

Un star system au Québec?; article. Jean-Paul Daoust. photo · *Jeu* 1987; No 43: p47–49.

DUCHESNE, JACQUES

Misères de l'édition théâtrale; reviews of plays. Lucie Robert. *Voix et images* Winter 1987; No 35: p339–342.

DUCLUZEAU, JEANNE

An historical novel on Acadians deported to France; review of *Le Chemin des Huit-Maisons*. Sally Ross. *Atlan Prov Book R* Nov-Dec 1987; Vol 14 No 4: p11.

DUCORNET, RIKKI

[Untitled]; review of *Entering Fire*. Oliver Conant. *NYT Book R* June 7, 1987: p30.

DUDEK, LOUIS

Montreal poets inspired by travel in hot countries; reviews of poetry books. Barbara Black. *MG* March 28, 1987: pE9.

Flashes of mortality; review of *Zembla's Rocks*. Ray Filip. *Books in Can* April 1987; Vol 16 No 3: p36.

Some beautiful moments but all too fleeting; reviews of poetry books. Maggie Helwig. *TS* Aug 15, 1987: M6.

Poetry: packing all the power into two of seven titles; reviews of poetry books. Robin Skelton. photo · *Quill & Quire* May 1987; Vol 53 No 5: p24.

The virtuous poet; review of *Zembla's Rocks*. Fraser Sutherland. *G&M* April 18, 1987: pC18.

DUET FOR THREE/Novel by Joan Barfoot

New in paper; reviews of novels. *TS* Aug 30, 1987: pA18.
[FIRST NOVELS: BOOK REVIEWS]

Ours as daughters; reviews of *Duet for Three* and *Flitterin' Judas*. Nancy Bailey. *Can Lit* Spring 1987; No 112: p143–145.

A magnificent greed; review of *Duet for Three*. Robb Forman Dew. *NYT Book R* April 5, 1987: p19.

DUFFY, DENNIS

Perfect hindsight; review of *Sounding the Iceberg*. Laurel Boone. *Books in Can* April 1987; Vol 16 No 3: p38–39

CanHistory?; review of *Sounding the Iceberg*. Allan Levine. *G&M* Feb 28, 1987: pE20.

Canadian historical fiction; review article about *Sounding the Iceberg*. Leslie Monkman. *Queen's Q* Autumn 1987; Vol 94 No 3: p630–640.
[HISTORICAL FICTION]

[Untitled]; review of *Sounding the Iceberg*. Clara Thomas. *U of Toronto Q* Fall 1987; Vol 57 No 1: p158–160.

DUFOUR, JOSÉE

Une petite fille qui ne manque pas de courage; review of *Le Testament de Madame Legendre*. Pierrette Dubé. *Can Child Lit* 1987; No 48: p86–87.

Le roman policier désarmé; review of *Vol à retardement*. René Gagné. *Can Child Lit* 1987; No 46: p85–86.

DUMAS, JACQUELINE

One miss, one hit; reviews of *And I'm Never Coming Back* and *Madam Piccolo and the Craziest Pickle Party Ever*. Sylvia Markle-Craine. *Can Child Lit* 1987; No 48: p100–102.

DUNCAN, DAVE

Geologists find gold in arts; article. Randy Fisher. Eva Innes. photo · *Fin Post* May 4, 1987: p22.

Oilpatch geologist mines for literary success; article. Kenneth McGoogan. photo · *CH* April 3, 1987: pC1.

DUNCAN, SARA JEANNETTE

Stories create magic moments for audience at Festival One; theatre review of *Dragon Snapper*. Reg Skene. *WFP* May 4, 1987: p29.

Pioneer lady on stage; article. Morley Walker. photo · *WFP* April 30, 1987: p26.

DUNMORE, SPENCER

I say, a hero too prim, too precious, eh wot?; review of *No Holds Barred*. Geoff Chapman. *TS* May 9, 1987: M4.

A corporate romp in Adland, N.Y.; review of *No Holds Barred*. William French. *G&M* March 14, 1987: pE19.

DUNN, SONJA

A trio of poets to tickle a child's fancy; reviews of children's poetry books. Adele Ashby. *Quill & Quire (Books for Young People)* June 1987; Vol 53 No 6: p10.

DUPRÉ, LOUISE

[Untitled]; review of *Chambres*. Anne-Marie Alonzo. *Estuaire* Winter 1986 87; No 43: p75–76.

Le récit à la NBJ; review of *La Nouvelle barre du jour*. Caroline Bayard. *Lettres québec* Summer 1987; No 46: p34–35.

La répétition de l'intime; reviews of poetry books. André Marquis. photo · *Lettres québec* Spring 1987; No 45: p44–46.

Deux récits de l'intelligence et du coeur; reviews of *Chambres* and *Catégoriques un deux et trois*. Jean Royer. *MD* Jan 3, 1987: pC4.

Le sentiment de la langue; reviews of 'Quand on a une langue on peut aller à Rome' and Les Changeurs de signes. Jean Royer. MD Feb 28, 1987: pC3.
[CANADIAN LITERARY PERIODICALS]

La vie littéraire; column. Jean Royer. MD April 4, 1987: pD2.
[POETRY READINGS]

[Untitled]; review of Chambres. Jacques Saint-Pierre. Moebius (special issue) Spring 1987; No 32: p120–121.

DUREAULT, VINCENT

Franco-Manitoban satire translates sense of deja vu; theatre review of Avant qu'les autres le fassent. Philip Clark. WFP Oct 17, 1987: p34.

Entertaining; letter to the editor. Richard McCarthy. WFP Nov 7, 1987: p7.

Cercle tries for last laugh first; article. Brad Oswald. photo · WFP Oct 16, 1987: p33.

DURHAM, JAMES

Festival One plays singularly successful; theatre reviews. Stephen Godfrey. photo · G&M May 8, 1987: pF9.
[FESTIVALS, DRAMA]

Picture of rebellious victim of cerebral palsy gripping, raises audience awareness; theatre review of Franklin. Reg Skene. WFP May 4, 1987: p29.

DUSSAULT, LOUISETTE

A box that could have stayed closed; theatre review of Pandora. Pat Donnelly. MG March 18, 1987: pD3.

Ouvrir la boîte à maux; theatre review of Pandora. Solange Lévesque. photo · Jeu 1987; No 44: p177–180.

DUSTSHIP GLORY/Novel by Andreas Schroeder

A monument to folly; review of Dustship Glory. Geoff Hancock. Can Forum Feb 1987; Vol 66 No 766: p39–40.
[FIRST NOVELS: BOOK REVIEWS]

Dust bowl to never land; review of Dustship Glory. Alan Shugard. Can Lit Winter 1987; No 115: p196–197.
[FIRST NOVELS: BOOK REVIEWS]

Recent Canadian fiction; reviews of novels. D.O. Spettigue. Queen's Q Summer 1987; Vol 94 No 2: p366–375.
[FIRST NOVELS: BOOK REVIEWS]

DUVAR, HUNTER

"O brave new world": colonialism in Hunter Duvar's De Roberval; article. Mark Blagrave. Can Drama 1987; Vol 13 No 2: p175–181.
[COLONIALISM; NATIVE CANADIANS IN LITERATURE]

DVORAK IN LOVE: A LIGHTHEARTED DREAM/Novel by Josef Skvorecky

A literary scherzo; review of Dvorak in Love. Marketa Goetz-Stankiewicz. illus · Can Forum Aug-Sept 1987; Vol 67 No 771: p41–43.

The latest novels; review of Dvorak in Love. Oliver Gorse. Idler March-April 1987; No 12: p58.

[Untitled]; review of Dvorak in Love. Peter Halewood. Rubicon Fall 1987; No 9: p165–166.

A soft spot for sousaphones; review of Dvorak in Love. Eva Hoffman. illus · NYT Book R Feb 22, 1987: p11.

Vanished consolations; reviews of Dvorak in Love and Mirákl. Roger Scruton. Times Lit Supp Jan 23, 1987; No 4373: p83.

DYKEVERSIONS/Short story anthology

Today's assignment: short fiction that's worth a long look; reviews of short story books. Douglas Hill. G&M March 14, 1987: pE19.
[ANTHOLOGIES: BOOK REVIEWS]

DZELARHONS/Indian legends retold by Anne Cameron

[Untitled]; review of Dzelarhons. Adelle Castelo. Quill & Quire March 1987; Vol 53 No 3: p73.

[Untitled]; review of Dzelarhons. Frances Duncan. Room of One's Own Sept 1987; Vol 11 No 4: p112–115.

Fine short stories examine contemporary domestic life; reviews of Dzelarhons and Afternoon Tea. Douglas Hill. G&M Jan 24, 1987: pE17.

A lesson from myths: live in harmony; review of Dzelarhons. Catherine Macleod. TS April 5, 1987: pA22.

[Untitled]; review of Dzelarhons. Sherie Posesorski. Books in Can June-July 1987; Vol 16 No 5: p22.

E.J. PRATT: THE MASTER YEARS 1927–1964/Biography by David G. Pitt

Poet's triumphant ascent presented with grace, insight; review of E.J. Pratt: The Master Years. Ken Adachi. photo · TS Dec 19, 1987: M4.

The likeable poet; review of E.J. Pratt: The Master Years. William French. G&M Dec 5, 1987: pC21.

E.J. PRATT: THE TRUANT YEARS 1882–1927/Biography by David G. Pitt

"Uncertain steerage"; review of E.J. Pratt: The Truant Years. Wendy Schissel. Ariel Jan 1987; Vol 18 No 1: p76–78.

EARLY, L.R.

[Untitled]; reviews of Archibald Lampman and John Metcalf. Dennis Duffy. Eng Studies in Can Sept 1987; Vol 13 No 3: p355–357.

Poet-confessor; review of Archibald Lampman. John Ower. Can Lit Winter 1987; No 115: p167–169.

EASY DOWN EASY/Play by Gordon Pinsent

A dream comes true for Pinsent with play he wrote and stars in; article. photo · MG July 23, 1987: pC10.

Barrie audiences responding to Pinsent play; column. Robert Crew. photo · TS July 27, 1987: pD1.

New Gordon Pinsent play embodies spirit of friend; article. Donna Shoemaker. photo · CH July 27, 1987: pB8.

ECONOMIC SEX/Novel by Ali-Janna Whyte

[Untitled]; review of Economic Sex. Richard Hamilton. Rubicon Spring 1987; No 8: p226.

Full stops; review of *Economic Sex*. Leon Surette. *Can Lit* Winter 1987; No 115: p245–246.
[FIRST NOVELS: BOOK REVIEWS]

ÉCLATS D'ÂME/Poems by Roland Lemieux

Cris et silences des poètes d'automne; review of *Éclats d'âme*. Benoît Lacroix. *MD* Dec 19, 1987: pD3.

ÉCOUTE, SULTANE/Poems by Anne-Marie Alonzo

La vitrine du livre; reviews. Guy Ferland. *MD* May 23, 1987: pD4.

La tentation du romanesque; reviews of poetry books. Richard Giguère. photo · *Lettres québec* Autumn 1987; No 47: p37–39.

Notes de lectures; reviews of *La Mort aurorale* and *Écoute, Sultane*. Jean Royer. *MD* May 23, 1987: pD2.

ÉCRIRE LA LUMIÈRE/Poems by Louise Warren

[Untitled]; review of *Écrire la lumière*. Hugues Corriveau. *Estuaire* Summer 1987; No 45: p59.

ÉCRITS DU CANADA FRANÇAIS/Periodical

Devenez mécène, abonnez-vous!; reviews of periodicals. Robert Melançon. *Liberté* June 1987; Vol 29 No 3: p80–87.
[CANADIAN LITERARY PERIODICALS]

La vitrine du livre; reviews. Jean Royer. photo · *MD* April 18, 1987: pD2.
[CANADIAN LITERARY PERIODICALS]

Des revues presque indispensables; reviews of periodicals. Adrien Thério. *Lettres québec* Autumn 1987; No 47: p63–65.
[CANADIAN LITERARY PERIODICALS]

ÉCRITS SUR LE FANTASTIQUE. BIBLIOGRAPHIE ANALYTIQUE DES ÉTUDES & ESSAIS SUR LE FANTASTIQUE PUBLIS ENTRE 1900 ET 1985 (LITTÉRATURE/CINÉMA/ART FANTASTIQUE)/Annotated bibliography by Norbert Spehner

Aaa! Aâh! Ha! que de belles catastrophes narratives!; reviews. Michel Lord. photo · *Lettres québec* Spring 1987; No 45: p32–35.

ÉCRIVAINS CONTEMPORAINS/Interview compilations

La vitrine du livre; reviews. Guy Ferland. *MD* June 20, 1987: pD4.
[CANADIAN LITERARY PERIODICALS]

Le goût de prolonger le dialogue avec les écrivains; review of *Écrivains contemporains, entretiens 4*. Lori Saint-Martin. photo · *MD* Nov 7, 1987: pD3.

LES ÉCRIVAINS S'ILLUSTRENT/Compilation of drawings by authors

Dessins d'écrivains; review of *Les Écrivains s'illustrent*. Jean Royer. *MD* March 21, 1987: pD2.

THE ECSTASY OF RITA JOE/Play by George Ryga

Wheels on fire: the train of thought in George Ryga's The Ecstasy of Rita Joe; article. Gary Boire. *Can Lit* Summer-Fall 1987; No 113–114: p62–74.

Soloist's view of Rita Joe grows; article. Donald Campbell. photo · *WFP* Oct 2, 1987: p21.

EDGAR POTATO/Children's story by Don Oickle

Meaningful nonsense; reviews of children's books. Adrienne Kertzer. *Can Lit* Winter 1987; No 115: p165–167.

EDMUNDSON, BRUCE

Knockouts; review of *Two Voices*. Jason Sherman. *G&M* Sept 26, 1987: pC22.

EDYTHE WITH A Y/Young adult novel by Mary Blakeslee

[Untitled]; reviews of *Edythe With a Y* and *It Isn't Easy Being Ms. Teeny Wonderful*. Patty Lawlor. *Quill & Quire (Books for Young People)* April 1987; Vol 53 No 4: p8.

EFFETS DE L'OEIL/Poems by Suzanne Paradis

[Untitled]; reviews of *Un goût de sel* and *Effets de l'oeil*. Hélène Thibaux. *Estuaire* Autumn 1987; No 46: p86–87.

EFFETS PERSONNELS SUIVI DE DOUZE JOURS DANS UNE NUIT/Poems by Pierre Morency

La tentation du romanesque; reviews of poetry books. Richard Giguère. photo · *Lettres québec* Autumn 1987; No 47: p37–39.

EHRART, PIERRE

Le trou de la serrure; review of *Tremblements du désir*. Guy Ferland. *MD* May 30, 1987: pD3.

EINSTEIN/Play by Gabriel Emanuel

Einstein a moving piece of theatre; theatre review. Marianne Ackerman. photo · *MG* May 1, 1987: pD4.

[Untitled]; theatre review of *Einstein*. Marianne Ackerman. *MG* May 15, 1987: pD6.

Selling doesn't mean selling out; article. Paul McKie. photo · *WFP* Oct 24, 1987: p22.
[TELEVISION AND CANADIAN LITERATURE]

ELEUSIS/Poems by Harold Rhenisch

Nursery rhyme, myth and dream; reviews of *Shaking the Dreamland Tree* and *Eleusis*. Gillian Harding-Russell. *NeWest R* Sept 1987; Vol 13 No 1: p17–18.

THE ELIZABETH STORIES/Short stories by Isabel Huggan

[Untitled]; review of *The Elizabeth Stories*. *New Yorker* Aug 31, 1987; Vol 63 No 28: p97–98.

I pledge allegiance to myself; review of *The Elizabeth Stories*. Ellen Currie. *NYT Book R* July 12, 1987: p11.

ELLIOTT, CHRIS LORNE

Culture Shock: not enough substance for two-act play; theatre review. Bill Brownstein. *MG* July 13, 1987: pB9.

ELLIOTT, GEORGE

Writer, photographer followed the 401's off-ramps to get story; article. photo · *WFP* Jan 21, 1987: p29.

ELLIOTT, PATRICIA

[Untitled]; reviews of poetry books. Lavinia Inbar. illus *Poetry Can R* Spring 1987; Vol 8 No 2–3: p51–53.

ELLIS, SARAH

[Untitled]; article. *G&M* Oct 31, 1987.
[AWARDS, LITERARY]

Tales for teenagers feature strong, viable family units; reviews of *The Baby Project* and *Payment in Death*. Jane Kent. *CH* April 12, 1987: pF7.

Learning to accept change and loss; review of *The Baby Project*. Margaret Steffler. *Can Child Lit* 1987; No 47: p90–91.

EMANUEL, GABRIEL

Einstein a moving piece of theatre; theatre review. Marianne Ackerman. photo · *MG* May 1, 1987: pD4.

[Untitled]; theatre review of *Einstein*. Marianne Ackerman. *MG* May 15, 1987: pD6.

Selling doesn't mean selling out; article. Paul McKie. photo · *WFP* Oct 24, 1987: p22.
[TELEVISION AND CANADIAN LITERATURE]

EMILY CARR/Play by Alan Richardson

Emily Carr paints a bland wash; theatre review. Robert Crew. photo · *TS* Nov 25, 1987: pB5.

New drama paints portrait of Emily Carr; column. Vit Wagner. photo · *TS* Nov 20, 1987: pE4.

THE EMPEROR'S PANDA/Children's novel by David Day

The language of fantasy; reviews of *The Emperor's Panda* and *Amanda Greenleaf Visits a Distant Star*. Jo-Ann Wallace. *Can Child Lit* 1987; No 47: p73–74

EMPIÈCEMENTS/Poems by Daniel Guenette

Comme un vent; reviews of poetry books. James P. Gilroy. *Can Lit* Winter 1987; No 115: p260–261.

THE EMPTY CHAIR/Young adult novel by Bess Kaplan

Struggles of adolescence; review of *The Empty Chair*. Helen Norrie. *WFP* April 11, 1987: p60.

Western publisher produces winners only; reviews of *Last Chance Summer* and *The Empty Chair*. Tim Wynne-Jones. *G&M* Feb 21, 1987: pE19.

THE ENCHANTED CARIBOU/Children's story by Elizabeth Cleaver

Meaningful nonsense; reviews of children's books. Adrienne Kertzer. *Can Lit* Winter 1987; No 115: p165–167.

THE ENCHANTED FOREST/Play by Leon Rooke

Back to the earth with baby, Mr. Big and the Fat Lady; theatre reviews of *The Good Baby* and *The Enchanted Forest*. Stephen Godfrey. photo · *G&M* July 18, 1987: pC1,C4.

ENCOUNTERS AND EXPLORATIONS: CANADIAN WRITERS AND EUROPEAN CRITICS/Critical essays anthology

[Untitled]; review of *Encounters and Explorations*. Hallvard Dahlie. *U of Toronto Q* Fall 1987; Vol 57 No 1: p156–158.

[Untitled]; reviews of critical works. Don Gutteridge. *Queen's Q* Summer 1987; Vol 94 No 2: p464–467.

[Untitled]; review of *Encounters and Explorations*. David Staines. *Amer R of Can Studies* Spring 1987; Vol 17 No 1: p117–118.

THE END OF ICE/Poems by Lesley Choyce

Iconographies; reviews of *Out of the Storm* and *The End of Ice*. Jack F. Stewart. *Can Lit* Spring 1987; No 112: p166–167.

ENFANTS D'HERMÈS/Poems by Patrick Coppens

Comme un vent; reviews of poetry books. James P. Gilroy. *Can Lit* Winter 1987; No 115: p260–261.

ENGEL, HOWARD

Aujourd'hui; column. *MD* Feb 16, 1987: p16.
[FICTION READINGS; WRITERS' WORKSHOPS]

New in paper; review of *A City Called July*. *TS* Aug 16, 1987: pA18.

Benny bumbles into a murder in the wilds; television review of *Murder Sees the Light*. Jim Bawden. photo · *TS* March 14, 1987: J6.
[TELEVISION AND CANADIAN LITERATURE]

Criminal proceedings; review of *A City Called July*. T.J. Binyon. *Times Lit Supp* July 17, 1987; No 4398: p778.

Murder Sees The Light best left in dark; television review. Mike Boone. *MG* March 13, 1987: pD6.
[TELEVISION AND CANADIAN LITERATURE]

Crime; review of *A City Called July*. Newgate Callendar. *NYT Book R* March 8, 1987: p29.

Kingsley triumphs in Silas Marner; television review of *Murder Sees the Light*. John Haslett Cuff. photo · *G&M* March 14, 1987: pE5.
[TELEVISION AND CANADIAN LITERATURE]

A shot in the park; essay. Howard Engel. illus · *G&M* March 14, 1987: pE1.
[TELEVISION AND CANADIAN LITERATURE]

Comic solutions; review of *A City Called July*. Roderick W. Harvey. *Can Lit* Winter 1987; No 115: p214–216.

Fiction for slow days when reading is the happiest sport; review of *Murder Sees the Light*. Douglas Hill. *G&M* Aug 1, 1987: pC15.

A salute to detective stories; article. Liam Lacey. photo · *G&M* Dec 8, 1987: pD7.

Expect the unexpected in off-beat murder mystery; television review of *Murder Sees the Light*. Doreen Martens. *WFP* March 13, 1987: p31.
[TELEVISION AND CANADIAN LITERATURE]

Paperback PIs battle crime; review of *A City Called July*. Kenneth McGoogan. photo · *CH* Sept 6, 1987: pE7.

Bumbling Benny takes new case; television review of *Murder Sees the Light*. Bill Musselwhite. photo · *CH* March 14, 1987: pF6.
[TELEVISION AND CANADIAN LITERATURE]

Tip sheet: storytellers will present a night for lovers, liars and lunatics; column. Susan Schwartz. photo · *MG* Feb 11, 1987: pD3.
[FICTION READINGS]

ENGEL, MARIAN

Maple Leaf memories in print; reviews of *The Bishop* and *The Glassy Sea*. Lew Gloin. *TS* July 12, 1987: pA18.

A humanistic vision of the lives of churchmen and women; reviews of *The Glassy Sea* and *The Bishop*. Douglas Hill. *G&M* Sept 12, 1987: pC17.

Marian Engel's family fictions: Lunatic Villas; article. Christl Verduyn. *New Q* Spring-Summer 1987; Vol 7 No 1–2: p274–283.
[THE FAMILY IN CANADIAN LITERATURE; FEMINIST WRITING AND CRITICISM; WOMEN IN LITERATURE]

ENGLISH-CANADIAN THEATRE/Critical work by Eugene Benson and L.W. Conolly

[Untitled]; review of *English-Canadian Theatre*. Rota Herzberg Lister. *Can Drama* 1987; Vol 13 No 2: p227–228.

A cogent view of Canadian theatre; review of *English-Canadian Theatre*. Margaret Penman. photo · *TS* Dec 27, 1987: pE18

ENNS, VICTOR JERRET

[Untitled]; review of *Correct in This Culture*. Leslie Nutting. *Poetry Can R* Fall 1987; Vol 9 No 1: p38.

ENTERING FIRE/Novel by Rikki Ducornet

[Untitled]; review of *Entering Fire*. Oliver Conant. *NYT Book R* June 7, 1987: p30.

EPP, RICHARD

Intimate Admiration has few insights, wooden dialogue; theatre review. Ray Conlogue. photo · *G&M* July 1, 1987: pC5.

Lethbridge writer's play to be staged at Stratford; article. Robert Crew. photo · *TS* March 2, 1987: pB3.

Intimate Admiration one big bore; theatre review. Robert Crew. photo · *TS* June 28, 1987: pC2.

[Untitled]; theatre review of *Intimate Admiration*. Keith Garebian. *Queen's Q* Autumn 1987; Vol 94 No 3: p753–755.

Neville to don makeup for new Canadian play; article about John Neville. Jamie Portman. photo · *CH* June 23, 1987: pB6.

Alberta playwright's work squanders talent; theatre review of *Intimate Admiration*. Jamie Portman. *CH* June 29, 1987: pC1.

EQUINOX/Novel by Kurt Maxwell

The plot thickens; review of *Equinox*. Jack Batten. *Books in Can* May 1987; Vol 16 No 4: p27–28.

Murder & mayhem: plot and details in a cop's life; reviews of *Gallows View* and *Equinox*. Margaret Cannon. photo · *G&M* May 23, 1987: pC23.

Heartless violence of terrorism explored in this numbing novel; review of *Equinox*. Joan McGrath. *TS* June 13, 1987: M4.

Book world: 'new' terrorists like their perks, author suggests; column. Beverley Slopen. *TS* May 10, 1987: pA22.

Would-be world-class thrillers need plots to be complete; reviews of *Equinox* and *Fire Eyes*. Philippe van Rjndt. photo · *Quill & Quire* April 1987; Vol 53 No 4: p28.

CIA gambits aren't what they used to be; review of *Equinox*. David Wimhurst. *MG* May 16, 1987: J8.

ERKUNDUNGEN, 26 KANADISCHE ERZÄHLER/Short story anthology

Une anthologie d'auteurs canadiens traduits en allemand; review of *Erkundungen, 26 kanadische Erzähler*. Diane-Monique Daviau. *Lettres québec* Summer 1987; No 46: p72–73.

ÉROSHIMA/Novel by Dany Laferrière

Une bombe dans la tête; review of *Éroshima*. Jean Royer. *MD* Oct 10, 1987: pD3.

ESCAPE FROM FANTASY GARDENS/Play by Mark Leiren-Young

Three new political plays; theatre reviews. Malcolm Page. *Can Drama* 1987; Vol 13 No 2: p224–226.

LES ESCLAVES/Novella by Jean-Yves Soucy

La vitrine du livre; reviews of fictional works. Guy Ferland. *MD* Dec 5, 1987: pD4.

ESSAIS INACTUELS/Essays by Pierre Vadeboncoeur

Le vrai penseur, un beau matin, prend son bâton de pèlerin; review of *Essais inactuels*. Jean Éthier-Blais. *MD* May 9, 1987: pD8.

ESSAYS ON SASKATCHEWAN WRITING/Critical essays collection

[Untitled]; review of *Essays on Saskatchewan Writing*. Martin Kuester. *Zeitschrift Kanada-Studien* 1987; Vol 7 No 1: p267–269.

ESSENTIAL WORDS: AN ANTHOLOGY OF JEWISH CANADIAN POETRY/Anthology

Destinations; reviews of *Essential Words* and *Voix-Off*. Marya Fiamengo. *Can Lit* Spring 1987; No 112: p112–114.
[ANTHOLOGIES: BOOK REVIEWS]

ESTUAIRE/Periodical

"Question de poésie": un colloque de la revue Estuaire le 20 novembre au salon du livre; article. *MD* Nov 16, 1987: p9.
[CANADIAN LITERARY PERIODICALS; CONFERENCES, LITERARY]

La revue des revues; reviews of periodicals. Guy Ferland. *MD* Sept 19, 1987: pD6.
[CANADIAN LITERARY PERIODICALS]

Devenez mécène, abonnez-vous!; reviews of periodicals. Robert Melançon. *Liberté* June 1987; Vol 29 No 3: p80–87.
[CANADIAN LITERARY PERIODICALS]

Ding et Dong; reviews of periodicals. Robert Melançon. *Liberté* Dec 1987; Vol 29 No 6: p122–129.
[CANADIAN LITERARY PERIODICALS]

Estuaire au carrefour des poésies; editorial Jean Royer. *Estuaire* Spring 1987; No 44: p5–8.
[CANADIAN LITERARY PERIODICALS]

ETCHEVERRY, JORGE

[Untitled]; reviews of poetry books. Anita Hurwitz. *Poetry Can R* Spring 1987; Vol 8 No 2–3: p50–51.

ETHERINGTON, FRANK

Theatre Direct probes urban kids' reality; theatre reviews of *The Snake Lady* and *Thin Ice*. Ray Conlogue. *G&M* April 29, 1987: pC7.

ÉTHIER-BLAIS, JEAN

Jean Éthier-Blais remporte le prix France-Québec 1987; article. *MD* June 12, 1987: p3.

Dans les poches; reviews of *Dictionnaire de moi-même* and *Mon cheval pour un royaume*. Guy Ferland. *MD* May 30, 1987: pD2

Prix et distinctions; list of award winners. Gaétan Lévesque. photo · *Lettres québec* Autumn 1987; No 47: p7.
[AWARDS, LITERARY; GOVERNOR GENERAL'S AWARDS]

[Untitled]; reviews of novels. Alice Parizeau. *MD* Nov 28, 1987: pD9.

Retour; letter to the editor. Luc Potvin. *MD* March 28, 1987: pA10.

Jean Éthier-Blais: "La littérature, c'est tout ce que nous avons"; article. Jean Royer. photo · *MD* Jan 24, 1987: pB1,B4.

[Untitled]; review of *Le Désert blanc*. Jacques Saint-Pierre. *Moebius (special issue)* Spring 1987; No 32: p121–123.

Trois voyages — petit, moyen et grand — du littératage à la littérature; reviews of short story books. Marie José Thériault. photo · *Lettres québec* Spring 1987; No 45: p30–32.
[ANTHOLOGIES: BOOK REVIEWS]

Les vacances d'un chroniqueur; letter to the editor. Henri Tranquille. *MD* July 27, 1987: p6.

ETHNIC-CANADIAN WRITING

Aujourd'hui; column. *MD* Feb 10, 1987: p10.
[WRITERS' WORKSHOPS]

Speculations: the ethnic music in Canadian poetry; column. Raymond Filip. *Poetry Can R* Fall 1987; Vol 9 No 1: p18.

The leopard's spots; article. George Woodcock. *Tor South Asian R* Spring 1987; Vol 5 No 3: p41–51.

ÉTIENNE, GÉRARD

La vie littéraire; column. Marc Morin. photo · *MD* Nov 28, 1987: pD12.
[CANADIAN LITERARY PERIODICALS]

ÉTUDES FRANÇAISES/Periodical

Analyse spectrale d'Études françaises; article. Bernard Beugnot. *Voix et images* Winter 1987; No 35: p278–284.
[CANADIAN LITERARY PERIODICALS]

Qui de neuf du côté universitaire?; reviews of periodicals. Carole David. *MD* Jan 17, 1987: pB5,B7.
[CANADIAN LITERARY PERIODICALS]

Un numéro d'Études françaises explore les rapports de la littérature et des médias; review. Carole David. *MD* May 9, 1987: pD2.
[CANADIAN LITERARY PERIODICALS]

Études françaises, vingt ans après; article. Laurent Mailhot. *Voix et images* Winter 1987; No 35: p284–287.

Poulin; review of *Études françaises (special issue)*. Anne Marie Miraglia. *Can Lit* Spring 1987; No 112: p152–154.
[CANADIAN LITERARY PERIODICALS]

Cartographies; review of *Études françaises*. Ralph Sarkonak. *Can Lit* Summer-Fall 1987; No 113–114: p244–245.
[CANADIAN LITERARY PERIODICALS]

ÉTUDES LITTÉRAIRES/Periodical

A fitting homage; review of *Études littéraire (special issue)*. Ellen Reisman Babby. *Essays on Can Writ* Spring 1987; No 34: p190–195.
[CANADIAN LITERARY PERIODICALS]

Qui de neuf du côté universitaire?; reviews of periodicals. Carole David. *MD* Jan 17, 1987: pB5,B7.
[CANADIAN LITERARY PERIODICALS]

De l'érudition: l'esprit et la lettre; reviews of periodicals. Suzanne Lamy. *Voix et images* Winter 1987; No 35: p342–346.
[CANADIAN LITERARY PERIODICALS]

[Untitled]; review of *Études littéraires*. Barbara McEwen. *Theatre Hist in Can* Fall 1987; Vol 8 No 2: p234–237.
[CANADIAN LITERARY PERIODICALS]

Études littéraires est-elle indispensable?; essay. Louise Milot. *Voix et images* Winter 1987; No 35: p267–271.
[CANADIAN LITERARY PERIODICALS]

Constantes et ruptures en recherche littéraire: le cas d'Études littéraires; article. Jean-Marcel Paquette. *Voix et images* Winter 1987; No 35: p271–277.
[CANADIAN LITERARY PERIODICALS]

La vitrine du livre; reviews. Jean Royer. *MD* March 14, 1987: pD4.
[CANADIAN LITERARY PERIODICALS]

EUROPE-CANADA LITERARY RELATIONS

Frankfurt follow-up; article. *Quill & Quire* Jan 1987; Vol 53 No 1: p18.
[CHILDREN'S LITERATURE]

Canadian books popular in Europe; article. *WFP* Oct 24, 1987: p32.

Novel exports; article. *CH* Oct 25, 1987: pE3.

A boost abroad for Canadian books; article. *G&M* Oct 24, 1987: pC12.

Export sales depend on Frankfurt presence; article. Hamish Cameron. photo · *Quill & Quire* Dec 1987; Vol 53 No 12: p10.
[CONFERENCES, LITERARY]

The effect of the international children's book industry on Canadian publishing endeavours for children and young people; article. Ronald A. Jobe. *Can Child Lit* 1987; No 47: p7–11.
[CANADIAN LITERARY PUBLISHING; CHILDREN'S LITERATURE; CONFERENCES, LITERARY]

Quebec publishers meet English Canada at Frankfurt; article. Jeanne Poulin. *Quill & Quire* Dec 1987; Vol 53 No 12: p11.
[CONFERENCES, LITERARY]

Nordic journey; essay. W.D. Valgardson. *Books in Can* Nov 1987; Vol 16 No 8: p3–4.
[CONFERENCES, LITERARY]

L.M. Montgomery: at home in Poland; article. Barbara Wachowicz. photo · *Can Child Lit* 1987; No 46: p7–35.
[DRAMATIC ADAPTATIONS OF CANADIAN LITERATURE; TRANSLATIONS OF CANADIAN LITERATURE]

EVANS, HUBERT

Hubert Evans — elder of the tribe; article. Betty Millway. photo · *Can Auth & Book* Winter 1987; Vol 62 No 2: p2–3.

EVASON, GREG

[Untitled]; reviews of poetry books. Shaunt Basmajian. *Cross Can Writ Q* 1987; Vol 9 No 3–4: p44,49.
[ANTHOLOGIES: BOOK REVIEWS]

EVERYTHING HAPPENS AT ONCE/Poems by Yvonne Trainer

[Untitled]; reviews of *My Round Table* and *Everything Happens at Once*. Rosemary Aubert. *Poetry Can R* Spring 1987; Vol 8 No 2–3: p48.

Western Canadian poets display talents in new volume; reviews of poetry books. G.P. Greenwood. *CH* July 5, 1987: pF7.

EXCERPTS FROM THE REAL WORLD/Poems by Robert Kroetsch

Realizing Kroetsch's poetry; reviews of *Excerpts from the Real World* and *Seed Catalogue*. Thomas B. Friedman. *Prairie Fire* Winter 1987–88; Vol 8 No 4: p95–98.

[Untitled]; review of *Excerpts from the Real World*. Beverly Harris. *Dandelion* Spring-Summer 1987; Vol 14 No 1: p81–84.

[Untitled]; review of *Excerpts from the Real World*. Louise Longo. *Books in Can* Jan-Feb 1987; Vol 16 No 1: p28.

EXILE HOME/EXILIO EN LA PATRIA/Poems by Lake Sagaris

Montreal poets inspired by travel in hot countries; reviews of poetry books. Barbara Black. *MG* March 28, 1987: pE9.

Slight drag but Cormorant takes off; reviews of *Slow Mist* and *Exile Home/Exilio En la Patria*. Keith Garebian. photo · *TS* March 28, 1987: M4.

The art of the impossible: two recent versions of translation; review of *Exile Home*. Christopher Levenson. *Arc* Fall 1987; No 19: p38–42.

[Untitled]; review of *Exile Home*. Karen Ruttan. *Poetry Can R* Fall 1987; Vol 9 No 1: p35.

Poetry and the loving Spanish tongue; reviews of poetry books. Fraser Sutherland. *G&M* May 30, 1987: pC21.
[ANTHOLOGIES: BOOK REVIEWS]

EXIT STAGE LEFT/Young adult novel by William Pasnak

Successful Alberta children's writers pen new works; article. Kenneth McGoogan. photo · *CH* Dec 18, 1987: pE7.

Fine books for in-betweens; reviews of young adult books. David Williamson. *WFP* Dec 5, 1987: p57.

EXPECTING RAIN/Poems by Stephen Scobie

Representation and celebration: Stephen Scobie's rain songs; review of *Expecting Rain*. Brian Edwards. *Essays on Can Writ* Spring 1987; No 34: p33–38.

EXTASE ET DÉCHIRURE/Essay by Claude Beausoleil

La culture de la confusion; reviews of *Extase et déchirure* and *L'Amour de la carte postale*. Réjean Beaudoin. *Liberté* Dec 1987; Vol 29 No 6: p107–113.

Des genres éclatés, près du "texte infini"; review of *Extase et déchirure*. Lori Saint-Martin. photo · *MD* Oct 17, 1987: pD3.

EXTRÊME LIVRE DES VOYAGES/Poems by Michel Van Schendel

La route sinue fortement; review of *Extrême livre des voyages*. Chantal Gamache. *Lettres québec* Autumn 1987; No 47: p70.

[Untitled]; review of *Extrême livre des voyages*. Pierre Ouellet. *Estuaire* Autumn 1987; No 46: p87–88.

EYE OF THE FATHER/Novel by David Williams

Rune-writer; review of *Eye of the Father*. William Latta. *Can Lit* Winter 1987; No 115: p191–193.

LA FÉE CALCINÉE/Novel by Daniel Gagnon

"La belle inconnue qui déambule depuis des siècles . . . "; review of *La Fée calcinée*. Jean Éthier-Blais. *MD* Nov 28, 1987: pD14.

La vitrine du livre; reviews. Guy Ferland. *MD* Nov 7, 1987: pD4.

FÉMININS SINGULIERS: PRATIQUES D'ÉCRITURE: BROSSARD, THÉORET/Critical work by Renée-Berthe Drapeau

[Untitled]; review of *Féminins singuliers*. Anne-Marie Picard. *U of Toronto Q* Fall 1987; Vol 57 No 1: p200–201.

FABLES FROM THE WOMEN'S QUARTERS/Poems by Claire Harris

[Untitled]; review of *Fables from the Women's Quarters*. Rhea Tregebov. *Fireweed* Winter 1987; No 24: p103–106.

FABLES OF BRUNSWICK AVENUE/Short stories by Katherine Govier

[Untitled]; reviews of short story collections. Carole Gerson. *Queen's Q* Summer 1987; Vol 94 No 2: p483–484

Memory & words; reviews of *Fables of Brunswick Avenue* and *Bottled Roses*. Michael Helm. *Can Lit* Spring 1987; No 112: p92–95.

THE FABULOUS DISGUISE OF OURSELVES/Poems by Jan Conn

Montreal poets inspired by travel in hot countries; reviews of poetry books. Barbara Black. *MG* March 28, 1987: pE9.

[Untitled]; review of *The Fabulous Disguise of Ourselves*. Charlotte Hussey. *Rubicon* Fall 1987; No 9: p163–164.

You ask me what I'm thinking; reviews of poetry books. M. Travis Lane. *Fiddlehead* Winter 1987; No 154: p95–104.

[Untitled]; reviews of *The Fabulous Disguise of Ourselves* and *The Power to Move*. Stephen Scobie. *Malahat R* June 1987; No 79: p166.

THE FABULOUS KELLEY/Play by Jim Betts

Dubois: Toronto's playwright-of-the-hour; theatre reviews. Marianne Ackerman. photo · *MG* May 5, 1987: pB6.

The Fabulous Kelley fails to fulfil promise; theatre review. Robert Crew. *TS* April 30, 1987: H3.

FACÉTIES/Short stories by Michel Francis Lagacé

Mourir comme un chat?; reviews of *Mourir comme un chat* and *Facéties*. Madeleine Ouellette-Michalska. *MD* July 4, 1987: pC6.

THE FACE OF JACK MUNRO/Poems by Tom Wayman

[Untitled]; review of *The Face of Jack Munro*. Gerald Hill. *Poetry Can R* Spring 1987; Vol 8 No 2–3: p46–47.

Looking for the face of Saturday night; review of *The Face of Jack Munro*. John Lent. *CV 2* Summer 1987; Vol 10 No 4: p52–54.

Poetry and solidarity — uneasy bedfellows?; review of *The Face of Jack Munro*. Diana Wegner. *Event* Summer 1987; Vol 16 No 2: p110–115.

LE FACTEUR RÉALITÉ/Play by René Gingras

[Untitled]; theatre review of *Le Facteur réalité*. Diane Pavlovic. photo · *Jeu* 1987; No 44: p112–113.

FADETTE. JOURNAL D'HENRIETTE DESSAULLES, 1874–1880/Journals by Henriette Dessaulles

Jalons pour une narratologie du journal intime: le statut du récit dans le Journal d'Henriette Dessaulles; article. Pierre Hébert. *Voix et images* Autumn 1987; Vol 13 No 1: p140–156.
[AUTOBIOGRAPHICAL WRITING; STRUCTURALIST WRITING AND CRITICISM]

Light words and humor about unions; reviews. Tim Wynne-Jones. *G&M* Oct 17, 1987: pE11.

FAGAN, CARY

[Untitled]; reviews. Beverley Daurio. *Cross Can Writ Q* 1987; Vol 9 No 2: p23.
[FIRST NOVELS: BOOK REVIEWS]

FAIERS, CHRIS

The people honour Faiers; article. *Quill & Quire* June 1987; Vol 53 No 6: p24.
[AWARDS, LITERARY]

[Untitled]; review of *Foot Through the Ceiling*. LeRoy Gorman. *Poetry Can R* Summer 1987; Vol 8 No 4: p32–33.

Seasons, time and memory; reviews of poetry books. Lesley McAllister. *TS* March 21, 1987: M5.

The Milton Acorn Memorial People's Poetry Award; article. Ted Plantos. illus · *Poetry Can R* Summer 1987; Vol 8 No 4: p17.
[AWARDS, LITERARY]

[Untitled]; reviews of poetry books. Martin Singleton. *Cross Can Writ Q* 1987; Vol 9 No 3–4: p38–39.

FAIRBANKS, CAROL

Prairie love; review of *Prairie Women*. Ann Leger Anderson. *Can Lit* Winter 1987; No 115: p249–251.

[Untitled]; reviews of *Varieties of Exile* and *Prairie Women*. Peter Buitenhuis. *Queen's Q* Summer 1987; Vol 94 No 2: p467–470.

[Untitled]; review of *Prairie Women*. Laurie Ricou. *U of Toronto Q* Fall 1987; Vol 57 No 1: p154–156.

[Untitled]; review of *Prairie Women*. Robert Thacker. *Amer R of Can Studies* Spring 1987; Vol 17 No 1: p113–115.

FAIRLEY, BARKER

Barker Fairley 1887–1986; obituary. Gary Michael Dault. *Can Lit* Summer-Fall 1987; No 113–114: p273–274.

Remembering the beginning: Barker Fairley on the origins of the Forum; interview. Hilda Kirkwood. illus · *Can Forum* Jan 1987; Vol 66 No 765: p6–8.
[CANADIAN LITERARY PERIODICALS]

FAIRY TALES

The fairy-tale elements in the early work of Mazo de la Roche; article. Heather Kirk. *Wascana R* Spring 1987; Vol 22 No 1: p3–17.

LE FAIT DE VIVRE OU D'AVOIR VU/Poems by François Charron

La démarche de François Charron; review of *Le Fait de vivre ou d'avoir vu*. Caroline Bayard. *Lettres québec* Winter 1986–87; No 44: p48–49.

La fiction du réel/le réel de la fiction; reviews of poetry books. André Brochu. *Voix et images* Winter 1987; No 35: p322–330.

[Untitled]; reviews of *Le Fait de vivre ou d'avoir vécu* and *La Chambre des miracles*. Hélène Dorion. *Estuaire* Summer 1987; No 45: p50–51.

LA FALAISE/Novel by Francine Lemay

Entre la maison, l'eau et le cosmos: l'écriture féminine; reviews of novels. Patricia Smart. *Voix et images* Winter 1987; No 35: p334–337.

THE FALCON BOW: AN ARCTIC LEGEND/Children's novel by James Houston

The folly of acting in anger; review of *The Falcon Bow*. Gillian Harding-Russell. *Can Child Lit* 1987; No 46: p74–75.

Native heritage is displayed in three timely books; reviews of children's books. Janice Kennedy. *MG* April 4, 1987: H11.

FALL OF THE HOUSE OF KREBBS/Play by Gary Stromsmoe

Events inspired new play; article. Kate Zimmerman. *CH* Sept 25, 1987: pF3.

Atmospheric nature is strength of play; theatre review of *Fall of the House of Krebbs*. Kate Zimmerman. photo · *CH* Oct 2, 1987: pE10.

FALLING TOGETHER/Poems by Lorne Daniel

Western Canadian poets display talents in new volume; reviews of poetry books. G.P. Greenwood. *CH* July 5, 1987: pF7.

[Untitled]; reviews of poetry books. Anita Hurwitz. *Poetry Can R* Spring 1987; Vol 8 No 2–3: p38–39.

FALSE FACE/Children's novel by Welwyn Wilton Katz

Past and present merge in painful, haunting tales; reviews of *False Face* and *Who Is Frances Rain?*. Peter Carver. photo · *Quill & Quire (Books for Young People)* Oct 1987; Vol 53 No 10: p10.
[FIRST NOVELS: BOOK REVIEWS]

Third time lucky for rising author; article. Kenneth Mc-Googan. photo · *CH* Nov 16, 1987: pB3.

The jolly fireplace's darker side; reviews of children's books. Joan McGrath. *TS* Nov 22, 1987: pC8.

FALUDY, GEORGE

Spleen may write the poem, but Layton's heart will speak tomorrow; reviews of poetry books. Trevor Ferguson. *MG* Sept 26, 1987: J11.

Columns of dark; review of *Selected Poems*. Henry Kreisel. *Can Lit* Winter 1987; No 115: p272–275.

FAMILIAR FACES/PRIVATE GRIEFS/Poems by Susan Ioannou

[Untitled]; reviews of poetry books. Lavinia Inbar. illus · *Poetry Can R* Spring 1987; Vol 8 No 2–3: p51–53.

THE FAMILY IN CANADIAN LITERATURE

Childhood experiences in The Loved and the Lost; article. Donald R. Bartlett. *New Q* Spring-Summer 1987; Vol 7 No 1–2: p294–300.

Heuresis: the mother-daughter theme in A Jest of God and Autumn Sonata; article. Michael Bird. *New Q* Spring-Summer 1987; Vol 7 No 1–2: p267–273.
[WOMEN IN LITERATURE]

Miracle, mystery, and authority: rereading The Double Hook; article. Glen Deer. *Open Letter* Summer 1987; Vol 6 No 8: p25–43.
[MYTHS AND LEGENDS IN CANADIAN LITERATURE]

Ernest Buckler's holy family; article. Leona M. Deorksen. *New Q* Spring-Summer 1987; Vol 7 No 1–2: p232–239.

Foreward. Kim Jernigan. *New Q* Spring-Summer 1987; Vol 7 No 1–2: p11–13.

Psychic violence: The Stone Angel and modern family life; article. Ed Jewinski. *New Q* Spring-Summer 1987; Vol 7 No 1–2: p255–266.
[MYTHS AND LEGENDS IN CANADIAN LITERATURE; WOMEN IN LITERATURE]

"To hell with the family!": an open letter to The New Quarterly; letter to the editor. W.J. Keith. *New Q* Spring-Summer 1987; Vol 7 No 1–2: p320–324.

Family relations in Alice Munro's fiction; article. W.R. Martin. *New Q* Spring-Summer 1987; Vol 7 No 1–2: p247–254.

Forward. Celia McLean. *New Q* Spring-Summer 1987; Vol 7 No 1–2: p229–231.

The writer-as-a-young-woman and her family: Montgomery's Emily; article. Judith Miller. *New Q* Spring-Summer 1987; Vol 7 No 1–2: p301–319.
[ARTIST FIGURE; WOMEN IN LITERATURE]

Between the world and the word: John Metcalf's "The Teeth of My Father"; article. Constance Rooke. *New Q* Spring-Summer 1987; Vol 7 No 1–2: p240–246.
[ARTIST FIGURE; METAFICTION]

Marian Engel's family fictions: Lunatic Villas; article. Christl Verduyn. *New Q* Spring-Summer 1987; Vol 7 No 1–2: p274–283.
[FEMINIST WRITING AND CRITICISM; WOMEN IN LITERATURE]

THE FAMILY ROMANCE/Critical essays by Eli Mandel

Style and substance; review of *The Family Romance*. Gary Draper. *Books in Can* May 1987; Vol 16 No 4: p29–31.

The critical art of Eli Mandel; review of *The Family Romance*. E.F. Dyck. *Prairie Fire* Autumn 1987; Vol 8 No 3: p98–101.

Mandel's two minds and Woodcock's single purpose; reviews of *The Family Romance* and *Northern Spring*. Doug Fetherling. photo · *Quill & Quire* May 1987; Vol 53 No 5: p20.

'Romance' a record by which poet puts theory into practice; review of *The Family Romance*. Maggie Helwig. photo · *TS* May 23, 1987: M4.

[Untitled]; review of *The Family Romance*. Robert Kroetsch. *Dandelion* Fall-Winter 1987; Vol 14 No 2: p145–147.

Mandel makes a sure-footed guide; review of *The Family Romance*. Robert Quickenden. *WFP* July 18, 1987: p54

FAMOUS LAST WORDS/Novel by Timothy Findley

CBC to dramatize Findley novel; article. *G&M* April 10, 1987: pC9.
[RADIO AND CANADIAN LITERATURE]

CBC Radio to dramatize Famous Last Words; article. *TS* April 10, 1987: pD20.
[RADIO AND CANADIAN LITERATURE]

Outcome of Bell Jar libel suit closely monitored by publishers; column. Ken Adachi. *TS* Jan 26, 1987: pD4.
[CENSORSHIP]

Findley novel a sell-out in London despite critical vitriol; article. Ken Adachi. *TS* April 6, 1987: pB1.
[INTERNATIONAL REVIEWS OF CANADIAN LITERATURE]

The off-the-wall writing on the wall; review of *Famous Last Words*. John Melmoth. *Times Lit Supp* April 24, 1987; No 4386: p435.

Mauberley's lies: fact and fiction in Timothy Findley's *Famous Last Words*; article. E.F. Shields. abstract · *J of Can Studies* Winter 1987–88; Vol 22 No 4: p44–59.
[HISTORICAL THEMES]

LES FANTÔMES DE MARTIN/Play by Gilbert Turp

a manque d'esprit(s) dans la maison!; theatre review of *Les Fantômes de Martin*. Robert Lévesque. *MD* Nov 26, 1987: p13.

FANTASY

Voyages of the mind; article, includes review of *The Darkest Road*. Peter Giffen. photo · *Maclean's* March 23, 1987; Vol 100 No 12: p66–67.
[SCIENCE FICTION]

FAREWELL TOUR/Short stories by Virgil Burnett

The human comedy; review of *Farewell Tour*. Brian Fawcett. *Books in Can* April 1987; Vol 16 No 3: p18.

Collection charms despite certain bias; review of *Farewell Tour*. Maggie Helwig. *TS* May 9, 1987: M10.

Today's assignment: short fiction that's worth a long look; reviews of short story books. Douglas Hill. *G&M* March 14, 1987: pE19.
[ANTHOLOGIES: BOOK REVIEWS]

[Untitled]; review of *Farewell Tour*. David Homel. *Quill & Quire* April 1987; Vol 53 No 4: p28.

FARHOUD, ABLA

Le théâtre qu'on joue; theatre reviews. André Dionne. illus photo · *Lettres québec* Spring 1987; No 45: p47–48.

FARMER JOE'S HOT DAY/Children's story by Nancy Wilcox Richards

Make way for a fine crop of picture-books; reviews of children's books. Adele Ashby. *Quill & Quire (Books for Young People)* Aug 1987; Vol 53 No 8: p6.

FAULKNER, LEIGH

[Untitled]; review of *Into Nests, Each Perfect as an Inner Ear!*. Glenn Hayes. *Poetry Can R* Spring 1987; Vol 8 No 2–3: p57–58.

FAWCETT, BRIAN

B.C. writer deliberately jars Jell-O minds; article. Ken Adachi. biog photo · *TS* March 7, 1987: M4.

Portrait of a society whose vision is shaped by television; review of *Cambodia*. Mary Ambrose. *G&M* July 25, 1987: pC15.

Cambodia: whose idea is this?; review article about *Cambodia*. Jeff Berg. *West Coast R* Spring 1987; Vol 21 No 4: p73–77.

[Untitled]; review of *Cambodia*. Clint Burnham. *Malahat R* June 1987; No 79: p156–157.

[Untitled]; review of *The Secret Journal of Alexander Mackenzie*. Lawrence Chanin. *Can Auth & Book* Summer 1987; Vol 62 No 4: p24.

A prose experiment; review of *Cambodia: A Book for People Who Find Television Too Slow*. Dennis Corcoran. *TS* Feb 15, 1987: pA18.

Brian Fawcett; interview. James Dennis Corcoran. photo · *Books in Can* May 1987; Vol 16 No 4: p38–40.

[Untitled]; reviews of novels. Beverley Daurio. *Cross Can Writ Q* 1987; Vol 9 No 3–4: p45–46.

Down the tube; review of *Cambodia*. Mary di Michele. *Books in Can* Jan-Feb 1987; Vol 16 No 1: p23.

Probing horror with footnotes; review of *Cambodia*. Seymour Hamilton. *CH* May 17, 1987: pE5.

[Untitled]; review of *Cambodia*. Geoff Heinricks. *Quill & Quire* June 1987; Vol 53 No 6: p31–32.

Moving pictures; review of *Cambodia*. Maggie Helwig. illus · *Can Forum* Aug-Sept 1987; Vol 67 No 771: p39–41.

Today's assignment: short fiction that's worth a long look; reviews of short story books. Douglas Hill. *G&M* March 14, 1987: pE19.
[ANTHOLOGIES: BOOK REVIEWS]

None of the above; letter to the editor. Anna Porter. *Books in Can* May 1987; Vol 16 No 4: p40.

Reading Brian Fawcett; reviews of *Cambodia* and *The Secret Journal of Alexander Mackenzie*. Norbert Ruebsaat. *Event* Summer 1987; Vol 16 No 2: p118–121.

Recent Canadian fiction; reviews of novels. D.O. Spettigue. *Queen's Q* Summer 1987; Vol 94 No 2: p366–375.
[FIRST NOVELS: BOOK REVIEWS]

FELICE: A TRAVELOGUE/Novel by Robert Harlow

Pissing in the parking lot; review of *Felice: A Travelogue*. Lawrence Mathews. *Essays on Can Writ* Winter 1987; No 35: p147–151.

(F.)LIP: A NEWSLETTER OF FEMINIST INNOVATIVE WRITING/Periodical

[Untitled]; review of *(f.)Lip*. Maggie Berg. *Rubicon* Fall 1987; No 9: p194–195.
[CANADIAN LITERARY PERIODICALS]

FÉLIX LECLERC, LE ROI HEUREUX/Biography by Jacques Bertin

[Untitled]; review of *Felix Leclerc, le roi heureux*. Nicole Décarie. *Moebius* Spring 1987; No 32: p125–127.

Mais Félix a préféré rester dans son île . . . ; article. Gilles Lesage. photo · *MD* Jan 28, 1987: p1,10.

Le Québec de Félix Leclerc. review of *Félix Leclerc, le roi heureux*. Jean Royer. *MD* Jan 24, 1987: pB3–B4.

LES FELUETTES OU LA RÉPÉTITION D'UN DRAME ROMANTIQUE/Play by Michel-Marc Bouchard

Homosexual passion, religious theatre crux of Les Feluettes; theatre review. Pat Donnelly. *MG* Sept 12, 1987: pD13.

[Untitled]; theatre reviews of *Tête à tête* and *Les Feluettes*. Pat Donnelly. *MG* Sept 18, 1987: pC8.

A work of power, imagination; article. Matthew Fraser. photo · G&M Nov 30, 1987: pC9.

Michel-Marc Bouchard: Roberval, 1912, j'avais 19 ans...; article. Robert Lévesque. photo · MD Sept 12, 1987: pC1–C2.

Bouchard et les feux de Roberval; theatre review of Les Feluettes. Robert Lévesque. photo · MD Sept 25, 1987: p13.

Les Feluettes seront en France en 1988; article. Robert Lévesque. photo · MD Nov 5, 1987: p13.
[FRANCE-CANADA LITERARY RELATIONS]

[Untitled]; theatre review of Les Feluettes. Robert Lévesque. MD Nov 27, 1987: p15.

[Untitled]; theatre reviews. Robert Lévesque. MD Dec 4, 1987: p15.

FEMINIST DRAMA

Female leads: search for feminism in the theatre; essay. Carol Bolt. illus · Can Forum June-July 1987; Vol 67 No 770: p37–40.

Feminists launch festival; article. Robert Crew. TS Jan 16, 1987: pD17.
[FESTIVALS, DRAMA]

Les femmes dans le théâtre du Québec et du Canada / Women in the theatre of Quebec and Canada; introduction. Louise H. Forsyth. Theatre Hist in Can (special issue) Spring 1987; Vol 8 No 1: p3–7.
[WOMEN WRITERS]

Idéologie féministe dans Le Temps sauvage et C'tait avant la guerre l'Anse Gilles; article. Monique Genuist. abstract · Theatre Hist in Can (special issue) Spring 1987; Vol 8 No 1: p49–58.

Autour du Théâtre expérimental des femmes; essay. Louise Laprade. illus · La Nouvelle barre du jour (special issue) March 1987; No 196: p82–86.

Isaac's cast puts its 500 years to good use; column. Vit Wagner. TS Nov 13, 1987: pE16.
[DRAMATIC READINGS; FESTIVALS, DRAMA; WOMEN WRITERS]

FEMINIST WRITING AND CRITICISM

On the margin: looking for a literary identity; article. Donna Bennett. illus · Can Forum April 1987; Vol 67 No 768: p17–25.
[CULTURAL IDENTITY]

Sous l'angle de la provocation ou quand la théorie imagine; essay. Louise Cotnoir. bibliog biog · La Nouvelle barre du jour (special issue) 1987; No 201–202: p81–94.

L'inframanifeste illimité; article. Jeanne Demers and Line McMurray. La Nouvelle barre du jour (special issue) 1987; No 194: p7–18.

Tableau chronologique des interventions à portée manifestaires qui ont marqué l'évolution du féminisme au Québec; bibliography. Jeanne Demers and Line McMurray. La Nouvelle barre du jour (special issue) 1987; No 194: p21–94.

Telling it over again: Atwood's art of parody; article. Barbara Godard. Can Poet Fall-Winter 1987; No 21: p1–30.
[MYTHS AND LEGENDS IN CANADIAN LITERATURE; STRUCTURALIST WRITING AND CRITICISM]

Laure Conan and Madame de La Fayette: rewriting the female plot; article. Mary Jean Green. Essays on Can Writ Spring 1987; No 34: p50–63.
[WOMEN WRITERS]

The religious roots of the feminine identity issue: Margaret Laurence's The Stone Angel and Margaret Atwood's Surfacing; article. Evelyn J. Hinz. abstract · J of Can Studies Spring 1987; Vol 22 No 1: p17–31.
[BIBLICAL MYTHS AND MYTHOLOGY; GOD IN LITERATURE]

Shape shifters: Canadian women novelists challenge tradition; article. Linda Hutcheon. illus · Can Forum Jan 1987; Vol 66 No 765: p26–32.
[ARTIST FIGURE; STRUCTURALIST WRITING AND CRITICISM; WOMEN WRITERS]

Sailing the oceans of the world; article. Lorna Irvine. New Q Spring-Summer 1987; Vol 7 No 1–2: p284–293.
[ARTIST FIGURE; WOMEN IN LITERATURE]

The spider and the rose: Aritha van Herk's No Fixed Address; article. Dorothy Jones. World Lit in Eng Spring 1987; Vol 27 No 1: p39–56.
[MYTHS AND LEGENDS IN CANADIAN LITERATURE; WOMEN IN LITERATURE]

The Bell Jar and Mrs. Blood: portraits of the artist as divided woman; article. Elizabeth Potvin. abstract · Atlantis Fall 1987; Vol 13 No 1: p38–46.
[ARTIST FIGURE; WOMEN IN LITERATURE]

Killed into art: Marjorie Pickthall and The Wood Carver's Wife; article. Diana M.A. Relke. biog · Can Drama 1987; Vol 13 No 2: p187–200.

La naissance d'une parole féminine autonome dans la littérature québécoise; article. Lucie Robert. abstract · Études lit Spring-Summer 1987; Vol 20 No 1: p99–110.
[WOMEN IN LITERATURE; WOMEN WRITERS]

The case for creative chaos: writing and gender; essay. Libby Scheier. photo · Poetry Can R Fall 1987; Vol 9 No 1: p8–9.

The re/membering of the female power in Lady Oracle; article. Roberta Sciff-Zamaro. Can Lit Spring 1987; No 112: p32–38.
[MYTHS AND LEGENDS IN CANADIAN LITERATURE]

Suzanne Lamy: le féminin au risque de la critique; article. Sherry Simon. Voix et images Autumn 1987; Vol 13 No 1: p52–64.
[STRUCTURALIST WRITING AND CRITICISM]

Repression, obsession and re-emergence in Hébert's Les Fous de Bassan; article. Kathryn Slott. Amer R of Can Studies Autumn 1987; Vol 17 No 3: p297–307.

Woman as object, women as subjects, & the consequences for narrative: Hubert Aquin's Neige noire and the impasse of post-modernism; article. Patricia Smart. Can Lit Summer-Fall 1987; No 113–114: p168–178.
[POSTMODERNIST WRITING AND CRITICISM]

Fiction et métissage ou écrire l'imaginaire du réel; essay. France Théoret. bibliog biog · La Nouvelle barre du jour (special issue) 1987; No 201–202: p65–78.
[POSTMODERNIST WRITING AND CRITICISM]

Marian Engel's family fictions: Lunatic Villas; article. Christl Verduyn. *New Q* Spring-Summer 1987; Vol 7 No 1–2: p274–283.
[THE FAMILY IN CANADIAN LITERATURE; WOMEN IN LITERATURE]

LA FEMME DE SABLE/Short stories by Madeleine Ouellette-Michalska

Dans les poches; reviews. Guy Ferland. *MD* Sept 26, 1987: pD6.

LA FEMME DE SATH/Novel by Andre-A. Michaud

Sous le signe du Scorpion, Andrée-A. Michaud nous convie aux confins de l'obsession; review of *La Femme de Sath.* Jean-Roch Boivin. *MD* June 6, 1987: pD3.
[FIRST NOVELS: BOOK REVIEWS]

THE FENCEPOST CHRONICLES/Short stories by W.P. Kinsella

Immigrant experience yields stream of interesting tales; reviews of *Tales from Firozsha Baag* and *The Fencepost Chronicles.* Barbara Black. *MG* May 30, 1987: J9.

[Untitled]; review of *The Fencepost Chronicles.* Mark Duncan. *Border Cross* Summer 1987; Vol 6 No 3: p23–24.

[Untitled]; review of *The Fencepost Chronicles.* Lenore Keeshig-Tobias. *Books in Can* Jan-Feb 1987; Vol 16 No 1: p25.

FENNARIO, DAVID

Billboard: McGonigal dinner set for Feb. 19; column. *WFP* Feb 3, 1987: p30.
[DRAMATIC READINGS]

FERGUSON, JEAN

Mini-comptes rendus; review of *Contes du pays de l'orignal.* François Paré. *Can Child Lit* 1987; No 47: p100–101.

FERLAND, MARCIEN

Riel play aims to right wrongs; article. Kevin Prokosh. photo · *WFP* March 5, 1987: p36.

FERNANDES, EUGENIE

Book captures emotional moment for child; reviews of *Big Sarah's Little Boots* and *A Difficult Day.* Joan Craven. *CH (Neighbors)* Oct 28, 1987: pA18.

Morgan, May, Melinda: new heroines offer humour and fantasy; reviews of children's books. Bernie Goedhart. *Quill & Quire (Books for Young People)* Oct 1987; Vol 53 No 10: p24.

The jolly fireplace's darker side; reviews of children's books. Joan McGrath. *TS* Nov 22, 1987: pC8.

FRON, JEAN

De l'ouest, des nouvelles et de l'histoire; reviews of short story books. Paulette Collet. photo · *Lettres québec* Summer 1987; No 46: p68–70.
[ANTHOLOGIES: BOOK REVIEWS]

FERRETTI, ANDRE

Les noeuds sacrés de l'âme, de la terre et du sang; reviews of novels. Réjean Beaudoin. *Liberté* Oct 1987; Vol 29 No 5: p106–114.

Aquin et Hypatie filant le parfait amour en Paganie; review of *Renaissance en Paganie.* Madeleine Ouellette-Michalska. photo · *MD* June 13, 1987: pD3.

Andrée Ferretti: "je ne peux être que politique, puisque je veux agir sur le monde"; article. Simone Piuze. photo · *MD* July 25, 1987: pC5.

FERRIER, IAN

First electronic novel hits computer screens; article. Heather Hill. photo · *MG* Aug 1, 1987: J9.
[PUBLISHING AND PUBLISHERS IN CANADA]

FERRON, JACQUES

"Les nouvelles de cousin Emmanuel": varieties of salvation and imagination in Ferron's Cotnoir; article. Brian Bartlett. *Studies in Can Lit* 1987; Vol 12 No 2: p177–186.

Par-delà la mort, le docteur Ferron continue de soigner nos âmes; review of *La Conférence inachevée.* Jean-Roch Boivin. photo · *MD* June 27, 1987: pC8.

La vitrine du livre; reviews. Guy Ferland. *MD* June 6, 1987: pD4.
[CANADIAN LITERARY PERIODICALS]

Le testament d'un artiste; review of *La Conférence inachevée.* Yolande Grisé. photo · *Lettres québec* Autumn 1987; No 47: p35–36.

Le Centre culturel de Longueuil prend le nom de Jacques Ferron; article. Jean Royer. photo · *MD* Oct 16, 1987: p15.

Tinamer ou le bon cet des choses; review of *L'Amlanchier.* Adrien Thério. *Lettres québec* Winter 1986–87; No 44: p77.

FERRON, MADELEINE

Madeleine Ferron au sommet de son talent; review of *Un Singulier amour.* Jean-Roch Boivin. photo · *MD* Sept 26, 1987: pD3.

[Untitled]; notice. Paul Cauchon. photo · *MD* Oct 9, 1987: p15.
[TELEVISION AND CANADIAN LITERATURE]

La vitrine du livre; reviews. Guy Ferland. *MD* Sept 12, 1987: pD4.

FERTILITY/Play by Leah Cherniak and Martha Ross

Talented comediennes energetic and funny; theatre review of *Fertility.* Robert Crew. *TS* March 6, 1987: pD21.

FESTIVALS, DRAMA

Festival on for young playwrights; article. *MG* Jan 14, 1987: pB5.
[DRAMATIC READINGS]

Festival of the Americas to stage 20 plays; article. *WFP* Feb 7, 1987: p20.

Fringe open for business; article. *CH* Jan 15, 1987: pC12.

Amateur theatre troupes gather for annual festival; article. *WFP* April 19, 1987: p17.

PTE invited to Olympics Arts Festival; article. *WFP* April 28, 1987: p33.

Cape Breton holding giant theatre festival; article. *WFP* May 8, 1987: p25.

Theatre festival envisioned; article. *WFP* May 15, 1987: p29.

Vancouver Fringe deadline looms; article. *CH* April 14, 1987: pD2.

Drama festival wraps up; article. *CH* May 12, 1987: pF9.

Backstage; column. *G&M* May 2, 1987: pC6.

Economic, social issues played out on the stage; article. *G&M* May 9, 1987: pC12.

Fair full of theatrics; article. *TS* April 16, 1987: pC15.

Kids fest going out with bang; article, includes theatre reviews. photo · *TS* May 15, 1987: pD11.

"Réalité-Jeunesse"; article. *MD* Aug 4, 1987: p11.

Theatre fun at festival; article. *CH* Aug 7, 1987: pE8.

Westerners rule ATP's second new play festival; article. *CH* Sept 4, 1987: pE4.

Fringe fest forms now available; article. *CH* Dec 16, 1987: pF4.

Political themes heavy in theatre fest; article. Marianne Ackerman. *MG* Feb 4, 1987: pB6.

Festival focus on multi-media events; article. Marianne Ackerman. *MG* April 8, 1987: pF1.

Check out drama fest for new theatre talent; article. Marianne Ackerman. photo · *MG* April 25, 1987: H7.
[WRITERS' WORKSHOPS]

Drama fest heads for grand finale; theatre reviews of *Jack of Hearts* and *Collideoscope*. Marianne Ackerman. photo · *MG* May 1, 1987: pD3.

[Untitled]; theatre review of *Le Vrai monde?*. Marianne Ackerman. *MG* May 1, 1987: pD6.

Off-stage drama in awards; article. Marianne Ackerman. *MG* May 4, 1987: pB9.
[AWARDS, LITERARY]

Festival of Americas: a rare feast of imaginative theatre; article. Marianne Ackerman. photo · *MG* May 23, 1987: H9.

Native actress returns to roots for inspiration; article. Marianne Ackerman. photo · *MG* May 29, 1987: pD2.

Theatre fest fever is spreading fast; article. Marianne Ackerman. photo · *MG* May 30, 1987: pC9.

Momentum picks up for Week 2 of theatre fest; article. Marianne Ackerman. photo · *MG* June 1, 1987: pD7.

[Untitled]; article. Marianne Ackerman. *MG* June 5, 1987: pD4.

Theatrefest: images and memories; article. Marianne Ackerman. photo · *MG* June 6, 1987: H10.

Les Québécois boudent les Africains; article. Carole Beaulieu. *MD* Sept 4, 1987: p16.

Gone with the Fringe: being there: a flying look at the 1987 Edmonton Fringe Theatre Festival; article. Nancy Bell. photo · *NeWest R* Oct 1987; Vol 13 No 2: p9-11.

Domestic drama that hits home; article, includes theatre reviews. John Bemrose. photo · *Maclean's* Aug 17, 1987; Vol 100 No 33: p49.

Playrites '87: ATP wades into new wave in theatre; article. Bob Blakey. photo · *CH* Jan 10, 1987: pB3.

ATP experiment pleased insiders; article. Bob Blakey. photo · *CH* Feb 14, 1987: pG1.

Weekend blitz will be ATP's litmus test; column. Brian Brennan. *CH* Feb 3, 1987: pF9.

Critics cite play festival's possibilities; article. Brian Brennan. *CH* Feb 14, 1987: pG4.

Festival features Alberta playwrights; article. Brian Brennan. *CH* Feb 19, 1987: pD4.

Canadian troupes will command the spotlight in '88; article. Brian Brennan. *CH* April 28, 1987: pC8.

Voyage théâtral dans la francophonie; article. Paul Cauchon. photo · *MD* Aug 29, 1987: pC3.

Feminists launch festival; article. Robert Crew. *TS* Jan 16, 1987: pD17.
[FEMINIST DRAMA]

Three Toronto plays premiere at Calgary fest; article, includes theatre reviews. Robert Crew. photo · *TS* Feb 10, 1987: pB4.

One-man Bethune show to tour China; column. Robert Crew. *TS* March 19, 1987: pE3.

Musical circus in tune with children's festival; column. Robert Crew. *TS* April 2, 1987: pG3.

PUC stops here for cabaret night; article. Robert Crew. *TS* April 24, 1987: pE12.
[DRAMATIC READINGS]

Italian troupe offers a touch of class; theatre review of *Together/Ensemble*. Robert Crew. *TS* May 13, 1987: pB3.

Taking the "kiddie stuff" seriously: the 1987 Edmonton International Children's Festival; article. Moira Day. photo · *NeWest R* Oct 1987; Vol 13 No 2: p6-8.
[CHILDREN'S DRAMA]

Fringe '87: the state of the art; article. Moira Day. photo · *NeWest R* Oct 1987; Vol 13 No 2: p12-13.

Playing linguistic musical chairs; article. Pat Donnelly. *MG* June 2, 1987: pD11.
[TRANSLATIONS OF CANADIAN LITERATURE]

Community theatre in festival limelight; article. Pat Donnelly. *MG* July 6, 1987: pB9.

Empty seats a shame as theatre fest hits midway point; article. Pat Donnelly. *MG* July 10, 1987: pD4.

Child's play? Far from it; article. Pat Donnelly. photo · *MG* July 31, 1987: pC1.
[CHILDREN'S DRAMA]

Stratford ahead of the game — and it's no overnight miracle; column. Pat Donnelly. *MG* Dec 10, 1987: pD6.

Rites returns ATP to its roots; article. Joyce Doolittle. photo · *NeWest R* April 1987; Vol 12 No 8: p16.

Réalité Jeunesse 87: de l'énergie à revendre; article. Marie-Claude Ducas. photo · *MD* Aug 10, 1987: p9.

Summer stock theatre sets stage for winter; column. Arnold Edinborough. photo · *Fin Post* Sept 21, 1987: p34.

Dispatches from the arts world, east and west; column. Arnold Edinborough. *Fin Post* Oct 26, 1987: p21.

Underdeveloped alliance; essay. Ian Filewod. photo · *Can Theatre R* Winter 1987; No 53: p39–42.
[POLITICAL WRITING]

Thémes et formes; article. Carole Frchette. Diane Pavlovic. photo · *Jeu* 1987; No 42: p40–48.
[POLITICAL WRITING; WOMEN WRITERS]

New-play festival deserves a curtain call; theatre reviews. Stephen Godfrey. photo · *G&M* Feb 10, 1987: pC5.

Festival One plays singularly successful; theatre reviews. Stephen Godfrey. photo · *G&M* May 8, 1987: pF9.

Vancouver Fringe springs surprises; article. Stephen Godfrey. photo · *G&M* Sept 15, 1987: pA21.

Quirks, interruptions don't deflate festival; article. Stephen Godfrey. photo · *G&M* Sept 22, 1987: pD5.

Extravaganzas, close calls and chaos, with imaginative windows on the arts; article. Stephen Godfrey. photo · *G&M* Dec 26, 1987: pC10.

Notes from the Fringe/1; article. Christa Grace-Warrick. photo · *Can Theatre R* Summer 1987; No 51: p79–80.

Inside the giant: Fringe for kids; article. Katherine IKoller. photo · *NeWest R* Oct 1987; Vol 13 No 2: p11.
[CHILDREN'S DRAMA]

Drama festival holds showcase; article. Paul Irish. *TS (Neighbours)* April 7, 1987: p21

'Best theatre in America' aim of festival; article. Deirdre Kelly. *G&M* May 28, 1987: pD1.

27 mars, journée mondiale du théâtre; column. Robert Lévesque. photo · *MD* March 24, 1987: p11.

Le Québec sera très présent au 2e Festival de théâtre des Amériques; article. Robert Lévesque. photo · *MD* April 8, 1987: p13.

André Brassard prend congé de mise en scène; column. Robert Lévesque. *MD* May 5, 1987: p11.

Ionesco soufflera ses 75 chandelles à Montréal; column. Robert Lévesque. *MD* May 12, 1987: p14.

[Untitled]; notice. Robert Lévesque. *MD* May 22, 1987: p15.

Montréal au centre des Amériques; article. Robert Lévesque. photo · *MD* May 23, 1987: pC1.

Jour un pour le 2e Festival des Amériques; column. Robert Lévesque. photo · *MD* May 26, 1987: p13.

Les anges dans nos campagnes; article. Robert Lévesque. *MD* June 4, 1987: p13.

Les théâtres d'été: au petit bonheur la blague; article. Robert Lévesque. photo · *MD* June 13, 1987: pC1,C10.

Limoges, principale vitrine du théâtre québécois en Europe; column. Robert Lévesque. photo · *MD* Sept 29, 1987: p13.
[AWARDS, LITERARY; CANADIAN LITERARY PERIODICALS]

Rachel Lortie prend les choses en mains; article. Robert Lévesque. *MD* Oct 2, 1987: p13.

Crowded theatres indicate success of Edmonton Fringe; article. Liam Lacey. *G&M* Aug 17, 1987: pC9.

Flashes of gold among the dross at Fringe festival; theatre reviews. Liam Lacey. *G&M* Aug 19, 1987: pC5.

Tall tales and home truths; article. Liam Lacey. photo · *G&M* Aug 22, 1987: pC3.

Des voix á découvrir; article. Pierre Lavoie. photo · *Jeu* 1987; No 44: p79–87.

Scarborough schools compete in Sears drama festival regionals; article. Alex Law. *TS (Neighbours)* April 14, 1987: p14.

Cedarbrae Collegiate's play to compete at Ontario finals; article. Alex Law. *TS (Neighbours)* May 5, 1987: p9.

Brampton, Etobicoke schools make it to drama festival finals; article. Alex Law. *TS (Neighbours)* May 5, 1987: p24.

Etobicoke, Brampton students win Sears drama festival honors; article. Alex Law. photo · *TS (Neighbours)* May 19, 1987: p19.

Milk International Children's Festival; article. Carol Lawlor. *Tor Life* May 1987; Vol 21 No 7: p107.

Notes from the Fringe/2; article. Malcolm Page. photo · *Can Theatre R* Summer 1987; No 51: p80–82.

Splendeurs et misres; article. Diane Pavlovic. Michel Vas. photo · *Jeu* 1987; No 42: p27–39.

Blyth musical succeeds where drama fails; theatre reviews of *Girls in the Gang* and *Bush Fire*. Jason Sherman. photo · *TS* Aug 7, 1987: pE10.

Metro high schools enter drama festival; article. Karen Shopsowitz. *TS (Neighbours)* Feb 10, 1987: p24.

Festival One offers hope for new wave of creative theatre; theatre reviews. Reg Skene. *WFP* May 11, 1987: p17.

Blyth spirit makes theatre festival labor of love; article. Tom Spears. photo · *TS* June 19, 1987: pD5.

F-words at Green Gables; article. Ann Thurlow. photo · *Maclean's* July 13, 1987; Vol 100 No 28: p49.
[DRAMATIC ADAPTATIONS OF CANADIAN LITERATURE]

Bloc-notes; column. Michel Vas. *Jeu* 1987; No 42: p190–191.

International kids' theatre festival hopes to touch child in everyone; article. Vit Wagner. *TS* May 8, 1987: pD11.

Isaac's cast puts its 500 years to good use; column. Vit Wagner. *TS* Nov 13, 1987: pE16.
[DRAMATIC READINGS; FEMINIST DRAMA; WOMEN WRITERS]

Festival eyes Brandon move; article. Morley Walker. photo · *WFP* April 23, 1987: p43.

The agitprop players; article. Chris Wood. photo · *Maclean's* June 8, 1987; Vol 100 No 23: p55.
[POLITICAL WRITING]

Play open to public but locale is secret; article. Kate Zimmerman. *CH* Jan 30, 1987: pC10.

Rabbit's experiment titillates; article. Kate Zimmerman. photo · *CH* Feb 9, 1987: pE6.

Local troupes catch the spirit; article. Kate Zimmerman. *CH* Aug 14, 1987: pD1.

Patience is a trademark of Fringe patrons; article. Kate Zimmerman. photo · *CH* Aug 17, 1987: pD7.

Fringe fun for families; article. Kate Zimmerman. *CH* Aug 18, 1987: pD5.

Weather takes toll on Fringe audiences; article. Kate Zimmerman. *CH* Aug 19, 1987: pD2

Calgary troupes draw fair share of plaudits at Fringe; article. Kate Zimmerman. *CH* Aug 21, 1987: pC1.

Fringe a fertile theatrical breeding ground; article. Kate Zimmerman. *CH* Aug 25, 1987: pD8.

FESTIVALS, LITERARY

Des écrivains acadiens et québécois en tournée; article. *MD* Feb 25, 1987: p8.

Children invited to poetry festival; article. *G&M* April 14, 1987: pC9.

"L'art à la rue": 150 artistes participeront au Festival d'art engagé de Montréal; article. *MD* June 2, 1987: p12.

Book fest celebrates homegrown writers; article. *TS* April 24, 1987: pE12.

Book festival begins; article. *MG* April 25, 1987: H12.

Westmount festival aims to bring local artists together; article. *MG* Sept 11, 1987: pC3.

Author Festival sneak preview; article. *Quill & Quire* Sept 1987; Vol 53 No 9: p72.

Poetry part of festival; article. *G&M* July 14, 1987: pC7.
[CHILDREN'S LITERATURE]

Paley, Moore at authors' festival; article. *G&M* Sept 2, 1987: pC6.

Panels on books, movies; article. *TS* Oct 11, 1987: pA22.
[FILM ADAPTATIONS OF CANADIAN LITERATURE]

Guillevec au 3e Festival national de poésie: "la voix privilégiée du beau"; article. *MD* Oct 13, 1987: p13.

Kid-lit fest on at ROM; article. *TS* Nov 13, 1987: pE18.
[CHILDREN'S LITERATURE; FESTIVALS, DRAMA]

Jewish Book Fair opens today; article. *TS* Nov 22, 1987: pC3.

Kid's book festival week to be proclaimed; article. *WFP (Weekly)* Nov 8, 1987: p15.

City author loved smell, feel of books as a child; article. *WFP* Nov 13, 1987: p36.

Writers head south for Festival Canada; article. *G&M* Oct 21, 1987: pC8.

Authors' festival film to air; article. *Quill & Quire* Oct 1987; Vol 53 No 10: p12.
[TELEVISION AND CANADIAN LITERATURE]

Science slant for annual festival; article. *Quill & Quire (Books for Young People)* Oct 1987; Vol 53 No 10: p8.
[CHILDREN'S LITERATURE]

English novelist praises Toronto festival; column. Ken Adachi. *TS* March 30, 1987: pF4.
[LATIN AMERICA-CANADA LITERARY RELATIONS]

Written word celebrated at National Book Festival; column. Ken Adachi. photo · *TS* April 20, 1987: pD2.

Authors' festival organizer coy about this year's lineup; column. Ken Adachi. photo · *TS* Aug 24, 1987: pB1.

Stephen Spender a highlight of authors' festival; article. Ken Adachi. *TS* Sept 24, 1987: pC1.

Harbourfront's authors festival opens with intriguing weekend; article, includes schedule. Ken Adachi. photo · *TS* Oct 16, 1987: pD12.

Latecomer to fiction-writing a talent to watch; column. Ken Adachi. photo · *TS* Oct 19, 1987: pC5.
[AWARDS, LITERARY]

Clever novelist confuses the critics; column. Ken Adachi. *TS* Oct 22, 1987: pB4.

Albee reads from first play in last act of great festival; column. Ken Adachi. *TS* Oct 26, 1987: pD5.

Interviews, literary 'gossip' slated for authors' festival; article. John Allemang. photo · *G&M* Sept 24, 1987: pD6.

Raising their glasses at the write angles; article. John Allemang. *G&M* Oct 17, 1987: pC14.

Last-minute readers and party-bound writers; article. John Allemang. photo · *G&M* Oct 21, 1987: pC9.
[AWARDS, LITERARY]

Some go to the Falls, Sariola goes to the 'burbs; article. John Allemang. *G&M* Oct 22, 1987: pD5.

Literary stock shows strong rate of return; article. John Allemang. *G&M* Oct 23, 1987: pD9.

Australian writer staying on for fall; article. John Allemang. *G&M* Oct 26, 1987: pC11.

Organizers up against a wall to get art fest off the ground; article. Bruce Bailey. photo · *MG* June 5, 1987: pD1.

Writers want out of OCO festival; article. Bob Blakey. *CH* March 20, 1987: pC3.
[WRITERS' ORGANIZATIONS]

Les maisons de la culture de Montréal accueillent la Quinzaine ontaroise; article. Sylvain Blanchard. *MD* Nov 4, 1987: p14.

Sculptor to help shape women's festival; article. Donald Campbell. *WFP* July 28, 1987: p28.

Quebec: festival national de la poésie; regional column. Antonio D'Alfonso. *Poetry Can R* Spring 1987; Vol 8 No 2–3: p22.

Olympic Arts Festival unveiled; article. Derek Ferguson. *TS* April 28, 1987: pG1.

Another brick in the wall; article. Ray Filip. *Books in Can* Aug-Sept 1987; Vol 16 No 6: p4–5.
[POLITICAL WRITING]

Dada processing; essay. Raymond Filip. *Books in Can* Nov 1987; Vol 16 No 8: p4–5.
[POETRY PERFORMANCE; POSTMODERNIST WRITING AND CRITICISM]

Poetry sweatshops add a new twist to Olympic tradition; column. William French. *G&M* March 3, 1987: pC7.
[CANADIAN LITERARY LANDMARKS; COMPETITIONS, LITERARY; POETRY READINGS]

Booking time for the issues; column. William French. *G&M* April 21, 1987: pD7.
[GOVERNMENT GRANTS FOR WRITERS/PUBLISHERS]

Authors talk about books as movies; article. Peter Goddard. *TS* Oct 20, 1987: H4.

A success story for children; article. Stephen Godfrey. photo · *G&M* May 18, 1987: pD9.

Wit, wisdom and tall tales take centrestage; article. Rick Groen. photo · *G&M* Oct 22, 1987: pD6.
[FILM ADAPTATIONS OF CANADIAN LITERATURE]

Underground arts surfacing for festival; article. Heather Hill. *MG* Sept 2, 1987: H1.

The write stuff in Toronto: literary fesival is world's largest; article. Heather Hill. photo · *MG* Oct 20, 1987: pE6.

Warnes warm to Cohen's material; column. Deirdre Kelly. *G&M* May 30, 1987: pC18.

Nation-wide book festival opens this weekend; article. Janice Kennedy. *MG* Nov 14, 1987: pD1.
[CHILDREN'S LITERATURE]

Eye for detail key to authors' festival; article. H.J. Kirchhoff. photo · *G&M* Oct 16, 1987: pB1–B2.

Authors' festival revisited; article. Martin Knelman. *Tor Life* Oct 1987; Vol 21 No 1[5]: 17.
[TELEVISION AND CANADIAN LITERATURE]

Les fantômes devront attendre . . . ; column. Robert Lévesque. *MD* Nov 10, 1987: p13,15.

Less is Moore for Brian; article. Liam Lacey. photo · *G&M* Oct 20, 1987: pD5.

Les artistes ontarois débarquent à Montréal; article. Françoise Lafleur. *MD* Nov 12, 1987: p13.

Une fête autour d'un conte; article. Françoise Lafleur. photo · *MD* Dec 16, 1987: p11.
[CHILDREN'S LITERATURE]

Deuxime festival national de la poésie 1986; article. André Marquis. photo · *Lettres québec* Winter 1986–87; No 44: p6.

Festival winds bring W.O. home; column. Kenneth McGoogan. *CH* March 1, 1987: pC8.
[AWARDS, LITERARY; CONFERENCES, LITERARY]

Writers plan on doing it with style; column. Kenneth Mc-Googan. *CH* March 22, 1987: pF5.
[AWARDS, LITERARY; COMPETITIONS, LITERARY]

Literary arts at Calgary Olympics; article. Kenneth McGoogan. *Quill & Quire* Feb 1987; Vol 53 No 2: p11.

U of A alumna wins novel contest; column. Kenneth Mc-Googan. *CH* April 2, 1987: pD14.
[AWARDS, LITERARY; POETRY READINGS]

Author interviews hit airwaves; column. Kenneth McGoogan. *CH* April 18, 1987: pE5.
[RADIO AND CANADIAN LITERATURE; WRITERS' ORGANIZATIONS]

Noted authors to attend; article. Kenneth McGoogan. *CH* April 28, 1987: pC7.

J.P. Donleavy here in '88; column. Kenneth McGoogan. *CH* July 26, 1987: pE5.
[AWARDS, LITERARY; CANADIAN LITERARY PERIODICALS; CANADIAN LITERARY PUBLISHING]

Festival attracts kids' writers; column. Kenneth McGoogan. *CH* Sept 20, 1987: pE6.
[AWARDS, LITERARY; CHILDREN'S LITERATURE]

Festival attracts glitterati; column. Kenneth McGoogan. *CH* Sept 27, 1987: pE6.
[FICTION READINGS; POETRY READINGS; WRITERS' ORGANIZATIONS]

Olympic readings scheduled; article. Kenneth McGoogan. *CH* Oct 1, 1987: pD1.

Alberta writers to fight 'censorship' bill; column. Kenneth McGoogan. *CH* Nov 29, 1987: pE6.
[CENSORSHIP; COMPETITIONS, LITERARY; WRITERS' ORGANIZATIONS]

Calgary attracting superstars to Olympic literary festival; article. Kenneth McGoogan. photo · *Quill & Quire* Oct 1987; Vol 53 No 10: p9.

Toronto's busy theatres merit superior magazine; column. Henry Mietkiewicz. *TS* May 20, 1987: pE3.

The west coast: the Spirit Quest Festival; regional column. Linda Rogers. *Poetry Can R* Fall 1987; Vol 9 No 1: p22.
[POETRY PERFORMANCE]

La vie littéraire; column. Jean Royer. photo · *MD* March 28, 1987: pD2.
[CONFERENCES, LITERARY; GOVERNMENT GRANTS FOR WRITERS/PUBLISHERS; RADIO AND CANADIAN LITERATURE; TELEVISION AND CANADIAN LITERATURE]

La vie littéraire; column. Jean Royer. *MD* April 25, 1987: pD2.
[AWARDS, LITERARY; CONFERENCES, LITERARY; FICTION READINGS; POETRY READINGS; RADIO AND CANADIAN LITERATURE; TELEVISION AND CANADIAN LITERATURE]

Le Festival national du livre est ouvert!; article. Jean Royer. *MD* April 28, 1987: p17.

La vie littéraire; column. Jean Royer. photo · *MD* May 30, 1987: pD2.
[AWARDS, LITERARY; CANADIAN LITERARY PUBLISHING; COMPETITIONS, LITERARY; RADIO AND CANADIAN LITERATURE; TELEVISION AND CANADIAN LITERATURE]

Le troisième Festival nationale de poésie; article. Jean Royer. photo · *MD* Sept 26, 1987: pD8.

La vie littéraire; column. Jean Royer. photo · *MD* Oct 10, 1987: pD2.
[CANADIAN LITERARY PUBLISHING; FRANCE-CANADA LITERARY RELATIONS]

Guillevic au Festival national de poésie: "Vous êtes plus francophones que les Français"; article. Jean Royer. *MD* Oct 14, 1987: p13.

Canadian writers fly south for fest; column. Thomas Schnurmacher. *MG* Oct 7, 1987: H1.
[UNITED STATES-CANADA LITERARY RELATIONS]

Book world: firm's growth is not merely a matter of luck; column. Beverley Slopen. *TS* Oct 4, 1987: pA20.
[PUBLISHING AND PUBLISHERS IN CANADA]

Laughing on the outside; essay. Phil Surguy. *Books in Can* Dec 1987; Vol 16 No 9: p4–5.

Big names and lesser lights make festival shine; article. Ann Vanderhoof. photo · *Quill & Quire* Jan 1987; Vol 53 No 1: p8–9.

Australia: of festivals and fringes; column. Barbara Williams. *Poetry Can R* Summer 1987; Vol 8 No 4: p28.

Familiarity and TV's stranglehold on life; reviews of children's books. Tim Wynne-Jones. *G&M* Nov 14, 1987: pE4.

Excursions; column. Betty Zyvatkauskas. illus · *G&M (Toronto Magazine)* Oct 1987; Vol 2 No 7: p31.

FETHERLING, DOUG

[Untitled]; review of *The Blue Notebook*. *Queen's Q* Summer 1987; Vol 94 No 2: p461–464.

New award celebrates Commonwealth writers; column. William French. photo · *G&M* Nov 17, 1987: pD7.
[AWARDS, LITERARY; WRITERS-IN-RESIDENCE]

[Untitled]; review of *The Blue Notebook*. Lynette Hunter. *British J of Can Studies* June 1987; Vol 2 No 1: p188–189.

In character; review of *The Blue Notebook*. Maurice Yacowar. *Can Lit* Spring 1987; No 112: p148–149.

LE FEU DES SOUCHES/Novel by Janine Tourville

À la rencontre des huguenots de Namur; review of *Le Feu des souches*. Alice Parizeau. *MD* Dec 12, 1987: pD4.
[FIRST NOVELS: BOOK REVIEWS]

LA FICTION DU RÉEL: POÈMES 1953–1975/Poems by Fernande Saint-Martin

La fiction du réel/le réel de la fiction; reviews of poetry books. André Brochu. *Voix et images* Winter 1987; No 35: p322–330.

Le réel et la fiction du réel; reviews of *Les Soirs rouges* (reprint) and *La Fiction du réel*. Richard Gigure. photo · *Lettres québec* Winter 1986–87; No 44: p38–40.

FICTION READINGS

Billboard: Whiteshell carnival starts today; column. *WFP* Feb 13, 1987: p36.

Aujourd'hui; column. *MD* Feb 16, 1987: p16.
[WRITERS' WORKSHOPS]

Aujourd'hui; column. *MD* March 16, 1987: p10.

Readings at NFB; article. *CH* Feb 20, 1987: pF7.
[POETRY READINGS]

Mainstreet Calgary; column. *CH (Neighbors)* March 26, 1987: pA4.

Harbourfront woos the literary-minded; article. *G&M* Jan 7, 1987: pC5.
[POETRY READINGS]

Harbourfront Readings Club; article. *Quill & Quire* March 1987; Vol 53 No 3: p60–61.
[POETRY READINGS]

Mainstreet Calgary; column. *CH (Neighbors)* May 13, 1987: pA6–A7.
[WRITERS' WORKSHOPS]

Canadian author to give reading; article. *TS (Neighbours)* April 21, 1987: p8.

Children's author to hold readings; article. *TS (Neighbours)* April 21, 1987: p15.

Spaced Out Library plans 'events'; article. *G&M* June 11, 1987: pD1.
[SCIENCE FICTION]

Aujourd'hui; column. *MD* April 7, 1987: p10.

Aujourd'hui; column. *MD* May 11, 1987: p10.

It's a date; column. *MG* April 3, 1987: pC10.

It's a date; column. *MG* Sept 18, 1987: pA9.

À surveiller; column. *MD* Sept 21, 1987: p8.

Billboard: Jon Sigurdson holds fall tea today; column. *WFP* Sept 26, 1987: p43.
[COMPETITIONS, LITERARY; WRITERS' ORGANIZATIONS]

Ondaatje opens reading series; article. photo · *CH* Sept 25, 1987: pF7.
[POETRY READINGS]

The Arc reading series; notice. *Arc* Fall 1987; No 19: p83.

It's a date; column. *MG* Oct 9, 1987: pD3.

It's a date; column. *MG* Nov 6, 1987: pC12.

Les lectures Skol: pour les dix ans de l'Union des écrivains; article. *MD* Oct 10, 1987: pD8.
[WRITERS' ORGANIZATIONS]

Billboard: Ukrainian youth holding policy meet; column. *WFP* Oct 9, 1987: p40.

Billboard: readings by authors slated for tomorrow; column. *WFP* Oct 20, 1987: p34.

Author plans reading; article. *WFP* Nov 21, 1987: p28.

Book launch planned; article. *WFP* Dec 4, 1987: p37.

Billboard: museum offers kids workshops on robotics; column. *WFP* Dec 28, 1987: p28.

Mainstreet Calgary; column. *CH (Neighbors)* Oct 7, 1987: pA14.

Mainstreet Calgary; column. *CH (Neighbors)* Oct 21, 1987: pA14–A15.

Mainstreet Calgary; column. *CH (Neighbors)* Oct 28, 1987: pA22–A23.
[WRITERS' WORKSHOPS]

Feminist quarterly honors Laurence; column. Ken Adachi. *TS* Nov 16, 1987: pC5.
[CANADIAN LITERARY PERIODICALS]

Nightspots: storytellers unite at La Ricane; column. Bill Brownstein. *MG* Jan 24, 1987: pD6.

Musical morality tales with a touch of magic; article. Robert Everett-Green. *G&M* May 12, 1987: pC10.

Davies conjures a musical ghost for children; article about *The Harper of the Stones*. William Littler. photo · *TS* May 9, 1987: J12.

More surprises from Kinsella; column. Kenneth McGoogan. *CH* Sept 13, 1987: pE5.

Festival attracts glitterati; column. Kenneth McGoogan. *CH* Sept 27, 1987: pE6.
[FESTIVALS, LITERARY; POETRY READINGS; WRITERS' ORGANIZATIONS]

La vie littéraire; column. Marc Morin. photo · *MD* Dec 19, 1987: pD2.
[AWARDS, LITERARY; POETRY READINGS]

La vie littéraire; column. Jean Royer. *MD* Feb 14, 1987: pC2.
[AWARDS, LITERARY; CANADIAN LITERARY PERIODICALS; COMPETITIONS, LITERARY; POETRY READINGS; RADIO AND CANADIAN LITERATURE]

La vie littéraire; column. Jean Royer. *MD* April 25, 1987: pD2.
[AWARDS, LITERARY; CONFERENCES, LITERARY; FESTIVALS, LITERARY; POETRY READINGS; RADIO AND CANADIAN LITERATURE; TELEVISION AND CANADIAN LITERATURE]

La vie littéraire; column. Jean Royer. photo · *MD* Sept 19, 1987: pD2.
[AWARDS, LITERARY; CONFERENCES, LITERARY; POETRY READINGS; PUBLISHING AND PUBLISHERS IN CANADA]

La vie littéraire; column. Jean Royer. photo · *MD* Oct 17, 1987: pD2.
[CANADIAN LITERARY PERIODICALS; COMPETITIONS, LITERARY; CONFERENCES, LITERARY; WRITERS' ORGANIZATIONS]

La vie littéraire; column. Jean Royer. *MD* Oct 24, 1987: pD2.
[CONFERENCES, LITERARY; POETRY READINGS; WRITERS' ORGANIZATIONS]

It's home-movie time — but let's just skip Debbie Does Dorion; column. Thomas Schnurmacher. *MG* Feb 10, 1987: pB6.

Tip sheet: storytellers will present a night for lovers, liars and lunatics; column. Susan Schwartz. photo · *MG* Feb 11, 1987: pD3.

Tip sheet: educator to speak on learning-disabled children; column. Susan Schwartz. *MG* March 11, 1987: pD10.

Tip sheet: doctor to speak on AIDS and food industry; column. Susan Schwartz. photo · *MG* April 1, 1987: pC10.

FICTION/Play by Bernar Hébert

[Untitled]; theatre review of *Fiction*. Diane Pavlovic. photo · *Jeu* 1987; No 44: p151–153.

THE FIELD/Children's play by Clem Martini

Actors' message not lost on kids; article. Sherri Clegg. photo · *CH* April 2, 1987: pD11.

FIELDING, JOY

Past formula; review of *The Deep End*. Margaret Jensen. *Can Lit* Winter 1987; No 115: p176–178.

FIELDWORK/Novel by Maureen Moore

Fatalities and feminism in Lotus Land; reviews of *Fieldwork* and *The Goldfish Bowl*. Margaret Cannon. *G&M* Aug 29, 1987: pC17.
[FIRST NOVELS: BOOK REVIEWS]

Heart of darkness; reviews of first novels. Janice Kulyk Keefer. *Books in Can* Dec 1987; Vol 16 No 9: p37–39.
[FIRST NOVELS: BOOK REVIEWS]

[Untitled]; reviews of *Doubtful Motives* and *Fieldwork*. Carolellen Norskey. *Quill & Quire* Sept 1987; Vol 53 No 9: p79.
[FIRST NOVELS: BOOK REVIEWS]

FIGURSKI, JAN

[Untitled]; reviews of poetry books. George Whipple. *Poetry Can R* Spring 1987; Vol 8 No 2–3: p53.

FILION, PIERRE

Dits et faits; column. photo · *Lettres québec* Spring 1987; No 45: p6–7.
[AWARDS, LITERARY; PUBLISHING AND PUBLISHERS IN CANADA; TRANSLATIONS OF CANADIAN LITERATURE; WRITERS' ORGANIZATIONS]

LA FILLE DE THOMAS VOGEL/Novel by Lise Vekeman

Les sentiers de la peur; review of *La Fille de Thomas Vogel*. Benoit Lacroix. *MD* Nov 7, 1987: pD3.

LES FILLES DE CALEB/Novel by Arlette Cousture

À Saint-Tite, la saga d'un patrimoine secret et sacré; column. Jean Éthier-Blais. photo · *MD* May 2, 1987: pD8.

Ce qui arrive, quant on écrit pour communiquer; review of *Le Cri de l'oie blanche*. Pierre Hébert. photo · *Lettres québec* Summer 1987; No 46: p24–25.

Caleb's juggernaut; article. Francine Pelletier. photo · *MG* Oct 31, 1987: J11.

LES FILLES DU 5–10–15/Play by Abla Farhoud

Le théâtre qu'on joue; theatre reviews. André Dionne. illus photo · *Lettres québec* Spring 1987; No 45: p47–48.

FILLES-MISSILES/Poems by Josée Yvon

La fiction du réel/le réel de la fiction; reviews of poetry books. André Brochu. *Voix et images* Winter 1987; No 35: p322–330.

FILLION, JACQUES

Un beau livre de réflexions; review of *L'Univers est fermé pour cause d'inventaire*. André Renaud. *Lettres québec* Summer 1987; No 46: p64–65.

FILM ADAPTATIONS OF CANADIAN LITERATURE

Filmmaker launches $260,000 lawsuit; article. *G&M* March 20, 1987: pD5.

Quebec director thrills 'n' chills; article about Yves Simoneau. photo · *TS* Feb 7, 1987: pG9.

Film-maker sues Cin Video; article. *MG* March 20, 1987: pC4.

Two Quebec films garner 22 Genie nominations; article. photo · *WFP* Feb 5, 1987: p38.

Decline of American Empire sweeps Genie Awards; article. *WFP* March 19, 1987: p40.

Les Fous de Bassan à Berlin; article. *MD* Feb 5, 1987: p6.

Decline of the American Empire wins top prizes at Genie awards; article. photo · *CH* March 19, 1987: pF6.

Film rights optioned for Ivory Swing; article. photo · *G&M* June 26, 1987: pD12.

Le Sourd dans la ville sera dans la course; article. *MD* July 14, 1987: p11.

Panels on books, movies; article. *TS* Oct 11, 1987: pA22.
[FESTIVALS, LITERARY]

Board buys rights to novels; article. *TS* Oct 18, 1987: pG4.

Un livre comme Hémon: secret, magique, introuvable; column. Jean Éthier-Blais. *MD* May 30, 1987: pD8.

Return of the native son; film review of *In the Shadow of the Wind*. Mark Abley. photo · *Maclean's* Jan 26, 1987; Vol 100 No 4: p54.

CBC variety keeps smiling despite budget cuts; column. Sid Adilman. *TS* Feb 26, 1987: pB1.

Devil, angel: Alliance has it covered; column. Sid Adilman. *TS* May 16, 1987: pG3.

Juicy real-life crime tales heat up fall book lists; column. Sid Adilman. *TS* Oct 3, 1987: J1.

A piece of the rock; film review of *In the Shadow of the Wind*. Bruce Bailey. photo · No 2–3: p53.

FILION, PIERRE

Dits et faits; column. photo · *Lettres québec* Spring 1987; No 45: p6–7.
[AWARDS, LITERARY; PUBLISHING AND PUBLISHERS IN CANADA; TRANSLATIONS OF CANADIAN LITERATURE; WRITERS' ORGANIZATIONS]

LA FILLE DE THOMAS VOGEL/Novel by Lise Vekeman

Les sentiers de la peur; review of *La Fille de Thomas Vogel*. Benoit Lacroix. *MD* Nov 7, 1987: pD3.

LES FILLES DE CALEB/Novel by Arlette Cousture

À Saint-Tite, la saga d'un patrimoine secret et sacré; column. Jean Éthier-Blais. photo · *MD* May 2, 1987: pD8.

Ce qui arrive, quant on écrit pour communiquer; review of *Le Cri de l'oie blanche*. Pierre Hébert. photo · *Lettres québec* Summer 1987; No 46: p24–25.

Caleb's juggernaut; article. Francine Pelletier. photo · *MG* Oct 31, 1987: J11.

LES FILLES DU 5–10–15/Play by Abla Farhoud

Le théâtre qu'on joue; theatre reviews. André Dionne. illus photo · *Lettres québec* Spring 1987; No 45: p47–48.

FILLES-MISSILES/Poems by Josée Yvon

La fiction du réel / le réel de la fiction; reviews of poetry books. André Brochu. *Voix et images* Winter 1987; No 35: p322–330.

FILLION, JACQUES

Un beau livre de réflexions; review of *L'Univers est fermé pour cause d'inventaire*. André Renaud. *Lettres québec* Summer 1987; No 46: p64–65.

FILM ADAPTATIONS OF CANADIAN LITERATURE

Filmmaker launches $260,000 lawsuit; article. *G&M* March 20, 1987: pD5.

Quebec director thrills 'n' chills; article about Yves Simoneau. photo · *TS* Feb 7, 1987: pG9.

Film-maker sues Cin Video; article. *MG* March 20, 1987: pC4.

Two Quebec films garner 22 Genie nominations; article. photo · *WFP* Feb 5, 1987: p38.

Decline of American Empire sweeps Genie awards; article. *WFP* March 19, 1987: p40.

Les Fous de Bassan à Berlin; article. *MD* Feb 5, 1987: p6.

Decline of American Empire wins top prizes at Genie Awards; article. photo · *CH* March 19, 1987: pF6.

Film rights optioned for Ivory Swing; article. photo · *G&M* June 26, 1987: pD12.

Le Sourd dans la ville sera dans la course; article. *MD* July 14, 1987: p11.

Panels on books, movies; article. *TS* Oct 11, 1987: pA22.
[FESTIVALS, LITERARY]

Board buys rights to novels; article. *TS* Oct 18, 1987: pG4.

Un livre comme Hémon: secret, magique, introuvable; column. Jean Éthier-Blais. *MD* May 30, 1987: pD8.

Return of the native son; film review of *In the Shadow of the Wind*. Mark Abley. photo · *Maclean's* Jan 26, 1987; Vol 100 No 4: p54.

CBC variety keeps smiling despite budget cuts; column. Sid Adilman. *TS* Feb 26, 1987: pB1.

Devil, angel: Alliance has it covered; column. Sid Adilman. *TS* May 16, 1987: pG3.

Juicy real-life crime tales heat up fall book lists; column. Sid Adilman. *TS* Oct 3, 1987: pJ1.

A piece of the rock; film review of *In the Shadow of the Wind*. Mark Abley. photo · *MG* Jan 10, 1987: pG3.

Dancing In The Dark: what happens when a homemaker cracks; film review. Bruce Bailey. photo · *MG* Jan 17, 1987: pD4.

The Genies: Le Déclin rises to the occasion; article. Bruce Bailey. photo · *MG* March 19, 1987: pB5.

John And The Missus misses despite commendable acting; film review. Ron Base. photo · *TS* Feb 6, 1987: pD8.

Empire strikes 8 Genies; article. Ron Base. photo · *TS* March 19, 1987: pE1.

Pinsent's presence overshadows film; film review of *John and the Missus*. Brian Brennan. photo · *CH* May 15, 1987: pE8.

Successful local novel to be made into film; article. Donald Campbell. Fortin's future; article. David Homel. *Quill & Quire* Oct 1987; Vol 53 No 10: p6.

A wealth of fine films lies waiting in Canadian novels; column. Joan Irwin. *TS* Jan 17, 1987: pG7.
[TELEVISION AND CANADIAN LITERATURE]

Olympic festival to open with Wheeler film; article. H.J. Kirchhoff. photo · *G&M* Dec 8, 1987: pD5.

Hits and Missus; article. Martin Knelman. biog photo · *Tor Life* Feb 1987; Vol 21 No 2: p29–31.

Les Fous de Bassan se cassent le bec sur un vrai mur; article. Robert Lévesque. *MD* Feb 25, 1987: p1,12.

Le sourd dans la ville, de Mireille Dansereau: près du roman mais loin de l'inspiration; film review. Robert Lévesque. *MD* Sept 19, 1987: pA7.

Roll 'em, cowboys; article. Liam Lacey. photo · *G&M* Aug 29, 1987: pC1.C3.

Une belle et dense histoire difficile à porter à l'écran; article. Francine Laurendeau. photo · *MD* Oct 24, 1987: pC1,C12.

Gordon Pinsent reminds us of our sense of place; editorial. James Lorimer. *Atlan Insight* May 1987; Vol 9 No 5: p3.

Literary extravaganza goes national; column. Kenneth McGoogan. *CH* April 5, 1987: pE5.
[AUTHORS, CANADIAN; WRITERS' ORGANIZATIONS; WRITERS' WORKSHOPS]

Get new year off to good start with Dancing In The Dark; film review. Paul McKie. photo · *WFP* Jan 4, 1987: p14.

Pinsent tells touching story; film review of *John and the Missus*. Paul McKie. photo · *WFP* April 19, 1987: p15.

Berton's memoirs due out in the fall; column. Henry Mietkiewicz. *TS* June 25, 1987: pF3.

Movie makers focusing on Canadian authors; column. Henry Mietkiewicz. photo · *TS* July 28, 1987: pC2.

Elegy for a dying village; film review of *John and the Missus*. Lawrence O'Toole. photo · *Maclean's* Feb 2, 1987; Vol 100 No 5: p78.

Decline rises to top Genie nominations; article. Greg Quill. photo · *TS* Feb 5, 1987: pF1.

Hollywood: some call it Quebec South; article. Linda Renaud. Anne Gregor. photo · *MG* Dec 19, 1987: pE7.

La vie littéraire; column. Jean Royer. photo · *MD* April 11, 1987: pD2.
[AWARDS, LITERARY; POETRY READINGS; RADIO AND CANADIAN LITERATURE; TELEVISION AND CANADIAN LITERATURE]

Le Matou d'Yves Beauchemin: du fait littéraire à la chaîne de productions-médias; article. Catherine Saouter. *Voix et images* Spring 1987; Vol 12 No 3: p393–402.
[TELEVISION AND CANADIAN LITERATURE]

Book world: Maggie Smith as Judith Hearne?; column. Beverley Slopen. *TS* Jan 25, 1987: pB6.
[AUTHORS, CANADIAN]

Book world: Owl magazine publisher wades into film field; column. Beverley Slopen. *TS* Sept 20, 1987: pA20.
[CHILDREN'S LITERATURE; PUBLISHING AND PUBLISHERS IN CANADA]

Book world: 'My year for films': Brian Moore; column. Beverley Slopen. photo · *TS* Nov 8, 1987: pA18.
[CHILDREN'S LITERATURE; PUBLISHING AND PUBLISHERS IN CANADA]

[The Rich Man]; theatre review. Lynne Van Luven. *NeWest R* Nov 1987; Vol 13 No 3: p18.
[DRAMATIC ADAPTATIONS OF CANADIAN LITERATURE]

Genies: daring to be different; article. Ina Warren. photo · *MG* March 17, 1987: pC10.

LE FILS D'ARIANE/Short stories by Micheline La France

La vitrine du livre; reviews of *À double sens* and *Le Fils d'Ariane*. Guy Ferland. *MD* Feb 14, 1987: pC2.

Un fil d'Ariane habilement tendu; review of *Le Fils d'Ariane*. Madeleine Ouellette-Michalska. photo · *MD* March 28, 1987: pD3.

Les vertus de la retenue et du silence; reviews of poetry books. Marie José Thériault. photo · *Lettres québec* Summer 1987; No 46: p30–32.

LA FIN DE L'HISTOIRE/Novel by Pierre Gravel

Deux fictions sur fond d'histoire; reviews of *La Fin de l'histoire* and *L'Amour de Jeanne*. Yvon Bernier. photo · *Lettres québec* Winter 1986–87; No 44: p31–33.

Qui a peur des héritiers de Papineau?; review of *La Fin de l'histoire*. Paul-André Comeau. *MD* March 14, 1987: pD7.

Écrire l'histoire ou histoire d'écrire; reviews of novels. Jacques Michon. *Voix et images* Spring 1987; Vol 12 No 3: p548–550.

LA FIN DES JEUX/Novel by Michel Gosselin

Les enfants du déclin; reviews of novels. Jacques Michon. *Voix et images* Winter 1987; No 35: p331–334.

FINDLEY, TIMOTHY

CBC to dramatize Findley novel; article. *G&M* April 10, 1987: pC9.
[RADIO AND CANADIAN LITERATURE]

CBC Radio to dramatize Famous Last Words; article. *TS* April 10, 1987: pD20.
[RADIO AND CANADIAN LITERATURE]

Periodical marketers pick Chrétien memoir as top book; article. *MG* Nov 18, 1987: pD1.
[AWARDS, LITERARY]

À surveiller; column. *MD* Nov 16, 1987: p8.

Marketers name top paperbacks; article. *TS* Nov 17, 1987: pF4.
[AWARDS, LITERARY]

Findley takes prize; article. *WFP* Nov 18, 1987: p50.
[AWARDS, LITERARY]

The Telling of Lies top of paperbacks; article. *CH* Nov 17, 1987: pE8.
[AWARDS, LITERARY]

Outcome of Bell Jar libel suit closely monitored by publishers; column. Ken Adachi. *TS* Jan 26, 1987: pD4.
[CENSORSHIP]

Findley novel a sell-out in London despite critical vitriol; article. Ken Adachi. *TS* April 6, 1987: pB1.
[INTERNATIONAL REVIEWS OF CANADIAN LITERATURE]

How English rose, prospered and begat new tongues; review of *The Telling of Lies*. Barbara Black. *MG* Dec 19, 1987: J13.

The very best of company: perceptions of a Canadian attitude towards war and nationalism in three contemporary plays; article. John S. Bolin. *Amer R of Can Studies* Autumn 1987; Vol 17 No 3: p309–322.
[CANADIAN DRAMA: HISTORY AND CRITICISM; CULTURAL IDENTITY]

[Untitled]; review of *The Telling of Lies*. Wilfred Cude. *Antigonish R* Winter 1987; No 68: p55–60.

My final hour: an address to the Philosophy Society, Trent University, Monday, 26 January 1987; essay. Timothy Findley. abstract · *J of Can Studies* Spring 1987; Vol 22 No 1: p5–16

Hyde is named Author of the Year; article. Matthew Fraser. photo · *G&M* Nov 17, 1987: pD7.
[AWARDS, LITERARY]

Authors talk about books as movies; article. Peter Goddard. *TS* Oct 20, 1987: H4.
[FESTIVALS, LITERARY]

Top flight practitioners of the craft of writing mysteries; review of *The Telling of Lies*. Douglas Hill. *G&M* Nov 21, 1987: pC21.

[Untitled]; review of *The Telling of Lies*. Catherine Hunter. *Malahat R (special issue)* March 1987; No 78: p148–151.

Murder & lies; reviews of *A Single Death* and *The Telling of Lies*. Linda Hutcheon. *Can Lit* Winter 1987; No 115: p225–227.

Apocalyptic imaginations: notes on Atwood's The Handmaid's Tale and Findley's Not Wanted on the Voyage; article. W.J. Keith. *Essays on Can Writ* Winter 1987; No 35: p123–134.
[THE APOCALYPSE; BIBLICAL MYTHS AND MYTHOLOGY; GOD IN LITERATURE; SATIRIC WRITING]

The off-the-wall writing on the wall; review of *Famous Last Words*. John Melmoth. *Times Lit Supp* April 24, 1987; No 4386: p435.

Mauberley's lies: fact and fiction in Timothy Findley's Famous Last Words; article. E.F. Shields. abstract · *J of Can Studies* Winter 1987–88; Vol 22 No 4: p44–59.
[HISTORICAL THEMES]

Photography "in camera"; article. Peter Sims. *Can Lit* Summer-Fall 1987; No 113–114: p145–166.

FIRE EYES/Novel by D.F. Bailey

Urban scrawl; reviews of first novels. Janice Kulyk Keefer. *Books in Can* Aug-Sept 1987; Vol 16 No 6: p33–34.
[FIRST NOVELS: BOOK REVIEWS]

Explosive debut made by writer; review of *Fire Eyes*. Michael Mirolla. photo · *CH* Sept 13, 1987: pE5.
[FIRST NOVELS: BOOK REVIEWS]

Not meant to be a thriller; letter to the editor. Bella Pomer. *Quill & Quire* June 1987; Vol 53 No 6: p4.

Would-be world-class thrillers need plots to be complete; reviews of *Equinox* and *Fire Eyes*. Philippe van Rjndt. photo · *Quill & Quire* April 1987; Vol 53 No 4: p28.

FIRE IN THE MORNING/Novel by Elizabeth Spencer

New & noteworthy; reviews of *The Voice at the Back Door* and *Fire in the Morning*. Patricia T. O'Connor. *NYT Book R* Feb 1, 1987: p32.

FIRE: AN EVANGELIC ROCK MUSICAL/Play by Paul Ledoux and David Young

[Untitled]; theatre review of *Fire*. Mark Abley. photo · *Maclean's* Jan 26, 1987; Vol 100 No 4: p55.

Musical Fire is a damp sparkler; theatre review. Brian Brennan. photo · *CH* Feb 14, 1987: pG4.

Rollicking rock and old-time religion stoke Fire; theatre review. Ray Conlogue. photo · *G&M* Jan 13, 1987: pC7.

Fire bites off a lot, chews most of it; theatre review of *Fire*. Wayne Grigsby. *MG* Jan 10, 1987: H7.

[Untitled]; theatre reviews of *Fire* and *Opium*. Wayne Grigsby. *MG* Jan 16, 1987: pD10.

[Fire]; theatre review. Susan Minsos. *NeWest R* April 1987; Vol 12 No 8: p17.

FIREWEED/Children's story by Margriet Ruurs

[Untitled]; review of *Fireweed*. Carolellen Norskey. *Quill & Quire (Books for Young People)* June 1987; Vol 53 No 6: p6,9.

FIREWEED/Periodical

Editorial. *Fireweed* Winter 1987; No 24: p5–7.
[CANADIAN LITERARY PERIODICALS]

FIREWORKS: THE BEST OF FIREWEED/Anthology

Best picks of feminism; review of *Fireworks*. Ruth Manson. *G&M* May 2, 1987: pC18.
[ANTHOLOGIES: BOOK REVIEWS]

FIRST NOVELS

Town and country; article. photo · *Books in Can* April 1987; Vol 16 No 3: p6–8.
[AWARDS, LITERARY]

For the sake of Clarity; letter to the editor. Annette Gordon. *Books in Can* Nov 1987; Vol 16 No 8: p40.

FIRST NOVELS: BOOK REVIEWS

New in paper; reviews of novels. *TS* Aug 30, 1987: pA18.

[Untitled]; review of *The Letter*. *Queen's Q* Winter 1987; Vol 94 No 4: p1067–1068.

Une famille dévorée par l'ennui et le néant de vie inutiles; review of *Les Dimanches sont mortels*. Jean Éthier-Blais. *MD* Nov 21, 1987: pD12.

A newcomer to Canadian crime fiction; review of *Gallows View*. Ken Adachi. *TS* April 19, 1987: pA19.

Risk-taking writer off to a good start; review of *The Butterfly Chair*. Ken Adachi. *TS* Nov 22, 1987: pC9.

Springtime, and some more Malouins; review of *Il y a toujours des printemps en Amérique*. Benoit Aubin. photo · *MG* Oct 31, 1987: J11.

Les Héritiers (prix Robert Cliche) et L'Écrit-vent; reviews. Noël Audet. photo · *Lettres québec* Autumn 1987; No 47: p19–21.

De la poésie la prose; review of *L'Hiver de Mira Christophe*. Noël Audet. photo · *Lettres québec* Winter 1986–87; No 44: p26–28.

[Untitled]; reviews of *Housebroken* and *Private Properties*. Sharon Batt. *Room of One's Own* Sept 1987; Vol 11 No 4: p109–112.

La ville toute verte, bordée de montagnes enneigées; review of *L'Hiver de Mira Christophe*. Réjean Beaudoin. *Liberté* April 1987; Vol 29 No 2: p118–124.

Le salut de Pierre Vallières; review of *Noces obscures*. Réjean Beaudoin. *Liberté* April 1987; Vol 29 No 2: p139–140.

A brutal inheritance; review of *The Butterfly Chair*. Celina Bell. *Maclean's* Dec 7, 1987; Vol 100 No 49: T8.

Montreal needle trade is setting for comic tale about working girl; review of *Damaged Goods*, includes profile. Barbara Black. photo · *MG* July 18, 1987: J9.

En poche, le premier roman de Yolande Villemaire: un thriller gigogne; review of *Meurtres à blanc*. Jean-Roch Boivin. photo · *MD* May 2, 1987: pD3.

Sous le signe du Scorpion, Andrée-A. Michaud nous convie aux confins de l'obsession; review of *La Femme de Sath*. Jean-Roch Boivin. *MD* June 6, 1987: pD3.

Un jeune couple de Québécois en quête du "ginseng de l'âme"; review of *Nichan*. Jean-Roch Boivin. photo · *MD* Sept 12, 1987: pD2.

Un roman bâclé qui fera fureur dans les supermarchés; review of *Probablement l'Espagne*. Jean-Roch Boivin. *MD* Nov 14, 1987: pD15.

Pour l'amour des grand-mères, des petites filles et des petits garons, de l'art, de Montréal et pour l'amour tout court; review of *Myriam première*. Jean-Roch Boivin. photo · *MD* Dec 12, 1987: pD3.

[Untitled]; review of *One Out of Four*. Steve Boyd. *CH* Jan 25, 1987: pE4.

Shallow griefs; review of *Back on Tuesday*. Diana Brydon. *Can Lit* Winter 1987; No 115: p194–195.

Éclats d'existence; review of *L'Hiver de Mira Christophe*. Lucie Côté. *MD* April 28, 1987: p17.

Crime; review of *To an Easy Grave*. Newgate Callendar. *NYT Book R* Jan 18, 1987: p23.

Murder & mayhem: tough guys on clean street; reviews of crime novels. Margaret Cannon. *G&M* Jan 3, 1987: pE15.

Murder & mayhem: Spenser's clones; review of *Crang Plays the Ace*. Margaret Cannon. photo · *G&M* April 25, 1987: pC19.

Murder & mayhem: plot and details in a cop's life; reviews of *Gallows View* and *Equinox*. Margaret Cannon. photo · *G&M* May 23, 1987: pC23.

Fatalities and feminism in Lotus Land; reviews of *Fieldwork* and *The Goldfish Bowl*. Margaret Cannon. *G&M* Aug 29, 1987: pC17.

Three new faces deserving discovery; reviews of crime novels. Margaret Cannon. photo · *G&M* Oct 17, 1987: pE4.

Surprising weight from the newcomers; reviews of *The Glorious East Wind* and *Ripper*. Margaret Cannon. *G&M* Nov 7, 1987: pC23.

Slain hitchhiker doesn't live up to writer's promise; reviews of *Sleep While I Sing* and *Sherlock Holmes and the Case of the Raleigh Legacy*. Paul Carbray. *MG* Feb 21, 1987: pB8.

[Untitled]; review of *A Long Night of Death*. Barbara Carey. *Books in Can* Jan-Feb 1987; Vol 16 No 1: p25.

Latin terror; review of *A Long Night of Death*. Pauline Carey. *G&M* Aug 22, 1987: pC14.

[Untitled]; reviews of *Flight Against Time* and *The Late Great Human Road Show*. Judith Carson. *Can Forum* Aug-Sept 1987; Vol 67 No 771: p48–49.

Past and present merge in painful, haunting tales; reviews of *False Face* and *Who Is Frances Rain?*. Peter Carver. photo · *Quill & Quire (Books for Young People)* Oct 1987; Vol 53 No 10: p10.

[Untitled]; review of *The Life of Helen Alone*. Adelle Castelo. *Quill & Quire* Jan 1987; Vol 53 No 1: p27–28.

Les bienfaits de la bombe; review of *Les Samourailles*. Jean-François Chassay. *MD* Dec 5, 1987: pD4.

Personnages en quête d'eux-mêmes; review of *Le Sexe des étoiles*. Jean-François Chassay. photo · *MD* Dec 12, 1987: pD4.

From mind to mind; reviews of *Night Studies* and *Wishbones*. H.W. Connor. *Can Lit* Spring 1987; No 112: p118–120.

[Untitled]; review of *Miss Abigail's Part*. Mary Lou Cornish. *Cross Can Writ Q* 1987; Vol 9 No 3–4: p49.

[Untitled]; review of *Miss Abigail's Part*. Maureen Corrigan. *NYT Book R* March 1, 1987: p20.

[Untitled]; reviews. Beverley Daurio. *Cross Can Writ Q* 1987; Vol 9 No 2: p23.

[Untitled]; review of *Gallows View*. Martin Dowding. *Quill & Quire* March 1987; Vol 53 No 3: p71.

Macabre parade of masks; review of *Our Hero in the Cradle of Confederation*. Sharon Drache. *G&M* July 11, 1987: pC14.

Stephen Reid's Jackrabbit Parole; review. Brian Fawcett. *West Coast R* Spring 1987; Vol 21 No 4: p78–80.

There's still room for the Great Mall Novel; review of *The Promised Land*. William French. photo · *G&M* March 19, 1987: pD1.

Novel about family tragedy a powerful debut; review of *The Butterfly Chair*. William French. illus · *G&M* Dec 3, 1987: pA25.

[Untitled]; review of *The Promised Land*. Cecelia Frey. *CH* May 17, 1987: pE5.

Women make difference in prairie family; review of *Under the House*. Cecelia Frey. *CH* July 19, 1987: pE4.

Une histoire de jeunesse; review of *Tableau de jeunesse*. Chantal Gamache. *MD* May 23, 1987: pD3.

Bugs, battles & ballet; reviews of *On Stage, Please* and *Redcoat*. James Gellert. *Can Lit* Winter 1987; No 115: p220–223.

Emily Nasrallah's first novel; review of *Flight Against Time*. Laura Groening. *Atlan Prov Book R* May-June 1987; Vol 14 No 2: p9.

Film's end; review of *The Disposables*. John Hamilton. *G&M* June 13, 1987: pC20.

[Untitled]; review of *Economic Sex*. Richard Hamilton. *Rubicon* Spring 1987; No 8: p226.

A monument to folly; review of *Dustship Glory*. Geoff Hancock. *Can Forum* Feb 1987; Vol 66 No 766: p39–40.

A dazzling novel that attempts to be masterpiece; review of *Selakhi*. Geoff Hancock. *TS* Nov 29, 1987: pA21.

Unkind but true: little skill in first novel; review of *Counterpoint*. Maggie Helwig. *TS* June 20, 1987: M7.

Publishers meet the demand with reissued crime classics; reviews of *The Night the Gods Smiled* and *One-Eyed Merchants*. Douglas Hill. *G&M* Feb 28, 1987: pE19.

[Untitled]; review of *The Letter*. Douglas Hill. *Books in Can* Jan-Feb 1987; Vol 16 No 1: p24.

The latest reports from the exotic worlds of fantasy; review of *The Summer Tree*. Douglas Hill. *G&M* July 11, 1987: pC13.

Small regional presses as saviors of cultural information; reviews of fictional works. Douglas Hill. *G&M* Oct 10, 1987: pC21.

Parody & legacy; reviews. Lorna Irvine. *Can Lit* Winter 1987; No 115: p264–267.

[Untitled]; review of *Sandinista*. Miriam Jones. *Rubicon* Fall 1987; No 9: p197–198.

Disappearing into Japan; review of *Almost Japanese*. Kathy Jones. *NYT Book R* Aug 16, 1987: p23.

An obsession for B.C.'s trees; review of *Looking for the Last Big Tree*. M.T. Kelly. photo · *G&M* Feb 7, 1987: pE19.

Impressive; review of *Under the House*. M.T. Kelly. *G&M* Feb 14, 1987: pE20.

Chilling view; review of *Dreams of an Unseen Planet*. H.J. Kirchhoff. *G&M* June 13, 1987: pC20.

World of wonders; reviews of first novels. Janice Kulyk Keefer. *Books in Can* May 1987; Vol 16 No 4: p37–38.

Cheap thrills; reviews of *The Last Hunter* and *Gallows View*. Janice Kulyk Keefer. *Books in Can* June-July 1987; Vol 16 No 5: p37–38.

Urban scrawl; reviews of first novels. Janice Kulyk Keefer. *Books in Can* Aug-Sept 1987; Vol 16 No 6: p33–34.

Me, myself, and I; reviews of first novels. Janice Kulyk Keefer. *Books in Can* Oct 1987; Vol 16 No 7: p35–36,38.

Local heroes; reviews of first novels. Janice Kulyk Keefer. *Books in Can* Nov 1987; Vol 16 No 8: p35,37.

Heart of darkness; reviews of first novels. Janice Kulyk Keefer. *Books in Can* Dec 1987; Vol 16 No 9: p37–39.

[Untitled]; review of *Me and Luke*. Patty Lawlor. *Quill & Quire (Books for Young People)* Oct 1987; Vol 53 No 10: p22.

Hitler's letter; review of *The Letter*. Robert G. Lawrence. *Can Lit* Winter 1987; No 115: p229–230.

Family continuum; review of *Miss Abigail's Part*. Andrea Lebowitz. *Can Lit* Winter 1987; No 115: p152–155.

L'effet science-fiction tous azimuts: la SF québécoise en 1986–1987; reviews of science fiction books and periodicals. Michel Lord. *Voix et images* Autumn 1987; Vol 13 No 1: p180–189.
[ANNOTATIONS, SHORT REVIEWS, BOOK LISTS; ANTHOLOGIES: BOOK REVIEWS; CANADIAN LITERARY PERIODICALS]

Entre la réussite et l'échec; reviews of science fiction books. Michel Lord. photo · *Lettres québec* Autumn 1987; No 47: p33–34.
[ANTHOLOGIES: BOOK REVIEWS]

A spot of skulduggery with an Asian flavor; review of *The Glorious East Wind*. Neil Louttit. *WFP* Dec 19, 1987: p51.

Grime and punishment; review of *Crang Plays the Ace*. Douglas Malcolm. *Books in Can* April 1987; Vol 16 No 3: p35.

Thriller mired in words; review of *Merlin's Web*. Elona Malterre. *CH* Nov 8, 1987: pE6.

[Untitled]; review of *Downfall People*. Frank Manley. *Books in Can* Jan-Feb 1987; Vol 16 No 1: p24–25.

All about women and relationships; reviews of *Housebroken* and *Frogs*. Lesley McAllister. *TS* Jan 3, 1987: M6.

Under dark cover of stark militarism; review of *A Long Night of Death*. Lesley McAllister. *TS* April 25, 1987: M7.

[Untitled]; reviews of *Under the House* and *A Forest for Zoe*. Lesley McAllister. *Cross Can Writ Q* 1987; Vol 9 No 3-4: p48–49.

Promising literary debut made by young mother; review of *The Woman Upstairs*. Kenneth McGoogan. biog photo · *CH* May 10, 1987: pE5.

Whodunits hit bookshelves in big way; review of *Gallows View*. Kenneth McGoogan. *CH* June 7, 1987: pE6.

[Untitled]; review of *The Butterfly Chair*. Joan McGrath. *Quill & Quire* Sept 1987; Vol 53 No 9: p78–79.

First novels set to different literary keys; reviews of *Crang Plays the Ace* and *Gallows View*. James Mennie. photo · *MG* April 11, 1987: pG6.

[Untitled]; review of *Miss Abigail's Part*. Mary Millar. *Queen's Q* Summer 1987; Vol 94 No 2: p477–478.

Léonce, Léonil . . . et Sept fois Jeanne; reviews of *Cette fois, Jeanne . . .* and *La Double vie de Léonce et Léonil*. Louise Milot. photo · *Lettres québec* Autumn 1987; No 47: p17–18.

Hostile Earth Mother insidiously subdues human colony; review of *Dreams of an Unseen Planet*. Michael Mirolla. photo · *MG* April 4, 1987: H10.

Explosive debut made by writer; review of *Fire Eyes*. Michael Mirolla. photo · *CH* Sept 13, 1987: pE5.

A mystery in Manitoba; review of *Who Is Frances Rain?*, Helen Norrie. *WFP* Dec 5, 1987: p57.

[Untitled]; review of *The Tiger's Daughter*. Carolellen Norskey. *Quill & Quire* July 1987; Vol 53 No 7: p65.

[Untitled]; review of *Counterpoint*. Carolellen Norskey. *Quill & Quire* Aug 1987; Vol 53 No 8: p30.

[Untitled]; reviews of *Doubtful Motives* and *Fieldwork*. Carolellen Norskey. *Quill & Quire* Sept 1987; Vol 53 No 9: p79.

Mysteries to feed the mind with varying tastes; reviews of *Crang Plays the Ace* and *To an Easy Grave*. John North. photo · *Quill & Quire* March 1987; Vol 53 No 3: p74.

[Untitled]; review of *The Hollow Woman*. John North. *Quill & Quire* June 1987; Vol 53 No 6: p32.

[Untitled]; review of *Merlin's Web*. John North. *Quill & Quire* Sept 1987; Vol 53 No 9: p79.

[Untitled]; review of *The Letter*. John North. *Quill & Quire* Jan 1987; Vol 53 No 1: p27.

[Untitled]; review of *Broken English*. John North. *Quill & Quire* Nov 1987; Vol 53 No 11: p24.

Une fille bien de son siècle; review of *Cette fois, Jeanne . . . .* Madeleine Ouellette-Michalska. *MD* Sept 5, 1987: pC9.

Une famille, un coin du monde, un pays; review of *Il y aura toujours des printemps en Amérique*. Alice Parizeau. *MD* Oct 3, 1987: pD3.

À la rencontre des huguenots de Namur; review of *Le Feu des souches*. Alice Parizeau. *MD* Dec 12, 1987: pD4.

Le syndrome du best-seller; review of *Sous la griffe du sida*. Alice Parizeau. photo · *MD* Dec 19, 1987: pD4.

[Untitled]; review of *The Tiger's Daughter*. Helen Porter. *Books in Can* Aug-Sept 1987; Vol 16 No 6: p29.

Novel's heroine searches for life after divorce; review of *The Life of Helen Alone*. Sherie Posesorski. *MG* Jan 24, 1987: pB8.

[Untitled]; review of *A Long Night of Death*. Rachel Rafelman. *Quill & Quire* Feb 1987; Vol 53 No 2: p17.

[Untitled]; review of *Under the House*. Rachel Rafelman. *Quill & Quire* April 1987; Vol 53 No 4: p29.

Le roman sans qualités; review of *L'Hiver de Mira Christophe*. Yvon Rivard. *Liberté* June 1987; Vol 29 No 3: p103.

[Untitled]; review of *The Glorious East Wind*. Peter Robinson. *Quill & Quire* Sept 1987; Vol 53 No 9: p79.

[Untitled]; review of *The Butterfly Chair*. Constance Rooke. *Malahat R* Dec 1987; No 81: p102.

[Untitled]; review of *Heroine*. Constance Rooke. *Malahat R* Dec 1987; No 81: p103.

Three absolute page-turners; reviews of *Crang Plays the Ace* and *Gallows View*. Janet Saunders. photo · *WFP* May 9, 1987: p56.

Dust bowl to never land; review of *Dustship Glory*. Alan Shugard. *Can Lit* Winter 1987; No 115: p196–197.

Recent Canadian fiction; reviews of novels. D.O. Spettigue. *Queen's Q* Summer 1987; Vol 94 No 2: p366–375.

[Untitled]; review of *Cette fois, Jeanne . . . .* Jacques St-Pierre. *Moebius* Summer 1987; No 33: p133–135.

[Untitled]; reviews of *Flavian's Fortune* and *The Story of Bobby O'Malley*. Charles R. Steele. *Queen's Q* Winter 1987; Vol 94 No 4: p1019–1022.

[Untitled]; review of *The Promised Land*. Thomas P. Sullivan. *Quill & Quire* May 1987; Vol 53 No 5: p20,22.

A daring invention of a new character; review of *Heroine*. Rosemary Sullivan. *G&M* Sept 19, 1987: pC19.

Full stops; review of *Economic Sex*. Leon Surette. *Can Lit* Winter 1987; No 115: p245–246.

The Rathbones' family skeletons; review of *Under the House*. Linda Taylor. *Times Lit Supp* Dec 18, 1987; No 4420: p1409.

[Untitled]; review of *Sandinista*. Larry Towell. *Queen's Q* Autumn 1987; Vol 94 No 3: p696–698.

[Untitled]; review of *One Out of Four*. Martin Townsend. *Quill & Quire* Feb 1987; Vol 53 No 2: p17.

Portrait of the artist as a middle-aged schlemiel; review of *Our Hero in the Cradle of Confederation*. Paul Tyndall. *Atlan Prov Book R* Sept-Oct 1987; Vol 14 No 3: p12.

[Untitled]; reviews of *The Cutting Season* and *A Nest of Singing Birds*. John A. Urquhart. *Prairie J of Can Lit* 1987; No 8: p50–54.

The summer before Browning died; review of *The Whirlpool*. Aritha van Herk. *Brick* Fall 1987; No 31: p15–17.

[Untitled]; reviews of *Vigil* and *The Whirlpool*. Alice Van Wart. *Can Forum* Aug-Sept 1987; Vol 67 No 771: p46–48.

Tale of growing up is a true standout; review of *The Woman Upstairs*. Morley Walker. *WFP* July 11, 1987: p57.

Crang: super-mouth sleuth; review of *Crang Plays the Ace*. Mike Walton. *TS* April 12, 1987: pA21.

A solid first effort from a Toronto cop; review of *The Glorious East Wind*. Mike Walton. photo · *TS* Dec 26, 1987: K7.

Killer stalks wet streets of Vancouver; review of *The Goldfish Bowl*. Paul Waters. *MG* Dec 24, 1987: L9.

Hong Kong is a jungle in Toronto cop's thriller; review of *The Glorious East Wind*. Paul Waters. *MG* Oct 31, 1987: J14.

[Untitled]; review of *The Lucky Ones*. David Willis. *Queen's Q* Summer 1987; Vol 94 No 2: p482–483.

[Untitled]; reviews. Janet Windeler. *Cross Can Writ Q* 1987; Vol 9 No 2: p25–26.

Fiction just loaded with personality; reviews of children's novels. Tim Wynne-Jones. photo · *G&M* Nov 28, 1987: pC22.

Dense, mystic tale requires much of reader; review of *Selakhi*. Thomas York. *CH* Dec 27, 1987: pE6.

FISH-HOOKS/Short stories by Reg Silvester

Peacetime; reviews of *Spectral Evidence* and *Fish-Hooks*. Keith Wilson. *Can Lit* Spring 1987; No 112: p154–156.

THE FISHERMAN'S REVENGE/Play by Michael Cook

[Untitled]; review of *The Fisherman's Revenge*. Bert Cowan. *Books in Can* March 1987; Vol 16 No 2: p25.

FISHMAN, MARTIN

Canadian playwrights give urban life short shrift, says one writer who didn't; article. Kevin Prokosh. *WFP* Jan 22, 1987: p35.

Exciting, refreshing City Limits tops theatre season; theatre review. Reg Skene. *WFP* Jan 24, 1987: p22.

THE FISHWHARF AND STEAMBOAT MEN/Play by R.C.A. Theatre collective

Collective concern; theatre reviews of *The Daily News* and *The Fishwharf and Steamboat Men*. Terry Goldie. photo · *Can Theatre R* Spring 1987; No 50: p81–83.

FITCH, SHEREE

A trio of poets to tickle a child's fancy; reviews of children's poetry books. Adele Ashby. *Quill & Quire (Books for Young People)* June 1987; Vol 53 No 6: p10.

FITZGERALD, JUDITH

[Untitled]; review of *Given Names*. Sharon Berg. *Poetry Can R* Spring 1987; Vol 8 No 2–3: p46.

Proof that poetry is not dead; review of *Diary of Desire*. Colline Caulder. *TS* Oct 25, 1987: pA18.

Desperately seeking Susan; essay. Judith Fitzgerald. photo · *TS* June 18, 1987: pD1,D4.

[Untitled]; review of *Whale Waddleby*. Dexter Peters. *TS* Feb 1, 1987: pA20.

FIVE FROM THE FRINGE/Play anthology

[Untitled]; review of *Five from the Fringe*. L.W. Conolly. *World Lit in Eng* Spring 1987; Vol 27 No 1: p56–58.
[ANTHOLOGIES: BOOK REVIEWS]

Dramatic fringe; reviews of *Five from the Fringe* and *Politics and the Playwright: George Ryga*. James Noonan. *Can Lit* Winter 1987; No 115: p235–238.
[ANTHOLOGIES: BOOK REVIEWS]

[Five from the Fringe]; review. Don Perkins. *NeWest R* April 1987; Vol 12 No 8: p18.
[ANTHOLOGIES: BOOK REVIEWS]

Beyond the Fringe; reviews of plays. Judith Rudakoff. *Books in Can* March 1987; Vol 16 No 2: p18.

FIVE NEW FACTS ABOUT GIORGIONE/Novel by Hugh Hood

Hugh Hood artfully rewrites history of Italian renaissance; review of *Five New Facts About Giorgione*. Mark Abley. *MG* Nov 7, 1987: K12.

Two novels offer pain — and incidental pleasures; reviews of *Death-Watch* and *Five Facts about Giorgione*. Ken Adachi. *TS* Aug 30, 1987: pA19.

Ghosts, gondolas and some fantastical imagining; review of *Five New Facts About Giorgione*. William French. photo · *G&M* Sept 1, 1987: pD7.

Delving into artistic mystery; review of *Five New Facts About Giorgione*. David Williamson. photo· *WFP* Dec 19, 1987: p50.

FLACK, BRIAN L.

[Untitled]; review of *With a Sudden & Terrible Clarity*. Theresa Hurley. *Quarry* Spring 1987; Vol 36 No 2: p109–111.

FLAVIAN'S FORTUNE/Novel by Alastair Macdonald

Lost innocents; reviews of *Nothing So Natural* and *Flavian's Fortune*. Peter Hinchcliffe. *Can Lit* Spring 1987; No 112: p90–91.

[Untitled]; reviews of *Flavian's Fortune* and *The Story of Bobby O'Malley*. Charles R. Steele. *Queen's Q* Winter 1987; Vol 94 No 4: p1019–1022.

FLESH AND PAPER/Poems by Suniti Namjoshi and Gillian Hanscombe

Male myths, obliterated lesbians and powerful dreams; reviews of poetry books. Fraser Sutherland. photo · *G&M* Feb 14, 1987: pE19.

LES FLEURS DE CATALPA/Poems by Madeleine Gagnon

Les géographies et le souffle chez Madeleine Gagnon; reviews of *Les Fleurs du Catalpa* and *L'Infante immmoriale*. Caroline Bayard. photo · *Lettres québec* Winter 1986–87; No 44: p46–47.

Entre la maison, l'eau et le cosmos: l'écriture féminine; reviews of novels. Patricia Smart. *Voix et images* Winter 1987; No 35: p334–337.

FLICKER AND HAWK/Poems by Patrick Friesen

[Untitled]; review of *Flicker and Hawk*. Paul Denham. *Books in Can* June-July 1987; Vol 16 No 5: p24.

Poets exhibit vast differences; reviews of *Flicker and Hawk* and *Skrag*. Robert Quickenden. *WFP* May 16, 1987: p70.

Poetry: packing all the power into two of seven titles; reviews of poetry books. Robin Skelton. photo · *Quill & Quire* May 1987; Vol 53 No 5: p24.

The impersonation of the irresistible; reviews of poetry books. Fraser Sutherland. *G&M* Sept 5, 1987: pC15.

A great book; review of *Flicker and Hawk*. Armin Wiebe. *Prairie Fire* Autumn 1987; Vol 8 No 3: p102–107.

FLIGHT AGAINST TIME/Novel by Emily Nasrallah

[Untitled]; reviews of *Flight Against Time* and *The Late Great Human Road Show*. Judith Carson. *Can Forum* Aug-Sept 1987; Vol 67 No 771: p48–49.
[FIRST NOVELS: BOOK REVIEWS]

Emily Nasrallah's first novel; review of *Flight Against Time*. Laura Groening. *Atlan Prov Book R* May-June 1987; Vol 14 No 2: p9.
[FIRST NOVELS: BOOK REVIEWS]

[Untitled]; review of *Flight Against Time*. Michele Melady. *Books in Can* May 1987; Vol 16 No 4: p21.

FLIGHT OF THE FALCON: SCOTT'S JOURNEY TO THE SOUTH POLE 1910–1912/Poems by J.A. Wainwright

Drama of failed pole trek unfulfilled; reviews of *Flight of the Falcon* and *Poems New and Selected*. Keith Garebian. *TS* Oct 31, 1987: M5.

[Untitled]; reviews of poetry books. Stephen Scobie. *Malahat R* Dec 1987; No 81: p104–106.

FLITTERIN' JUDAS/Novel by Victoria Branden

Ours as daughters; reviews of *Duet for Three* and *Flitterin' Judas*. Nancy Bailey. *Can Lit* Spring 1987; No 112: p143–145.

FLOOD, JOHN

Common language in private words; reviews of poetry books. Maggie Helwig. *TS* Aug 8, 1987: M10.

The pastoral myth and its observers; reviews of poetry books. Fraser Sutherland. *G&M* Sept 26, 1987: pC23.

FLORENCE/Play by Marcel Dub

Stage version of early Radio-Canada drama works well; theatre review of *Florence*. Marianne Ackerman. *MG* April 1, 1987: pD8.

Le théâtre qu'on joue; theatre reviews. André Dionne. photo · *Lettres québec* Summer 1987; No 46: p47–48.

FLOWERS OF DARKNESS/Novel by Matt Cohen

The wonders and pleasures of fictional empire-building; reviews of novels by Matt Cohen. Douglas Hill. photo · *G&M* Jan 3, 1987: pE15.

FOGEL, STANLEY

[Untitled]; reviews of critical works. Ronald B. Hatch. *Eng Studies in Can* March 1987; Vol 13 No 1: p107–115.

Erasures; review of *A Tale of Two Countries*. Mark S. Madoff. *Can Lit* Spring 1987; No 112: p185–186.

FOLKLORE

Woman preserved province's folklore; article about Helen Creighton. *CH* Dec 26, 1987: pD1.

FOLLES ALLIES THEATRE COLLECTIVE

Théâtre didactique; reviews of *Mademoiselle Autobody* and *Sortie de secours*. Lucie Robert. *Voix et images* Autumn 1987; Vol 13 No 1: p196–198.

THE FONTAINEBLEAU DREAM MACHINE/Poems by Roy Kiyooka

Roy Kiyooka's The Fontainebleau Dream Machine: a reading; article. Eva-Marie Kröler. *Can Lit* Summer-Fall 1987; No 113-114: p47-58.
[SURREALISM]

FOOL'S GOLD/Novel by Ted Wood

Criminal proceedings; review of *Fool's Gold*. T.J. Binyon. *Times Lit Supp* April 17, 1987; No 4385: p411.

FOON, DENNIS

Some advances, some retreats in theatre season selections; column. Ray Conlogue. photo · *G&M* Aug 28, 1987: pD8.

Contrived character flaws Zaydok; theatre review. Stephen Godfrey. photo · *G&M* Oct 28, 1987: pC5.

Entrances and exits; column. Mark Leiren-Young. photo · *Can Theatre R* Fall 1987; No 52: p91-94.
[AWARDS, LITERARY]

Plays probe evils of prejudice; article. Kevin Prokosh. photo · *WFP* Feb 3, 1987: p32.

Mini-reviews; reviews of children's stories. Mary Rubio. *Can Child Lit* 1987; No 46: p105-109.

Invisible Kids suffers from poor focus; theatre review. Reg Skene. *WFP* Feb 5, 1987: p37

Race relations documentary emotion-packed experience; theatre review of *Skin*. Reg Skene. *WFP* Feb 6, 1987: p29.

FOOT THROUGH THE CEILING/Poems by Chris Faiers

[Untitled]; review of *Foot Through the Ceiling*. LeRoy Gorman. *Poetry Can R* Summer 1987; Vol 8 No 4: p32-33.

Seasons, time and memory; reviews of poetry books. Lesley McAllister. *TS* March 21, 1987: M5.

[Untitled]; reviews of poetry books. Martin Singleton. *Cross Can Writ Q* 1987; Vol 9 No 3-4: p38-39.

UNE FORÊT POUR ZOÉ/A FOREST FOR ZOE/Novel by Louise Maheux-Forcier

Castles of childhood; review of *A Forest for Zoe*. Margaret Belcher. *Can Lit* Winter 1987; No 115: p208-209.

A rich, feminist novel from Quebec; reviews of *A Forest for Zoe* and *After the Fact*. Geoff Hancock. *TS* Feb 15, 1987: pA19.

Shadows of a dream; review of *A Forest for Zoe*. Brent Ledger. *Books in Can* June-July 1987; Vol 16 No 5: p17-18.

[Untitled]; reviews of *Under the House* and *A Forest for Zoe*. Lesley McAllister. *Cross Can Writ Q* 1987; Vol 9 No 3-4: p48-49.
[FIRST NOVELS: BOOK REVIEWS]

A friendship; review of *A Forest for Zoe*. Sherie Posesorski. *G&M* Jan 10, 1987: pE17.

FORCÉMENT DANS LA TÊTE/Poems by Hugues Corriveau

Forcément de l'amour; reviews of *Forcément dans la tête* and *De ce nom de l'amour*. Deloris Williams. *Can Lit* Summer-Fall 1987; No 113-114: p233-235.

A FOREST FOR ZOE

See UNE FORÊT POUR ZOÉ/A FOREST FOR ZOE/Novel by Louise Maheux-Forcier

FOREST, JEAN

Comme un vent; reviews of poetry books. James P. Gilroy. *Can Lit* Winter 1987; No 115: p260-261.

Les enfants du déclin; reviews of novels. Jacques Michon. *Voix et images* Winter 1987; No 35: p331-334.

FOREVER YOUNG/Play by Theatre Brats collective

Kids speak on their own behalf; theatre review of *Forever Young*. Ray Conlogue. photo · *G&M* Jan 3, 1987: pE8.

FORGETTING HOW TO FLY/Poems by Mark Lowey

Thistledown presents prairie poets in full bloom; reviews of poetry books. Christopher Wiseman. *CH* May 24, 1987: pE6.

FORRESTER, HELEN

People; column. *Maclean's* April 13, 1987; Vol 100 No 15: p24.

Tune in, turn on, drop out: truckin' back to the '60s with Esquire; reviews of *Lime Street at Two* and *The Next Best Thing*. Barbara Black. *MG* July 4, 1987: J9.

Romantic novel set in India is typical of Canadian writer's British penchant; review of *The Moneylenders of Shahpur*. Peggy Curran. *MG* Aug 8, 1987: J3.

English poverty parlayed into perfect prose; biographical article. Candas Jane Dorsey. photo · *Quill & Quire* May 1987; Vol 53 No 5: p23.

FORTIN, CLYNE

[Untitled]; review of *Au coeur de l'instant*. Hélène Thibaux. *Estuaire* Winter 1986-87; No 43: p76.

FORTUNATE EXILE/Poems by Irving Layton

With these older poets, the strengths are intrinsic; reviews of poetry books. Judith Fitzgerald. photo · *TS* Dec 20, 1987: pE6.

Poetic successes; reviews of *The Difficulty of Living on Other Planets* and *Fortunate Exile*. Joel Yanofsky. illus · *MG* Dec 19, 1987: J11.

FOSS, MICHAEL

[Untitled]; review of *Looking for the Last Big Tree*. Douglas Hill. *Books in Can* Jan-Feb 1987; Vol 16 No 1: p25-26.

An obsession for B.C.'s trees; review of *Looking for the Last Big Tree*. M.T. Kelly. photo · *G&M* Feb 7, 1987: pE19.
[FIRST NOVELS: BOOK REVIEWS]

FOSTER, NORM

Promising comedy weighed down by serious issues; theatre review of *The Melville Boys*. Brian Brennan. *CH* April 11, 1987: pF2.

Comedy with a clever twist; theatre review of *The Melville Boys*. Ray Conlogue. photo · *G&M* Feb 27, 1987: pD11.

Heart-warming tale limited but likeable; theatre review of *The Melville Boys*. Robert Crew. *TS* Feb 27, 1987: pD21.

[Untitled]; review of *My Darling Judith*. Kathryn Harley. *Maclean's* Oct 19, 1987; Vol 100 No 42: p70.

Sinners' cast in over its head; theatre review. Alex Law. *TS (Neighbours)* June 16, 1987: p22.

Dinner theatre play leaves bland aftertaste; theatre review of *The Melville Boys*. Randal McIlroy. *WFP* Nov 4, 1987: p43.

[Untitled]; review of *The Melville Boys*. Linda M. Peake. *Books in Can* March 1987; Vol 16 No 2: p25.

[Untitled]; reviews of plays. Judith Rudakoff. *Can Theatre R* Summer 1987; No 51: p86–87.

Playwright finds unlikable cast proving popular; article. Kate Zimmerman. *CH* Sept 4, 1987: pE1.

Dinner farce lacking consistency; theatre review of *Sinners*. Kate Zimmerman. *CH* Sept 6, 1987: pE6.

FOSTER, TONY

Trio named to receive awards from Canadian authors' group; article. photo · *WFP* May 14, 1987: p46.
[AWARDS, LITERARY]

[Untitled]; review of *Rue du Bac*. B.K. Adams. *Books in Can* Oct 1987; Vol 16 No 7: p24.

Three new twists on old and favorite spy themes; review of *Rue du Bac*. Margaret Cannon. *G&M* Sept 12, 1987: pC19.

Foster's life even richer than the stories he writes; article. H.J. Kirchhoff. photo · *G&M* Nov 19, 1987: pA31.

Bizarre tale dark, quirky and Rendell; review of *Rue du Bac*. Kenneth McGoogan. *CH* Oct 4, 1987: pE6.

This international thriller is like a long, winding and ultimately pointless safari; review of *Rue du Bac*. James Mennie. *MG* Oct 3, 1987: J13.

FOTHERGILL, ROBERT

[Untitled]; review of *Detaining Mr. Trotsky*. John Bemrose. *Maclean's* Nov 9, 1987; Vol 100 No 45: p70.

Making saint of Trotsky pays off for play; theatre review of *Detaining Mr. Trotsky*. Ray Conlogue. photo · *G&M* Oct 23, 1987: pD13.

Taut Trotsky play an intelligent debut; theatre review of *Detaining Mr. Trotsky*. Robert Crew. *TS* Oct 22, 1987: pB1.

Trotsky 'tough act to follow' for playwright; article. Liam Lacey. photo · *G&M* Nov 12, 1987: pA31.

Jacob Two-Two star hits 'big time' at age 7; column. Vit Wagner. *TS* Oct 16, 1987: pD10.

FOUR SEASONS FOR TOBY/THEO ET LES QUATRES SAISONS/Children's story by Dorothy Joan Harris

[Untitled]; review of *Four Seasons for Toby*. Linda Granfield. *Quill & Quire (Books for Young People)* April 1987; Vol 53 No 4: p9.

FOURNIER, DANIELLE

Forcément de l'amour; reviews of *Forcément dans la tête* and *De ce nom de l'amour*. Deloris Williams. *Can Lit* Summer-Fall 1987; No 113–114: p233–235.

FOURNIER, MARCEL

[Untitled]; reviews of critical works. B.-Z. Shek. *U of Toronto Q* Fall 1987; Vol 57 No 1: p192–199.

FOURNIER, PIERRE-ANDRÉ

Pourquoi a-t-on peur de Maude?; theatre review of *"JAMMÉE, les nerfs! les nerfs!"*. Patricia Badoux. photo · *MD* May 7, 1987: p13.

Le Conseil de la santé récupère une pièce boudée par l'hôpital Louis-H. Lafontaine; article. Renée Rowan. photo · *MD* April 30, 1987: p13.

THE FOURPOSTER/Play by Jan de Hartog

Comedy enjoyable despite bad acoustics, set changes; theatre review of *The Fourposter*. Alex Law. *TS (Neighbours)* March 10, 1987: p14.

LES FOUS DE BASSAN/Novel by Anne Hébert

Filmmaker launches $260,000 lawsuit; article. *G&M* March 20, 1987: pD5.
[FILM ADAPTATIONS OF CANADIAN LITERATURE]

Film-maker sues Cin Video; article. *MG* March 20, 1987: pC4.
[FILM ADAPTATIONS OF CANADIAN LITERATURE]

Les Fous de Bassan à Berlin; article. *MD* Feb 5, 1987: p6.
[FILM ADAPTATIONS OF CANADIAN LITERATURE]

Return of the native son; film review of *In the Shadow of the Wind*. Mark Abley. photo · *Maclean's* Jan 26, 1987; Vol 100 No 4: p54.
[FILM ADAPTATIONS OF CANADIAN LITERATURE]

A piece of the rock; film review of *In the Shadow of the Wind*. Bruce Bailey. photo · *MG* Jan 10, 1987: pG3.
[FILM ADAPTATIONS OF CANADIAN LITERATURE]

Les Fous de Bassan se cassent le bec sur un vrai mur; article. Robert Lévesque. *MD* Feb 25, 1987: p1,12.
[FILM ADAPTATIONS OF CANADIAN LITERATURE]

Repression, obsession and re-emergence in Hébert's Les Fous de Bassan; article. Kathryn Slott. *Amer R of Can Studies* Autumn 1987; Vol 17 No 3: p297–307.
[FEMINIST WRITING AND CRITICISM]

FOWLER, MARIAN

She's living exactly the way she wants; article. Alison Gordon. photo · *TS* May 24, 1987: pD1–D2.

Book world: from unhappy housewife to busy biographer; column. Beverley Slopen. photo · *TS* May 24, 1987: pA18.

FOX, GAIL

[Untitled]; review of *The Deepening of the Colours*. Mary di Michele. *Books in Can* May 1987; Vol 16 No 4: p23.

[Untitled]; reviews of *Stoning the Moon* and *The Deepening of the Colours*. Susan Huntley Elderkin. *Quarry* Summer 1987; Vol 36 No 3: p76–79.

Painful scrutiny of relationships; reviews of poetry books. Patricia Keeney Smith. *TS* May 30, 1987: M9.

FOXMAN, STUART

Relations & families; review of *Time of Their Lives*. George Woodcock. *Can Lit* Summer-Fall 1987; No 113–114: p235–239.

FRÉCHETTE, JOSÉ

Un coup d'essai qui est aussi un coup de maître!; review of *Le Père de Lisa*. Jean-Roch Boivin. *MD* Nov 28, 1987: pD11.

La vitrine du livre; reviews. Guy Ferland. *MD* Nov 14, 1987: pD16.
[ANTHOLOGIES: BOOK REVIEWS]

FRADETTE, BENOÎT

Un homme dont les semelles étaient de vent; review of *L'Écrit-vent*. Jean Éthier-Blais. *MD* May 16, 1987: pD8.

Les Héritiers (prix Robert Cliche) et L'Écrit-vent; reviews. Noël Audet. photo · *Lettres québec* Autumn 1987; No 47: p19–21.
[FIRST NOVELS: BOOK REVIEWS]

FRAGMENTS D'UNE LETTRE D'ADIEU LUS PAR DES GOLOGUES/Play by Normand Chaurette

Deux pièces en forme d'interrogatoire; reviews of *Being at Home with Claude* and *Fragments d'une lettre d'adieu lus par des géologues*. André-G. Bourassa. photo · *Lettres québec* Spring 1987; No 45: p50–51.

Des dramaturges ayant en commun l'usage du français; theatre review of *Fragments d'une lettre d'adieu lus par des géologues*. Robert Lévesque. *MD* Sept 9, 1987: p13.

Les jeunes loups; reviews. Lucie Robert. *Voix et images* Spring 1987; Vol 12 No 3: p561–564.
[CANADIAN LITERARY PERIODICALS]

FRANÇOIS DUVALET/Novel by Maurice de Goumois

La forêt dans le roman "ontarois"; article. Yolande Grisé. abstract · *Études can* 1987; No 23: p109–122.
[MYTHS AND LEGENDS IN CANADIAN LITERATURE; NATURE IN CANADIAN LITERATURE]

FRANCE-CANADA LITERARY RELATIONS

Le personnage français dans quelques romans québécois contemporains; article. Neil B. Bishop. *Voix et images* Autumn 1987; Vol 13 No 1: p82–103.

La poésie québécoise dénaturée dans la capitale française; essay. Jean-François Doré. *MD* Dec 5, 1987: pC2.
[AUDIO-VISUALS AND CANADIAN LITERATURE]

Promenade au Salon du livre; article. Guy Ferland. *MD* Nov 24, 1987: p13.
[CHILDREN'S LITERATURE]

Canadian writers make headlines in France; column. William French. photo · *G&M* Dec 22, 1987: pD5.

Les Feluettes seront en France en 1988; article. Robert Lévesque. photo · *MD* Nov 5, 1987: p13.

Le Seuil diffusera des auteurs du Boréal; article. Marie Laurier. photo · *MD* Oct 1, 1987: p13.
[CANADIAN LITERARY PUBLISHING]

Antoine Gallimard, petit-fils de Gaston et fils de Claude; article. Marie Laurier. photo · *MD* Dec 14, 1987: p9.

L'autonomisation de la "littérature nationale" au XIXe siècle; article. Maurice Lemire. abstract · *Études lit* Spring-Summer 1987; Vol 20 No 1: p75–98.
[CANADIAN LITERATURE (19TH CENTURY): HISTORY AND CRITICISM; COLONIALISM; CULTURAL IDENTITY; RELIGIOUS THEMES]

Deux échos québécois de grands romans épistolaires du dix-huitième siècle français; article. Monique Moser-Verrey. *Voix et images* Spring 1987; Vol 12 No 3: p512–514,516–522.

La vie littéraire; column. Jean Royer. photo · *MD* Oct 10, 1987: pD2.
[CANADIAN LITERARY PUBLISHING; FESTIVALS, LITERARY]

Entre France et Québec: des lieux, des liens, une voix; article. Monique La Rue. *Voix et images* Autumn 1987; Vol 13 No 1: p42–45.

Littérature québécoise d'hier et d'aujourd'hui on en parle je vous donne des addresses; editorial. Adrien Thério. *Lettres québec* Summer 1987; No 46: p10–12.
[CANADIAN LITERARY PERIODICALS]

400,000$; editorial. Adrien Thério. *Lettres québec* Winter 1986–87; No 44: p10–11.
[AWARDS, LITERARY]

FRANCOEUR, LUCIEN

Quatre musiciens à la rescousse de Francoeur; article. Jean-François Doré. photo · *MD* June 11, 1987: p17.

FRANKLYN/Play by James Durham

Festival One plays singularly successful; theatre reviews. Stephen Godfrey. photo · *G&M* May 8, 1987: pF9.
[FESTIVALS, DRAMA]

Picture of rebellious victim of cerebral palsy gripping, raises audience awareness; theatre review of *Franklyn*. Reg Skene. *WFP* May 4, 1987: p29.

FRASER, BRAD

Young writer explores time-honored themes; theatre review of *Young Art*. John Fitzgerald. photo · *G&M* Jan 17, 1987: pE13.

Tale hampered by small stage; theatre review of *Young Art*. Henry Mietkiewicz. photo · *TS* Jan 18, 1987: pG3

FRASER, KEATH

Latecomer to fiction-writing a talent to watch; column. Ken Adachi. photo · *TS* Oct 19, 1987: pC5.
[AWARDS, LITERARY; FESTIVALS, LITERARY]

FRASER, SYLVIA

An autobiography like few you've read; review of *My Father's House*. Ken Adachi. photo · *TS* Sept 27, 1987: pA23.

Daddy's little girl; review of *My Father's House*. John Bemrose. *Maclean's* Oct 26, 1987; Vol 100 No 43: p52h

Misery of incest drove novelist to divide her personality; column. June Callwood. *G&M* Sept 30, 1987: pA2.

Incest victim recounts anguish, horror in novel; article. Rod Currie. photo · *WFP* Nov 9, 1987: p19.

Repressing abuse: the crime against Sylvia; review of *My Father's House*. Janet Hamilton. photo · *Quill & Quire* Aug 1987; Vol 53 No 8: p33.

Daddy's girl; article. Barbara MacKay. photo · *Books in Can* Oct 1987; Vol 16 No 7: p3.

Sylvia Fraser frees the Minotaur at the heart of her own labyrinth; review of *My Father's House*. Marion McCormick. photo · *MG* Oct 3, 1987: J11.

Fraser stirs deep fears to provide understanding; review of *My Father's House*. Susan Scott. *CH* Oct 25, 1987: pE5.

Book world: incest victim created a 'twin' to survive; column. Beverley Slopen. photo · *TS* June 21, 1987: pA22.

Incest 'split' writer; article. Brenda Southam. photo · *CH* Oct 31, 1987: pB7.

An acute eye trained on a nasty subject; review of *My Father's House*. Nancy Wigston. photo · *G&M* Sept 12, 1987: pC17.

FRATICELLI, RINA

Rina Fraticelli named producer at film board; article. *TS* March 10, 1987: pC4.

Some method to madness in hiring of Fraticelli as new NFB women's studio head; article. Bruce Bailey. photo · *MG* May 11, 1987: pB5.

Studio D faces big job small budget; article. Lois Sweet. photo · *TS* May 4, 1987: pC1,C3.

FRECHETTE, JEAN-MARC

Chronique: soliloques; reviews of poetry books. Marguerite Andersen. *Poetry Can R* Spring 1987; Vol 8 No 2–3: p23–24.

La fiction du réel / le réel de la fiction; reviews of poetry books. André Brochu. *Voix et images* Winter 1987; No 35: p322–330.

Songe, révolte et manifeste; reviews of poetry books. Robert Yergeau. photo · *Lettres québec* Spring 1987; No 45: p38–39.

FRECHETTE, LOUISE

Une écriture qui se cherche encore; review of *L'Écran brisé*. Madeleine Ouellette-Michalska. *MD* July 25, 1987: pC6.

FREEMAN, BILL

School's out, and books are in; reviews of children's books. Janice Kennedy. *MG* July 4, 1987: J9.

Freeman and Crook offer adventure and mystery in serial form; reviews of *Danger on the Tracks* and *Payment in Death*. Joan McGrath. photo · *Quill & Quire (Books for Young People)* April 1987; Vol 53 No 4: p9.

A little help on the dull days; reviews of children's books. Joan McGrath. *TS* Aug 2, 1987: pC11.

Living in the past; reviews of children's novels. Mary Ainslie Smith. *Books in Can* June-July 1987; Vol 16 No 5: p35–37.

FREEMAN, NANCY

From city to country; review of *Sandy*. David W. Atkinson. *Can Child Lit* 1987; No 46: p89–90.

THE FRENCH NOVEL OF QUEBEC/Critical work by Maurice Gagnon

[Untitled]; review of *The French Novel of Quebec*. Fritz Peter Kirsch. *Zeitschrift Kanada-Studien* 1987; Vol 7 No 1: p265–266.

FRENCH, DAVID

Small, nostalgic play is an unexpected delight; theatre review of *Salt-Water Moon*. Brian Brennan. photo · *CH* Jan 18, 1987: pE1.

Piggery production circumvents Salt Water Moon pitfalls; theatre review. Pat Donnelly. *MG* Aug 15, 1987: pE15.

Noises Off and Jitters: two comedies of backstage life; article. Albert-Reiner Glaap. *Can Drama* 1987; Vol 13 No 2: p210–215.

David French and the theatre of speech; article. Anne Nothof. *Can Drama* 1987; Vol 13 No 2: p216–223.

Actor captures depths of play's leading character; theatre review of *Salt-Water Moon*. Reg Skene. *WFP* Jan 8, 1987: p33.

FRENCH, WILLIAM

Editor French wins president's award; article. *MG* July 2, 1987: pE4.
[AWARDS, LITERARY]

FRENCH-CANADIAN LITERATURE

See QUEBEC DRAMA (FRENCH LANGUAGE): HISTORY AND CRITICISM; QUEBEC LITERATURE (FRENCH LANGUAGE): HISTORY AND CRITICISM

FRENCH-CANADIAN THEATER/Critical work by Jonathan M. Weiss

[Untitled]; reviews of *Theatre and Politics in Modern Quebec* and *French-Canadian Theater*. L.E. Doucette. *U of Toronto Q* Fall 1987; Vol 57 No 1: p186–189.

FRENETTE, CHRISTIANE

La fiction du réel / le réel de la fiction; reviews of poetry books. André Brochu. *Voix et images* Winter 1987; No 35: p322–330.

[Untitled]; review of *Indigo nuit*. Guy Marchamps. *Estuaire* Winter 1986–87; No 43: p76–77.

LA FREQUE DE MUSSOLINI/Play by Filippo Salvatore

Transculture; reviews of poetry books. Viviana Comensoli. *Can Lit* Spring 1987; No 112: p120–123.

FRICK, ALICE

A megalomania for radio drama; reviews of *All the Bright Company* and *Image in the Mind*. Bronwyn Drainie. photo · *G&M* Nov 28, 1987: pC19.
[ANTHOLOGIES: BOOK REVIEWS]

Book world: 'My year for films': Brian Moore; column. Beverley Slopen. photo · *TS* Nov 8, 1987: pA18.
[CHILDREN'S LITERATURE; FILM ADAPTATIONS OF CANADIAN LITERATURE; PUBLISHING AND PUBLISHERS IN CANADA]

LES FRIDOLINADES/Play by Gratien Gélinas

De la fronde au bazooka; editorial. Rolande Allard-Lacerte. *MD* Jan 19, 1987: p14.

Des Boches à Fridolin; letter to the editor. H.-Paul Delimal. *MD* Jan 17, 1987: pB2.

Ageless Fridolin skits leave crowd euphoric; theatre review of *Les Fridolinades*. Pat Donnelly. photo · *MG* Nov 27, 1987: pC1.

[Untitled]; theatre reviews. Pat Donnelly. *MG* Nov 27, 1987: pC7.

[Untitled]; theatre reviews. Pat Donnelly. *MG* Dec 4, 1987: pC6.

Fridolin's as funny as ever; theatre review of *Les Fridolinades*. Matthew Fraser. photo · *G&M* Jan 27, 1987: pC5.

Gratien Gélinas: le retour de Fridolin; article. Robert Lévesque. illus photo · *MD* Jan 10, 1987: pB1,B4.

Des Fridolinades sorties de leur temps; theatre review of *Les Fridolinades*. Robert Lévesque. photo · *MD* Jan 14, 1987: p6.

Québec: Alexandre Hausvater quitte la Quinzaine théâtrale; column. Robert Lévesque. *MD* April 14, 1987: p12.

Qui sera le directeur artistique du TPQ?; column. Robert Lévesque. *MD* Nov 17, 1987: p11.

FRIESEN, PATRICK

[Untitled]; review of *Flicker and Hawk*. Paul Denham. *Books in Can* June-July 1987; Vol 16 No 5: p24.

Intriguing idea poses performance problems; review of *Anna*. Randal McIlroy. *WFP* June 28, 1987: p24.
[POETRY PERFORMANCE]

Poets exhibit vast differences; reviews of *Flicker and Hawk* and *Skrag*. Robert Quickenden. *WFP* May 16, 1987: p70.

Winnipeg poet envisages role as quiet healer; article. Barbara Robson. photo · *WFP* April 3, 1987: p30.

Poetry: packing all the power into two of seven titles; reviews of poetry books. Robin Skelton. photo · *Quill & Quire* May 1987; Vol 53 No 5: p24.

The impersonation of the irresistible; reviews of poetry books. Fraser Sutherland. *G&M* Sept 5, 1987: pC15.

A great book; review of *Flicker and Hawk*. Armin Wiebe. *Prairie Fire* Autumn 1987; Vol 8 No 3: p102–107.

FROGS & OTHER STORIES/Short stories by Diane Schoemperlen

[Untitled]; reviews. Beverley Daurio. *Cross Can Writ Q* 1987; Vol 9 No 2: p23.
[FIRST NOVELS: BOOK REVIEWS]

[Untitled]; review of *Frogs*. Beth Duthie. *CH* Jan 25, 1987: pE4.

Everything by thought waves; reviews of short story collections. Patricia Matson. *Event* March 1987; Vol 16 No 1: p97–100.

All about women and relationships; reviews of *Housebroken* and *Frogs*. Lesley McAllister. *TS* Jan 3, 1987: M6.
[FIRST NOVELS: BOOK REVIEWS]

A frog he would a-wooing go; review of *Frogs*. Marjorie Retzleff. *Matrix* Fall 1987; No 25: p75–76.

New Albertan fiction; reviews of *Green Eyes, Dukes and Kings* and *Frogs*. M.L. Scott. *NeWest R* Summer 1987; Vol 12 No 10: p12.

The lively art; reviews of *Double Exposures* and *Frogs*. Kent Thompson. *Fiddlehead* Winter 1987; No 154: p87–91.

FROM THE DARK WOOD (POEMS 1977–83)/Poems by Victor Coleman

[Untitled]; reviews of *My Round Table* and *Everything Happens at Once*. Rosemary Aubert. *Poetry Can R* Spring 1987; Vol 8 No 2–3: p48.

[Untitled]; review of *From the Dark Wood*. Beverley Daurio. *Poetry Can R* Spring 1987; Vol 8 No 2–3: p47.

FRUTKIN, MARK

Recent poetry; reviews of poetry books. Terrence Craig. *Atlan Prov Book R* Feb-March 1987; Vol 14 No 1: p18.

Four poets; reviews of poetry books. Randall Maggs. *Can Lit* Winter 1987; No 115: p280–284.

FRYE, NORTHROP

Frye, Wieland are among arts awards winners; article. photo · *G&M* Sept 23, 1987: pC7.
[AWARDS, LITERARY]

TO Arts Awards; article. *Quill & Quire* Dec 1987; Vol 53 No 12: p14.
[AWARDS, LITERARY]

Arts awards lack flash and glamour; column. Sid Adilman. *TS* Oct 17, 1987: H2.
[AWARDS, LITERARY]

Landscape with politicians; review of *Northrop Frye: A Vision of the New World*. William T. Booth. *Essays on Can Writ* Winter 1987; No 35: p117–122.

People; column. Yvonne Cox. photo · *Maclean's* Oct 26, 1987; Vol 100 No 43: p34.

A unique way of seeing the world; column. Robert Fulford. *TS* Sept 26, 1987: M5.

Stars of the city, year two; photographic portfolio. Edward Gajdel. *Tor Life* Oct 1987; Vol 21 No 1[5]: 89–95.

Fingers was a real wizard at keyboards, not smalltalk; biographical article. George Gamester. *TS* Nov 12, 1987: pA2.

The Prospero figure: Northrop Frye's magic criticism; article. Maggie Helwig. *Can Forum* Oct 1987; Vol 67 No 772: p28–32.

[Untitled]; review of *Northrop Frye: A Vision of the New World*. Michael Hurley. *Queen's Q* Spring 1987; Vol 94 No 1: p219–222.

St. Agnes' Eve; or, criticism becomes part of literature; fictional essay. Martin Kevan. *Essays on Can Writ* Winter 1987; No 35: p37–56.
[CANADIAN LITERATURE: STUDY AND TEACHING]

[Untitled]; review of *Northrop Frye: A Vision of the New World*. Mark Kingwell. *Rubicon* Spring 1987; No 8: p193–195.

From the Frye pen into the foyer; article. Martin Knelman. photo · *Tor Life* Aug 1987; Vol 21 No 11: p10.
[AWARDS, LITERARY]

[Untitled]; review of *Northrop Frye: A Vision of the New World*. Lauriat Lane, Jr. *Eng Studies in Can* Sept 1987; Vol 13 No 3: p349–352.

Toronto honors the best with annual arts awards; article. Greg Quill. photo · *TS* Sept 23, 1987: pF1.
[AWARDS, LITERARY]

FÜHRER, CHARLOTTE

The other Montrealers; review of *The Mysteries of Montreal*. Michèle Lacombe. *Essays on Can Writ* Spring 1987; No 34: p180–184.

LA FUITE IMMOBILE/STANDING FLIGHT/Novel by Gilles Archambault

Introspection; review of *Standing Flight*. Pauline Carey. *G&M* Jan 31, 1987: pE18.

[Untitled]; reviews of *Standing Flight* and *The Legacy*. Cary Fagan. *Cross Can Writ Q* 1987; Vol 9 No 2: p24–25.

Two Quebec novels in translation; reviews of *Standing Flight* and *The Legacy*. Theresia Quigley. *Fiddlehead* Summer 1987; No 152: p95–98.

Recent Canadian fiction; reviews of novels. D.O. Spettigue. *Queen's Q* Summer 1987; Vol 94 No 2: p366–375.
[FIRST NOVELS: BOOK REVIEWS]

FULFORD, ROBERT

Robert Fulford quits Saturday Night post; article. *CH* June 25, 1987: pD1.
[CANADIAN LITERARY PERIODICALS]

Milestones; column. *TS* June 28, 1987: pB6.

Saturday Night's editor Fulford quits; article. *MG* June 25, 1987: pE1.
[CANADIAN LITERARY PERIODICALS]

Robert Fulford accepts post at university; article. *TS* Aug 20, 1987: pA7.

Collins buys Fulford memoirs; article. *TS* Sept 13, 1987: pA22.

Star explains his Nerd method; column. *WFP* July 16, 1987: p21.

Fulford appointed; article. *WFP* Aug 21, 1987: p20.

Fulford at U of T; article. *CH* Aug 21, 1987: pC12.

He never leaves home, with or without it; article. photo · *G&M (Toronto Magazine)* Aug 1987; Vol 2 No 5: p8.

Memoirs bring $80,000; article. photo · *G&M* Sept 12, 1987: pC10.

Passages; column. *Maclean's* Aug 31, 1987; Vol 100 No 35: p4.

Collins gets Fulford memoirs; article. *Quill & Quire* Oct 1987; Vol 53 No 10: p11–12.

Saturday Night loses a guy who loves his craft; column. Ken Adachi. *TS* June 25, 1987: pF1.

Saturday Night film dispiriting; column. Ken Adachi. photo · *TS* Sept 7, 1987: pB2.
[AUDIO-VISUALS AND CANADIAN LITERATURE; CANADIAN LITERARY PERIODICALS]

Radio's Scales of Justice seen as possible CTV series; column. Sid Adilman. *TS* Dec 30, 1987: pB1.
[CANADIAN LITERARY PERIODICALS]

Saturday Night editor has few regrets as new career opens; column. Stevie Cameron. *G&M* Aug 20, 1987: pA2.

The end of Fulford's era; article. Doug Fetherling. *Maclean's* July 6, 1987; Vol 100 No 27: p53.
[CANADIAN LITERARY PERIODICALS]

Dropout plans to drop in; letter to the editor. Peter D. James. photo · *G&M* Aug 29, 1987: pD7

Robert Fulford resigns as editor of Saturday Night; article. Liam Lacey. photo · *G&M* June 25, 1987: pD1.
[CANADIAN LITERARY PERIODICALS]

Contemplating dens; article. Donna Jean MacKinnon. photo · *TS* Oct 18, 1987: pC1,C6.

Fulford leaves his Saturday Night post; article. Henry Mietkiewicz. photo · *TS* June 25, 1987: pA2.
[CANADIAN LITERARY PERIODICALS]

Writers praise Robert Fulford; article. Henry Mietkiewicz. photo · *TS* June 26, 1987: pE25.
[AUTHORS, CANADIAN]

Mr. Saturday Night; biographical article. Leslie Scrivener. photo · *TS* July 5, 1987: pD1–D2.
[CANADIAN LITERARY PERIODICALS]

Magazine's literary mentor leaves with mixed emotions; article. Leslie Scrivener. photo · *CH* July 12, 1987: pE6.
[CANADIAN LITERARY PERIODICALS]

Saturday Night does its job well; letter to the editor. David Zapparoli. *TS* July 20, 1987: pA16.
[CANADIAN LITERARY PERIODICALS]

FULFORD, ROBIN

Class's reaction a bitter lesson for playwright; article. *CH* Oct 20, 1987: pC9.

Gay murder explored, unexplained; theatre review of *Steel Kiss*. Liam Lacey. *G&M* Oct 5, 1987: pD11.

The laugh's on apartheid in one-man show; column. Vit Wagner. photo · *TS* Sept 25, 1987: pE6.

Intensity exhausting in ugly Steel Kiss; theatre review. Vit Wagner. *TS* Oct 2, 1987: pE12.

Death in High Park inspiration for play; article. Deborah Wilson. photo · *G&M* Oct 17, 1987: pA13.

FULTON, KEITH LOUISE

Name power: local poet wrestles with words, increase in feminist knowledge; article. Barbara Robson. photo · *WFP* Oct 13, 1987: p33.

THE FUSION FACTOR/Children's novel by Carol Matas

[Untitled]; reviews of *The Fusion Factor* and *Zanu*. Leslie McGrath. *Quill & Quire (Books for Young People)* June 1987; Vol 53 No 6: p9–10.

[Untitled]; reviews of *The Fusion Factor* and *Zanu*. Mavis Reimer. *Border Cross* Spring 1987; Vol 6 No 2: p25.

How suspense dies when it is misused; reviews of young adult novels. Tim Wynne-Jones. *G&M* Aug 8, 1987: pC19.

FYFFE, LAURIE

Domestic drama that hits home; article, includes theatre reviews. John Bemrose. photo · *Maclean's* Aug 17, 1987; Vol 100 No 33: p49.
[FESTIVALS, DRAMA]

Blyth musical succeeds where drama fails; theatre reviews of *Girls in the Gang* and *Bush Fire*. Jason Sherman. photo · *TS* Aug 7, 1987: pE10.

LES GÉANTS DE BLIZZARD/Children's novel by Denis Côté

Les clichés du futur; review of *Les Géants de Blizzard*. Chantal de Grandpré. *Can Child Lit* 1987; No 46: p68–70.

GÉRIN-LAJOIE, ANTOINE

Faire de la terre ou faire la guerre? L'intertexte napoléonien dans le roman de défrichement québécois; article. Robert Major. abstract · *Études can* 1987; No 23: p71–86.
[COLONIAL LITERATURE]

GABORIAU, LINDA

Bear gives lesson in keeping identity; theatre review of *I Am a Bear!*. Randal McIlroy. *WFP* Oct 10, 1987: p48.

Actor drawn to play by novelty, challenge of playing a bear; article. Brad Oswald. *WFP* Oct 7, 1987: p39.

GABRIELLE ROY ET MARGARET LAURENCE: DEUX CHEMINS, UNE RECHERCHE/Critical work by Terrance Hughes

La vitrine du livre; review of *Gabrielle Roy et Margaret Laurence: deux chemins, une recherche*. Guy Ferland. *MD* Aug 8, 1987: pC6.

GABRIELLE ROY/Critical work by M.G. Hesse

Bonds of dignity; review of *Gabrielle Roy*. Paul Socken. *Can Lit* Winter 1987; No 115: p193–194.

GAETZ, DAYLE

Mini-reviews; reviews of children's books. Margaret Paré. *Can Child Lit* 1987; No 45: p93–96.

GAGNON, CÉCILE

Round table: responses, notes and queries; column. *Can Child Lit* 1987; No 45: p98–99.
[AWARDS, LITERARY; CONFERENCES, LITERARY]

Quand un ours polaire dérive vers le sud; reviews of children's stories by Cécile Gagnon. Solange Boudreau. *Can Child Lit* 1987; No 47: p62–63.

L'embarras du choix; review of *Un Chien, un vélo et des pizzas*. Dominique Demers. *MD* Nov 28, 1987: pD6.

GAGNON, DANIEL

Aujourd'hui; column. *MD* April 7, 1987: p10.
[FICTION READINGS]

Aujourd'hui; column. *MD* May 28, 1987: p12.
[WRITERS' ORGANIZATIONS]

"La belle inconnue qui déambule depuis des siècles . . ."; review of *La Fée calcinée*. Jean Éthier-Blais. *MD* Nov 28, 1987: pD14.

La vitrine du livre; reviews. Guy Ferland. *MD* Nov 7, 1987: pD4.

Écrire l'histoire ou histoire d'écrire; reviews of novels. Jacques Michon. *Voix et images* Spring 1987; Vol 12 No 3: p548–550.

[Untitled]; reviews of *Mon mari le docteur* and *Américane*. Jacques St-Pierre. *Moebius* Winter 1987; No 31: p139–140.

GAGNON, JEAN CHAPDELAINE

Jean Chapdelaine Gagnon: dans l'apprentissage des langues; review of *Dans l'attente d'une aube*. Gérald Gaudet. *MD* Oct 3, 1987: pD3.

[Untitled]; reviews of *Langues d'aimer* and *Le Tant-à-coeur*. Jacques Paquin. *Estuaire* Summer 1987; No 45: p49–50.

Désert, attente, silence; reviews of poetry books. Robert Yergeau. photo · *Lettres québec* Autumn 1987; No 47: p44–45.

GAGNON, MADELEINE

Les géographies et le souffle chez Madeleine Gagnon; reviews of *Les Fleurs du Catalpa* and *L'Infante immmoriale*. Caroline Bayard. photo · *Lettres québec* Winter 1986–87; No 44: p46–47.

[Untitled]; notice. Paul Cauchon. *MD* Dec 11, 1987: p13.
[TELEVISION AND CANADIAN LITERATURE]

[Untitled]; review of *L'Infante immémoriale*. Antonio D'Alfonso. *Estuaire* Summer 1987; No 45: p54–55.

Rêverie sur l'eau; review of *Au pays des gouttes*. Jurate Kaminskas. *Can Child Lit* 1987; No 47: p75–76.

Prix et distinctions; list of award winners. Gaétan Lévesque. photo · *Lettres québec* Autumn 1987; No 47: p7.
[AWARDS, LITERARY; GOVERNOR GENERAL'S AWARDS]

La vie littéraire; column. Jean Royer. photo · *MD* June 13, 1987: pD2.
[AWARDS, LITERARY; COMPETITIONS, LITERARY; POETRY READINGS; RADIO AND CANADIAN LITERATURE; TELEVISION AND CANADIAN LITERATURE; WRITERS' ORGANIZATIONS]

La vie littéraire; column. Jean Royer. *MD* Oct 3, 1987: pD2.
[AWARDS, LITERARY; CANADIAN LITERARY PUBLISHING; POETRY READINGS; WRITERS' WORKSHOPS]

Deux nouveaux académéciens; article. Jean Royer. *MD* Oct 19, 1987: p9.
[AWARDS, LITERARY]

Entre la maison, l'eau et le cosmos: l'écriture féminine; reviews of novels. Patricia Smart. *Voix et images* Winter 1987; No 35: p334–337.

GAGNON, MAURICE

[Untitled]; reviews of *Doubtful Motives* and *A Body Surrounded by Water*. Paul Cabray. *MG* Aug 15, 1987: L2.

Murder & mayhem: the English style of the whodunits; reviews of *A Body Surrounded by Water* and *Doubtful Motives*. Margaret Cannon. photo · *G&M* July 18, 1987: pC17.

[Untitled]; review of *The French Novel of Quebec*. Fritz Peter Kirsch. *Zeitschrift Kanada-Studien* 1987; Vol 7 No 1: p265–266.

[Untitled]; reviews of *Doubtful Motives* and *Fieldwork*. Carolellen Norskey. *Quill & Quire* Sept 1987; Vol 53 No 9: p79.
[FIRST NOVELS: BOOK REVIEWS]

Crime novels provide a study in contrasts; reviews of *Doubtful Motives* and *A Body Surrounded by Water*. David Williamson. photo · *WFP* Aug 1, 1987: p50.

GAGNON, SIEGFRIED

Help! Kirk! Star Trek image being tarnished!; theatre review of *Gilles Vachon: Incendiaire*. Pat Donnelly. *MG* Aug 13, 1987: pE16.

[Untitled]; theatre review of *Gilles Vachon: Incendiaire*. Pat Donnelly. *MG* Aug 14, 1987: pC8.

Quelque chose d'Aurore . . . ; theatre review of *Gilles Vachon: Incendiaire*. Robert Lévesque. *MD* Aug 19, 1987: p11.

Une histoire cousue de fils araignées; theatre review of *Gilles Vachon: Incendiaire*. Solange Lévesque. photo · *Jeu* 1987; No 45: p216–217.

GAGNON-THIBAUDEAU, MARTHE

Le syndrome du best-seller; review of *Sous la griffe du sida*. Alice Parizeau. photo · *MD* Dec 19, 1987: pD4.
[FIRST NOVELS: BOOK REVIEWS]

GAINING GROUND: EUROPEAN CRITICS ON CANADIAN LITERATURE/Critical essays

On strategies; review of *Gaining Ground*. Stanley S. Atherton. *Can Lit* Winter 1987; No 115: p184–186.

Views from afar; review of *Gaining Ground*. Sylvia Söderlind. *Essays on Can Writ* Winter 1987; No 35: p111–116.

[Untitled]; review of *Gaining Ground*. David Staines. *Eng Studies in Can* March 1987; Vol 13 No 1: p119–120.

A view from outside; review of *Gaining Ground*. Bruce Whiteman. *Prairie Fire* Winter 1987–88; Vol 8 No 4: p99–100.

GALAHAD SCHWARTZ AND THE COCKROACH ARMY/Children's novel by Morgan Nyberg

Fiction just loaded with personality; reviews of children's novels. Tim Wynne-Jones. photo · *G&M* Nov 28, 1987: pC22.
[FIRST NOVELS: BOOK REVIEWS]

GALLANT, MAVIS

The New Yorker lists at this season some books by its contributors published during the year; article. *New Yorker* Dec 21, 1987; Vol 63 No 44: p100–101.

The aporias of Lily Littel: Mavis Gallant's "Acceptance of Their Ways"; article. Helmut Bonheim. *Ariel* Oct 1987; Vol 18 No 4: p69–78.

Capital appreciation; review of *Overhead in a Balloon*. Lindsay Duguid. *Times Lit Supp* Sept 25, 1987; No 4408: p1052.

Canadian writers make headlines in France; column. William French. photo · *G&M* Dec 22, 1987: pD5.
[FRANCE-CANADA LITERARY RELATIONS]

Fairly good times: an interview with Mavis Gallant. Barbara Gabriel. *Can Forum* Feb 1987; Vol 66 No 766: p23–27.

[Untitled]; review of *Home Truths*. Thomas Healy. *British J of Can Studies* June 1987; Vol 2 No 1: p183–184.

Today's assignment: short fiction that's worth a long look; reviews of short story books. Douglas Hill. *G&M* March 14, 1987: pE19.
[ANTHOLOGIES: BOOK REVIEWS]

The last time I smelled Paris; article. Caryn James. photo · *NYT Book R* March 15, 1987: p7.

[Untitled]; review of *Paris Notebooks*. Janice Kulyk Keefer. *U of Toronto Q* Fall 1987; Vol 57 No 1: p168–170.

Dates and details in Mavis Gallant's "Its Image On The Mirror"; article. W.J. Keith. *Studies in Can Lit* 1987; Vol 12 No 1: p156–159.

[Untitled]; review of *Paris Notebooks*. Guido Monzano. *Idler* March-April 1987; No 12: p60–61.

[Untitled]; review of *Paris Notebooks*. Ken Mouré. *Rubicon* Fall 1987; No 9: p155–157.

New & noteworthy; review of *Home Truths*. Patricia T. O'Connor. photo · *NYT Book R* Feb 22, 1987: p34.

One step ahead of the zeitgeist; review of *Overhead in a Balloon*. Phyllis Rose. *NYT Book R* March 15, 1987: p7.

GALLOWS VIEW/Novel by Peter Robinson

A newcomer to Canadian crime fiction; review of *Gallows View*. Ken Adachi. *TS* April 19, 1987: pA19.
[FIRST NOVELS: BOOKS REVIEWS]

Murder & mayhem: plot and details in a cop's life; reviews of *Gallows View* and *Equinox*. Margaret Cannon. photo · *G&M* May 23, 1987: pC23.

[Untitled]; review of *Gallows View*. Martin Dowding. *Quill & Quire* March 1987; Vol 53 No 3: p71.
[FIRST NOVELS: BOOK REVIEWS]

Cheap thrills; reviews of *The Last Hunter* and *Gallows View*. Janice Kulyk Keefer. *Books in Can* June-July 1987; Vol 16 No 5: p37–38.
[FIRST NOVELS: BOOK REVIEWS]

Whodunits hit bookshelves in big way; review of *Gallows View*. Kenneth McGoogan. *CH* June 7, 1987: pE6.
[FIRST NOVELS: BOOK REVIEWS]

First novels set to different literary keys; reviews of *Crang Plays the Ace* and *Gallows View*. James Mennie. photo · *MG* April 11, 1987: pG6.
[FIRST NOVELS: BOOK REVIEWS]

Three absolute page-turners; reviews of *Crang Plays the Ace* and *Gallows View*. Janet Saunders. photo · *WFP* May 9, 1987: p56.
[FIRST NOVELS: BOOK REVIEWS]

Book world: Grolier moves into children's fiction; column. Beverley Slopen. *TS* March 22, 1987: pA20.
[CHILDREN'S LITERATURE; PUBLISHING AND PUBLISHERS IN CANADA]

THE GARDEN GOING ON WITHOUT US/Poems by Lorna Crozier

The poet's double gift; review of *The Garden Going On without Us*. Catherine Hunter. *Prairie Fire* Spring 1987; Vol 8 No 1: p78–82.

Understanding zero; review of *The Garden Going On without Us*. Frances W. Kaye. *Can Lit* Winter 1987; No 115: p138–139.

THE GARDEN OF ELOISE LOON/Short stories by Edna Alford

[Untitled]; review of *The Garden of Eloise Loon*. Audrey Andrews. *Dandelion* Spring-Summer 1987; Vol 14 No 1: p89–91.

Other voices; review article about *The Garden of Eloise Loon*. Jason Sherman. biog · *Books in Can* Jan-Feb 1987; Vol 16 No 1: p31–32.

GARIPY, MARC

Autour d'une "noyade orchestrale"; review of *La Mort aurorale*. Jean-Pierre Issenhuth. *Liberté* Dec 1987; Vol 29 No 6: p154–155.

Notes de lectures; reviews of *La Mort aurorale* and *Écoute, Sultane*. Jean Royer. *MD* May 23, 1987: pD2.

GARNEAU, HECTOR de SAINT-DENYS

The U.S.: foundation poets & personal views; comparative column. David Donnell. *Poetry Can R* Fall 1987; Vol 9 No 1: p25.

L'apprentissage de Saint-Denys Garneau; article. Philippe Haeck. *Voix et images* Autumn 1987; Vol 13 No 1: p115–122.

Figures, summaries, questions; article. Philippe Haeck. trans · *Ellipse* 1987; No 37: p6–15.

Roger Bellemare: de la musique sur des poèmes de Miron et Anne Hébert; article. Jean Royer. photo · *MD* May 20, 1987: p12.

Pour un portrait de Saint-Denys Garneau; review of *Le Choix de Jacques Blais dans l'oeuvre de Saint-Denys Garneau*. Jean Royer. *MD* May 23, 1987: pD2

GARNEAU, MICHEL

La "Coalition de 1%" rencontrera Bourassa; article. Angèle Dagenais. photo · *MD* Dec 4, 1987: p13.
[GOVERNMENT GRANTS FOR WRITERS/PUBLISHERS]

Le milieu artistique encouragé par les intentions libérales; article. Angèle Dagenais. photo · *MD* Dec 15, 1987: p11.
[GOVERNMENT GRANTS FOR WRITERS/PUBLISHERS]

Harnessing poetry; reviews of *Blind Painting* and *Small Horses & Intimate Beasts*. Philip Lanthier. *Can Lit* Winter 1987; No 115: p140–142.

[Untitled]; reviews of *Small Horses & Intimate Beasts* and *Blind Painting*. David Leahy. *Queen's Q* Spring 1987; Vol 94 No 1: p189–191.

Problems; review of *Small Horses and Intimate Beasts*. Sue Matheson. *Prairie Fire* Summer 1987; Vol 8 No 2: p68–69.

La vie littéraire; column. Jean Royer. photo · *MD* Oct 10, 1987: pD2.
[CANADIAN LITERARY PUBLISHING; FESTIVALS, LITERARY; FRANCE-CANADA LITERARY RELATIONS]

[Untitled]; reviews of *Blind Painting* and *Small Horses & Intimate Beasts*. Andrew Vaisius. *Poetry Can R* Spring 1987; Vol 8 No 2–3: p59.

GARNER, BETTY SANDERS

[Untitled]; reviews of poetry books. George Whipple. *Poetry Can R* Spring 1987; Vol 8 No 2–3: p53.

GARROCHS EN PARADIS/Play by Antonine Maillet

Le théâtre qu'on joue; theatre reviews. André Dionne. photo · *Lettres québec* Winter 1986–87; No 44: p53–54.

GATES, EDWARD

The poems of Edward Gates; introduction. Allan Cooper. *Germination* Spring 1987; Vol 10 No 2: p27–28.

GAUDET, GERALD

Du désir à l'écriture ou vice versa; review of *Lignes de nuit*. Régis Normandeau. *Lettres québec* Summer 1987; No 46: p70.

[Untitled]; reviews of poetry books. Jacques Saint-Pierre. *Moebius* Spring 1987; No 32: p128–130.

Questionner et rêver; review of *Voix d'écrivains: entretiens*. Paul G. Socken. *Can Lit* Spring 1987; No 112: p171–172.

[Untitled]; review of *Lignes de nuit*. Hélène Thibaux. *Estuaire* Spring 1987; No 44: p81–82.

GAUDREAULT-LABRECQUE, MADELEINE

Simplicité et dynamisme; review of *Alerte ce soir à 22 heures*. Kenneth W. Meadwell. *Can Child Lit* 1987; No 45: p70–71.

Dans la gueule du loup; review of *Gueule-de-loup*. Léonard Rosmarin. *Can Child Lit* 1987; No 45: p63–64.

GAULT, CONNIE

Billboard: museum offers kids workshops on robotics; column. *WFP* Dec 28, 1987: p28.
[FICTION READINGS]

[Untitled]; reviews of short story collections. Pauline Carey. *Cross Can Writ Q* 1987; Vol 9 No 3–4: p46–47.

[Untitled]; review of *Some of Eve's Daughters*. Cecelia Frey. *CH* June 7, 1987: pE6.

GAUTHIER, BERTRAND

Les malheurs de Rosalie ou l'éloge de l'enfance; reviews of children's books. Dominique Demers. *MD* May 2, 1987: pD3.

Les 10 ans de La Courte Échelle; article. Dominique Demers. photo · *MD* Sept 26, 1987: pD6.

Littérature jeunesse; reviews of children's books. Domique Demers. *MD* Oct 10, 1987: pD6.

Plus adulte que les adultes; review of *Ani Croche*. Marie Naudin. *Can Child Lit* 1987; No 45: p61–62.

GAUTHIER, GILLES

Bear gives lesson in keeping identity; theatre review of *I Am a Bear!*. Randal McIlroy. *WFP* Oct 10, 1987: p48.

Actor drawn to play by novelty, challenge of playing a bear; article. Brad Oswald. *WFP* Oct 7, 1987: p39.

GAUVIN, LISE

Deux échos québécois de grands romans épistolaires du dix-huitième siècle français; article. Monique Moser-Verrey. *Voix et images* Spring 1987; Vol 12 No 3: p512–514,516–522.
[FRANCE-CANADA LITERARY RELATIONS]

GAUVREAU, CLAUDE

The automatist movement of Montreal: towards non-figuration in painting, dance, and poetry; article. Ray Ellenwood. illus · *Can Lit* Summer-Fall 1987; No 113–114: p11–27.
[SURREALISM]

La modernité: des formes qui (s')inquiètent; reviews of critical works. Agnès Whitfield. photo · *Lettres québec* Summer 1987; No 46: p56–58.

GAY, JAMES

A bad poet rates title; letter to the editor. Margaret McBurney. Mary Byers. *G&M* July 29, 1987: pA7.

GAY, MARIE-LOUISE

Littérature jeunesse; reviews of children's books. Domique Demers. *MD* Oct 10, 1987: pD6

Title tattle; column. Martin Dowding. *Quill & Quire (Books for Young People)* Dec 1987; Vol 53 No 12: p3.
[FILM ADAPTATIONS OF CANADIAN LITERATURE; TELEVISION AND CANADIAN LITERATURE]

From giant snakes to punk pigeons: escapism at its best; reviews of children's stories. Bernie Goedhart. *Quill & Quire (Books for Young People)* June 1987; Vol 53 No 6: p5.

School's out, and books are in; reviews of children's books. Janice Kennedy. *MG* July 4, 1987: J9.

Inventive illustrator works magic with a rainy day; article. Sandra Martin. illus photo · *G&M* July 4, 1987: pC5.

Mini-reviews; reviews of children's stories. Mary Rubio. *Can Child Lit* 1987; No 46: p105–109.

Three noble stories; review of *Rainy Day Magic*. Tim Wynne-Jones. *G&M* May 30, 1987: pC21.

GAY, MICHEL

L'Union des écrivains québécois, c'est quoi?; interview with Michel Gay. photo · *Lettres québec* Spring 1987; No 45: p16–21.
[WRITERS' ORGANIZATIONS]

GAY, PAUL

[Untitled]; review of *La Vitalité littéraire de l'Ontario français*. L.E. Doucette. *U of Toronto Q* Fall 1987; Vol 57 No 1: p206–207.

GEDDES, GARY

L'Actualite picks up six magazine awards; article. Ken Adachi. *TS* May 22, 1987: pE21.
[AWARDS, LITERARY; CANADIAN LITERARY PERIODICALS]

Loss and renewal: Changes of State by Gary Geddes; review. Dwayne Brenna. *NeWest R* Sept 1987; Vol 13 No 1: p18.

Stories of the West best when satirical; review of *The Unsettling of the West*. Keith Garebian. photo · *TS* May 24, 1987: pA19.

[Untitled]; review of *Changes of State*. Robert Gibbs. *Poetry Can R* Fall 1987; Vol 9 No 1: p33–34.

Narrative tendencies; reviews of poetry books. Phil Hall. *Waves* Winter 1987; Vol 15 No 3: p84–88.

[Untitled]; review of *Changes of State*. Laurence Hutchman. *Rubicon* Spring 1987; No 8: p190–193.

Tiger poems; reviews of poetry books. M. Travis Lane. *Fiddlehead* Autumn 1987; No 153: p88–91.

[Untitled]; review of *Changes of State*. Louise Longo. *Books in Can* Jan-Feb 1987; Vol 16 No 1: p27–28.

[Untitled]; reviews of poetry books. Stephen Scobie. *Malahat R* Dec 1987; No 81: p104–106.

[Untitled]; review of *The Unsettling of the West*. Bob Wakulich. *CH* May 31, 1987: pF5.

In the mode; reviews of short story collections. Allan Weiss. *Books in Can* April 1987; Vol 16 No 3: p30–31.

[Untitled]; reviews of poetry books. Bruce Whiteman. *Cross Can Writ Q* 1987; Vol 9 No 2: p21–22,26.

[Untitled]; review of *Changes of State*. Elizabeth Woods. *Malahat R* June 1987; No 79: p166–168.

GEDGE, PAULINE

Sward draws blood; letter to the editor. John Patrick Gillese. *Can Auth & Book* Spring 1987; Vol 62 No 3: p2.

[Untitled]; letter to the editor. Jean B. Greig. *Can Auth & Book* Spring 1987; Vol 62 No 3: p2.

[Untitled]; review of *The Twelfth Transforming*. Robert Sward. *Can Auth & Book* Winter 1987; Vol 62 No 2: p23.

GEEKS IN LOVE/Play by Jeffrey Hirschfield

Off-the-wall play hit with audience; theatre review of *Geeks in Love*. Kate Zimmerman. *CH* March 1, 1987: pC5.

GÉLINAS, GRATIEN

Aujourd'hui; column. *MD* Feb 25, 1987: p12.

Arts conference to target municipal funding support; article. *CH* May 20, 1987: pF3.

À surveiller; column. *MD* Nov 4, 1987: p12.

De la fronde au bazooka; editorial. Rolande Allard-Lacerte. *MD* Jan 19, 1987: p14.

Des Boches à Fridolin; letter to the editor. H.-Paul Delimal. *MD* Jan 17, 1987: pB2.

Le théâtre qu'on joue; theatre reviews. André Dionne. photo · *Lettres québec* Summer 1987; No 46: p47–48.

Gélinas and Oligny: a match made in theatrical heaven; theatre review of *La Passion de Narcisse Mondoux*. Pat Donnelly. photo · *MG* Jan 20, 1987: pD11.

From English to French to English; article. Pat Donnelly. photo · *MG* Sept 5, 1987: pC6.

[Untitled]; theatre reviews. Pat Donnelly. *MG* Sept 11, 1987: pC8.

Ageless Fridolin skits leave crowd euphoric; theatre review of *Les Fridolinades*. Pat Donnelly. photo · *MG* Nov 27, 1987: pC1.

[Untitled]; theatre reviews. Pat Donnelly. *MG* Nov 27, 1987: pC7.

[Untitled]; theatre reviews. Pat Donnelly. *MG* Dec 4, 1987: pC6.

Fridolin's as funny as ever; theatre review of *Les Fridolinades*. Matthew Fraser. photo · *G&M* Jan 27, 1987: pC5.

Büchner, Marivaux, Shephard, Gélinas: un mois théâtral chargé; column. Robert Lévesque. photo · *MD* Jan 6, 1987: p4.

Gratien Gélinas: le retour de Fridolin; article. Robert Lévesque. illus photo · *MD* Jan 10, 1987: pB1,B4

Des Fridolinades sorties de leur temps; theatre review of *Les Fridolinades*. Robert Lévesque. photo · *MD* Jan 14, 1987: p6.

Québec: Alexandre Hausvater quitte la Quinzaine théâtrale; column. Robert Lévesque. *MD* April 14, 1987: p12.

Qui sera le directeur artistique du TPQ?; column. Robert Lévesque. *MD* Nov 17, 1987: p11.

La vie littéraire; column. Jean Royer. photo · *MD* May 30, 1987: pD2.

[AWARDS, LITERARY; CANADIAN LITERARY PUBLISHING; COMPETITIONS, LITERARY; FESTIVALS, LITERARY; RADIO AND CANADIAN LITERATURE; TELEVISION AND CANADIAN LITERATURE]

GENDRON, MARC

Deux échos québécois de grands romans épistolaires du dix-huitième siècle français; article. Monique Moser-Verrey. *Voix et images* Spring 1987; Vol 12 No 3: p512–514,516–522.
[FRANCE-CANADA LITERARY RELATIONS]

GENTLEMAN, DOROTHY CORBETT

Small press reviews; reviews of poetry books. Shaunt Basmajian. *Cross Can Writ Q* 1987; Vol 9 No 1: p25.

[Untitled]; reviews of *The Proper Lover* and *Above the Tilted Earth*. Barbara Carey. *Poetry Can R* Summer 1987; Vol 8 No 4: p34.

GERMAIN, DORIC

Cycles; reviews of *L'Oeil interrompu* and *Poison*. Mark Benson. *Can Lit* Spring 1987; No 112: p136–138.

GERMANY-CANADA LITERARY RELATIONS

Cartographie: l'Allemagne québécoise; article. Diane Pavlovic. bibliog photo · *Jeu* 1987; No 43: p77–110.
[QUEBEC DRAMA (FRENCH LANGUAGE): HISTORY AND CRITICISM]

Kanada made me; article. Horst Wittmann. *Books in Can* Oct 1987; Vol 16 No 7: p3–4.

GERTRUDE AND OPHELIA/Play by Margaret Clarke

Theatre company faces stiff test; article. Brad Oswald. photo · *WFP* Sept 23, 1987: p44.

GERVAIS, C.H. (MARTY)

[Untitled]; review of *Letters from the Equator*. Phil Hall. *Books in Can* Aug-Sept 1987; Vol 16 No 6: p28.

GERVAIS, GUY

"Le monde en un seul mot"; review of *Verbe silence*. Jean Royer. *MD* May 30, 1987: pD5.

GERVAIS, LUC

V.S.O.P. pale imitation of a play; theatre review. Pat Donnelly. *MG* Oct 16, 1987: pC7.

Avis aux consommateurs; theatre review of *V.S.O.P.*. Robert Lévesque. photo · *MD* Oct 16, 1987: p15.

GETTING MARRIED IN BUFFALO JUMP/Novel by Susan Charlotte Haley

The fight for love and truth hampered by riddle of past; reviews of *Between Men* and *Getting Married in Buffalo Jump*. Ken Adachi. photo · *TS* Oct 17, 1987: M4.

Frontier women: two tales in search of the perfect marriage; reviews of *Between Men* and *Getting Married in Buffalo Jump*. Ruby Andrew. photo · *Quill & Quire* Sept 1987; Vol 53 No 9: p76.

Anglos, Ukrainians, Indians mesh cultures in novel set in Alberta; review of *Getting Married in Buffalo Jump*. Barbara Black. *MG* Aug 29, 1987: J3.

Marriage and violence Western-Canadian style; reviews of *Getting Married in Buffalo Jump* and *The Dancing Chicken*. William French. photo · *G&M* Nov 19, 1987: pA25.

Wedding in wheat; review of *Getting Married in Buffalo Jump*. Douglas Glover. *Books in Can* Oct 1987; Vol 16 No 7: p32,34.

Love with the right farm hand; review of *Getting Married in Buffalo Jump*. Sue Hubbell. *NYT Book R* Aug 16, 1987: p22.

Delicacy, humor mark wry novel; review of *Getting Married in Buffalo Jump*. Dave Margoshes. *CH* Oct 11, 1987: pE6.

Shadow of violence seems out of place in deft, lightly comic novel; review of *Getting Married in Buffalo Jump*. David Williamson. *WFP* Sept 5, 1987: p58.

THE GHOST SHIPS THAT DIDN'T BELONG/Children's novel by Lynn Manuel

Formulaic mysteries to attract unenthusiastic readers; reviews of *The Ghost Ships That Didn't Belong* and *The Secret of Sunset House*. Bessie Condos Egan. *Quill & Quire* (Books for Young People) June 1987; Vol 53 No 6: p6.

GIBBS, ROBERT

Maritime letters; reviews. Carrie MacMillan. *Can Lit* Spring 1987; No 112: p189–192.

GIBSON, GRAEME

People; column. Yvonne Cox. *Maclean's* March 9, 1987; Vol 100 No 10: p48.

L'obsession de l'impossible; review of *Mouvement sans fin*. Jean-Pierre Issenhuth. *Liberté* June 1987; Vol 29 No 3: p105–106.

GIBSON, WILLIAM

Future and past histories: repeating winning formulae simply not on the cards; review of *Burning Chrome*. Douglas Barbour. *TS* March 7, 1987: M4.

New video law keeps Vancouver's accent on lust; column. John Masters. *TS* Jan 10, 1987: K4.

Bringing sci-fi down to Earth; article. Henry Mietkiewicz. illus · *TS* May 24, 1987: pC1.
[SCIENCE FICTION]

THE GIFT ANGEL/Children's story by Airdrie Thomsen

Snoring, smuggling, and snuggling; reviews of children's stories. Susan Perren. *Quill & Quire (Books for Young People)* Dec 1987; Vol 53 No 12: p8.

GILBERT LA ROCQUE: L'CRITURE DU RÈVE/Critical essays

Black lyricist; review of *Gilbert La Rocque: l'écriture du rêve*. P. Merivale. *Can Lit* Spring 1987; No 112: p124–126.

GILBERT, SKY

ATP's Postman Rings Once is a risk within a larger risk; article. Bob Blakey. *CH* Jan 30, 1987: pC1.

Tame gay play marked by low-camp theatrics; theatre review of *The Postman Rings Once*. Brian Brennan. photo · *CH* Feb 1, 1987: pC6.

Play review endorsed; letter to the editor. Edna Brown. *CH* Feb 8, 1987: pB4.

The Postman Rings Once too often; theatre review. Ray Conlogue. photo · *G&M* Oct 8, 1987: pD5.

Three Toronto plays premiere at Calgary fest; article, includes theatre reviews. Robert Crew. photo · *TS* Feb 10, 1987: pB4.
[FESTIVALS, DRAMA]

Theatrelife takes typecasting to the limit; article about Graham Harley. Robert Crew. photo · *TS* March 27, 1987: pD14.

Theatrelife exposes raw side of the stage; theatre review. Robert Crew. photo · *TS* March 30, 1987: pB3.

New-play festival deserves a curtain call; theatre reviews. Stephen Godfrey. photo · *G&M* Feb 10, 1987: pC5.
[FESTIVALS, DRAMA]

CBC explores impact of AIDS on the arts; article. Liam Lacey. *G&M* April 11, 1987: pE3.

Theatrelife stylish, ingenious; theatre review. Liam Lacey. photo · *G&M* April 1, 1987: pC5.

Artist gives surreal play haunting backdrop; column. Vit Wagner. *TS* Oct 2, 1987: pE12.

Lana Turner steals the show; theatre review of *The Postman Rings Once*. Vit Wagner. photo · *TS* Oct 9, 1987: pE9.

GILKES, MARGARET

Novel recalls author's wartime experiences; article. *MG* Jan 12, 1987: pC2.

Remembrance Day spurs London terror memories; article. Dave Haynes. photo · *CH* Nov 11, 1987: pB1.

GILLES VACHON: INCENDIAIRE/Play by Siegfried Gagnon

Help! Kirk! Star Trek image being tarnished!; theatre review of *Gilles Vachon: Incendiaire*. Pat Donnelly. *MG* Aug 13, 1987: pE16.

[Untitled]; theatre review of *Gilles Vachon: Incendiaire*. Pat Donnelly. *MG* Aug 14, 1987: pC8.

Quelque chose d'Aurore . . . ; theatre review of *Gilles Vachon: Incendiaire*. Robert Lévesque. *MD* Aug 19, 1987: p11.

Une histoire cousue de fils araignées; theatre review of *Gilles Vachon: Incendiaire*. Solange Lévesque. photo · *Jeu* 1987; No 45: p216–217.

GILMAN, PHOEBE

Mini-reviews; reviews of children's books. Margaret Paré. *Can Child Lit* 1987; No 45: p93–96.

GILMOUR, DAVID

Juicy real-life crime tales heat up fall book lists; column. Sid Adilman. *TS* Oct 3, 1987: J1.
[FILM ADAPTATIONS OF CANADIAN LITERATURE]

Shallow griefs; review of *Back on Tuesday*. Diana Brydon. *Can Lit* Winter 1987; No 115: p194–195.
[FIRST NOVELS: BOOK REVIEW]

[Untitled]; reviews. Beverley Daurio. *Cross Can Writ Q* 1987; Vol 9 No 2: p23.
[FIRST NOVELS: BOOK REVIEWS]

GINGRAS, RENÉ

[Untitled]; theatre review of *Le Facteur réalité*. Diane Pavlovic. photo · *Jeu* 1987; No 44: p112–113.

GIRLS CAN! BOYS CAN!/Children's play by Dolly Reisman

Play discourages children from sexual stereotyping; article. Beverley Ware. photo · *TS (Neighbors)* Aug 11, 1987: p6.

Play about equality of the sexes impressing Metro area children; article. Beverley Ware. *TS (Neighbors)* Aug 18, 1987: p20.

GIRLS IN THE GANG/Play by Raymond Storey

Domestic drama that hits home; article, includes theatre reviews. John Bemrose. photo · *Maclean's* Aug 17, 1987; Vol 100 No 33: p49.
[FESTIVALS, DRAMA]

Girls a slick, witty musical; theatre review of *Girls in the Gang*. Ray Conlogue. photo · *G&M* July 2, 1987: pD3.

Blyth musical succeeds where drama fails; theatre reviews of *Girls in the Gang* and *Bush Fire*. Jason Sherman. photo · *TS* Aug 7, 1987: pE10.

GIROUX, ROBERT

La répétition de l'intime; reviews of poetry books. André Marquis. photo · *Lettres québec* Spring 1987; No 45: p44–46.

GIVEN NAMES: NEW AND SELECTED POEMS 1972–1985/Poems by Judith Fitzgerald

[Untitled]; review of *Given Names*. Sharon Berg. *Poetry Can R* Spring 1987; Vol 8 No 2–3: p46

GIVNER, JOAN

Dandelion uncovers new voice; column. Kenneth McGoogan. photo · *CH* Feb 1, 1987: pC8.
[AWARDS, LITERARY; CANADIAN LITERARY PERIODICALS; POETRY READINGS]

THE GLASS AIR/Poems by P.K. Page

Diamond panes; review of *The Glass Air*. Sandra Hutchison. *Can Lit* Summer-Fall 1987; No 113–114: p247–249.

[Untitled]; review of *The Glass Air*. M.K. Louis. *Malahat R (special issue)* March 1987; No 78: p156–158.

GLASS, JOANNA McCLELLAND

Piggery kicks off '87 seasons with warm and witty winner; theatre review of *Artichoke*. Marianne Ackerman. *MG* June 29, 1987: pD9.

[Untitled]; theatre review of *Artichoke*. Marianne Ackerman. *MG* July 3, 1987: pC10.

Play's memorable but its production is rather less so; theatre review of *Play Memory*. Robert Crew. photo · *TS* July 3, 1987: pD21.

[Untitled]; theatre review of *Play Memory*. Keith Garebian. *Queen's Q* Autumn 1987; Vol 94 No 3: p755–757.

Glass's *Play Memory* is sober look at alcoholism; theatre review. Liam Lacey. photo · *G&M* July 3, 1987: pD11.

Playwright torn between two countries; article. Henry Mietkiewicz. photo · *TS* June 30, 1987: pE2.

Credit Valley's Artichoke has l: p93–96.

GILMOUR, DAVID

Juicy real-life crime tales heat up fall book lists; column. Sid Adilman. *TS* Oct 3, 1987: J1.
[FILM ADAPTATIONS OF CANADIAN LITERATURE]

Shallow griefs; review of *Back on Tuesday*. Diana Brydon. *Can Lit* Winter 1987; No 115: p194–195.
[FIRST NOVELS: BOOK REVIEW]

[Untitled]; reviews. Beverley Daurio. *Cross Can Writ Q* 1987; Vol 9 No 2: p23.
[FIRST NOVELS: BOOK REVIEWS]

GINGRAS, RENÉ

[Untitled]; theatre review of *Le Facteur réalitots of heart; theatre review. Lynn Moore. photo · *TS (Neighbours)* Feb 24, 1987: p16.

[Untitled]; reviews. Lisbie Rae. *Can Drama* 1987; Vol 13 No 2: p229–231.
[ANTHOLOGIES: BOOK REVIEWS]

GLASSCO, JOHN

Photography "in camera"; article. Peter Sims. *Can Lit* Summer-Fall 1987; No 113–114: p145–166.

THE GLASSY SEA/Novel by Marian Engel

Maple Leaf memories in print; reviews of *The Bishop* and *The Glassy Sea*. Lew Gloin. *TS* July 12, 1987: pA18.

A humanistic vision of the lives of churchmen and women; reviews of *The Glassy Sea* and *The Bishop*. Douglas Hill. *G&M* Sept 12, 1987: pC17.

GLICKMAN, SUSAN

[Untitled]; review of *The Power to Move*. Carolyn Bond. *Quarry* Fall 1987; Vol 36 No 4: p83–86.

[Untitled]; review of *The Power to Move*. Barbara Carey. *Books in Can* May 1987; Vol 16 No 4: p23–24.

You ask me what I'm thinking; reviews of poetry books. M. Travis Lane. *Fiddlehead* Winter 1987; No 154: p95–104.

[Untitled]; reviews of *The Fabulous Disguise of Ourselves* and *The Power to Move*. Stephen Scobie. *Malahat R* June 1987; No 79: p166.

THE GLORIOUS EAST WIND/Novel by K.G.E. Konkel

Surprising weight from the newcomers; reviews of *The Glorious East Wind* and *Ripper*. Margaret Cannon. *G&M* Nov 7, 1987: pC23.
[FIRST NOVELS: BOOK REVIEWS]

Local heroes; reviews of first novels. Janice Kulyk Keefer. *Books in Can* Nov 1987; Vol 16 No 8: p35,37.
[FIRST NOVELS: BOOK REVIEWS]

A spot of skulduggery with an Asian flavor; review of *The Glorious East Wind*. Neil Louttit. *WFP* Dec 19, 1987: p51.
[FIRST NOVELS: BOOK REVIEWS]

[Untitled]; review of *The Glorious East Wind*. Peter Robinson. *Quill & Quire* Sept 1987; Vol 53 No 9: p79.
[FIRST NOVELS: BOOK REVIEWS]

A solid first effort from a Toronto cop; review of *The Glorious East Wind*. Mike Walton. photo · *TS* Dec 26, 1987: K7.
[FIRST NOVELS: BOOK REVIEWS]

Hong Kong is a jungle in Toronto cop's thriller; review of *The Glorious East Wind*. Paul Waters. *MG* Oct 31, 1987: J14.
[FIRST NOVELS: BOOK REVIEWS]

UN GOÛT DE SEL/Poems by Suzanne Paradis

[Untitled]; reviews of *Un goût de sel* and *Effets de l'oeil*. Hélène Thibaux. *Estuaire* Autumn 1987; No 46: p86–87.

GOD IN LITERATURE

The religious roots of the feminine identity issue: Margaret Laurence's The Stone Angel and Margaret Atwood's Surfacing; article. Evelyn J. Hinz. abstract · *J of Can Studies* Spring 1987; Vol 22 No 1: p17–31.
[BIBLICAL MYTHS AND MYTHOLOGY; FEMINIST WRITING AND CRITICISM]

Apocalyptic imaginations: notes on Atwood's The Handmaid's Tale and Findley's Not Wanted on the Voyage; article. W.J. Keith. *Essays on Can Writ* Winter 1987; No 35: p123–134.
[THE APOCALYPSE; BIBLICAL MYTHS AND MYTHOLOGY; SATIRIC WRITING]

GODBOUT, JACQUES

Écrire l'histoire ou histoire d'écrire; reviews of novels. Jacques Michon. *Voix et images* Spring 1987; Vol 12 No 3: p548–550.

Le second déclin de l'empire américain; review of *Une Histoire américaine*. Louise Milot. photo · *Lettres québec* Winter 1986–87; No 44: p22–25

GODFREY, DAVE

The I and the eye in the desert: the political and philosophical key to Dave Godfrey's The New Ancestors; article. A.C. Morrell. *Studies in Can Lit* 1987; Vol 12 No 2: p264–272.

GODFREY, MARTYN

[Untitled]; reviews of *Edythe With a Y* and *It Isn't Easy Being Ms. Teeny Wonderful*. Patty Lawlor. *Quill & Quire (Books for Young People)* April 1987; Vol 53 No 4: p8.

Youth writers flourish in Alberta; article. Kenneth McGoogan. photo · *CH* Feb 21, 1987: pG1.
[AUTHORS, CANADIAN; CHILDREN'S LITERATURE]

Experts offered the write advice; article. Kenneth McGoogan. photo · *CH* April 6, 1987: pD6.
[CONFERENCES, LITERARY]

A little help on the dull days; reviews of children's books. Joan McGrath. *TS* Aug 2, 1987: pC11.

A touching, but unsentimental story; review of *Plan B Is Total Panic*. Lyle Weis. *Can Child Lit* 1987; No 45: p72–73.

Fine books for in-betweens; reviews of young adult books. David Williamson. *WFP* Dec 5, 1987: p57.

Lite-lit for children has arrived; reviews of children's books. Tim Wynne-Jones. *G&M* March 7, 1987: pE19.

GODIN, GÉRALD

Poet-politician wins literary prize; article. *G&M* Nov 20, 1987: pD11.
[AWARDS, LITERARY]

Pas d'atout mais du coeur; review of *SoirS sans AtouT*. Réjean Beaudoin. *Liberté* Feb 1987; Vol 29 No 1: p153–154.

[Untitled]; review of *SoirS sans AtouT*. Claude Beausoleil. *Estuaire* Winter 1986–87; No 43: p77.

Le Duvernay à Gérald Godin, le Victor-Morin à André Brassard; article. Sylvain Blanchard. *MD* Oct 9, 1987: p13–14.
[AWARDS, LITERARY]

La vitrine du livre; reviews. Guy Ferland. *MD* Aug 29, 1987: pC12.

26 ans d'criture, deux trajectoires opposes; reviews of *L'écouté* and *SoirS sans AtouT*. André Marquis. photo · *Lettres québec* Winter 1986–87; No 44: p42–43.

La vie littéraire; column. Marc Morin. *MD* Oct 31, 1987: pD2.
[COMPETITIONS, LITERARY; POETRY READINGS; WRITERS' ORGANIZATIONS]

La voix familière de Gérald Godin; review of *Ils ne demandaient qu'à brûler*. Jean Royer. photo · *MD* Sept 12, 1987: pD3.

GODIN, MARCEL

Des contes et des nouvelles pour rêver; reviews of short story books. Dominique Garand. *Voix et images* Spring 1987; Vol 12 No 3: p551–555.
[ANTHOLOGIES: BOOK REVIEWS]

Trois voyages — petit, moyen et grand — du littératage à la littérature; reviews of short story books. Marie José Thériault. photo · *Lettres québec* Spring 1987; No 45: p30–32.
[ANTHOLOGIES: BOOK REVIEWS]

GODS AND OTHER MORTALS/Poems by Helen Humphreys

[Untitled]; reviews of poetry books. Sheila Martindale. *Cross Can Writ Q* 1987; Vol 9 No 2: p20–21.

GOING TO THE DOGS/Novel by Russell McRae

Local heroes; reviews of first novels. Janice Kulyk Keefer. *Books in Can* Nov 1987; Vol 16 No 8: p35,37.
[FIRST NOVELS: BOOK REVIEWS]

THE GOLDFISH BOWL/Novel by Laurence Gough

Fatalities and feminism in Lotus Land; reviews of *Fieldwork* and *The Goldfish Bowl*. Margaret Cannon. *G&M* Aug 29, 1987: pC17.
[FIRST NOVELS· BOOK REVIEWS]

Heart of darkness; reviews of first novels. Janice Kulyk Keefer. *Books in Can* Dec 1987; Vol 16 No 9: p37–39.
[FIRST NOVELS: BOOK REVIEWS]

Killer stalks wet streets of Vancouver; review of *The Goldfish Bowl*. Paul Waters. *MG* Dec 24, 1987: L9.
[FIRST NOVELS: BOOK REVIEWS]

GOLDIE AND THE SEA/Children's story by Judith Saltman

Annabel and Goldie go to the sea, Josephine goes to school; reviews of *Can You Catch Josephine?* and *Goldie and the Sea*. Susan Perren. *Quill & Quire (Books for Young People)* Oct 1987; Vol 53 No 10: p18–19.

GOLDSMITH, OLIVER

[Untitled]; review of *Autobiography of Oliver Goldsmith*. Maurice Lebel. *Études can* June 1987; No 22: p134–136.

[Untitled]; review of *Autobiography of Oliver Goldsmith*. George Woodcock. *Can Lit* Spring 1987; No 112: p224–225.

GOM, LEONA

Mainstreet Calgary; column. *CH (Neighbors)* Nov 11, 1987: pA15,A18.
[POETRY READINGS]

[Untitled]; article. *G&M* Oct 31, 1987.
[AWARDS, LITERARY]

Trial by experience; reviews of *Letters from Some Islands* and *Private Properties*. Bert Almon. *Can Lit* Winter 1987; No 115: p206–208.

[Untitled]; reviews of *Housebroken* and *Private Properties*. Sharon Batt. *Room of One's Own* Sept 1987; Vol 11 No 4: p109–112.
[FIRST NOVELS: BOOK REVIEWS]

[Untitled]; reviews. Beverley Daurio. *Cross Can Writ Q* 1987; Vol 9 No 2: p23.
[FIRST NOVELS: BOOK REVIEWS]

Between the sexes; reviews of poetry books. Mary di Michele. *Books in Can* March 1987; Vol 16 No 2: p31–32.

[Untitled]; reviews of poetry books. Anita Hurwitz. *Poetry Can R* Spring 1987; Vol 8 No 2–3: p38–39.

All about women and relationships; reviews of *Housebroken* and *Frogs*. Lesley McAllister. *TS* Jan 3, 1987: M6.
[FIRST NOVELS: BOOK REVIEWS]

[Untitled]; reviews of *Private Properties* and *Second Nature*. Stephen Scobie. *Malahat R (special issue)* March 1987; No 78: p153–154.

Wit and humor mark poetry; reviews of *Second Nature* and *Private Properties*. Andrew Wreggitt. *CH* Jan 11, 1987: pF4.

GONE THE BURNING SUN/Play by Ken Mitchell

One-man Bethune show to tour China; column. Robert Crew. *TS* March 19, 1987: pE3.
[FESTIVALS, DRAMA]

Portrait of Bethune strong on passion; theatre review of *Gone the Burning Sun*. Robert Crew. photo · *TS* March 27, 1987: pD22.

TWP to take Bethune show to China; column. Liam Lacey. photo · *G&M* March 20, 1987: pD10.

Author, actor combine to make Sun a success; theatre review of *Gone the Burning Sun*. Liam Lacey. photo · *G&M* March 27, 1987: pD9.

Prairie spaces in the big city: western theatre in Toronto; theatre reviews. Margaret Gail Osachoff. *NeWest R* Oct 1987; Vol 13 No 2: p18–19.

Moose Jaw meets Mao; article. Maggie Siggins. biog photo · *G&M* March 21, 1987: pE1,E6.
[CHINA-CANADA LITERARY RELATIONS]

THE GOOD BABY/Play by Leon Rooke

Back to the earth with baby, Mr. Big and the Fat Lady; theatre reviews of *The Good Baby* and *The Enchanted Forest*. Stephen Godfrey. photo · *G&M* July 18, 1987: pC1,C4.

GOOD HUMOUR MAN/Short story anthology

Book launch planned; article. *WFP* Dec 4, 1987: p37.
[FICTION READINGS]

A GOOD PLACE TO COME FROM/Short stories by Morley Torgov

Season's greetings: companies take cues from holidays past; article. Brian Brennan. photo · *CH* Nov 22, 1987: pA11.
[DRAMATIC ADAPTATIONS OF CANADIAN LITERATURE]

GOODBYE HAROLD, GOOD LUCK/Short stories by Audrey Thomas

The country of the human heart; review of *Goodbye Harold, Good Luck*. Diana Austin. *Fiddlehead* Spring 1987; No 151: p107–110.

Country manners; reviews of *The Progress of Love* and *Goodbye Harold, Good Luck*. Julie Beddoes. *Brick* Winter 1987; No 29: p24–27.

Story postponed; review of *Goodbye Harold, Good Luck*. Margery Fee. *Can Lit* Winter 1987; No 115: p218–220.

[Untitled]; reviews of short story collections. Carole Gerson. *Queen's Q* Summer 1987; Vol 94 No 2: p483–484.

How short story writers can gain their literary credibility; review of *Goodbye Harold, Good Luck*. Douglas Hill. *G&M* April 18, 1987: pC17.

GOSSELIN, MICHEL

Les enfants du déclin; reviews of novels. Jacques Michon. *Voix et images* Winter 1987; No 35: p331–334.

GOTHIC/Poems by David Day

Crimes of the heart; reviews of *Gothic* and *The Animals Within*. Al Purdy. *Books in Can* April 1987; Vol 16 No 3: p32,34.

Poetry of love at its purest; reviews of poetry books. Paul Roberts. *TS* Aug 15, 1987: M10.

GOTTESMAN, MEIR

Reaching out to little children through books; article. Michael McAteer. photo · *TS* Dec 12, 1987: M15.
[JEWISH-CANADIAN WRITING]

GOUGH, LAURENCE

Fatalities and feminism in Lotus Land; reviews of *Fieldwork* and *The Goldfish Bowl*. Margaret Cannon. *G&M* Aug 29, 1987: pC17.
[FIRST NOVELS: BOOK REVIEWS]

Heart of darkness; reviews of first novels. Janice Kulyk Keefer. *Books in Can* Dec 1987; Vol 16 No 9: p37–39.
[FIRST NOVELS: BOOK REVIEWS]

Killer stalks wet streets of Vancouver; review of *The Goldfish Bowl*. Paul Waters. *MG* Dec 24, 1987: L9.
[FIRST NOVELS: BOOK REVIEWS]

GOUGH, WILLIAM

All this and quality, too; review of *The Last White Man in Panama*. Andrew Allentuck. *WFP* Oct 24, 1987: p54.

A decade of great thrillers continues with two treasures; reviews of *Swann: A Mystery* and *The Last White Man in Panama*. Margaret Cannon. *G&M* Sept 26, 1987: pC23.

[Untitled]; reviews of *The Proper Lover* and *Above the Tilted Earth*. Barbara Carey. *Poetry Can R* Summer 1987; Vol 8 No 4: p34.

One slick thriller — and another that's not so slick; review of *The Last White Man in Panama*. Geoff Chapman. *TS* Oct 18, 1987: pC8.

Fun and games with sharp-tongued Tracey; column. John Haslett Cuff. *G&M* May 2, 1987: pC4.

[Untitled]; review of *The Last White Man in Panama*. Geoff Heinricks. *Quill & Quire* Sept 1987; Vol 53 No 9: p79.

Romantic adventure set in Panama City is as thin as the celluloid it's written for; review of *The Last White Man in Panama*. P. Scott Lawrence. photo · *MG* Nov 7, 1987: K12.

Francis has winner in new whodunit; review of *The Last White Man in Panama*. Kenneth McGoogan. *CH* Nov 1, 1987: pE6.

Young poets on display; reviews of poetry books. Robert Quickenden. photo · *WFP* March 14, 1987: p52.

Mistaken identity; letter to the editor. Nicholas Rice. *G&M* Oct 9, 1987: pA6.

LA GOUTTE/Children's play by Joel da Silva

Du théâtre comme dans un moulin; article. Angèle Dagenais. photo · *MD* Nov 11, 1987: p11.

Music, theatre union needs fine tuning; theatre reviews of *Le Dernier quatuor d'un homme sourd* and *La Goutte*. Pat Donnelly. *MG* Nov 18, 1987: pD3.

GOVERNMENT GRANTS FOR WRITERS/PUBLISHERS

Ottawa notebook: at times our Prime Minister can be a very elusive man; column. photo · *TS* March 22, 1987: pA6.
[LIBRARY SERVICES AND CANADIAN LITERATURE]

Authors collect for library use; article. *MG* March 18, 1987: pB4.
[LIBRARY SERVICES AND CANADIAN LITERATURE]

Authors get paid for titles in libraries; article. *WFP* Feb 13, 1987: p31.
[LIBRARY SERVICES AND CANADIAN LITERATURE]

Authors get long-promised cheques; article. *WFP* March 18, 1987: p38.
[LIBRARY SERVICES AND CANADIAN LITERATURE]

50 artistes se partagent $354,000; article. *MD* Feb 4, 1987: p22.

Prêts en bibliothèque: les auteurs reoivent leurs premiers chèques; article. *MD* March 18, 1987: p17.
[LIBRARY SERVICES AND CANADIAN LITERATURE]

Publishing subsidies face axe; article. *CH* Jan 8, 1987: pE8.

Library-book royalties winging way to writers; article. *CH* March 18, 1987: pC11.
[LIBRARY SERVICES AND CANADIAN LITERATURE]

Writers eager for list; article. *WFP* April 24, 1987: p33.
[LIBRARY SERVICES AND CANADIAN LITERATURE]

Manitoba publishers look for bail-out; article. *WFP* July 16, 1987: p36.
[PUBLISHING AND PUBLISHERS IN CANADA]

20 writers share Toronto awards; article. *G&M* July 14, 1987: pC5.

Arts Councils' programs for writers — an overview; list of grant programs. *Cross Can Writ Q* 1987; Vol 9 No 3–4: p36,64.

A momentous day for writers; column. Ken Adachi. *TS* March 16, 1987: pB1.
[LIBRARY SERVICES AND CANADIAN LITERATURE]

Retain subsidies, publisher urges; article. Dave Blaikie. *G&M* April 29, 1987: pC8.

[Untitled]; essay. Anne Burke. photo · *Cross Can Writ Q* 1987; Vol 9 No 3–4: p22–23.

Federal book program finally official; article. Hamish Cameron. *Quill & Quire* Jan 1987; Vol 53 No 1: p13.

[Untitled]; essay. Lesley Choyce. photo · *Cross Can Writ Q* 1987; Vol 9 No 3–4: p25–26.

Literary funding in Quebec; article. Anne Cimon. *Cross Can Writ Q* 1987; Vol 9 No 3–4: p31,64.

La "Coalition de 1%" rencontrera Bourassa; article. Angèle Dagenais. photo · *MD* Dec 4, 1987: p13.

Le milieu artistique encouragé par les intentions libérales; article. Angèle Dagenais. photo · *MD* Dec 15, 1987: p11.

Taken for granted?; article about the Canada Council. Matthew Fraser. illus photo · *G&M* Feb 28, 1987: pE1,E5

A red-letter day for Canadian writers; column. William French. *G&M* March 10, 1987: pD7.
[LIBRARY SERVICES AND CANADIAN LITERATURE]

Booking time for the issues; column. William French. *G&M* April 21, 1987: pD7.
[FESTIVALS, LITERARY]

Public Lending Right debate takes new twist; column. William French. *G&M* Nov 10, 1987: pD7.
[LIBRARY SERVICES AND CANADIAN LITERATURE]

Sound ship in a sea of malice; column about the Canada Council. Robert Fulford. photo · *TS* March 28, 1987: M5.

Ottawa struggles to ensure authors get their due; article. Carol Goar. illus · *MG* Dec 4, 1987: pB3.
[COPYRIGHT; LIBRARY SERVICES AND CANADIAN LITERATURE]

Subsidies and writers: two views are debated; article. Stephen Godfrey. *G&M* April 29, 1987: pC5.

Authors group fought for public lending right; letter to the editor. Della Golland-Lui. *TS* April 6, 1987: pA16.
[LIBRARY SERVICES AND CANADIAN LITERATURE; WRITERS' ORGANIZATIONS]

[Untitled]; essay. David Halliday. photo · *Cross Can Writ Q* 1987; Vol 9 No 3–4: p23.

Cheque mates; article about the Ontario Arts Council. Martin Hunter. illus · *Tor Life* June 1987; Vol 21 No 9: p52,86–90,93,95–96.

Art for art & and truth; editorial. Susan Ioannou. *Cross Can Writ Q* 1987; Vol 9 No 3–4: p37,64.

The other side of the coin; editorial. Christopher Levenson. *Arc* Spring 1987; No 18: p4–7.
[CULTURAL IDENTITY]

[Untitled]; essay. Bernice Lever. photo · *Cross Can Writ Q* 1987; Vol 9 No 3–4: p26.

[Untitled]; essay. Gwendolyn MacEwen. photo · *Cross Can Writ Q* 1987; Vol 9 No 3–4: p22.

[Untitled]; essay. Claire Mackay. photo · *Cross Can Writ Q* 1987; Vol 9 No 3–4: p24.

Breaking the myths about the Canada Council: literary officer Robert Richard's inside view of Council operations; article. Blaine Marchand. *Cross Can Writ Q* 1987; Vol 9 No 3–4: p28–29,57.

[Untitled]; essay. Tom Marshall. *Cross Can Writ Q* 1987; Vol 9 No 3–4: p24.

Storm brewing in literary heaven; column. Kenneth McGoogan. *CH* Jan 11, 1987: pF4.
[WRITERS' ORGANIZATIONS]

Literary arts foundation doles out another $190,000; article. Kenneth McGoogan. *CH* March 11, 1987: pD2.

Alberta foundation a boon to the arts; article. Kenneth McGoogan. *Quill & Quire* Feb 1987; Vol 53 No 2: p10–11.

Calgary writers take top honors; column. Kenneth McGoogan. *CH* April 9, 1987: pE7.
[AWARDS, LITERARY]

Poets fare best under payment scheme, says chairman; article. Kenneth McGoogan. *CH* May 1, 1987: pE4.
[LIBRARY SERVICES AND CANADIAN LITERATURE]

Writers, publishers, libraries rejoice; column. Kenneth McGoogan. *CH2* June 14, 1987: pE6.
[AWARDS, LITERARY]

Libraries given bulk of grants; article. Kenneth McGoogan. *CH* Aug 27, 1987: pC5.

Foundation awards new round of grants; article. Kenneth McGoogan. *CH* Dec 10, 1987: pF2.

Freedom from culture: liberating the Canadian literary world from the subversion of government subsidy; essay. John Metcalf. photo · *Cross Can Writ Q* 1987; Vol 9 No 3–4: p27,53–57.

Literary life-support systems & the Ontario Arts Council; article. Ted Plantos. photo · *Cross Can Writ Q* 1987; Vol 9 No 3–4: p30–31,59–60.

Government sabotaging its own cultural initiatives; article. Jamie Portman. photo · *CH* Aug 8, 1987: pF3.
[PUBLISHING AND PUBLISHERS IN CANADA]

Canada Council 30 years old; article. Jamie Portman. *TS* Dec 17, 1987: pC2.

Council funds fostered arts across nation; article about the Canada Council. Jamie Portman. *CH* Dec 15, 1987: pC1.

How I wasted Canada Council money — and wrote a thousand poems; essay. Al Purdy. photo · *Cross Can Writ Q* 1987; Vol 9 No 3–4: p34–35,58–59.

[Untitled]; essay. Janis Rapoport. photo · *Cross Can Writ Q* 1987; Vol 9 No 3–4: p24–25.

Library-use payments not trumpeted; article. Barbara Robson. *WFP* April 1, 1987: p35.

Novelist, poet Kroetsch receives top payment under library fee plan; article. Barbara Robson. *WFP* April 22, 1987: p38.
[LIBRARY SERVICES AND CANADIAN LITERATURE]

La vie littéraire; column. Jean Royer. photo · *MD* March 28, 1987: pD2.
[CONFERENCES, LITERARY; FESTIVALS, LITERARY; RADIO AND CANADIAN LITERATURE; TELEVISION AND CANADIAN LITERATURE]

[Untitled]; letter to the editor. Sarah Sheard. Diane Morton. *Tor Life* Oct 1987; Vol 21 No 1[5]: 12.

Book world: 'I swear by Apollo' and CIA; column. Beverley Slopen. *TS* April 12, 1987: pA20.
[GREAT BRITAIN-CANADA LITERARY RELATIONS]

Letter to the Canada Council; essay. Anne Swannell. *Cross Can Writ Q* 1987; Vol 9 No 3–4: p35.

Dits et faits; column. Adrien Thério. photo · *Lettres québec* Summer 1987; No 46: p6.
[AUTHORS, CANADIAN; CANADIAN LITERARY PUBLISHING; CONFERENCES, LITERARY; LIBRARY SERVICES AND CANADIAN LITERATURE]

Bloc-notes; column. Michel Vaïs. photo · *Jeu* 1987; No 45: p227–231.
[AWARDS, LITERARY; WRITERS' ORGANIZATIONS]

PLR: writers registered and sampling under way; article. Ann Vanderhoof. *Quill & Quire* Feb 1987; Vol 53 No 2: p14.
[LIBRARY SERVICES AND CANADIAN LITERATURE]

A jury of her peers; article about the Canada Council. Ann Wilson. photo · *Can Theatre R* Summer 1987; No 51: p4–8.

Patronage Canadian style; essay. George Woodcock. photo · *Cross Can Writ Q* 1987; Vol 9 No 3–4: p32–33,57–58.

[Untitled]; essay. Elizabeth Woods. *Cross Can Writ Q* 1987; Vol 9 No 3–4: p23.

Writers get their cheques; article. Kathryn Young. *G&M* March 18, 1987: pC3.
[LIBRARY SERVICES AND CANADIAN LITERATURE]

GOVERNOR GENERAL'S AWARDS

Manitoba writer in running; article. *WFP* April 30, 1987: p28.

Hat trick; article. *WFP* May 1, 1987: p33.
[CANADIAN LITERARY PUBLISHING]

Munro short story collection wins award; article. *WFP* May 29, 1987: p34.

Two Calgarians in running for literary awards; article. *CH* May 1, 1987: pE2.

For the record; column. photo · *CH* May 31, 1987: pB4.

Passages; column. *Maclean's* June 8, 1987; Vol 100 No 23: p4.

The Governor General's Awards: winners, finalists, and juries. *Can Theatre R* Summer 1987; No 51: p16.

Awards finalists announced; article. *G&M* May 1, 1987: pC5.

Le prix du Gouverneur général à Yvon Rivard; article. *MD* May 28, 1987: p2.

Montrealer English non-fiction finalist; article. *MG* May 1, 1987: pD1.

Governor General's Award to Munro amid poetry protest; article. photo · *MG* May 28, 1987: pC1.

Governor General's award winners; article. *Quill & Quire* July 1987; Vol 53 No 7: p53–54.

GG shortlist in January; article. *Quill & Quire* Dec 1987; Vol 53 No 12: p14.

Frye finally wins elusive award for best non-fiction book of '86; article. Ken Adachi. photo · *TS* May 28, 1987: H1.

Frye in good position to take Governor-General's prize; column. Ken Adachi. photo · *TS* April 30, 1987: H1.
[AUTHORS, CANADIAN]

Pollock is tops again; article. Brian Brennan. photo · *CH* May 27, 1987: pA1.

People; column. Yvonne Cox. photo · *Maclean's* June 8, 1987; Vol 100 No 23: p46.

The hand that feeds; article. Alan Filewod. photo · *Can Theatre R* Summer 1987; No 51: p9–15.

Poetic licence: G-G's list: what? No women poets?; column. Judith Fitzgerald. *TS* May 10, 1987: pA23.

Making short work of an award winner; column. William French. *G&M* Dec 8, 1987: pD5.
[AWARDS, LITERARY]

Yvon Rivard et Northrop Frye parmi les lauréats des prix du gouverneur général; article. Robert Lévesque. photo · *MD* May 28, 1987: p13.

Prix et distinctions; list of award winners. Gaétan Lévesque. photo · *Lettres québec* Autumn 1987; No 47: p7.
[AWARDS, LITERARY]

La vie littéraire; column. Marc Morin. *MD* Dec 12, 1987: pD2.
[POETRY READINGS]

Munro wins third Governor General's Award; article. Jamie Portman. photo · *CH* May 28, 1987: pC9.

Award nomination 'petrifies' Prairie storyteller; article. Barbara Robson. photo · *WFP* May 23, 1987: p21–22.

Munro wins top literary prize; article. Lisa Rochon. photo · *G&M* May 28, 1987: pD1.

Le CDA dévoile la liste des finalistes; article. Jean Royer. photo · *MD* April 30, 1987: p13.

La vie littéraire; column. Jean Royer. photo · *MD* June 6, 1987: pD2.
[INTERNATIONAL REVIEWS OF CANADIAN LITERATURE; RADIO AND CANADIAN LITERATURE; TELEVISION AND CANADIAN LITERATURE]

Bloc-notes; column. Michel Vaïs. *Jeu* 1987; No 44: p215–218.
[COMPETITIONS, LITERARY; CONFERENCES, LITERARY; RADIO AND CANADIAN LITERATURE]

THE GOVERNOR OF PRINCE EDWARD ISLAND/Short stories by Rick Bowers

Literary 'docudrama' captures the essence; review of *The Orangeman*. Roger Hall. photo · *G&M* Feb 14, 1987: pE19.

People and P.E.I.; review of *The Governor of Prince Edward Island*. Frank J. Ledwell. *Atlan Prov Book R* Feb-March 1987; Vol 14 No 1: p9.

Poignant tales of P.E.I. life give pleasure; review of *The Governor of Prince Edward Island*. Robert M. Seller. *CH* April 5, 1987: pE5.

GOVIER, KATHERINE

[Untitled]; review of *Between Men*. *Can Forum* Nov 1987; Vol 67 No 773: p38.

The fight for love and truth hampered by riddle of past; reviews of *Between Men* and *Getting Married in Buffalo Jump*. Ken Adachi. photo · *TS* Oct 17, 1987: M4.

Frontier women: two tales in search of the perfect marriage; reviews of *Between Men* and *Getting Married in Buffalo Jump*. Ruby Andrew. photo · *Quill & Quire* Sept 1987; Vol 53 No 9: p76.

Unlikely characters populate realistic Calgary urbanscape; review of *Between Men*. Lucinda Chodan. photo · *MG* Oct 24, 1987: J13.

Mawkish history; review of *Between Men*. William French. *G&M* Sept 26, 1987: pC21.

[Untitled]; reviews of short story collections. Carole Gerson. *Queen's Q* Summer 1987; Vol 94 No 2: p483–484.

Memory & words; reviews of *Fables of Brunswick Avenue* and *Bottled Roses*. Michael Helm. *Can Lit* Spring 1987; No 112: p92–95.

Katherine Govier; interview. Brent Ledger. photo · *Books in Can* Nov 1987; Vol 16 No 8: p39–40.

Heart of the city; review of *Between Men*. Kenneth McGoogan. *Books in Can* Aug-Sept 1987; Vol 16 No 6: p18–19.

Book puts Calgary on literary map; review of *Between Men*. Kenneth McGoogan. photo · *CH* Sept 5, 1987: H7.

More surprises from Kinsella; column. Kenneth McGoogan. *CH* Sept 13, 1987: pE5.

[Untitled]; review of *Fables of Brunswick Avenue*. Stephen Regan. *British J of Can Studies* June 1987; Vol 2 No 1: p185–187.

A mating of east and west; review of *Between Men*. Mary W. Riskin. *Maclean's* Oct 12, 1987; Vol 100 No 41: p56h

Novel's reach exceeds its grasp; review of *Between Men*. David Williamson. photo · *WFP* Sept 26, 1987: p64.

GOWAN, ELSIE PARK

CKUA: radio drama and regional theatre; article. Howard Fink. abstract · *Theatre Hist in Can* Fall 1987; Vol 8 No 2: p221–233.
[RADIO AND CANADIAN LITERATURE]

Elsie Park Gowan: distinctively Canadian; article. Anton Wagner. abstract bibliog biog · *Theatre Hist in Can (special issue)* Spring 1987; Vol 8 No 1: p68–82.

GRACE, GREGORY

Ministries of grace; review of *A Sacrifice of Fire*. M. Travis Lane. *Fiddlehead* Spring 1987; No 151: p110–115.

[Untitled]; review of *A Sacrifice of Fire*. Brian Vanderlip. *Poetry Can R* Spring 1987; Vol 8 No 2–3: p43–44.

GRAINES DE FÉES/Poems by Dyane Léger

Dyane Léger, l'enfant terrible d'Acadie; reviews of *Graines de fées* and *Sorcière du vent!*. Gérard Étienne. photo · *MD* July 4, 1987: pC7.

GRANDBOIS, ALAIN

Les Îles de la nuit d'Alain Grandbois: clôture du monde et ouverture du verbe; article. Alexandre Amprimoz. *Can Lit* Spring 1987; No 112: p64–70.

LES GRANDES CORVÉES BEAUCERONNES/Novel by Jeanne Pomerleau

La vitrine du livre; reviews. Guy Ferland. *MD* Aug 29, 1987: pC12.

Ah! les Beaucerons!; review of *Les Grandes corvées beauceronnes*. Benoît Lacroix. *MD* Sept 19, 1987: pD2.

LES GRANDES MARES/SPRING TIDES/Novel by Jacques Poulin

[Untitled]; review of *Spring Tides*. Barbara Leckie. *Rubicon* Spring 1987; No 8: p195–197.

[Untitled]; review of *Spring Tides*. Peter S. Noble. *British J of Can Studies* June 1987; Vol 2 No 1: p182

A crowded Eden; review of *Spring Tides*. Theresia Quigley. *Fiddlehead* Autumn 1987; No 153: p102–103.

Recent Canadian fiction; reviews of novels. D.O. Spettigue. *Queen's Q* Summer 1987; Vol 94 No 2: p366–375. [FIRST NOVELS: BOOK REVIEWS]

A teddy bear's tale; review of *Spring Tides*. Jeannette Urbas. *Can Forum* Jan 1987; Vol 66 No 765: p39–40.

GRANDFATHER HERON FINDS A FRIEND/Children's story by Dayle Gaetz

Mini-reviews; reviews of children's books. Margaret Paré. *Can Child Lit* 1987; No 45: p93–96.

LES GRANDS DÉSORDRES/Novel by Marie Cardinal

De la drogue, de la passion de l'absolu et de l'amour dont toujours tout reste à dire; review of *Les Grands désordres*. Jean-Roch Boivin. photo · *MD* Oct 24, 1987: pD5.

GRAVEL, FRANÇOIS

Benito, vierge et rêveur de profession; review of *Benito*. Réjean Beaudoin. *Liberté* Oct 1987; Vol 29 No 5: p163.

Benito ou la confirmation d'un talent de romancier; review of *Benito*. Yvon Bernier. photo · *Lettres québec* Autumn 1987; No 47: p24–25.

L'histoire d'un homme qui voulait la paix; review of *Benito*. Jean-Roch Boivin. photo · *MD* May 16, 1987: pD3.

À l'impossible certains sont tenus; reviews of *Benito* and *Aaa, Aâh, Ha ou les amours malaisées*. Pierre Hébert. *Voix et images* Autumn 1987; Vol 13 No 1: p192–194.

L'evasion et l'education; review of *La Note de passage*. Robert Viau. *Can Child Lit* 1987; No 48: p95–97.

GRAVEL, PIERRE

Deux fictions sur fond d'histoire; reviews of *La Fin de l'histoire* and *L'Amour de Jeanne*. Yvon Bernier. photo · *Lettres québec* Winter 1986–87; No 44: p31–33.

Qui a peur des héritiers de Papineau?; review of *La Fin de l'histoire*. Paul-André Comeau. *MD* March 14, 1987: pD7.

Écrire l'histoire ou histoire d'écrire; reviews of novels. Jacques Michon. *Voix et images* Spring 1987; Vol 12 No 3: p548–550.

GRAVES, WARREN

Actor hopes Rubbish exudes innocent joy; biographical article. Bob Blakey. photo · *CH* April 3, 1987: pC11.

The Last Real Summer a 'warm,' faded memory; article. Keith Bolender. *TS (Neighbours)* Jan 27, 1987: p20.

'Memory play' takes woman to childhood; article. Alex Law. *TS (Neighbors)* Nov 24, 1987: p16.

This play doesn't come to life; theatre review of *The Last Real Summer*. Alex Law. *TS (Neighbors)* Dec 8, 1987: p19.

Audience relishes stale farce; theatre review of *The Hand That Cradles the Rock*. Kate Zimmerman. *CH* May 3, 1987: pE2.

GRAY, GENE

Tired dreams and holy fools; theatre review of *Unexpected Moves*. Ray Conlogue. photo · *G&M* Oct 28, 1987: pC7.

Unexpected Moves jaunty little comedy; theatre review. Robert Crew. photo · *TS* Oct 28, 1987: pE2.

GRAY, JOHN

The very best of company: perceptions of a Canadian attitude towards war and nationalism in three contemporary plays; article. John S. Bolin. *Amer R of Can Studies* Autumn 1987; Vol 17 No 3: p309–322. [CANADIAN DRAMA: HISTORY AND CRITICISM; CULTURAL IDENTITY]

Language and structure in Billy Bishop Goes To War; article. Jean MacIntyre. *Can Drama* 1987; Vol 13 No 1: p50–59.

Playwright goes to war on conservative theatre; article. Martin Morrow. *CH* Oct 31, 1987: H4.

GREAT BRITAIN-CANADA LITERARY RELATIONS

The mermaid inn: when BritLit meets CanLit; essay. Katherine Govier. photo · *G&M* Jan 17, 1987: pD6.

Canadian content in England; essay. Monica Hughes. *Quill & Quire (Books for Young People)* April 1987; Vol 53 No 4: p4.

Book world: 'I swear by Apollo' and CIA; column. Beverley Slopen. *TS* April 12, 1987: pA20. [GOVERNMENT GRANTS FOR WRITERS/PUBLISHERS]

THE GREAT WAR OF WORDS: BRITISH, AMERICAN, AND CANADIAN PROPAGANDA AND FICTION, 1914–1933/Critical work by Peter Buitenhuis

[Untitled]; review of *The Great War of Words*. Martin Dowding. *Quill & Quire* Nov 1987; Vol 53 No 11: p25.

Propagandists had huge impact; article. John Ferri. *TS* Nov 8, 1987: pA16.

First World War propaganda undermined truth about second; article. John Ferri. photo · *CH* Nov 11, 1987: pA5.

Fighting words; review of *The Great War of Words*. David Glassco. *Can Forum* Nov 1987; Vol 67 No 773: p36–37.

Writers of the 'foul literature of glory'; review of *The Great War of Words*. Sandra Martin. *G&M* Oct 24, 1987: pC19.

Hyping the good fight; review of *The Great War of Words*. Desmond Morton. *Books in Can* Nov 1987; Vol 16 No 8: p14–15.

Writers at war found wanting; review of *The Great War of Words*. Robert Saunders. *WFP* Nov 7, 1987: p54.

GREEN EYES, DUKES & KINGS/Short stories by Michael Rawdon

[Untitled]; review of *Green Eyes, Dukes & Kings*. *Queen's Q* Spring 1987; Vol 94 No 1: p253–254.

Rare/fear; reviews of *Green Eyes, Dukes & Kings* and *The Book of Fears*. Thomas Gerry. *Can Lit* Spring 1987; No 112: p107–108

New Albertan fiction; reviews of *Green Eyes, Dukes & Kings* and *Frogs*. M.L. Scott. *NeWest R* Summer 1987; Vol 12 No 10: p12.

THE GREEN GABLES DETECTIVES/Young adult novel by Eric Wilson

[Untitled]; review of *The Green Gables Detectives*. Fran Geitzler. *CH* Dec 6, 1987: pD9.

[Untitled]; reviews of *The Green Gables Detectives* and *The Loon Lake Murders*. Linda Granfield. *Quill & Quire (Books for Young People)* Aug 1987; Vol 53 No 8: p5–6.

The New World and the Old World for children; review of *The Green Gables Detectives*. Rosi Jory. *Atlan Prov Book R* Nov-Dec 1987; Vol 14 No 4: p4.

Baby of the family gets respect raising flock of Canada geese; reviews of children's books. Janice Kennedy. *MG* Oct 3, 1987: J13.

GREEN, H. GORDON

[Untitled]; review of *The Devil Is Innocent*. David A. Reid. *Quill & Quire* Jan 1987; Vol 53 No 1: p27.

GREEN, JIM

[Untitled]; reviews of *The Louis Riel Organ & Piano Co.* and *The North Book*. John F. Vardon. *Poetry Can R* Spring 1987; Vol 8 No 2–3: p47.

GREEN, JOHN F.

[Untitled]; review of *There's a Dragon in My Closet*. Teresa Cowan. *Quill & Quire (Books for Young People)* April 1987; Vol 53 No 4: p5.

World of fantasy important to kids Oshawa writer says; article. Alex Law. photo · *TS (Neighbours)* Feb 24, 1987: p16.

Thrills and chills: hints for Hallowe'en reading; reviews of children's books. Joan McGrath. illus · *Quill & Quire (Books for Young People)* Oct 1987; Vol 53 No 10: p8.
[ANTHOLOGIES: BOOK REVIEWS]

Mini-reviews; reviews of children's stories. Mary Rubio. *Can Child Lit* 1987; No 46: p105–109.

Escape from reality; review of *There's a Dragon in My Closet*. Tim Wynne-Jones. *G&M* April 18, 1987: pC18.

GREEN, TERENCE M.

[*The Woman Who Is the Midnight Wind*]; review. Alison Sutherland. *Atlan Prov Book R* May-June 1987; Vol 14 No 2: p9.

The price of progress; review of *The Woman Who Is the Midnight Wind*. Joel Yanofsky. *Books in Can* June-July 1987; Vol 16 No 5: p18–19.

GREENAPPLE STREET BLUES/Children's novel by Ted Staunton

[Untitled]; review of *Greenapple Street Blues*. Joan McGrath. *Quill & Quire (Books for Young People)* Oct 1987; Vol 53 No 10: p19,22.

GREENWOOD, BARBARA

Little's achievements simply huge; reviews of *Little by Little* and *Her Special Vision*. Joan McGrath. *TS* Nov 29, 1987: pA21.

GREENWOOD, L.B.

Slain hitchhiker doesn't live up to writer's promise; reviews of *Sleep While I Sing* and *Sherlock Holmes and the Case of the Raleigh Legacy*. Paul Carbray. *MG* Feb 21, 1987: pB8.
[FIRST NOVELS: BOOK REVIEWS]

GRIFF GETS A HAND AND OTHER STORIES/ Children's stories by Kit Hood et al

Taking the Degrassi kids from screen to page; reviews of *Casey Draws the Line* and *Griff Gets a Hand*. Frieda Wishinsky. photo · *Quill & Quire (Books for Young People)* June 1987; Vol 53 No 6: p3.

GRIFF MAKES A DATE AND OTHER STORIES/ Children's stories by Kit Hood et al

From box to book; reviews of *Lisa Makes the Headlines* and *Griff Makes a Date*. Laurie Bildfell. *Can Child Lit* 1987; No 46: p93–94.

LES GRIFFES DE L'EMPIRE/Young adult novel by Camille Bouchard

Faiblesses d'un roman ambitieux; review of *Les Griffes de l'empire*. Alexandre Amprimoz. *Can Child Lit* 1987; No 47: p86–87.

GRIFFITHS, LINDA

Linda Griffiths gives NTS reading tonight; article. Pat Donnelly. photo · *MG* Nov 2, 1987: pB13.
[DRAMATIC READINGS]

GRIGNON, CLAUDE-HENRI

[Untitled]; review of *Un Homme et son péché*. André Marquis. *Moebius (special issue)* Spring 1987; No 32: p119–120.

Grignon plurilingue; article. Magessa O'Reilly. *Voix et images* Autumn 1987; Vol 13 No 1: p123–139.
[STRUCTURALIST WRITING AND CRITICISM]

Un homme plein d'artifices; review of *Un Homme et son péché* (critical edition). Adrien Thério. photo · *Lettres québec* Spring 1987; No 45: p62–63.

GROULX, LIONEL-ADOLPHE

Dits et faits; column. Adrien Thério. photo · *Lettres québec* Summer 1987; No 46: p6.
[AUTHORS, CANADIAN; CANADIAN LITERARY PUBLISHING; CONFERENCES, LITERARY; GOVERNMENT GRANTS FOR WRITERS/PUBLISHERS; LIBRARY SERVICES AND CANADIAN LITERATURE]

Une première traduction de L'Appel de la race; review of *The Iron Wedge*. Adrien Thério. *Lettres québec* Winter 1986–87; No 44: p85.

[Untitled]; review of *The Iron Wedge*. George Woodcock. *Can Lit* Winter 1987; No 115: p290.

GROVE, FREDERICK PHILIP

A wealth of provocative and inspiring literary criticism; reviews. Douglas Hill. *G&M* Sept 5, 1987: pC13.
[ANTHOLOGIES: BOOK REVIEWS]

Grove's "Nationhood" and the European immigrant; article. Enoch Padolsky. abstract · *J of Can Studies* Spring 1987; Vol 22 No 1: p32–50.
[CULTURAL IDENTITY; IMMIGRANTS IN CANADIAN LITERATURE]

"The eternal feminine" and the clothing motif in Grove's fiction; article. Elizabeth Potvin. *Studies in Can Lit* 1987; Vol 12 No 2: p222–238.
[WOMEN IN LITERATURE]

Grove's "Stella"; article. K.P. Stich. illus · *Can Lit* Summer-Fall 1987; No 113–114: p258–262.

GRYN, GOLDIE OLSZYNKO

[Untitled]; reviews of *Come into My Room* and *Hey World, Here I Am!*. Adele Ashby. *Quill & Quire (Books for Young People)* April 1987; Vol 53 No 4: p5.

Sam McGee leads the way in showing the potential of poetry; reviews of children's poetry books. Janice Kennedy. *MG* March 7, 1987: H10.

GRYSKI, CAMILLA

Chitchat; column. Maria Casas. *Quill & Quire (Books for Young People)* June 1987; Vol 53 No 6: p3.

GUAY, JEAN-PIERRE

L'épormyable élan; article. Jacques Folch-Ribas. *Liberté* Aug 1987; Vol 29 No 4: p128–129.

Les quarante ans d'un écrivain québécois; review of *Journal 2, août 1985 —avril 1986*. Yolande Grisé. photo · *Lettres québec* Spring 1987; No 45: p54–55.

La vie littéraire; column. Jean Royer. *MD* April 4, 1987: pD2.
[POETRY READINGS]

[Untitled]; reviews of *Journal*. Jacques St-Pierre. *Moebius* Summer 1987; No 33: p140–142.

GUNETTE, DANIEL

Chronique: soliloques; reviews of poetry books. Marguerite Andersen. *Poetry Can R* Spring 1987; Vol 8 No 2–3: p23–24.

Comme un vent; reviews of poetry books. James P. Gilroy. *Can Lit* Winter 1987; No 115: p260–261.

GUEULE-DE-LOUP/Children's novel by Madeleine Gaudreault-Labrecque

Dans la gueule du loup; review of *Gueule-de-loup*. Léonard Rosmarin. *Can Child Lit* 1987; No 45: p63–64.

GUITARD, AGNÈS

La vitrine du livre; reviews. Guy Ferland. *MD* May 9, 1987: pD4.

GUNNARS, KRISTJANA

[Untitled]; review of *The Night Workers of Ragnarök*. Paul Faulkner. *Quarry* Spring 1987; Vol 36 No 2: p116–117.

GUNNERY, SYLVIA

Living to tell the tale: survival guides for adolescent readers; reviews of *Can You Promise Me Spring?* and *We're Friends, Aren't We?*. Joanne Buckley. *Can Child Lit* 1987; No 46: p78–79.

[Untitled]; review of *We're Friends, Aren't We?*. Lawrence Jackson. *Can Auth & Book* Winter 1987; Vol 62 No 2: p24.

GURR, DAVID

[Untitled]; review of *The Ring Master*. Oliver Conant. *NYT Book R* Nov 1, 1987: p24.

A framework for history; review of [I]The Ring Master. Alberto Manguel. photo · *G&M* Nov 14, 1987: pE1.

GUSTAFSON, RALPH

With these older poets, the strengths are intrinsic; reviews of poetry books. Judith Fitzgerald. photo · *TS* Dec 20, 1987: pE6.

Landscapes & eyes; reviews of poetry books. Karl Jirgens. *Can Lit* Spring 1987; No 112: p192–193.

The dying generations; reviews of poetry books. Dermot McCarthy. *Essays on Can Writ* Spring 1987; No 34: p24–32.

GUTTERIDGE, DON

Old photographs and the documentary imperative; essay. Don Gutteridge. *Can Lit* Summer-Fall 1987; No 113–114: p253–258.

Adventure in corners of Canada; reviews of *St. Vitus Dance* and *Our Hero in the Cradle of Confederation*. Hugh McKellar. *TS* Aug 23, 1987: pA20.

GUY DELAHAYE ET LA MODERNITÉ LITTÉRAIRE/ Critical work by Robert Lahaise

Guy Delahaye, un gamin mélancolique, sourire aux lèvres; column. Jean Éthier-Blais. *MD* Sept 12, 1987: pD8.

La vitrine du livre; review of *Guy Delahaye et la modernité littéraire*. Guy Ferland. *MD* July 25, 1987: pC6.

Le "médecin de Nelligan"; review of *Guy Delahaye et la modernité littéraire*. Marcel Fournier. *MD* Aug 29, 1987: pC14.

LES HÉRITIERS/Novel by Louise Doyon

Les Héritiers (prix Robert Cliche) et L'Écrit-vent; reviews. Noël Audet. photo · *Lettres québec* Autumn 1987; No 47: p19–21.
[FIRST NOVELS: BOOK REVIEWS]

HA! HA!/Play by Réjean Ducharme

[Untitled]; review of *Ha! Ha!*. Marc Côté. *Books in Can* March 1987; Vol 16 No 2: p25.

HAAS, MAARA

[Untitled]; review of *On Stage with Maara Haas*. Barbara Florio Graham. *Can Auth & Book* Spring 1987; Vol 62 No 3: p24

HALEY, SUSAN CHARLOTTE

The fight for love and truth hampered by riddle of past; reviews of *Between Men* and *Getting Married in Buffalo Jump*. Ken Adachi. photo · *TS* Oct 17, 1987: M4.

Toronto firm dramatizes U.S. tales; column. Sid Adilman. *TS* Jan 7, 1987: pF1.
[TELEVISION AND CANADIAN LITERATURE]

Frontier women: two tales in search of the perfect marriage; reviews of *Between Men* and *Getting Married in Buffalo Jump*. Ruby Andrew. photo · *Quill & Quire* Sept 1987; Vol 53 No 9: p76.

Anglos, Ukrainians, Indians mesh cultures in novel set in Alberta; review of *Getting Married in Buffalo Jump*. Barbara Black. *MG* Aug 29, 1987: J3.

Marriage and violence Western-Canadian style; reviews of *Getting Married in Buffalo Jump* and *The Dancing Chicken*. William French. photo · *G&M* Nov 19, 1987: pA25.

Wedding in wheat; review of *Getting Married in Buffalo Jump*. Douglas Glover. *Books in Can* Oct 1987; Vol 16 No 7: p32,34.

Love with the right farm hand; review of *Getting Married in Buffalo Jump*. Sue Hubbell. *NYT Book R* Aug 16, 1987: p22.

Delicacy, humor mark wry novel; review of *Getting Married in Buffalo Jump*. Dave Margoshes. *CH* Oct 11, 1987: pE6.

First novel turned into TV movie; column. Kenneth McGoogan. *CH* May 3, 1987: pE6.
[CONFERENCES, LITERARY; TELEVISION AND CANADIAN LITERATURE]

[Untitled]; reviews of *The Cutting Season* and *A Nest of Singing Birds*. John A. Urquhart. *Prairie J of Can Lit* 1987; No 8: p50–54.
[FIRST NOVELS: BOOK REVIEWS]

Shadow of violence seems out of place in deft, lightly comic novel; review of *Getting Married in Buffalo Jump*. David Williamson. *WFP* Sept 5, 1987: p58.

HALIBURTON, THOMAS CHANDLER

Clockmaker; review of *Recollections of Nova Scotia: The Clockmaker*. Richard A. Davies. *Can Lit* Spring 1987; No 112: p123–124.

Reappraisals; review of *The Thomas Chandler Haliburton Symposium*. R.L. McDougall. *Can Lit* Spring 1987; No 112: p186–188.

HALL, PHIL

[Untitled]; reviews of poetry books. Anita Hurwitz. *Poetry Can R* Spring 1987; Vol 8 No 2–3: p50–51.

HALLORAN, GORDON

Six Palm Trees hilarious, moving family tale; theatre review. Lisa Rochon. photo · *G&M* July 9, 1987: pD6.

HALVORSON, MARILYN

Domingo gave opera company a $40,000 break; column. Sid Adilman. *TS* March 13, 1987: pC19.

Cowboys don't cry . . . except on a movie set; article. Eric Dawson. photo · *TS* Aug 26, 1987: pD1.
[FILM ADAPTATIONS OF CANADIAN LITERATURE]

Rewrites upset author; article. Eric Dawson. *CH* Aug 27, 1987: pC2.
[FILM ADAPTATIONS OF CANADIAN LITERATURE]

Title tattle; column. Martin Dowding. *Quill & Quire (Books for Young People)* Dec 1987; Vol 53 No 12: p3.
[FILM ADAPTATIONS OF CANADIAN LITERATURE; TELEVISION AND CANADIAN LITERATURE]

Book's author original talent; letter to the editor. Mike Kapiczowski. *CH* Oct 13, 1987: pA6.

Olympic festival to open with Wheeler film; article. H.J. Kirchhoff. photo · *G&M* Dec 8, 1987: pD5.
[FILM ADAPTATIONS OF CANADIAN LITERATURE]

Roll 'em, cowboys; article. Liam Lacey. photo · *G&M* Aug 29, 1987: pC1.C3.
[FILM ADAPTATIONS OF CANADIAN LITERATURE]

Youth writers flourish in Alberta; article. Kenneth McGoogan. photo · *CH* Feb 21, 1987: pG1.
[AUTHORS, CANADIAN; CHILDREN'S LITERATURE]

[Untitled]; review of *Nobody Said It Would Be Easy*. Joan McGrath. *Quill & Quire (Books for Young People)* April 1987; Vol 53 No 4: p10.

Beatrix Potter better than ever; reviews of *Nobody Said It Would Be Easy* and *Log Jam*. Joan McGrath. *TS* April 25, 1987: M4.

Authors ease teen angst in the wilds of Alberta; reviews of young adult novels. Susan Scott. photo · *CH* April 23, 1987: pD1.

Roughing it in the bush; reviews of children's books. Mary Ainslie Smith. *Books in Can* Aug-Sept 1987; Vol 16 No 6: p34–36.

Calls to the wild; reviews of young adult novels. Tim Wynne-Jones. *G&M* May 2, 1987: pC19.

HAMBLET, EDWIN

[Untitled]; review of *Littérature canadienne francophone*. Eloise A. Brière. *Amer R of Can Studies* Winter 1987–88; Vol 17 No 4: p449–450.

HAMMERLOCKE/Novel by Jack Barnao (pseud.)

Murder & mayhem: tough guys on clean street; reviews of crime novels. Margaret Cannon. *G&M* Jan 3, 1987: pE15.
[FIRST NOVELS: BOOK REVIEWS]

HAMMERSTROKE/Poems by Don Domanski

Recent poetry; reviews of poetry books. Terrence Craig. *Atlan Prov Book R* Feb-March 1987; Vol 14 No 1: p18

Domanski, Harris, Hutchman; reviews of poetry books. Barry Dempster. *Poetry Can R* Summer 1987; Vol 8 No 4: p31.

[Untitled]; review of *Hammerstroke*. Louise Longo. *Quill & Quire* March 1987; Vol 53 No 3: p74–75.

Rush job, high gloss and high-risk realism; reviews of poetry books. Fraser Sutherland. *G&M* March 21, 1987: pE18.

HAMMOND, MARIE-LYNN

Radio job 'a chance to fulfil a fantasy'; article. Liam Laled]; reviews of poetry books. Anita Hurwitz. *Poetry Can R* Spring 1987; Vol 8 No 2–3: p50–51.

THE HAND THAT CRADLES THE ROCK/Play by Warren Graves

Audience relishes stale farce; theatre review of *The Hand That Cradles the Rock*. Kate Zimmerman. *CH* May 3, 1987: pE2.

A HANDFUL OF TIME/Young adult novel by Kit Pearson

[Untitled]; review of *A Handful of Time*. Annette Goldsmith. *Quill & Quire (Books for Young People)* April 1987; Vol 53 No 4: p10.

School's out, and books are in; reviews of children's books. Janice Kennedy. *MG* July 4, 1987: J9.

Current crop of kids' books is brighter than spring gardens; reviews of *Pop Bottles* and *A Handful of Time*. Joan McGrath. *TS* May 24, 1987: pA19.

Authors ease teen angst in the wilds of Alberta; reviews of young adult novels. Susan Scott. photo · *CH* April 23, 1987: pD1.

Living in the past; reviews of children's novels. Mary Ainslie Smith. *Books in Can* June-July 1987; Vol 16 No 5: p35–37.

Much more than a love story; reviews of *Salmonberry Wine* and *A Handful of Time*. Tim Wynne-Jones. *G&M* June 27, 1987: pE20.

THE HANDMAID'S TALE/LA SERVANTE ÉCARLATE/ Novel by Margaret Atwood

A Swiftian sermon; review of *The Handmaid's Tale*. Ildikó de Papp Carrington. *Essays on Can Writ* Spring 1987; No 34: p127–132.

[Untitled]; review of *The Handmaid's Tale*. Michel Fabre. *Études can* June 1987; No 22: p136–138.

[Untitled]; review of *The Handmaid's Tale*. Michel Fabre. *Afram* Jan 1987; No 24: p54–56.

On Atwood; essay. David Halliday. *Waves* Spring 1987; Vol 15 No 4: p51–54.

Apocalyptic imaginations: notes on Atwood's The Handmaid's Tale and Findley's Not Wanted on the Voyage; article. W.J. Keith. *Essays on Can Writ* Winter 1987; No 35: p123–134.
[THE APOCALYPSE; BIBLICAL MYTHS AND MYTHOLOGY; GOD IN LITERATURE; SATIRIC WRITING]

Margaret Atwood's The Handmaid's Tale and the dystopian tradition; article. Amin Malak. *Can Lit* Spring 1987; No 112: p9–16.
[UTOPIA/DYSTOPIA]

[Untitled]; review of *La Servante écarlate*. Marc Morin. *MD* Nov 28, 1987: pD8.

New & noteworthy; review of *The Handmaid's Tale*. Patricia T. O'Connor. photo · *NYT Book R* Feb 8, 1987: p38.

HANNAH, DON

Going down the road; article. Mark Czarnecki. biog photo · *Books in Can* March 1987; Vol 16 No 2: p13.

HANSCOMBE, GILLIAN

Male myths, obliterated lesbians and powerful dreams; reviews of poetry books. Fraser Sutherland. photo · *G&M* Feb 14, 1987: pE19.

THE HARBINGERS/Poems by Douglas Barbour

Trimly clipped and barboured; reviews of *Visible Visions* and *The Harbingers*. Louis K. MacKendrick. *Essays on Can Writ* Spring 1987; No 34: p39–43.

HARD CONFESSIONS/Short stories by Alexandre Amprimoz

Fabulist fictions fail to get passing grade; review of *Hard Confessions*. Norman Sigurdson. *WFP* Oct 31, 1987: p52.

Little magic; review of *Hard Confessions*. Antanas Sileika. *G&M* Dec 12, 1987: pE9.

HARDWIRED ANGEL/Novel by Nora Abercrombie and Candas Jane Dorsey

Wacky novel competition hits bottom with a thud; review of *Hardwired Angel*. William French. *G&M* Aug 25, 1987: pD7.

[Untitled]; review of *Hardwired Angel*. Norman Sigurdson. *Quill & Quire* Dec 1987; Vol 53 No 12: p25.

Winner is a real stinker; review of *Hardwired Angel*. Morley Walker. *WFP* Sept 5, 1987: p58.

HARLOW, ROBERT

Pissing in the parking lot; review of *Felice: A Travelogue*. Lawrence Mathews. *Essays on Can Writ* Winter 1987; No 35: p147–151.

HAROU, LISE

La passion selon Lise Harou; review of *À propos de Maude*. Jean Royer. *MD* Jan 10, 1987: pB3.

HARRIS, CLAIRE

Guild honors Pollock, van Herk; article. *G&M* May 13, 1987: pC5.
[AWARDS, LITERARY]

Writers Guild of Alberta awards; article. *Quill & Quire* July 1987; Vol 53 No 7: p54.
[AWARDS, LITERARY]

Calgary poet takes $1,000 award; article. *G&M* July 20, 1987: pC9.
[AWARDS, LITERARY]

Mainstreet Calgary; column. *CH (Neighbors)* Dec 2, 1987: pA11, A14–A15.
[POETRY READINGS]

Mainstreet Calgary; column. *CH (Neighbors)* Dec 9, 1987: pA17–A18.
[COMPETITIONS, LITERARY; POETRY READINGS]

Recent poetry; reviews of poetry books. Terrence Craig. *Atlan Prov Book R* Feb-March 1987; Vol 14 No 1: p18.

Narrative tendencies; reviews of poetry books. Phil Hall. *Waves* Winter 1987; Vol 15 No 3: p84–88.

J.P. Donleavy here in '88; column. Kenneth McGoogan. *CH* July 26, 1987: pE5.
[AWARDS, LITERARY; CANADIAN LITERARY PERIODICALS; CANADIAN LITERARY PUBLISHING; FESTIVALS, LITERARY]

[Untitled]; review of *Fables from the Women's Quarters*. Rhea Tregebov. *Fireweed* Winter 1987; No 24: p103–106.

HARRIS, DOROTHY JOAN

[Untitled]; review of *Four Seasons for Toby*. Linda Granfield. *Quill & Quire (Books for Young People)* April 1987; Vol 53 No 4: p9.

HARRIS, MICHAEL

Domanski, Harris, Hutchman; reviews of poetry books. Barry Dempster. *Poetry Can R* Summer 1987; Vol 8 No 4: p31.

[Untitled]; review of *In Transit*. David Manicom. *Rubicon* Spring 1987; No 8: p173–176.

HARRISON, CLAIRE

Claire Harrison plaide en faveur des romans Harlequin; article. France Lafuste. photo · *MD* Dec 12, 1987: pD1,D12.
[ROMANTIC FICTION]

HARRISON, KEITH

A question of taste; reviews of *After Six Days* and *Mario*. Noreen Golfman. *Can Lit* Spring 1987; No 112: p104–107.

HARRY, MARGARET

Sara[h] Jackson's book works; reviews of books by Sarah Jackson. Alexa Thompson. *Atlan Prov Book R* Sept-Oct 1987; Vol 14 No 3: p15.

HART, MATTHEW

Writers must be critical of own work, novelist says; article. Phil Johnson. photo · *TS (Neighbors)* Sept 22, 1987: p20.
[WRITERS-IN-RESIDENCE]

HARTOG, DIANA

[Untitled]; article. *G&M* Oct 31, 1987.
[AWARDS, LITERARY]

[Untitled]; review of *Candy from Strangers*. Susan Glickman. *Poetry Can R* Spring 1987; Vol 8 No 2–3: p42–43.

Western Canadian poets display talents in new volume; reviews of poetry books. G.P. Greenwood. *CH* July 5, 1987: pF7.

[Untitled]; reviews of *Candy from Strangers* and *Second Nature*. Roberta Morris. *Cross Can Writ Q* 1987; Vol 9 No 3–4: p42.

Male myths, obliterated lesbians and powerful dreams; reviews of poetry books. Fraser Sutherland. photo · *G&M* Feb 14, 1987: pE19.

Diana Hartog: poetry beyond revision; review of *Candy from Strangers*. Lola Lemire Tostevin. *Brick* Winter 1987; No 29: p9–13.

HARVEY, KEN J.

Ken Harvey's very short stories; review of *No Lies*. Sheldon Currie. *Atlan Prov Book R* Feb-March 1987; Vol 14 No 1: p16.

HASELEY, DENNIS

Snoring, smuggling, and snuggling; reviews of children's stories. Susan Perren. *Quill & Quire (Books for Young People)* Dec 1987; Vol 53 No 12: p8.

HAVE YOU SEEN JOSEPHINE?/Children's story by Stéphane Poulin

Excellent books for the very young; review of *Have You Seen Josephine?*. Helen Norrie. *WFP* July 11, 1987: p57.

Mini-reviews; reviews of children's stories. Mary Rubio. *Can Child Lit* 1987; No 46: p105–109.

HAVEMANN, ERNST

A farm at Raraba; letter to the editor. Mark Andel. *Atlantic* May 1987; Vol 259 No 5: p14.

[Untitled]; review of *Bloodsong*. Michael Bloom. *NYT Book R* Aug 23, 1987: p16.

A conversation with Ernst Havemann; interview. Joan Givner. biog · *Wascana R* Fall 1987; Vol 22 No 2: p41–52.

Crossing the bar; review of *Bloodsong*. John Goddard. *Books in Can* Dec 1987; Vol 16 No 9: p33,35.

Moving tales of homelands left behind; reviews of *Bloodsong* and *Tales from Firozsha Baag*. Janet Hamilton. photo · *Quill & Quire* June 1987; Vol 53 No 6: p32.

Inside South Africa, fictionally; article, includes review of *Bloodsong*. Ross Klatte. photo · *CH* July 26, 1987: pE5.

Ernst Havemann; interview. Irene Mock. photo · *Books in Can* Dec 1987; Vol 16 No 9: p39–40.

[Untitled]; letter to the editor. Paul Quinnet. *Atlantic* May 1987; Vol 259 No 5: p14

Reflecting South Africa; review of *Bloodsong*. John Shingler. photo · *MG* Oct 3, 1987: J12.

Paperclips: bush league authors . . . much depends on Visser . . . prosaic retirement; column. Beverley Slopen. *Quill & Quire* Dec 1987; Vol 53 No 12: p20.

South African stories convey clear moral vision; review of *Bloodsong*. Morley Walker. *WFP* Sept 26, 1987: p64.

THE HAWRYLIW PROCESS/Novel by Robert Allen

A note on The Hawryliw Process; article. Philip Lanthier. *Matrix* Fall 1987; No 25: p39–40.

HEADFRAME/Long poem by Birk Sproxton

Flin Flons; review of *Headframe*. Robert Hilles. *Prairie Fire* Autumn 1987; Vol 8 No 3: p109–112.

Songs of innocence and experience — the hometown in us all; reviews of *Headframe* and *No Fixed Address*. Scott Jeffrey. *NeWest R* Summer 1987; Vol 12 No 10: p13.

HEADING OUT: THE NEW SASKATCHEWAN POETS/ Poetry anthology

Looking beyond the landscape; review of *Heading Out*. E.F. Dyck. *Books in Can* April 1987; Vol 16 No 3: p34.
[ANTHOLOGIES: BOOK REVIEWS]

Flaws, good work mark collections; reviews of *The Slidingback Hills* and *Heading Out*. Mark Jarman. *CH* April 26, 1987: pE5.
[ANTHOLOGIES: BOOK REVIEWS]

[Heading Out]; review. Peter Stoicheff. *NeWest R* Sept 1987; Vol 13 No 1: p17.
[ANTHOLOGIES: BOOK REVIEWS]

[Untitled]; reviews of *Heading Out* and *Relations: Family Portraits*. Janet Windeler. *Cross Can Writ Q* 1987; Vol 9 No 3–4: p42–43.
[ANTHOLOGIES: BOOK REVIEWS]

HEAR US O LORD FROM HEAVEN THY DWELLING PLACE/Short stories by Malcolm Lowry

Lowry links Greek myth with cautionary tale; reviews of *Malcolm Lowry: Vancouver Days* and *Hear Us O Lord from Heaven Thy Dwelling Place*. Ken Adachi. photo · *TS* July 11, 1987: M4.

THE HEART OF THE MACHINE/Novel by Ian Ferrier

First electronic novel hits computer screens; article. Heather Hill. photo · *MG* Aug 1, 1987: J9.
[PUBLISHING AND PUBLISHERS IN CANADA]

HEARTBREAKS ALONG THE ROAD

See DE L'AMOUR DANS LA FERRAILLE/HEARTBREAKS ALONG THE ROAD/Novel by Roch Carrier

HEARTWOOD/Poems by Gerald Hill

Four poets; reviews of poetry books. Randall Maggs. *Can Lit* Winter 1987; No 115: p280–284.

First books from five regional presses; reviews of poetry books. Colin Morton. *Arc* Spring 1987; No 18: p52–59.

HEAT LIGHTNING/Poems by Robert Hogg

[Untitled]; reviews of poetry books. Martin Singleton. *Cross Can Writ Q* 1987; Vol 9 No 2: p19–20.

HEAVY MINOU/Play by Rachel Moisan

Talk-rock musical sizzles with energy and staging is slick; theatre review of *Heavy Minou*. Pat Donnelly. photo · *MG* Nov 17, 1987: pE7.

HEAVY SEASONING & HEAVENLY BODIES/Poems by Jan Figurski

[Untitled]; reviews of poetry books. George Whipple. *Poetry Can R* Spring 1987; Vol 8 No 2–3: p53.

HÉBERT, ANNE

Filmmaker launches $260,000 lawsuit; article. *G&M* March 20, 1987: pD5.
[FILM ADAPTATIONS OF CANADIAN LITERATURE]

Film-maker sues Cin Video; article. *MG* March 20, 1987: pC4.
[FILM ADAPTATIONS OF CANADIAN LITERATURE]

Les Fous de Bassan à Berlin; article. *MD* Feb 5, 1987: p6.
[FILM ADAPTATIONS OF CANADIAN LITERATURE]

Le Sourd dans la ville sera dans la course; article. *MD* July 14, 1987: p11.
[FILM ADAPTATIONS OF CANADIAN LITERATURE]

Poet-politician wins literary prize; article. *G&M* Nov 20, 1987: pD11.
[AWARDS, LITERARY]

Return of the native son; film review of *In the Shadow of the Wind*. Mark Abley. photo · *Maclean's* Jan 26, 1987; Vol 100 No 4: p54.
[FILM ADAPTATIONS OF CANADIAN LITERATURE]

A piece of the rock; film review of *In the Shadow of the Wind*. Bruce Bailey. photo · *MG* Jan 10, 1987: pG3.
[FILM ADAPTATIONS OF CANADIAN LITERATURE]

Anne Hébert, Wilfrid Lemoyne, Ginette Anfousse reoivent les premiers prix Fleury-Mesplet; article. Paul Cauchon. photo · *MD* Nov 20, 1987: p13–14.
[AWARDS, LITERARY]

[Untitled]; review of *L'Oeuvre romanesque de Marie-Claire Blais*. Élène Cliche. *Voix et images* Winter 1987; No 35: p318–321.

Le Salon du livre de Québec: c'est parti!; article. Hélène de Billy. photo · *MD* April 29, 1987: p13.
[AWARDS, LITERARY; CONFERENCES, LITERARY]

Mais Anne Hébert était là; article. Hélène de Billy. *MD* May 4, 1987: p9–10.

Idéologie féministe dans Le Temps sauvage et C'tait avant la guerre l'Anse Gilles; article. Monique Genuist. abstract · *Theatre Hist in Can (special issue)* Spring 1987; Vol 8 No 1: p49–58.
[FEMINIST DRAMA]

Le Sourd dans la ville, de Mireille Dansereau, est bien accueilli à la Mostra de Venise; article. Jean-Noël Gillet. *MD* Sept 9, 1987: p13.
[FILM ADAPTATIONS OF CANADIAN LITERATURE]

[Untitled]; review of *Anne Hébert: architexture romanesque*. Mary Jean Green. *Amer R of Can Studies* Spring 1987; Vol 17 No 1: p115–116.

Schéma actantiel d'un pseudo-récit: le Torrent d'Anne Hébert; article. Laure Hesbois. *Voix et images* Autumn 1987; Vol 13 No 1: p104–114.
[STRUCTURALIST WRITING AND CRITICISM]

Les Fous de Bassan se cassent le bec sur un vrai mur; article. Robert Lévesque. *MD* Feb 25, 1987: p1,12.
[FILM ADAPTATIONS OF CANADIAN LITERATURE]

Le sourd dans la ville, de Mireille Dansereau: près du roman mais loin de l'inspiration; film review. Robert Lévesque. *MD* Sept 19, 1987: pA7.
[FILM ADAPTATIONS OF CANADIAN LITERATURE]

[Untitled]; review of *Anne Hébert: architexture romanesque*. Jean Marmier. *Études can* June 1987; No 22: p133–134.

Son trac le plus fou, Anne Hébert le ressent devant la page blanche; article. Johanne Roy. photo · *MD* May 1, 1987: p12.
[CONFERENCES, LITERARY]

Bonne anné, Anne Hébert!; editorial. Jean Royer. *MD* Jan 5, 1987: p10.

Roger Bellemare: de la musique sur des poèmes de Miron et Anne Hébert; article. Jean Royer. photo · *MD* May 20, 1987: p12.

Repression, obsession and re-emergence in Hébert's Les Fous de Bassan; article. Kathryn Slott. *Amer R of Can Studies* Autumn 1987; Vol 17 No 3: p297–307.
[FEMINIST WRITING AND CRITICISM]

HÉBERT, BERNAR

[Untitled]; theatre review of *Fiction*. Diane Pavlovic. photo · *Jeu* 1987; No 44: p151–153.

HÉBERT, François

François Hébert, moraliste sans morale; reviews of *L'Homme aux maringouins* and *Le Dernier chant de l'avant-dernier dodo*. Jean Royer. *MD* Feb 7, 1987: pB3.

François Hébert: un auteur derrière sa pipe; article. Jean Royer. photo · *MD* Feb 14, 1987: pC1,C6.

HÉBERT, MAURICE

Des revues presque indispensables; reviews of periodicals. Adrien Thério. *Lettres québec* Autumn 1987; No 47: p63–65.
[CANADIAN LITERARY PERIODICALS]

HEIDBREDER, ROBERT

Meaningful nonsense; reviews of children's books. Adrienne Kertzer. *Can Lit* Winter 1987; No 115: p165–167.

HEKKANEN, ERNEST

Stories of the medieval in the present day; reviews of *Beneath the Western Slopes* and *Medieval Hour in the Author's Mind*. Clark Blaise. *Quill & Quire* June 1987; Vol 53 No 6: p34.

Morbid stories confront human spirit; review of *Medieval Hour in the Author's Mind*. Cecelia Frey. *CH* June 21, 1987: pE5.

Powerful imagery impresses; review of *Medieval Hour in the Author's Mind*. Maggie Helwig. *TS* June 28, 1987: pA18.

HELLBOUND TRAIN/Play by Roxanne Hill

Two one-person shows long on self-indulgence; theatre review of *Hellbound Train*. Vit Wagner. *TS* Nov 11, 1987: H5.

HELLER, LIANE

[Untitled]; reviews of *Who's to Say?* and *Shaking the Dreamland Tree*. Susan Glickman. *Poetry Can R* Summer 1987; Vol 8 No 4: p32.

Young poets on display; reviews of poetry books. Robert Quickenden. photo · *WFP* March 14, 1987: p52.

[Untitled]; reviews of poetry books. Martin Singleton. *Cross Can Writ Q* 1987; Vol 9 No 3–4: p38–39.

HELMET OF FLESH/Novel by Scott Symons

Scott Symons and the strange case of Helmet of Flesh; article. Peter Buitenhuis. *West Coast R* Spring 1987; Vol 21 No 4: p59–72.

[Untitled]; review of *Helmet of Flesh*. Jones. *Rubicon* Spring 1987; No 8: p199–202.

The immoralist; review of *Helmet of Flesh*. Sam Solecki. *Can Lit* Winter 1987; No 115: p146–148.

HELWIG, DAVID

Sainty, beloved bishop relives past as he lies dying; review of *The Bishop*. Barbara Black. *MG* Sept 19, 1987: J8

Maple Leaf memories in print; reviews of *The Bishop* and *The Glassy Sea*. Lew Gloin. *TS* July 12, 1987: pA18.

A humanistic vision of the lives of churchmen and women; reviews of *The Glassy Sea* and *The Bishop*. Douglas Hill. *G&M* Sept 12, 1987: pC17.

Death with the proper shaman; review of *The Bishop*. John Leggett. *NYT Book R* Jan 11, 1987: p23.

HELWIG, MAGGIE

Four poets; reviews of poetry books. Randall Maggs. *Can Lit* Winter 1987; No 115: p280–284.

HÉMON, LOUIS

Les trois Marias; article. *MD* April 16, 1987: p15.
[CANADIAN LITERARY LANDMARKS]

Guérin publie Louis Hémon; article. *MD* Aug 26, 1987: p11.

Le Musée Louis-Hémon voile "l'hymen" de Maria Chapdelaine; article. *MD* Nov 28, 1987: pA7.
[CANADIAN LITERARY LANDMARKS]

Furore raised over statue; article. photo · *CH* Dec 3, 1987: pF5.

Un livre comme Hémon: secret, magique, introuvable; column. Jean Éthier-Blais. *MD* May 30, 1987: pD8.
[FILM ADAPTATIONS OF CANADIAN LITERATURE]

L'illustration de Maria Chapdelaine: les lectures de Suzor-Côté et Clarence Gagnon; article. Sylvie Bernier. illus · *Can Lit* Summer-Fall 1987; No 113–114: p76–90.

Les connivences implicites entre le texte et l'image: le cas Maria Chapdelaine; article. Gabrielle Gourdeau. *Can Lit* Summer-Fall 1987; No 113–114: p93–107.

D'autres classiques; letter to the editor. Joséphine Pouliot. *MD* June 16, 1987: p10.

La vie littéraire; column. Jean Royer. photo · *MD* Jan 10, 1987: pB2.
[AWARDS, LITERARY; POETRY READINGS; RADIO AND CANADIAN LITERATURE; TELEVISION AND CANADIAN LITERATURE; WRITERS' WORKSHOPS]

[Untitled]; reviews of *Itinéraire de Liverpool à Québec* and *Colloque Louis Hémon*. B.-Z. Shek. *U of Toronto Q* Fall 1987; Vol 57 No 1: p179–182.

HENDEN, NEIL

[Untitled]; reviews of poetry books. James McElroy. *Poetry Can R* Fall 1987; Vol 9 No 1: p36.

[Untitled]; review of *Donkey Dance*. Howard Tessler. *Rubicon* Fall 1987; No 9: p202–203.

HENEY, JOAN

But where is the poetry?; reviews of *Road Dances* and *Counterpane*. Bruce Whiteman. *Essays on Can Writ* Spring 1987; No 34: p48–49.

HER SPECIAL VISION/Biography by Barbara Greenwood and Audrey McKim

Little's achievements simply huge; reviews of *Little by Little* and *Her Special Vision*. Joan McGrath. *TS* Nov 29, 1987: pA21.

HERBERT, JOHN

Büchner in Canada: Woyzeck and the development of English-Canadian theatre; article. Jerry Wasserman. abstract photo · *Theatre Hist in Can* Fall 1987; Vol 8 No 2: p181–192.
[CANADIAN DRAMA: HISTORY AND CRITICISM; POLITICAL WRITING]

HERE'S TO HIGH HEELS/Poems by Patricia Elliott

[Untitled]; reviews of poetry books. Lavinia Inbar. illus · *Poetry Can R* Spring 1987; Vol 8 No 2–3: p51–53.

A HERO TRAVELS LIGHT/Short stories by Lilly Barnes

Zig-zag management; reviews of *Nadine* and *A Hero Travels Light*. Anthony S. Brennan. *Fiddlehead* Winter 1987; No 154: p91–95.

Cruel events; review of *A Hero Travels Light*. Pauline Carey. *G&M* Jan 24, 1987: pE18.

[Untitled]; review of *A Hero Travels Light*. Candace Carman. *Books in Can* Jan-Feb 1987; Vol 16 No 1: p25.

Childhood endured across frontiers; review of *A Hero Travels Light*. Maggie Helwig. *TS* Feb 21, 1987: M6.

HEROINE/Novel by Gail Scott

Me, myself, and I; reviews of first novels. Janice Kulyk Keefer. *Books in Can* Oct 1987; Vol 16 No 7: p35–36,38.
[FIRST NOVELS: BOOK REVIEWS]

[Untitled]; review of *Heroine*. Constance Rooke. *Malahat R* Dec 1987; No 81: p103.
[FIRST NOVELS: BOOK REVIEWS]

A daring invention of a new character; review of *Heroine*. Rosemary Sullivan. *G&M* Sept 19, 1987: pC19.
[FIRST NOVELS: BOOK REVIEWS]

HERTEL, FRANÇOIS

François Hertel (1905–1985); obituary. Jean Éthier-Blais. *Can Lit* Spring 1987; No 112: p218–221.

La statue de François Hertel; review of *Hertel, l'homme et l'oeuvre*. Réjean Beaudoin. *Liberté* Feb 1987; Vol 29 No 1: p100–104.

Un oeil ouvert sur le monde, l'autre ferm sur soi; review of *Hertel, l'homme et l'oeuvre*. Yolande Gris. photo · *Lettres québec* Winter 1986–87; No 44: p60–61.

[Untitled]; review of *Hertel, l'homme et l'oeuvre*. Robert Major. *U of Toronto Q* Fall 1987; Vol 57 No 1: p185–186

À propos de Jean Tétreau, Hertel l'homme et l'oeuvre; review. Guylaine Massoutre. *Voix et images* Spring 1987; Vol 12 No 3: p527–530.

La vie littéraire; column. Jean Royer. photo · *MD* May 16, 1987: pD2.
[AWARDS, LITERARY; CONFERENCES, LITERARY; PUBLISHING AND PUBLISHERS IN CANADA; RADIO AND CANADIAN LITERATURE; TELEVISION AND CANADIAN LITERATURE]

Dits et faits; column. Adrien Thério. photo · *Lettres québec* Summer 1987; No 46: p6.
[AUTHORS, CANADIAN; CANADIAN LITERARY PUBLISHING; CONFERENCES, LITERARY; GOVERNMENT GRANTS FOR WRITERS/PUBLISHERS; LIBRARY SERVICES AND CANADIAN LITERATURE]

[Untitled]; review of *Hertel, l'homme et l'oeuvre*. Agnes Whitfield. *Queen's Q* Autumn 1987; Vol 94 No 3: p687–688.

HERTEL, L'HOMME ET L'OEUVRE/Critical work by Jean Tétreau

La statue de François Hertel; review of *Hertel, l'homme et l'oeuvre*. Réjean Beaudoin. *Liberté* Feb 1987; Vol 29 No 1: p100–104.

Un oeil ouvert sur le monde, l'autre ferm sur soi; review of *Hertel, l'homme et l'oeuvre*. Yolande Gris. photo · *Lettres québec* Winter 1986–87; No 44: p60–61.

[Untitled]; review of *Hertel, l'homme et l'oeuvre*. Robert Major. *U of Toronto Q* Fall 1987; Vol 57 No 1: p185–186.

À propos de Jean Tétreau, Hertel l'homme et l'oeuvre; review. Guylaine Massoutre. *Voix et images* Spring 1987; Vol 12 No 3: p527–530.

[Untitled]; review of *Hertel, l'homme et l'oeuvre*. Agnes Whitfield. *Queen's Q* Autumn 1987; Vol 94 No 3: p687–688.

HERTZ, KENNETH V.

Airline scrambling to send poet home; article. photo · *MG* May 29, 1987: pA3.

Parkinson's victim: new hope for survival; article. Nicholas Regush. photo · *MG* April 24, 1987: pA1,A5.

Victim of Parkinson's is too weak for surgery; article. Nicholas Regush. *MG* May 21, 1987: pA1.

Poet Hertz too weak for surgery in Mexico; article. Nicholas Regush. photo · *MG* May 28, 1987: pA1,A5.

Feeding on glimmers of hope; article. Nicholas Regush. photo · *MG* May 30, 1987: pB1.

Poet still hoping for last-chance surgery; article. Nicholas Regush. *MG* June 1, 1987: pA3.

Montreal poet hopes for second shot at surgery; article. Nicholas Regush. *MG* Oct 28, 1987: pA6.

Cairo professor in Westmount synagogue as guest speaker; column. Thomas Schnurmacher. *MG* April 30, 1987: pE2.
[POETRY READINGS]

Meatball Al guards pearly gates in adolescent farce; column. Thomas Schnurmacher. *MG* May 7, 1987: pD12.

HESSE, M.G.

Bonds of dignity; review of *Gabrielle Roy*. Paul Socken. *Can Lit* Winter 1987; No 115: p193–194.

LES HEURES/Poems by Fernand Ouellette

Ouellette et Royer: depuis la mort jusqu'à l'amour . . . ; reviews of *Les Heures* and *Depuis l'amour*. Jean Éthier-Blais. *MD* June 27, 1987: pC9.

[Untitled]; review of *Les Heures*. Pierre-Justin Déry. *Estuaire* Summer 1987; No 45: p55–57.

La vitrine du livre; reviews. Jean Royer. *MD* April 11, 1987: pD2.
[CANADIAN LITERARY PERIODICALS]

"Regarder le monde et découvrir ce qui attend de naître": Fernand Ouellette et le retour de la poésie; article. Jean Royer. photo · *MD* June 13, 1987: pD1,D8.

L'amour la mort; reviews of poetry books. Robert Yergeau. photo · *Lettres québec* Summer 1987; No 46: p37–38.

HEUREUSEMENT, ICI IL Y A LA GUERRE/Poems by Normand de Bellefeuille

La vitrine du livre; reviews of *Hommes* and *Heureusement, ici il y a la guerre*. Guy Ferland. *MD* Oct 17, 1987: pD4.

HEWARD, JOHN

[Untitled]; review of *Instructions*. Stephen Scobie. *Malahat R* Dec 1987; No 81: p106.

HEY WORLD, HERE I AM!/Children's poems by Jean Little

[Untitled]; reviews of *Come into My Room* and *Hey World, Here I Am!*. Adele Ashby. *Quill & Quire (Books for Young People)* April 1987; Vol 53 No 4: p5.

Sam McGee leads the way in showing the potential of poetry; reviews of children's poetry books. Janice Kennedy. *MG* March 7, 1987: H10.

Christine 'truly enjoyed' this book; review of *Hey World, Here I Am!*. Christine Sekulic. *TS* Feb 1, 1987: pA20.

Wit, enjoyment and urgency; reviews of children's poetry books. Tim Wynne-Jones. *G&M* Feb 7, 1987: pE19.

HEYN, GREGORY

Insight Theatre offers 2 plays; article. *TS (Neighbors)* July 28, 1987: p16.

Insight Theatre shows get better and better; theatre review of *Whispers of Moonlight*. Robert Davis. *TS (Neighbors)* Aug 11, 1987: p16.

Visually impaired tread the boards; article. Phil Johnson. photo · *TS (Neighbors)* July 28, 1987: p16.

HIBBERT, ALUN

Beyond the Fringe; reviews of plays. Judith Rudakoff. *Books in Can* March 1987; Vol 16 No 2: p18.

HICKS, CAITLIN

Six Palm Trees hilarious, moving family tale; theatre review. Lisa Rochon. photo · *G&M* July 9, 1987: pD6

HICKS, JOHN V.

Seeker & finder; reviews of *Canada Gees Mate for Life* and *Rootless Tree*. Bruce Whiteman. *Can Lit* Winter 1987; No 115: p148–150.

HIDDEN GOLD MYSTERY/Young adult novel by Marion Crook

[Untitled]; review of *Hidden Gold Mystery*. Peter Carver. *Quill & Quire (Books for Young People)* June 1987; Vol 53 No 6: p10.

How suspense dies when it is misused; reviews of young adult novels. Tim Wynne-Jones. *G&M* Aug 8, 1987: pC19.

HIEBERT, PAUL

Hiebert's Sarah spread a lot of glee; article. photo · *TS* Sept 9, 1987: pB2.

Sarah Binks creator Hiebert dies at 95; obituary. *MG* Sept 8, 1987: pB5.

Humorist Hiebert won Leacock medal; obituary. photo · *WFP* Sept 8, 1987: p10.

The father of Sarah Binks; editorial. *WFP* Sept 9, 1987: p6.

Hiebert remembered as wise man, humorist; article. *WFP* Sept 9, 1987: p36.

Humorist won medal for his fictional poet; obituary. *CH* Sept 8, 1987: pC3.

Manitoba humorist won Leacock award; obituary. photo *G&M* Sept 8, 1987: pA19.

Passages; column. *Maclean's* Sept 21, 1987; Vol 100 No 38: p4.

Paul Hiebert author wrote Sarah Binks; obituary. Paul Bilodeau. photo · *TS* Sept 7, 1987: pA7.

Paul Hiebert, 1892–1987; obituary. Paul Denham. *NeWest R* Oct 1987; Vol 13 No 2: p1.

Editorial. Brenda Riches. *Grain* Winter 1987; Vol 15 No 4: p5.

HIGGINSON, SHIRLEY

Make way for a fine crop of picture-books; reviews of children's books. Adele Ashby. *Quill & Quire (Books for Young People)* Aug 1987; Vol 53 No 8: p6.

HIGH WIRE SPIDER/Children's poems by George Swede

A trio of poets to tickle a child's fancy; reviews of children's poetry books. Adele Ashby. *Quill & Quire (Books for Young People)* June 1987; Vol 53 No 6: p10.

Wit, enjoyment and urgency; reviews of children's poetry books. Tim Wynne-Jones. *G&M* Feb 7, 1987: pE19.

HIGHWAY, TOMSON

Highway play due in city; article. *WFP* June 26, 1987: p35. [AWARDS, LITERARY]

Friends, relatives book flight for play; article. *WFP* Sept 18, 1987: p31.

Rotary Club stages art show; column. *WFP* Oct 31, 1987: p33. [DRAMATIC READINGS]

Rez role based on '71 rape; article. *WFP* Nov 27, 1987: p37.

Uneven but energetic look at life as a native woman; theatre review of *Aria*. Ray Conlogue. *G&M* March 12, 1987: pC7.

Mikado, B-Movie big Dora winners; article. Ray Conlogue. photo · *G&M* June 23, 1987: pD8. [AWARDS, LITERARY]

Mixing spirits, bingo and genius; article. Ray Conlogue. photo · *G&M* Nov 21, 1987: pC5.

The Rez Sisters lacks a satisfying resolution; theatre review. Ray Conlogue. photo · *G&M* Nov 26, 1987: pA29.

Like a chameleon Kliest breathes life into Aria's women; theatre review of *Aria*. Robert Crew. photo · *TS* March 6, 1987: pD11.

The Mikado hits a high note with seven Dora Awards; article. Robert Crew. photo · *TS* June 23, 1987: pE3. [AWARDS, LITERARY]

Rez Sisters inviting you out for bingo; article. Rosie DiManno. photo · *TS* Nov 20, 1987: pE3.

The trickster theatre of Tomson Highway; article. Daniel David Moses. biog · *Can Fic Mag (special issue)* 1987; No 60: p83–88.
[MYTHS AND LEGENDS IN CANADIAN LITERATURE]

Writer turns back on Bach; biographical article. Kevin Prokosh. photo · *WFP* Oct 31, 1987: p21,31.

Making the prairie connection; theatre reviews. Reg Skene. *NeWest R* Dec 1987; Vol 13 No 4: p16.

Legends on the stage; article. Drew Taylor. photo · *Maclean's* Oct 19, 1987; Vol 100 No 42: p69.
[NATIVE-CANADIAN WRITING AND WRITERS]

Helped on way; letter to the editor. Kathy Watson. photo · *WFP* Nov 29, 1987: p6.

HILL, GERALD

Four poets; reviews of poetry books. Randall Maggs. *Can Lit* Winter 1987; No 115: p280–284.

First books from five regional presses; reviews of poetry books. Colin Morton. *Arc* Spring 1987; No 18: p52–59.

HILL, ROXANNE

Two one-person shows long on self-indulgence; theatre review of *Hellbound Train*. Vit Wagner. *TS* Nov 11, 1987: H5.

HILLIS, DORIS

Two ways of making poetry; reviews of *The Prismatic Eye* and *Walking Slow*. Paul Barclay. *Prairie Fire* Summer 1987; Vol 8 No 2: p56–59.

Landscapes & eyes; reviews of poetry books. Karl Jirgens. *Can Lit* Spring 1987; No 112: p192–193.

A HINGE OF SPRING/Poems by Patience Wheatley

[Untitled]; review of *A Hinge of Spring*. Karen Ruttan. *Poetry Can R* Fall 1987; Vol 9 No 1: p32–33.

HIRED HANDS/Poems by John B. Lee

Writing life; reviews of *Hired Hands* and *What Feathers Are For*. Arthur Adamson. *Can Lit* Winter 1987; No 115: p230–232.

HIRSCHFIELD, JEFFREY

Off-the-wall play hit with audience; theatre review of *Geeks in Love*. Kate Zimmerman. *CH* March 1, 1987: pC5.

UNE HISTOIRE AMÉRICAINE/Novel by Jacques Godbout

Écrire l'histoire ou histoire d'écrire; reviews of novels. Jacques Michon. *Voix et images* Spring 1987; Vol 12 No 3: p548–550.

Le second déclin de l'empire américain; review of *Une Histoire américaine*. Louise Milot. photo · *Lettres québec* Winter 1986–87; No 44: p22–25.

HISTORICAL FICTION

Somewhere — in the Canadian past; essay. Barbara Greenwood. photo · *Can Child Lit* 1987; No 48: p66–68.

Imagining history: the romantic background of George Bowering's Burning Water; article. Edward Lobb. *Studies in Can Lit* 1987; Vol 12 No 1: p112–128.

Canadian historical fiction; review article about *Sounding the Iceberg*. Leslie Monkman. *Queen's Q* Autumn 1987; Vol 94 No 3: p630–640.

Historicity in historical fiction: Burning Water and The Temptations Of Big Bear; article. Carla Visser. *Studies in Can Lit* 1987; Vol 12 No 1: p90–111.

HISTORICAL THEMES

La forêt dans l'oeuvre de Louis Caron: une puissance libératrice; article. Georges L. Bérubé. abstract · *Études can* 1987; No 23: p123–133.
[NATURE IN CANADIAN LITERATURE]

Canadian (tw)ink: surviving the white-outs; article. Gary Boire. *Essays on Can Writ* Winter 1987; No 35: p1–16.
[COLONIALISM; MODERNIST WRITING AND CRITICISM; NATIVE CANADIANS IN LITERATURE]

Die Depression der dreiBiger Jahre im amerikanischen und kanadischen Roman; article. Dieter Meindl. abstract · *Zeitschrift Kanada-Studien* 1987; Vol 7 No 1: p193–204.

Mauberley's lies: fact and fiction in Timothy Findley's Famous Last Words; article. E.F. Shields. abstract · *J of Can Studies* Winter 1987–88; Vol 22 No 4: p44–59.

THE HISTORY OF THE VILLAGE OF THE SMALL HUTS/Play series by Michael Hollingsworth

His historical send-up is 10-year project; article. Liam Lacey. photo · *G&M* May 2, 1987: pC5.

THE HOCKEY SWEATER/Children's story by Roch Carrier

Hockey sweaters and picture books: matching the external image with the inner content; review of *The Hockey Sweater*. Marie-Louise Gay. *Can Child Lit* 1987; No 45: p90–91.

HOCKEYBAT HARRIS/Children's novel by Geoffrey Bilson

[Untitled]; letter to the editor. Geoffrey Bilson. *Can Child Lit* 1987; No 45: p98.

HODGINS, JACK

Ondaatje opens reading series; article. photo · *CH* Sept 25, 1987: pF7.
[FICTION READINGS; POETRY READINGS]

Jack Hodgins is famous for his extravagant tales about the unpredictable characters of Vancouver Island . . . ; review of *The Honorary Patron*. Mark Abley. photo · *MG* Sept 26, 1987: J9.

New novel moves into realism; review of *The Honorary Patron*. Ken Adachi. photo · *TS* Oct 3, 1987: M4.

Hodgins still has the knack; review of *The Honorary Patron*. Donna Coates. photo · *CH* Nov 8, 1987: pE6.

People; column. Yvonne Cox. photo · *Maclean's* Oct 5, 1987; Vol 100 No 40: p56.

A fond look back at the books of autumn; reviews of *The Honorary Patron* and *Swann: A Mystery*. Arnold Edinborough. *Fin Post* Nov 2, 1987: p24.

Mired in reality; review of *The Honorary Patron*. William French. *G&M* Sept 19, 1987: pC17.

Hodgins brings his island into the literary limelight; article. Stephen Godfrey. photo · *G&M* Sept 19, 1987: pC1.

[Untitled]; letter. Anne Hébert. photo · *Brick (special issue)* Summer 1987; No 30: p41–42.

The power of love; review of *The Honorary Patron*. Ronald B. Hatch. *Can Forum* Oct 1987; Vol 67 No 772: p39–40.

Today's assignment: short fiction that's worth a long look; reviews of short story books. Douglas Hill. *G&M* March 14, 1987: pE19.
[ANTHOLOGIES: BOOK REVIEWS]

Jack Hodgins and the sources of invention; article. W.J. Keith. *Essays on Can Writ* Spring 1987; No 34: p81–91.

Humorous Hodgins takes a conventional turn; review of *The Honorary Patron*. Brent Ledger. photo · *Quill & Quire* Aug 1987; Vol 53 No 8: p30.

Too little too late; review of *The Honorary Patron*. Alberto Manguel. *Books in Can* Aug-Sept 1987; Vol 16 No 6: p14.

Return to lotus land; review of *The Honorary Patron*. Susan Swan. *Maclean's* Oct 26, 1987; Vol 100 No 43: p52f

The invention of Jack Hodgins; article. Eleanor Wachtel. photo · *Books in Can* Aug-Sept 1987; Vol 16 No 6: p6–10.

Hodgins loses sense of humor; review of *The Honorary Patron*. David Williamson. photo · *WFP* Oct 24, 1987: p54.

HOGAN-WALKER, MICHELLE

[Untitled]; reviews of poetry books. Elizabeth Woods. *Poetry Can R* Spring 1987; Vol 8 No 2–3: p49.

HOGG, ROBERT

[Untitled]; reviews of poetry books. Martin Singleton. *Cross Can Writ Q* 1987; Vol 9 No 2: p19–20.

HOLD THE RAIN IN YOUR HANDS/Poems by Glen Sorestad

Something in common; reviews of poetry books. Cary Fagan. *Prairie Fire* Spring 1987; Vol 8 No 1: p83–87.

HOLDEN, HÉLÈNE

Aujourd'hui; column. *MD* May 11, 1987: p10.
[FICTION READINGS]

South African journalist finds a tragic answer to question of apartheid; reviews of *Intimate Strangers* and *After the Fact*. Barbara Black. *MG* Feb 7, 1987: pB9.

Airing Canlit chestnuts; review of *After the Fact*. Elizabeth Brady. *Fiddlehead* Autumn 1987; No 153: p103–106.

A rich, feminist novel from Quebec; reviews of *A Forest for Zoe* and *After the Fact*. Geoff Hancock. *TS* Feb 15, 1987: pA19.

A novel approach to presenting her work; column. Thomas Schnurmacher. *MG* May 5, 1987: pB6.

Tip sheet: . . . writers meet; column. Susan Schwartz. photo · *MG* Oct 14, 1987: pC9.
[WRITERS' ORGANIZATIONS]

[Untitled]; review of *After the Fact*. Lorna Scoville. *CH* May 3, 1987: pE6.

Après la guerre; review of *After the Fact*. George Tombs. *MD* June 20, 1987: pD6.

Overpowering ambiguity; review of *After the Fact*. David Williamson. *WFP* April 11, 1987: p60.

HOLLINGSWORTH, MARGARET

War Babies: du théâtre féroce; theatre review. Marie-France Bomais. photo · *MD (L'Express de Toronto)* March 17, 1987: p4.

Playwright avoids 'giving answers'; article. Ray Conlogue. photo · *G&M* March 2, 1987: pD9.

Shuttling between layers of reality; theatre review of *War Babies*. Ray Conlogue. photo · *G&M* March 4, 1987: pC8.

Intelligent writer lost in translating to drama; theatre review of *War Babies*. Robert Crew. photo · *TS* March 4, 1987: pB3.

[Untitled]; review of *Willful Acts*. Linda M. Peake. *Theatre Hist in Can (special issue)* Spring 1987; Vol 8 No 1: p126–129.

HOLLINGSWORTH, MICHAEL

Michael Hollingsworth: making history; interview. Paul Bettis. photo · *Can Theatre R* Fall 1987; No 52: p36–44.

Spoof of Canadian history a riot of fun; theatre review of *The Mackenzie/Papineau Rebellion*. Robert Crew. photo · *TS* April 16, 1987: pC15.

His historical send-up is 10-year project; article. Liam Lacey. photo · *G&M* May 2, 1987: pC5.

Historical satire highly original, funny; theatre review of *The Mackenzie/Papineau Rebellion*. Liam Lacey. photo · *G&M* April 16, 1987: pD6.

THE HOLLOW WOMAN/Novel by Simon Ritchie

Crime; review of *The Hollow Woman*. Newgate Callendar. *NYT Book R* March 29, 1987: p25.

Murder & mayhem: tough guys on clean street; reviews of crime novels. Margaret Cannon. *G&M* Jan 3, 1987: pE15.
[FIRST NOVELS: BOOK REVIEWS]

Urban scrawl; reviews of first novels. Janice Kulyk Keefer. *Books in Can* Aug-Sept 1987; Vol 16 No 6: p33–34.
[FIRST NOVELS: BOOK REVIEWS]

Top felon worth troop of bumblers; review of *The Hollow Woman*. Hugh McKellar. *TS* April 18, 1987: M4.

[Untitled]; review of *The Hollow Woman*. John North. *Quill & Quire* June 1987; Vol 53 No 6: p32.

HOMAGE TO VICTOR JARA/Poems by Patrick White

[Untitled]; reviews of poetry books. Bruce Hunter. *Cross Can Writ Q* 1987; Vol 9 No 3–4: p40–42.

Grief & memory; reviews of poetry books. Peter Stenberg. *Can Lit* Spring 1987; No 112: p169–171.

HOME TRUTHS/Short stories by Mavis Gallant

[Untitled]; review of *Home Truths*. Thomas Healy. *British J of Can Studies* June 1987; Vol 2 No 1: p183–184.

New & noteworthy; review of *Home Truths*. Patricia T. O'Connor. photo · *NYT Book R* Feb 22, 1987: p34

HOMECOMING/Short stories by Veronica Ross

[Untitled]; review of *Homecoming*. D. French. *Books in Can* Nov 1987; Vol 16 No 8: p24.

Betrayal runs through short story collection; review of *Homecoming*. Ranjini Mendis. *CH* Dec 6, 1987: pD8.

UN HOMME ET SON PÉCHÉ/Novel by Claude-Henri Grignon

[Untitled]; review of *Un Homme et son péché*. André Marquis. *Moebius (special issue)* Spring 1987; No 32: p119–120.

Grignon plurilingue; article. Magessa O'Reilly. *Voix et images* Autumn 1987; Vol 13 No 1: p123–139.
[STRUCTURALIST WRITING AND CRITICISM]

Un homme plein d'artifices; review of *Un Homme et son péché* (critical edition). Adrien Thério. photo · *Lettres québec* Spring 1987; No 45: p62–63.

UN HOMME PAISIBLE/Short stories by Donald Alarie

La vitrine du livre; reviews. Jean Royer. *MD* March 14, 1987: pD4.
[CANADIAN LITERARY PERIODICALS]

HOMMES/Novel by Carole Massé

La vitrine du livre; reviews of *Hommes* and *Heureusement, ici il y a la guerre*. Guy Ferland. *MD* Oct 17, 1987: pD4.

HONG KONG POEMS/Poems by Gary Geddes

[Untitled]; reviews of poetry books. Stephen Scobie. *Malahat R* Dec 1987; No 81: p104–106.

THE HONORARY PATRON/Novel by Jack Hodgins

Jack Hodgins is famous for his extravagant tales about the unpredictable characters of Vancouver Island . . . ; review of *The Honorary Patron*. Mark Abley. photo · *MG* Sept 26, 1987: J9.

New novel moves into realism; review of *The Honorary Patron*. Ken Adachi. photo · *TS* Oct 3, 1987: M4.

Hodgins still has the knack; review of *The Honorary Patron*. Donna Coates. photo · *CH* Nov 8, 1987: pE6.

A fond look back at the books of autumn; reviews of *The Honorary Patron* and *Swann: A Mystery*. Arnold Edinborough. *Fin Post* Nov 2, 1987: p24.

Mired in reality; review of *The Honorary Patron*. William French. *G&M* Sept 19, 1987: pC17.

The power of love; review of *The Honorary Patron*. Ronald B. Hatch. *Can Forum* Oct 1987; Vol 67 No 772: p39–40.

Humorous Hodgins takes a conventional turn; review of *The Honorary Patron*. Brent Ledger. photo · *Quill & Quire* Aug 1987; Vol 53 No 8: p30.

Too little too late; review of *The Honorary Patron*. Alberto Manguel. *Books in Can* Aug-Sept 1987; Vol 16 No 6: p14.

Return to lotus land; review of *The Honorary Patron*. Susan Swan. *Maclean's* Oct 26, 1987; Vol 100 No 43: p52f

Hodgins loses sense of humor; review of *The Honorary Patron*. David Williamson. photo · *WFP* Oct 24, 1987: p54.

HOOD, HUGH

Hugh Hood artfully rewrites history of Italian renaissance; review of *Five New Facts About Giorgione*. Mark Abley. *MG* Nov 7, 1987: K12.

Two novels offer pain — and incidental pleasures; reviews of *Death-Watch* and *Five Facts about Giorgione*. Ken Adachi. *TS* Aug 30, 1987: pA19.

Ghosts, gondolas and some fantastical imagining; review of *Five New Facts About Giorgione*. William French. photo · *G&M* Sept 1, 1987: pD7.

[Untitled]; review of *August Nights*. Thomas Gerry. *Rubicon* Spring 1987; No 8: p208–210.

[Untitled]; reviews of *August Nights* and *Jokes for the Apocalypse*. Lesley McAllister. *Cross Can Writ Q* 1987; Vol 9 No 2: p24.

David Suzuki set to tell his story in Metamorphosis; column. Henry Mietkiewicz. *TS* April 12, 1987: pC3.
[WRITERS-IN-RESIDENCE]

Part six of twelve; review of *The Motor Boys in Ottawa*. I.M. Owen. *Idler* Jan-Feb 1987; No 11: p47–49.

Delving into artistic mystery; review of *Five New Facts About Giorgione*. David Williamson. photo · *WFP* Dec 19, 1987: p50.

HOOD, KIT

From box to book; reviews of *Lisa Makes the Headlines* and *Griff Makes a Date*. Laurie Bildfell. *Can Child Lit* 1987; No 46: p93–94.

Fine books for in-betweens; reviews of young adult books. David Williamson. *WFP* Dec 5, 1987: p57.

Taking the Degrassi kids from screen to page; reviews of *Casey Draws the Line* and *Griff Gets a Hand*. Frieda Wishinsky. photo · *Quill & Quire (Books for Young People)* June 1987; Vol 53 No 6: p3.

HORODYSKI, MARY

We have to shout; review of *Mr Spock Do You Read Me?*. Angela Marie Medwid. *CV 2* Summer 1987; Vol 10 No 4: p55–58.

Chapbooks range from good to silly; reviews of poetry books. Robert Quickenden. *WFP* Jan 31, 1987: p55.

HORS CHAMP/Poems by Hélène Dorion

[Untitled]; review of *Hors champ*. Hélène Thibaux. *Estuaire* Spring 1987; No 44: p81.

HORWOOD, HAROLD

Where it's near; review of *Remembering Summer*. Gideon Forman. *Books in Can* April 1987; Vol 16 No 3: p22.

Recapturing flower-power days; review of *Remembering Summer*. William French. *G&M* Feb 12, 1987: pC1.

A reminder 'of the covenant that binds man to moth and star'; review of *Dancing on the Shore*. William French. *G&M* Sept 17, 1987: pD1

God's little acreage; review of *Dancing on the Shore*. Janice Kulyk Keefer. *Books in Can* Dec 1987; Vol 16 No 9: p23–24.

[Untitled]; review of *Remembering Summer*. John Moore. *Quill & Quire* June 1987; Vol 53 No 6: p33.

[Untitled]; review of *Dancing on the Shore*. Norman Sigurdson. *Quill & Quire* Sept 1987; Vol 53 No 9: p80.

Universe probed from the shore; review of *Dancing on the Shore*. Penny Williams. *CH* Oct 18, 1987: pC7.

Novel doesn't make it; review of *Remembering Summer*. David Williamson. *WFP* July 25, 1987: p33.

HOSANNA/Play by Michel Tremblay

Hosanna on high to the queen; theatre review. Robert Crew. photo · *TS* May 27, 1987: pE3.

Hosanna ages with grace and style; theatre review. Liam Lacey. photo · *G&M* May 27, 1987: pC10.

HOSPITAL, JANETTE TURNER

Film rights optioned for Ivory Swing; article. photo · *G&M* June 26, 1987: pD12.
[FILM ADAPTATIONS OF CANADIAN LITERATURE]

Brian Moore's Jesuit priest travels into heart of darkness; reviews of novels. Barbara Black. *MG* March 7, 1987: H11.

[Untitled]; reviews of fictional works. Beverley Daurio. *Cross Can Writ Q* 1987; Vol 9 No 1: p18–19.

Berton's memoirs due out in the fall; column. Henry Mietkiewicz. *TS* June 25, 1987: pF3.
[FILM ADAPTATIONS OF CANADIAN LITERATURE]

[Untitled]; review of *Dislocations*. Martha Ann Mueller. *Queen's Q* Autumn 1987; Vol 94 No 3: p692–694.

New & noteworthy; review of *Borderline*. Patricia T. O'Connor. *NYT Book R* May 10, 1987: p34.

[Untitled]; review of *Dislocations*. Katrina Preece. *Malahat R (special issue)* March 1987; No 78: p151–152.

HOUDE, NICOLE

La vie littéraire; column. Jean Royer. photo · *MD* May 23, 1987: pD2.
[CULTURAL IDENTITY; RADIO AND CANADIAN LITERATURE; TELEVISION AND CANADIAN LITERATURE; WRITERS' ORGANIZATIONS]

Entre la maison, l'eau et le cosmos: l'écriture féminine; reviews of novels. Patricia Smart. *Voix et images* Winter 1987; No 35: p334–337.

HOUR OF THE PEARL/Poems by Rhona McAdam

Thistledown presents prairie poets in full bloom; reviews of poetry books. Christopher Wiseman. *CH* May 24, 1987: pE6.

A HOUSE FAR FROM HOME/Children's novel by Budge Wilson

[Untitled]; review of *A House Far from Home*. Linda Granfield. *Quill & Quire (Books for Young People)* June 1987; Vol 53 No 6: p10.

HOUSEBROKEN/Novel by Leona Gom

[Untitled]; reviews of *Housebroken* and *Private Properties*. Sharon Batt. *Room of One's Own* Sept 1987; Vol 11 No 4: p109–112.
[FIRST NOVELS: BOOK REVIEWS]

[Untitled]; reviews. Beverley Daurio. *Cross Can Writ Q* 1987; Vol 9 No 2: p23.
[FIRST NOVELS: BOOK REVIEWS]

All about women and relationships; reviews of *Housebroken* and *Frogs*. Lesley McAllister. *TS* Jan 3, 1987: M6.
[FIRST NOVELS: BOOK REVIEWS]

HOUSTON, JAMES

The north and its artistic images: a provocative view; review of *Ice Swords*. Thomas Gerry. *Can Child Lit* 1987; No 45: p59–61.

The folly of acting in anger; review of *The Falcon Bow*. Gillian Harding-Russell. *Can Child Lit* 1987; No 46: p74–75.

Native heritage is displayed in three timely books; reviews of children's books. Janice Kennedy. *MG* April 4, 1987: H11.

Book world: Owl magazine publisher wades into film field; column. Beverley Slopen. *TS* Sept 20, 1987: pA20.
[CHILDREN'S LITERATURE; FILM ADAPTATIONS OF CANADIAN LITERATURE; PUBLISHING AND PUBLISHERS IN CANADA]

Back to the future; reviews of children's books. Mary Ainsley Smith. *Books in Can* March 1987; Vol 16 No 2: p37–39.

HOW TO READ FACES/Poems by Heather Spears

[Untitled]; review of *How to Read Faces*. Barbara Carey. *Books in Can* June-July 1987; Vol 16 No 5: p25.

[Untitled]; review of *How to Read Faces*. Stephen Scobie. *Malahat R* Sept 1987; No 80: p140–141.

[Untitled]; review of *How to Read Faces*. Elizabeth Woods. *Poetry Can R* Fall 1987; Vol 9 No 1: p37.

HOWE, JOSEPH

The Anchorage series proceedings: the Sir Charles G.D. Roberts and Joseph Howe symposia; reviews of *The Sir Charles G.D. Roberts Symposium* and *The Joseph Howe Symposium*. Laurel Boone. *Essays on Can Writ* Spring 1987; No 34: 196–201.

HOWELLS, CORAL ANN

[Untitled]; review of *Private and Fictional Words*. Keith Garebian. *Quill & Quire* Oct 1987; Vol 53 No 10: p23–24

Relevant writing; reviews of *Private and Fictional Words* and *More Stories by Canadian Women*. Ann Holloway. *G&M* Nov 28, 1987: pC22.
[ANTHOLOGIES: BOOK REVIEWS]

[Untitled]; review of *Private and Fictionalized Words*. Margaret McGraw. *Books in Can* Nov 1987; Vol 16 No 8: p24.

Totally impenetrable prose; review of *Private and Fictional Words*. Morley Walker. *WFP* Oct 17, 1987: p61.

HUBERT AQUIN OU LA QUÊTE INTERROMPUE/Critical work by Pierre-Yves Mocquais

[Untitled]; review of *Hubert Aquin ou la quête interrompue.* Janet M. Paterson. *U of Toronto Q* Fall 1987; Vol 57 No 1: p182–183.

HUDSON, NOEL

[Untitled]; reviews. Anne Cimon. *Cross Can Writ Q* 1987; Vol 9 No 3–4: p47–48.

Parody & legacy; reviews. Lorna Irvine. *Can Lit* Winter 1987; No 115: p264–267.
[FIRST NOVELS: BOOK REVIEWS]

[Untitled]; review of *Mobile Homes.* Richard Lanoie. *Rubicon* Spring 1987; No 8: p215.

Everything by thought waves; reviews of short story collections. Patricia Matson. *Event* March 1987; Vol 16 No 1: p97–100.

[Untitled]; review of *Mobile Homes.* Dona Sturmanis. *Can Auth & Book* Spring 1987; Vol 62 No 3: p25.

HUGGAN, ISABEL

[Untitled]; review of *The Elizabeth Stories. New Yorker* Aug 31, 1987; Vol 63 No 28: p97–98.

I pledge allegiance to myself; review of *The Elizabeth Stories.* Ellen Currie. *NYT Book R* July 12, 1987: p11.

Do we really escape?; article. Kim Heron. photo · *NYT Book R* July 12, 1987: p11.

Book world: a tip of the hat to small presses; column. Beverley Slopen. photo · *TS* Aug 9, 1987: pA20.
[CANADIAN LITERARY PUBLISHING]

HUGHES, MONICA

Guild honors Pollock, van Herk; article. *G&M* May 13, 1987: pC5.
[AWARDS, LITERARY]

Writers Guild of Alberta awards; article. *Quill & Quire* July 1987; Vol 53 No 7: p54.
[AWARDS, LITERARY]

Books nominated for U.S. award; article. *Quill & Quire (Books for Young People)* Oct 1987; Vol 53 No 10: p8.
[AWARDS, LITERARY]

Canadian content in England; essay. Monica Hughes. *Quill & Quire (Books for Young People)* April 1987; Vol 53 No 4: p4.
[GREAT BRITAIN-CANADA LITERARY RELATIONS]

[Untitled]; review of *The Dream Catcher.* Callie Israel. *Quill & Quire (Books for Young People)* June 1987; Vol 53 No 6: p4,6.

Midsummer doldrums are relieved with engaging, artful activity book; review of *Log Jam.* Janice Kennedy. *MG* Aug 1, 1987: J9.

Youth writers flourish in Alberta; article. Kenneth McGoogan. photo · *CH* Feb 21, 1987: pG1.
[AUTHORS, CANADIAN; CHILDREN'S LITERATURE]

Beatrix Potter better than ever; reviews of *Nobody Said It Would Be Easy* and *Log Jam.* Joan McGrath. *TS* April 25, 1987: M4.

There and back again; review of *Blaine's Way.* Mary Pritchard. *Can Child Lit* 1987; No 46: p66–67.

Authors ease teen angst in the wilds of Alberta; reviews of young adult novels. Susan Scott. photo · *CH* April 23, 1987: pD1.

Science fiction story probes relationships; review of *The Dream Catcher.* Susan Scott. *CH* July 12, 1987: pE4.

Roughing it in the bush; reviews of children's books. Mary Ainslie Smith. *Books in Can* Aug-Sept 1987; Vol 16 No 6: p34–36.

Calls to the wild; reviews of young adult novels. Tim Wynne-Jones. *G&M* May 2, 1987: pC19.

HUGHES, TERRANCE

La vitrine du livre; review of *Gabrielle Roy et Margaret Laurence: deux chemins, une recherche.* Guy Ferland. *MD* Aug 8, 1987: pC6.

HUMPHREYS, HELEN

[Untitled]; reviews of poetry books. Sheila Martindale. *Cross Can Writ Q* 1987; Vol 9 No 2: p20–21.

HUNTER, BERNICE THURMAN

[Untitled]; review of *Margaret in the Middle.* Sarah Smithies. *TS* Jan 18, 1987: pC8.

Bernice Thurman Hunter: a world of wonder from her own past; article. Charles Wilkins. photo · *Quill & Quire (Books for Young People)* Oct 1987; Vol 53 No 10: p12.

HUNTER, BRUCE

Mainstreet Calgary; column. *CH (Neighbors)* Feb 26, 1987: pA5.
[POETRY READINGS]

[Untitled]; reviews of *The Beekeeper's Daughter* and *Midnight Found You Dancing.* Robert Hilles. *Poetry Can R* Spring 1987; Vol 8 No 2–3: p41

The space of images; reviews of poetry books. Lavinia Inbar. *Can Lit* Summer-Fall 1987; No 113–114: p245–247.

HUTCHINS, HAZEL J.

Youth writers flourish in Alberta; article. Kenneth McGoogan. photo · *CH* Feb 21, 1987: pG1.
[AUTHORS, CANADIAN; CHILDREN'S LITERATURE]

Snoring, smuggling, and snuggling; reviews of children's stories. Susan Perren. *Quill & Quire (Books for Young People)* Dec 1987; Vol 53 No 12: p8.

Magical wishes . . . old tales to savour . . . musical rainbow; review of tape version of *The Three and Many Wishes of Jason Reid.* Richard Perry. *Quill & Quire (Books for Young People)* Dec 1987; Vol 53 No 12: p6.

HUTCHISON, BRUCE

Bruce Hutchison — senior scribe; biographical article. Richard W. Cooper. photo · *Can Auth & Book* Spring 1987; Vol 62 No 3: p5–6.

HUTCHISON, JAMES

Chapbooks range from good to silly; reviews of poetry books. Robert Quickenden. *WFP* Jan 31, 1987: p55.

HUTCHMAN, LAURENCE

Domanski, Harris, Hutchman; reviews of poetry books. Barry Dempster. *Poetry Can R* Summer 1987; Vol 8 No 4: p31.

[Untitled]; review of *Blue Riders*. Gerald Doerksen. *Rubicon* Spring 1987; No 8: p222–223.

In voice; reviews of poetry books. Richard Stevenson. *Can Lit* Spring 1987; No 112: p167–169.

HYDE, ANTHONY

Periodical marketers pick Chrétien memoir as top book; article. *MG* Nov 18, 1987: pD1.
[AWARDS, LITERARY]

Findley takes prize; article. *WFP* Nov 18, 1987: p50.
[AWARDS, LITERARY]

The Telling of Lies top of paperbacks; article. *CH* Nov 17, 1987: pE8.
[AWARDS, LITERARY]

Anthony Hyde follows Red Fox; article. Barbara Black. photo · *MG* May 23, 1987: J9.

Hyde is named Author of the Year; article. Matthew Fraser. photo · *G&M* Nov 17, 1987: pD7.
[AWARDS, LITERARY]

A fox shows off its cunning; review of tape version of *The Red Fox*. Frank Jones. *TS* Sept 26, 1987: M4.
[AUDIO-VISUALS AND CANADIAN LITERATURE]

Pair of thrillers . . . giving the Devil his due . . . sci-fi fare; review of tape version of *The Red Fox*. Richard Perry. photo · *Quill & Quire* Aug 1987; Vol 53 No 8: p38.
[AUDIO-VISUALS AND CANADIAN LITERATURE]

HYDE, CHRISTOPHER

Crime writers who use the macabre to maximum effect; review of *Whisperland*. Margaret Cannon. photo · *G&M* Nov 21, 1987: pC23.

[Untitled]; review of *Jericho Falls*. John North. *Quill & Quire* Feb 1987; Vol 53 No 2: p17.

I AM A BEAR!/Children's play by Gilles Gauthier and Linda Gaboriau

Bear gives lesson in keeping identity; theatre review of *I Am a Bear!*. Randal McIlroy. *WFP* Oct 10, 1987: p48.

Actor drawn to play by novelty, challenge of playing a bear; article. Brad Oswald. *WFP* Oct 7, 1987: p39.

I AM MARY DUNNE/Novel by Brian Moore

Board buys rights to novels; article. *TS* Oct 18, 1987: pG4.
[FILM ADAPTATIONS OF CANADIAN LITERATURE]

I AM YOURS/Play by Judith Thompson

Love among the ruins; theatre review of *I Am Yours*. John Bemrose. *Maclean's* Nov 30, 1987; Vol 100 No 48: p65.

I Am Yours wages a comedy war of women; theatre review. Ray Conlogue. photo · *G&M* Nov 18, 1987: pC6.

Thompson play true to form; theatre review of *I Am Yours*. Robert Crew. photo · *TS* Nov 18, 1987: pB1.

[Untitled]; theatre reviews. Gina Mallet. *G&M (Toronto Magazine)* Nov 1987; Vol 2 No 8: p29.

I HAVE TO GO!/Children's story by Robert Munsch

Mini-reviews; reviews of children's stories. Mary Rubio. *Can Child Lit* 1987; No 46: p105–109.

I LOVE MY MOM/Children's story by Caroline Bell

Snoring, smuggling, and snuggling; reviews of children's stories. Susan Perren. *Quill & Quire (Books for Young People)* Dec 1987; Vol 53 No 12: p8.

I SAID TO SAM/Children's poems by Gwen Molnar

Make way for a fine crop of picture-books; reviews of children's books. Adele Ashby. *Quill & Quire (Books for Young People)* Aug 1987; Vol 53 No 8: p6.

I SING FOR MY DEAD IN GERMAN/Poems by Audrey Poetker

Young poets on display; reviews of poetry books. Robert Quickenden. photo · *WFP* March 14, 1987: p52.

Grief and love; review of *I Sing for My Dead in German*. Brenda Suderman. *Prairie Fire* Autumn 1987; Vol 8 No 3: p115–117.

I WANT A DOG/Children's story by Dayal Kaur Khalsa

A girl's best friend is her skate; review of *I Want a Dog*. Roz Chast. *NYT Book R* Nov 8, 1987: p32.

Morgan, May, Melinda: new heroines offer humour and fantasy; reviews of children's books. Bernie Goedhart. *Quill & Quire (Books for Young People)* Oct 1987; Vol 53 No 10: p24.

Youngsters get choice of beautiful books; reviews. Helen Norrie. *WFP* Dec 5, 1987: p57.

I WAS A 15-YEAR-OLD BLIMP/Young adult novel by Patti Stren

Teenage eating problems; review of *I Was a 15-Year-Old Blimp*. Sofiah Friesen. *Can Child Lit* 1987; No 46: p84.

THE ICE EATERS/Novel by Bruce Allen Powe

Much hard sledding through the North; review of *The Ice Eaters*. Max Layton. *G&M* Nov 14, 1987: pE3.

Arctic vs Toronto clash of cultures; review of *The Ice Eaters*. Roberta Morris. *TS* Dec 20, 1987: pE6.

[Untitled]; review of *The Ice Eaters*. Norman Sigurdson. *Quill & Quire* Sept 1987; Vol 53 No 9: p79.

ICE SWORDS/Children's story by James Houston

The north and its artistic images: a provocative view; review of *Ice Swords*. Thomas Gerry. *Can Child Lit* 1987; No 45: p59–61.

ICI RESTENT EN PAIX/Play by Jacques Duchesne

Misères de l'édition théâtrale; reviews of plays. Lucie Robert. *Voix et images* Winter 1987; No 35: p339–342.

IDA AND THE WOOL SMUGGLERS/Children's story by Sue Ann Alderson

Snoring, smuggling, and snuggling; reviews of children's stories. Susan Perren. *Quill & Quire (Books for Young People)* Dec 1987; Vol 53 No 12: p8.

IDENTITY

See CULTURAL IDENTITY

THE IDLER/Periodical

Little literary magazine packs loads of pleasure; article. Nick Auf der Maur. *MG* June 19, 1987: pA2.
[CANADIAN LITERARY PERIODICALS]

Mag's humor may have done it in; article. David Trigueiro. *CH* Dec 18, 1987: pA4.
[CANADIAN LITERARY PERIODICALS]

THE IDLER/Play by Ian Weir

Charming comedy toys with the work ethic; theatre review of *The Idler*. Stephen Godfrey. photo · *G&M* Sept 29, 1987: pD5.

IKONA, GUNA

Poet-artist at Cedarbrae library; article. *TS (Neighbours)* March 24, 1987: p15.
[POETRY READINGS]

IL Y A DES NUITS QUE NOUS HABITONS TOUS/Poems by Claude Beausoleil

La fiction du réel/le réel de la fiction; reviews of poetry books. André Brochu. *Voix et images* Winter 1987; No 35: p322–330.

Il y a des poèmes que nous habitons tous; reviews of poetry books. Robert Yergeau. *Lettres québec* Winter 1986–87; No 44: p36–37.

IL Y A TOUJOURS DES PRINTEMPS EN AMÉRIQUE/Novel by Louis-Martin Tard

Springtime, and some more Malouins; review of *Il y a toujours des printemps en Amérique*. Benoit Aubin. photo · *MG* Oct 31, 1987: J11.
[FIRST NOVELS: BOOK REVIEWS]

Une famille, un coin du monde, un pays; review of *Il y aura toujours des printemps en Amérique*. Alice Parizeau. *MD* Oct 3, 1987: pD3.
[FIRST NOVELS: BOOK REVIEWS]

I'LL BE BACK BEFORE MIDNIGHT/Play by Peter Colley

The Piggery scores a direct hit with scary-funny Canadian play; theatre review of *I'll Be Back Before Midnight*. Pat Donnelly. *MG* July 21, 1987: pD2.

I'LL MAKE YOU SMALL/Children's story by Tim Wynne-Jones

The big menace; reviews of *I'll Make You Small* and *Mischief City*. Sandra Martin. *G&M* Jan 17, 1987: pE18.

Thrills and chills: hints for Hallowe'en reading; reviews of children's books. Joan McGrath. illus · *Quill & Quire (Books for Young People)* Oct 1987; Vol 53 No 10: p8.
[ANTHOLOGIES: BOOK REVIEWS]

LES ILES DE LA NUIT/Poems by Alain Grandbois

Les Îles de la nuit d'Alain Grandbois: clôture du monde et ouverture du verbe; article. Alexandre Amprimoz. *Can Lit* Spring 1987; No 112: p64–70.

ILLUSIONS/Novel by Charlotte Vale Allen

Summer reading for quiet times; review of *Illusions*. Lew Gloin. photo · *TS* Aug 9, 1987: pA21.

[Untitled]; review of *Illusions*. Ann Jansen. *Quill & Quire* June 1987; Vol 53 No 6: p32

Escapes into feminine victimization; review of *Illusions*. Ruth Manson. *G&M* July 25, 1987: pC16.

ILS NE DEMANDAIENT QU'À BRÛLER: POÈMES, 1960–1986/Poems by Gérald Godin

La vitrine du livre; reviews. Guy Ferland. *MD* Aug 29, 1987: pC12.

La voix familière de Gérald Godin; review of *Ils ne demandaient qu'à brûler*. Jean Royer. photo · *MD* Sept 12, 1987: pD3.

ILSA, QUEEN OF THE NAZI LOVE CAMP/Play by One Yellow Rabbit Theatre collective

Rabbit writers team up to parody anti-Semitism; article. Kate Zimmerman. photo · *CH* May 28, 1987: pC15.

Timid pussyfooting defuses play's satirical intent; theatre review of *Ilsa, Queen of the Nazi Love Camp*. Kate Zimmerman. *CH* May 30, 1987: pF5.

IMAGE IN THE MIND: CBC RADIO DRAMA 1944–1954/Critical work by Alice Frick

A megalomania for radio drama; reviews of *All the Bright Company* and *Image in the Mind*. Bronwyn Drainie. photo · *G&M* Nov 28, 1987: pC19.
[ANTHOLOGIES: BOOK REVIEWS]

Book world: 'My year for films': Brian Moore; column. Beverley Slopen. photo · *TS* Nov 8, 1987: pA18.
[CHILDREN'S LITERATURE; FILM ADAPTATIONS OF CANADIAN LITERATURE; PUBLISHING AND PUBLISHERS IN CANADA]

THE IMMACULATE PERCEPTION/Poems by Christopher Dewdney

"Footprints in the snow which stop"; review of *The Immaculate Perception*. Gillian Harding-Russell. *Event* March 1987; Vol 16 No 1: p105–106.

[Untitled]; review of *The Immaculate Perception*. Louise Longo. *Quill & Quire* March 1987; Vol 53 No 3: p75.

[Untitled]; review of *The Immaculate Perception*. Peter O'Brien. *Rubicon* Fall 1987; No 9: p187–190.

Painful scrutiny of relationships; reviews of poetry books. Patricia Keeney Smith. *TS* May 30, 1987: M9.

Poetry, science, mind and religion; reviews of poetry books. Fraser Sutherland. photo · *G&M* Jan 31, 1987: pE19.

IMMIGRANT WRITING AND WRITERS

Who are the immigrant writers and what have they done?; essay. Rosemary Sullivan. *G&M* Oct 17, 1987: pE1.

IMMIGRANTS IN CANADIAN LITERATURE

Grove's "Nationhood" and the European immigrant; article. Enoch Padolsky. abstract · *J of Can Studies* Spring 1987; Vol 22 No 1: p32–50.
[CULTURAL IDENTITY]

IMMUNE TO GRAVITY/Poems by Mary di Michele

Fine lines & fractures; review of *Immune to Gravity*. Ron Miles. *Can Lit* Spring 1987; No 112: p183–185.

THE IMPOSSIBLE SUM OF OUR TRADITIONS: REFLECTIONS ON CANADIAN LITERATURE/Critical essays by Malcolm Ross

[Untitled]; review of *The Impossible Sum of Our Traditions*. Douglas Daymond. *World Lit in Eng* Autumn 1987; Vol 27 No 2: p264–269.

[Untitled]; reviews of critical works. Don Gutteridge. *Queen's Q* Summer 1987; Vol 94 No 2: p464–467.

[Untitled]; reviews of *Studies in Literature and the Humanities* and *The Impossible Sum of Our Traditions* W.J. Keith. *U of Toronto Q* Fall 1987; Vol 57 No 1: p145–148.

[Untitled]; review of *The Impossible Sum of Our Traditions*. Vernon R. Lindquist. *Amer R of Can Studies* Autumn 1987; Vol 17 No 3: p353–354.

IMPROMPTUS/Poems by Ralph Gustafson

The dying generations; reviews of poetry books. Dermot McCarthy. *Essays on Can Writ* Spring 1987; No 34: p24–32.

IN THE FEMININE: WOMEN AND WORDS/LES FEMMES ET LES MOTS CONFERENCE PROCEEDINGS 1983/Conference report

[Untitled]; review of *In the Feminine*. Janice Kulyk Keefer. *U of Toronto Q* Fall 1987; Vol 57 No 1: p201–203.
[CONFERENCE REPORTS: REVIEWS AND ARTICLES]

Body & language; review of *In the Feminine*. Thelma McCormack. *Can Lit* Winter 1987; No 115: p142–144.

IN THE SECOND PERSON/Poems by Smaro Kamboureli

Communication deluxe; review of *In the Second Person*. John Donlan. *CV 2* Spring 1987; Vol 10 No 3: p58–60.

[Untitled]; reviews of *In the Second Person* and *Double Standards*. Joan Ruvinsky. *Rubicon* Spring 1987; No 8: p178–181.

IN THE SHADOW OF THE VULTURE/Novel by George Ryga

Underwing; reviews of *In the Shadow of the Vulture* and *The Quarter-Pie Window*. Ronald B. Hatch. *Can Lit* Spring 1987; No 112: p95–97.

IN THE SKIN OF A LION/Novel by Michael Ondaatje

Fact and fiction make an impressive novel; review of *In the Skin of a Lion*. Ken Adachi. photo · *TS* May 30, 1987: M4.

Ondaatje's latest novel winning raves in Britain; column. Ken Adachi. photo · *TS* Aug 31, 1987: pB5.
[INTERNATIONAL REVIEWS OF CANADIAN LITERATURE]

View from the bridge; review of *In the Skin of a Lion*. John Bemrose. *Maclean's* June 8, 1987; Vol 100 No 23: U10.

Michael Ondaatje gives Toronto its early voice; review of *In the Skin of a Lion*. Lindsay Brown. photo · *MG* June 20, 1987: J9.

Free-fall fiction; review of *In the Skin of a Lion*. William French. *G&M* May 23, 1987: pC21.

Worlds in collision; review of *In the Skin of a Lion*. Michael Hulse. *Times Lit Supp* Sept 4, 1987; No 4405: p948

Ondaatje fuses poetry & history; review of *In the Skin of a Lion*. Marni Jackson. photo · *Chatelaine* Sept 1987; Vol 60 No 9: p10.

Structure eludes Ondaatje's imagination; review of *In the Skin of a Lion*. Mark Anthony Jarman. *CH* Aug 23, 1987: pE4.

Mr. Small isn't here. Have an iguana!; review of *In the Skin of a Lion*. Carolyn Kizer. illus · *NYT Book R* Sept 27, 1987: p12–13.

Serendipity; review of *In the Skin of a Lion*. Linda Leith. illus · *Can Forum* Aug-Sept 1987; Vol 67 No 771: p35–37.

[Untitled]; review of *In the Skin of a Lion*. Alberto Manguel. *Tor Life* May 1987; Vol 21 No 7: p105.

Missed connections; review of *In the Skin of a Lion*. Tom Marshall. *Books in Can* June-July 1987; Vol 16 No 5: p16.

Michael Ondaatje's new novel rocks its way to market; column. Henry Mietkiewicz. *TS* May 21, 1987: pF2.

In the skin of Michael Ondaatje: giving voice to a social conscience; review article about *In the Skin of a Lion*. Barbara Turner. photo · *Quill & Quire* May 1987; Vol 53 No 5: p21–22.

[Untitled]; review of *In the Skin of a Lion*. Aritha van Herk. *Malahat R* Sept 1987; No 80: p134–137.

Michael Ondaatje turns in a memorable performance; review of *In the Skin of a Lion*. David Williamson. photo · *WFP* Aug 29, 1987: p52.

IN THE SPIRIT OF THE TIMES/Poems by Ken Norris

[Untitled]; review of *In the Spirit of the Times*. Rod Anderson. *Poetry Can R* Spring 1987; Vol 8 No 2–3: p43.

Between the sexes; reviews of poetry books. Mary di Michele. *Books in Can* March 1987; Vol 16 No 2: p31–32.

Tellings; reviews of poetry books. Susan Rudy Dorscht. *Can Lit* Winter 1987; No 115: p257–260.

[Untitled]; reviews of *In the Spirit of the Times* and *One Night*. Andrew Flynn. *Rubicon* Spring 1987; No 8: p202–205.

IN THE VILLAGE OF ALIAS/Short stories by Fraser Sutherland

Against the reasoning mind; reviews of *In the Village of Alias* and *Vibrations in Time*. Jon Kertzer. *Fiddlehead* Autumn 1987; No 153: p97–100.

IN TRANSIT/Poems by Michael Harris

Domanski, Harris, Hutchman; reviews of poetry books. Barry Dempster. *Poetry Can R* Summer 1987; Vol 8 No 4: p31.

[Untitled]; review of *In Transit*. David Manicom. *Rubicon* Spring 1987; No 8: p173–176.

INCOGNITO/Short stories by David Young

Raising two worthy books from the dead; reviews of *Kicking Against the Pricks* and *Incognito*. William French. photo · *G&M* Feb 24, 1987: pD7.

THE INCREDIBLE JOURNEY/Children's novel by Sheila Burnford

[Untitled]; review of *The Incredible Journey*. Brooke Willmott. *TS* March 15, 1987: H6.

INCUBATION/Novel by Gerard Bessette

Bar hopping; review of *Incubation*. Rui Umezawa. *G&M* June 20, 1987: pC19.

INDIANS IN CANADIAN LITERATURE

See NATIVE CANADIANS IN LITERATURE

THE INDIGO DRESS AND OTHER STORIES/Short stories by Rona Murray

Women with a past; review of *The Indigo Dress*. Anne Denoon. *Books in Can* May 1987; Vol 16 No 4: p16.

Narrative authority and the economy of secrets; review of *The Indigo Dress*. Janet Giltrow. *Event* Summer 1987; Vol 16 No 2: p121–124.

INDIGO NUIT/Poems by Christiane Frenette

La fiction du réel/le réel de la fiction; reviews of poetry books. André Brochu. *Voix et images* Winter 1987; No 35: p322–330.

[Untitled]; review of *Indigo nuit*. Guy Marchamps. *Estuaire* Winter 1986–87; No 43: p76–77.

LES INITIÉS DE LA POINTE-AUX-CAGEUX/Children's novel by Paul de Grosbois

Un beau roman historique; review of *Les Initiés de la Pointe-aux-Cageux*. Dennis Essar. *Can Child Lit* 1987; No 48: p98–100.

INLAND PASSAGE AND OTHER STORIES/Short stories by Jane Rule

[Untitled]; reviews of short story collections. Carole Gerson. *Queen's Q* Summer 1987; Vol 94 No 2: p483–484.

INNES, CHRISTOPHER

Dramatic fringe; reviews of *Five from the Fringe* and *Politics and the Playwright: George Ryga*. James Noonan. *Can Lit* Winter 1987; No 115: p235–238.
[ANTHOLOGIES: BOOK REVIEWS]

INSIDE A MOSQUITO NET/Poems by Vernon Mooers

Noticing three poets; reviews of poetry books. Terrence Craig. *Atlan Prov Book R* May-June 1987; Vol 14 No 2: p10.

INSIDE OUT/Play by Pamela Boyd

[Untitled]; reviews. Lisbie Rae. *Can Drama* 1987; Vol 13 No 2: p229–231.
[ANTHOLOGIES: BOOK REVIEWS]

INSPECTING THE VAULTS/Short stories by Eric Mc-Cormack

A new and nervy short story writer; review of *Inspecting the Vaults*. Ken Adachi. *TS* Feb 1, 1987: pB7.

Art of darkness; review of *Inspecting the Vaults*. Edna Alford. *Books in Can* May 1987; Vol 16 No 4: p26–27

A voyage into the countries of the mind; review of *Inspecting the Vaults*. Dennis Duffy. photo · *G&M* Feb 21, 1987: pE19.

Stories strange, disturbing; review of *Inspecting the Vaults*. Donald Floyd. *WFP* April 18, 1987: p50.

Excellent illusions, cloying clichés in short-story collections; reviews of *Afternoon Tea* and *Inspecting the Vaults*. Brent Ledger. photo · *Quill & Quire* March 1987; Vol 53 No 3: p72.

[Untitled]; review of *Inspecting the Vaults*. David Manicom. *Rubicon* Fall 1987; No 9: p150–152.

[Untitled]; review of *Inspecting the Vaults*. Steven Slosberg. *NYT Book R* Sept 20, 1987: p26.

Kafka, Addams family creep into these tales of the macabre; review of *Inspecting the Vaults*. Joel Yanofsky. photo · *MG* Feb 7, 1987: pB7.

INSTANT-PHÉNIX/Poems by Gatien Lapointe

La fiction du réel/le réel de la fiction; reviews of poetry books. André Brochu. *Voix et images* Winter 1987; No 35: p322–330.

INSTRUCTIONS/Long poem by John Heward

[Untitled]; review of *Instructions*. Stephen Scobie. *Malahat R* Dec 1987; No 81: p106.

LES INTERDITS/Short stories by Daniel Marcoux

La vitrine du livre; reviews of fictional works. Guy Ferland. *MD* Dec 5, 1987: pD4.

INTERNATIONAL REVIEWS OF CANADIAN LITERATURE

U.S. critics rave over Anne of Green Gables sequel; article. photo · *MG* May 26, 1987: pD10.
[TELEVISION AND CANADIAN LITERATURE]

Mixed reviews for Duddy as musical breathes anew; article. photo · *G&M* Sept 30, 1987: pC7.
[DRAMATIC ADAPTATIONS OF CANADIAN LITERATURE]

Philadelphia gives resurrection of Richler's Duddy Kravitz mixed reviews; article. *WFP* Oct 2, 1987: p24.
[DRAMATIC ADAPTATIONS OF CANADIAN LITERATURE]

J.D. Salinger's biography too tame to cause ripples; column. Ken Adachi. *TS* Feb 2, 1987: pD2.

Findley novel a sell-out in London despite critical vitriol; article. Ken Adachi. *TS* April 6, 1987: pB1.

Ondaatje's latest novel winning raves in Britain; column. Ken Adachi. photo · *TS* Aug 31, 1987: pB5.

Mixed reviews for Tamara; article. Salem Alaton. *G&M* Dec 4, 1987: pD9.

Tamara gets a rave in New York Times; column. Robert Crew. *TS* Dec 3, 1987: pB1.

Tamara, Tamara, they'll love it Tamara; column. Robert Crew. *TS* Dec 4, 1987: pD27.

Film stars stage celebrity bashes; column. Dave Haynes. *WFP* June 19, 1987: p21.

Robert Lepage impose son Vinci dans la Ville lumière; column. Robert Lévesque. photo · *MD* Dec 8, 1987: p11.

CanLit's queen gets one cold shoulder from U.S.; article. Richard Marin. illus · *MG* Jan 31, 1987: pB7.

[Untitled]; reviews of foreign books and periodicals about Canadian literature. Laurie Ricou. *Can Lit* Summer-Fall 1987; No 113–114: p274–275.

La vie littéraire; column. Jean Royer. photo · *MD* May 2, 1987: pD2.
[AWARDS, LITERARY; RADIO AND CANADIAN LITERATURE; TELEVISION AND CANADIAN LITERATURE; WRITERS' ORGANIZATIONS]

La vie littéraire; column. Jean Royer. photo · *MD* June 6, 1987: pD2.
[GOVERNOR GENERAL'S AWARDS; RADIO AND CANADIAN LITERATURE; TELEVISION AND CANADIAN LITERATURE]

Le réception critique du Matou; article. Frances J. Summers. *Voix et images* Spring 1987; Vol 12 No 3: p383–392.

Give my regards to Hell's Kitchen; essay. Peter Eliot Weiss. photo · *Can Theatre R* Fall 1987; No 52: p89–91.

INTERNATIONAL WRITERS' ORGANIZATIONS

International writers' organization concerned with Canada's porn laws; article. *WFP* May 16, 1987: p56.
[CENSORSHIP]

50e congrès u Pen Club; article. *MD* May 12, 1987: p13.

Prisoners and PEN; article. *Quill & Quire* Jan 1987; Vol 53 No 1: p18

International P.E.N.: a world association of writers; article. Marguerite Andersen. *Poetry Can R* Spring 1987; Vol 8 No 2–3: p27.

Critics agree on one thing: peace is paramount; article. Brian Brennan. photo · *CH* Dec 10, 1987: pF1.

Writing: the pain & the pleasure; essay. Timothy Findley. illus · *TS* March 21, 1987: M1,M5.
[CENSORSHIP]

La vie littéraire; column. Jean Royer. photo · *MD* April 18, 1987: pD2.
[RADIO AND CANADIAN LITERATURE; TELEVISION AND CANADIAN LITERATURE]

La vie littéraire; column. Jean Royer. photo · *MD* Sept 26, 1987: pD2.
[AUDIO-VISUALS AND CANADIAN LITERATURE; CONFERENCES, LITERARY; PUBLISHING AND PUBLISHERS IN CANADA; WRITERS' ORGANIZATION]

Crime in the Crimea . . . where glasnost and mystery meet; essay. Eric Wright. photo · *Quill & Quire* Sept 1987; Vol 53 No 9: p75.
[CONFERENCES, LITERARY]

INTERTIDAL LIFE/Novel by Audrey Thomas

Sailing the oceans of the world; article. Lorna Irvine. *New Q* Spring-Summer 1987; Vol 7 No 1–2: p284–293.
[ARTIST FIGURE; FEMINIST WRITING AND CRITICISM; WOMEN IN LITERATURE]

INTIMATE ADMIRATION/Play by Richard Epp

Intimate Admiration has few insights, wooden dialogue; theatre review. Ray Conlogue. photo · *G&M* July 1, 1987: pC5.

Intimate Admiration one big bore; theatre review. Robert Crew. photo · *TS* June 28, 1987: pC2.

[Untitled]; theatre review of *Intimate Admiration*. Keith Garebian. *Queen's Q* Autumn 1987; Vol 94 No 3: p753–755.

Neville to don makeup for new Canadian play; article about John Neville. Jamie Portman. photo · *CH* June 23, 1987: pB6.

Alberta playwright's work squanders talent; theatre review of *Intimate Admiration*. Jamie Portman. *CH* June 29, 1987: pC1.

INTIMATE INVASION

See A CREVE LES YEUX, A CREVE LE COEUR/INTIMATE INVASION — A CONCERNED LOOK AT PORNOGRAPHY/Play by Théâtre Parminou collective

INTIMATE STRANGERS: NEW STORIES FROM QUEBEC/Anthology

Quebec nurses its surrealists; review of *Intimate Strangers*. Ken Adachi. photo · *TS* June 13, 1987: M4.
[ANTHOLOGIES: BOOK REVIEWS]

South African journalist finds a tragic answer to question of apartheid; reviews of *Intimate Strangers* and *After the Fact*. Barbara Black. *MG* Feb 7, 1987: pB9.

Strength from Quebec; review of *Intimate Strangers*. H. Kirchhoff. photo · *G&M* Jan 31, 1987: pE18.
[ANTHOLOGIES: BOOK REVIEWS]

[Untitled]; review of *Intimate Strangers*. Brent Ledger. *Quill & Quire* Feb 1987; Vol 53 No 2: p17.
[ANTHOLOGIES: BOOK REVIEWS]

Quebec's literary lights shed old traditions; review of *Intimate Strangers*. Michael Mirolla. *CH* March 8, 1987: pE5.
[ANTHOLOGIES: BOOK REVIEWS]

Children of the world; review of *Intimate Strangers*. I.M. Owen. *Books in Can* Jan-Feb 1987; Vol 16 No 1: p17–18.
[ANTHOLOGIES: BOOK REVIEWS]

A mixed bag of short stories; reviews of short story anthologies. Norman Sigurdson. *WFP* Feb 28, 1987: p54.
[ANTHOLOGIES: BOOK REVIEWS]

INTO NESTS, EACH PERFECT AS AN INNER EAR!/Poems by Leigh Faulkner

[Untitled]; review of *Into Nests, Each Perfect as an Inner Ear!*. Glenn Hayes. *Poetry Can R* Spring 1987; Vol 8 No 2–3: p57–58.

[Untitled]; theatre review of *It Must Be Sunday*. Danielle Salvail. photo · *Jeu* 1987; No 42: p156–158.

IT TAKES ALL KINDS/Poems by Raymond Souster

[Untitled]; review of *It Takes All Kinds*. Bert Almon. *Poetry Can R* Spring 1987; Vol 8 No 2–3: p44–45.

In principio; reviews. Laurel Boone. *Can Lit* Winter 1987; No 115: p209–211.
[CONFERENCE REPORTS: REVIEWS AND ARTICLES]

[Untitled]; reviews of poetry books. Bruce Whiteman. *Cross Can Writ Q* 1987; Vol 9 No 2: p21–22,26

ITALIA PERVERSA/Novel trilogy by Richard Appignanesi

Confusion as high art; review of *Italia Perversa*. Joel Yanofsky. photo · *MG* Aug 8, 1987: J2.

ITALIAN-CANADIAN WRITING AND WRITERS

La poétique de la mort: la poésie italo-canadienne et italo-québécoise aujourd'hui; article. Alexandre Amprimoz. *Studies in Can Lit* 1987; Vol 12 No 2: p161–176.

For the record; letter to the editor. C.D. Minni. *Books in Can* Jan-Feb 1987; Vol 16 No 1: p38.
[CONFERENCES, LITERARY]

ITINÉRAIRE DE LIVERPOOL À QUÉBEC/Journals by Louis Hémon

[Untitled]; reviews of *Itinéraire de Liverpool à Québec* and *Colloque Louis Hémon*. B.-Z. Shek. *U of Toronto Q* Fall 1987; Vol 57 No 1: p179–182.

THE IVORY SWING/Novel by Janette Turner Hospital

Film rights optioned for Ivory Swing; article. photo · *G&M* June 26, 1987: pD12.
[FILM ADAPTATIONS OF CANADIAN LITERATURE]

Berton's memoirs due out in the fall; column. Henry Mietkiewicz. *TS* June 25, 1987: pF3.
[FILM ADAPTATIONS OF CANADIAN LITERATURE]

J'AI BESOIN DE PERSONNE/Children's novel by Reynald Cantin

Littérature jeunesse; reviews of children's books. Dominique Demers. *MD* Nov 21, 1987: pD6.

J'AI CHAUD/Children's story by Cécile Gagnon

Quand un ours polaire dérive vers le sud; reviews of children's stories by Cécile Gagnon. Solange Boudreau. *Can Child Lit* 1987; No 47: p62–63.

J'AI FAIM/Children's story by Cécile Gagnon

Quand un ours polaire dérive vers le sud; reviews of children's stories by Cécile Gagnon. Solange Boudreau. *Can Child Lit* 1987; No 47: p62–63.

JÉZABEL/Play by Denise Boucher

La guerre de religion de Denise Boucher; column. Robert Lévesque. photo · *MD* Jan 13, 1987: p6.
[DRAMATIC READINGS]

JACK OF HEARTS/Play by Rochelle Bruneau

Drama fest heads for grand finale; theatre reviews of *Jack of Hearts* and *Collideoscope*. Marianne Ackerman. photo · *MG* May 1, 1987: pD3.
[FESTIVALS, DRAMA]

The effort is there but results disappoint; theatre review of *Jack of Hearts*. Pat Donnelly. *MG* July 18, 1987: pD8.

JACK, DONALD

Behind that mournful face there truly is a sad person; review of *This One's on Me*. Christopher Braden. photo · *TS* Nov 14, 1987: M4.

Bandy Papers mix bizarre humor with just a touch of the tragic; review of *This One's on Me*. Tom Saunders. *WFP* Nov 7, 1987: p54.

[Untitled]; review of *This One's on Me*. Thomas P. Sullivan. *Quill & Quire* Nov 1987; Vol 53 No 11: p25.

JACKRABBIT PAROLE/Novel by Stephen Reid

Stephen Reid's Jackrabbit Parole; review. Brian Fawcett. *West Coast R* Spring 1987; Vol 21 No 4: p78–80.
[FIRST NOVELS: BOOK REVIEWS]

JACKSON, SARAH

Sarah Jackson's book works; reviews of books by Sarah Jackson. Alexa Thompson. *Atlan Prov Book R* Sept-Oct 1987; Vol 14 No 3: p15.

JACOB'S LITTLE GIANT/Children's novel by Barbara Smucker

Baby of the family gets respect raising flock of Canada geese; reviews of children's books. Janice Kennedy. *MG* Oct 3, 1987: J13.

Big responsibilities theme of tall tale and growing-up story; reviews of *The Doll* and *Jacob's Little Giant*. Joan McGrath. photo · *Quill & Quire (Books for Young People)* Aug 1987; Vol 53 No 8: p11.

A title that will grab teenagers; reviews of children's books. Joan McGrath. *TS* Oct 25, 1987: pA18.

[Untitled]; review of *Jacob's Little Giant*. Dianne Millar. *CH* Dec 6, 1987: pD9.

JACOB TWO-TWO AND THE DINOSAUR/Children's novel by Mordecai Richler

Richler sicks PM on Jacob; article. photo · *WFP* June 19, 1987: p35.

[Untitled]; review of *Jacob Two-Two and the Dinosaur*. Peter Carver. *Quill & Quire (Books for Young People)* April 1987; Vol 53 No 4: p9.

Jacob Two-Two returns with pet dinosaur and new villain; article. Victor Dabby. *CH* June 14, 1987: pE1.

Jacob meets Dippy the dinosaur; article. Christopher Hume. *TS* May 26, 1987: pG1.

Jacob Two-Two in love; review of *Jacob Two-Two and the Dinosaur*. Brian D. Johnson. photo · *Maclean's* June 1, 1987; Vol 100 No 22: p52.

Jacob Two-Two returns in another grand adventure; review of *Jacob Two-Two and the Dinosaur.* Janice Kennedy. *MG* May 30, 1987: J7.

[Untitled]; review of *Jacob Two-Two and the Dinosaur.* Francine Prose. *NYT Book R* Oct 18, 1987: p38.

Roughing it in the bush; reviews of children's books. Mary Ainslie Smith. *Books in Can* Aug-Sept 1987; Vol 16 No 6: p34–36

Triumphant return; reviews of *Jacob Two-Two and the Dinosaur* and *Pop Bottles.* Tim Wynne-Jones. *G&M* June 13, 1987: pC19.

[AWARDS, LITERARY]

JACOB TWO-TWO MEETS THE HOODED FANG/ Children's novel by Mordecai Richler

Jacob Two-Two meets The Fang in zippy musical; theatre review. Ray Conlogue. photo · *G&M* Oct 26, 1987: pC11.

[DRAMATIC ADAPTATIONS OF CANADIAN LITERATURE]

Child subversion reigns in delightful play; theatre review of *Jacob Two-Two Meets the Hooded Fang.* Neil Harris. *WFP* Nov 13, 1987: p37.

Fast-paced kids' tale is simply irresistible; theatre review of *Jacob Two-Two Meets the Hooded Fang.* Christopher Hume. photo · *TS* Oct 23, 1987: pE8.

[DRAMATIC ADAPTATIONS OF CANADIAN LITERATURE]

[Untitled]; theatre reviews. Gina Mallet. *G&M (Toronto Magazine)* Nov 1987; Vol 2 No 8: p29.

Child power injects fun into play; article. Brad Oswald. photo · *WFP* Nov 13, 1987: p37.

[DRAMATIC ADAPTATIONS OF CANADIAN LITERATURE]

JACOB, LOUIS

Les noeuds sacrés de l'âme, de la terre et du sang; reviews of novels. Réjean Beaudoin. *Liberté* Oct 1987; Vol 29 No 5: p106–114.

JACOB, SUZANNE

Aujourd'hui; column. *MD* Feb 13, 1987: p20.

À surveiller; column. *MD* Sept 24, 1987: p12.

La passion cuisinée; review of *La Passion selon Galatée.* Réjean Beaudoin. *Liberté* June 1987; Vol 29 No 3: p90–94.

Une passion d'auteure; review of *La Passion selon Galatée.* Louise Milot. photo · *Lettres québec* Summer 1987; No 46: p21–23.

Pour l'amour d'un puzzle; review of *La Passion selon Galatée.* Madeleine Ouellette-Michalska. *MD* March 14, 1987: pD3.

[Untitled]; review of *La Passion selon Galatée.* Jean Royer. *MD* Jan 30, 1987: p7.

Suzanne Jacob: les grand boulevards intérieurs; article. Jean Royer. photo · *MD* Jan 31, 1987: pB1.

JACOBS, MARIA

Writing life; reviews of *Hired Hands* and *What Feathers Are For.* Arthur Adamson. *Can Lit* Winter 1987; No 115: p230–232.

[Untitled]; reviews of poetry books. Barbara Carey. *Cross Can Writ Q* 1987; Vol 9 No 1: p23–24.

Jacobs, Lever, Marriott; reviews of poetry books. Barry Dempster. *Poetry Can R* Spring 1987; Vol 8 No 2–3: p35.

The family business; reviews of *What Feathers Are For* and *Squid Inc 86.* Kim Van Vliet. *Waves* Spring 1987; Vol 15 No 4: p88–91.

JAKOBER, MARIE

[Untitled]; review of *Sandinista.* Miriam Jones. *Rubicon* Fall 1987; No 9: p197–198.

[FIRST NOVELS: BOOK REVIEWS]

Politics & paradise; review of *Sandinista.* C. Kanaganayakam. *Can Lit* Winter 1987; No 115: p270–272.

[Untitled]; review of *Sandinista.* Larry Towell. *Queen's Q* Autumn 1987; Vol 94 No 3: p696–698.

[FIRST NOVELS: BOOK REVIEWS]

JAMES, JANET CRAIG

Print power, a book for children; review of *Jeremy Gates and the Magic Key.* Linda Pearse. *Atlan Prov Book R* Feb-March 1987; Vol 14 No 1: p14.

Living in the past; reviews of children's novels. Mary Ainslie Smith. *Books in Can* June-July 1987; Vol 16 No 5: p35–37.

"JAMME, LES NERFS! LES NERFS!"/Play by Pierre-André Fournier and Suzanne Beaucaire

Pourquoi a-t-on peur de Maude?; theatre review of "JAMMÉE, les nerfs! les nerfs!". Patricia Badoux. photo · *MD* May 7, 1987: p13.

Le Conseil de la santé récupère une pièce boudée par l'hôpital Louis-H. Lafontaine; article. Renée Rowan. photo · *MD* April 30, 1987: p13.

JANES, J. ROBERT

How I spent my summer mystery; reviews of young adult novels by J. Robert Janes. James Gellert. *Can Child Lit* 1987; No 48: p93–95.

JANES, PERCY

Allowances must be made; review of *A Collection of Short Stories.* Kent Thompson. *Atlan Prov Book R* Sept-Oct 1987; Vol 14 No 3: p12.

LE JARDIN DES DÉLICES/Novel by Roch Carrier

Carnivalesque and parody in Le Jardin des délices; article. John Lennox. *Can Lit* Spring 1987; No 112: p48–58.

[CARNIVALIZATION]

JARMAN, MARK ANTHONY

[Untitled]; review of *Killing the Swan.* Stephen Scobie. *Malahat R (special issue)* March 1987; No 78: p154.

Dancing with snowflakes: monologue with the silent author; article. Charles R. Steele. *Dandelion* Spring-Summer 1987; Vol 14 No 1: p72–80.

JASMIN, CLAUDE

Aujourd'hui; column. *MD* Feb 23, 1987: p16.

Activity books kids will enjoy; reviews of *Dragon Sandwiches* and *The Dragon and Other Laurentian Tales*. TS Dec 20, 1987: pE8.

Claude, Clemence . . . et qui d'autre?; editorial. Rolande Allard-Lacerte. MD July 27, 1987: p6.
[TELEVISION AND CANADIAN LITERATURE]

Délivrez-nous de Claude Jasmin!; letter to the editor. Jean-Roch Boivin. MD Oct 6, 1987: p8.

Médiocrité; letter to the editor. Jean Ferguson. MD Feb 24, 1987: p8.
[TELEVISION AND CANADIAN LITERATURE]

A question of taste; reviews of *After Six Days* and *Mario*. Noreen Golfman. Can Lit Spring 1987; No 112: p104–107.

School's out, and books are in; reviews of children's books. Janice Kennedy. MG July 4, 1987: J9.

Traditional tales made new again with super illustrations; reviews of *The Dragon* and *The Lucky Old Woman*. Eva Martin. *Quill & Quire (Books for Young People)* Aug 1987; Vol 53 No 8: p7.

La vie littéraire; column. Jean Royer. photo · MD Jan 10, 1987: pB2.
[AWARDS, LITERARY; POETRY READINGS; RADIO AND CANADIAN LITERATURE; TELEVISION AND CANADIAN LITERATURE; WRITERS' WORKSHOPS]

La vie littéraire; column. Jean Royer. MD Jan 17, 1987: pB2.
[AWARDS, LITERARY; CONFERENCES, LITERARY; RADIO AND CANADIAN LITERATURE; TELEVISION AND CANADIAN LITERATURE]

La vie littéraire; column. Jean Royer. photo · MD March 14, 1987: pD4.
[AWARDS, LITERARY; POETRY READINGS; RADIO AND CANADIAN LITERATURE; TELEVISION AND CANADIAN LITERATURE]

Recent Canadian fiction; reviews of novels. D.O. Spettigue. *Queen's Q* Summer 1987; Vol 94 No 2: p366–375.
[FIRST NOVELS: BOOK REVIEWS]

JASMIN/JASMINE/Young adult novel by Jan Truss

Pour les adolescents: quatre mains et deux solitudes; reviews of young adult novels. Dominique Demers. photo · MD Dec 19, 1987: pD6–D7.

JASPER, PAT

Four poets; reviews of poetry books. Randall Maggs. *Can Lit* Winter 1987; No 115: p280–284.

JE BOUDE/Children's story by Ginette Anfousse

Le retour de Jiji et Pichou; review of *Je boude*. Sandra Beckett. *Can Child Lit* 1987; No 47: p77–78.

LE JEU ILLOCUTOIRE/Critical work by Agnès Whitfield

La vitrine du livre; reviews of *Le Je(u) illocutoire* and *XYZ*. Guy Ferland. MD Aug 1, 1987: pC6.
[CANADIAN LITERARY PERIODICALS]

JEFFERY, LAWRENCE

Best food forward in the theatre world; article. Ray Conlogue. G&M Jan 10, 1987: pE3.

Clashes of tone mute play's voice; theatre review of *Precipice*. Ray Conlogue. photo · G&M Jan 14, 1987: pC8.

Weak play an aberration for theatre; theatre review of *Precipice*. Robert Crew. photo · TS Jan 14, 1987: pF4.

JENNINGS, EVE

From box to book; reviews of *Lisa Makes the Headlines* and *Griff Makes a Date*. Laurie Bildfell. *Can Child Lit* 1987; No 46: p93–94.

Fine books for in-betweens; reviews of young adult books. David Williamson. WFP Dec 5, 1987: p57.

Taking the Degrassi kids from screen to page; reviews of *Casey Draws the Line* and *Griff Gets a Hand*. Frieda Wishinsky. photo · *Quill & Quire (Books for Young People)* June 1987; Vol 53 No 6: p3.

JENNY'S NEIGHBOURS/Children's story by Richard Thompson

From giant snakes to punk pigeons: escapism at its best; reviews of children's stories. Bernie Goedhart. *Quill & Quire (Books for Young People)* June 1987; Vol 53 No 6: p5.

JENSEN, MARGARET ANN

[Untitled]; review of *Love's Sweet Return*. Angela Miles. *Atlantis* Fall 1987; Vol 13 No 1: p185–187.

JEREMY GATES AND THE MAGIC KEY/Children's novel by Janet Craig James

Print power, a book for children; review of *Jeremy Gates and the Magic Key*. Linda Pearse. *Atlan Prov Book R* Feb-March 1987; Vol 14 No 1: p14.

Living in the past; reviews of children's novels. Mary Ainslie Smith. *Books in Can* June-July 1987; Vol 16 No 5: p35–37.

JERICHO FALLS/Novel by Christopher Hyde

[Untitled]; review of *Jericho Falls*. John North. *Quill & Quire* Feb 1987; Vol 53 No 2: p17.

A JEST OF GOD/Novel by Margaret Laurence

Heuresis: the mother-daughter theme in A Jest of God and Autumn Sonata; article. Michael Bird. *New Q* Spring-Summer 1987; Vol 7 No 1–2: p267–273.
[THE FAMILY IN CANADIAN LITERATURE; WOMEN IN LITERATURE]

Image juxtaposition in A Jest Of God; article. B.A. Legendre. *Studies in Can Lit* 1987; Vol 12 No 1: p53–68.
[BIBLICAL MYTHS AND MYTHOLOGY]

JEU: CAHIERS DE THÉÂTRE/Periodical

La vitrine du livre; reviews. Guy Ferland. MD June 6, 1987: pD4.
[CANADIAN LITERARY PERIODICALS]

La revue des revues; reviews of periodicals. Guy Ferland. MD Sept 19, 1987: pD6.
[CANADIAN LITERARY PERIODICALS]

Limoges, principale vitrine du théâtre québécois en Europe; column. Robert Lévesque. photo · MD Sept 29, 1987: p13.
[AWARDS, LITERARY; CANADIAN LITERARY PERIODICALS; FESTIVALS, DRAMA]

Les jeunes loups; reviews. Lucie Robert. *Voix et images* Spring 1987; Vol 12 No 3: p561–564.
[CANADIAN LITERARY PERIODICALS]

De qui se moque Le Devoir?; editorial. Michel Vaïs. photo · *Jeu* 1987; No 45: p7–9.
[AWARDS, LITERARY; CANADIAN LITERARY PERIODICALS; WRITERS' ORGANIZATIONS]

JEWEL/Play by Joan Macleod

Jewel shines with unexpected qualities; theatre review of *Jewel*. Ray Conlogue. photo · *G&M* April 27, 1987: pC12.

Gem of a Jewel needs strong actress; theatre review of *Jewel*. Robert Crew. photo · *TS* April 28, 1987: pG3.

Prairie spaces in the big city: western theatre in Toronto; theatre reviews. Margaret Gail Osachoff. *NeWest R* Oct 1987; Vol 13 No 2: p18–19.

JEWISH-CANADIAN WRITING AND WRITERS

Reaching out to little children through books; article. Michael McAteer. photo · *TS* Dec 12, 1987: M15.

JILES, PAULETTE

Ranging from colored bleakness to breeziness; reviews of novels by Paulette Jiles. Ken Adachi. photo · *TS* Feb 28, 1987: M4.

[Untitled]; reviews of *Flight Against Time* and *The Late Great Human Road Show*. Judith Carson. *Can Forum* Aug-Sept 1987; Vol 67 No 771: p48–49.
[FIRST NOVELS: BOOK REVIEWS]

[Untitled]; reviews of novels. Beverley Daurio. *Cross Can Writ Q* 1987; Vol 9 No 3–4: p45–46.

Paulette Jiles' fictional strategies; reviews of *Sitting in the Club Car Drinking Rum and Karma-Kola* and *The Late Great Human Road Show*. Roslyn Dixon. *Event* Summer 1987; Vol 16 No 2: p127–130.

Apocalyptic consumers; review of *The Late Great Human Road Show*. Cecelia Frey. photo · *CH* March 15, 1987: pE5.

Starting over; reviews of *The Late Great Human Road Show* and *Sitting in the Club Car Drinking Rum and Karma-Kola*. David Helwig. *Books in Can* Jan-Feb 1987; Vol 16 No 1: p15.

My favourite Canadian poem; article. Susan Ioannou. *Cross Can Writ Q* 1987; Vol 9 No 1: p11,21.

Paulette Jiles; interview. Eleanor Wachtel. photo · *Books in Can* Jan-Feb 1987; Vol 16 No 1: p36–38.

JITTERS/Play by David French

Noises Off and Jitters: two comedies of backstage life; article. Albert-Reiner Glaap. *Can Drama* 1987; Vol 13 No 2: p210–215.

JO'S SEARCH/Young adult novel by Paul Kropp

Lite-lit for children has arrived; reviews of children's books. Tim Wynne-Jones. *G&M* March 7, 1987: pE19.

JOCELYN, MATTHEW

Age of reason: play with eight senior actors seeks to dispel myths on aging; article. Stasia Evasuk. photo · *TS* Aug 31, 1987: pC3.

JOHN AND THE MISSUS/Play by Gordon Pinsent

Newfoundland on the back burner; article. Bruce Bailey. photo · *MG* April 18, 1987: pC3.

John and the Missus is slow, but sincere; film review. Bruce Bailey. *MG* April 18, 1987: pC3.

John And The Missus misses despite commendable acting; film review. Ron Base. photo · *TS* Feb 6, 1987: pD8.
[FILM ADAPTATIONS OF CANADIAN LITERATURE]

Burgess touch refreshes yet another Roman tale; reviews of *Dancing in the Dark* and *John and the Missus*. Barbara Black. *MG* April 11, 1987: pG7.

Pinsent's presence overshadows film; film review of *John and the Missus*. Brian Brennan. photo · *CH* May 15, 1987: pE8.
[FILM ADAPTATIONS OF CANADIAN LITERATURE]

Hits and Missus; article. Martin Knelman. biog photo · *Tor Life* Feb 1987; Vol 21 No 2: p29–31.
[FILM ADAPTATIONS OF CANADIAN LITERATURE]

Gordon Pinsent reminds us of our sense of place; editorial. James Lorimer. *Atlan Insight* May 1987; Vol 9 No 5: p3.
[FILM ADAPTATIONS OF CANADIAN LITERATURE]

Pinsent tells touching story; film review of *John and the Missus*. Paul McKie. photo · *WFP* April 19, 1987: p15.
[FILM ADAPTATIONS OF CANADIAN LITERATURE]

Elegy for a dying village; film review of *John and the Missus*. Lawrence O'Toole. photo · *Maclean's* Feb 2, 1987; Vol 100 No 5: p78.
[FILM ADAPTATIONS OF CANADIAN LITERATURE]

JOHN METCALF/Critical work by Barry Cameron

[Untitled]; reviews of *Archibald Lampman* and *John Metcalf*. Dennis Duffy. *Eng Studies in Can* Sept 1987; Vol 13 No 3: p355–357.

JOHNSON, JANE

A little help on the dull days; reviews of children's books. Joan McGrath. *TS* Aug 2, 1987: pC11.

JOHNSON, LINDA WIKENE

[Untitled]; review of *Showcase Animals*. Elizabeth Maloney. *Rubicon* Fall 1987; No 9: p186–187.

JOHNSTON, ANDREW

Imaginative kids' plays hit the spot; theatre reviews of *The Knocks* and *Coeur à coeur*. Pat Donnelly. *MG* April 9, 1987: pE8.

JOHNSTON, BASIL H.

Indian culture dying fast; article. Phil Johnson. photo · *TS (Neighbors)* Oct 13, 1987: p16.
[NATIVE CANADIAN WRITERS AND WRITING]

The magic of myth and love of legend; reviews of children's books. Tim Wynne-Jones. *G&M* July 25, 1987: pC17.

JOHNSTON, GEORGE

Three talks with George Johnston; interview. William Blissett. biog · *Malahat R (special issue)* March 1987; No 78: p37–51.

George Johnston's poems: letters of a friend; article. Elizabeth Brewster. *Malahat R (special issue)* March 1987; No 78: p136–146.

Happy Enough: the poetry of George Johnston; article. Harvey De Roo. *Malahat R (special issue)* March 1987; No 78: p106–131.

How it strikes a philologist: George Johnston's translation of saga prose; article. Peter Foote. *Malahat R (special issue)* March 1987; No 78: p92–97.

GJ at Victoria: from Acta to Auk; article. Jay Macpherson. *Malahat R (special issue)* March 1987; No 78: p52–56.

Dear George,; essay. Robert L. McDougall. *Malahat R (special issue)* March 1987; No 78: p27–32.

Notes on re-reading George Johnston; article. P.K. Page. *Malahat R (special issue)* March 1987; No 78: p67–72.

George Johnston's The Saga Of Gisli; article. John Tucker. *Malahat R (special issue)* March 1987; No 78: p83–91.

JOHNSTON, MIKE

Teenage amateur theatre group produces play at 'real' theatre; article. Robert Davis. photo · *TS (Neighbours)* Feb 10, 1987: p26.

JOHNSTON, WAYNE

[Untitled]; reviews of *Flavian's Fortune* and *The Story of Bobby O'Malley*. Charles R. Steele. *Queen's Q* Winter 1987; Vol 94 No 4: p1019–1022.

JOHNSTONE, KEITH

Playwright reaps laughs from reality; article. Elliott Gould. photo · *CH* May 22, 1987: pF1.

Johnstone's Beast rants, bewilders; theatre review of *The Beast with Five Fingers*. Kate Zimmerman. *CH* May 24, 1987: pE5.

JOKES FOR THE APOCALYPSE/Novellas by David Carpenter

[Untitled]; reviews of *August Nights* and *Jokes for the Apocalypse*. Lesley McAllister. *Cross Can Writ Q* 1987; Vol 9 No 2: p24.

JONASSAINT, JEAN

[Untitled]; review of *Le Pouvoir des mots, les maux du pouvoir*. Suzanne Crosta. *U of Toronto Q* Fall 1987; Vol 57 No 1: p212–214.

JONES

In voice; reviews of poetry books. Richard Stevenson. *Can Lit* Spring 1987; No 112: p167–169.

JONES, CATHY

Wacky Cathy Jones returns; theatre review of *Wedding in Texas and Other Stories*. Robert Crew. photo · *TS* Feb 18, 1987: pE3.

Women to watch in the Maritimes; article. Sue MacLeod. Donalee Moulton-Barrett. photo · *Chatelaine* April 1987; Vol 60 No 4: p114,116,118,120.

JONES, D.G.

Two windows: an interview with D.G. Jones. Bruce Meyer. bibliog biog photo · *Poetry Can R* Spring 1987; Vol 8 No 1–2: p3–5.

JONES, DENNIS

There's more at stake than military balance; column. Nick Auf der Maur. *MG* April 29, 1987: pA2.

JORDAN, G.P.

Pulp science fiction: slick adventures in a moral void; reviews of *Clone Patrol* and *Satellite Skyjack*. Eva Martin. *Quill & Quire (Books for Young People)* June 1987; Vol 53 No 6: p8.

THE JOSEPH HOWE SYMPOSIUM/Conference report

The Anchorage series proceedings: the Sir Charles G.D. Roberts and Joseph Howe symposia; reviews of *The Sir Charles G.D. Roberts Symposium* and *The Joseph Howe Symposium*. Laurel Boone. *Essays on Can Writ* Spring 1987; No 34: 196–201.

JOUDRY, PATRICIA

Book store aims to please the theatre and movie crowd; article. Marianne Ackerman. *MG* Feb 17, 1987: pE8.
[BOOK TRADE IN CANADA; CANADIAN LITERARY PERIODICALS]

UNE JOURNÉE DE SOPHIE LACHANCE/Children's play by Isabelle Myre

Mini-comptes rendus; reviews of *Legs et Bizou/Legs and Bizou* and *Une Journée de Sophie Lachance*. Claudine Lesage. *Can Child Lit* 1987; No 46: p110.

JOURNAL DE BORD DU GAMIN DES TÉNÈBRES/Poems by Louis-Philippe Corbeil

A spokesman for his time; review of *Journal de bord du gamin des ténèbres*. Guy Gauthier. *Prairie Fire* Autumn 1987; Vol 8 No 3: p113–115.

LE JOURNAL INTIME D'ANI CROCHE/Children's novel by Bertrand Gauthier

Les malheurs de Rosalie ou l'éloge de l'enfance; reviews of children's books. Dominique Demers. *MD* May 2, 1987: pD3.

JOURNAL OF CANADIAN POETRY/Periodical

Tempus fugit, but not in poetry; article. *TS* Aug 23, 1987: pA20.
[CANADIAN LITERARY PERIODICALS]

JOURNAL/Journals by Jean-Pierre Guay

Les quarante ans d'un écrivain québécois; review of *Journal 2, août 1985—avril 1986*. Yolande Grisé. photo · *Lettres québec* Spring 1987; No 45: p54–55.

[Untitled]; reviews of *Journal*. Jacques St-Pierre. *Moebius* Summer 1987; No 33: p140–142.

JUSQU'À LA MOËLLE DES FIÈVRES/Poems by Clarisse Tremblay

[Untitled]; review of *Jusqu'à la moëlle des fièvres*. Lucie Bourassa. *Estuaire* Summer 1987; No 45: p58–59.

KÉROSÈNE/Periodical

Trois premiers numéros: Le Beffroi, Filigrane, Kérosène; reviews. Robert Melançon. *Liberté* April 1987; Vol 29 No 2: p125–128.
[CANADIAN LITERARY PERIODICALS]

KAM, WINSTON

Play's premise unfulfilled; theatre review of *Bachelor-Man*. Robert Crew. *TS* Nov 13, 1987: pE26.

[Untitled]; letter to the editor. Scott Fairweather. *TS* Dec 4, 1987: pD10.

Bachelor uses intriguing techniques; theatre review of *Bachelor-Man*. Liam Lacey. photo · *G&M* Nov 14, 1987: pC8.

Blowing bubbles with Simone and Sartre; column. Vit Wagner. photo · *TS* Nov 6, 1987: pE4.
[TRANSLATIONS OF CANADIAN LITERATURE]

KAMBOURELI, SMARO

Communication deluxe; review of *In the Second Person*. John Donlan. *CV 2* Spring 1987; Vol 10 No 3: p58–60.

[Untitled]; reviews of *In the Second Person* and *Double Standards*. Joan Ruvinsky. *Rubicon* Spring 1987; No 8: p178–181.

Sounding the difference: an interview with Smaro Kamboureli and Lola Tostevin. Janice Williamson. illus · *Can Forum* Jan 1987; Vol 66 No 765: p33–38.

KAMOURASKA/Novel by Anne Hébert

Mini-comptes rendus; review of *L'Arbre mort*. François Paré. *Can Child Lit* 1987; No 45: p96–97.

KANE, MARGO

Native actress returns to roots for inspiration; article. Marianne Ackerman. photo · *MG* May 29, 1987: pD2.
[FESTIVALS, DRAMA]

KAPLAN, BESS

City author loved smell, feel of books as a child; article. *WFP* Nov 13, 1987: p36.
[FESTIVALS, LITERARY]

Struggles of adolescence; review of *The Empty Chair*. Helen Norrie. *WFP* April 11, 1987: p60.

Western publisher produces winners only; reviews of *Last Chance Summer* and *The Empty Chair*. Tim Wynne-Jones. *G&M* Feb 21, 1987: pE19.

KAREN KEEPS HER WORD AND OTHER STORIES/ Children's stories by Kit Hood et al

Fine books for in-betweens; reviews of young adult books. David Williamson. *WFP* Dec 5, 1987: p57.

KASPER, VANCY

[Untitled]; review of *Mother I'm So Glad You Taught Me How to Dance*. Gideon Forman. *Books in Can* Aug-Sept 1987; Vol 16 No 6: p28.

KATANA/Novel by Paul Ohl

Un roman historique remarquable: Katana; review. Yvon Bernier. photo · *Lettres québec* Summer 1987; No 46: p18–19.

Un roman d'érudition au souffle immense; review of *Katana*. Jean-Rock Boivin. photo · *MD* March 28, 1987: pD3.

Katana, épopée fascinante dont le héros est le Japon; article. Gil Courtemanche. photo · *MD* March 28, 1987: pD1,D8.

L'âme japonaise de Paul Ohl; article. Jean Royer. photo · *MD* March 5, 1987: p9.

KATIE'S ALLIGATOR GOES TO DAYCARE/Children's story by Ann Decter

[Untitled]; reviews of *Katie's Alligator Goes to Daycare* and *Tom Doesn't Visit Us Any More*. Adele Ashby. *Quill & Quire (Books for Young People)* Dec 1987; Vol 53 No 12: p8–9

KATTAN, NAÏM

Un univers peuplé d'éternels voyageurs sans bagages; column. Jean Éthier-Blais. photo · *MD* Nov 14, 1987: pD19.

Meaning and craft; review of *Le Repos et l'oubli*. Sharon Drache. photo · *G&M* May 30, 1987: pC21.

Prenez et lisez . . . ; review of *Le Repos et l'oubli*. Maurice Lebel. *MD* Dec 5, 1987: pD4.

Le dualisme de Naïm Kattan; review of *Le Repos et l'oubli*. André Renaud. photo · *Lettres québec* Autumn 1987; No 47: p52–53.

Naïm Kattan: "J'ai choisi Montréal pour vivre en français"; article. Jean Royer. photo · *MD* April 25, 1987: pD5.

La vie littéraire; column. Jean Royer. photo · *MD* Sept 19, 1987: pD2.
[AWARDS, LITERARY; CONFERENCES, LITERARY; FICTION READINGS; POETRY READINGS; PUBLISHING AND PUBLISHERS IN CANADA]

Naïm Kattan de Bagdad à Montréal; review of *Le Repos et l'oubli*. Lori Saint-Martin. photo · *MD* June 6, 1987: pD2.

KATZ, WELWYN WILTON

London writer wins international award; article. *TS* March 20, 1987: pD21.
[AWARDS, LITERARY]

Ontario writer wins children's book award; article. *CH* March 21, 1987: pA20.
[AWARDS, LITERARY]

Past and present merge in painful, haunting tales; reviews of *False Face* and *Who Is Frances Rain?*. Peter Carver. photo · *Quill & Quire (Books for Young People)* Oct 1987; Vol 53 No 10: p10.
[FIRST NOVELS: BOOK REVIEWS]

Third time lucky for rising author; article. Kenneth McGoogan. photo · *CH* Nov 16, 1987: pB3.

The jolly fireplace's darker side; reviews of children's books. Joan McGrath. *TS* Nov 22, 1987: pC8.

When is a book not a book? The novels of Welwyn Wilton Katz; article. Marianne Micros. *Can Child Lit* 1987; No 47: p23–28.

Book world: a 'nice little hobby' that finally paid off; column. Beverley Slopen. photo · *TS* May 3, 1987: pA25.

London writer awarded children's book prize; article. Tim Wynne-Jones. photo · *G&M* March 20, 1987: pD5.
[AWARDS, LITERARY]

KAVANAGII, ED

The language of fantasy; reviews of *The Emperor's Panda* and *Amanda Greenleaf Visits a Distant Star*. Jo-Ann Wallace. *Can Child Lit* 1987; No 47: p73–74.

KAY, GUY GAVRIEL

[Untitled]; review of *The Darkest Road*. Douglas Barbour. *Malahat R* June 1987; No 79: p160–161.

Voyages of the mind; article, includes review of *The Darkest Road*. Peter Giffen. photo · *Maclean's* March 23, 1987; Vol 100 No 12: p66–67.
[FANTASY; SCIENCE FICTION]

The latest reports from the exotic worlds of fantasy; review of *The Summer Tree*. Douglas Hill. *G&M* July 11, 1987: pC13.
[FIRST NOVELS. BOOK REVIEWS]

Tapestry times three; review of *The Darkest Road*. P. Scott Lawrence. photo · *MG* March 7, 1987: H11.

[Untitled]; review of *The Darkest Road*. Alberto Manguel. *Tor Life* March 1987; Vol 21 No 4: p93,95.

Fantasy becomes winning author's reality; article. Kenneth McGoogan. photo · *CH* March 17, 1987: pC7.

'Brightly woven' the right words; review of *The Darkest Road*. Henry Mietkiewicz. *TS* April 5, 1987: pA22.

Flaws mar a major fantasy; review of *The Darkest Road*. Tom Oleson. photo · *WFP* June 13, 1987: p58.

KAZUK, A.R.

Random musings of a middle-aged middle-class male; reviews of poetry books. Lesley McAllister. *TS* Oct 10, 1987: M4.

KEITH, W.J.

[Untitled]; review of *Canadian Literature in English*. L.W. Conolly. *Theatre Hist in Can* Fall 1987; Vol 8 No 2: p247–249.

[Untitled]; review of *Canadian Literature in English*. John Orange. *U of Windsor R* Spring-Summer 1987; Vol 20 No 2: p92–94.

KELLY, M.T.

Revenge of the native; review of *A Dream Like Mine*. John Bemrose. photo · *Maclean's* Nov 9, 1987; Vol 100 No 45: p64g

Dreaming for our children; column. Mary di Michele. *Poetry Can R* Fall 1987; Vol 9 No 1: p19.

Kelly's taut, grim narrative; review of *A Dream Like Mine*. Judith Fitzgerald. *TS* Nov 22, 1987: pC9.

The impossible dream; review of *A Dream Like Mine*. Terry Goldie. *Books in Can* Nov 1987; Vol 16 No 8: p30–31.

Irked by criticism; letter to the editor. Shelagh Grant. *G&M* Aug 6, 1987: pA6.

Reporter trips over angles of 'light' Indian story; review of *A Dream Like Mine*. Marion McCormick. *MG* Nov 21, 1987: J12.

The real story behind the story; review of *A Dream Like Mine*. T.F. Rigelhof. photo · *G&M* Oct 24, 1987: pC19.

[Untitled]; review of *A Dream Like Mine*. Norman Sigurdson. *Quill & Quire* Dec 1987; Vol 53 No 12: p24–25

Unpleasant, harsh novel probes social ills; review of *A Dream Like Mine*. John Vance Snow. photo · *CH* Nov 29, 1987: pE6.

KEMP, PENNY

[Untitled]; review of *Travelling Light*. Mary di Michele. *Poetry Can R* Summer 1987; Vol 8 No 4: p35.

[Untitled]; reviews of poetry books. Sheila Martindale. *Cross Can Writ Q* 1987; Vol 9 No 2: p20–21.

Penny Kemp: creating the world she inhabits; article. Patricia Keeney Smith. photo · *Cross Can Writ Q* 1987; Vol 9 No 2: p8–9,28–29.

KERRISDALE ELEGIES/Long poem by George Bowering

Stealing the text: George Bowering's Kerrisdale Elegies and Dennis Cooley's Bloody Jack; article. Smaro Kamboureli. *Can Lit* Winter 1987; No 115: p9–23.
[CANADIAN LONG POEM; STRUCTURALIST WRITING AND CRITICISM]

KERSLAKE, SUSAN

Rare/fear; reviews of *Green Eyes, Dukes & Kings* and *The Book of Fears*. Thomas Gerry. *Can Lit* Spring 1987; No 112: p107–108.

Short shrift for novel's art; review of *Penumbra*. Nanette Norris. *Essays on Can Writ* Spring 1987; No 34: p136–139.

KESSLER, DEIRDRE

Three stories for children; reviews of children's books. Veronica Leonard. *Atlan Prov Book R* Nov-Dec 1987; Vol 14 No 4: p1.

Mini-reviews; reviews of children's stories. Mary Rubio. *Can Child Lit* 1987; No 47: p96–99.

KHALO, MICHEL

La vitrine du livre; reviews. Guy Ferland. *MD* June 20, 1987: pD4.
[CANADIAN LITERARY PERIODICALS]

École buissonnière; review of *L'Académie du désir*. Madeleine Ouellette-Michalska. *MD* Oct 31, 1987: pD3.

KHALSA, DAYAL KAUR

A girl's best friend is her skate; review of *I Want a Dog*. Roz Chast. *NYT Book R* Nov 8, 1987: p32.

Morgan, May, Melinda: new heroines offer humour and fantasy; reviews of children's books. Bernie Goedhart. *Quill & Quire (Books for Young People)* Oct 1987; Vol 53 No 10: p24.

Convincing and colourful; review of *Tales of a Gambling Grandma*. Marlene Kadar. *Can Child Lit* 1987; No 47: p91–92.

Children's author enjoys growing readership; interview with Dayal Kaur Khalsa. Elisabeth Kalbfuss. photo · *MG* Dec 24, 1987: L2.

Funny books are a joy to find; reviews of *An Armadillo Is Not a Pillow* and *Tales of a Gambling Grandma.* Helen Norrie. *WFP* Feb 14, 1987: p60.

Youngsters get choice of beautiful books; reviews. Helen Norrie. *WFP* Dec 5, 1987: p57.

Now great-grandma gets to cry wolf, too; column. Thomas Schnurmacher. *MG* Dec 16, 1987: pF1.

Rare joy and simple truth; reviews of *Tales of a Gambling Grandma* and *Love You Forever.* Tim Wynne-Jones. *G&M* Jan 24, 1987: pE19.

KICKING AGAINST THE PRICKS/Essays by John Metcalf

Raising two worthy books from the dead; reviews of *Kicking Against the Pricks* and *Incognito.* William French. photo · *G&M* Feb 24, 1987: pD7.

KIDDER, WAYNE

New troupe doesn't shun controversy; article. Sherri Clegg. *CH* April 10, 1987: pE1.

Troupe's first venture brave but flat; theatre review of *The Worlds of William Korth.* Kate Zimmerman. photo · *CH* April 16, 1987: pE5.

KILLING THE SWAN/Poems by Mark Anthony Jarman

[Untitled]; review of *Killing the Swan.* Stephen Scobie. *Malahat R (special issue)* March 1987; No 78: p154.

KILODNEY, CRAD

Satirist courts 'humorless' Toronto; article. Mark Bastien. photo · *TS* July 13, 1987: pC3.

Writer who can't come in from the cold; article. Gary Lautens. *TS* Nov 30, 1987: pA3.

KIMM, D.

La vitrine du livre; review of *Ô solitude!.* Guy Ferland. *MD* Dec 19, 1987: pD6.

KING LEARY/Novel by Paul Quarrington

King Leary is a type of literary hat trick; review. William French. photo · *G&M* Oct 20, 1987: pD5.

Hockey's puckish wit; review of *King Leary.* Brian D. Johnson. *Maclean's* Nov 9, 1987; Vol 100 No 45: p64h

Paul Quarrington: a good sport in life and letters; article, includes review of *King Leary.* Paul Kennedy. photo · *Quill & Quire* Sept 1987; Vol 53 No 9: p77.

Smooth skating; review of *King Leary.* Douglas Malcolm. *Books in Can* Oct 1987; Vol 16 No 7: p27.

Legendary Leaf proved inspiration to Toronto novelist; article. Kenneth McGoogan. *CH* Dec 7, 1987: pB6.

An end-to-end rush; review of *King Leary.* Scott Taylor. *WFP* Nov 14, 1987: p50.

It's fiction, but it's unmistakably 'King'; review of *King Leary.* Mike Walton. photo · *TS* Oct 18, 1987: pC8.

King Leary: his ego is as big as a rink, and his heart hard as a puck; review. Joel Yanofsky. *MG* Oct 24, 1987: J13.

THE KING OF AMERICA/Play by Alan Williams

Challenging the commonplaces; introduction to play excerpt from *The King of America.* Rory Runnells. *Prairie Fire* Spring 1987; Vol 8 No 1: p56.

Williams' King Of America intelligent, rich and funny; theatre review. Reg Skene. *WFP* May 3, 1987: p15.

KING, DAVID

Reviewer was right; article. *WFP* July 3, 1987: p17.
[AWARDS, LITERARY]

A madcap journey out to the Backyard; theatre review of *Backyard Beguine,* includes profile. Stephen Godfrey. photo · *G&M* April 8, 1987: pC7.

Entrances and exits; column. Mark Leiren-Young. photo · *Can Theatre R* Fall 1987; No 52: p91–94.
[AWARDS, LITERARY]

THE KINGDOM OF LOUDASCANBE/Children's play by Kim Renders

Director a natural for New Canadian Kid; column. Vit Wagner. *TS* Dec 18, 1987: pD12.

KINGSBURY, DONALD

Montrealer's 'time bus' tours superpowers' war zone; review of *The Moon Goddess and the Son.* Michael Carin. *MG* Feb 14, 1987: pB8.

KINSELLA, W.P.

Kinsella wins Leacock medal; article. *WFP* April 25, 1987: p27.
[AWARDS, LITERARY]

Kinsella wins Leacock award; article. *Quill & Quire* June 1987; Vol 53 No 6: p24.
[AWARDS, LITERARY]

Foreward; editorial. *Malahat R (special issue)* March 1987; No 78: p1–4.
[CENSORSHIP]

Kinsella collects the Leacock medal; article. *G&M* April 24, 1987: pC5.
[AWARDS, LITERARY]

'My year for awards'; article. *G&M* April 25, 1987: pC5.
[AWARDS, LITERARY]

Booksellers honor Globe editor; article. *G&M* June 30, 1987: pD7.
[AWARDS, LITERARY]

B.C.'s Kinsella wins Leacock humor award; article. *TS* April 24, 1987: pE22.
[AWARDS, LITERARY]

Mainstreet Calgary; column. *CH (Neighbors)* Oct 7, 1987: pA14.
[FICTION READINGS]

Kinsella finds the pathos in ordinary lives; review of *Red Wolf, Red Wolf.* Ken Adachi. *TS* Sept 6, 1987: pA19.

Immigrant experience yields stream of interesting tales; reviews of *Tales from Firozsha Baag* and *The Fencepost Chronicles*. Barbara Black. *MG* May 30, 1987: J9.

Kinsella should stretch his fancy; review of *Red Wolf, Red Wolf*. Barbara Black. photo · *MG* Sept 12, 1987: I6.

Kinsella promotes book, but slips into baseball; article. Donald Campbell. photo · *WFP* Sept 15, 1987: p29.

[Untitled]; reviews of short story collections. Pauline Carey. *Cross Can Writ Q* 1987; Vol 9 No 3–4: p46–47.

Leacock celebration honors medal winner; column. Zena Cherry. *G&M* May 26, 1987: pD12.
[AWARDS, LITERARY]

People; column. Yvonne Cox. *Maclean's* May 18, 1987; Vol 100 No 20: p36.
[AWARDS, LITERARY]

[Untitled]; review of *The Fencepost Chronicles*. Mark Duncan. *Border Cross* Summer 1987; Vol 6 No 3: p23–24.

[Untitled]; review of *The Alligator Report*. Cary Fagan. *Books in Can* April 1987; Vol 16 No 3: p24.

Gators, jugglers and the gerbil that ate L.A.; review of *The Alligator Report*. William French. illus · *G&M* Feb 19, 1987: pC1.

Middle class under fire; review of *Red Wolf, Red Wolf*. William French. photo · *G&M* Sept 3, 1987: pC1.

At home in left field; article. Stephen Godfrey. photo · *G&M* April 25, 1987: pC1, C5.

[Untitled]; review of *The Alligator Report*. Alice Gur-Arie. *Quill & Quire* May 1987; Vol 53 No 5: p20.

Diamond & daydream; review of *The Iowa Baseball Confederacy*. Allen E. Hye. *Can Lit* Winter 1987; No 115: p162–164.

[Untitled]; review of *The Fencepost Chronicles*. Lenore Keeshig-Tobias. *Books in Can* Jan-Feb 1987; Vol 16 No 1: p25.

First novel turned into TV movie; column. Kenneth McGoogan. *CH* May 3, 1987: pE6.
[CONFERENCES, LITERARY; TELEVISION AND CANADIAN LITERATURE]

McDonald scores with Canada's booksellers; article. Kenneth McGoogan. *CH* June 30, 1987: pE1.
[AWARDS, LITERARY]

Kinsella displays new range; review of *Red Wolf, Red Wolf*. Kenneth McGoogan. photo · *CH* Aug 30, 1987: pE4.

More surprises from Kinsella; column. Kenneth McGoogan. *CH* Sept 13, 1987: pE5.

Kinsella's losers triumph; review of *The Alligator Report*. Lorna Scoville. photo · *CH* March 29, 1987: pE5.

Book world: the man who stole millions; column. Beverley Slopen. *TS* April 19, 1987: pA18.

Book world: writers sell selves to the booksellers; column. Beverley Slopen. *TS* July 5, 1987: pA18.
[AWARDS, LITERARY]

[Untitled]; review of *Red Wolf, Red Wolf*. Martin Townsend. *Quill & Quire* Sept 1987; Vol 53 No 9: p79.

Tributes to two writers; review of *The Alligator Report*. David Williamson. *WFP* March 7, 1987: p70.

Writing for fun and profit; review of *Red Wolf, Red Wolf*. David Williamson. photo · *WFP* Sept 19, 1987: p64.

KIYOOKA, ROY

Roy Kiyooka's The Fontainebleau Dream Machine: a reading; article. Eva-Marie Kröler. *Can Lit* Summer-Fall 1987; No 113–114: p47–58.
[SURREALISM]

KLEIN, A.M.

Esoteric callings; review of *A.M. Klein: Literary Essays and Reviews*. Sharon Drache. *G&M* May 16, 1987: pC19.

Dire l'exode: l'oeuvre d'A.M. Klein; article. Cedric May. *Ellipse* 1987; No 37: p57–69.

Overworked motif is just new kind of exploitation; review of *Contact Prints*. David Williamson. *WFP* June 27, 1987: p58.

KLIMOV, ALEXIS

[Untitled]; reviews. Raymond Martin. *Moebius* Winter 1987; No 31: p164–166.

KNIGHT, M.L.

[Untitled]; review of *Overlooking the Red Jail*. Mark Everard. *Books in Can* June-July 1987; Vol 16 No 5: p22.

KNISTER, RAYMOND

Death by drowning; letter to the editor. Imogen Knister Givens. *Books in Can* Aug-Sept 1987; Vol 16 No 6: p38.

Death by drowning; essay. Dorothy Livesay. illus · *Books in Can* April 1987; Vol 16 No 3: p15–16.

[Untitled]; letter to the editor. Alice Munro. *Books in Can* Aug-Sept 1987; Vol 16 No 6: p38–39.

THE KNOCKS/Children's play by Andrew Johnston

Imaginative kids' plays hit the spot; theatre reviews of *The Knocks* and *Coeur à coeur*. Pat Donnelly. *MG* April 9, 1987: pE8.

KODACHROMES AT MIDDAY/Poems by Gilean Douglas

Still lifes; reviews of poetry books. Laurence Hutchman. *Can Lit* Winter 1987; No 115: p263–264.

KOGAWA, JOY

[Untitled]; review of *Woman in the Woods*. Anne Cimon. *Rubicon* Spring 1987; No 8: p215–216.

Still lifes; reviews of poetry books. Laurence Hutchman. *Can Lit* Winter 1987; No 115: p263–264.

Joy Kogawa: a need to reach out . . . ; biographical article. Anna Kohn. photo · *Cross Can Writ Q* 1987; Vol 9 No 2: p6–7, 28.

Interview with Joy Kogawa. Leslie Komori. *Fireweed* Winter 1987; No 24: p63–66.

Speaking the silence: Joy Kogawa's Obasan; article. Gary Willis. *Studies in Can Lit* 1987; Vol 12 No 2: p239–250.

Other cultures featured in tales for youths; reviews of *The Unmasking of 'Ksan* and *Naomi's Road*. Kate Zimmerman. *CH* July 19, 1987: pE4.

THE KOMAGATA MARU INCIDENT/Play by Sharon Pollock

Looking back at a tragedy; theatre review of *The Komagata Maru Incident*. Liam Lacey. *G&M* April 2, 1987: pC5.

KONKEL, K.G.E.

Toronto policeman writes books when not on patrol; article. *WFP* Nov 19, 1987: p51.

Street cop Chuck Konkel is also K.G.E. Konkel, novelist; article. Jack Cahill. photo · *TS* Oct 18, 1987: pD7.

Surprising weight from the newcomers; reviews of *The Glorious East Wind* and *Ripper*. Margaret Cannon. *G&M* Nov 7, 1987: pC23.
[FIRST NOVELS: BOOK REVIEWS]

People; column. Yvonne Cox. *Maclean's* Nov 16, 1987; Vol 100 No 46: p64.

Author of exotic Asian thriller isn't your average Toronto cop; article. H.J. Kirchhoff. photo · *G&M* Nov 7, 1987: pC14.

Local heroes; reviews of first novels. Janice Kulyk Keefer. *Books in Can* Nov 1987; Vol 16 No 8: p35,37.
[FIRST NOVELS: BOOK REVIEWS]

A spot of skulduggery with an Asian flavor; review of *The Glorious East Wind*. Neil Louttit. *WFP* Dec 19, 1987: p51.
[FIRST NOVELS: BOOK REVIEWS]

[Untitled]; review of *The Glorious East Wind*. Peter Robinson. *Quill & Quire* Sept 1987; Vol 53 No 9: p79.
[FIRST NOVELS: BOOK REVIEWS]

A solid first effort from a Toronto cop; review of *The Glorious East Wind*. Mike Walton. photo · *TS* Dec 26, 1987: K7.
[FIRST NOVELS: BOOK REVIEWS]

Hong Kong is a jungle in Toronto cop's thriller; review of *The Glorious East Wind*. Paul Waters. *MG* Oct 31, 1987: J14.
[FIRST NOVELS: BOOK REVIEWS]

KORMAN, GORDON

Brief notes; article. *Quill & Quire* March 1987; Vol 53 No 3: p67.

Chit chat; column. Maria Casas. *Quill & Quire (Books for Young People)* April 1987; Vol 53 No 4: p3.
[CHILDREN'S LITERATURE; CHINA-CANADA LITERARY RELATIONS; WRITERS-IN-RESIDENCE]

People; column. Yvonne Cox. *Maclean's* May 4, 1987; Vol 100 No 18: p54.

Gordon Korman: entertaining as ever; review of *Don't Care High*. Sonja Dunn. *Can Child Lit* 1987; No 46: p83.

KORN, RACHEL

Grief & memory; reviews of poetry books. Peter Stenberg. *Can Lit* Spring 1987; No 112: p169–171.

KOUHI, ELIZABETH

Women and things; review of *Melancholy Ain't No Baby*. Cary Fagan. *Prairie Fire* Summer 1987; Vol 8 No 2: p70–71.

KOVALSKI, MARYANN

Alligator Pie leads way to healthy kid-lit market; article. *WFP* Nov 9, 1987: p24.
[CHILDREN'S LITERATURE]

Make way for a fine crop of picture-books; reviews of children's books. Adele Ashby. *Quill & Quire (Books for Young People)* Aug 1987; Vol 53 No 8: p6.

Drawing power; article. Christopher Hume. illus photo · *TS* Nov 1, 1987: pC1,C5.
[CHILDREN'S LITERATURE]

Gammer Gurton leaps from early English stage into the 20th century; reviews of children's books. Janice Kennedy. *MG* Nov 21, 1987: J13.

A title that will grab teenagers; reviews of children's books. Joan McGrath. *TS* Oct 25, 1987: pA18.

[Untitled]; review of *The Wheels on the Bus*. Gen Weinmayr. *CH* Dec 6, 1987: pD9.

KRAUSE, JUDITH

The elephant: a federal or provincial responsibility?; review of *What We Bring Home*. Paul Denham. illus · *NeWest R* Summer 1987; Vol 12 No 10: p14.

[Untitled]; reviews of poetry books. Sheila Martindale. *Cross Can Writ Q* 1987; Vol 9 No 2: p20–21.

First books from five regional presses; reviews of poetry books. Colin Morton. *Arc* Spring 1987; No 18: p52–59.

An auspicious debut; review of *What We Bring Home*. Richard Stevenson. *Prairie Fire* Summer 1987; Vol 8 No 2: p60–62.

KREINER, PHILIP

Comic novel about the North is as sharp as frostbite; review of *Contact Prints*. Barbara Black. *MG* June 13, 1987: J8.

Dissension in the backyard of Canada's frozen near north; review of *Contact Prints*. Geoff Hancock. photo · *TS* May 3, 1987: pA24.

A gritty tale of a teacher's turmoil among the Cree; review of *Contact Prints*. Philip Kreiner. photo · *G&M* April 9, 1987: pC1.

[Untitled]; review of *Contact Prints*. Brent Ledger. *Quill & Quire* May 1987; Vol 53 No 5: p20.

Through a lens darkly; review of *Contact Prints*. Douglas Malcolm. *Books in Can* May 1987; Vol 16 No 4: p28.

KREISEL, HENRY

It's a date; column. *MG* Nov 6, 1987: pC12.
[FICTION READINGS]

[Untitled]; reviews of *Robert Kroetsch* and *Another Country*. Russell Brown. *U of Toronto Q* Fall 1987; Vol 57 No 1: p161–166.

[Untitled]; review of *Another Country*. Peter Halewood. *Rubicon* Spring 1987; No 8: p218–219.

Sex and Politics: parody in the bedrooms of the province; theatre review. David A. Powell. *NeWest R* Nov 1987; Vol 13 No 3: p18.

[Untitled]; review of *Another Country*. F.L. Radford. *World Lit in Eng* Spring 1987; Vol 27 No 1: p60–62.

[The Rich Man]; theatre review. Lynne Van Luven. *NeWest R* Nov 1987; Vol 13 No 3: p18.

[DRAMATIC ADAPTATIONS OF CANADIAN LITERATURE]

Humane vision; review of *Another Country*. Frank W. Watt. *Can Lit* Winter 1987; No 115: p202–203.

The triumphant exile; review of *Another Country*. George Woodcock. *Essays on Can Writ* Winter 1987; No 35: p82–87.

KRISTAL DREAMS/Children's play by David Pody

Anti-drug play goes to school; article. Beverley Mitchell. photo · *MG* Nov 18, 1987: pE7

KRIZANC, JOHN

Mixed reviews for Tamara; article. Salem Alaton. *G&M* Dec 4, 1987: pD9.

[INTERNATIONAL REVIEWS OF CANADIAN LITERATURE]

Bright lights, Big Apple; article. Larry Black. photo · *Maclean's* Dec 7, 1987; Vol 100 No 49: p69–70.

People; column. Yvonne Cox. *Maclean's* Dec 21, 1987; Vol 100 No 51: p30.

Tamara producers work on Casa Loma '88; article. Robert Crew. *TS* Dec 2, 1987: pB4.

Tamara gets a rave in New York Times; column. Robert Crew. *TS* Dec 3, 1987: pB1.

[INTERNATIONAL REVIEWS OF CANADIAN LITERATURE]

Tamara, Tamara, they'll love it Tamara; column. Robert Crew. *TS* Dec 4, 1987: pD27.

[Untitled]; review of *Prague*. Keith Garebian. *Quill & Quire* June 1987; Vol 53 No 6: p31.

To tell the truth; review of *Prague*. John Gilbert. *Books in Can* March 1987; Vol 16 No 2: p17.

Tamara New York; article. Peter Goddard. photo · *TS* Nov 22, 1987: pC1,C4.

"The truth must out": the political plays of John Krizanc; article. Richard Paul Knowles. *Can Drama* 1987; Vol 13 No 1: p27–33.

[POLITICAL WRITING]

Theatre of Future would lack only stage and script; theatre review of *Tamara*. Lewis H. Lapham. photo · *G&M* Dec 12, 1987: pC12.

Tamara: intrigue, champagne et amuse-gueules; article. Maurice Tourigny. photo · *MD* Nov 14, 1987: pC6.

KROETSCH, ROBERT

Billboard: Knox Church stages neighborhood party; column. *WFP* Sept 19, 1987: p43.

Antipodean travels with Robert Kroetsch; essay. Douglas Barbour. *Prairie Fire* Winter 1987–88; Vol 8 No 4: p24,26–32.

Selections from Errata; essay. George Bowering. *Prairie Fire* Winter 1987–88; Vol 8 No 4: p6,8.

[Untitled]; reviews of *Robert Kroetsch* and *Another Country*. Russell Brown. *U of Toronto Q* Fall 1987; Vol 57 No 1: p161–166.

The vernacular muse in prairie poetry (Part 3); article. Dennis Cooley. *Prairie Fire* Summer 1987; Vol 8 No 2: p49–53.

[PRAIRIE POETRY AND POETS]

A deconstructive narratology; reading Robert Kroetsch's Alibi; article. Susan Rudy Dorscht. *Open Letter* Summer 1987; Vol 6 No 8: p78–83.

[METAFICTION; STRUCTURALIST WRITING AND CRITICISM]

Trope as topos in the poetry of Robert Kroetsch; review article about *Advice to My Friends*. E.F. Dyck. *Prairie Fire* Winter 1987–88; Vol 8 No 4: p86,88–93.

Novelist as trickster: the magical presence of Gabriel García Márquez in Robert Kroetsch's What The Crow Said; article. Brian Edwards. *Essays on Can Writ* Spring 1987; No 34: p92–110.

[LATIN AMERICA-CANADA LITERARY RELATIONS; MAGIC REALISM; POSTMODERNIST WRITING AND CRITICISM; STRUCTURALIST WRITING AND CRITICISM]

A mazing grace: the writings of Robert Kroetsch; article. Robert Enright. *Border Cross* Summer 1987; Vol 6 No 3: p29–30.

Realizing Kroetsch's poetry; reviews of *Excerpts from the Real World* and *Seed Catalogue*. Thomas B. Friedman. *Prairie Fire* Winter 1987–88; Vol 8 No 4: p95–98.

Reading Robert Kroetsch in Italy; article. Alessandro Gebbia. *Prairie Fire* Winter 1987–88; Vol 8 No 4: p83–85.

'Meditation on a snowy morning': a conversation with Robert Kroetsch. Kristjana Gunnars. photo · *Prairie Fire* Winter 1987–88; Vol 8 No 4: p54–62.64–67.

[Untitled]; review of *Excerpts from the Real World*. Beverly Harris. *Dandelion* Spring-Summer 1987; Vol 14 No 1: p81–84.

The alibis of Kroetsch and Butler; introduction to Alibi Drawings. Terrence Heath. *Border Cross* Summer 1987; Vol 6 No 3: p31–32.

Discourse of the other; review of *Advice to My Friends*. Paul Hjartarson. *Can Lit* Winter 1987; No 115: p135–138.

The Twayning of Robert Kroetsch; review of *Robert Kroetsch*. Martin Kuester. *Prairie Fire* Winter 1987–88; Vol 8 No 4: p101–105.

[Untitled]; review of *Excerpts from the Real World*. Louise Longo. *Books in Can* Jan-Feb 1987; Vol 16 No 1: p28.

Novelist, poet Kroetsch receives top payment under library fee plan; article. Barbara Robson. *WFP* April 22, 1987: p38.

[GOVERNMENT GRANTS FOR WRITERS/PUBLISHERS; LIBRARY SERVICES AND CANADIAN LITERATURE]

Photography "in camera"; article. Peter Sims. *Can Lit* Summer-Fall 1987; No 113–114: p145–166.

(No parrot/no crow/no parrot); essay. Aritha van Herk. *Prairie Fire* Winter 1987–88; Vol 8 No 4: p12,14–20.

[Untitled]; review of *Seed Catalogue*. Bruce Whiteman. *Poetry Can R* Summer 1987; Vol 8 No 4: p34–35.

KROPP, PAUL

A little help on the dull days; reviews of children's books. Joan McGrath. *TS* Aug 2, 1987: pC11.

Lite-lit for children has arrived; reviews of children's books. Tim Wynne-Jones. *G&M* March 7, 1987: pE19.

KUKLA, KAILA

One miss, one hit; reviews of *And I'm Never Coming Back* and *Madam Piccolo and the Craziest Pickle Party Ever*. Sylvia Markle-Craine. *Can Child Lit* 1987; No 48: p100–102.

KULYK KEEFER, JANICE

Nova Scotia writer wins CBC short story contest; article. *TS* Jan 14, 1987: pF2.
[AWARDS, LITERARY]

New faces; survey article. photo · *TS* March 7, 1987: K1-K4.
[AUTHORS, CANADIAN]

Keefer wins short story award for the second consecutive year; article. *WFP* Jan 14, 1987: p42.
[AWARDS, LITERARY]

Keefer collects literary prize; article. *G&M* Jan 14, 1987: pC7.
[AWARDS, LITERARY]

One-woman writing machine finds fewer distractions in N.S.; article. *MG* Dec 12, 1987: I12.

[Untitled]; reviews of *The Paris-Napoli Express* and *White of the Lesser Angels*. Elizabeth Brewster. *Event* March 1987; Vol 16 No 1: p103–104.

Calling attention to the Maritimes; review of *Under Eastern Eyes*. Dennis Duffy. *G&M* Nov 21, 1987: pC23.

[Untitled]; reviews of short story collections. David Helwig. *Queen's Q* Winter 1987; Vol 94 No 4: p1022–1024.

Isolation helps nurture Keefer's writing; article. H.J. Kirchhoff. photo · *G&M* Oct 28, 1987: pC5.

Exile & belonging: two Maritime poets; reviews of *White of the Lesser Angels* and *Tiger in the Skull*. Richard Lemm. *Atlan Prov Book R* May-June 1987; Vol 14 No 2: p10.

[Untitled]; review of *White of the Lesser Angels*. Tom Marshall. *U of Windsor R* Fall-Winter 1987; Vol 20 No 1: p94–95.

Images of motherhood; review of *The Paris-Napoli Express*. A.C. Morrell. *Fiddlehead* Summer 1987; No 152: p91–95.

[Untitled]; reviews of *The Need of Wanting Always* and *The Paris-Napoli Express*. S.A. Newman. *Cross Can Writ Q* 1987; Vol 9 No 1: p20.

Kulyk Keefer's rising star: five books in three genres in one year; article, includes reviews. Nancy Robb. photo · *Quill & Quire* July 1987; Vol 53 No 7: p69–70.

Rush job, high gloss and high-risk realism; reviews of poetry books. Fraser Sutherland. *G&M* March 21, 1987: pE18.

Oranges and onions; reviews of *White of the Lesser Angels* and *The Abbotsford Guide to India*. Fred Wah. *Books in Can* March 1987; Vol 16 No 2: p32,34.

KURAPEL, ALBERTO

Les anges dans nos campagnes; article. Robert Lévesque. *MD* June 4, 1987: p13.
[FESTIVALS, DRAMA]

'Oiseau' feeds on violent love — 'Neruda' long 2-hour stretch; theatre reviews of *Un Oiseau vivant dans la gueule* and *Off Off Off*. Francine Pelletier. *MG* June 3, 1987: pB4.

KUSHNER, DONN

Renaissance man Donn Kushner a delightful challenge for children; article. Bernie Goedhart. photo · *Quill & Quire (Books for Young People)* Dec 1987; Vol 53 No 12: p1,3.

Gammer Gurton leaps from early English stage into the 20th century; reviews of children's books. Janice Kennedy. *MG* Nov 21, 1987: J13.

A dragon stands on guard; review of *A Book Dragon*. Joan McGrath. *TS* Dec 20, 1987: pE5.

L'ACADÉMIE DU DÉSIR/Novel by Michel Khalo

La vitrine du livre; reviews. Guy Ferland. *MD* June 20, 1987: pD4.
[CANADIAN LITERARY PERIODICALS]

École buissonnière; review of *L'Académie du désir*. Madeleine Ouellette-Michalska. *MD* Oct 31, 1987: pD3.

L'ACCÉLÉRATEUR D'INTENSITÉ suivi de ON NE SAIT PAS SI C'EST ÉCRIT AVANT OU APRÈS LA GRANDE CONFLAGRATION/Poems by André Roy

André Roy, "l'écouteur des choses tristes"; review of *L'Accélérateur d'intensité*. Gérald Gaudet. photo · *MD* Dec 5, 1987: pD9.

L'AMLANCHIER/Story by Jacques Ferron

Tinamer ou le bon cet des choses; review of *L'Amlanchier*. Adrien Thério. *Lettres québec* Winter 1986–87; No 44: p77.

L'AMOUR DE JEANNE/Novel by Alice Parizeau

Deux fictions sur fond d'histoire; reviews of *La Fin de l'histoire* and *L'Amour de Jeanne*. Yvon Bernier. photo · *Lettres québec* Winter 1986–87; No 44: p31-33

L'AMOUR DE LA CARTE POSTALE/Essay by Madeleine Ouellette-Michalska

La culture de la confusion; reviews of *Extase et déchirure* and *L'Amour de la carte postale*. Réjean Beaudoin. *Liberté* Dec 1987; Vol 29 No 6: p107–113.

La vitrine du livre; reviews. Guy Ferland. *MD* May 9, 1987: pD4.

[Untitled]; review of *L'Amour de la carte postale*. Robert Giroux. *Moebius* Summer 1987; No 33: p146–148.

Un essai original sur l'impérialisme culturel; review of *L'Amour de la carte postale*. Lori Saint-Martin. *MD* May 30, 1987: pD3.

[Untitled]; introduction. Adrien Thério. photo · *Lettres québec* Autumn 1987; No 47: p55.

L'AMOUR EN DÉROUTE

See **CRIMINALS IN LOVE/L'AMOUR EN DÉROUTE/Play by George F. Walker**

L'ANNÉE DE LA SCIENCE-FICTION ET DU FANTASTIQUE QUÉBÉCOIS 1986/Anthology

Entre la réussite et l'échec; reviews of science fiction books. Michel Lord. photo · *Lettres québec* Autumn 1987; No 47: p33–34.
[ANTHOLOGIES: BOOK REVIEWS; FIRST NOVELS: BOOK REVIEWS]

L'ANNEAU DU GUÉPARD/Young adult novel by David Schinkel and Yves Beauchesne

Pour les adolescents: quatre mains et deux solitudes; reviews of young adult novels. Dominique Demers. photo · *MD* Dec 19, 1987: pD6–D7.

L'ANTHOLOGIE DES ÉCRIVAINS LAVALLOIS D'AUJOURD'HUI/Anthology

La vie littéraire; column. Marc Morin. *MD* Dec 5, 1987: pD2.
[CANADIAN LITERARY PUBLISHING; CONFERENCES, LITERARY; POETRY READINGS; WRITERS' ORGANIZATIONS]

L'APPEL DE LA RACE/THE IRON WEDGE/Novel by Lionel-Adolphe Groulx

Une première traduction de L'Appel de la race; review of *The Iron Wedge*. Adrien Thério. *Lettres québec* Winter 1986–87; No 44: p85.

[Untitled]; review of *The Iron Wedge*. George Woodcock. *Can Lit* Winter 1987; No 115: p290.

L'APROPOS/Periodical

La vitrine du livre; reviews. Jean Royer. *MD* April 11, 1987: pD2.
[CANADIAN LITERARY PERIODICALS]

L'ARBRE MORT/Children's story by Louise Beaudin and François Caumartin

Mini-comptes rendus; review of *L'Arbre mort*. François Paré. *Can Child Lit* 1987; No 45: p96–97.

L'AUBE DE SUSE/Novel by Jean Forest

Les enfants du déclin; reviews of novels. Jacques Michon. *Voix et images* Winter 1987; No 35: p331–334.

L'AUDACE DES MAINS/Poems by Louise Cotnoir

[Untitled]; review of *L'Audace des mains*. Louise Blouin. *Estuaire* Autumn 1987; No 46: p83.

L'AUTRE RIVAGE

See **THE OTHER SHORE/L'AUTRE RIVAGE/Poems by Antonio D'Alfonso**

L'AVÉNEMENT DE LA MODERNITÉ CULTURELLE AU QUÉBEC/Critical essays collection

[Untitled]; review of *L'Avénement de la modernité culturelle au Québec*. Pierre Guillaume. *Études can* June 1987; No 22: p132.

[Untitled]; reviews of critical works. B.-Z. Shek. *U of Toronto Q* Fall 1987; Vol 57 No 1: p192–199.

L'AVENTURE, LA MÉSAVENTURE/Short story anthology

Au rayon de la nouvelle: l'écriture sur commande; reviews of *Qui a peur de?* . . . and *L'Aventure, la mésaventure*. Jean-Roch Boivin. photo · *MD* Dec 24, 1987: pC11.
[ANTHOLOGIES: BOOK REVIEWS]

La vitrine du livre; reviews of *Le Québec en poésie* and *L'Aventure, la mésaventure*. Guy Ferland. *MD* Nov 28, 1987: pD11.
[ANTHOLOGIES: BOOK REVIEWS]

L'ÉCOUTÉ: POÈMES 1960–1983/Poems by Cécile Cloutier

26 ans d'écriture, deux trajectoires opposes; reviews of *L'écouté* and *SoirS sans AtouT*. André Marquis. photo · *Lettres québec* Winter 1986–87; No 44: p42–43.

[Untitled]; review of *L'Écouté*. Bernard Pozier. *Estuaire* Winter 1986–87; No 43: p75.

Poésie: trois rétrospectives; reviews of poetry books. Jean Royer. photo · *MD* Feb 9, 1987: p11.

L'ÉCRAN BRISÉ/Novel by Louise Frechette

Une écriture qui se cherche encore; review of *L'Écran brisé*. Madeleine Ouellette-Michalska. *MD* July 25, 1987: pC6.

L'ÉCRIT-VENT/Novel by Benoît Fradette

Un homme dont les semelles étaient de vent; review of *L'Écrit-vent*. Jean Éthier-Blais. *MD* May 16, 1987: pD8.

Les Héritiers (prix Robert Cliche) et L'Écrit-vent; reviews. Noël Audet. photo · *Lettres québec* Autumn 1987; No 47: p19–21.
[FIRST NOVELS: BOOK REVIEWS]

L'ÉCRIT PRIMAL/Periodical

La vitrine du livre; reviews. Jean Royer. photo · *MD* April 4, 1987: pD2.
[CANADIAN LITERARY PERIODICALS]

L'ÉDITION LITTÉRAIRE AU QUÉBEC DE 1940 À 1960/Historical survey

[Untitled]; review of *L'Édition littéraire au Québec de 1940 à 1960*. Robert Schwartzwald. *Études lit* Spring-Summer 1987; Vol 20 No 1: p193–199.

L'ENJEU DU MANIFESTE/LE MANIFESTE EN JEU/Essay by Line McMurray and Jeanne Demers

Manifeste: au jeu; review of *L'Enjeu du manifeste/le manifeste en jeu*. Bruno Roy. *Moebius* Spring 1987; No 32: p133–136.

"Crois ou meurs": à quand le manifeste vidéo-clip?; review of *L'Enjeu du manifeste/le manifeste en jeu*. Lori Saint-Martin. photo · *MD* April 18, 1987: pD2.

Le jeu du manifeste littéraire; review of *L'Enjeu du manifeste/Le manifeste en jeu*. Agnès Whitfield. *Lettres québec* Autumn 1987; No 47: p51–52

L'ENTRÉE DANS LA MODERNITÉ: SCIENCE, CULTURE ET SOCIÉTÉ AU QUÉBEC/Critical work by Marcel Fournier

[Untitled]; reviews of critical works. B.-Z. Shek. *U of Toronto Q* Fall 1987; Vol 57 No 1: p192–199.

L'ENVOLEUR DE CHEVAUX ET AUTRE CONTES/Short stories by Marie José Thériault

Des contes et des nouvelles pour rêver; reviews of short story books. Dominique Garand. *Voix et images* Spring 1987; Vol 12 No 3: p551–555.
[ANTHOLOGIES: BOOK REVIEWS]

D'abominables délices; review of *L'Envoleur de chevaux et autres contes*. Michel Lord. *Lettres québec* Winter 1986–87; No 44: p81.

L'ERGASTULE/Novel by Nicole Langlois

L'imagination au pouvoir, la grammaire en déroute; review of *L'Ergastule*. Jean-Roch Boivin. *MD* July 11, 1987: pC7.

L'ESPAGNOLE ET LA PÉKINOISE/Children's story by Gabrielle Roy

Une ultime vision de l'idéal; review of *L'Espagnole et la Pékinoise*. Robert Viau. *Can Child Lit* 1987; No 47: p88–89.

L'ÉTRANGE MONUMENT DU DÉSERT LIBYQUE/Novel by Claude D'Astous

Entre la réussite et l'échec; reviews of science fiction books. Michel Lord. photo · *Lettres québec* Autumn 1987; No 47: p33–34.
[ANTHOLOGIES: BOOK REVIEWS; FIRST NOVELS: BOOK REVIEWS]

L'HABIT DE NEIGE

See THOMAS' SNOWSUIT/L'HABIT DE NEIGE/Children's story by Robert Munsch

L'HÉRITAGE/Novel by Victor-Lévy Beaulieu

Un beau roman; review of *L'Héritage*. Alice Parizeau. photo · *MD* Dec 12, 1987: pD5.

L'HEUREUX, CHRISTINE

Chouette: des livres, des jeux, des jouets; article. Dominique Demers. photo · *MD* Dec 5, 1987: pD6.
[CHILDREN'S LITERATURE; PUBLISHING AND PUBLISHERS IN CANADA]

L'HIVER AU COEUR/Short stories by André Major

La vie est bien faite, dit Vendredi, et juste en somme!; column, includes prose excerpt from *L'Hiver au coeur*. Jean Éthier-Blais. *MD* April 4, 1987: pD8.

Le métier d'écrire; review of *L'Hiver au coeur*. Réjean Beaudoin. *Liberté* Aug 1987; Vol 29 No 4: p110–114.

[Untitled]; review of *L'Hiver au coeur*. Nicole Décarie. *Moebius* Summer 1987; No 33: p133.

Les vertus de la retenue et du silence; reviews of poetry books. Marie José Thériault. photo · *Lettres québec* Summer 1987; No 46: p30–32.

L'HIVER DE MIRA CHRISTOPHE/Novel by Pierre Nepveau

De la poésie la prose; review of *L'Hiver de Mira Christophe*. Noël Audet. photo · *Lettres québec* Winter 1986–87; No 44: p26–28.
[FIRST NOVELS: BOOK REVIEWS]

La ville toute verte, bordée de montagnes enneigées; review of *L'Hiver de Mira Christophe*. Réjean Beaudoin. *Liberté* April 1987; Vol 29 No 2: p118–124.
[FIRST NOVELS: BOOK REVIEWS]

[Untitled]; review article about *L'Hiver de Mira Christophe*. Robert Berrouët-Oriol. *Moebius* Winter 1987; No 31: p143–148.

Éclats d'existence; review of *L'Hiver de Mira Christophe*. Lucie Côté. *MD* April 28, 1987: p17.
[FIRST NOVELS: BOOK REVIEWS]

Couples; reviews of novels. Jacques Michon. *Voix et images* Autumn 1987; Vol 13 No 1: p189–192.

Le roman sans qualités; review of *L'Hiver de Mira Christophe*. Yvon Rivard. *Liberté* June 1987; Vol 29 No 3: p103.
[FIRST NOVELS: BOOK REVIEWS]

L'HOMME AUX MARINGOUINS/Novel by François Hébert

François Hébert, moraliste sans morale; reviews of *L'Homme aux maringouins* and *Le Dernier chant de l'avant-dernier dodo*. Jean Royer. *MD* Feb 7, 1987: pB3.

L'HOMME DE HONG KONG/Short stories by Hélène Rioux

Tous feux teints; review of *L'Homme de Hong Kong*. Marie José Thériault. *Lettres québec* Winter 1986–87; No 44: p34–35.

L'HOMME GRIS suivi de ÉVA ET ÉVELYNE/Play by Marie Laberge

Misères de l'édition théâtrale; reviews of plays. Lucie Robert. *Voix et images* Winter 1987; No 35: p339–342.

L'HUITIÈME JOUR/THE EIGHTH DAY/Novel by Antonine Maillet

Après les mille et une nuits; review of *Le Huitime jour*. Pierre Hébert. photo · *Lettres québec* Winter 1986–87; No 44: p29–30.

L'HYDRE À DEUX COEURS/Poems by Marcelle Roy

Chronique: soliloques; reviews of poetry books. Marguerite Andersen. *Poetry Can R* Spring 1987; Vol 8 No 2–3: p23–24.

[Untitled]; review of *L'Hydre à deux coeurs*. Louise Blouin. *Estuaire* Summer 1987; No 45: p57.

L'ILE JOYEUSE/ISLE OF JOY/Novel by Louise Maheux-Forcier

Hard memory; review of *Isle of Joy*. Sherie Posesorski. *G&M* Aug 22, 1987: pC14.

L'INCONCEPTION/Play by Robert Marinier

Théâtre au masculin; reviews of plays. Jane Moss. *Can Lit* Spring 1987; No 112: p180–183.

L'INCUNABLE/Periodical

Pauvre choix; letter to the editor. Roger Moisan. *MD* Feb 7, 1987: pA18.
[CANADIAN LITERARY PERIODICALS]

La vie littéraire; column. Marc Morin. photo · *MD* Nov 28, 1987: pD12.
[CANADIAN LITERARY PERIODICALS]

La vie littéraire; column. Jean Royer. *MD* Jan 31, 1987: pB2.
[CANADIAN LITERARY PERIODICALS; COMPETITIONS, LITERARY; RADIO AND CANADIAN LITERATURE; TELEVISION AND CANADIAN LITERATURE]

La vitrine du livre; reviews. Jean Royer. photo · *MD* March 28, 1987: pD2.
[CANADIAN LITERARY PERIODICALS]

L'INFANTE IMMMORIALE/Poems by Madeleine Gagnon

Les géographies et le souffle chez Madeleine Gagnon; reviews of *Les Fleurs du Catalpa* and *L'Infante immmoriale*. Caroline Bayard. photo · *Lettres québec* Winter 1986–87; No 44: p46–47.

[Untitled]; review of *L'Infante immémoriale*. Antonio D'Alfonso. *Estuaire* Summer 1987; No 45: p54–55.

L'INFLUENCE D'UN LIVRE/Novel by Philippe-Aubert de Gaspé

Tout texte fondateur en cache un autre!; reviews of *Les Révélations du crime* and *L'Influence d'un livre*. Patrick Imbert. *Lettres québec* Autumn 1987; No 47: p58–60.

L'INSTITUTION LITTÉRAIRE/Conference report

[Untitled]; reviews of critical works. B.-Z. Shek. *U of Toronto Q* Fall 1987; Vol 57 No 1: p192–199.

La structure de la grande machine faire des livres; review of *L'Institution littéraire*. Adrien Thério. *Lettres québec* Winter 1986–87; No 44: p84.
[CONFERENCE REPORTS: REVIEWS AND ARTICLES]

L'IRONIE DE LA FORME: ESSAI SUR "L'ÉLAN D'AMÉRIQUE D'ANDRÉ LANGEVIN/Critical work by Marie-Andrée Beaudet

La modernité: des formes qui (s')inquiètent; reviews of critical works. Agnès Whitfield. photo · *Lettres québec* Summer 1987; No 46: p56–58.

L'IRRÉSOLUE/Poems by Daniel Gunette

Chronique: soliloques; reviews of poetry books. Marguerite Andersen. *Poetry Can R* Spring 1987; Vol 8 No 2–3: p23–24.

L'ITINERARIO DEL SENSO NELLA NARRATIVA DI MALCOLM LOWRY/Critical work by Elsa Linguanti

Demon of analogy; review of *L'Itinerario del senso nella narrativa di Malcolm Lowry*. Richard Cavell. *Can Lit* Spring 1987; No 112: p87–88.

L'OBOMSAWIN/Novel by Daniel Poliquin

Ontarois entre deux langues; reviews of *Nouvelles de la capitale* and *L'Obomsawin*. Lori Saint-Martin. *MD* Dec 12, 1987: pD4.

L'OBSDANTE OBÈSE ET AUTRES AGGRESSIONS/ Short stories by Gilles Archambault

Le malin plaisir de déplaire; review of *L'Obsédante obèse*. Réjean Beaudoin. *Liberté* Oct 1987; Vol 29 No 5: p161–162.

Gilles Archambault et l'art de la sourdine; review of *L'Obsédante obèse et autres agressions*. Jean-Roch Boivin. photo · *MD* June 20, 1987: pD3.

La vitrine du livre; reviews. Guy Ferland. *MD* May 23, 1987: pD4.

Un livre pour tester la conscience; review of *L'Obsédante obèse*. Marie José Thériault. photo · *Lettres québec* Autumn 1987; No 47: p30–31.

L'OEIL INTERROMPUE/Novel by Michel Dallaire

Cycles; reviews of *L'Oeil interrompu* and *Poison*. Mark Benson. *Can Lit* Spring 1987; No 112: p136–138.

L'OEUVRE ROMANESQUE DE MARIE-CLAIRE BLAIS/Critical work by Françoise Laurent

[Untitled]; review of *L'Oeuvre romanesque de Marie-Claire Blais*. Élène Cliche. *Voix et images* Winter 1987; No 35: p318–321.

Lire et relire Marie-Claire Blais; review of *L'Oeuvre romanesque de Marie-Claire Blais*. Chantal Gamache. *Lettres québec* Spring 1987; No 45: p52.

[Untitled]; review of *L'Oeuvre romanesque de Marie-Claire Blais*. Annette Hayward. *U of Toronto Q* Fall 1987; Vol 57 No 1: p183–184.

La vitrine du livre; reviews. Jean Royer. photo · *MD* March 28, 1987: pD2.
[CANADIAN LITERARY PERIODICALS]

L'OUEST EN NOUVELLES/Short story anthology

De l'ouest, des nouvelles et de l'histoire; reviews of short story books. Paulette Collet. photo · *Lettres québec* Summer 1987; No 46: p68–70.
[ANTHOLOGIES: BOOK REVIEWS]

L'OURS ET LE KANGAROU/Novel by Roch Carrier

Theatre encore; reviews of *L'Ours et le kangourou* and *Au septième ciel*. Carrol F. Coates. *Can Lit* Winter 1987; No 115: p255–257.

Rencontre tonnante; review of *L'Ours et le kangourou*. Claude Sabourin. *Lettres québec* Winter 1986–87; No 44: p82.

L'UNIVERS EST FERMÉ POUR CAUSE D'INVENTOIRE/Essay by Jacques Fillion

Un beau livre de réflexions; review of *L'Univers est fermé pour cause d'inventaire*. André Renaud. *Lettres québec* Summer 1987; No 46: p64–65.

L'USAGE DU RÉEL suivi de EXERCISES DE TIR/Poems by Robert Yergeau

[Untitled]; review of *L'Usage du réel*. Hélène Dorion. *Estuaire* Winter 1986–87; No 43: p79.

Écrire sur l'écrire; review of *L'Usage du réel*. Régis Normandeau. *Lettres québec* Spring 1987; No 45: p64.

[Untitled]; reviews of poetry books. Jacques St-Pierre. *Moebius* Winter 1987; No 31: p137–139.

LÉGER, DYANE

Dyane Léger, l'enfant terrible d'Acadie; reviews of *Graines de fées* and *Sorcière du vent!*. Gérard Étienne. photo · *MD* July 4, 1987: pC7.

LÈVRES URBAINES/Periodical

Notes de lecture; reviews of periodicals. Jean Royer. *MD* March 21, 1987: pC7.
[CANADIAN LITERARY PERIODICALS]

Notes de lecture; reviews of periodicals. Jean Royer. *MD* March 21, 1987: pD8.
[CANADIAN LITERARY PERIODICALS]

LA FRANCE, MICHELINE

Micheline La France et les fils de sa trame; interview. Jean-Roch Boivin. photo · *Lettres québec* Summer 1987; No 46: p32–33.

La vitrine du livre; reviews of *À double sens* and *Le Fils d'Ariane*. Guy Ferland. *MD* Feb 14, 1987: pC2.

Un fil d'Ariane habilement tendu; review of *Le Fils d'Ariane*. Madeleine Ouellette-Michalska. photo · *MD* March 28, 1987: pD3.

La vie littéraire; column. Jean Royer. photo · *MD* May 23, 1987: pD2.
[CULTURAL IDENTITY; RADIO AND CANADIAN LITERATURE; TELEVISION AND CANADIAN LITERATURE; WRITERS' ORGANIZATIONS]

Les vertus de la retenue et du silence; reviews of poetry books. Marie José Thériault. photo · *Lettres québec* Summer 1987; No 46: p30–32.

LA ROCQUE, GILBERT

Dans les poches; reviews. Guy Ferland. *MD* Sept 26, 1987: pD6.

Focalisation, voyeurisme et scène originaire dans Serge d'entre les morts; article. Alain Piette. *Voix et images* Spring 1987; Vol 12 No 3: p497–511.
[STRUCTURALIST WRITING AND CRITICISM]

LABBÉ, JOSETTE

À la recherche de tendresse; review of *Les Vingt-quatre heures du clan*. Alice Parizeau. *MD* Dec 24, 1987: pC11.

LABERGE, MARIE

Experimental theatre: only some works; theatre review of *Nouvelles pour le théâtre*. Marianne Ackerman. *MG* Feb 5, 1987: pE6.

Le Night Cap Bar a minor thriller that tries to be more; theatre review. Marianne Ackerman. *MG* April 9, 1987: pE8.

Le théâtre qu'on joue; theatre reviews. André Dionne. photo · *Lettres québec* Summer 1987; No 46: p47–48.

Oublier could have been a lot of things but misses chance; theatre review. Pat Donnelly. photo · *MG* Nov 4, 1987: pB9.

La vitrine du livre; reviews. Guy Ferland. *MD* May 30, 1987: pD4.

Idéologie féministe dans Le Temps sauvage et C'tait avant la guerre l'Anse Gilles; article. Monique Genuist. abstract · *Theatre Hist in Can (special issue)* Spring 1987; Vol 8 No 1: p49–58.
[FEMINIST DRAMA]

"Nouvelles pour le théâtre"; column. Robert Lévesque. *MD* Jan 27, 1987: p5.

Moisson d'avril; column. Robert Lévesque. photo · *MD* March 31, 1987: p17.

Je serai Robert Thomas ou rien . . . ; theatre review of *Le Night Cap Bar*. Robert Lévesque. photo · *MD* April 9, 1987: p13.

Le théâtre du Rire joue gagnant; column. Robert Lévesque. *MD* Oct 13, 1987: p11.
[AWARDS, LITERARY]

Oublier ou ne pas oublier; article. Robert Lévesque. photo · *MD* Oct 31, 1987: pC1,C3.

L'insoutenable dureté de l'être; theatre review of *Oublier*. Robert Lévesque. photo · *MD* Nov 4, 1987: p13.

[Untitled]; theatre reviews of *Oublier* and *Tête à tête*. Robert Lévesque. *MD* Nov 6, 1987: p15.

[Untitled]; theatre review of *Oublier*. Robert Lévesque. photo · *MD* Nov 13, 1987: p15.

[Untitled]; theatre reviews. Robert Lévesque. *MD* Dec 4, 1987: p15.

Misères de l'édition théâtrale; reviews of plays. Lucie Robert. *Voix et images* Winter 1987; No 35: p339–342.

Suspense au fond du gouffre; theatre review of *Le Night Cap Bar*. Michel Vaïs. photo · *Jeu* 1987; No 44: p175–177.

LABERGE, PIERRE

[Untitled]; review of *Pris de présence*. Réjean Bonenfant. *Estuaire* Autumn 1987; No 46: p84–85.

La métamorphose du quotidien; reviews of poetry books. André Marquis. photo · *Lettres québec* Autumn 1987; No 47: p41–43.

LACHAPELLE, CÔME

Désert, attente, silence; reviews of poetry books. Robert Yergeau. photo · *Lettres québec* Autumn 1987; No 47: p44–45.

LADIES OF THE HOUSE/Short stories by Sandra Birdsell

The Lafreniere family of Agassiz; reviews of *Night Travellers* and *Ladies of the House*. J.K. Johnstone. illus · *NeWest R* April 1987; Vol 12 No 8: p12.

LADY ORACLE/Novel by Margaret Atwood

George, Leda, and a poured concrete balcony: a study of three aspects of the evolution of Lady Oracle; article. Carol L. Beran. *Can Lit* Spring 1987; No 112: p18–28.
[ARTIST FIGURE]

The re/membering of the female power in Lady Oracle; article. Roberta Sciff-Zamaro. *Can Lit* Spring 1987; No 112: p32–38.
[FEMINIST WRITING AND CRITICISM; MYTHS AND LEGENDS IN CANADIAN LITERATURE]

LAFERRIÈRE, DANY

Le Laferrière nouveau; article. Robert Lévesque. photo · *MD* Sept 30, 1987: p13.

Dany Laferrière: "le talent a m'irait!"; article. Robert Lévesque. photo · *MD* Oct 10, 1987: pD3.

Dany's destiny; article. Francine Pelletier. photo · *MG* Dec 24, 1987: L8.

En attendant la bombe; column. Nathalie Petrowski. *MD* Oct 3, 1987: pC2.

Une bombe dans la tête; review of *Éroshima*. Jean Royer. *MD* Oct 10, 1987: pD3.

LAFOND, GUY

[Untitled]; review of *La Nuit émeraude*. Dana Mockevïciuté. *Moebius* Summer 1987; No 33: p139.

LAGACÉ, MICHEL FRANCIS

Mourir comme un chat?; reviews of *Mourir comme un chat* and *Facéties*. Madeleine Ouellette-Michalska. *MD* July 4, 1987: pC6.

LAIIAISE, ROBERT

Guy Delahaye, un gamin mélancolique, sourire aux lèvres; column. Jean Éthier-Blais. *MD* Sept 12, 1987: pD8.

La vitrine du livre; review of *Guy Delahaye et la modernité littéraire*. Guy Ferland. *MD* July 25, 1987: pC6.

Le "médecin de Nelligan"; review of *Guy Delahaye et la modernité littéraire*. Marcel Fournier. *MD* Aug 29, 1987: pC14.

LALONDE, ROBERT

Conservatisme; reviews of novels. Neil B. Bishop. *Can Lit* Winter 1987; No 115: p169–172.

Japrisot à La Licorne, Strauss à Fred-Barry; column. Robert Lévesque. *MD* Feb 3, 1987: p7.

Robert Lalonde: un théâtre de risques et sans compromis; article. Robert Lévesque. photo · *MD* April 4, 1987: pC1,C8.

L'originalité et l'oralité; reviews of *Coq à deux têtes* and *Les Terres du songe*. Jean Royer. *MD* May 30, 1987: pD3.

LAMARCHE, GUSTAVE

Le Père Gustave Lamarche s'éteint; obituary. Renée Rowan. photo · *MD* Oct 13, 1987: p3.

La poésie spirituelle de Gustave Lamarche; article. Jean Royer. photo · *MD* Oct 17, 1987: pD2.

Bloc-notes; column. Michel Vaïs. photo · *Jeu* 1987; No 45: p227–231.
[AWARDS, LITERARY; GOVERNMENT GRANTS FOR WRITERS/PUBLISHERS; WRITERS' ORGANIZATIONS]

LAMOTHE, RAYMONDE

La vitrine du livre; reviews of *Retour II: journal d'émotions* and *N'eût été cet été nu*. Guy Ferland. *MD* July 11, 1987: pC6.

Les fruits de mon imagination; letter to the editor. Raymonde Lamothe. *MD* Aug 19, 1987: p8.

Nudisme et fiction; letter to the editor. Michel Vaïs. *MD* Aug 13, 1987: p8.

LAMPMAN, ARCHIBALD

[Untitled]; reviews of *Archibald Lampman* and *John Metcalf*. Dennis Duffy. *Eng Studies in Can* Sept 1987; Vol 13 No 3: P355–357.

[Untitled]; letter to the editor. Victoria Ellison. *Books in Can* Nov 1987; Vol 16 No 8: p40.

Avant-propos/Forward; editorial article in French and in English translation. Patricia Godbout. *Ellipse* 1987; No 38: p4–7.

Le mérite d'Archibald Lampman; article. D.G. Jones. trans · *Ellipse* 1987; No 38: p89–95.

Poet-confessor; review of *Archibald Lampman*. John Ower. *Can Lit* Winter 1987; No 115: p167–169.

The story of an affinity: Lampman's "The Frogs" and Tennyson's "The Lotos-Eaters"; article. John Ower. *Can Lit* Winter 1987; No 115: p285–289.

LAMY, JULES

De l'ouest, des nouvelles et de l'histoire; reviews of short story books. Paulette Collet. photo · *Lettres québec* Summer 1987; No 46: p68–70.
[ANTHOLOGIES: BOOK REVIEWS]

LAMY, SUZANNE

Décès de Suzanne Lamy; obituary. *MD* Feb 26, 1987: p3.

La voix minimale; article. Jacques Brault. *Voix et images* Autumn 1987; Vol 13 No 1: p66–69.

Suzanne Lamy; obituary. Jacques Folch-Ribas. *Liberté* June 1987; Vol 29 No 3: p103.

Bibliographie de Suzanne Lamy; bibliography. Pascale Noizet. *Voix et images* Autumn 1987; Vol 13 No 1: p70–80.

Avatars d'un pacte amoureux; article. Alain Piette. *Voix et images* Autumn 1987; Vol 13 No 1: p46–51.

Suzanne Lamy: elle était le double d'Ariane et un théoricienne passionnée; obituary. Jean Royer. photo · *MD* Feb 28, 1987: pC3.

Entre France et Québec: des lieux, des liens, une voix; article. Monique La Rue. *Voix et images* Autumn 1987; Vol 13 No 1: p42–45.
[FRANCE-CANADA LITERARY RELATIONS]

Suzanne Lamy, pour une morale de la critique; article. Lori Saint-Martin. *Voix et images* Autumn 1987; Vol 13 No 1: p29–40.

Suzanne Lamy: le féminin au risque de la critique; article. Sherry Simon. *Voix et images* Autumn 1987; Vol 13 No 1: p52–64.
[FEMINIST WRITING AND CRITICISM; STRUCTURALIST WRITING AND CRITICISM]

Hommage à Suzanne Lamy; obituary. Adrien Thério. photo · *Lettres québec* Summer 1987; No 46: p8.
[CANADIAN LITERARY PERIODICALS]

Suzanne Lamy. D'un texte l'autre; introduction. Andrée Yanacopoulo. *Voix et images* Autumn 1987; Vol 13 No 1: p8.

LANA LUST: THE BITCH STOPS HERE/Play by Kent Staines

Flashes of gold among the dross at Fringe festival; theatre reviews. Liam Lacey. *G&M* Aug 19, 1987: pC5.
[FESTIVALS, DRAMA]

THE LAND CALLED MORNING/Children's play anthology

Native dramas; review of *The Land Called Morning*. Thomas Gerry. *Can Child Lit* 1987; No 46: p97–98.
[ANTHOLOGIES: BOOK REVIEWS]

LANDRY-THERIAULT, JEANNINE

An interview with Jeannine Landry-Theriault. Martine Jacquot. biog photo · *Fiddlehead* Summer 1987; No 152: p72–75.

LANDSBERG, MICHELE

Author warns of racism in classics; article. *CH* May 20, 1987: pF2.

Passionate and practical; review of *Michele Landsberg's Guide to Children's Books*. Mary G. Hamilton. *Can Child Lit* 1987; No 46: p64–65.

LANDSLIDES: SELECTED POEMS 1975–1985/Poems by Don Coles

[Untitled]; review of *Landslides*. Stephen Brockwell. *Rubicon* Fall 1987; No 9: p182–184.

Meddling with time; review of *Landslides*. Rita Donovan. *Fiddlehead* Summer 1987; No 152: p100–104.

Confident voices heard through poetry collections; reviews of poetry books. Christopher Wiseman. *CH* Feb 8, 1987: pE5.

LANE, PATRICK

Billboard: libraries to sell books for three days; column. *WFP* Nov 3, 1987: p19.
[POETRY READINGS]

[Untitled]; review of *Selected Poems*. Barbara Carey. *Books in Can* Dec 1987; Vol 16 No 9: p29–30.

Lane is chained to rock of reality; review of *Selected Poems*. Sid Marty. *CH* Dec 13, 1987: pC8.

LANGEVIN, ANDRÉ

La modernité: des formes qui (s')inquiètent; reviews of critical works. Agnès Whitfield. photo · *Lettres québec* Summer 1987; No 46: p56–58.

LANGEVIN, GILBERT

La fiction du réel/le réel de la fiction; reviews of poetry books. André Brochu. *Voix et images* Winter 1987; No 35: p322–330.

La vie littéraire; column. Marc Morin. *MD* Nov 14, 1987: pD14.
[AWARDS, LITERARY; CHILDREN'S LITERATURE; POETRY READINGS]

Songe, révolte et manifeste; reviews of poetry books. Robert Yergeau. photo · *Lettres québec* Spring 1987; No 45: p38–39.

LANGLOIS, NICOLE

L'imagination au pouvoir, la grammaire en déroute; review of *L'Ergastule*. Jean-Roch Boivin. *MD* July 11, 1987: pC7.

LANGNER, PAT

Appealing performer wasted in aimless ghost town saga; theatre review of *Tag in a Ghost Town*. Ray Conlogue. photo · *G&M* May 15, 1987: pD10.

Tag makes your hair stand on end; theatre review of *Tag in a Ghost Town*. Henry Mietkiewicz. *TS* May 15, 1987: pD11.

Prairie spaces in the big city: western theatre in Toronto; theatre reviews. Margaret Gail Osachoff. *NeWest R* Oct 1987; Vol 13 No 2: p18–19.

LANGUES D'AIMER/Poems by Jean Chapdelaine Gagnon

[Untitled]; reviews of *Langues d'aimer* and *Le Tant-à-coeur*. Jacques Paquin. *Estuaire* Summer 1987; No 45: p49–50.

LAPOINTE, GATIEN

La fiction du réel/le réel de la fiction; reviews of poetry books. André Brochu. *Voix et images* Winter 1987; No 35: p322–330.

Dits et faits; column. Adrien Thério. photo · *Lettres québec* Summer 1987; No 46: p6.
[AUTHORS, CANADIAN; CANADIAN LITERARY PUBLISHING; CONFERENCES, LITERARY; GOVERNMENT GRANTS FOR WRITERS/PUBLISHERS; LIBRARY SERVICES AND CANADIAN LITERATURE]

LAPOINTE, PAUL-MARIE

Paul-Marie Lapointe chez Seghers; review of *Paul-Marie Lapointe*. André-G. Bourassa. *Lettres québec* Summer 1987; No 46: p77–78

La poésie de Paul-Marie Lapointe; review of *Paul-Marie Lapointe*. Jean Fisette. *Voix et images* Autumn 1987; Vol 13 No 1: p174–178.

Paul-Marie Lapointe, poète d'aujourd'hui; article. Jean Royer. photo · *MD* April 18, 1987: pD1,D3.

LAPP, CLAUDIA E.

[Untitled]; review of *Cloud Gate*. Anne Cimon. *Rubicon* Spring 1987; No 8: p221–222.

[Untitled]; review of *Cloud Gate*. Karen Ruttan. *Poetry Can R* Spring 1987; Vol 8 No 2–3: p40.

LARKIN, PHYLLIS

[Untitled]; reviews of poetry books. George Whipple. *Poetry Can R* Spring 1987; Vol 8 No 2–3: p53.

LAROCQUE, PIERRE A.

Opéra-fête: the power of the image; article. Solange Lévesque. photo trans · *Can Theatre R* Spring 1987; No 50: p20–25.

LAROSE, JEAN

Jean Larose: un dialogue entre l'Écrit et l'Oral; column. Jean Éthier-Blais. *MD* Sept 26, 1987: pD8.

La vitrine du livre; reviews. Guy Ferland. *MD* Sept 12, 1987: pD4.

LAROUCHE-THIBAULT, MONIQUE

Conservatisme; reviews of novels. Neil B. Bishop. *Can Lit* Winter 1987; No 115: p169–172.

LARUE, MONIQUE

La vitrine du livre; reviews. Guy Ferland. *MD* March 7, 1987: pB2.
[CANADIAN LITERARY PERIODICALS]

LASCAUX/Novel by Normand de Bellefeuille

[Untitled]; reviews of *Lascaux* and *Catégoriques un deux trois*. Richard Boutin. *Estuaire* Summer 1987; No 45: p52–54.

THE LAST BLEWOINTMENT ANTHOLOGY: VOLUME ONE/Anthology

Blewointment: rites of passage; review of *The Last Blewointment Anthology: Volume One*. Len Early. *Essays on Can Writ* Winter 1987; No 35: p178–181.
[ANTHOLOGIES: BOOK REVIEWS]

THE LAST BUS/Play by Raymond Storey

Smooth ride on The Last Bus; theatre review. Stephen Godfrey. photo · *G&M* Feb 16, 1987: pD9.

[The Last Bus]; theatre review. Susan Minsos. *NeWest R* April 1987; Vol 12 No 8: p17.

[Untitled]; theatre review of *The Last Bus*. Mark Schoenberg. photo · *Maclean's* Feb 23, 1987; Vol 100 No 8: p55.

LAST CHANCE SUMMER/Young adult novel by Diana J. Wieler

Literary extravaganza goes national; column. Kenneth McGoogan. *CH* April 5, 1987: pE5.
[AUTHORS, CANADIAN; FILM ADAPTATIONS OF CANADIAN LITERATURE; WRITERS' ORGANIZATIONS; WRITERS' WORKSHOPS]

What troubles troubled kids; review of *Last Chance Summer*. Douglas Thorpe. *Can Child Lit* 1987; No 46: p86–87.

Western publisher produces winners only; reviews of *Last Chance Summer* and *The Empty Chair*. Tim Wynne-Jones. *G&M* Feb 21, 1987: pE19.

THE LAST ECHO/Novel by Byrna Barclay

Anybody home; reviews of *The Last Echo* and *Wise-Ears*. Linda Rogers. *Can Lit* Winter 1987; No 115: p204–205.

THE LAST HUNTER/Novel by Fred Cederberg

Cheap thrills; reviews of *The Last Hunter* and *Gallows View*. Janice Kulyk Keefer. *Books in Can* June-July 1987; Vol 16 No 5: p37–38.
[FIRST NOVELS: BOOK REVIEWS]

THE LAST REAL SUMMER/Play by Warren Graves

The Last Real Summer a 'warm,' faded memory; article. Keith Bolender. *TS (Neighbours)* Jan 27, 1987: p20.

'Memory play' takes woman to childhood; article. Alex Law. *TS (Neighbors)* Nov 24, 1987: p16.

This play doesn't come to life; theatre review of *The Last Real Summer*. Alex Law. *TS (Neighbors)* Dec 8, 1987: p19.

THE LAST SEASON/Novel by Roy McGregor

Hockey drama kicks off new Canadian TV season; column. Jim Bawden. photo · *TS* Jan 2, 1987: pD21.
[TELEVISION AND CANADIAN LITERATURE]

Ambitious hockey saga fails to score; television review of *The Last Season*. John Haslett Cuff. photo · *G&M* Jan 3, 1987: pE5.
[TELEVISION AND CANADIAN LITERATURE]

THE LAST VOYAGE OF THE DEVIL'S WHEEL/ Children's play by Jim Betts

Last Voyage appeals to all; theatre review of *The Last Voyage of the Devil's Wheel*. Pat Donnelly. photo · *MG* Dec 16, 1987: pF3.

THE LAST WAR/Young adult novel by Martyn Godfrey

Lite-lit for children has arrived; reviews of children's books. Tim Wynne-Jones. *G&M* March 7, 1987: pE19

THE LAST WHITE MAN IN PANAMA/Novel by William Gough

All this and quality, too; review of *The Last White Man in Panama*. Andrew Allentuck. *WFP* Oct 24, 1987: p54.

A decade of great thrillers continues with two treasures; reviews of *Swann: A Mystery* and *The Last White Man in Panama*. Margaret Cannon. *G&M* Sept 26, 1987: pC23.

One slick thriller — and another that's not so slick; review of *The Last White Man in Panama*. Geoff Chapman. *TS* Oct 18, 1987: pC8.

[Untitled]; review of *The Last White Man in Panama*. Geoff Heinricks. *Quill & Quire* Sept 1987; Vol 53 No 9: p79.

Romantic adventure set in Panama City is as thin as the celluloid it's written for; review of *The Last White Man in Panama*. P. Scott Lawrence. photo · *MG* Nov 7, 1987: K12.

Francis has winner in new whodunit; review of *The Last White Man in Panama*. Kenneth McGoogan. *CH* Nov 1, 1987: pE6.

THE LAST WILL AND TESTAMENT OF LOLITA/Play by Nightwood Theatre collective

The humor saves Lolita, but it's strained; theatre review of *The Last Will and Testament of Lolita*. Christopher Hume. *TS* June 5, 1987: pE19.

Lolita grows up to get last laughs; article. Henry Mietkiewicz. *TS* May 29, 1987: pE13.

THE LATE BLUMER/Play by John Lazarus

Late Blumer's a step behind; theatre review. Brian Brennan. photo · *CH (Sunday Magazine)* Jan 13, 1987: pD5.

THE LATE GREAT HUMAN ROAD SHOW/Novel by Paulette Jiles

Ranging from colored bleakness to breeziness; reviews of novels by Paulette Jiles. Ken Adachi. photo · *TS* Feb 28, 1987: M4.

[Untitled]; reviews of *Flight Against Time* and *The Late Great Human Road Show*. Judith Carson. *Can Forum* Aug-Sept 1987; Vol 67 No 771: p48–49.
[FIRST NOVELS: BOOK REVIEWS]

[Untitled]; reviews of novels. Beverley Daurio. *Cross Can Writ Q* 1987; Vol 9 No 3–4: p45–46.

Paulette Jiles' fictional strategies; reviews of Sitting in the Club Car Drinking Rum and Karma-Kola and *The Late Great Human Road Show*. Roslyn Dixon. *Event* Summer 1987; Vol 16 No 2: p127–130.

Apocalyptic consumers; review of *The Late Great Human Road Show*. Cecelia Frey. photo · *CH* March 15, 1987: pE5.

Starting over; reviews of *The Late Great Human Road Show* and *Sitting in the Club Car Drinking Rum and Karma-Kola*. David Helwig. *Books in Can* Jan-Feb 1987; Vol 16 No 1: p15.

LATIF-GHATTAS, MONA

[Untitled]; review of *Quarante voiles pour un exil*. Claude Beausoleil. *Estuaire* Spring 1987; No 44: p82.

[Untitled]; review of *Quarante voiles pour un exil*. Paul Desgreniers. *Moebius* Winter 1987; No 31: p142–143.

La vitrine du livre; reviews. Jean Royer. photo · *MD* March 21, 1987: pD2.
[CANADIAN LITERARY PERIODICALS]

LATIN AMERICA-CANADA LITERARY RELATIONS

English novelist praises Toronto festival; column. Ken Adachi. *TS* March 30, 1987: pF4.
[FESTIVALS, LITERARY]

A South American education; essay. Mary di Michele. illus · *Books in Can* Aug-Sept 1987; Vol 16 No 6: p3.

Novelist as trickster: the magical presence of Gabriel García Márquez in Robert Kroetsch's What The Crow Said; article. Brian Edwards. *Essays on Can Writ* Spring 1987; No 34: p92–110.
[MAGIC REALISM; POSTMODERNIST WRITING AND CRITICISM; STRUCTURALIST WRITING AND CRITICISM]

LATRAVERSE, PLUME

Une vie de Patachon bien sympathique; reviews of *D'ailleurs et d'ici* and *Contes gouttes ou le pays d'un reflet*. Yolande Grisé. photo · *Lettres québec* Summer 1987; No 46: p59–60.

Plume: écrire pour sauver sa peau; article. Nathalie Petrowski. photo · *MD* Feb 20, 1987: pB1,B7.

LAURENCE, MARGARET

Novelist Margaret Laurence dead of lung cancer at age 60; obituary. *TS* Jan 6, 1987: pA1.

Laurence memorial service Friday; article. *TS* Jan 7, 1987: pF1.

Milestones; column. photo · *TS* Jan 11, 1987: H6.

Manitoba town honors Laurence; article. *TS* Jan 12, 1987: pC3.

MPPs pay tribute to Laurence; article. *TS* Jan 13, 1987: pA8.

Film tribute to Margaret Laurence; article. *TS* Jan 13, 1987: pB1.
[AUDIO-VISUALS AND CANADIAN LITERATURE]

Novelist Laurence dies at 60; notice. *MG* Jan 6, 1987: pA1.

Margaret Laurence dies of cancer; obituary. photo · *MG* Jan 6, 1987: pB13.

Margaret Laurence; editorial. *MG* Jan 7, 1987: pB2.

Laurence's girlhood home an arts centre; article. biog photo · *MG* Jan 7, 1987: pE5.
[CANADIAN LITERARY LANDMARKS]

Grief, memory and hope at Laurence memorial; article. *MG* Jan 10, 1987: pB8.

Lakefield service honors Laurence; article. *MG* Jan 19, 1987: pD5

Margaret Laurence; editorial. *WFP* Jan 8, 1987: p6.

Excerpts from Laurence novels to be read at memorial service; article. *WFP* Jan 9, 1987: p15.

Laurence memorial service planned at U of M; article. *WFP* Jan 10, 1987: p23.

Laurence's work defended; article. *WFP* Jan 14, 1987: p39.

Author eulogized; article. *WFP* Jan 19, 1987: p13.

Laurence spent last months securing funds for the blind; article. photo · *WFP* Jan 20, 1987: p30.

NFB honors Laurence; article. *WFP* Jan 22, 1987: p36.

Memorial conference; article. *WFP* Feb 13, 1987: p29.
[CONFERENCES, LITERARY]

Tribute to Laurence; article. *WFP* March 6, 1987: p22.

Billboard: Christian women's club plans lunch program; column. *WFP* March 8, 1987: p12.
[AUDIO-VISUALS AND CANADIAN LITERATURE]

Décès de la romancière Margaret Laurence; obituary. photo · *MD* Jan 7, 1987: p7.

For the record; obituary. photo · *CH* Jan 11, 1987: pB5.

Author's beliefs saluted; article. photo · *CH* Jan 19, 1987: pE6.

Memorial service set for Laurence; article. *G&M* Jan 8, 1987: pC1.

Books still raise eyebrows in Laurence's hometown; article. *G&M* Jan 10, 1987: pE6.

Laurence recalled as model pupil; article. *G&M* Jan 12, 1987: pC9.

Town remembers Margaret Laurence; article. *G&M* Jan 19, 1987: pC9.

Films to be shown at Laurence tribute; article. *G&M* Jan 20, 1987: pD9.
[AUDIO-VISUALS AND CANADIAN LITERATURE]

Deceased author's support helped project for the blind; article. *G&M* Jan 20, 1987: pD14.

Margaret Laurence, 1926–1987; obituary. *Books in Can* Jan-Feb 1987; Vol 16 No 1: p3.

Passages; column. *Maclean's* Jan 19, 1987; Vol 100 No 3: p4.

Laurence memorial opened; article. *WFP* June 24, 1987: p26.
[CANADIAN LITERARY LANDMARKS]

Rainbow brings smile; article. *WFP* June 26, 1987: p42.
[CANADIAN LITERARY LANDMARKS]

Canadian studies news and notes; column. *J of Can Studies* Summer 1987; Vol 22 No 2: p210–211.
[CONFERENCES, LITERARY]

Dits et faits; column. photo · *Lettres québec* Spring 1987; No 45: p6–7.
[AWARDS, LITERARY; PUBLISHING AND PUBLISHERS IN CANADA; TRANSLATIONS OF CANADIAN LITERATURE; WRITERS' ORGANIZATIONS]

Laurence home made historical site; article. *MG* June 26, 1987: pC2.
[CANADIAN LITERARY LANDMARKS]

Canadian Studies news and notes; column. *J of Can Studies* Fall 1987; Vol 22 No 3: p162.

New Laurence fund plans peace benefit; article. *G&M* Dec 30, 1987: pC5.

Images of '87: the deaths; article. photo · *Maclean's* Dec 21, 1987; Vol 100 No 51: p48.

Fund promotes late author's concerns; article. *CH* Dec 31, 1987: pD5.

Margaret Laurence left a wonderful legacy; letter to the editor. I. Aagaard. *TS* Jan 10, 1987: pB3.

[Untitled]; letter to the editor. Susan Abeles. *G&M* Jan 21, 1987: pA7.

Margaret Laurence dead at 60: revered writer remembered for her humanity as well as books; article. Ken Adachi. biog photo · *TS* Jan 6, 1987: pD1–D2.

Tears flow as piper's lament eulogizes Margaret Laurence; article. Ken Adachi. photo · *TS* Jan 10, 1987: pA6.

"I've done what I set out to do; I have nothing to regret"; essay. Ken Adachi. photo · *CH* Jan 7, 1987: pD3.

Feminist quarterly honors Laurence; column. Ken Adachi. *TS* Nov 16, 1987: pC5.
[CANADIAN LITERARY PERIODICALS; FICTION READINGS]

CBC variety keeps smiling despite budget cuts; column. Sid Adilman. *TS* Feb 26, 1987: pB1.
[FILM ADAPTATIONS OF CANADIAN LITERATURE]

Carlton's closing for major renovations; column. Sid Adilman. *TS* Dec 29, 1987: pE1.

Staunch few attend Laurence memorial; article. Jane Armstrong. photo · *WFP* Jan 11, 1987: p2

The diviner; essay. Don Bailey. *Brick* Winter 1987; No 29: p6–9.

Matrimony; review of *Mother and Daughter Relationships in the Manawaka Works of Margaret Laurence*. Connie Bellamy. *Essays on Can Writ* Winter 1987; No 35: p93–99.

Heuresis: the mother-daughter theme in A Jest of God and Autumn Sonata; article. Michael Bird. *New Q* Spring-Summer 1987; Vol 7 No 1–2: p267–273.
[THE FAMILY IN CANADIAN LITERATURE; WOMEN IN LITERATURE]

Margaret Laurence 1926–1987: prairie, ancestors, woman; article. Anne Burke. *Cross Can Writ Q* 1987; Vol 9 No 2: p16–17,29.

Margaret Laurence in England; essay. Barry Callaghan. photo · *Books in Can* March 1987; Vol 16 No 2: p9–12.

The legacy of Margaret Laurence; article. Michael Cardy. *Can Auth & Book* Summer 1987; Vol 62 No 4: p3.
[CENSORSHIP]

Neepawa mourns Laurence; article. Adrian Chamberlain. photo · *WFP* Jan 6, 1987: p1,4.

Laurence clung to roots; obituary. Rod Currie. photo · *WFP* Jan 6, 1987: p21.

Margaret Laurence dead at 60; obituary. Rod Currie. photo · *CH* Jan 6, 1987: pD5.

Laurence service; letter to the editor. Brian Curtis. photo · *WFP* Jan 26, 1987: p6.
[CANADIAN LITERARY LANDMARKS]

The best part of going out; editorial. Paul Denham. *NeWest R* Oct 1987; Vol 13 No 2: p1.
[CANADIAN LITERARY LANDMARKS]

Writer's women among most memorable in Canadian fiction; obituary. Donn Downey. photo · *G&M* Jan 6, 1987: pA11.

La vitrine du livre; review of *Gabrielle Roy et Margaret Laurence: deux chemins, une recherche*. Guy Ferland. *MD* Aug 8, 1987: pC6.

A life of eloquence and radicalism; obituary. Timothy Findley. photo · *Maclean's* Jan 19, 1987; Vol 100 No 3: p52–53.

My final hour: an address to the Philosophy Society, Trent University, Monday, 26 January 1987; essay. Timothy Findley. abstract · *J of Can Studies* Spring 1987; Vol 22 No 1: p5–16.

Poetry sweatshops add a new twist to Olympic tradition; column. William French. *G&M* March 3, 1987: pC7.
[CANADIAN LITERARY LANDMARKS; COMPETITIONS, LITERARY; FESTIVALS, LITERARY; POETRY READINGS]

A salute to a writer of rare integrity; article. William French. photo · *G&M* Jan 6, 1987: pC5.

A moving tribute to a great writer; article. William French. photo · *G&M* Jan 10, 1987: pE6.

Anti-smoking message is right on target; column. William French. *G&M* April 14, 1987: pC7.
[WRITERS' ORGANIZATIONS]

Timely celebrations of women's achievements; column. William French. photo · *G&M* Dec 1, 1987: pD5.

Orphan from Neepawa; editorial article. Robert Fulford. illus · *Sat Night* May 1987; Vol 102 No 5: p5–6.

Laurence's hour; letter to the editor. William A. Gilbert. *G&M* Feb 2, 1987: pA6.

Personal recollections of controversy that made Margaret Laurence weep; article. John Goddard. photo · *MG* Jan 10, 1987: pB8.
[CENSORSHIP]

The rhythms of ritual in Margaret Laurence's The Tomorrow-Tamer; article. James Harrison. *World Lit in Eng* Autumn 1987; Vol 27 No 2: p245–252.

The religious roots of the feminine identity issue: Margaret Laurence's The Stone Angel and Margaret Atwood's Surfacing; article. Evelyn J. Hinz. abstract · *J of Can Studies* Spring 1987; Vol 22 No 1: p17–31.
[BIBLICAL MYTHS AND MYTHOLOGY; FEMINIST WRITING AND CRITICISM; GOD IN LITERATURE]

Writer's obit upstaged by Reagan's operation; letter to the editor. Helena Hughes. *TS* Jan 8, 1987: pA12.

'Natural writer' mourned; article. Christopher Hume. *TS* Jan 6, 1987: pD1.

Laurence kept finger on pulse of humanity; column. Elaine Husband. *CH* Jan 21, 1987: pA8.

NFB films spark memories of Margaret Laurence; column. Elaine Husband. *CH* Jan 28, 1987: pA10.

Heartfelt service; letter to the editor. Martha Jackson. *G&M* Jan 27, 1987: pA6.

Psychic violence: The Stone Angel and modern family life; article. Ed Jewinski. *New Q* Spring-Summer 1987; Vol 7 No 1–2: p255–266.
[THE FAMILY IN CANADIAN LITERATURE; MYTHS AND LEGENDS IN CANADIAN LITERATURE; WOMEN IN LITERATURE]

[Untitled]; letter to the editor. Nenke Jongkind. *G&M* Jan 27, 1987: pA6.

Margaret Laurence's legacy; letter to the editor. Andrea Journeaux. *Maclean's* March 9, 1987; Vol 100 No 10: p6.

"Uncertain Flowering" an overlooked short story by Margaret Laurence; article. W.J. Keith. *Can Lit* Spring 1987; No 112: p202–205.

The diviner's gift: in celebration of Margaret Laurence; essay. Hilda Kirkwood. *Can Forum* Feb 1987; Vol 66 No 766: p5–6.

Writers revive censorship-pornography debate; article. Liam Lacey. photo · *G&M* June 1, 1987: pC9.
[AUTHORS, CANADIAN; CENSORSHIP; WOMEN WRITERS; WRITERS' ORGANIZATIONS]

Image juxtaposition in A Jest Of God; article. B.A. Legendre. *Studies in Can Lit* 1987; Vol 12 No 1: p53–68.
[BIBLICAL MYTHS AND MYTHOLOGY]

Neepawa forgives its most famous citizen; article. Dan Lett. photo · *TS* Oct 18, 1987: pD5.
[CANADIAN LITERARY LANDMARKS]

Roots; letter to the editor. J.D. Marnoch. photo · *WFP* Jan 16, 1987: p6.

A Way Out may not thrill residents of Beausejour; column. Doreen Martens. *WFP* March 14, 1987: p23.
[TELEVISION AND CANADIAN LITERATURE]

Margaret Laurence; essay. Jack McClelland. bibliog photo · *Quill & Quire* Feb 1987; Vol 53 No 2: p9.

Tribute to author planned; article. Kenneth McGoogan. photo · *CH* Jan 16, 1987: pF1.

Culture director's tribute to author captured sentiment; column. Kenneth McGoogan. photo · *CH* Jan 27, 1987: pB6.
[AUDIO-VISUALS AND CANADIAN LITERATURE; POETRY READINGS]

Fiery MacLennan defends late Margaret Laurence; article. Kenneth McGoogan. *CH* May 31, 1987: pF2.

Margaret Laurence slaked a human thirst; column. Bruce McLeod. *TS* Jan 13, 1987: pA15.

Laurence deserves honor; letter to the editor. Jim McMurtry. *G&M* Jan 21, 1987: pA7.

Writer another victim of tobacco industry; letter to the editor. Carol Muchison. *TS* Jan 14, 1987: pA14.

Laurence tribute deserved better from The Journal; television review. Bill Musselwhite. *CH* Jan 7, 1987: pD4.

Margaret Laurence 1926–1987; obituary. W.H. New. *Can Lit* Spring 1987; No 112: p221–223.

Revolting teddies . . . time-travelling tot . . . rhymes macabre; reviews of tape versions of *The Olden Days Coat* and *Auntie's Knitting a Baby*. Richard Perry. photo · *Quill & Quire (Books for Young People)* Oct 1987; Vol 53 No 10: p14

New ventures; editorial article. Michael Peterman. *J of Can Studies* Winter 1987–88; Vol 22 No 4: p3–4.

Laurence selected own funeral music; article. Tracey Shreiber. *WFP* Jan 8, 1987: p33.

Photography "in camera"; article. Peter Sims. *Can Lit* Summer-Fall 1987; No 113–114: p145–166.

Actress draws powerful portraits of heroines in Laurence's work; theatre review of *The Women of Margaret Laurence*. Reg Skene. *WFP* May 14, 1987: p46.
[DRAMATIC ADAPTATIONS OF CANADIAN LITERATURE]

Book world: 'I swear by Apollo' and CIA; column. Beverley Slopen. *TS* April 12, 1987: pA20.
[GOVERNMENT GRANTS FOR WRITERS/PUBLISHERS; GREAT BRITAIN-CANADA LITERARY RELATIONS]

Canada needs writers like Margaret Laurence; essay. Keith Spicer. photo · *MG* Jan 8, 1987: pB3.
[CENSORSHIP]

[Untitled]; letter to the editor. Ruhi E. Tuzlak. *G&M* Jan 21, 1987: pA7.

Board fought banning; letter to the editor. John A. Young. photo · *G&M* Dec 19, 1987: pD7.
[CENSORSHIP]

Margaret Laurence 1926–1987; obituary. Dale Zieroth. *Event* March 1987; Vol 16 No 1: p7.

LAURENT, FRANÇOISE

[Untitled]; review of *L'Oeuvre romanesque de Marie-Claire Blais*. Élène Cliche. *Voix et images* Winter 1987; No 35: p318–321.

Lire et relire Marie-Claire Blais; review of *L'Oeuvre romanesque de Marie-Claire Blais*. Chantal Gamache. *Lettres québec* Spring 1987; No 45: p52.

[Untitled]; review of *L'Oeuvre romanesque de Marie-Claire Blais*. Annette Hayward. *U of Toronto Q* Fall 1987; Vol 57 No 1: p183–184.

La vitrine du livre; reviews. Jean Royer. photo · *MD* March 28, 1987: pD2.
[CANADIAN LITERARY PERIODICALS]

LAUZON, DOMINIQUE

Dominique Lauzon ou une étonnante vivacité; introduction. Hugues Corriveau. *Estuaire* Spring 1987; No 44: p51–52.

Dominique Lauzon: "Dans une zone si fragile de lui-même"; interview. Gérald Gaudet. *Estuaire* Spring 1987; No 44: p57–60.

La vie littéraire; column. Jean Royer. *MD* April 4, 1987: pD2.
[POETRY READINGS]

LAVALLÉE, RONALD

Local novelist's Red River saga strikes chord among Europeans; article. *WFP* Dec 18, 1987: p36.

Des mythes canadiens comme les Français les aiment; review of *Tchipayuk ou le chemin du loup*. Jean Éthier-Blais. photo · *MD* Dec 19, 1987: pD10.

La vitrine du livre; review of *Tchipayuk ou le chemin du loup*. Guy Ferland. *MD* Oct 31, 1987: pD4.

Les débuts parisiens d'un jeune Manitobain; article. Guy Ferland. photo · *MD* Nov 21, 1987: pD1, D12.

TV reporter in Winnipeg suddenly a hit with historical novel on Metis in French; article. Don Macdonald. photo · *G&M* Dec 21, 1987: pC10.

LAVIGNE, LOUIS-DOMINIQUE

Le Sous-sol des anges ou les années de braise; theatre review. Angèle Dagenais. photo · *MD* Dec 15, 1987: p11.

LAW, ALEXANDER

Crime; review of *To an Easy Grave*. Newgate Callendar. *NYT Book R* Jan 18, 1987: p23.
[FIRST NOVELS: BOOK REVIEWS]

Murder & mayhem: tough guys on clean street; reviews of crime novels. Margaret Cannon. *G&M* Jan 3, 1987: pE15.
[FIRST NOVELS: BOOK REVIEWS]

Mysteries to feed the mind with varying tastes; reviews of *Crang Plays the Ace* and *To an Easy Grave*. John North. photo · *Quill & Quire* March 1987; Vol 53 No 3: p74.
[FIRST NOVELS: BOOK REVIEWS]

LAWRENCE, KAREN

New faces; survey article. photo · *TS* March 7, 1987: K1-K4.
[AUTHORS, CANADIAN]

Windsor writer wins $3,000 in first-novel contest; article. *WFP* April 4, 1987: p28.
[AWARDS, LITERARY]

Town and country; article. photo · *Books in Can* April 1987; Vol 16 No 3: p6–8.
[AWARDS, LITERARY; FIRST NOVELS]

WHS/BiC award; article. photo · *Quill & Quire* May 1987; Vol 53 No 5: p12.
[AWARDS, LITERARY]

Lawrence captures $3,000 literary prize; article. *G&M* April 3, 1987: pD9.
[AWARDS, LITERARY]

Karen Lawrence wins first-novel competition; article. photo · *TS* April 3, 1987: pD22.
[AWARDS, LITERARY]

Life of Helen Alone wins novel prize; article. *MG* April 3, 1987: pC2.
[AWARDS, LITERARY]

[Untitled]; review of *The Life of Helen Alone*. Adelle Castelo. *Quill & Quire* Jan 1987; Vol 53 No 1: p27–28.
[FIRST NOVELS: BOOK REVIEWS]

Prize-winning writer basks in attention; article. H.J. Kirchhoff. photo · *G&M* April 18, 1987: pC7.

U of A alumna wins novel contest; column. Kenneth McGoogan. *CH* April 2, 1987: pD14.
[AWARDS, LITERARY; FESTIVALS, LITERARY; POETRY READINGS]

Novel's heroine searches for life after divorce; review of *The Life of Helen Alone*. Sherie Posesorski. *MG* Jan 24, 1987: pB8.
[FIRST NOVELS: BOOK REVIEWS]

LAYTON, IRVING

In ordinary life we don't assume we know anyone; article. Ken Adachi. *TS* Sept 19, 1987: M5.
[CANADIAN LITERATURE: BIOGRAPHY]

At 75, Canada's 'worrier poet' still scorns restraint; article. James Adams. photo · *CH* Dec 29, 1987: pC9.

[Untitled]; letter to the editor. Anne Cimon. *Books in Can* Jan-Feb 1987; Vol 16 No 1: p38.

Spleen may write the poem, but Layton's heart will speak tomorrow; reviews of poetry books. Trevor Ferguson. *MG* Sept 26, 1987: J11.

No respect; letter to the editor. Ray Filip. *Books in Can* April 1987; Vol 16 No 3: p40.

Poetic licence: with best wishes, to Irving Layton; column. Judith Fitzgerald. *TS* May 31, 1987: pA23.

With these older poets, the strengths are intrinsic; reviews of poetry books. Judith Fitzgerald. photo · *TS* Dec 20, 1987: pE6.

Zarathustran; review of *Waiting for the Messiah*. Graham Forst. *Can Lit* Spring 1987; No 112: p109–110.

Forgive him, Lord, he's just a bit confused; letter to the editor. Jack Gold. *MG* March 17, 1987: pB2.

[Untitled]; review of *Dance with Desire*. Harold Heft. *Rubicon* Spring 1987; No 8: p184–185.

[Untitled]; review of *Dance with Desire*. Liane Heller. *Cross Can Writ Q* 1987; Vol 9 No 1: p22–23.

[Untitled]; review of *Waiting for the Messiah*. Peter Herman. *Rubicon* Spring 1987; No 8: p181–183.

O dear!; letter to the editor. Marion Johnson. *Books in Can* Jan-Feb 1987; Vol 16 No 1: p38.

Lazarovitch to Layton; review of *Irving Layton: A Portrait*. Ben Jones. *Can Lit* Winter 1987; No 115: p160–162.

Layton's Holocaust view nonsense; letter to the editor. Allen A. Lang. *MG* March 17, 1987: pB2.

Loquacious Layton a joy to hear; television review of *Poet: Irving Layton Observed*. Doreen Martens. photo · *WFP* July 25, 1987: p47.
[TELEVISION AND CANADIAN LITERATURE]

Winkler catches Layton on film; article. Paul McKie. photo · *WFP* Feb 27, 1987: p33.
[AUDIO-VISUALS AND CANADIAN LITERATURE]

The artist behind Irving Layton's bravado; television review of *Poet: Irving Layton Observed*. Henry Mietkiewicz. photo · *TS* July 30, 1987: H5.
[TELEVISION AND CANADIAN LITERATURE]

On the carpet: a memoir of Layton and Callaghan; column. David O'Rourke. photo · *Poetry Can R* Fall 1987; Vol 9 No 1: p14–15.

"Irving Layton speaking"; interview. Al Purdy. photo · *Waves* Winter 1987; Vol 15 No 3: p5–13.

Great Montrealer Hugh MacLennan feted at Racket Club; column. Thomas Schnurmacher. *MG* March 13, 1987: H1.

Canadian writers fly south for fest; column. Thomas Schnurmacher. *MG* Oct 7, 1987: H1.
[FESTIVALS, LITERARY; UNITED STATES-CANADA LITERARY RELATIONS]

Tip sheet: forum will focus on AIDS, media; column. Susan Schwartz. *MG* June 17, 1987: H2.
[POETRY READINGS]

Tip sheet: . . . Irving Layton; column. Susan Schwartz. photo · *MG* Dec 9, 1987: pE14.
[POETRY READINGS]

Elspeth Cameron and Irving Layton; reviews of *Irving Layton: A Portrait* and *Waiting for the Messiah*. Patricia Keeney Smith. *U of Toronto Q* Spring 1987; Vol 56 No 3: p467–470.

Poetic successes; reviews of *The Difficulty of Living on Other Planets* and *Fortunate Exile*. Joel Yanofsky. illus · *MG* Dec 19, 1987: J11.

LAZARUS, JOHN

Late Blumer's a step behind; theatre review. Brian Brennan. photo · *CH (Sunday Magazine)* Jan 13, 1987: pD5.

[Village of Idiots]; theatre review. Jan Truss. *NeWest R* Feb 1987; Vol 12 No 6: p16.

LE FRANC, MARIE

Introduction par Marie Le Franc de la forêt en littérature québécoise; article. Madeleine Ducrocq-Poirier. abstract · *Études can* 1987; No 23: p87–92.
[WILDERNESS WRITING]

LE MAY, PAMPHILE

Quebec author Lemay gets exhibit; article. Heather Hill. *MG* March 17, 1987: pC10.

La vie littéraire; column. Jean Royer. *MD* March 7, 1987: pB2.
[AWARDS, LITERARY; CANADIAN LITERARY PUBLISHING; POETRY READINGS; RADIO AND CANADIAN LITERATURE; TELEVISION AND CANADIAN LITERATURE; WRITERS' ORGANIZATIONS]

La vitrine du livre; reviews. Jean Royer. *MD* March 14, 1987: pD4.
[CANADIAN LITERARY PERIODICALS]

LE POOL THEATRE COLLECTIVE

Le théâtre qu'on joue; theatre reviews. André Dionne. illus photo · *Lettres québec* Spring 1987; No 45: p47–48.

[Untitled]; theatre review of *It Must Be Sunday*. Danielle Salvail. photo · *Jeu* 1987; No 42: p156–158.

LEACOCK, STEPHEN

The gift of humorous bifocals; review of *Stephen Leacock: A Reappraisal*. Clive Doucet. photo · *G&M* Aug 1, 1987: pC16.

Professor loved booze but had sense of humor; biographical article. George Gamester. *TS* Sept 17, 1987: pA2.

[Untitled]; review of *Stephen Leacock: A Reappraisal*. Carl Spadoni. *Queen's Q* Winter 1987; Vol 94 No 4: p1028–1030.
[CONFERENCE REPORTS: REVIEWS AND ARTICLES]

Riding off in all directions; review of *Leacock: A Biography*. Carl Spadoni. *Essays on Can Writ* Winter 1987; No 35: p74–81.

The narrator, the reader, and Mariposa: the cost of preserving the status quo in Sunshine Sketches Of A Little Town; article. Francis Zichy. abstract · *J of Can Studies* Spring 1987; Vol 22 No 1: p51–65.
[SATIRIC WRITING]

LEACOCK: A BIOGRAPHY/Biography by Albert and Theresa Moritz

Riding off in all directions; review of *Leacock: A Biography*. Carl Spadoni. *Essays on Can Writ* Winter 1987; No 35: p74–81.

THE LEAGUE OF NIGHT AND FOG/Novel by David Morrell

During or after, war is still hell; review of *The League of Night and Fog*. Philippe van Rjndt. *TS* July 11, 1987: M4.

LEAPING UP SLIDING AWAY/Short stories by Kent Thompson

Short short stories by Kent Thompson; review of *Leaping Up Sliding Away*. Roger MacDonald. *Atlan Prov Book R* Feb-March 1987; Vol 14 No 1: p18.

In the mode; reviews of short story collections. Allan Weiss. *Books in Can* April 1987; Vol 16 No 3: p30–31.

LEARN, BETH

[Untitled]; reviews of poetry books. Anne Burke. *Poetry Can R* Summer 1987; Vol 8 No 4: p38.

LEARNING BY HEART/Short stories by Margot Livesey

Matter-of-fact visions; reviews of *Learning by Heart* and *Queen of the Headaches*. Hilda Kirkwood. *Can Forum* Jan 1987; Vol 66 No 765: p39.

[Untitled]; review of *Learning by Heart*. Mary S. Ladky. *Rubicon* Fall 1987; No 9: p201–202.

[Untitled]; review of *Learning by Heart*. Frances Ruhlen McConnel. illus · *NYT Book R* Aug 2, 1987: p16

LEARNING ON THE JOB/Poems by Robert Currie

[Untitled]; reviews of poetry books. Anne Archer. *Queen's Q* Winter 1987; Vol 94 No 4: p1042–1043.

Tellings; reviews of poetry books. Susan Rudy Dorscht. *Can Lit* Winter 1987; No 115: p257–260.

[Untitled]; reviews of poetry books. Tom Marshall. *Cross Can Writ Q* 1987; Vol 9 No 1: p24–25.

LEBEAU, SUZANNE

With passion, intensity and style; review of *Les Petits pouvoirs*. Hélène Beauchamp. *Can Child Lit* 1987; No 45: p65–68.

LEBLANC, LOUISE

Un laboratoire d'écriture ludique; review of *Popcorn*. Dorothy Leigh-Lizotte. *MD* April 28, 1987: p17.

LECKER, ROBERT

[Untitled]; reviews of *Robert Kroetsch* and *Another Country*. Russell Brown. *U of Toronto Q* Fall 1987; Vol 57 No 1: p161–166.

The Twayning of Robert Kroetsch; review of *Robert Kroetsch*. Martin Kuester. *Prairie Fire* Winter 1987–88; Vol 8 No 4: p101–105.

LECKIE, ROSS

First books from five regional presses; reviews of poetry books. Colin Morton. *Arc* Spring 1987; No 18: p52–59.

LECLERC, FÉLIX

Leclerc recuperating after a coronary scare; article. *MG* Nov 11, 1987: pF1.

Singer, poet Leclerc home from hospital; article. *MG* Nov 18, 1987: pD1.

Un homme qui s'intéressait aux créateurs; article. *MD* Nov 3, 1987: p4.

Quebec poet better; article. *WFP* Nov 12, 1987: p88.

Leclerc improving; article. *G&M* Nov 12, 1987: pA30.

[Untitled]; review of *Felix Leclerc, le roi heureux*. Nicole Décarie. *Moebius* Spring 1987; No 32: p125–127.

Félix Leclerc aux soins coronariens; article. Robert Lévesque. photo · *MD* Nov 9, 1987: p1,10.

Félix Leclerc reste toujours chancelant; article. Robert Lévesque. *MD* Nov 10, 1987: p1,12.

L'Académie canadienne française accueille Félix; article. Marie Laurier. photo · *MD* Dec 24, 1987: pA7.
[AWARDS, LITERARY]

Mais Félix a préféré rester dans son île . . . ; article. Gilles Lesage. photo · *MD* Jan 28, 1987: p1,10.

Le Québec de Félix Leclerc. review of *Félix Leclerc, le roi heureux*. Jean Royer. *MD* Jan 24, 1987: pB3–B4.

LECLERC, RACHEL

[Untitled]; review of *Vivre n'est pas clair*. Hugues Corriveau. *Estuaire* Spring 1987; No 44: p83.

L'amour la mort; reviews of poetry books. Robert Yergeau. photo · *Lettres québec* Summer 1987; No 46: p37–38.

LECOMPTE, LUC

Des livres ou des poètes?; reviews of *La Chevelure de Bérénice* and *Ces étirements du regard*. André Marquis. photo · *Lettres québec* Summer 1987; No 46: p35–36.

[Untitled]; reviews of poetry books. Jacques Saint-Pierre. *Moebius* Spring 1987; No 32: p128–130.

LEDBETTER, KEN

[Untitled]; reviews. Janet Windeler. *Cross Can Writ Q* 1987; Vol 9 No 2: p25–26.
[FIRST NOVELS: BOOK REVIEWS]

LEDOUX, PAUL

[Untitled]; theatre review of *Fire*. Mark Abley. photo · *Maclean's* Jan 26, 1987; Vol 100 No 4: p55.

Musical Fire is a damp sparkler; theatre review. Brian Brennan. photo · *CH* Feb 14, 1987: pG4.

Rollicking rock and old-time religion stoke Fire; theatre review. Ray Conlogue. photo · *G&M* Jan 13, 1987: pC7.

Fire bites off a lot, chews most of it; theatre review of *Fire*. Wayne Grigsby. *MG* Jan 10, 1987: H7.

[Untitled]; theatre reviews of *Fire* and *Opium*. Wayne Grigsby. *MG* Jan 16, 1987: pD10.

[Fire]; theatre review. Susan Minsos. *NeWest R* April 1987; Vol 12 No 8: p17.

LEDWELL, FRANK J.

Frank Ledwell's colloquial ease; review of *The North Shore of Home*. Thomas B. O'Grady. *Atlan Prov Book R* Feb-March 1987; Vol 14 No 1: p17.

LEE, DENNIS

Billboard: Transcona Streamliners schedule guest speaker; column. *WFP* Oct 26, 1987: p14.

Authors to speak in Scarborough; article. *TS (Neighbors)* Nov 10, 1987: p19.

Authors speak at Oakville school tonight; article. *TS (Neighbors)* Nov 17, 1987: p10.

A garden of adult verse; review of *The Difficulty of Living on Other Planets*. John Bemrose. *Maclean's* Nov 16, 1987; Vol 100 No 46: p64b

Lee's whimsy cuts into heavy issues; article. Rosie DiManno. photo · *TS* Nov 1, 1987: pC2.

Playful poetry for adults, 'what a subversive idea'; article. Deirdre Kelly. photo · *G&M* Nov 3, 1987: pD8.

Lee cooks up Alligator Pie for adults; review of *The Difficulty of Living on Other Planets*. Kenneth McGoogan. *CH* Nov 8, 1987: pE6.

Book world: inside Iran: a woman's prison-like existence; column. Beverley Slopen. photo · *TS* Aug 2, 1987: pC10.

Ballads and ditties for grown-ups; reviews of poetry books. Fraser Sutherland. illus · *G&M* Nov 7, 1987: pC21.

Poetic successes; reviews of *The Difficulty of Living on Other Planets* and *Fortunate Exile*. Joel Yanofsky. illus · *MG* Dec 19, 1987: J11.

LEE, JOHN B.

Writing life; reviews of *Hired Hands* and *What Feathers Are For*. Arthur Adamson. *Can Lit* Winter 1987; No 115: p230–232.

[Untitled]; reviews of poetry books. Anita Hurwitz. *Poetry Can R* Spring 1987; Vol 8 No 2–3: p38–39.

The Milton Acorn Memorial People's Poetry Award; article. Ted Plantos. illus · *Poetry Can R* Summer 1987; Vol 8 No 4: p17.
[AWARDS, LITERARY]

THE LEGACY

See **QUAND J'AURAI PAY TON VISAGE/THE LEGACY/Novel by Claire Martin**

LEGAULT, ANNE

Munro short story collection wins award; article. *WFP* May 29, 1987: p34.
[GOVERNOR GENERAL'S AWARDS]

Le prix du Gouverneur général à Yvon Rivard; article. *MD* May 28, 1987: p2.
[GOVERNOR GENERAL'S AWARDS]

Governor General's Award to Munro amid poetry protest; article. photo · *MG* May 28, 1987: pC1.
[GOVERNOR GENERAL'S AWARDS]

Governor General's award winners; article. *Quill & Quire* July 1987; Vol 53 No 7: p53–54.
[GOVERNOR GENERAL'S AWARDS]

Frye finally wins elusive award for best non-fiction book of '86; article. Ken Adachi. photo · *TS* May 28, 1987: H1.
[GOVERNOR GENERAL'S AWARDS]

Yvon Rivard et Northrop Frye parmi les lauréats des prix du gouverneur général; article. Robert Lévesque. photo · *MD* May 28, 1987: p13.
[GOVERNOR GENERAL'S AWARDS]

Prix et distinctions; list of award winners. Gaétan Lévesque. photo · *Lettres québec* Autumn 1987; No 47: p7.
[AWARDS, LITERARY; GOVERNOR GENERAL'S AWARDS]

[Untitled]; theatre review of *La Visite des sauvages*. Stphane Lpine. photo · *Jeu* 1987; No 42: p141–147.

Munro wins third Governor General's Award; article. Jamie Portman. photo · *CH* May 28, 1987: pC9.
[GOVERNOR GENERAL'S AWARDS]

Munro wins top literary prize; article. Lisa Rochon. photo · *G&M* May 28, 1987: pD1.
[GOVERNOR GENERAL'S AWARDS]

La vie littéraire; column. Jean Royer. photo · *MD* June 6, 1987: pD2.
[GOVERNOR GENERAL'S AWARDS; INTERNATIONAL REVIEWS OF CANADIAN LITERATURE; RADIO AND CANADIAN LITERATURE; TELEVISION AND CANADIAN LITERATURE]

Bloc-notes; column. Michel Vaïs. *Jeu* 1987; No 44: p215–218.
[COMPETITIONS, LITERARY; CONFERENCES, LITERARY; GOVERNOR GENERAL'S AWARDS; RADIO AND CANADIAN LITERATURE]

THE LEGEND OF CALGARY — A TALL TALE/Story by Linda Wasom-Ellam

Legend of Calgary no ordinary tall tale; column. Joan Craven. *CH (Neighbors)* July 8, 1987: pA8.

LEGG, THOMAS

Legg pulls off one-man show; theatre review of *A Terrible Beauty*. Sherri Clegg. *CH* April 4, 1987: pB6.

Storyteller weaves gripping tales; column. Patrick Tivy. illus · *CH* April 3, 1987: pC2.

LEGS ET BIZOU/LEGS AND BIZOU/Children's story by Frances Cherry

Mini-comptes rendus; reviews of *Legs et Bizou/Legs and Bizou* and *Une Journée de Sophie Lachance*. Claudine Lesage. *Can Child Lit* 1987; No 46: p110.

LEIREN-YOUNG, MARK

Three new political plays; theatre reviews. Malcolm Page. *Can Drama* 1987; Vol 13 No 2: p224–226.

LEITCH LENNOX, ADELAIDE

A.L. Lennox, 66, author; obituary. *TS* Oct 27, 1987: pA21.

Author Lennox dies; obituary. *WFP* Oct 28, 1987: p42

LEMAIRE, MICHEL

De Bellefeuille, Nepveu, Lemaire, Royer; reviews of poetry books. Jean-Pierre Issenhuth. *Liberté* Aug 1987; Vol 29 No 4: p78–87.

LEMAY, FRANCINE

Entre la maison, l'eau et le cosmos: l'écriture féminine; reviews of novels. Patricia Smart. *Voix et images* Winter 1987; No 35: p334–337.

LEMELIN, ROGER

Roger Lemelin publié en format de poche; article. *MD* June 3, 1987: p12.

[Untitled]; reviews of novels. Alice Parizeau. *MD* Nov 28, 1987: pD9.

LEMIEUX, MICHÈLE

La magie du livre pour enfants; review of *Quel est ce bruit?*. Dominique Demers. *MD* July 4, 1987: pC5.

LEMIEUX, ROLAND

Cris et silences des poètes d'automne; review of *Éclats d'âme*. Benoît Lacroix. *MD* Dec 19, 1987: pD3.

LEMOINE, STEWART

Horror spoof keeps audience on edge; theatre review of *The Vile Governess & Other Psychodramas*. Ray Conlogue. photo · *G&M* Sept 10, 1987: pD3.

Wild, wacky Vile Governess a delicious spoof of Ibsen angst; theatre review of *The Vile Governess & Other Psychodramas*. Robert Crew. photo · *TS* Sept 11, 1987: pE11.

Beyond the Fringe: Stewart Lemoine's off-the-wall humor has finally moved east; article. Liam Lacey. photo · *G&M* Sept 23, 1987: pC10.

LEPAGE, ROBERT

Prepare for sincerely ridiculous as new-look Carmen is unveiled; article. Marianne Ackerman. photo · *MG* April 23, 1987: pE3.

"O.K. on change!"; article. Lorraine Camerlain. photo · *Jeu* 1987; No 45: p83–97.

Questions sur des questions; essay. Lorraine Camerlain. photo · *Jeu* 1987; No 45: p164–168.

Questions sur une démarche; essay. Jean-Luce Denis. photo · *Jeu* 1987; No 45: p159–163.

One-man Vinci tour de force for Lepage; theatre review. Pat Donnelly. *MG* June 5, 1987: pD2.

Lepage play romps away with festival Grand Prize; article. Pat Donnelly. *MG* June 8, 1987: pD7.
[AWARDS, LITERARY]

"L'arte un veicolo": entretien avec Robert Lepage; interview. Carole Frchette. Lorraine Camerlain. photo · *Jeu* 1987; No 42: p109–126.

Cultural epic is must-see theatre; theatre review of *La Trilogie des dragons*. Wayne Grigsby. *MG* Jan 17, 1987: pC5.

Moisson d'avril; column. Robert Lévesque. photo · *MD* March 31, 1987: p17.

Le grand retour de Murielle Dutil dans Le Temps d'une vie; column. Robert Lévesque. *MD* April 7, 1987: p12.

Le grand prix va à Robert Lepage; article. Robert Lévesque. photo · *MD* June 8, 1987: p1,8.

Le retour du "Chien mexicain"; column. Robert Lévesque. *MD* June 9, 1987: p11.

Robert Lepage, de Nyon en Avignon; article. Robert Lévesque. photo · *MD* Aug 6, 1987: p11.

[AWARDS, LITERARY]

Prix et distinctions; list of award winners. Gaétan Lévesque. photo · *Lettres québec* Autumn 1987; No 47: p7.

[AWARDS, LITERARY; GOVERNOR GENERAL'S AWARDS]

Tenir l'univers dans sa main; article. Solange Lévesque. photo · *Jeu* 1987; No 45: p111–120.

Robert Lepage, globe-trotter; column. Robert Lévesque. photo · *MD* Oct 20, 1987: p13,15.

[CONFERENCES, LITERARY]

Yvette Brind'amour reoit le prix Molson du Conseil des arts; column. Robert Lévesque. *MD* Nov 3, 1987: p13.

Robert Lepage impose son Vinci dans la Ville lumière; column. Robert Lévesque. photo · *MD* Dec 8, 1987: p11.

[INTERNATIONAL REVIEWS OF CANADIAN LITERATURE]

Des personnages qui s'imposent aussi bien à Londres qu'à Montréal; article. Daniel Latouche. photo · *MD* Sept 5, 1987: pC4.

Du hasard et de la nécessité: genèse de l'oeuvre; essay. Pierre Lavoie. photo · *Jeu* 1987; No 45: p169–170.

Points de repère: entretiens avec les créateurs; interview with the Théâtre Repère collective. Pierre Lavoie. Lorraine Camerlain. photo · *Jeu* 1987; No 45: p177–208.

Robert Lepage: new filters for creation; interview, includes introduction. Paul Lefebvre. photo · *Can Theatre R* Fall 1987; No 52: p30–35.

Harmonie et contrepoint; article. Solange Lvesque. photo · *Jeu* 1987; No 42: p100–108.

Reconstitution de "La Trilogie"; article. Diane Pavlovic. photo · *Jeu* 1987; No 45: p40–82.

Le sable et les étoiles; article. Diane Pavlovic. photo · *Jeu* 1987; No 45: p121–140.

Figures: portraits en dix tableaux; article. Diane Pavlovic. photo · *Jeu* 1987; No 45: p141–158.

Du décollage l'envol; article. Diane Pavlovic. illus photo · *Jeu* 1987; No 42: p86–99.

Magie et mysticisme: comment (ne pas) expliquer l'inexplicable; essay. Philippe Soldevila. photo · *Jeu* 1987; No 45: p171–176

Remise des prix d'excellence de la culture; article. Julie Stanton. photo · *MD* Oct 27, 1987: p11.

[AWARDS, LITERARY]

Entre le jouet de pacotille et la voûte céleste: le voyage des personnages à travers les objets; article. Michel Vaïs. photo · *Jeu* 1987; No 45: p98–110.

LEPAGE, ROLAND

Plenty of life left in this classic; theatre review of *Le Temps d'une vie*. Pat Donnelly. *MG* Sept 18, 1987: pC10.

LePAN, DOUGLAS

With these older poets, the strengths are intrinsic; reviews of poetry books. Judith Fitzgerald. photo · *TS* Dec 20, 1987: pE6.

LEPROHON, J.L.

Imperfect conquests; reviews of *The Manor House of De Villeray* and *Le Tour du Québec par deux enfants*. Anthony Raspa. *Can Lit* Winter 1987; No 115: p172–174.

[CANADIAN LITERARY PERIODICALS]

LESBIAN TRIPTYCH/Short stories by Jovette Marchessault

Putrefying sore; reviews of fictional works. Kathryn Chittick. *Can Lit* Spring 1987; No 112: p128–129.

LET'S NOT REMEMBER EVERYTHING: THREE STORIES/Short stories by Cary Fagan

[Untitled]; reviews. Beverley Daurio. *Cross Can Writ Q* 1987; Vol 9 No 2: p23.

[FIRST NOVELS: BOOK REVIEWS]

LETARTE, GENEVIÈVE

Solitaire, voyeuse et voyante; article. Paul Cauchon. photo · *MD* Nov 6, 1987: p15.

La vie littéraire; column. Jean Royer. *MD* Feb 7, 1987: pB2.

[COMPETITIONS, LITERARY; CONFERENCES, LITERARY; POETRY READINGS; PUBLISHING AND PUBLISHERS IN CANADA; TELEVISION AND CANADIAN LITERATURE; WRITERS' WORKSHOPS]

LETENDRE, MARIE-HÉLÈNE

[Untitled]; theatre review of *À la recherche de M.*. Diane Pavlovic. photo · *Jeu* 1987; No 42: p167–168.

LETINSKY CAFE/Play by Louise Cloutier

Letinsky Cafe dishes out fantasy play focusing on ghost of Marilyn Monroe; theatre review. Philip Clark. *WFP* Feb 7, 1987: p23.

LETTER FROM WINGFIELD FARM/Play by Dan Needles

Acting sparkles in insulting play; theatre review of *Letter from Wingfield Farm*. Randal McIlroy. *WFP* Nov 26, 1987: p79.

Just good fun; letter to the editor. Heather Mousseau. *WFP* Dec 6, 1987: p6.

Comedy hits Canadian vein; article. Brad Oswald. photo · *WFP* Nov 25, 1987: p43.

LETTER TO A DISTANT FATHER/Poems by Kenneth Radu

Random musings of a middle-aged middle-class male; reviews of poetry books. Lesley McAllister. *TS* Oct 10, 1987: M4.

THE LETTER/Novel by W. Gunther Plaut

[Untitled]; review of *The Letter*. *Queen's Q* Winter 1987; Vol 94 No 4: p1067–1068.
[FIRST NOVELS: BOOK REVIEWS]

[Untitled]; review of *The Letter*. Douglas Hill. *Books in Can* Jan-Feb 1987; Vol 16 No 1: p24.
[FIRST NOVELS: BOOK REVIEWS]

Hitler's letter; review of *The Letter*. Robert G. Lawrence. *Can Lit* Winter 1987; No 115: p229–230.
[FIRST NOVELS: BOOK REVIEWS]

[Untitled]; review of *The Letter*. John North. *Quill & Quire* Jan 1987; Vol 53 No 1: p27.
[FIRST NOVELS: BOOK REVIEWS]

LETTERS FROM SOME ISLANDS/Poems by Anne Marriott

Trial by experience; reviews of *Letters from Some Islands* and *Private Properties*. Bert Almon. *Can Lit* Winter 1987; No 115: p206–208.

[Untitled]; reviews of poetry books. Barbara Carey. *Cross Can Writ Q* 1987; Vol 9 No 1: p23–24.

Jacobs, Lever, Marriott; reviews of poetry books. Barry Dempster. *Poetry Can R* Spring 1987; Vol 8 No 2–3: p35.

B.C. international — in search of new subjects and forms; reviews. Gillian Harding-Russell. *Event* Summer 1987; Vol 16 No 2: p125–127.

LETTERS FROM THE EQUATOR/Poems by C.H. (Marty) Gervais

[Untitled]; review of *Letters from the Equator*. Phil Hall. *Books in Can* Aug-Sept 1987; Vol 16 No 6: p28.

LETTRES D'ITALIE/Letters by Denise Boucher

De l'Italie, de l'art et de la civilisation; review of *Lettres d'Italie*. Jean-Roch Boivin. photo · *MD* Sept 19, 1987: pD3.

LETTRES D'UNE AUTRE/Novel by Lise Gauvin

Deux échos québécois de grands romans épistolaires du dix-huitième siècle français; article. Monique Moser-Verrey. *Voix et images* Spring 1987; Vol 12 No 3: p512–514,516–522.
[FRANCE-CANADA LITERARY RELATIONS]

LEVENSON, CHRISTOPHER

[Untitled]; review of *Arriving at Night*. Philip Kokotailo. *U of Windsor R* Spring-Summer 1987; Vol 20 No 2: p90–92.

[Untitled]; reviews of poetry books. Stephen Morrissey. *Poetry Can R* Fall 1987; Vol 9 No 1: p32.

LEVER, BERNICE

[Untitled]; reviews of poetry books. Barbara Carey. *Cross Can Writ Q* 1987; Vol 9 No 1: p23–24.

Jacobs, Lever, Marriott; reviews of poetry books. Barry Dempster. *Poetry Can R* Spring 1987; Vol 8 No 2–3: p35.

LÉVESQUE, RAYMOND

Une vie de Patachon bien sympathique; reviews of *D'ailleurs et d'ici* and *Contes gouttes ou le pays d'un reflet*. Yolande Grisé. photo · *Lettres québec* Summer 1987; No 46: p59–60.

Bozo et les bas-culottes; theatre review of *La Waitress*. Marc Morin. photo · *MD* Feb 25, 1987: p8.

La vitrine du livre; reviews. Jean Royer. photo · *MD* March 21, 1987: pD2.
[CANADIAN LITERARY PERIODICALS]

LEVINE, NORMAN

Just what was said: an analytical approach to the Hansen 'hoopla'; column. *G&M* Feb 21, 1987: pD6.

Kanada made me; article. Horst Wittmann. *Books in Can* Oct 1987; Vol 16 No 7: p3–4.
[GERMANY-CANADA LITERARY RELATIONS]

LIBERTÉ/Periodical

La vitrine du livre; reviews. Guy Ferland. *MD* March 7, 1987: pB2.
[CANADIAN LITERARY PERIODICALS]

La vitrine du livre; reviews. Guy Ferland. *MD* June 6, 1987: pD4.
[CANADIAN LITERARY PERIODICALS]

La revue des revues; reviews of periodicals. Guy Ferland. *MD* Sept 19, 1987: pD6.
[CANADIAN LITERARY PERIODICALS]

Pretentieux? Idéalistes? Elitistes?; article. François Hébert. *Liberté* Feb 1987; Vol 29 No 1: p159–160.
[CANADIAN LITERARY PERIODICALS]

De l'érudition: l'esprit et la lettre; reviews of periodicals. Suzanne Lamy. *Voix et images* Winter 1987; No 35: p342–346.
[CANADIAN LITERARY PERIODICALS]

Imperfect conquests; reviews of *The Manor House of De Villeray* and *Le Tour du Québec par deux enfants*. Anthony Raspa. *Can Lit* Winter 1987; No 115: p172–174.
[CANADIAN LITERARY PERIODICALS]

La vie littéraire; column. Jean Royer. *MD* Jan 31, 1987: pB2.
[CANADIAN LITERARY PERIODICALS; COMPETITIONS, LITERARY; RADIO AND CANADIAN LITERATURE; TELEVISION AND CANADIAN LITERATURE]

La vie littéraire; column. Jean Royer. *MD* Feb 28, 1987: pC2.
[AWARDS, LITERARY; CANADIAN LITERARY PERIODICALS; CANADIAN LITERARY PUBLISHING; CONFERENCES, LITERARY; RADIO AND CANADIAN LITERATURE]

La vitrine du livre; reviews. Jean Royer. *MD* April 11, 1987: pD2.
[CANADIAN LITERARY PERIODICALS]

LIBRARY SERVICES AND CANADIAN LITERATURE

Ottawa notebook: at times our Prime Minister can be a very elusive man; column. photo · *TS* March 22, 1987: pA6.
[GOVERNMENT GRANTS FOR WRITERS/PUBLISHERS]

Authors collect for library use; article. *MG* March 18, 1987: pB4.
[GOVERNMENT GRANTS FOR WRITERS/PUBLISHERS]

Authors get paid for titles in libraries; article. *WFP* Feb 13, 1987: p31.
[GOVERNMENT GRANTS FOR WRITERS/PUBLISHERS]

Authors get long-promised cheques; article. *WFP* March 18, 1987: p38.
[GOVERNMENT GRANTS FOR WRITERS/PUBLISHERS]

Prêts en bibliothèque: les auteurs reoivent leurs premiers chèques; article. *MD* March 18, 1987: p17.
[GOVERNMENT GRANTS FOR WRITERS/PUBLISHERS]

Library-book royalties winging way to writers; article. *CH* March 18, 1987: pC11.
[GOVERNMENT GRANTS TO WRITERS/PUBLISHERS]

Writers eager for list; article. *WFP* April 24, 1987: p33.
[GOVERNMENT GRANTS FOR WRITERS/PUBLISHERS]

Round table: responses, notes and queries; column. *Can Child Lit* 1987; No 47: p102–103.
[AWARDS, LITERARY; WRITERS' ORGANIZATIONS]

Library gets works; article. *WFP* Aug 8, 1987: p37.

Grant earmarked for PEI papers; article. *G&M* Dec 17, 1987: pC1.

Moodie collection acquired by NLC; article. *Quill & Quire* Nov 1987; Vol 53 No 11: p19.

A momentous day for writers; column. Ken Adachi. *TS* March 16, 1987: pB1.
[GOVERNMENT GRANTS FOR WRITERS/PUBLISHERS]

Professional writers aid aspiring authors from Ontario libraries; article. Ian Bailey. *WFP* Nov 20, 1987: p38.
[WRITERS-IN-RESIDENCE]

Writers-in-libraries program well under way; article. Martin Dowding. *Quill & Quire* July 1987; Vol 53 No 7: p62–63.

National Library acquires 'a real treasure trove'; article. Matthew Fraser. photo · *G&M* Oct 7, 1987: pC7.

A red-letter day for Canadian writers; column. William French. *G&M* March 10, 1987: pD7.
[GOVERNMENT GRANTS FOR WRITERS/PUBLISHERS]

Writers lend their expertise; column. William French. *G&M* June 23, 1987: pD5.
[WRITERS-IN-RESIDENCE]

Public Lending Right debate takes new twist; column. William French. *G&M* Nov 10, 1987: pD7.
[GOVERNMENT GRANTS FOR WRITERS/PUBLISHERS]

Ottawa struggles to ensure authors get their due; article. Carol Goar. illus · *MG* Dec 4, 1987: pB3.
[COPYRIGHT; GOVERNMENT GRANTS FOR WRITERS/PUBLISHERS]

Authors group fought for public lending right; letter to the editor. Della Golland-Lui. *TS* April 6, 1987: pA16.
[GOVERNMENT GRANTS FOR WRITERS/PUBLISHERS; WRITERS' ORGANIZATIONS]

Library gets 19th-century windfall featuring Canadian literary legend; article. Heather Hill. illus · *MG* Aug 7, 1987: pA1,A4.

Abuse of copyright; letter to the editor. Richard Lemm. *G&M* Dec 1, 1987: pA6.
[COPYRIGHT]

Poets fare best under payment scheme, says chairman; article. Kenneth McGoogan. *CH* May 1, 1987: pE4.
[GOVERNMENT GRANTS FOR WRITERS/PUBLISHERS]

History turning to dust: institute races time to microfilm ravaged literature; article. Jamie Portman. *CH* Oct 28, 1987: pD1.

Authors and libraries; letter to the editor. John S. Ridout. *G&M* Nov 4, 1987: pA6.

Library-use payments not trumpeted; article. Barbara Robson. *WFP* April 1, 1987: p35.

Novelist, poet Kroetsch receives top payment under library fee plan; article. Barbara Robson. *WFP* April 22, 1987: p38.
[GOVERNMENT GRANTS FOR WRITERS/PUBLISHERS]

Book world: Ojibwa's diary led to biography; column. Beverley Slopen. *TS* Nov 29, 1987: pA20.

Dits et faits; column. Adrien Thério. photo · *Lettres québec* Summer 1987; No 46: p6.
[AUTHORS, CANADIAN; CANADIAN LITERARY PUBLISHING; CONFERENCES, LITERARY; GOVERNMENT GRANTS FOR WRITERS/PUBLISHERS]

PLR: writers registered and sampling under way; article. Ann Vanderhoof. *Quill & Quire* Feb 1987; Vol 53 No 2: p14.
[GOVERNMENT GRANTS FOR WRITERS/PUBLISHERS]

Writers get their cheques; article. Kathryn Young. *G&M* March 18, 1987: pC3.
[GOVERNMENT GRANTS FOR WRITERS/PUBLISHERS]

LIFE AFTER HOCKEY/Play by Kenneth Brown

Red Deer College Arts Centre: life after hockey?; article. Carolyn Dearden. photo · *NeWest R* Feb 1987; Vol 12 No 6: p15–16.

The great Canadian dream; article. Kevin Prokosh. photo · *WFP* March 18, 1987: p35.

Hockey metaphor fails to make dramatic point; theatre review of *Life After Hockey*. Reg Skene. *WFP* March 19, 1987: p41.

THE LIFE OF HELEN ALONE/Novel by Karen Lawrence

[Untitled]; review of *The Life of Helen Alone*. Adelle Castelo. *Quill & Quire* Jan 1987; Vol 53 No 1: p27–28.
[FIRST NOVELS: BOOK REVIEWS]

Novel's heroine searches for life after divorce; review of *The Life of Helen Alone*. Sherie Posesorski. *MG* Jan 24, 1987: pB8.
[FIRST NOVELS: BOOK REVIEWS]

THE LIFE OF HOPE/Novel by Paul Quarrington

Versions of St. Hope; review of *The Life of Hope*. John Ferns. *Can Lit* Spring 1987; No 112: p114–115.

THE LIGHT IN THE PIAZZA/Novel by Elizabeth Spencer

Other Americas; reviews of *The Light in the Piazza* and *Voyage to the Other Extreme*. Michael Greenstein. *Can Lit* Spring 1987; No 112: p97–100.

LIGHT, JOANNE

Noticing three poets; reviews of poetry books. Terrence Craig. *Atlan Prov Book R* May-June 1987; Vol 14 No 2: p10.

LIGNES DE NUIT/Poems by Gérald Gaudet

Du désir à l'écriture ou vice versa; review of *Lignes de nuit*. Régis Normandeau. *Lettres québec* Summer 1987; No 46: p70.

[Untitled]; reviews of poetry books. Jacques Saint-Pierre. *Moebius* Spring 1987; No 32: p128–130.

[Untitled]; review of *Lignes de nuit*. Hélène Thibaux. *Estuaire* Spring 1987; No 44: p81–82.

LIITOJA, HILLAR

Bold style masks some flimsy ideas; theatre review of *This Is What Happens In Orangeville*. Marianne Ackerman. *MG* June 5, 1987: pD2.

Hillar Liitoja: chaos and control; article. Nigel Hunt. photo · *Can Theatre R* Fall 1987; No 52: p45–49.

Force of evil unveiled in play about murder; theatre review of *This Is What Happens in Orangeville*. Liam Lacey. photo · *G&M* Jan 31, 1987: pE4.

LES LILAS FLEURISSENT À VARSOVIE/THE LILACS ARE BLOOMING IN WARSAW/Novel by Alice Parizeau

La vie littéraire; column. Jean Royer. photo · *MD* May 30, 1987: pD2.

[AWARDS, LITERARY; CANADIAN LITERARY PUBLISHING; COMPETITIONS, LITERARY; FESTIVALS, LITERARY; RADIO AND CANADIAN LITERATURE; TELEVISION AND CANADIAN LITERATURE]

LILBURN, TIM

[Untitled]; review of *Names of God*. Margaret Avison. *Books in Can* May 1987; Vol 16 No 4: p23.

Magnificent voice of the poetic mad; review of *Names of God*. Maggie Helwig. *TS* April 11, 1987: M4.

The celebrations of Tim Lilburn; review of *Names of God*. Jane Urquhart. *Brick* Fall 1987; No 31: p39–40.

LILL, WENDY

[Untitled]; reviews. Lisbie Rae. *Can Drama* 1987; Vol 13 No 2: p229–231.

[ANTHOLOGIES: BOOK REVIEWS]

LILY OF THE MOHAWKS/Play by Patricia Rodriguez

Tale of Indian mystic a challenge to stage; article. photo · *G&M* Feb 27, 1987: pD12.

Producer brings tale of 17th-century Indian princess to stage; article. photo · *WFP* Feb 27, 1987: p37.

Sam Gesser tries again with Lily; article. Marianne Ackerman. photo · *MG* Feb 21, 1987: pD1.

Sense of guilt driving force behind thinly sketched Lily; theatre review of *Lily of the Mohawks*. Marianne Ackerman. *MG* Feb 27, 1987: pC2.

Sainte Kateri et le mythe du bon sauvage; theatre review of *Lily of the Mohawks*. Paul Lefebvre. photo · *MD* March 4, 1987: p6.

LILY: A RHAPSODY IN RED/Novel by Heather Robertson

Lilly & Willie; review of *Lily: A Rhapsody in Red*. Linda Lamont-Stewart. *Can Lit* Winter 1987; No 115: p275–277.

LIME STREET AT TWO/Novel by Helen Forrester

Tune in, turn on, drop out: truckin' back to the '60s with Esquire; reviews of *Lime Street at Two* and *The Next Best Thing*. Barbara Black. *MG* July 4, 1987: J9.

LINGUANTI, ELSA

Demon of analogy; review of *L'Itinerario del senso nella narrativa di Malcolm Lowry*. Richard Cavell. *Can Lit* Spring 1987; No 112: p87–88.

LISA MAKES THE HEADLINES AND OTHER STORIES/Children's stories by Kit Hood et al

From box to book; reviews of *Lisa Makes the Headlines* and *Griff Makes a Date*. Laurie Bildfell. *Can Child Lit* 1987; No 46: p93–94.

LISA/Children's novel by Carol Matas

Gammer Gurton leaps from early English stage into the 20th century; reviews of children's books. Janice Kennedy. *MG* Nov 21, 1987: J13.

[Untitled]; review of *Lisa*. Kenneth Oppel. *Quill & Quire (Books for Young People)* Dec 1987; Vol 53 No 12: p6.

A LITERARY AND LINGUISTIC HISTORY OF NEW BRUNSWICK/LANGUES ET LITTÉRATURES AU NOUVEAU-BRUNSWICK/Survey

[Untitled]; review of *A Literary and Linguistic History of New Brunswick*. *Queen's Q* Winter 1987; Vol 94 No 4: p1070–1071.

[Untitled]; review of *Langues et littératures au Nouveau-Brunswick*. L.E. Doucette. *U of Toronto Q* Fall 1987; Vol 57 No 1: p207–209.

A LITERARY FRIENDSHIP: THE CORRESPONDENCE OF RALPH GUSTAFSON AND W.W.E. ROSS/Compilation of letters

[Untitled]; reviews of critical works. Ronald B. Hatch. *Eng Studies in Can* March 1987; Vol 13 No 1: p107–115.

LITTÉRATURE CANADIENNE FRANCOPHONE/Survey by Edwin Hamblet

[Untitled]; review of *Littérature canadienne francophone*. Eloise A. Brière. *Amer R of Can Studies* Winter 1987–88; Vol 17 No 4: p449–450.

LITTLE BLUE BEN/Children's story by Phoebe Gilman

Mini-reviews; reviews of children's books. Margaret Paré. *Can Child Lit* 1987; No 45: p93–96.

LITTLE BY LITTLE: A WRITER'S EDUCATION/Autobiography by Jean Little

There's a lot more here than a little by Little; review of *Little by Little*. Callie Israel. photo · *Quill & Quire (Books for Young People)* Dec 1987; Vol 53 No 12: p3.

Little's achievements simply huge; reviews of *Little by Little* and *Her Special Vision*. Joan McGrath. *TS* Nov 29, 1987: pA21.

THE LITTLE MAGAZINE IN CANADA 1925–1980: ITS ROLE IN THE DEVELOPMENT OF MODERNISM AND POSTMODERNISM IN CANADIAN POETRY/Critical work by Ken Norris

[Untitled]; reviews of critical works. Ronald B. Hatch. *Eng Studies in Can* March 1987; Vol 13 No 1: p107–115.

LITTLE, JEAN

[Untitled]; reviews of *Come into My Room* and *Hey World, Here I Am!*. Adele Ashby. *Quill & Quire (Books for Young People)* April 1987; Vol 53 No 4: p5.

Dog in the attic; review of *Different Dragons*. Peter Blake. *Times Lit Supp* May 15, 1987; No 4389: p529.

Chit chat; column. Maria Casas. *Quill & Quire (Books for Young People)* Aug 1987; Vol 53 No 8: p3.

Title tattle; column. Martin Dowding. *Quill & Quire (Books for Young People)* Dec 1987; Vol 53 No 12: p3.
[FILM ADAPTATIONS OF CANADIAN LITERATURE; TELEVISION AND CANADIAN LITERATURE]

Wars with internal dragons; reviews of *Lost and Found* and *Different Dragons*. Frances Frazer. *Can Child Lit* 1987; No 45: p91–93.

Canadian content in England; essay. Monica Hughes. *Quill & Quire (Books for Young People)* April 1987; Vol 53 No 4: p4.
[GREAT BRITAIN-CANADA LITERARY RELATIONS]

There's a lot more here than a little by Little; review of *Little by Little*. Callie Israel. photo · *Quill & Quire (Books for Young People)* Dec 1987; Vol 53 No 12: p3.

Sam McGee leads the way in showing the potential of poetry; reviews of children's poetry books. Janice Kennedy. *MG* March 7, 1987: H10.

Readers, writers of tomorrow; column. Joan McGrath. *TS* July 5, 1987: pA18.
[BOOK TRADE IN CANADA]

Little's achievements simply huge; reviews of *Little by Little* and *Her Special Vision*. Joan McGrath. *TS* Nov 29, 1987: pA21.

Paperbacks in brief; review of *Lost and Found*. Stephanie Nettell. *Times Lit Supp* May 15, 1987; No 4389: p529.

Christine 'truly enjoyed' this book; review of *Hey World, Here I Am!*. Christine Sekulic. *TS* Feb 1, 1987: pA20.

Wit, enjoyment and urgency; reviews of children's poetry books. Tim Wynne-Jones. *G&M* Feb 7, 1987: pE19.

My Cousin's director brings you tears next; article. Rita Zekas. photo · *TS* Oct 18, 1987: pG6.
[TELEVISION AND CANADIAN LITERATURE]

LITURGY OF LIGHT/Poems by Stavros Tsimicalis

[Untitled]; review of *Liturgy of Light*. Corrado Federici. *Poetry Can R* Summer 1987; Vol 8 No 4: p36.

Seasons, time and memory; reviews of poetry books. Lesley McAllister. *TS* March 21, 1987: M5.

LIVES OF GIRLS AND WOMEN/Novel by Alice Munro

The rival bards; article. Lorraine M. York. *Can Lit* Spring 1987; No 112: p211–216.

LIVESAY, DOROTHY

Ondaatje opens reading series; article. photo · *CH* Sept 25, 1987: pF7.
[FICTION READINGS; POETRY READINGS]

Poet explores social issues; article. *CH* Nov 17, 1987: pE8.
[POETRY READINGS]

Dorothy Livesay: a rare breed of woman; biographical article. Ken Adachi. photo · *TS* June 28, 1987: pA19.

[Untitled]; review of *The Self-Completing Tree*. Audrey Andrews. *CH* Sept 27, 1987: pF.6.

The self-completing poet; review of *The Self-Completing Tree*. Phil Hall. illus · *Can Forum* Aug-Sept 1987; Vol 67 No 771: p37–39.

[Untitled]; review of *Dorothy Livesay*. Lorna Irvine. *Amer R of Can Studies* Winter 1987–88; Vol 17 No 4: p452–453.

Quilting — a spiral of experience; review of *Dorothy Livesay*. R. Alex Kizuk. *Can Poet* Fall-Winter 1987; No 21: p110–115.

Death by drowning; letter to the editor. Imogen Knister Givens. *Books in Can* Aug-Sept 1987; Vol 16 No 6: p38.

Lives of the poet; review of *The Self-Completing Tree*. David Latham. *Books in Can* April 1987; Vol 16 No 3: p27–28.

Infinite song; review of *The Self-Completing Tree*. Louise Longo. *Waves* Spring 1987; Vol 15 No 4: p84–87.

Livesay's selected seasons — a heady brew; review of *The Self-Completing Tree*. Ann Munton. *Event* Summer 1987; Vol 16 No 2: p133–137.

[Untitled]; review of *A Public and Private Voice*. Margaret Gail Osachoff. *U of Windsor R* Spring-Summer 1987; Vol 20 No 2: p94–97.
[CONFERENCE REPORTS: REVIEWS AND ARTICLES]

The Livesay papers; review of *The Papers of Dorothy Livesay*. Catherine Sheldrick Ross. *Can Poet* Fall-Winter 1987; No 21: p116–117.

[Untitled]; review of *The Self-Completing Tree*. Libby Scheier. *Cross Can Writ Q* 1987; Vol 9 No 3–4: p39–40.

[Untitled]; reviews of *The Self-Completing Tree* and *The Collected Poems*. Stephen Scobie. *Malahat R (special issue)* March 1987; No 78: p154–155.

LIVESEY, MARGOT

Matter-of-fact visions; reviews of *Learning by Heart* and *Queen of the Headaches*. Hilda Kirkwood. *Can Forum* Jan 1987; Vol 66 No 765: p39.

[Untitled]; review of *Learning by Heart*. Mary S. Ladky. *Rubicon* Fall 1987; No 9: p201–202.

[Untitled]; review of *Learning by Heart*. Frances Ruhlen McConnel. illus · *NYT Book R* Aug 2, 1987: p16.

LOBSTER IN MY POCKET/Children's story by Deirdre Kessler

Three stories for children; reviews of children's books. Veronica Leonard. *Atlan Prov Book R* Nov-Dec 1987; Vol 14 No 4: p1.

Mini-reviews; reviews of children's stories. Mary Rubio. *Can Child Lit* 1987; No 47: p96–99.

LOCHHEAD, DOUGLAS

[Untitled]; review of *Tiger in the Skull*. *Queen's Q* Winter 1987; Vol 94 No 4: p1068–1069.

In principio; reviews. Laurel Boone. *Can Lit* Winter 1987; No 115: p209–211.
[CONFERENCE REPORTS: REVIEWS AND ARTICLES]

Tiger poems; reviews of poetry books. M. Travis Lane. *Fiddlehead* Autumn 1987; No 153: p88–91.

Exile & belonging: two Maritime poets; reviews of *White of the Lesser Angels* and *Tiger in the Skull*. Richard Lemm. *Atlan Prov Book R* May-June 1987; Vol 14 No 2: p10.

[Untitled]; review of *Tiger in the Skull*. Robin Skelton. *Poetry Can R* Spring 1987; Vol 8 No 2–3: p42.

Mapping inner and outer selves; review of *Tiger in the Skull* and *Dogstones*. Fraser Sutherland. *G&M* Feb 28, 1987: pE18.

[Untitled]; reviews of poetry books. Bruce Whiteman. *Cross Can Writ Q* 1987; Vol 9 No 2: p21–22,26.

LOG JAM/Young adult novel by Monica Hughes

Midsummer doldrums are relieved with engaging, artful activity book; review of *Log Jam*. Janice Kennedy. *MG* Aug 1, 1987: J9.

Beatrix Potter better than ever; reviews of *Nobody Said It Would Be Easy* and *Log Jam*. Joan McGrath. *TS* April 25, 1987: M4.

Authors ease teen angst in the wilds of Alberta; reviews of young adult novels. Susan Scott. photo · *CH* April 23, 1987: pD1.

Roughing it in the bush; reviews of children's books. Mary Ainslie Smith. *Books in Can* Aug-Sept 1987; Vol 16 No 6: p34–36.

Calls to the wild; reviews of young adult novels. Tim Wynne-Jones. *G&M* May 2, 1987: pC19.

THE LONELY PASSION OF JUDITH HEARNE/Novel by Brian Moore

Book world: Maggie Smith as Judith Hearne?; column. Beverley Slopen. *TS* Jan 25, 1987: pB6.
[AUTHORS, CANADIAN; FILM ADAPTATIONS OF CANADIAN LITERATURE]

A LONG NIGHT OF DEATH/Novel by Alberto Balcarce

[Untitled]; review of *A Long Night of Death*. Barbara Carey. *Books in Can* Jan-Feb 1987; Vol 16 No 1: p25.
[FIRST NOVELS: BOOK REVIEWS]

Latin terror; review of *A Long Night of Death*. Pauline Carey. *G&M* Aug 22, 1987: pC14.
[FIRST NOVELS: BOOK REVIEWS]

Under dark cover of stark militarism; review of *A Long Night of Death*. Lesley McAllister. *TS* April 25, 1987: M7.
[FIRST NOVELS: BOOK REVIEWS]

[Untitled]; review of *A Long Night of Death*. Rachel Rafelman. *Quill & Quire* Feb 1987; Vol 53 No 2: p17.
[FIRST NOVELS: BOOK REVIEWS]

LONG, CYNTHIA

From mind to mind; reviews of *Night Studies* and *Wishbones*. H.W. Connor. *Can Lit* Spring 1987; No 112: p118–120.
[FIRST NOVELS: BOOK REVIEWS]

LONGCHAMPS, RENAUD

Une Amérique d'arrière-cour; review of *Américane*. Jacques Michon. *MD* Oct 17, 1987: pD3–D4.

Renaud Longchamps: le vertige derrière la découverte; article. Jean Royer. photo · *MD* April 4, 1987: pD3.

[Untitled]; reviews of *Mon mari le docteur* and *Américane*. Jacques St-Pierre. *Moebius* Winter 1987; No 31: p139–140.

LOOKING FOR THE LAST BIG TREE/Novel by Michael Foss

[Untitled]; review of *Looking for the Last Big Tree*. Douglas Hill. *Books in Can* Jan-Feb 1987; Vol 16 No 1: p25–26.

An obsession for B.C.'s trees; review of *Looking for the Last Big Tree*. M.T. Kelly. photo · *G&M* Feb 7, 1987: pE19.
[FIRST NOVELS: BOOK REVIEWS]

LOOKING UP/Poems by J. Alvin Speers

[Untitled]; reviews of poetry books. Anne Cimon. *Poetry Can R* Spring 1987; Vol 8 No 2–3: p62.

THE LOON LAKE MURDERS/Young adult novel by Robert Sutherland

[Untitled]; reviews of *The Green Gables Detectives* and *The Loon Lake Murders*. Linda Granfield. *Quill & Quire (Books for Young People)* Aug 1987; Vol 53 No 8: p5–6.

LOST AND FOUND/Children's story by Jean Little

Wars with internal dragons; reviews of *Lost and Found* and *Different Dragons*. Frances Frazer. *Can Child Lit* 1987; No 45: p91–93.

Paperbacks in brief; review of *Lost and Found*. Stephanie Nettell. *Times Lit Supp* May 15, 1987; No 4389: p529.

THE LOUIS RIEL ORGAN & PIANO COMPANY/Poems by Frank Davey

Parlour pump organs and prairie cafes; reviews of *Waiting for Saskatchewan* and *The Louis Riel Organ & Piano Company*. Phillip Lanthier. *NeWest R* April 1987; Vol 12 No 8: p13,15.

[Untitled]; reviews of *The Louis Riel Organ & Piano Co.* and *The North Book*. John F. Vardon. *Poetry Can R* Spring 1987; Vol 8 No 2–3: p47.

"Citizens-in-language"; reviews of *The Louis Riel Organ & Piano Co.* and *Waiting for Saskatchewan*. Lorraine York. *Essays on Can Writ* Winter 1987; No 35: p171–177.

LOUIS, JOSEPH

[Untitled]; review of *Madelaine*. Nicole de Montbrun. *Quill & Quire* June 1987; Vol 53 No 6: p32–33.

LOUISE ET LA NOUVELLE JULIE/Novel by Marc Gendron

Deux échos québécois de grands romans épistolaires du dix-huitième siècle français; article. Monique Moser-Verrey. *Voix et images* Spring 1987; Vol 12 No 3: p512–514,516–522.
[FRANCE-CANADA LITERARY RELATIONS]

LOVE'S SWEET RETURN: THE HARLEQUIN STORY/ Critical work by Margaret Ann Jensen

[Untitled]; review of *Love's Sweet Return*. Angela Miles. *Atlantis* Fall 1987; Vol 13 No 1: p185–187.

LOVE IS A LONG SHOT/Novel by Ted Allan

Rewriting the past; article. Paul Stuewe. *Books in Can* Aug-Sept 1987; Vol 16 No 6: p13–14.

LOVE YOU FOREVER/Children's story by Robert Munsch

Rare joy and simple truth; reviews of *Tales of a Gambling Grandma* and *Love You Forever*. Tim Wynne-Jones. *G&M* Jan 24, 1987: pE19.

THE LOVED AND THE LOST/Novel by Morley Callaghan

Childhood experiences in The Loved and the Lost; article. Donald R. Bartlett. *New Q* Spring-Summer 1987; Vol 7 No 1–2: p294–300.
[THE FAMILY IN CANADIAN LITERATURE]

LOVHERS/Poems by Nicole Brossard

[Untitled]; review of *Lovhers*. Eva Tihanyi. *Poetry Can R* Spring 1987; Vol 8 No 2–3: p40–41.

LOVING YOU IS LIKE TRYING TO SING ALONG WITH FRANK SINATRA/Play by Bryden Macdonald

Puppetry the great strength of this Peter and the Wolf; theatre review of *Loving You Is Like Trying to Sing Along with Frank Sinatra*. Ray Conlogue. *G&M* April 24, 1987: pC7.

LOWEY, MARK

Poets propelled by Thistledown; article. Kenneth McGoogan. *CH* April 12, 1987: pF2.
[CANADIAN LITERARY PUBLISHING]

Thistledown presents prairie poets in full bloom; reviews of poetry books. Christopher Wiseman. *CH* May 24, 1987: pE6.

LOWRY, MALCOLM

Lowry links Greek myth with cautionary tale; reviews of *Malcolm Lowry: Vancouver Days* and *Hear Us O Lord from Heaven Thy Dwelling Place*. Ken Adachi. photo · *TS* July 11, 1987: M4.

The descent into hell of Jacques Laruelle: chapter I of Under The Volcano; article. David Falk. *Can Lit* Spring 1987; No 112: p72–83.
[ARTIST FIGURE; CONFESSIONAL WRITING]

Conflicting memories of a friend about to self-destruct; review of *Malcolm Lowry: Vancouver Days*. William French. photo · *G&M* June 18, 1987: pD1.

Memories of Malcolm Lowry; column. William French. illus · *G&M* Aug 18, 1987: pD7.

[Untitled]; review of *Malcolm Lowry: Vancouver Days*. Shelagh Garland. *Books in Can* Dec 1987; Vol 16 No 9: p26.

UBC plans Lowry symposium; article. Stephen Godfrey. *G&M* April 30, 1987: pC1.
[CONFERENCES, LITERARY]

[Untitled]; review of *Malcolm Lowry: Vancouver Days*. Jay Ruzesky. *Malahat R* Dec 1987; No 81: p109–110.

Rereading Lowry's "Lunar Caustic"; article. Mark Thomas. *Can Lit* Spring 1987; No 112: p195–197.

Critical programmes; reviews of *Malcolm Lowry* and *Four Contemporary Novelists*. Paul Tiessen. *Can Lit* Winter 1987; No 115: p157–159.

The mystique of mezcal; article. Sue Vice. *Can Lit* Spring 1987; No 112: p197–202.

Lowry's B.C. connection examined; review of *Malcolm Lowry: Vancouver Days*. Thomas York. *CH* June 28, 1987: pF8.

LOZEAU, ALBERT

Avant-propos/Forward; editorial article in French and in English translation. Patricia Godbout. *Ellipse* 1987; No 38: p4–7

A poet at his window: Albert Lozeau; article. Laurent Mailhot. trans · *Ellipse* 1987; No 38: p45–53.

LÉTAIF, NADINE

[Untitled]; review of *Les Métamorphoses d'Ishtar*. André Roy. *Estuaire* Autumn 1987; No 46: p85.

LUCIEN/Play by Marshall Button

Mill life provided fuel for persona; article. Kate Zimmerman. photo · *CH* Nov 2, 1987: pB6.

THE LUCKY OLD WOMAN/Children's story by Robin Muller

Baby of the family gets respect raising flock of Canada geese; reviews of children's books. Janice Kennedy. *MG* Oct 3, 1987: J13.

[Untitled]; review of *The Lucky Old Woman*. Judy Magnuson. *CH* Dec 6, 1987: pD9.

Traditional tales made new again with super illustrations; reviews of *The Dragon* and *The Lucky Old Woman*. Eva Martin. *Quill & Quire (Books for Young People)* Aug 1987; Vol 53 No 8: p7.

A title that will grab teenagers; reviews of children's books. Joan McGrath. *TS* Oct 25, 1987: pA18.

Familiarity and TV's stranglehold on life; reviews of children's books. Tim Wynne-Jones. *G&M* Nov 14, 1987: pE4.
[FESTIVALS, LITERARY]

THE LUCKY ONES/Novel by Donald Purcell

[Untitled]; review of *The Lucky Ones*. David Willis. *Queen's Q* Summer 1987; Vol 94 No 2: p482–483.
[FIRST NOVELS: BOOK REVIEWS]

LUDWIG ZELLER: A CELEBRATION/Poem by Ludwig Zeller

Translators feast on Pheasant; column. William French. illus · *G&M* Sept 22, 1987: pD5.

LUNATIC VILLAS/Novel by Marian Engel

Marian Engel's family fictions: Lunatic Villas; article. Christl Verduyn. *New Q* Spring-Summer 1987; Vol 7 No 1–2: p274–283.
[THE FAMILY IN CANADIAN LITERATURE; FEMINIST WRITING AND CRITICISM; WOMEN IN LITERATURE]

LUNN, JAMES

Vancouver man wins pulp prize; article. Kenneth McGoogan. *CH* Nov 11, 1987: pA18.
[AWARDS, LITERARY]

LUNN, JANET

U.S.-born writer wins book award; article. *WFP* April 29, 1987: p41.
[AWARDS, LITERARY]

Lunn, Gay, Reid, Poulin garner kids' book awards; article. *Quill & Quire (Books for Young People)* June 1987; Vol 53 No 6: p4.
[AWARDS, LITERARY]

Council award goes to Lunn; article. *G&M* April 30, 1987: pC1.
[AWARDS, LITERARY]

Le Conseil des arts du Canada attribue ses prix de littérature-jeunesse; article. *MD* April 28, 1987: p14.
[AWARDS, LITERARY]

Ontario writer wins Canada Council prize; article. *TS* April 28, 1987: pG4.
[AWARDS, LITERARY]

Apt appraisal; article. *Quill & Quire* Aug 1987; Vol 53 No 8: p27.
[AWARDS, LITERARY]

Janet Lunn's time/space travellers; article. James Harrison. *Can Child Lit* 1987; No 46: p60–63.

La vie littéraire; column. Jean Royer. photo · *MD* May 2, 1987: pD2.
[AWARDS, LITERARY; INTERNATIONAL REVIEWS OF CANADIAN LITERATURE; RADIO AND CANADIAN LITERATURE; TELEVISION AND CANADIAN LITERATURE; WRITERS' ORGANIZATIONS]

Living in the past; reviews of children's novels. Mary Ainslie Smith. *Books in Can* June-July 1987; Vol 16 No 5: p35–37.

Satisfying prizes; column. Tim Wynne-Jones. *G&M* May 16, 1987: pC19.
[AWARDS, LITERARY]

LUSCOMBE, GEORGE

Mr. Jelly Roll falls short of its goal; theatre review. photo · *TS* May 1, 1987: pD24.

LUSH, RICHARD

Frost shadows; reviews of poetry books. Andrew Taylor. *Can Lit* Winter 1987; No 115: p197–199.

LYDIA/Play by Paula Wing

Paula Wing's Lydia is filled with love, joy and rich spirit; column. Robert Crew. *TS* Nov 8, 1987: pC2.

Director says Lorca tragedy a timeless tale; column. Vit Wagner. photo · *TS* Oct 30, 1987: pE4

LYNCH, MICHAEL

CBC explores impact of AIDS on the arts; article. Liam Lacey. *G&M* April 11, 1987: pE3.

LYPCHUK, DONNA

Much to do with very little; theatre review of *Tragedy of Manners*. Ray Conlogue. *G&M* Oct 5, 1987: pD11.

It's tragic but there goes old Queen St. neighborhood; theatre review of *Tragedy of Manners*. Robert Crew. photo · *TS* Oct 4, 1987: pC2.

Criticism misdirected; letter to the editor. Deborah Porter. *G&M* Oct 28, 1987: pA6.

LES MÉMOIRES ARTIFICIELLES/Poems by Michael Delisle

[Untitled]; reviews of *Les Mémoires artificielles* and *Les Changeurs de signes*. Jacques Paquin. *Estuaire* Autumn 1987; No 46: p83–84.

LES MÉTAMORPHOSES D'ISHTAR/Poems by Nadine Ltaif

[Untitled]; review of *Les Métamorphoses d'Ishtar*. André Roy. *Estuaire* Autumn 1987; No 46: p85.

MacARTHUR PARK/Play by Mike Johnston

Teenage amateur theatre group produces play at 'real' theatre; article. Robert Davis. photo · *TS (Neighbours)* Feb 10, 1987: p26.

MacCORMACK, KAREN

Each to her own rhythm; reviews of poetry books. Lesley McAllister. *TS* July 25, 1987: M5.

MacDONALD, ALASTAIR

Lost innocents; reviews of *Nothing So Natural* and *Flavian's Fortune*. Peter Hinchcliffe. *Can Lit* Spring 1987; No 112: p90–91.

[Untitled]; reviews of *Flavian's Fortune* and *The Story of Bobby O'Malley*. Charles R. Steele. *Queen's Q* Winter 1987; Vol 94 No 4: p1019–1022.

MacDONALD, BRYDEN

Puppetry the great strength of this Peter and the Wolf; theatre review of *Loving You Is Like Trying to Sing Along with Frank Sinatra*. Ray Conlogue. *G&M* April 24, 1987: pC7.

MacDONALD, JAKE

[Untitled]; reviews. Anne Cimon. *Cross Can Writ Q* 1987; Vol 9 No 3–4: p47–48.

[Untitled]; reviews of *The Bridge Out of Town* and *A Model Lover*. Clifford G. Holland. *Queen's Q* Summer 1987; Vol 94 No 2: p472–474.

[Untitled]; review of *The Bridge Out of Town*. Ruth Manson. *Quill & Quire* March 1987; Vol 53 No 3: p71.

MacEWEN, GWENDOLYN

Milestones; column. *TS* Dec 6, 1987: pB6.

Activity books kids will enjoy; reviews of *Dragon Sandwiches* and *The Dragon and Other Laurentian Tales*. *TS* Dec 20, 1987: pE8.

Author MacEwen dies at 46; obituary. *MG* Dec 2, 1987: H2.

Writer dead at 46; obituary. *WFP* Dec 3, 1987: p48.

Poet won Governor-General's Award; obituary. *G&M* Dec 2, 1987: pA10.

Passages; obituary. *Maclean's* Dec 14, 1987; Vol 100 No 50: p4.

Writer dies at home; obituary. photo · *CH* Dec 2, 1987: pD2.

For the record; obituary. *CH* Dec 6, 1987: pB6.

Poet Gwendolyn MacEwen dead; obituary. Ken Adachi. photo · *TS* Dec 1, 1987: H1.

[Untitled]; reviews of *Noman's Land* and *Queen of the Headaches*. Anne Cimon. *Cross Can Writ Q* 1987; Vol 9 No 1: p20–21.

MacEwen and McKay; reviews of *Afterworlds* and *Sanding Down This Rocking Chair on a Windy Night*. Barry Dempster. *Poetry Can R* Fall 1987; Vol 9 No 1: p29–30.

So you think poetry no longer exists for readers?; reviews of *Afterworlds* and *Sanding Down This Rocking Chair on a Windy Night*. Judith Fitzgerald. photo · *TS* May 3, 1987: pA24.

Anarchy and afterthoughts; review of *Afterworlds*. Susan Glickman. *Books in Can* June-July 1987; Vol 16 No 5: p26.

Home rituals; review of *Noman's Land*. Sherrill Grace. *Can Lit* Spring 1987; No 112: p102–104.

MacEwen possessed a talent that was fragile, precocious; article. M.T. Kelly. photo · *G&M* Dec 2, 1987: pC5.

Generous and open; letter to the editor. Tim McNamara. photo · *G&M* Dec 19, 1987: pD7.

[Untitled]; reviews of *Afterworlds* and *Sanding Down This Rocking Chair on a Windy Night*. Barbara Powell. *Wascana R* Fall 1987; Vol 22 No 2: p88–91.

[Untitled]; letter to the editor. Susan Schelle. *G&M* Dec 19, 1987: pD7.

[Untitled]; review of *Afterworlds*. Stephen Scobie. *Malahat R* June 1987; No 79: p168.

Poetry: packing all the power into two of seven titles; reviews of poetry books. Robin Skelton. photo · *Quill & Quire* May 1987; Vol 53 No 5: p24.

Literary tricks and the larger concerns; reviews of *Delayed Mercy* and *Afterworlds*. Fraser Sutherland. photo · *G&M* Aug 8, 1987: pC19.

Familiarity and TV's stranglehold on life; reviews of children's books. Tim Wynne-Jones. *G&M* Nov 14, 1987: pE4.
[FESTIVALS, LITERARY]

MacGREGOR, ROY

Hockey drama kicks off new Canadian TV season; column. Jim Bawden. photo · *TS* Jan 2, 1987: pD21.
[TELEVISION AND CANADIAN LITERATURE]

MacIVOR, DANIEL

See Bob Run dark ride into subconscious; theatre review. Pat Donnelly. *MG* Oct 1, 1987: pE7.

A funny look at a bad girl; theatre review of *See Bob Run*. Liam Lacey. photo · *G&M* July 22, 1987: pC6.

Teen hitchhikes back to childhood horror; theatre review of *See Bob Run*. Henry Mietkiewicz. photo · *TS* July 23, 1987: pB4.

MACK LE ROUGE/Children's novel by David Schinkel and Yves Beauchesne

Littérature jeunesse; reviews of children's books. Dominique Demers. *MD* Nov 21, 1987: pD6.

MACKAY, CLAIRE

Chit chat; column. Maria Casas. *Quill & Quire (Books for Young People)* April 1987; Vol 53 No 4: p3.
[CHILDREN'S LITERATURE; CHINA-CANADA LITERARY RELATIONS; WRITERS-IN-RESIDENCE]

Pour les adolescents: quatre mains et deux solitudes; reviews of young adult novels. Dominique Demers. photo · *MD* Dec 19, 1987: pD6–D7.

Creative Workshops for Children encourage young writers to produce; article. Paul Irish. *TS (Neighbours)* May 5, 1987: p18.

McDonald scores with Canada's booksellers; article. Kenneth McGoogan. *CH* June 30, 1987: pE1.
[AWARDS, LITERARY]

Readers, writers of tomorrow; column. Joan McGrath. *TS* July 5, 1987: pA18.
[BOOK TRADE IN CANADA]

Book world: where the $$$ land — legally; column. Beverley Slopen. *TS* March 1, 1987: pA15.
[PUBLISHING AND PUBLISHERS IN CANADA; WRITERS-IN-RESIDENCE]

THE MACKENZIE/PAPINEAU REBELLION (A PUNCH AND JUDY SHOW)/Play by Michael Hollingsworth

Spoof of Canadian history a riot of fun; theatre review of *The Mackenzie/Papineau Rebellion*. Robert Crew. photo · *TS* April 16, 1987: pC15.

Historical satire highly original, funny; theatre review of *The Mackenzie/Papineau Rebellion*. Liam Lacey. photo · *G&M* April 16, 1987: pD6.

MacLENNAN, HUGH

Novelist wins apartment fight; article. *TS* Jan 9, 1987: pD20.

Novelist Hugh MacLennan honored by Princeton University; article. *TS* Jan 21, 1987: pD3.
[AWARDS, LITERARY]

Author won't have to leave his apartment; article. photo · *MG* Jan 9, 1987: pA3.

Novelist MacLennan winner of prestigious award from Princeton; article. photo · *MG* Jan 20, 1987: pD10.
[AWARDS, LITERARY]

MacLennan allowed to stay in apartment; article. *WFP* Jan 10, 1987: p28.

Author wins medal; article. *WFP* Jan 21, 1987: p32.
[AWARDS, LITERARY]

Say that again?; column. photo · *CH* March 29, 1987: pA4.

Princeton honors Hugh MacLennan; article. *G&M* Jan 21, 1987: pC7.
[AWARDS, LITERARY]

Barometer's rising the curtain in Halifax; article. *TS* Sept 26, 1987: pG10.

The rumor mill grinds: Chrétien to the NDP?; column. Nick Auf der Maur. *MG* March 4, 1987: pA2.

People; column. Yvonne Cox. photo · *Maclean's* Jan 26, 1987; Vol 100 No 4: p48.
[AWARDS, LITERARY]

Neptune Theatre's Barometer Rising too faithful to book; theatre review. Matthew Fraser. *G&M* Nov 9, 1987: pD9.
[DRAMATIC ADAPTATIONS OF CANADIAN LITERATURE]

Anti-smoking message is right on target; column. William French. *G&M* April 14, 1987: pC7.
[WRITERS' ORGANIZATIONS]

MacLennan, the lion of CanLit, turns 80; article. Heather Hill. biog photo · *MG* March 20, 1987: pA1,A5.

Visionary author retains warmth and wit at 80; article. Heather Hill. photo · *CH* March 24, 1987: pD1.

Writers revive censorship-pornography debate; article. Liam Lacey. photo · *G&M* June 1, 1987: pC9.
[AUTHORS, CANADIAN; CENSORSHIP; WOMEN WRITERS; WRITERS' ORGANIZATIONS]

Maritime letters; reviews. Carrie MacMillan. *Can Lit* Spring 1987; No 112: p189–192.

Fiery MacLennan defends late Margaret Laurence; article. Kenneth McGoogan. *CH* May 31, 1987: pF2.

Death on the waterfront; theatre review of *Barometer Rising*, includes profile. Stephen Pedersen. photo · *Maclean's* Nov 23, 1987; Vol 100 No 47: p57.
[DRAMATIC ADAPTATIONS OF CANADIAN LITERATURE]

Halifax blast commemorated in effective stage production; theatre review of *Barometer Rising*. Jamie Portman. *CH* Nov 12, 1987: pD2.
[DRAMATIC ADAPTATIONS OF CANADIAN LITERATURE]

A sound beyond hearing; article. Tom Regan. photo · *Atlan Insight* Dec 1987; Vol 9 No 12: p19–21.
[DRAMATIC ADAPTATIONS OF CANADIAN LITERATURE]

"Suddenly, you wake up and you're 80"; biographical article. Oakland Ross. photo · *G&M* April 18, 1987: pC1.

On fiction, TV and losers; article. Oakland Ross. photo · *G&M* April 18, 1987: pC1.

Great Montrealer Hugh MacLennan feted at Racket Club; column. Thomas Schnurmacher. *MG* March 13, 1987: H1.

Tip sheet: . . . writers meet; column. Susan Schwartz. photo · *MG* Oct 14, 1987: pC9.
[WRITERS' ORGANIZATIONS]

MacLennan happy with plans to stage his Barometer Rising; article. Derrick Toth. photo · *CH* Sept 26, 1987: pG1.
[DRAMATIC ADAPTATIONS OF CANADIAN LITERATURE]

MacLEOD, ALISTAIR

Mainstreet Calgary; column. *CH (Neighbors)* Oct 21, 1987: pA14–A15.
[FICTION READINGS]

Mainstreet Calgary; column. *CH (Neighbors)* Oct 28, 1987: pA22–A23.
[FICTION READINGS; WRITERS' WORKSHOPS]

[Untitled]; reviews of short story collections. David Helwig. *Queen's Q* Winter 1987; Vol 94 No 4: p1022–1024.

MACLEOD, FRANCIS

Children's fantasy fails to fulfil promise; theatre review of *A Princess Comes of Age*. Neil Harris. *WFP* Nov 21, 1987: p22.

MACLEOD, JOAN

Jewel shines with unexpected qualities; theatre review of *Jewel*. Ray Conlogue. photo · *G&M* April 27, 1987: pC12.

Toronto, Mississippi is well worth a visit; theatre review. Ray Conlogue. photo · *G&M* Oct 7, 1987: pC8.

Gem of a Jewel needs strong actress; theatre review of *Jewel*. Robert Crew. photo · *TS* April 28, 1987: pG3.

Play talks to handicapped via Elvis; article. Robert Crew. photo · *TS* Oct 2, 1987: pE12.

Toronto, Mississippi a heartfelt new play; theatre review. Robert Crew. *TS* Oct 7, 1987: pD1.

Prairie spaces in the big city: western theatre in Toronto; theatre reviews. Margaret Gail Osachoff. *NeWest R* Oct 1987; Vol 13 No 2: p18–19.

MAD QUEEN OF MORDRA

See BILLY AND THE BUBBLESHIP/MAD QUEEN OF MORDRA/Children's novel by Elwy Yost

MADAME PICCOLO AND THE CRAZIEST PICKLE PARTY EVER/Children's story by Kaila Kukla

One miss, one hit; reviews of *And I'm Never Coming Back* and *Madam Piccolo and the Craziest Pickle Party Ever*. Sylvia Markle-Craine. *Can Child Lit* 1987; No 48: p100–102.

MADELAINE/Novel by Joseph Louis

[Untitled]; review of *Madelaine*. Nicole de Montbrun. *Quill & Quire* June 1987; Vol 53 No 6: p32–33.

MADEMOISELLE AUTOBODY/Play by Folles Alliées Theatre collective

Théâtre didactique; reviews of *Mademoiselle Autobody* and *Sortie de secours*. Lucie Robert. *Voix et images* Autumn 1987; Vol 13 No 1: p196–198.

MADOTT, DARLENE

[Untitled]; review of *Bottled Roses*. *Queen's Q* Spring 1987; Vol 94 No 1: p253.

Memory & words; reviews of *Fables of Brunswick Avenue* and *Bottled Roses*. Michael Helm. *Can Lit* Spring 1987; No 112: p92–95.

MAGIC REALISM

Novelist as trickster: the magical presence of Gabriel García Márquez in Robert Kroetsch's What The Crow Said; article. Brian Edwards. *Essays on Can Writ* Spring 1987; No 34: p92–110.

[LATIN AMERICA-CANADA LITERARY RELATIONS; POSTMODERNIST WRITING AND CRITICISM; STRUCTURALIST WRITING AND CRITICISM]

MAGIE D'UN JOUR DE PLUIE/RAINY DAY MAGIC/ Children's story by Marie-Louise Gay

Littérature jeunesse; reviews of children's books. Domique Demers. *MD* Oct 10, 1987: pD6.

School's out, and books are in; reviews of children's books. Janice Kennedy. *MG* July 4, 1987: J9.

Three noble stories; review of *Rainy Day Magic*. Tim Wynne-Jones. *G&M* May 30, 1987: pC21.

MAGINI, ROGER

La vitrine du livre; review of *Saint Cooperblack*. Guy Ferland. *MD* Jan 31, 1987: pB2.

Les vertus de la retenue et du silence; reviews of poetry books. Marie José Thériault. photo · *Lettres québec* Summer 1987; No 46: p30–32.

MAHE, IRENE

French play tackles social problems; theatre review of *Les Tremblay 2*. Philip Clark. *WFP* April 4, 1987: p23.

MAHEU, GILLES

Ne s'improvise pas improvisateur qui veut!; column. Paul Cauchon. *MD* Jan 21, 1987: p7.

[TELEVISION AND CANADIAN LITERATURE]

Gilles Maheu: corps à corps; article. Diane Pavlovic. photo trans · *Can Theatre R* Fall 1987; No 52: p22–29.

MAHEU-FORCIER, LOUISE

Castles of childhood; review of *A Forest for Zoe*. Margaret Belcher. *Can Lit* Winter 1987; No 115: p208–209.

A rich, feminist novel from Quebec; reviews of *A Forest for Zoe* and *After the Fact*. Geoff Hancock. *TS* Feb 15, 1987: pA19.

[Untitled]; reviews of *Under the House* and *A Forest for Zoe*. Lesley McAllister. *Cross Can Writ Q* 1987; Vol 9 No 3–4: p48–49.

[FIRST NOVELS: BOOK REVIEWS]

A friendship; review of *A Forest for Zoe*. Sherie Posesorski. *G&M* Jan 10, 1987: pE17.

Hard memory; review of *Isle of Joy*. Sherie Posesorski. *G&M* Aug 22, 1987: pC14.

Half-mad bohemian lyricism; review of *Amadou*. Anatanas Sileika. *G&M* Dec 26, 1987: pC23.

MAHLER ET AUTRES MATIÈRES/Poems by Pierre Nepveu

De Bellefeuille, Nepveu, Lemaire, Royer; reviews of poetry books. Jean-Pierre Issenhuth. *Liberté* Aug 1987; Vol 29 No 4: p78–87.

MAILLET, ANDRÉE

Andrée Maillet: bien écrire dans la fierté des origines; column. Jean Éthier-Blais. photo · *MD* Sept 19, 1987: pD8.

MAILLET, ANTONINE

Author Maillet named to council; article. *WFP* Jan 30, 1987: p33.

Mitterand nomme Antonine Maillet au Haut Conseil de la francophonie; article. photo · *MD* Jan 28, 1987: p6.

Aujourd'hui; column. *MD* May 4, 1987: p8.

En Acadie, Antonine Maillet sert de guide à Mitterand; article. photo · *MD* Sept 5, 1987: pA2.

Stuffed with legends; review of *The Devil Is Loose!*. Roberta Buchanan. *Can Lit* Winter 1987; No 115: p213–214.

La Sagouine: home to stay; article. Sue Calhoun. photo · *Atlan Insight* April 1987; Vol 9 No 4: p19–21.

[DRAMATIC ADAPTATIONS OF CANADIAN LITERATURE]

La Sagouine: un regard perant et lucide, source d'espoir; article. Paulette Collet. *Can Drama* 1987; Vol 13 No 1: p43–49.

A singular scrubwoman; article about Viola Leger. Ray Conlogue. photo · *G&M* May 2, 1987: pC1,C5.

Le théâtre qu'on joue; theatre reviews. André Dionne. photo · *Lettres québec* Winter 1986–87; No 44: p53–54.

New Maillet play slow getting off the mark; theatre review of *Margot la Folle*. Pat Donnelly. *MG* Oct 7, 1987: H4.

La Sagouine shows drawing power of good story well-told; theatre review. Pat Donnelly. *MG* Nov 6, 1987: pC1.

Death theme recurs in Maillet play; theatre review of *Margot la Folle*. Matthew Fraser. photo · *G&M* Oct 12, 1987: pC9.

Celebrity statu leaves Maillet 'street-wise'; column. William French. *G&M* Aug 13, 1987: pD1.

Rollicking tale captures spirit of Acadian life; review of *Mariaagélas*. Cecelia Frey. photo · *CH* Jan 4, 1987: pE4.

Après les mille et une nuits; review of *Le Huitime jour*. Pierre Hébert. photo · *Lettres québec* Winter 1986–87; No 44: p29–30.

Pélagie-la-Charrette and the carnivalesque; article. Robin Howells. *British J of Can Studies* June 1987; Vol 2 No 1: p48–60.

[CARNIVALIZATION]

Acadians in English; review of *Mariaagélas*. Allison Mitcham. *Fiddlehead* Spring 1987; No 151: p120–122.

The bible and myth in Antonine Maillet's Pélagie-la-Charrette; article. Paul G. Socken. *Studies in Can Lit* 1987; Vol 12 No 2: p187–198.

[VIOLENCE IN CANADIAN LITERATURE]

MAILLET, MARGUERITE

New Brunswick letters; review of *The Bicentennial Lectures on New Brunswick Literature*. Alan R. Young. *Can Lit* Spring 1987; No 112: p146–148.

LA MAISON DU REMOUS/Novel by Nicole Houde

Entre la maison, l'eau et le cosmos: l'écriture féminine; reviews of novels. Patricia Smart. *Voix et images* Winter 1987; No 35: p334–337.

MAJOR CANADIAN AUTHORS: A CRITICAL INTRO-DUCTION/Survey by David Stouck

[Untitled]; reviews of critical works. Ronald B. Hatch. *Eng Studies in Can* March 1987; Vol 13 No 1: p107–115.

MAJOR, ANDRÉ

La vie est bien faite, dit Vendredi, et juste en somme!; column, includes prose excerpt from *L'Hiver au coeur*. Jean Éthier-Blais. *MD* April 4, 1987: pD8.

Le métier d'écrire; review of *L'Hiver au coeur*. Réjean Beaudoin. *Liberté* Aug 1987; Vol 29 No 4: p110–114.

[Untitled]; review of *L'Hiver au coeur*. Nicole Décarie. *Moebius* Summer 1987; No 33: p133

Les vertus de la retenue et du silence; reviews of poetry books. Marie José Thériault. photo · *Lettres québec* Summer 1987; No 46: p30–32.

MAJOR, HENRIETTE

Rus in urbe: un concept classique pour enfants modernes; review of *Si l'herbe poussait sur les toits*. Pauline Pocknell. *Can Child Lit* 1987; No 47: p79–81.

MAJOR, KEVIN

Major's realistic epistles to Springsteen; review of *Dear Bruce Springsteen*. Peter Carver. photo · *Quill & Quire (Books for Young People)* Aug 1987; Vol 53 No 8: p4.

Dear Bruce Springsteen one author's fan letter; article. Rosie DiManno. *TS* Oct 2, 1987: pE23.

Baby of the family gets respect raising flock of Canada geese; reviews of children's books. Janice Kennedy. *MG* Oct 3, 1987: J13.

A title that will grab teenagers; reviews of children's books. Joan McGrath. *TS* Oct 25, 1987: pA18.

Novels deal with family breakup; reviews of *The Doll* and *Dear Bruce Springsteen*. Helen Norrie. *WFP* Dec 5, 1987: p57.

Fiction just loaded with personality; reviews of children's novels. Tim Wynne-Jones. photo · *G&M* Nov 28, 1987: pC22.
[FIRST NOVELS: BOOK REVIEWS]

A MAJORITY OF TWO/Play by Alun Hibbert

Beyond the Fringe; reviews of plays. Judith Rudakoff. *Books in Can* March 1987; Vol 16 No 2: p18.

MAJZELS, ROBERT

Liz says she laughed at the fat jokes; column. Thomas Schnurmacher. *MG* Oct 9, 1987: pC1.
[DRAMATIC READINGS]

MALCOLM LOWRY/Critical work by Ronald Binns

[Untitled]; reviews of critical works. Ronald B. Hatch. *Eng Studies in Can* March 1987; Vol 13 No 1: p107–115.

Critical programmes; reviews of *Malcolm Lowry* and *Four Contemporary Novelists*. Paul Tiessen. *Can Lit* Winter 1987; No 115: p157–159.

MALCOLM LOWRY: VANCOUVER DAYS/Compilation

Lowry links Greek myth with cautionary tale; reviews of *Malcolm Lowry: Vancouver Days* and *Hear Us O Lord from Heaven Thy Dwelling Place*. Ken Adachi. photo · *TS* July 11, 1987: M4.

Conflicting memories of a friend about to self-destruct; review of *Malcolm Lowry: Vancouver Days*. William French. photo · *G&M* June 18, 1987: pD1.

[Untitled]; review of *Malcolm Lowry: Vancouver Days*. Shelagh Garland. *Books in Can* Dec 1987; Vol 16 No 9: p26.

[Untitled]; review of *Malcolm Lowry: Vancouver Days*. Jay Ruzesky. *Malahat R* Dec 1987; No 81: p109–110.

Lowry's B.C. connection examined; review of *Malcolm Lowry: Vancouver Days*. Thomas York. *CH* June 28, 1987: pF8.

MALENFANT, PAUL CHANEL

[Untitled]; reviews of *Les Noms du père* and *Coq à deux têtes*. Jean Chapdelaine Gagnon. *Estuaire* Autumn 1987; No 46: p85–86.

L'originalité et l'oralité; reviews of *Coq à deux têtes* and *Les Terres du songe*. Jean Royer. *MD* May 30, 1987: pD3.

MALLET, MARILÚ

[Untitled]; review of *Voyage to the Other Extreme*. *Queen's Q* Spring 1987; Vol 94 No 1: p251.

La question des journaux intimes; article. Lise Gauvin. *Études fran* Winter 1987; Vol 22 No 3: p101–115.
[AUTOBIOGRAPHICAL WRITING, RADIO AND CANADIAN LITERATURE]

Other Americas; reviews of *The Light in the Piazza* and *Voyage to the Other Extreme*. Michael Greenstein. *Can Lit* Spring 1987; No 112: p97–100.

La vie littéraire; column. Marc Morin. *MD* Nov 14, 1987: pD14.
[AWARDS, LITERARY; CHILDREN'S LITERATURE; POETRY READINGS]

MALTMAN, KIM

Kinetic space; reviews of poetry books. Robert James Merrett. *Can Lit* Summer-Fall 1987; No 113–114: p241–243.

The voice of truth in Kim Maltman's *Softened Violence*; review article. Louise Simon. *Quarry* Winter 1987; Vol 36 No 1: p125–130.

MAMA'S GOING TO BUY YOU A MOCKINGBIRD/ Children's novel by Jean Little

My Cousin's director brings you tears next; article. Rita Zekas. photo · *TS* Oct 18, 1987: pG6.
[TELEVISION AND CANADIAN LITERATURE]

MAN AT STELLACO RIVER/Poems by Andrew Wreggitt

At the margins of disaster; review of *Man at Stellaco River*. Don Kerr. *Prairie Fire* Spring 1987; Vol 8 No 1: p88–90.

MANDEL, ELI

Eli Mandel in hospital; article. *G&M* Feb 3, 1987: pC5.

Reading Series features poet/critic Eli Mandel; article. *TS* Feb 1, 1987: pE9.
[POETRY READINGS]

Eli Mandel appearance at Harbourfront cancelled; article. *TS* Feb 2, 1987: H1.
[POETRY READINGS]

Big bash for book; article. *WFP* Jan 16, 1987: p31.

Mandel in hospital; article. *WFP* Feb 4, 1987: p36.

Style and substance; review of *The Family Romance*. Gary Draper. *Books in Can* May 1987; Vol 16 No 4: p29–31.

The critical art of Eli Mandel; review of *The Family Romance*. E.F. Dyck. *Prairie Fire* Autumn 1987; Vol 8 No 3: p98–101.

Mandel's two minds and Woodcock's single purpose; reviews of *The Family Romance* and *Northern Spring*. Doug Fetherling. photo · *Quill & Quire* May 1987; Vol 53 No 5: p20.

'Romance' a record by which poet puts theory into practice; review of *The Family Romance*. Maggie Helwig. photo · *TS* May 23, 1987: M4.

[Untitled]; review of *The Family Romance*. Robert Kroetsch. *Dandelion* Fall-Winter 1987; Vol 14 No 2: p145–147.

Mandel makes a sure-footed guide; review of *The Family Romance*. Robert Quickenden. *WFP* July 18, 1987: p54.

MANLEY, FRANK

[Untitled]; review of *Precious Stones*. Sparling Mills. *Poetry Can R* Fall 1987; Vol 9 No 1: p30.

THE MANOR HOUSE OF DE VILLERAY/Novel by J.L. Leprohon

Imperfect conquests; reviews of *The Manor House of De Villeray* and *Le Tour du Québec par deux enfants*. Anthony Raspa. *Can Lit* Winter 1987; No 115: p172–174.
[CANADIAN LITERARY PERIODICALS]

A MANUAL FOR LYING DOWN/Poems by Richard Lush

Frost shadows; reviews of poetry books. Andrew Taylor. *Can Lit* Winter 1987; No 115: p197–199.

MANUEL, LYNN

Formulaic mysteries to attract unenthusiastic readers; reviews of *The Ghost Ships That Didn't Belong* and *The Secret of Sunset House*. Bessie Condos Egan. *Quill & Quire (Books for Young People)* June 1987; Vol 53 No 6: p6.

MANY MIRRORS MANY FACES/Poems by Shulamis Yelin

[Untitled]; reviews of poetry books. Shaunt Basmajian. *Cross Can Writ Q* 1987; Vol 9 No 2: p22.

[Untitled]; reviews of poetry books. Andrew Parkin. *Poetry Can R* Fall 1987; Vol 9 No 1: p37.
[ANTHOLOGIES: BOOK REVIEWS]

MAO TS-TOUNG OU SOIRES DE MUSIQUE AU CONSULAT/Play by Jean-Pierre Ronfard

TNE's Mao charming highly visual theatre; theatre review of *Mao Ts Toung, ou soire de musique au consulat*. Marianne Ackerman. *MG* Feb 28, 1987: pG5.

[Untitled]; theatre review of *Mao Tse Toung ou soires de musique au consulat*. Marianne Ackerman. *MG* March 20, 1987: pC7.

Ronfard et les traces de Mao, Nadon et les frasques de Lorenzaccio; column. Robert Lévesque. *MD* Feb 17, 1987: p7.

[Untitled]; theatre reviews. Robert Lévesque. photo · *MD* March 13, 1987: p15.

Mao, sa révolution et nous; theatre review of *Mao Tsé-toung ou soirées de musique au consulat*. Paul Lefebvre. photo · *MD* March 3, 1987: p5.

[Untitled]; theatre review of *Mao Tsé Toung ou soirée de musique au consulat*. Louise Vigeant. photo · *Jeu* 1987; No 43: p156–159.

THE MARBLE HEAD AND OTHER POEMS/Poems by Ludwig Zeller

[Untitled]; reviews of poetry books. Stephen Morrissey. *Poetry Can R* Fall 1987; Vol 9 No 1: p32.

MARCIIAND, CLÉMENT

Le réel et la fiction du réel; reviews of *Les Soirs rouges* (reprint) and *La Fiction du rel*. Richard Gigure. photo · *Lettres québec* Winter 1986–87; No 44: p38–40.

MARCHAND, JACQUES

La palme à Ollivier et à Ouellette; article. photo · *MD* Nov 18, 1987: p11.
[AWARDS, LITERARY]

Les noeuds sacrés de l'âme, de la terre et du sang; reviews of novels. Réjean Beaudoin. *Liberté* Oct 1987; Vol 29 No 5: p106–114.

L'impossible fuite et les tragiques exigences de l'amour entre deux frères; review of *Le Premier mouvement*. Jean-Roch Boivin. *MD* Aug 8, 1987: pC7.

La vitrine du livre; review of *Le Premier mouvement*. Guy Ferland. *MD* June 13, 1987: pD4.

MARCHER DANS OUTREMONT OU AILLEURS/Poems by Paul Chamberland

Une mystique du désir; review of *Marcher dans Outremont ou ailleurs*. Jean-Roch Boivin. photo · *MD* June 13, 1987: pD3.

La vitrine du livre; reviews. Guy Ferland. *MD* May 23, 1987: pD4.

MARCHESSAULT, JOVETTE

Free premiere set for Fireworks; article. *TS* April 12, 1987: pC6.
[AUDIO-VISUALS AND CANADIAN LITERATURE]

À surveiller; column. *MD* Oct 30, 1987: p12.

"Donner naissance à des choses grandes et imparfaites"; review of *Des Cailloux blancs pour les forêts obscures*. Jean-Roch Boivin. photo · *MD* Oct 31, 1987: pD3.

Putrefying sore; reviews of fictional works. Kathryn Chittick. *Can Lit* Spring 1987; No 112: p128–129.

La vitrine du livre; reviews. Guy Ferland. *MD* Sept 19, 1987: pD4.

Jovette Marchessault: le roman de la réconciliation; article. Jean Royer. photo · *MD* Oct 8, 1987: p15

MARCOUX, DANIEL

La vitrine du livre; reviews of fictional works. Guy Ferland. *MD* Dec 5, 1987: pD4.

MARGARET ATWOOD: A FEMINIST POETICS/Critical work by Frank Davey

An Atwood anatomy; review of *Margaret Atwood: A Feminist Poetics*. Jerome H. Rosenberg. *Essays on Can Writ* Winter 1987; No 35: p88–92.

MARGARET IN THE MIDDLE/Children's novel by Bernice Thurman Hunter

[Untitled]; review of *Margaret in the Middle*. Sarah Smithies. *TS* Jan 18, 1987: pC8.

MARGOSHES, DAVE

[Untitled]; review of *Small Regrets*. Alice Gur-Arie. *Quill & Quire* Jan 1987; Vol 53 No 1: p28.

Uneven gaps; review of *Small Regrets*. Hilda Kirkwood. *Waves* Spring 1987; Vol 15 No 4: p77–79.

Enduring a thankless existence with father; reviews of *Black Swan* and *Small Regrets*. Hugh McKellar. *TS* Jan 31, 1987: M4.

Stories vivid, unpleasant—and memorable; reviews of short story books. John Mills. *Fiddlehead* Autumn 1987; No 153: p91–95.

In the mode; reviews of short story collections. Allan Weiss. *Books in Can* April 1987; Vol 16 No 3: p30–31.

MARGOT LA FOLLE/Play by Antonine Maillet

New Maillet play slow getting off the mark; theatre review of *Margot la Folle*. Pat Donnelly. *MG* Oct 7, 1987: H4.

Death theme recurs in Maillet play; theatre review of *Margot la Folle*. Matthew Fraser. photo · *G&M* Oct 12, 1987: pC9.

MARIA CHAPDELAINE/Novel by Louis Hmon

Un livre comme Hémon: secret, magique, introuvable; column. Jean Éthier-Blais. *MD* May 30, 1987: pD8.
[FILM ADAPTATIONS OF CANADIAN LITERATURE]

L'illustration de Maria Chapdelaine: les lectures de Suzor-Côté et Clarence Gagnon; article. Sylvie Bernier. illus · *Can Lit* Summer-Fall 1987; No 113–114: p76–90.

Les connivences implicites entre le texte et l'image: le cas Maria Chapdelaine; article. Gabrielle Gourdeau. *Can Lit* Summer-Fall 1987; No 113–114: p93–107.

D'autres classiques; letter to the editor. Joséphine Pouliot. *MD* June 16, 1987: p10.

MARIAAGÉLAS/Novel by Antonine Maillet

Rollicking tale captures spirit of Acadian life; review of *Mariaagélas*. Cecelia Frey. photo · *CH* Jan 4, 1987: pE4.

Acadians in English; review of *Mariaagélas*. Allison Mitcham. *Fiddlehead* Spring 1987; No 151: p120–122.

MARILYN (JOURNAL INTIME DE MARGARET MACPHERSON)/Play by Jean-Pierre Ronfard

Marilyn situation poignant but where's the drama?; theatre review of *Marilyn (journal intime de Margaret Macpherson)*. Pat Donnelly. photo · *MG* Oct 15, 1987: pE12.

Théâtre ouvert et théâtre intime; theatre review of *Marilyn (journal intime de Margaret Macpherson)*. Robert Lévesque. *MD* Oct 14, 1987: p14.

MARINIER, ROBERT

Théâtre au masculin; reviews of plays. Jane Moss. *Can Lit* Spring 1987; No 112: p180–183.

MARIO/Novel by Claude Jasmin

A question of taste; reviews of *After Six Days* and *Mario*. Noreen Golfman. *Can Lit* Spring 1987; No 112: p104–107.

Recent Canadian fiction; reviews of novels. D.O. Spettigue. *Queen's Q* Summer 1987; Vol 94 No 2: p366–375.
[FIRST NOVELS: BOOK REVIEWS]

MARITIME PROVINCES WRITING

See **ATLANTIC PROVINCES DRAMA; ATLANTIC PROVINCES LITERATURE: BIBLIOGRAPHY; ATLANTIC PROVINCES WRITING AND WRITERS**

MARITIME SONG/Play by Marni Walsh

Maritime Song needs a tune-up; theatre review. Alex Law. *TS (Neighbors)* Sept 22, 1987: p26.

Maritime Song has promise, lacks cohesion; theatre review. Alex Law. photo · *TS (Neighbors)* Sept 22, 1987: p13.

MARK OF CAIN/Play by Peter Colley

Stage thriller condensed for Lunchbox crowds; article. Kate Zimmerman. *CH* Oct 30, 1987: pE8.

MARLATT, DAPHNE

Mainstreet Calgary; column. *CH (Neighbors)* April 1, 1987: pA4.
[POETRY READINGS; WRITERS' WORKSHOPS]

Literary extravaganza goes national; column. Kenneth McGoogan. *CH* April 5, 1987: pE5.
[AUTHORS, CANADIAN; FILM ADAPTATIONS OF CANADIAN LITERATURE; WRITERS' ORGANIZATIONS; WRITERS' WORKSHOPS]

MARLYN, JOHN

Sandor, Alex and the rest: multiplication of the subject in John Marlyn's Under the Ribs of Death; article. Julie Beddoes. *Open Letter* Summer 1987; Vol 6 No 8: p5–14.

MARRIOTT, ANNE

Trial by experience; reviews of *Letters from Some Islands* and *Private Properties*. Bert Almon. *Can Lit* Winter 1987; No 115: p206–208

[Untitled]; reviews of poetry books. Barbara Carey. *Cross Can Writ Q* 1987; Vol 9 No 1: p23–24.

Jacobs, Lever, Marriott; reviews of poetry books. Barry Dempster. *Poetry Can R* Spring 1987; Vol 8 No 2–3: p35.

B.C. international — in search of new subjects and forms; reviews. Gillian Harding-Russell. *Event* Summer 1987; Vol 16 No 2: p125–127.

MARSHALL, TOM

[Untitled]; reviews of novels. Beverley Daurio. *Cross Can Writ Q* 1987; Vol 9 No 3–4: p45–46.

Getting physical; reviews of *Dance of the Particles* and *Playing with Fire*. Paul Denham. *Essays on Can Writ* Spring 1987; No 34: p44–47.

Love and sin in Rosedale; review of *Adele at the End of the Day*. Elaine Kahn. *TS* April 19, 1987: pA18.

Vivid imagination drives novel's slender plot line; review of *Adele at the End of the Day*. P. Scott Lawrence. photo · *MG* April 11, 1987: pG5.

Daring novel rewarding read; review of *Adele at the End of the Day*. Kenneth McGoogan. *CH* April 26, 1987: pE5.

Mother and son; review of *Adele at the End of the Day*. Kenneth McGoogan. *Books in Can* April 1987; Vol 16 No 3: p20.

[Untitled]; review of *Adele at the End of the Day*. Constance Rooke. *Malahat R* June 1987; No 79: p161.

[Untitled]; review of *Adele at the End of the Day*. Richard Streiling. *Quill & Quire* March 1987; Vol 53 No 3: p71.

A search for the perfect pairing; review of *Adele at the End of the Day*. David Williamson. photo · *WFP* April 25, 1987: p54.

A novel a poet can write; review of *Adele at the End of the Day*. Thomas S. Woods. *G&M* May 30, 1987: pC19.

MARTEL, SUZANNE

[Untitled]; review of *Nos amis, robots*. Chris Pattinson. *TS* Feb 8, 1987: pC8.

MARTIN MEETS THE PIRATES AND OTHER STORIES/Children's stories by Kit Hood et al

Fine books for in-betweens; reviews of young adult books. David Williamson. *WFP* Dec 5, 1987: p57.

MARTIN, CLAIRE

[Untitled]; reviews of *Standing Flight* and *The Legacy*. Cary Fagan. *Cross Can Writ Q* 1987; Vol 9 No 2: p24–25.

Two Quebec novels in translation; reviews of *Standing Flight* and *The Legacy*. Theresia Quigley. *Fiddlehead* Summer 1987; No 152: p95–98.

Recent Canadian fiction; reviews of novels. D.O. Spettigue. *Queen's Q* Summer 1987; Vol 94 No 2: p366–375.
[FIRST NOVELS: BOOK REVIEWS]

MARTIN, DONALD

[Untitled]; review of *One Out of Four*. Steve Boyd. *CH* Jan 25, 1987: pE4.
[FIRST NOVELS: BOOK REVIEWS]

[Untitled]; review of *One Out of Four*. Martin Townsend. *Quill & Quire* Feb 1987; Vol 53 No 2: p17.

MARTIN, RAYMOND

La métamorphose du quotidien; reviews of poetry books. André Marquis. photo · *Lettres québec* Autumn 1987; No 47: p41–43.

La poésie n'est pas une science mais une parole; reviews of *Le Tombeau d'Adélina Albert* and *Qu'en carapaces de mes propres ailes*. Jean Royer. *MD* April 25, 1987: pD4.

MARTINEZ, ERIK

[Untitled]; review of *Tequila Sunrise*. Antonio D'Alfonso. *Poetry Can R* Spring 1987; Vol 8 No 2–3: p36–37.

MARTINI, CLEM

Actors' message not lost on kids; article. Sherri Clegg. photo · *CH* April 2, 1987: pD11.

THE MARTYROLOGY/Long poem by bpNichol

Words move unrestrained and with joy across pages; review of *The Martyrology* (Book Six). Lesley McAllister. *TS* June 20, 1987: M4.

MARYSE/Novel by Francine Noël

Paradigme, palimpseste, pastiche, parodie dans Maryse de Francine Noël; article. Anne Élaine Cliche. *Voix et images* Spring 1987; Vol 12 No 3: p430–438.
[STRUCTURALIST WRITING AND CRITICISM]

La vitrine du livre; reviews. Guy Ferland. *MD* March 7, 1987: pB2.
[CANADIAN LITERARY PERIODICALS]

MASQUES OF MORALITY: FEMALES IN FICTION/Critical work by Johan Lyall Aitken

[Untitled]; review of *Masques of Morality*. Tracy Shepherd Matheson. *Books in Can* Oct 1987; Vol 16 No 7: p21.

[Untitled]; review of *Masques of Morality*. Anne E. Russell. *Quill & Quire* Oct 1987; Vol 53 No 10: p23.

LES MASQUES/Novel by Gilbert La Rocque

Dans les poches; reviews. Guy Ferland. *MD* Sept 26, 1987: pD6.

MASS, CAROLE

La vitrine du livre; reviews of *Hommes* and *Heureusement, ici il y a la guerre*. Guy Ferland. *MD* Oct 17, 1987: pD4.

MASSING, CONNI

Last of the makeovers; theatre review of *The Thin Edge*. Don Perkins. *NeWest R* Feb 1987; Vol 12 No 6: p17.

THE MASTER OF THE MILL/Novel by Frederick Philip Grove

Grove's "Stella"; article. K.P. Stich. illus · *Can Lit* Summer-Fall 1987; No 113–114: p258–262.

MATAS, CAROL

Gammer Gurton leaps from early English stage into the 20th century; reviews of children's books. Janice Kennedy. *MG* Nov 21, 1987: J13.

[Untitled]; reviews of *The Fusion Factor* and *Zanu*. Leslie McGrath. *Quill & Quire (Books for Young People)* June 1987; Vol 53 No 6: p9–10.

Time travel series maintains quality; review of *Me, Myself and I*. Helen Norrie. *WFP* Dec 5, 1987: p57.

[Untitled]; review of *Lisa*. Kenneth Oppel. *Quill & Quire (Books for Young People)* Dec 1987; Vol 53 No 12: p6.

[Untitled]; reviews of *The Fusion Factor* and *Zanu*. Mavis Reimer. *Border Cross* Spring 1987; Vol 6 No 2: p25.

Back to the future; reviews of children's books. Mary Ainsley Smith. *Books in Can* March 1987; Vol 16 No 2: p37–39.

How suspense dies when it is misused; reviews of young adult novels. Tim Wynne-Jones. *G&M* Aug 8, 1987: pC19.

MATHIEU, PIERRE

Pierre Mathieu: le silence rompu; interview. Robert Viau. bibliog photo · *Lettres québec* Autumn 1987; No 47: p46–48.

LES MATINS DU NOUVEAU MONDE/Novel by Yves Berger

Amérique, utopie; review of *Les Matins du Nouveau Monde*. Jacques Folch-Ribas. *Liberté* June 1987; Vol 29 No 3: p106–107.

MATIVAT, DANIEL

La place de l'humain; review of *Ram le Robot*. Renee A. Kingcaid. *Can Child Lit* 1987; No 45: p87–90.

LE MATOU/THE ALLEY CAT/Novel by Yves Beauchemin

[Untitled]; review of *The Alley Cat*. *Queen's Q* Spring 1987; Vol 94 No 1: p252.

L'inscription du littéraire dans Le Matou d'Yves Beauchemin; article. Micheline Beauregard. abstract · *Études lit* Spring-Summer 1987; Vol 20 No 1: p131–147.
[METAFICTION]

The Yankee devils!; review of *The Alley Cat*. Bob Coleman. *NYT Book R* Jan 11, 1987: p14.

[Untitled]; review of *The Alley Cat*. Charles Foran. *Rubicon* Spring 1987; No 8: p176–178.

Beauchemin's The Alley Cat as modern myth; article. Constantina Mitchell. *Amer R of Can Studies* Winter 1987–88; Vol 17 No 4: p409–418.
[MYTHS AND LEGENDS IN CANADIAN LITERATURE; POLITICAL WRITING]

Le Matou d'Yves Beauchemin: du fait littéraire à la chaîne de productions-médias; article. Catherine Saouter. *Voix et images* Spring 1987; Vol 12 No 3: p393–402.
[FILM ADAPTATIONS OF CANADIAN LITERATURE; TELEVISION AND CANADIAN LITERATURE]

Le réception critique du Matou; article. Frances J. Summers. *Voix et images* Spring 1987; Vol 12 No 3: p383–392.
[INTERNATIONAL REVIEWS OF CANADIAN LITERATURE]

Floating signs; review of *The Alley Cat*. John Thieme. *Can Lit* Summer-Fall 1987; No 113–114: p249–251.

MATTHEW AND THE MIDNIGHT MONEY VAN/ Children's story by Allen Morgan

From giant snakes to punk pigeons: escapism at its best; reviews of children's stories. Bernie Goedhart. *Quill & Quire (Books for Young People)* June 1987; Vol 53 No 6: p5.

Mini-reviews; reviews of children's stories. Mary Rubio. *Can Child Lit* 1987; No 47: p96–99.

MATTHEW AND THE MIDNIGHT TOW TRUCK/ Children's story by Allen Morgan

Meaningful nonsense; reviews of children's books. Adrienne Kertzer. *Can Lit* Winter 1987; No 115: p165–167.

Asimov robotics . . . orchestral overtures . . . marvellous Munsch; reviews of tape versions of children's books. Richard Perry. photo · *Quill & Quire (Books for Young People)* Aug 1987; Vol 53 No 8: p10.
[AUDIO-VISUALS AND CANADIAN LITERATURE]

MAXWELL, KURT

The plot thickens; review of *Equinox*. Jack Batten. *Books in Can* May 1987; Vol 16 No 4: p27–28.

Murder & mayhem: plot and details in a cop's life; reviews of *Gallows View* and *Equinox*. Margaret Cannon. photo · *G&M* May 23, 1987: pC23.

Heartless violence of terrorism explored in this numbing novel; review of *Equinox*. Joan McGrath. *TS* June 13, 1987: M4.

Book world: 'new' terrorists like their perks, author suggests; column. Beverley Slopen. *TS* May 10, 1987: pA22.

Would-be world-class thrillers need plots to be complete; reviews of *Equinox* and *Fire Eyes*. Philippe van Rjndt. photo · *Quill & Quire* April 1987; Vol 53 No 4: p28.

CIA gambits aren't what they used to be; review of *Equinox*. David Wimhurst. *MG* May 16, 1987: J8.

MAYNE, SEYMOUR

[Untitled]; review of *Children of Abel*. Barbara Carey. *Books in Can* March 1987; Vol 16 No 2: p27.

[Untitled]; review of *Children of Abel*. Harold Jack Heft. *Rubicon* Fall 1987; No 9: p176–177.

[Untitled]; reviews of poetry books. Stephen Morrissey. *Poetry Can R* Fall 1987; Vol 9 No 1: p32.

"Give me melancholy or give me death"; reviews of *Children of Abel* and *The Moving Light*. Harry Prest. *U of Windsor R* Fall-Winter 1987; Vol 20 No 1: p95–98

MAYSE, SUSAN

Three new faces deserving discovery; reviews of crime novels. Margaret Cannon. photo · *G&M* Oct 17, 1987: pE4.

Thriller mired in words; review of *Merlin's Web*. Elona Malterre. *CH* Nov 8, 1987: pE6.
[FIRST NOVELS: BOOK REVIEWS]

[Untitled]; review of *Merlin's Web*. John North. *Quill & Quire* Sept 1987; Vol 53 No 9: p79.
[FIRST NOVELS: BOOK REVIEWS]

McADAM, RHONA

Poets propelled by Thistledown; article. Kenneth McGoogan. *CH* April 12, 1987: pF2.
[CANADIAN LITERARY PUBLISHING]

Thistledown presents prairie poets in full bloom; reviews of poetry books. Christopher Wiseman. *CH* May 24, 1987: pE6.

McALLISTER, LESLEY

TV's generation suffers detachment; reviews of *The Blue House* and *Not Noir*. Colline Caulder. *TS* Nov 28, 1987: M5.

Book was fiction and pice fictitious too; letter to the editor. Beverley Daurio. *TS* Dec 27, 1987: pB2.

Small regional presses as saviors of cultural information; reviews of fictional works. Douglas Hill. *G&M* Oct 10, 1987: pC21.
[FIRST NOVELS: BOOK REVIEWS]

McCAFFERY, STEVE

Dr. Sadhu's semi-opticks, or how to write a virtual-novel by the book: Steve McCaffery's Panopticon; article. Rafael Barreto-Rivera. *Open Letter (special issue)* Fall 1987; Vol 6 No 9: p39–47.
[POSTMODERNIST WRITING AND CRITICISM]

Panoptical artifice; article. Charles Bernstein. *Open Letter (special issue)* Fall 1987; Vol 6 No 9: p9–15.
[POSTMODERNIST WRITING AND CRITICISM]

Grammatology & economy; article. Michael Coffey. photo · *Open Letter (special issue)* Fall 1987; Vol 6 No 9: p27–38.
[POSTMODERNIST WRITING AND CRITICISM; STRUCTURALIST WRITING AND CRITICISM]

The sonic graffitist: Steve McCaffery as improvisor; article. Paul Dutton. photo · *Open Letter (special issue)* Fall 1987; Vol 6 No 9: p17–25.
[SOUND POETRY]

[Untitled]; review of *North of Intention*. Keith Garebian. *Quill & Quire* July 1987; Vol 53 No 7: p66.

Semiotic song; review of *North of Intention*. Stephen Luxton. *Matrix* Fall 1987; No 25: p77–79.

Steve McCaffery's Panopticon; article. William McPheron. photo · *Open Letter (special issue)* Fall 1987; Vol 6 No 9: p49–54.
[METAFICTION; POSTMODERNIST WRITING AND CRITICISM; STRUCTURALIST WRITING AND CRITICISM]

Introduction. bpNichol. *Open Letter (special issue)* Fall 1987; Vol 6 No 9: p7.

The annotated, anecdoted, beginnings of a critical checklist of the published works of Steve McCaffery; bibliography, includes introduction. bpNichol. *Open Letter (special issue)* Fall 1987; Vol 6 No 9: p67–92.

High ideas from a split end; review of *North of Intention*. Paul Stuewe. *G&M* July 11, 1987: pC15.

Opaque criticism; letter to the editor. Sophie Thomas. *G&M* July 25, 1987: pD7.

[Untitled]; review of *North of Intention*. Bruce Whiteman. *Books in Can* Oct 1987; Vol 16 No 7: p21.

McCLURE/Play by Monroe Scott

An exaggeration; letter to the editor. Rod Booth. *Maclean's* Nov 30, 1987; Vol 100 No 48: p4.

[Untitled]; review of *McClure*. Kathryn Harley. *Maclean's* Nov 9, 1987; Vol 100 No 45: p70.

McCORMACK, ERIC

A new and nervy short story writer; review of *Inspecting the Vaults*. Ken Adachi. *TS* Feb 1, 1987: pB7.

Art of darkness; review of *Inspecting the Vaults*. Edna Alford. *Books in Can* May 1987; Vol 16 No 4: p26–27.

A voyage into the countries of the mind; review of *Inspecting the Vaults*. Dennis Duffy. photo · *G&M* Feb 21, 1987: pE19.

Stories strange, disturbing; review of *Inspecting the Vaults*. Donald Floyd. *WFP* April 18, 1987: p50.

Excellent illusions, cloying clichés in short-story collections; reviews of *Afternoon Tea* and *Inspecting the Vaults*. Brent Ledger. photo · *Quill & Quire* March 1987; Vol 53 No 3: p72.

[Untitled]; review of *Inspecting the Vaults*. David Manicom. *Rubicon* Fall 1987; No 9: p150–152.

[Untitled]; review of *Inspecting the Vaults*. Constance Rooke. *Malahat R* Dec 1987; No 81: p101.

[Untitled]; review of *Inspecting the Vaults*. Steven Slosberg. *NYT Book R* Sept 20, 1987: p26.

Kafka, Addams family creep into these tales of the macabre; review of *Inspecting the Vaults*. Joel Yanofsky. photo · *MG* Feb 7, 1987: pB7.

McCRAE, JOHN

Home of soldier-poet is memorial; article. biog · *TS* Oct 24, 1987: pE38.
[CANADIAN LITERARY LANDMARKS]

Two ceremonies planned to honor Guelph author of Flanders poem; article. Christina Jonas. *TS* Nov 9, 1987: pD34.

McFADDEN, DAVID

Canadian Quixote flogs death; review of *Canadian Sunset*. Audrey Andrews. *CH* April 18, 1987: pE5.

Is this the ultimate CanLit novel?; review of *Canadian Sunset*. Pauline Carey. *G&M* Feb 28, 1987: pE20.

Believing is seeing; review of *Canadian Sunset*. Mark Czarnecki. *Books in Can* Jan-Feb 1987; Vol 16 No 1: p19–20.

[Untitled]; reviews of novels. Beverley Daurio. *Cross Can Writ Q* 1987; Vol 9 No 3–4: p45–46.

McFadden's dilemma; article. Brian Fawcett. illus · *Books in Can* March 1987; Vol 16 No 2: p3–5.

The dying generations; reviews of poetry books. Dermot McCarthy. *Essays on Can Writ* Spring 1987; No 34: p24–32.

[Untitled]; review of *Canadian Sunset*. Richard Streiling. *Quill & Quire* Jan 1987; Vol 53 No 1: p27.

McGEHEE, PETER

Contest winner makes waves with short story called Goldfish; article. Paul Warnick. *TS* Aug 2, 1987: pA2.

McGREGOR, ROY

Ambitious hockey saga fails to score; television review of *The Last Season*. John Haslett Cuff. photo · *G&M* Jan 3, 1987: pE5. [TELEVISION AND CANADIAN LITERATURE]

McHUGH, FIONA

Gammer Gurton leaps from early English stage into the 20th century; reviews of children's books. Janice Kennedy. *MG* Nov 21, 1987: J13.

Literary lions linger in libraries; reviews of children's books. Joan McGrath. *TS* Dec 20, 1987: pE5.

A quality spin-off; review of *The Anne of Green Gables Storybook*. Linda Pearse. *Atlan Prov Book R* Nov-Dec 1987; Vol 14 No 4: p4.

McINNES, GRAHAM

Polished prose from diplomat; biographical article. William French. photo · *G&M* Jan 27, 1987: pC5.

McINNIS, NADINE

[Untitled]; review of *Shaking the Dreamland Tree*. Margaret Dyment. *Arc* Fall 1987; No 19: p61–65.

[Untitled]; reviews of *Who's to Say?* and *Shaking the Dreamland Tree*. Susan Glickman. *Poetry Can R* Summer 1987; Vol 8 No 4: p32.

Nursery rhyme, myth and dream; reviews of *Shaking the Dreamland Tree* and *Eleusis*. Gillian Harding-Russell. *NeWest R* Sept 1987; Vol 13 No 1: p17–18.

Young poets on display; reviews of poetry books. Robert Quickenden. photo · *WFP* March 14, 1987: p52.

McKAY, DON

MacEwen and McKay; reviews of *Afterworlds* and *Sanding Down This Rocking Chair on a Windy Night*. Barry Dempster. *Poetry Can R* Fall 1987; Vol 9 No 1: p29–30.

So you think poetry no longer exists for readers?; reviews of *Afterworlds* and *Sanding Down This Rocking Chair on a Windy Night*. Judith Fitzgerald. photo · *TS* May 3, 1987: pA24.

[Untitled]; review of *Sanding Down This Rocking Chair on a Windy Night*. David Manicom. *Rubicon* Fall 1987; No 9: p184–185.

Lord of the wings; review of *Sanding Down This Rocking Chair on a Windy Night*. John Oughton. *Books in Can* June-July 1987; Vol 16 No 5: p12–13.

[Untitled]; reviews of *Afterworlds* and *Sanding Down This Rocking Chair on a Windy Night*. Barbara Powell. *Wascana R* Fall 1987; Vol 22 No 2: p88–91.

Poetry: packing all the power into two of seven titles; reviews of poetry books. Robin Skelton. photo · *Quill & Quire* May 1987; Vol 53 No 5: p24.

The pastoral myth and its observers; reviews of poetry books. Fraser Sutherland. *G&M* Sept 26, 1987: pC23.

McKENZIE, NADINE

Discours-fleuve; reviews of *Le Coupeur de têtes* and *Les Deux soeurs*. Marguerite Andersen. *Can Lit* Winter 1987; No 115: p182–184.

Straining credulity; review of *Le Coupeur de têtes*. Ann Carson. *Prairie Fire* Summer 1987; Vol 8 No 2: p75–76.

McKIM, AUDREY

Little's achievements simply huge; reviews of *Little by Little* and *Her Special Vision*. Joan McGrath. *TS* Nov 29, 1987: pA21.

McKINLAY, MICHAEL D.C.

Ambitious drama falls short of the mark; theatre reviews of *Penguins* and *Sliding for Home*. Stephen Godfrey. photo · *G&M* Nov 26, 1987: pA25.

McMANUS, BRUCE

Bruce McManus, playwright; introduction to play excerpt from *Schedules*. Doug Arrell. *Prairie Fire* Spring 1987; Vol 8 No 1: p50.

Gas Station to stage breezy theatre fare for summer crowd; article. Brad Oswald. *WFP* June 27, 1987: p31.

Scenes from a relationship; theatre review of *Schedules*. Don Perkins. *NeWest R* Dec 1987; Vol 13 No 4: p17.

Funny play fails to fulfil promise; theatre review of *Schedules*. Reg Skene. *WFP* Jan 23, 1987: p31.

Crafty lust: a prof[i]le of Bruce McManus. Reg Skene. *Border Cross* Summer 1987; Vol 6 No 3: p53–57.

Dogs with No Tails delivers pain, laughs; theatre review. Reg Skene. *WFP* July 4, 1987: p40.

Playwright's opening night began with car that bombed; article. Morley Walker. photo · *WFP* March 29, 1987: p14.

McMASTER, BETH

Kids play key role in Storybook tale; theatre review of *Stick with Molasses*. Kate Zimmerman. photo · *CH* Feb 2, 1987: pB6.

McMASTER, SUSAN

[Untitled]; reviews of poetry books. Shaunt Basmajian. *Cross Can Writ Q* 1987; Vol 9 No 2: p22.

[Untitled]; review of *Dark Galaxies*. Anne Burke. *Poetry Can R* Spring 1987; Vol 8 No 2–3: p51.

Poetry's eye; review of *Dark Galaxies*. Margaret Dyment. *Arc* Spring 1987; No 18: p18–22.

Dark galaxies: the poetry of Susan McMaster; interview. Lydia Fensom. *Quarry* Fall 1987; Vol 36 No 4: p78–82.

Seasons, time and memory; reviews of poetry books. Lesley McAllister. *TS* March 21, 1987: M5.

McMURRAY, LINE

Manifeste: au jeu; review of *L'Enjeu du manifeste/le manifeste en jeu*. Bruno Roy. *Moebius* Spring 1987; No 32: p133–136.

"Crois ou meurs": à quand le manifeste vidéo-clip?; review of *L'Enjeu du manifeste/le manifeste en jeu*. Lori Saint-Martin. photo · *MD* April 18, 1987: pD2.

Le jeu du manifeste littéraire; review of *L'Enjeu du manifeste/Le manifeste en jeu*. Agnès Whitfield. *Lettres québec* Autumn 1987; No 47: p51–52.

McNAIR, RICK

What's happening; notice. illus · *CH* April 10, 1987: pE7.

McNAMARA, EUGENE

"Give me melancholy or give me death"; reviews of *Children of Abel* and *The Moving Light*. Harry Prest. *U of Windsor R* Fall-Winter 1987; Vol 20 No 1: p95-98.

Editor's introduction. Joseph A. Quinn. photo · *U of Windsor R* Fall-Winter 1987; Vol 20 No 1: p2.

[Untitled]; review of *The Moving Light*. Stephen Scobie. *Malahat R* Sept 1987; No 80: p140.

Peacetime; reviews of *Spectral Evidence* and *Fish-Hooks*. Keith Wilson. *Can Lit* Spring 1987; No 112: p154-156.

McRAE, RUSSELL

Local heroes; reviews of first novels. Janice Kulyk Keefer. *Books in Can* Nov 1987; Vol 16 No 8: p35,37.
[FIRST NOVELS: BOOK REVIEWS]

Book world: when a publicist needs a lawyer . . . ; column. Beverley Slopen. *TS* Nov 15, 1987: pA22.

McWHIRTER, GEORGE

Brave novel needs power of a narrative; review of *Cage*. Ken Adachi. *TS* June 21, 1987: pA23.

[Untitled]; review of *Cage*. Shelagh Garland. *Books in Can* Oct 1987; Vol 16 No 7: p24.

[Untitled]; review of *Cage*. Gail Greenwood. *CH* Sept 27, 1987: pE6.

A gringo's view of Mexico; review of *Cage*. T.F. Rigelhof. *G&M* July 18, 1987: pC17.

ME AND LUKE/Novel by Audrey O'Hearn

[Untitled]; review of *Me and Luke*. Patty Lawlor. *Quill & Quire (Books for Young People)* Oct 1987; Vol 53 No 10: p22.
[FIRST NOVELS: BOOK REVIEWS]

ME, MYSELF AND I/Children's novel by Carol Matas

Time travel series maintains quality; review of *Me, Myself and I*. Helen Norrie. *WFP* Dec 5, 1987: p57.

THE MEANING OF GARDENS/Poems by Paul Savoie

Common language in private words; reviews of poetry books. Maggie Helwig. *TS* Aug 8, 1987: M10.

MEDIEVAL HOUR IN THE AUTHOR'S MIND/Short stories by Ernest Hekkanen

Stories of the medieval in the present day; reviews of *Beneath the Western Slopes* and *Medieval Hour in the Author's Mind*. Clark Blaise. *Quill & Quire* June 1987; Vol 53 No 6: p34.

Morbid stories confront human spirit; review of *Medieval Hour in the Author's Mind*. Cecelia Frey. *CH* June 21, 1987: pE5.

Powerful imagery impresses; review of *Medieval Hour in the Author's Mind*. Maggie Helwig. *TS* June 28, 1987: pA18.

MEDITATIONS: 50 SESTINAS/Poems by Fred Cogswell

[Untitled]; review of *Meditations*. Glenn Hayes. *Poetry Can R* Spring 1987; Vol 8 No 2-3: p58-59.

Structures of meditation; reviews of *Meditations* and *Midnight Found You Dancing*. Michael Thorpe. *Fiddlehead* Spring 1987; No 151: p115-120.

MEETING THE NORTH/Poems by Joanne Light

Noticing three poets; reviews of poetry books. Terrence Craig. *Atlan Prov Book R* May-June 1987; Vol 14 No 2: p10.

MELANCHOLY AIN'T NO BABY/Poems by Patricia Young

Women and things; review of *Melancholy Ain't No Baby*. Cary Fagan. *Prairie Fire* Summer 1987; Vol 8 No 2: p70-71.

[Untitled]; review of *Melancholy Ain't No Baby*. Maurice Mierau. *Rubicon* Spring 1987; No 8: p220-221.

[Untitled]; review of *Melancholy Ain't No Baby*. Jane Munro. *Poetry Can R* Summer 1987; Vol 8 No 4: p34.

Frost shadows; reviews of poetry books. Andrew Taylor. *Can Lit* Winter 1987; No 115: p197-199.

MELANÇON, ROBERT

Paul-Marie Lapointe chez Seghers; review of *Paul-Marie Lapointe*. André-G. Bourassa. *Lettres québec* Summer 1987; No 46: p77-78.

[Untitled]; reviews of *Blind Painting* and *All the Polarities*. Estelle Dansereau. *Quarry* Summer 1987; Vol 36 No 3: p82-86.

La poésie de Paul-Marie Lapointe; review of *Paul-Marie Lapointe*. Jean Fisette. *Voix et images* Autumn 1987; Vol 13 No 1: p174-178.

Harnessing poetry; reviews of *Blind Painting* and *Small Horses & Intimate Beasts*. Philip Lanthier. *Can Lit* Winter 1987; No 115: p140-142.

[Untitled]; reviews of *Small Horses & Intimate Beasts* and *Blind Painting*. David Leahy. *Queen's Q* Spring 1987; Vol 94 No 1: p189-191.

[Untitled]; review of *Blind Painting*. Peter Malden. *Rubicon* Fall 1987; No 9: p170-173.

[Untitled]; reviews of *Blind Painting* and *Small Horses & Intimate Beasts*. Andrew Vaisius. *Poetry Can R* Spring 1987; Vol 8 No 2-3: p59.

MELFI, MARY

[Untitled]; reviews of poetry books. Anne Burke. *Poetry Can R* Summer 1987; Vol 8 No 4: p38.

[Untitled]; review of *A Dialogue with Masks*. Charlotte Hussey. *Rubicon* Spring 1987; No 8: p205-208.

MELLING, O.R.

It's how it should have happened; review of *The Singing Stone*. Kieran Kealy. *Can Child Lit* 1987; No 47: p71-72.

MELODY FARM/Play by Ken Mitchell

Melody Farm feels like two plays trying to be one; theatre reviews of *Melody Farm* and *Biting Nails*. Stephen Godfrey. photo · *G&M* Feb 18, 1987: pC7.

[Untitled]; theatre review of *Melody Farm*. Ron Marken. *Maclean's* Feb 23, 1987; Vol 100 No 8: p55.

THE MELVILLE BOYS/Play by Norm Foster

Promising comedy weighed down by serious issues; theatre review of *The Melville Boys*. Brian Brennan. *CH* April 11, 1987: pF2.

Comedy with a clever twist; theatre review of *The Melville Boys*. Ray Conlogue. photo · *G&M* Feb 27, 1987: pD11.

Heart-warming tale limited but likeable; theatre review of *The Melville Boys*. Robert Crew. *TS* Feb 27, 1987: pD21.

Dinner theatre play leaves bland aftertaste; theatre review of *The Melville Boys*. Randal McIlroy. *WFP* Nov 4, 1987: p43.

[Untitled]; review of *The Melville Boys*. Linda M. Peake. *Books in Can* March 1987; Vol 16 No 2: p25.

[Untitled]; reviews of plays. Judith Rudakoff. *Can Theatre R* Summer 1987; No 51: p86–87.

MEMOIR/SARAH ET LE CRI DE LA LANGOUSTE/Play by John Murrell

Le grand retour de Murielle Dutil dans Le Temps d'une vie; column. Robert Lévesque. *MD* April 7, 1987: p12.

MEMOIRS OF A BOOK-MOLESTING CHILDHOOD AND OTHER ESSAYS/Essays by Adele Wiseman

Wiseman wrote a moving memoir; review of *Memoirs of a Book-Molesting Childhood*. Ken Adachi. *TS* Nov 15, 1987: pA23.

A wonderful way to go; review of *Memoirs of a Book-Molesting Childhood*. Cary Fagan. *Books in Can* Dec 1987; Vol 16 No 9: p32–33.

Those accidents of truth that sneak up; review of *Memoirs of a Book-Molesting Childhood*. Marion Quednau. *G&M* Dec 26, 1987: pC23.

MEMORY BOARD/Novel by Jane Rule

Tale of eternal triangle reads like a tract; review of *Memory Board*. John Goddard. *MG* Nov 14, 1987: J10.

Mixed doubles; review of *Memory Board*. Terry Goldie. *Books in Can* Nov 1987; Vol 16 No 8: p19–20.

A sensitive tale focusing on aging; review of *Memory Board*. Geoff Hancock. photo · *TS* Nov 21, 1987: M4.

Knots of age and sex; review of *Memory Board*. Janette Turner Hospital. *G&M* Oct 17, 1987: pE5.

[Untitled]; review of *Memory Board*. Sharon J. Hunt. *Quarry* Fall 1987; Vol 36 No 4: p87–88.

The fixed point of love; review of *Memory Board*. Alberto Manguel. *Maclean's* Oct 19, 1987; Vol 100 No 42: p60b

Fascinating trio comes to grips with aging; review of *Memory Board*. Dave Margoshes. *CH* Nov 29, 1987: pE6.

[Untitled]; review of *Memory Board*. Constance Rooke. *Malahat R* Dec 1987; No 81: p102.

LA MÉNAGERIE/Children's stories by Jocelyne Villeneuve

Leons du monde animal; review of *La Ménagerie*. Michel Gaulin. *Can Child Lit* 1987; No 45: p86–87.

Le sable et les étoiles; article. Diane Pavlovic. photo · *Jeu* 1987; No 45: p121–140.

MENAUD, MAÎTRE-DRAVEUR/Novel by Félix-Antoine Savard

Menaud prophète: et si Joson n'était pas mort . . . ; column. Jean Éthier-Blais. photo · *MD* Oct 3, 1987: pD8.

MERLIN'S WEB/Novel by Susan Mayse

Three new faces deserving discovery; reviews of crime novels. Margaret Cannon. photo · *G&M* Oct 17, 1987: pE4.

Plotting against the royals; reviews of *Broken English* and *Merlin's Web*. Brian Kappler. *MG* Nov 7, 1987: K13.

Thriller mired in words; review of *Merlin's Web*. Elona Malterre. *CH* Nov 8, 1987: pE6.
[FIRST NOVELS: BOOK REVIEWS]

[Untitled]; review of *Merlin's Web*. John North. *Quill & Quire* Sept 1987; Vol 53 No 9: p79.
[FIRST NOVELS: BOOK REVIEWS]

MERRIL, JUDITH

Author's ready to hand out advice; article. H.J. Kirchhoff. photo · *G&M* May 6, 1987: pC6.
[WRITERS-IN-RESIDENCE]

MERRY CHRISTMAS ANGEL STAR/Play by Marni Walsh

Angel Star a sweet treat but not much substance; theatre review of *Merry Christmas Angel Star*. Alex Law. *TS (Neighbors)* Dec 1, 1987: p19.

THE MERZBOOK: KURT SCHWITTERS POEMS/Poems by Colin Morton

Women are the root of all change; reviews of *The Unravelling* and *The Merzbook*. Lesley McAllister. photo · *TS* Nov 14, 1987: M4.

Poets view China, Dada; reviews of *China: Shockwaves* and *The Merzbook*. Robert Quickenden. *WFP* Dec 5, 1987: p56.

[Untitled]; reviews of poetry books. Stephen Scobie. *Malahat R* Dec 1987; No 81: p104–106.

METAFICTION

L'inscription du littéraire dans Le Matou d'Yves Beauchemin; article. Micheline Beauregard. abstract · *Études lit* Spring-Summer 1987; Vol 20 No 1: p131–147.

A deconstructive narratology; reading Robert Kroetsch's Alibi; article. Susan Rudy Dorscht. *Open Letter* Summer 1987; Vol 6 No 8: p78–83.
[STRUCTURALIST WRITING AND CRITICISM]

Steve McCaffery's Panopticon; article. William McPheron. photo · *Open Letter (special issue)* Fall 1987; Vol 6 No 9: p49–54.
[POSTMODERNIST WRITING AND CRITICISM; STRUCTURALIST WRITING AND CRITICISM]

Between the world and the word: John Metcalf's "The Teeth of My Father"; article. Constance Rooke. *New Q* Spring-Summer 1987; Vol 7 No 1–2: p240–246.
[ARTIST FIGURE; THE FAMILY IN CANADIAN LITERATURE]

METAL HEAD/Young adult novel by William Bell

A little help on the dull days; reviews of children's books. Joan McGrath. *TS* Aug 2, 1987: pC11.

METCALF, JOHN

Aujourd'hui; column. *MD* March 16, 1987: p10.
[FICTION READINGS]

[Untitled]; review of *Adult Entertainment*. Scot Bishop. *Rubicon* Fall 1987; No 9: p196–197.

[Untitled]; reviews of short story collections. Pauline Carey. *Cross Can Writ Q* 1987; Vol 9 No 3–4: p46–47.

[Untitled]; reviews of *Archibald Lampman* and *John Metcalf*. Dennis Duffy. *Eng Studies in Can* Sept 1987; Vol 13 No 3: p355–357.

Raising two worthy books from the dead; reviews of *Kicking Against the Pricks* and *Incognito*. William French. photo · *G&M* Feb 24, 1987: pD7.

[Untitled]; review of *Adult Entertainment*. Oliver Gorse. *Idler* March-April 1987; No 12: p60.

Fighting words; biographical article. Brent Ledger. photo · *Books in Can* April 1987; Vol 16 No 3: p9–10,12–14.

Metcalf chairs debate; column. Kenneth McGoogan. *CH* March 8, 1987: pE5.
[BOOK REVIEWING]

[Untitled]; review of *Adult Entertainment*. Mary Millar. *Queen's Q* Winter 1987; Vol 94 No 4: p1024–1026.

Sticks and stones; letter to the editor. Colin Morton. *Books in Can* June-July 1987; Vol 16 No 5: p39.

[Untitled]; letter to the editor. John Moss. *Books in Can* June-July 1987; Vol 16 No 5: p39–40.

Between the world and the word: John Metcalf's "The Teeth of My Father"; article. Constance Rooke. *New Q* Spring-Summer 1987; Vol 7 No 1–2: p240–246.
[ARTIST FIGURE; THE FAMILY IN CANADIAN LITERATURE; METAFICTION]

Tip sheet: educator to speak on learning-disabled children; column. Susan Schwartz. *MG* March 11, 1987: pD10.
[FICTION READINGS]

MEUNIER, CLAUDE

Les Voisins: scènes de la vie de banlieue; article. Paul Cauchon. photo · *MD* Sept 25, 1987: p15.
[TELEVISION AND CANADIAN LITERATURE]

MEURTRES À BLANC/Novel by Yolande Villemaire

En poche, le premier roman de Yolande Villemaire: un thriller gigogne; review of *Meurtres à blanc*. Jean-Roch Boivin. photo · *MD* May 2, 1987: pD3.
[FIRST NOVELS: BOOK REVIEWS]

MICHAELS, ANNE

[Untitled]; review of *The Weight of Oranges*. Paul Dutton. *Quill & Quire* Jan 1987; Vol 53 No 1: p32.

[Untitled]; review of *The Weight of Oranges*. Anne Todkill. *Quarry* Winter 1987; Vol 36 No 1: p131–133.

MICHAUD, ANDRÉE-A.

Sous le signe du Scorpion, Andrée-A. Michaud nous convie aux confins de l'obsession; review of *La Femme de Sath*. Jean-Roch Boivin. *MD* June 6, 1987: pD3.
[FIRST NOVELS: BOOK REVIEWS]

"Écrire pour se donner ce qu'on n'a pas dans la vraie vie"; article. Jean Royer. photo · *MD* June 6, 1987: pD3.

MICHAUD, JACQUES

La vie littéraire; column. Jean Royer. *MD* April 25, 1987: pD2.
[AWARDS, LITERARY; CONFERENCES, LITERARY; FESTIVALS, LITERARY; FICTION READINGS; POETRY READINGS; RADIO AND CANADIAN LITERATURE; TELEVISION AND CANADIAN LITERATURE]

MICHELE LANDSBERG'S GUIDE TO CHILDREN'S BOOKS/Critical work by Michele Landsberg

Passionate and practical; review of *Michele Landsberg's Guide to Children's Books*. Mary G. Hamilton. *Can Child Lit* 1987; No 46: p64–65.

MICONE, MARCO

Masques, personnages et personnes; reviews of plays. André-G. Bourassa. photo · *Lettres québec* Summer 1987; No 46: p51–52.

Le théâtre qu'on joue; theatre reviews. André Dionne. illus photo · *Lettres québec* Spring 1987; No 45: p47–48.

[Untitled]; theatre review of *Bilico*. Diane Pavlovic. photo · *Jeu* 1987; No 42: p149–151.

Marco Micone propose la cohabitation; article. Jean Royer. photo · *MD* March 17, 1987: p14.
[CULTURAL I2ENTITY]

La vitrine du livre; reviews. Jean Royer. *MD* April 11, 1987: pD2.
[CANADIAN LITERARY PERIODICALS]

MICROPHONES/Poems by A.R. Kazuk

Random musings of a middle-aged middle-class male; reviews of poetry books. Lesley McAllister. *TS* Oct 10, 1987: M4.

MIDNIGHT FOUND YOU DANCING/Poems by John Smith

[Untitled]; reviews of *The Beekeeper's Daughter* and *Midnight Found You Dancing*. Robert Hilles. *Poetry Can R* Spring 1987; Vol 8 No 2–3: p41.

The space of images; reviews of poetry books. Lavinia Inbar. *Can Lit* Summer-Fall 1987; No 113–114: p245–247.

Structures of meditation; reviews of *Meditations* and *Midnight Found You Dancing*. Michael Thorpe. *Fiddlehead* Spring 1987; No 151: p115–120.

MILES, KIRK

Musical comedy written as a true labor of love; article. Kate Zimmerman. photo · *CH* Dec 4, 1987: pE2.

MILLAN, JIM

Family drama lacks depth; theatre review of *South of Heaven*. Ray Conlogue. photo · *G&M* Nov 23, 1987: pC12.

Talented young writer fails to take off this time; theatre review of *South of Heaven*. Robert Crew. photo · *TS* Nov 20, 1987: pE26.

Isaac's cast puts its 500 years to good use; column. Vit Wagner. *TS* Nov 13, 1987: pE16.
[DRAMATIC READINGS; FEMINIST DRAMA; FESTIVALS, DRAMA; WOMEN WRITERS]

MILLAR, T.P.

Freudian farce; review of *Who's Afraid of Sigmund Freud?*. Kay Stockholder. *Can Lit* Spring 1987; No 112: p162–164.

MILLER, MURIEL

Passages; obituary. *Maclean's* April 20, 1987; Vol 100 No 16: p4.

Confederation poets; reviews. Ronald B. Hatch. *Can Lit* Winter 1987; No 115: p223–225.

UN MILLIER D'OISEAUX

See ONE THOUSAND CRANES / UN MILLIER D'OISEAUX/Children's play by Colin Thomas

MILLIONS OF CANADIANS/Play by Tom Crichton

Flashes of gold among the dross at Fringe festival; theatre reviews. Liam Lacey. *G&M* Aug 19, 1987: pC5.
[FESTIVALS, DRAMA]

MILLS, SPARLING

[Untitled]; reviews of *My Round Table* and *Everything Happens at Once*. Rosemary Aubert. *Poetry Can R* Spring 1987; Vol 8 No 2–3: p48.

[Untitled]; reviews of poetry books. Barbara Carey. *Cross Can Writ Q* 1987; Vol 9 No 1: p23–24.

MILNER, ARTHUR

Politics, playwriting and Zero Hour; interview with Arthur Milner. Larry McDonald. photo · *Can Theatre R* Winter 1987; No 53: p43–48.

MILTON ACORN: THE UNCOLLECTED ACORN/ Poems by Milton Acorn

Into the depths of Milton Acorn's passion; review of *Milton Acorn: The Uncollected Acorn*. Colin Lowndes. photo · *G&M* March 21, 1987: pE18.

THE MINERVA PROGRAM/LE PROGRAMME MINERVE/Young adult novel by Claire Mackay

Pour les adolescents: quatre mains et deux solitudes; reviews of young adult novels. Dominique Demers. photo · *MD* Dec 19, 1987: pD6–D7.

MINNI, C.D.

[Untitled]; review of *Other Selves*. Richard Lanoie. *Rubicon* Spring 1987; No 8: p221

[Untitled]; review of *Other Selves*. Dona Sturmanis. *Can Auth & Book* Winter 1987; Vol 62 No 2: p23–24.

MIRÁKL/Novel by Josef Skvorecky

Josef Skvorecky; letter to the editor. Jan Culík. *Times Lit Supp* Feb 6, 1987; No 4375: p137.

Vanished consolations; reviews of *Dvorak in Love* and *Mirákl*. Roger Scruton. *Times Lit Supp* Jan 23, 1987; No 4373: p83.

MIRON, GASTON

Roger Bellemare: de la musique sur des poèmes de Miron et Anne Hébert; article. Jean Royer. photo · *MD* May 20, 1987: p12.

MISCHIEF CITY/Children's poems by Tim Wynne-Jones

The big menace; reviews of *I'll Make You Small* and *Mischief City*. Sandra Martin. *G&M* Jan 17, 1987: pE18.

MISS ABIGAIL'S PART: OR VERSION AND DIVERSION/Novel by Judith Ann Terry

[Untitled]; review of *Miss Abigail's Part*. Mary Lou Cornish. *Cross Can Writ Q* 1987; Vol 9 No 3–4: p49.
[FIRST NOVELS: BOOK REVIEWS]

[Untitled]; review of *Miss Abigail's Part*. Maureen Corrigan. *NYT Book R* March 1, 1987: p20.
[FIRST NOVELS: BOOK REVIEWS]

Family continuum; review of *Miss Abigail's Part*. Andrea Lebowitz. *Can Lit* Winter 1987; No 115: p152–155.
[FIRST NOVELS: BOOK REVIEWS]

[Untitled]; review of *Miss Abigail's Part*. Mary Millar. *Queen's Q* Summer 1987; Vol 94 No 2: p477–478.
[FIRST NOVELS: BOOK REVIEWS]

MISS BALMORAL OF THE BAYVIEW/Play by Colleen Curran

Domestic drama that hits home; article, includes theatre reviews. John Bemrose. photo · *Maclean's* Aug 17, 1987; Vol 100 No 33: p49.
[FESTIVALS, DRAMA]

Cabarets, readings, workshops have Stratford in full swing; theatre review of *Miss Balmoral of the Bayview*. Robert Crew. photo · *TS* July 19, 1987: pC2.

MISTER JELLY ROLL/Play by George Luscombe and Larry Cox

Mr. Jelly Roll falls short of its goal; theatre review. photo · *TS* May 1, 1987: pD24.

MISTRY, ROHINTON

New jewel in Canada's literary crown; review of *Tales from Firozsha Baag*. Ken Adachi. photo · *TS* April 18, 1987: M4.

Short stories lay bare peoples' foibles, passions; review of *Tales from Firozsha Baag*. J. Leslie Ball. *CH* July 5, 1987: pF7.

Immigrant experience yields stream of interesting tales; reviews of *Tales from Firozsha Baag* and *The Fencepost Chronicles*. Barbara Black. *MG* May 30, 1987: J9.

Moving tales of homelands left behind; reviews of *Bloodsong* and *Tales from Firozsha Baag*. Janet Hamilton. photo · *Quill & Quire* June 1987; Vol 53 No 6: p32.

[Untitled]; review of *Tales from Firozsha Baag*. Louis K. Mac-Kendrick. *Books in Can* Aug-Sept 1987; Vol 16 No 6: p25–26.

Rohinton Mistry; interview. Nancy Wigston. photo · *Books in Can* June-July 1987; Vol 16 No 5: p38–39.

The vision of the self-exiled; review of *Tales from Firozsha Baag*. Nancy Wigston. photo · *G&M* May 2, 1987: pC17.

MITCHAM, ALLISON

[Untitled]; review of *The Northern Imagination*. John Ferns. *British J of Can Studies* June 1987; Vol 2 No 1: p187–188.

MITCHELL, KEN

[Untitled]; reviews of *Through the Nan Da Gate* and *Death Is an Anxious Mother*. Nancy Batty. *Dandelion* Spring-Summer 1987; Vol 14 No 1: p84–87.

[Untitled]; review of *Through the Nan Da Gate*. Barbara Carey. *Books in Can* March 1987; Vol 16 No 2: p27–28.

One-man Bethune show to tour China; column. Robert Crew. *TS* March 19, 1987: pE3.
[FESTIVALS, DRAMA]

Portrait of Bethune strong on passion; theatre review of *Gone the Burning Sun*. Robert Crew. photo · *TS* March 27, 1987: pD22.

Melody Farm feels like two plays trying to be one; theatre reviews of *Melody Farm* and *Biting Nails*. Stephen Godfrey. photo · *G&M* Feb 18, 1987: pC7.

TWP to take Bethune show to China; column. Liam Lacey. photo · *G&M* March 20, 1987: pD10.

Author, actor combine to make Sun a success; theatre review of *Gone the Burning Sun*. Liam Lacey. photo · *G&M* March 27, 1987: pD9.

[Untitled]; theatre review of *Melody Farm*. Ron Marken. *Maclean's* Feb 23, 1987; Vol 100 No 8: p55.

[Untitled]; reviews of poetry books. James McElroy. *Poetry Can R* Fall 1987; Vol 9 No 1: p36.

Prairie spaces in the big city: western theatre in Toronto; theatre reviews. Margaret Gail Osachoff. *NeWest R* Oct 1987; Vol 13 No 2: p18–19.

Moose Jaw meets Mao; article. Maggie Siggins. biog photo · *G&M* March 21, 1987: pE1,E6.
[CHINA-CANADA LITERARY RELATIONS]

Snapshots of China; review of *Through the Nan Da Gate*. Sally Swenson. *Arc* Spring 1987; No 18: p70–71.

MITCHELL, NICK

Black comedy neither dark nor funny; theatre review of *Mum*. Randal McIlroy. *WFP* March 6, 1987: p20.

Playwright, 37, credits absurd inquisitiveness for surrealistic drama; article. Kevin Prokosh. photo · *WFP* March 6, 1987: p20.

MITCHELL, W.O.

W.O. Mitchell returning to west after productive years in Windsor; article. *WFP* May 22, 1987: p39.

After 8 years, W.O. Mitchell is heading west; article. *G&M* May 21, 1987: pD1.
[WRITERS-IN-RESIDENCE]

Mitchell's messy hair just right; article. *WFP* Oct 9, 1987: p31.

[Untitled]; theatre review of *Royalty Is Royalty*. John Bemrose. *Maclean's* Oct 19, 1987; Vol 100 No 42: p70.

W.O. Mitchell's creative thoughts turn to plays; article. Donald Campbell. photo · *WFP* Oct 8, 1987: p42.

Black Bonspiel presents a devil of a problem; theatre review of *The Black Bonspiel of Wullie MacCrimmon*. Ray Conlogue. photo · *G&M* April 18, 1987: pC7.

[Untitled]; review of *Autobiographical and Biographical Writing in the Commonwealth*. Héliane Daziron. *Afram* Jan 1987; No 24: p75.

Delightful play; letter to the editor. Gitta Fricke. photo · *WFP* Oct 20, 1987: p6.

W.O. Mitchell from The Alien to The Vanishing Point; article. W.J. Keith. *World Lit in Eng* Autumn 1987; Vol 27 No 2: p252–262.

Festival winds bring W.O. home; column. Kenneth McGoogan. *CH* March 1, 1987: pC8.
[AWARDS, LITERARY; CONFERENCES, LITERARY; FESTIVALS, LITERARY]

W.O. Mitchell's Crocus cronies shine on stage; theatre review of *Royalty Is Royalty*. Jamie Portman. *CH* Oct 15, 1987: pF1.

Mitchell praises academic life; article. Susan Schwartz. photo · *MG* Dec 5, 1987: J13.

Making the prairie connection; theatre reviews. Reg Skene. *NeWest R* Dec 1987; Vol 13 No 4: p16.

MOBILE HOMES/Short stories by Noel Hudson

[Untitled]; reviews. Anne Cimon. *Cross Can Writ Q* 1987; Vol 9 No 3–4: p47–48.

Parody & legacy; reviews. Lorna Irvine. *Can Lit* Winter 1987; No 115: p264–267.
[FIRST NOVELS: BOOK REVIEWS]

[Untitled]; review of *Mobile Homes*. Richard Lanoie. *Rubicon* Spring 1987; No 8: p215.

Everything by thought waves; reviews of short story collections. Patricia Matson. *Event* March 1987; Vol 16 No 1: p97–100.

[Untitled]; review of *Mobile Homes*. Dona Sturmanis. *Can Auth & Book* Spring 1987; Vol 62 No 3: p25.

MOCHON, JACQUELINE DÉRY

Hésitation; review of *Clara*. Frédéric Charbonneau. *Lettres québec* Autumn 1987; No 47: p70.

MOCQUAIS, PIERRE-YVES

[Untitled]; review of *Hubert Aquin ou la quête interrompue*. Janet M. Paterson. *U of Toronto Q* Fall 1987; Vol 57 No 1: p182–183.

A MODEL LOVER/Short stories by H.R. Percy

[Untitled]; reviews of *The Swell Season* and *A Model Lover*. Pauline Carey. *Cross Can Writ Q* 1987; Vol 9 No 1: p19–20.

[Untitled]; review of *A Model Lover*. Michael Helm. *Rubicon* Spring 1987; No 8: p224–225.

[Untitled]; reviews of *The Bridge Out of Town* and *A Model Lover*. Clifford G. Holland. *Queen's Q* Summer 1987; Vol 94 No 2: p472–474.

Circle games; reviews of fictional works. Barbara Leckie. *Can Lit* Winter 1987; No 115: p278–280.

[Untitled]; review of *A Model Lover*. C.H. Little. *Can Auth & Book* Winter 1987; Vol 62 No 2: p23.

Passions and ironies; review of *A Model Lover*. Alan R. Young. *Fiddlehead* Summer 1987; No 152: p98–100.

MODERN CANADIAN CHILDREN'S BOOKS/Critical work by Judith Saltman

A little help on the dull days; reviews of children's books. Joan McGrath. *TS* Aug 2, 1987: pC11.

Saltman's superior guide good news about Canadian books; review of *Modern Canadian Children's Books*. Irma Mc-Donough Milnes. photo · *Quill & Quire (Books for Young People)* April 1987; Vol 53 No 4: p1,3.

Roughing it in the bush; reviews of children's books. Mary Ainslie Smith. *Books in Can* Aug-Sept 1987; Vol 16 No 6: p34–36.

MODERNIST WRITING AND CRITICISM

Canadian (tw)ink: surviving the white-outs; article. Gary Boire. *Essays on Can Writ* Winter 1987; No 35: p1–16.
[COLONIALISM; HISTORICAL THEMES; NATIVE CANADIANS IN LITERATURE]

MOEBIUS/Periodical

Moebius ou l'ironie du repli; editorial. *Moebius* Winter 1987; No 31: p1–2.
[CANADIAN LITERARY PERIODICALS]

Moebius ou les vertus paradoxales de l'athéisme; column. Carole David. photo · *MD* April 11, 1987: pD3.
[CANADIAN LITERARY PERIODICALS]

La vitrine du livre; reviews. Jean Royer. photo · *MD* March 28, 1987: pD2.
[CANADIAN LITERARY PERIODICALS]

MOHER, FRANK

Ambitious drama falls short of the mark; theatre reviews of *Penguins* and *Sliding for Home*. Stephen Godfrey. photo · *G&M* Nov 26, 1987: pA25.

Collective creativity — working Odd Jobs; article. Anne Nothof. photo · *Can Drama* 1987; Vol 13 No 1: p34–42.

[Untitled]; review of *Odd Jobs*. Linda M. Peake. *Books in Can* March 1987; Vol 16 No 2: p25–26.

[Untitled]; reviews of plays. Judith Rudakoff. *Can Theatre R* Summer 1987; No 51: p86–87.

MOIRA'S BIRTHDAY/Children's story by Robert Munsch

[Untitled]; review of *Moira's Birthday*. Jan Dobbins. *CH* Dec 6, 1987: pD9.

[Untitled]; review of *Moira's Birthday*. Frieda Wishinsky. *Quill & Quire (Books for Young People)* Dec 1987; Vol 53 No 12: p6,8.

MOISAN, CLÉMENT

La vitrine du livre; reviews of *Poètes québécois contemporains* and *Comparaison et raison*. Guy Ferland. *MD* Oct 10, 1987: pD4.
[ANTHOLOGIES: BOOK REVIEWS]

MOISAN, RACHEL

Talk-rock musical sizzles with energy and staging is slick; theatre review of *Heavy Minou*. Pat Donnelly. photo · *MG* Nov 17, 1987: pE7.

MOLNAR, GWEN

Make way for a fine crop of picture-books; reviews of children's books. Adele Ashby. *Quill & Quire (Books for Young People)* Aug 1987; Vol 53 No 8: p6.

MON AMI PIERROT. POÈMES POUR ENFANTS/ Children's poems by Jean-Yves Roy

Poèmes et rimes pour émerveiller; review of *Mon ami Pierrot*. François Paré. *Can Child Lit* 1987; No 46: p100–101.

MON CHEVAL POUR UN ROYAUME/Novel by Jacques Poulin

Dans les poches; reviews of *Dictionnaire de moi-même* and *Mon cheval pour un royaume*. Guy Ferland. *MD* May 30, 1987: pD2.

MON MARI LE DOCTEUR/Novel by Daniel Gagnon

Écrire l'histoire ou histoire d'écrire; reviews of novels. Jacques Michon. *Voix et images* Spring 1987; Vol 12 No 3: p548–550.

[Untitled]; reviews of *Mon mari le docteur* and *Américane*. Jacques St-Pierre. *Moebius* Winter 1987; No 31: p139–140.

THE MONEYLENDERS OF SHAHPUR/Novel by Helen Forrester (pseud.)

The romance of the Far East; review of *The Moneylenders of Shahpur*. James P. Carley. *G&M* July 25, 1987: pC15.

Romantic novel set in India is typical of Canadian writer's British penchant; review of *The Moneylenders of Shahpur*. Peggy Curran. *MG* Aug 8, 1987: J3.

Cultural collisions fascinate; review of *The Moneylenders of Shahpur*. Susan Scott. *CH* April 12, 1987: pF7.

MONGEAU, FRANCE

Montreal women split poetry prize; article. *MG* March 10, 1987: pD9.
[AWARDS, LITERARY]

Prix et distinctions; list of award winners. photo · *Lettres québec* Summer 1987; No 46: p7.
[AWARDS, LITERARY]

Carole David et France Mongeau lauréates du prix Nelligan 1986; article. Jean Royer. photo · *MD* March 10, 1987: p11.
[AWARDS, LITERARY]

La vie littéraire; column. Jean Royer. photo · *MD* March 14, 1987: pD4.

[AWARDS, LITERARY; POETRY READINGS; RADIO AND CANADIAN LITERATURE; TELEVISION AND CANADIAN LITERATURE]

MONICA'S MOTHER SAID NO!/Children's story by Shirley Day

[Untitled]; review of *Monica's Mother Said No!*. Adele Ashby. *Quill & Quire (Books for Young People)* Dec 1987; Vol 53 No 12: p9.

Mini-reviews; reviews of children's stories. Mary Rubio. *Can Child Lit* 1987; No 47: p96–99.

MONSTER CHEESE/Children's story by Steve Wolfson

Mini-reviews; reviews of children's stories. Mary Rubio. *Can Child Lit* 1987; No 46: p105–109.

MONTAGUE, MASANI (CHARMAINE)

Breakout's only strength is in its message; theatre review. Alex Law. photo · *TS (Neighbours)* March 31, 1987: p18.

MONTGOMERY, LUCY MAUD

Disney to show Anne sequel seven months before Canada; article. *WFP* Feb 14, 1987: p23.
[TELEVISION AND CANADIAN LITERATURE]

CBS wins 5 Peabody awards; article. *G&M* April 28, 1987: pC9.
[TELEVISION AND CANADIAN LITERATURE]

Anne pockets Peabody award; article. *TS* April 26, 1987: pC7.
[TELEVISION AND CANADIAN LITERATURE]

'Green Gables' wins award; article. *MG* April 28, 1987: pA14.

U.S. critics rave over Anne of Green Gables sequel; article. photo · *MG* May 26, 1987: pD10.
[INTERNATIONAL REVIEWS OF CANADIAN LITERATURE; TELEVISION AND CANADIAN LITERATURE]

Green Gables sequel a winner; article. *MG* Oct 7, 1987: H1.
[TELEVISION AND CANADIAN LITERATURE]

Anne a U.S. favorite; article. *WFP* Oct 7, 1987: p41.
[TELEVISION AND CANADIAN LITERATURE]

Sequel reaps awards; article. *CH* Oct 7, 1987: pD2.
[TELEVISION AND CANADIAN LITERATURE]

Two awards given to Anne's sequel; article. *G&M* Oct 7, 1987: pC7.
[TELEVISION AND CANADIAN LITERATURE]

Grant earmarked for PEI papers; article. *G&M* Dec 17, 1987: pC1.
[LIBRARY SERVICES AND CANADIAN LITERATURE]

The girl she never was; biographical article. Mark Abley. photo · *Sat Night* Nov 1987; Vol 102 No 11: p52–54,56,58–59.

Anne's author faced darkness; review of *The Selected Journals of Lucy Maud Montgomery, Volume Two*. Ken Adachi. *TS* Dec 6, 1987: pC8.

Anne sequel likely to outdraw original; article. Bill Anderson. photo · *WFP* Dec 1, 1987: p34.
[TELEVISION AND CANADIAN LITERATURE]

Anne of Green Gables — the Sequel; television review. Jim Bawden. photo · *TS* Dec 5, 1987: pF1,F12.
[TELEVISION AND CANADIAN LITERATURE]

P.E.I.'s spirited redhead returns; article. Bob Blakey. photo · *CH* Dec 2, 1987: pD1.
[TELEVISION AND CANADIAN LITERATURE]

Anne II: Canadians' love affair resumes; article. Mike Boone. photo · *MG* Dec 4, 1987: pC1.
[TELEVISION AND CANADIAN LITERATURE]

Brilliantly crafted Green Gables sequel Follows naturally; television review. Mike Boone. *MG* Dec 4, 1987: pC8.
[TELEVISION AND CANADIAN LITERATURE]

Anne to be adapted for ballet; article. Donald Campbell. *WFP* Nov 26, 1987: p83.

Anne sequel takes too many liberties; letter to the editor. Maida Campbell. photo · *G&M* Dec 26, 1987: pD7.

Slick Anne sequel takes no chances with success; television review. John Haslett Cuff. photo · *G&M* Dec 5, 1987: pC5.
[TELEVISION AND CANADIAN LITERATURE]

Dans les poches; reviews. Guy Ferland. *MD* Sept 26, 1987: pD6.

Anne's secret quality keeps her coming back; column. Robert Fulford. *TS* Dec 5, 1987: pF1.
[TELEVISION AND CANADIAN LITERATURE]

LMM: finding a voice; review of *The Selected Journals of L.M. Montgomery*. Coral Ann Howells. *Can Child Lit* 1987; No 45: p79–81.

Anne of Green Gables in translation; review of *Anne . . . la Maison aux pignons verts*. Martine Jacquot. *Atlan Prov Book R* Feb-March 1987; Vol 14 No 1: p13.

Anne of Green Gables grows up; article. Brian D. Johnson. Barbara MacAndrew. photo · *Maclean's* Dec 7, 1987; Vol 100 No 49: p46–48,50.
[TELEVISION AND CANADIAN LITERATURE]

Anne's back home, safe and sound; theatre review of *Anne of Green Gables*. Deirdre Kelly. photo · *G&M* June 29, 1987: pC9.
[DRAMATIC ADAPTATIONS OF CANADIAN LITERATURE]

Gammer Gurton leaps from early English stage into the 20th century; reviews of children's books. Janice Kennedy. *MG* Nov 21, 1987: J13.

[Untitled]; television review of *Anne of Green Gables — The Sequel*. Martin Knelman. photo · *Tor Life* Dec 1987; Vol 21 No 18: p131.

[Untitled]; review of *Anne . . . La Maison aux pignons verts*. Eva-Marie Kröler. *Can Lit* Winter 1987; No 115: p290.

Looking for Lucy Maud; article. Kathy Large. *Atlan Insight* June 1987; Vol 9 No 6: p48–49.

Group brings back Anne of Green Gables; article. Muriel Leeper. *TS (Neighbours)* April 7, 1987: p21.
[DRAMATIC ADAPTATIONS OF CANADIAN LITERATURE]

Anne of Green Gables opens with lively spirit; theatre review. Muriel Leeper. *TS (Neighbours)* April 28, 1987: p14.
[DRAMATIC ADAPTATIONS OF CANADIAN LITERATURE]

Murdoch ahead in Booker race; article. photo · *G&M* Sept 25, 1987: pD11.
[AWARDS, LITERARY]

Board buys rights to novels; article. *TS* Oct 18, 1987: pG4.
[FILM ADAPTATIONS OF CANADIAN LITERATURE]

Penelope Lively wins Booker prize; article. *TS* Oct 30, 1987: pE22.
[AWARDS, LITERARY]

British author beats out Brian Moore for Booker; article. *MG* Oct 30, 1987: pC9.
[AWARDS, LITERARY]

Penelope Lively décroche le Booker Prize; article. *MD* Oct 30, 1987: p14.
[AWARDS, LITERARY]

Lively wins Booker Prize; article. *CH* Oct 31, 1987: H4.
[AWARDS, LITERARY]

Moore moves ahead in race for Booker; article. *G&M* Oct 27, 1987: pD7.
[AWARDS, LITERARY]

[Untitled]; review of *The Color of Blood*. *New Yorker* Oct 19, 1987; Vol 63 No 35: p120.

Something gravely missing in Brian Moore's last novel; review of *The Color of Blood*. Ken Adachi. photo · *TS* Sept 5, 1987: M4.

Latecomer to fiction-writing a talent to watch; column. Ken Adachi. photo · *TS* Oct 19, 1987: pC5.
[AWARDS, LITERARY; FESTIVALS, LITERARY]

Clever novelist confuses the critics; column. Ken Adachi. *TS* Oct 22, 1987: pB4.
[FESTIVALS, LITERARY]

Devil, angel: Alliance has it covered; column. Sid Adilman. *TS* May 16, 1987: pG3.
[FILM ADAPTATIONS OF CANADIAN LITERATURE]

Expansion blamed for red ink at CBC's sales division; column. Sid Adilman. *TS* Nov 2, 1987: pC4.
[CANADIAN LITERARY PERIODICALS]

Polish nightmares; review of *The Color of Blood*. Neal Ascherson. illus · *New York R of Books* Dec 17, 1987; Vol 34 No 20: p44,46,48.

A clash of crimsons; review of *The Color of Blood*. John Bemrose. *Maclean's* Oct 19, 1987; Vol 100 No 42: p60f

Brian Moore's Jesuit priest travels into heart of darkness; reviews of novels. Barbara Black. *MG* March 7, 1987: H11.

Moore shatters illusion in the search for spiritual survival; review of *The Color of Blood*. Patricia Bradbury. photo · *Quill & Quire* Aug 1987; Vol 53 No 8: p29.

Le primat et le patriote; review of *La Couleur du sang*. Paul-André Comeau. *MD* Dec 12, 1987: pD8.

Under the red robe; review of *The Color of Blood*. Anne-Marie Conway. *Times Lit Supp* Oct 2, 1987; No 4409: p1073.

People; column. Yvonne Cox. photo · *Maclean's* Nov 2, 1987; Vol 100 No 44: p48.

Film draws engaging portrait; column. John Haslett Cuff. photo · *G&M* July 23, 1987: pD3.

Realpolitik of the spirit; article. Sarah Ferrell. photo · *NYT Book R* Sept 27, 1987: p11.

Moore didn't finish his suspense novel; review of *The Color of Blood*. Catherine Ford. *CH* Sept 5, 1987: H7.

The holy murder; review of *The Color of Blood*. William French. *G&M* Sept 5, 1987: pC13.

For God's sake; review of *The Color of Blood*. Douglas Glover. *Books in Can* Oct 1987; Vol 16 No 7: p18.

Brian Moore: this is your life; article. Martin Knelman. *Tor Life* June 1987; Vol 21 No 9: p19.
[TELEVISION AND CANADIAN LITERATURE]

Less is Moore for Brian; article. Liam Lacey. photo · *G&M* Oct 20, 1987: pD5.
[FESTIVALS, LITERARY]

Laurels in literature; article. Alberto Manguel. *Maclean's* Nov 2, 1987; Vol 100 No 44: p52a-52b.
[AWARDS, LITERARY]

Sorceries; review of *Black Robe*. Kerry McSweeney. *Essays on Can Writ* Spring 1987; No 34: p111-118.

Documentary profiles witty author; television review of *The Lonely Passion of Brian Moore*. Henry Mietkiewicz. photo · *TS* July 22, 1987: pD3.
[TELEVISION AND CANADIAN LITERATURE]

Moore's latest disappointing; review of *The Color of Blood*. Tom Oleson. photo · *WFP* Sept 5, 1987: p58.

Hollywood: some call it Quebec South; article. Linda Renaud. Anne Gregor. photo · *MG* Dec 19, 1987: pE7.
[FILM ADAPTATIONS OF CANADIAN LITERATURE]

[Untitled]; review of *The Color of Blood*. Constance Rooke. *Malahat R* Dec 1987; No 81: p101-102.

Cardinal Bem on the run; review of *The Color of Blood*. Clancy Sigal. *NYT Book R* Sept 27, 1987: p11.

Book world: Maggie Smith as Judith Hearne?; column. Beverley Slopen. *TS* Jan 25, 1987: pB6.
[AUTHORS, CANADIAN; FILM ADAPTATIONS OF CANADIAN LITERATURE]

Book world: 'My year for films': Brian Moore; column. Beverley Slopen. photo · *TS* Nov 8, 1987: pA18.
[CHILDREN'S LITERATURE; FILM ADAPTATIONS OF CANADIAN LITERATURE; PUBLISHING AND PUBLISHERS IN CANADA]

[Untitled]; review of *The Color of Blood*. Robert Stewart. illus · *MG* Sept 5, 1987: J1.

Critical programmes; reviews of *Malcolm Lowry* and *Four Contemporary Novelists*. Paul Tiessen. *Can Lit* Winter 1987; No 115: p157-159.

MOORE, MAUREEN

Fatalities and feminism in Lotus Land; reviews of *Fieldwork* and *The Goldfish Bowl*. Margaret Cannon. *G&M* Aug 29, 1987: pC17.
[FIRST NOVELS: BOOK REVIEWS]

Heart of darkness; reviews of first novels. Janice Kulyk Keefer. *Books in Can* Dec 1987; Vol 16 No 9: p37-39.
[FIRST NOVELS: BOOK REVIEWS]

[Untitled]; reviews of *Doubtful Motives* and *Fieldwork*. Car-olellen Norskey. *Quill & Quire* Sept 1987; Vol 53 No 9: p79.
[FIRST NOVELS: BOOK REVIEWS]

MOORE, MAVOR

Dits et faits; column. photo · *Lettres québec* Spring 1987; No 45: p6–7.
[AWARDS, LITERARY; PUBLISHING AND PUBLISHERS IN CANADA; TRANSLATIONS OF CANADIAN LITERATURE; WRITERS' ORGANIZA-TIONS]

MOORE, ROGER

Recent poetry; reviews of poetry books. Terrence Craig. *Atlan Prov Book R* Feb-March 1987; Vol 14 No 1: p18.

[Untitled]; review of *Broken Ghosts*. Brian Vanderlip. *Poetry Can R* Fall 1987; Vol 9 No 1: p38.

MORE STORIES BY CANADIAN WOMEN/Anthology

Gender aside, a strong collection of stories by Canadian women; review of *More Stories by Canadian Women*. Keith Garebian. *TS* Oct 31, 1987: M11.
[ANTHOLOGIES: BOOK REVIEWS]

Relevant writing; reviews of *Private and Fictional Words* and *More Stories by Canadian Women*. Ann Holloway. *G&M* Nov 28, 1987: pC22.
[ANTHOLOGIES: BOOK REVIEWS]

Making connections; review of *More Stories by Canadian Women*. W.H. New. *Books in Can* Oct 1987; Vol 16 No 7: p31–32.
[ANTHOLOGIES: BOOK REVIEWS]

MORE TALES FROM THE IGLOO/Children's book by Agnes Nanogak

[Untitled]; review of *More Tales from the Igloo*. *Queen's Q* Winter 1987; Vol 94 No 4: p1073.

Native heritage is displayed in three timely books; reviews of children's books. Janice Kennedy. *MG* April 4, 1987: H11.

MORE, ROBERT

Persistence pays off for determined actor-writer; article. Brian Brennan. photo · *CH* March 6, 1987: pF1.

Fare can't be taken at face value; theatre review of *Possibly Yours*. Brian Brennan. photo · *CH* March 10, 1987: pC7.

MORENCY, JEAN

La fiction de nos devanciers; reviews of *Le Roman québécois de 1944 1965* and *Un Roman du regard*. Agnès Whitfield. photo · *Lettres québec* Winter 1986–87; No 44: p56–58.

MORENCY, PIERRE

La tentation du romanesque; reviews of poetry books. Rich-ard Giguère. photo · *Lettres québec* Autumn 1987; No 47: p37–39.

MORGAN THE MAGNIFICENT/Children's novel by Ian Wallace

Morgan, May, Melinda: new heroines offer humour and fantasy; reviews of children's books. Bernie Goedhart. *Quill & Quire (Books for Young People)* Oct 1987; Vol 53 No 10: p24.

Daring diner date jogs writer; column. Kenneth McGoogan. photo · *CH* Dec 20, 1987: pE6.

'Daring girl' who captured author's heart stars in book; article. Leslie Scrivener. biog photo · *TS* Dec 6, 1987: pD5.

Dreams of magical change; review of *Morgan the Magnificent*. Tim Wynne-Jones. *G&M* Dec 19, 1987: pC26.

MORGAN, ALLEN

From giant snakes to punk pigeons: escapism at its best; reviews of children's stories. Bernie Goedhart. *Quill & Quire (Books for Young People)* June 1987; Vol 53 No 6: p5.

Meaningful nonsense; reviews of children's books. Adrienne Kertzer. *Can Lit* Winter 1987; No 115: p165–167

Paperbacks offer good value; review of *Nicole's Boat*. Helen Norrie. *WFP* May 23, 1987: p74.

Asimov robotics . . . orchestral overtures . . . marvellous Munsch; reviews of tape versions of children's books. Rich-ard Perry. photo · *Quill & Quire (Books for Young People)* Aug 1987; Vol 53 No 8: p10.
[AUDIO-VISUALS AND CANADIAN LITERATURE]

Mini-reviews; reviews of children's stories. Mary Rubio. *Can Child Lit* 1987; No 47: p96–99.

MORGAN, ROBERT

Italian troupe offers a touch of class; theatre review of *Together/Ensemble*. Robert Crew. *TS* May 13, 1987: pB3.
[FESTIVALS, DRAMA]

Ernest and Ernestine are funny and familiar; theatre review of *The Anger of Ernest and Ernestine*. Liam Lacey. photo · *G&M* May 28, 1987: pD6.

Well-wrought Anger comedy marred only by false-note finale; theatre review of *The Anger in Ernest and Ernestine*. Henry Mietkiewicz. photo · *TS* May 29, 1987: pE12.

MORITZ, A.F.

[Untitled]; reviews of poetry books. Martin Singleton. *Cross Can Writ Q* 1987; Vol 9 No 2: p19–20.

MORITZ, ALBERT

Riding off in all directions; review of *Leacock: A Biography*. Carl Spadoni. *Essays on Can Writ* Winter 1987; No 35: p74–81.

MORITZ, THERESA

Riding off in all directions; review of *Leacock: A Biography*. Carl Spadoni. *Essays on Can Writ* Winter 1987; No 35: p74–81.

MORRELL, DAVID

During or after, war is still hell; review of *The League of Night and Fog*. Philippe van Rjndt. *TS* July 11, 1987: M4.

MORRIS, ROBERTA

[Untitled]; review of *Vigil*. Gloria Hildebrandt. *Books in Can* May 1987; Vol 16 No 4: p21.

[Untitled]; reviews of *Vigil* and *The Whirlpool*. Alice Van Wart. *Can Forum* Aug-Sept 1987; Vol 67 No 771: p46–48.
[FIRST NOVELS: BOOK REVIEWS]

MORRITT, HOPE

Book world: Japan likes Toronto 'letters'; column. Beverley Slopen. *TS* May 17, 1987: pA16.

MORSE, L.A.

Win some, lose some; letter to the editor. Terence M. Green. *Books in Can* Aug-Sept 1987; Vol 16 No 6: p40.
[AWARDS, LITERARY]

Win some, lose some more; letter to the editor. Jack Jensen. *Books in Can* Nov 1987; Vol 16 No 8: p40.
[AWARDS, LITERARY]

LA MORT AURORALE: POÈMES ET PROSE/Poems and prose by Marc Garipy

Autour d'une "noyade orchestrale"; review of *La Mort aurorale*. Jean-Pierre Issenhuth. *Liberté* Dec 1987; Vol 29 No 6: p154–155.

Notes de lectures; reviews of *La Mort aurorale* and *Écoute, Sultane*. Jean Royer. *MD* May 23, 1987: pD2.

MORTAL SINS/Novel by Anna Porter

Black Sheep time; review of *Mortal Sins*. Margaret Cannon. photo · *G&M* Nov 14, 1987: pE4.

Under the Nazi shadow; review of *Mortal Sins*. Gillian Mac-Kay. *Maclean's* Nov 23, 1987; Vol 100 No 47: p54a

[Untitled]; review of *Mortal Sins*. John North. *Quill & Quire* Oct 1987; Vol 53 No 10: p22.

MORTIMER/Children's story by Robert Munsch

Meaningful nonsense; reviews of children's books. Adrienne Kertzer. *Can Lit* Winter 1987; No 115: p165–167.

MORTMAN, DORIS

Bad women make good pop novels; article. *WFP* July 28, 1987: p27.

MORTON, COLIN

Women are the root of all change; reviews of *The Unravelling* and *The Merzbook*. Lesley McAllister. photo · *TS* Nov 14, 1987: M4.

Poets view China, Dada; reviews of *China: Shockwaves* and *The Merzbook*. Robert Quickenden. *WFP* Dec 5, 1987: p56.

[Untitled]; reviews of poetry books. Stephen Scobie. *Malahat R* Dec 1987; No 81: p104–106.

Frost shadows; reviews of poetry books. Andrew Taylor. *Can Lit* Winter 1987; No 115: p197–199.

MOSER, MARIE

Mainstreet Calgary; column. *CH (Neighbors)* May 13, 1987: pA6–A7.
[FICTION READINGS; WRITERS' WORKSHOPS]

Getting on a literary roulette wheel; reviews of fictional works. Trevor Ferguson. *MG* Nov 14, 1987: J11.
[FIRST NOVELS: BOOK REVIEWS]

Unkind but true: little skill in first novel; review of *Counterpoint*. Maggie Helwig. *TS* June 20, 1987: M7.
[FIRST NOVELS: BOOK REVIEWS]

Ancestors inspire novelist; column. Kenneth McGoogan. biog photo · *CH* May 31, 1987: pF5.

[Untitled]; review of *Counterpoint*. Carolellen Norskey. *Quill & Quire* Aug 1987; Vol 53 No 8: p30.
[FIRST NOVELS: BOOK REVIEWS]

MOSS, JOHN

A flowering spring and a simplistic guide; reviews of *Northern Spring* and *A Reader's Guide to the Canadian Novel* (second edition). Ken Adachi. photo · *TS* Aug 1, 1987: M4.

MOTHER AND DAUGHTER RELATIONSHIPS IN THE MANAWAKA WORLD OF MARGARET LAURENCE/Critical work by Margaret M. Buss

Matrimony; review of *Mother and Daughter Relationships in the Manawaka Works of Margaret Laurence*. Connie Bellamy. *Essays on Can Writ* Winter 1987; No 35: p93–99.

MOTHER I'M SO GLAD YOU TAUGHT ME HOW TO DANCE/Poems by Vancy Kasper

[Untitled]; review of *Mother I'm So Glad You Taught Me How to Dance*. Gideon Forman. *Books in Can* Aug-Sept 1987; Vol 16 No 6: p28.

THE MOTOR BOYS IN OTTAWA/Novel by Hugh Hood

Part six of twelve; review of *The Motor Boys in Ottawa*. I.M. Owen. *Idler* Jan-Feb 1987; No 11: p47–49.

MOURIR COMME UN CHAT/Short stories by Claude-Emmanuelle Yance

Mourir comme un chat?; reviews of *Mourir comme un chat* and *Facéties*. Madeleine Ouellette-Michalska. *MD* July 4, 1987: pC6.

Deux livres pour partir en voyage; reviews of *Mourir comme un chat* and *Banc de Brume*. Marie José Thériault. photo · *Lettres québec* Autumn 1987; No 47: p31–32.

THE MOURNFUL DEMEANOR OF LIEUTENANT BORUVKA/Short stories by Josef Skvorecky

Detective with the blues; review of *The Mournful Demeanor of Lieutenant Boruvka*. Mark Abley. photo · *Maclean's* Sept 14, 1987; Vol 100 No 37: T12.

Lieut. Boruvka Czechs in to the case; review of *The Mournful Demeanor of Lieutenant Boruvka*. Barbara Black. photo · *MG* Oct 17, 1987: J13.

Czech detective a belated delight; review of *The Mournful Demeanor of Lieutenant Boruvka*. William French. *G&M* Sept 10, 1987: pD1.

[Untitled]; review of *The Mournful Demeanour of Lieutenant Boruvka*. William Grimes. *NYT Book R* Sept 6, 1987: p16.

Lost in translation; review of *The Mournful Demeanor of Lieutenant Boruvka*. Alberto Manguel. *Books in Can* June-July 1987; Vol 16 No 5: p13–14.

[Untitled]; review of *The Mournful Demeanor of Lieutenant Boruvka*. Peter Robinson. *Quill & Quire* June 1987; Vol 53 No 6: p33.

Detective with a difference; review of *The Mournful Demeanor of Lieutenant Boruvka*. Tom Saunders. photo · *WFP* Sept 26, 1987: p64.

MOUVEMENT SANS FIN

See PERPETUAL MOTION/MOUVEMENT SANS FIN/ Novel by Graeme Gibson

MOVING LANDSCAPE/Poems by Pasquale Verdicchio

Roman heartbeat; reviews of *The Other Shore* and *Moving Landscape*. Louise McKinney. *Can Lit* Winter 1987; No 115: p232–234.

THE MOVING LIGHT/Poems by Eugene McNamara

"Give me melancholy or give me death"; reviews of *Children of Abel* and *The Moving Light*. Harry Prest. *U of Windsor R* Fall-Winter 1987; Vol 20 No 1: p95–98.

[Untitled]; review of *The Moving Light*. Stephen Scobie. *Malahat R* Sept 1987; No 80: p140.

MOWAT, FARLEY

U.S. may kill 1952 law used to bar Mowat; article. *TS* Feb 19, 1987: pA16.

Congressmen seek end to 'Farley Mowat' law; article. photo · *CH* Feb 19, 1987: pB4.

Farley Mowat gets U.S. again; column. Allan Fotheringham. *CH* Oct 29, 1987: pA8.

U.S. school bans use of Farley Mowat book; column. William French. *G&M* May 12, 1987: pC7.
[AUTHORS, CANADIAN; CENSORSHIP]

Book about a funny dog; review of *The Dog Who Wouldn't Be*. Marla Maudsley. *TS* March 1, 1987: pA17.

Actor studies each role with director's eye; article. Jamie Portman. photo · *CH* Oct 8, 1987: pF5.

Farley Mowat's writing for fun now; article. Leslie Scrivener. photo · *TS* Oct 18, 1987: pD1–D2.

LE MOYNE PICOTÉ/Novel by Agnès Guitard

La vitrine du livre; reviews. Guy Ferland. *MD* May 9, 1987: pD4.

MR SPOCK DO YOU READ ME?/Poems by Mary Horodyski

We have to shout; review of *Mr Spock Do You Read Me?*. Angela Marie Medwid. *CV 2* Summer 1987; Vol 10 No 4: p55–58.

Chapbooks range from good to silly; reviews of poetry books. Robert Quickenden. *WFP* Jan 31, 1987: p55.

MR. THINGAMAGOO AND OTHER NONSENSE VERSE/Children's poems by Shirley Higginson

Make way for a fine crop of picture-books; reviews of children's books. Adele Ashby. *Quill & Quire (Books for Young People)* Aug 1987; Vol 53 No 8: p6.

MRS. BLOOD/Novel by Audrey Thomas

The Bell Jar and Mrs. Blood: portraits of the artist as divided woman; article. Elizabeth Potvin. abstract · *Atlantis* Fall 1987; Vol 13 No 1: p38–46.
[ARTIST FIGURE; FEMINIST WRITING AND CRITICISM; WOMEN IN LITERATURE]

MRS. DUNPHY'S DOG/Children's story by Catharine O'Neill

[Untitled]; review of *Mrs. Dunphy's Dog*. Susan Perren. *Quill & Quire (Books for Young People)* Aug 1987; Vol 53 No 8: p6–7.

[Untitled]; review of *Mrs. Dunphy's Dog*. Dana Watson. *CH* Dec 6, 1987: pD9.

MUKHERJEE, BHARATI

Fear cancels tour; article. *WFP* May 29, 1987: p31.

[Untitled]; review of *The Tiger's Daughter*. Carolellen Norskey. *Quill & Quire* July 1987; Vol 53 No 7: p65.
[FIRST NOVELS: BOOK REVIEWS]

[Untitled]; review of *The Tiger's Daughter*. Helen Porter. *Books in Can* Aug-Sept 1987; Vol 16 No 6: p29.
[FIRST NOVELS: BOOK REVIEWS]

Book world: Air India bombing 'a Canadian tragedy'; column. Beverley Slopen. *TS* Feb 8, 1987: pG9.

MULHALLEN, KAREN

Quilted patch; reviews of poetry books. Uma Parameswaran. Teresa Mallam. *Can Lit* Spring 1987; No 112: p176–179.

MULLER, ROBIN

Baby of the family gets respect raising flock of Canada geese; reviews of children's books. Janice Kennedy. *MG* Oct 3, 1987: J13.

[Untitled]; review of *The Lucky Old Woman*. Judy Magnuson. *CH* Dec 6, 1987: pD9.

Traditional tales made new again with super illustrations; reviews of *The Dragon* and *The Lucky Old Woman*. Eva Martin. *Quill & Quire (Books for Young People)* Aug 1987; Vol 53 No 8: p7.

A title that will grab teenagers; reviews of children's books. Joan McGrath. *TS* Oct 25, 1987: pA18.

Familiarity and TV's stranglehold on life; reviews of children's books. Tim Wynne-Jones. *G&M* Nov 14, 1987: pE4.
[FESTIVALS, LITERARY]

MUM/Play by Nick Mitchell

Playwright, 37, credits absurd inquisitiveness for surrealistic drama; article. Kevin Prokosh. photo · *WFP* March 6, 1987: p20.

MUNRO, ALICE

Just what was said: an analytical approach to the Hansen 'hoopla'; column. *G&M* Feb 21, 1987: pD6.

Munro short story collection wins award; article. *WFP* May 29, 1987: p34.
[GOVERNOR GENERAL'S AWARDS]

For the record; column. photo · *CH* May 31, 1987: pB4.
[GOVERNOR GENERAL'S AWARDS]

Le prix du Gouverneur général à Yvon Rivard; article. *MD* May 28, 1987: p2.
[GOVERNOR GENERAL'S AWARDS]

Governor General's Award to Munro amid poetry protest; article. photo · *MG* May 28, 1987: pC1.
[GOVERNOR GENERAL'S AWARDS]

Governor General's award winners; article. *Quill & Quire* July 1987; Vol 53 No 7: p53–54.
[GOVERNOR GENERAL'S AWARDS]

J.D. Salinger's biography too tame to cause ripples; column. Ken Adachi. *TS* Feb 2, 1987: pD2.
[INTERNATIONAL REVIEWS OF CANADIAN LITERATURE]

Frye finally wins elusive award for best non-fiction book of '86; article. Ken Adachi. photo · *TS* May 28, 1987: H1.
[GOVERNOR GENERAL'S AWARDS]

[Untitled]; review of *The Progress of Love*. Allan Austin. *World Lit in Eng* Spring 1987; Vol 27 No 1: p58–59.

Country manners; reviews of *The Progress of Love* and *Goodbye Harold, Good Luck*. Julie Beddoes. *Brick* Winter 1987; No 29: p24–27.

People; column. Yvonne Cox. photo · *Maclean's* June 8, 1987; Vol 100 No 23: p46.
[GOVERNOR GENERAL'S AWARDS]

[Untitled]; reviews of fictional works. Beverley Daurio. *Cross Can Writ Q* 1987; Vol 9 No 1: p18–19.

Symbols of transformation: Alice Munro's "Mrs. Cross and Mrs. Kidd"; article. Héliane Daziron. *Open Letter* Summer 1987; Vol 6 No 8: p15–24.
[STRUCTURALIST WRITING AND CRITICISM]

Respect for the facts; review of *The Progress of Love*. Anne Duchêne. *Times Lit Supp* Jan 30, 1987; No 4374: p109.

[Untitled]; review of *The Progress of Love*. Oliver Gorse. *Idler* March-April 1987; No 12: p59–60.

New & noteworthy; review of *The Progress of Love*. George Johnson. *NYT Book R* Aug 30, 1987: p34.

Yvon Rivard et Northrop Frye parmi les lauréats des prix du gouverneur général; article. Robert Lévesque. photo · *MD* May 28, 1987: p13.
[GOVERNOR GENERAL'S AWARDS]

Family relations in Alice Munro's fiction; article. W.R. Martin. *New Q* Spring-Summer 1987; Vol 7 No 1–2: p247–254.
[THE FAMILY IN CANADIAN LITERATURE]

[Untitled]; review of *The Progress of Love*. Mary Millar. *Queen's Q* Winter 1987; Vol 94 No 4: p1015–1017.

Munro wins third Governor General's Award; article. Jamie Portman. photo · *CH* May 28, 1987: pC9.
[GOVERNOR GENERAL'S AWARDS]

Munro wins top literary prize; article. Lisa Rochon. photo · *G&M* May 28, 1987: pD1.
[GOVERNOR GENERAL'S AWARDS]

[Untitled]; review of *The Progress of Love*. Constance Rooke. *Malahat R (special issue)* March 1987; No 78: p152.

Photography "in camera"; article. Peter Sims. *Can Lit* Summer-Fall 1987; No 113–114: p145–166.

Munro's progress; review of *The Progress of Love*. Robert Thacker. *Can Lit* Winter 1987; No 115: p239–242.

The rival bards; article. Lorraine M. York. *Can Lit* Spring 1987; No 112: p211–216.

"Gulfs" and "connections": the fiction of Alice Munro; article. Lorraine York. *Essays on Can Writ* Winter 1987; No 35: p135–146.
[ISOLATION THEME]

MUNRO, JANE

Tellings; reviews of poetry books. Susan Rudy Dorscht. *Can Lit* Winter 1987; No 115: p257–260.

Narrative tendencies; reviews of poetry books. Phil Hall. *Waves* Winter 1987; Vol 15 No 3: p84–88.

B.C. international — in search of new subjects and forms; reviews. Gillian Harding-Russell. *Event* Summer 1987; Vol 16 No 2: p125–127.

[Untitled]; reviews of poetry books. Sheila Martindale. *Cross Can Writ Q* 1987; Vol 9 No 2: p20–21.

MUNSCH, ROBERT

Munsch, Reimer win Metcalf awards; article. *Quill & Quire* July 1987; Vol 53 No 7: p53.
[AWARDS, LITERARY]

Stage is Munsch's desk for rewrites; article. photo · *WFP* Nov 26, 1987: p81.

Roof-raiser; article. photo · *CH* Nov 27, 1987: pC8.

Chit chat; column. Maria Casas. *Quill & Quire (Books for Young People)* April 1987; Vol 53 No 4: p3.
[CHILDREN'S LITERATURE; CHINA-CANADA LITERARY RELATIONS; WRITERS-IN-RESIDENCE]

Books offer children world of adventure; reviews. Joan Craven. *CH (Neighbors)* April 1, 1987: pA7.
[AUDIO-VISUALS AND CANADIAN LITERATURE]

The raconteur of the day-care set; article. Trish Crawford. photo · *TS* Aug 9, 1987: pD1–D2.
[STORYTELLING]

Littérature jeunesse; reviews of children's books. Domique Demers. *MD* Oct 10, 1987: pD6.

[Untitled]; review of *Moira's Birthday*. Jan Dobbins. *CH* Dec 6, 1987: pD9.

Munsch tells it like it is for kids; article. Christopher Hume. *TS* Feb 6, 1987: pD19.

Robert Munsch readying sore tonsils for Montreal shows; article. Janice Kennedy. photo · *MG* Oct 22, 1987: pC1.

1988; article. Jane Kent. photo · *CH* Dec 29, 1987: pB4.

CAA opposes pornography bill; article. Fred Kerner. *Quill & Quire* Aug 1987; Vol 53 No 8: p24.
[AWARDS, LITERARY; CENSORSHIP; WRITERS' ORGANIZATIONS]

Meaningful nonsense; reviews of children's books. Adrienne Kertzer. *Can Lit* Winter 1987; No 115: p165–167.

The world according to Munsch; article. Liam Lacey. biog photo · *G&M* Jan 24, 1987: pE1.

Children's play provides dizzy gaiety, excitement; theatre review of *Snowsuits, Birthdays, & Giants!*. Randal McIlroy. *WFP* Dec 20, 1987: p21.

Children's play not child's play; article. Brad Oswald. *WFP* Dec 16, 1987: p38.
[DRAMATIC ADAPTATIONS OF CANADIAN LITERATURE]

Mini-reviews; reviews of children's stories. Mary Rubio. *Can Child Lit* 1987; No 46: p105–109.

Japanese steal show at children's festival; review. Reg Skene. *WFP* May 27, 1987: p36.

[Untitled]; review of *Moira's Birthday*. Frieda Wishinsky. *Quill & Quire (Books for Young People)* Dec 1987; Vol 53 No 12: p6,8.

Rare joy and simple truth; reviews of *Tales of a Gambling Grandma* and *Love You Forever*. Tim Wynne-Jones. *G&M* Jan 24, 1987: pE19.

Triumphant return; reviews of *Jacob Two-Two and the Dinosaur* and *Pop Bottles*. Tim Wynne-Jones. *G&M* June 13, 1987: pC19.
[AWARDS, LITERARY]

MURDER FOR SALE/Play by Stephen Cooper

Murder for Sale turns mystery into song and dance; theatre review. Pat Donnelly. *MG* June 6, 1987: H10.

MURDER IN THE DARK: SHORT FICTIONS AND PROSE POEMS/Prose by Margaret Atwood

Troupe's translation of Atwood promises more than it delivers; review of dance based on *Murder in the Dark*. Michael Crabb. *TS* June 7, 1987: pG2.

Innovation and athletic interpretation mingle in Dutch treatment of Atwood; review of dance based on *Murder in the Dark*. Lisa Rochon. *G&M* June 8, 1987: pC10.

MURDER IN THE MARKET/Young adult novel by J. Robert Janes

How I spent my summer mystery; reviews of young adult novels by J. Robert Janes. James Gellert. *Can Child Lit* 1987; No 48: p93–95.

MURDER PATTERN/Play by Herman Voaden

Editor's notebook; editorial. John Flood. *Northward J* 1987; No 42: p2.

MURDER SEES THE LIGHT/Novel by Howard Engel

Benny bumbles into a murder in the wilds; television review of *Murder Sees the Light*. Jim Bawden. photo · *TS* March 14, 1987: J6.
[TELEVISION AND CANADIAN LITERATURE]

Murder Sees The Light best left in dark; television review. Mike Boone. *MG* March 13, 1987: pD6.
[TELEVISION AND CANADIAN LITERATURE]

Kingsley triumphs in Silas Marner; television review of *Murder Sees the Light*. John Haslett Cuff. photo · *G&M* March 14, 1987: pE5.
[TELEVISION AND CANADIAN LITERATURE]

A shot in the park; essay. Howard Engel. illus · *G&M* March 14, 1987: pE1.
[TELEVISION AND CANADIAN LITERATURE]

Fiction for slow days when reading is the happiest sport; review of *Murder Sees the Light*. Douglas Hill. *G&M* Aug 1, 1987: pC15.

Expect the unexpected in off-beat murder mystery; television review of *Murder Sees the Light*. Doreen Martens. *WFP* March 13, 1987: p31.
[TELEVISION AND CANADIAN LITERATURE]

Bumbling Benny takes new case; television review of *Murder Sees the Light*. Bill Musselwhite. photo · *CH* March 14, 1987: pF6.
[TELEVISION AND CANADIAN LITERATURE]

MURPHY, COLLEEN

Destinations strays off course despite strong cast, director; theatre review of *All Other Destinations Are Cancelled*. Ray Conlogue. photo · *G&M* Feb 25, 1987: pC10.

New Canadian drama needs leaner approach; theatre review of *All Other Destinations Are Cancelled*. Robert Crew. photo · *TS* Feb 25, 1987: pF3.

Editor's notebook; editorial. John Flood. *Northward J* 1987; No 42: p2.

MURPHY, MIKE [pseud.]

The company he keeps; review of *Ned 'n' Me*. Peter Gard. *Atlan Prov Book R* Sept-Oct 1987; Vol 14 No 3: p13.

MURRAY, RONA

Women with a past; review of *The Indigo Dress*. Anne Denoon. *Books in Can* May 1987; Vol 16 No 4: p16.

Narrative authority and the economy of secrets; review of *The Indigo Dress*. Janet Giltrow. *Event* Summer 1987; Vol 16 No 2: p121–124.

MURRELL, JOHN

Calgary playwright honored; article. *G&M* Jan 30, 1987: pD5.
[AWARDS, LITERARY]

Playwright Murrell wins Chalmers award; article. *WFP* Jan 31, 1987: p26.
[AWARDS, LITERARY]

Murrell play wins '86 Chalmers; article. *CH* Jan 30, 1987: pC9.
[AWARDS, LITERARY]

Trio named to receive awards from Canadian authors' group; article. photo · *WFP* May 14, 1987: p46.
[AWARDS, LITERARY]

Murrell lauded; article. *CH* May 14, 1987: pC12.
[AWARDS, LITERARY]

Authors honour their best; article. *Quill & Quire* June 1987; Vol 53 No 6: p24.
[AWARDS, LITERARY]

Authors association honors Purdy, Murrell and Foster; article. photo · *G&M* May 14, 1987: pC3.
[AWARDS, LITERARY]

Literary winners announced; article. *TS* May 13, 1987: pB4.
[AWARDS, LITERARY]

Canadian Authors Association leaves fiction prize unawarded; article. photo · *MG* May 15, 1987: pD8.
[AWARDS, LITERARY]

The very best of company: perceptions of a Canadian attitude towards war and nationalism in three contemporary plays; article. John S. Bolin. *Amer R of Can Studies* Autumn 1987; Vol 17 No 3: p309–322.
[CANADIAN DRAMA: HISTORY AND CRITICISM; CULTURAL IDENTITY]

Murrell wins top theatre award; article. Robert Crew. photo · *TS* Jan 30, 1987: pD21.
[AWARDS, LITERARY]

CAA opposes pornography bill; article. Fred Kerner. *Quill & Quire* Aug 1987; Vol 53 No 8: p24.
[AWARDS, LITERARY; CENSORSHIP; WRITERS' ORGANIZATIONS]

Le grand retour de Murielle Dutil dans Le Temps d'une vie; column. Robert Lévesque. *MD* April 7, 1987: p12.

Fine art of writing: Banff Centre nurtures authors, playwrights, screenwriters; article. Kenneth McGoogan. photo · *CH* May 16, 1987: pC1.
[WRITERS' WORKSHOPS]

Murrell to write play for Stratford; article. Jamie Portman. *CH* Oct 7, 1987: pD2.

MUSGRAVE, SUSAN

Dancing Chicken more of a turkey, reviewer finds; review. Ken Adachi. *TS* Nov 8, 1987: pA19.

Voice of one's own; review of *Cocktails at the Mausoleum*. Richard Bevis. *Can Lit* Winter 1987; No 115: p186–188.

Marriage and violence Western-Canadian style; reviews of *Getting Married in Buffalo Jump* and *The Dancing Chicken*. William French. photo · *G&M* Nov 19, 1987: pA25.

Songs of the sea-witch; article. John Goddard. photo · *Sat Night* July 1987; Vol 102 No 7: p23–29.

Musgrave makes it with love, sex, death; review of *The Dancing Chicken*. Janet Hamilton. photo · *Quill & Quire* Oct 1987; Vol 53 No 10: p22.

[Untitled]; review of *Cocktails at the Mausoleum*. Marilyn J. Rose. *U of Windsor R* Spring-Summer 1987; Vol 20 No 2: p97–101.

A career of love; article. Leslie Scrivener. photo · *TS* Nov 8, 1987: pD1–D2.

Paperclips: the Lovesick ladies . . . a writer's parole . . . Eden changes hands; column. Beverley Slopen. *Quill & Quire* June 1987; Vol 53 No 6: p28.

An unsuccessful satire; review of *The Dancing Chicken*. Joan Thomas. *WFP* Nov 28, 1987: p58.

Different strokes; review of *The Dancing Chicken*. Eleanor Wachtel. *Books in Can* Dec 1987; Vol 16 No 9: p19–20.

MUSIC AT THE HEART OF THINKING/Poems by Fred Wah

Red Deer Press series champions western writers; reviews of poetry books. Murdoch Burnett. *CH* Dec 13, 1987: pC11.

MY BEDTIME RHYME/Children's poems by Jane Johnson

A little help on the dull days; reviews of children's books. Joan McGrath. *TS* Aug 2, 1987: pC11.

MY DAD TAKES CARE OF ME/Children's story by Patricia Quinlan

From giant snakes to punk pigeons: escapism at its best; reviews of children's stories. Bernie Goedhart. *Quill & Quire (Books for Young People)* June 1987; Vol 53 No 6: p5.

Mini-reviews; reviews of children's stories. Mary Rubio. *Can Child Lit* 1987; No 46: p105–109.

MY DARLING JUDITH/Play by Norm Foster

[Untitled]; review of *My Darling Judith*. Kathryn Harley. *Maclean's* Oct 19, 1987; Vol 100 No 42: p70.

MY FATHER'S HOUSE: A MEMOIR OF INCEST AND HEALING/Autobiography by Sylvia Fraser

An autobiography like few you've read; review of *My Father's House*. Ken Adachi. photo · *TS* Sept 27, 1987: pA23.

Daddy's little girl; review of *My Father's House*. John Bemrose. *Maclean's* Oct 26, 1987; Vol 100 No 43: p52h

Incest victim recounts anguish, horror in novel; article. Rod Currie. photo · *WFP* Nov 9, 1987: p19.

Repressing abuse: the crime against Sylvia; review of *My Father's House*. Janet Hamilton. photo · *Quill & Quire* Aug 1987; Vol 53 No 8: p33.

Daddy's girl; article. Barbara MacKay. photo · *Books in Can* Oct 1987; Vol 16 No 7: p3.

Sylvia Fraser frees the Minotaur at the heart of her own labyrinth; review of *My Father's House*. Marion McCormick. photo · *MG* Oct 3, 1987: J11.

Fraser stirs deep fears to provide understanding; review of *My Father's House*. Susan Scott. *CH* Oct 25, 1987: pE5.

Book world: incest victim created a 'twin' to survive; column. Beverley Slopen. photo · *TS* June 21, 1987: pA22.

Incest 'split' writer; article. Brenda Southam. photo · *CH* Oct 31, 1987: pB7.

An acute eye trained on a nasty subject; review of *My Father's House*. Nancy Wigston. photo · *G&M* Sept 12, 1987: pC17.

MY ROUND TABLE/Poems by Sparling Mills

[Untitled]; reviews of poetry books. Barbara Carey. *Cross Can Writ Q* 1987; Vol 9 No 1: p23–24.

MYRE, ISABELLE

Mini-comptes rendus; reviews of *Legs et Bizou/Legs and Bizou* and *Une Journée de Sophie Lachance*. Claudine Lesage. *Can Child Lit* 1987; No 46: p110.

MYRIAM PREMIÈRE/Novel by Francine Noël

Pour l'amour des grand-mères, des petites filles et des petits garons, de l'art, de Montréal et pour l'amour tout court; review of *Myriam première*. Jean-Roch Boivin. photo · *MD* Dec 12, 1987: pD3.
[FIRST NOVELS: BOOK REVIEWS]

Le deuxième roman de Francine Noël; article. Marie Laurier. photo · *MD* Nov 18, 1987: p11.

THE MYSTERIES OF MONTREAL: MEMOIRS OF A MIDWIFE/Novel by Charlotte Führer

The other Montrealers; review of *The Mysteries of Montreal*. Michèle Lacombe. *Essays on Can Writ* Spring 1987; No 34: p180–184.

MYSTERY HOUSE/Children's novel by Jean Booker

Family ties and mysteries; reviews of children's novels. Joan McGrath. *Quill & Quire (Books for Young People)* Dec 1987; Vol 53 No 12: p10.

MYSTERY LIGHTS AT BLUE HARBOUR/Children's novel by Budge Wilson

Family ties and mysteries; reviews of children's novels. Joan McGrath. *Quill & Quire (Books for Young People)* Dec 1987; Vol 53 No 12: p10.

MYTHS AND LEGENDS IN CANADIAN LITERATURE
See also BIBLICAL MYTHS AND MYTHOLOGY

Miracle, mystery, and authority: rereading The Double Hook; article. Glen Deer. *Open Letter* Summer 1987; Vol 6 No 8: p25–43.
[THE FAMILY IN CANADIAN LITERATURE]

Telling it over again: Atwood's art of parody; article. Barbara Godard. *Can Poet* Fall-Winter 1987; No 21: p1–30.
[FEMINIST WRITING AND CRITICISM; STRUCTURALIST WRITING AND CRITICISM]

La forêt dans le roman "ontarois"; article. Yolande Grisé. abstract · *Études can* 1987; No 23: p109–122.
[NATURE IN CANADIAN LITERATURE]

Psychic violence: The Stone Angel and modern family life; article. Ed Jewinski. *New Q* Spring-Summer 1987; Vol 7 No 1–2: p255–266.
[THE FAMILY IN CANADIAN LITERATURE; WOMEN IN LITERATURE]

The spider and the rose: Aritha van Herk's No Fixed Address; article. Dorothy Jones. *World Lit in Eng* Spring 1987; Vol 27 No 1: p39–56.
[FEMINIST WRITING AND CRITICISM; WOMEN IN LITERATURE]

Trieste and George Bowering's Burning Water; article. Eva-Marie Kröler. *Open Letter* Summer 1987; Vol 6 No 8: p44–54.

Rummaging in the sewing basket of the gods: Sheila Watson's "Antigone"; article. Judith Miller. *Studies in Can Lit* 1987; Vol 12 No 2: p212–221.

Beauchemin's The Alley Cat as modern myth; article. Constantina Mitchell. *Amer R of Can Studies* Winter 1987–88; Vol 17 No 4: p409–418.
[POLITICAL WRITING]

The trickster theatre of Tomson Highway; article. Daniel David Moses. biog · *Can Fic Mag (special issue)* 1987; No 60: p83–88.

Food and power: Homer, Carroll, Atwood and others; article. Mervyn Nicholson. *Mosaic* Summer 1987; Vol 20 No 3: p37–55.

The re/membering of the female power in Lady Oracle; article. Roberta Sciff-Zamaro. *Can Lit* Spring 1987; No 112: p32–38.
[FEMINIST WRITING AND CRITICISM]

Image and mood: recent poems by Michael Bullock; article. Jack F. Stewart. *Can Lit* Winter 1987; No 115: p107–121.
[SURREALISM]

N'EÛT ÉTÉ CET ÉTÉ NU/Novel by Raymonde Lamothe

La vitrine du livre; reviews of *Retour II: journal d'émotions* and *N'eût été cet été nu*. Guy Ferland. *MD* July 11, 1987: pC6.

Les fruits de mon imagination; letter to the editor. Raymonde Lamothe. *MD* Aug 19, 1987: p8.

Nudisme et fiction; letter to the editor. Michel Vaïs. *MD* Aug 13, 1987: p8.

NADINE/Novel by Matt Cohen

New in paper; reviews of novels. *TS* Aug 30, 1987: pA18.
[FIRST NOVELS: BOOK REVIEWS]

Zig-zag management; reviews of *Nadine* and *A Hero Travels Light*. Anthony S. Brennan. *Fiddlehead* Winter 1987; No 154: p91–95.

[Untitled]; review of *Nadine*. Karen Rile. *NYT Book R* Aug 9, 1987: p20.

Recent Canadian fiction; reviews of novels. D.O. Spettigue. *Queen's Q* Summer 1987; Vol 94 No 2: p366–375.
[FIRST NOVELS: BOOK REVIEWS]

The sweet taste of digression; review of *Nadine*. George Woodcock. *Event* March 1987; Vol 16 No 1: p95–97.

A NAME FOR HIMSELF: A BIOGRAPHY OF THOMAS HEAD RADDALL/Biography by Joyce Barkhouse

Thomas H. Raddall, a decade later; reviews of *The Dreamers* and *A Name for Himself*. Andrew Seaman. *Atlan Prov Book R* Feb-March 1987; Vol 14 No 1: p19.

NAMES OF GOD/Poems by Tim Lilburn

[Untitled]; review of *Names of God*. Margaret Avison. *Books in Can* May 1987; Vol 16 No 4: p23

Magnificent voice of the poetic mad; review of *Names of God*. Maggie Helwig. *TS* April 11, 1987: M4.

The celebrations of Tim Lilburn; review of *Names of God*. Jane Urquhart. *Brick* Fall 1987; No 31: p39–40.

NAMJOSHI, SUNITI

Male myths, obliterated lesbians and powerful dreams; reviews of poetry books. Fraser Sutherland. photo · *G&M* Feb 14, 1987: pE19.

NANOGAK, AGNES

[Untitled]; review of *More Tales from the Igloo*. *Queen's Q* Winter 1987; Vol 94 No 4: p1073.

Native heritage is displayed in three timely books; reviews of children's books. Janice Kennedy. *MG* April 4, 1987: H11.

NAOMI'S ROAD/Children's novel by Joy Kogawa

Other cultures featured in tales for youths; reviews of *The Unmasking of 'Ksan* and *Naomi's Road*. Kate Zimmerman. *CH* July 19, 1987: pE4.

NARDOCCHIO, ELAINE F.

[Untitled]; review of *Theatre and Politics in Modern Quebec*. Denis Carrier. *Theatre Hist in Can* Fall 1987; Vol 8 No 2: p243–245.

[Untitled]; reviews of *Theatre and Politics in Modern Quebec* and *French-Canadian Theater*. L.E. Doucette. *U of Toronto Q* Fall 1987; Vol 57 No 1: p186–189.

[Untitled]; review of *Theatre and Politics in Modern Quebec*. Debra Martens. *Rubicon* Fall 1987; No 9: p177–179.

Drama summary; review of *Theatre and Politics in Modern Québec*. Jane Moss. *Can Lit* Winter 1987; No 115: p175–176.

[Untitled]; review of *Theatre and Politics in Modern Quebec*. Renate Usmiani. *Can Theatre R* Spring 1987; No 50: p84–85.

Vue lointaine d'un Québec pas si moderne; review of *Theatre and Politics in Modern Québec*. Louise Vigeant. *Jeu* 1987; No 45: p222–223.

[Untitled]; review of *Theatre and Politics in Modern Quebec*. Jonathan M. Weiss. *Amer R of Can Studies* Autumn 1987; Vol 17 No 3: p358–359.

A NARROW VISION: DUNCAN CAMPBELL SCOTT AND THE ADMINISTRATION OF INDIAN AFFAIRS IN CANADA/Historical work by E. Brian Titley

Scott and Indian Affairs; review of *A Narrow Vision*. Stan Dragland. *Can Poet* Fall-Winter 1987; No 21: p103–109.

Duncan Campbell Scott: a poet who put down Indians; review of *A Narrow Vision*. John Goddard. photo · *MG* Aug 1, 1987: J7.

The poet who ran Indian Affairs; review of *A Narrow Vision*. Allan Levine. photo · *G&M* Feb 28, 1987: pE17.

NASH, ROGER

[Untitled]; reviews of *Psalms from the Suburbs* and *Sympathetic Magic*. Doug Watling. *Poetry Can R* Spring 1987; Vol 8 No 2–3: p51.

NASRALLAH, EMILY

[Untitled]; reviews of *Flight Against Time* and *The Late Great Human Road Show*. Judith Carson. *Can Forum* Aug-Sept 1987; Vol 67 No 771: p48–49.
[FIRST NOVELS: BOOK REVIEWS]

Emily Nasrallah's first novel; review of *Flight Against Time*. Laura Groening. *Atlan Prov Book R* May-June 1987; Vol 14 No 2: p9.
[FIRST NOVELS: BOOK REVIEWS]

[Untitled]; review of *Flight Against Time*. Michele Melady. *Books in Can* May 1987; Vol 16 No 4: p21.

NATIONAL THEATRE SCHOOL COLLECTIVE

NTS's Dog Day a hazard in more ways than one; theatre review. Pat Donnelly. *MG* Dec 19, 1987: pE6.

NATIVE CANADIANS IN LITERATURE

"O brave new world": colonialism in Hunter Duvar's De Roberval; article. Mark Blagrave. *Can Drama* 1987; Vol 13 No 2: p175–181.
[COLONIALISM]

Canadian (tw)ink: surviving the white-outs; article. Gary Boire. *Essays on Can Writ* Winter 1987; No 35: p1–16.
[COLONIALISM; HISTORICAL THEMES; MODERNIST WRITING AND CRITICISM]

La forêt dans l'oeuvre littéraire et picturale d'Emily Carr; article. Jean-Marcel Duciaume. abstract biog · *Études can* 1987; No 23: p135–145.
[NATURE IN CANADIAN LITERATURE]

Une oeuvre multiforme: les livres d'Yves Thériault pour adolescents; article. Claude Romney. bibliog · *Can Child Lit* 1987; No 47: p12–22.

The Indian in contemporary North American drama; article. Péter Szaffkó. *Can Drama* 1987; Vol 13 No 2: p182–186.

L'Indien imaginaire: de Buffalo Bill à la "sagamité"; article. Clément Trudel. photo · *MD* Aug 29, 1987: pC13.

THE NATIVE IN LITERATURE/Critical essays

[Untitled]; review of *The Native in Literature*. Sandy Greer. *Quill & Quire* June 1987; Vol 53 No 6: p35.

NATIVE-CANADIAN WRITING AND WRITERS

Indian culture dying fast; article. Phil Johnson. photo · *TS (Neighbors)* Oct 13, 1987: p16.

Introduction: an anthology of Canadian Native fiction; editorial article. Thomas King. *Can Fic Mag (special issue)* 1987; No 60: p4–10.

Three cultures, one issue; essay. Jan Selman. photo · *Can Theatre R* Winter 1987; No 53: p11–19.

Legends on the stage; article. Drew Taylor. photo · *Maclean's* Oct 19, 1987; Vol 100 No 42: p69.

THE NATURAL HISTORY OF WATER: A CLOSE READING/Poems by David Donnell

[Untitled]; review of *The Natural History of Water*. Gerald Hill. *Poetry Can R* Spring 1987; Vol 8 No 2–3: p45.

A design-conscious guy; reviews of *Settlements* and *The Natural History of Water*. Jan Horner. *CV 2* Spring 1987; Vol 10 No 3: p61–66.

[Untitled]; reviews of poetry books. Tom Marshall. *Cross Can Writ Q* 1987; Vol 9 No 1: p24–25.

NATURE IN CANADIAN LITERATURE

La forêt dans l'oeuvre de Louis Caron: une puissance libératrice; article. Georges L. Bérubé. abstract · *Études can* 1987; No 23: p123–133.
[HISTORICAL THEMES]

Snow as reality and trope in Canadian literature; article. Rosalie Murphy Baum. *Amer R of Can Studies* Autumn 1987; Vol 17 No 3: p323–333.

La forêt dans l'oeuvre littéraire et picturale d'Emily Carr; article. Jean-Marcel Duciaume. abstract biog · *Études can* 1987; No 23: p135–145.
[NATIVE CANADIANS IN LITERATURE]

La forêt dans le roman "ontarois"; article. Yolande Grisé. abstract · *Études can* 1987; No 23: p109–122.
[MYTHS AND LEGENDS IN CANADIAN LITERATURE]

La forêt dans l'oeuvre imaginaire de Marie-Claire Blais; article. Irène Oore. abstract · *Études can* 1987; No 23: p93–108.

La forêt chez les écrivains anglophones; article. Danièle Pitavy. abstract · *Études can* 1987; No 23: p147–157.
[BRITISH COLUMBIA WRITING AND WRITERS; CANADIAN IMAGINATION; COLONIAL LITERATURE]

The forest and the trees; article. Rosemary Sullivan. *Brick* Winter 1987; No 29: p43–46.
[CANADIAN LANDSCAPE; NATURE IN CANADIAN LITERATURE]

The dark pines of the mind: the symbol of the forest in Canadian literature; article. Rosemary Sullivan. abstract · *Études can* 1987; No 23: p173–182.
[NATURE IN CANADIAN LITERATURE; WILDERNESS WRITING]

NE BLÂMEZ JAMAIS LES BEDOUINS/DON'T BLAME THE BEDOUINS/Play by René-Daniel Dubois

Dubois' Bedouins run riot through prairie theatre; theatre review of *Don't Blame the Bedouins*. Stephen Godfrey. photo · *G&M* Dec 3, 1987: pA25.

Bedouins voluminous toy chest filled with witty, wordy delight; theatre review of *Don't Blame the Bedouins*. Randal McIlroy. *WFP* Nov 13, 1987: p35.

NEALE, WILLIAM SCOTT

[Untitled]; reviews of poetry books. James McElroy. *Poetry Can R* Fall 1987; Vol 9 No 1: p36.

NECESSARY SECRETS/Journals by Elizabeth Smart

Elizabeth Smart's journals: dress rehearsal for a novel; review of *Necessary Secrets*. Brent Ledger. photo · *Quill & Quire* Feb 1987; Vol 53 No 2: p16.

Elizabeth Smart: love left her battered, but not wrecked; review of *Necessary Secrets*. Marion McCormick. photo · *MG* Jan 10, 1987: pB8.

Fool for love; review of *Necessary Secrets*. Audrey Thomas. photo · *Books in Can* April 1987; Vol 16 No 3: p17–18.

[Untitled]; review of *Necessary Secrets*. Iris Winston. *CH* May 31, 1987: pF5.

NED 'N' ME/Short stories by Mike Murphy

The company he keeps; review of *Ned 'n' Me*. Peter Gard. *Atlan Prov Book R* Sept-Oct 1987; Vol 14 No 3: p13.

THE NEED OF WANTING ALWAYS/Novel by Gertrude Story

Red crayon; review of *The Need of Wanting Always*. Anne Hicks. *Can Lit* Spring 1987; No 112: p91–92.

Charting discoveries; review of *The Need of Wanting Always*. Daniel Lenoski. photo · *NeWest R* Nov 1987; Vol 13 No 3: p13,17.

[Untitled]; reviews of *The Need of Wanting Always* and *The Paris-Napoli Express*. S.A. Newman. *Cross Can Writ Q* 1987; Vol 9 No 1: p20.

NEEDLES, DAN

Acting sparkles in insulting play; theatre review of *Letter from Wingfield Farm*. Randal McIlroy. *WFP* Nov 26, 1987: p79.

Just good fun; letter to the editor. Heather Mousseau. *WFP* Dec 6, 1987: p6.

Comedy hits Canadian vein; article. Brad Oswald. photo · *WFP* Nov 25, 1987: p43.

NEIGE NOIRE/Novel by Hubert Aquin

Woman as object, women as subjects, & the consequences for narrative: Hubert Aquin's Neige noire and the impasse of post-modernism; article. Patricia Smart. *Can Lit* Summer-Fall 1987; No 113–114: p168–178.
[FEMINIST WRITING AND CRITICISM; POSTMODERNIST WRITING AND CRITICISM]

NELLIGAN 1879–1941: BIOGRAPHIE/Biography by Paul Wyczynski

Le Nelligan de Wyczynski: un si beau cadeau; review. Jean Éthier-Blais. photo · *MD* Dec 24, 1987: pC13.

Paul Wyczynski signe une "somme nelliganienne"; review of *Nelligan*. Marie Laurier. photo · *MD* Nov 28, 1987: pD11.

NELLIGAN N'ÉTAIT PAS FOU!/Critical work by Bernard Courteau

Nelligan n'était pas fou, il acceptait seulement de passer pour ce fou qui s'appelait Nelligan; review of *Nelligan n'était pas fou!*. Réjean Robidoux. *Lettres québec* Winter 1986–87; No 44: p74–76.

NELLIGAN, ÉMILE EDWIN

Le Nelligan de Wyczynski: un si beau cadeau; review. Jean Éthier-Blais. photo · *MD* Dec 24, 1987: pC13.

Paul Wyczynski signe une "somme nelliganienne"; review of *Nelligan*. Marie Laurier. photo · *MD* Nov 28, 1987: pD11.

La vie littéraire; column. Jean Royer. photo · *MD* March 28, 1987: pD2.
[CONFERENCES, LITERARY; FESTIVALS, LITERARY; GOVERNMENT GRANTS FOR WRITERS/PUBLISHERS; RADIO AND CANADIAN LITERATURE; TELEVISION AND CANADIAN LITERATURE]

NELSON, AUDREY

[Untitled]; review of *The Wart on My Finger*. Susan Perren. *Quill & Quire (Books for Young People)* June 1987; Vol 53 No 6: p11.

NEPVEU, PIERRE

De la poésie la prose; review of *L'Hiver de Mira Christophe*. Noël Audet. photo · *Lettres québec* Winter 1986–87; No 44: p26–28.
[FIRST NOVELS: BOOK REVIEWS]

La ville toute verte, bordée de montagnes enneigées; review of *L'Hiver de Mira Christophe*. Réjean Beaudoin. *Liberté* April 1987; Vol 29 No 2: p118–124.
[FIRST NOVELS: BOOK REVIEWS]

[Untitled]; review article about *L'Hiver de Mira Christophe*. Robert Berrouët-Oriol. *Moebius* Winter 1987; No 31: p143–148.

Éclats d'existence; review of *L'Hiver de Mira Christophe*. Lucie Côté. *MD* April 28, 1987: p17.
[FIRST NOVELS: BOOK REVIEWS]

De Bellefeuille, Nepveu, Lemaire, Royer; reviews of poetry books. Jean-Pierre Issenhuth. *Liberté* Aug 1987; Vol 29 No 4: p78–87.

Couples; reviews of novels. Jacques Michon. *Voix et images* Autumn 1987; Vol 13 No 1: p189–192.

Le roman sans qualités; review of *L'Hiver de Mira Christophe*. Yvon Rivard. *Liberté* June 1987; Vol 29 No 3: p103.
[FIRST NOVELS: BOOK REVIEWS]

NESBITT, ROB

Oakville poet, 21, carves career out of experiences on the road; article. Mike Beggs. photo · *TS (Neighbors)* Aug 4, 1987: p13.

A NEST OF SINGING BIRDS/Novel by Susan Charlotte Haley

Toronto firm dramatizes U.S. tales; column. Sid Adilman. *TS* Jan 7, 1987: pF1.
[TELEVISION AND CANADIAN LITERATURE]

First novel turned into TV movie; column. Kenneth McGoogan. *CH* May 3, 1987: pE6.
[CONFERENCES, LITERARY; TELEVISION AND CANADIAN LITERATURE]

[Untitled]; reviews of *The Cutting Season* and *A Nest of Singing Birds*. John A. Urquhart. *Prairie J of Can Lit* 1987; No 8: p50–54.
[FIRST NOVELS: BOOK REVIEWS]

THE NEW ANCESTORS/Novel by Dave Godfrey

The I and the eye in the desert: the political and philosophical key to Dave Godfrey's The New Ancestors; article. A.C. Morrell. *Studies in Can Lit* 1987; Vol 12 No 2: p264–272.

NEW WORKS I/Play anthology

[Untitled]; review of *New Works I*. Lynne van Luven. *Can Theatre R* Winter 1987; No 53: p81–82.
[ANTHOLOGIES: BOOK REVIEWS]

NEW, W.H.

[Untitled]; review of *Dreams of Speech and Violence*. James Acheson. *Amer R of Can Studies* Autumn 1987; Vol 17 No 3: p352–353.

[Untitled]; review of *Dreams of Speech and Violence*. Keith Garebian. *Quill & Quire* June 1987; Vol 53 No 6: p35.

[Untitled]; review of *Dreams of Speech and Violence*. Patricia Morley. *Books in Can* Aug-Sept 1987; Vol 16 No 6: p25.

NEWEST PLAYS BY WOMEN/Anthology

[Untitled]; reviews. Lisbie Rae. *Can Drama* 1987; Vol 13 No 2: p229–231.
[ANTHOLOGIES: BOOK REVIEWS]

NEWLOVE, JOHN

[Untitled]; reviews of poetry books. Anne Archer. *Queen's Q* Winter 1987; Vol 94 No 4: p1042–1043.

[Untitled]; review of *The Night the Dog Smiled*. David Manicom. *Rubicon* Fall 1987; No 9: p199–200.

[Untitled]; review of *The Night the Dog Smiled*. Stephen Morrissey. *Poetry Can R* Spring 1987; Vol 8 No 2–3: p36.

[Untitled]; review of *The Night the Dog Smiled*. Andrew Wreggitt. *Event* March 1987; Vol 16 No 1: p107–108.

THE NEXT BEST THING/Novel by John Ralston Saul

Tune in, turn on, drop out: truckin' back to the '60s with Esquire; reviews of *Lime Street at Two* and *The Next Best Thing*. Barbara Black. *MG* July 4, 1987: J9.

Danger! A trained assassin at work; review of *The Next Best Thing*. Geoff Chapman. *TS* June 14, 1987: pA18

NI LE LIEU NI L'HEURE/Short stories by Gilles Pellerin

Ici, maintenant et autrement; review of *Ni le lieu ni l'heure*. Réjean Beaudoin. *Liberté* Aug 1987; Vol 29 No 4: p125–126.

La vitrine du livre; reviews. Jean Royer. *MD* March 14, 1987: pD4.
[CANADIAN LITERARY PERIODICALS]

Les vertus de la retenue et du silence; reviews of poetry books. Marie José Thériault. photo · *Lettres québec* Summer 1987; No 46: p30–32.

NICHAN/Novel by Christian Beaulieu

Un jeune couple de Québécois en quête du "ginseng de l'âme"; review of *Nichan*. Jean-Roch Boivin. photo · *MD* Sept 12, 1987: pD2.
[FIRST NOVELS: BOOK REVIEWS]

NICHOL, bp

Directional devices; review of *Once: A Lullaby*. Jan Dalley. *Times Lit Supp* April 3, 1987; No 4383: p356.

[Untitled]; reviews of *Canada Gees Mate for Life* and *Zygal*. Phil Hall. *Poetry Can R* Fall 1987; Vol 9 No 1: p34.

Words move unrestrained and with joy across pages; review of *The Martyrology* (Book Six). Lesley McAllister. *TS* June 20, 1987: M4.

Ontario report: a rite to remember; regional column. Steven Smith. *Poetry Can R* Spring 1987; Vol 8 No 2–3: p24.
[POETRY READINGS]

NICHOL, JAMES W.

Murder mystery hatched in eerie isolated farmhouse; article. Brian Brennan. *CH* March 13, 1987: pC1.

Hackneyed pot-boiler contains few surprises; theatre review of *And When I Wake*. Brian Brennan. photo · *CH* March 15, 1987: pE2.

TC performance gave entertainment; letter to the editor. D.A. Brink. *CH* April 7, 1987: pA6.

NICOLE'S BOAT: A GOOD-NIGHT/Children's story by Allen Morgan

Paperbacks offer good value; review of *Nicole's Boat*. Helen Norrie. *WFP* May 23, 1987: p74.

LE NIGHT CAP BAR/Play by Marie Laberge

Le Night Cap Bar a minor thriller that tries to be more; theatre review. Marianne Ackerman. *MG* April 9, 1987: pE8.

Le théâtre qu'on joue; theatre reviews. André Dionne. photo · *Lettres québec* Summer 1987; No 46: p47–48.

La vitrine du livre; reviews. Guy Ferland. *MD* May 30, 1987: pD4.

Je serai Robert Thomas ou rien . . . ; theatre review of *Le Night Cap Bar*. Robert Lévesque. photo · *MD* April 9, 1987: p13.

Suspense au fond du gouffre; theatre review of *Le Night Cap Bar*. Michel Vaïs. photo · *Jeu* 1987; No 44: p175–177.

NIGHT DRIVING/Short stories by Peter Behrens

[Untitled]; review of *Night Driving*. *Quill & Quire* March 1987; Vol 53 No 3: p71–72.

Life slices; review of *Night Driving*. Laszlo Buhasz. *G&M* June 6, 1987: pC19.

These 'night drivers' travel stark roads that enjoy neither beginning nor an end; review of *Night Driving*. Michael Carin. photo · *MG* April 25, 1987: H12.

Interesting stories reach into dark depths; review of *Night Driving*. Mark Jarman. *CH* May 31, 1987: pF5.

With used scars on their sleeves; review of *Night Driving*. Tom Spears. *TS* April 11, 1987: M8.

Tough, taut short stories; review of *Night Driving*. Morley Walker. *WFP* May 2, 1987: p84.

Travelling light; review of *Night Driving*. Allan Weiss. *Books in Can* April 1987; Vol 16 No 3: p36–37.

NIGHT LIGHT: STORIES OF AGING/Short story anthology

Age and the masters of short fiction; review of *Night Light*. Pauline Carey. *G&M* Jan 10, 1987: pE14.
[ANTHOLOGIES: BOOK REVIEWS]

[Untitled]; review of *Night Light*. Barbara Carey. *Quill & Quire* Jan 1987; Vol 53 No 1: p26–27.
[ANTHOLOGIES: BOOK REVIEWS]

NIGHT STUDIES/Novel by Constance Beresford-Howe

From mind to mind; reviews of *Night Studies* and *Wishbones*. H.W. Connor. *Can Lit* Spring 1987; No 112: p118–120.
[FIRST NOVELS: BOOK REVIEWS]

THE NIGHT THE DOG SMILED/Poems by John Newlove

[Untitled]; reviews of poetry books. Anne Archer. *Queen's Q* Winter 1987; Vol 94 No 4: p1042–1043.

[Untitled]; review of *The Night the Dog Smiled*. David Manicom. *Rubicon* Fall 1987; No 9: p199–200.

[Untitled]; review of *The Night the Dog Smiled*. Stephen Morrissey. *Poetry Can R* Spring 1987; Vol 8 No 2–3: p36.

[Untitled]; review of *The Night the Dog Smiled*. Andrew Wreggitt. *Event* March 1987; Vol 16 No 1: p107–108.

THE NIGHT THE GODS SMILED/Novel by Eric Wright

Publishers meet the demand with reissued crime classics; reviews of *The Night the Gods Smiled* and *One-Eyed Merchants*. Douglas Hill. *G&M* Feb 28, 1987: pE19.
[FIRST NOVELS: BOOK REVIEWS]

NIGHT TRAVELLERS/Short stories by Sandra Birdsell

The Lafreniere family of Agassiz; reviews of *Night Travellers* and *Ladies of the House*. J.K. Johnstone. illus · *NeWest R* April 1987; Vol 12 No 8: p12.

THE NIGHT WORKERS OF RAGNARÖK/Poems by Kristjana Gunnars

[Untitled]; review of *The Night Workers of Ragnarök*. Paul Faulkner. *Quarry* Spring 1987; Vol 36 No 2: p116–117.

THE NIGHTMARE ALPHABET/Poems by Sean O Huigin

Ballads and ditties for grown-ups; reviews of poetry books. Fraser Sutherland. illus · *G&M* Nov 7, 1987: pC21.

NIGHTWOOD THEATRE COLLECTIVE

The humor saves Lolita, but it's strained; theatre review of *The Last Will and Testament of Lolita*. Christopher Hume. *TS* June 5, 1987: pE19.

Lolita grows up to get last laughs; article. Henry Mietkiewicz. *TS* May 29, 1987: pE13.

NIGHTY-KNIGHT/Poems by Mona Elaine Adilman

Small press reviews; reviews of poetry books. Shaunt Basmajian. *Cross Can Writ Q* 1987; Vol 9 No 1: p25.

[Untitled]; reviews of poetry books. Anne Cimon. *Poetry Can R* Spring 1987; Vol 8 No 2–3: p62.

NIHMEY, JOHN

Book world: when a publicist needs a lawyer . . . ; column. Beverley Slopen. *TS* Nov 15, 1987: pA22.

Relations & families; review of *Time of Their Lives*. George Woodcock. *Can Lit* Summer-Fall 1987; No 113–114: p235–239.

THE NINE DAYS QUEEN/Young adult novel by Karleen Bradford

History comes alive; review of *The Nine Days Queen*. Marjory Body. *Can Child Lit* 1987; No 48: p85–86.

NINE MEN WHO LAUGHED/Short stories by Austin Clarke

[Untitled]; review of *Nine Men Who Laughed*. Valerie Wilson Wesley. *NYT Book R* Aug 23, 1987: p16–17.

NO' XYA'/Play by David Diamond

Aboriginal issue takes centre stage; theatre review of *No' Xya'*. Stephen Godfrey. photo · *G&M* Nov 7, 1987: pC3.

Three new political plays; theatre reviews. Malcolm Page. *Can Drama* 1987; Vol 13 No 2: p224–226.

NO CONTINGENCIES/Poems by Ayanna Black

Each to her own rhythm; reviews of poetry books. Lesley McAllister. *TS* July 25, 1987: M5.

NO CYCLE/Play cycle by Harry Standjofski

No Cycle is a deeply searching celebration of life in the 1980s; theatre review. Pat Donnelly. photo · *MG* Dec 12, 1987: pD20.

NO FIXED ADDRESS: AN AMOROUS JOURNEY/Novel by Aritha van Herk

[Untitled]; reviews of fictional works. Beverley Daurio. *Cross Can Writ Q* 1987; Vol 9 No 1: p18–19.

Songs of innocence and experience — the hometown in us all; reviews of *Headframe* and *No Fixed Address*. Scott Jeffrey. *NeWest R* Summer 1987; Vol 12 No 10: p13.

The spider and the rose: Aritha van Herk's No Fixed Address; article. Dorothy Jones. *World Lit in Eng* Spring 1987; Vol 27 No 1: p39–56.
[FEMINIST WRITING AND CRITICISM; MYTHS AND LEGENDS IN CANADIAN LITERATURE; WOMEN IN LITERATURE]

Circle games; reviews of fictional works. Barbara Leckie. *Can Lit* Winter 1987; No 115: p278–280.

Arachne's progress; review of *No Fixed Address*. Stephen Scobie. *Brick* Winter 1987; No 29: p37–40.

NO FIXED ADMISSION/Novel by Jacqui Smyth

Putrefying sore; reviews of fictional works. Kathryn Chittick. *Can Lit* Spring 1987; No 112: p128–129.

More saturated with colour; review of *No Fixed Admission*. Peter Slade. *NeWest R* Feb 1987; Vol 12 No 6: p18.

NO HOLDS BARRED/Novel by Spencer Dunmore

I say, a hero too prim, too precious, eh wot?; review of *No Holds Barred*. Geoff Chapman. *TS* May 9, 1987: M4.

A corporate romp in Adland, N.Y.; review of *No Holds Barred*. William French. *G&M* March 14, 1987: pE19.

NO LIES AND OTHER STORIES/Short stories by Ken J. Harvey

Ken Harvey's very short stories; review of *No Lies*. Sheldon Currie. *Atlan Prov Book R* Feb-March 1987; Vol 14 No 1: p16.

NO LONGER NORTH/Poems by John Flood

Common language in private words; reviews of poetry books. Maggie Helwig. *TS* Aug 8, 1987: M10.

The pastoral myth and its observers; reviews of poetry books. Fraser Sutherland. *G&M* Sept 26, 1987: pC23.

NO ONE WE KNOW/Poems by Rhea Tregebov

The mutability of memory: Rhea Tregebov's No One We Know; review. Barbara Carey. *Quarry* Summer 1987; Vol 36 No 3: p70–75.

Each to her own rhythm; reviews of poetry books. Lesley McAllister. *TS* July 25, 1987: M5.

[Untitled]; reviews of poetry books. Martin Singleton. *Cross Can Writ Q* 1987; Vol 9 No 3–4: p38–39.

NOBLE, CHARLES

Quilted patch; reviews of poetry books. Uma Parameswaran. Teresa Mallam. *Can Lit* Spring 1987; No 112: p176–179.

Witty plenitude; review of *Afternoon Starlight*. Douglas Reimer. *Prairie Fire* Spring 1987; Vol 8 No 1: p91–93.

NOBODY ASKED ME/Young adult novel by Elizabeth Brochmann

Romance and rebellion in young adult fiction; reviews of *Nobody Asked Me* and *Storm Child*. Sarah Ellis. *Can Child Lit* 1987; No 46: p87–89.

NOBODY SAID IT WOULD BE EASY/Young adult novel by Marilyn Halvorson

[Untitled]; review of *Nobody Said It Would Be Easy*. Joan McGrath. *Quill & Quire (Books for Young People)* April 1987; Vol 53 No 4: p10.

Beatrix Potter better than ever; reviews of *Nobody Said It Would Be Easy* and *Log Jam*. Joan McGrath. *TS* April 25, 1987: M4.

Authors ease teen angst in the wilds of Alberta; reviews of young adult novels. Susan Scott. photo · *CH* April 23, 1987: pD1.

Roughing it in the bush; reviews of children's books. Mary Ainslie Smith. *Books in Can* Aug-Sept 1987; Vol 16 No 6: p34–36.

Calls to the wild; reviews of young adult novels. Tim Wynne-Jones. *G&M* May 2, 1987: pC19.

NOCES OBSCURES/Novel by Pierre Vallieres

Le salut de Pierre Vallières; review of *Noces obscures*. Réjean Beaudoin. *Liberté* April 1987; Vol 29 No 2: p139–140.
[FIRST NOVELS: BOOK REVIEWS]

Un roman de jeunesse de Pierre Vallières; review of *Noces obscures*. Jacques Michon. *MD* May 16, 1987: pD3,D8.

NOCHER, FRANÇOIS

Talky treatment for Chekhov's life; theatre review of *Tchekhov Tchekova*. Pat Donnelly. photo · *MG* Jan 24, 1987: pC8.

Bouleversante Patricia Nolin; theatre review of *Tchekhov Tchekhova*. Robert Lévesque. photo · *MD* Jan 29, 1987: p5.

[Untitled]; theatre review of *Tchekhov Tchekhova*. Robert Lévesque. *MD* Jan 30, 1987: p7.

[Untitled]; theatre review of *Tchekhov Tchekhova*. Robert Lévesque. *MD* Feb 6, 1987: p7.

[Untitled]; theatre review of *Tchekhov Tchekhova*. Stéphane Lépine. photo · *Jeu* 1987; No 42: p161–164.

NOËL, FRANCINE

Pour l'amour des grand-mères, des petites filles et des petits garçons, de l'art, de Montréal et pour l'amour tout court; review of *Myriam première*. Jean-Roch Boivin. photo · *MD* Dec 12, 1987: pD3.
[FIRST NOVELS: BOOK REVIEWS]

Paradigme, palimpseste, pastiche, parodie dans Maryse de Francine Noël; article. Anne Élaine Cliche. *Voix et images* Spring 1987; Vol 12 No 3: p430–438.
[STRUCTURALIST WRITING AND CRITICISM]

La vitrine du livre; reviews. Guy Ferland. *MD* March 7, 1987: pB2.
[CANADIAN LITERARY PERIODICALS]

Le deuxième roman de Francine Noël; article. Marie Laurier. photo · *MD* Nov 18, 1987: p11.

NOEL COWARD: A PORTRAIT/Play by Peter Pringle

Geminis are sad reminder of TV's glory days; column. Mike Boone. *MG* Dec 9, 1987: pF3.
[TELEVISION AND CANADIAN LITERATURE]

'Coward' classy but disappoints as theatre; theatre review of *Noel Coward: A Portrait*. Pat Donnelly. photo · *MG* Nov 26, 1987: H5.

[Untitled]; theatre reviews. Pat Donnelly. *MG* Nov 27, 1987: pC7.

[Untitled]; theatre reviews. Pat Donnelly. *MG* Dec 4, 1987: pC6.

To Sir Noel, with affection; theatre review of *Noel Coward: A Portrait*. Deirdre Kelly. photo · *G&M* July 3, 1987: pD9.

Sir Noël Pringle ou Sir Noël Coward?; theatre review of *Noel Coward: A Portrait*. Marc Morin. photo · *MD* Nov 26, 1987: p15.

NOMAN'S LAND/Novel by Gwendolyn MacEwen

[Untitled]; reviews of *Noman's Land* and *Queen of the Headaches*. Anne Cimon. *Cross Can Writ Q* 1987; Vol 9 No 1: p20–21.

Home rituals; review of *Noman's Land*. Sherrill Grace. *Can Lit* Spring 1987; No 112: p102–104.

LES NOMS DU PÈRE SUIVI DE LIEUX DITS: ITALIQUE/Poems by Paul Chanel Malenfant

[Untitled]; reviews of *Les Noms du père* and *Coq à deux têtes*. Jean Chapdelaine Gagnon. *Estuaire* Autumn 1987; No 46: p85–86.

NON, JE NE SUIS PAS N/Children's story by Rita Scalabrini

Un conte philosophique; review of *Non, je ne suis pas né*. Lynn Penrod. *Can Child Lit* 1987; No 45: p81–82.

LE NORD LECTRIQUE/Novel by Jean-Pierre April

Aaa! Aâh! Ha! que de belles catastrophes narratives!; reviews. Michel Lord. photo · *Lettres québec* Spring 1987; No 45: p32–35.

NORRIS, KEN

[Untitled]; review of *In the Spirit of the Times*. Rod Anderson. *Poetry Can R* Spring 1987; Vol 8 No 2–3: p43.

Montreal poets inspired by travel in hot countries; reviews of poetry books. Barbara Black. *MG* March 28, 1987: pE9

[Untitled]; review of *Islands*. Marc Côté. *Books in Can* Dec 1987; Vol 16 No 9: p31.

Between the sexes; reviews of poetry books. Mary di Michele. *Books in Can* March 1987; Vol 16 No 2: p31–32.

Tellings; reviews of poetry books. Susan Rudy Dorscht. *Can Lit* Winter 1987; No 115: p257–260.

[Untitled]; reviews of *In the Spirit of the Times* and *One Night*. Andrew Flynn. *Rubicon* Spring 1987; No 8: p202–205.

[Untitled]; reviews of critical works. Ronald B. Hatch. *Eng Studies in Can* March 1987; Vol 13 No 1: p107–115.

Landscapes & eyes; reviews of poetry books. Karl Jirgens. *Can Lit* Spring 1987; No 112: p192–193.

Three poets dare to reject labelling; reviews of poetry books. Patricia Smith. *TS* July 4, 1987: M4.

A plumber of bathetic depths; reviews of *Islands* and *The Collected Poems of George Whalley*. Fraser Sutherland. photo · *G&M* July 18, 1987: pC15.

THE NORTH BOOK/Poems by Jim Green

[Untitled]; reviews of *The Louis Riel Organ & Piano Co.* and *The North Book*. John F. Vardon. *Poetry Can R* Spring 1987; Vol 8 No 2–3: p47.

NORTH LIGHT/Poems by Jack Brooks

[Untitled]; reviews of poetry books. Anne Cimon. *Poetry Can R* Spring 1987; Vol 8 No 2–3: p62.

NORTH OF INTENTION/Critical essays by Steve McCaffery

[Untitled]; review of *North of Intention*. Keith Garebian. *Quill & Quire* July 1987; Vol 53 No 7: p66.

Semiotic song; review of *North of Intention*. Stephen Luxton. *Matrix* Fall 1987; No 25: p77–79.

High ideas from a split end; review of *North of Intention*. Paul Stuewe. *G&M* July 11, 1987: pC15.

Opaque criticism; letter to the editor. Sophie Thomas. *G&M* July 25, 1987: pD7.

[Untitled]; review of *North of Intention*. Bruce Whiteman. *Books in Can* Oct 1987; Vol 16 No 7: p21.

THE NORTH SHORE OF HOME/Poems and prose by Frank J. Ledwell

Frank Ledwell's colloquial ease; review of *The North Shore of Home*. Thomas B. O'Grady. *Atlan Prov Book R* Feb-March 1987; Vol 14 No 1: p17.

THE NORTHERN IMAGINATION: A STUDY OF NORTHERN CANADIAN LITERATURE/Critical work by Allison Mitcham

[Untitled]; review of *The Northern Imagination*. John Ferns. *British J of Can Studies* June 1987; Vol 2 No 1: p187–188.

NORTHERN POEMS: WHERE THE HEART CATCHES ITS BREATH/Poems by Robert Billings

[Untitled]; reviews of *The Revels* and *Northern Poems: Where the Heart Catches Its Breath*. Gary Draper. *Poetry Can R* Spring 1987; Vol 8 No 2–3: p37.

THE NORTHERN RED OAK: POEMS FOR AND ABOUT MILTON ACORN/Poetry anthology

[Untitled]; review of *The Northern Red Oak*. Bruce Whiteman. *Books in Can* Oct 1987; Vol 16 No 7: p26.
[ANTHOLOGIES: BOOK REVIEWS]

NORTHERN SPRING: THE FLOWERING OF CANADIAN LITERATURE/Critical essays by George Woodcock

A flowering spring and a simplistic guide; reviews of *Northern Spring* and *A Reader's Guide to the Canadian Novel* (second edition). Ken Adachi. photo · *TS* Aug 1, 1987: M4.

Mandel's two minds and Woodcock's single purpose; reviews of *The Family Romance* and *Northern Spring*. Doug Fetherling. photo · *Quill & Quire* May 1987; Vol 53 No 5: p20.

A wealth of provocative and inspiring literary criticism; reviews. Douglas Hill. *G&M* Sept 5, 1987: pC13.
[ANTHOLOGIES: BOOK REVIEWS]

NORTHROP FRYE: A VISION OF THE NEW WORLD/Critical work by David Cook

Landscape with politicians; review of *Northrop Frye: A Vision of the New World*. William T. Booth. *Essays on Can Writ* Winter 1987; No 35: p117–122.

[Untitled]; review of *Northrop Frye: A Vision of the New World*. Michael Hurley. *Queen's Q* Spring 1987; Vol 94 No 1: p219–222.

[Untitled]; review of *Northrop Frye: A Vision of the New World*. Mark Kingwell. *Rubicon* Spring 1987; No 8: p193–195.

[Untitled]; review of *Northrop Frye: A Vision of the New World*. Lauriat Lane, Jr. *Eng Studies in Can* Sept 1987; Vol 13 No 3: p349–352.

NORTHWARD JOURNAL/Periodical

Editor's notebook; editorial. John Flood. *Northward J* 1987; No 41: p2.
[CANADIAN LITERARY PERIODICALS]

NORWOOD, ROBERT

Religion, place, & self in early twentieth-century Canada: Robert Norwood's poetry; article. Alex Kizuk. *Can Lit* Winter 1987; No 115: p66–77.
[BIBLICAL MYTHS AND MYTHOLOGY; RELIGIOUS THEMES]

NOS AMIS, ROBOTS/Children's novel by Suzanne Martel

[Untitled]; review of *Nos amis, robots*. Chris Pattinson. *TS* Feb 8, 1987: pC8.

NOT ENOUGH WOMEN/Novel by Ken Ledbetter

[Untitled]; reviews. Janet Windeler. *Cross Can Writ Q* 1987; Vol 9 No 2: p25–26.
[FIRST NOVELS: BOOK REVIEWS]

NOT NOIR/Poems by Kate Van Dusen

TV's generation suffers detachment; reviews of *The Blue House* and *Not Noir*. Colline Caulder. *TS* Nov 28, 1987: M5.

[Untitled]; review of *Not Noir*. Stephen Scobie. *Malahat R* Dec 1987; No 81: p108.

NOT WANTED ON THE VOYAGE/Novel by Timothy Findley

Apocalyptic imaginations: notes on Atwood's The Handmaid's Tale and Findley's Not Wanted on the Voyage; article. W.J. Keith. *Essays on Can Writ* Winter 1987; No 35: p123–134.
[THE APOCALYPSE; BIBLICAL MYTHS AND MYTHOLOGY; GOD IN LITERATURE; SATIRIC WRITING]

LA NOTE DE PASSAGE/Novel by François Gravel

L'evasion et l'education; review of *La Note de passage*. Robert Viau. *Can Child Lit* 1987; No 48: p95–97.

NOTHING SO NATURAL/Novel by Jim Curry

Lost innocents; reviews of *Nothing So Natural* and *Flavian's Fortune*. Peter Hinchcliffe. *Can Lit* Spring 1987; No 112: p90–91.

NOTRE-DAME DU COLPORTAGE/Novel by Georges Cartier

Un polar polyphonique à la recherche du temps perdu; review of *Notre-Dame du colportage*. Jean-Roch Boivin. *MD* Dec 5, 1987: pD3.

NOUS PASSIONS/Poems by Marie Bélisle

[Untitled]; review of *Nous passions*. Antonio D'Alfonso. *Estuaire* Summer 1987; No 45: p49.

LE NOUVEL ÉLOÏZES/Periodical

La revue des revues; reviews of periodicals. Guy Ferland. *MD* Sept 19, 1987: pD6.
[CANADIAN LITERARY PERIODICALS]

LA NOUVELLE BARRE DU JOUR/Periodical

Le récit à la NBJ; review of *La Nouvelle barre du jour*. Caroline Bayard. *Lettres québec* Summer 1987; No 46: p34–35.

[Untitled]; review of *La Nouvelle barre du jour* (special issue). Ginette Castro. *Études can* June 1987; No 22: p131.
[CANADIAN LITERARY PERIODICALS]

Devenez mécène, abonnez-vous!; reviews of periodicals. Robert Melançon. *Liberté* June 1987; Vol 29 No 3: p80–87.
[CANADIAN LITERARY PERIODICALS]

La littérature est inactuelle; reviews of *La Nouvelle barre du jour* and *Le Beffroi*. Robert Melançon. *Liberté* Aug 1987; Vol 29 No 4: p102–108.

Le sentiment de la langue; reviews of *"Quand on a une langue on peut aller à Rome"* and *Les Changeurs de signes*. Jean Royer. *MD* Feb 28, 1987: pC3.
[CANADIAN LITERARY PERIODICALS]

La vie littéraire; column. Jean Royer. photo · *MD* Sept 26, 1987: pD2.
[AUDIO-VISUALS AND CANADIAN LITERATURE; CONFERENCES, LITERARY; INTERNATIONAL WRITERS' ORGANIZATIONS; PUBLISHING AND PUBLISHERS IN CANADA; WRITERS' ORGANIZATION]

NOUVELLES DE LA CAPITALE/Short stories by Daniel Poliquin

La vitrine du livre; reviews. Guy Ferland. *MD* Nov 21, 1987: pD4.

Ontarois entre deux langues; reviews of *Nouvelles de la capitale* and *L'Obomsawin*. Lori Saint-Martin. *MD* Dec 12, 1987: pD4.

NOUVELLES POUR LE THÉÂTRE/Plays by Marie Cardinal et al

Experimental theatre: only some works; theatre review of *Nouvelles pour le théâtre*. Marianne Ackerman. *MG* Feb 5, 1987: pE6.

NOYES, STEVE

[Untitled]; reviews of poetry books. Anne Archer. *Queen's Q* Winter 1987; Vol 94 No 4: p1042–1043.

[Untitled]; reviews of poetry books. Anne Burke. *Poetry Can R* Summer 1987; Vol 8 No 4: p38.

Tellings; reviews of poetry books. Susan Rudy Dorscht. *Can Lit* Winter 1987; No 115: p257–260.

[Untitled]; reviews of poetry books. Stephen Morrissey. *Poetry Can R* Spring 1987; Vol 8 No 2–3: p49.

First books from five regional presses; reviews of poetry books. Colin Morton. *Arc* Spring 1987; No 18: p52–59.

LA NUIT ÉMERAUDE/Poems by Guy Lafond

[Untitled]; review of *La Nuit émeraude*. Dana Mockevïciuté. *Moebius* Summer 1987; No 33: p139.

LA NUIT DES P'TITS COUTEAUX/Play by Suzanne Aubry

Masques, personnages et personnes; reviews of plays. André-G. Bourassa. photo · *Lettres québec* Summer 1987; No 46: p51–52.

Night of Little Knives aims its barbs at cults; theatre review of *La Nuit des p'tits couteaux*. Matthew Fraser. photo · *G&M* Jan 19, 1987: pC9.

Aubry play superb theatre; theatre review of *La Nuit des p'tits couteaux*. Wayne Grigsby. *MG* Jan 16, 1987: pD2.

NUMBERS/Play by Peter Spear

Polygons to cavort on stage; article. Kate Zimmerman. photo · *CH* Nov 26, 1987: pC1.

Musical's lyrics at odds with uncomplicated story; theatre review of *Numbers*. Kate Zimmerman. *CH* Nov 29, 1987: pE3.

NYBERG, MORGAN

Fiction just loaded with personality; reviews of children's novels. Tim Wynne-Jones. photo · *G&M* Nov 28, 1987: pC22.
[FIRST NOVELS: BOOK REVIEWS]

O'BRIEN, JACK

Author O'Brien plays to win; article. Susan Kastner. *TS* Oct 11, 1987: pD1.

O'FLAHERTY, PATRICK

Small regional presses as saviors of cultural information; reviews of fictional works. Douglas Hill. *G&M* Oct 10, 1987: pC21.
[FIRST NOVELS: BOOK REVIEWS]

O'GRADY, STANDISH

Preliminaries for a life of Standish O'Grady; biographical article. Brian Trehearne. *Can Poet* Fall-Winter 1987; No 21: p81–92.

O'HEARN, AUDREY

[Untitled]; review of *Me and Luke*. Patty Lawlor. *Quill & Quire (Books for Young People)* Oct 1987; Vol 53 No 10: p22.
[FIRST NOVELS: BOOK REVIEWS]

O'NEILL, CATHARINE

[Untitled]; review of *Mrs. Dunphy's Dog*. Susan Perren. *Quill & Quire (Books for Young People)* Aug 1987; Vol 53 No 8: p6–7.

[Untitled]; review of *Mrs. Dunphy's Dog*. Dana Watson. *CH* Dec 6, 1987: pD9.

O'SULLIVAN, DENNIS

Dennis O'Sullivan: la disjonction entre la vie et l'écran; article. Paul Lefebvre. photo · *Jeu* 1987; No 44: p142–143.

[Untitled]; theatre review of *Montréal, série noire*. Diane Pavlovic. photo · *Jeu* 1987; No 44: p139–141.

O'SULLIVAN, DONNA

[Untitled]; reviews of poetry books. Shaunt Basmajian. *Cross Can Writ Q* 1987; Vol 9 No 3–4: p44,49.
[ANTHOLOGIES: BOOK REVIEWS]

THE O CANADA POEMS/Poems by Mary Melfi

[Untitled]; reviews of poetry books. Anne Burke. *Poetry Can R* Summer 1987; Vol 8 No 4: p38.

O HUIGIN, SEAN

Ballads and ditties for grown-ups; reviews of poetry books. Fraser Sutherland. illus · *G&M* Nov 7, 1987: pC21.

OAB 1/Poems by Robert Zend

Zendmark; review of *Oab 1*. Karl Jirgens. *Can Lit* Summer-Fall 1987; No 113–114: p217–219.

OBASAN/Novel by Joy Kogawa

Speaking the silence: Joy Kogawa's Obasan; article. Gary Willis. *Studies in Can Lit* 1987; Vol 12 No 2: p239–250.

LES OBJETS PARLENT/Play by Jean-Pierre Ronfard

[Untitled]; theatre reviews of *La Tour* and *Les Objets parlent*. Solange Lévesque. photo · *Jeu* 1987; No 43: p145–147.

THE OCCUPATION OF HEATHER ROSE/Play by Wendy Lill

[Untitled]; reviews. Lisbie Rae. *Can Drama* 1987; Vol 13 No 2: p229–231.
[ANTHOLOGIES: BOOK REVIEWS]

ODD JOBS/Play by Frank Moher

Collective creativity — working Odd Jobs; article. Anne Nothof. photo · *Can Drama* 1987; Vol 13 No 1: p34–42.

[Untitled]; review of *Odd Jobs*. Linda M. Peake. *Books in Can* March 1987; Vol 16 No 2: p25–26.

[Untitled]; reviews of plays. Judith Rudakoff. *Can Theatre R* Summer 1987; No 51: p86–87.

LES OEUVRES DE CRÉATION ET LE FRANÇAIS AU QUÉBEC/Conference report

De se dire; review of *Les Oeuvres de création et le français au Québec*. Paul G. Socken. *Can Lit* Winter 1987; No 115: p164–165.
[CONFERENCE REPORTS: REVIEWS AND ARTICLES]

OFF EARTH/Poems by John Robert Colombo

Random musings of a middle-aged middle-class male; reviews of poetry books. Lesley McAllister. *TS* Oct 10, 1987: M4.

Ballads and ditties for grown-ups; reviews of poetry books. Fraser Sutherland. illus · *G&M* Nov 7, 1987: pC21.

OFF OFF OFF OU SUR LE TOIT DE PABLO NERUDA/Play by Alberto Kurapel

Les anges dans nos campagnes; article. Robert Lévesque. *MD* June 4, 1987: p13.
[FESTIVALS, DRAMA]

'Oiseau' feeds on violent love — 'Neruda' long 2-hour stretch; theatre reviews of *Un Oiseau vivant dans la gueule* and *Off Off Off*. Francine Pelletier. *MG* June 3, 1987: pB4.

OGLE, ROBERT J.

A priest taking life one day at a time; article. Michael McAteer. photo · *TS* May 23, 1987: M17

OHL, PAUL

Un roman historique remarquable: Katana; review. Yvon Bernier. photo · *Lettres québec* Summer 1987; No 46: p18–19.

Un roman d'érudition au souffle immense; review of *Katana*. Jean-Rock Boivin. photo · *MD* March 28, 1987: pD3.

Katana, épopée fascinante dont le héros est le Japon; article. Gil Courtemanche. photo · *MD* March 28, 1987: pD1,D8.

L'âme japonaise de Paul Ohl; article. Jean Royer. photo · *MD* March 5, 1987: p9.

OIKLE, DON

Meaningful nonsense; reviews of children's books. Adrienne Kertzer. *Can Lit* Winter 1987; No 115: p165–167.

UN OISEAU VIVANT DANS LA GUEULE/Play by Jeanne-Mance Delisle

Masques, personnages et personnes; reviews of plays. André-G. Bourassa. photo · *Lettres québec* Summer 1987; No 46: p51–52.

La vitrine du livre; reviews. Guy Ferland. *MD* May 9, 1987: pD4.

Des personnages et un langage qui se déchirent; review of *Un Oiseau vivant dans la gueule*. Chantal Gamache. photo · *MD* Oct 24, 1987: pD3.

'Oiseau' feeds on violent love — 'Neruda' long 2-hour stretch; theatre reviews of *Un Oiseau vivant dans la gueule* and *Off Off Off*. Francine Pelletier. *MG* June 3, 1987: pB4.

THE OLD DANCE: LOVE STORIES OF ONE KIND OR ANOTHER/Short story anthology

Stories painful and fresh; review of *The Old Dance*. Patricia Bradbury. *Quill & Quire* Jan 1987; Vol 53 No 1: p28.
[ANTHOLOGIES: BOOK REVIEWS]

[Untitled]; review of *The Old Dance*. Mark Duncan. *Border Cross* Spring 1987; Vol 6 No 2: p29–30.
[ANTHOLOGIES: BOOK REVIEWS]

Anthology samples Prairie writing; review of *The Old Dance*. Dave Margoshes. *CH* Feb 22, 1987: pE6.
[ANTHOLOGIES: BOOK REVIEWS]

The Wife of Bath today — games of love; review of *The Old Dance*. Alex Pett. *Event* March 1987; Vol 16 No 1: p100–102.

A mixed bag of short stories; reviews of short story anthologies. Norman Sigurdson. *WFP* Feb 28, 1987: p54.
[ANTHOLOGIES: BOOK REVIEWS]

THE OLD WORLD AND THE NEW: LITERARY PERSPECTIVES OF GERMAN-SPEAKING CANADIANS/Anthology

German contexts in Canadian literature; review of *The Old World and the New*. K.P. Stich. *Essays on Can Writ* Spring 1987; No 34: p185–189.
[ANTHOLOGIES: BOOK REVIEWS]

THE OLDEN DAYS COAT/Children's story by Margaret Laurence

Revolting teddies . . . time-travelling tot . . . rhymes macabre; reviews of tape versions of *The Olden Days Coat* and *Auntie's Knitting a Baby*. Richard Perry. photo · *Quill & Quire (Books for Young People)* Oct 1987; Vol 53 No 10: p14

OLLIVIER, MILE

La palme à Ollivier et à Ouellette; article. photo · *MD* Nov 18, 1987: p11.
[AWARDS, LITERARY]

Une épopée des Caraïbes; review of *La Discorde aux cent voix*. Noël Audet. *Lettres québec* Spring 1987; No 45: p24–26.

La vie littéraire; column. Jean Royer. *MD* Feb 28, 1987: pC2.
[AWARDS, LITERARY; CANADIAN LITERARY PERIODICALS; CANADIAN LITERARY PUBLISHING; CONFERENCES, LITERARY; RADIO AND CANADIAN LITERATURE]

La vie littéraire; column. Jean Royer. photo · *MD* June 6, 1987: pD2.
[GOVERNOR GENERAL'S AWARDS; INTERNATIONAL REVIEWS OF CANADIAN LITERATURE; RADIO AND CANADIAN LITERATURE; TELEVISION AND CANADIAN LITERATURE]

ON BEING A MARITIME WRITER/Lectures by Hugh MacLennan

Maritime letters; reviews. Carrie MacMillan. *Can Lit* Spring 1987; No 112: p189–192.

ON MIDDLE GROUND/Novella anthology

To make a short story long; review of *On Middle Ground*. Cary Fagan. *Books in Can* Aug-Sept 1987; Vol 16 No 6: p19–20.
[ANTHOLOGIES: BOOK REVIEWS]

Collection highlights neglected genre; review of *On Middle Ground*. G.P. Greenwood. *CH* Oct 4, 1987: pE6.
[ANTHOLOGIES: BOOK REVIEWS]

[Untitled]; review of *On Middle Ground*. Carolellen Norskey. *Quill & Quire* Sept 1987; Vol 53 No 9: p78.
[ANTHOLOGIES: BOOK REVIEWS]

ON STAGE WITH MAARA HAAS/Poems and prose by Maara Haas

[Untitled]; review of *On Stage with Maara Haas*. Barbara Florio Graham. *Can Auth & Book* Spring 1987; Vol 62 No 3: p24.

ON STAGE, PLEASE/Children's novel by Veronica Tennant

Bugs, battles & ballet; reviews of *On Stage, Please* and *Redcoat*. James Gellert. *Can Lit* Winter 1987; No 115: p220–223.
[FIRST NOVELS: BOOK REVIEWS]

ON TO POEM 400/Poems by J. Alvin Speers

[Untitled]; reviews of poetry books. Anita Hurwitz. *Poetry Can R* Spring 1987; Vol 8 No 2–3: p50–51.

ONCE: A LULLABY/Children's poem by bpNichol

Directional devices; review of *Once: A Lullaby*. Jan Dalley. *Times Lit Supp* April 3, 1987; No 4383: p356.

ONDAATJE, MICHAEL

It's a date; column. *MG* Sept 18, 1987: pA9.
[FICTION READINGS]

À surveiller; column. *MD* Sept 21, 1987: p8.
[FICTION READINGS]

Toronto artists win recognition; article. *WFP* Sept 23, 1987: p46.
[AWARDS, LITERARY]

Ondaatje opens reading series; article. photo · *CH* Sept 25, 1987: pF7.
[FICTION READINGS; POETRY READINGS]

Frye, Wieland are among arts awards winners; article. photo · *G&M* Sept 23, 1987: pC7.
[AWARDS, LITERARY]

Arts award winners to give lectures; article. *TS* Oct 6, 1987: pF1.

Toronto Arts Week wants to say thanks to you; article. *TS* Oct 9, 1987: pE3.

TO Arts Awards; article. *Quill & Quire* Dec 1987; Vol 53 No 12: p14.
[AWARDS, LITERARY]

Fact and fiction make an impressive novel; review of *In the Skin of a Lion*. Ken Adachi. photo · *TS* May 30, 1987: M4.

Arts awards lack flash and glamour; column. Sid Adilman. *TS* Oct 17, 1987: H2.
[AWARDS, LITERARY]

View from the bridge; review of *In the Skin of a Lion*. John Bemrose. *Maclean's* June 8, 1987; Vol 100 No 23: U10.

Michael Ondaatje gives Toronto its early voice; review of *In the Skin of a Lion*. Lindsay Brown. photo · *MG* June 20, 1987: J9.

[Untitled]; review of *Spider Blues*. Graham Carr. *Poetry Can R* Spring 1987; Vol 8 No 2–3: p61–62.

Musicians jazz up Ondaatje poetry; column. Val Clery. *TS* Nov 26, 1987: pB3.

People; column. Yvonne Cox. photo · *Maclean's* Oct 26, 1987; Vol 100 No 43: p34.

Free-fall fiction; review of *In the Skin of a Lion*. William French. *G&M* May 23, 1987: pC21.

Stars of the city, year two; photographic portfolio. Edward Gajdel. *Tor Life* Oct 1987; Vol 21 No 1[5]: 89–95.

Solecki's Ondaatje; review of *Spider Blues*. Susan Gingell. *Can Lit* Summer-Fall 1987; No 113–114: p214–217.

A note on Ondaatje's "Peter": a creative myth; article. Gillian Harding-Russell. *Can Lit* Spring 1987; No 112: p205–211.

[Untitled]; review of *Spider Blues*. R.F. Gillian Harding-Russell. *U of Toronto Q* Fall 1987; Vol 57 No 1: p166–168.

Worlds in collision; review of *In the Skin of a Lion*. Michael Hulse. *Times Lit Supp* Sept 4, 1987; No 4405: p948.

Ondaatje fuses poetry & history; review of *In the Skin of a Lion*. Marni Jackson. photo · *Chatelaine* Sept 1987; Vol 60 No 9: p10.

Structure eludes Ondaatje's imagination; review of *In the Skin of a Lion*. Mark Anthony Jarman. *CH* Aug 23, 1987: pE4.

Mr. Small isn't here. Have an iguana!; review of *In the Skin of a Lion*. Carolyn Kizer. illus · *NYT Book R* Sept 27, 1987: p12–13.

Serendipity; review of *In the Skin of a Lion*. Linda Leith. illus · *Can Forum* Aug-Sept 1987; Vol 67 No 771: p35–37.

[Untitled]; review of *In the Skin of a Lion*. Alberto Manguel. *Tor Life* May 1987; Vol 21 No 7: p105.

Missed connections; review of *In the Skin of a Lion*. Tom Marshall. *Books in Can* June-July 1987; Vol 16 No 5: p16.

Michael Ondaatje's new novel rocks its way to market; column. Henry Mietkiewicz. *TS* May 21, 1987: pF2.

Musicians breathe life into poems; review. Mark Miller. photo · *G&M* Nov 30, 1987: pC11.

Toronto honors the best with annual arts awards; article. Greg Quill. photo · *TS* Sept 23, 1987: pF1.
[AWARDS, LITERARY]

Photography "in camera"; article. Peter Sims. *Can Lit* Summer-Fall 1987; No 113–114: p145–166.

[Untitled]; review of *Spider Blues*. Peter Stevens. *Queen's Q* Autumn 1987; Vol 94 No 3: p717–719.

In the skin of Michael Ondaatje: giving voice to a social conscience; review article about *In the Skin of a Lion*. Barbara Turner. photo · *Quill & Quire* May 1987; Vol 53 No 5: p21–22.

From the land of the terrifically believable; article. Mark A. Uhlig. photo · *NYT Book R* Sept 27, 1987: p13.

[Untitled]; review of *In the Skin of a Lion*. Aritha van Herk. *Malahat R* Sept 1987; No 80: p134–137.

Michael Ondaatje turns in a memorable performance; review of *In the Skin of a Lion*. David Williamson. photo · *WFP* Aug 29, 1987: p52

Tennant gets top award for costume and design; article. Rita Zekas. *TS* Oct 14, 1987: pE1.
[AWARDS, LITERARY]

Herrndorf is the sum of his arts; article about Peter Herrndorf. Antonia Zerbisias. photo · *TS* Oct 10, 1987: H1,H3.
[AWARDS, LITERARY]

ONE NIGHT AT THE INDIGO HOTEL/Poems by Robert Allen

Montreal poets inspired by travel in hot countries; reviews of poetry books. Barbara Black. *MG* March 28, 1987: pE9.

Poets in search of praise; reviews of *One Night at the Indigo Hotel* and *The Bones of Their Occasion*. Keith Garebian. *TS* May 16, 1987: M4.

ONE NIGHT/Long poem by Ken Norris

[Untitled]; reviews of *In the Spirit of the Times* and *One Night*. Andrew Flynn. *Rubicon* Spring 1987; No 8: p202–205.

Landscapes & eyes; reviews of poetry books. Karl Jirgens. *Can Lit* Spring 1987; No 112: p192–193.

ONE OUT OF FOUR/Novel by Donald Martin

[Untitled]; review of *One Out of Four*. Steve Boyd. *CH* Jan 25, 1987: pE4.
[FIRST NOVELS: BOOK REVIEWS]

[Untitled]; review of *One Out of Four*. Martin Townsend. *Quill & Quire* Feb 1987; Vol 53 No 2: p17.

ONE THOUSAND CRANES/UN MILLIER D'OISEAUX/Children's play by Colin Thomas

[Untitled]; review of *One Thousand Cranes*. David Booth. *Quill & Quire (Books for Young People)* June 1987; Vol 53 No 6: p11.

Tandis qu'on négocie au sommet, un millier d'oiseaux chantent la paix; theatre review of *Un Millier d'oiseaux*. Angèle Dagenais. photo · *MD* Dec 11, 1987: p11.

Oiseaux makes nuclear point without traumatizing kids; theatre review of *Un Millier d'oiseaux*. Pat Donnelly. *MG* Dec 19, 1987: pE9.

ONE YELLOW RABBIT THEATRE COLLECTIVE

Rabbit writers team up to parody anti-Semitism; article. Kate Zimmerman. photo · *CH* May 28, 1987: pC15.

Timid pussyfooting defuses play's satirical intent; theatre review of *Ilsa, Queen of the Nazi Love Camp*. Kate Zimmerman. *CH* May 30, 1987: pF5.

ONE-EYED MERCHANTS/Novel by Kathleen Timms

Publishers meet the demand with reissued crime classics; reviews of *The Night the Gods Smiled* and *One-Eyed Merchants*. Douglas Hill. *G&M* Feb 28, 1987: pE19.
[FIRST NOVELS: BOOK REVIEWS]

THE ONLY MINORITY IS THE BOURGEOISIE/Poems by Krisantha Sri Bhaggiyadatta

Hard time, maximum time; reviews of *The Only Minority Is the Bourgeoisie* and *Doing Time*. Marlene Philip. *Tor South Asian R* Spring 1987; Vol 5 No 3: p28–34.

ONTARIO WRITING AND WRITERS

Defying linear deification — contemporary Toronto visual poetry; article. J.W. Curry. illus · *Cross Can Writ Q* 1987; Vol 9 No 3–4: p6–8.
[CONCRETE POETRY; POSTMODERNIST WRITING AND CRITICISM]

Literary Ontario: a regional irony; editorial. Ted Plantos. *Cross Can Writ Q* 1987; Vol 9 No 2: p2.
[REGIONALISM IN CANADIAN LITERATURE]

OPEN WINDOWS/Poems by Gabriel Safdie

[Untitled]; review of *Open Windows*. Gerald Doerksen. *Rubicon* Spring 1987; No 8: p223–224.

[Untitled]; review of *Open Windows*. Gerald Hill. *Poetry Can R* Fall 1987; Vol 9 No 1: p37.

OPIUM/Play by Carbon 14 Theatre collective

[Untitled]; theatre review of *Opium*. Danièle Le Blanc. photo · *Jeu* 1987; No 43: p155–156.

Evocative, but laced with ennui; theatre review of *Opium*. Ray Conlogue. photo · *G&M* Jan 14, 1987: pC7.

Carbone 14 does it again; theatre review of *Opium*. Wayne Grigsby. *MG* Jan 12, 1987: pB8.

[Untitled]; theatre reviews of *Fire* and *Opium*. Wayne Grigsby. *MG* Jan 16, 1987: pD10.

Les pièges de l'esthétique; theatre review of *Opium*. Robert Lévesque. photo · *MD* Jan 16, 1987: p7.

OPPENHEIM, JOANNE

[Untitled]; review of *You Can't Catch Me!*. Maeve Binchy. *NYT Book R* March 1, 1987: p31.

OPUS ONE/Poetry anthology

[Untitled]; reviews. Andrew Parkin. *Poetry Can R* Summer 1987; Vol 8 No 4: p36–37.
[ANTHOLOGIES: BOOK REVIEWS; CANADIAN LITERARY PERIODICALS]

ORAL POETRY

See POETRY PERFORMANCE; POETRY READINGS; SOUND POETRY

THE ORANGEMAN: THE LIFE AND TIMES OF OGLE GOWAN/Novel by Don Akenson

The man who made Ontario Orange; review of *The Orangeman*. Richard Campbell. photo · *TS* Feb 8, 1987: pG8

[Untitled]; review of *The Orangeman*. Peter D. James. *Quill & Quire* Feb 1987; Vol 53 No 2: p17.

[Untitled]; review of *The Orangeman*. Royce MacGillivray. *Books in Can* Jan-Feb 1987; Vol 16 No 1: p27.

So-called fiction serves no purpose; letter to the editor. Leslie H. Saunders. *TS* March 24, 1987: pA20.

ORCA'S SONG/Children's story by Anne Cameron

[Untitled]; reviews of *Orca's Song* and *Raven Returns the Water*. Eva Martin. *Quill & Quire (Books for Young People)* Oct 1987; Vol 53 No 10: p23.

The magic of myth and love of legend; reviews of children's books. Tim Wynne-Jones. *G&M* July 25, 1987: pC17.

OSBORNE, JOANNE

[The Rich Man]; theatre review. Lynne Van Luven. *NeWest R* Nov 1987; Vol 13 No 3: p18.
[DRAMATIC ADAPTATIONS OF CANADIAN LITERATURE]

OSTENSO, MARTHA

Possessing the promised land; editorial. Paul Denham. *NeWest R* Nov 1987; Vol 13 No 3: p1.

[Untitled]; letter to the editor. Margaret Gail Osachoff. *NeWest R* Dec 1987; Vol 13 No 4: p1.

OTHER SELVES/Short stories by C.D. Minni

[Untitled]; review of *Other Selves*. Richard Lanoie. *Rubicon* Spring 1987; No 8: p221.

[Untitled]; review of *Other Selves*. Dona Sturmanis. *Can Auth & Book* Winter 1987; Vol 62 No 2: p23–24.

THE OTHER SHORE/L'AUTRE RIVAGE/Poems by Antonio D'Alfonso

Un Italien au Québec: cet autre rivage jamais atteint; column. Jean Éthier-Blais. *MD* Oct 24, 1987: pD8.

[Untitled]; review of *The Other Shore*. Corrado Federici. *Poetry Can R* Spring 1987; Vol 8 No 2–3: p45–46.

Roman heartbeat; reviews of *The Other Shore* and *Moving Landscape*. Louise McKinney. *Can Lit* Winter 1987; No 115: p232–234.

[Untitled]; review of *The Other Shore*. Steve Noyes. *Rubicon* Spring 1987; No 8: p219.

Antonio d'Alfonso ou "l'érotisme des mots"; review of *L'Autre rivage*. Jean Royer. photo · *MD* June 20, 1987: pD2.

[Untitled]; reviews. Janet Windeler. *Cross Can Writ Q* 1987; Vol 9 No 2: p25–26.
[FIRST NOVELS: BOOK REVIEWS]

OTHER VOICES/Anthology

[Untitled]; reviews. Anne Cimon. *Cross Can Writ Q* 1987; Vol 9 No 3–4: p47–48.

Skin deep; review of *Other Voices*. Ray Filip. *Books in Can* Oct 1987; Vol 16 No 7: p28–29.
[ANTHOLOGIES: BOOK REVIEWS]

[Untitled]; review of *Other Voices*. Winston Smith. *Rubicon* Fall 1987; No 9: p160–163.
[ANTHOLOGIES: BOOK REVIEWS]

OTTO, MARYLEAH

[Untitled]; reviews of *Katie's Alligator Goes to Daycare* and *Tom Doesn't Visit Us Any More*. Adele Ashby. *Quill & Quire (Books for Young People)* Dec 1987; Vol 53 No 12: p8–9.

OUBLIER/Play by Marie Laberge

Oublier could have been a lot of things but misses chance; theatre review. Pat Donnelly. photo · *MG* Nov 4, 1987: pB9.

Le théâtre du Rire joue gagnant; column. Robert Lévesque. *MD* Oct 13, 1987: p11.
[AWARDS, LITERARY]

Oublier ou ne pas oublier; article. Robert Lévesque. photo · *MD* Oct 31, 1987: pC1,C3.

L'insoutenable dureté de l'être; theatre review of *Oublier*. Robert Lévesque. photo · *MD* Nov 4, 1987: p13.

[Untitled]; theatre reviews of *Oublier* and *Tête à tête*. Robert Lévesque. *MD* Nov 6, 1987: p15.

[Untitled]; theatre review of *Oublier*. Robert Lévesque. photo · *MD* Nov 13, 1987: p15.

[Untitled]; theatre reviews. Robert Lévesque. *MD* Dec 4, 1987: p15.

OUELLET, JACQUES

La vitrine du livre; reviews. Guy Ferland. *MD* May 23, 1987: pD4.

La métamorphose du quotidien; reviews of poetry books. André Marquis. photo · *Lettres québec* Autumn 1987; No 47: p41–43.

OUELLETTE, FERNAND

Poet, theatre great among winners of Prix du Québec; article. *MG* Nov 10, 1987: pB4.
[AWARDS, LITERARY]

La palme à Ollivier et à Ouellette; article. photo · *MD* Nov 18, 1987: p11.
[AWARDS, LITERARY]

Ouellette et Royer: depuis la mort jusqu'à l'amour . . . ; reviews of *Les Heures* and *Depuis l'amour*. Jean Éthier-Blais. *MD* June 27, 1987: pC9

Le prix David va à Fernand Ouellette; article. Sylvain Blanchard. photo · *MD* Nov 5, 1987: p15.
[AWARDS, LITERARY]

[Untitled]; review of *Les Heures*. Pierre-Justin Déry. *Estuaire* Summer 1987; No 45: p55–57.

Le corps vibrant de désir; interview with Fernand Ouellette. Gérald Gaudet. photo · *Lettres québec* Winter 1986–87; No 44: p16–21.

La vie littéraire; column. Marc Morin. *MD* Dec 12, 1987: pD2.
[GOVERNOR GENERAL'S AWARDS; POETRY READINGS]

La vitrine du livre; reviews. Jean Royer. *MD* April 11, 1987: pD2.
[CANADIAN LITERARY PERIODICALS]

"Regarder le monde et découvrir ce qui attend de naître": Fernand Ouellette et le retour de la poésie; article. Jean Royer. photo · *MD* June 13, 1987: pD1,D8.

Le Léon-Gérin à Louis-Edmond Hamelin; le Marie-Victorin à Pierre Deslongchamps; article. Julie Stanton. photo · *MD* Nov 10, 1987: p13.
[AWARDS, LITERARY]

L'amour la mort; reviews of poetry books. Robert Yergeau. photo · *Lettres québec* Summer 1987; No 46: p37–38.

OUELLETTE-MICHALSKA, MADELEINE

La culture de la confusion; reviews of *Extase et déchirure* and *L'Amour de la carte postale*. Réjean Beaudoin. *Liberté* Dec 1987; Vol 29 No 6: p107–113.

La vitrine du livre; reviews. Guy Ferland. *MD* May 9, 1987: pD4.

La vitrine du livre; reviews. Guy Ferland. *MD* May 2, 1987: pD4.

Dans les poches; reviews. Guy Ferland. *MD* Sept 26, 1987: pD6.

Vivre de sa plume au Québec; interview with Madeleine Ouellette-Michalska. Gérald Gaudet. photo · *Lettres québec* Spring 1987; No 45: p12–14.

[Untitled]; review of *L'Amour de la carte postale*. Robert Giroux. *Moebius* Summer 1987; No 33: p146–148.

Un essai original sur l'impérialisme culturel; review of *L'Amour de la carte postale*. Lori Saint-Martin. *MD* May 30, 1987: pD3.

[Untitled]; introduction. Adrien Thério. photo · *Lettres québec* Autumn 1987; No 47: p55.

OUR HERO IN THE CRADLE OF CONFEDERATION/ Novel by J.J. Steinfeld

Macabre parade of masks; review of *Our Hero in the Cradle of Confederation*. Sharon Drache. *G&M* July 11, 1987: pC14.
[FIRST NOVELS: BOOK REVIEWS]

Me, myself, and I; reviews of first novels. Janice Kulyk Keefer. *Books in Can* Oct 1987; Vol 16 No 7: p35–36,38.
[FIRST NOVELS: BOOK REVIEWS]

Adventure in corners of Canada; reviews of *St. Vitus Dance* and *Our Hero in the Cradle of Confederation*. Hugh McKellar. *TS* Aug 23, 1987: pA20.

Portrait of the artist as a middle-aged schlemiel; review of *Our Hero in the Cradle of Confederation*. Paul Tyndall. *Atlan Prov Book R* Sept-Oct 1987; Vol 14 No 3: p12.
[FIRST NOVELS: BOOK REVIEWS]

OUT OF THE STORM/Poems by Michael Thorpe

Iconographies; reviews of *Out of the Storm* and *The End of Ice*. Jack F. Stewart. *Can Lit* Spring 1987; No 112: p166–167.

OUT OF THE WILLOW TREES/Poems and prose by Peter Stevens

[Untitled]; review of *Out of the Willow Trees*. Stephen Brockwell. *Rubicon* Spring 1987; No 8: p225–226.

[Untitled]; review of *Out of the Willow Trees*. Allan Markin. *Poetry Can R* Fall 1987; Vol 9 No 1: p33.

THE OUTSIDE CHANCE OF MAXIMILIAN GLICK/ Novel by Morley Torgov

Glick clicks at last; article. Stephen Godfrey. photo · *G&M* Dec 5, 1987: pC1,C5.
[FILM ADAPTATIONS OF CANADIAN LITERATURE]

OUTTA SIGHT/Young adult novel by Mary Blakeslee

[Untitled]; review of *Outta Sight*. Patty Lawlor. *Quill & Quire (Books for Young People)* Aug 1987; Vol 53 No 8: p7.

OUZOUNIAN, RICHARD

Ouzounian visits; article. *WFP* June 26, 1987: p35.

Getting back on the theatrical track; article. photo · *Maclean's* April 20, 1987; Vol 100 No 16: p47–48.

Neptune cooks up a delicious satire; theatre review of *Tartuffe*. Ray Conlogue. photo · *G&M* April 17, 1987: pC7.

Neptune Theatre's Barometer Rising too faithful to book; theatre review. Matthew Fraser. *G&M* Nov 9, 1987: pD9.
[DRAMATIC ADAPTATIONS OF CANADIAN LITERATURE]

Ouzounian finds a niche in Halifax; article. Matthew Fraser. photo · *G&M* Dec 21, 1987: pC9.

The Gipper and The Jaw spice up Tartuffe; article. Robert Martin. photo · *G&M* April 10, 1987: pC9.

Canadian content updates classic 17th-century satire; theatre review of *Tartuffe*. Tom McDougall. photo · *CH* April 13, 1987: pF3.

Moliere's farce gets modern twist; television review of *Tartuffe*. Paul McKie. photo · *WFP* Oct 1, 1987: p40

Death on the waterfront; theatre review of *Barometer Rising*, includes profile. Stephen Pedersen. photo · *Maclean's* Nov 23, 1987; Vol 100 No 47: p57.
[DRAMATIC ADAPTATIONS OF CANADIAN LITERATURE]

A sound beyond hearing; article. Tom Regan. photo · *Atlan Insight* Dec 1987; Vol 9 No 12: p19–21.
[DRAMATIC ADAPTATIONS OF CANADIAN LITERATURE]

Book world: a tip of the hat to small presses; column. Beverley Slopen. photo · *TS* Aug 9, 1987: pA20.
[CANADIAN LITERARY PUBLISHING]

OVERGROUND/Play by Alice Ronfard

Ionesco soufflera ses 75 chandelles à Montréal; column. Robert Lévesque. *MD* May 12, 1987: p14.
[FESTIVALS, DRAMA]

Stark theatrical visions lose focus in pile of sordid detail; theatre review of *Overground*. Francine Pelletier. *MG* May 26, 1987: pD11.

Une auteure qui se découvrira; theatre review of *Overground*. Jean-Robert Rémillard. *Liberté* Dec 1987; Vol 29 No 6: p156.

OVERHEAD IN A BALLOON: STORIES OF PARIS/Short stories by Mavis Gallant

The New Yorker lists at this season some books by its contributors published during the year; article. *New Yorker* Dec 21, 1987; Vol 63 No 44: p100–101.

Capital appreciation; review of *Overhead in a Balloon*. Lindsay Duguid. *Times Lit Supp* Sept 25, 1987; No 4408: p1052.

One step ahead of the zeitgeist; review of *Overhead in a Balloon*. Phyllis Rose. *NYT Book R* March 15, 1987: p7.

OVERLOOKING THE RED JAIL/Short stories by M.L. Knight

[Untitled]; review of *Overlooking the Red Jail*. Mark Everard. *Books in Can* June-July 1987; Vol 16 No 5: p22.

OWL/Periodical

Could be disaster story for children's magazine; article. Renate Lerch. *Fin Post* Oct 5, 1987: p3.
[CANADIAN LITERARY PERIODICALS]

THE OXFORD BOOK OF CANADIAN SHORT STORIES IN ENGLISH/Anthology

Embracing the wilderness; reviews of *The Oxford Book of Canadian Short Stories in English* and *Bluebeard's Egg*. John Clute. *Times Lit Supp* June 12, 1987; No 4393: p626.
[ANTHOLOGIES: BOOK REVIEWS]

Story anthologies: the tried, the true, and the best of the new; reviews of short story anthologies. Brent Ledger. photo · *Quill & Quire* Jan 1987; Vol 53 No 1: p29.
[ANTHOLOGIES: BOOK REVIEWS]

Sin of omission; letter to the editor. Alice Munro. *Books in Can* April 1987; Vol 16 No 3: p40.

Sins of omission; review of *The Oxford Book of Canadian Short Stories in English*. Allan Weiss. *Books in Can* Jan-Feb 1987; Vol 16 No 1: p21–22.
[ANTHOLOGIES: BOOK REVIEWS]

THE OXFORD ILLUSTRATED LITERARY GUIDE TO CANADA/Reference guide

A preference for reference; article. *Quill & Quire* July 1987; Vol 53 No 7: p10.

Christmas books; review of *The Oxford Illustrated Literary Guide to Canada*. illus · *MG* Dec 5, 1987: J1-J3.

On the street where they lived; review of *The Oxford Illustrated Literary Guide to Canada*. Ken Adachi. photo · *TS* Nov 29, 1987: pA21.

Literary minutiae; review of *The Oxford Illustrated Literary Guide to Canada*. William French. *G&M* Nov 28, 1987: pC19.

Taking a survey of the world; review of *The Oxford Illustrated Literary Guide to Canada*. Tom Oleson. *WFP* Dec 12, 1987: p50.

Guiding the way to our literary history and geography; review of *The Oxford Illustrated Literary Guide to Canada*. Larry Scanlan. photo · *Quill & Quire* Dec 1987; Vol 53 No 12: p21.

Many happy returns; review of *The Oxford Illustrated Literary Guide to Canada*. Paul Stuewe. *Books in Can* Nov 1987; Vol 16 No 8: p12–14.

PÉLAGIE-LA-CHARRETTE/Novel by Antonine Maillet

Pélagie-la-Charrette and the carnivalesque; article. Robin Howells. *British J of Can Studies* June 1987; Vol 2 No 1: p48–60.
[CARNIVALIZATION]

The bible and myth in Antonine Maillet's Pélagie-la-Charrette; article. Paul G. Socken. *Studies in Can Lit* 1987; Vol 12 No 2: p187–198.
[VIOLENCE IN CANADIAN LITERATURE]

PÉPÈRE GOGUEN LOUP DE MER/Children's story by Jean Pérronet

Two illustrated Acadian books; reviews of *Pépère Goguen loup de mer*. Martine Jacquot. *Atlan Prov Book R* Nov-Dec 1987; Vol 14 No 4: p11.

LE PÈRE DE LISA/Novel by José Fréchette

Un coup d'essai qui est aussi un coup de maître!; review of *Le Père de Lisa*. Jean-Roch Boivin. *MD* Nov 28, 1987: pD11.

La vitrine du livre; reviews. Guy Ferland. *MD* Nov 14, 1987: pD16.
[ANTHOLOGIES: BOOK REVIEWS]

PÉRRONET, JEAN

Two illustrated Acadian books; reviews of *Pépère Goguen loup de mer*. Martine Jacquot. *Atlan Prov Book R* Nov-Dec 1987; Vol 14 No 4: p11.

PAGE, P.K.

Page on places and things pure pleasure; review of *Brazilian Journal*. Ken Adachi. photo · *TS* June 27, 1987: M4.

[Untitled]; review of *Brazilian Journal*. Ruby Andrew. *Quill & Quire* May 1987; Vol 53 No 5: p22,24.

The ambassador's wife; review of *Brazilian Journal*. John Bemrose. illus · *Maclean's* Aug 10, 1987; Vol 100 No 32: p51.

P.K. Page: traveller, conjuror, journeyman; article. Marjorie Body. photo · *Cross Can Writ Q* 1987; Vol 9 No 2: p4–5,28.

[Untitled]; review of *Brazilian Journal*. Adelle Castelo. *Idler* Sept-Oct 1987; No 14: p49.

Tropical dreaming; review of *Brazilian Journal*. William French. *G&M* June 27, 1987: pE17.

Insulting an author; letter to the editor. Robert Fulford. *G&M* July 17, 1987: pA6.

The poet in the pink palace; review article about *Brazilian Journal*. George Galt. photo · *Sat Night* Sept 1987; Vol 102 No 9: p61–63.

Diamond panes; review of *The Glass Air*. Sandra Hutchison. *Can Lit* Summer-Fall 1987; No 113–114: p247–249.

[Untitled]; review of *Brazilian Journal*. M.K. Louis. *Malahat R* June 1987; No 79: p162–164.

[Untitled]; review of *The Glass Air*. M.K. Louis. *Malahat R* (special issue) March 1987; No 78: p156–158.

Publishers serve up some dismal fare; letter to the editor. Anna Pottier. photo · *G&M* July 8, 1987: pA7.
[PUBLISHING AND PUBLISHERS IN CANADA]

Poetical protest; letter to the editor. Anna Pottier. *G&M* July 27, 1987: pA6.

Paperclips: publishing on-stage . . . P.K. Page's love song to Brazil; column. Beverley Slopen. photo · *Quill & Quire* May 1987; Vol 53 No 5: p14.

Poet records two years in paradise; review of *Brazilian Journal*. John Vance Snow. *CH* Aug 30, 1987: pE4.

Lady of the house; review of *Brazilian Journal*. Barbara Wade Rose. *Books in Can* June-July 1987; Vol 16 No 5: p29–30.

Brazil dreaming; review of *Brazilian Journal*. William Weintraub. illus · *MG* July 25, 1987: J7.

PALIN, VIVIAN

Festival One plays singularly successful; theatre reviews. Stephen Godfrey. photo · *G&M* May 8, 1987: pF9.
[FESTIVALS, DRAMA]

Stories create magic moments for audience at Festival One; theatre review of *Dragon Snapper*. Reg Skene. *WFP* May 4, 1987: p29.

Pioneer lady on stage; article. Morley Walker. photo · *WFP* April 30, 1987: p26.

PALMER, JOHN

Palmer play shows surprising sweetness; theatre review of *A Day at the Beach*. Ray Conlogue. photo · *G&M* Dec 12, 1987: pC8.

A Day at the Beach still has a way to go; theatre review. Robert Crew. *TS* Dec 7, 1987: pC4.

Semmelweiss role just what doctor ordered; column. Vit Wagner. photo · *TS* Dec 4, 1987: pD7.

PANDORA OU MON P'TIT PAPA/Play by Louisette Dussault

A box that could have stayed closed; theatre review of *Pandora*. Pat Donnelly. *MG* March 18, 1987: pD3.

Ouvrir la boîte à maux; theatre review of *Pandora*. Solange Lévesque. photo · *Jeu* 1987; No 44: p177–180.

PANNETON, PHILIPPE

See RINGUET

PANOPTICON/Long poem by Steve McCaffery

Dr. Sadhu's semi-opticks, or how to write a virtual-novel by the book: Steve McCaffery's Panopticon; article. Rafael Barreto-Rivera. *Open Letter (special issue)* Fall 1987; Vol 6 No 9: p39–47.
[POSTMODERNIST WRITING AND CRITICISM]

Panoptical artifice; article. Charles Bernstein. *Open Letter (special issue)* Fall 1987; Vol 6 No 9: p9–15.
[POSTMODERNIST WRITING AND CRITICISM]

Steve McCaffery's Panopticon; article. William McPheron. photo · *Open Letter (special issue)* Fall 1987; Vol 6 No 9: p49–54.
[METAFICTION; POSTMODERNIST WRITING AND CRITICISM; STRUCTURALIST WRITING AND CRITICISM]

PAPER ROSES/Poems by Rachel Korn

Grief & memory; reviews of poetry books. Peter Stenberg. *Can Lit* Spring 1987; No 112: p169–171.

PAPERNY, MYRA

Paperny takes giant step with new novel; biographical article. Kenneth McGoogan. photo · *CH* Feb 21, 1987: pG1.

THE PAPERS OF DOROTHY LIVESAY: A RESEARCH TOOL/Catalogue

The Livesay papers; review of *The Papers of Dorothy Livesay*. Catherine Sheldrick Ross. *Can Poet* Fall-Winter 1987; No 21: p116–117.

THE PAPERS OF SAMUEL MARCHBANKS/Humorous essays by Robertson Davies

Early espièglerie; review of *The Papers of Samuel Marchbanks*. Richard Deveson. *Times Lit Supp* Oct 16, 1987; No 4411: p1137.

Magpie mind; review of *The Papers of Samuel Marchbanks*. Nicholas Hudson. *Can Lit* Spring 1987; No 112: p88–90.

PAPERS/Play by Alan Stratton

[Untitled]; review of *Papers*. Bert Cowan. *Books in Can* March 1987; Vol 16 No 2: p26.

[Untitled]; reviews of plays. Judith Rudakoff. *Can Theatre R* Summer 1987; No 51: p86–87.

PAQUIN, WILFRID

[Untitled]; review of *Arthur de Bussières, poète, et l'École littéraire de Montréal*. David M. Hayne. *U of Toronto Q* Fall 1987; Vol 57 No 1: p178–179.

PAQUIN-BACK, GHISLAINE

Un livre tendre; review of *Crac!*. Ghislaine Monoré-Johnson. *Can Child Lit* 1987; No 48: p97–98.

PARADIS, SUZANNE

[Untitled]; reviews of *Un goût de sel* and *Effets de l'oeil*. Hélène Thibaux. *Estuaire* Autumn 1987; No 46: p86–87.

PARASOLS/Play by Théâtre de la Marmaille collective

Disturbing play incoherent; theatre review of *Parasols*. Reg Skene. *WFP* May 1, 1987: p35.

PARDON ME, MOM/Children's story by Gail Chislett

Mini-reviews; reviews of children's books. Margaret Paré. *Can Child Lit* 1987; No 45: p93–96.

PARIS NOTEBOOKS: ESSAYS AND REVIEWS/Prose by Mavis Gallant

[Untitled]; review of *Paris Notebooks*. Janice Kulyk Keefer. *U of Toronto Q* Fall 1987; Vol 57 No 1: p168–170.

[Untitled]; review of *Paris Notebooks*. Guido Monzano. *Idler* March-April 1987; No 12: p60–61.

[Untitled]; review of *Paris Notebooks*. Ken Mouré. *Rubicon* Fall 1987; No 9: p155–157.

THE PARIS-NAPOLI EXPRESS/Short stories by Janice Kulyk Keefer

[Untitled]; reviews of *The Paris-Napoli Express* and *White of the Lesser Angels*. Elizabeth Brewster. *Event* March 1987; Vol 16 No 1: p103–104.

[Untitled]; reviews of short story collections. David Helwig. *Queen's Q* Winter 1987; Vol 94 No 4: p1022–1024.

Images of motherhood; review of *The Paris-Napoli Express*. A.C. Morrell. *Fiddlehead* Summer 1987; No 152: p91–95.

[Untitled]; reviews of *The Need of Wanting Always* and *The Paris-Napoli Express*. S.A. Newman. *Cross Can Writ Q* 1987; Vol 9 No 1: p20.

PARIZEAU, ALICE

Aujourd'hui; column. *MD* April 27, 1987: p10.

Blizzard . . . : un sommet dans l'art d'Alice Parizeau; review of *Blizzard sur Québec*. Jean Éthier-Blais. *MD* Dec 5, 1987: pD10.

Deux fictions sur fond d'histoire; reviews of *La Fin de l'histoire* and *L'Amour de Jeanne*. Yvon Bernier. photo · *Lettres québec* Winter 1986–87; No 44: p31–33.

Un roman à la gloire de l'Hydro-Québec; review of *Blizzard sur Québec*. Jean-Roch Boivin. *MD* Nov 21, 1987: pD3.

[Untitled]; notice. Paul Cauchon. *MD* Dec 4, 1987: p15.
[TELEVISION AND CANADIAN LITERATURE]

La vie littéraire; column. Jean Royer. photo · *MD* May 30, 1987: pD2.
[AWARDS, LITERARY; CANADIAN LITERARY PUBLISHING; COMPETITIONS, LITERARY; FESTIVALS, LITERARY; RADIO AND CANADIAN LITERATURE; TELEVISION AND CANADIAN LITERATURE]

PARKER, GEORGE L.

[Untitled]; review of *The Beginnings of the Book Trade in Canada*. Herbert Rosengarten. *Eng Studies in Can* June 1987; Vol 13 No 2: p220–224.

Early Canadian publishing; review of *The Beginnings of the Book Trade in Canada*. Marjory Whitelaw. *Atlan Prov Book R* Feb-March 1987; Vol 14 No 1: p16.

THE PARROT WHO COULD/Short stories by Robin Skelton

Sardonic commentary; review of *The Parrot Who Could*. Sherie Posesorski. *G&M* Aug 8, 1987: pC18.

[Untitled]; reviews of *Telling the Tale* and *The Parrot Who Could*. Norman Sigurdson. *Books in Can* Nov 1987; Vol 16 No 8: p25–26.

[Untitled]; review of *The Parrot Who Could*. Martin Townsend. *Quill & Quire* July 1987; Vol 53 No 7: p65.

PARTI PRIS ET L'ENJEU DU RÉCIT/Critical work by Marcel Roy

La vitrine du livre; reviews. Guy Ferland. *MD* May 2, 1987: pD4.

PASNAK, WILLIAM

Successful Alberta children's writers pen new works; article. Kenneth McGoogan. photo · *CH* Dec 18, 1987: pE7.

Fine books for in-betweens; reviews of young adult books. David Williamson. *WFP* Dec 5, 1987: p57.

PASS, JOHN

Something in common; reviews of poetry books. Cary Fagan. *Prairie Fire* Spring 1987; Vol 8 No 1: p83–87.

PASSAGES/Periodical

La revue des revues; reviews of periodicals. Guy Ferland. *MD* Sept 19, 1987: pD6.
[CANADIAN LITERARY PERIODICALS]

La vitrine du livre; reviews. Jean Royer. photo · *MD* April 18, 1987: pD2.
[CANADIAN LITERARY PERIODICALS]

LA PASSION DE NARCISSE MONDOUX/Play by Gratien Gélinas

Le théâtre qu'on joue; theatre reviews. André Dionne. photo · *Lettres québec* Summer 1987; No 46: p47–48.

Gélinas and Oligny: a match made in theatrical heaven; theatre review of *La Passion de Narcisse Mondoux*. Pat Donnelly. photo · *MG* Jan 20, 1987: pD11.

[Untitled]; theatre reviews. Pat Donnelly. *MG* Sept 11, 1987: pC8.

LA PASSION SELON GALATE/Novel by Suzanne Jacob

La passion cuisinée; review of *La Passion selon Galatée*. Réjean Beaudoin. *Liberté* June 1987; Vol 29 No 3: p90–94.

Une passion d'auteure; review of *La Passion selon Galatée*. Louise Milot. photo · *Lettres québec* Summer 1987; No 46: p21–23.

Pour l'amour d'un puzzle; review of *La Passion selon Galatée*. Madeleine Ouellette-Michalska. *MD* March 14, 1987: pD3.

[Untitled]; review of *La Passion selon Galatée*. Jean Royer. *MD* Jan 30, 1987: p7.

Suzanne Jacob: les grand boulevards intérieurs; article. Jean Royer. photo · *MD* Jan 31, 1987: pB1.

PATERSON, ANDREW JAMES

Solving the perfect culture crime; article. John Bentley Mays. photo · *G&M* Jan 1, 1987: pC3.

PATERSON, JANET M.

[Untitled]; review of *Anne Hébert: architexture romanesque*. Mary Jean Green. *Amer R of Can Studies* Spring 1987; Vol 17 No 1: p115–116.

[Untitled]; review of *Anne Hébert: architexture romanesque*. Jean Marmier. *Études can* June 1987; No 22: p133–134.

LA PATTE DANS LE SAC/Children's novel by Sylvie Desrosiers

Les malheurs de Rosalie ou l'éloge de l'enfance; reviews of children's books. Dominique Demers. *MD* May 2, 1987: pD3.

PATTERSON, ANDREW J.

Film's end; review of *The Disposables*. John Hamilton. *G&M* June 13, 1987: pC20.
[FIRST NOVELS: BOOK REVIEWS]

PAUL-MARIE LAPOINTE/Critical work by Robert Melançon

Paul-Marie Lapointe chez Seghers; review of *Paul-Marie Lapointe*. André-G. Bourassa. *Lettres québec* Summer 1987; No 46: p77–78.

La poésie de Paul-Marie Lapointe; review of *Paul-Marie Lapointe*. Jean Fisette. *Voix et images* Autumn 1987; Vol 13 No 1: p174–178.

PAXTON, MAUREEN

Activity books kids will enjoy; reviews of *Dragon Sandwiches* and *The Dragon and Other Laurentian Tales*. TS Dec 20, 1987: pE8.

Familiarity and TV's stranglehold on life; reviews of children's books. Tim Wynne-Jones. G&M Nov 14, 1987: pE4.
[FESTIVALS, LITERARY]

PAYERLE, GEORGE

Billboard: Ukrainian youth holding policy meet; column. WFP Oct 9, 1987: p40.
[FICTION READINGS]

Alcoholic vet's story drives home the horror; review of *Unknown Soldier*. Don Gillmor. photo · MG Oct 17, 1987: J12.

Cliched veteran profoundly human; review of *Unknown Soldier*. Maggie Helwig. TS Oct 10, 1987: M8.

Unlikely romantic; review of *Unknown Soldier*. T.F. Rigelhof. G&M Dec 12, 1987: pE5.

Winners have wounds, too; review of *Unknown Soldier*. Scott Van Wynsberghe. WFP Oct 31, 1987: p52.

[Untitled]; review of *Unknown Soldier*. Allan Weiss. *Books in Can* Aug-Sept 1987; Vol 16 No 6: p26.

Death and dying dogs old soldier; review of *Unknown Soldier*. Thomas York. CH Oct 25, 1987: pE5.

PAYMENT IN DEATH/Young adult novel by Marion Crook

Tales for teenagers feature strong, viable family units; reviews of *The Baby Project* and *Payment in Death*. Jane Kent. CH April 12, 1987: pF7.

Freeman and Crook offer adventure and mystery in serial form; reviews of *Danger on the Tracks* and *Payment in Death*. Joan McGrath. photo · *Quill & Quire (Books for Young People)* April 1987; Vol 53 No 4: p9.

How suspense dies when it is misused; reviews of young adult novels. Tim Wynne-Jones. G&M Aug 8, 1987: pC19.

LE PAYS NATAL/Critical essays by Max Dorsinville

La vue comparatiste; review of *Le Pays natal*. C. Bouygues. *Can Lit* Winter 1987; No 115: p211–213.

UN PAZARO ES UN POEMA/Poetry anthology

Poetry and the loving Spanish tongue; reviews of poetry books. Fraser Sutherland. G&M May 30, 1987: pC21.
[ANTHOLOGIES: BOOK REVIEWS]

PEARSON, KIT

[Untitled]; review of *A Handful of Time*. Annette Goldsmith. *Quill & Quire (Books for Young People)* April 1987; Vol 53 No 4: p10.

School's out, and books are in; reviews of children's books. Janice Kennedy. MG July 4, 1987: J9.

Current crop of kids' books is brighter than spring gardens; reviews of *Pop Bottles* and *A Handful of Time*. Joan McGrath. TS May 24, 1987: pA19

Authors ease teen angst in the wilds of Alberta; reviews of young adult novels. Susan Scott. photo · CH April 23, 1987: pD1.

Living in the past; reviews of children's novels. Mary Ainslie Smith. *Books in Can* June-July 1987; Vol 16 No 5: p35–37.

Much more than a love story; reviews of *Salmonberry Wine* and *A Handful of Time*. Tim Wynne-Jones. G&M June 27, 1987: pE20.

Apple-pie beds and water bombs; review of *The Daring Game*. Lorraine M. York. *Can Child Lit* 1987; No 46: p79–81.

PEINTURE AVEUGLE/BLIND PAINTING/Poems by Robert Melançon

[Untitled]; reviews of *Blind Painting* and *All the Polarities*. Estelle Dansereau. *Quarry* Summer 1987; Vol 36 No 3: p82–86.

Harnessing poetry; reviews of *Blind Painting* and *Small Horses & Intimate Beasts*. Philip Lanthier. *Can Lit* Winter 1987; No 115: p140–142.

[Untitled]; reviews of *Small Horses & Intimate Beasts* and *Blind Painting*. David Leahy. *Queen's Q* Spring 1987; Vol 94 No 1: p189–191.

[Untitled]; review of *Blind Painting*. Peter Malden. *Rubicon* Fall 1987; No 9: p170–173.

[Untitled]; reviews of *Blind Painting* and *Small Horses & Intimate Beasts*. Andrew Vaisius. *Poetry Can R* Spring 1987; Vol 8 No 2–3: p59.

PELLERIN, GILLES

Ici, maintenant et autrement; review of *Ni le lieu ni l'heure*. Réjean Beaudoin. *Liberté* Aug 1987; Vol 29 No 4: p125–126.

La vitrine du livre; reviews. Jean Royer. MD March 14, 1987: pD4.
[CANADIAN LITERARY PERIODICALS]

Les vertus de la retenue et du silence; reviews of poetry books. Marie José Thériault. photo · *Lettres québec* Summer 1987; No 46: p30–32.

PELLETIER, JEAN

Coup De Soleil isn't great theatre, but it's a nice winter break; theatre review. Pat Donnelly. MG Jan 23, 1987: pC5.

PENGUINS/Play by Michael McKinley

Ambitious drama falls short of the mark; theatre reviews of *Penguins* and *Sliding for Home*. Stephen Godfrey. photo · G&M Nov 26, 1987: pA25.

PENNER, FRED

Kids' entertainer Penner plans three shows here; article. Janice Kennedy. photo · MG Nov 19, 1987: pE7.

PENUMBRA/Novel by Susan Kerslake

Short shrift for novel's art; review of *Penumbra*. Nanette Norris. *Essays on Can Writ* Spring 1987; No 34: p136–139.

PENUMBRA/Play by Linda Zwicker

Playwright's debut shows promise; theatre review of *Penumbra*. Brian Brennan. photo · CH Jan 20, 1987: pA10.

Three Toronto plays premiere at Calgary fest; article, includes theatre reviews. Robert Crew. photo · *TS* Feb 10, 1987: pB4.
[FESTIVALS, DRAMA]

New-play festival deserves a curtain call; theatre reviews. Stephen Godfrey. photo · *G&M* Feb 10, 1987: pC5.
[FESTIVALS, DRAMA]

PERCY, H.R.

Oak tree is weak base of H.R. Percy's tangled tales; review of *Tranter's Tree*. Lindsay Brown. photo · *MG* July 25, 1987: J8.

[Untitled]; reviews of *The Swell Season* and *A Model Lover*. Pauline Carey. *Cross Can Writ Q* 1987; Vol 9 No 1: p19–20.

Bill Percy turns his back on the sea; biographical article. Judith Fitzgerald. photo · *TS* June 21, 1987: pD8.

Historical novel starring oak tree a shade too slow; review of *Tranter's Tree*. William French. photo · *G&M* June 11, 1987: pD1.

[Untitled]; review of *A Model Lover*. Michael Helm. *Rubicon* Spring 1987; No 8: p224–225.

[Untitled]; reviews of *The Bridge Out of Town* and *A Model Lover*. Clifford G. Holland. *Queen's Q* Summer 1987; Vol 94 No 2: p472–474.

Circle games; reviews of fictional works. Barbara Leckie. *Can Lit* Winter 1987; No 115: p278–280.

[Untitled]; review of *A Model Lover*. C.H. Little. *Can Auth & Book* Winter 1987; Vol 62 No 2: p23.

A lovely, polished tree tale; review of *Tranter's Tree*. Joan McGrath. *TS* June 7, 1987: pG11.

Bred in the bark; review of *Tranter's Tree*. I.M. Owen. *Books in Can* May 1987; Vol 16 No 4: p19.

[Untitled]; review of *Tranter's Tree*. Thomas P. Sullivan. *Quill & Quire* May 1987; Vol 53 No 5: p22.

Fine writing saves novel; review of *Tranter's Tree*. David Williamson. *WFP* July 11, 1987: p57.

Passions and ironies; review of *A Model Lover*. Alan R. Young. *Fiddlehead* Summer 1987; No 152: p98–100.

THE PERFECT CIRCUS/Novel by Frederick Biro

[Untitled]; review of *The Perfect Circus*. Joan McGrath. *Quill & Quire* March 1987; Vol 53 No 3: p72–73.

PERICLES PRINCE OF TYRE BY WILLIAM SHAKES-PEARE/Play by René-Daniel Dubois

Dubois: Toronto's playwright-of-the-hour; theatre reviews. Marianne Ackerman. photo · *MG* May 5, 1987: pB6.

Drama's daring new voice; theatre review of *Pericles Prince of Tyre by William Shakespeare*. John Bemrose. photo · *Maclean's* April 27, 1987; Vol 100 No 17: p61.

Mystifying show looks at nature of art, magic; theatre review of *Pericles Prince of Tyre by William Shakespeare*. Ray Conlogue. photo · *G&M* April 10, 1987: pC6

Dubois' Pericles not perfect but impressive nonetheless; theatre review of *Pericles Prince of Tyre by William Shakespeare*. Robert Crew. photo · *TS* April 10, 1987: pD20.

PERPETUAL MOTION/MOUVEMENT SANS FIN/Novel by Graeme Gibson

L'obsession de l'impossible; review of *Mouvement sans fin*. Jean-Pierre Issenhuth. *Liberté* June 1987; Vol 29 No 3: p105–106.

PERRAULT, PIERRE

Un homme qui s'intéressait aux créateurs; article. *MD* Nov 3, 1987: p4.

La vie littéraire; column. Jean Royer. photo · *MD* June 20, 1987: pD2.
[AUTHORS, CANADIAN; POETRY READINGS; RADIO AND CANADIAN LITERATURE; TELEVISION AND CANADIAN LITERATURE]

PERRON, JEAN

[Untitled]; review of *Rock desperado*. Lucie Bourassa. *Estuaire* Winter 1986–87; No 43: p77.

PERSPECTIVES ON MORDECAI RICHLER/Critical essays collection

[Untitled]; review of *Perspectives on Mordecai Richler*. *Queen's Q* Winter 1987; Vol 94 No 4: p1066–1067.

[Untitled]; review of *Perspectives on Mordecai Richler*. Arnold E. Davidson. *Amer R of Can Studies* Summer 1987; Vol 17 No 2: p257–259.

Beyond the merely competent; reviews of critical works. Larry McDonald. *Atlan Prov Book R* Sept-Oct 1987; Vol 14 No 3: p11.
[CANADIAN LITERARY PERIODICALS]

PETCH, STEVE

Typical folks tell powerful internment story; theatre review of *Another Morning*. Stephen Godfrey. photo · *G&M* April 24, 1987: pC5.

PETERMAN, MICHAEL

[Untitled]; review of *Robertson Davies*. John H. Ferres. *Amer R of Can Studies* Winter 1987–88; Vol 17 No 4: p450–452.

[Untitled]; reviews of *Robertson Davies* and *Robertson Davies, Playwright*. D.O. Spettigue. *Queen's Q* Autumn 1987; Vol 94 No 3: p722–724.

LE PETIT UNIVERS DE R.P./Play by Normand Daoust

Le théâtre qu'on joue; theatre reviews. André Dionne. photo · *Lettres québec* Winter 1986–87; No 44: p53–54.

[Untitled]; theatre review of *Le Petit univers de R.P.*. Claude Poissant. photo · *Jeu* 1987; No 42: p148–149.

LA PETITE NOIRCEUR/Critical essays by Jean Larose

Jean Larose: un dialogue entre l'Écrit et l'Oral; column. Jean Éthier-Blais. *MD* Sept 26, 1987: pD8.

La vitrine du livre; reviews. Guy Ferland. *MD* Sept 12, 1987: pD4.

LES PETITS POUVOIRS/Children's play by Suzanne Lebeau

With passion, intensity and style; review of *Les Petits pouvoirs*. Hélène Beauchamp. *Can Child Lit* 1987; No 45: p65–68.

PETROFF, LEO

Leo Petroff poet, pressman fought for czar; obituary. Vincent Ball. photo · *TS* Jan 25, 1987: pA20.

LA PEUR DU GRAND AMOUR/Critical work by Louise Poissant

La droite amoureuse rallume ses brasiers; reviews of *La Peur du Grand Amour* and *La Corrida de l'amour*. Chantal Théry. *Lettres québec* Winter 1986–87; No 44: p69–71.

PEUT-TU ATTRAPER JOSEPHINE?/CAN YOU CATCH JOSEPHINE?/Children's story by Stéphane Poulin

[Untitled]; review of *Can You Catch Josephine?*. Abigail Cramer. *CH* Dec 6, 1987: pD9.

La vitrine du livre; review of *Peux-tu attraper Joséphine*. Guy Ferland. *MD* Sept 26, 1987: pD4.

Three stories for children; reviews of children's books. Veronica Leonard. *Atlan Prov Book R* Nov-Dec 1987; Vol 14 No 4: p1.

A title that will grab teenagers; reviews of children's books. Joan McGrath. *TS* Oct 25, 1987: pA18.

Youngsters get choice of beautiful books; reviews. Helen Norrie. *WFP* Dec 5, 1987: p57.

Annabel and Goldie go to the sea, Josephine goes to school; reviews of *Can You Catch Josephine?* and *Goldie and the Sea*. Susan Perren. *Quill & Quire (Books for Young People)* Oct 1987; Vol 53 No 10: p18–19.

Mini-reviews; reviews of children's stories. Mary Rubio. *Can Child Lit* 1987; No 47: p96–99.

A cat's brilliant new escapade; review of *Can You Catch Josephine?*. Tim Wynne-Jones. *G&M* Sept 19, 1987: pC19.

PFAUS, B.

Joyless in Jubilee?; review of *Alice Munro*. Lorraine M. York. *Essays on Can Writ* Spring 1987; No 34: p157–161.

PHILLIPS, EDWARD

Buried On Sunday wins Ellis award; article. *WFP* May 27, 1987: p36.
[AWARDS, LITERARY]

Crime winners no mystery; article. *Quill & Quire* June 1987; Vol 53 No 6: p26.
[AWARDS, LITERARY]

Crime pays for Arthur winners; article. *G&M* May 23, 1987: pC14.
[AWARDS, LITERARY]

À surveiller; column. *MD* Sept 23, 1987: p10.

How my novel of manners won the prize for crime; essay. Edward Phillips. illus · *MG* June 27, 1987: I3.
[AWARDS, LITERARY]

Edward Phillips; interview. Nancy Wigston. photo · *Books in Can* April 1987; Vol 16 No 3: p39–40.

PIAZZA, FRANÇOIS

Portrait de Piazza au coeur de la ville; review of *Blues Note*. Jean Royer. photo · *MD* Jan 17, 1987: pB3.

PICHÉ, ALPHONSE

La violence de la mort; review of *Sursis*. Gérald Gaudet. *MD* Dec 12, 1987: pD3.

The poetry of Alphonse Piché 1946–1982; article. Kathleen M. O'Donnell. *U of Windsor R* Spring-Summer 1987; Vol 20 No 2: p75–81.

PICKTHALL, MARJORIE

Killed into art: Marjorie Pickthall and The Wood Carver's Wife; article. Diana M.A. Relke. biog · *Can Drama* 1987; Vol 13 No 2: p187–200.
[FEMINIST WRITING AND CRITICISM]

PIECES OF MAP, PIECES OF MUSIC/Poems by Robert Bringhurst

[Untitled]; review of *Pieces of Map, Pieces of Music*. Ron Clark. *Wascana R* Spring 1987; Vol 22 No 1: p92–95.

Breathing in tune and time; review of *Pieces of Map, Pieces of Music*. Gwladys V. Downes. *Event* Summer 1987; Vol 16 No 2: p115–118.

[Untitled]; review of *Pieces of Map, Pieces of Music*. Peter O'Brien. *Rubicon* Fall 1987; No 9: p203–204.

[Untitled]; review of *Pieces of Map, Pieces of Music*. Ken Stange. *Poetry Can R* Summer 1987; Vol 8 No 4: p35–36.

Poetry, science, mind and religion; reviews of poetry books. Fraser Sutherland. photo · *G&M* Jan 31, 1987: pE19.

PIECES OF THE JIGSAW PUZZLE/Anthology of children's poetry and prose

Cultural heritage; review of *Pieces of the Jigsaw Puzzle*. Regine Haensel. *Prairie Fire* Autumn 1987; Vol 8 No 3: p120–122.
[ANTHOLOGIES: BOOK REVIEWS]

PILING BLOOD/Poems by Al Purdy

The dying generations; reviews of poetry books. Dermot McCarthy. *Essays on Can Writ* Spring 1987; No 34: p24–32.

PILON, JEAN-GUY

Le sénateur Paul David et 18 autres Québécois recevront l'Ordre national; article. *MD* Dec 24, 1987: pA3.

PINDER, LESLIE HALL

Women make difference in prairie family; review of *Under the House*. Cecelia Frey. *CH* July 19, 1987: pE4.
[FIRST NOVELS: BOOK REVIEWS]

Impressive; review of *Under the House*. M.T. Kelly. *G&M* Feb 14, 1987: pE20.
[FIRST NOVELS: BOOK REVIEWS]

World of wonders; reviews of first novels. Janice Kulyk Keefer. *Books in Can* May 1987; Vol 16 No 4: p37–38.
[FIRST NOVELS: BOOK REVIEWS]

[Untitled]; reviews of *Under the House* and *A Forest for Zoe*. Lesley McAllister. *Cross Can Writ Q* 1987; Vol 9 No 3–4: p48–49.
[FIRST NOVELS: BOOK REVIEWS]

[Untitled]; review of *Under the House*. Rachel Rafelman. *Quill & Quire* April 1987; Vol 53 No 4: p29.

Book world: a tip of the hat to small presses; column. Beverley Slopen. photo · *TS* Aug 9, 1987: pA20.
[CANADIAN LITERARY PUBLISHING]

The Rathbones' family skeletons; review of *Under the House*. Linda Taylor. *Times Lit Supp* Dec 18, 1987; No 4420: p1409.
[FIRST NOVELS: BOOK REVIEWS]

PINSENT, GORDON

A dream comes true for Pinsent with play he wrote and stars in; article. photo · *MG* July 23, 1987: pC10.

Newfoundland on the back burner; article. Bruce Bailey. photo · *MG* April 18, 1987: pC3.

John and the Missus is slow, but sincere; film review. Bruce Bailey. *MG* April 18, 1987: pC3.

John And The Missus misses despite commendable acting; film review. Ron Base. photo · *TS* Feb 6, 1987: pD8.
[FILM ADAPTATIONS OF CANADIAN LITERATURE]

Burgess touch refreshes yet another Roman tale; reviews of *Dancing in the Dark* and *John and the Missus*. Barbara Black. *MG* April 11, 1987: pG7.

Pinsent's presence overshadows film; film review of *John and the Missus*. Brian Brennan. photo · *CH* May 15, 1987: pE8.
[FILM ADAPTATIONS OF CANADIAN LITERATURE]

Barrie audiences responding to Pinsent play; column. Robert Crew. photo · *TS* July 27, 1987: pD1

The restless dreamer from the Rock; article. Brian D. Johnson. photo · *Maclean's* Feb 2, 1987; Vol 100 No 5: p76–78.

Hits and Missus; article. Martin Knelman. biog photo · *Tor Life* Feb 1987; Vol 21 No 2: p29–31.
[FILM ADAPTATIONS OF CANADIAN LITERATURE]

Gordon Pinsent reminds us of our sense of place; editorial. James Lorimer. *Atlan Insight* May 1987; Vol 9 No 5: p3.
[FILM ADAPTATIONS OF CANADIAN LITERATURE]

Pinsent tells touching story; film review of *John and the Missus*. Paul McKie. photo · *WFP* April 19, 1987: p15.
[FILM ADAPTATIONS OF CANADIAN LITERATURE]

Elegy for a dying village; film review of *John and the Missus*. Lawrence O'Toole. photo · *Maclean's* Feb 2, 1987; Vol 100 No 5: p78.
[FILM ADAPTATIONS OF CANADIAN LITERATURE]

Doubts and fears of a writing actor; essay. Gordon Pinsent. photo · *TS* Jan 24, 1987: pG1.

New Gordon Pinsent play embodies spirit of friend; article. Donna Shoemaker. photo · *CH* July 27, 1987: pB8.

A PIONEER PLACE/Poems by Betty Sanders Garner

[Untitled]; reviews of poetry books. George Whipple. *Poetry Can R* Spring 1987; Vol 8 No 2–3: p53.

PIROT, ALISON LOHANS

Living to tell the tale: survival guides for adolescent readers; reviews of *Can You Promise Me Spring?* and *We're Friends, Aren't We?*. Joanne Buckley. *Can Child Lit* 1987; No 46: p78–79.

[Untitled]; review of *Can You Promise Me Spring?*. Betty Dyck. *Can Auth & Book* Spring 1987; Vol 62 No 3: p25.

PITT, DAVID G.

Poet's triumphant ascent presented with grace, insight; review of *E.J. Pratt: The Master Years*. Ken Adachi. photo · *TS* Dec 19, 1987: M4.

The likeable poet; review of *E.J. Pratt: The Master Years*. William French. *G&M* Dec 5, 1987: pC21.

Pitt on Pratt: a match made in Newfoundland; article. Nancy Robb. photo · *Quill & Quire* Aug 1987; Vol 53 No 8: p31.

"Uncertain steerage"; review of *E.J. Pratt: The Truant Years*. Wendy Schissel. *Ariel* Jan 1987; Vol 18 No 1: p76–78.

PITTMAN, AL

How Newfie named Porky just died for TV fame; biographical article. George Gamester. *TS* June 25, 1987: pA2.

PLAGES/Short story anthology

Des regards qui s'attardent; review of *Plages*. Chantal Gamache. *MD* April 4, 1987: pD3.
[ANTHOLOGIES: BOOK REVIEWS]

PLAN B IS TOTAL PANIC/Young adult novel by Martyn Godfrey

A touching, but unsentimental story; review of *Plan B Is Total Panic*. Lyle Weis. *Can Child Lit* 1987; No 45: p72–73.

PLANÉRIA/Anthology of children's stories

Du réel à l'imaginaire; review of *Planéria*. René Gagné. *Can Child Lit* 1987; No 47: p94–95.
[ANTHOLOGIES: BOOK REVIEWS]

PLANTE, RAYMOND

U.S.-born writer wins book award; article. *WFP* April 29, 1987: p41.
[AWARDS, LITERARY]

Lunn, Gay, Reid, Poulin garner kids' book awards; article. *Quill & Quire (Books for Young People)* June 1987; Vol 53 No 6: p4.
[AWARDS, LITERARY]

Council award goes to Lunn; article. *G&M* April 30, 1987: pC1.
[AWARDS, LITERARY]

Le Conseil des arts du Canada attribue ses prix de littérature-jeunesse; article. *MD* April 28, 1987: p14.
[AWARDS, LITERARY]

Ontario writer wins Canada Council prize; article. *TS* April 28, 1987: pG4.
[AWARDS, LITERARY]

Dix années de littérature pour jeunes Québécois; article. Dominique Demers. photo · *MD* Nov 14, 1987: pD10.
[CANADIAN LITERARY PUBLISHING; CHILDREN'S LITERATURE]

Prix et distinctions; list of award winners. Gaétan Lévesque. photo · *Lettres québec* Autumn 1987; No 47: p7.
[AWARDS, LITERARY; GOVERNOR GENERAL'S AWARDS]

La vie littéraire; column. Jean Royer. photo · *MD* May 2, 1987: pD2.

[AWARDS, LITERARY; INTERNATIONAL REVIEWS OF CANADIAN LITERATURE; RADIO AND CANADIAN LITERATURE; TELEVISION AND CANADIAN LITERATURE; WRITERS' ORGANIZATIONS]

Satisfying prizes; column. Tim Wynne-Jones. *G&M* May 16, 1987: pC19.

[AWARDS, LITERARY]

PLAUT, W. GUNTHER

[Untitled]; review of *The Letter*. *Queen's Q* Winter 1987; Vol 94 No 4: p1067–1068.

[FIRST NOVELS: BOOK REVIEWS]

[Untitled]; review of *The Letter*. Douglas Hill. *Books in Can* Jan-Feb 1987; Vol 16 No 1: p24.

[FIRST NOVELS: BOOK REVIEWS]

Hitler's letter; review of *The Letter*. Robert G. Lawrence. *Can Lit* Winter 1987; No 115: p229–230.

[FIRST NOVELS: BOOK REVIEWS]

[Untitled]; review of *The Letter*. John North. *Quill & Quire* Jan 1987; Vol 53 No 1: p27.

[FIRST NOVELS: BOOK REVIEWS]

PLAY MEMORY/Play by Joanna McClelland Glass

Play's memorable but its production is rather less so; theatre review of *Play Memory*. Robert Crew. photo · *TS* July 3, 1987: pD21.

[Untitled]; theatre review of *Play Memory*. Keith Garebian. *Queen's Q* Autumn 1987; Vol 94 No 3: p755–757.

Glass's Play Memory is sober look at alcoholism; theatre review. Liam Lacey. photo · *G&M* July 3, 1987: pD11.

[Untitled]; reviews. Lisbie Rae. *Can Drama* 1987; Vol 13 No 2: p229–231.

[ANTHOLOGIES: BOOK REVIEWS]

THE PLAY OF LANGUAGE AND SPECTACLE: A STRUCTURAL READING OF SELECTED TEXTS BY GABRIELLE ROY/Critical work by Ellen Reisman Babby

Roy's language; review of *The Play of Language and Spectacle*. Paul G. Socken. *Can Lit* Spring 1987; No 112: p194.

PLAYING WITH FIRE/Poems by Tom Marshall

Getting physical; reviews of *Dance of the Particles* and *Playing with Fire*. Paul Denham. *Essays on Can Writ* Spring 1987; No 34: p44–47.

PLOWRIGHT, TERESA

Chilling view; review of *Dreams of an Unseen Planet*. H.J. Kirchhoff. *G&M* June 13, 1987: pC20.

[FIRST NOVELS: BOOK REVIEWS]

Me, myself, and I; reviews of first novels. Janice Kulyk Keefer. *Books in Can* Oct 1987; Vol 16 No 7: p35–36,38.

[FIRST NOVELS: BOOK REVIEWS]

Hostile Earth Mother insidiously subdues human colony; review of *Dreams of an Unseen Planet*. Michael Mirolla. photo · *MG* April 4, 1987: H10.

[FIRST NOVELS: BOOK REVIEWS]

POÈMES 1 (MÉMOIRE, LA POÉSIE CE MATIN, L'EN-DESSOUS L'ADMIRABLE)/Poems by Jacques Brault

[Untitled]; review of *Poèmes 1*. Jean Chapdelaine Gagnon. *Estuaire* Spring 1987; No 44: p79–80.

Brault, Fischer, Liscano; review of *Poèmes 1*. Jean-Pierre Issenhuth. *Liberté* June 1987; Vol 29 No 3: p74–79.

Poésie: trois rétrospectives; reviews of poetry books. Jean Royer. photo · *MD* Feb 9, 1987: p11.

Brault ou la mémoire du poème; review of *Poèmes 1*. Robert Yergeau. photo · *Lettres québec* Spring 1987; No 45: p40–41.

POÈMES: SIGNE ET RUMEUR, L'OUTRE-VIE, AUTO-PORTRAITS, INDITS/Poems by Marie Uguay

[Untitled]; review of *Poèmes*. Hélène Dorion. *Estuaire* Spring 1987; No 44: p83–84.

Marie Uguay, Mandelstam, Luzi; review of *Poèmes*. Jean-Pierre Issenhuth. *Liberté* April 1987; Vol 29 No 2: p86–94.

La répétition de l'intime; reviews of poetry books. André Marquis. photo · *Lettres québec* Spring 1987; No 45: p44–46.

Poésie: trois rétrospectives; reviews of poetry books. Jean Royer. photo · *MD* Feb 9, 1987: p11.

LA POÉSIE QUÉBÉCOISE CONTEMPORAINE/Anthology

La vitrine du livre; reviews. Guy Ferland. *MD* Nov 14, 1987: pD16.

[ANTHOLOGIES: BOOK REVIEWS]

POÈTES QUÉBÉCOIS CONTEMPORAINS/Poetry anthology

La vitrine du livre; reviews of *Poètes québécois contemporains* and *Comparaison et raison*. Guy Ferland. *MD* Oct 10, 1987: pD4.

[ANTHOLOGIES: BOOK REVIEWS]

PODY, DAVID

Anti-drug play goes to school; article. Beverley Mitchell. photo · *MG* Nov 18, 1987: pE7.

POEMS NEW AND SELECTED/Poems by Henry Beissel

Drama of failed pole trek unfulfilled; reviews of *Flight of the Falcon* and *Poems New and Selected*. Keith Garebian. *TS* Oct 31, 1987: M5.

From ivy-covered professors; reviews of poetry books. Fraser Sutherland. *G&M* Oct 17, 1987: pF9.

POEMS RELEASED ON A NUCLEAR WIND/Poems by Allan Cooper

[Untitled]; review of *Poems Released on a Nuclear Wind*. Barbara Carey. *Books in Can* Dec 1987; Vol 16 No 9: p30–31.

POEMS: COLLECTED, UNPUBLISHED AND NEW/ Poems by Wilfred Watson

[Untitled]; review of *Poems*. George Woodcock. *Poetry Can R* Spring 1987; Vol 8 No 2–3: p56–57.

POETKER, AUDREY

Young poets on display; reviews of poetry books. Robert Quickenden. photo · *WFP* March 14, 1987: p52.

Grief and love; review of *I Sing for My Dead in German*. Brenda Suderman. *Prairie Fire* Autumn 1987; Vol 8 No 3: p115–117.

POETRY PERFORMANCE

Dada processing; essay. Raymond Filip. *Books in Can* Nov 1987; Vol 16 No 8: p4–5.
[FESTIVALS, LITERARY; POSTMODERNIST WRITING AND CRITICISM]

Intriguing idea poses performance problems; review of *Anna*. Randal McIlroy. *WFP* June 28, 1987: p24.

The west coast: the Spirit Quest Festival; regional column. Linda Rogers. *Poetry Can R* Fall 1987; Vol 9 No 1: p22.
[FESTIVALS, LITERARY]

La vie littéraire; column. Jean Royer. *MD* Sept 12, 1987: pD2.
[AWARDS, LITERARY; CONFERENCES, LITERARY; POETRY READINGS]

Ontario report: advancing & retreating with Ontario Lit.; regional column. Steven Smith. *Poetry Can R* Summer 1987; Vol 8 No 4: p22.
[RADIO AND CANADIAN LITERATURE]

Sound poetry: serious play; article. Richard Truhlar. illus · *Cross Can Writ Q* 1987; Vol 9 No 3–4: p16–18.
[SOUND POETRY]

POETRY READINGS

Reading series features poet/critic Eli Mandel; article. *TS* Feb 1, 1987: pE9.

Eli Mandel appearance at Harbourfront cancelled; article. *TS* Feb 2, 1987: H1.

Love poetry reading for Valentine's Day; article. *TS* Feb 13, 1987: pD21.

Wakes for Acorn; article. *TS* March 1, 1987: pC4.

Billboard: U of M Suzuki program holds workshop; column. *WFP* Feb 19, 1987: p36.

Billboard: Red Cross seeks return of unused canes, crutches; column. *WFP* March 9, 1987: p21.
[COMPETITIONS, LITERARY]

Billboard: genealogical society meets tonight at 7:30 in museum; column. *WFP* March 19, 1987: p39.

Aujourd'hui; column. *MD* Feb 26, 1987: p20.

Lectures au Pluriel; article. *MD* March 24, 1987: p15.

Readings at NFB; article. *CH* Feb 20, 1987: pF7.
[FICTION READINGS]

Mainstreet Calgary; column. *CH (Neighbors)* Feb 26, 1987: pA5.

Mainstreet Calgary; column. *CH (Neighbors)* March 11, 1987: pA8–A9.

Harbourfront woos the literary-minded; article. *G&M* Jan 7, 1987: pC5.
[FICTION READINGS]

Poet-artist at Cedarbrae library; article. *TS (Neighbours)* March 24, 1987: p15.

Harbourfront Readings Club; article. *Quill & Quire* March 1987; Vol 53 No 3: p60–61.
[FICTION READINGS]

Mainstreet Calgary; column. *CH (Neighbors)* April 1, 1987: pA4.
[WRITERS' WORKSHOPS]

À surveiller; column. *MD* Sept 18, 1987: p12

Ondaatje opens reading series; article. photo · *CH* Sept 25, 1987: pF7.
[FICTION READINGS]

The Arc reading series; notice. *Arc* Fall 1987; No 19: p83.

Community calendar; column. *TS* July 3, 1987: pB2.

Louise de Gonzague Pelletier à Place aux poètes; article. *MD* Dec 2, 1987: p14.
[AWARDS, LITERARY]

Billboard: libraries to sell books for three days; column. *WFP* Nov 3, 1987: p19.

Author to read; article. *CH* Nov 10, 1987: pD3.

Mainstreet Calgary; column. *CH (Neighbors)* Nov 11, 1987: pA15, A18.

Poet explores social issues; article. *CH* Nov 17, 1987: pE8.

Mainstreet Calgary; column. *CH (Neighbors)* Nov 18, 1987: pA15–A16.

Mainstreet Calgary; column. *CH (Neighbors)* Nov 25, 1987: pA8.

Mainstreet Calgary; column. *CH (Neighbors)* Dec 2, 1987: pA11, A14–A15.

Mainstreet Calgary; column. *CH (Neighbors)* Dec 9, 1987: pA17–A18.
[COMPETITIONS, LITERARY]

East Coast report: Labrador and the gift of tongues; column. Lesley Choyce. *Poetry Can R* Spring 1987; Vol 8 No 1–2: p14–15.

Poetry sweatshops add a new twist to Olympic tradition; column. William French. *G&M* March 3, 1987: pC7.
[CANADIAN LITERARY LANDMARKS; COMPETITIONS, LITERARY; FESTIVALS, LITERARY]

The poetry sweatshop; article. Liane Heller. photo · *Cross Can Writ Q* 1987; Vol 9 No 1: p5–6,28.
[COMPETITIONS, LITERARY]

A whole lotta scribblin' goin' on; article about Poetry Sweatshop. Urjo Kareda. photo · *G&M (Toronto Magazine)* March 1987; Vol 1 No 12: p12–13.
[COMPETITIONS, LITERARY]

Literary giants got rotten reviews; column. Kenneth McGoogan. *CH* Jan 18, 1987: pE4.
[CANADIAN LITERARY PERIODICALS]

Culture director's tribute to author captured sentiment; column. Kenneth McGoogan. photo · *CH* Jan 27, 1987: pB6.
[AUDIO-VISUALS AND CANADIAN LITERATURE]

Dandelion uncovers new voice; column. Kenneth McGoogan. photo · *CH* Feb 1, 1987: pC8.
[AWARDS, LITERARY; CANADIAN LITERARY PERIODICALS]

POETRY TORONTO/Periodical

Poetry magazine holds rummage sale; article. *TS* Sept 30, 1987: pD1.

[CANADIAN LITERARY PERIODICALS]

POETS WHO DON'T DANCE/Poems by Shaunt Basmajian

[Untitled]; review of *Poets Who Don't Dance*. Rod Anderson. *Poetry Can R* Spring 1987; Vol 8 No 2–3: p58.

Grief & memory; reviews of poetry books. Peter Stenberg. *Can Lit* Spring 1987; No 112: p169–171.

LES POIDS DES POLITIQUES: LIVRES, LECTURE ET LITTÉRATURE/Critical essays collection

La vitrine du livre; reviews. Guy Ferland. *MD* Nov 7, 1987: pD4.

LE POISON DANS L'EAU/Novel by Christine Brouillet

La vitrine du livre; reviews. Guy Ferland. *MD* May 9, 1987: pD4.

[Untitled]; review of *Le Poison dans l'eau*. Alberto Manguel. *Books in Can* Nov 1987; Vol 16 No 8: p24–25.

POISON/Novel by Doric Germain

Cycles; reviews of *L'Oeil interrompu* and *Poison*. Mark Benson. *Can Lit* Spring 1987; No 112: p136–138.

POISSANT, ALAIN

Auprès de ma blonde, qu'il fait bon, fait bon . . . ; review of *La Blonde d'Yvon*. Jean-Roch Boivin. *MD* Oct 17, 1987: pD3.

POISSANT, CLAUDE

Director, cast work wonders; theatre review of *Ce qui reste du désir*. Marianne Ackerman. photo · *MG* March 18, 1987: pD3.

Le théâtre qu'on joue; theatre reviews. André Dionne. photo · *Lettres québec* Summer 1987; No 46: p47–48.

Grandeur et misère: le retour du père sur la scène québécoise; article. Carole Fréchette. photo · *Jeu* 1987; No 45: p17–35.

[QUEBEC DRAMA (FRENCH LANGUAGE): HISTORY AND CRITICISM]

Heureusement pour le théâtre, l'argent n'a pas d'odeur; article. Paul Lefebvre. photo · *MD* March 14, 1987: pC3.

Bloc-notes; column. Michel Vaïs. photo · *Jeu* 1987; No 45: p227–231.

[AWARDS, LITERARY; GOVERNMENT GRANTS FOR WRITERS/PUBLISHERS; WRITERS' ORGANIZATIONS]

POISSANT, LOUISE

La droite amoureuse rallume ses brasiers; reviews of *La Peur du Grand Amour* and *La Corrida de l'amour*. Chantal Thry. *Lettres québec* Winter 1986–87; No 44: p69–71.

THE POLAR BEAR EXPRESS/Short stories by Lesley Battler

Getting on a literary roulette wheel; reviews of fictional works. Trevor Ferguson. *MG* Nov 14, 1987: J11.

[FIRST NOVELS: BOOK REVIEWS]

POLIQUIN, DANIEL

La vitrine du livre; reviews. Guy Ferland. *MD* Nov 21, 1987: pD4.

Ontarois entre deux langues; reviews of *Nouvelles de la capitale* and *L'Obomsawin*. Lori Saint-Martin. *MD* Dec 12, 1987: pD4.

POLITICAL WRITING

Political poetry — a rejoinder; essay. John Baglow. *Arc* Spring 1987; No 18: p72–74.

Out of the collectives; article. David Barnet. photo · *Can Theatre R* Winter 1987; No 53: p5–6.

In the neighbourhood of my heart; essay. Don Bouzek. photo · *Can Theatre R* Winter 1987; No 53: p20–25.

[WRITERS' WORKSHOPS]

A note on political poems; editorial. Allan Cooper. *Germination* Fall 1987; Vol 11 No 1: p25.

U.S. report: political poems & personal visions; comparative column. David Donnell. *Poetry Can R* Summer 1987; Vol 8 No 4: p26.

The political dramaturgy of the Mummers Troupe; article. Alan Filewod. *Can Drama* 1987; Vol 13 No 1: p60–71.

The ideological formation of political theatre in Canada; article. Alan Filewod. abstract · *Theatre Hist in Can* Fall 1987; Vol 8 No 2: p254–263.

[CANADIAN DRAMA: HISTORY AND CRITICISM; COLONIALISM]

Popular theatre; editorial. Alan Filewod. *Can Theatre R* Winter 1987; No 53: p3.

Underdeveloped alliance; essay. Ian Filewod. photo · *Can Theatre R* Winter 1987; No 53: p39–42.

[FESTIVALS, DRAMA]

Another brick in the wall; article. Ray Filip. *Books in Can* Aug-Sept 1987; Vol 16 No 6: p4–5.

[FESTIVALS, LITERARY]

Thémes et formes; article. Carole Fréchette. Diane Pavlovic. photo · *Jeu* 1987; No 42: p40–48.

[FESTIVALS, DRAMA; WOMEN WRITERS]

Ballrooms and boardroom tables; essay. Amanda Hale. photo · *Can Theatre R* Winter 1987; No 53: p29–32.

"The truth must out": the political plays of John Krizanc; article. Richard Paul Knowles. *Can Drama* 1987; Vol 13 No 1: p27–33.

The editor replies; Christopher Levenson. *Arc* Spring 1987; No 18: p75–77.

Now more than ever; article. Judith Mastai. photo · *Can Theatre R* Winter 1987; No 53: p7–10.

Super(stack) inspiration; essay. Laurie-Ann McGauley. photo · *Can Theatre R* Winter 1987; No 53: p35–38.

Beauchemin's The Alley Cat as modern myth; article. Constantina Mitchell. *Amer R of Can Studies* Winter 1987–88; Vol 17 No 4: p409–418.

[MYTHS AND LEGENDS IN CANADIAN LITERATURE]

Via Newfoundland and Africa; essay. Rhonda Payne. photo · *Can Theatre R* Winter 1987; No 53: p26–28.

Constitution d'une avant-garde littéraire; article. Jacques Pelletier. abstract · *Études lit* Spring-Summer 1987; Vol 20 No 1: p111–130.
[CANADIAN LITERARY PERIODICALS; POSTMODERNIST WRITING AND CRITICISM; QUEBEC LITERATURE (FRENCH LANGUAGE): HISTORY AND CRITICISM]

Tom Wayman's work poetry; article. Grant Shilling. *Poetry Can R* Spring 1987; Vol 8 No 2–3: p20–21.

Büchner in Canada: Woyzeck and the development of English-Canadian theatre; article. Jerry Wasserman. abstract photo · *Theatre Hist in Can* Fall 1987; Vol 8 No 2: p181–192.
[CANADIAN DRAMA: HISTORY AND CRITICISM]

The agitprop players; article. Chris Wood. photo · *Maclean's* June 8, 1987; Vol 100 No 23: p55.
[FESTIVALS, DRAMA]

POLITICS AND THE PLAYWRIGHT: GEORGE RYGA/ Critical work by Christopher Innes

Dramatic fringe; reviews of *Five from the Fringe* and *Politics and the Playwright: George Ryga*. James Noonan. *Can Lit* Winter 1987; No 115: p235–238.
[ANTHOLOGIES: BOOK REVIEWS]

THE POLITICS OF THE IMAGINATION: A LIFE OF F.R. SCOTT/Biography by Sandra Djwa

Portrait of an extraordinary man: a vibrant and influential presence in our intellectual and political life; review of *The Politics of the Imagination*. Ken Adachi. photo · *TS* Nov 21, 1987: M4.

The monument; review of *The Politics of the Imagination*. Louis Dudek. illus · *G&M* Nov 21, 1987: pC23.

F.R. Scott: just portrayal of a poetic humanist; review of *The Politics of the Imagination*. Doug Fetherling. photo · *Quill & Quire* Sept 1987; Vol 53 No 9: p80.

A very public life; review of *The Politics of the Imagination*. John Hutcheson. *Can Forum* Oct 1987; Vol 67 No 772: p40–41.

Evolution of an intellectual; review of *The Politics of the Imagination*. Allen Mills. photo · *WFP* Nov 14, 1987: p50.

F.R. Scott: his life was his finest hour; review of *The Politics of the Imagination*. Joel Yanofsky. photo · *MG* Nov 14, 1987: J9.

POLK, JAMES

Stage fright; article. Marc Côté. *Books in Can* June-July 1987; Vol 16 No 5: p3,5.

Vanity Press experiences first-play problems; theatre review. Ray Conlogue. *G&M* March 14, 1987: pE10.

Book world: Clarkson brings pool of goodwill to M&S job; column. Beverley Slopen. *TS* March 15, 1987: pA22.
[AWARDS, LITERARY; PUBLISHING AND PUBLISHERS IN CANADA]

Paperclips: publishing on-stage . . . P.K. Page's love song to Brazil; column. Beverley Slopen. photo · *Quill & Quire* May 1987; Vol 53 No 5: p14.

POLLAK, VÉRA

Une enfant du siècle au "monde merveilleux du kitsch du coeur"; review of *Rose-Rouge*. Jean-Roch Boivin. *MD* Aug 29, 1987: p11–12.

POLLOCK, SHARON

Writer explores mother's suicide; article. photo · *WFP* Feb 4, 1987: p35.

Billboard: fitness program for all ages; column. *WFP* Feb 24, 1987: p52.
[DRAMATIC READINGS]

Munro short story collection wins award; article. *WFP* May 29, 1987: p34.
[GOVERNOR GENERAL'S AWARDS]

What's happening; notice. photo · *CH* April 3, 1987: pC6–C7.

Guild honors Pollock, van Herk; article. *G&M* May 13, 1987: pC5.
[AWARDS, LITERARY]

Le prix du Gouverneur général à Yvon Rivard; article. *MD* May 28, 1987: p2.
[GOVERNOR GENERAL'S AWARDS]

Governor General's Award to Munro amid poetry protest; article. photo · *MG* May 28, 1987: pC1.
[GOVERNOR GENERAL'S AWARDS]

Governor General's award winners; article. *Quill & Quire* July 1987; Vol 53 No 7: p53–54.
[GOVERNOR GENERAL'S AWARDS]

Writers Guild of Alberta awards; article. *Quill & Quire* July 1987; Vol 53 No 7: p54.
[AWARDS, LITERARY]

Author plans play; article. *WFP* Dec 18, 1987: p38.

Frye finally wins elusive award for best non-fiction book of '86; article. Ken Adachi. photo · *TS* May 28, 1987: H1.
[GOVERNOR GENERAL'S AWARDS]

Pollock's Egg won't be done in time for festival; article. Bob Blakey. photo · *CH* June 18, 1987: pD7.

Pollock play makes debut on TC stage in '88 season; article. Brian Brennan. photo · *CH* April 23, 1987: pD1.

Pollock is tops again; article. Brian Brennan. photo · *CH* May 27, 1987: pA1.
[GOVERNOR GENERAL'S AWARDS]

City thespian lands role in HMS Pinafore; column. Brian Brennan. *CH* Sept 22, 1987: pC9.

Remembrance of things past; review of *Doc*. Marc Côté. *Books in Can* March 1987; Vol 16 No 2: p1718.

Sculptor to help shape women's festival; article. Donald Campbell. *WFP* July 28, 1987: p28.
[FESTIVALS, LITERARY]

[Untitled]; review of *Doc*. Cindy Cowan. *Can Theatre R* Fall 1987; No 52: p95–96.

Blood Relations script at fault; theatre review. Robert Davis. photo · *TS (Neighbours)* April 7, 1987: p16.

Passionate playwright; interview with Sharon Pollock. Marie Hohtanz. photo · *CH (Sunday Magazine)* Nov 29, 1987: p6–10.

Lizzie Borden story staged in Pickering; article. Paul Irish. *TS (Neighbours)* March 24, 1987: p14.

Sharon Pollock: personal frictions; review of *Doc*. Richard Paul Knowles. *Atlan Prov Book R* Feb-March 1987; Vol 14 No 1: p19.

Yvon Rivard et Northrop Frye parmi les lauréats des prix du gouverneur général; article. Robert Lévesque. photo · *MD* May 28, 1987: p13.
[GOVERNOR GENERAL'S AWARDS]

Looking back at a tragedy; theatre review of *The Komagata Maru Incident*. Liam Lacey. *G&M* April 2, 1987: pC5.

Production of Blood Relations offers electric performances; theatre review. Alex Law. photo · *TS (Neighbours)* April 7, 1987: p16.

[Untitled]; review of *Doc*. Randee Loucks. *Dandelion* Fall-Winter 1987; Vol 14 No 2: p147–150.

Sharon Pollock; interview. Robin Metcalfe. photo · *Books in Can* March 1987; Vol 16 No 2: p39–40.

Munro wins third Governor General's Award; article. Jamie Portman. photo · *CH* May 28, 1987: pC9.
[GOVERNOR GENERAL'S AWARDS]

[Untitled]; reviews. Lisbie Rae. *Can Drama* 1987; Vol 13 No 2: p229–231.
[ANTHOLOGIES: BOOK REVIEWS]

Munro wins top literary prize; article. Lisa Rochon. photo · *G&M* May 28, 1987: pD1.
[GOVERNOR GENERAL'S AWARDS]

MTC shows ability with Doc production; theatre review. Reg Skene. *WFP* Feb 6, 1987: p29.

Schools' forced funding cutbacks can't quell Quest; article. Kate Zimmerman. photo · *CH* Oct 22, 1987: pD1.

POMERLEAU, JEANNE

La vitrine du livre; reviews. Guy Ferland. *MD* Aug 29, 1987: pC12.

Ah! les Beaucerons!; review of *Les Grandes corvées beauceronnes*. Benoît Lacroix. *MD* Sept 19, 1987: pD2.

POMEROY, ELSIE MAY

Torn between love and loyalty; reviews of *Sir Charles God Damn* and Sir Charles G.D. Roberts: A Biography. David McFadden. photo · *Brick* Fall 1987; No 31: p55–59.

POMME RECOUNTS/Children's story by Louise Pomminville

Garden tale helps cancer children; article. E.J. Gordon. photo · *MG* Aug 25, 1987: pC6.

LES POMMIERS EN FLEURS/FORBIDDEN TREES/Play by Serge Sirois

"Nouvelles pour le théâtre"; column. Robert Lévesque. *MD* Jan 27, 1987: p5.

POMMINVILLE, LOUISE

Garden tale helps cancer children; article. E.J. Gordon. photo · *MG* Aug 25, 1987: pC6.

POP BOTTLES/Children's novel by Ken Roberts

Current crop of kids' books is brighter than spring gardens; reviews of *Pop Bottles* and *A Handful of Time*. Joan McGrath. *TS* May 24, 1987: pA19.

Triumphant return; reviews of *Jacob Two-Two and the Dinosaur* and *Pop Bottles*. Tim Wynne-Jones. *G&M* June 13, 1987: pC19.
[AWARDS, LITERARY]

POPCORN/Novel by Louis Leblanc

Un laboratoire d'écriture ludique; review of *Popcorn*. Dorothy Leigh-Lizotte. *MD* April 28, 1987: p17.

THE PORT DALHOUSIE STORIES/Novel by Dennis Tourbin

The tribulations of these teens are a trial for readers; review of *The Port Dalhousie Stories*. William French. illud · *G&M* April 23, 1987: pC1.

[Untitled]; review of *The Port Dalhousie Stories*. D. French. *Books in Can* Nov 1987; Vol 16 No 8: p25.

PORTER, ANNA

Black Sheep time; review of *Mortal Sins*. Margaret Cannon. photo · *G&M* Nov 14, 1987: pE4.

Tough publisher tackles new mystery; article. Rod Currie. photo · *WFP* Dec 1, 1987: p32.

Under the Nazi shadow; review of *Mortal Sins*. Gillian MacKay. *Maclean's* Nov 23, 1987; Vol 100 No 47: p54a

[Untitled]; review of *Mortal Sins*. John North. *Quill & Quire* Oct 1987; Vol 53 No 10: p22.

PORTER, HELEN

Storyteller relives her youth; article. Leslie Scrivener. photo · *TS* Dec 20, 1987: pD6.
[STORYTELLING]

THE POSSIBILITIES OF CHINESE TROUT/Poems by Greg Simison

[Untitled]; review of *The Possibilities of Chinese Trout*. Brian Vanderlip. *Poetry Can R* Fall 1987; Vol 9 No 1: p34–35.

Confident voices heard through poetry collections; reviews of poetry books. Christopher Wiseman. *CH* Feb 8, 1987: pE5.

POSSIBLES/Periodical

La vitrine du livre; reviews of periodicals. Guy Ferland. *MD* Sept 5, 1987: pC8.
[CANADIAN LITERARY PERIODICALS]

La vitrine du livre; reviews. Jean Royer. photo · *MD* March 21, 1987: pD2.
[CANADIAN LITERARY PERIODICALS]

POSSIBLY YOURS/Play by Robert More

Persistence pays off for determined actor-writer; article. Brian Brennan. photo · *CH* March 6, 1987: pF1.

Fare can't be taken at face value; theatre review of *Possibly Yours*. Brian Brennan. photo · *CH* March 10, 1987: pC7.

POST-SIXTIES NOCTURNE/Poems by Pier Giorgio di Cicco

Excesses; reviews of poetry books. Eva Tihanyi. *Can Lit* Winter 1987; No 115: p200–202.

THE POSTMAN RINGS ONCE/Play by Sky Gilbert

ATP's Postman Rings Once is a risk within a larger risk; article. Bob Blakey. *CH* Jan 30, 1987: pC1.

Tame gay play marked by low-camp theatrics; theatre review of *The Postman Rings Once*. Brian Brennan. photo · *CH* Feb 1, 1987: pC6.

Play review endorsed; letter to the editor. Edna Brown. *CH* Feb 8, 1987: pB4.

The Postman Rings Once too often; theatre review. Ray Conlogue. photo · *G&M* Oct 8, 1987: pD5.

Three Toronto plays premiere at Calgary fest; article, includes theatre reviews. Robert Crew. photo · *TS* Feb 10, 1987: pB4.
[FESTIVALS, DRAMA]

New-play festival deserves a curtain call; theatre reviews. Stephen Godfrey. photo · *G&M* Feb 10, 1987: pC5.
[FESTIVALS, DRAMA]

Lana Turner steals the show; theatre review of *The Postman Rings Once*. Vit Wagner. photo · *TS* Oct 9, 1987: pE9.

POSTMODERNIST WRITING AND CRITICISM

See also **METAFICTION**

Dr. Sadhu's semi-opticks, or how to write a virtual-novel by the book: Steve McCaffery's Panopticon; article. Rafael Barreto-Rivera. *Open Letter (special issue)* Fall 1987; Vol 6 No 9: p39–47.

Panoptical artifice; article. Charles Bernstein. *Open Letter (special issue)* Fall 1987; Vol 6 No 9: p9–15.

The state of theatre: avant-garde advances bewilder actors, critics; article. Brian Brennan. photo · *CH* Oct 18, 1987: pC4.

Grammatology & economy; article. Michael Coffey. photo · *Open Letter (special issue)* Fall 1987; Vol 6 No 9: p27–38.
[STRUCTURALIST WRITING AND CRITICISM]

West coast recollections; article. Judith Copithorne. *Cross Can Writ Q* 1987; Vol 9 No 3–4: p10.
[BRITISH COLUMBIA WRITING AND WRITERS]

Sous l'angle de la provocation ou quand la théorie imagine; essay. Louise Cotnoir. bibliog biog · *La Nouvelle barre du jour (special issue)* 1987; No 201–202: p81–94

Defying linear deification — contemporary Toronto visual poetry; article. J.W. Curry. illus · *Cross Can Writ Q* 1987; Vol 9 No 3–4: p6–8.
[CONCRETE POETRY; ONTARIO WRITING AND WRITERS]

Novelist as trickster: the magical presence of Gabriel García Márquez in Robert Kroetsch's What The Crow Said; article. Brian Edwards. *Essays on Can Writ* Spring 1987; No 34: p92–110.
[LATIN AMERICA-CANADA LITERARY RELATIONS; MAGIC REALISM; STRUCTURALIST WRITING AND CRITICISM]

Data processing; essay. Raymond Filip. *Books in Can* Nov 1987; Vol 16 No 8: p4–5.
[FESTIVALS, LITERARY; POETRY PERFORMANCE]

Poetry in motion — new dimensions in creating with computers; article. Marco Fraticelli. illus · *Cross Can Writ Q* 1987; Vol 9 No 3–4: p19–20.

Art for art & and truth; editorial. Susan Ioannou. *Cross Can Writ Q* 1987; Vol 9 No 3–4: p37,64.

Steve McCaffery's Panopticon; article. William McPheron. photo · *Open Letter (special issue)* Fall 1987; Vol 6 No 9: p49–54.
[METAFICTION; STRUCTURALIST WRITING AND CRITICISM]

Présentation; editorial. Clément Moisan. Denis Saint-Jacques. *Études lit* Spring-Summer 1987; Vol 20 No 1: p9–16.
[CANADIAN LITERATURE: STUDY AND TEACHING; STRUCTURALIST WRITING AND CRITICISM]

L'être et le paraître: une question du XVIIe siècle posée aujourd'hui; article. Diane Pavlovic. photo · *Jeu* 1987; No 44: p154–168.
[AUDIO-VISUALS AND CANADIAN LITERATURE]

Constitution d'une avant-garde littéraire; article. Jacques Pelletier. abstract · *Études lit* Spring-Summer 1987; Vol 20 No 1: p111–130.
[CANADIAN LITERARY PERIODICALS; POLITICAL WRITING; QUEBEC LITERATURE (FRENCH LANGUAGE): HISTORY AND CRITICISM]

From known to invention; editorial. Ted Plantos. *Cross Can Writ Q* 1987; Vol 9 No 3–4: p2.

Of poets and hackers: notes on Canadian post-modern poets; article. Don Precosky. *Studies in Can Lit* 1987; Vol 12 No 1: p146–155.
[CANADIAN POETRY: HISTORY AND CRITICISM]

Woman as object, women as subjects, & the consequences for narrative: Hubert Aquin's Neige noire and the impasse of post-modernism; article. Patricia Smart. *Can Lit* Summer-Fall 1987; No 113–114: p168–178.
[FEMINIST WRITING AND CRITICISM]

Experiskinno poetry — then and now; editorial article. George Swede. photo · *Cross Can Writ Q* 1987; Vol 9 No 3–4: p3–5.
[CANADIAN LITERARY PERIODICALS; CANADIAN LITERARY PUBLISHING]

Fiction et métissage ou écrire l'imaginaire du réel; essay. France Théoret. bibliog biog · *La Nouvelle barre du jour (special issue)* 1987; No 201–202: p65–78.
[FEMINIST WRITING AND CRITICISM]

You are what you write; essay. Richard Truhlar. *Poetry Can R* Fall 1987; Vol 9 No 1: p12.

POTREBENKO, HELEN

Two ways of making poetry; reviews of *The Prismatic Eye* and *Walking Slow*. Paul Barclay. *Prairie Fire* Summer 1987; Vol 8 No 2: p56–59.

[Untitled]; review of *Sometimes They Sang*. Phil Hall. *Books in Can* June-July 1987; Vol 16 No 5: p21–22.

Grief & memory; reviews of poetry books. Peter Stenberg. *Can Lit* Spring 1987; No 112: p169–171.

POTTER, GERRY

[The Rich Man]; theatre review. Lynne Van Luven. *NeWest R* Nov 1987; Vol 13 No 3: p18.
[DRAMATIC ADAPTATIONS OF CANADIAN LITERATURE]

POULIN, GABRIELLE

[Untitled]; review of *All the Way Home*. Peter S. Noble. *British J of Can Studies* June 1987; Vol 2 No 1: p182–183.

POULIN, JACQUES

Dans les poches; reviews of *Dictionnaire de moi-même* and *Mon cheval pour un royaume*. Guy Ferland. *MD* May 30, 1987: pD2.

Dans les poches; reviews. Guy Ferland. *MD* Sept 26, 1987: pD6.

[Untitled]; review of *Spring Tides*. Barbara Leckie. *Rubicon* Spring 1987; No 8: p195–197.

Poulin; review of *Études françaises (special issue)*. Anne Marie Miraglia. *Can Lit* Spring 1987; No 112: p152–154.
[CANADIAN LITERARY PERIODICALS]

[Untitled]; review of *Spring Tides*. Peter S. Noble. *British J of Can Studies* June 1987; Vol 2 No 1: p182.

A crowded Eden; review of *Spring Tides*. Theresia Quigley. *Fiddlehead* Autumn 1987; No 153: p102–103.

Recent Canadian fiction; reviews of novels. D.O. Spettigue. *Queen's Q* Summer 1987; Vol 94 No 2: p366–375.
[FIRST NOVELS: BOOK REVIEWS]

A teddy bear's tale; review of *Spring Tides*. Jeannette Urbas. *Can Forum* Jan 1987; Vol 66 No 765: p39–40.

POULIN, STÉPHANE

[Untitled]; review of *Can You Catch Josephine?*. Abigail Cramer. *CH* Dec 6, 1987: pD9.

Children's-book artists love their work; article. Ann Duncan. photo · *MG* Nov 14, 1987: pD1

There's not much money in kids' books; article. Ann Duncan. photo · *MG* Nov 14, 1987: pD1.

La vitrine du livre; review of *Peux-tu attraper Joséphine*. Guy Ferland. *MD* Sept 26, 1987: pD4.

Stéphane Poulin's sensitive approach to life and art; article. Bernie Goedhart. photo · *Quill & Quire (Books for Young People)* Aug 1987; Vol 53 No 8: p1,8.

Native heritage is displayed in three timely books; reviews of children's books. Janice Kennedy. *MG* April 4, 1987: H11.

Three stories for children; reviews of children's books. Veronica Leonard. *Atlan Prov Book R* Nov-Dec 1987; Vol 14 No 4: p1.

A title that will grab teenagers; reviews of children's books. Joan McGrath. *TS* Oct 25, 1987: pA18.

Excellent books for the very young; review of *Have You Seen Josephine?*. Helen Norrie. *WFP* July 11, 1987: p57.

Youngsters get choice of beautiful books; reviews. Helen Norrie. *WFP* Dec 5, 1987: p57.

Annabel and Goldie go to the sea, Josephine goes to school; reviews of *Can You Catch Josephine?* and *Goldie and the Sea*. Susan Perren. *Quill & Quire (Books for Young People)* Oct 1987; Vol 53 No 10: p18–19.

Mini-reviews; reviews of children's stories. Mary Rubio. *Can Child Lit* 1987; No 46: p105–109.

Mini-reviews; reviews of children's stories. Mary Rubio. *Can Child Lit* 1987; No 47: p96–99.

A cat's brilliant new escapade; review of *Can You Catch Josephine?*. Tim Wynne-Jones. *G&M* Sept 19, 1987: pC19.

POULSEN, DAVID A.

Satisfying youth mystery also portrays way of life; review of *The Cowboy Kid*. Susan Scott. photo · *CH* July 11, 1987: pE10.

POUPART, JEAN-MARIE

Le suicide comme métaphore; review of *Beaux draps*. Jean-Roch Boivin. *MD* May 30, 1987: pD3.

La vitrine du livre; review of *Beaux draps*. Guy Ferland. *MD* May 16, 1987: pD4.

Un jour de rage, Jean-Marie Poupart s'est mis dans de "beaux draps"; article. Jean Royer. photo · *MD* June 6, 1987: pD4.

POUR QUARRIR L'ABSOLU/Poems by Denuis Saint-Yves

Songe, révolte et manifeste; reviews of poetry books. Robert Yergeau. photo · *Lettres québec* Spring 1987; No 45: p38–39.

POUR N'IMPORTE QUI/Poems by Rachel Saulnier

Two illustrated Acadian books; reviews of *Pépère Goguen loup de mer*. Martine Jacquot. *Atlan Prov Book R* Nov-Dec 1987; Vol 14 No 4: p11.

POURQUOI PAS DIX?/Novel by Georges Allaire

Un choix délibéré pour la vie; review of *Pourquoi pas dix?*. Jacques-G. Ruelland. *MD* Nov 14, 1987: pD15.

LA POURSUITE/Novel by Dominique Blondeau

Cette fleur qui veut occuper tout la place; review of *La Poursuite*. Jean Éthier-Blais. *MD* May 23, 1987: pD8.

Être adolescent, aujourd'hui; review of *La Poursuite*. Pierre Hébert. photo · *Lettres québec* Spring 1987; No 45: p28–29.

[Untitled]; review of *La Poursuite*. Hélène Rioux. *Moebius* Winter 1987; No 31: p135–137.

LE POUVOIR DES MOTS, LES MAUX DU POUVOIR: DES ROMANCIERS HAITIENS DE L'EXIL/Critical work by Jean Jonassaint

[Untitled]; review of *Le Pouvoir des mots, les maux du pouvoir*. Suzanne Crosta. *U of Toronto Q* Fall 1987; Vol 57 No 1: p212–214.

"Un bless qui se sauve"; review of *Le Pouvoir des mots, les maux du pouvoir*. Chantal Gamache. *Lettres québec* Winter 1986–87; No 44: p83.
[ANTHOLOGIES: BOOK REVIEWS]

POWASSAN'S DRUM: POEMS OF DUNCAN CAMP-BELL SCOTT/Poems by Duncan Campbell Scott

Confederation poets; reviews. Ronald B. Hatch. *Can Lit* Winter 1987; No 115: p223–225.

POWE, B.W.

New faces; survey article. photo · *TS* March 7, 1987: K1-K4.
[AUTHORS, CANADIAN]

POWE, BRUCE ALLEN

People; column. Yvonne Cox. *Maclean's* Nov 23, 1987; Vol 100 No 47: p46.

Much hard sledding through the North; review of *The Ice Eaters*. Max Layton. *G&M* Nov 14, 1987: pE3.

Arctic vs Toronto clash of cultures; review of *The Ice Eaters*. Roberta Morris. *TS* Dec 20, 1987: pE6.

On Sundays this businessman writes; article. Leslie Scrivener. photo · *TS* Dec 6, 1987: pD1–D2.

[Untitled]; review of *The Ice Eaters*. Norman Sigurdson. *Quill & Quire* Sept 1987; Vol 53 No 9: p79.

THE POWER PLAYS: [GOSSIP; FILTHY RICH; THE ART OF WAR]/Plays by George F. Walker

Dramatic trilogies; review of *The Power Plays*. L.W. Conolly. *Can Lit* Spring 1987; No 112: p110–112.

THE POWER TO MOVE/Poems by Susan Glickman

[Untitled]; review of *The Power to Move*. Carolyn Bond. *Quarry* Fall 1987; Vol 36 No 4: p83–86.

[Untitled]; review of *The Power to Move*. Barbara Carey. *Books in Can* May 1987; Vol 16 No 4: p23–24.

You ask me what I'm thinking; reviews of poetry books. M. Travis Lane. *Fiddlehead* Winter 1987; No 154: p95–104

[Untitled]; reviews of *The Fabulous Disguise of Ourselves* and *The Power to Move*. Stephen Scobie. *Malahat R* June 1987; No 79: p166.

POZIER, BERNARD

La vie littéraire; column. Jean Royer. *MD* May 9, 1987: pD2.
[CONFERENCES, LITERARY; POETRY READINGS; RADIO AND CANADIAN LITERATURE; TELEVISION AND CANADIAN LITERATURE]

PRÉFONTAINE, YVES

Désert, attente, silence; reviews of poetry books. Robert Yergeau. photo · *Lettres québec* Autumn 1987; No 47: p44–45.

PRAGMATIQUE DE LA POÉSIE QUÉBÉCOISE/Critical essays collection

La poésie du point de vue de la réception; review of *Pragmatique de la poésie québécoise*. Jean Fisette. *Voix et images* Winter 1987; No 35: p314–318.

Nouvelles frontières thériques; review of *Pragmatique de la poésie québécoise*. Agnès Whitfield. *Lettres québec* Spring 1987; No 45: p53–54.

PRAGUE/Play by John Krizanc

[Untitled]; review of *Prague*. Keith Garebian. *Quill & Quire* June 1987; Vol 53 No 6: p31.

To tell the truth; review of *Prague*. John Gilbert. *Books in Can* March 1987; Vol 16 No 2: p17.

PRAIRIE DRAGONS/Children's play by Sharon Pollock

Schools' forced funding cutbacks can't quell Quest; article. Kate Zimmerman. photo · *CH* Oct 22, 1987: pD1.

PRAIRIE FICTION

Under a prairie muse: ten years of Manitoba fiction; survey article. David Williamson. *Prairie Fire* Autumn 1987; Vol 8 No 3: p79–85.

PRAIRIE JOURNAL OF CANADIAN LITERATURE/Periodical

[Untitled]; reviews. Andrew Parkin. *Poetry Can R* Summer 1987; Vol 8 No 4: p36–37.
[ANTHOLOGIES: BOOK REVIEWS; CANADIAN LITERARY PERIODICALS]

PRAIRIE JUNGLE: SONGS, POEMS AND STORIES FOR CHILDREN/Anthology

A delightful anthology; review of *Prairie Jungle*. Ronnie Kennedy. *Can Child Lit* 1987; No 45: p57–58.
[ANTHOLOGIES: BOOK REVIEWS]

PRAIRIE POETRY AND POETS

The prairies: AltaSaskMan; regional column. Mick Burrs. *Poetry Can R* Fall 1987; Vol 9 No 1: p22.

The vernacular muse in prairie poetry (Part 3); article. Dennis Cooley. *Prairie Fire* Summer 1987; Vol 8 No 2: p49–53.

The vernacular muse in prairie poetry (conclusion); article. Dennis Cooley. *Prairie Fire* Autumn 1987; Vol 8 No 3: p88–94.

The vernacular muse in prairie poetry (Part Two); article. Dennis Cooley. *Prairie Fire* Spring 1987; Vol 8 No 1: p60–70.

The rhetoric of the prairie formula-poem; article. E.F. Dyck. *Prairie Fire* Spring 1987; Vol 8 No 1: p71–77.

The exact shape of distance; article. Patrick Lane. *NeWest R* Sept 1987; Vol 13 No 1: p2–3,19.

PRAIRIE WOMEN: IMAGES IN AMERICAN AND CANADIAN FICTION/Critical work by Carol Fairbanks

Prairie love; review of *Prairie Women*. Ann Leger Anderson. *Can Lit* Winter 1987; No 115: p249–251.

[Untitled]; reviews of *Varieties of Exile* and *Prairie Women*. Peter Buitenhuis. *Queen's Q* Summer 1987; Vol 94 No 2: p467–470.

[Untitled]; review of *Prairie Women*. Laurie Ricou. *U of Toronto Q* Fall 1987; Vol 57 No 1: p154–156.

[Untitled]; review of *Prairie Women*. Robert Thacker. *Amer R of Can Studies* Spring 1987; Vol 17 No 1: p113–115.

PRAIRIE WRITING AND WRITERS

Winnipeg theatre in the eighties: moving towards a theatrical culture; article. Doug Arrell. *Prairie Fire* Autumn 1987; Vol 8 No 3: p52–57.

Writing Saskatchewan — a literary symposium; article. Dennis Gruending. photo · *NeWest R* Nov 1987; Vol 13 No 3: p9–11.
[CONFERENCES, LITERARY]

De la littérature franco-manitobaine: being a very short history of Franco-Manitoban writing; survey article. J.R. Léveillé. illus · *Prairie Fire* Autumn 1987; Vol 8 No 3: p58–69.

LES PRATIQUES CULTURELLES DES QUÉBÉCOIS: UNE AUTRE IMAGE DE NOUS-MÊMES/Essays

Portrait du Québécois au repos; review of *Les Pratiques culturelles des Québécois*. Lori Saint-Martin. *MD* April 25, 1987: pD4.

[Untitled]; reviews of critical works. B.-Z. Shek. *U of Toronto Q* Fall 1987; Vol 57 No 1: p192–199.

PRATT, E.J.

Poet's triumphant ascent presented with grace, insight; review of *E.J. Pratt: The Master Years*. Ken Adachi. photo · *TS* Dec 19, 1987: M4.

Fort and forest: instability in the symbolic code of E.J. Pratt's Brebeuf and His Brethren; article. Frank Davey. abstract · *Études can* 1987; No 23: p183–194.
[RELIGIOUS THEMES]

The likeable poet; review of *E.J. Pratt: The Master Years*. William French. *G&M* Dec 5, 1987: pC21

Pitt on Pratt: a match made in Newfoundland; article. Nancy Robb. photo · *Quill & Quire* Aug 1987; Vol 53 No 8: p31.

"Uncertain steerage"; review of *E.J. Pratt: The Truant Years*. Wendy Schissel. *Ariel* Jan 1987; Vol 18 No 1: p76–78.

PRECIOUS STONES AND OTHER POEMS/Poems by Frank Manley

[Untitled]; review of *Precious Stones*. Sparling Mills. *Poetry Can R* Fall 1987; Vol 9 No 1: p30.

PRECIPICE/Play by Lawrence Jeffery

Clashes of tone mute play's voice; theatre review of *Precipice*. Ray Conlogue. photo · *G&M* Jan 14, 1987: pC8.

Weak play an aberration for theatre; theatre review of *Precipice*. Robert Crew. photo · *TS* Jan 14, 1987: pF4.

LE PREMIER MOUVEMENT/Novel by Jacques Marchand

Les noeuds sacrés de l'âme, de la terre et du sang; reviews of novels. Réjean Beaudoin. *Liberté* Oct 1987; Vol 29 No 5: p106–114.

L'impossible fuite et les tragiques exigences de l'amour entre deux frères; review of *Le Premier mouvement*. Jean-Roch Boivin. *MD* Aug 8, 1987: pC7.

La vitrine du livre; review of *Le Premier mouvement*. Guy Ferland. *MD* June 13, 1987: pD4.

PREWETT, FRANK

A Canadian in the Garsington circle: Frank Prewett's literary friendships; biographical article. Andrew Coppolino. *Studies in Can Lit* 1987; Vol 12 No 2: p273–289.

PRIEST, ROBERT

Priest is Toronto's pied piper of poetry; article. Peter Goddard. illus · *TS* Jan 9, 1987: pD3.

Today's model; article. Christopher Hume. photo · *TS* Jan 9, 1987: pD4.

Bongo and McToots play along when Boinks bop in on our galaxy; article. Craig MacInnis. photo · *TS* Jan 9, 1987: pD3.

Mini-reviews; reviews of children's books. Margaret Paré. *Can Child Lit* 1987; No 45: p93–96.

[Untitled]; reviews of poetry books. Douglas Smith. *Poetry Can R* Spring 1987; Vol 8 No 2–3: p39–40.
[ANTHOLOGIES: BOOK REVIEWS]

A PRINCESS COMES OF AGE/Children's play by Francis Macleod

Children's fantasy fails to fulfil promise; theatre review of *A Princess Comes of Age*. Neil Harris. *WFP* Nov 21, 1987: p22.

PRINCESS FROWNSALOT/Children's story by John Bianchi

Baby of the family gets respect raising flock of Canada geese; reviews of children's books. Janice Kennedy. *MG* Oct 3, 1987: J13.

Familiarity and TV's stranglehold on life; reviews of children's books. Tim Wynne-Jones. *G&M* Nov 14, 1987: pE4.
[FESTIVALS, LITERARY]

PRINGLE, PETER

Geminis are sad reminder of TV's glory days; column. Mike Boone. *MG* Dec 9, 1987: pF3.
[TELEVISION AND CANADIAN LITERATURE]

'Coward' classy but disappoints as theatre; theatre review of *Noel Coward: A Portrait*. Pat Donnelly. photo · *MG* Nov 26, 1987: H5.

[Untitled]; theatre reviews. Pat Donnelly. *MG* Nov 27, 1987: pC7.

[Untitled]; theatre reviews. Pat Donnelly. *MG* Dec 4, 1987: pC6.

To Sir Noel, with affection; theatre review of *Noel Coward: A Portrait*. Deirdre Kelly. photo · *G&M* July 3, 1987: pD9.

Sir Noël Pringle ou Sir Noël Coward?; theatre review of *Noel Coward: A Portrait*. Marc Morin. photo · *MD* Nov 26, 1987: p15.

LE PRINTEMPS, MONSIEUR DESLAURIERS/Play by René-Daniel Dubois

Le Printemps cool flash but no sizzle; theatre review of *Le Printemps, monsieur Deslauriers*. Marianne Ackerman. photo · *MG* April 14, 1987: pB8.

'Titanic encounter' typifies rising star's style; theatre review of *Le Printemps, monsieur Deslauriers*. Ray Conlogue. photo · *G&M* April 16, 1987: pD3.

Le théâtre qu'on joue; theatre reviews of *Le Printemps, monsieur Deslauriers* and *Le Vrai monde?*. André Dionne. photo · *Lettres québec* Autumn 1987; No 47: p49–50.

Grandeur et misère: le retour du père sur la scène québécoise; article. Carole Fréchette. photo · *Jeu* 1987; No 45: p17–35.
[QUEBEC DRAMA (FRENCH LANGUAGE): HISTORY AND CRITICISM]

Dubois chez Duceppe: les années de plomb de l'après-référendum; article. Robert Lévesque. photo · *MD* April 25, 1987: pC1,C10.

Un printemps clair-obscur; theatre review of *Le Printemps, monsieur Deslauriers*. Solange Lévesque. photo · *Jeu* 1987; No 44: p180–182.

La Russie de Basile, le Québec de Dubois; review of *Le Printemps, monsieur Deslauriers*. Robert Lévesque. photo · *MD* Oct 10, 1987: pD6.

PRIS DE PRESENCE/Poems by Pierre Laberge

[Untitled]; review of *Pris de présence*. Réjean Bonenfant. *Estuaire* Autumn 1987; No 46: p84–85.

La métamorphose du quotidien; reviews of poetry books. André Marquis. photo · *Lettres québec* Autumn 1987; No 47: p41–43.

THE PRISMATIC EYE/Poems by Doris Hillis

Two ways of making poetry; reviews of *The Prismatic Eye* and *Walking Slow*. Paul Barclay. *Prairie Fire* Summer 1987; Vol 8 No 2: p56–59.

Landscapes & eyes; reviews of poetry books. Karl Jirgens. *Can Lit* Spring 1987; No 112: p192–193

PRIVATE AND FICTIONAL WORDS: CANADIAN WOMEN NOVELISTS OF THE 1970s AND 1980s/Critical work by Coral Ann Howells

[Untitled]; review of *Private and Fictional Words*. Keith Garebian. *Quill & Quire* Oct 1987; Vol 53 No 10: p23–24.

Relevant writing; reviews of *Private and Fictional Words* and *More Stories by Canadian Women*. Ann Holloway. *G&M* Nov 28, 1987: pC22.
[ANTHOLOGIES: BOOK REVIEWS]

[Untitled]; review of *Private and Fictionalized Words*. Margaret McGraw. *Books in Can* Nov 1987; Vol 16 No 8: p24.

Totally impenetrable prose; review of *Private and Fictional Words*. Morley Walker. *WFP* Oct 17, 1987: p61.

THE PRIVATE LATITUDES/Poems by Gordon Rodgers

Noticing three poets; reviews of poetry books. Terrence Craig. *Atlan Prov Book R* May-June 1987; Vol 14 No 2: p10.

PRIVATE PROPERTIES/Poems by Leona Gom

Trial by experience; reviews of *Letters from Some Islands* and *Private Properties*. Bert Almon. *Can Lit* Winter 1987; No 115: p206–208.

[Untitled]; reviews of *Housebroken* and *Private Properties*. Sharon Batt. *Room of One's Own* Sept 1987; Vol 11 No 4: p109–112.
[FIRST NOVELS: BOOK REVIEWS]

Between the sexes; reviews of poetry books. Mary di Michele. *Books in Can* March 1987; Vol 16 No 2: p31–32.

[Untitled]; reviews of poetry books. Anita Hurwitz. *Poetry Can R* Spring 1987; Vol 8 No 2–3: p38–39.

[Untitled]; reviews of *Private Properties* and *Second Nature*. Stephen Scobie. *Malahat R (special issue)* March 1987; No 78: p153–154.

Wit and humor mark poetry; reviews of *Second Nature* and *Private Properties*. Andrew Wreggitt. *CH* Jan 11, 1987: pF4.

LE PRIX DU LAIT/Poems by François Tourigny

[Untitled]; review of *Le Prix du lait*. Bernard Pozier. *Estuaire* Summer 1987; No 45: p58.

PROBABLE FICTIONS: ALICE MUNRO'S NARRATIVE ACTS/Critical essays anthology

[Untitled]; reviews of *Probable Fictions* and *The Art of Alice Munro*. Winnifred M. Bogaards. *Eng Studies in Can* March 1987; Vol 13 No 1: p115–119.

PROBABLEMENT L'ESPAGNE/Novel by Claude Charron

Un roman bâclé qui fera fureur dans les supermarchés; review of *Probablement l'Espagne*. Jean-Roch Boivin. *MD* Nov 14, 1987: pD15.
[FIRST NOVELS: BOOK REVIEWS]

[Untitled]; review of *Probablement l'Espagne*. Pierre Gobeil. *Moebius* Autumn 1987; No 34: p123–125.

Claude Charron, complice de la liberté; article. Isabelle Paré. photo · *MD* Nov 14, 1987: pD13.

THE PROGRESS OF LOVE/Short stories by Alice Munro

J.D. Salinger's biography too tame to cause ripples; column. Ken Adachi. *TS* Feb 2, 1987: pD2.
[INTERNATIONAL REVIEWS OF CANADIAN LITERATURE]

[Untitled]; review of *The Progress of Love*. Allan Austin. *World Lit in Eng* Spring 1987; Vol 27 No 1: p58–59.

Country manners; reviews of *The Progress of Love* and *Goodbye Harold, Good Luck*. Julie Beddoes. *Brick* Winter 1987; No 29: p24–27.

[Untitled]; reviews of fictional works. Beverley Daurio. *Cross Can Writ Q* 1987; Vol 9 No 1: p18–19.

Respect for the facts; review of *The Progress of Love*. Anne Duchêne. *Times Lit Supp* Jan 30, 1987; No 4374: p109.

[Untitled]; review of *The Progress of Love*. Oliver Gorse. *Idler* March-April 1987; No 12: p59–60.

New & noteworthy; review of *The Progress of Love*. George Johnson. *NYT Book R* Aug 30, 1987: p34.

[Untitled]; review of *The Progress of Love*. Mary Millar. *Queen's Q* Winter 1987; Vol 94 No 4: p1015–1017.

[Untitled]; review of *The Progress of Love*. Constance Rooke. *Malahat R (special issue)* March 1987; No 78: p152.

Munro's progress; review of *The Progress of Love*. Robert Thacker. *Can Lit* Winter 1987; No 115: p239–242.

PROGRESS OF MADNESS/Poems by Mary Anderson

[Untitled]; reviews of poetry books. Anne Burke. *Poetry Can R* Summer 1987; Vol 8 No 4: p38.

THE PROMISED LAND/Novel by Martin Waxman

There's still room for the Great Mall Novel; review of *The Promised Land*. William French. photo · *G&M* March 19, 1987: pD1.
[FIRST NOVELS: BOOK REVIEWS]

[Untitled]; review of *The Promised Land*. Cecelia Frey. *CH* May 17, 1987: pE5.
[FIRST NOVELS: BOOK REVIEWS]

Urban scrawl; reviews of first novels. Janice Kulyk Keefer. *Books in Can* Aug-Sept 1987; Vol 16 No 6: p33-34.
[FIRST NOVELS: BOOK REVIEWS]

Comic novel falls flat; review of *The Promised Land*. Norman Sigurdson. photo · *WFP* May 2, 1987: p84.
[FIRST NOVELS: BOOK REVIEWS]

Book world: where the $$$ land — legally; column. Beverley Slopen. *TS* March 1, 1987: pA15.
[PUBLISHING AND PUBLISHERS IN CANADA; WRITERS-IN-RESIDENCE]

[Untitled]; review of *The Promised Land*. Thomas P. Sullivan. *Quill & Quire* May 1987; Vol 53 No 5: p20,22.
[FIRST NOVELS: BOOK REVIEWS]

THE PROPER LOVER/Poems by William Gough

[Untitled]; reviews of *The Proper Lover* and *Above the Tilted Earth*. Barbara Carey. *Poetry Can R* Summer 1987; Vol 8 No 4: p34.

Young poets on display; reviews of poetry books. Robert Quickenden. photo · *WFP* March 14, 1987: p52.

PROSSER, DAVID

Kingston editor retains theatre critics' award; article. Pat Donnelly. *MG* Oct 5, 1987: pB15.
[AWARDS, LITERARY]

PROULX, BERNARD

L'instinct territorial; review of *Le Roman du territoire*. Robert Major. *Voix et images* Autumn 1987; Vol 13 No 1: p162-165.

PROULX, MONIQUE

Personnages en quête d'eux-mêmes; review of *Le Sexe des étoiles*. Jean-François Chassay. photo · *MD* Dec 12, 1987: pD4.
[FIRST NOVELS: BOOK REVIEWS]

Monique Proulx: comme un gratte-ciel; article. Guy Ferland. photo · *MD* Dec 31, 1987: pC9.

La vie littéraire; column. Marc Morin. photo · *MD* Dec 19, 1987: pD2.
[AWARDS, LITERARY; FICTION READINGS; POETRY READINGS]

PROVENCHER, ANNE-MARIE

Experimental theatre: only some works; theatre review of *Nouvelles pour le théâtre*. Marianne Ackerman. *MG* Feb 5, 1987: pE6.

Le théâtre qu'on joue; theatre reviews. André Dionne. photo · *Lettres québec* Winter 1986-87; No 44: p53-54.

Face to face with the actor; theatre review of *La Tour*. Josette Féral. photo trans · *Can Theatre R* Spring 1987; No 50: p78-81.

"Nouvelles pour le théâtre"; column. Robert Lévesque. *MD* Jan 27, 1987: p5.

[Untitled]; theatre reviews of *La Tour* and *Les Objets parlent*. Solange Lévesque. photo · *Jeu* 1987; No 43: p145-147.

PSALMS FROM THE SUBURBS/Poems by Roger Nash

[Untitled]; reviews of *Psalms from the Suburbs* and *Sympathetic Magic*. Doug Watling. *Poetry Can R* Spring 1987; Vol 8 No 2-3: p51.

A PUBLIC AND PRIVATE VOICE: ESSAYS ON THE LIFE AND WORK OF DOROTHY LIVESAY/Conference report

[Untitled]; review of *A Public and Private Voice*. Margaret Gail Osachoff. *U of Windsor R* Spring-Summer 1987; Vol 20 No 2: p94-97.
[CONFERENCE REPORTS: REVIEWS AND ARTICLES]

PUBLISHING AND PUBLISHERS IN CANADA

See also CANADIAN LITERARY PUBLISHING

Anne McClelland leaves publishing firm; article. *TS* March 23, 1987: pB1.

Publicity man goes as publisher wields axe; article. *MG* Jan 21, 1987: pF8.

Albertan writes book on women in business; article. photo · *MG* Jan 26, 1987: pC2.

Top authors praise McClelland as he leaves publishing; article. photo · *MG* Feb 20, 1987: pC1.

New McClelland and Stewart owner fires long-time publicist, other staff; article. *WFP* Jan 21, 1987: p34.

McClelland severing ties with publishing; article. photo · *WFP* Feb 20, 1987: p19.

Jack McClelland prend sa retraite; article. *MD* Feb 23, 1987: p10.

Jack McClelland bids farewell to publishing world; article. *CH* Feb 20, 1987: pF2.

Walter resigns from publishing firm; article. *G&M* May 9, 1987: pC4.

Literati in love; article about Janet Turnbull. illus · *G&M* (Toronto Magazine) June 1987; Vol 2 No 3: p38,46.

Tundra publisher wins Orpen award; article. *G&M* June 20, 1987: pC11.
[AWARDS, LITERARY]

Roger Lemelin publié en format de poche; article. *MD* June 3, 1987: p12.

Dits et faits; column. photo · *Lettres québec* Spring 1987; No 45: p6-7.
[AWARDS, LITERARY; TRANSLATIONS OF CANADIAN LITERATURE; WRITERS' ORGANIZATIONS]

Firm to offer Canadian books in big print; article. *MG* April 24, 1987: pD10.

Alberta publishing developer dies at 55; obituary of Ken McVey. *WFP* July 10, 1987: p21.
[WRITERS' ORGANIZATIONS]

Manitoba publishers look for bail-out; article. *WFP* July 16, 1987: p36.
[GOVERNMENT GRANTS FOR WRITERS/PUBLISHERS]

Vote of confidence for Ragweed Press; article. *G&M* July 24, 1987: pD5.

Bernard Valiquette, éditeur: "le vin, le vent, la vie . . . "; column. Jean Éthier-Blais. *MD* June 20, 1987: pD8.

Firings at McClelland unsettle book community; column. Ken Adachi. *TS* Jan 19, 1987: pD1.

No blockbusters in spring lists; preview of spring book list. Ken Adachi. *TS* Feb 15, 1987: pA19.

McClelland quits publishing with characteristic class; column. Ken Adachi. photo · *TS* Feb 20, 1987: pD23.

The gofers are gaining control; article about women publishers. Ken Adachi. photo · *TS* March 21, 1987: M3.

Memoirs major theme in this fall's line-up but enough variety to suit everyone's taste; preview of fall book list. Ken Adachi. photo · *TS* Aug 29, 1987: M4.

Everything's coming up roses for busy Canadian publishers; article. Ken Adachi. photo · *TS* Sept 22, 1987: pC2.
[AUTHORS, CANADIAN]

Firings at M&S puzzle executives; article. Salem Alaton. *G&M* Jan 20, 1987: pD9.

The secret of her success; article about Anna Porter. John Allemang. photo · *G&M (Toronto Magazine)* Aug 1987; Vol 2 No 5: p36–39,63,65,67.

Writer won't let blindness slow him down; article. Jay Bryan. photo · *MG* July 2, 1987: pC1.

The spring lists: prices holding steady in a shaky world; preview of spring book list. Hamish Cameron. photo · *Quill & Quire* Feb 1987; Vol 53 No 2: p5–6.

Bertelsmann deals Doubleday to Porter; article. Hamish Cameron. photo · *Quill & Quire* Feb 1987; Vol 53 No 2: p8.

Making the rights move: why publishers are paying so much more; article. Hamish Cameron. photo · *Quill & Quire* March 1987; Vol 53 No 3: p8,10.
[AGENTS, LITERARY; AUTHORS, CANADIAN]

Seal added to Porter acquisitions; article. Hamish Cameron. *Quill & Quire* April 1987; Vol 53 No 4: p14.

McClelland retires, no more encores; article. Hamish Cameron. photo · *Quill & Quire* April 1987; Vol 53 No 4: p14.

New publishing career takes Clarkson 'beyond adrenalin'; column about Adrienne Clarkson. Stevie Cameron. *G&M* July 23, 1987: pA2.

French writers survive here, Quebecers told; article about Les Éditions du blé. Donald Campbell. photo · *WFP* July 22, 1987: p36.

Québec 10/10: bientôt 100 titres; essay. Roch Carrier. photo · *MD* Nov 14, 1987: pD20.

Clarkson: I want to make book publishing pay; interview with Adrienne Clarkson. Susan Carson. photo · *MG* Dec 7, 1987: pB12.

Tough publisher tackles new mystery; article. Rod Currie. photo · *WFP* Dec 1, 1987: p32.

Chouette: des livres, des jeux, des jouets; article. Dominique Demers. photo · *MD* Dec 5, 1987: pD6.
[CHILDREN'S LITERATURE]

The fall line-up: political pundits, literary lore, and sports strategies; previes of fall book list. Martin Dowding. photo · *Quill & Quire* July 1987; Vol 53 No 7: p10,12,14,16.

The top 50; article. Harriet Eisenkraft. *Tor Life* May 1987; Vol 21 No 7: p50–53,72,74,77.

Fiducious says: He who tax reading, will sit on reader's attacks; editorial. Robert Enright. *Border Cross* Spring 1987; Vol 6 No 2: p4.

La domination française préoccupe davantage les éditeurs; article. Guy Ferland. photo · *MD* Nov 24, 1987: p13.

McClelland's exit ends chapter in Canadian publishing; article. William French. photo · *G&M* Feb 20, 1987: pD5.

Disasters, memoirs, news headline spring book list; preview of spring book list. William French. *G&M* March 12, 1987: pC1.

Canadian readers may be all booked up this fall; preview of fall book list. William French. photo · *G&M* Aug 20, 1987: pC1.

Fiction's favorites show their colors for fall; preview of fall book list. William French. *G&M* Aug 21, 1987: pC9.

Getting an early start in the book game; column. William French. *G&M* Nov 24, 1987: pD5.

Jolts suggest that publishing is no longer a trade for the gentle folk; article. William French. photo · *G&M* Dec 26, 1987: pC21.

Alone at the microphone, Jack McClelland takes a final bow; article. Robert Fulford. photo · *Sat Night* June 1987; Vol 102 No 6: p56.

Le livre de poche au Québec: la grande histoire de petits livres; article. Jean Chapdelaine Gagnon. photo · *MD* Oct 24, 1987: pD1,D8.

Authors paying for book tariff; column. Peter Hadekel. *MG* Feb 17, 1987: pC1.

Now M&S wants a profit on its books; article. Heather Hill. photo · *MG* Feb 28, 1987: pB4.

Tundra turns 20; article. Heather Hill. photo · *MG* May 2, 1987: H13.
[CHILDREN'S LITERATURE]

May Cutler wins publishing award; article. Heather Hill. *MG* June 23, 1987: pC10.

Fall books: raft of recycles on wave of high advances; preview of fall book list. Heather Hill. photo · *MG* July 4, 1987: J7.

First electronic novel hits computer screens; article. Heather Hill. photo · *MG* Aug 1, 1987: J9.

Celebs help publishing house launch fall season; article. Heather Hill. *MG* Aug 28, 1987: pC1.
[AUTHORS, CANADIAN]

The name of Roseau grows in Quebec book market; article. David Homel. *Quill & Quire* March 1987; Vol 53 No 3: p58.
[TRANSLATIONS OF CANADIAN LITERATURE]

Editions Fides: keeping the faith at 50; article. David Homel. photo · *Quill & Quire* April 1987; Vol 53 No 4: p18.

The good fight; article about May Cutler. David Homel. photo · *Books in Can* Dec 1987; Vol 16 No 9: p8–10.
[CHILDREN'S LITERATURE]

Fiery 'disaster' forces publisher to retrace steps; article. Deborah Jones. photo · *G&M* July 21, 1987: pC7.

What business do publishers think they're in?; article. Jack Kapica. illus · *G&M* Nov 14, 1987: pE1.

Ragweed publisher goes against the PEI tide; article about Libby Oughton. Deirdre Kelly. photo · *G&M* July 14, 1987: pC5.

Megamergers rock book publishers; article. Kenneth Kidd. photo · *TS* June 14, 1987: pF1–F2.

'Severance Santa' visits Methuen 'wake'; article. H.J. Kirchhoff. *G&M* Dec 12, 1987: pC3.

Deneau Publishers seeks reorganization; column. H.J. Kirchhoff. *G&M* Dec 29, 1987: pC8.
[CENSORSHIP; WRITERS' ORGANIZATIONS]

Jack: the sequel; article about Jack McClelland. Martin Knelman. photo · *Tor Life* May 1987; Vol 21 No 7: p13.

L'édition ontaroise: un monde à découvrir; article. Françoise Lafleur. *MD* Nov 19, 1987: p13.
[CANADIAN LITERARY PERIODICALS]

Carole Levert: pas besoin de s'appeler Maggie pour être éditrice; article. France Lafuste. photo · *MD* Dec 31, 1987: pC9–C10.

Le demi-siècle de Fides; article. Marie Laurier. *MD* March 10, 1987: p11.

Fides a 50 ans; article. Marie Laurier. photo · *MD* March 14, 1987: pD1–D2.

Fides édite la liste de ses livres depuis 1937; article. Marie Laurier. photo · *MD* March 23, 1987: p3.

Lévesque s'oppose vigoureusement à une surtaxe pour les biens culturels; article. Marie Laurier. *MD* April 11, 1987: pA3.

Direct marketing writes Harlequin's own happy ending to romance wars; article. Rebate Lerch. illus photo · *Fin Post* Oct 26, 1987: p23.
[ROMANTIC FICTION]

A good book blurb helps a lot. Is it right?; article. Dorothy Lipovenko. *G&M* Dec 26, 1987: pB1–B2.

Writers confront publishing odds; article. Katherine Macklem. photo · *MG* Sept 28, 1987: pB9.
[WOMEN WRITERS]

Brevity, soul and wit; article. Alberto Manguel. photo · *Maclean's* Sept 21, 1987; Vol 100 No 38: p53–54.
[CANADIAN SHORT STORY: HISTORY AND CRITICISM]

The secret sharer; article. Alberto Manguel. illus · *Sat Night* July 1987; Vol 102 No 7: p39–41.
[AUTHORS, CANADIAN]

Hot money and grizzly tales hit the presses this spring; preview of spring book list. Kenneth McGoogan. *CH* Feb 6, 1987: pD1.

Banff Centre lands novelist; column. Kenneth McGoogan. *CH* Feb 22, 1987: pE6.
[CANADIAN LITERARY PERIODICALS; WRITERS' WORKSHOPS]

McClelland's retirement marks end of an era; article. Kenneth McGoogan. photo · *CH* Feb 24, 1987: pF5.

Western voice strengthened in publishers association; article. Kenneth McGoogan. photo · *CH* March 24, 1987: pD1.

Autumn promises Canadian book bonanza; preview of fall book list. Kenneth McGoogan. *CH* June 21, 1987: pE5.

Literary world loses a champion; column. Kenneth McGoogan. *CH* July 12, 1987: pE4.
[AWARDS, LITERARY; CONFERENCES, LITERARY; SCIENCE FICTION; WRITERS' WORKSHOPS]

Fall promises plethora from publishers; preview of fall book list. Kenneth McGoogan. photo · *CH* July 14, 1987: pB6.

La passion de Louise Courteau; article. Simone Piuze. photo · *MD* March 21, 1987: pD1,D8.

Government sabotaging its own cultural initiatives; article. Jamie Portman. photo · *CH* Aug 8, 1987: pF3.
[GOVERNMENT GRANTS FOR WRITERS/PUBLISHERS]

Publishers serve up some dismal fare; letter to the editor. Anna Pottier. photo · *G&M* July 8, 1987: pA7.

Prairie Publishers Group disbanding after five years; article. Barbara Robson. *WFP* March 4, 1987: p33.

L'année littéraire 86: René, Jacques et les autres . . . ; survey article. Jean Royer. photo · *MD* Jan 10, 1987: pB1,B5.

La vie littéraire; column. Jean Royer. photo · *MD* Jan 24, 1987: pB2.
[AWARDS, LITERARY; POETRY READINGS; RADIO AND CANADIAN LITERATURE; WRITERS' WORKSHOPS]

La vie littéraire; column. Jean Royer. *MD* Feb 7, 1987: pB2.
[COMPETITIONS, LITERARY; CONFERENCES, LITERARY; POETRY READINGS; TELEVISION AND CANADIAN LITERATURE; WRITERS' WORKSHOPS]

La vie littéraire; column. Jean Royer. photo · *MD* May 16, 1987: pD2.
[AWARDS, LITERARY; CONFERENCES, LITERARY; RADIO AND CANADIAN LITERATURE; TELEVISION AND CANADIAN LITERATURE]

La rentrée littéraire; preview of fall book list. Jean Royer. photo · *MD* Sept 12, 1987: pD1,D8.

La vie littéraire; column. Jean Royer. photo · *MD* Sept 19, 1987: pD2.
[AWARDS, LITERARY; CONFERENCES, LITERARY; FICTION READINGS; POETRY READINGS]

La vie littéraire; column. Jean Royer. photo · *MD* Sept 26, 1987: pD2.
[AUDIO-VISUALS AND CANADIAN LITERATURE; CONFERENCES, LITERARY; INTERNATIONAL WRITERS' ORGANIZATIONS; WRITERS' ORGANIZATION]

Looking forward to the fall list for kids; preview of fall book list. Diana Shepherd. *Quill & Quire (Books for Young People)* Aug 1987; Vol 53 No 8: p3–4,10.

Book world: McClelland moves to quash 'secret' biography; column. Beverley Slopen. photo · *TS* Feb 12, 1987: pF1.

Book world: where the $$$ land — legally; column. Beverley Slopen. *TS* March 1, 1987: pA15.
[WRITERS-IN-RESIDENCE]

Book world: Clarkson brings pool of goodwill to M&S job; column. Beverley Slopen. *TS* March 15, 1987: pA22.
[AWARDS, LITERARY]

Book world: Grolier moves into children's fiction; column. Beverley Slopen. *TS* March 22, 1987: pA20.
[CHILDREN'S LITERATURE]

Paperclips: helping U.S. librarians fill their shelves . . . the party animal; column. Beverley Slopen. photo · *Quill & Quire* Feb 1987; Vol 53 No 2: p7.
[AUTHORS, CANADIAN]

Paperclips: 25 years of minding McClelland's business . . . political yarns; column. Beverley Slopen. photo · *Quill & Quire* April 1987; Vol 53 No 4: p12.

Book world: Collins (Murdoch) fine-tunes a new purchase; column. Beverley Slopen. *TS* July 12, 1987: pA18.

Book world: Owl magazine publisher wades into film field; column. Beverley Slopen. *TS* Sept 20, 1987: pA20.
[CHILDREN'S LITERATURE; FILM ADAPTATIONS OF CANADIAN LITERATURE]

Book world: firm's growth is not merely a matter of luck; column. Beverley Slopen. *TS* Oct 4, 1987: pA20.
[FESTIVALS, LITERARY]

Book world: 'My year for films': Brian Moore; column. Beverley Slopen. photo · *TS* Nov 8, 1987: pA18.
[CHILDREN'S LITERATURE; FILM ADAPTATIONS OF CANADIAN LITERATURE]

Paperclips: impressive feminists . . . vampire visionary . . . crossing the border; column. Beverley Slopen. photo · *Quill & Quire* Oct 1987; Vol 53 No 10: p15.

Micheline Tremblay relance une entreprise au passé prestigieux; article. Claude Turcotte. photo · *MD* March 2, 1987: p9.

'Female ferrets and crime-busting babes'; reviews of paperback books. Mike Walton. *TS* Feb 8, 1987: pG9.

'You can't have too much romance'; essay. Joel Yanofsky. illus · *MG* May 2, 1987: H11.
[ROMANTIC FICTION]

A bookman bids farewell; article about Jack McClelland. Pamela Young. photo · *Maclean's* March 2, 1987; Vol 100 No 9: p50.

PURCELL, DONALD

[Untitled]; review of *The Lucky Ones*. David Willis. *Queen's Q* Summer 1987; Vol 94 No 2: p482–483.
[FIRST NOVELS: BOOK REVIEWS]

PURDY, AL

Trio named to receive awards from Canadian authors' group; article. photo · *WFP* May 14, 1987: p46.
[AWARDS, LITERARY]

Munro short story collection wins award; article. *WFP* May 29, 1987: p34.
[GOVERNOR GENERAL'S AWARDS]

Murrell lauded; article. *CH* May 14, 1987: pC12.
[AWARDS, LITERARY]

Authors honour their best; article. *Quill & Quire* June 1987; Vol 53 No 6: p24.
[AWARDS, LITERARY]

Authors association honors Purdy, Murrell and Foster; article. photo · *G&M* May 14, 1987: pC3.
[AWARDS, LITERARY]

Le prix du Gouverneur général à Yvon Rivard; article. *MD* May 28, 1987: p2.
[GOVERNOR GENERAL'S AWARDS]

Literary winners announced; article. *TS* May 13, 1987: pB4.
[AWARDS, LITERARY]

Canadian Authors Association leaves fiction prize unawarded; article. photo · *MG* May 15, 1987: pD8.
[AWARDS, LITERARY]

Governor General's Award to Munro amid poetry protest; article. photo · *MG* May 28, 1987: pC1.
[GOVERNOR GENERAL'S AWARDS]

Governor General's award winners; article. *Quill & Quire* July 1987; Vol 53 No 7: p53–54.
[GOVERNOR GENERAL'S AWARDS]

Frye finally wins elusive award for best non-fiction book of '86; article. Ken Adachi. photo · *TS* May 28, 1987: H1.
[GOVERNOR GENERAL'S AWARDS]

Friends bring poet back to life at wake; article. John Allemang. photo · *G&M* March 23, 1987: pC12.

[Untitled]; review of *The Collected Poem*. Bert Almon. *Poetry Can R* Summer 1987; Vol 8 No 4: p32.

The best in poetry; letter to the editor. Dorothy Farmiloe. photo · *G&M* Jan 17, 1987: pD7.

Giant steps; review of *Collected Poems*. George Galt. *Books in Can* Jan-Feb 1987; Vol 16 No 1: p16–17.

[Untitled]; reviews of poetry books. Bruce Hunter. *Cross Can Writ Q* 1987; Vol 9 No 3–4: p40–42.

[Untitled]; review of *The Collected Poems*. Laurence Hutchman. *Rubicon* Fall 1987; No 9: p179–182.

St. Al and the heavenly bodies; review of *The Collected Poems*. D.G. Jones. *Brick* Winter 1987; No 29: p14–20.

CAA opposes pornography bill; article. Fred Kerner. *Quill & Quire* Aug 1987; Vol 53 No 8: p24.
[AWARDS, LITERARY; CENSORSHIP; WRITERS' ORGANIZATIONS]

Yvon Rivard et Northrop Frye parmi les lauréats des prix du gouverneur général; article. Robert Lévesque. photo · *MD* May 28, 1987: p13.
[GOVERNOR GENERAL'S AWARDS]

[Untitled]; review of *The Collected Poems*. Tom Marshall. *Queen's Q* Summer 1987; Vol 94 No 2: p475–477.

The dying generations; reviews of poetry books. Dermot McCarthy. *Essays on Can Writ* Spring 1987; No 34: p24–32.

Munro wins third Governor General's Award; article. Jamie Portman. photo · *CH* May 28, 1987: pC9.
[GOVERNOR GENERAL'S AWARDS]

Munro wins top literary prize; article. Lisa Rochon. photo · *G&M* May 28, 1987: pD1.
[GOVERNOR GENERAL'S AWARDS]

QUÉBEC CANADA FRANCE: LE CANADA LITTÉRAIRE À LA CROISE DES CULTURES/Critical work by Stéphane Sarkany

De la sociologie des cultures la bibliologie; review of *Québec Canada France*. Patrick Imbert. *Lettres québec* Winter 1986–87; No 44: p78.

QUEBEC DRAMA (ENGLISH LANGUAGE): HISTORY AND CRITICISM

A critic takes a final bow: some general reflections on Quebec theatre scene; essay. Marianne Ackerman. photo · *MG* July 4, 1987: pC10.

QUEBEC DRAMA (FRENCH LANGUAGE): HISTORY AND CRITICISM

The Quebec invasion: French connection has 'le tout Toronto' abuzz; article. Marianne Ackerman. photo · *MG* May 5, 1987: pB6.

Grandeur et misère: le retour du père sur la scène québécoise; article. Carole Fréchette. photo · *Jeu* 1987; No 45: p17–35.

Théâtre; survey review article. Jean Cléo Godin. *U of Toronto Q* Fall 1987; Vol 57 No 1: p74–77.

La rentrée théâtrale; article. Robert Lévesque. photo · *MD* Sept 12, 1987: pC1–C2.

Dragons, Feluettes et Vrai monde; survey article. Robert Lévesque. photo · *MD* Dec 31, 1987: pC1,C12.

Sexual games: hypertheatricality and homosexuality in recent Quebec plays; article. Jane Moss. *Amer R of Can Studies* Autumn 1987; Vol 17 No 3: p287–296.

Cartographie: l'Allemagne québécoise; article. Diane Pavlovic. bibliog photo · *Jeu* 1987; No 43: p77–110.
[GERMANY-CANADA LITERARY RELATIONS]

QUEBEC LITERATURE (FRENCH LANGUAGE): HISTORY AND CRITICISM

A world of books in Quebec; survey article. illus photo · *MG* Nov 21, 1987: J11.
[AWARDS, LITERARY; CANADIAN LITERARY PUBLISHING]

Diachronie des styles de la poésie québécoise, 1960–80; article. Ivor A. Arnold. *Studies in Can Lit* 1987; Vol 12 No 1: p3–14.

Anthologies de poésie québécoise; survey article. François Dumont. *Voix et images* Spring 1987; Vol 12 No 3: p486–492,494–496.

Romans; survey review article. Pierre Hébert. *U of Toronto Q* Fall 1987; Vol 57 No 1: p22–32.

Fresh names on the Quebec literary front; article. David Homel. photo · *Quill & Quire* Oct 1987; Vol 53 No 10: p4,6

Constitution d'une avant-garde littéraire; article. Jacques Pelletier. abstract · *Études lit* Spring-Summer 1987; Vol 20 No 1: p111–130.
[CANADIAN LITERARY PERIODICALS; POLITICAL WRITING; POSTMODERNIST WRITING AND CRITICISM]

Poésie; survey review article. Robert Yergeau. *U of Toronto Q* Fall 1987; Vol 57 No 1: p50–62.

QUEBEC VOICES: THREE PLAYS/Play anthology

A wealth of provocative and inspiring literary criticism; reviews. Douglas Hill. *G&M* Sept 5, 1987: pC13.
[ANTHOLOGIES: BOOK REVIEWS]

LA QUÉBÉCOITE/Novel by Regine Robin

The text as crossroads; review of *La Québécoite*. Ralph Sarkonak. *Can Lit* Spring 1987; No 112: p100–102.

QUEDNAU, MARION

Risk-taking writer off to a good start; review of *The Butterfly Chair*. Ken Adachi. *TS* Nov 22, 1987: pC9.
[FIRST NOVELS: BOOK REVIEWS]

A brutal inheritance; review of *The Butterfly Chair*. Celina Bell. *Maclean's* Dec 7, 1987; Vol 100 No 49: T8.
[FIRST NOVELS: BOOK REVIEWS]

Novel about family tragedy a powerful debut; review of *The Butterfly Chair*. William French. illus · *G&M* Dec 3, 1987: pA25.
[FIRST NOVELS: BOOK REVIEWS]

[Untitled]; review of *The Butterfly Chair*. Joan McGrath. *Quill & Quire* Sept 1987; Vol 53 No 9: p78–79.
[FIRST NOVELS: BOOK REVIEWS]

[Untitled]; review of *The Butterfly Chair*. Constance Rooke. *Malahat R* Dec 1987; No 81: p102.
[FIRST NOVELS: BOOK REVIEWS]

THE QUEEN'S SECRET/Novel by Charles Templeton

[Untitled]; review of *The Queen's Secret*. Douglas Malcolm. *Books in Can* Jan-Feb 1987; Vol 16 No 1: p26.

Book world: 'new' terrorists like their perks, author suggests; column. Beverley Slopen. *TS* May 10, 1987: pA22.

QUEEN OF THE HEADACHES/Short stories by Sharon Butala

[Untitled]; reviews of *Noman's Land* and *Queen of the Headaches*. Anne Cimon. *Cross Can Writ Q* 1987; Vol 9 No 1: p20–21.

Matter-of-fact visions; reviews of *Learning by Heart* and *Queen of the Headaches*. Hilda Kirkwood. *Can Forum* Jan 1987; Vol 66 No 765: p39.

The essence of the prairies; review of *Queen of the Headaches*. Margaret Owen. *Prairie Fire* Summer 1987; Vol 8 No 2: p63–65.

QUEL EST CE BRUIT?/Children's story by Michèle Lemieux

La magie du livre pour enfants; review of *Quel est ce bruit?*. Dominique Demers. *MD* July 4, 1987: pC5.

QUI A PEUR DE? . . . /Short story anthology

Au rayon de la nouvelle: l'écriture sur commande; reviews of *Qui a peur de?* . . . and *L'Aventure, la mésaventure*. Jean-Roch Boivin. photo · *MD* Dec 24, 1987: pC11.
[ANTHOLOGIES: BOOK REVIEWS]

La vitrine du livre; reviews. Guy Ferland. *MD* Nov 7, 1987: pD4.

QUI OSE REGARDER/Poems by Jacques Ouellet

La vitrine du livre; reviews. Guy Ferland. *MD* May 23, 1987: pD4.

La métamorphose du quotidien; reviews of poetry books. André Marquis. photo · *Lettres québec* Autumn 1987; No 47: p41–43.

QUILL & QUIRE/Periodical

L'Actualite picks up six magazine awards; article. Ken Adachi. *TS* May 22, 1987: pE21.
[AWARDS, LITERARY; CANADIAN LITERARY PERIODICALS]

QUINLAN, PATRICIA

From giant snakes to punk pigeons: escapism at its best; reviews of children's stories. Bernie Goedhart. *Quill & Quire (Books for Young People)* June 1987; Vol 53 No 6: p5.

Mini-reviews; reviews of children's stories. Mary Rubio. *Can Child Lit* 1987; No 46: p105–109.

QUINTAL, PATRICK

[Untitled]; letter to the editor. Mario Boivin. *Jeu* 1987; No 43: p181.

[Untitled]; editorial reply. Pierre Rousseau. *Jeu* 1987; No 43: p181.

LE RÉCIF DU PRINCE/Novel by Jacques Savoie

Conservatisme; reviews of novels. Neil B. Bishop. *Can Lit* Winter 1987; No 115: p169–172.

Les enfants du déclin; reviews of novels. Jacques Michon. *Voix et images* Winter 1987; No 35: p331–334.

LE RÉPÉTITION/Poems by Denise Desautels

La fiction du réel/le réel de la fiction; reviews of poetry books. André Brochu. *Voix et images* Winter 1987; No 35: p322–330

LES RÉVÉLATIONS DU CRIME OU CAMBRAY ET SES COMPLICES/Novel by François-Réal Angers

Tout texte fondateur en cache un autre!; reviews of *Les Révélations du crime* and *L'Influence d'un livre*. Patrick Imbert. *Lettres québec* Autumn 1987; No 47: p58–60.

R.C.A. THEATRE COLLECTIVE

Collective concern; theatre reviews of *The Daily News* and *The Fishwharf and Steamboat Men*. Terry Goldie. photo · *Can Theatre R* Spring 1987; No 50: p81–83.

RACIAL ATTITUDES IN ENGLISH-CANADIAN FICTION, 1905–1980/Critical work by Terrence Craig

Fiction and racial attitudes; review of *Racial Attitudes in English-Canadian Fiction, 1905–1980*. Margaret Harry. *Atlan Prov Book R* Nov-Dec 1987; Vol 14 No 4: p10.

RADDALL, THOMAS H.

Home from the sea; article. Laurel Boone. photo · *Books in Can* June-July 1987; Vol 16 No 5: p3.

Title tattle; column. Martin Dowding. *Quill & Quire (Books for Young People)* Dec 1987; Vol 53 No 12: p3.
[FILM ADAPTATIONS OF CANADIAN LITERATURE; TELEVISION AND CANADIAN LITERATURE]

Three stories for children; reviews of children's books. Veronica Leonard. *Atlan Prov Book R* Nov-Dec 1987; Vol 14 No 4: p1.

Youngsters get choice of beautiful books; reviews. Helen Norrie. *WFP* Dec 5, 1987: p57.

Thomas H. Raddall, a decade later; reviews of *The Dreamers* and *A Name for Himself*. Andrew Seaman. *Atlan Prov Book R* Feb-March 1987; Vol 14 No 1: p19.

Yesterday's heroes; review of *The Dreamers*. Joanne Tompkins. *Books in Can* June-July 1987; Vol 16 No 5: p32–33.

RADIO AND CANADIAN LITERATURE

Radio reviews; letter to the editor. *Quill & Quire* April 1987; Vol 53 No 4: p3.

CBC to dramatize Findley novel; article. *G&M* April 10, 1987: pC9.

CBC Radio to dramatize Famous Last Words; article. *TS* April 10, 1987: pD20.

Les écrivains souhaitent une meilleure "couverture" des médias; article. *MD* Nov 14, 1987: pD15.
[CONFERENCES, LITERARY; TELEVISION AND CANADIAN LITERATURE]

Ondaatje's latest novel winning raves in Britain; column. Ken Adachi. photo · *TS* Aug 31, 1987: pB5.
[INTERNATIONAL REVIEWS OF CANADIAN LITERATURE]

Shakespeare meets the Butterfly in rerun heaven; column. Mike Boone. *MG* April 29, 1987: H2.

Ceux et celles qui nous disent qui lire; article. Paul Cauchon. *MD* May 2, 1987: pD1,D8.
[TELEVISION AND CANADIAN LITERATURE]

CKUA: radio drama and regional theatre; article. Howard Fink. abstract · *Theatre Hist in Can* Fall 1987; Vol 8 No 2: p221–233.

La question des journaux intimes; article. Lise Gauvin. *Études fran* Winter 1987; Vol 22 No 3: p101–115.
[AUTOBIOGRAPHICAL WRITING]

Books program; letter to the editor. Estelle Gee. *G&M* Oct 29, 1987: pA6.

Take books off CBC's shelf; letter to the editor. Joan Halam-Andres. *G&M* Oct 17, 1987: pD7.

Methuen staffers go in all directions; column. H.J. Kirchhoff. *G&M* Dec 24, 1987: pC3.

The mermaid inn: the poor relation of the arts; essay. Alberto Manguel. photo · *G&M* Oct 3, 1987: pD6.

Manitobans get month in spotlight on CBC TV, radio; column. Doreen Martens. *WFP* Feb 23, 1987: p14.
[TELEVISION AND CANADIAN LITERATURE]

Recalling the best of CBC radio drama; article. Ian Mayer. *G&M* Nov 14, 1987: pC20.

Author interviews hit airwaves; column. Kenneth McGoogan. *CH* April 18, 1987: pE5.
[FESTIVALS, LITERARY; WRITERS' ORGANIZATIONS]

Les ondes littéraires; list of radio and television programs. Marc Morin. *MD* Oct 31, 1987: pD2.
[TELEVISION AND CANADIAN LITERATURE]

Les ondes littéraire; list of radio and television programs. Marc Morin. *MD* Nov 7, 1987: pD2.
[TELEVISION AND CANADIAN LITERATURE]

Les ondes littéraires; list of radio and television programs. Marc Morin. *MD* Nov 14, 1987: pD14.
[TELEVISION AND CANADIAN LITERATURE]

Les ondes littéraires; list of radio and television programs. Marc Morin. *MD* Nov 21, 1987: pD2.
[TELEVISION AND CANADIAN LITERATURE]

Les ondes littéraires; list of radio and television programs. Marc Morin. *MD* Nov 28, 1987: pD12.
[TELEVISION AND CANADIAN LITERATURE]

Les ondes littéraires; list of radio and television programs. Marc Morin. *MD* Dec 5, 1987: pD2.
[TELEVISION AND CANADIAN LITERATURE]

Les ondes littéraires; list of radio and television programs. Marc Morin. *MD* Dec 12, 1987: pD2.
[TELEVISION AND CANADIAN LITERATURE]

Les ondes littéraires; list of radio and television programs. Marc Morin. *MD* Dec 24, 1987: pC10.
[TELEVISION AND CANADIAN LITERATURE]

Les ondes littéraires; list of radio and television programs. Marc Morin. *MD* Dec 31, 1987: pC10.
[TELEVISION AND CANADIAN LITERATURE]

Les ondes littéraires; list of radio and television programs. Marc Morin. *MD* Dec 19, 1987: pD2.

CBC's Vanishing Point; letter to the editor. Sandra Rabinovitch. *G&M* Nov 3, 1987: pA6.

La vie littéraire; column. Jean Royer. photo · *MD* Jan 10, 1987: pB2.
[AWARDS, LITERARY; POETRY READINGS; TELEVISION AND CANADIAN LITERATURE; WRITERS' WORKSHOPS]

La vie littéraire; column. Jean Royer. *MD* Jan 17, 1987: pB2.
[AWARDS, LITERARY; CONFERENCES, LITERARY; TELEVISION AND CANADIAN LITERATURE]

La vie littéraire; column. Jean Royer. photo · *MD* Jan 24, 1987: pB2.
[AWARDS, LITERARY; POETRY READINGS; PUBLISHING AND PUBLISHERS IN CANADA; WRITERS' WORKSHOPS]

La vie littéraire; column. Jean Royer. *MD* Jan 31, 1987: pB2.
[CANADIAN LITERARY PERIODICALS; COMPETITIONS, LITERARY; TELEVISION AND CANADIAN LITERATURE]

La vie littéraire; column. Jean Royer. *MD* Feb 14, 1987: pC2.
[AWARDS, LITERARY; CANADIAN LITERARY PERIODICALS; COMPETITIONS, LITERARY; FICTION READINGS; POETRY READINGS]

La vie littéraire; column. Jean Royer. *MD* Feb 28, 1987: pC2.
[AWARDS, LITERARY; CANADIAN LITERARY PERIODICALS; CANADIAN LITERARY PUBLISHING; CONFERENCES, LITERARY]

La vie littéraire; column. Jean Royer. *MD* March 7, 1987: pB2.
[AWARDS, LITERARY; CANADIAN LITERARY PUBLISHING; POETRY READINGS; TELEVISION AND CANADIAN LITERATURE; WRITERS' ORGANIZATIONS]

La vie littéraire; column. Jean Royer. photo · *MD* March 14, 1987: pD4.
[AWARDS, LITERARY; POETRY READINGS; TELEVISION AND CANADIAN LITERATURE]

La vie littéraire; column. Jean Royer. photo · *MD* March 21, 1987: pD2.
[AWARDS, LITERARY; CANADIAN LITERARY PUBLISHING; COMPETITIONS, LITERARY; POETRY READINGS; TELEVISION AND CANADIAN LITERATURE]

La vie littéraire; column. Jean Royer. photo · *MD* March 28, 1987: pD2.
[CONFERENCES, LITERARY; FESTIVALS, LITERARY; GOVERNMENT GRANTS FOR WRITERS/PUBLISHERS; TELEVISION AND CANADIAN LITERATURE]

La vie littéraire; column. Jean Royer. photo · *MD* April 11, 1987: pD2.
[AWARDS, LITERARY; FILM ADAPTATIONS OF CANADIAN LITERATURE; POETRY READINGS; TELEVISION AND CANADIAN LITERATURE]

La vie littéraire; column. Jean Royer. photo · *MD* April 18, 1987: pD2.
[INTERNATIONAL WRITERS' ORGANIZATIONS; TELEVISION AND CANADIAN LITERATURE]

La vie littéraire; column. Jean Royer. *MD* April 25, 1987: pD2.
[AWARDS, LITERARY; CONFERENCES, LITERARY; FESTIVALS, LITERARY; FICTION READINGS; POETRY READINGS; TELEVISION AND CANADIAN LITERATURE]

La vie littéraire; column. Jean Royer. photo · *MD* May 2, 1987: pD2.
[AWARDS, LITERARY; INTERNATIONAL REVIEWS OF CANADIAN LITERATURE; TELEVISION AND CANADIAN LITERATURE; WRITERS' ORGANIZATIONS]

La vie littéraire; column. Jean Royer. *MD* May 9, 1987: pD2.
[CONFERENCES, LITERARY; POETRY READINGS; TELEVISION AND CANADIAN LITERATURE]

La vie littéraire; column. Jean Royer. photo · *MD* May 16, 1987: pD2.
[AWARDS, LITERARY; CONFERENCES, LITERARY; PUBLISHING AND PUBLISHERS IN CANADA; TELEVISION AND CANADIAN LITERATURE]

La vie littéraire; column. Jean Royer. photo · *MD* May 23, 1987: pD2.
[CULTURAL IDENTITY; TELEVISION AND CANADIAN LITERATURE; WRITERS' ORGANIZATIONS]

La vie littéraire; column. Jean Royer. photo · *MD* May 30, 1987: pD2.
[AWARDS, LITERARY; CANADIAN LITERARY PUBLISHING; COMPETITIONS, LITERARY; FESTIVALS, LITERARY; TELEVISION AND CANADIAN LITERATURE]

La vie littéraire; column. Jean Royer. photo · *MD* June 6, 1987: pD2.
[GOVERNOR GENERAL'S AWARDS; INTERNATIONAL REVIEWS OF CANADIAN LITERATURE; TELEVISION AND CANADIAN LITERATURE]

La vie littéraire; column. Jean Royer. photo · *MD* June 13, 1987: pD2.
[AWARDS, LITERARY; COMPETITIONS, LITERARY; POETRY READINGS; TELEVISION AND CANADIAN LITERATURE; WRITERS' ORGANIZATIONS]

La vie littéraire; column. Jean Royer. photo · *MD* June 20, 1987: pD2.
[AUTHORS, CANADIAN; POETRY READINGS; TELEVISION AND CANADIAN LITERATURE]

Les ondes littéraires; list of radio and television programmes. Jean Royer. *MD* Sept 12, 1987: pD2.
[TELEVISION AND CANADIAN LITERATURE]

Les ondes littéraires; list of radio and television programmes. Jean Royer. *MD* Sept 19, 1987: pD2.
[TELEVISION AND CANADIAN LITERATURE]

Les ondes littéraires; list of radio and television programmes. Jean Royer. *MD* Sept 26, 1987: pD2.
[TELEVISION AND CANADIAN LITERATURE]

Les ondes littéraires; list of radio and television programs. Jean Royer. *MD* Oct 3, 1987: pD2.
[TELEVISION AND CANADIAN LITERATURE]

Les ondes littéraires; list of radio and television programs. Jean Royer. *MD* Oct 10, 1987: pD2.
[TELEVISION AND CANADIAN LITERATURE]

Les ondes littéraires; list of radio and television programs. Jean Royer. *MD* Oct 17, 1987: pD2.
[TELEVISION AND CANADIAN LITERATURE]

Les ondes littéraires; list of radio and television programs. Jean Royer. *MD* Oct 24, 1987: pD2.
[TELEVISION AND CANADIAN LITERATURE]

Aural dilemmas; radio review of *Sextet*. Jason Sherman. *Books in Can* March 1987; Vol 16 No 2: p5–7.

Paperclips: booksellers take to the air . . . noteworthy biographer for Gould; column. Beverley Slopen. *Quill & Quire* Jan 1987; Vol 53 No 1: p11.

Ontario report: advancing & retreating with Ontario Lit.; regional column. Steven Smith. *Poetry Can R* Summer 1987; Vol 8 No 4: p22.
[POETRY PERFORMANCE]

Bloc-notes; column. Michel Vaïs. *Jeu* 1987; No 44: p215–218.
[COMPETITIONS, LITERARY; CONFERENCES, LITERARY; GOVERNOR GENERAL'S AWARDS]

RADU, KENNETH

Random musings of a middle-aged middle-class male; reviews of poetry books. Lesley McAllister. *TS* Oct 10, 1987: M4.

RAFIE, PASCALE

Zany Toupie Wildwood an escape story made to measure for its outdoor space; theatre review. Marianne Ackerman. photo · *MG* July 2, 1987: pE5.

La grande virée à Wildwood; column. Robert Lévesque. photo · *MD* June 16, 1987: p13.

La fièvre du lundi matin; theatre review of *Toupie Wildwood*. Robert Lévesque. *MD* June 25, 1987: p13.

LE RAIL/Play by Gilles Maheu

Ne s'improvise pas improvisateur qui veut!; column. Paul Cauchon. *MD* Jan 21, 1987: p7.
[TELEVISION AND CANADIAN LITERATURE]

RAINY DAY MAGIC

See **MAGIE D'UN JOUR DE PLUIE/RAINY DAY MAGIC/ Children's story by Marie-Louise Gay**

RAINY DAY MAGIC/Children's story by Marie-Louise Gay

From giant snakes to punk pigeons: escapism at its best; reviews of children's stories. Bernie Goedhart. *Quill & Quire (Books for Young People)* June 1987; Vol 53 No 6: p5.

Mini-reviews; reviews of children's stories. Mary Rubio. *Can Child Lit* 1987; No 46: p105–109.

RAM LE ROBOT/Children's novel by Daniel Mativat and Marie-Andre Boucher

La place de l'humain; review of *Ram le Robot*. Renee A. Kingcaid. *Can Child Lit* 1987; No 45: p87–90.

LES RAPPORTS CULTURELS ENTRE LE QUÉBEC ET LES ÉTATS-UNIS/Critical essays anthology

[Untitled]; review of *Les Rapports culturels entre le Québec et les États-Unis*. C.D. Rolfe. *British J of Can Studies* June 1987; Vol 2 No 1: p167–168.

RATS IN THE SLOOP/Children's novel by Nan Doerksen

Fiction for children: history and mystery; reviews of *Rats in the Sloop* and *Shivers in Your Nightshirt*. Dorothy Perkyns. *Atlan Prov Book R* Feb-March 1987; Vol 14 No 1: p14.
[ANTHOLOGIES: BOOK REVIEWS]

RAVEL, AVIVA

Ravel reading is pay-what-you-can; article. *TS* April 26, 1987: pC7.
[DRAMATIC READINGS]

RAVEN RETURNS THE WATER/Children's story by Anne Cameron

[Untitled]; reviews of *Orca's Song* and *Raven Returns the Water*. Eva Martin. *Quill & Quire (Books for Young People)* Oct 1987; Vol 53 No 10: p23.

The magic of myth and love of legend; reviews of children's books. Tim Wynne-Jones. *G&M* July 25, 1987: pC17.

RAWDON, MICHAEL

[Untitled]; review of *Green Eyes, Dukes & Kings*. *Queen's Q* Spring 1987; Vol 94 No 1: p253–254.

Rare/fear; reviews of *Green Eyes, Dukes & Kings* and *The Book of Fears*. Thomas Gerry. *Can Lit* Spring 1987; No 112: p107–108.

New Albertan fiction; reviews of *Green Eyes, Dukes and Kings* and *Frogs*. M.L. Scott. *NeWest R* Summer 1987; Vol 12 No 10: p12.

RAY, WAYNE

[Untitled]; reviews of poetry books. Shaunt Basmajian. *Cross Can Writ Q* 1987; Vol 9 No 3–4: p44,49.
[ANTHOLOGIES: BOOK REVIEWS]

[Untitled]; reviews of poetry books. Elizabeth Woods. *Poetry Can R* Spring 1987; Vol 8 No 2–3: p49.

RAZZELL, MARY

Salmonberry Wine a rare concoction of complex issues and gutsy realism; review. Peter Carver. photo · *Quill & Quire (Books for Young People)* April 1987; Vol 53 No 4: p3.

Roughing it in the bush; reviews of children's books. Mary Ainslie Smith. *Books in Can* Aug-Sept 1987; Vol 16 No 6: p34–36.

Much more than a love story; reviews of *Salmonberry Wine* and *A Handful of Time*. Tim Wynne-Jones. *G&M* June 27, 1987: pE20.

A READER'S GUIDE TO THE CANADIAN NOVEL/Critical work by John Moss

A flowering spring and a simplistic guide; reviews of *Northern Spring* and *A Reader's Guide to the Canadian Novel* (second edition). Ken Adachi. photo · *TS* Aug 1, 1987: M4.

REALISM IN CANADIAN LITERATURE

Hyperrealism: Michel Tremblay and Franz Xaver Kroetz; article. Renate Usmiani. *Can Drama* 1987; Vol 13 No 2: p201–209.

REANEY, JAMES

Musical morality tales with a touch of magic; article. Robert Everett-Green. *G&M* May 12, 1987: pC10.
[FICTION READINGS]

Three Desks: a turning point in James Reaney's drama; article. Tim McNamara. *Queen's Q* Spring 1987; Vol 94 No 1: p15–32.

REBAR, KELLY

Domestic drama that hits home; article, includes theatre reviews. John Bemrose. photo · *Maclean's* Aug 17, 1987; Vol 100 No 33: p49.
[FESTIVALS, DRAMA]

Dilemma in Bordertown; theatre review of *Bordertown Cafe*. Ray Conlogue. photo · *G&M* July 4, 1987: pC9.

Blyth's Cafe dishes up cliches; theatre review of *Bordertown Cafe*. Robert Crew. *TS* June 26, 1987: pE4.

Play lacks strong shape; theatre review of *Bordertown Cafe*. Randal McIlroy. *WFP* Oct 2, 1987: p19.

Border play proves timely; article. Brad Oswald. photo · *WFP* Sept 30, 1987: p41.

Alberta play bombs at Blyth festival; theatre review of *Bordertown Cafe*. Jamie Portman. *CH* July 2, 1987: pF1.

Prairie playwright: Kelly Rebar's characters have roots in Canadian soil; article. Kevin Prokosh. photo · *WFP* Sept 19, 1987: p29.

Making the prairie connection; theatre reviews. Reg Skene. *NeWest R* Dec 1987; Vol 13 No 4: p16.

THE REBEL ANGELS/Novel by Robertson Davies

The Rebel Angels: Robertson Davies and the novel of ideas; article. James Mulvihill. *Eng Studies in Can* June 1987; Vol 13 No 2: p182–194.

REBEL YELL/Young adult novel by Martyn Godfrey

A little help on the dull days; reviews of children's books. Joan McGrath. *TS* Aug 2, 1987: pC11.

RECOLLECTIONS OF NOVA SCOTIA: THE CLOCKMAKER/Short stories by Thomas Chandler Haliburton

Clockmaker; review of *Recollections of Nova Scotia: The Clockmaker*. Richard A. Davies. *Can Lit* Spring 1987; No 112: p123–124.

RECOVERING CANADA'S FIRST NOVELIST: PROCEEDINGS FROM THE JOHN RICHARDSON CONFERENCE/Conference report

More than forty-nine parallels; review of *Recovering Canada's First Novelist*. Dennis Duffy. *Essays on Can Writ* Spring 1987; No 34: p170–173.

RECYCLING/Poems by Pat Jasper

Four poets; reviews of poetry books. Randall Maggs. *Can Lit* Winter 1987; No 115: p280–284.

THE RED FOX/Novel by Anthony Hyde

Pair of thrillers . . . giving the Devil his due . . . sci-fi fare; review of tape version of *The Red Fox*. Richard Perry. photo · *Quill & Quire* Aug 1987; Vol 53 No 8: p38.
[AUDIO-VISUALS AND CANADIAN LITERATURE]

A fox shows off its cunning; review of tape version of *The Red Fox*. Frank Jones. *TS* Sept 26, 1987: M4.
[AUDIO-VISUALS AND CANADIAN LITERATURE]

RED FOX/Novel by Sir Charles G.D. Roberts

An important animal story; review of *Red Fox*. Richard C. Davis. *Can Child Lit* 1987; No 47: p82–84

[Untitled]; review of *Red Fox*. Deborah Kind. *TS* Oct 25, 1987: H6.

RED WOLF, RED WOLF/Short stories by W.P. Kinsella

Kinsella finds the pathos in ordinary lives; review of *Red Wolf, Red Wolf*. Ken Adachi. *TS* Sept 6, 1987: pA19.

Kinsella should stretch his fancy; review of *Red Wolf, Red Wolf*. Barbara Black. photo · *MG* Sept 12, 1987: I6.

Middle class under fire; review of *Red Wolf, Red Wolf*. William French. photo · *G&M* Sept 3, 1987: pC1.

Kinsella displays new range; review of *Red Wolf, Red Wolf*. Kenneth McGoogan. photo · *CH* Aug 30, 1987: pE4.

[Untitled]; review of *Red Wolf, Red Wolf*. Martin Townsend. *Quill & Quire* Sept 1987; Vol 53 No 9: p79.

Writing for fun and profit; review of *Red Wolf, Red Wolf*. David Williamson. photo · *WFP* Sept 19, 1987: p64.

REDCOAT/Young adult novel by Gregory Sass

Bugs, battles & ballet; reviews of *On Stage, Please* and *Redcoat*. James Gellert. *Can Lit* Winter 1987; No 115: p220–223.
[FIRST NOVELS: BOOK REVIEWS]

REDDIN, DAVID

Scarborough librarian turns children's author; article. Paul Irish. photo · *TS (Neighbors)* Dec 8, 1987: p10.

REEVES-STEVENS, GARFIELD

[Untitled]; review of *Children of the Shroud*. John North. *Quill & Quire* Sept 1987; Vol 53 No 9: p79.

Novel needs a miracle; review of *Children of the Shroud*. Scott Van Wynsberghe. *WFP* Oct 10, 1987: p30.

REFLET PLURIEL/Poems by Hédi Bouraoui

Chronique: Bouraoui, Cahiers blues; reviews of *Reflet pluriel* and French periodical featuring French-Canadian literature. Marguerite Andersen. *Poetry Can R* Fall 1987; Vol 9 No 1: p16.

REFUS GLOBAL/TOTAL REFUSAL: THE COMPLETE 1948 MANIFESTO OF THE MONTREAL AUTOMA-TISTS/Compilation

The automatist movement of Montreal: towards non-figuration in painting, dance, and poetry; article. Ray Ellenwood. illus · *Can Lit* Summer-Fall 1987; No 113–114: p11–27.
[SURREALISM]

[Untitled]; review of *Total Refusal*. Karl Jirgens. *Books in Can* June-July 1987; Vol 16 No 5: p21.

REGIONALISM IN CANADIAN LITERATURE

The U.S.: regions & districts as labels; comparative column. David Donnell. *Poetry Can R* Spring 1987; Vol 8 No 2–3: p29.

Literary Ontario: a regional irony; editorial. Ted Plantos. *Cross Can Writ Q* 1987; Vol 9 No 2: p2.
[ONTARIO WRITING AND WRITERS]

[Untitled]; letter to the editor. Al Purdy. *Cross Can Writ Q* 1987; Vol 9 No 3–4: p64.

REIBETANZ, JOHN

[Untitled]; review of *Ashbourn*. Thomas Dilworth. *U of Windsor R* Spring-Summer 1987; Vol 20 No 2: p88–90.

[Untitled]; review of *Ashbourn*. Jeffery Donaldson. *Rubicon* Fall 1987; No 9: p169–170.

[Untitled]; review of *Ashbourn*. Gideon Forman. *Books in Can* June-July 1987; Vol 16 No 5: p24.

REID, MONTY

A choice of codes; reviews of poetry books. Thomas Gerry. illus · *NeWest R* Nov 1987; Vol 13 No 3: p16–17.

Kinetic space; reviews of poetry books. Robert James Merrett. *Can Lit* Summer-Fall 1987; No 113–114: p241–243.

REID, STEPHEN

Convict-writer wins praise but parole board unimpressed; article. photo · *WFP* Jan 22, 1987: p30.

Stephen Reid's Jackrabbit Parole; review. Brian Fawcett. *West Coast R* Spring 1987; Vol 21 No 4: p78–80.
[FIRST NOVELS: BOOK REVIEWS]

Songs of the sea-witch; article. John Goddard. photo · *Sat Night* July 1987; Vol 102 No 7: p23–29.

Paperclips: the Lovesick ladies . . . a writer's parole . . . Eden changes hands; column. Beverley Slopen. *Quill & Quire* June 1987; Vol 53 No 6: p28.

Book world: the publisher who caught 'Spy Catcher'; column. Beverley Slopen. *TS* June 7, 1987: pG10.

REIMER, ISABEL

Munsch, Reimer win Metcalf awards; article. *Quill & Quire* July 1987; Vol 53 No 7: p53.
[AWARDS, LITERARY]

Author spent prize money early; article. Donald Campbell. photo · *WFP* June 24, 1987: p27.
[AWARDS, LITERARY]

CAA opposes pornography bill; article. Fred Kerner. *Quill & Quire* Aug 1987; Vol 53 No 8: p24.
[AWARDS, LITERARY; CENSORSHIP; WRITERS' ORGANIZATIONS]

REISMAN, DOLLY

Play discourages children from sexual stereotyping; article. Beverley Ware. photo · *TS (Neighbors)* Aug 11, 1987: p6.

Play about equality of the sexes impressing Metro area children; article. Beverley Ware. *TS (Neighbors)* Aug 18, 1987: p20.

LE RELAIS ABITIBIEN/Novel by Claude Boisvert et al

La vitrine du livre; reviews. Guy Ferland. *MD* May 30, 1987: pD4.

RELATIONS: FAMILY PORTRAITS/Poetry anthology

[Untitled]; review of *Relations*. Ellie Barton. *Quarry* Fall 1987; Vol 36 No 4: p86–87.
[ANTHOLOGIES: BOOK REVIEWS]

[Untitled]; reviews. Andrew Parkin. *Poetry Can R* Summer 1987; Vol 8 No 4: p36–37.
[ANTHOLOGIES: BOOK REVIEWS; CANADIAN LITERARY PERIODICALS]

[Untitled]; reviews of *Heading Out* and *Relations: Family Portraits*. Janet Windeler. *Cross Can Writ Q* 1987; Vol 9 No 3–4: p42–43.
[ANTHOLOGIES: BOOK REVIEWS]

RELIGIOUS THEMES

Fort and forest: instability in the symbolic code of E.J. Pratt's Brebeuf and His Brethren; article. Frank Davey. abstract · *Études can* 1987; No 23: p183–194.

Religion, place, & self in early twentieth-century Canada: Robert Norwood's poetry; article. Alex Kizuk. *Can Lit* Winter 1987; No 115: p66–77.
[BIBLICAL MYTHS AND MYTHOLOGY]

L'autonomisation de la "littérature nationale" au XIXe siècle; article. Maurice Lemire. abstract · *Études lit* Spring-Summer 1987; Vol 20 No 1: p75–98.
[CANADIAN LITERATURE (19TH CENTURY): HISTORY AND CRITICISM; COLONIALISM; CULTURAL IDENTITY; FRANCE-CANADA LITERARY RELATIONS]

REMBRANDT BROWN/Play by Blake Brooker

One Yellow Rabbit great; letter to the editor. Ruth Thompson. *CH* June 15, 1987: pA6.

Tale of economic woe became family affair; article. Kate Zimmerman. *CH* April 23, 1987: pD3.

Misery of unemployment hits home in poetic play; theatre review of *Rembrandt Brown*. Kate Zimmerman. *CH* April 25, 1987: pD3.

REMEMBER ME/Play by Michel Tremblay

Théâtre au masculin; reviews of plays. Jane Moss. *Can Lit* Spring 1987; No 112: p180–183.

REMEMBERING SUMMER/Novel by Harold Horwood

Where it's near; review of *Remembering Summer*. Gideon Forman. *Books in Can* April 1987; Vol 16 No 3: p22.

Recapturing flower-power days; review of *Remembering Summer*. William French. *G&M* Feb 12, 1987: pC1.

[Untitled]; review of *Remembering Summer*. John Moore. *Quill & Quire* June 1987; Vol 53 No 6: p33.

Novel doesn't make it; review of *Remembering Summer*. David Williamson. *WFP* July 25, 1987: p33.

RENAISSANCE EN PAGANIE/Novel by Andre Ferretti

Les noeuds sacrés de l'âme, de la terre et du sang; reviews of novels. Réjean Beaudoin. *Liberté* Oct 1987; Vol 29 No 5: p106–114.

Aquin et Hypatie filant le parfait amour en Paganie; review of *Renaissance en Paganie*. Madeleine Ouellette-Michalska. photo · *MD* June 13, 1987: pD3.

RENDERS, KIM

Director a natural for New Canadian Kid; column. Vit Wagner. *TS* Dec 18, 1987: pD12.

REPERTOIRE DES ÉCRIVAINS FRANCOPHONES DES CANTONS DE L'EST/Catalogue

La vitrine du livre; reviews. Jean Royer. photo · *MD* April 18, 1987: pD2.
[CANADIAN LITERARY PERIODICALS]

LE REPOS ET L'OUBLI/Essays by Naïm Kattan

Meaning and craft; review of *Le Repos et l'oubli*. Sharon Drache. photo · *G&M* May 30, 1987: pC21.

Prenez et lisez . . . ; review of *Le Repos et l'oubli*. Maurice Lebel. *MD* Dec 5, 1987: pD4.

Le dualisme de Naïm Kattan; review of *Le Repos et l'oubli*. André Renaud. photo · *Lettres québec* Autumn 1987; No 47: p52–53.

Naïm Kattan de Bagdad à Montréal; review of *Le Repos et l'oubli*. Lori Saint-Martin. photo · *MD* June 6, 1987: pD2.

REQUIEM EN SAULE PLEUREUR/Short stories by Rose Deprés

La relève poétique en Acadie?; review of *Requiem en saule pleureur*. Caroline Bayard. *Lettres québec* Spring 1987; No 45: p43.

RESIDENT ALIEN/Short stories by Clark Blaise

[Untitled]; review of *Resident Alien*. *Queen's Q* Spring 1987; Vol 94 No 1: p254.

Whereness; review of *Resident Alien*. Catherine Sheldrick Ross. *Can Lit* Spring 1987; No 112: p164–165

RESNICK, PHILIP

[Untitled]; review of *The Centaur's Mountain*. Corrado Federici. *Poetry Can R* Summer 1987; Vol 8 No 4: p33.

RETOUR II: JOURNAL D'ÉMOTIONS/Journals by Paquerette Villeneuve

La vitrine du livre; reviews of *Retour II: journal d'émotions* and *N'eût été cet été nu*. Guy Ferland. *MD* July 11, 1987: pC6.

THE REVELS/Poems by Robert Billings

[Untitled]; reviews of *The Revels* and *Northern Poems: Where the Heart Catches Its Breath*. Gary Draper. *Poetry Can R* Spring 1987; Vol 8 No 2–3: p37.

[Untitled]; reviews of poetry books. Martin Singleton. *Cross Can Writ Q* 1987; Vol 9 No 2: p19–20.

REVIEWS OF BOOKS

See ANNOTATIONS, SHORT REVIEWS, BOOK LISTS

THE REVIVAL/Play by Sandra Birdsell

"The missing story"; introduction to play excerpt from *The Revival*. Kim McCaw;. *Prairie Fire* Spring 1987; Vol 8 No 1: p42–43.

REVUE D'HISTOIRE LITTÉRAIRE DU QUÉBEC ET DU CANADA FRANÇAIS (NUMBER 13): HISTOIRE DE MENAUD/Critical essays collection

Menaud prophète: et si Joson n'était pas mort . . . ; column. Jean Éthier-Blais. photo · *MD* Oct 3, 1987: pD8.

Des revues presque indispensables; reviews of periodicals. Adrien Thério. *Lettres québec* Autumn 1987; No 47: p63–65.
[CANADIAN LITERARY PERIODICALS]

REVUE D'HISTOIRE LITTÉRAIRE DU QUÉBEC ET DU CANADA FRANÇAIS (NUMBER TWELVE): FRONTIÈRES/Critical essays collection

Sommaires; reviews. Adrien Thério. *Lettres québec* Summer 1987; No 46: p80.

THE REZ SISTERS/Play by Tomson Highway

Rez role based on '71 rape; article. *WFP* Nov 27, 1987: p37.

The Rez Sisters lacks a satisfying resolution; theatre review. Ray Conlogue. photo · *G&M* Nov 26, 1987: pA29.

Rez Sisters inviting you out for bingo; article. Rosie DiManno. photo · *TS* Nov 20, 1987: pE3.

The trickster theatre of Tomson Highway; article. Daniel David Moses. biog · *Can Fic Mag (special issue)* 1987; No 60: p83–88.
[MYTHS AND LEGENDS IN CANADIAN LITERATURE]

Making the prairie connection; theatre reviews. Reg Skene. *NeWest R* Dec 1987; Vol 13 No 4: p16.

RHENISCH, HAROLD

Nursery rhyme, myth and dream; reviews of *Shaking the Dreamland Tree* and *Eleusis*. Gillian Harding-Russell. *NeWest R* Sept 1987; Vol 13 No 1: p17–18.

RHYME OR CRIME?/Poems by J. Alvin Speers

[Untitled]; reviews of poetry books. Andrew Parkin. *Poetry Can R* Fall 1987; Vol 9 No 1: p37.
[ANTHOLOGIES: BOOK REVIEWS]

THE RICH MAN/Novel by Henry Kreisel

[The Rich Man]; theatre review. Lynne Van Luven. *NeWest R* Nov 1987; Vol 13 No 3: p18.
[DRAMATIC ADAPTATIONS OF CANADIAN LITERATURE]

RICHARDS, DAVID ADAMS

Maritime letters; reviews. Carrie MacMillan. *Can Lit* Spring 1987; No 112: p189–192.

Recent Canadian fiction; reviews of novels. D.O. Spettigue. *Queen's Q* Summer 1987; Vol 94 No 2: p366–375.
[FIRST NOVELS: BOOK REVIEWS]

RICHARDS, MARY WILCOX

Make way for a fine crop of picture-books; reviews of children's books. Adele Ashby. *Quill & Quire (Books for Young People)* Aug 1987; Vol 53 No 8: p6.

RICHARDSON, ALAN

Emily Carr paints a bland wash; theatre review. Robert Crew. photo · *TS* Nov 25, 1987: pB5.

New drama paints portrait of Emily Carr; column. Vit Wagner. photo · *TS* Nov 20, 1987: pE4.

RICHARDSON, MAJOR JOHN

More than forty-nine parallels; review of *Recovering Canada's First Novelist*. Dennis Duffy. *Essays on Can Writ* Spring 1987; No 34: p170–173.

RICHLER, MORDECAI

Duddy revised; article. *WFP* April 23, 1987: p44.
[DRAMATIC ADAPTATIONS OF CANADIAN LITERATURE]

Richler sicks PM on Jacob; article. photo · *WFP* June 19, 1987: p35.

A revised Duddy to open in U.S.; article. *G&M* April 23, 1987: pC3.
[DRAMATIC ADAPTATIONS OF CANADIAN LITERATURE]

Mixed reviews for Duddy as musical breathes anew; article. photo · *G&M* Sept 30, 1987: pC7.
[DRAMATIC ADAPTATIONS OF CANADIAN LITERATURE; INTERNATIONAL REVIEWS OF CANADIAN LITERATURE]

Mordecai Richler, aussi invité d'honneur; article. photo · *MD* Nov 14, 1987: pD4.

Richler switches to Penguin Books; article. *TS* Nov 30, 1987: pC5.

Philadelphia gives resurrection of Richler's Duddy Kravitz mixed reviews; article. *WFP* Oct 2, 1987: p24.
[DRAMATIC ADAPTATIONS OF CANADIAN LITERATURE; INTERNATIONAL REVIEWS OF CANADIAN LITERATURE]

Richler drops line; article. *WFP* Nov 13, 1987: p33.

Free trade deal won't threaten culture: Richler; article. *G&M* Nov 19, 1987: pA28.
[CULTURAL IDENTITY]

[Untitled]; review of *Perspectives on Mordecai Richler*. *Queen's Q* Winter 1987; Vol 94 No 4: p1066–1067.

Feminist quarterly honors Laurence; column. Ken Adachi. *TS* Nov 16, 1987: pC5.
[CANADIAN LITERARY PERIODICALS; FICTION READINGS]

An interview with Mordecai Richler. Michael Benazon. photo · *Matrix* Spring 1987; No 24: p39–49.

People; column. Marsha Boulton. *Maclean's* Aug 10, 1987; Vol 100 No 32: p43.
[DRAMATIC ADAPTATIONS OF CANADIAN LITERATURE]

Theatre notes; column. Brian Brennan. *CH* May 11, 1987: pC6.
[DRAMATIC ADAPTATIONS OF CANADIAN LITERATURE; WRITERS' WORKSHOPS]

[Untitled]; review of *Jacob Two-Two and the Dinosaur*. Peter Carver. *Quill & Quire (Books for Young People)* April 1987; Vol 53 No 4: p9.

The Philadelphia experiment: a disaster in Canada, Duddy tries again in U.S.; article. Lucinda Chodan. photo · *MG* Sept 29, 1987: pB5.
[DRAMATIC ADAPTATIONS OF CANADIAN LITERATURE]

How to sell free trade? Bash Ontario, Richler says; article. Martin Cohn. photo · *TS* Nov 19, 1987: pA1,A8.
[CULTURAL IDENTITY]

Jacob Two-Two meets The Fang in zippy musical; theatre review. Ray Conlogue. photo · *G&M* Oct 26, 1987: pC11.
[DRAMATIC ADAPTATIONS OF CANADIAN LITERATURE]

Jacob Two-Two returns with pet dinosaur and new villain; article. Victor Dabby. *CH* June 14, 1987: pE1.

[Untitled]; review of *Perspectives on Mordecai Richler*. Arnold E. Davidson. *Amer R of Can Studies* Summer 1987; Vol 17 No 2: p257–259.

Child subversion reigns in delightful play; theatre review of *Jacob Two-Two Meets the Hooded Fang*. Neil Harris. *WFP* Nov 13, 1987: p37.

Richler lays aside sharp stiletto to write Jacob Two-Two; article. Heather Hill. photo · *MG* May 25, 1987: pF5.

French book fair aims for more anglophones; article. Heather Hill. *MG* Nov 6, 1987: pC1.
[CONFERENCES, LITERARY]

Jacob meets Dippy the dinosaur; article. Christopher Hume. *TS* May 26, 1987: pG1.

Fast-paced kids' tale is simply irresistible; theatre review of *Jacob Two-Two Meets the Hooded Fang*. Christopher Hume. photo · *TS* Oct 23, 1987: pE8.
[DRAMATIC ADAPTATIONS OF CANADIAN LITERATURE]

Jacob Two-Two in love; review of *Jacob Two-Two and the Dinosaur*. Brian D. Johnson. photo · *Maclean's* June 1, 1987; Vol 100 No 22: p52.

Warnes warm to Cohen's material; column. Deirdre Kelly. *G&M* May 30, 1987: pC18.
[FESTIVALS, LITERARY]

Jacob Two-Two returns in another grand adventure; review of *Jacob Two-Two and the Dinosaur*. Janice Kennedy. *MG* May 30, 1987: J7.

Richler revels in kidlit success; article. H.J. Kirchhoff. photo · *G&M* June 10, 1987: pC5.

[Untitled]; theatre reviews. Gina Mallet. *G&M (Toronto Magazine)* Nov 1987; Vol 2 No 8: p29.

Tammy saw cats on wings; column. Doreen Martens. *WFP* Aug 12, 1987: p21.
[DRAMATIC ADAPTATIONS OF CANADIAN LITERATURE]

Beyond the merely competent; reviews of critical works. Larry McDonald. *Atlan Prov Book R* Sept-Oct 1987; Vol 14 No 3: p11.
[CANADIAN LITERARY PERIODICALS]

Richler toasts any deal that puts it to Ontario; article. Juliet O'Neill. photo · *CH* Nov 19, 1987: pA18.
[CULTURAL IDENTITY]

Child power injects fun into play; article. Brad Oswald. photo · *WFP* Nov 13, 1987: p37.
[DRAMATIC ADAPTATIONS OF CANADIAN LITERATURE]

[Untitled]; review of *Jacob Two-Two and the Dinosaur*. Francine Prose. *NYT Book R* Oct 18, 1987: p38.

Miami Vice's Don Johnson a Stowe-away in resort town; column. Thomas Schnurmacher. *MG* Jan 21, 1987: pF6.
[DRAMATIC ADAPTATIONS OF CANADIAN LITERATURE]

Great Montrealer Hugh MacLennan feted at Racket Club; column. Thomas Schnurmacher. *MG* March 13, 1987: H1.

Star Trek's Capt. Kirk beaming up to Montreal; column. Thomas Schnurmacher. *MG* Aug 11, 1987: pC8.
[DRAMATIC ADAPTATIONS OF CANADIAN LITERATURE]

Author Jacobson has more than the gift of the gab; column. Thomas Schnurmacher. *MG* Dec 4, 1987: pC1.

Photography "in camera"; article. Peter Sims. *Can Lit* Summer-Fall 1987; No 113–114: p145–166.

Roughing it in the bush; reviews of children's books. Mary Ainslie Smith. *Books in Can* Aug-Sept 1987; Vol 16 No 6: p34–36.

A deeper sense of outrage, an afternoon with Mordecai Richler; interview. Eric Wright. *Descant (special issue)* Spring-Summer 1987; Vol 18 No 1–2: p168–173.

Triumphant return; reviews of *Jacob Two-Two and the Dinosaur* and *Pop Bottles*. Tim Wynne-Jones. *G&M* June 13, 1987: pC19.
[AWARDS, LITERARY]

RIEGER, JOHN

[Untitled]; review of *Schizotexte*. Quendrith Johnson. *Rubicon* Spring 1987; No 8: p186–187.

[Untitled]; review of *Schizotexte*. Sparling Mills. *Poetry Can R* Summer 1987; Vol 8 No 4: p38.

RIEN À VOIR/Play by Bernard-J. Andrés

Le théâtre qu'on joue; theatre reviews. André Dionne. illus photo · *Lettres québec* Spring 1987; No 45: p47–48.

[Untitled]; theatre review of *Rien voir*. Diane Pavlovic. *Jeu* 1987; No 42: p170.

THE RING MASTER/Novel by David Gurr

[Untitled]; review of *The Ring Master*. Oliver Conant. *NYT Book R* Nov 1, 1987: p24.

A framework for history; review of [I]The Ring Master. Alberto Manguel. photo · *G&M* Nov 14, 1987: pE1.

RINGTAIL/Children's story by Patricia Sillers

A fun bunch of books to read and look at; reviews of *Big Sarah's Little Boots* and *Ringtail*. Frieda Wishinsky. *Quill & Quire (Books for Young People)* Aug 1987; Vol 53 No 8: p3.

RINGUET

Le silence de Trente arpents; article. Javier García Méndez. *Voix et images* Spring 1987; Vol 12 No 3: p452–469.
[STRUCTURALIST WRITING AND CRITICISM]

Si Ringuet n'avait pas regardé l'atlas; review of *Le Choix de Jean Panneton dans l'oeuvre de Ringuet*. Madeleine Ouellette-Michalska. photo · *MD* Sept 19, 1987: pD3.

RINGWOOD, GWEN PHARIS

CKUA: radio drama and regional theatre; article. Howard Fink. abstract · *Theatre Hist in Can* Fall 1987; Vol 8 No 2: p221–233.
[RADIO AND CANADIAN LITERATURE]

The dowser character in the plays of Gwen Pharis Ringwood; article. Denyse Lynde. *Ariel* Jan 1987; Vol 18 No 1: p27–37.

RINTOUL, HARRY

Refugees premiere set; article. *WFP* Nov 20, 1987: p33.

RIOUX, HÉLÈNE

Tous feux teints; review of *L'Homme de Hong Kong*. Marie José Thériault. *Lettres québec* Winter 1986–87; No 44: p34–35.

RIPPER/Novel by Mark Clark

Surprising weight from the newcomers; reviews of *The Glorious East Wind* and *Ripper*. Margaret Cannon. *G&M* Nov 7, 1987: pC23.
[FIRST NOVELS: BOOK REVIEWS]

Jack the Ripper is wealthy MD in thriller with social conscience; review of *Ripper*. Peggy Curran. *MG* Nov 7, 1987: K13.

Plotting against the royals; reviews of *Broken English* and *Merlin's Web*. Brian Kappler. *MG* Nov 7, 1987: K13.

RISING TIDE THEATRE COLLECTIVE

Interest in politics led Butt to work in theatre; article about Donna Butt. *WFP* May 16, 1987: p21.

Collective concern; theatre reviews of *The Daily News* and *The Fishwharf and Steamboat Men*. Terry Goldie. photo · *Can Theatre R* Spring 1987; No 50: p81–83.

RISKIN, MARY W.

Mainstreet Calgary; column. *CH (Neighbors)* May 13, 1987: pA6–A7.
[FICTION READINGS; WRITERS' WORKSHOPS]

Appointments; column. *Quill & Quire* June 1987; Vol 53 No 6: p26.
[WRITERS' ORGANIZATIONS]

Me, myself, and I; reviews of first novels. Janice Kulyk Keefer. *Books in Can* Oct 1987; Vol 16 No 7: p35–36,38.
[FIRST NOVELS: BOOK REVIEWS]

Promising literary debut made by young mother; review of *The Woman Upstairs*. Kenneth McGoogan. biog photo · *CH* May 10, 1987: pE5.
[FIRST NOVELS: BOOK REVIEWS]

Reader left with agreeable sense of déjà vu; reviews of *Beneath the Western Slopes* and *The Woman Upstairs*. Hugh McKellar. *TS* Aug 9, 1987: pA21.

Tale of growing up is a true standout; review of *The Woman Upstairs*. Morley Walker. *WFP* July 11, 1987: p57.
[FIRST NOVELS: BOOK REVIEWS]

RITCHIE, SIMON

Crime; review of *The Hollow Woman*. Newgate Callendar. *NYT Book R* March 29, 1987: p25.

Murder & mayhem: tough guys on clean street; reviews of crime novels. Margaret Cannon. *G&M* Jan 3, 1987: pE15.
[FIRST NOVELS: BOOK REVIEWS]

Urban scrawl; reviews of first novels. Janice Kulyk Keefer. *Books in Can* Aug-Sept 1987; Vol 16 No 6: p33–34.
[FIRST NOVELS: BOOK REVIEWS]

Top felon worth troop of bumblers; review of *The Hollow Woman*. Hugh McKellar. *TS* April 18, 1987: M4.

[Untitled]; review of *The Hollow Woman*. John North. *Quill & Quire* June 1987; Vol 53 No 6: p32.

RITTER, ERIKA

Erika Ritter quits Dayshift; article. *TS* March 15, 1987: pC5.

Ritter quits Dayshift; article. *WFP* March 14, 1987: p21.

Ritter quitting; article. *CH* March 15, 1987: pE2.

Erika Ritter: a shlep as bewildered as her audience; article. Lucinda Chodan. photo · *MG* Oct 31, 1987: pD13.

Author's favorite comic pieces 'came in an unbidden moment'; article. Kenneth McGoogan. photo · *CH* Oct 23, 1987: pF1.

RIVARD, YVON

Munro short story collection wins award; article. *WFP* May 29, 1987: p34.
[GOVERNOR GENERAL'S AWARDS]

Le prix du Gouverneur général à Yvon Rivard; article. *MD* May 28, 1987: p2.
[GOVERNOR GENERAL'S AWARDS]

Governor General's Award to Munro amid poetry protest; article. photo · *MG* May 28, 1987: pC1.
[GOVERNOR GENERAL'S AWARDS]

Governor General's award winners; article. *Quill & Quire* July 1987; Vol 53 No 7: p53–54.
[GOVERNOR GENERAL'S AWARDS]

Les lectures Skol: pour les dix ans de l'Union des écrivains; article. *MD* Oct 10, 1987: pD8.
[FICTION READINGS; WRITERS' ORGANIZATIONS]

Frye finally wins elusive award for best non-fiction book of '86; article. Ken Adachi. photo · *TS* May 28, 1987: H1.
[GOVERNOR GENERAL'S AWARDS]

Machine romanesque; review of *Les Silences du corbeau*. Jacques Julien. *Can Lit* Winter 1987; No 115: p227–229.

Yvon Rivard et Northrop Frye parmi les lauréats des prix du gouverneur général; article. Robert Lévesque. photo · *MD* May 28, 1987: p13.
[GOVERNOR GENERAL'S AWARDS]

Prix et distinctions; list of award winners. Gaétan Lévesque. photo · *Lettres québec* Autumn 1987; No 47: p7.
[AWARDS, LITERARY; GOVERNOR GENERAL'S AWARDS]

[Untitled]; reviews. Raymond Martin. *Moebius* Winter 1987; No 31: p164–166.

Savoir garder ses distances; review of *Les Silences du corbeau*. Louise Milot. photo · *Lettres québec* Spring 1987; No 45: p22–23.

Munro wins third Governor General's Award; article. Jamie Portman. photo · *CH* May 28, 1987: pC9.
[GOVERNOR GENERAL'S AWARDS]

Munro wins top literary prize; article. Lisa Rochon. photo · *G&M* May 28, 1987: pD1.
[GOVERNOR GENERAL'S AWARDS]

La vie littéraire; column. Jean Royer. photo · *MD* June 6, 1987: pD2.
[GOVERNOR GENERAL'S AWARDS; INTERNATIONAL REVIEWS OF CANADIAN LITERATURE; RADIO AND CANADIAN LITERATURE; TELEVISION AND CANADIAN LITERATURE]

La vie littéraire; column. Jean Royer. photo · *MD* Oct 17, 1987: pD2.
[CANADIAN LITERARY PERIODICALS; COMPETITIONS, LITERARY; CONFERENCES, LITERARY; FICTION READINGS; WRITERS' ORGANIZATIONS]

Impasses ou issues? L'imaginaire masculin face à la femme; reviews of *Les Silences du corbeau* and *À double sens*. Patricia Smart. *Voix et images* Spring 1987; Vol 12 No 3: p555–560.

ROAD DANCES/Poems by Joan Heney

But where is the poetry?; reviews of *Road Dances* and *Counterpane*. Bruce Whiteman. *Essays on Can Writ* Spring 1987; No 34: p48–49

ROAD TO THE STILT HOUSE/Novel by David Adams Richards

Maritime letters; reviews. Carrie MacMillan. *Can Lit* Spring 1987; No 112: p189–192.

Recent Canadian fiction; reviews of novels. D.O. Spettigue. *Queen's Q* Summer 1987; Vol 94 No 2: p366–375.
[FIRST NOVELS: BOOK REVIEWS]

ROBART, ROSE

Mini-reviews; reviews of children's stories. Mary Rubio. *Can Child Lit* 1987; No 46: p105–109.

ROBERT KROETSCH/Critical work by Robert Lecker

[Untitled]; reviews of *Robert Kroetsch* and *Another Country*. Russell Brown. *U of Toronto Q* Fall 1987; Vol 57 No 1: p161–166.

The Twayning of Robert Kroetsch; review of *Robert Kroetsch*. Martin Kuester. *Prairie Fire* Winter 1987–88; Vol 8 No 4: p101–105.

ROBERT LOVELACE: AN EXAMINATION OF AN INDIVIDUAL MIND AND ITS LIMITS/Poems by Donna O'Sullivan

[Untitled]; reviews of poetry books. Shaunt Basmajian. *Cross Can Writ Q* 1987; Vol 9 No 3–4: p44,49.
[ANTHOLOGIES: BOOK REVIEWS]

ROBERTS, KEN

Current crop of kids' books is brighter than spring gardens; reviews of *Pop Bottles* and *A Handful of Time*. Joan McGrath. *TS* May 24, 1987: pA19.

Triumphant return; reviews of *Jacob Two-Two and the Dinosaur* and *Pop Bottles*. Tim Wynne-Jones. *G&M* June 13, 1987: pC19.
[AWARDS, LITERARY]

ROBERTS, SIR CHARLES G.D.

Sir Charles G.D. Roberts: post biography; article. John Coldwell Adams. *Can Poet* Fall-Winter 1987; No 21: p77–80.

A New Brunswick Roberts; review of *The Collected Poems of Sir Charles G.D. Roberts*. D.M.R. Bentley. *Can Lit* Spring 1987; No 112: p133–136.

The Anchorage series proceedings: the Sir Charles G.D. Roberts and Joseph Howe symposia; reviews of *The Sir Charles G.D. Roberts Symposium* and *The Joseph Howe Symposium*. Laurel Boone. *Essays on Can Writ* Spring 1987; No 34: 196–201.

An important animal story; review of *Red Fox*. Richard C. Davis. *Can Child Lit* 1987; No 47: p82–84.

"The old kinship of earth": science, man and nature in the animal stories of Charles G.D. Roberts; article. Thomas R. Dunlap. abstract · *J of Can Studies* Spring 1987; Vol 22 No 1: p104–120.
[ANIMAL STORIES]

[Untitled]; review of *Red Fox*. Deborah Kind. *TS* Oct 25, 1987: H6.

Torn between love and loyalty; reviews of *Sir Charles God Damn* and *Sir Charles G.D. Roberts: A Biography*. David McFadden. photo · *Brick* Fall 1987; No 31: p55–59.

[Untitled]; reviews of *The Collected Poems of Sir Charles G.D. Roberts* and *Sir Charles God Damn*. Mary McGillivray. *Queen's Q* Winter 1987; Vol 94 No 4: p1039–1042.

[Untitled]; interview with Sir Charles G.D. Roberts. Lorne Pierce. *Can Poet* Fall-Winter 1987; No 21: p63–76.

Lorne Pierce's 1927 interview with Charles G.D. Roberts (as reported by Margaret Lawrence); introduction. Terry Whalen. *Can Poet* Fall-Winter 1987; No 21: p59–62.

ROBERTSON DAVIES, PLAYWRIGHT: A SEARCH FOR THE SELF ON THE CANADIAN STAGE/Critical work by Susan Stone-Blackburn

[Untitled]; review of *Robertson Davies, Playwright*. Diane Bessai. *Ariel* April 1987; Vol 18 No 2: p101–104.

[Untitled]; review of *Robertson Davies, Playwright*. S.F. Gallagher. *Eng Studies in Can* June 1987; Vol 13 No 2: p234–237.

[Untitled]; review of *Robertson Davies, Playwright*. Michael Peterman. *Theatre Hist in Can* Fall 1987; Vol 8 No 2: p249–252.

[Untitled]; reviews of *Robertson Davies* and *Robertson Davies, Playwright*. D.O. Spettigue. *Queen's Q* Autumn 1987; Vol 94 No 3: p722–724.

ROBERTSON DAVIES/Critical work by Michael Peterman

[Untitled]; review of *Robertson Davies*. John H. Ferres. *Amer R of Can Studies* Winter 1987–88; Vol 17 No 4: p450–452.

[Untitled]; reviews of *Robertson Davies* and *Robertson Davies, Playwright*. D.O. Spettigue. *Queen's Q* Autumn 1987; Vol 94 No 3: p722–724.

ROBERTSON, HEATHER

It's a date; column. *MG* April 3, 1987: pC10.
[FICTION READINGS]

Montreal spy connection adds spice to the latest Mackenzie King novel; article. Barbara Black. photo · *MG* April 11, 1987: pG6.

Aspiring writers take their books to the library; article. Phil Johnson. photo · *TS (Neighbors)* Sept 22, 1987: p20.
[WRITERS-IN-RESIDENCE]

Lilly & Willie; review of *Lily: A Rhapsody in Red*. Linda Lamont-Stewart. *Can Lit* Winter 1987; No 115: p275–277.

Author calls free-trade deal a disaster; article. Linda Matchan. photo · *CH* Oct 11, 1987: pE7.
[CULTURAL IDENTITY]

Writer fears free trade will kill her career; article. Linda Mitcham. photo · *WFP* Oct 9, 1987: p36.
[CULTURAL IDENTITY]

Tip sheet: doctor to speak on AIDS and food industry; column. Susan Schwartz. photo · *MG* April 1, 1987: pC10.
[FICTION READINGS]

ROBIDOUX, RÉJEAN

La vitrine du livre; reviews. Guy Ferland. *MD* Nov 14, 1987: pD16.
[ANTHOLOGIES: BOOK REVIEWS]

ROBIN, REGINE

À l'heure du glasnost comment exorciser le social-réalisme . . . ; article. Paul-André Comeau. photo · *MD* Aug 1, 1987: pC5.

The text as crossroads; review of *La Québécoite*. Ralph Sarkonak. *Can Lit* Spring 1987; No 112: p100–102.

ROBINS, JOHN D.

Fishing tales made all Canada laugh; biographical article. Donald Jones. photo · *TS* July 18, 1987: M3.

ROBINSON, BRAD

[Untitled]; review of *Afternoon Tea*. Shelagh Garland. *Books in Can* May 1987; Vol 16 No 4: p20.

Poor George and Jessie, poor reader; review of *Afternoon Tea*. Maggie Helwig. *TS* Feb 28, 1987: M6.

Fine short stories examine contemporary domestic life; reviews of *Dzelarhons* and *Afternoon Tea*. Douglas Hill. *G&M* Jan 24, 1987: pE17.

Excellent illusions, cloying clichés in short-story collections; reviews of *Afternoon Tea* and *Inspecting the Vaults*. Brent Ledger. photo · *Quill & Quire* March 1987; Vol 53 No 3: p72.

Book world: a little-known bestseller; column. Beverley Slopen. *TS* Jan 11, 1987: pA16.

ROBINSON, GAIL

Melody Farm feels like two plays trying to be one; theatre reviews of *Melody Farm* and *Biting Nails*. Stephen Godfrey. photo · *G&M* Feb 18, 1987: pC7.

ROBINSON, PETER

A newcomer to Canadian crime fiction; review of *Gallows View*. Ken Adachi. *TS* April 19, 1987: pA19.
[FIRST NOVELS: BOOKS REVIEWS]

Murder & mayhem: plot and details in a cop's life; reviews of *Gallows View* and *Equinox*. Margaret Cannon. photo · *G&M* May 23, 1987: pC23.

[Untitled]; review of *Gallows View*. Martin Dowding. *Quill & Quire* March 1987; Vol 53 No 3: p71.
[FIRST NOVELS: BOOK REVIEWS]

Cheap thrills; reviews of *The Last Hunter* and *Gallows View*. Janice Kulyk Keefer. *Books in Can* June-July 1987; Vol 16 No 5: p37–38.
[FIRST NOVELS: BOOK REVIEWS]

Whodunits hit bookshelves in big way; review of *Gallows View*. Kenneth McGoogan. *CH* June 7, 1987: pE6.
[FIRST NOVELS: BOOK REVIEWS]

First novels set to different literary keys; reviews of *Crang Plays the Ace* and *Gallows View*. James Mennie. photo · *MG* April 11, 1987: pG6.
[FIRST NOVELS: BOOK REVIEWS]

Three absolute page-turners; reviews of *Crang Plays the Ace* and *Gallows View*. Janet Saunders. photo · *WFP* May 9, 1987: p56.
[FIRST NOVELS: BOOK REVIEWS]

Book world: Grolier moves into children's fiction; column. Beverley Slopen. *TS* March 22, 1987: pA20.
[CHILDREN'S LITERATURE; PUBLISHING AND PUBLISHERS IN CANADA]

ROBINSON, SPIDER

Writer, dancer take TransCanada mystery tour; article. photo · *WFP* July 14, 1987: p33.

An unsolvable maze; review of *Time Pressure*. Chuck Biggs. *WFP* Dec 12, 1987: p50.

'It hurts' to leave Halifax, writer discovers; article. Deborah Jones. photo · *G&M* June 24, 1987: pC5.

Novel shelved for sharp scrutiny of the sixties; column. H.J. Kirchhoff. *G&M* Dec 19, 1987: pC17.

Bringing sci-fi down to Earth; article. Henry Mietkiewicz. illus · *TS* May 24, 1987: pC1.
[SCIENCE FICTION]

Spider Robinson's time traveller lands in rural N.S.; review of *Time Pressure*. Michael Mirolla. *MG* Dec 24, 1987: L8.

ROCHON, ESTHER

Prix et distinctions; list of award winners. photo · *Lettres québec* Summer 1987; No 46: p7.
[AWARDS, LITERARY]

Esther Rochon: une écriture "cool"; review of *Le Traversier*. Jean-Roch Boivin. photo · *MD* April 18, 1987: pD3.

[Untitled]; review of *Le Traversier*. Gaétan Breton. *Moebius* Summer 1987; No 33: p135–136.

La quête de la pensée la pensée de la quête; review of *Le Traversier*. Michel Lord. photo · *Lettres québec* Summer 1987; No 46: p28–29.

Le grand prix Logidisque de la science-fiction et du fantastique est attribué à Esther Rochon; article. Jean Royer. photo · *MD* April 14, 1987: p11.
[AWARDS, LITERARY; SCIENCE FICTION]

ROCK DESPERADO/Poems by Jean Perron

[Untitled]; review of *Rock desperado*. Lucie Bourassa. *Estuaire* Winter 1986–87; No 43: p77.

ROCK IS DEAD/Play by Alan Williams

Indecisive play fails to elicit empathy for young characters; theatre review of *Rock Is Dead*. Randal McIlroy. *WFP* July 25, 1987: p48.

RODGERS, GORDON

Noticing three poets; reviews of poetry books. Terrence Craig. *Atlan Prov Book R* May-June 1987; Vol 14 No 2: p10.

RODGERS, GUY

Drama fest heads for grand finale; theatre reviews of *Jack of Hearts* and *Collideoscope*. Marianne Ackerman. photo · *MG* May 1, 1987: pD3.
[FESTIVALS, DRAMA]

RODRIGUEZ, PATRICIA

Tale of Indian mystic a challenge to stage; article. photo · *G&M* Feb 27, 1987: pD12.

Producer brings tale of 17th-century Indian princess to stage; article. photo · *WFP* Feb 27, 1987: p37.

Sam Gesser tries again with Lily; article. Marianne Ackerman. photo · *MG* Feb 21, 1987: pD1.

Sense of guilt driving force behind thinly sketched Lily; theatre review of *Lily of the Mohawks*. Marianne Ackerman. *MG* Feb 27, 1987: pC2.

Sainte Kateri et le mythe du bon sauvage; theatre review of *Lily of the Mohawks*. Paul Lefebvre. photo · *MD* March 4, 1987: p6.

LES ROGERS/Play by Robert Bellefeuille et al

Théâtre au masculin; reviews of plays. Jane Moss. *Can Lit* Spring 1987; No 112: p180–183.

ROHMER, RICHARD

Rohmer spins good yarn; review of *Rommel and Patton*. Fred Cleverley. *WFP* Jan 10, 1987: p66.

Rohmer brews mystery from fact and fiction; review of *Rommel and Patton*. Bill Hart. *CH* March 22, 1987: pF5.

[Untitled]; review of *Rommel and Patton*. Douglas Malcolm. *Books in Can* April 1987; Vol 16 No 3: p24–25.

UN ROMAN DU REGARD: LA MONTAGNE SECRÈTE DE GABRIELLE ROY/Critical work by Jean Morency

La fiction de nos devanciers; reviews of *Le Roman québécois de 1944 à 1965* and *Un Roman du regard*. Agnès Whitfield. photo · *Lettres québec* Winter 1986–87; No 44: p56–58.

LE ROMAN DU TERRITOIRE/Critical work by Bernard Proulx

L'instinct territorial; review of *Le Roman du territoire*. Robert Major. *Voix et images* Autumn 1987; Vol 13 No 1: p162–165.

LE ROMAN QUÉBÉCOIS DE 1944 À 1965: SYMPTÔMES DU COLONIALISME ET SIGNES DE LIBRATION/Critical work by Maurice Arguin

La fiction de nos devanciers; reviews of *Le Roman québécois de 1944 à 1965* and *Un Roman du regard*. Agnès Whitfield. photo · *Lettres québec* Winter 1986–87; No 44: p56–58.

ROMANTIC FICTION

[Untitled]; letter to the editor. Andrée Gagnon. *Lettres québec* Spring 1987; No 45: p7.

Claire Harrison plaide en faveur des romans Harlequin; article. France Lafuste. photo · *MD* Dec 12, 1987: pD1,D12.

Direct marketing writes Harlequin's own happy ending to romance wars; article. Rebate Lerch. illus photo · *Fin Post* Oct 26, 1987: p23.
[PUBLISHING AND PUBLISHERS IN CANADA]

Bestsellers on TV, and a sunny summer romance; column. Diana Shepherd. *Quill & Quire* Sept 1987; Vol 53 No 9: p72.
[TELEVISION AND CANADIAN LITERATURE]

'You can't have too much romance'; essay. Joel Yanofsky. illus · *MG* May 2, 1987: H11.
[PUBLISHING AND PUBLISHERS IN CANADA]

ROMMEL AND PATTON/Novel by Richard Rohmer

Rohmer spins good yarn; review of *Rommel and Patton*. Fred Cleverley. *WFP* Jan 10, 1987: p66.

Rohmer brews mystery from fact and fiction; review of *Rommel and Patton*. Bill Hart. *CH* March 22, 1987: pF5.

[Untitled]; review of *Rommel and Patton*. Douglas Malcolm. *Books in Can* April 1987; Vol 16 No 3: p24–25.

RONFARD, ALICE

Ionesco soufflera ses 75 chandelles à Montréal; column. Robert Lévesque. *MD* May 12, 1987: p14.
[FESTIVALS, DRAMA]

Stark theatrical visions lose focus in pile of sordid detail; theatre review of *Overground*. Francine Pelletier. *MG* May 26, 1987: pD11.

Une auteure qui se découvrira; theatre review of *Overground*. Jean-Robert Rémillard. *Liberté* Dec 1987; Vol 29 No 6: p156.

RONFARD, JEAN-PIERRE

Experimental theatre: only some works; theatre review of *Nouvelles pour le théâtre*. Marianne Ackerman. *MG* Feb 5, 1987: pE6

TNE's Mao charming highly visual theatre; theatre review of *Mao Ts Toung, ou soire de musique au consulat*. Marianne Ackerman. *MG* Feb 28, 1987: pG5.

[Untitled]; theatre review of *Mao Tse Toung ou soires de musique au consulat*. Marianne Ackerman. *MG* March 20, 1987: pC7.

[Untitled]; notice. Paul Cauchon. photo · *MD* Oct 9, 1987: p15.
[TELEVISION AND CANADIAN LITERATURE]

"Nouvelles pour le théâtre"; column. Robert Lévesque. *MD* Jan 27, 1987: p5.

Ronfard et les traces de Mao, Nadon et les frasques de Lorenzaccio; column. Robert Lévesque. *MD* Feb 17, 1987: p7.

[Untitled]; theatre reviews. Robert Lévesque. photo · *MD* March 13, 1987: p15.

[Untitled]; theatre reviews of *La Tour* and *Les Objets parlent*. Solange Lévesque. photo · *Jeu* 1987; No 43: p145–147.

Denise Filiatrault revient au théâtre; column. Robert Lévesque. *MD* April 28, 1987: p14.

André Brassard prend congé de mise en scène; column. Robert Lévesque. *MD* May 5, 1987: p11.
[FESTIVALS, DRAMA]

Théâtre ouvert et théâtre intime; theatre review of *Marilyn (journal intime de Margaret Macpherson)*. Robert Lévesque. *MD* Oct 14, 1987: p14.

Mao, sa révolution et nous; theatre review of *Mao Tsé-toung ou soirées de musique au consulat*. Paul Lefebvre. photo · *MD* March 3, 1987: p5.

(Im)pure theatre; article. Louise Vigeant. photo trans · *Can Theatre R* Spring 1987; No 50: p14–19.

[Untitled]; theatre review of *Mao Tsé Toung ou soirée de musique au consulat*. Louise Vigeant. photo · *Jeu* 1987; No 43: p156–159.

ROOKE, LEON

Congratulations!; notice. Bernice Lever. *Waves* Winter 1987; Vol 15 No 3: p89.
[AWARDS, LITERARY]

ROOTLESS TREE/Poems by John V. Hicks

Seeker & finder; reviews of *Canada Gees Mate for Life* and *Rootless Tree*. Bruce Whiteman. *Can Lit* Winter 1987; No 115: p148–150.

ROSCOE, PATRICK

Stories of the medieval in the present day; reviews of *Beneath the Western Slopes* and *Medieval Hour in the Author's Mind*. Clark Blaise. *Quill & Quire* June 1987; Vol 53 No 6: p34.

New author weaves poetic stories into magical fantasy; review of *Beneath the Western Slopes*. Cecelia Frey. *CH* Sept 20, 1987: pE6.

Writer leads us on his Mexican magical mystery tour; review of *Beneath the Western Slopes*. P. Scott Lawrence. photo · *MG* July 18, 1987: J8.

Reader left with agreeable sense of déjà vu; reviews of *Beneath the Western Slopes* and *The Woman Upstairs*. Hugh McKellar. *TS* Aug 9, 1987: pA21.

[Untitled]; review of *Beneath the Western Slopes*. Constance Rooke. *Malahat R* Sept 1987; No 80: p137.

ROSE-ROUGE/Novel by Véra Pollak

Une enfant du siècle au "monde merveilleux du kitsch du cœur"; review of *Rose-Rouge*. Jean-Roch Boivin. *MD* Aug 29, 1987: p11–12.

ROSEN, SHELDON

The play's the thing, despite thieves, greed and flops; article. Stephen Godfrey. photo · *G&M* Aug 8, 1987: pC1.

ROSS, MALCOLM

[Untitled]; review of *The Impossible Sum of Our Traditions*. Douglas Daymond. *World Lit in Eng* Autumn 1987; Vol 27 No 2: p264–269.

[Untitled]; reviews of critical works. Don Gutteridge. *Queen's Q* Summer 1987; Vol 94 No 2: p464–467.

[Untitled]; reviews of *Studies in Literature and the Humanities* and *The Impossible Sum of Our Traditions* W.J. Keith. *U of Toronto Q* Fall 1987; Vol 57 No 1: p145–148.

[Untitled]; review of *The Impossible Sum of Our Traditions*. Vernon R. Lindquist. *Amer R of Can Studies* Autumn 1987; Vol 17 No 3: p353–354.

New Brunswick letters; review of *The Bicentennial Lectures on New Brunswick Literature*. Alan R. Young. *Can Lit* Spring 1987; No 112: p146–148.

ROSS, MARTHA

Talented comediennes energetic and funny; theatre review of *Fertility*. Robert Crew. *TS* March 6, 1987: pD21.

The Mikado hits a high note with seven Dora Awards; article. Robert Crew. photo · *TS* June 23, 1987: pE3.
[AWARDS, LITERARY]

Neville to extend stay at Stratford for a year; column. Robert Crew. *TS* June 24, 1987: pF1.
[AWARDS, LITERARY]

Ernest and Ernestine are funny and familiar; theatre review of *The Anger of Ernest and Ernestine*. Liam Lacey. photo · *G&M* May 28, 1987: pD6.

Well-wrought Anger comedy marred only by false-note finale; theatre review of *The Anger in Ernest and Ernestine*. Henry Mietkiewicz. photo · *TS* May 29, 1987: pE12.

John Fraser new Saturday Night editor; column. Henry Mietkiewicz. *TS* July 17, 1987: pE23.
[CANADIAN LITERARY PERIODICALS]

ROSS, VERONICA

[Untitled]; review of *Homecoming*. D. French. *Books in Can* Nov 1987; Vol 16 No 8: p24.

Betrayal runs through short story collection; review of *Homecoming*. Ranjini Mendis. *CH* Dec 6, 1987: pD8.

ROSS, W.E. DAN

Nurse novelist Dan Ross admits his characters often confuse him; article. *WFP* April 4, 1987: p20.

Author Ross admits he gets mixed up; article. *MG* April 4, 1987: H11.

ROTSTEIN, NANCY-GAY

[Untitled]; review of *China Shockwaves*. Barbara Carey. *Books in Can* June-July 1987; Vol 16 No 5: p23.

Poet tries to capture true cadence of China; article. Eric Dawson. photo · *CH* Dec 10, 1987: pF5.

Poets view China, Dada; reviews of *China: Shockwaves* and *The Merzbook*. Robert Quickenden. *WFP* Dec 5, 1987: p56.

ROUGH PASSAGE/Novel by Paddy Webb

[Untitled]; reviews of *Rough Passage* and *April Raintree*. Judith Russell. *Queen's Q* Spring 1987; Vol 94 No 1: p191–193.

ROULSTON, KEITH

[Another Season's Promise]; theatre review. Susan Minsos. *NeWest R* Dec 1987; Vol 13 No 4: p17.

ROY, ANDRÉ

André Roy ou l'invention d'un littéral métaphysique; introduction. Marie-Andrée Beaudet. *Estuaire* Spring 1987; No 44: p63–66.

[Untitled]; review of *Becoming Light*. Marc Côté. *Books in Can* Dec 1987; Vol 16 No 9: p31.

André Roy: on n'écrit pas impunément; interview. Jean-Paul Daoust. *Estuaire* Spring 1987; No 44: p71–78.

Les mots retrouvent tous leurs pouvoirs; review of *C'est encore le solitaire qui parle*. Gérald Gaudet. photo · *MD* Sept 5, 1987: pC9.

André Roy, "l'écouteur des choses tristes"; review of *L'Accélérateur d'intensité*. Gérald Gaudet. photo · *MD* Dec 5, 1987: pD9.

La Fondations des Forges couronne André Roy; article. Jean Royer. photo · *MD* Sept 23, 1987: p11.
[AWARDS, LITERARY]

ROY, DANIEL

Tramp takes the safe route; television review of *Tramp at the Door*. John Haslett Cuff. photo · *G&M* Jan 1, 1987: pC1.
[TELEVISION AND CANADIAN LITERATURE]

ROY, GABRIELLE

Gabrielle Roy travelled from an impoverished household in Manitoba . . . ; review of *Enchantment and Sorrow*. Marianne Ackerman. illus · *MG* Nov 28, 1987: J9.

A lesson in how to look at life and virtues of love and courage; review of *Enchantment and Sorrow*. Ken Adachi. photo · *TS* Nov 14, 1987: M4.

Gabrielle Roy: a compelling glimpse of an enchanting life; review of *Enchantment and Sorrow*. Ruby Andrew. photo · *Quill & Quire* Dec 1987; Vol 53 No 12: p23.

Roy's candid memoirs recall joy and sorrow; review of *Enchantment and Sorrow*. Audrey Andrews. photo · *CH* Dec 20, 1987: pE6.

A fitting homage; review of *Études littéraire* (special issue). Ellen Reisman Babby. *Essays on Can Writ* Spring 1987; No 34: p190–195.
[CANADIAN LITERARY PERIODICALS]

[Untitled]; review of *La Détresse et l'enchantement*. Jean-V. Dufresne. *MD* Nov 28, 1987: pD8.

La vitrine du livre; review of *Gabrielle Roy et Margaret Laurence: deux chemins, une recherche*. Guy Ferland. *MD* Aug 8, 1987: pC6.

Echoes of a tin flute; review of *Enchantment and Sorrow*. Anne Holloway. *Maclean's* Nov 23, 1987; Vol 100 No 47: p54d, 54f

Restaurant dining room evokes early Quebec era; article. Annabelle King. *MG* Nov 28, 1987: I5.

Entering infinity; review of *Enchantment and Sorrow*. I.M. Owen. *Books in Can* Dec 1987; Vol 16 No 9: p17–18.

The tribulations of an author; review of *Enchantment and Sorrow*. Tom Saunders. photo · *WFP* Dec 19, 1987: p51.

Book world: a tip of the hat to small presses; column. Beverley Slopen. photo · *TS* Aug 9, 1987: pA20.
[CANADIAN LITERARY PUBLISHING]

Roy's language; review of *The Play of Language and Spectacle*. Paul G. Socken. *Can Lit* Spring 1987; No 112: p194.

Bonds of dignity; review of *Gabrielle Roy*. Paul Socken. *Can Lit* Winter 1987; No 115: p193–194.

Living inspirations; review of *Enchantment and Sorrow*. Ronald Sutherland. photo · *G&M* Dec 26, 1987: pC23.

Une ultime vision de l'idéal; review of *L'Espagnole et la Pékinoise*. Robert Viau. *Can Child Lit* 1987; No 47: p88–89.

La fiction de nos devanciers; reviews of *Le Roman québécois de 1944 à 1965* and *Un Roman du regard*. Agnès Whitfield. photo · *Lettres québec* Winter 1986–87; No 44: p56–58.

ROY, JEAN-YVES

Poèmes et rimes pour émerveiller; review of *Mon ami Pierrot*. François Paré. *Can Child Lit* 1987; No 46: p100–101.

ROY, MARCELLE

Chronique: soliloques; reviews of poetry books. Marguerite Andersen. *Poetry Can R* Spring 1987; Vol 8 No 2–3: p23–24.

[Untitled]; review of *L'Hydre à deux coeurs*. Louise Blouin. *Estuaire* Summer 1987; No 45: p57.

ROY, MAX

La vitrine du livre; reviews. Guy Ferland. *MD* May 2, 1987: pD4

ROYALTY IS ROYALTY/Play by W.O. Mitchell

[Untitled]; theatre review of *Royalty Is Royalty*. John Bemrose. *Maclean's* Oct 19, 1987; Vol 100 No 42: p70.

W.O. Mitchell's creative thoughts turn to plays; article. Donald Campbell. photo · *WFP* Oct 8, 1987: p42.

Delightful play; letter to the editor. Gitta Fricke. photo · *WFP* Oct 20, 1987: p6.

W.O. Mitchell's Crocus cronies shine on stage; theatre review of *Royalty Is Royalty*. Jamie Portman. *CH* Oct 15, 1987: pF1.

Making the prairie connection; theatre reviews. Reg Skene. *NeWest R* Dec 1987; Vol 13 No 4: p16.

ROYER, JEAN

Week-end; column. *MD* April 18, 1987: pA10.

La palme à Ollivier et à Ouellette; article. photo · *MD* Nov 18, 1987: p11.
[AWARDS, LITERARY]

Ouellette et Royer: depuis la mort jusqu'à l'amour . . . ; reviews of *Les Heures* and *Depuis l'amour*. Jean Éthier-Blais. *MD* June 27, 1987: pC9.

[Untitled]; review of *Le Chemin brulé*. Antonio D'Alfonso. · *Estuaire* Winter 1986–87; No 43: p77–78.

[Untitled]; review of *Depuis l'amour*. Jean Chapdelaine Gagnon. *Estuaire* Summer 1987; No 45: p57–58.

De Bellefeuille, Nepveu, Lemaire, Royer; reviews of poetry books. Jean-Pierre Issenhuth. *Liberté* Aug 1987; Vol 29 No 4: p78–87.

L'amour la mort; reviews of poetry books. Robert Yergeau. photo · *Lettres québec* Summer 1987; No 46: p37–38.

Il y a des poèmes que nous habitons tous; reviews of poetry books. Robert Yergeau. *Lettres québec* Winter 1986–87; No 44: p36–37.

RUBESS, BANUTA

Billboard: U of M holds seminar on role of stress, immune system in voles; column. *WFP* Jan 20, 1987: p28.

Billboard: archeology, botany in Greece will be featured in colloquium; column. *WFP* Jan 21, 1987: p30.
[WRITERS' WORKSHOPS]

Theatre Direct probes urban kids' reality; theatre reviews of *The Snake Lady* and *Thin Ice*. Ray Conlogue. *G&M* April 29, 1987: pC7.

The Mikado hits a high note with seven Dora Awards; article. Robert Crew. photo · *TS* June 23, 1987: pE3.
[AWARDS, LITERARY]

Teens need to see play on vital issue; column. Lois Sweet. *TS* April 20, 1987: pC1.

RUE DU BAC/Novel by Tony Foster

[Untitled]; review of *Rue du Bac*. B.K. Adams. *Books in Can* Oct 1987; Vol 16 No 7: p24.

Three new twists on old and favorite spy themes; review of *Rue du Bac*. Margaret Cannon. *G&M* Sept 12, 1987: pC19.

Bizarre tale dark, quirky and Rendell; review of *Rue du Bac*. Kenneth McGoogan. *CH* Oct 4, 1987: pE6.

This international thriller is like a long, winding and ultimately pointless safari; review of *Rue du Bac*. James Mennie. *MG* Oct 3, 1987: J13.

RUEBSAAT, NORBERT

Listening for space; review of audio tapes by Norbert Ruebsaat. Irene Niechoda. *Event* Summer 1987; Vol 16 No 2: p130–132.

RUEL, FRANÇINE

Music, theatre union needs fine tuning; theatre reviews of *Le Dernier quatuor d'un homme sourd* and *La Goutte*. Pat Donnelly. *MG* Nov 18, 1987: pD3.

Quatre personnages en quête d'une pièce; theatre review of *Le Dernier quatuor d'un homme sourd*. Robert Lévesque. photo · *MD* Nov 20, 1987: p13.

RULE, JANE

[Untitled]; reviews of short story collections. Carole Gerson. *Queen's Q* Summer 1987; Vol 94 No 2: p483–484.

Tale of eternal triangle reads like a tract; review of *Memory Board*. John Goddard. *MG* Nov 14, 1987: J10.

Mixed doubles; review of *Memory Board*. Terry Goldie. *Books in Can* Nov 1987; Vol 16 No 8: p19–20.

A sensitive tale focusing on aging; review of *Memory Board*. Geoff Hancock. photo · *TS* Nov 21, 1987: M4.

Knots of age and sex; review of *Memory Board*. Janette Turner Hospital. *G&M* Oct 17, 1987: pE5.

[Untitled]; review of *Memory Board*. Sharon J. Hunt. *Quarry* Fall 1987; Vol 36 No 4: p87–88.

The fixed point of love; review of *Memory Board*. Alberto Manguel. *Maclean's* Oct 19, 1987; Vol 100 No 42: p60b

Fascinating trio comes to grips with aging; review of *Memory Board*. Dave Margoshes. *CH* Nov 29, 1987: pE6.

Imprecise intertwinings; review of *This Is Not for You*. Jane O'Grady. *Times Lit Supp* June 26, 1987; No 4395: p698.

[Untitled]; review of *Memory Board*. Constance Rooke. *Malahat R* Dec 1987; No 81: p102.

Laughing on the outside; essay. Phil Surguy. *Books in Can* Dec 1987; Vol 16 No 9: p4–5.
[FESTIVALS, LITERARY]

RUN, MADRINA, RUN/Novel by Dorothy Wingrove

World of wonders; reviews of first novels. Janice Kulyk Keefer. *Books in Can* May 1987; Vol 16 No 4: p37–38.
[FIRST NOVELS: BOOK REVIEWS]

RUSH, JERRY

[The Bones of Their Occasion]; review. Robert Currie. photo · *NeWest R* Dec 1987; Vol 13 No 4: p15.

Poets in search of praise; reviews of *One Night at the Indigo Hotel* and *The Bones of Their Occasion*. Keith Garebian. *TS* May 16, 1987: M4.

RUSSIA-CANADA LITERARY RELATIONS

La littérature du Québec en URSS; article. Irina Kouznétsova. photo · *Lettres québec* Summer 1987; No 46: p71–72.

RUURS, MARGRIET

[Untitled]; review of *Fireweed*. Carolellen Norskey. *Quill & Quire (Books for Young People)* June 1987; Vol 53 No 6: p6,9.

RYGA, GEORGE

Playwright Ryga tough, committed; article. *MG* Nov 20, 1987: pC1.

Playwright George Ryga dies at 55; obituary. *TS* Nov 19, 1987: pB7.

George Ryga praised; article. *TS* Nov 20, 1987: pE26.

Canadian author-playwright dies; obituary. photo · *WFP* Nov 19, 1987: p49.

Cancer claims author-playwright George Ryga; obituary. *CH* Nov 19, 1987: pC3.

For the record; obituary. photo · *CH* Nov 22, 1987: pB5.

Canadian author wrote The Ecstasy of Rita Joe; obituary. photo · *G&M* Nov 19, 1987: pA23.

Passages; obituary. *Maclean's* Nov 30, 1987; Vol 100 No 48: p4.

Wheels on fire: the train of thought in George Ryga's The Ecstasy of Rita Joe; article. Gary Boire. *Can Lit* Summer-Fall 1987; No 113–114: p62–74.

Soloist's view of Rita Joe grows; article. Donald Campbell. photo · *WFP* Oct 2, 1987: p21.

Gifted playwright never lost sense of compassion, outrage; article. Ray Conlogue. photo · *G&M* Nov 20, 1987: pD5.

Underwing; reviews of *In the Shadow of the Vulture* and *The Quarter-Pie Window*. Ronald B. Hatch. *Can Lit* Spring 1987; No 112: p95–97.

A last column, and a farewell to a great friend; article. Elaine Husband. photo · *CH* Dec 16, 1987: pA8.

Le théâtre québécoise triomphe maintenant dans les grandes salles; column. Robert Lévesque. photo · *MD* Dec 1, 1987: p11.

Dramatic fringe; reviews of *Five from the Fringe* and *Politics and the Playwright: George Ryga*. James Noonan. *Can Lit* Winter 1987; No 115: p235–238.
[ANTHOLOGIES: BOOK REVIEWS]

Büchner in Canada: Woyzeck and the development of English-Canadian theatre; article. Jerry Wasserman. abstract photo · *Theatre Hist in Can* Fall 1987; Vol 8 No 2: p181–192.
[CANADIAN DRAMA: HISTORY AND CRITICISM; POLITICAL WRITING]

LE SABORD/Periodical

La vitrine du livre; reviews. Jean Royer. photo · *MD* April 4, 1987: pD2.
[CANADIAN LITERARY PERIODICALS]

THE SACRED BEECH AND OTHER POEMS FROM WALES/Poems by Beryl Baigent

[Untitled]; reviews of poetry books. Anita Hurwitz. *Poetry Can R* Spring 1987; Vol 8 No 2–3: p50–51.

A SACRIFICE OF FIRE: EXPEDITIONS INTO THE INTERIOR/Poems by Gregory Grace

Ministries of grace; review of *A Sacrifice of Fire*. M. Travis Lane. *Fiddlehead* Spring 1987; No 151: p110–115.

[Untitled]; review of *A Sacrifice of Fire*. Brian Vanderlip. *Poetry Can R* Spring 1987; Vol 8 No 2–3: p43–44.

SACRIFICES/Novel by Ven Begamudré

World of wonders; reviews of first novels. Janice Kulyk Keefer. *Books in Can* May 1987; Vol 16 No 4: p37–38.
[FIRST NOVELS: BOOK REVIEWS]

[Untitled]; review of *Sacrifices*. Daniel McBride. *Tor South Asian R* Summer 1987; Vol 6 No 1: p83–85.

THE SAD AND FABULOUS DAYS OF MS G./Play by Kirk Miles

Musical comedy written as a true labor of love; article. Kate Zimmerman. photo · *CH* Dec 4, 1987: pE2.

SAFDIE, GABRIEL

[Untitled]; review of *Open Windows*. Gerald Doerksen. *Rubicon* Spring 1987; No 8: p223–224.

[Untitled]; review of *Open Windows*. Gerald Hill. *Poetry Can R* Fall 1987; Vol 9 No 1: p37.

SAGARIS, LAKE

Montreal poets inspired by travel in hot countries; reviews of poetry books. Barbara Black. *MG* March 28, 1987: pE9.

Slight drag but Cormorant takes off; reviews of *Slow Mist* and *Exile Home/Exilio En la Patria*. Keith Garebian. photo · *TS* March 28, 1987: M4.

The art of the impossible: two recent versions of translation; review of *Exile Home*. Christopher Levenson. *Arc* Fall 1987; No 19: p38–42.

Chileans fight militarism with poetry, music; article. James Muretich. photo · *CH* July 24, 1987: pF1

Violence a theme of life in Chile; article. Elsie Ross. photo · *CH* July 27, 1987: pA5.

[Untitled]; review of *Exile Home*. Karen Ruttan. *Poetry Can R* Fall 1987; Vol 9 No 1: p35.

Poetry and the loving Spanish tongue; reviews of poetry books. Fraser Sutherland. *G&M* May 30, 1987: pC21.
[ANTHOLOGIES: BOOK REVIEWS]

LA SAGOUINE/Novel by Antonine Maillet

La Sagouine: home to stay; article. Sue Calhoun. photo · *Atlan Insight* April 1987; Vol 9 No 4: p19–21.
[DRAMATIC ADAPTATIONS OF CANADIAN LITERATURE]

La Sagouine shows drawing power of good story well-told; theatre review. Pat Donnelly. *MG* Nov 6, 1987: pC1.

SAGWYN, DEBORAH TURNEY

Legend of Calgary no ordinary tall tale; column. Joan Craven. *CH (Neighbors)* July 8, 1987: pA8.

SAIA, LOUIS

Les Voisins: scènes de la vie de banlieue; article. Paul Cauchon. photo · *MD* Sept 25, 1987: p15.
[TELEVISION AND CANADIAN LITERATURE]

SAINT COOPERBLACK/Short stories by Roger Magini

La vitrine du livre; review of *Saint Cooperblack*. Guy Ferland. *MD* Jan 31, 1987: pB2.

Les vertus de la retenue et du silence; reviews of poetry books. Marie José Thériault. photo · *Lettres québec* Summer 1987; No 46: p30–32.

SAINT-DENIS, JANOU

La vie littéraire; column. Jean Royer. photo · *MD* May 2, 1987: pD2.
[AWARDS, LITERARY; INTERNATIONAL REVIEWS OF CANADIAN LITERATURE; RADIO AND CANADIAN LITERATURE; TELEVISION AND CANADIAN LITERATURE; WRITERS' ORGANIZATIONS]

SAINT-MARTIN, FERNANDE

La fiction du réel/le réel de la fiction; reviews of poetry books. André Brochu. *Voix et images* Winter 1987; No 35: p322–330.

Fernande Saint-Martin: une "grammaire" du langage visuel; article. Angèle Dagenais. photo · *MD* April 4, 1987: pC1,C8.

Le réel et la fiction du réel; reviews of *Les Soirs rouges* (reprint) and *La Fiction du réel*. Richard Gigure. photo · *Lettres québec* Winter 1986–87; No 44: p38–40.

SAINT-PIERRE, ANNETTE

Racisme et complexes dans l'ouest; review of *Sans bon sang*. Paulette Collet. photo · *Lettres québec* Autumn 1987; No 47: p68–69.

SAINT-YVES, DENUIS

Songe, révolte et manifeste; reviews of poetry books. Robert Yergeau. photo · *Lettres québec* Spring 1987; No 45: p38–39.

SALE, MEDORA

Crime pays for Arthur winners; article. *G&M* May 23, 1987: pC14.
[AWARDS, LITERARY]

SALIVAROVA, ZDENA

Small regional presses as saviors of cultural information; reviews of fictional works. Douglas Hill. *G&M* Oct 10, 1987: pC21.
[FIRST NOVELS: BOOK REVIEWS]

SALLOUM, SHERYL

Lowry's B.C. connection examined; review of *Malcolm Lowry: Vancouver Days*. Thomas York. *CH* June 28, 1987: pF8.

SALMONBERRY WINE/Young adult novel by Mary Razzell

Salmonberry Wine a rare concoction of complex issues and gutsy realism; review. Peter Carver. photo · *Quill & Quire (Books for Young People)* April 1987; Vol 53 No 4: p3.

Roughing it in the bush; reviews of children's books. Mary Ainslie Smith. *Books in Can* Aug-Sept 1987; Vol 16 No 6: p34–36.

Much more than a love story; reviews of *Salmonberry Wine* and *A Handful of Time*. Tim Wynne-Jones. *G&M* June 27, 1987: pE20.

SALT-WATER MOON/Play by David French

Small, nostalgic play is an unexpected delight; theatre review of *Salt-Water Moon*. Brian Brennan. photo · *CH* Jan 18, 1987: pE1.

Piggery production circumvents Salt Water Moon pitfalls; theatre review. Pat Donnelly. *MG* Aug 15, 1987: pE15.

Actor captures depths of play's leading character; theatre review of *Salt-Water Moon*. Reg Skene. *WFP* Jan 8, 1987: p33.

SALTMAN, JUDITH

A little help on the dull days; reviews of children's books. Joan McGrath. *TS* Aug 2, 1987: pC11.

Saltman's superior guide good news about Canadian books; review of *Modern Canadian Children's Books*. Irma McDonough Milnes. photo · *Quill & Quire (Books for Young People)* April 1987; Vol 53 No 4: p1,3.

Annabel and Goldie go to the sea, Josephine goes to school; reviews of *Can You Catch Josephine?* and *Goldie and the Sea*. Susan Perren. *Quill & Quire (Books for Young People)* Oct 1987; Vol 53 No 10: p18–19.

Roughing it in the bush; reviews of children's books. Mary Ainslie Smith. *Books in Can* Aug-Sept 1987; Vol 16 No 6: p34–36.

SALUTIN, RICK

Play retells story of 1837 rebellion; article. Lynne Ainsworth. photo · *TS (Neighbours)* June 30, 1987: p19.

Some go to the Falls, Sariola goes to the 'burbs; article. John Allemang. *G&M* Oct 22, 1987: pD5.
[FESTIVALS, LITERARY]

Farmer's Rebellion stands test of time; theatre review of *1837: The Farmers' Revolt*. Ray Conlogue. *G&M* Dec 8, 1987: pD7.

1837 revolt hits centre stage; article. Robert Davis. photo · *TS (Neighbors)* Aug 11, 1987: p16.

[Untitled]; letter to the editor. Dan Gawthrop. *G&M* Nov 21, 1987: pD7.

Authors talk about books as movies; article. Peter Goddard. *TS* Oct 20, 1987: H4.
[FESTIVALS, LITERARY]

A smoking gun response from Salutin; column. Mavor Moore. *G&M* Aug 8, 1987: pC3.

No fear of castration; letter to the editor. C.J. Sullivan. *G&M* Nov 20, 1987: pA6.

Summer theatre takes on a new twist; article. Betty Zyvatkauskas. photo · *G&M* July 11, 1987: pE7.

THE SALVATION OF YASCH SIEMENS/Novel by Armin Wiebe

Successful local novel to be made into film; article. Donald Campbell. *WFP* Sept 26, 1987: p30.
[FILM ADAPTATIONS OF CANADIAN LITERATURE]

SALVATORE, FILIPPO

Transculture; reviews of poetry books. Viviana Comensoli. *Can Lit* Spring 1987; No 112: p120–123.

SAMCHUK, ULAS

Writer was best known for Ukrainian trilogy; obituary. *G&M* July 14, 1987: pD10.

LES SAMOURAILLES/Novel by France Boisvert

Les bienfaits de la bombe; review of *Les Samourailles*. Jean-François Chassay. *MD* Dec 5, 1987: pD4.
[FIRST NOVELS: BOOK REVIEWS]

SANDING DOWN THIS ROCKING CHAIR ON A WINDY NIGHT/Poems by Don McKay

MacEwen and McKay; reviews of *Afterworlds* and *Sanding Down This Rocking Chair on a Windy Night*. Barry Dempster. *Poetry Can R* Fall 1987; Vol 9 No 1: p29–30.

So you think poetry no longer exists for readers?; reviews of *Afterworlds* and *Sanding Down This Rocking Chair on a Windy Night*. Judith Fitzgerald. photo · *TS* May 3, 1987: pA24.

[Untitled]; review of *Sanding Down This Rocking Chair on a Windy Night*. David Manicom. *Rubicon* Fall 1987; No 9: p184–185.

Lord of the wings; review of *Sanding Down This Rocking Chair on a Windy Night*. John Oughton. *Books in Can* June-July 1987; Vol 16 No 5: p12–13.

[Untitled]; reviews of *Afterworlds* and *Sanding Down This Rocking Chair on a Windy Night*. Barbara Powell. *Wascana R* Fall 1987; Vol 22 No 2: p88–91.

Poetry: packing all the power into two of seven titles; reviews of poetry books. Robin Skelton. photo · *Quill & Quire* May 1987; Vol 53 No 5: p24.

The pastoral myth and its observers; reviews of poetry books. Fraser Sutherland. *G&M* Sept 26, 1987: pC23.

SANDINISTA/Novel by Marie Jakober

[Untitled]; review of *Sandinista*. Miriam Jones. *Rubicon* Fall 1987; No 9: p197–198.
[FIRST NOVELS: BOOK REVIEWS]

Politics & paradise; review of *Sandinista*. C. Kanaganayakam. *Can Lit* Winter 1987; No 115: p270–272.
[FIRST NOVELS: BOOK REVIEWS]

[Untitled]; review of *Sandinista*. Larry Towell. *Queen's Q* Autumn 1987; Vol 94 No 3: p696–698.
[FIRST NOVELS: BOOK REVIEWS]

SANDOR, ANNA

Fun and games with sharp-tongued Tracey; column. John Haslett Cuff. *G&M* May 2, 1987: pC4.

SANDY/Young adult novel by Nancy Freeman

From city to country; review of *Sandy*. David W. Atkinson. *Can Child Lit* 1987; No 46: p89–90.

LE SANG DU SOUVENIR/Short stories by Jacques Brossard

L'inquiétante étrangeté des récits de Jacques Brossard; review of *Le Sang du souvenir*. Jacques Michon. *MD* Sept 5, 1987: pC7.

SANGER, PETER

Ghazal-maker; review of *Sea Run*. Phyllis Webb. *Can Lit* Spring 1987; No 112: p156–157.

SANS BON SANG/Novel by Annette Saint-Pierre

Racisme et complexes dans l'ouest; review of *Sans bon sang*. Paulette Collet. photo · *Lettres québec* Autumn 1987; No 47: p68–69.

SANSCHAGRIN, JOCELINE

Les malheurs de Rosalie ou l'éloge de l'enfance; reviews of children's books. Dominique Demers. *MD* May 2, 1987: pD3.

SAPERGIA, BARBARA

Interview with Barbara Sapergia: her plays, her concerns, her influences. Doris Hillis. photo · *NeWest R* Oct 1987; Vol 13 No 2: p2–4

SARAH ET LE CRI DE LA LANGOUSTE

See **MEMOIR/SARAH ET LE CRI DE LA LANGOUSTE/ Play by John Murrell**

SARKANY, STPHANE

De la sociologie des cultures la bibliologie; review of *Québec Canada France*. Patrick Imbert. *Lettres québec* Winter 1986–87; No 44: p78.

SASS, GREGORY

Bugs, battles & ballet; reviews of *On Stage, Please* and *Redcoat*. James Gellert. *Can Lit* Winter 1987; No 115: p220–223.
[FIRST NOVELS: BOOK REVIEWS]

SATELLITE SKYJACK/Children's novel by G.P. Jordan

Pulp science fiction: slick adventures in a moral void; reviews of *Clone Patrol* and *Satellite Skyjack*. Eva Martin. *Quill & Quire (Books for Young People)* June 1987; Vol 53 No 6: p8.

SATIRIC WRITING

Apocalyptic imaginations: notes on Atwood's The Handmaid's Tale and Findley's Not Wanted on the Voyage; article. W.J. Keith. *Essays on Can Writ* Winter 1987; No 35: p123–134.
[THE APOCALYPSE; BIBLICAL MYTHS AND MYTHOLOGY; GOD IN LITERATURE]

The narrator, the reader, and Mariposa: the cost of preserving the status quo in Sunshine Sketches Of A Little Town; article. Francis Zichy. abstract · *J of Can Studies* Spring 1987; Vol 22 No 1: p51–65.

SATURDAY NIGHT/Periodical

Saturday Night: 100 ans et des plumes; article. *MD* Jan 7, 1987: p8.
[CANADIAN LITERARY PERIODICALS]

Black buys Saturday Night magazine; article. photo · *WFP* June 19, 1987: p24.
[CANADIAN LITERARY PERIODICALS]

Fulford bails out as editor in Saturday Night takeover; article. photo · *WFP* June 25, 1987: p19.
[CANADIAN LITERARY PERIODICALS]

Black buys Saturday Night; article. *CH* June 19, 1987: pF2.
[CANADIAN LITERARY PERIODICALS]

Robert Fulford quits Saturday Night post; article. *CH* June 25, 1987: pD1.
[CANADIAN LITERARY PERIODICALS]

Saturday Night's editor Fulford quits; article. *MG* June 25, 1987: pE1.
[CANADIAN LITERARY PERIODICALS]

New owner running into problems trying to get staff for Saturday Night; article. *TS* July 5, 1987: pA12.
[CANADIAN LITERARY PERIODICALS]

Black completes deal to buy Saturday Night; article. *TS* July 9, 1987: pA3.
[CANADIAN LITERARY PERIODICALS]

Black takes over Saturday Night; article. *MG* July 9, 1987: pD7.
[CANADIAN LITERARY PERIODICALS]

Conrad Black met enfin la main sur Saturday Night; article. *MD* July 9, 1987: p9.
[CANADIAN LITERARY PERIODICALS]

Magazine's new editor to earn 'unprecedented' salary; article. *WFP* July 7, 1987: p28.
[CANADIAN LITERARY PERIODICALS]

Magazine purchase completed; article. *WFP* July 9, 1987: p15.
[CANADIAN LITERARY PERIODICALS]

Fraser new editor; article. *WFP* July 17, 1987: p34.
[CANADIAN LITERARY PERIODICALS]

Saturday Night shakeup unlikely, new editor says; article. *WFP* July 18, 1987: p31.
[CANADIAN LITERARY PERIODICALS]

Six-figure salary rumored for Saturday Night's new editor; article. *CH* July 7, 1987: pC6.
[CANADIAN LITERARY PERIODICALS]

Black closes Saturday Night deal; article. photo · *CH* July 9, 1987: pF2.
[CANADIAN LITERARY PERIODICALS]

Fraser accepts post at Saturday Night; article. *CH* July 17, 1987: pF10.
[CANADIAN LITERARY PERIODICALS]

Saturday Night deal goes through; article. *G&M* July 9, 1987: pD5.
[CANADIAN LITERARY PERIODICALS]

Saturday Night's Macfarlane leaves 'with great regret'; article. *G&M* July 10, 1987: pD5.
[CANADIAN LITERARY PERIODICALS]

L'Actualite picks up six magazine awards; article. Ken Adachi. *TS* May 22, 1987: pE21.
[AWARDS, LITERARY; CANADIAN LITERARY PERIODICALS]

But will Black respect Saturday Night on Sunday morning?; column. Ken Adachi. *TS* June 19, 1987: pD23.
[CANADIAN LITERARY PERIODICALS]

Saturday Night film dispiriting; column. Ken Adachi. photo · *TS* Sept 7, 1987: pB2.
[AUDIO-VISUALS AND CANADIAN LITERATURE; CANADIAN LITERARY PERIODICALS]

Magazine to have face lift; column. Ken Adachi. photo · *TS* Dec 15, 1987: pG4.
[CANADIAN LITERARY PERIODICALS]

Radio's Scales of Justice seen as possible CTV series; column. Sid Adilman. *TS* Dec 30, 1987: pB1.
[CANADIAN LITERARY PERIODICALS]

Saturday Night editor envisions moe changes; article. Ian Bailey. photo · *WFP* Dec 21, 1987: p35.
[CANADIAN LITERARY PERIODICALS]

Saturday Night's new editor champing at bit; article. Ian Bailey. photo · *CH* Dec 22, 1987: pD8.
[CANADIAN LITERARY PERIODICALS]

Telling tales on Saturday Night; column. George Bain. *Maclean's* July 27, 1987; Vol 100 No 30: p44.
[CANADIAN LITERARY PERIODICALS]

Saturday Night intriguing tale of intrigue; letter to the editor. Pierre Berton. *TS* July 8, 1987: pA18.
[CANADIAN LITERARY PERIODICALS]

Saturday Night branches out in search of publishing profits; article. Pat Brennan. photo · *TS* Jan 6, 1987: pE1.
[CANADIAN LITERARY PERIODICALS]

Saturday Night observes 100th birthday; article. Rod Currie. *WFP* Jan 6, 1987: p26.
[CANADIAN LITERARY PERIODICALS]

Saturday Night's first century; editorial. Christopher Dafoe. *WFP* Jan 18, 1987: p6.
[CANADIAN LITERARY PERIODICALS]

The end of Fulford's era; article. Doug Fetherling. *Maclean's* July 6, 1987; Vol 100 No 27: p53.
[CANADIAN LITERARY PERIODICALS]

Saturday Night changes will take time to implement; column. William French. photo · *G&M* Dec 15, 1987: pD5.
[CANADIAN LITERARY PERIODICALS]

Old heck; column. Robert Fulford. illus · *Sat Night* Nov 1987; Vol 102 No 11: p7–8,10–11.
[CANADIAN LITERARY PERIODICALS]

Saturday Night celebrates sobriety; article. Peter Goddard. photo · *TS* Jan 6, 1987: pD4.
[CANADIAN LITERARY PERIODICALS]

Conrad Black deal to buy Saturday Night said up in air; article. Richard Gwyn. *TS* July 3, 1987: pA1,A4.
[CANADIAN LITERARY PERIODICALS]

What's Black and White and may or may not be read all over?; article. David Hayes. photo · *Tor Life* Dec 1987; Vol 21 No 18: p54–60,108,110–111.
[CANADIAN LITERARY PERIODICALS]

Pages for the powerful; article. Brian D. Johnson. photo · *Maclean's* Jan 19, 1987; Vol 100 No 3: p62.
[CANADIAN LITERARY PERIODICALS]

Conrad Black purchases Saturday Night magazine; article. Kenneth Kidd. *TS* June 19, 1987: pF1.
[CANADIAN LITERARY PERIODICALS]

John Fraser: child star; article. Martin Knelman. photo · *Tor Life* Dec 1987; Vol 21 No 18: p12.
[CANADIAN LITERARY PERIODICALS]

Robert Fulford resigns as editor of Saturday Night; article. Liam Lacey. photo · *G&M* June 25, 1987: pD1.
[CANADIAN LITERARY PERIODICALS]

Saturday Night sale unsure, search for editor continues; article. Liam Lacey. *G&M* July 4, 1987: pC4.
[CANADIAN LITERARY PERIODICALS]

Sale of magazine stalled over debt; article. Jonathan Manthorpe. *CH* July 4, 1987: pC6.
[CANADIAN LITERARY PERIODICALS]

Splash of grey heralds Saturday Night centenary; article. John Bentley Mays. photo · *G&M* Jan 5, 1987: pC9.
[CANADIAN LITERARY PERIODICALS]

Fraser to be editor of Saturday Night; article. John Bentley Mays. photo · *G&M* July 17, 1987: pD11.
[CANADIAN LITERARY PERIODICALS]

100-year-old magazine filled with literary gems; column. Kenneth McGoogan. *CH* Jan 25, 1987: pE4.
[CANADIAN LITERARY PERIODICALS]

Fulford leaves his Saturday Night post; article. Henry Mietkiewicz. photo · *TS* June 25, 1987: pA2.
[CANADIAN LITERARY PERIODICALS]

Publisher to cut Sauve anecdote in book of gossip; column. Henry Mietkiewicz. *TS* July 10, 1987: pE23.
[CANADIAN LITERARY PERIODICALS]

John Fraser new Saturday Night editor; column. Henry Mietkiewicz. *TS* July 17, 1987: pE23.
[CANADIAN LITERARY PERIODICALS]

Mr. Saturday Night; biographical article. Leslie Scrivener. photo · *TS* July 5, 1987: pD1–D2.
[CANADIAN LITERARY PERIODICALS]

Magazine's literary mentor leaves with mixed emotions; article. Leslie Scrivener. photo · *CH* July 12, 1987: pE6.
[CANADIAN LITERARY PERIODICALS]

Saturday Night fiasco shakes your faith in tycoonery; humorous essay. Joey Slinger. *TS* July 7, 1987: pA6.
[CANADIAN LITERARY PERIODICALS]

Book world: anti-Khomeini plotter's story told in new book; column. Beverley Slopen. *TS* Sept 6, 1987: pA18.
[AUDIO-VISUALS AND CANADIAN LITERATURE; AUTHORS, CANADIAN; CANADIAN LITERARY PERIODICALS]

Book world: the Bay saga: before Vol. 3 comes Vol. 2 1/2; column. Beverley Slopen. *TS* Nov 22, 1987: pC8.
[CANADIAN LITERARY PERIODICALS]

Black October; article. Michael Totzke. *Tor Life* Sept 1987; Vol 21 No 13: p17.
[CANADIAN LITERARY PERIODICALS]

Saturday Night does its job well; letter to the editor. David Zapparoli. *TS* July 20, 1987: pA16.
[CANADIAN LITERARY PERIODICALS]

SATURDAY NIGHTS AT THE RITZ/Poems by Howard Tessler

[Untitled]; reviews of poetry books. Anne Burke. *Poetry Can R* Summer 1987; Vol 8 No 4: p38.

[Untitled]; review of *Saturday Nights at the Ritz*. David Manicom. *Rubicon* Spring 1987; No 8: p216–217.

SAUL, JOHN RALSTON

Tune in, turn on, drop out: truckin' back to the '60s with Esquire; reviews of *Lime Street at Two* and *The Next Best Thing*. Barbara Black. *MG* July 4, 1987: J9.

Danger! A trained assassin at work; review of *The Next Best Thing*. Geoff Chapman. *TS* June 14, 1987: pA18.

Canadian writers make headlines in France; column. William French. photo · *G&M* Dec 22, 1987: pD5.
[FRANCE-CANADA LITERARY RELATIONS]

The peril of Mexico; article. John Godfrey. *Fin Post* Nov 30, 1987: p14.

Liz barges down the Nile in triumph; column. Thomas Schnurmacher. *MG* April 21, 1987: pC11.

SAULNIER, RACHEL

Two illustrated Acadian books; reviews of *Pépère G=* [CANADIAN LITERARY PERIODICALS]

100-year-old magazine filled with literary gems; column. Kenneth McGoogan. *CH* Jan 25, 1987: pE4.
[CANADIAN LITERARY PERIODICALS]

Fulford leaves his Saturday Night post; article. Henry Mietkiewicz. photo · *TS* June 25, 1987: pA2.
[CANADIAN LITERARY PERIODICALS]

Publisher to cut Sauve anecdote in book of gossip; column. Henry Mietkiewicz. *TS* July 10, 1987: pE23.
[CANADIAN LITERARY PERIODICALS]

John Fraser new Saturday Night editor; column. Henry Mietkiewicz. *TS* July 17, 1987: pE23.
[CANADIAN LITERARY PERIODICALS]

Mr. Saturday Night; biographical article. Leslie Scrivener. photo · *TS* July 5, 1987: pD1–D2.
[CANADIAN LITERARY PERIODICALS]

Magazine's literary mentor leaves with mixed emotions; article. Leslie Scrivener. photo · *CH* July 12, 1987: pE6.
[CANADIAN LITERARY PERIODICALS]

Saturday Night fiasco shakes your faith in tycoonery; humorous essay. Joey Slinger. *TS* July 7, 1987: pA6.
[CANADIAN LITERARY PERIODICALS]

Book world: anti-Khomeini plooguen loup de mer. Martine Jacquot. *Atlan Prov Book R* Nov-Dec 1987; Vol 14 No 4: p11.

SAVARD, FÉLIX-ANTOINE

Menaud prophète: et si Joson n'était pas mort . . . ; column. Jean Éthier-Blais. photo · *MD* Oct 3, 1987: pD8.

SAVARD, MARIE

La vie littéraire; column. Marc Morin. *MD* Dec 12, 1987: pD2.
[GOVERNOR GENERAL'S AWARDS; POETRY READINGS]

La vie littéraire; column. Jean Royer. *MD* Feb 21, 1987: pB2.
[CANADIAN LITERARY PUBLISHING; COMPETITIONS, LITERARY; POETRY READINGS; TELEVISION AND CANADIAN LITERATURE; WRITERS' ORGANIZATIONS]

SAVARD, MICHEL

Maniaques depressifs; reviews of poetry books. Mark Benson. *Can Lit* Spring 1987; No 112: p138–141.

SAVOIE, JACQUES

Conservatisme; reviews of novels. Neil B. Bishop. *Can Lit* Winter 1987; No 115: p169–172.

Les enfants du déclin5P255; Vol 9 No 3–4: p44,49.
[ANTHOLOGIES: BOOK REVIEWS]

SCENES OF THE CRIME/Poems by William Scott Neale

[Untitled]; reviews of poetry books. James McElroy. *Poetry Can R* Fall 1987; Vol 9 No 1: p36.

SCHEDULES OF SILENCE: THE COLLECTED LONGER POEMS 1960–1986/Poems by J. Michael Yates

The reader's duties; review of *Schedules of Silence*. Fraser Sutherland. *G&M* June 6, 1987: pC19.

SCHEDULES/Play by Bruce McManus

Scenes from a relationship; theatre review of *Schedules*. Don Perkins. *NeWest R* Dec 1987; Vol 13 No 4: p17.

Funny play fails to fulfil promise; theatre review of *Schedules*. Reg Skene. *WFP* Jan 23, 1987: p31.

SCHEIER, LIBBY

Some beautiful moments but all too fleeting; reviews of poetry books. Maggie Helwig. *TS* Aug 15, 1987: M6.

[Untitled]; reviews of *Candy from Strangers* and *Second Nature*. Roberta Morris. *Cross Can Writ Q* 1987; Vol 9 No 3–4: p42.

[Untitled]; reviews of *Private Properties* and *Second Nature*. Stephen Scobie. *Malahat R (special issue)* March 1987; No 78: p153–154.

[Untitled]; review of *Second Nature*. Richard Streiling. *Quill & Quire* March 1987; Vol 53 No 3: p75.

[Untitled]; review of *Second Nature*. Bronwen Wallace. *Poetry Can R* Spring 1987; Vol 8 No 2–3: p37–38.

Victims of a bleak universe; reviews of poetry books. Bruce Whiteman. *Books in Can* Jan-Feb 1987; Vol 16 No 1: p22–23.

Wit and humor mark poetry; reviews of *Second Nature* and *Private Properties*. Andrew Wreggitt. *CH* Jan 11, 1987: pF4.

SCHINKEL, DAVID

Littérature jeunesse; reviews of children's books. Dominique Demers. *MD* Nov 21, 1987: pD6.

Pour les adolescents: quatre mains et deux solitudes; reviews of young adult novels. Dominique Demers. photo · *MD* Dec 19, 1987: pD6–D7.

SCHIZOTEXTE/Poems by John Rieger et al

[Untitled]; review of *Schizotexte*. Quendrith Johnson. *Rubicon* Spring 1987; No 8: p186–187.

[Untitled]; review of *Schizotexte*. Sparling Mills. *Poetry Can R* Summer 1987; Vol 8 No 4: p38.

SCHOEMPERLEN, DIANE

Guild honors Pollock, van Herk; article. *G&M* May 13, 1987: pC5.
[AWARDS, LITERARY]

Writers Guild of Alberta awards; article. *Quill & Quire* July 1987; Vol 53 No 7: p54.
[AWARDS, LITERARY]

[Untitled]; reviews. Beverley Daurio. *Cross Can Writ Q* 1987; Vol 9 No 2: p23.
[FIRST NOVELS: BOOK REVIEWS]

[Untitled]; review of *Frogs*. Beth Duthie. *CH* Jan 25, 1987: pE4.

Everything by thought waves; reviews of short story collections. Patricia Matson. *Event* March 1987; Vol 16 No 1: p97–100.

All about women and relationships; reviews of *Housebroken* and *Frogs*. Lesley McAllister. *TS* Jan 3, 1987: M6.
[FIRST NOVELS: BOOK REVIEWS]

A frog he would a-wooing go; review of *Frogs*. Marjorie Retzleff. *Matrix* Fall 1987; No 25: p75–76.

New Albertan fiction; reviews of *Green Eyes, Dukes and Kings* and *Frogs*. M.L. Scott. *NeWest R* Summer 1987; Vol 12 No 10: p12.

The lively art; reviews of *Double Exposures* and *Frogs*. Kent Thompson. *Fiddlehead* Winter 1987; No 154: p87–91

SCHROEDER, ANDREAS

A monument to folly; review of *Dustship Glory*. Geoff Hancock. *Can Forum* Feb 1987; Vol 66 No 766: p39–40.
[FIRST NOVELS: BOOK REVIEWS]

Dust bowl to never land; review of *Dustship Glory*. Alan Shugard. *Can Lit* Winter 1987; No 115: p196–197.
[FIRST NOVELS: BOOK REVIEWS]

Recent Canadian fiction; reviews of novels. D.O. Spettigue. *Queen's Q* Summer 1987; Vol 94 No 2: p366–375.
[FIRST NOVELS: BOOK REVIEWS]

SCHUYLER, LINDA

From box to book; reviews of *Lisa Makes the Headlines* and *Griff Makes a Date*. Laurie Bildfell. *Can Child Lit* 1987; No 46: p93–94.

Fine books for in-betweens; reviews of young adult books. David Williamson. *WFP* Dec 5, 1987: p57.

Taking the Degrassi kids from screen to page; reviews of *Casey Draws the Line* and *Griff Gets a Hand*. Frieda Wishinsky. photo · *Quill & Quire (Books for Young People)* June 1987; Vol 53 No 6: p3.

SCIENCE FICTION

Spaced Out Library plans 'events'; article. *G&M* June 11, 1987: pD1.
[FICTION READINGS]

Un prix Logidisque pour la sf et le fantastique; article. *MD* April 7, 1987: p11.
[AWARDS, LITERARY]

Voyages of the mind; article, includes review of *The Darkest Road*. Peter Giffen. photo · *Maclean's* March 23, 1987; Vol 100 No 12: p66–67.
[FANTASY]

Literary world loses a champion; column. Kenneth McGoogan. *CH* July 12, 1987: pE4.
[AWARDS, LITERARY; CONFERENCES, LITERARY; PUBLISHING AND PUBLISHERS IN CANADA; WRITERS' WORKSHOPS]

Bringing sci-fi down to Earth; article. Henry Mietkiewicz. illus · *TS* May 24, 1987: pC1.

Le grand prix Logidisque de la science-fiction et du fantastique est attribué à Esther Rochon; article. Jean Royer. photo · *MD* April 14, 1987: p11.
[AWARDS, LITERARY]

SCIROCCO: POÈMES/Poems by Fulvio Caccia

Transculture; reviews of poetry books. Viviana Comensoli. *Can Lit* Spring 1987; No 112: p120–123.

SCOBIE, STEPHEN

Representation and celebration: Stephen Scobie's rain songs; review of *Expecting Rain*. Brian Edwards. *Essays on Can Writ* Spring 1987; No 34: p33–38.

Stephen Scobie; interview. Margarey Fee. biog · *Can Lit* Winter 1987; No 115: p81–102.

SCOTT, DUNCAN CAMPBELL

Scott and Indian Affairs; review of *A Narrow Vision*. Stan Dragland. *Can Poet* Fall-Winter 1987; No 21: p103–109.

Duncan Campbell Scott: a poet who put down Indians; review of *A Narrow Vision*. John Goddard. photo · *MG* Aug 1, 1987: J7.

Confederation poets; reviews. Ronald B. Hatch. *Can Lit* Winter 1987; No 115: p223–225.

The poet who ran Indian Affairs; review of *A Narrow Vision*. Allan Levine. photo · *G&M* Feb 28, 1987: pE17.

Bipolar paths of desire: D.C. Scott's poetic and narrative structures; article. Lyle P. Weis. *Studies in Can Lit* 1987; Vol 12 No 1: p35–53.

SCOTT, F.R.

[Untitled]; letter. Milton Acorn. *Brick (special issue)* Summer 1987; No 30: p58.

Feminist quarterly honors Laurence; column. Ken Adachi. *TS* Nov 16, 1987: pC5.

[CANADIAN LITERARY PERIODICALS; FICTION READINGS]

Portrait of an extraordinary man: a vibrant and influential presence in our intellectual and political life; review of *The Politics of the Imagination*. Ken Adachi. photo · *TS* Nov 21, 1987: M4.

[Untitled]; biographical articles. Margaret Atwood. *Brick (special issue)* Summer 1987; No 30: 50–51.

[Untitled]; biographical articles. Edward Aust. *Brick (special issue)* Summer 1987; No 30: passim.

[Untitled]; biographical articles. Thomas Berger. *Brick (special issue)* Summer 1987; No 30: passim.

[Untitled]; biographical articles. Florence Bird. *Brick (special issue)* Summer 1987; No 30: passim.

[Untitled]; essay. Leonard Cohen. *Brick (special issue)* Summer 1987; No 30: p56.

[Untitled]; biographical articles. Louis Dudek. *Brick (special issue)* Summer 1987; No 30: passim.

The monument; review of *The Politics of the Imagination*. Louis Dudek. illus · *G&M* Nov 21, 1987: pC23.

[Untitled]; biographical articles. Leon Edel. *Brick (special issue)* Summer 1987; No 30: passim.

Spleen may write the poem, but Layton's heart will speak tomorrow; reviews of poetry books. Trevor Ferguson. *MG* Sept 26, 1987: J11

[Untitled]; prose excerpt from *Quince Jam*. Jacques Ferron. *Brick (special issue)* Summer 1987; No 30: p57.

F.R. Scott: just portrayal of a poetic humanist; review of *The Politics of the Imagination*. Doug Fetherling. photo · *Quill & Quire* Sept 1987; Vol 53 No 9: p80.

[Untitled]; biographical articles. Eugene Forsey. *Brick (special issue)* Summer 1987; No 30: passim.

[Untitled]; biographical articles. Graham Fraser. *Brick (special issue)* Summer 1987; No 30: passim.

[Untitled]; biographical articles. Michael Gnarowski. *Brick (special issue)* Summer 1987; No 30: passim.

[Untitled]; biographical articles. King Gordon. *Brick (special issue)* Summer 1987; No 30: passim.

[Untitled]; biographical articles. Ruth Gordon. *Brick (special issue)* Summer 1987; No 30: passim.

Editorial. Elizabeth Grove-White. photo · *Brick (special issue)* Summer 1987; No 30: p51.

[Untitled]; biographical articles. Ralph Gustafson. *Brick (special issue)* Summer 1987; No 30: passim.

[Untitled]; letter. Anne Hébert. photo · *Brick (special issue)* Summer 1987; No 30: p41–42.

[Untitled]; biographical article. Helen Drummond Henderson. *Brick (special issue)* Summer 1987; No 30: p19.

[Untitled]; biographical articles. Michiel Horn. *Brick (special issue)* Summer 1987; No 30: passim.

A very public life; review of *The Politics of the Imagination*. John Hutcheson. *Can Forum* Oct 1987; Vol 67 No 772: p40–41.

[Untitled]; biographical articles. Donald Johnston. *Brick (special issue)* Summer 1987; No 30: passim.

[Untitled]; biographical articles. D.G. Jones. *Brick (special issue)* Summer 1987; No 30: passim.

[Untitled]; biographical articles. Stanley Knowles. *Brick (special issue)* Summer 1987; No 30: passim.

Ideas sheds light on eclectic career; radio review. Liam Lacey. *G&M* April 7, 1987: pC7.

[Untitled]; biographical articles. Irving Layton. *Brick (special issue)* Summer 1987; No 30: passim.

[Untitled]; biographical articles. Hugh MacLennan. *Brick (special issue)* Summer 1987; No 30: passim.

[Untitled]; biographical articles. J.R. Mallory. *Brick (special issue)* Summer 1987; No 30: passim.

[Untitled]; biographical articles. Seymour Mayne. *Brick (special issue)* Summer 1987; No 30: passim.

[Untitled]; biographical article. Donald McSween. *Brick (special issue)* Summer 1987; No 30: p61.

Evolution of an intellectual; review of *The Politics of the Imagination*. Allen Mills. photo · *WFP* Nov 14, 1987: p50.

[Untitled]; biographical articles. Anne Moreau. *Brick (special issue)* Summer 1987; No 30: passim.

[Untitled]; essay. John Newlove. *Brick (special issue)* Summer 1987; No 30: p58.

[Untitled]; biographical articles. P.K. Page. *Brick (special issue)* Summer 1987; No 30: passim.

[Untitled]; biographical articles. Michael Pitfield. *Brick (special issue)* Summer 1987; No 30: passim.

[Untitled]; biographical articles. Timothy Porteous. *Brick (special issue)* Summer 1987; No 30: passim.

[Untitled]; biographical articles. Al Purdy. *Brick (special issue)* Summer 1987; No 30: passim.

[Untitled]; biographical articles. Keith Richardson. *Brick (special issue)* Summer 1987; No 30: passim.

[Untitled]; autobiographical essays. F.R. Scott. *Brick (special issue)* Summer 1987; No 30: passim.

[Untitled]; biographical articles. Marian Dale Scott. *Brick (special issue)* Summer 1987; No 30: passim.

[Untitled]; biographical articles. Ann Scotton. *Brick (special issue)* Summer 1987; No 30: passim.

Book world: championing books called 'out of print'; column. Beverley Slopen. *TS* Dec 20, 1987: pE5.

Differing with Dudek; letter to the editor. Susan Stromberg Stein. photo · *G&M* Dec 26, 1987: pD7.

[Untitled]; biographical articles. Ronald Sutherland. *Brick (special issue)* Summer 1987; No 30: passim.

The mermaid inn: on Frank Scott's veranda; essay. Ronald Sutherland. photo · *G&M* Aug 1, 1987: pD6.

[Untitled]; biographical articles. Walter Tarnapolski. *Brick (special issue)* Summer 1987; No 30: passim.

[Untitled]; biographical articles. Audrey Thomas. *Brick (special issue)* Summer 1987; No 30: passim.

On the occasion of Frank Scott's seventieth birthday; essay. Pierre Trudeau. photo · *Brick (special issue)* Summer 1987; No 30: p47–48.

[Untitled]; biographical articles. Frank Underhill. *Brick (special issue)* Summer 1987; No 30: passim.

[Untitled]; biographical articles. Robert Weaver. *Brick (special issue)* Summer 1987; No 30: passim.

[Untitled]; biographical articles. Phyllis Webb. *Brick (special issue)* Summer 1987; No 30: passim.

F.R. Scott: his life was his finest hour; review of *The Politics of the Imagination.* Joel Yanofsky. photo · *MG* Nov 14, 1987: J9.

SCOTT, GAIL

Me, myself, and I; reviews of first novels. Janice Kulyk Keefer. *Books in Can* Oct 1987; Vol 16 No 7: p35–36,38.
[FIRST NOVELS: BOOK REVIEWS]

[Untitled]; review of *Heroine.* Constance Rooke. *Malahat R* Dec 1987; No 81: p103.
[FIRST NOVELS: BOOK REVIEWS]

A daring invention of a new character; review of *Heroine.* Rosemary Sullivan. *G&M* Sept 19, 1987: pC19.
[FIRST NOVELS: BOOK REVIEWS]

SCOTT, MONROE

An exaggeration; letter to the editor. Rod Booth. *Maclean's* Nov 30, 1987; Vol 100 No 48: p4.

[Untitled]; review of *McClure.* Kathryn Harley. *Maclean's* Nov 9, 1987; Vol 100 No 45: p70.

SCOTT, PETER DALE

Book world: championing books called 'out of print'; column. Beverley Slopen. *TS* Dec 20, 1987: pE5.

SEA RUN: NOTES ON JOHN THOMPSON'S STILT JACK/Critical work by Peter Sanger

Ghazal-maker; review of *Sea Run.* Phyllis Webb. *Can Lit* Spring 1987; No 112: p156–157.

SEARS, DÉJANET

Gonna take a sentimental journey; theatre review of *Africa Solo.* Ray Conlogue. photo · *G&M* Nov 18, 1987: pC7.

Blowing bubbles with Simone and Sartre; column. Vit Wagner. photo · *TS* Nov 6, 1987: pE4.
[TRANSLATIONS OF CANADIAN LITERATURE]

Africa Solo works best when related in song; theatre review. Vit Wagner. photo · *TS* Nov 13, 1987: pE26.

SEAWEED IN YOUR STOCKING: STORIES AND POEMS BY NOVA SCOTIAN WRITERS/Anthology of children's poems and prose

A stocking stuffer anthology; review of *Seaweed in Your Stocking.* Carol Anne Wien. *Can Child Lit* 1987; No 47: p92–93.
[ANTHOLOGIES: BOOK REVIEWS]

SECOND NATURE/Poems by Libby Scheier

Some beautiful moments but all too fleeting; reviews of poetry books. Maggie Helwig. *TS* Aug 15, 1987: M6.

[Untitled]; reviews of *Candy from Strangers* and *Second Nature.* Roberta Morris. *Cross Can Writ Q* 1987; Vol 9 No 3–4: p42.

[Untitled]; reviews of *Private Properties* and *Second Nature.* Stephen Scobie. *Malahat R (special issue)* March 1987; No 78: p153–154.

[Untitled]; review of *Second Nature.* Richard Streiling. *Quill & Quire* March 1987; Vol 53 No 3: p75.

[Untitled]; review of *Second Nature.* Bronwen Wallace. *Poetry Can R* Spring 1987; Vol 8 No 2–3: p37–38.

Victims of a bleak universe; reviews of poetry books. Bruce Whiteman. *Books in Can* Jan-Feb 1987; Vol 16 No 1: p22–23.

Wit and humor mark poetry; reviews of *Second Nature* and *Private Properties.* Andrew Wreggitt. *CH* Jan 11, 1987: pF4.

LE SECRET DE LAMORANDIÈRE/Young adult novel by Bertrand Simard

Sus aux trafiquants de stupéfiants!; review of *Le Secret de Lamorandière.* Pierre Gérin. *Can Child Lit* 1987; No 48: p90–91.

Mystery for young readers; review of *Le Secret de Lamorandière.* Martine Jacquot. *Atlan Prov Book R* Sept-Oct 1987; Vol 14 No 3: p7.

THE SECRET JOURNAL OF ALEXANDER MACKENZIE/Short stories by Brian Fawcett

[Untitled]; review of *The Secret Journal of Alexander Mackenzie.* Lawrence Chanin. *Can Auth & Book* Summer 1987; Vol 62 No 4: p24.

Reading Brian Fawcett; reviews of *Cambodia* and *The Secret Journal of Alexander Mackenzie.* Norbert Ruebsaat. *Event* Summer 1987; Vol 16 No 2: p118–121.

Recent Canadian fiction; reviews of novels. D.O. Spettigue. *Queen's Q* Summer 1987; Vol 94 No 2: p366–375.
[FIRST NOVELS: BOOK REVIEWS]

THE SECRET OF SUNSET HOUSE/Children's novel by Sharon Siamon

Formulaic mysteries to attract unenthusiastic readers; reviews of *The Ghost Ships That Didn't Belong* and *The Secret of Sunset House*. Bessie Condos Egan. *Quill & Quire (Books for Young People)* June 1987; Vol 53 No 6: p6.

SÉDIMENTS/Periodical

Philosophie et littérature en revue(s): genres et styles mêlés; reviews of *Le Beffroi* and *Sédiments*. Ginette Michaud. *Liberté* April 1987; Vol 29 No 2: p129–133.
[CANADIAN LITERARY PERIODICALS]

L'air du temps; review of *Sédiments 1986*. Jacques Pelletier. *Voix et images* Spring 1987; Vol 12 No 3: p524–527.
[CANADIAN LITERARY PERIODICALS]

SEE BOB RUN/Play by Daniel MacIvor

See Bob Run dark ride into subconscious; theatre review. Pat Donnelly. *MG* Oct 1, 1987: pE7.

A funny look at a bad girl; theatre review of *See Bob Run*. Liam Lacey. photo · *G&M* July 22, 1987: pC6.

Teen hitchhikes back to childhood horror; theatre review of *See Bob Run*. Henry Mietkiewicz. photo · *TS* July 23, 1987: pB4.

SEED CATALOGUE/Poems by Robert Kroetsch

Realizing Kroetsch's poetry; reviews of *Excerpts from the Real World* and *Seed Catalogue*. Thomas B. Friedman. *Prairie Fire* Winter 1987–88; Vol 8 No 4: p95–98.

[Untitled]; review of *Seed Catalogue*. Bruce Whiteman. *Poetry Can R* Summer 1987; Vol 8 No 4: p34–35.

SELAKHI/Novel by Sean Virgo

A dazzling novel that attempts to be masterpiece; review of *Selakhi*. Geoff Hancock. *TS* Nov 29, 1987: pA21.
[FIRST NOVELS: BOOK REVIEWS]

Heart of darkness; reviews of first novels. Janice Kulyk Keefer. *Books in Can* Dec 1987; Vol 16 No 9: p37–39.
[FIRST NOVELS: BOOK REVIEWS]

Dense, mystic tale requires much of reader; review of *Selakhi*. Thomas York. *CH* Dec 27, 1987: pE6.
[FIRST NOVELS: BOOK REVIEWS]

THE SELECTED JOURNALS OF LUCY MAUD MONTGOMERY/Compilation

Anne's author faced darkness; review of *The Selected Journals of Lucy Maud Montgomery, Volume Two*. Ken Adachi. *TS* Dec 6, 1987: pC8.

LMM: finding a voice; review of *The Selected Journals of L.M. Montgomery*. Coral Ann Howells. *Can Child Lit* 1987; No 45: p79–81.

SELECTED POEMS 1933–1980/Poems by George Faludy

Columns of dark; review of *Selected Poems*. Henry Kreisel. *Can Lit* Winter 1987; No 115: p272–275.

SELECTED POEMS II: POEMS SELECTED AND NEW 1976–1986/Poems by Margaret Atwood

[Untitled]; review of *Selected Poems II*. Tom Marshall. *Poetry Can R* Spring 1987; Vol 8 No 2–3: p40.

Victims of a bleak universe; reviews of poetry books. Bruce Whiteman. *Books in Can* Jan-Feb 1987; Vol 16 No 1: p22–23.

SELECTED POEMS/Poems by Patrick Lane

[Untitled]; review of *Selected Poems*. Barbara Carey. *Books in Can* Dec 1987; Vol 16 No 9: p29–30.

Lane is chained to rock of reality; review of *Selected Poems*. Sid Marty. *CH* Dec 13, 1987: pC8.

THE SELF-COMPLETING TREE: SELECTED POEMS/Poems by Dorothy Livesay

[Untitled]; review of *The Self-Completing Tree*. Audrey Andrews. *CH* Sept 27, 1987: pE6.

The self-completing poet; review of *The Self-Completing Tree*. Phil Hall. illus · *Can Forum* Aug-Sept 1987; Vol 67 No 771: p37–39.

Lives of the poet; review of *The Self-Completing Tree*. David Latham. *Books in Can* April 1987; Vol 16 No 3: p27–28.

Infinite song; review of *The Self-Completing Tree*. Louise Longo. *Waves* Spring 1987; Vol 15 No 4: p84–87.

Livesay's selected seasons — a heady brew; review of *The Self-Completing Tree*. Ann Munton. *Event* Summer 1987; Vol 16 No 2: p133–137.

[Untitled]; review of *The Self-Completing Tree*. Libby Scheier. *Cross Can Writ Q* 1987; Vol 9 No 3–4: p39–40.

[Untitled]; reviews of *The Self-Completing Tree* and *The Collected Poems*. Stephen Scobie. *Malahat R (special issue)* March 1987; No 78: p154–155.

SERGE D'ENTRE LES MORTS/Novel by Gilbert La Rocque

Focalisation, voyeurisme et scène originaire dans Serge d'entre les morts; article. Alain Piette. *Voix et images* Spring 1987; Vol 12 No 3: p497–511.
[STRUCTURALIST WRITING AND CRITICISM]

LA SERVANTE ÉCARLATE

See THE HANDMAID'S TALE/LA SERVANTE ÉCARLATE/Novel by Margaret Atwood

SERVICE, ROBERT W.

The U.S.: foundation poets & personal views; comparative column. David Donnell. *Poetry Can R* Fall 1987; Vol 9 No 1: p25.

Sam McGee leads the way in showing the potential of poetry; reviews of children's poetry books. Janice Kennedy. *MG* March 7, 1987: H10.

Cool tale captures mystique of North; review of *The Cremation of Sam McGee*; Maggie D. McClelland. *CH* Feb 25, 1987: pE1.

New images for old favourites; review of *The Cremation of Sam McGee*. Diane Watson. *Can Child Lit* 1987; No 48: p87–90.

SETTLEMENT LITERATURE

See COLONIAL LITERATURE

SEVENTY-ONE POEMS FOR PEOPLE/Poems by George Bowering

For people; review of *Seventy-One Poems for People*. Noah Zacharin. *Can Lit* Spring 1987; No 112: p145–146.

SEX AND POLITICS/Play by William Chadwick

Sex and Politics: parody in the bedrooms of the province; theatre review. David A. Powell. *NeWest R* Nov 1987; Vol 13 No 3: p18.

SEX TIPS FOR MODERN GIRLS/Play by Peter Eliot Weiss et al

Lunchbox hopes farce will score; article. Brian Brennan. photo · *CH* Sept 25, 1987: pF1.

Sex Tips tastefully, cleverly staged; theatre review of *Sex Tips for Modern Girls*. Brian Brennan. photo · *CH* Sept 29, 1987: pD7.

LE SEXE DES ÉTOILES/Novel by Monique Proulx

Personnages en quête d'eux-mêmes; review of *Le Sexe des étoiles*. Jean-François Chassay. photo · *MD* Dec 12, 1987: pD4.
[FIRST NOVELS: BOOK REVIEWS]

SEXTET: PLAYS BY WOMEN ON CBC RADIO, 1986/Play anthology

[Untitled]; review of *Sextet*. Malcolm Page. *Theatre Hist in Can (special issue)* Spring 1987; Vol 8 No 1: p129–133.
[ANTHOLOGIES: BOOK REVIEWS]

SHADOW IN HAWTHORN BAY/Children's novel by Janet Lunn

Living in the past; reviews of children's novels. Mary Ainslie Smith. *Books in Can* June-July 1987; Vol 16 No 5: p35–37.

SHAKING THE DREAMLAND TREE/Poems by Nadine McInnis

[Untitled]; review of *Shaking the Dreamland Tree*. Margaret Dyment. *Arc* Fall 1987; No 19: p61–65.

[Untitled]; reviews of *Who's to Say?* and *Shaking the Dreamland Tree*. Susan Glickman. *Poetry Can R* Summer 1987; Vol 8 No 4: p32.

Nursery rhyme, myth and dream; reviews of *Shaking the Dreamland Tree* and *Eleusis*. Gillian Harding-Russell. *NeWest R* Sept 1987; Vol 13 No 1: p17–18.

Young poets on display; reviews of poetry books. Robert Quickenden. photo · *WFP* March 14, 1987: p52.

A SHAPELY FIRE: CHANGING THE LITERARY LANDSCAPE/Anthology

A change of climate; review of *A Shapely Fire*. Alberto Manguel. *Books in Can* Nov 1987; Vol 16 No 8: p33–34.
[ANTHOLOGIES: BOOK REVIEWS]

SHEARD, SARAH

Disappearing into Japan; review of *Almost Japanese*. Kathy Jones. *NYT Book R* Aug 16, 1987: p23.
[FIRST NOVELS: BOOK REVIEWS]

SHEBA AND SOLOMON/Poems by Karen Mulhallen

Quilted patch; reviews of poetry books. Uma Parameswaran. Teresa Mallam. *Can Lit* Spring 1987; No 112: p176–179.

SHEILA WATSON AND THE DOUBLE HOOK/Critical essays anthology

Resident & alien; review of *Sheila Watson and The Double Hook*. Michael Peterman. *Can Lit* Winter 1987; No 115: p144–146.

SHERLOCK HOLMES AND THE CASE OF THE RALEIGH LEGACY/Novel by L.B. Greenwood

Slain hitchhiker doesn't live up to writer's promise; reviews of *Sleep While I Sing* and *Sherlock Holmes and the Case of the Raleigh Legacy*. Paul Carbray. *MG* Feb 21, 1987: pB8.
[FIRST NOVELS: BOOK REVIEWS]

SHIELDS, CAROL

Author plans reading; article. *WFP* Nov 21, 1987: p28.

Author unaware latest book mystery; article. Donald Campbell. photo · *WFP* Sept 29, 1987: p29.

A decade of great thrillers continues with two treasures; reviews of *Swann: A Mystery* and *The Last White Man in Panama*. Margaret Cannon. *G&M* Sept 26, 1987: pC23.

A fond look back at the books of autumn; reviews of *The Honorary Patron* and *Swann: A Mystery*. Arnold Edinborough. *Fin Post* Nov 2, 1987: p24.

Nouvelles du centre; article. Michel Fabre. *Afram* June 1987; No 25: p1–2.

Shields fashions mystery; review of *Swann: A Mystery*. Cecelia Frey. photo · *CH* Nov 22, 1987: pA16.

Mystery that truly mystifies; review of *Swann: A Mystery*. Geoff Hancock. *TS* Oct 18, 1987: pC9.

Poetic justice; review of *Swann: A Mystery*. Brent Ledger. *Books in Can* Oct 1987; Vol 16 No 7: p15–16.

The mystery of Mary Swann, poet, farmwife and murder victim, is more like a comedy of manners; review of *Swann: A Mystery*. Marion McCormick. photo · *MG* Oct 31, 1987: J12.

Bigger canvas suits Shields; review of *Swann: A Mystery*. Norman Sigurdson. photo · *WFP* Oct 17, 1987: p61.

Carol Shields: raising everyday lives to the level of art; review of *Swann: A Mystery*. Norman Sigurdson. photo · *Quill & Quire* Nov 1987; Vol 53 No 11: p21.

SHIVERS IN YOUR NIGHTSHIRT/Anthology of children's stories

Thrills and chills: hints for Hallowe'en reading; reviews of children's books. Joan McGrath. illus · *Quill & Quire (Books for Young People)* Oct 1987; Vol 53 No 10: p8.
[ANTHOLOGIES: BOOK REVIEWS]

Fiction for children: history and mystery; *reviews* of *Rats in the Sloop* and *Shivers in Your Nightshirt*. Dorothy Perkyns. *Atlan Prov Book R* Feb-March 1987; Vol 14 No 1: p14.
[ANTHOLOGIES: BOOK REVIEWS]

THE SHORT HOCKEY CAREER OF AMAZING JANY/ Children's story by Robert Priest

Mini-reviews; reviews of children's books. Margaret Paré. *Can Child Lit* 1987; No 45: p93–96.

THE SHORT TREE AND THE BIRD THAT COULD NOT SING/Children's story by Dennis Foon

Mini-reviews; reviews of children's stories. Mary Rubio. *Can Child Lit* 1987; No 46: p105–109.

SHOWCASE ANIMALS/Poems by Linda Wikene Johnson

[Untitled]; review of *Showcase Animals*. Elizabeth Maloney. *Rubicon* Fall 1987; No 9: p186–187.

SI L'HERBE POUSSAIT SUR LES TOITS/Children's story by Henriette Major

Rus in urbe: un concept classique pour enfants modernes; review of *Si l'herbe poussait sur les toits*. Pauline Pocknell. *Can Child Lit* 1987; No 47: p79–81.

SIAMON, SHARON

Formulaic mysteries to attract unenthusiastic readers; reviews of *The Ghost Ships That Didn't Belong* and *The Secret of Sunset House*. Bessie Condos Egan. *Quill & Quire (Books for Young People)* June 1987; Vol 53 No 6: p6.

SIBUM, NORM

The Hungarian's place; review of *10 Poems*. Charles Watts. *Brick* Winter 1987; No 29: p55–60

LES SILENCES DU CORBEAU/Novel by Yvon Rivard

Machine romanesque; review of *Les Silences du corbeau*. Jacques Julien. *Can Lit* Winter 1987; No 115: p227–229.

[Untitled]; reviews. Raymond Martin. *Moebius* Winter 1987; No 31: p164–166.

Savoir garder ses distances; review of *Les Silences du corbeau*. Louise Milot. photo · *Lettres québec* Spring 1987; No 45: p22–23.

Impasses ou issues? L'imaginaire masculin face à la femme; reviews of *Les Silences du corbeau* and *À double sens*. Patricia Smart. *Voix et images* Spring 1987; Vol 12 No 3: p555–560.

SILK TRAIL/Poems by Andrew Suknaski

[Untitled]; review of *Silk Trail*. Bert Almon. *Poetry Can R* Spring 1987; Vol 8 No 2–3: p62.

SILLERS, PATRICIA

A fun bunch of books to read and look at; reviews of *Big Sarah's Little Boots* and *Ringtail*. Frieda Wishinsky. *Quill & Quire (Books for Young People)* Aug 1987; Vol 53 No 8: p3.

SILVESTER, REG

Peacetime; reviews of *Spectral Evidence* and *Fish-Hooks*. Keith Wilson. *Can Lit* Spring 1987; No 112: p154–156.

SIMARD, BERTRAND

Sus aux trafiquants de stupéfiants!; review of *Le Secret de Lamorandière*. Pierre Gérin. *Can Child Lit* 1987; No 48: p90–91.

Mystery for young readers; review of *Le Secret de Lamorandière*. Martine Jacquot. *Atlan Prov Book R* Sept-Oct 1987; Vol 14 No 3: p7.

SIMISON, GREG

[Untitled]; review of *The Possibilities of Chinese Trout*. Brian Vanderlip. *Poetry Can R* Fall 1987; Vol 9 No 1: p34–35.

Confident voices heard through poetry collections; reviews of poetry books. Christopher Wiseman. *CH* Feb 8, 1987: pE5.

SIMMIE, LOIS

Sam McGee leads the way in showing the potential of poetry; reviews of children's poetry books. Janice Kennedy. *MG* March 7, 1987: H10.

Two sensitive poets; reviews of *Some Talk Magic* and *An Armadillo Is Not a Pillow*. Sylvia Middlebro'. Tom Middlebro'. *Can Child Lit* 1987; No 46: p99–100.

Funny books are a joy to find; reviews of *An Armadillo Is Not a Pillow* and *Tales of a Gambling Grandma*. Helen Norrie. *WFP* Feb 14, 1987: p60.

Revolting teddies . . . time-travelling tot . . . rhymes macabre; reviews of tape versions of *The Olden Days Coat* and *Auntie's Knitting a Baby*. Richard Perry. photo · *Quill & Quire (Books for Young People)* Oct 1987; Vol 53 No 10: p14

Wit, enjoyment and urgency; reviews of children's poetry books. Tim Wynne-Jones. *G&M* Feb 7, 1987: pE19.

SIMON'S SURPRISE/Children's story by Ted Staunton

Mini-reviews; reviews of children's stories. Mary Rubio. *Can Child Lit* 1987; No 46: p105–109.

SINGING AGAINST THE WIND/Poems by Rienzi Crusz

[Untitled]; reviews of *Singing Against the Wind* and *A Time for Loving*. Francis Mansbridge. *Poetry Can R* Fall 1987; Vol 9 No 1: p30.

Crusz; review of *Singing Against the Wind*. Mathew Zachariah. *Can Lit* Spring 1987; No 112: p188–189.

THE SINGING STONE/Young adult novel by O.R. Melling

It's how it should have happened; review of *The Singing Stone*. Kieran Kealy. *Can Child Lit* 1987; No 47: p71–72.

A SINGLE DEATH/Novel by Eric Wright

Murder & lies; reviews of *A Single Death* and *The Telling of Lies*. Linda Hutcheon. *Can Lit* Winter 1987; No 115: p225–227.

UN SINGULIER AMOUR/Short stories by Madeleine Ferron

Madeleine Ferron au sommet de son talent; review of *Un Singulier amour*. Jean-Roch Boivin. photo · *MD* Sept 26, 1987: pD3.

La vitrine du livre; reviews. Guy Ferland. *MD* Sept 12, 1987: pD4.

SINNERS/Play by Norm Foster

Sinners' cast in over its head; theatre review. Alex Law. *TS (Neighbours)* June 16, 1987: p22.

Playwright finds unlikable cast proving popular; article. Kate Zimmerman. *CH* Sept 4, 1987: pE1.

Dinner farce lacking consistency; theatre review of *Sinners*. Kate Zimmerman. *CH* Sept 6, 1987: pE6.

THE SIR CHARLES G.D. ROBERTS SYMPOSIUM/Conference report

The Anchorage series proceedings: the Sir Charles G.D. Roberts and Joseph Howe symposia; reviews of *The Sir Charles G.D. Roberts Symposium* and *The Joseph Howe Symposium*. Laurel Boone. *Essays on Can Writ* Spring 1987; No 34: 196–201.

SIR CHARLES G.D. ROBERTS: A BIOGRAPHY/Biography by Elsie May Pomeroy

Torn between love and loyalty; reviews of *Sir Charles God Damn* and *Sir Charles G.D. Roberts: A Biography*. David McFadden. photo · *Brick* Fall 1987; No 31: p55–59.

SIR CHARLES GOD DAMN: THE LIFE OF SIR CHARLES G.D. ROBERTS/Biography by John Coldwell Adams

[Untitled]; review of *Sir Charles God Damn*. Christopher Armitage. *Amer R of Can Studies* Winter 1987–88; Vol 17 No 4: p439–440.

Torn between love and loyalty; reviews of *Sir Charles God Damn* and *Sir Charles G.D. Roberts: A Biography*. David McFadden. photo · *Brick* Fall 1987; No 31: p55–59.

[Untitled]; reviews of *The Collected Poems of Sir Charles G.D. Roberts* and *Sir Charles God Damn*. Mary McGillivray. *Queen's Q* Winter 1987; Vol 94 No 4: p1039–1042

SIROIS, SERGE

"Nouvelles pour le théâtre"; column. Robert Lévesque. *MD* Jan 27, 1987: p5.

SISKALAO/Play by Patrick Quintal

[Untitled]; letter to the editor. Mario Boivin. *Jeu* 1987; No 43: p181.

[Untitled]; editorial reply. Pierre Rousseau. *Jeu* 1987; No 43: p181.

SITTING IN THE CLUB CAR DRINKING RUM AND KARMA-COLA: A MANUAL OF ETIQUETTE FOR LADIES CROSSING CANADA BY TRAIN/Novel by Paulette Jiles

Ranging from colored bleakness to breeziness; reviews of novels by Paulette Jiles. Ken Adachi. photo · *TS* Feb 28, 1987: M4.

Paulette Jiles' fictional strategies; reviews of *Sitting in the Club Car Drinking Rum and Karma-Kola* and *The Late Great Human Road Show*. Roslyn Dixon. *Event* Summer 1987; Vol 16 No 2: p127–130.

Starting over; reviews of *The Late Great Human Road Show* and *Sitting in the Club Car Drinking Rum and Karma-Kola*. David Helwig. *Books in Can* Jan-Feb 1987; Vol 16 No 1: p15.

SIX PALM TREES/Play by Gordon Halloran and Caitlin Hicks

Six Palm Trees hilarious, moving family tale; theatre review. Lisa Rochon. photo · *G&M* July 9, 1987: pD6.

SKELTON AT 60/Compilation

[Untitled]; review of *Skelton at 60*. Keith Garebian. *Quill & Quire* Feb 1987; Vol 53 No 2: p18.

National debt; letter to the editor. Joe Rosenblatt. *Books in Can* Jan-Feb 1987; Vol 16 No 1: p38.

SKELTON, ROBIN

[Untitled]; review of *Skelton at 60*. Keith Garebian. *Quill & Quire* Feb 1987; Vol 53 No 2: p18.

[Untitled]; review of *Distances*. Luella Kerr. *Poetry Can R* Fall 1987; Vol 9 No 1: p35–36.

Sardonic commentary; review of *The Parrot Who Could*. Sherie Posesorski. *G&M* Aug 8, 1987: pC18.

The thrill of reading intoxicating stories; review of *Telling the Tale*. T.F. Rigelhof. *G&M* Sept 5, 1987: pC13.

National debt; letter to the editor. Joe Rosenblatt. *Books in Can* Jan-Feb 1987; Vol 16 No 1: p38.

[Untitled]; reviews of *Telling the Tale* and *The Parrot Who Could*. Norman Sigurdson. *Books in Can* Nov 1987; Vol 16 No 8: p25–26.

[Untitled]; review of *The Parrot Who Could*. Martin Townsend. *Quill & Quire* July 1987; Vol 53 No 7: p65.

THE SKIN OF A SONG/Poems by Russell Thornton

[Untitled]; reviews of poetry books. Shaunt Basmajian. *Cross Can Writ Q* 1987; Vol 9 No 3–4: p44,49.
[ANTHOLOGIES: BOOK REVIEWS]

[Untitled]; review of *The Skin of a Song*. Peter Herman. *Rubicon* Fall 1987; No 9: p198–199.

The impersonation of the irresistible; reviews of poetry books. Fraser Sutherland. *G&M* Sept 5, 1987: pC15.

SKIN/Play by Dennis Foon

Plays probe evils of prejudice; article. Kevin Prokosh. photo · *WFP* Feb 3, 1987: p32.

Race relations documentary emotion-packed experience; theatre review of *Skin*. Reg Skene. *WFP* Feb 6, 1987: p29.

SKRAG/Poems by David Arnason

Poets exhibit vast differences; reviews of *Flicker and Hawk* and *Skrag*. Robert Quickenden. *WFP* May 16, 1987: p70.

From ivy-covered professors; reviews of poetry books. Fraser Sutherland. *G&M* Oct 17, 1987: pE9.

SKULL RIDERS/Play by Jesse Glenn Bodyan

Beyond the Fringe; reviews of plays. Judith Rudakoff. *Books in Can* March 1987; Vol 16 No 2: p18.

SKVORECKY, JOSEF

New publications; notice. *Quill & Quire* June 1987; Vol 53 No 6: p16.

It's a date; column. *MG* Oct 9, 1987: pD3.
[FICTION READINGS]

À surveiller; column. *MD* Oct 13, 1987: p10.

Detective with the blues; review of *The Mournful Demeanor of Lieutenant Boruvka*. Mark Abley. photo · *Maclean's* Sept 14, 1987; Vol 100 No 37: T12.

Lieut. Boruvka Czechs in to the case; review of *The Mournful Demeanor of Lieutenant Boruvka*. Barbara Black. photo · *MG* Oct 17, 1987: J13.

[Untitled]; reviews of *The Swell Season* and *A Model Lover*. Pauline Carey. *Cross Can Writ Q* 1987; Vol 9 No 1: p19–20.

Josef Skvorecky; letter to the editor. Jan Culík. *Times Lit Supp* Feb 6, 1987; No 4375: p137.

Czech detective a belated delight; review of *The Mournful Demeanor of Lieutenant Boruvka*. William French. *G&M* Sept 10, 1987: pD1.

A literary scherzo; review of *Dvorak in Love*. Marketa Goetz-Stankiewicz. illus · *Can Forum* Aug-Sept 1987; Vol 67 No 771: p41–43.

The latest novels; review of *Dvorak in Love*. Oliver Gorse. *Idler* March-April 1987; No 12: p58.

[Untitled]; review of *The Mournful Demeanour of Lieutenant Boruvka*. William Grimes. *NYT Book R* Sept 6, 1987: p16.

[Untitled]; review of *Dvorak in Love*. Peter Halewood. *Rubicon* Fall 1987; No 9: p165–166

A soft spot for sousaphones; review of *Dvorak in Love*. Eva Hoffman. illus · *NYT Book R* Feb 22, 1987: p11.

An interview with Josef Skvorecky. Barbara Leckie. bibliog biog photo · *Rubicon* Fall 1987; No 9: p106–127.

Lost in translation; review of *The Mournful Demeanor of Lieutenant Boruvka*. Alberto Manguel. *Books in Can* June-July 1987; Vol 16 No 5: p13–14.

[Untitled]; review of *The Mournful Demeanor of Lieutenant Boruvka*. Peter Robinson. *Quill & Quire* June 1987; Vol 53 No 6: p33.

Detective with a difference; review of *The Mournful Demeanor of Lieutenant Boruvka*. Tom Saunders. photo · *WFP* Sept 26, 1987: p64.

Vanished consolations; reviews of *Dvorak in Love* and *Mirákl*. Roger Scruton. *Times Lit Supp* Jan 23, 1987; No 4373: p83.

An uncensored view; interview with Josef Skvorecky. Eva Seidner. photo · *Maclean's* May 11, 1987; Vol 100 No 19: T3-T4.

Interview with Joseph Skvorecky. Alan Twigg. *Dandelion* Fall-Winter 1987; Vol 14 No 2: p136–142.

SLASH/Young adult novel by Jeannette C. Armstrong

Intense tale; review of *Slash*. M.T. Kelly. *G&M* June 6, 1987: pC19.

SLEEP WHILE I SING/Novel by L.R. Wright

Criminal proceedings; review of *Sleep While I Sing*. T.J. Binyon. *Times Lit Supp* Aug 21, 1987; No 4403: p910.

Criminal proceedings; review of *Sleep While I Sing*. T.J. Binyon. *Times Lit Supp* Oct 9, 1987; No 4410: p1124.

Slain hitchhiker doesn't live up to writer's promise; reviews of *Sleep While I Sing* and *Sherlock Holmes and the Case of the Raleigh Legacy*. Paul Carbray. *MG* Feb 21, 1987: pB8.
[FIRST NOVELS: BOOK REVIEWS]

SLIDING FOR HOME/Play by Frank Moher

Ambitious drama falls short of the mark; theatre reviews of *Penguins* and *Sliding for Home*. Stephen Godfrey. photo · *G&M* Nov 26, 1987: pA25.

THE SLIDINGBACK HILLS/Poems by Peter Trower

[Untitled]; reviews of poetry books. Bruce Hunter. *Cross Can Writ Q* 1987; Vol 9 No 3-4: p40–42.

Flaws, good work mark collections; reviews of *The Slidingback Hills* and *Heading Out*. Mark Jarman. *CH* April 26, 1987: pE5.
[ANTHOLOGIES: BOOK REVIEWS]

A SLOW LIGHT/Poems by Ross Leckie

First books from five regional presses; reviews of poetry books. Colin Morton. *Arc* Spring 1987; No 18: p52–59.

SLOW MIST/Poems by Vincenzo Albanese

Montreal poets inspired by travel in hot countries; reviews of poetry books. Barbara Black. *MG* March 28, 1987: pE9.

Slight drag but Cormorant takes off; reviews of *Slow Mist* and *Exile Home/Exilio En la Patria*. Keith Garebian. photo · *TS* March 28, 1987: M4.

SMALL CLAIMS/Short stories by Jill Ciment

The absurd majesty of desires; review of *Small Claims*. Sherie Posesorski. *G&M* Jan 31, 1987: pE20.

SMALL HORSES & INTIMATE BEASTS/Poems by Michel Garneau

Harnessing poetry; reviews of *Blind Painting* and *Small Horses & Intimate Beasts*. Philip Lanthier. *Can Lit* Winter 1987; No 115: p140–142.

[Untitled]; reviews of *Small Horses & Intimate Beasts* and *Blind Painting*. David Leahy. *Queen's Q* Spring 1987; Vol 94 No 1: p189–191.

Problems; review of *Small Horses & Intimate Beasts*. Sue Matheson. *Prairie Fire* Summer 1987; Vol 8 No 2: p68–69.

[Untitled]; reviews of *Blind Painting* and *Small Horses & Intimate Beasts*. Andrew Vaisius. *Poetry Can R* Spring 1987; Vol 8 No 2–3: p59.

SMALL REGRETS/Short stories by Dave Margoshes

[Untitled]; review of *Small Regrets*. Alice Gur-Arie. *Quill & Quire* Jan 1987; Vol 53 No 1: p28.

Uneven gaps; review of *Small Regrets*. Hilda Kirkwood. *Waves* Spring 1987; Vol 15 No 4: p77–79.

Enduring a thankless existence with father; reviews of *Black Swan* and *Small Regrets*. Hugh McKellar. *TS* Jan 31, 1987: M4.

Stories vivid, unpleasant — and memorable; reviews of short story books. John Mills. *Fiddlehead* Autumn 1987; No 153: p91–95.

In the mode; reviews of short story collections. Allan Weiss. *Books in Can* April 1987; Vol 16 No 3: p30–31.

SMALL WORLDS/Poems by John B. Lee

[Untitled]; reviews of poetry books. Anita Hurwitz. *Poetry Can R* Spring 1987; Vol 8 No 2–3: p38–39.

SMART, CAROLYN

[Untitled]; reviews of *Stoning the Moon* and *The Deepening of the Colours*. Susan Huntley Elderkin. *Quarry* Summer 1987; Vol 36 No 3: p76–79.

Painful scrutiny of relationships; reviews of poetry books. Patricia Keeney Smith. *TS* May 30, 1987: M9.

SMART, ELIZABETH

[Untitled]; review of *Autobiographies*. Patricia Bradbury. *Quill & Quire* Nov 1987; Vol 53 No 11: p27.

Love and art; letter to the editor. Jacqueline Dumas. *Books in Can* June-July 1987; Vol 16 No 5: p40.

Researching Elizabeth Smart; letter to the editor. Sally Ann Kellar. *TS* July 5, 1987: pD3.

Elizabeth Smart's journals: dress rehearsal for a novel; review of *Necessary Secrets*. Brent Ledger. photo · *Quill & Quire* Feb 1987; Vol 53 No 2: p16

Elizabeth Smart: love left her battered, but not wrecked; review of *Necessary Secrets*. Marion McCormick. photo · *MG* Jan 10, 1987: pB8.

Rubinek to write novel on escape from Nazis; column. Henry Mietkiewicz. photo · *TS* June 2, 1987: pG3.

Conventional wisdom; letter to the editor. Susan Swan. *Books in Can* Oct 1987; Vol 16 No 7: p40.

Fool for love; review of *Necessary Secrets*. Audrey Thomas. photo · *Books in Can* April 1987; Vol 16 No 3: p17–18.

[Untitled]; review of *Necessary Secrets*. Iris Winston. *CH* May 31, 1987: pF5.

SMILEY, RUTH

Audience plays out dilemmas in drama; article. Shannon Hall. photo · *CH* Nov 22, 1987: pG8.

SMITH, DONALD

Black lyricist; review of *Gilbert La Rocque: l'écriture du rêve*. P. Merivale. *Can Lit* Spring 1987; No 112: p124–126.

SMITH, JOHN

[Untitled]; reviews of *The Beekeeper's Daughter* and *Midnight Found You Dancing*. Robert Hilles. *Poetry Can R* Spring 1987; Vol 8 No 2–3: p41.

The space of images; reviews of poetry books. Lavinia Inbar. *Can Lit* Summer-Fall 1987; No 113–114: p245–247.

Structures of meditation; reviews of *Meditations* and *Midnight Found You Dancing*. Michael Thorpe. *Fiddlehead* Spring 1987; No 151: p115–120.

SMITH, JOHN

City's first and only 'poet laureate' died a pauper on Elm St.; biographical article. Donald Jones. illus · *TS* Nov 21, 1987: M3.

SMITH, RAY

Somewhere in time; review of *Century*. Barry Dempster. illus · *Can Forum* Aug-Sept 1987; Vol 67 No 771: p45–46.

[Untitled]; reviews of short story collections. David Helwig. *Queen's Q* Winter 1987; Vol 94 No 4: p1022–1024.

David Suzuki set to tell his story in Metamorphosis; column. Henry Mietkiewicz. *TS* April 12, 1987: pC3.
[WRITERS-IN-RESIDENCE]

Author reveal's book's skeleton; review of *Century*. Michael Mirolla. *CH* Jan 4, 1987: pE4.

Ray Smith's world; reviews of *Century* and *The Montreal Story Tellers*. T.F. Rigelhof. *Atlan Prov Book R* Feb-March 1987; Vol 14 No 1: p17.

[Untitled]; review of *Century*. Ann Scowcroft. *Rubicon* Fall 1987; No 9: p153–155.

Ray Smith's stories are prodding and perplexing; review of *Century*. David Williamson. *WFP* March 21, 1987: p58.

SMITH, STEVEN

[Untitled]; reviews of *Blind Zone* and *Wenkchemna*. Dennis Duffy. *Poetry Can R* Spring 1987; Vol 8 No 2–3: p45.

Excesses; reviews of poetry books. Eva Tihanyi. *Can Lit* Winter 1987; No 115: p200–202.

SMITH, T.H.

Pacific coast adventure; review of *Cry to the Night Wind*. Dave Jenkinson. *Can Child Lit* 1987; No 47: p67–68.

SMUCKER, BARBARA

Round table: responses, notes and queries; column. *Can Child Lit* 1987; No 47: p102–103.
[AWARDS, LITERARY; LIBRARY SERVICES AND CANADIAN LITERATURE; WRITERS' ORGANIZATIONS]

Chit chat; column. Maria Casas. *Quill & Quire (Books for Young People)* Aug 1987; Vol 53 No 8: p3.

History lessons; review of *White Mist*. Gwyneth Evans. *Can Child Lit* 1987; No 45: p55–57.

Baby of the family gets respect raising flock of Canada geese; reviews of children's books. Janice Kennedy. *MG* Oct 3, 1987: J13.

Big responsibilities theme of tall tale and growing-up story; reviews of *The Doll* and *Jacob's Little Giant*. Joan McGrath. photo · *Quill & Quire (Books for Young People)* Aug 1987; Vol 53 No 8: p11.

A title that will grab teenagers; reviews of children's books. Joan McGrath. *TS* Oct 25, 1987: pA18.

[Untitled]; review of *Jacob's Little Giant*. Dianne Millar. *CH* Dec 6, 1987: pD9.

SMYTH, DONNA E.

[Untitled]; review of *Subversive Elements*. Thelma McCormack. *Atlantis* Fall 1987; Vol 13 No 1: p191–193.

SMYTH, JACQUI

Putrefying sore; reviews of fictional works. Kathryn Chittick. *Can Lit* Spring 1987; No 112: p128–129.

Songs of innocence and experience — the hometown in us all; reviews of *Headframe* and *No Fixed Address*. Scott Jeffrey. *NeWest R* Summer 1987; Vol 12 No 10: p13.

More saturated with colour; review of *No Fixed Admission*. Peter Slade. *NeWest R* Feb 1987; Vol 12 No 6: p18.

THE SNAKE LADY/Play by Frank Etherington

Theatre Direct probes urban kids' reality; theatre reviews of *The Snake Lady* and *Thin Ice*. Ray Conlogue. *G&M* April 29, 1987: pC7.

SNEYD, LOLA

Canadian author to read for children; article. *TS (Neighbors)* July 28, 1987: p3.

SNOWSUITS, BIRTHDAYS, & GIANTS!/Children's play by Robert Munsch

Children's play provides dizzy gaiety, excitement; theatre review of *Snowsuits, Birthdays, & Giants!*. Randal McIlroy. *WFP* Dec 20, 1987: p21.

SOAP-BOX SUDS/Poems by J. Alvin Speers

[Untitled]; reviews of poetry books. Shaunt Basmajian. *Cross Can Writ Q* 1987; Vol 9 No 2: p22.

LA SOCIÉTÉ DES MÉTIS/Play by Normand Chaurette

Des estivants sans été; theatre review of *La Société de Métis*. Robert Lévesque. *MD* Sept 29, 1987: p13.

SOCIAL BUTTERFLY/Poems by Sarah Jackson

Sarah Jackson's book works; reviews of books by Sarah Jackson. Alexa Thompson. *Atlan Prov Book R* Sept-Oct 1987; Vol 14 No 3: p15.

SOFTENED VIOLENCE/Poems by Kim Maltman

The voice of truth in Kim Maltman's Softened Violence; review article. Louise Simon. *Quarry* Winter 1987; Vol 36 No 1: p125–130.

LES SOIRS ROUGES/Poems by Clment Marchand

Le réel et la fiction du réel; reviews of *Les Soirs rouges* (reprint) and *La Fiction du réel*. Richard Gigure. photo · *Lettres québec* Winter 1986–87; No 44: p38–40.

SOIRS SANS ATOUT/Poems by Gérald Godin

Pas d'atout mais du coeur; review of *Soirs sans AtouT*. Réjean Beaudoin. *Liberté* Feb 1987; Vol 29 No 1: p153–154.

[Untitled]; review of *SoirS sans AtouT*. Claude Beausoleil. *Estuaire* Winter 1986–87; No 43: p77.

26 ans d'criture, deux trajectoires opposes; reviews of *L'cout* and *SoirS sans AtouT*. André Marquis. photo · *Lettres québec* Winter 1986–87; No 44: p42–43.

SOLDIER GIRL/Novel by Margaret Gilkes

Novel recalls author's wartime experiences; article. *MG* Jan 12, 1987: pC2.

SOLEIL ET RIPAILLE/Poems by Paul Savoie

La métamorphose du quotidien; reviews of poetry books. André Marquis. photo · *Lettres québec* Autumn 1987; No 47: p41–43.

SOLIDARITY FOREVER?/Play by Chris Creighton-Kelly

Three new political plays; theatre reviews. Malcolm Page. *Can Drama* 1987; Vol 13 No 2: p224–226.

SOLITUDE ROMPUE/Critical essays collection

Hommage à David Hayne; review of *Solitude rompue*. Lucie Robert. photo · *Lettres québec* Spring 1987; No 45: p68.

SOME FRIENDS OF MINE/Short stories by Ernesto R. Cuevas

Walls of prose; review of *Some Friends of Mine*. Jason Sherman. *G&M* Nov 14, 1987: pE11.

SOME OF EVE'S DAUGHTERS/Short stories by Connie Gault

[Untitled]; reviews of short story collections. Pauline Carey. *Cross Can Writ Q* 1987; Vol 9 No 3–4: p46–47.

[Untitled]; review of *Some of Eve's Daughters*. Cecelia Frey. *CH* June 7, 1987: pE6.

SOME TALK MAGIC/Poems by Penny Kemp

[Untitled]; reviews of poetry books. Sheila Martindale. *Cross Can Writ Q* 1987; Vol 9 No 2: p20–21.

SOMEBODY SOMEBODY'S COMING/Play by Fred Ward

New play at Centaur is strong medicine — and a strange mixture; theatre review of *Somebody Somebody's Returning*. Marianne Ackerman. *MG* Feb 6, 1987: pD1.

SOMETIMES THE DISTANCE/Poems by Bernice Lever

[Untitled]; reviews of poetry books. Barbara Carey. *Cross Can Writ Q* 1987; Vol 9 No 1: p23–24.

Jacobs, Lever, Marriott; reviews of poetry books. Barry Dempster. *Poetry Can R* Spring 1987; Vol 8 No 2–3: p35.

SOMETIMES THEY SANG/Novel by Helen Potrebenko

[Untitled]; review of *Sometimes They Sang*. Phil Hall. *Books in Can* June-July 1987; Vol 16 No 5: p21–22.

SONG OF THIS PLACE/Play by Joy Coghill

Play born out of obsession; article. Stephen Godfrey. photo · *G&M* Sept 12, 1987: pC9.

Another playwright foiled by Emily Carr; theatre review of *Song of This Place*. Stephen Godfrey. photo · *G&M* Sept 18, 1987: pD11.

SONGS FROM THE STAR MOTEL/Poems by Ian Adam

Red Deer Press series champions western writers; reviews of poetry books. Murdoch Burnett. *CH* Dec 13, 1987: pC11.

SORCIÈRE DU VENT!/Poems by Dyane Léger

Dyane Léger, l'enfant terrible d'Acadie; reviews of *Graines de fées* and *Sorcière du vent!*. Gérard Étienne. photo · *MD* July 4, 1987: pC7.

SORESTAD, GLEN

Something in common; reviews of poetry books. Cary Fagan. *Prairie Fire* Spring 1987; Vol 8 No 1: p83–87.

SORTIE D'ELLE(S) MUTANTE/Novel by Germaine Beaulieu

La vitrine du livre; reviews. Guy Ferland. *MD* Aug 29, 1987: pC12.

SORTIE DE SECOURS/Play by Théâtre Petit à Petit collective

Théâtre didactique; reviews of *Mademoiselle Autobody* and *Sortie de secours*. Lucie Robert. *Voix et images* Autumn 1987; Vol 13 No 1: p196–198.

SOUCY, JEAN-YVES

La vitrine du livre; reviews of fictional works. Guy Ferland. *MD* Dec 5, 1987: pD4.

LE SOUFFLE DE L'HARMATTAN/Novel by Sylvain Trudel

Pourquoi le manque de croyances peut vous faire mourir de soif; review of *Le Souffle de l'Harmattan*. Pierre Hébert. photo · *Lettres québec* Autumn 1987; No 47: p22–23.

Couples; reviews of novels. Jacques Michon. *Voix et images* Autumn 1987; Vol 13 No 1: p189–192.

SOUL SEARCHING/Poems by Dennis Cooley

Red Deer Press series champions western writers; reviews of poetry books. Murdoch Burnett. *CH* Dec 13, 1987: pC11.

SOULIÈRES, ROBERT

Round table: responses, notes and queries; column. *Can Child Lit* 1987; No 45: p98–99.
[AWARDS, LITERARY; CONFERENCES, LITERARY]

Valeurs ludiques et valeurs fonctionelles: Le Visiteur du soir de Robert Soulières; article. Alexandre Amprimoz. Sante A. Viselli. *Can Child Lit* 1987; No 45: p6–13.
[CRIME FICTION; STRUCTURALIST WRITING AND CRITICISM]

Dix années de littérature pour jeunes Québécois; article. Dominique Demers. photo · *MD* Nov 14, 1987: pD10.
[CANADIAN LITERARY PUBLISHING; CHILDREN'S LITERATURE]

La vie littéraire; column. Marc Morin. *MD* Nov 14, 1987: pD14.
[AWARDS, LITERARY; CHILDREN'S LITERATURE; POETRY READINGS]

SOUND POETRY

The sonic graffitist: Steve McCaffery as improvisor; article. Paul Dutton. photo · *Open Letter (special issue)* Fall 1987; Vol 6 No 9: p17–25.

Sound poetry: serious play; article. Richard Truhlar. illus · *Cross Can Writ Q* 1987; Vol 9 No 3–4: p16–18.
[POETRY PERFORMANCE]

SOUNDING THE ICEBERG: AN ESSAY ON CANADIAN HISTORICAL NOVELS/Critical work by Dennis Duffy

Perfect hindsight; review of *Sounding the Iceberg*. Laurel Boone. *Books in Can* April 1987; Vol 16 No 3: p38–39.

CanHistory?; review of *Sounding the Iceberg*. Allan Levine. *G&M* Feb 28, 1987: pE20.

Canadian historical fiction; review article about *Sounding the Iceberg*. Leslie Monkman. *Queen's Q* Autumn 1987; Vol 94 No 3: p630–640.
[HISTORICAL FICTION]

[Untitled]; review of *Sounding the Iceberg*. Clara Thomas. *U of Toronto Q* Fall 1987; Vol 57 No 1: p158–160.

LE SOURD DANS LA VILLE/DEAF TO THE CITY/Novel by Anne Hébert

Le Sourd dans la ville sera dans la course; article. *MD* July 14, 1987: p11.
[FILM ADAPTATIONS OF CANADIAN LITERATURE]

Dans les poches; reviews of paperback books. Guy Ferland. *MD* Oct 31, 1987: pD6.

Le Sourd dans la ville, de Mireille Dansereau, est bien accueilli à la Mostra de Venise; article. Jean-Noël Gillet. *MD* Sept 9, 1987: p13.
[FILM ADAPTATIONS OF CANADIAN LITERATURE]

Le sourd dans la ville, de Mireille Dansereau: près du roman mais loin de l'inspiration; film review. Robert Lévesque. *MD* Sept 19, 1987: pA7.
[FILM ADAPTATIONS OF CANADIAN LITERATURE]

Une belle et dense histoire difficile à porter à l'écran; article. Francine Laurendeau. photo · *MD* Oct 24, 1987: pC1,C12.
[FILM ADAPTATIONS OF CANADIAN LITERATURE]

Steeped in lechery; review of *Deaf to the City*. Paul West. illus · *NYT Book R* Sept 20, 1987: p12–13.

SOUS LA GRIFFE DU SIDA/Novel by Marthe Gagnon-Thibaudeau

Le syndrome du best-seller; review of *Sous la griffe du sida*. Alice Parizeau. photo · *MD* Dec 19, 1987: pD4.
[FIRST NOVELS: BOOK REVIEWS]

SOUS LE SIGNE DU PHÉNIX, ENTRETIENS AVEC 15 CRATEURS ITALO-QUÉBÉCOIS/Interview compilation

Transculture; reviews of poetry books. Viviana Comensoli. *Can Lit* Spring 1987; No 112: p120–123.

LE SOUS-SOL DES ANGES/Play by Louis-Dominique Lavigne

Le Sous-sol des anges ou les années de braise; theatre review. Angèle Dagenais. photo · *MD* Dec 15, 1987: p11.

SOUSTER, RAYMOND

[Untitled]; review of *It Takes All Kinds*. Bert Almon. *Poetry Can R* Spring 1987; Vol 8 No 2–3: p44–45.

In principio; reviews. Laurel Boone. *Can Lit* Winter 1987; No 115: p209–211.
[CONFERENCE REPORTS: REVIEWS AND ARTICLES]

[Untitled]; reviews of poetry books. Bruce Whiteman. *Cross Can Writ Q* 1987; Vol 9 No 2: p21–22,26.

SOUTH OF HEAVEN/Play by Jim Millan

Family drama lacks depth; theatre review of *South of Heaven*. Ray Conlogue. photo · *G&M* Nov 23, 1987: pC12.

Talented young writer fails to take off this time; theatre review of *South of Heaven*. Robert Crew. photo · *TS* Nov 20, 1987: pE26.

Isaac's cast puts its 500 years to good use; column. Vit Wagner. *TS* Nov 13, 1987: pE16.
[DRAMATIC READINGS; FEMINIST DRAMA; FESTIVALS, DRAMA; WOMEN WRITERS]

SOUTHEASTERLY/Poems by Andrew Wreggitt

[Untitled]; review of *Southeasterly*. John Bemrose. *Books in Can* Oct 1987; Vol 16 No 7: p26–27.

Some beautiful moments but all too fleeting; reviews of poetry books. Maggie Helwig. *TS* Aug 15, 1987: M6.

Poetry: packing all the power into two of seven titles; reviews of poetry books. Robin Skelton. photo · *Quill & Quire* May 1987; Vol 53 No 5: p24.

The pastoral myth and its observers; reviews of poetry books. Fraser Sutherland. *G&M* Sept 26, 1987: pC23.

Thistledown presents prairie poets in full bloom; reviews of poetry books. Christopher Wiseman. *CH* May 24, 1987: pE6.

SP/ELLES: POETRY BY CANADIAN WOMEN/POÉSIE DES FEMMES CANADIENNES/Anthology

In the name of the Mother; review of *SP/ELLES*. Barbara Carey. *Books in Can* Jan-Feb 1987; Vol 16 No 1: p20–21.
[ANTHOLOGIES: BOOK REVIEWS]

[Untitled]; review of *SP/ELLES*. Paul Dutton. *Quill & Quire* Feb 1987; Vol 53 No 2: p20.
[ANTHOLOGIES: BOOK REVIEWS]

Male myths, obliterated lesbians and powerful dreams; reviews of poetry books. Fraser Sutherland. photo · *G&M* Feb 14, 1987: pE19.

THE SPACE A NAME MAKES/Poems by Rosemary Sullivan

Common language in private words; reviews of poetry books. Maggie Helwig. *TS* Aug 8, 1987: M10.

[Untitled]; reviews of poetry books. Sheila Martindale. *Cross Can Writ Q* 1987; Vol 9 No 2: p20–21.

SPEAKING FOR MYSELF: CANADIAN WRITERS IN INTERVIEW/Interview compilation

Interviews with Canadian fiction writers; review of *Speaking for Myself*. Joseph Griffin. *Atlan Prov Book R* May-June 1987; Vol 14 No 2: p11.

Minding their q's and a's; review of *Speaking for Myself*. Alan Twigg. *Books in Can* May 1987; Vol 16 No 4: p31–32.

SPEAR, PETER

Polygons to cavort on stage; article. Kate Zimmerman. photo · *CH* Nov 26, 1987: pC1.

Musical's lyrics at odds with uncomplicated story; theatre review of *Numbers*. Kate Zimmerman. *CH* Nov 29, 1987: pE3.

SPEARE, JEAN

[Untitled]; review of *A Candle for Christmas*. Rosemary L. Bray. *NYT Book R* Dec 6, 1987: p81.

Mini-reviews; reviews of children's stories. Mary Rubio. *Can Child Lit* 1987; No 46: p105–109.

SPEARS, HEATHER

Sullivan honored for poetry book; article. *G&M* May 9, 1987: pC4.
[AWARDS, LITERARY]

[Untitled]; review of *How to Read Faces*. Barbara Carey. *Books in Can* June-July 1987; Vol 16 No 5: p25.

[Untitled]; review of *How to Read Faces*. Stephen Scobie. *Malahat R* Sept 1987; No 80: p140–141.

[Untitled]; review of *How to Read Faces*. Elizabeth Woods. *Poetry Can R* Fall 1987; Vol 9 No 1: p37.

SPECTRAL EVIDENCE/Short stories by Eugene McNamara

Peacetime; reviews of *Spectral Evidence* and *Fish-Hooks*. Keith Wilson. *Can Lit* Spring 1987; No 112: p154–156.

SPEERS, J. ALVIN

[Untitled]; reviews of poetry books. Shaunt Basmajian. *Cross Can Writ Q* 1987; Vol 9 No 2: p22.

[Untitled]; reviews of poetry books. Anne Burke. *Poetry Can R* Summer 1987; Vol 8 No 4: p38.

[Untitled]; reviews of poetry books. Anne Cimon. *Poetry Can R* Spring 1987; Vol 8 No 2–3: p62.

[Untitled]; reviews of poetry books. Anita Hurwitz. *Poetry Can R* Spring 1987; Vol 8 No 2–3: p50–51.

[Untitled]; reviews of poetry books. Andrew Parkin. *Poetry Can R* Fall 1987; Vol 9 No 1: p37.
[ANTHOLOGIES: BOOK REVIEWS]

SPENCER, ELIZABETH

Other Americas; reviews of *The Light in the Piazza* and *Voyage to the Other Extreme*. Michael Greenstein. *Can Lit* Spring 1987; No 112: p97–100.

New & noteworthy; reviews of *The Voice at the Back Door* and *Fire in the Morning*. Patricia T. O'Connor. *NYT Book R* Feb 1, 1987: p32

SPIDER BLUES: ESSAYS ON MICHAEL ONDAATJE/ Critical essays

[Untitled]; review of *Spider Blues*. Graham Carr. *Poetry Can R* Spring 1987; Vol 8 No 2–3: p61–62.

Solecki's Ondaatje; review of *Spider Blues*. Susan Gingell. *Can Lit* Summer-Fall 1987; No 113–114: p214–217.

[Untitled]; review of *Spider Blues*. R.F. Gillian Harding-Russell. *U of Toronto Q* Fall 1987; Vol 57 No 1: p166–168.

[Untitled]; review of *Spider Blues*. Peter Stevens. *Queen's Q* Autumn 1987; Vol 94 No 3: p717–719.

A SPIDER IN THE HOUSE/Play by Brian Tremblay

Tragic affair comes to life at Curtain Club; article. photo · *TS (Neighbors)* Nov 24, 1987: p22.

Curtain Club play needs to show more emotional thigh; theatre review of *A Spider in the House*. Alex Law. *TS (Neighbors)* Dec 1, 1987: p19.

SPIES FOR DINNER/Young adult novel by J. Robert Janes

How I spent my summer mystery; reviews of young adult novels by J. Robert Janes. James Gellert. *Can Child Lit* 1987; No 48: p93–95.

SPIRIT IN THE RAINFOREST/Children's novel by Eric Wilson

Canadian-set mysteries; reviews of children's novels by Eric Wilson. Sheila Ward. *Can Child Lit* 1987; No 48: p91–93.

SPIT DELANEY'S ISLAND/Short stories by Jack Hodgins

Today's assignment: short fiction that's worth a long look; reviews of short story books. Douglas Hill. *G&M* March 14, 1987: pE19.
[ANTHOLOGIES: BOOK REVIEWS]

SPRING TIDES

See LES GRANDES MARES/SPRING TIDES/Novel by Jacques Poulin

SPROTCH ET LE TUYAU MANQUANT/Children's novel by Stéphane Drolet

La vitrine du livre; review of *Sprotch et le tuyau manquant*. Guy Ferland. *MD* July 18, 1987: pC6.

SPROXTON, BIRK

Flin Flons; review of *Headframe*. Robert Hilles. *Prairie Fire* Autumn 1987; Vol 8 No 3: p109–112.

Songs of innocence and experience — the hometown in us all; reviews of *Headframe* and *No Fixed Address*. Scott Jeffrey. *NeWest R* Summer 1987; Vol 12 No 10: p13.

ReTracing prairie voices: a conversation with Birk Sproxton. Martin Kuester. photo · *Prairie Fire* Summer 1987; Vol 8 No 2: p4–10.

SQUATTERS' ISLAND/Novel by W.D. Barcus

World of wonders; reviews of first novels. Janice Kulyk Keefer. *Books in Can* May 1987; Vol 16 No 4: p37–38.
[FIRST NOVELS: BOOK REVIEWS]

SQUID INC. 86/Poetry anthology

[Untitled]; reviews of *Squid Inc. 86* and *The Buda Books Poetry Series*. Shaunt Basmajian. *Cross Can Writ Q* 1987; Vol 9 No 3–4: p43.

Umbrellas for a torrent of Canadian poems; reviews of poetry anthologies. Fraser Sutherland. *G&M* March 28, 1987: pE19.
[ANTHOLOGIES: BOOK REVIEWS]

The family business; reviews of *What Feathers Are For* and *Squid Inc 86*. Kim Van Vliet. *Waves* Spring 1987; Vol 15 No 4: p88–91.

ST-PIERRE, BERTIN

Un texte dense et beau; theatre review of *Le Testament*. Jean Cléo Godin. photo · *Jeu* 1987; No 44: p191–192.

ST-PIERRE, CHRISTIANE

Short stories from Caraquet; review of *Sur les pas de la mer*. Sally Ross. *Atlan Prov Book R* May-June 1987; Vol 14 No 2: p9.

ST. PIERRE, PAUL

Growing up in the saddle; review of *Boss of the Namko Drive*. Chris Ferns. *Can Child Lit* 1987; No 47: p81–82.

ST. VITUS DANCE/Novel by Don Gutteridge

Adventure in corners of Canada; reviews of *St. Vitus Dance* and *Our Hero in the Cradle of Confederation*. Hugh McKellar. *TS* Aug 23, 1987: pA20.

STAINES, KENT

Flashes of gold among the dross at Fringe festival; theatre reviews. Liam Lacey. *G&M* Aug 19, 1987: pC5.
[FESTIVALS, DRAMA]

A STAND OF JACKPINE: TWO DOZEN CANADIAN SONNETS/Poems by Milton Acorn and James Deahl

[Untitled]; reviews of *The Uncollected Acorn* and *A Stand of Jackpine*. David Leahy. *Rubicon* Fall 1987; No 9: p167–168.

STANDING FLIGHT

See LA FUITE IMMOBILE/STANDING FLIGHT/Novel by Gilles Archambault

STANDJOFSKI, HARRY

Centaur actor turns playwright; article. *MG* Jan 29, 1987: pC13.

No Cycle is a deeply searching celebration of life in the 1980s; theatre review. Pat Donnelly. photo · *MG* Dec 12, 1987: pD20

STANTON, JULIE

[Untitled]; review of *À vouloir vaincre l'absence*. Hélène Thibaux. *Estuaire* Winter 1986–87; No 43: p78–79.

STARING QUINCY RUMPEL/Children's novel by Betty Waterton

If at first you don't succeed; review of *Starring Quincy Rumpel*. Brenda M. Schmidt. *Can Child Lit* 1987; No 46: p81–82.

STAUNTON, TED

[Untitled]; review of *Greenapple Street Blues*. Joan McGrath. *Quill & Quire (Books for Young People)* Oct 1987; Vol 53 No 10: p19,22.

Mini-reviews; reviews of children's stories. Mary Rubio. *Can Child Lit* 1987; No 46: p105–109.

STEEL KISS/Play by Robin Fulford

Class's reaction a bitter lesson for playwright; article. *CH* Oct 20, 1987: pC9.

Gay murder explored, unexplained; theatre review of *Steel Kiss*. Liam Lacey. *G&M* Oct 5, 1987: pD11.

The laugh's on apartheid in one-man show; column. Vit Wagner. photo · *TS* Sept 25, 1987: pE6.

Intensity exhausting in ugly Steel Kiss; theatre review. Vit Wagner. *TS* Oct 2, 1987: pE12.

Death in High Park inspiration for play; article. Deborah Wilson. photo · *G&M* Oct 17, 1987: pA13.

STEINFELD, J.J.

Macabre parade of masks; review of *Our Hero in the Cradle of Confederation*. Sharon Drache. *G&M* July 11, 1987: pC14.
[FIRST NOVELS: BOOK REVIEWS]

Me, myself, and I; reviews of first novels. Janice Kulyk Keefer. *Books in Can* Oct 1987; Vol 16 No 7: p35–36,38.
[FIRST NOVELS: BOOK REVIEWS]

Adventure in corners of Canada; reviews of *St. Vitus Dance* and *Our Hero in the Cradle of Confederation*. Hugh McKellar. *TS* Aug 23, 1987: pA20.

Portrait of the artist as a middle-aged schlemiel; review of *Our Hero in the Cradle of Confederation*. Paul Tyndall. *Atlan Prov Book R* Sept-Oct 1987; Vol 14 No 3: p12.
[FIRST NOVELS: BOOK REVIEWS]

STENSON, FRED

Ondaatje opens reading series; article. photo · *CH* Sept 25, 1987: pF7.
[FICTION READINGS; POETRY READINGS]

Festival attracts kids' writers; column. Kenneth McGoogan. *CH* Sept 20, 1987: pE6.
[AWARDS, LITERARY; CHILDREN'S LITERATURE; FESTIVALS, LITERARY]

STEPHANSSON, STEPHAN GUDMUNDSSON

What's happening: Stephansson's home site of crafts fair; column. photo · *CH* June 12, 1987: pF6–F7.

STEPHEN LEACOCK: A REAPPRAISAL/Conference report

The gift of humorous bifocals; review of *Stephen Leacock: A Reappraisal*. Clive Doucet. photo · *G&M* Aug 1, 1987: pC16.

STEVEN, LE HÉRAULT/Novel by Victor-Lévy Beaulieu

Le livre d'Abel; review of *Steven le Hérault*. Neil B. Bishop. *Can Lit* Spring 1987; No 112: p126–128.

To be continued; review of *Steven, le Hérault*. Wayne Grady. *Books in Can* June-July 1987; Vol 16 No 5: p20.

[Untitled]; review of *Steven, le Hérault*. John Gregory. *Quill & Quire* April 1987; Vol 53 No 4: p28.

Squandered craft; review of *Steven le Hérault*. Thomas S. Woods. *G&M* Sept 19, 1987: pC17.

STEVENS, PETER

[Untitled]; review of *Out of the Willow Trees*. Stephen Brockwell. *Rubicon* Spring 1987; No 8: p225–226.

[Untitled]; review of *Out of the Willow Trees*. Allan Markin. *Poetry Can R* Fall 1987; Vol 9 No 1: p33.

STEVENSON, RICHARD

First books from five regional presses; reviews of poetry books. Colin Morton. *Arc* Spring 1987; No 18: p52–59.

STEVENSON, WILLIAM

Was this book written with Ollie in mind?; review of *Booby Trap*. Max Crittenden. *TS* July 19, 1987: pA20.

[Untitled]; review of *Booby Trap*. John North. *Quill & Quire* July 1987; Vol 53 No 7: p65.

Upper-case action and epic adventure; review of *Booby Trap*. Chris Scott. photo · *G&M* Aug 22, 1987: pC16.

STICK WITH MOLASSES/Play by Beth McMaster

Kids play key role in Storybook tale; theatre review of *Stick with Molasses*. Kate Zimmerman. photo · *CH* Feb 2, 1987: pB6.

STICKLAND, EUGENE

Darkness casts a powerful spell; theatre review of *Darkness on the Edge of Town*. H.J. Kirchhoff. photo · *G&M* May 15, 1987: pD8.

Disciplined acting shines in play etched in despair; theatre review of *Darkness on the Edge of Town*. Henry Mietkiewicz. *TS* May 12, 1987: pF4

Prairie spaces in the big city: western theatre in Toronto; theatre reviews. Margaret Gail Osachoff. *NeWest R* Oct 1987; Vol 13 No 2: p18–19.

STINSON, KATHY

Chitchat; column. Maria Casas. *Quill & Quire (Books for Young People)* April 1987; Vol 53 No 4: p3.
[CHILDREN'S LITERATURE; CHINA-CANADA LITERARY RELATIONS; WRITERS-IN-RESIDENCE]

Canadian content in England; essay. Monica Hughes. *Quill & Quire (Books for Young People)* April 1987; Vol 53 No 4: p4.
[GREAT BRITAIN-CANADA LITERARY RELATIONS]

STOKES, DENNIS

[Untitled]; reviews of poetry books. Shaunt Basmajian. *Cross Can Writ Q* 1987; Vol 9 No 3–4: p44,49.
[ANTHOLOGIES: BOOK REVIEWS]

THE STONE ANGEL/Novel by Margaret Laurence

CBC variety keeps smiling despite budget cuts; column. Sid Adilman. *TS* Feb 26, 1987: pB1.
[FILM ADAPTATIONS OF CANADIAN LITERATURE]

The religious roots of the feminine identity issue: Margaret Laurence's The Stone Angel and Margaret Atwood's Surfacing; article. Evelyn J. Hinz. abstract · *J of Can Studies* Spring 1987; Vol 22 No 1: p17–31.
[BIBLICAL MYTHS AND MYTHOLOGY; FEMINIST WRITING AND CRITICISM; GOD IN LITERATURE]

Psychic violence: The Stone Angel and modern family life; article. Ed Jewinski. *New Q* Spring-Summer 1987; Vol 7 No 1–2: p255–266.
[THE FAMILY IN CANADIAN LITERATURE; MYTHS AND LEGENDS IN CANADIAN LITERATURE; WOMEN IN LITERATURE]

A STONE WATERMELON/Short stories by Lois Braun

[Untitled]; review of *A Stone Watermelon*. Ruby Andrew. *Quill & Quire* April 1987; Vol 53 No 4: p28–29.

[Untitled]; review of *A Stone Watermelon*. Howard Curle. *Border Cross* Summer 1987; Vol 6 No 3: p21.

Prairie writer displays poise and assurance in book of short stories; review of *A Stone Watermelon*. William French. photo · *G&M* March 5, 1987: pD1.

Victims left poised, petrified; review of *A Stone Watermelon*. Cecelia Frey. *CH* April 12, 1987: pF7.

[Untitled]; review of *A Stone Watermelon*. Isabel Huggan. *Books in Can* April 1987; Vol 16 No 3: p25.

Engaging stories by newcomer; review of *A Stone Watermelon*. John Parr. *TS* March 29, 1987: pA19.

[Untitled]; review of *A Stone Watermelon*. Constance Rooke. *Malahat R* June 1987; No 79: p156.

Fiction debut is impressive; review of *A Stone Watermelon*. David Williamson. photo · *WFP* Feb 7, 1987: p59.

STONE-BLACKBURN, SUSAN

[Untitled]; review of *Robertson Davies, Playwright*. Diane Bessai. *Ariel* April 1987; Vol 18 No 2: p101–104.

[Untitled]; review of *Robertson Davies, Playwright*. S.F. Gallagher. *Eng Studies in Can* June 1987; Vol 13 No 2: p234–237.

[Untitled]; review of *Robertson Davies, Playwright*. Michael Peterman. *Theatre Hist in Can* Fall 1987; Vol 8 No 2: p249–252.

[Untitled]; reviews of *Robertson Davies* and *Robertson Davies, Playwright*. D.O. Spettigue. *Queen's Q* Autumn 1987; Vol 94 No 3: p722–724.

STONING THE MOON/Poems by Carolyn Smart

[Untitled]; reviews of *Stoning the Moon* and *The Deepening of the Colours*. Susan Huntley Elderkin. *Quarry* Summer 1987; Vol 36 No 3: p76–79.

Painful scrutiny of relationships; reviews of poetry books. Patricia Keeney Smith. *TS* May 30, 1987: M9.

STOP/Periodical

La revue des revues; reviews of periodicals. Guy Ferland. *MD* Sept 19, 1987: pD6.
[CANADIAN LITERARY PERIODICALS]

STOREY, RAYMOND

Domestic drama that hits home; article, includes theatre reviews. John Bemrose. photo · *Maclean's* Aug 17, 1987; Vol 100 No 33: p49.
[FESTIVALS, DRAMA]

Girls a slick, witty musical; theatre review of *Girls in the Gang*. Ray Conlogue. photo · *G&M* July 2, 1987: pD3.

Smooth ride on The Last Bus; theatre review. Stephen Godfrey. photo · *G&M* Feb 16, 1987: pD9.

[The Last Bus]; theatre review. Susan Minsos. *NeWest R* April 1987; Vol 12 No 8: p17.

[Untitled]; theatre review of *The Last Bus*. Mark Schoenberg. photo · *Maclean's* Feb 23, 1987; Vol 100 No 8: p55.

Blyth musical succeeds where drama fails; theatre reviews of *Girls in the Gang* and *Bush Fire*. Jason Sherman. photo · *TS* Aug 7, 1987: pE10.

STORM CHILD/Young adult novel by Brenda Bellingham

Romance and rebellion in young adult fiction; reviews of *Nobody Asked Me* and *Storm Child*. Sarah Ellis. *Can Child Lit* 1987; No 46: p87–89.

STORM GLASS/Short stories by Jane Urquhart

Jane Urquhart's stand-up talent; review of *Storm Glass*. Ken Adachi. *TS* June 7, 1987: pG11.

Jane Urquhart's short stories in the landscape of the poet; review of *Storm Glass*. Patricia Bradbury. photo · *Quill & Quire* July 1987; Vol 53 No 7: p64

Getting on a literary roulette wheel; reviews of fictional works. Trevor Ferguson. *MG* Nov 14, 1987: J11.
[FIRST NOVELS: BOOK REVIEWS]

Through the looking glass; review of *Storm Glass*. Timothy Findley. *Books in Can* June-July 1987; Vol 16 No 5: p14.

A shimmering crop of short stories from 'other' places; review of *Storm Glass*. William French. *G&M* June 25, 1987: pD1.

[Untitled]; review of *Storm Glass*. Michael Kenyon. *Malahat R* Sept 1987; No 80: p137–138.

STORM RIDER/Young adult novel by Joan S. Weir

Horse stories tell of struggles to achieve personal worth; reviews of *Storm Rider* and *Summer Goes Riding*. Callie Israel. photo · *Quill & Quire (Books for Young People)* Oct 1987; Vol 53 No 10: p16.

THE STORY OF BOBBY O'MALLEY/Novel by Wayne Johnston

[Untitled]; reviews of *Flavian's Fortune* and *The Story of Bobby O'Malley*. Charles R. Steele. *Queen's Q* Winter 1987; Vol 94 No 4: p1019–1022.

STORY, GERTRUDE

[Untitled]; review of *Black Swan*. Weyman Chan. *Dandelion* Spring-Summer 1987; Vol 14 No 1: p87–89.

[Untitled]; review of *Black Swan*. Gideon Forman. *Books in Can* May 1987; Vol 16 No 4: p20–21.

Red crayon; review of *The Need of Wanting Always*. Anne Hicks. *Can Lit* Spring 1987; No 112: p91–92.

A true voice; review of *Black Swan*. Hilda Kirkwood. *Waves* Spring 1987; Vol 15 No 4: p74–76.

[Untitled]; review of *Black Swan*. Mary S. Ladky. *Rubicon* Fall 1987; No 9: p200–201.

Charting discoveries; review of *The Need of Wanting Always*. Daniel Lenoski. photo · *NeWest R* Nov 1987; Vol 13 No 3: p13,17.

Enduring a thankless existence with father; reviews of *Black Swan* and *Small Regrets*. Hugh McKellar. *TS* Jan 31, 1987: M4.

Stories vivid, unpleasant—and memorable; reviews of short story books. John Mills. *Fiddlehead* Autumn 1987; No 153: p91–95.

[Untitled]; reviews of *The Need of Wanting Always* and *The Paris-Napoli Express*. S.A. Newman. *Cross Can Writ Q* 1987; Vol 9 No 1: p20.

STORYBOARD/Poems by Pierre Desruisseaux

Il y a des poèmes que nous habitons tous; reviews of poetry books. Robert Yergeau. *Lettres québec* Winter 1986–87; No 44: p36–37.

STORYTELLING

The raconteur of the day-care set; article. Trish Crawford. photo · *TS* Aug 9, 1987: pD1–D2.

Age of reason: she's a giant among storytellers; column about Alice Kane. Stasia Evasuk. photo · *TS* March 23, 1987: pC2.

Tale of tales; article about Kay Stone. Barbara Robson. photo · *WFP* Dec 6, 1987: p18.

Storyteller's credo: 'I rearrange reality'; article about Fred Hill. Leslie Scrivener. photo · *TS* Aug 16, 1987: pD1,D5.

Storyteller relives her youth; article. Leslie Scrivener. photo · *TS* Dec 20, 1987: pD6.

Storytellers unlimited; article. Anne Spencer. photo · *Can Auth & Book* Summer 1987; Vol 62 No 4: p6.

Once upon a time . . . ; article. Kate Zimmerman. photo · *CH* May 31, 1987: pF1.

STOUCK, DAVID

[Untitled]; reviews of critical works. Ronald B. Hatch. *Eng Studies in Can* March 1987; Vol 13 No 1: p107–115.

STRAIGHT AHEAD/BLIND DANCERS/Plays by Charles Tidler

Simple folk wax poetic in wordy one-act plays; theatre review of *Straight Ahead/Blind Dancers*. Vit Wagner. photo · *TS* Nov 27, 1987: pD12.

A STRANGE MANUSCRIPT FOUND IN A COPPER CYLINDER/Novel by James De Mille

James de Mille's strange manuscript; review of *A Strange Manuscript Found in a Copper Cylinder*. Janice Kulyk Keefer. *Atlan Prov Book R* May-June 1987; Vol 14 No 2: p12.

The restoration of CanLit; article, includes review. Marion McCormick. photo · *MG* March 7, 1987: H10.
[CANADIAN LITERARY PUBLISHING; CANADIAN LITERATURE: BIBLIOGRAPHY]

Copper-plating a strange fantasy; review of *A Strange Manuscript Found in a Copper Cylinder*. Paul Roberts. *TS* July 4, 1987: M10.

A STRANGER TO MY TIME: ESSAYS BY AND ABOUT FREDERICK PHILIP GROVE/Compilation

A wealth of provocative and inspiring literary criticism; reviews. Douglas Hill. *G&M* Sept 5, 1987: pC13.
[ANTHOLOGIES: BOOK REVIEWS]

STRATFORD, PHILIP

[Untitled]; reviews of *Blind Painting* and *All the Polarities*. Estelle Dansereau. *Quarry* Summer 1987; Vol 36 No 3: p82–86.

[Untitled]; reviews of critical works. Don Gutteridge. *Queen's Q* Summer 1987; Vol 94 No 2: p464–467.

Prix et distinctions; list of award winners. Gaétan Lévesque. photo · *Lettres québec* Autumn 1987; No 47: p7.
[AWARDS, LITERARY; GOVERNOR GENERAL'S AWARDS]

On both hands; review of *All the Polarities*. Patricia Merivale. *Can Lit* Summer-Fall 1987; No 113–114: p207–212

STRATTON, ALLAN

Billboard: women's group holding dessert party; column. *WFP* Nov 29, 1987: p18.
[DRAMATIC READINGS]

[Untitled]; review of *Papers*. Bert Cowan. *Books in Can* March 1987; Vol 16 No 2: p26.

TV evangelism thriller merits rerun on radio; theatre review of *The 101 Miracles of Hope Chance*. Stephen Godfrey. *G&M* Dec 7, 1987: pD9.

Evangelical lampoon offers lightweight fun; theatre review of *The 101 Miracles of Hope Chance*. Randal McIlroy. *WFP* Nov 20, 1987: p35.

PTL debacle timely for writer; article. Brad Oswald. photo · *WFP* Nov 19, 1987: p49.

[Untitled]; reviews of plays. Judith Rudakoff. *Can Theatre R* Summer 1987; No 51: p86–87.

STRAW CUPID/Poems by Karen MacCormack

Each to her own rhythm; reviews of poetry books. Lesley McAllister. *TS* July 25, 1987: M5.

STREN, PATTI

Teenage eating problems; review of *I Was a 15-Year-Old Blimp*. Sofiah Friesen. *Can Child Lit* 1987; No 46: p84.

STROMSMOE, GARY

Events inspired new play; article. Kate Zimmerman. *CH* Sept 25, 1987: pF3.

Atmospheric nature is strength of play; theatre review of *Fall of the House of Krebbs*. Kate Zimmerman. photo · *CH* Oct 2, 1987: pE10.

STRUCTURALIST WRITING AND CRITICISM

Valeurs ludiques et valeurs fonctionelles: Le Visiteur du soir de Robert Soulières; article. Alexandre Amprimoz. Sante A. Viselli. *Can Child Lit* 1987; No 45: p6–13.
[CRIME FICTION]

Fred Wah: poet as theor(h)et(or)ician; article. Pamela Banting. *Open Letter* Spring 1987; Vol 6 No 7: p5–20.

Paradigme, palimpseste, pastiche, parodie dans Maryse de Francine Noël; article. Anne Élaine Cliche. *Voix et images* Spring 1987; Vol 12 No 3: p430–438.

Grammatology & economy; article. Michael Coffey. photo · *Open Letter (special issue)* Fall 1987; Vol 6 No 9: p27–38.
[POSTMODERNIST WRITING AND CRITICISM]

Symbols of transformation: Alice Munro's "Mrs. Cross and Mrs. Kidd"; article. Héliane Daziron. *Open Letter* Summer 1987; Vol 6 No 8: p15–24.

A deconstructive narratology; reading Robert Kroetsch's Alibi; article. Susan Rudy Dorscht. *Open Letter* Summer 1987; Vol 6 No 8: p78–83.
[METAFICTION]

Novelist as trickster: the magical presence of Gabriel García Márquez in Robert Kroetsch's What The Crow Said; article. Brian Edwards. *Essays on Can Writ* Spring 1987; No 34: p92–110.
[LATIN AMERICA-CANADA LITERARY RELATIONS; MAGIC REALISM; POSTMODERNIST WRITING AND CRITICISM]

Robertson Davies' dialogic imagination; article. Barbara Godard. *Essays on Can Writ* Spring 1987; No 34: p64–80.
[CARNIVALIZATION]

Telling it over again: Atwood's art of parody; article. Barbara Godard. *Can Poet* Fall-Winter 1987; No 21: p1–30.
[FEMINIST WRITING AND CRITICISM; MYTHS AND LEGENDS IN CANADIAN LITERATURE]

Jalons pour une narratologie du journal intime: le statut du récit dans le Journal d'Henriette Dessaulles; article. Pierre Hébert. *Voix et images* Autumn 1987; Vol 13 No 1: p140–156.
[AUTOBIOGRAPHICAL WRITING]

Schéma actantiel d'un pseudo-récit: le Torrent d'Anne Hébert; article. Laure Hesbois. *Voix et images* Autumn 1987; Vol 13 No 1: p104–114.

Shape shifters: Canadian women novelists challenge tradition; article. Linda Hutcheon. illus · *Can Forum* Jan 1987; Vol 66 No 765: p26–32.
[ARTIST FIGURE; FEMINIST WRITING AND CRITICISM; WOMEN WRITERS]

Stealing the text: George Bowering's Kerrisdale Elegies and Dennis Cooley's Bloody Jack; article. Smaro Kamboureli. *Can Lit* Winter 1987; No 115: p9–23.
[CANADIAN LONG POEM]

Le silence de Trente arpents; article. Javier García Méndez. *Voix et images* Spring 1987; Vol 12 No 3: p452–469.

Thematic criticism, literary nationalism, and the critic's new clothes; article. T.D. MacLulich. *Essays on Can Writ* Winter 1987; No 35: p17–36.
[CANADIAN LITERARY: STUDY AND TEACHING; CULTURAL IDENTITY]

Steve McCaffery's Panopticon; article. William McPheron. photo · *Open Letter (special issue)* Fall 1987; Vol 6 No 9: p49–54.
[METAFICTION; POSTMODERNIST WRITING AND CRITICISM]

L'autonomisation de la littérature: sa taxinomie, ses seuils, sa sémiotique; article. Joseph Melançon. abstract · *Études lit* Spring-Summer 1987; Vol 20 No 1: p17–43

Présentation; editorial. Clément Moisan and Denis Saint-Jacques. *Études lit* Spring-Summer 1987; Vol 20 No 1: p9–16.
[CANADIAN LITERATURE: STUDY AND TEACHING; POSTMODERNIST WRITING AND CRITICISM]

Grignon plurilingue; article. Magessa O'Reilly. *Voix et images* Autumn 1987; Vol 13 No 1: p123–139.

Focalisation, voyeurisme et scène originaire dans Serge d'entre les morts; article. Alain Piette. *Voix et images* Spring 1987; Vol 12 No 3: p497–511.

Effets sonores et signification dans les Belles-soeurs de Michel Tremblay; article. Alvina Ruprecht. *Voix et images* Spring 1987; Vol 12 No 3: p439–451.

Par-delà la censure, les séductions du vrai; article. Fernande Saint-Martin. *Moebius (special issue)* Spring 1987; No 32: p97–105.
[CENSORSHIP]

Theory comes out of the closet; essay. Ralph Sarkonak. *Can Lit* Spring 1987; No 112: p61–63.

Suzanne Lamy: le féminin au risque de la critique; article. Sherry Simon. *Voix et images* Autumn 1987; Vol 13 No 1: p52–64.
[FEMINIST WRITING AND CRITICISM]

STUDIES IN CANADIAN LITERATURE/Periodical

Beyond the merely competent; reviews of critical works. Larry McDonald. *Atlan Prov Book R* Sept-Oct 1987; Vol 14 No 3: p11.
[CANADIAN LITERARY PERIODICALS]

STUDIES IN LITERATURE AND THE HUMANITIES/ Critical essays by George Whalley

[Untitled]; review of *Studies in Literature and the Humanities*. J.R. de J. Jackson. *Eng Studies in Can* June 1987; Vonadian women novelists challenge tradition; article. Linda Hutcheon. illus · *Can Forum* Jan 1987; Vol 66 No 765: p26–32.
[ARTIST FIGURE; FEMINIST WRITING AND CRITICISM; WOMEN WRITERS]

Stealing the text: George Bowering's Kerrisdale Elegies and Dennis Cooley's Bloody Jack; article. Smaro Kamboureli. *Can Lit* Winter 1987; No 115: p9–23.
[CANADIAN LONG POEM]

Le silence de Trente arpents; article. Javier García Méndez. *Voix et images* Spring 1987; Vol 12 No 3: p452–469.

Thematic criticism, literary nationalism, and the critic's new clothes; article. T.D. MacLulich. *Essays on Can Writ* Winter 1987; No 35: p17–36.
[CANADIAN LITERARY: STUDY AND TEACHING; CULTURAL IDENTITY]

Steve McCaffery's Panopticon; article. William McPheron. photo · *Open Letter (special issue)* Fall 1987; Vol 6 No 9: p49–54.
[METAFICTION; POSTMODERNIST WRITING AND CRITICISM]

L'autonomisation de la littérature: sa taxinomie, ses seuils, sa sémiotique; article. Joseph Melançon. abstract λ 13 No 2: p229–234.

[Untitled]; reviews of *Studies in Literature and the Humanities* and *The Impossible Sum of Our Traditions* W.J. Keith. *U of Toronto Q* Fall 1987; Vol 57 No 1: p145–148.

SUB/VERSION: CANADIAN FICTIONS BY WOMEN/ Critical work by Lorna Irvine

[Untitled]; review of *Sub/version*. Nancy Bailey. *World Lit in Eng* Autumn 1987; Vol 27 No 2: p262–264.

Beyond the merely competent; reviews of critical works. Larry McDonald. *Atlan Prov Book R* Sept-Oct 1987; Vol 14 No 3: p11.
[CANADIAN LITERARY PERIODICALS]

[Untitled]; review of *Sub/version*. Christl Verduyn. *Amer R of Can Studies* Summer 1987; Vol 17 No 2: p259–260.

SUBJECT INDEX TO CANADIAN POETRY IN ENGLISH FOR CHILDREN AND YOUNG PEOPLE/Reference guide

Books for librarians; review of ATION = [AWARDS, LITERARY]

Common language in private words; reviews of poetry books. Maggie Helwig. *TS* Aug 8, 1987: M10.

[Untitled]; reviews of poetry books. Sheila Martindale. *Cross Can Writ Q* 1987; Vol 9 No 2: p20–21.

Rubinek to write novel on escape from Nazis; column. Henry Mietkiewicz. photo · *TS* June 2, 1987: pG3.

SUMMER GOES RIDING/Young adult novel by Jan Truss

Horse stories tell of struggles to achieve personal worth; reviews of *Storm Rider* and *Summer Goes Riding*. Callie Israel. photo · *Quill & Quire (Books for Young People)* Oct 1987; Vol 53 No 10: p16.

Successful Alberta children's writers pen new works; article. Kenneth McGoogan. photo · *CH* Dec 18, 1987: pE7.

SUMMER OF DISCOVERY/Children's novel by Eric Wilson

Canadian-set mysteries; reviews of children's novels by Eric Wilson. Sheila Ward. *Can Child Lit* 1987; No 48: p91–93.

SUMMER OF THE GREATER YELLOWLEGS/Short stories by Patrick O'Flaherty

Small regional presses as saviors of cultural information; reviews of fictional works. Douglas Hill. *G&M* Oct 10, 1987: pC21.
[FIRST NOVELS: BOOK REVIEWS]

THE SUMMER TREE/Novel by Guy Gavriel Kay

The latest reports from the exotic worlds of fantasy; review of *The Summer Tree*. Douglas Hill. *G&M* July 11, 1987: pC13.
[FIRST NOVELS: BOOK REVIEWS]

SUMMERS, JARON

Columns prompt readers to write; column. William French. *G&M* April 7, 1987: pC7.

Book world: radical right illumined; column. Beverley Slopen. *TS* Oct 18, 1987: pC8.

SUNSHINE SKETCHES OF A LITTLE TOWN/Short stories by Stephen Leacock

The narrator, the reader, and Mariposa: the cost of preserving the status quo in Sunshine Sketches Of A Little Town; article. Francis Zichy. abstract · *J of Can Studies* Spring 1987; Vol 22 No 1: p51–65.
[SATIRIC WRITING]

SUR LES PAS DE LA MER/Short stories by Christiane St-Pierre

Short stories from Caraquet; review of *Sur les pas de la mer*. Sally Ross. *Atlan Prov Book R* May-June 1987; Vol 14 No 2: p9.

SURFACING/Novel by Margaret Atwood

The religious roots of the feminine identity issue: Margaret Laurence's The Stone Angel and Margaret Atwood's Surfacing; article. Evelyn J. Hinz. abstract · *J of Can Studies* Spring 1987; Vol 22 No 1: p17–31.
[BIBLICAL MYTHS AND MYTHOLOGY; FEMINIST WRITING AND CRITICISM; GOD IN LITERATURE]

SURPRENDRE LES VOIX/Critical essays by André Belleau

Belleau; review of *Surprendre les voix*. Robert Melançon. *Liberté* April 1987; Vol 29 No 2: p137–139.

André Belleau: une voix reconnaissable entre toutes; review of *Surprendre les voix*. Lori Saint-Martin. photo · *MD* Jan 24, 1987: pB3.

SURRÉALISME ET LITTÉRATURE QUÉBÉCOISE

See **SURREALISM AND QUEBEC LITERATURE: HISTORY OF A CULTURAL REVOLUTION/SURRÉALISME ET LITTÉRATURE QUÉBÉCOISE. HISTOIRE D'UNE RÉVOLUTION CULTURELLE/Survey by André-G. Bourassa**

SURREALISM

The automatist movement of Montreal: towards non-figuration in painting, dance, and poetry; article. Ray Ellenwood. illus · *Can Lit* Summer-Fall 1987; No 113–114: p11–27.

Roy Kiyooka's The Fontainebleau Dream Machine: a reading; article. Eva-Marie Kröler. *Can Lit* Summer-Fall 1987; No 113–114: p47–58.

Image and mood: recent poems by Michael Bullock; article. Jack F. Stewart. *Can Lit* Winter 1987; No 115: p107–121.
[MYTHS AND LEGENDS IN CANADIAN LITERATURE]

SURREALISM AND QUEBEC LITERATURE: HISTORY OF A CULTURAL REVOLUTION/SURRÉALISME ET LITTÉRATURE QUÉBÉCOISE. HISTOIRE D'UNE RÉVOLUTION CULTURELLE/Survey by André-G. Bourassa

Pour transformer l'essence même de la pensée; review of *Surréalisme et littérature québécoise*. Lori Saint-Martin. *MD* Oct 31, 1987: pD3.

SURSIS/Poems by Alphone Piché

La violence de la mort; review of *Sursis*. Gérald Gaudet. *MD* Dec 12, 1987: pD3.

LE SURVEILLANT/Short stories by Gaétan Brulotte

L'étrangeté du quotidien; review of *Le Surveillant*. Réjean Beaudoin. *Liberté* June 1987; Vol 29 No 3: p104–105.

SUTHERLAND, FRASER

Against the reasoning mind; reviews of *In the Village of Alias* and *Vibrations in Time*. Jon Kertzer. *Fiddlehead* Autumn 1987; No 153: p97–100.

SUTHERLAND, JOHN

The tradition: John Sutherland, 1919–1956; column. Bruce Whiteman. *Poetry Can R* Summer 1987; Vol 8 No 4: p10.
[CANADIAN LITERARY PERIODICALS]

SUTHERLAND, ROBERT

[Untitled]; reviews of *The Green Gables Detectives* and *The Loon Lake Murders*. Linda Granfield. *Quill & Quire (Books for Young People)* Aug 1987; Vol 53 No 8: p5–6.

SWANN: A MYSTERY/Novel by Carol Shields

Author unaware latest book mystery; article. Donald Campbell. photo · *WFP* Sept 29, 1987: p29.

A decade of great thrillers continues with two treasures; reviews of *Swann: A Mystery* and *The Last White Man in Panama*. Margaret Cannon. *G&M* Sept 26, 1987: pC23.

Shields fashions mystery; review of *Swann: A Mystery*. Cecelia Frey. photo · *CH* Nov 22, 1987: pA16.

Mystery that truly mystifies; review of *Swann: A Mystery*. Geoff Hancock. *TS* Oct 18, 1987: pC9.

Poetic justice; review of *Swann: A Mystery*. Brent Ledger. *Books in Can* Oct 1987; Vol 16 No 7: p15–16.

The mystery of Mary Swann, poet, farmwife and murder victim, is more like a comedy of manners; review of *Swann: A Mystery*. Marion McCormick. photo · *MG* Oct 31, 1987: J12.

Bigger canvas suits Shields; review of *Swann: A Mystery*. Norman Sigurdson. photo · *WFP* Oct 17, 1987: p61.

Carol Shields: raising everyday lives to the level of art; review of *Swann: A Mystery*. Norman Sigurdson. photo · *Quill & Quire* Nov 1987; Vol 53 No 11: p21.

SWARD, ROBERT

[Untitled]; reviews of poetry books. Douglas Smith. *Poetry Can R* Spring 1987; Vol 8 No 2–3: p39–40.
[ANTHOLOGIES: BOOK REVIEWS]

SWEDE, GEORGE

A trio of poets to tickle a child's fancy; reviews of children's poetry books. Adele Ashby. *Quill & Quire (Books for Young People)* June 1987; Vol 53 No 6: p10.

Wit, enjoyment and urgency; reviews of children's poetry books. Tim Wynne-Jones. *G&M* Feb 7, 1987: pE19.

THE SWEET SECOND SUMMER OF KITTY MALONE/Novel by Matt Cohen

The wonders and pleasures of fictional empire-building; reviews of novels by Matt Cohen. Douglas Hill. photo · *G&M* Jan 3, 1987: pE15.

THE SWELL SEASON/Short stories by Josef Skvorecky

[Untitled]; reviews of *The Swell Season* and *A Model Lover*. Pauline Carey. *Cross Can Writ Q* 1987; Vol 9 No 1: p19–20.

SWIFT CURRENT/Periodical

[Untitled]; review of *Inspecting the Vaults*. Constance Rooke. *Malahat R* Dec 1987; No 81: p101.

SYMONS, SCOTT

Scott Symons and the strange case of Helmet of Flesh; article. Peter Buitenhuis. *West Coast R* Spring 1987; Vol 21 No 4: p59–72.

[Untitled]; review of *Helmet of Flesh*. Jones. *Rubicon* Spring 1987; No 8: p199–202.

The immoralist; review of *Helmet of Flesh*. Sam Solecki. *Can Lit* Winter 1987; No 115: p146–148.

SYMPATHETIC MAGIC/Poems by Paul Cameron Brown

[Untitled]; reviews of *Psalms from the Suburbs* and *Sympathetic Magic*. Doug Watling. *Poetry Can R* Spring 1987; Vol 8 No 2–3: p51.

LE SYNDROME DE CÉZANNE/Play by Normand Canac-Marquis

Syndrome obscure yet polished; theatre review of *Le Syndrome de Cézanne*. Pat Donnelly. *MG* March 5, 1987: pD13.

[Untitled]; theatre reviews. Robert Lévesque. photo · *MD* March 13, 1987: p15.

Mécanique violente et masques aimables; theatre review of *Le Syndrome de Cézanne*. Paul Lefebvre. photo · *MD* Feb 23, 1987: p10.

[Untitled]; theatre review of *Le Syndrome de Cézanne*. Paul Lefebvre. *MD* Feb 27, 1987: p7.

SZUMIGALSKI, ANNE

Billboard: U of M Suzuki program holds workshop; column. *WFP* Feb 19, 1987: p36.
[POETRY READINGS]

Billboard: genealogical society meets tonight at 7:30 in museum; column. *WFP* March 19, 1987: p39.
[POETRY READINGS]

City approves writer residency for poet-author; article. *WFP* Sept 10, 1987: p3.
[WRITERS-IN-RESIDENCE]

Funding fuss shocks writer-in-residence; article. Donald Campbell. photo · *WFP* Oct 6, 1987: p32.
[WRITERS-IN-RESIDENCE]

Writer's earnings questioned; article. David Roberts. *WFP* Sept 9, 1987: p1,4.
[WRITERS-IN-RESIDENCE]

[Untitled]; review of *Dogstones*. Richard Streiling. *Quill & Quire* Feb 1987; Vol 53 No 2: p20.

Mapping inner and outer selves; review of *Tiger in the Skull* and *Dogstones*. Fraser Sutherland. *G&M* Feb 28, 1987: pE18.

Victims of a bleak universe; reviews of poetry books. Bruce Whiteman. *Books in Can* Jan-Feb 1987; Vol 16 No 1: p22–23.

[Untitled]; review of *Dogstones*. George Woodcock. *Poetry Can R* Summer 1987; Vol 8 No 4: p37–38.

TABLEAUX DE JEUNESSE/Novel by Dominique Drouin

Une histoire de jeunesse; review of *Tableau de jeunesse*. Chantal Gamache. *MD* May 23, 1987: pD3.
[FIRST NOVELS: BOOK REVIEWS]

La vitrine du livre; reviews. Jean Royer. *MD* March 14, 1987: pD4.
[CANADIAN LITERARY PERIODICALS]

TÂCHE DE NAISSANCE/Poems by Jean Charlebois

La fiction du réel/le réel de la fiction; reviews of poetry books. André Brochu. *Voix et images* Winter 1987; No 35: p322–330.

TAG IN A GHOST TOWN/Play by Pat Langner

Appealing performer wasted in aimless ghost town saga; theatre review of *Tag in a Ghost Town*. Ray Conlogue. photo · *G&M* May 15, 1987: pD10.

Tag makes your hair stand on end; theatre review of *Tag in a Ghost Town*. Henry Mietkiewicz. *TS* May 15, 1987: pD11.

Prairie spaces in the big city: western theatre in Toronto; theatre reviews. Margaret Gail Osachoff. *NeWest R* Oct 1987; Vol 13 No 2: p18–19.

A TAIL BETWEEN TWO CITIES/Children's story by Andrea Wayne von Konigslow

[Untitled]; review of *A Tail Between Two Cities*. Bernie Goedhart. *Quill & Quire (Books for Young People)* Dec 1987; Vol 53 No 12: p9.

A TALE OF TWO COUNTRIES: CONTEMPORARY FICTION IN CANADA AND THE UNITED STATES/Critical work by Stanley Fogel

[Untitled]; reviews of critical works. Ronald B. Hatch. *Eng Studies in Can* March 1987; Vol 13 No 1: p107–115.

Erasures; review of *A Tale of Two Countries*. Mark S. Madoff. *Can Lit* Spring 1987; No 112: p185–186.

TALES FROM FIROZSHA BAAG/Short stories by Rohinton Mistry

New jewel in Canada's literary crown; review of *Tales from Firozsha Baag*. Ken Adachi. photo · *TS* April 18, 1987: M4.

Short stories lay bare peoples' foibles, passions; review of *Tales from Firozsha Baag*. J. Leslie Ball. *CH* July 5, 1987: pF7.

Immigrant experience yields stream of interesting tales; reviews of *Tales from Firozsha Baag* and *The Fencepost Chronicles*. Barbara Black. *MG* May 30, 1987: J9.

Moving tales of homelands left behind; reviews of *Bloodsong* and *Tales from Firozsha Baag*. Janet Hamilton. photo · *Quill & Quire* June 1987; Vol 53 No 6: p32.

[Untitled]; review of *Tales from Firozsha Baag*. Louis K. MacKendrick. *Books in Can* Aug-Sept 1987; Vol 16 No 6: p25–26.

The vision of the self-exiled; review of *Tales from Firozsha Baag*. Nancy Wigston. photo · *G&M* May 2, 1987: pC17.

TALES OF A GAMBLING GRANDMA/Children's stories by Dayar Kaur Khalsa

Convincing and colourful; review of *Tales of a Gambling Grandma*. Marlene Kadar. *Can Child Lit* 1987; No 47: p91–92.

Funny books are a joy to find; reviews of *An Armadillo Is Not a Pillow* and *Tales of a Gambling Grandma*. Helen Norrie. *WFP* Feb 14, 1987: p60.

Rare joy and simple truth; reviews of *Tales of a Gambling Grandma* and *Love You Forever*. Tim Wynne-Jones. *G&M* Jan 24, 1987: pE19.

TALES UNTIL DAWN: THE WORLD OF A CAPE BRETON GAELIC STORY-TELLER/Compilation

Cleverness will prevail; review of *Tales Until Dawn*. Wilfred Cude. photo · *Atlan Prov Book R* Nov-Dec 1987; Vol 14 No 4: p7.

TALKING WATER, TALKING FIRE/Poems by Jim Tallosi

A choice of codes; reviews of poetry books. Thomas Gerry. illus · *NeWest R* Nov 1987; Vol 13 No 3: p16–17.

Kinetic space; reviews of poetry books. Robert James Merrett. *Can Lit* Summer-Fall 1987; No 113–114: p241–243.

TALLOSI, JIM

A choice of codes; reviews of poetry books. Thomas Gerry. illus · *NeWest R* Nov 1987; Vol 13 No 3: p16–17.

Kinetic space; reviews of poetry books. Robert James Merrett. *Can Lit* Summer-Fall 1987; No 113–114: p241–243.

TAMAHNOUS THEATRE COLLECTIVE

Cocaine use to be probed in B.C. play; article. *WFP* July 26, 1987: p16.

TAMARA/Play by John Krizanc

Mixed reviews for Tamara; article. Salem Alaton. *G&M* Dec 4, 1987: pD9.
[INTERNATIONAL REVIEWS OF CANADIAN LITERATURE]

Bright lights, Big Apple; article. Larry Black. photo · *Maclean's* Dec 7, 1987; Vol 100 No 49: p69–70.

Tamara producers work on Casa Loma '88; article. Robert Crew. *TS* Dec 2, 1987: pB4.

Tamara gets a rave in New York Times; column. Robert Crew. *TS* Dec 3, 1987: pB1.
[INTERNATIONAL REVIEWS OF CANADIAN LITERATURE]

Tamara, Tamara, they'll love it Tamara; column. Robert Crew. *TS* Dec 4, 1987: pD27.

Tamara New York; article. Peter Goddard. photo · *TS* Nov 22, 1987: pC1,C4.

Theatre of Future would lack only stage and script; theatre review of *Tamara*. Lewis H. Lapham. photo · *G&M* Dec 12, 1987: pC12.

Tamara: intrigue, champagne et amuse-gueules; article. Maurice Tourigny. photo · *MD* Nov 14, 1987: pC6

LE TANT-À-COEUR/Poems by Jean Chapdelaine Gagnon

[Untitled]; reviews of *Langues d'aimer* and *Le Tant-à-coeur*. Jacques Paquin. *Estuaire* Summer 1987; No 45: p49–50.

TARD, LOUIS-MARTIN

Springtime, and some more Malouins; review of *Il y a toujours des printemps en Amérique*. Benoit Aubin. photo · *MG* Oct 31, 1987: J11.
[FIRST NOVELS: BOOK REVIEWS]

[Untitled]; notice. Paul Cauchon. *MD* Dec 4, 1987: p15.
[TELEVISION AND CANADIAN LITERATURE]

"Un jour, j'écrirai un livre sur le Québec": Louis-Martin Tard a tenu sa promesse; article. Marie Laurier. photo · *MD* Oct 3, 1987: pD1,D8.

Une famille, un coin du monde, un pays; review of *Il y aura toujours des printemps en Amérique*. Alice Parizeau. *MD* Oct 3, 1987: pD3.
[FIRST NOVELS: BOOK REVIEWS]

TARDIF, LAURENCE

Poetic, spell-binding Caryopse is theatre for thinking person; theatre review of *Caryopse ou le monde entier*. Pat Donnelly. *MG* Oct 30, 1987: pC2.

TARTUFFE/Play by Richard Ouzounian

Getting back on the theatrical track; article. photo · *Maclean's* April 20, 1987; Vol 100 No 16: p47–48.

Neptune cooks up a delicious satire; theatre review of *Tartuffe*. Ray Conlogue. photo · *G&M* April 17, 1987: pC7.

The Gipper and The Jaw spice up Tartuffe; article. Robert Martin. photo · *G&M* April 10, 1987: pC9.

Canadian content updates classic 17th-century satire; theatre review of *Tartuffe*. Tom McDougall. photo · *CH* April 13, 1987: pF3.

Moliere's farce gets modern twist; television review of *Tartuffe*. Paul McKie. photo · *WFP* Oct 1, 1987: p40.

TASHLIN, FRANK

Bear gives lesson in keeping identity; theatre review of *I Am a Bear!*. Randal McIlroy. *WFP* Oct 10, 1987: p48.

Actor drawn to play by novelty, challenge of playing a bear; article. Brad Oswald. *WFP* Oct 7, 1987: p39.

TAYLOR, CORA

Billboard: Jon Sigurdson holds fall tea today; column. *WFP* Sept 26, 1987: p43.
[COMPETITIONS, LITERARY; FICTION READINGS; WRITERS' ORGANIZATIONS]

Books nominated for U.S. award; article. *Quill & Quire (Books for Young People)* Oct 1987; Vol 53 No 10: p8.
[AWARDS, LITERARY]

Big responsibilities theme of tall tale and growing-up story; reviews of *The Doll* and *Jacob's Little Giant*. Joan McGrath. photo · *Quill & Quire (Books for Young People)* Aug 1987; Vol 53 No 8: p11.

Novels deal with family breakup; reviews of *The Doll* and *Dear Bruce Springsteen*. Helen Norrie. *WFP* Dec 5, 1987: p57.

Albertan's time travel tale offers reassurance; review of *The Doll*. Susan Scott. photo · *CH* Sept 27, 1987: pE6.

Hard perspectives on traumatic family break-ups; review of *The Doll*. Tim Wynne-Jones. *G&M* Oct 3, 1987: pC22.

TAYLOR, GLADYS

Albertan writes book on women in business; article. photo · *MG* Jan 26, 1987: pC2.
[PUBLISHING AND PUBLISHERS IN CANADA]

TCHEKHOV TCHEKHOVA/Play by François Nocher

Talky treatment for Chekhov's life; theatre review of *Tchekov Tchekova*. Pat Donnelly. photo · *MG* Jan 24, 1987: pC8.

Bouleversante Patricia Nolin; theatre review of *Tchekhov Tchekhova*. Robert Lévesque. photo · *MD* Jan 29, 1987: p5.

[Untitled]; theatre review of *Tchekhov Tchekhova*. Robert Lévesque. *MD* Jan 30, 1987: p7.

[Untitled]; theatre review of *Tchekhov Tchekhova*. Robert Lévesque. *MD* Feb 6, 1987: p7.

[Untitled]; theatre review of *Tchekhov Tchekhova*. Stphane Lpine. photo · *Jeu* 1987; No 42: p161–164.

TCHIPAYUK OU LE CHEMIN DU LOUP/Novel by Ronald Lavallée

Local novelist's Red River saga strikes chord among Europeans; article. *WFP* Dec 18, 1987: p36.

Des mythes canadiens comme les Français les aiment; review of *Tchipayuk ou le chemin du loup*. Jean Éthier-Blais. photo · *MD* Dec 19, 1987: pD10.

La vitrine du livre; review of *Tchipayuk ou le chemin du loup*. Guy Ferland. *MD* Oct 31, 1987: pD4.

TV reporter in Winnipeg suddenly a hit with historical novel on Metis in French; article. Don Macdonald. photo · *G&M* Dec 21, 1987: pC10.

A TEACUP IN A FIELD/Poems by Michelle Hogan-Walker

[Untitled]; reviews of poetry books. Elizabeth Woods. *Poetry Can R* Spring 1987; Vol 8 No 2–3: p49.

TEARS OF A DINOSAUR/Play by Blake Brooker

Friends blend skills into theatre piece; article. Kate Zimmerman. *CH* Nov 22, 1987: pA15.

TEATRO SOUS-SOL COLLECTIVE

Stratford ahead of the game — and it's no overnight miracle; column. Pat Donnelly. *MG* Dec 10, 1987: pD6.
[FESTIVALS, DRAMA]

TEICHROB, KEVIN

Turtle Jazz excruciating; theatre review. Ray Conlogue. photo · *G&M* June 27, 1987: pE8.

TELEVISION AND CANADIAN LITERATURE

Local film stretched to eight-part TV series; article. *WFP* Jan 17, 1987: p21.

Disney to show Anne sequel seven months before Canada; article. *WFP* Feb 14, 1987: p23.

U.S. to see Anne sequel first; article. *CH* Feb 15, 1987: pE3.

Novel slated for TV; article. *WFP* April 9, 1987: p45.

Robertson Davies novel to become TV mini-series; article. *CH* April 9, 1987: pE2.

CBS wins 5 Peabody awards; article. *G&M* April 28, 1987: pC9.

Davies' hit novel to be TV mini-series; article. photo · *TS* April 8, 1987: pD1.

Anne pockets Peabody award; article. *TS* April 26, 1987: pC7.

'Green Gables' wins award; article. *MG* April 28, 1987: pA14.

U.S. critics rave over Anne of Green Gables sequel; article. photo · *MG* May 26, 1987: pD10.
[INTERNATIONAL REVIEWS OF CANADIAN LITERATURE]

Canadian content still 80 per cent but CBC starts prime-time reruns; article. photo · *MG* June 30, 1987: pC8.

Birdsell drama wrapped; article. *WFP* Sept 25, 1987: p29.

Green Gables sequel a winner; article. *MG* Oct 7, 1987: H1.

Les écrivains souhaitent une meilleure "couverture" des médias; article. *MD* Nov 14, 1987: pD15.
[CONFERENCES, LITERARY; RADIO AND CANADIAN LITERATURE]

Anne a U.S. favorite; article. *WFP* Oct 7, 1987: p41.

Sequel reaps awards; article. *CH* Oct 7, 1987: pD2.

Two awards given to Anne's sequel; article. *G&M* Oct 7, 1987: pC7.

Authors' festival film to air; article. *Quill & Quire* Oct 1987; Vol 53 No 10: p12.
[FESTIVALS, LITERARY]

It's good to see and hear feisty Callaghan; television review of *Morley Callaghan: First Person Singular*. Ken Adachi. photo · *TS* March 24, 1987: pC6.

Authors ham it up on TV special; column. Ken Adachi. photo · *TS* Oct 12, 1987: pB5.
[AUTHORS, CANADIAN]

Toronto firm dramatizes U.S. tales; column. Sid Adilman. *TS* Jan 7, 1987: pF1.

Domingo gave opera company a $40,000 break; column. Sid Adilman. *TS* March 13, 1987: pC19.

Claude, Clemence . . . et qui d'autre?; editorial. Rolande Allard-Lacerte. *MD* July 27, 1987: p6.

Anne sequel likely to outdraw original; article. Bill Anderson. photo · *WFP* Dec 1, 1987: p34.

Hockey drama kicks off new Canadian TV season; column. Jim Bawden. photo · *TS* Jan 2, 1987: pD21.

Benny bumbles into a murder in the wilds; television review of *Murder Sees the Light*. Jim Bawden. photo · *TS* March 14, 1987: J6.

Atwood at the cottage; column. Jim Bawden. *TS* April 2, 1987: pG2.

Anne of Green Gables — the Sequel; television review. Jim Bawden. photo · *TS* Dec 5, 1987: pF1,F12.

Portraits of patriarchs; television review of *First Person Singular*. John Bemrose. photo · *Maclean's* March 30, 1987; Vol 100 No 13: p63.

P.E.I.'s spirited redhead returns; article. Bob Blakey. photo · *CH* Dec 2, 1987: pD1.

Murder Sees The Light best left in dark; television review. Mike Boone. *MG* March 13, 1987: pD6.

Anne II: Canadians' love affair resumes; article. Mike Boone. photo · *MG* Dec 4, 1987: pC1.

Brilliantly crafted Green Gables sequel Follows naturally; television review. Mike Boone. *MG* Dec 4, 1987: pC8.

Geminis are sad reminder of TV's glory days; column. Mike Boone. *MG* Dec 9, 1987: pF3.

Anne sequel takes too many liberties; letter to the editor. Maida Campbell. photo · *G&M* Dec 26, 1987: pD7.

Ne s'improvise pas improvisateur qui veut!; column. Paul Cauchon. *MD* Jan 21, 1987: p7.

Cause toujours ma Clémence . . . ; article. Paul Cauchon. photo · *MD* April 10, 1987: p13.

Ceux et celles qui nous disent qui lire; article. Paul Cauchon. *MD* May 2, 1987: pD1,D8.
[RADIO AND CANADIAN LITERATURE]

Les Voisins: scènes de la vie de banlieue; article. Paul Cauchon. photo · *MD* Sept 25, 1987: p15.

[Untitled]; notice. Paul Cauchon. photo · *MD* Oct 9, 1987: p15.

[Untitled]; notice. Paul Cauchon. *MD* Dec 4, 1987: p15.

[Untitled]; notice. Paul Cauchon. *MD* Dec 11, 1987: p13.

Kingsley triumphs in Silas Marner; television review of *Murder Sees the Light*. John Haslett Cuff. photo · *G&M* March 14, 1987: pE5.

Tramp takes the safe route; television review of *Tramp at the Door*. John Haslett Cuff. photo · *G&M* Jan 1, 1987: pC1.

Ambitious hockey saga fails to score; television review of *The Last Season*. John Haslett Cuff. photo · *G&M* Jan 3, 1987: pE5.

Gambles hedged with returns. article. John Haslett Cuff. *G&M* May 30, 1987: pC3.

Mini-series bred from Davies' novel; article. John Haslett Cuff. photo · *G&M* April 8, 1987: pC7.

Film draws engaging portrait; column. John Haslett Cuff. photo · *G&M* July 23, 1987: pD3.

'Compelling' stories from Mrs. Gouzenko; television review of *Voices on the Water*. John Haslett Cuff. *G&M* Oct 17, 1987: pC3.

Slick Anne sequel takes no chances with success; television review. John Haslett Cuff. photo · *G&M* Dec 5, 1987: pC5.

Title tattle; column. Martin Dowding. *Quill & Quire (Books for Young People)* Dec 1987; Vol 53 No 12: p3.
[FILM ADAPTATIONS OF CANADIAN LITERATURE]

A shot in the park; essay. Howard Engel. illus · *G&M* March 14, 1987: pE1.

Médiocrité; letter to the editor. Jean Ferguson. *MD* Feb 24, 1987: p8.

Anne's secret quality keeps her coming back; column. Robert Fulford. *TS* Dec 5, 1987: pF1.

Wrong network; letter to the editor. Mimi Fullerton. *G&M* Oct 19, 1987: pA6.

A wealth of fine films lies waiting in Canadian novels; column. Joan Irwin. *TS* Jan 17, 1987: pG7.
[FILM ADAPTATIONS OF CANADIAN LITERATURE]

"Adieu Albert, je t'aimais bien, tu sais!"; letter to the editor. Claude Jasmin. *MD* Feb 14, 1987: pA10.

Anne of Green Gables grows up; article. Brian D. Johnson. Barbara MacAndrew. photo · *Maclean's* Dec 7, 1987; Vol 100 No 49: p46–48,50.

Brian Moore: this is your life; article. Martin Knelman. *Tor Life* June 1987; Vol 21 No 9: p19.

Authors' festival revisited; article. Martin Knelman. *Tor Life* Oct 1987; Vol 21 No 1[5]: 17.
[FESTIVALS, LITERARY]

[Untitled]; television review of *Anne of Green Gables — The Sequel*. Martin Knelman. photo · *Tor Life* Dec 1987; Vol 21 No 18: p131.

Morley Callaghan, past & present; television review of *Morley Callaghan: First Person Singular*. Gina Mallet. photo · *Chatelaine* April 1987; Vol 60 No 4: p22.

[Untitled]; letter to the editor. Alberto Manguel. *G&M* Oct 17, 1987: pD7.

Manitobans get month in spotlight on CBC TV, radio; column. Doreen Martens. *WFP* Feb 23, 1987: p14.
[RADIO AND CANADIAN LITERATURE]

Expect the unexpected in off-beat murder mystery; television review of *Murder Sees the Light*. Doreen Martens. *WFP* March 13, 1987: p31.

A Way Out may not thrill residents of Beausejour; column. Doreen Martens. *WFP* March 14, 1987: p23.

Washing Machine give hilarious twist to technophobia tale; television review. Doreen Martens. photo · *WFP* March 21, 1987: p25.

Choreographer's dance fantasy pieces dramatic, sensuous; column. Doreen Martens. *WFP* March 23, 1987: p17.

Loquacious Layton a joy to hear; television review of *Poet: Irving Layton Observed*. Doreen Martens. photo · *WFP* July 25, 1987: p47.

First novel turned into TV movie; column. Kenneth McGoogan. *CH* May 3, 1987: pE6.
[CONFERENCES, LITERARY]

All Sales Final subtle family drama focusing on lost romance, death; column. Paul McKie. photo · *WFP* Oct 17, 1987: p30.

Selling doesn't mean selling out; article. Paul McKie. photo · *WFP* Oct 24, 1987: p22.

Niagara Falls boring television; television review. Paul McKie. photo · *WFP* Nov 9, 1987: p22.

Anne sequel wonderfully fresh fare amid TV drudgery; television review of *Anne of Green Gables: The Sequel*. Paul McKie. photo · *WFP* Dec 4, 1987: p35.

Documentary profiles witty author; television review of *The Lonely Passion of Brian Moore*. Henry Mietkiewicz. photo · *TS* July 22, 1987: pD3.

The artist behind Irving Layton's bravado; television review of *Poet: Irving Layton Observed*. Henry Mietkiewicz. photo · *TS* July 30, 1987: H5.

Les ondes littéraires; list of radio and television programs. Marc Morin. *MD* Oct 31, 1987: pD2.
[RADIO AND CANADIAN LITERATURE]

Les ondes littéraire; list of radio and television programs. Marc Morin. *MD* Nov 7, 1987: pD2.
[RADIO AND CANADIAN LITERATURE]

Les ondes littéraires; list of radio and television programs. Marc Morin. *MD* Nov 14, 1987: pD14.
[RADIO AND CANADIAN LITERATURE]

Les ondes littéraires; list of radio and television programs. Marc Morin. *MD* Nov 21, 1987: pD2.
[RADIO AND CANADIAN LITERATURE]

Les ondes littéraires; list of radio and television programs. Marc Morin. *MD* Nov 28, 1987: pD12.
[RADIO AND CANADIAN LITERATURE]

Les ondes littéraires; list of radio and television programs. Marc Morin. *MD* Dec 5, 1987: pD2.
[RADIO AND CANADIAN LITERATURE]

Les ondes littéraires; list of radio and television programs. Marc Morin. *MD* Dec 12, 1987: pD2.
[RADIO AND CANADIAN LITERATURE]

Les ondes littéraires; list of radio and television programs. Marc Morin. *MD* Dec 24, 1987: pC10.
[RADIO AND CANADIAN LITERATURE]

Les ondes littéraires; list of radio and television programs. Marc Morin. *MD* Dec 31, 1987: pC10.
[RADIO AND CANADIAN LITERATURE]

Les ondes littéraires; list of radio and television programs. Marc Morin. *MD* Dec 19, 1987: pD2.

Bumbling Benny takes new case; television review of *Murder Sees the Light*. Bill Musselwhite. photo · *CH* March 14, 1987: pF6.

La littérature en perte de vitesse!; letter to the editor. Yves Préfontaine. *MD* Aug 12, 1987: p8.

Vrai et faux; letter to the editor. Robert Roy. *MD* Jan 8, 1987: p8.

La vie littéraire; column. Jean Royer. photo · *MD* Jan 3, 1987: pC2.
[CULTURAL IDENTITY; WRITERS' ORGANIZATIONS]

La vie littéraire; column. Jean Royer. photo · *MD* Jan 10, 1987: pB2.
[AWARDS, LITERARY; POETRY READINGS; RADIO AND CANADIAN LITERATURE; WRITERS' WORKSHOPS]

Q-S congédiera Jasmin mais gardera l'émission; article. Jean Royer. *MD* Jan 15, 1987: p6.

La vie littéraire; column. Jean Royer. *MD* Jan 17, 1987: pB2.
[AWARDS, LITERARY; CONFERENCES, LITERARY; RADIO AND CANADIAN LITERATURE]

La vie littéraire; column. Jean Royer. *MD* Jan 31, 1987: pB2.
[CANADIAN LITERARY PERIODICALS; COMPETITIONS, LITERARY; RADIO AND CANADIAN LITERATURE]

La vie littéraire; column. Jean Royer. *MD* Feb 7, 1987: pB2.
[COMPETITIONS, LITERARY; CONFERENCES, LITERARY; POETRY READINGS; PUBLISHING AND PUBLISHERS IN CANADA; WRITERS' WORKSHOPS]

La vie littéraire; column. Jean Royer. *MD* Feb 14, 1987: pC2.
[AWARDS, LITERARY; CANADIAN LITERARY PERIODICALS; COMPETITIONS, LITERARY; FICTION READINGS; POETRY READINGS; RADIO AND CANADIAN LITERATURE]

La vie littéraire; column. Jean Royer. *MD* Feb 21, 1987: pB2.
[CANADIAN LITERARY PUBLISHING; COMPETITIONS, LITERARY; POETRY READINGS; WRITERS' ORGANIZATIONS]

La vie littéraire; column. Jean Royer. *MD* Feb 28, 1987: pC2.
[AWARDS, LITERARY; CANADIAN LITERARY PERIODICALS; CANADIAN LITERARY PUBLISHING; CONFERENCES, LITERARY; RADIO AND CANADIAN LITERATURE]

La vie littéraire; column. Jean Royer. *MD* March 7, 1987: pB2.
[AWARDS, LITERARY; CANADIAN LITERARY PUBLISHING; POETRY READINGS; RADIO AND CANADIAN LITERATURE; WRITERS' ORGANIZATIONS]

La vie littéraire; column. Jean Royer. photo · *MD* March 14, 1987: pD4.
[AWARDS, LITERARY; POETRY READINGS; RADIO AND CANADIAN LITERATURE]

La vie littéraire; column. Jean Royer. photo · *MD* March 21, 1987: pD2.
[AWARDS, LITERARY; CANADIAN LITERARY PUBLISHING; COMPETITIONS, LITERARY; POETRY READINGS; RADIO AND CANADIAN LITERATURE]

La vie littéraire; column. Jean Royer. photo · *MD* March 28, 1987: pD2.
[CONFERENCES, LITERARY; FESTIVALS, LITERARY; GOVERNMENT GRANTS FOR WRITERS/PUBLISHERS; RADIO AND CANADIAN LITERATURE]

La vie littéraire; column. Jean Royer. photo · *MD* April 11, 1987: pD2.
[AWARDS, LITERARY; FILM ADAPTATIONS OF CANADIAN LITERATURE; POETRY READINGS; RADIO AND CANADIAN LITERATURE]

La vie littéraire; column. Jean Royer. photo · *MD* April 18, 1987: pD2.
[INTERNATIONAL WRITERS' ORGANIZATIONS; RADIO AND CANADIAN LITERATURE]

La vie littéraire; column. Jean Royer. *MD* April 25, 1987: pD2.
[AWARDS, LITERARY; CONFERENCES, LITERARY; FESTIVALS, LITERARY; FICTION READINGS; POETRY READINGS; RADIO AND CANADIAN LITERATURE]

La vie littéraire; column. Jean Royer. photo · *MD* May 2, 1987: pD2.
[AWARDS, LITERARY; INTERNATIONAL REVIEWS OF CANADIAN LITERATURE; RADIO AND CANADIAN LITERATURE; WRITERS' ORGANIZATIONS]

La vie littéraire; column. Jean Royer. *MD* May 9, 1987: pD2.
[CONFERENCES, LITERARY; POETRY READINGS; RADIO AND CANADIAN LITERATURE]

La vie littéraire; column. Jean Royer. photo · *MD* May 16, 1987: pD2.
[AWARDS, LITERARY; CONFERENCES, LITERARY; PUBLISHING AND PUBLISHERS IN CANADA; RADIO AND CANADIAN LITERATURE]

La vie littéraire; column. Jean Royer. photo · *MD* May 23, 1987: pD2.
[CULTURAL IDENTITY; RADIO AND CANADIAN LITERATURE; WRITERS' ORGANIZATIONS]

La vie littéraire; column. Jean Royer. photo · *MD* May 30, 1987: pD2.
[AWARDS, LITERARY; CANADIAN LITERARY PUBLISHING; COMPETITIONS, LITERARY; FESTIVALS, LITERARY; RADIO AND CANADIAN LITERATURE]

La vie littéraire; column. Jean Royer. photo · *MD* June 6, 1987: pD2.
[GOVERNOR GENERAL'S AWARDS; INTERNATIONAL REVIEWS OF CANADIAN LITERATURE; RADIO AND CANADIAN LITERATURE]

La vie littéraire; column. Jean Royer. photo · *MD* June 13, 1987: pD2.
[AWARDS, LITERARY; COMPETITIONS, LITERARY; POETRY READINGS; RADIO AND CANADIAN LITERATURE; WRITERS' ORGANIZATIONS]

Quatre Saisons laisse tomber son émission littéraire; article. Jean Royer. *MD* June 17, 1987: p13.

La vie littéraire; column. Jean Royer. photo · *MD* June 20, 1987: pD2.
[AUTHORS, CANADIAN; POETRY READINGS; RADIO AND CANADIAN LITERATURE]

Les ondes littéraires; list of radio and television programmes. Jean Royer. *MD* Sept 12, 1987: pD2.
[RADIO AND CANADIAN LITERATURE]

Les ondes littéraires; list of radio and television programmes. Jean Royer. *MD* Sept 19, 1987: pD2.
[RADIO AND CANADIAN LITERATURE]

Les ondes littéraires; list of radio and television programmes. Jean Royer. *MD* Sept 26, 1987: pD2.
[RADIO AND CANADIAN LITERATURE]

Les ondes littéraires; list of radio and television programs. Jean Royer. *MD* Oct 3, 1987: pD2.
[RADIO AND CANADIAN LITERATURE]

Les ondes littéraires; list of radio and television programs. Jean Royer. *MD* Oct 10, 1987: pD2.
[RADIO AND CANADIAN LITERATURE]

Les ondes littéraires; list of radio and television programs. Jean Royer. *MD* Oct 17, 1987: pD2.
[RADIO AND CANADIAN LITERATURE]

Les ondes littéraires; list of radio and television programs. Jean Royer. *MD* Oct 24, 1987: pD2.
[RADIO AND CANADIAN LITERATURE]

Le Matou d'Yves Beauchemin: du fait littéraire à la chaîne de productions-médias; article. Catherine Saouter. *Voix et images* Spring 1987; Vol 12 No 3: p393–402.
[FILM ADAPTATIONS OF CANADIAN LITERATURE]

Bestsellers on TV, and a sunny summer romance; column. Diana Shepherd. *Quill & Quire* Sept 1987; Vol 53 No 9: p72.
[ROMANTIC FICTION]

Book world: winners or losers? Wait for returns; column. Beverley Slopen. *TS* Feb 22, 1987: pA18.

Male director adds richness to short-story filming, author says; article. Morley Walker. photo · *WFP* March 19, 1987: p42.

My Cousin's director brings you tears next; article. Rita Zekas. photo · *TS* Oct 18, 1987: pG6.

THE TELLING OF LIES/Novel by Timothy Findley

How English rose, prospered and begat new tongues; review of *The Telling of Lies*. Barbara Black. *MG* Dec 19, 1987: J13.

[Untitled]; review of *The Telling of Lies*. Wilfred Cude. *Antigonish R* Winter 1987; No 68: p55–60.

Top flight practitioners of the craft of writing mysteries; review of *The Telling of Lies*. Douglas Hill. *G&M* Nov 21, 1987: pC21.

[Untitled]; review of *The Telling of Lies*. Catherine Hunter. *Malahat R (special issue)* March 1987; No 78: p148–151

Murder & lies; reviews of *A Single Death* and *The Telling of Lies*. Linda Hutcheon. *Can Lit* Winter 1987; No 115: p225–227.

TELLING THE TALE/Short stories by Robin Skelton

The thrill of reading intoxicating stories; review of *Telling the Tale*. T.F. Rigelhof. *G&M* Sept 5, 1987: pC13.

[Untitled]; reviews of *Telling the Tale* and *The Parrot Who Could*. Norman Sigurdson. *Books in Can* Nov 1987; Vol 16 No 8: p25–26.

TEMPLETON, CHARLES

CNE goers always knew that Chuck was a hustler; biographical article. George Gamester. *TS* Sept 3, 1987: pA2.

[Untitled]; review of *The Queen's Secret*. Douglas Malcolm. *Books in Can* Jan-Feb 1987; Vol 16 No 1: p26.

Paperclips: Rivoche's robots . . . on the cookbook beat . . . Templeton's teddy; column. Beverley Slopen. *Quill & Quire* March 1987; Vol 53 No 3: p64.

Book world: 'new' terrorists like their perks, author suggests; column. Beverley Slopen. *TS* May 10, 1987: pA22.

LE TEMPS D'UNE PAIX/Play by Claude Deschênes and Camille Deschênes

Le Temps d'une paix est transposé au théâtre; article. *MD* Aug 1, 1987: pC3.

LE TEMPS D'UNE VIE/Play by Roland Lepage

Plenty of life left in this classic; theatre review of *Le Temps d'une vie*. Pat Donnelly. *MG* Sept 18, 1987: pC10.

LE TEMPS EST AU NOIR/Play by Robert Claing

Le théâtre qu'on joue; theatre reviews. André Dionne. photo · *Lettres québec* Winter 1986–87; No 44: p53–54.

LE TEMPS SAUVAGE/Play by Anne Hébert

Idéologie féministe dans Le Temps sauvage et C'tait avant la guerre l'Anse Gilles; article. Monique Genuist. abstract · *Theatre Hist in Can (special issue)* Spring 1987; Vol 8 No 1: p49–58.
[FEMINIST DRAMA]

THE TEMPTATIONS OF BIG BEAR/Novel by Rudy Wiebe

Historicity in historical fiction: Burning Water and The Temptations Of Big Bear; article. Carla Visser. *Studies in Can Lit* 1987; Vol 12 No 1: p90–111.
[HISTORICAL FICTION]

TEMPTONGA: THE REDDEST WOMAN IN THE WORLD/Play by Ida Carnevali

Temptonga doesn't let audience in on the plot; theatre review. Henry Mietkiewicz. photo · *TS* April 10, 1987: pD12.

TEN TANDEM VIA YORK/Poetry anthology

[Untitled]; reviews of poetry books. Shaunt Basmajian. *Cross Can Writ Q* 1987; Vol 9 No 3–4: p44,49.
[ANTHOLOGIES: BOOK REVIEWS]

TENNANT, VERONICA

Bugs, battles & ballet; reviews of *On Stage, Please* and *Redcoat*. James Gellert. *Can Lit* Winter 1987; No 115: p220–223.
[FIRST NOVELS: BOOK REVIEWS]

TEQUILA SUNRISE/Poems by Erik Martinez

[Untitled]; review of *Tequila Sunrise*. Antonio D'Alfonso. *Poetry Can R* Spring 1987; Vol 8 No 2–3: p36–37.

LES TERRES DU SONGE/Poems by Robert Lalonde

L'originalité et l'oralité; reviews of *Coq à deux têtes* and *Les Terres du songe*. Jean Royer. *MD* May 30, 1987: pD3.

A TERRIBLE BEAUTY (THE NONSENSE OF WAR)/Play by Thomas Legg

Legg pulls off one-man show; theatre review of *A Terrible Beauty*. Sherri Clegg. *CH* April 4, 1987: pB6.

TERRORISME ET BEAUTÉ/Novel by Alexis Klimov

[Untitled]; reviews. Raymond Martin. *Moebius* Winter 1987; No 31: p164–166.

TERRORISTES D'AMOUR suivi de JOURNAL D'UNE FICTION/Poems by Carole David

[Untitled]; review of *Terroristes d'amour*. Jean-Paul Daoust. *Estuaire* Spring 1987; No 44: p80.

[Untitled]; review of *Terroristes d'amour*. Jean Royer. *MD* March 13, 1987: p15.

TERRY, JUDITH ANN

[Untitled]; review of *Miss Abigail's Part*. Mary Lou Cornish. *Cross Can Writ Q* 1987; Vol 9 No 3–4: p49.
[FIRST NOVELS: BOOK REVIEWS]

[Untitled]; review of *Miss Abigail's Part*. Maureen Corrigan. *NYT Book R* March 1, 1987: p20.
[FIRST NOVELS: BOOK REVIEWS]

Family continuum; review of *Miss Abigail's Part*. Andrea Lebowitz. *Can Lit* Winter 1987; No 115: p152–155.
[FIRST NOVELS: BOOK REVIEWS]

[Untitled]; review of *Miss Abigail's Part*. Mary Millar. *Queen's Q* Summer 1987; Vol 94 No 2: p477–478.
[FIRST NOVELS: BOOK REVIEWS]

TESSERACTS/Short story anthology

SF for survival; review of *Tesseracts*. Douglas Barbour. *Can Lit* Spring 1987; No 112: p141–143.

TESSLER, HOWARD

[Untitled]; reviews of poetry books. Anne Burke. *Poetry Can R* Summer 1987; Vol 8 No 4: p38.

[Untitled]; review of *Saturday Nights at the Ritz*. David Manicom. *Rubicon* Spring 1987; No 8: p216–217.

LE TESTAMENT DE MADAME LEGENDRE/Children's novel by Josée Dufour

Une petite fille qui ne manque pas de courage; review of *Le Testament de Madame Legendre*. Pierrette Dubé. *Can Child Lit* 1987; No 48: p86–87.

LE TESTAMENT/Play by Bertin St-Pierre

Un texte dense et beau; theatre review of *Le Testament*. Jean Cléo Godin. photo · *Jeu* 1987; No 44: p191–192.

TÊTE À TÊTE/Play by Ralph Burdman

Marriage of true minds; theatre review of *Tête à tête*. John Bemrose. photo · *Maclean's* Sept 21, 1987; Vol 100 No 38: p50.

Tete-a-Tete worthwhile for its wit and elegance; theatre review. Ray Conlogue. photo · *G&M* Nov 13, 1987: pD13.

Play dares to add levity to legacy; theatre review of *Tête à tête*. Robert Crew. photo · *TS* Nov 15, 1987: pC2.

From English to French to English; article. Pat Donnelly. photo · *MG* Sept 5, 1987: pC6.

Lightweight Tête-à-Tête an evening of intimacy; theatre review. Pat Donnelly. *MG* Sept 10, 1987: pC14.

[Untitled]; theatre reviews. Pat Donnelly. *MG* Sept 11, 1987: pC8.

[Untitled]; theatre reviews of *Tête à tête* and *Les Feluettes*. Pat Donnelly. *MG* Sept 18, 1987: pC8.

[Untitled]; theatre review of *Tête à tête*. Solange Lévesque. photo · *Jeu* 1987; No 43: p167–168.

[Untitled]; theatre reviews of *Oublier* and *Tête à tête*. Robert Lévesque. *MD* Nov 6, 1987: p15.

Une centième au Café de la Place; article. Robert Lévesque. photo · *MD* Dec 3, 1987: p13

[Untitled]; theatre reviews. Gina Mallet. *G&M (Toronto Magazine)* Nov 1987; Vol 2 No 8: p29.

Blowing bubbles with Simone and Sartre; column. Vit Wagner. photo · *TS* Nov 6, 1987: pE4.
[TRANSLATIONS OF CANADIAN LITERATURE]

TÉTREAU, JEAN

La statue de François Hertel; review of *Hertel, l'homme et l'oeuvre*. Réjean Beaudoin. *Liberté* Feb 1987; Vol 29 No 1: p100–104.

Un oeil ouvert sur le monde, l'autre ferm sur soi; review of *Hertel, l'homme et l'oeuvre*. Yolande Gris. photo · *Lettres québec* Winter 1986–87; No 44: p60–61.

[Untitled]; review of *Hertel, l'homme et l'oeuvre*. Robert Major. *U of Toronto Q* Fall 1987; Vol 57 No 1: p185–186.

À propos de Jean Tétreau, Hertel l'homme et l'oeuvre; review. Guylaine Massoutre. *Voix et images* Spring 1987; Vol 12 No 3: p527–530.

[Untitled]; review of *Hertel, l'homme et l'oeuvre*. Agnes Whitfield. *Queen's Q* Autumn 1987; Vol 94 No 3: p687–688.

TEXTURES EN TEXTES/Poems by Germaine Beaulieu

[Untitled]; review of *Textures en textes*. Anne-Marie Alonzo. *Estuaire* Spring 1987; No 44: p79.

[Untitled]; reviews of poetry books. Jacques St-Pierre. *Moebius* Winter 1987; No 31: p137–139.

THEATRE BRATS COLLECTIVE

Kids speak on their own behalf; theatre review of *Forever Young*. Ray Conlogue. photo · *G&M* Jan 3, 1987: pE8.

THÉÂTRE DE LA MARMAILLE COLLECTIVE

Disturbing play incoherent; theatre review of *Parasols*. Reg Skene. *WFP* May 1, 1987: p35

LE THÉÂTRE POUR ENFANTS AU QUÉBEC: 1950–1980/Critical work by Hlne Beauchamp

[Untitled]; review of *Le Théâtre pour enfants au Québec: 1950–1980*. Gilbert David. *Jeu* 1987; No 42: p176–179.

Une analyse éclairante du théâtre pour enfants; review of *Le Théâtre pour enfants au Québec*. Elvine Gignac-Pharand. *Can Child Lit* 1987; No 46: p95–96.

THEATRE AND POLITICS IN MODERN QUEBEC/Critical work by Elaine F. Nardocchio

[Untitled]; review of *Theatre and Politics in Modern Quebec*. Denis Carrier. *Theatre Hist in Can* Fall 1987; Vol 8 No 2: p243–245.

[Untitled]; reviews of *Theatre and Politics in Modern Quebec* and *French-Canadian Theater*. L.E. Doucette. *U of Toronto Q* Fall 1987; Vol 57 No 1: p186–189.

[Untitled]; review of *Theatre and Politics in Modern Quebec*. Debra Martens. *Rubicon* Fall 1987; No 9: p177–179.

Drama summary; review of *Theatre and Politics in Modern Québec*. Jane Moss. *Can Lit* Winter 1987; No 115: p175–176.

[Untitled]; review of *Theatre and Politics in Modern Quebec*. Renate Usmiani. *Can Theatre R* Spring 1987; No 50: p84–85.

Vue lointaine d'un Québec pas si moderne; review of *Theatre and Politics in Modern Québec*. Louise Vigeant. *Jeu* 1987; No 45: p222–223.

[Untitled]; review of *Theatre and Politics in Modern Quebec*. Jonathan M. Weiss. *Amer R of Can Studies* Autumn 1987; Vol 17 No 3: p358–359.

THÉÂTRE PARMINOU COLLECTIVE

Parminou parmi nous; article. *MD* Oct 22, 1987: p15

Le Théâtre Parminou: une année bien remplie; article. *MD* Nov 13, 1987: p15

Play examines porn issues; theatre review of *Intimate Invasion*. Brian Brennan. *CH* Nov 6, 1987: pE8

Actors explore effects of porn; article. Brad Oswald. photo · *WFP* Sept 9, 1987: p36

Porn purveyors assailed in play; theatre review of *Intimate Invasion*. Kate Zimmerman. *CH* Nov 15, 1987: pF2

THEATRE PASSE MURAILLE COLLECTIVE

Play retells story of 1837 rebellion; article. Lynne Ainsworth. photo · *TS (Neighbours)* June 30, 1987: p19.

Farmer's Rebellion stands test of time; theatre review of *1837: The Farmers' Revolt*. Ray Conlogue. *G&M* Dec 8, 1987: pD7.

1837 revolt hits centre stage; article. Robert Davis. photo · *TS (Neighbors)* Aug 11, 1987: p16.

Pythagoras's problem; theatre review of *Pythagoras — The Mystery*. Liam Lacey. photo · *G&M* July 23, 1987: pD5.

Pythagoras mystery makes audience play archeologist; theatre review of *Pythagoras — The Mystery*. Henry Mietkiewicz. *TS* July 24, 1987: pE9.

Summer theatre takes on a new twist; article. Betty Zyvatkauskas. photo · *G&M* July 11, 1987: pE7.

THÉÂTRE PETIT À PETIT COLLECTIVE

[Untitled]; theatre review of *Bain public*. Pierre Lavoie. photo · *Jeu* 1987; No 42: p168–169

Théâtre didactique; reviews of *Mademoiselle Autobody* and *Sortie de secours*. Lucie Robert. *Voix et images* Autumn 1987; Vol 13 No 1: p196–198

THÉÂTRE REPÈRE COLLECTIVE

Des dragons sur la colline; article. *MD* Feb 25, 1987: p9

"O.K. on change!"; article. Lorraine Camerlain. photo · *Jeu* 1987; No 45: p83–97

Questions sur des questions; essay. Lorraine Camerlain. photo · *Jeu* 1987; No 45: p164–168

Questions sur une démarche; essay. Jean-Luce Denis. photo · *Jeu* 1987; No 45: p159–163

Tenir l'univers dans sa main; article. Solange Lévesque. photo · *Jeu* 1987; No 45: p111–120

Du hasard et de la nécessité: genèse de l'oeuvre; essay. Pierre Lavoie. photo · *Jeu* 1987; No 45: p169–170

Points de repère: entretiens avec les créateurs; interview with the Théâtre Repère collective. Pierre Lavoie. Lorraine Camerlain. photo · *Jeu* 1987; No 45: p177–208

Reconstitution de "La Trilogie"; article. Diane Pavlovic. photo · *Jeu* 1987; No 45: p40–82

Le sable et les étoiles; article. Diane Pavlovic. photo · *Jeu* 1987; No 45: p121–140

Magie et mysticisme: comment (ne pas) expliquer l'inexplicable; essay. Philippe Soldevila. photo · *Jeu* 1987; No 45: p171–176

Entre le jouet de pacotille et la voûte céleste: le voyage des personnages à travers les objets; article. Michel Vaïs. photo · *Jeu* 1987; No 45: p98–110

THEATRELIFE/Play by Sky Gilbert

Theatrelife takes typecasting to the limit; article about Graham Harley. Robert Crew. photo · *TS* March 27, 1987: pD14.

Theatrelife exposes raw side of the stage; theatre review. Robert Crew. photo · *TS* March 30, 1987: pB3.

Theatrelife stylish, ingenious; theatre review. Liam Lacey. photo · *G&M* April 1, 1987: pC5.

THÉORET, FRANCE

[Untitled]; review of *Féminins singuliers*. Anne-Marie Picard. *U of Toronto Q* Fall 1987; Vol 57 No 1: p200–201.

La vitrine du livre; reviews. Jean Royer. photo · *MD* March 21, 1987: pD2.
[CANADIAN LITERARY PERIODICALS]

THERE'S A DRAGON IN MY CLOSET/Children's story by John F. Green

[Untitled]; review of *There's a Dragon in My Closet*. Teresa Cowan. *Quill & Quire (Books for Young People)* April 1987; Vol 53 No 4: p5.

Thrills and chills: hints for Hallowe'en reading; reviews of children's books. Joan McGrath. illus · *Quill & Quire (Books for Young People)* Oct 1987; Vol 53 No 10: p8.
[ANTHOLOGIES: BOOK REVIEWS]

Mini-reviews; reviews of children's stories. Mary Rubio. *Can Child Lit* 1987; No 46: p105–109.

Escape from reality; review of *There's a Dragon in My Closet*. Tim Wynne-Jones. *G&M* April 18, 1987: pC18.

THÉRIAULT, MARIE JOSÉ

Des contes et des nouvelles pour rêver; reviews of short story books. Dominique Garand. *Voix et images* Spring 1987; Vol 12 No 3: p551–555.
[ANTHOLOGIES: BOOK REVIEWS]

D'abominables dlices; review of *L'Envoleur de chevaux et autres contes*. Michel Lord. *Lettres québec* Winter 1986–87; No 44: p81.

THÉRIAULT, YVES

Une bibliographie indispensable; review of *Bibliographie analytique d'Yves Thériault, 1940–1984*. Anthony Purdy. *Can Child Lit* 1987; No 45: p54–55.

Une oeuvre multiforme: les livres d'Yves Thériault pour adolescents; article. Claude Romney. bibliog · *Can Child Lit* 1987; No 47: p12–22.
[NATIVE CANADIANS IN LITERATURE]

Sommaires; reviews. Adrien Thério. *Lettres québec* Summer 1987; No 46: p80.

THESEN, SHARON

Lowry's mouths; review of *Confabulations*. Ronald Binns. *Can Lit* Spring 1987; No 112: p85–87.

Confabulation; review of *Confabulations*. Sherrill Grace. illus · *Essays on Can Writ* Spring 1987; No 34: p18–23.

THEY SHALL INHERIT THE EARTH/Novel by Morley Callaghan

[They Shall Inherit the Earth]; review. Dorothy Livesay. *Brick* Winter 1987; No 29: p47–48.

THIESSEN, VERN

Festival One plays singularly successful; theatre reviews. Stephen Godfrey. photo · *G&M* May 8, 1987: pF9.
[FESTIVALS, DRAMA]

Courier's inner conflict makes terrific theatre; theatre review of *The Courier*. Reg Skene. *WFP* May 7, 1987: p43.

THE THIN EDGE/Play by Conni Massing

Last of the makeovers; theatre review of *The Thin Edge*. Don Perkins. *NeWest R* Feb 1987; Vol 12 No 6: p17.

THIN ICE/Play by Banuta Rubess and Beverley Cooper

Theatre Direct probes urban kids' reality; theatre reviews of *The Snake Lady* and *Thin Ice*. Ray Conlogue. *G&M* April 29, 1987: pC7.

Teens need to see play on vital issue; column. Lois Sweet. *TS* April 20, 1987: pC1.

THIN POEMS/Poems by James Hutchison

Chapbooks range from good to silly; reviews of poetry books. Robert Quickenden. *WFP* Jan 31, 1987: p55.

THIS IS NOT FOR YOU/Novel by Jane Rule

Imprecise intertwinings; review of *This Is Not for You*. Jane O'Grady. *Times Lit Supp* June 26, 1987; No 4395: p698.

THIS IS WHAT HAPPENS IN ORANGEVILLE/Play by Hillar Liitoja

Bold style masks some flimsy ideas; theatre review of *This Is What Happens In Orangeville*. Marianne Ackerman. *MG* June 5, 1987: pD2.

Force of evil unveiled in play about murder; theatre review of *This Is What Happens in Orangeville*. Liam Lacey. photo · *G&M* Jan 31, 1987: pE4.

THIS ONE'S ON ME: THE BANDY PAPERS/Novel by Donald Jack

Behind that mournful face there truly is a sad person; review of *This One's on Me*. Christopher Braden. photo · *TS* Nov 14, 1987: M4.

Bandy Papers mix bizarre humor with just a touch of the tragic; review of *This One's on Me*. Tom Saunders. *WFP* Nov 7, 1987: p54.

[Untitled]; review of *This One's on Me*. Thomas P. Sullivan. *Quill & Quire* Nov 1987; Vol 53 No 11: p25.

THIS WON'T LAST FOREVER/Poems by Colin Morton

Frost shadows; reviews of poetry books. Andrew Taylor. *Can Lit* Winter 1987; No 115: p197–199.

THOMAS' SNOWSUIT/L'HABIT DE NEIGE/Children's story by Robert Munsch

Littérature jeunesse; reviews of children's books. Domique Demers. *MD* Oct 10, 1987: pD6.

THE THOMAS CHANDLER HALIBURTON SYMPO-SIUM/Conference report

Reappraisals; review of *The Thomas Chandler Haliburton Symposium*. R.L. McDougall. *Can Lit* Spring 1987; No 112: p186–188.

THOMAS, AUDREY

Only pen and paper for author; article. photo · *TS* April 4, 1987: pF8.

Latecomer to fiction-writing a talent to watch; column. Ken Adachi. photo · *TS* Oct 19, 1987: pC5.
[AWARDS, LITERARY; FESTIVALS, LITERARY]

Last-minute readers and party-bound writers; article. John Allemang. photo · *G&M* Oct 21, 1987: pC9.
[AWARDS, LITERARY; FESTIVALS, LITERARY]

The country of the human heart; review of *Goodbye Harold, Good Luck*. Diana Austin. *Fiddlehead* Spring 1987; No 151: p107–110.

Country manners; reviews of *The Progress of Love* and *Goodbye Harold, Good Luck*. Julie Beddoes. *Brick* Winter 1987; No 29: p24–27.

Story postponed; review of *Goodbye Harold, Good Luck*. Margery Fee. *Can Lit* Winter 1987; No 115: p218–220.

[Untitled]; reviews of short story collections. Carole Gerson. *Queen's Q* Summer 1987; Vol 94 No 2: p483–484.

How short story writers can gain their literary credibility; review of *Goodbye Harold, Good Luck*. Douglas Hill. *G&M* April 18, 1987: pC17.

Sailing the oceans of the world; article. Lorna Irvine. *New Q* Spring-Summer 1987; Vol 7 No 1–2: p284–293.
[ARTIST FIGURE; FEMINIST WRITING AND CRITICISM; WOMEN IN LITERATURE]

The Bell Jar and Mrs. Blood: portraits of the artist as divided woman; article. Elizabeth Potvin. abstract · *Atlantis* Fall 1987; Vol 13 No 1: p38–46.
[ARTIST FIGURE; FEMINIST WRITING AND CRITICISM; WOMEN IN LITERATURE]

THOMAS, COLIN

[Untitled]; review of *One Thousand Cranes*. David Booth. *Quill & Quire (Books for Young People)* June 1987; Vol 53 No 6: p11.

Tandis qu'on négocie au sommet, un millier d'oiseaux chantent la paix; theatre review of *Un Millier d'oiseaux*. Angèle Dagenais. photo · MD Dec 11, 1987: p11.

Oiseaux makes nuclear point without traumatizing kids; theatre review of *Un Millier d'oiseaux*. Pat Donnelly. MG Dec 19, 1987: pE9.

THOMPSON, DAVID

Three new faces deserving discovery; reviews of crime novels. Margaret Cannon. photo · G&M Oct 17, 1987: pE4.

Plotting against the royals; reviews of *Broken English* and *Merlin's Web*. Brian Kappler. MG Nov 7, 1987: K13.

Local heroes; reviews of first novels. Janice Kulyk Keefer. *Books in Can* Nov 1987; Vol 16 No 8: p35,37.
[FIRST NOVELS: BOOK REVIEWS]

[Untitled]; review of *Broken English*. John North. *Quill & Quire* Nov 1987; Vol 53 No 11: p24.
[FIRST NOVELS: BOOK REVIEWS]

THOMPSON, JUDITH

Love among the ruins; theatre review of *I Am Yours*. John Bemrose. *Maclean's* Nov 30, 1987; Vol 100 No 48: p65.

I Am Yours wages a comedy war of women; theatre review. Ray Conlogue. photo · G&M Nov 18, 1987: pC6.

Thompson play true to form; theatre review of *I Am Yours*. Robert Crew. photo · TS Nov 18, 1987: pB1.

Trying to crack the big time; article. Deirdre Kelly. photo · G&M April 7, 1987: pC7.

[Untitled]; theatre reviews. Gina Mallet. *G&M (Toronto Magazine)* Nov 1987; Vol 2 No 8: p29.

Play likely to be tough viewing; article. Brad Oswald. photo · WFP Nov 7, 1987: p23.

THOMPSON, KENT

Short short stories by Kent Thompson; review of *Leaping Up Sliding Away*. Roger MacDonald. *Atlan Prov Book R* Feb-March 1987; Vol 14 No 1: p18.

In the mode; reviews of short story collections. Allan Weiss. *Books in Can* April 1987; Vol 16 No 3: p30-31.

THOMPSON, LEE BRISCOE

[Untitled]; review of *Dorothy Livesay*. Lorna Irvine. *Amer R of Can Studies* Winter 1987-88; Vol 17 No 4: p452-453.

Quilting — a spiral of experience; review of *Dorothy Livesay*. R. Alex Kizuk. *Can Poet* Fall-Winter 1987; No 21: p110-115.

THOMPSON, PEGGY

Brides in Space launched on a mission impossible; theatre review of *Brides in Space*. Stephen Godfrey. photo · G&M Jan 15, 1987: pD1.

THOMPSON, RICHARD

Chit chat; column. Maria Casas. *Quill & Quire (Books for Young People)* Oct 1987; Vol 53 No 10: p8.

From giant snakes to punk pigeons: escapism at its best; reviews of children's stories. Bernie Goedhart. *Quill & Quire (Books for Young People)* June 1987; Vol 53 No 6: p5.

THOMSEN, AIRDRIE

Snoring, smuggling, and snuggling; reviews of children's stories. Susan Perren. *Quill & Quire (Books for Young People)* Dec 1987; Vol 53 No 12: p8.

THORNTON, RUSSELL

[Untitled]; reviews of poetry books. Shaunt Basmajian. *Cross Can Writ Q* 1987; Vol 9 No 3-4: p44,49.
[ANTHOLOGIES: BOOK REVIEWS]

[Untitled]; review of *The Skin of a Song*. Peter Herman. *Rubicon* Fall 1987; No 9: p198-199.

The impersonation of the irresistible; reviews of poetry books. Fraser Sutherland. G&M Sept 5, 1987: pC15.

THORPE, MICHAEL

Iconographies; reviews of *Out of the Storm* and *The End of Ice*. Jack F. Stewart. *Can Lit* Spring 1987; No 112: p166-167.

THE THREE AND MANY WISHES OF JASON REID/ Children's story by Hazel J. Hutchins

Magical wishes . . . old tales to savour . . . musical rainbow; review of tape version of *The Three and Many Wishes of Jason Reid*. Richard Perry. *Quill & Quire (Books for Young People)* Dec 1987; Vol 53 No 12: p6

THREE DESKS/Play by James Reaney

Three Desks: a turning point in James Reaney's drama; article. Tim McNamara. *Queen's Q* Spring 1987; Vol 94 No 1: p15-32.

THREE LIVES IN MINE/Autobiography by Grace Irwin

Toronto author praises three of 'God's good men'; review of *Three Lives in Mine*. Heather Hill. photo · MG March 28, 1987: pE8.

THE THREE ROBERTS ON CHILDHOOD/Poems by Robert Priest, Robert Sward, and Robert Zend

[Untitled]; reviews of poetry books. Douglas Smith. *Poetry Can R* Spring 1987; Vol 8 No 2-3: p39-40.
[ANTHOLOGIES: BOOK REVIEWS]

THROUGH THE NAN DA GATE/Poems by Ken Mitchell

[Untitled]; reviews of *Through the Nan Da Gate* and *Death Is an Anxious Mother*. Nancy Batty. *Dandelion* Spring-Summer 1987; Vol 14 No 1: p84-87.

[Untitled]; review of *Through the Nan Da Gate*. Barbara Carey. *Books in Can* March 1987; Vol 16 No 2: p27-28.

[Untitled]; reviews of poetry books. James McElroy. *Poetry Can R* Fall 1987; Vol 9 No 1: p36.

Snapshots of China; review of *Through the Nan Da Gate*. Sally Swenson. *Arc* Spring 1987; No 18: p70-71.

THURSTON, HARRY

Landscapes & eyes; reviews of poetry books. Karl Jirgens. *Can Lit* Spring 1987; No 112: p192-193.

TIBO, GILLES

Children's-book artists love their work; article. Ann Duncan. photo · *MG* Nov 14, 1987: pD1.

TICKLEACE/Periodical

Sheer 'persistence' keeps literary magazine alive; article. Joan Sullivan. *G&M* Nov 23, 1987: pC9.
[CANADIAN LITERARY PERIODICALS]

Newfoundland and Labrador: TickleAce poised; regional column. Martin Ware. *Poetry Can R* Summer 1987; Vol 8 No 4: p12.
[CANADIAN LITERARY PERIODICALS]

TIDLER, CHARLES

Simple folk wax poetic in wordy one-act plays; theatre review of *Straight Ahead/Blind Dancers*. Vit Wagner. photo · *TS* Nov 27, 1987: pD12.

THE TIGER'S DAUGHTER/Novel by Bharati Mukherjee

[Untitled]; review of *The Tiger's Daughter*. Carolellen Norskey. *Quill & Quire* July 1987; Vol 53 No 7: p65.
[FIRST NOVELS: BOOK REVIEWS]

[Untitled]; review of *The Tiger's Daughter*. Helen Porter. *Books in Can* Aug-Sept 1987; Vol 16 No 6: p29.
[FIRST NOVELS: BOOK REVIEWS]

TIGER IN THE SKULL: NEW AND SELECTED POEMS 1959–1985/Poems by Douglas Lochhead

[Untitled]; review of *Tiger in the Skull*. *Queen's Q* Winter 1987; Vol 94 No 4: p1068–1069.

In principio; reviews. Laurel Boone. *Can Lit* Winter 1987; No 115: p209–211.
[CONFERENCE REPORTS: REVIEWS AND ARTICLES]

Tiger poems; reviews of poetry books. M. Travis Lane. *Fiddlehead* Autumn 1987; No 153: p88–91.

Exile & belonging: two Maritime poets; reviews of *White of the Lesser Angels* and *Tiger in the Skull*. Richard Lemm. *Atlan Prov Book R* May-June 1987; Vol 14 No 2: p10.

[Untitled]; review of *Tiger in the Skull*. Robin Skelton. *Poetry Can R* Spring 1987; Vol 8 No 2–3: p42.

Mapping inner and outer selves; review of *Tiger in the Skull* and *Dogstones*. Fraser Sutherland. *G&M* Feb 28, 1987: pE18.

[Untitled]; reviews of poetry books. Bruce Whiteman. *Cross Can Writ Q* 1987; Vol 9 No 2: p21–22,26.

TIGHTROPE TIME (AIN'T NOTHIN' BUT AN ITTY BITTY MADNESS BETWEEN TWILIGHT AND DAWN)/Play by Walter Borden

Tightrope Time a poetic one-man show that spans black history of Nova Scotia; theatre review. Pat Donnelly. photo · *MG* Sept 10, 1987: pC14.

[Untitled]; theatre reviews. Pat Donnelly. *MG* Sept 11, 1987: pC8.

Walter Borden en 12 temps . . . ; theatre review of *Tightrope Time*. Marc Morin. *MD* Sept 15, 1987: p11.

A TIME FOR LOVING/Poems by Rienzi Crusz

[Untitled]; review of *A Time for Loving*. Paul Denham. *Books in Can* June-July 1987; Vol 16 No 5: p24–25.

[Untitled]; reviews of *Singing Against the Wind* and *A Time for Loving*. Francis Mansbridge. *Poetry Can R* Fall 1987; Vol 9 No 1: p30.

TIME IN THE AIR/Novel by Rachel Wyatt

Up in the air; review of *Time in the Air*. Coral Ann Howells. *Can Lit* Winter 1987; No 115: p150–152.

[Untitled]; review of *Time in the Air*. Kathy Kelly. *Quarry* Winter 1987; Vol 36 No 1: p133–135.

[Untitled]; review of *Time in the Air*. Debra Martens. *Room of One's Own* Sept 1987; Vol 11 No 4: p115–118.

[Untitled]; review of *Time in the Air*. Marcienne Rocard. *Études can* June 1987; No 22: p138–139

Perils of a double life; review of *Time in the Air*. Norman Sigurdson. *WFP* Jan 10, 1987: p66.

TIME OF THEIR LIVES: THE DIONNE TRAGEDY/Novel by John Nihmey and Stuart Foxman

Book world: when a publicist needs a lawyer . . . ; column. Beverley Slopen. *TS* Nov 15, 1987: pA22.

Relations & families; review of *Time of Their Lives*. George Woodcock. *Can Lit* Summer-Fall 1987; No 113–114: p235–239.

TIME PRESSURE/Novel by Spider Robinson

An unsolvable maze; review of *Time Pressure*. Chuck Biggs. *WFP* Dec 12, 1987: p50.

Spider Robinson's time traveller lands in rural N.S.; review of *Time Pressure*. Michael Mirolla. *MG* Dec 24, 1987: L8.

TIMMS, KATHLEEN

Publishers meet the demand with reissued crime classics; reviews of *The Night the Gods Smiled* and *One-Eyed Merchants*. Douglas Hill. *G&M* Feb 28, 1987: pE19.
[FIRST NOVELS: BOOK REVIEWS]

THE TIN FLUTE

See **BONHEUR D'OCCASION/THE TIN FLUTE/Novel by Gabrielle Roy**

TIPS FOR DANCING THE TANGO/Poems by Sarah Jackson

Sarah Jackson's book works; reviews of books by Sarah Jackson. Alexa Thompson. *Atlan Prov Book R* Sept-Oct 1987; Vol 14 No 3: p15.

TITLEY, E. BRIAN

Scott and Indian Affairs; review of *A Narrow Vision*. Stan Dragland. *Can Poet* Fall-Winter 1987; No 21: p103–109.

Duncan Campbell Scott: a poet who put down Indians; review of *A Narrow Vision*. John Goddard. photo · *MG* Aug 1, 1987: J7.

The poet who ran Indian Affairs; review of *A Narrow Vision*. Allan Levine. photo · *G&M* Feb 28, 1987: pE17.

TO AN EASY GRAVE/Novel by Alexander Law

Crime; review of *To an Easy Grave*. Newgate Callendar. *NYT Book R* Jan 18, 1987: p23.
[FIRST NOVELS: BOOK REVIEWS]

Murder & mayhem: tough guys on clean street; reviews of crime novels. Margaret Cannon. *G&M* Jan 3, 1987: pE15.
[FIRST NOVELS: BOOK REVIEWS]

Mysteries to feed the mind with varying tastes; reviews of *Crang Plays the Ace* and *To an Easy Grave*. John North. photo · *Quill & Quire* March 1987; Vol 53 No 3: p74.
[FIRST NOVELS: BOOK REVIEWS]

TODAY I AM A FOUNTAIN PEN/Play by Israel Horovitz

Play needs time to be digested; theatre review of *Today I Am a Fountain Pen*. Brian Brennan. *CH* Dec 1, 1987: pD3.

TOES IN MY NOSE/Children's poems by Sheree Fitch

A trio of poets to tickle a child's fancy; reviews of children's poetry books. Adele Ashby. *Quill & Quire (Books for Young People)* June 1987; Vol 53 No 6: p10.

TOGANE, MOHAMUD S.

[Untitled]; reviews of poetry books. Anne Archer. *Queen's Q* Winter 1987; Vol 94 No 4: p1042–1043.

A Somali voice in cold Canada; review of *The Bottle and the Bushman*. Harold Barratt. *Fiddlehead* Summer 1987; No 152: p89–91.

[Untitled]; review of *The Bottle and the Bushman*. Jacqueline Damato. *Can Auth & Book* Winter 1987; Vol 62 No 2: p24.

[Untitled]; reviews of poetry books. Stephen Morrissey. *Poetry Can R* Spring 1987; Vol 8 No 2–3: p49.

[Untitled]; review of *The Bottle and the Bushman*. Howard Tessler. *Rubicon* Fall 1987; No 9: p195–196.

TOGETHER/ENSEMBLE/Children's play by David S. Craig and Robert Morgan

Italian troupe offers a touch of class; theatre review of *Together/Ensemble*. Robert Crew. *TS* May 13, 1987: pB3.
[FESTIVALS, DRAMA]

TOM DOESN'T VISIT US ANY MORE/Children's story by Maryleah Otto

[Untitled]; reviews of *Katie's Alligator Goes to Daycare* and *Tom Doesn't Visit Us Any More*. Adele Ashby. *Quill & Quire (Books for Young People)* Dec 1987; Vol 53 No 12: p8–9.

LE TOMBEAU D'ADLINA ALBERT/Poems by Robert Yergeau

Mort, vie et écriture; review of *Le Tombeau d'Adélina Albert*. Régis Normandeau. photo · *Lettres québec* Autumn 1987; No 47: p69.

La poésie n'est pas une science mais une parole; reviews of *Le Tombeau d'Adélina Albert* and *Qu'en carapaces de mes propres ailes*. Jean Royer. *MD* April 25, 1987: pD4.

THE TOMORROW-TAMER/Short stories by Margaret Laurence

The rhythms of ritual in Margaret Laurence's The Tomorrow-Tamer; article. James Harrison. *World Lit in Eng* Autumn 1987; Vol 27 No 2: p245–252.

THE TONGUE STILL DANCES/Poems by Robert Gibbs

Maritime letters; reviews. Carrie MacMillan. *Can Lit* Spring 1987; No 112: p189–192.

TONGUES OF MEN AND ANGELS/Poems by Maggie Helwig

Four poets; reviews of poetry books. Randall Maggs. *Can Lit* Winter 1987; No 115: p280–284

THE TOP OF THE HEART/Poems by Lesley Choyce

The space of images; reviews of poetry books. Lavinia Inbar. *Can Lit* Summer-Fall 1987; No 113–114: p245–247.

[Untitled]; review of *The Top of the Heart*. Sparling Mills. *Poetry Can R* Spring 1987; Vol 8 No 2–3: p41–42.

TOPPINGS, MICHAEL

[Untitled]; review of *Schizotexte*. Quendrith Johnson. *Rubicon* Spring 1987; No 8: p186–187.

[Untitled]; review of *Schizotexte*. Sparling Mills. *Poetry Can R* Summer 1987; Vol 8 No 4: p38.

TORGOV, MORLEY

Season's greetings: companies take cues from holidays past; article. Brian Brennan. photo · *CH* Nov 22, 1987: pA11.
[DRAMATIC ADAPTATIONS OF CANADIAN LITERATURE]

Play needs time to be digested; theatre review of *Today I Am a Fountain Pen*. Brian Brennan. *CH* Dec 1, 1987: pD3.

Glick clicks at last; article. Stephen Godfrey. photo · *G&M* Dec 5, 1987: pC1,C5.
[FILM ADAPTATIONS OF CANADIAN LITERATURE]

TORONTO LIFE/Periodical

Herrndorf is the sum of his arts; article about Peter Herrndorf. Antonia Zerbisias. photo · *TS* Oct 10, 1987: H1,H3.
[AWARDS, LITERARY]

THE TORONTO SOUTH ASIAN REVIEW/Periodical

Five years of TSAR; editorial. *Tor South Asian R* Spring 1987; Vol 5 No 3: p1–2.
[CANADIAN LITERARY PERIODICALS]

TORONTO, MISSISSIPPI/Play by Joan MacLeod

Toronto, Mississippi is well worth a visit; theatre review. Ray Conlogue. photo · *G&M* Oct 7, 1987: pC8.

Play talks to handicapped via Elvis; article. Robert Crew. photo · *TS* Oct 2, 1987: pE12.

Toronto, Mississippi a heartfelt new play; theatre review. Robert Crew. *TS* Oct 7, 1987: pD1.

LE TORRENT/THE TORRENT/Novella by Anne Hébert

Schéma actantiel d'un pseudo-récit: le Torrent d'Anne Hébert; article. Laure Hesbois. *Voix et images* Autumn 1987; Vol 13 No 1: p104–114.
[STRUCTURALIST WRITING AND CRITICISM]

TOSTEVIN, LOLA LEMIRE

[Untitled]; review of *Double Standards*. Jane Munro. *Poetry Can R* Spring 1987; Vol 8 No 2–3: p44.

[Untitled]; reviews of *In the Second Person* and *Double Standards*. Joan Ruvinsky. *Rubicon* Spring 1987; No 8: p178–181.

Sounding the difference: an interview with Smaro Kamboureli and Lola Tostevin. Janice Williamson. illus · *Can Forum* Jan 1987; Vol 66 No 765: p33–38.

TOUGAS, DANIEL

Franco-Manitoban satire translates sense of deja vu; theatre review of *Avant qu'les autres le fassent*. Philip Clark. *WFP* Oct 17, 1987: p34.

Entertaining; letter to the editor. Richard McCarthy. *WFP* Nov 7, 1987: p7.

Cercle tries for last laugh first; article. Brad Oswald. photo · *WFP* Oct 16, 1987: p33.

TOUPIE WILDWOOD/Play by Pascale Rafie

Zany Toupie Wildwood an escape story made to measure for its outdoor space; theatre review. Marianne Ackerman. photo · *MG* July 2, 1987: pE5.

La grande virée à Wildwood; column. Robert Lévesque. photo · *MD* June 16, 1987: p13.

La fièvre du lundi matin; theatre review of *Toupie Wildwood*. Robert Lévesque. *MD* June 25, 1987: p13.

LA TOUR DE CAP-CHAT/Children's story by Ginette Anfousse

Littérature jeunesse; reviews of children's books. Dominique Demers. *MD* Nov 21, 1987: pD6.

LE TOUR DU QUÉBEC PAR DEUX ENFANTS: UN ROMAN D'ÉDUCATION/Novel by E. Bertil

Imperfect conquests; reviews of *The Manor House of De Villeray* and *Le Tour du Québec par deux enfants*. Anthony Raspa. *Can Lit* Winter 1987; No 115: p172–174.
[CANADIAN LITERARY PERIODICALS]

LA TOUR/Play by Anne-Marie Provencher

Le théâtre qu'on joue; theatre reviews. André Dionne. photo · *Lettres québec* Winter 1986–87; No 44: p53–54.

Face to face with the actor; theatre review of *La Tour*. Josette Féral. photo trans · *Can Theatre R* Spring 1987; No 50: p78–81.

[Untitled]; theatre reviews of *La Tour* and *Les Objets parlent*. Solange Lévesque. photo · *Jeu* 1987; No 43: p145–147.

TOURBIN, DENNIS

The tribulations of these teens are a trial for readers; review of *The Port Dalhousie Stories*. William French. illud · *G&M* April 23, 1987: pC1.

[Untitled]; review of *The Port Dalhousie Stories*. D. French. *Books in Can* Nov 1987; Vol 16 No 8: p25

TOURIGNY, François

[Untitled]; review of *Le Prix du lait*. Bernard Pozier. *Estuaire* Summer 1987; No 45: p58.

TOURISTS/Novel by Richard B. Wright

Fear and loathing in Yucatan; review of *Tourists*. John Mills. *Essays on Can Writ* Spring 1987; No 34: p133–135.

TOURVILLE, JANINE

À la rencontre des huguenots de Namur; review of *Le Feu des souches*. Alice Parizeau. *MD* Dec 12, 1987: pD4.
[FIRST NOVELS: BOOK REVIEWS]

TOUTE LA TERRE À DVORER/Novel by André Vachon

Les noeuds sacrés de l'âme, de la terre et du sang; reviews of novels. Réjean Beaudoin. *Liberté* Oct 1987; Vol 29 No 5: p106–114.

Le cru et le cuit; review of *Toute la terre à dévorer*. Ginette Michaud. *Liberté* Aug 1987; Vol 29 No 4: p115–120.

Quand la "réalité" risque de l'emporter sur la fiction; review of *Toute la terre à dévorer*. Louise Milot. photo · *Lettres québec* Autumn 1987; No 47: p15–16.

André Vachon: le rappel d'une fable ancienne; review of *Toute la terre à dévorer*. Madeleine Ouellette-Michalska. photo · *MD* May 23, 1987: pD3.

TRACE: PRAIRIE WRITERS ON WRITING/Prose anthology

ReTracing prairie voices: a conversation with Birk Sproxton. Martin Kuester. photo · *Prairie Fire* Summer 1987; Vol 8 No 2: p4–10.

[Untitled]; review of *Trace*. Martin Kuester. *Zeitschrift Kanada-Studien* 1987; Vol 7 No 1: p272–274.

[Untitled]; review of *Trace*. Andrew Vaisius. *Poetry Can R* Fall 1987; Vol 9 No 1: p33.
[ANTHOLOGIES: BOOK REVIEWS]

THE TRADITION/Poems by A.F. Moritz

[Untitled]; reviews of poetry books. Martin Singleton. *Cross Can Writ Q* 1987; Vol 9 No 2: p19–20.

TRAGEDY OF MANNERS/Play by Donna Lypchuk

Much to do with very little; theatre review of *Tragedy of Manners*. Ray Conlogue. *G&M* Oct 5, 1987: pD11.

It's tragic but there goes old Queen St. neighborhood; theatre review of *Tragedy of Manners*. Robert Crew. photo · *TS* Oct 4, 1987: pC2.

Criticism misdirected; letter to the editor. Deborah Porter. *G&M* Oct 28, 1987: pA6.

TRAILL, CATHARINE PARR

Canada the way it used to be; review of *Canadian Crusoes*. M.T. Kelly. *G&M* Jan 10, 1987: pE17.

Catharine Parr Traill; letter to the editor. Norma Martin. *G&M* Feb 28, 1987: pD7.

[Untitled]; review of *Canadian Crusoes*. Michael Peterman. *U of Toronto Q* Fall 1987; Vol 57 No 1: p160–161.

TRAINER, YVONNE

[Untitled]; reviews of *My Round Table* and *Everything Happens at Once*. Rosemary Aubert. *Poetry Can R* Spring 1987; Vol 8 No 2–3: p48.

Western Canadian poets display talents in new volume; reviews of poetry books. G.P. Greenwood. *CH* July 5, 1987: pF7.

LES TRAINS D'EXILS/Novel by Réjean Bonenfant and Louis Jacob

Les noeuds sacrés de l'âme, de la terre et du sang; reviews of novels. Réjean Beaudoin. *Liberté* Oct 1987; Vol 29 No 5: p106–114.

Un roman biparental lourd de bonnes intentions; review of *Les Trains d'exils*. Jean-Roch Boivin. *MD* July 25, 1987: pC7.

TRANSLATIONS OF CANADIAN LITERATURE

Birdsell early pick; article. *WFP* Feb 13, 1987: p27.

Hopes and Dreams translate into award; article. *G&M* May 18, 1987: pD9.
[AWARDS, LITERARY]

Council hands out translation prizes; article. *G&M* June 2, 1987: pC7.
[AWARDS, LITERARY]

Dits et faits; column. photo · *Lettres québec* Spring 1987; No 45: p6–7.
[AWARDS, LITERARY; PUBLISHING AND PUBLISHERS IN CANADA; WRITERS' ORGANIZATIONS]

Playing linguistic musical chairs; article. Pat Donnelly. *MG* June 2, 1987: pD11.
[FESTIVALS, DRAMA]

Traduire c'est trahir, disent les Italiens; mais certains le font avec un tel bonheur!; article. Evelyn Dumas. photo · *MD* June 6, 1987: pD1,D8.

Fadette, de Saint-Hyacinthe à Toronto; article. Evelyn Dumas. *MD* June 6, 1987: pD7.

Translating words into action; article about literary translation. Matthew Fraser. illus · *G&M* Feb 7, 1987: pE1,E4.

Translations of children's books in Canada; article. André Gagnon. bibliog · *Can Child Lit* 1987; No 45: p14–53.
[CHILDREN'S LITERATURE: BIBLIOGRAPHY]

Translations; survey review article. Barbara Godard. *U of Toronto Q* Fall 1987; Vol 57 No 1: p77–98.

Can computers take on the task of translating?; article. Gord Graham. *Quill & Quire* March 1987; Vol 53 No 3: p68.

The name of Roseau grows in Quebec book market; article. David Homel. *Quill & Quire* March 1987; Vol 53 No 3: p58.
[PUBLISHING AND PUBLISHERS IN CANADA]

Verse translation in Canada; editorial article. Christopher Levenson. *Arc* Fall 1987; No 19: p4–6.

Lots of tribulations in doing translation; letter to the editor. Michelle Robinson. *G&M* March 4, 1987: pA7.

La vie littéraire; column. Jean Royer. photo · *MD* May 30, 1987: pD2.
[AWARDS, LITERARY; CANADIAN LITERARY PUBLISHING; COMPETITIONS, LITERARY; FESTIVALS, LITERARY; RADIO AND CANADIAN LITERATURE; TELEVISION AND CANADIAN LITERATURE]

Book world: will they leave the boss' book on sale?; column. Beverley Slopen. *TS* Nov 1, 1987: H6.

Une collecion qui part de bon pied; article. Adrien Thério. *Lettres québec* Summer 1987; No 46: p77.

L.M. Montgomery: at home in Poland; article. Barbara Wachowicz. photo · *Can Child Lit* 1987; No 46: p7–35.
[DRAMATIC ADAPTATIONS OF CANADIAN LITERATURE; EUROPE-CANADA LITERARY RELATIONS]

Blowing bubbles with Simone and Sartre; column. Vit Wagner. photo · *TS* Nov 6, 1987: pE4.

THE TRANSPARENCE OF NOVEMBER/SNOW/Poems by Roo Borson and Kim Maltman

Kinetic space; reviews of poetry books. Robert James Merrett. *Can Lit* Summer-Fall 1987; No 113–114: p241–243.

TRANTER'S TREE/Novel by H.R. Percy

Oak tree is weak base of H.R. Percy's tangled tales; review of *Tranter's Tree*. Lindsay Brown. photo · *MG* July 25, 1987: J8.

Historical novel starring oak tree a shade too slow; review of *Tranter's Tree*. William French. photo · *G&M* June 11, 1987: pD1.

A lovely, polished tree tale; review of *Tranter's Tree*. Joan McGrath. *TS* June 7, 1987: pG11.

Bred in the bark; review of *Tranter's Tree*. I.M. Owen. *Books in Can* May 1987; Vol 16 No 4: p19.

[Untitled]; review of *Tranter's Tree*. Thomas P. Sullivan. *Quill & Quire* May 1987; Vol 53 No 5: p22.

Fine writing saves novel; review of *Tranter's Tree*. David Williamson. *WFP* July 11, 1987: p57.

TRAVELLING LIGHT/Poems by Penny Kemp

[Untitled]; review of *Travelling Light*. Mary di Michele. *Poetry Can R* Summer 1987; Vol 8 No 4: p35.

TRAVELLING TO FIND A REMEDY/Poems by Claire Harris

Recent poetry; reviews of poetry books. Terrence Craig. *Atlan Prov Book R* Feb-March 1987; Vol 14 No 1: p18.

Narrative tendencies; reviews of poetry books. Phil Hall. *Waves* Winter 1987; Vol 15 No 3: p84–88.

LE TRAVERSIER/Short stories by Esther Rochon

Esther Rochon: une écriture "cool"; review of *Le Traversier*. Jean-Roch Boivin. photo · *MD* April 18, 1987: pD3.

[Untitled]; review of *Le Traversier*. Gaétan Breton. *Moebius* Summer 1987; No 33: p135–136.

La quête de la pensée la pensée de la quête; review of *Le Traversier*. Michel Lord. photo · *Lettres québec* Summer 1987; No 46: p28–29.

THE TREES JUST MOVED INTO A SEASON OF OTHER SHAPES/Poems by Jane Munro

Tellings; reviews of poetry books. Susan Rudy Dorscht. *Can Lit* Winter 1987; No 115: p257–260.

B.C. international — in search of new subjects and forms; reviews. Gillian Harding-Russell. *Event* Summer 1987; Vol 16 No 2: p125–127.

[Untitled]; reviews of poetry books. Sheila Martindale. *Cross Can Writ Q* 1987; Vol 9 No 2: p20–21.

TREGEBOV, RHEA

The mutability of memory: Rhea Tregebov's No One We Know; review. Barbara Carey. *Quarry* Summer 1987; Vol 36 No 3: p70–75.

Each to her own rhythm; reviews of poetry books. Lesley McAllister. *TS* July 25, 1987: M5.

[Untitled]; reviews of poetry books. Martin Singleton. *Cross Can Writ Q* 1987; Vol 9 No 3–4: p38–39.

LES TREMBLAY 2/Play by Claude Dorge and Irene Mahe

French play tackles social problems; theatre review of *Les Tremblay 2*. Philip Clark. *WFP* April 4, 1987: p23.

TREMBLAY, BRIAN

Tragic affair comes to life at Curtain Club; article. photo · *TS* (Neighbors) Nov 24, 1987: p22.

Curtain Club play needs to show more emotional thigh; theatre review of *A Spider in the House*. Alex Law. *TS* (Neighbors) Dec 1, 1987: p19.

TREMBLAY, CLARISSE

[Untitled]; review of *Jusqu'à la moëlle des fièvres*. Lucie Bourassa. *Estuaire* Summer 1987; No 45: p58–59.

TREMBLAY, MICHEL

Peering into the soul of French Canada; article. photo · *Maclean's* April 13, 1987; Vol 100 No 15: p46.

Aujourd'hui; column. *MD* April 24, 1987: p10.

Un homme qui s'intéressait aux créateurs; article. *MD* Nov 3, 1987: p4.

Invité d'honneur; article. *MD* Nov 14, 1987: pD1.

Michel Tremblay's 19th play superbly crafted — call it even a masterpiece; theatre review of *Le Vrai monde?*. Marianne Ackerman. photo · *MG* April 18, 1987: pC1.

[Untitled]; theatre review of *Le Vrai monde?*. Marianne Ackerman. *MG* April 24, 1987: pD8.

[Untitled]; theatre review of *Le Vrai monde?*. Marianne Ackerman. *MG* May 1, 1987: pD6.
[FESTIVALS, DRAMA]

Des Nouvelles d'Edouard: Michel Tremblay's fugal composition; article. Ellen Reisman Babby. *Amer R of Can Studies* Winter 1987–88; Vol 17 No 4: p383–394.

"Ce morceau de chair inexpliqué qu'il faut bien appeler le coeur…"; review of *La Coeur découverte*. Yvon Bernier. photo · *Lettres québec* Spring 1987; No 45: p26–27.

Tremblay looks in the mirror and doesn't like what he sees; theatre review of *Le Vrai monde?*. Ray Conlogue. photo · *G&M* Oct 2, 1987: pD10.

Hosanna on high to the queen; theatre review. Robert Crew. photo · *TS* May 27, 1987: pE3.

Un star system au Québec?; article. Jean-Paul Daoust. photo · *Jeu* 1987; No 43: p47–49.

Le théâtre qu'on joue; theatre reviews of *Le Printemps, monsieur Deslauriers* and *Le Vrai monde?*. André Dionne. photo · *Lettres québec* Autumn 1987; No 47: p49–50.

Stylish direction freshens Bonjour; theatre review of *Bonjour, là, bonjour*. Pat Donnelly. photo · *MG* Nov 25, 1987: H4.

[Untitled]; theatre reviews. Pat Donnelly. *MG* Nov 27, 1987: pC7.

[Untitled]; theatre reviews. Pat Donnelly. *MG* Dec 4, 1987: pC6.

Grandeur et misère: le retour du père sur la scène québécoise; article. Carole Fréchette. photo · *Jeu* 1987; No 45: p17–35.
[QUEBEC DRAMA (FRENCH LANGUAGE): HISTORY AND CRITICISM]

A playwright bares his soul; theatre review of *Le Vrai monde?*. Matthew Fraser. photo · *G&M* April 25, 1987: pC5.

[Untitled]; review of *Le Coeur découvert*. Michel Gosselin. *Moebius* Winter 1987; No 31: p141–142.

Au coeur de l'imaginaire; theatre review of *Le Vrai monde?*. Madeleine Greffard. photo · *Liberté* Dec 1987; Vol 29 No 6: p146–147.

French book fair aims for more anglophones; article. Heather Hill. *MG* Nov 6, 1987: pC1.
[CONFERENCES, LITERARY]

27 mars, journée mondiale du théâtre; column. Robert Lévesque. photo · *MD* March 24, 1987: p11.
[FESTIVALS, DRAMA]

Moisson d'avril; column. Robert Lévesque. photo · *MD* March 31, 1987: p17.

Le grand règlement de comptes de Michel Tremblay; theatre review of *Le Vrai monde?*. Robert Lévesque. photo · *MD* April 6, 1987: p11.

Le retour magistral de Tremblay; theatre review of *Le Vrai monde?*. Richard Lévesque. photo · *MD* April 16, 1987: p15.

Limoges, principale vitrine du théâtre québécois en Europe; column. Robert Lévesque. photo · *MD* Sept 29, 1987: p13.
[AWARDS, LITERARY; CANADIAN LITERARY PERIODICALS; FESTIVALS, DRAMA]

Tremblay chez les plus grands; article. Robert Lévesque. photo · *MD* Oct 8, 1987: p13.

Un parc, quelques rues et deux quartiers; article. Robert Lévesque. photo · *MD* Nov 14, 1987: pD1,D3.

Une apocalypse du désassorti; theatre review of *Bonjour, là, bonjour*. Robert Lévesque. photo · *MD* Nov 24, 1987: p11.

[Untitled]; theatre reviews. Robert Lévesque. *MD* Dec 4, 1987: p15.

Hosanna ages with grace and style; theatre review. Liam Lacey. photo · *G&M* May 27, 1987: pC10.

Out of this world; review of *Le Coeur découvert*. Alberto Manguel. *Books in Can* April 1987; Vol 16 No 3: p31–32.

[Untitled]; review of *Albertine, in Five Times*. Alberto Manguel. *Books in Can* May 1987; Vol 16 No 4: p22.

Couples; reviews of novels. Jacques Michon. *Voix et images* Autumn 1987; Vol 13 No 1: p189–192.

Théâtre au masculin; reviews of plays. Jane Moss. *Can Lit* Spring 1987; No 112: p180–183.

[Untitled]; review of *Albertine, in Five Times*. Carolellen Norskey. *Quill & Quire* June 1987; Vol 53 No 6: p31.

Reality, fiction mix in new Tremblay play; theatre review of *Le Vrai monde?*. Margarur du père sur la scène québécoise; article. Carole Fréchette. photo · *Jeu* 1987; No 45: p17–35.
[QUEBEC DRAMA (FRENCH LANGUAGE): HISTORY AND CRITICISM]

A playwright bares his soul; theatre review of *Le Vrai monde?*. Matthew Fraser. photo · *G&M* April 25, 1987: pC5.

[Untitled]; review of *Le Coeur découvert*. Michel Gosselin. *Moebius* Winter 1987; No 31: p141–142.

Au coeur de l'imaginaire; theatre review of *Le Vrai monde?*. Madeleine Greffard. photo · *Liberté* Dec 1987; Vol 29 No 6: p146–147.

French book fair aims for more anglophones; article. Heather Hill. *MG* Nov 6, 1987: pC1.
[CONFERENCES, LITERARY]

27 mars, journée mondiale du théâtre; column. Robert Lévesque. photo · *MD* March 24, 1987: p11.
[FESTIVALS, DRAMA]

Moisson d'avril; column. Robert Lévesque. photo · *MD* March 31, 1987: p17.

Le grand règleet Penman. *TS* Oct 4, 1987: pC4.

Du déjà goûté quelque part; theatre review of *Le Vrai monde?*. Jean-Robert Rémillard. *Liberté* Dec 1987; Vol 29 No 6: p145–146.

Tremblay at P'tit Bonheur, 1982–1985; article. Lisbie Rae. photo · *Can Drama* 1987; Vol 13 No 1: p1–26.

La vitrine du livre; reviews. Jean Royer. photo · *MD* April 4, 1987: pD2.
[CANADIAN LITERARY PERIODICALS]

Effets sonores et signification dans les Belles-soeurs de Michel Tremblay; article. Alvina Ruprecht. *Voix et images* Spring 1987; Vol 12 No 3: p439–451.
[STRUCTURALIST WRITING AND CRITICISM]

Narcisse se regarde dans l'eau jusqu'à y plonger . . . ; theatre review of *Le Vrai monde?*. Jean-Guy Sabourin. *Liberté* Dec 1987; Vol 29 NF255 *Jeu* 1987; No 45: p164–168.

Questions sur une démarche; essay. Jean-Luce Denis. photo · *Jeu* 1987; No 45: p159–163.

Cultural epic is must-see theatre; theatre review of *La Trilogie des dragons*. Wayne Grigsby. *MG* Jan 17, 1987: pC5.

Tenir l'univers dans sa main; article. Solange Lévesque. photo · *Jeu* 1987; No 45: p111–120.

Des personnages qui s'imposent aussi bien à Londres qu'à Montréal; article. Daniel Latouche. photo · *MD* Sept 5, 1987: pC4.

Du hasard et de la nécessité: genèse de l'oeuvre; essay. Pierre Lavoie. photo · *Jeu* 1987; No 45: p169–170.

Reconstitution de "La Trilogie"; article. Diane Pavlovic. photo · *Jeu* 1987; No 45: p40–82.

Magie et mysticisme: comment (ne pas) expliquer l'inexplicable; essay. Philippe Soldevila. photo · *Jeu* 1987; No 45: p171–176.

Entre le jouet de pacotille et la voûte céleste: le voyage des personnages à travers les objets; article. Michel Vaïs. photo · *Jeu* 1987; No 45: p98–110.

TROIS/Periodical

La vitrine du livre; reviews of *Trois* and *Vice Versa*. Guy Ferland. *MD* July 4, 1987: pC6.
[CANADIAN LITERARY PERIODICALS]

De l'érudition: l'esprit et la lettre; reviews of periodicals. Suzanne Lamy. *Voix et images* Winter 1987; No 35: p342–346.
[CANADIAN LITERARY PERIODICALS]

Ding et Dong; reviews of periodicals. Robert Melançon. *Liberté* Dec 1987; Vol 29 No 6: p122–129.
[CANADIAN LITERARY PERIODICALS]

LE TROISIÈME FILS DU PROFESSEUR YOUROLOV /Play by René Daniel Dubois

Du côté du rococo . . . ; theatre review of *Le Troisième fils du professeur Yourolov*. Robert Lévesque. *MD* Sept 23, 1987: p11.

[Untitled]; theatre review of *Le Troisième fils du professeur Yourolov*. Robert Lévesque. *MD* Oct 2, 1987: p15.

TROTTIER, PIERRE

Des livres ou des poètes?; reviews of *La Chevelure de Bérénice* and *Ces étirements du regard*. André Marquis. photo · *Lettres québec* Summer 1987; No 46: p35–36.

[Untitled]; reviews of poetry books. Jacques Saint-Pierre. *Moebius* Spring 1987; No 32: p128–130.

TROUBLES IN PARADISE/Poems by James Whittall

[Untitled]; reviews of poetry books. Shaunt Basmajian. *Cross Can Writ Q* 1987; Vol 9 No 3–4: p44,49.
[ANTHOLOGIES: BOOK REVIEWS]

[Untitled]; reviews of poetry books. Andrew Parkin. *Poetry Can R* Fall 1987; Vol 9 No 1: p37.
[ANTHOLOGIES: BOOK REVIEWS]

TROWER, PETER

[Untitled]; reviews of poetry books. Bruce Hunter. *Cross Can Writ Q* 1987; Vol 9 No 3–4: p40–42.

Flaws, good work mark collections; reviews of *The Slidingback Hills* and *Heading Out*. Mark Jarman. *CH* April 26, 1987: pE5.
[ANTHOLOGIES: BOOK REVIEWS]

TRUDEL, SYLVAIN

Sylvain Trudel remporte le Prix Molson; article. Angèle Dagenais. photo · *MD* Nov 11, 1987: p11.
[AWARDS, LITERARY]

Pourquoi le manque de croyances peut vous faire mourir de soif; review of *Le Souffle de l'Harmattan*. Pierre Hébert. photo · *Lettres québec* Autumn 1987; No 47: p22–23.

Couples; reviews of novels. Jacques Michon. *Voix et images* Autumn 1987; Vol 13 No 1: p189–192.

TRUJILLO, RENATO

[Untitled]; review of *Behind the Orchestra*. Raymond Filip. *Books in Can* Nov 1987; Vol 16 No 8: p26

TRUSS, JAN

Pour les adolescents: quatre mains et deux solitudes; reviews of young adult novels. Dominique Demers. photo · *MD* Dec 19, 1987: pD6–D7.

Horse stories tell of struggles to achieve personal worth; reviews of *Storm Rider* and *Summer Goes Riding*. Callie Israel. photo · *Quill & Quire (Books for Young People)* Oct 1987; Vol 53 No 10: p16.

McDonald scores with Canada's booksellers; article. Kenneth McGoogan. *CH* June 30, 1987: pE1.
[AWARDS, LITERARY]

Successful Alberta children's writers pen new works; article. Kenneth McGoogan. photo · *CH* Dec 18, 1987: pE7.

Readers, writers of tomorrow; column. Joan McGrath. *TS* July 5, 1987: pA18.
[BOOK TRADE IN CANADA]

TSIMICALIS, STAVROS

[Untitled]; review of *Liturgy of Light*. Corrado Federici. *Poetry Can R* Summer 1987; Vol 8 No 4: p36.

Seasons, time and memory; reviews of poetry books. Lesley McAllister. *TS* March 21, 1987: M5.

TUCKER, OTTO

Humour from the heart; review of *A Collection of Stories*. Tom Dawe. *Atlan Prov Book R* Sept-Oct 1987; Vol 14 No 3: p13.

TUPPENCE HA'PENNY IS A NICKEL/Novel by Francis X. Atherton

Lively story of immigrants needs a sequel; review of *Tuppence Ha'penny Is a Nickel*. Joan McGrath. *TS* Aug 30, 1987: pA19.

Fine writing about a tale worth telling; review of *Tuppence Ha'penny Is a Nickel*. Thomas S. Woods. *G&M* Sept 12, 1987: pC19.

TURCOTTE, ELISE

[Untitled]; review of *La Voix de Carla*. Antonio D'Alfonso. *Estuaire* Autumn 1987; No 46: p89–90.

La vitrine du livre; reviews. Guy Ferland. *MD* June 6, 1987: pD4.
[CANADIAN LITERARY PERIODICALS]

La tentation du romanesque; reviews of poetry books. Richard Giguère. photo · *Lettres québec* Autumn 1987; No 47: p37–39.

TURP, GILBERT

A manque d'esprit(s) dans la maison!; theatre review of *Les Fantômes de Martin*. Robert Lévesque. *MD* Nov 26, 1987: p13.

TURTLE JAZZ/Play by Kevin Teichrob

Turtle Jazz excruciating; theatre review. Ray Conlogue. photo · *G&M* June 27, 1987: pE8.

THE TWELFTH TRANSFORMING/Novel by Pauline Gedge

Sward draws blood; letter to the editor. John Patrick Gillese. *Can Auth & Book* Spring 1987; Vol 62 No 3: p2.

[Untitled]; letter to the editor. Jean B. Greig. *Can Auth & Book* Spring 1987; Vol 62 No 3: p2.

[Untitled]; review of *The Twelfth Transforming*. Robert Sward. *Can Auth & Book* Winter 1987; Vol 62 No 2: p23.

TWELVE LANDSCAPES/Poems by Ralph Gustafson

Landscapes & eyes; reviews of poetry books. Karl Jirgens. *Can Lit* Spring 1987; No 112: p192–193.

TWENTY ELEVEN A.C.: A FABLE/Poems by Sarah Jackson

Sara[h] Jackson's book works; reviews of books by Sarah Jackson. Alexa Thompson. *Atlan Prov Book R* Sept-Oct 1987; Vol 14 No 3: p15.

TWIGG, ALAN

Literary giants got rotten reviews; column. Kenneth McGoogan. *CH* Jan 18, 1987: pE4.
[CANADIAN LITERARY PERIODICALS; POETRY READINGS]

TWO VOICES/Short stories by Bruce Edmundson

Knockouts; review of *Two Voices*. Jason Sherman. *G&M* Sept 26, 1987: pC22.

TYNES, MAXINE

Taking the measure of Maxine; article. Sharon Fraser. photo · *Atlan Insight* Sept 1987; Vol 9 No 9: p16–18.

Maxine Tynes' first book of poems; review of *Borrowed Beauty*. Joanne Light. photo · *Atlan Prov Book R* Sept-Oct 1987; Vol 14 No 3: p14.

UGUAY, MARIE

[Untitled]; review of *Poèmes*. Hélène Dorion. *Estuaire* Spring 1987; No 44: p83–84.

Marie Uguay, Mandelstam, Luzi; review of *Poèmes*. Jean-Pierre Issenhuth. *Liberté* April 1987; Vol 29 No 2: p86–94.

Poésie: trois rétrospectives; reviews of poetry books. Jean Royer. photo · *MD* Feb 9, 1987: p11.

La vie littéraire; column. Jean Royer. photo · *MD* March 14, 1987: pD4.
[AWARDS, LITERARY; POETRY READINGS; RADIO AND CANADIAN LITERATURE; TELEVISION AND CANADIAN LITERATURE]

La vie littéraire; column. Jean Royer. photo · *MD* Sept 19, 1987: pD2.
[AWARDS, LITERARY; CONFERENCES, LITERARY; FICTION READINGS; POETRY READINGS; PUBLISHING AND PUBLISHERS IN CANADA]

UKETORININ/Poems by Wayne Ray

[Untitled]; reviews of poetry books. Shaunt Basmajian. *Cross Can Writ Q* 1987; Vol 9 No 3–4: p44,49.
[ANTHOLOGIES: BOOK REVIEWS]

THE UNCOLLECTED ACORN: POEMS, 1950–1986/ Poems by Milton Acorn

Passion without precision; review of *The Uncollected Acorn*. George Elliott Clarke. *Atlan Prov Book R* May-June 1987; Vol 14 No 2: p11.

Standing up for himself; reviews of *The Uncollected Acorn* and *Whiskey Jack*. Paul Denham. *Books in Can* June-July 1987; Vol 16 No 5: p30,32.

[Untitled]; reviews of *The Uncollected Acorn* and *A Stand of Jackpine*. David Leahy. *Rubicon* Fall 1987; No 9: p167–168.

Acorn's poems pro-life; review of *The Uncollected Acorn*. Lesley McAllister. *TS* June 13, 1987: M4.

Poetry: packing all the power into two of seven titles; reviews of poetry books. Robin Skelton. photo · *Quill & Quire* May 1987; Vol 53 No 5: p24.

UNDER EASTERN EYES: A CRITICAL READING OF MARITIME FICTION/Critical work by Janice Kulyk Keefer

Calling attention to the Maritimes; review of *Under Eastern Eyes*. Dennis Duffy. *G&M* Nov 21, 1987: pC23.

UNDER THE HOUSE/Novel by Leslie Hall Pinder

Women make difference in prairie family; review of *Under the House*. Cecelia Frey. *CH* July 19, 1987: pE4.
[FIRST NOVELS: BOOK REVIEWS]

Impressive; review of *Under the House*. M.T. Kelly. *G&M* Feb 14, 1987: pE20.
[FIRST NOVELS: BOOK REVIEWS]

World of wonders; reviews of first novels. Janice Kulyk Keefer. *Books in Can* May 1987; Vol 16 No 4: p37–38.
[FIRST NOVELS: BOOK REVIEWS]

[Untitled]; reviews of *Under the House* and *A Forest for Zoe*. Lesley McAllister. *Cross Can Writ Q* 1987; Vol 9 No 3–4: p48–49.
[FIRST NOVELS: BOOK REVIEWS]

[Untitled]; review of *Under the House*. Rachel Rafelman. *Quill & Quire* April 1987; Vol 53 No 4: p29.

The Rathbones' family skeletons; review of *Under the House*. Linda Taylor. *Times Lit Supp* Dec 18, 1987; No 4420: p1409.
[FIRST NOVELS: BOOK REVIEWS]

UNDER THE RIBS OF DEATH/Novel by John Marlyn

Sandor, Alex and the rest: multiplication of the subject in John Marlyn's Under the Ribs of Death; article. Julie Beddoes. *Open Letter* Summer 1987; Vol 6 No 8: p5–14.

UNDER THE VOLCANO/Novel by Malcolm Lowry

The descent into hell of Jacques Laruelle: chapter I of Under The Volcano; article. David Falk. *Can Lit* Spring 1987; No 112: p72–83.
[ARTIST FIGURE; CONFESSIONAL WRITING]

UNDRESSING THE DARK/Poems by Barbara Carey

Between the sexes; reviews of poetry books. Mary di Michele. *Books in Can* March 1987; Vol 16 No 2: p31–32.

Seasons, time and memory; reviews of poetry books. Lesley McAllister. *TS* March 21, 1987: M5.

[Untitled]; review of *Undressing the Dark*. Karen Ruttan. *Poetry Can R* Summer 1987; Vol 8 No 4: p37.

[Untitled]; reviews of poetry books. Martin Singleton. *Cross Can Writ Q* 1987; Vol 9 No 3–4: p38–39.

UNEXPECTED MOVES/Play by Gene Gray

Tired dreams and holy fools; theatre review of *Unexpected Moves*. Ray Conlogue. photo · *G&M* Oct 28, 1987: pC7.

Unexpected Moves jaunty little comedy; theatre review. Robert Crew. photo · *TS* Oct 28, 1987: pE2.

THE UNICORN MOON/Play by Christopher Covert

Play is sheer magic; theatre review of *The Unicorn Moon*. Muriel Leeper. *TS (Neighbors)* Nov 17, 1987: p14.

Unicorns and princesses hit Scarborough stage; article. Muriel Leeper. photo · *TS (Neighbors)* Oct 27, 1987: p10.

UNISON LIGHT/Poems by Phil Hall

[Untitled]; reviews of poetry books. Anita Hurwitz. *Poetry Can R* Spring 1987; Vol 8 No 2–3: p50–51.

UNITED STATES-CANADA LITERARY RELATIONS

"All we North Americans": literary culture and the continentalist ideal, 1919–1939; article. Graham Carr. *Amer R of Can Studies* Summer 1987; Vol 17 No 2: p145–157.
[CANADIAN LITERATURE (20TH CENTURY): HISTORY AND CRITICISM; COLONIALISM; CULTURAL IDENTITY]

The U.S.: regions & districts as labels; comparative column. David Donnell. *Poetry Can R* Spring 1987; Vol 8 No 2–3: p29.

Canada's a hit with this group; article. Michael Farber. *MG* Oct 9, 1987: pA3.
[CONFERENCES, LITERARY]

Canadian writers fly south for fest; column. Thomas Schnurmacher. *MG* Oct 7, 1987: H1.
[FESTIVALS, LITERARY]

UNKNOWN SOLDIER/Novel by George Payerle

Alcoholic vet's story drives home the horror; review of *Unknown Soldier*. Don Gillmor. photo · *MG* Oct 17, 1987: J12.

Cliched veteran profoundly human; review of *Unknown Soldier*. Maggie Helwig. *TS* Oct 10, 1987: M8.

Unlikely romantic; review of *Unknown Soldier*. T.F. Rigelhof. *G&M* Dec 12, 1987: pE5.

Winners have wounds, too; review of *Unknown Soldier*. Scott Van Wynsberghe. *WFP* Oct 31, 1987: p52.

[Untitled]; review of *Unknown Soldier*. Allan Weiss. *Books in Can* Aug-Sept 1987; Vol 16 No 6: p26.

Death and dying dogs old soldier; review of *Unknown Soldier*. Thomas York. *CH* Oct 25, 1987: pE5.

THE UNMASKING OF 'KSAN/Children's novel by Eric Wilson

Canadian-set mysteries; reviews of children's novels by Eric Wilson. Sheila Ward. *Can Child Lit* 1987; No 48: p91–93.

Other cultures featured in tales for youths; reviews of *The Unmasking of 'Ksan* and *Naomi's Road*. Kate Zimmerman. *CH* July 19, 1987: pE4.

THE UNRAVELLING/Poems by Gay Allison

Women are the root of all change; reviews of *The Unravelling* and *The Merzbook*. Lesley McAllister. photo · *TS* Nov 14, 1987: M4.

UNREST BOUND/Poems by Liliane Welch

[Untitled]; reviews of poetry books. Anita Hurwitz. *Poetry Can R* Spring 1987; Vol 8 No 2–3: p50–51.

THE UNSETTLING OF THE WEST/Short stories by Gary Geddes

Stories of the West best when satirical; review of *The Unsettling of the West*. Keith Garebian. photo · *TS* May 24, 1987: pA19.

[Untitled]; review of *The Unsettling of the West*. Bob Wakulich. *CH* May 31, 1987: pF5.

In the mode; reviews of short story collections. Allan Weiss. *Books in Can* April 1987; Vol 16 No 3: p30–31.

UP YOUR ALLEY/Play by Seymour Blicker

Up Your Alley is a jangle of conflicting styles; theatre review. Ray Conlogue. photo · *G&M* Jan 15, 1987: pD4.
[DRAMATIC ADAPTATIONS OF CANADIAN LITERATURE]

Curtain rises on new play, new theatre; theatre review of *Up Your Alley*. Wayne Grigsby. *MG* Jan 12, 1987: pB5.

URGENCES/Periodical

Devenez mécène, abonnez-vous!; reviews of periodicals. Robert Melançon. *Liberté* June 1987; Vol 29 No 3: p80–87.
[CANADIAN LITERARY PERIODICALS]

URQUHART, JANE

Jane Urquhart's stand-up talent; review of *Storm Glass*. Ken Adachi. *TS* June 7, 1987: pG11.

Brian Moore's Jesuit priest travels into heart of darkness; reviews of novels. Barbara Black. *MG* March 7, 1987: H11.

Jane Urquhart's short stories in the landscape of the poet; review of *Storm Glass*. Patricia Bradbury. photo · *Quill & Quire* July 1987; Vol 53 No 7: p64.

Getting on a literary roulette wheel; reviews of fictional works. Trevor Ferguson. *MG* Nov 14, 1987: J11.
[FIRST NOVELS: BOOK REVIEWS]

Through the looking glass; review of *Storm Glass*. Timothy Findley. *Books in Can* June-July 1987; Vol 16 No 5: p14.

A shimmering crop of short stories from 'other' places; review of *Storm Glass*. William French. *G&M* June 25, 1987: pD1.

Novel loses its energy in whirlpool; review of *The Whirlpool*. Cecelia Frey. *CH* Jan 11, 1987: pF4.

[Untitled]; review of *Storm Glass*. Michael Kenyon. *Malahat R* Sept 1987; No 80: p137–138.

[Untitled]; review of *The Whirlpool*. Sherie Posesorski. *Books in Can* Jan-Feb 1987; Vol 16 No 1: p26.
[FIRST NOVELS: BOOK REVIEWS]

The summer before Browning died; review of *The Whirlpool*. Aritha van Herk. *Brick* Fall 1987; No 31: p15–17.
[FIRST NOVELS: BOOK REVIEWS]

[Untitled]; reviews of *Vigil* and *The Whirlpool*. Alice Van Wart. *Can Forum* Aug-Sept 1987; Vol 67 No 771: p46–48.
[FIRST NOVELS: BOOK REVIEWS]

UTOPIA/DYSTOPIA

L'utopie comme refus de la réalité; essay. Pierre Bertrand. *Moebius* Summer 1987; No 33: p65–69.

Requiem pour l'utopie; essay. Jean-Claude Dussault. *Moebius* Summer 1987; No 33: p25–28.

Margaret Atwood's The Handmaid's Tale and the dystopian tradition; article. Amin Malak. *Can Lit* Spring 1987; No 112: p9–16.

V.S.O.P./Play by Luc Gervais

V.S.O.P. pale imitation of a play; theatre review. Pat Donnelly. *MG* Oct 16, 1987: pC7.

Avis aux consommateurs; theatre review of *V.S.O.P.*. Robert Lévesque. photo · *MD* Oct 16, 1987: p15

VACHON, ANDRÉ

Les noeuds sacrés de l'âme, de la terre et du sang; reviews of novels. Réjean Beaudoin. *Liberté* Oct 1987; Vol 29 No 5: p106–114.

Le cru et le cuit; review of *Toute la terre à dévorer*. Ginette Michaud. *Liberté* Aug 1987; Vol 29 No 4: p115–120.

Quand la "réalité" risque de l'emporter sur la fiction; review of *Toute la terre à dévorer*. Louise Milot. photo · *Lettres québec* Autumn 1987; No 47: p15–16.

André Vachon: le rappel d'une fable ancienne; review of *Toute la terre à dévorer*. Madeleine Ouellette-Michalska. photo · *MD* May 23, 1987: pD3.

VADEBONCOEUR, PIERRE

Prix et distinctions; list of award winners. photo · *Lettres québec* Summer 1987; No 46: p7.
[AWARDS, LITERARY]

Le vrai penseur, un beau matin, prend son bâton de pèlerin; review of *Essais inactuels*. Jean Éthier-Blais. *MD* May 9, 1987: pD8.

Pierre Vadeboncoeur remporte le prix Canada-Suisse; article. Jean Royer. photo · *MD* March 31, 1987: p17.
[AWARDS, LITERARY]

VAGABONDAGES/Periodical

Reconnaissance à André Roy; review of *Vagabondages*. Jean-Pierre Issenhuth. *Liberté* Oct 1987; Vol 29 No 5: p162–163.
[CANADIAN LITERARY PERIODICALS]

VAIVEM/Short stories by Laura Bulger

Relating the newcomers' pain; article. Sarah Jane Growe. photo · *TS* Jan 8, 1987: pD1,D4.

VALAIS, GILLES [pseud.]

Discours-fleuve; reviews of *Le Coupeur de têtes* and *Les Deux soeurs*. Marguerite Andersen. *Can Lit* Winter 1987; No 115: p182–184.

VALGARDSON, W.D.

Narrative tendencies; reviews of poetry books. Phil Hall. *Waves* Winter 1987; Vol 15 No 3: p84–88.

[Untitled]; review of *The Carpenter of Dreams*. Ann Knight. *Poetry Can R* Spring 1987; Vol 8 No 2–3: p44.

My trip to Iceland; essay. W.D. Valgardson. *Books in Can* Jan-Feb 1987; Vol 16 No 1: p4,6–7.

VALLÉE, CATHERINE

Suspense à la Quinzaine de Québec; column. Robert Lévesque. *MD* Sept 22, 1987: p11.

[DRAMATIC READINGS]

VALLIÈRES, PIERRE

Le salut de Pierre Vallières; review of *Noces obscures*. Réjean Beaudoin. *Liberté* April 1987; Vol 29 No 2: p139–140.

[FIRST NOVELS: BOOK REVIEWS]

Entrevue de Pierre Vallières; interview. Dominique Garand. *Moebius (special issue)* Spring 1987; No 32: p5–21.

Un roman de jeunesse de Pierre Vallières; review of *Noces obscures*. Jacques Michon. *MD* May 16, 1987: pD3,D8.

VAMPIRES IN OTTAWA/Children's novel by Eric Wilson

Canadian-set mysteries; reviews of children's novels by Eric Wilson. Sheila Ward. *Can Child Lit* 1987; No 48: p91–93.

VAN DUSEN, KATE

TV's generation suffers detachment; reviews of *The Blue House* and *Not Noir*. Colline Caulder. *TS* Nov 28, 1987: M5.

[Untitled]; review of *Not Noir*. Stephen Scobie. *Malahat R* Dec 1987; No 81: p108.

VAN HERK, ARITHA

Guild honors Pollock, van Herk; article. *G&M* May 13, 1987: pC5.

[AWARDS, LITERARY]

Writers Guild of Alberta awards; article. *Quill & Quire* July 1987; Vol 53 No 7: p54.

[AWARDS, LITERARY]

[Untitled]; reviews of fictional works. Beverley Daurio. *Cross Can Writ Q* 1987; Vol 9 No 1: p18–19.

The spider and the rose: Aritha van Herk's *No Fixed Address*; article. Dorothy Jones. *World Lit in Eng* Spring 1987; Vol 27 No 1: p39–56.

[FEMINIST WRITING AND CRITICISM; MYTHS AND LEGENDS IN CANADIAN LITERATURE; WOMEN IN LITERATURE]

Circle games; reviews of fictional works. Barbara Leckie. *Can Lit* Winter 1987; No 115: p278–280.

Arachne's progress; review of *No Fixed Address*. Stephen Scobie. *Brick* Winter 1987; No 29: p37–40.

VAN SCHENDEL, MICHEL

La route sinue fortement; review of *Extrême livre des voyages*. Chantal Gamache. *Lettres québec* Autumn 1987; No 47: p70.

[Untitled]; review of *Extrême livre des voyages*. Pierre Ouellet. *Estuaire* Autumn 1987; No 46: p87–88.

VANASSE, ANDRÉ

La mondialisation de la culture menace la littérature des nations francophone; article. photo · *MD* Dec 30, 1987: p11.

Le complexe de Jonas; review of *La Vie à rebours*. Jean-Roch Boivin. photo · *MD* Dec 19, 1987: pD3.

La vitrine du livre; reviews. Guy Ferland. *MD* Nov 21, 1987: pD4.

VANCOUVER AND ITS WRITERS: A GUIDE TO VANCOUVER'S LITERARY LANDMARKS/Reference guide by Alan Twigg

Literary giants got rotten reviews; column. Kenneth McGoogan. *CH* Jan 18, 1987: pE4.

[CANADIAN LITERARY PERIODICALS; POETRY READINGS]

VANCOUVER FICTION/Anthology

Vancouver mind; reviews of *Vancouver Short Stories* and *Vancouver Fiction*. David Stouck. *Can Lit* Spring 1987; No 112: p157–159.

[ANTHOLOGIES: BOOK REVIEWS]

VANCOUVER POETRY/Poetry anthology

Van lit; reviews of *Vancouver: Soul of a City* and *Vancouver Poetry*. Margaret Doyle. *Can Lit* Winter 1987; No 115: p188–190.

[ANTHOLOGIES: BOOK REVIEWS]

[Untitled]; review of *Vancouver Poetry*. Glenn Hayes. *Poetry Can R* Fall 1987; Vol 9 No 1: p36–37.

[ANTHOLOGIES: BOOK REVIEWS]

[Untitled]; review of *Vancouver Poetry*. Elizabeth Woods. *Malahat R (special issue)* March 1987; No 78: p158–159.

[ANTHOLOGIES: BOOK REVIEWS]

VANCOUVER SHORT STORIES/Anthology

Vancouver mind; reviews of *Vancouver Short Stories* and *Vancouver Fiction*. David Stouck. *Can Lit* Spring 1987; No 112: p157–159.

[ANTHOLOGIES: BOOK REVIEWS]

VANCOUVER: SOUL OF A CITY/Anthology

Van lit; reviews of *Vancouver: Soul of a City* and *Vancouver Poetry*. Margaret Doyle. *Can Lit* Winter 1987; No 115: p188–190.

[ANTHOLOGIES: BOOK REVIEWS]

VANDERHAEGHE, GUY

Violence and narrative metalepsis in Guy Vanderhaeghe's fiction; article. Tom Gerry. *Studies in Can Lit* 1987; Vol 12 No 2: p199–211.
[VIOLENCE IN CANADIAN LITERATURE]

THE VANISHING POINT/Novel by W.O. Mitchell

W.O. Mitchell from The Alien to The Vanishing Point; article. W.J. Keith. *World Lit in Eng* Autumn 1987; Vol 27 No 2: p252–262.

VANITY PRESS/Play by James Polk

Stage fright; article. Marc Côté. *Books in Can* June-July 1987; Vol 16 No 5: p3,5.

Vanity Press experiences first-play problems; theatre review. Ray Conlogue. *G&M* March 14, 1987: pE10.

Book world: Clarkson brings pool of goodwill to M&S job; column. Beverley Slopen. *TS* March 15, 1987: pA22.
[AWARDS, LITERARY; PUBLISHING AND PUBLISHERS IN CANADA]

Paperclips: publishing on-stage . . . P.K. Page's love song to Brazil; column. Beverley Slopen. photo · *Quill & Quire* May 1987; Vol 53 No 5: p14.

LES VANQUEURS

See **WINNERS/LES VAINQUEURS/Young adult novel by Mary-Ellen Lang Collura**

VARIETIES OF EXILE: THE CANADIAN EXPERIENCE/ Critical essays by Hallvard Dahlie

[Untitled]; reviews of *Varieties of Exile* and *Prairie Women*. Peter Buitenhuis. *Queen's Q* Summer 1987; Vol 94 No 2: p467–470.

Languages of exile; review of *Varieties of Exile*. David Dowling. *Can Lit* Winter 1987; No 115: p216–218.

[Untitled]; review of *Varieties of Exile*. August J. Fry. *British J of Can Studies* June 1987; Vol 2 No 1: p180–181.

[Untitled]; review of *Varieties of Exile*. D.B. Jewison. *U of Toronto Q* Fall 1987; Vol 57 No 1: p151–154.

Literary 'exiles' came to Canada from choice, not need; review of *Varieties of Exile*. Marion McCormick. *MG* Jan 3, 1987: pB8.

[Untitled]; review of *Varieties of Exile*. Barry Thorne. *Eng Studies in Can* Dec 1987; Vol 13 No 4: p480–483.

VEKEMAN, LISE

Les sentiers de la peur; review of *La Fille de Thomas Vogel*. Benoit Lacroix. *MD* Nov 7, 1987: pD3.

VENRIGHT, STEVE

[Untitled]; reviews. Beverley Daurio. *Cross Can Writ Q* 1987; Vol 9 No 2: p23.
[FIRST NOVELS: BOOK REVIEWS]

[Untitled]; review of *Visitations*. Maurice Mierau. *Rubicon* Spring 1987; No 8: p217–218.

[Untitled]; reviews of poetry books. Stephen Morrissey. *Poetry Can R* Spring 1987; Vol 8 No 2–3: p49.

VERBE SILENCE/Poems by Guy Gervais

"Le monde en un seul mot"; review of *Verbe silence*. Jean Royer. *MD* May 30, 1987: pD5

LES VERBES SEULS/Poems by Louise Desjardins

Maniaques depressifs; reviews of poetry books. Mark Benson. *Can Lit* Spring 1987; No 112: p138–141.

VERDICCHIO, PASQUALE

Roman heartbeat; reviews of *The Other Shore* and *Moving Landscape*. Louise McKinney. *Can Lit* Winter 1987; No 115: p232–234.

VERNON, LORRAINE

The poems of Lorraine Vernon; introduction. Allan Cooper. *Germination* Fall 1987; Vol 11 No 1: p41.

VERY LAST FIRST TIME/Children's story by Jan Andrews

The Canadian north; review of *Very Last First Time*. Mary Ellen Binder. *Can Child Lit* 1987; No 45: p82–86.

Picture-power; reviews of *Very Last First Time* and *Zoom Away*. Jon C. Scott. *Can Lit* Spring 1987; No 112: p159–162.

VIAU, ROGER

Radiographie urbaine; review of *Au milieu, la montagne*. Jean-François Chassay. photo · *MD* Oct 24, 1987: pD3.

Dans les poches; reviews. Guy Ferland. *MD* Sept 26, 1987: pD6.

Le prolétariat montréalais cras; review of *Au milieu la montagne*. Patrick Imbert. photo · *Lettres québec* Winter 1986–87; No 44: p63–64.

VIBRATIONS IN TIME/Short stories by David Watmough

Against the reasoning mind; reviews of *In the Village of Alias* and *Vibrations in Time*. Jon Kertzer. *Fiddlehead* Autumn 1987; No 153: p97–100.

[Untitled]; reviews. Janet Windeler. *Cross Can Writ Q* 1987; Vol 9 No 2: p25–26.
[FIRST NOVELS: BOOK REVIEWS]

VICE VERSA/Periodical

Quelle culture politique existe au Québec? Une conférence-débat du magazine Vice versa; article. *MD* Feb 25, 1987: p9.
[CANADIAN LITERARY PERIODICALS]

Book store aims to please the theatre and movie crowd; article. Marianne Ackerman. *MG* Feb 17, 1987: pE8.
[BOOK TRADE IN CANADA; CANADIAN LITERARY PERIODICALS]

La vitrine du livre; reviews of *Trois* and *Vice Versa*. Guy Ferland. *MD* July 4, 1987: pC6.
[CANADIAN LITERARY PERIODICALS]

[Untitled]; review of *Albertine, in Five Times*. Alberto Manguel. *Books in Can* May 1987; Vol 16 No 4: p22.

La vie littéraire; column. Jean Royer. *MD* Feb 14, 1987: pC2.
[AWARDS, LITERARY; CANADIAN LITERARY PERIODICALS; COMPETITIONS, LITERARY; FICTION READINGS; POETRY READINGS; RADIO AND CANADIAN LITERATURE]

La vie littéraire; column. Jean Royer. photo · *MD* Oct 17, 1987: pD2.

[CANADIAN LITERARY PERIODICALS; COMPETITIONS, LITERARY; CONFERENCES, LITERARY; FICTION READINGS; WRITERS' ORGANIZATIONS]

LA VIE À REBOURS/Novel by André Vanasse

Le complexe de Jonas; review of *La Vie à rebours*. Jean-Roch Boivin. photo · *MD* Dec 19, 1987: pD3.

La vitrine du livre; reviews. Guy Ferland. *MD* Nov 21, 1987: pD4.

LA VIE D'ARTISTE/Novel by Louis Caron

[Untitled]; reviews of novels. Alice Parizeau. *MD* Nov 28, 1987: pD9.

LES VIEUX M'ONT CONTÉ/Folklore compilation

Folktales; review of *Les Vieux m'ont conté*. Gerald Thomas. *Can Lit* Winter 1987; No 115: p242–245.

VIGIL/Novel by Roberta Morris

[Untitled]; review of *Vigil*. Gloria Hildebrandt. *Books in Can* May 1987; Vol 16 No 4: p21.

[Untitled]; reviews of *Vigil* and *The Whirlpool*. Alice Van Wart. *Can Forum* Aug-Sept 1987; Vol 67 No 771: p46–48.

[FIRST NOVELS: BOOK REVIEWS]

VIGNEAULT, GILLES

Un doctorat de Laval à Gilles Vigneault; article. *MD* Feb 18, 1987: p4.

Un homme qui s'intéressait aux créateurs; article. *MD* Nov 3, 1987: p4.

Poet-politician wins literary prize; article. *G&M* Nov 20, 1987: pD11.

[AWARDS, LITERARY]

Le Duvernay à Gérald Godin, le Victor-Morin à André Brassard; article. Sylvain Blanchard. *MD* Oct 9, 1987: p13–14.

[AWARDS, LITERARY]

Anne Hébert, Wilfrid Lemoyne, Ginette Anfousse reoivent les premiers prix Fleury-Mesplet; article. Paul Cauchon. photo · *MD* Nov 20, 1987: p13–14.

[AWARDS, LITERARY]

Gilles Vigneault: que nos maîtres redeviennent des maîtres à penser; article. France Lafuste. photo · *MD* Dec 19, 1987: pC1,C12.

THE VILE GOVERNESS & OTHER PSYCHODRAMAS/ Plays by Stewart Lemoine

Horror spoof keeps audience on edge; theatre review of *The Vile Governess & Other Psychodramas*. Ray Conlogue. photo · *G&M* Sept 10, 1987: pD3.

Wild, wacky Vile Governess a delicious spoof of Ibsen angst; theatre review of *The Vile Governess & Other Psychodramas*. Robert Crew. photo · *TS* Sept 11, 1987: pE11.

VILLAGE OF IDIOTS/Play by John Lazarus

[Village of Idiots]; theatre review. Jan Truss. *NeWest R* Feb 1987; Vol 12 No 6: p16.

VILLARD, MARC

La surface du monde; review of *Carnage pâle*. André Roy. *Estuaire* Winter 1986–87; No 43: p79–80.

VILLEMAIRE, YOLANDE

En poche, le premier roman de Yolande Villemaire: un thriller gigogne; review of *Meurtres à blanc*. Jean-Roch Boivin. photo · *MD* May 2, 1987: pD3.

[FIRST NOVELS: BOOK REVIEWS]

Du privé au politique: la Constellation du Cygne de Yolande Villemaire; article. Suzanne Lamy. *Voix et images* Autumn 1987; Vol 13 No 1: p18–28.

VILLENEUVE, JOCELYNE

Leons du monde animal; review of *La Ménagerie*. Michel Gaulin. *Can Child Lit* 1987; No 45: p86–87.

VILLENEUVE, PAQUERETTE

La vitrine du livre; reviews of *Retour II: journal d'émotions* and *N'eût été cet été nu*. Guy Ferland. *MD* July 11, 1987: pC6.

VINCI/Play by Robert Lepage

One-man Vinci tour de force for Lepage; theatre review. Pat Donnelly. *MG* June 5, 1987: pD2.

Le grand retour de Murielle Dutil dans Le Temps d'une vie; column. Robert Lévesque. *MD* April 7, 1987: p12.

Robert Lepage impose son Vinci dans la Ville lumière; column. Robert Lévesque. photo · *MD* Dec 8, 1987: p11.

[INTERNATIONAL REVIEWS OF CANADIAN LITERATURE]

Harmonie et contrepoint; article. Solange Lvesque. photo · *Jeu* 1987; No 42: p100–108.

Du décollage l'envol; article. Diane Pavlovic. illus photo · *Jeu* 1987; No 42: p86–99.

LES VINGT-QUATRE HEURES DU CLAN/Novel by Josette Labbé

À la recherche de tendresse; review of *Les Vingt-quatre heures du clan*. Alice Parizeau. *MD* Dec 24, 1987: pC11.

VIOLENCE IN CANADIAN LITERATURE

Violence and narrative metalepsis in Guy Vanderhaeghe's fiction; article. Tom Gerry. *Studies in Can Lit* 1987; Vol 12 No 2: p199–211.

VIRGIN SCIENCE/Poems by Pier Giorgio di Cicco

[Untitled]; review of *Virgin Science*. Brian Fawcett. *Books in Can* Jan-Feb 1987; Vol 16 No 1: p28.

Poetry, science, mind and religion; reviews of poetry books. Fraser Sutherland. photo · *G&M* Jan 31, 1987: pE19.

[Untitled]; review of *Virgin Science*. George Woodcock. *Poetry Can R* Spring 1987; Vol 8 No 2–3: p38.

VIRGO, SEAN

A dazzling novel that attempts to be masterpiece; review of *Selakhi*. Geoff Hancock. *TS* Nov 29, 1987: pA21.

[FIRST NOVELS: BOOK REVIEWS]

Heart of darkness; reviews of first novels. Janice Kulyk Keefer. *Books in Can* Dec 1987; Vol 16 No 9: p37–39.
[FIRST NOVELS: BOOK REVIEWS]

Dense, mystic tale requires much of reader; review of *Selakhi*. Thomas York. *CH* Dec 27, 1987: pE6.
[FIRST NOVELS: BOOK REVIEWS]

VISIBLE VISIONS: THE SELECTED POEMS OF DOUGLAS BARBOUR/Poems by Douglas Barbour

Trimly clipped and barboured; reviews of *Visible Visions* and *The Harbingers*. Louis K. MacKendrick. *Essays on Can Writ* Spring 1987; No 34: p39–43.

VISITATIONS/Poems by Steve Venright

[Untitled]; reviews. Beverley Daurio. *Cross Can Writ Q* 1987; Vol 9 No 2: p23.
[FIRST NOVELS: BOOK REVIEWS]

[Untitled]; review of *Visitations*. Maurice Mierau. *Rubicon* Spring 1987; No 8: p217–218.

[Untitled]; reviews of poetry books. Stephen Morrissey. *Poetry Can R* Spring 1987; Vol 8 No 2–3: p49.

VISITATIONS/Short stories by Elizabeth Brewster

No need to explain; review of *Visitations*. Anne Denoon. *Books in Can* Aug-Sept 1987; Vol 16 No 6: p21,24.

[Untitled]; review of *Visitations*. M.A. Thompson. *Quarry* Summer 1987; Vol 36 No 3: p80–82

Sharing touching reveries; review of *Visitations*. Thomas S. Woods. *G&M* July 11, 1987: pC14.

LA VISITE DES SAUVAGES/Play by Anne Legault

[Untitled]; theatre review of *La Visite des sauvages*. Stphane Lpine. photo · *Jeu* 1987; No 42: p141–147.

LE VISITEUR DU SOIR/Young adult novel by Robert Soulires

Valeurs ludiques et valeurs fonctionelles: Le Visiteur du soir de Robert Soulières; article. Alexandre Amprimoz. Sante A. Viselli. *Can Child Lit* 1987; No 45: p6–13.
[CRIME FICTION; STRUCTURALIST WRITING AND CRITICISM]

LA VITALITÉ LITTÉRAIRE DE L'ONTARIO FRANÇAIS, PREMIER PANORAMA/Critical work by Paul Gay

[Untitled]; review of *La Vitalité littéraire de l'Ontario français*. L.E. Doucette. *U of Toronto Q* Fall 1987; Vol 57 No 1: p206–207.

VIVRE N'EST PAS CLAIR/Poems by Rachel Leclerc

[Untitled]; review of *Vivre n'est pas clair*. Hugues Corriveau. *Estuaire* Spring 1987; No 44: p83.

L'amour la mort; reviews of poetry books. Robert Yergeau. photo · *Lettres québec* Summer 1987; No 46: p37–38.

VIZINCZEY, STEPHEN

Book world: 'My year for films': Brian Moore; column. Beverley Slopen. photo · *TS* Nov 8, 1987: pA18.
[CHILDREN'S LITERATURE; FILM ADAPTATIONS OF CANADIAN LITERATURE; PUBLISHING AND PUBLISHERS IN CANADA]

VLASSIE, KATHERINE

Getting on a literary roulette wheel; reviews of fictional works. Trevor Ferguson. *MG* Nov 14, 1987: J11.
[FIRST NOVELS: BOOK REVIEWS]

Heart of darkness; reviews of first novels. Janice Kulyk Keefer. *Books in Can* Dec 1987; Vol 16 No 9: p37–39.
[FIRST NOVELS: BOOK REVIEWS]

Greek immigrants populate collection; article. Doreen Martens. *WFP* Oct 23, 1987: p32.

VOADEN, HERMAN

Emily Carr play; letter to the editor. William Angus. *G&M* Sept 29, 1987: pA6.

'Grand old man' Voaden sees play revived at 84; article. William Clark. photo · *TS* April 5, 1987: pD6.

Editor's notebook; editorial. John Flood. *Northward J* 1987; No 42: p2.

Drama views/perspectives dramatiques: Herman Voaden's Murder Pattern: 1936 and 1987; article. Sherrill E. Grace. *Can Drama* 1987; Vol 13 No 1: p117–119.

THE VOICE AT THE BACK DOOR/Novel by Elizabeth Spencer

New & noteworthy; reviews of *The Voice at the Back Door* and *Fire in the Morning*. Patricia T. O'Connor. *NYT Book R* Feb 1, 1987: p32.

VOICES AND VISIONS: INTERVIEWS WITH SASKATCHEWAN WRITERS/Interview compilation

Seeing voices; reviews of *Voices and Visions* and *Voices of Deliverance*. Patricia Köser. *Can Lit* Summer-Fall 1987; No 113–114: p239–241.

[Untitled]; review of *Voices & Visions*. Clea Notar. *Rubicon* Spring 1987; No 8: p214.

VOICES OF DELIVERANCE: INTERVIEWS WITH QUEBEC AND ACADIAN WRITERS/Interview compilation

[Untitled]; review of *Voices of Deliverance*. Paul Albert Cyr. *Amer R of Can Studies* Autumn 1987; Vol 17 No 3: p354–355.

Seeing voices; reviews of *Voices and Visions* and *Voices of Deliverance*. Patricia Köser. *Can Lit* Summer-Fall 1987; No 113–114: p239–241.

Francophones on writing; review of *Voices of Deliverance*. Michèle Lacombe. *Essays on Can Writ* Winter 1987; No 35: p105–110.

[Untitled]; review of *Voices of Deliverance*. Peter S. Noble. *British J of Can Studies* June 1987; Vol 2 No 1: p181–182.

VOILA, C'EST MOI: C'EST RIEN, J'ANGOISSE/Short stories by Anne Dandurand

La vitrine du livre; reviews of fictional works. Guy Ferland. *MD* Dec 5, 1987: pD4.

LES VOISINS/Play by Claude Meunier and Louis Saia

Les Voisins: scènes de la vie de banlieue; article. Paul Cauchon. photo · *MD* Sept 25, 1987: p15.
[TELEVISION AND CANADIAN LITERATURE]

VOIX D'CRIVAINS/Interview compilation

Questionner et rêver; review of *Voix d'écrivains: entretiens*. Paul G. Socken. *Can Lit* Spring 1987; No 112: p171–172.

LA VOIX DE CARLA/Poems by lise Turcotte

[Untitled]; review of *La Voix de Carla*. Antonio D'Alfonso. *Estuaire* Autumn 1987; No 46: p89–90.

La vitrine du livre; reviews. Guy Ferland. *MD* June 6, 1987: pD4.
[CANADIAN LITERARY PERIODICALS]

La tentation du romanesque; reviews of poetry books. Richard Giguère. photo · *Lettres québec* Autumn 1987; No 47: p37–39.

VOIX ET IMAGES/Periodical

D'où vient Voix et images?; article. Jacques Allard. *Voix et images* Winter 1987; No 35: p294–303.
[CANADIAN LITERARY PERIODICALS]

De Voix et images du pays à Voix et images: 20 ans déjà; editorial. Bernard-J. Andrès. *Voix et images* Autumn 1987; Vol 13 No 1: p5–6.
[CANADIAN LITERARY PERIODICALS]

La littérature québécoise à Voix et images: créneau ou ghetto?; article. Bernard Andrès. *Voix et images* Winter 1987; No 35: p303–312.
[CANADIAN LITERARY PERIODICALS]

Qui de neuf du côté universitaire?; reviews of periodicals. Carole David. *MD* Jan 17, 1987: pB5,B7.
[CANADIAN LITERARY PERIODICALS]

La vitrine du livre; reviews. Guy Ferland. *MD* June 20, 1987: pD4.
[CANADIAN LITERARY PERIODICALS]

Les voix des Amériques; review of *Voix et images* (special issue). Chantal Gamache. *MD* March 21, 1987: pD2.
[CANADIAN LITERARY PERIODICALS]

L'intérêt de Voix & images pour les aventures culturelles de notre société; review. Chantal Gamache. *MD* April 25, 1987: pD3.
[CANADIAN LITERARY PERIODICALS]

En toute simplicité; review of *Voix et images*. Chantal Gamache. photo · *MD* Nov 7, 1987: pD3.
[CANADIAN LITERARY PERIODICALS]

Current Canadian studies; column. Victor A. Konrad. *Amer R of Can Studies* Autumn 1987; Vol 17 No 3: p360–366.
[ANNOTATIONS, SHORT REVIEWS, ; CANADIAN LITERARY PERIODICALS]

Voix et images 36; review. Gaëtan Lévesque. *Lettres québec* Autumn 1987; No 47: p66.
[CANADIAN LITERARY PERIODICALS]

La vie littéraire; column. Jean Royer. *MD* Feb 28, 1987: pC2.
[AWARDS, LITERARY; CANADIAN LITERARY PERIODICALS; CANADIAN LITERARY PUBLISHING; CONFERENCES, LITERARY; RADIO AND CANADIAN LITERATURE]

La vitrine du livre; reviews. Jean Royer. *MD* March 14, 1987: pD4.
[CANADIAN LITERARY PERIODICALS]

UNE VOIX POUR ODILE/Novel by France Thoret

La vitrine du livre; reviews. Jean Royer. photo · *MD* March 21, 1987: pD2.
[CANADIAN LITERARY PERIODICALS]

VOL À RETARDEMENT: LES ENQUÊTES DE GLORIA/Children's novel by Josée Dufour

Le roman policier désarmé; review of *Vol à retardement*. René Gagné. *Can Child Lit* 1987; No 46: p85–86.

LE VOL DU VOLEUR DE JOB/Play by Teatro Sous-sol collective

Stratford ahead of the game — and it's no overnight miracle; column. Pat Donnelly. *MG* Dec 10, 1987: pD6.
[FESTIVALS, DRAMA]

VOLKSWAGEN BLUES/Novel by Jacques Poulin

Dans les poches; reviews. Guy Ferland. *MD* Sept 26, 1987: pD6.

VON KONIGSLOW, ANDREA WAYNE

[Untitled]; review of *A Tail Between Two Cities*. Bernie Goedhart. *Quill & Quire* (Books for Young People) Dec 1987; Vol 53 No 12: p9.

VOYAGE D'HIVER/Novel by Jean Éthier-Blais

[Untitled]; reviews of novels. Alice Parizeau. *MD* Nov 28, 1987: pD9.

VOYAGE TO THE OTHER EXTREME/Short stories by Maril Mallet

[Untitled]; review of *Voyage to the Other Extreme*. *Queen's Q* Spring 1987; Vol 94 No 1: p251.

Other Americas; reviews of *The Light in the Piazza* and *Voyage to the Other Extreme*. Michael Greenstein. *Can Lit* Spring 1987; No 112: p97–100.

LES VOYANTS/Novel by Robert Baillie

[Untitled]; review of *Les Voyants*. Sylvie-L. Bergeron. *Moebius* Summer 1987; No 33: p137–139.

LE VRAI MONDE?/Play by Michel Tremblay

Michel Tremblay's 19th play superbly crafted — call it even a masterpiece; theatre review of *Le Vrai monde?*. Marianne Ackerman. photo · *MG* April 18, 1987: pC1.

[Untitled]; theatre review of *Le Vrai monde?*. Marianne Ackerman. *MG* April 24, 1987: pD8.

[Untitled]; theatre review of *Le Vrai monde?*. Marianne Ackerman. *MG* May 1, 1987: pD6.
[FESTIVALS, DRAMA]

Tremblay looks in the mirror and doesn't like what he sees; theatre review of *Le Vrai monde?*. Ray Conlogue. photo · *G&M* Oct 2, 1987: pD10.

Le théâtre qu'on joue; theatre reviews of *Le Printemps, monsieur Deslauriers* and *Le Vrai monde?*. André Dionne. photo · *Lettres québec* Autumn 1987; No 47: p49–50.

Grandeur et misère: le retour du père sur la scène québécoise; article. Carole Fréchette. photo · *Jeu* 1987; No 45: p17–35.
[QUEBEC DRAMA (FRENCH LANGUAGE): HISTORY AND CRITICISM]

A playwright bares his soul; theatre review of *Le Vrai monde?*. Matthew Fraser. photo · *G&M* April 25, 1987: pC5.

Au coeur de l'imaginaire; theatre review of *Le Vrai monde?*. Madeleine Greffard. photo · *Liberté* Dec 1987; Vol 29 No 6: p146–147.

27 mars, journée mondiale du théâtre; column. Robert Lévesque. photo · *MD* March 24, 1987: p11.
[FESTIVALS, DRAMA]

Le grand règlement de comptes de Michel Tremblay; theatre review of *Le Vrai monde?*. Robert Lévesque. photo · *MD* April 6, 1987: p11.

Le retour magistral de Tremblay; theatre review of *Le Vrai monde?*. Richard Lévesque. photo · *MD* April 16, 1987: p15.

Reality, fiction mix in new Tremblay play; theatre review of *Le Vrai monde?*. Margaret Penman. *TS* Oct 4, 1987: pC4.

Du déjà goûté quelque part; theatre review of *Le Vrai monde?*. Jean-Robert Rémillard. *Liberté* Dec 1987; Vol 29 No 6: p145–146.

Narcisse se regarde dans l'eau jusqu'à y plonger . . . ; theatre review of *Le Vrai monde?*. Jean-Guy Sabourin. *Liberté* Dec 1987; Vol 29 No 6: p144–145.

The laugh's on apartheid in one-man show; column. Vit Wagner. photo · *TS* Sept 25, 1987: pE6.

WADDINGTON, MIRIAM

Tiger poems; reviews of poetry books. M. Travis Lane. *Fiddlehead* Autumn 1987; No 153: p88–91.

[Untitled]; review of *Collected Poems*. Tom Marshall. *Queen's Q* Summer 1987; Vol 94 No 2: p474–475.

A green world; review of *Collected Poems*. Eva Tihanyi. *Waves* Winter 1987; Vol 15 No 3: p78–80.

WADE, BRYAN

Making image theatre; article. James O'Regan. *Can Theatre R* Spring 1987; No 50: p10–13.

WAH, FRED

Fred Wah: poet as theor(h)et(or)ician; article. Pamela Banting. *Open Letter* Spring 1987; Vol 6 No 7: p5–20.
[STRUCTURALIST WRITING AND CRITICISM]

Red Deer Press series champions western writers; reviews of poetry books. Murdoch Burnett. *CH* Dec 13, 1987: pC11.

Parlour pump organs and prairie cafes; reviews of *Waiting for Saskatchewan* and *The Louis Riel Organ & Piano Company*. Phillip Lanthier. *NeWest R* April 1987; Vol 12 No 8: p13,15.

Culture director's tribute to author captured sentiment; column. Kenneth McGoogan. photo · *CH* Jan 27, 1987: pB6.
[AUDIO-VISUALS AND CANADIAN LITERATURE; POETRY READINGS]

[Untitled]; review of *Waiting for Saskatchewan*. Erin Mouré. *Rubicon* Spring 1987; No 8: p187–189.

Don't sit around language: an interview with Fred Wah. Lola Lemire Tostevin. *Poetry Can R* Fall 1987; Vol 9 No 1: p3–5.

"Citizens-in-language"; reviews of *The Louis Riel Organ & Piano Co.* and *Waiting for Saskatchewan*. Lorraine York. *Essays on Can Writ* Winter 1987; No 35: p171–177.

WAINWRIGHT, J.A.

Drama of failed pole trek unfulfilled; reviews of *Flight of the Falcon* and *Poems New and Selected*. Keith Garebian. *TS* Oct 31, 1987: M5.

[Untitled]; reviews of poetry books. Stephen Scobie. *Malahat R* Dec 1987; No 81: p104–106.

WAITING FOR SASKATCHEWAN/Poems by Fred Wah

Parlour pump organs and prairie cafes; reviews of *Waiting for Saskatchewan* and *The Louis Riel Organ & Piano Company*. Phillip Lanthier. *NeWest R* April 1987; Vol 12 No 8: p13,15.

[Untitled]; review of *Waiting for Saskatchewan*. Erin Mouré. *Rubicon* Spring 1987; No 8: p187–189.

"Citizens-in-language"; reviews of *The Louis Riel Organ & Piano Co.* and *Waiting for Saskatchewan*. Lorraine York. *Essays on Can Writ* Winter 1987; No 35: p171–177.

WAITING FOR THE MESSIAH: REFLECTIONS ON MY EARLY DAYS/Autobiography by Irving Layton

Zarathustran; review of *Waiting for the Messiah*. Graham Forst. *Can Lit* Spring 1987; No 112: p109–110.

[Untitled]; review of *Waiting for the Messiah*. Peter Herman. *Rubicon* Spring 1987; No 8: p181–183.

Elspeth Cameron and Irving Layton; reviews of *Irving Layton: A Portrait* and *Waiting for the Messiah*. Patricia Keeney Smith. *U of Toronto Q* Spring 1987; Vol 56 No 3: p467–470.

LA WAITRESS/Play by Raymond Lvesque

Bozo et les bas-culottes; theatre review of *La Waitress*. Marc Morin. photo · *MD* Feb 25, 1987: p8.

WALKER, GEORGE F.

Satan with a sword; article. John Bemrose. photo · *Maclean's* May 25, 1987; Vol 100 No 21: p55.

[Untitled]; theatre review of *Beautiful City*. John Bemrose. photo · *Maclean's* Oct 19, 1987; Vol 100 No 42: p70.

A triumph of Gothic comedy; theatre review of *Zastrozzi*. Ray Conlogue. photo · *G&M* May 14, 1987: pC3.

Walker has left the city but the city hasn't left him; article. Ray Conlogue. photo · *G&M* Sept 19, 1987: pC1,C4

Flaws show in Beautiful City; theatre review. Ray Conlogue. photo · *G&M* Oct 1, 1987: pD5.

French version of Walker play riddled with extra problems; theatre review of *L'Amour en deroute*. Ray Conlogue. photo · *G&M* Nov 16, 1987: pD12.

Dramatic trilogies; review of *The Power Plays*. L.W. Conolly. *Can Lit* Spring 1987; No 112: p110–112.

Zastrozzi returns in splended form; theatre review. Robert Crew. photo · *TS* May 14, 1987: pF3.

Play's real anger diluted: potential George Walker firecracker fizzles into sentimentality; theatre review of *Beautiful City*. Robert Crew. photo · *TS* Oct 1, 1987: pE1.

Chain letter; article. Martin Knelman. illus · *Tor Life* May 1987; Vol 21 No 7: p11.

[Untitled]; theatre review of *Zastrozzi*. Martin Knelman. *Tor Life* June 1987; Vol 21 No 9: p115.

Sword plays: it's fight for the right to parry; article. Henry Mietkiewicz. photo · *TS* May 8, 1987: pD3.

Magic of popular play is lost in translation; theatre review of *L'Amour en DeRoute*. Margaret Penman. *TS* Nov 16, 1987: pB6.

Curse of the shopping class; article. Vit Wagner. photo · *TS* Sept 25, 1987: pE1,E3.

Blowing bubbles with Simone and Sartre; column. Vit Wagner. photo · *TS* Nov 6, 1987: pE4.
[TRANSLATIONS OF CANADIAN LITERATURE]

WALKING SLOW/Poems by Helen Potrebenko

Two ways of making poetry; reviews of *The Prismatic Eye* and *Walking Slow*. Paul Barclay. *Prairie Fire* Summer 1987; Vol 8 No 2: p56–59.

Grief & memory; reviews of poetry books. Peter Stenberg. *Can Lit* Spring 1987; No 112: p169–171.

WALLACE, IAN

Billboard: Whiteshell carnival starts today; column. *WFP* Feb 13, 1987: p36.
[FICTION READINGS]

Morgan, May, Melinda: new heroines offer humour and fantasy; reviews of children's books. Bernie Goedhart. *Quill & Quire (Books for Young People)* Oct 1987; Vol 53 No 10: p24.

Daring diner date jogs writer; column. Kenneth McGoogan. photo · *CH* Dec 20, 1987: pE6.

'Daring girl' who captured author's heart stars in book; article. Leslie Scrivener. biog photo · *TS* Dec 6, 1987: pD5.

Dreams of magical change; review of *Morgan the Magnificent*. Tim Wynne-Jones. *G&M* Dec 19, 1987: pC26.

WALSH, MARNI

Wanted! One detective show; theatre review of *Wanted!*. Robert Davis. photo · *TS (Neighbours)* May 26, 1987: p19.

Maritime Song needs a tune-up; theatre review. Alex Law. *TS (Neighbors)* Sept 22, 1987: p26.

Maritime Song has promise, lacks cohesion; theatre review. Alex Law. photo · *TS (Neighbors)* Sept 22, 1987: p13.

Angel Star a sweet treat but not much substance; theatre review of *Merry Christmas Angel Star*. Alex Law. *TS (Neighbors)* Dec 1, 1987: p19.

WALSHE, ROBERT

World's waiting for second Walshe novel; column. Ken Adachi. *TS* July 20, 1987: pB7.

WANTED!/Play by Marni Walsh and Steven Baker

Wanted! One detective show; theatre review of *Wanted!*. Robert Davis. photo · *TS (Neighbours)* May 26, 1987: p19.

WAR BABIES/Play by Margaret Hollingsworth

War Babies: du théâtre féroce; theatre review. Marie-France Bomais. photo · *MD (L'Express de Toronto)* March 17, 1987: p4.

Playwright avoids 'giving answers'; article. Ray Conlogue. photo · *G&M* March 2, 1987: pD9.

Shuttling between layers of reality; theatre review of *War Babies*. Ray Conlogue. photo · *G&M* March 4, 1987: pC8.

Intelligent writer lost in translating to drama; theatre review of *War Babies*. Robert Crew. photo · *TS* March 4, 1987: pB3.

WAR IN CANADIAN LITERATURE

Canadian servicemen's memoirs of the Second World War; article. Michael A. Mason. *Mosaic* Fall 1987; Vol 20 No 4: p11–22.
[AUTOBIOGRAPHICAL WRITING]

WARD, FRED

New play at Centaur is strong medicine — and a strange mixture; theatre review of *Somebody Somebody's Returning*. Marianne Ackerman. *MG* Feb 6, 1987: pD1.

Don't get the wrong idea — writer Ward's an original; article. Marianne Ackerman. photo · *MG* Feb 11, 1987: pB7.

WARD, NORMAN

What would you do as PM?; article. Jim Foster. *TS* Nov 8, 1987: pD7.

WARREN, LOUISE

[Untitled]; review of *Écrire la lumière*. Hugues Corriveau. *Estuaire* Summer 1987; No 45: p59.

THE WART ON MY FINGER/Children's story by Audrey Nelson

[Untitled]; review of *The Wart on My Finger*. Susan Perren. *Quill & Quire (Books for Young People)* June 1987; Vol 53 No 6: p11.

WASOM-ELLAM, LINDA

Legend of Calgary no ordinary tall tale; column. Joan Craven. *CH (Neighbors)* July 8, 1987: pA8.

WATERTON, BETTY

If at first you don't succeed; review of *Starring Quincy Rumpel*. Brenda M. Schmidt. *Can Child Lit* 1987; No 46: p81–82.

WATMOUGH, DAVID

The gaucherie and confusion of early manhood; review of *The Year of Fears*. Pauline Carey. *G&M* Oct 17, 1987: pE4.

Against the reasoning mind; reviews of *In the Village of Alias* and *Vibrations in Time*. Jon Kertzer. *Fiddlehead* Autumn 1987; No 153: p97–100.

[Untitled]; reviews. Janet Windeler. *Cross Can Writ Q* 1987; Vol 9 No 2: p25–26.
[FIRST NOVELS: BOOK REVIEWS]

WATSON, SHEILA

Miracle, mystery, and authority: rereading The Double Hook; article. Glen Deer. *Open Letter* Summer 1987; Vol 6 No 8: p25–43.
[THE FAMILY IN CANADIAN LITERATURE; MYTHS AND LEGENDS IN CANADIAN LITERATURE]

Rummaging in the sewing basket of the gods: Sheila Watson's "Antigone"; article. Judith Miller. *Studies in Can Lit* 1987; Vol 12 No 2: p212–221.
[MYTHS AND LEGENDS IN CANADIAN LITERATURE]

Resident & alien; review of *Sheila Watson and The Double Hook*. Michael Peterman. *Can Lit* Winter 1987; No 115: p144–146.

Fiction, break, silence: language. Sheila Watson's The Double Hook; article. Margaret E. Turner. *Ariel* April 1987; Vol 18 No 2: p65–78.
[CULTURAL IDENTITY]

WATSON, WILFRED

[Untitled]; review of *Poems*. George Woodcock. *Poetry Can R* Spring 1987; Vol 8 No 2–3: p56–57.

WATT, FRANK W.

From ivy-covered professors; reviews of poetry books. Fraser Sutherland. *G&M* Oct 17, 1987: pE9.

WAVES/Periodical

Editor's note. Bernice Lever. *Waves* Spring 1987; Vol 15 No 4: p94.
[CANADIAN LITERARY PERIODICALS]

WAXMAN, MARTIN

Oh, for the good old days; letter to the editor. Judith Fitzgerald. *Quill & Quire* July 1987; Vol 53 No 7: p6.

There's still room for the Great Mall Novel; review of *The Promised Land*. William French. photo · *G&M* March 19, 1987: pD1.
[FIRST NOVELS: BOOK REVIEWS]

Columns prompt readers to write; column. William French. *G&M* April 7, 1987: pC7.

[Untitled]; review of *The Promised Land*. Cecelia Frey. *CH* May 17, 1987: pE5.
[FIRST NOVELS: BOOK REVIEWS]

Urban scrawl; reviews of first novels. Janice Kulyk Keefer. *Books in Can* Aug-Sept 1987; Vol 16 No 6: p33–34.
[FIRST NOVELS: BOOK REVIEWS]

Comic novel falls flat; review of *The Promised Land*. Norman Sigurdson. photo · *WFP* May 2, 1987: p84.
[FIRST NOVELS: BOOK REVIEWS]

Book world: where the $$$ land — legally; column. Beverley Slopen. *TS* March 1, 1987: pA15.
[PUBLISHING AND PUBLISHERS IN CANADA; WRITERS-IN-RESIDENCE]

[Untitled]; review of *The Promised Land*. Thomas P. Sullivan. *Quill & Quire* May 1987; Vol 53 No 5: p20,22.
[FIRST NOVELS: BOOK REVIEWS]

WAYMAN, TOM

Waiting for Wayman to get off work; article. Phil Hall. *Quarry* Fall 1987; Vol 36 No 4: p73–77.

[Untitled]; review of *The Face of Jack Munro*. Gerald Hill. *Poetry Can R* Spring 1987; Vol 8 No 2–3: p46–47.

Looking for the face of Saturday night; review of *The Face of Jack Munro*. John Lent. *CV 2* Summer 1987; Vol 10 No 4: p52–54.

Tom Wayman's work poetry; article. Grant Shilling. *Poetry Can R* Spring 1987; Vol 8 No 2–3: p20–21.
[POLITICAL WRITING]

Poetry and solidarity — uneasy bedfellows?; review of *The Face of Jack Munro*. Diana Wegner. *Event* Summer 1987; Vol 16 No 2: p110–115.

WE'RE FRIENDS, AREN'T WE?/Young adult novel by Sylvia Gunnery

Living to tell the tale: survival guides for adolescent readers; reviews of *Can You Promise Me Spring?* and *We're Friends, Aren't We?*. Joanne Buckley. *Can Child Lit* 1987; No 46: p78–79.

[Untitled]; review of *We're Friends, Aren't We?*. Lawrence Jackson. *Can Auth & Book* Winter 1987; Vol 62 No 2: p24.

WEATHERING IT/Poems by Douglas LePan

With these older poets, the strengths are intrinsic; reviews of poetry books. Judith Fitzgerald. photo · *TS* Dec 20, 1987: pE6

WEAVER, ROBERT

Magazine to have face lift; column. Ken Adachi. photo · *TS* Dec 15, 1987: pG4.
[CANADIAN LITERARY PERIODICALS]

WEBB, PADDY

[Untitled]; reviews of *Rough Passage* and *April Raintree*. Judith Russell. *Queen's Q* Spring 1987; Vol 94 No 1: p191–193.

WEBB, PHYLLIS

Mainstreet Calgary; column. *CH (Neighbors)* April 1, 1987: pA4.
[POETRY READINGS; WRITERS' WORKSHOPS]

"Proceeding before the amorous invisible": Phyllis Webb and the Ghazal; article. Susan Glickman. *Can Lit* Winter 1987; No 115: p48–61.

WEDDING IN TEXAS AND OTHER STORIES/Play by Cathy Jones

Wacky Cathy Jones returns; theatre review of *Wedding in Texas and Other Stories*. Robert Crew. photo · *TS* Feb 18, 1987: pE3.

WEIER, JOHN

Chapbooks range from good to silly; reviews of poetry books. Robert Quickenden. *WFP* Jan 31, 1987: p55.

THE WEIGHT OF ORANGES/Poems by Anne Michaels

[Untitled]; review of *The Weight of Oranges*. Paul Dutton. *Quill & Quire* Jan 1987; Vol 53 No 1: p32.

[Untitled]; review of *The Weight of Oranges*. Anne Todkill. *Quarry* Winter 1987; Vol 36 No 1: p131–133.

WEINER, ANDREW

Andrew Weiner; interview. Terence M. Green. photo · *Books in Can* Oct 1987; Vol 16 No 7: p38–40.

Book world: what about Frankfurt? A hemline dilemma; column. Beverley Slopen. *TS* Sept 13, 1987: pA22.

WEIR, IAN

Charming comedy toys with the work ethic; theatre review of *The Idler*. Stephen Godfrey. photo · *G&M* Sept 29, 1987: pD5.

WEIR, JOAN S.

Horse stories tell of struggles to achieve personal worth; reviews of *Storm Rider* and *Summer Goes Riding*. Callie Israel. photo · *Quill & Quire (Books for Young People)* Oct 1987; Vol 53 No 10: p16.

WEISS, ANNE-MARIE

[Untitled]; review of *Schizotexte*. Quendrith Johnson. *Rubicon* Spring 1987; No 8: p186–187.

[Untitled]; review of *Schizotexte*. Sparling Mills. *Poetry Can R* Summer 1987; Vol 8 No 4: p38.

WEISS, JONATHAN M.

[Untitled]; reviews of *Theatre and Politics in Modern Quebec* and *French-Canadian Theater*. L.E. Doucette. *U of Toronto Q* Fall 1987; Vol 57 No 1: p186–189.

WEISS, PETER ELIOT

Lunchbox hopes farce will score; article. Brian Brennan. photo · *CH* Sept 25, 1987: pF1.

Sex Tips tastefully, cleverly staged; theatre review of *Sex Tips for Modern Girls*. Brian Brennan. photo · *CH* Sept 29, 1987: pD7.

WELCH, LILIANE

[Untitled]; reviews of poetry books. Anita Hurwitz. *Poetry Can R* Spring 1987; Vol 8 No 2–3: p50–51.

Poetry as cheirography; essay. Liliane Welch. illus · *Poetry Can R* Spring 1987; Vol 8 No 1–2: p8–9.

WENKCHEMNA/Poems by Jon Whyte

[Untitled]; reviews of *Blind Zone* and *Wenkchemna*. Dennis Duffy. *Poetry Can R* Spring 1987; Vol 8 No 2–3: p45.

WEST COAST REVIEW/Periodical

Index to volume 19/4 — volume 21/4. *West Coast R* Spring 1987; Vol 21 No 4: p83–88.
[CANADIAN LITERARY PERIODICALS]

WHALE WADDLEBY/Children's poems by Judith Fitzgerald

[Untitled]; review of *Whale Waddleby*. Dexter Peters. *TS* Feb 1, 1987: pA20.

WHALLEY, GEORGE

[Untitled]; review of *Studies in Literature and the Humanities*. J.R. de J. Jackson. *Eng Studies in Can* June 1987; Vol 13 No 2: p229–234.

[Untitled]; reviews of *Studies in Literature and the Humanities* and *The Impossible Sum of Our Traditions* W.J. Keith. *U of Toronto Q* Fall 1987; Vol 57 No 1: p145–148.

You ask me what I'm thinking; reviews of poetry books. M. Travis Lane. *Fiddlehead* Winter 1987; No 154: p95–104.

[Untitled]; review of *The Collected Poems of George Whalley*. David Lewis. *Queen's Q* Winter 1987; Vol 94 No 4: p1045–1047.

Three poets dare to reject labelling; reviews of poetry books. Patricia Smith. *TS* July 4, 1987: M4.

A plumber of bathetic depths; reviews of *Islands* and *The Collected Poems of George Whalley*. Fraser Sutherland. photo · *G&M* July 18, 1987: pC15.

WHAT'S BRED IN THE BONE/Novel by Robertson Davies

Novel slated for TV; article. *WFP* April 9, 1987: p45.
[TELEVISION AND CANADIAN LITERATURE]

Robertson Davies novel to become TV mini-series; article. *CH* April 9, 1987: pE2.
[TELEVISION AND CANADIAN LITERATURE]

Davies' hit novel to be TV mini-series; article. photo · *TS* April 8, 1987: pD1.
[TELEVISION AND CANADIAN LITERATURE]

Mini-series bred from Davies' novel; article. John Haslett Cuff. photo · *G&M* April 8, 1987: pC7.
[TELEVISION AND CANADIAN LITERATURE]

[Untitled]; review of *What's Bred in the Bone*. Margaret Keith. *Northward J* 1987; No 43: p43–46.

WHAT FEATHERS ARE FOR/Poems by Maria Jacobs

Writing life; reviews of *Hired Hands* and *What Feathers Are For*. Arthur Adamson. *Can Lit* Winter 1987; No 115: p230–232.

[Untitled]; reviews of poetry books. Barbara Carey. *Cross Can Writ Q* 1987; Vol 9 No 1: p23–24.

Jacobs, Lever, Marriott; reviews of poetry books. Barry Dempster. *Poetry Can R* Spring 1987; Vol 8 No 2–3: p35.

The family business; reviews of *What Feathers Are For* and *Squid Inc 86*. Kim Van Vliet. *Waves* Spring 1987; Vol 15 No 4: p88–91.

WHAT THE CROW SAID/Novel by Robert Kroetsch

Novelist as trickster: the magical presence of Gabriel García Márquez in Robert Kroetsch's What The Crow Said; article. Brian Edwards. *Essays on Can Writ* Spring 1987; No 34: p92–110.
[LATIN AMERICA-CANADA LITERARY RELATIONS; MAGIC REALISM; POSTMODERNIST WRITING AND CRITICISM; STRUCTURALIST WRITING AND CRITICISM]

WHAT WE BRING HOME/Poems by Judith Krause

The elephant: a federal or provincial responsibility?; review of *What We Bring Home*. Paul Denham. illus · *NeWest R* Summer 1987; Vol 12 No 10: p14.

[Untitled]; reviews of poetry books. Sheila Martindale. *Cross Can Writ Q* 1987; Vol 9 No 2: p20–21.

First books from five regional presses; reviews of poetry books. Colin Morton. *Arc* Spring 1987; No 18: p52–59.

An auspicious debut; review of *What We Bring Home*. Richard Stevenson. *Prairie Fire* Summer 1987; Vol 8 No 2: p60–62.

WHEATLEY, PATIENCE

[Untitled]; review of *A Hinge of Spring*. Karen Ruttan. *Poetry Can R* Fall 1987; Vol 9 No 1: p32–33.

THE WHEELS ON THE BUS/Children's story by Maryann Kovalski

Make way for a fine crop of picture-books; reviews of children's books. Adele Ashby. *Quill & Quire (Books for Young People)* Aug 1987; Vol 53 No 8: p6.

Gammer Gurton leaps from early English stage into the 20th century; reviews of children's books. Janice Kennedy. *MG* Nov 21, 1987: J13.

A title that will grab teenagers; reviews of children's books. Joan McGrath. *TS* Oct 25, 1987: pA18.

[Untitled]; review of *The Wheels on the Bus*. Gen Weinmayr. *CH* Dec 6, 1987: pD9.

WHEN I'M BIG/Play by Rob Wipond and Allen Booth

Short plays confront man's helplessness; theatre review of *When I'm Big*. Vit Wagner. *TS* Dec 1, 1987: H4.

Duo borrows big from Smothers Brothers' style; column. Vit Wagner. *TS* Nov 27, 1987: pD12.

WHEN THE STONES FLY UP/Poems by Dale Zieroth

A choice of codes; reviews of poetry books. Thomas Gerry. illus · *NeWest R* Nov 1987; Vol 13 No 3: p16–17.

Frost shadows; reviews of poetry books. Andrew Taylor. *Can Lit* Winter 1987; No 115: p197–199.

THE WHIRLPOOL/Novel by Jane Urquhart

Brian Moore's Jesuit priest travels into heart of darkness; reviews of novels. Barbara Black. *MG* March 7, 1987: H11.

Novel loses its energy in whirlpool; review of *The Whirlpool*. Cecelia Frey. *CH* Jan 11, 1987: pF4.

[Untitled]; review of *The Whirlpool*. Sherie Posesorski. *Books in Can* Jan-Feb 1987; Vol 16 No 1: p26.
[FIRST NOVELS: BOOK REVIEWS]

The summer before Browning died; review of *The Whirlpool*. Aritha van Herk. *Brick* Fall 1987; No 31: p15–17.
[FIRST NOVELS: BOOK REVIEWS]

[Untitled]; reviews of *Vigil* and *The Whirlpool*. Alice Van Wart. *Can Forum* Aug-Sept 1987; Vol 67 No 771: p46–48.
[FIRST NOVELS: BOOK REVIEWS]

WHISKEY JACK/Poems by Milton Acorn

Standing up for himself; reviews of *The Uncollected Acorn* and *Whiskey Jack*. Paul Denham. *Books in Can* June-July 1987; Vol 16 No 5: p30,32.

Acorn: swept up in imagery; review of *Whiskey Jack*. Maggie Helwig. photo · *TS* Feb 8, 1987: pG8.

Rush job, high gloss and high-risk realism; reviews of poetry books. Fraser Sutherland. *G&M* March 21, 1987: pE18.

WHISKEY SIX CADENZA/Play by Sharon Pollock

[Untitled]; reviews. Lisbie Rae. *Can Drama* 1987; Vol 13 No 2: p229–231.
[ANTHOLOGIES: BOOK REVIEWS]

WHISPERLAND/Novel by Christopher Hyde

Crime writers who use the macabre to maximum effect; review of *Whisperland*. Margaret Cannon. photo · *G&M* Nov 21, 1987: pC23.

WHISPERS OF MOONLIGHT/Play by Gregory Heyn

Insight Theatre shows get better and better; theatre review of *Whispers of Moonlight*. Robert Davis. *TS (Neighbors)* Aug 11, 1987: p16.

WHITE BITING DOG/Play by Judith Thompson

Play likely to be tough viewing; article. Brad Oswald. photo · *WFP* Nov 7, 1987: p23.

THE WHITE DOGS OF TEXAS/Play by Alan Williams

White Dogs exposes harmful legacy of rational thought; theatre review of *The White Dogs of Texas*. Reg Skene. *WFP* April 28, 1987: p32.

WHITE MIST/Children's story by Barbara Smucker

History lessons; review of *White Mist*. Gwyneth Evans. *Can Child Lit* 1987; No 45: p55–57.

WHITE OF THE LESSER ANGELS/Poems by Janice Kulyk Keefer

[Untitled]; reviews of *The Paris-Napoli Express* and *White of the Lesser Angels*. Elizabeth Brewster. *Event* March 1987; Vol 16 No 1: p103–104.

Exile & belonging: two Maritime poets; reviews of *White of the Lesser Angels* and *Tiger in the Skull*. Richard Lemm. *Atlan Prov Book R* May-June 1987; Vol 14 No 2: p10.

[Untitled]; review of *White of the Lesser Angels*. Tom Marshall. *U of Windsor R* Fall-Winter 1987; Vol 20 No 1: p94–95.

Rush job, high gloss and high-risk realism; reviews of poetry books. Fraser Sutherland. *G&M* March 21, 1987: pE18.

Oranges and onions; reviews of *White of the Lesser Angels* and *The Abbotsford Guide to India*. Fred Wah. *Books in Can* March 1987; Vol 16 No 2: p32,34.

WHITE, PATRICK

[Untitled]; reviews of poetry books. Bruce Hunter. *Cross Can Writ Q* 1987; Vol 9 No 3–4: p40–42.

Grief & memory; reviews of poetry books. Peter Stenberg. *Can Lit* Spring 1987; No 112: p169–171.

WHITEMAN, BRUCE

Excesses; reviews of poetry books. Eva Tihanyi. *Can Lit* Winter 1987; No 115: p200–202.

WHITFIELD, AGNÈS

La vitrine du livre; reviews of *Le Je(u) illocutoire* and *XYZ*. Guy Ferland. *MD* Aug 1, 1987: pC6.
[CANADIAN LITERARY PERIODICALS]

WHITTAKER'S THEATRE/Theatre reviews by Herbert Whittaker

[Untitled]; review of *Whittaker's Theatre*. Richard Plant. *Can Theatre R* Winter 1987; No 53: p79–80.

WHITTAKER, HERBERT

[Untitled]; review of *Whittaker's Theatre*. Richard Plant. *Can Theatre R* Winter 1987; No 53: p79–80.

WHITTALL, JAMES

[Untitled]; reviews of poetry books. Shaunt Basmajian. *Cross Can Writ Q* 1987; Vol 9 No 3–4: p44,49.
[ANTHOLOGIES: BOOK REVIEWS]

[Untitled]; reviews of poetry books. Andrew Parkin. *Poetry Can R* Fall 1987; Vol 9 No 1: p37.
[ANTHOLOGIES: BOOK REVIEWS]

WHO'S AFRAID OF SIGMUND FREUD?/Novel by T.P. Millar

Freudian farce; review of *Who's Afraid of Sigmund Freud?*. Kay Stockholder. *Can Lit* Spring 1987; No 112: p162–164.

WHO'S TO SAY?/Poems by Liane Heller

[Untitled]; reviews of *Who's to Say?* and *Shaking the Dreamland Tree*. Susan Glickman. *Poetry Can R* Summer 1987; Vol 8 No 4: p32.

Young poets on display; reviews of poetry books. Robert Quickenden. photo · *WFP* March 14, 1987: p52.

[Untitled]; reviews of poetry books. Martin Singleton. *Cross Can Writ Q* 1987; Vol 9 No 3–4: p38–39.

WHO HIDES IN THE PARK/Children's poem by Warab Aska

Mini-reviews; reviews of children's books. Margaret Paré. *Can Child Lit* 1987; No 45: p93–96.

WHO IS FRANCES RAIN?/Young adult novel by Margaret Buffie

Past and present merge in painful, haunting tales; reviews of *False Face* and *Who Is Frances Rain?*. Peter Carver. photo · *Quill & Quire (Books for Young People)* Oct 1987; Vol 53 No 10: p10.
[FIRST NOVELS: BOOK REVIEWS]

Chit chat; column. Maria Casas. *Quill & Quire (Books for Young People)* Oct 1987; Vol 53 No 10: p8.

Literary lions linger in libraries; reviews of children's books. Joan McGrath. *TS* Dec 20, 1987: pE5.

A mystery in Manitoba; review of *Who Is Frances Rain?*, Helen Norrie. *WFP* Dec 5, 1987: p57.
[FIRST NOVELS: BOOK REVIEWS]

WHYTE, ALI-JANNA

[Untitled]; review of *Economic Sex*. Richard Hamilton. *Rubicon* Spring 1987; No 8: p226.

Full stops; review of *Economic Sex*. Leon Surette. *Can Lit* Winter 1987; No 115: p245–246.
[FIRST NOVELS: BOOK REVIEWS]

WHYTE, JON

[Untitled]; reviews of *Blind Zone* and *Wenkchemna*. Dennis Duffy. *Poetry Can R* Spring 1987; Vol 8 No 2–3: p45.

WIEBE, ARMIN

Successful local novel to be made into film; article. Donald Campbell. *WFP* Sept 26, 1987: p30.
[FILM ADAPTATIONS OF CANADIAN LITERATURE]

WIEBE, RUDY

Nouvelles du centre; article. Michel Fabre. *Afram* June 1987; No 25: p1–2.

Oral Wiebe; interview with Rudy Wiebe. Wolfgang Hochbruck. *Zeitschrift Kanada-Studien* 1987; Vol 7 No 1: p251–254.

Writers' event grows on young people; column. Kenneth McGoogan. *CH* March 29, 1987: pE5.
[CONFERENCES, LITERARY; WRITERS' WORKSHOPS]

Historicity in historical fiction: Burning Water and The Temptations Of Big Bear; article. Carla Visser. *Studies in Can Lit* 1987; Vol 12 No 1: p90–111.
[HISTORICAL FICTION]

WIELER, DIANA J.

Literary extravaganza goes national; column. Kenneth McGoogan. *CH* April 5, 1987: pE5.
[AUTHORS, CANADIAN; FILM ADAPTATIONS OF CANADIAN LITERATURE; WRITERS' ORGANIZATIONS; WRITERS' WORKSHOPS]

What troubles troubled kids; review of *Last Chance Summer*. Douglas Thorpe. *Can Child Lit* 1987; No 46: p86–87.

Western publisher produces winners only; reviews of *Last Chance Summer* and *The Empty Chair*. Tim Wynne-Jones. *G&M* Feb 21, 1987: pE19.

WILD CHILD/Play by Flix Mirbt

Making image theatre; article. James O'Regan. *Can Theatre R* Spring 1987; No 50: p10–13.

WILD GEESE/Novel by Martha Ostenso

Possessing the promised land; editorial. Paul Denham. *NeWest R* Nov 1987; Vol 13 No 3: p1.

[Untitled]; letter to the editor. Margaret Gail Osachoff. *NeWest R* Dec 1987; Vol 13 No 4: p1.

WILD NIGHT/Young adult novel by Martyn Godfrey

A little help on the dull days; reviews of children's books. Joan McGrath. *TS* Aug 2, 1987: pC11.

WILDERNESS WRITING

Introduction par Marie Le Franc de la forêt en littérature québécoise; article. Madeleine Ducrocq-Poirier. abstract · *Études can* 1987; No 23: p87–92.

Taking to the woods: of myths, metaphors and poets; article. Barbara Godard. abstract · *Études can* 1987; No 23: p159–171.
[CONFEDERATION POETRY AND POETS; CULTURAL IDENTITY]

The dark pines of the mind: the symbol of the forest in Canadian literature; article. Rosemary Sullivan. abstract · *Études can* 1987; No 23: p173–182.
[NATURE IN CANADIAN LITERATURE]

WILKINSON, ANNE

The tradition: "Her long duty cut short": on Anne Wilkinson; column. Bruce Whiteman. *Poetry Can R* Fall 1987; Vol 9 No 1: p10.

WILL TO LIFE/Poems by Sarah Jackson and Margaret Harry

Sarah Jackson's book works; reviews of books by Sarah Jackson. Alexa Thompson. *Atlan Prov Book R* Sept-Oct 1987; Vol 14 No 3: p15.

WILLFUL ACTS/Plays by Margaret Hollingsworth

[Untitled]; review of *Willful Acts*. Linda M. Peake. *Theatre Hist in Can (special issue)* Spring 1987; Vol 8 No 1: p126–129.

WILLIAMS BENNETT, JO ANNE

[Untitled]; review of *Downfall People*. Frank Manley. *Books in Can* Jan-Feb 1987; Vol 16 No 1: p24–25.
[FIRST NOVELS: BOOK REVIEWS]

WILLIAMS, ALAN

Students get Rude about acting; article. *G&M* July 30, 1987: pD6.

Brilliant comic leaves us gasping; column. Robert Fulford. photo · *TS* June 20, 1987: M5.

Daredevil dramatist slips out of focus; theatre review of *Dixieland's Night of Shame*. Stephen Godfrey. photo · *G&M* May 9, 1987: pC5

Festival One plays singularly successful; theatre reviews. Stephen Godfrey. photo · *G&M* May 8, 1987: pF9.
[FESTIVALS, DRAMA]

Tall tales and home truths; article. Liam Lacey. photo · *G&M* Aug 22, 1987: pC3.
[FESTIVALS, DRAMA]

Indecisive play fails to elicit empathy for young characters; theatre review of *Rock Is Dead*. Randal McIlroy. *WFP* July 25, 1987: p48.

Inspired comic shares sharp observations; theatre review of *Dixieland's Night of Shame*. Henry Mietkiewicz. photo · *TS* June 2, 1987: pG3.

Challenging the commonplaces; introduction to play excerpt from *The King of America*. Rory Runnells. *Prairie Fire* Spring 1987; Vol 8 No 1: p56.

White Dogs exposes harmful legacy of rational thought; theatre review of *The White Dogs of Texas*. Reg Skene. *WFP* April 28, 1987: p32.

Williams' King Of America intelligent, rich and funny; theatre review. Reg Skene. *WFP* May 3, 1987: p15.

Theatrical satire hits target; theatre review of *Dixieland's Night of Shame*. Reg Skene. *WFP* May 8, 1987: p23.

WILLIAMS, DAVID

Rune-writer; review of *Eye of the Father*. William Latta. *Can Lit* Winter 1987; No 115: p191–193.

WILLIAMS, HARLAND

Lickety split! He's hoping kids' books will zoom him to top; article. Phil Johnson. *TS (Neighbors)* Nov 3, 1987: p8.

WILLIE THE SQUOWSE/Children's story by Ted Allan

'Squowse' sparkles for kids; theatre review of *Willie the Squowse*. Ray Conlogue. photo · *G&M* Dec 11, 1987: pD6.
[DRAMATIC ADAPTATIONS OF CANADIAN LITERATURE]

Delightfully tiny Willie makes a big impression; theatre review of *Willie the Squowse*. Christopher Hume. photo · *TS* Dec 11, 1987: pD14.
[DRAMATIC ADAPTATIONS OF CANADIAN LITERATURE]

WILSON, BUDGE

[Untitled]; review of *A House Far from Home*. Linda Granfield. *Quill & Quire (Books for Young People)* June 1987; Vol 53 No 6: p10.

Family ties and mysteries; reviews of children's novels. Joan McGrath. *Quill & Quire (Books for Young People)* Dec 1987; Vol 53 No 12: p10.

WILSON, ERIC

Chit chat; column. Maria Casas. *Quill & Quire (Books for Young People)* April 1987; Vol 53 No 4: p3.
[CHILDREN'S LITERATURE; CHINA-CANADA LITERARY RELATIONS; WRITERS-IN-RESIDENCE]

[Untitled]; review of *The Green Gables Detectives*. Fran Geitzler. *CH* Dec 6, 1987: pD9.

[Untitled]; reviews of *The Green Gables Detectives* and *The Loon Lake Murders*. Linda Granfield. *Quill & Quire (Books for Young People)* Aug 1987; Vol 53 No 8: p5–6.

The New World and the Old World for children; review of *The Green Gables Detectives*. Rosi Jory. *Atlan Prov Book R* Nov-Dec 1987; Vol 14 No 4: p4.

Baby of the family gets respect raising flock of Canada geese; reviews of children's books. Janice Kennedy. *MG* Oct 3, 1987: J13.

Canadian-set mysteries; reviews of children's novels by Eric Wilson. Sheila Ward. *Can Child Lit* 1987; No 48: p91–93.

Other cultures featured in tales for youths; reviews of *The Unmasking of 'Ksan* and *Naomi's Road*. Kate Zimmerman. *CH* July 19, 1987: pE4.

WILSON, SERGE

Week-end; column. *MD* April 18, 1987: pA10.

Dix années de littérature pour jeunes Québécois; article. Dominique Demers. photo · *MD* Nov 14, 1987: pD10.
[CANADIAN LITERARY PUBLISHING; CHILDREN'S LITERATURE]

THE WIMP AND THE JOCK/Young adult novel by John Ibbitson

Lite-lit for children has arrived; reviews of children's books. Tim Wynne-Jones. *G&M* March 7, 1987: pE19.

WINDFLOWER: POEMS OF BLISS CARMAN/Poems by Bliss Carman

Confederation poets; reviews. Ronald B. Hatch. *Can Lit* Winter 1987; No 115: p223–225.

WING, PAULA

Paula Wing's Lydia is filled with love, joy and rich spirit; column. Robert Crew. *TS* Nov 8, 1987: pC2.

Director says Lorca tragedy a timeless tale; column. Vit Wagner. photo · *TS* Oct 30, 1987: pE4.

WINGROVE, DOROTHY

World of wonders; reviews of first novels. Janice Kulyk Keefer. *Books in Can* May 1987; Vol 16 No 4: p37–38.
[FIRST NOVELS: BOOK REVIEWS]

WINNERS/LES VAINQUEURS/Young adult novel by Mary-Ellen Lang Collura

Littérature jeunesse; reviews of children's books. Domique Demers. *MD* Oct 10, 1987: pD6.

WINNING/Play by David Bolt

Lacrosse road trips inspired Bolt's play; article. Bob Blakey. photo · *CH* Jan 24, 1987: pA11

Play lacks clear plot; theatre review of *Winning*. Brian Brennan. photo · *CH* Jan 26, 1987: pB6.

Three Toronto plays premiere at Calgary fest; article, includes theatre reviews. Robert Crew. photo · *TS* Feb 10, 1987: pB4.
[FESTIVALS, DRAMA]

New-play festival deserves a curtain call; theatre reviews. Stephen Godfrey. photo · *G&M* Feb 10, 1987: pC5.
[FESTIVALS, DRAMA]

WINTER PROPHECIES/Poems by Ralph Gustafson

With these older poets, the strengths are intrinsic; reviews of poetry books. Judith Fitzgerald. photo · *TS* Dec 20, 1987: pE6.

WIPOND, ROB

Short plays confront man's helplessness; theatre review of *When I'm Big*. Vit Wagner. *TS* Dec 1, 1987: H4.

Duo borrows big from Smothers Brothers' style; column. Vit Wagner. *TS* Nov 27, 1987: pD12.

WISE-EARS/Novel by Nancy Bauer

Anybody home; reviews of *The Last Echo* and *Wise-Ears*. Linda Rogers. *Can Lit* Winter 1987; No 115: p204–205.

Recent Canadian fiction; reviews of novels. D.O. Spettigue. *Queen's Q* Summer 1987; Vol 94 No 2: p366–375.
[FIRST NOVELS: BOOK REVIEWS]

WISEMAN, ADELE

Writing program a splendid notion; column. Ken Adachi. photo · *TS* July 6, 1987: pD5.
[WRITERS' WORKSHOPS]

Wiseman wrote a moving memoir; review of *Memoirs of a Book-Molesting Childhood*. Ken Adachi. *TS* Nov 15, 1987: pA23.

A wonderful way to go; review of *Memoirs of a Book-Molesting Childhood*. Cary Fagan. *Books in Can* Dec 1987; Vol 16 No 9: p32–33.

Banff Centre lands novelist; column. Kenneth McGoogan. *CH* Feb 22, 1987: pE6.
[CANADIAN LITERARY PERIODICALS; PUBLISHING AND PUBLISHERS IN CANADA; WRITERS' WORKSHOPS]

Fine art of writing: Banff Centre nurtures authors, playwrights, screenwriters; article. Kenneth McGoogan. photo · *CH* May 16, 1987: pC1.
[WRITERS' WORKSHOPS]

Those accidents of truth that sneak up; review of *Memoirs of a Book-Molesting Childhood*. Marion Quednau. *G&M* Dec 26, 1987: pC23.

WISHBONES/Novel by Cynthia Long

From mind to mind; reviews of *Night Studies* and *Wishbones*. H.W. Connor. *Can Lit* Spring 1987; No 112: p118–120.
[FIRST NOVELS: BOOK REVIEWS]

THE WITCH/Poems by Jorge Etcheverry

[Untitled]; reviews of poetry books. Anita Hurwitz. *Poetry Can R* Spring 1987; Vol 8 No 2–3: p50–51.

WITH A SUDDEN & TERRIBLE CLARITY/Novel by Brian L. Flack

[Untitled]; review of *With a Sudden & Terrible Clarity*. Theresa Hurley. *Quarry* Spring 1987; Vol 36 No 2: p109–111.

WITTGENSTEIN ELEGIES/Poems by Jan Zwicky

[Untitled]; review of *Wittgenstein Elegies*. Anne Burke. *Poetry Can R* Spring 1987; Vol 8 No 2–3: p47.

Confident voices heard through poetry collections; reviews of poetry books. Christopher Wiseman. *CH* Feb 8, 1987: pE5.

WOLFSON, STEVE

Mini-reviews; reviews of children's stories. Mary Rubio. *Can Child Lit* 1987; No 46: p105–109.

WOMAN'S TONGUE/Short stories by Hazel D. Campbell

Putrefying sore; reviews of fictional works. Kathryn Chittick. *Can Lit* Spring 1987; No 112: p128–129.

WOMAN IN THE WOODS/Poems by Joy Kogawa

[Untitled]; review of *Woman in the Woods*. Anne Cimon. *Rubicon* Spring 1987; No 8: p215–216.

Still lifes; reviews of poetry books. Laurence Hutchman. *Can Lit* Winter 1987; No 115: p263–264.

THE WOMAN UPSTAIRS/Novel by Mary W. Riskin

Me, myself, and I; reviews of first novels. Janice Kulyk Keefer. *Books in Can* Oct 1987; Vol 16 No 7: p35–36,38.
[FIRST NOVELS: BOOK REVIEWS]

Promising literary debut made by young mother; review of *The Woman Upstairs*. Kenneth McGoogan. biog photo · *CH* May 10, 1987: pE5.
[FIRST NOVELS: BOOK REVIEWS]

Reader left with agreeable sense of déjà vu; reviews of *Beneath the Western Slopes* and *The Woman Upstairs*. Hugh McKellar. *TS* Aug 9, 1987: pA21.
[FIRST NOVELS: BOOK REVIEWS]

Tale of growing up is a true standout; review of *The Woman Upstairs*. Morley Walker. *WFP* July 11, 1987: p57.
[FIRST NOVELS: BOOK REVIEWS]

THE WOMAN WHO IS THE MIDNIGHT WIND/Short stories by Terence M. Green

[The Woman Who Is the Midnight Wind]; review. Alison Sutherland. *Atlan Prov Book R* May-June 1987; Vol 14 No 2: p9.

The price of progress; review of *The Woman Who Is the Midnight Wind*. Joel Yanofsky. *Books in Can* June-July 1987; Vol 16 No 5: p18–19.

WOMEN IN LITERATURE

Heuresis: the mother-daughter theme in A Jest of God and Autumn Sonata; article. Michael Bird. *New Q* Spring-Summer 1987; Vol 7 No 1–2: p267–273.
[THE FAMILY IN CANADIAN LITERATURE]

Female images in some (mostly Canadian) children's books; article. Frances Duncan. *Room of One's Own* Sept 1987; Vol 11 No 4: p11–24.
[CHILDREN'S LITERATURE]

Sailing the oceans of the world; article. Lorna Irvine. *New Q* Spring-Summer 1987; Vol 7 No 1–2: p284–293.
[ARTIST FIGURE; FEMINIST WRITING AND CRITICISM]

Psychic violence: The Stone Angel and modern family life; article. Ed Jewinski. *New Q* Spring-Summer 1987; Vol 7 No 1–2: p255–266.
[THE FAMILY IN CANADIAN LITERATURE; MYTHS AND LEGENDS IN CANADIAN LITERATURE]

The spider and the rose: Aritha van Herk's No Fixed Address; article. Dorothy Jones. *World Lit in Eng* Spring 1987; Vol 27 No 1: p39–56.
[FEMINIST WRITING AND CRITICISM; MYTHS AND LEGENDS IN CANADIAN LITERATURE]

The writer-as-a-young-woman and her family: Montgomery's Emily; article. Judith Miller. *New Q* Spring-Summer 1987; Vol 7 No 1–2: p301–319.
[ARTIST FIGURE; THE FAMILY IN CANADIAN LITERATURE]

The Bell Jar and Mrs. Blood: portraits of the artist as divided woman; article. Elizabeth Potvin. abstract · *Atlantis* Fall 1987; Vol 13 No 1: p38–46.
[ARTIST FIGURE; FEMINIST WRITING AND CRITICISM]

"The eternal feminine" and the clothing motif in Grove's fiction; article. Elizabeth Potvin. *Studies in Can Lit* 1987; Vol 12 No 2: p222–238.

La naissance d'une parole féminine autonome dans la littérature québécoise; article. Lucie Robert. abstract · *Études lit* Spring-Summer 1987; Vol 20 No 1: p99–110.
[FEMINIST WRITING AND CRITICISM; WOMEN WRITERS]

Marian Engel's family fictions: Lunatic Villas; article. Christl Verduyn. *New Q* Spring-Summer 1987; Vol 7 No 1–2: p274–283.
[THE FAMILY IN CANADIAN LITERATURE; FEMINIST WRITING AND CRITICISM; WOME*TS* Aug 9, 1987: pA21.

Tale of growing up is a true standout; review of *The Woman Upstairs*. Morley Walker. *WFP* July 11, 1987: p57.
[FIRST NOVELS: BOOK REVIEWS]

THE WOMEN OF MARGARET LAURENCE/Play adaptation by Juliana Saxton

Actress draws powerful portraits of heroines in Laurence's work; theatre review of *The Women of Margaret Laurence*. Reg Skene. *WFP* May 14, 1987: p46.
[DRAMATIC ADAPTATIONS OF CANADIAN LITERATURE]

WOMEN WRITERS

Les femmes dans le théâtre du Québec et du Canada / Women in the theatre of Quebec and Canada; introduction. Louise H. Forsyth. *Theatre Hist in Can (special issue)* Spring 1987; Vol 8 No 1: p3–7.
[FEMINIST DRAMA]

Thèmes et formes; article. Carole Frchette. Diane Pavlovic. photo · *Jeu* 1987; No 42: p40–48.
[FESTIVALS, DRAMA; POLITICAL WRITING]

Laure Conan and Madame de La Fayette: rewriting the female plot; article. Mary Jean Green. *Essays on Can Writ* Spring 1987; No 34: p50–63.
[FEMINIST WRITING AND CRITICISM]

55 No 1: p99–110.
[FEMINIST WRITING AND CRITICISM; WOMEN IN LITERATURE]

On the necessity of criticising criticism; essay. Ann Saddlemyer. abstract · *Theatre Hist in Can (special issue)* Spring 1987; Vol 8 No 1: p135–140.

Our women artists face discrimination; column. Lois Sweet. *TS* Jan 26, 1987: pC1.

Isaac's cast puts its 500 years to good use; column. Vit Wagner. *TS* Nov 13, 1987: pE16.
[DRAMATIC READINGS; FEMINIST DRAMA; FESTIVALS, DRAMA]

THE WOOD CARVER'S WIFE/Play by Marjorie Pickthall

Killed into art: Marjorie Pickthall and The Wood Carver's Wife; article. Diana M.A. Relke. biog · *Can Drama* 1987; Vol 13 No 2: p187–200.
[FEMINIST WRITING AND CRITICISM]

WOOD, TED

Crime novelist to speak Thursday; article. *TS (Neighbors)* Dec 8, 1987: p14.

Criminal proceedings; review of *Fool's Gold*. T.J. Binyon. *Times Lit Supp* April 17, 1987; No 4385: p411.

Murder & mayhem: tough guys on clean street; reviews of crime novels. Margaret Cannon. *G&M* Jan 3, 1987: pE15.
[FIRST NOVELS: BOOK REVIEWS]

Pickering crime writer hopes to steal award; article. Alex Law. photo · *TS (Neighbours)* May 19, 1987: p17.
[AWARDS, LITERARY]

[Untitled]; review of *Corkscrew*. Norman Sigurdson. *Quill & Quire* Nov 1987; Vol 53 No 11: p24–25.

WOOD, TOM

B-Movie wins laughs with gags, old lines; theatre review of *B-Movie, the Play*. Brian Brennan. *CH* Sept 19, 1987: pD6.

Story of hit play's fade-out reads like a B-Movie script; article. Ray Conlogue. photo · *G&M* April 16, 1987: pD1.

Mikado, B-Movie big Dora winners; article. Ray Conlogue. photo · *G&M* June 23, 1987: pD8.
[AWARDS, LITERARY]

B-Movie's devilish wit proves nothing succeeds like excess; theatre review of *B-Movie, The Play*. Robert Crew. photo · *TS* Jan 23, 1987: pD18.

B-Movie the play gets flood of offers; column. Robert Crew. photo · *TS* Feb 11, 1987: pF1.

Neville to extend stay at Stratford for a year; column. Robert Crew. *TS* June 24, 1987: pF1.
[AWARDS, LITERARY]

Funny theatre piece says life imitates movie life; article. Rod Currie. *CH* Jan 24, 1987: pA11.

B-Movie could extend run but 'that would be suicide'; article. Mira Friedlander. photo · *TS* March 13, 1987: pC11.

B-Movie features Grade-A laughs; theatre review. Liam Lacey. photo · *G&M* Jan 22, 1987: pC3.

Playwright recalls double-bill dementia; essay. Tom Wood. photo · *TS* Jan 23, 1987: pD3.

Author skewers films' popularity in new ATP play; article. Kate Zimmerman. photo · *CH* Sept 11, 1987: pF1.

WOODCOCK, GEORGE

George Woodcock's glassy prose banishes pain, passion; review of *Beyond the Blue Mountains*. Mark Abley. photo · *MG* Dec 31, 1987: pB7.

A flowering spring and a simplistic guide; reviews of *Northern Spring* and *A Reader's Guide to the Canadian Novel* (second edition). Ken Adachi. photo · *TS* Aug 1, 1987: M4.

There are times when you must go home again; review of *Beyond the Blue Mountains*. Ken Adachi. photo · *TS* Nov 28, 1987: M4.

Mandel's two minds and Woodcock's single purpose; reviews of *The Family Romance* and *Northern Spring*. Doug Fetherling. photo · *Quill & Quire* May 1987; Vol 53 No 5: p20.

The driven writer; review of *Beyond the Blue Mountains*. William French. *G&M* Nov 21, 1987: pC21.

A wealth of provocative and inspiring literary criticism; reviews. Douglas Hill. *G&M* Sept 5, 1987: pC13.
[ANTHOLOGIES: BOOK REVIEWS]

WOOLLATT, RICHARD

Small press reviews; reviews of poetry books. Shaunt Basmajian. *Cross Can Writ Q* 1987; Vol 9 No 1: p25.

[Untitled]; reviews of poetry books. George Whipple. *Poetry Can R* Spring 1987; Vol 8 No 2–3: p53.

THE WORDS TO SAY IT/Autobiography by Marie Cardinal

In the eye of abjection: Marie Cardinal's The Words to Say It; article. Patricia Elliot. *Mosaic* Fall 1987; Vol 20 No 4: p71–81.
[AUTOBIOGRAPHICAL WRITING]

WORDSEED: AN ANTHOLOGY OF POETRY AND PROSE/Anthology

[Untitled]; review of *Wordseed*. Rod Anderson. *Poetry Can R* Spring 1987; Vol 8 No 2–3: p50.
[ANTHOLOGIES: BOOK REVIEWS]

[Untitled]; review of *Wordseed*. Margaret Drage. *Cross Can Writ Q* 1987; Vol 9 No 2: p22.
[ANTHOLOGIES: BOOK REVIEWS]

WORK FOR A MILLION/Novel by Eve Zaremba

Three new faces deserving discovery; reviews of crime novels. Margaret Cannon. photo · *G&M* Oct 17, 1987: pE4.

THE WORLDS OF WILLIAM KORTH/Play by Wayne Kidder

Troupe's first venture brave but flat; theatre review of *The Worlds of William Korth*. Kate Zimmerman. photo · *CH* April 16, 1987: pE5

WREGGITT, ANDREW

[Untitled]; review of *Southeasterly*. John Bemrose. *Books in Can* Oct 1987; Vol 16 No 7: p26–27.

Some beautiful moments but all too fleeting; reviews of poetry books. Maggie Helwig. *TS* Aug 15, 1987: M6.

At the margins of disaster; review of *Man at Stellaco River*. Don Kerr. *Prairie Fire* Spring 1987; Vol 8 No 1: p88–90.

Poets propelled by Thistledown; article. Kenneth McGoogan. *CH* April 12, 1987: pF2.
[CANADIAN LITERARY PUBLISHING]

Poetry: packing all the power into two of seven titles; reviews of poetry books. Robin Skelton. photo · *Quill & Quire* May 1987; Vol 53 No 5: p24.

The pastoral myth and its observers; reviews of poetry books. Fraser Sutherland. *G&M* Sept 26, 1987: pC23.

Thistledown presents prairie poets in full bloom; reviews of poetry books. Christopher Wiseman. *CH* May 24, 1987: pE6.

WRIGHT, ERIC

Inspector Salter of Green Gables; review of *A Body Surrounded by Water*. Ken Adachi. *TS* July 12, 1987: pA19.

[Untitled]; review of *A Body Surrounded by Water*. Ruby Andrew. *Quill & Quire* Oct 1987; Vol 53 No 10: p22–23.

[Untitled]; reviews of *Doubtful Motives* and *A Body Surrounded by Water*. Paul Cabray. *MG* Aug 15, 1987: L2.

Murder & mayhem: the English style of the whodunits; reviews of *A Body Surrounded by Water* and *Doubtful Motives*. Margaret Cannon. photo · *G&M* July 18, 1987: pC17.

People; column. Yvonne Cox. *Maclean's* Aug 17, 1987; Vol 100 No 33: p44.

Main course: murder; article about murder-mystery weekends. Robert Crew. photo · *TS* Aug 1, 1987: pE1,E3.

Publishers meet the demand with reissued crime classics; reviews of *The Night the Gods Smiled* and *One-Eyed Merchants*. Douglas Hill. *G&M* Feb 28, 1987: pE19.
[FIRST NOVELS: BOOK REVIEWS]

Murder & lies; reviews of *A Single Death* and *The Telling of Lies*. Linda Hutcheon. *Can Lit* Winter 1987; No 115: p225–227.

[Untitled]; review of *A Body Surrounded by Water*. Douglas Malcolm. *Books in Can* Aug-Sept 1987; Vol 16 No 6: p25.

From P.E.I. to Big Apple; review of *A Body Surrounded by Water*. Kenneth McGoogan. *CH* Aug 2, 1987: pC8.

Crime novels provide a study in contrasts; reviews of *Doubtful Motives* and *A Body Surrounded by Water*. David Williamson. photo · *WFP* Aug 1, 1987: p50.

WRIGHT, L.R.

Criminal proceedings; review of *Sleep While I Sing*. T.J. Binyon. *Times Lit Supp* Aug 21, 1987; No 4403: p910.

Criminal proceedings; review of *Sleep While I Sing*. T.J. Binyon. *Times Lit Supp* Oct 9, 1987; No 4410: p1124.

Slain hitchhiker doesn't live up to writer's promise; reviews of *Sleep While I Sing* and *Sherlock Holmes and the Case of the Raleigh Legacy*. Paul Carbray. *MG* Feb 21, 1987: pB8.
[FIRST NOVELS: BOOK REVIEWS]

Win some, lose some; letter to the editor. Terence M. Green. *Books in Can* Aug-Sept 1987; Vol 16 No 6: p40.
[AWARDS, LITERARY]

Win some, lose some more; letter to the editor. Jack Jensen. *Books in Can* Nov 1987; Vol 16 No 8: p40.
[AWARDS, LITERARY]

Canada's queen of crime fiction; biographical article. Rona Maynard. photo · *Chatelaine* April 1987; Vol 60 No 4: p108–109.

First novel turned into TV movie; column. Kenneth McGoogan. *CH* May 3, 1987: pE6.
[CONFERENCES, LITERARY; TELEVISION AND CANADIAN LITERATURE]

Mystery woman; biographical article. Eleanor Wachtel. photo · *Books in Can* June-July 1987; Vol 16 No 5: p6–9.

WRIGHT, RICHARD B.

Fear and loathing in Yucatan; review of *Tourists*. John Mills. *Essays on Can Writ* Spring 1987; No 34: p133–135.

WRITERS' ORGANIZATIONS

See also **INTERNATIONAL WRITERS' ORGANIZATIONS**

Aujourd'hui; column. *MD* March 31, 1987: p16.

Serious writers invited to meeting; article. *TS (Neighbours)* Feb 17, 1987: p11.

Correction; notice. *Quill & Quire* March 1987; Vol 53 No 3: p64.

Billboard: cyclo-thon set for Assiniboine; column. *WFP* May 28, 1987: p38.
[WRITERS' WORKSHOPS]

Appointments; column. *Quill & Quire* June 1987; Vol 53 No 6: p26.

Aujourd'hui; column. *MD* May 28, 1987: p12.

Dits et faits; column. photo · *Lettres québec* Spring 1987; No 45: p6–7.
[AWARDS, LITERARY; PUBLISHING AND PUBLISHERS IN CANADA; TRANSLATIONS OF CANADIAN LITERATURE]

L'Union des écrivains québécois, c'est quoi?; interview with Michel Gay. photo · *Lettres québec* Spring 1987; No 45: p16–21.

Authors association boosts children's stories; article. *TS* April 15, 1987: pD1.
[AWARDS, LITERARY]

Round table: responses, notes and queries; column. *Can Child Lit* 1987; No 47: p102–103.
[AWARDS, LITERARY; LIBRARY SERVICES AND CANADIAN LITERATURE]

La Société des écrivains proteste contre la nomination d'un troisième poète lauréat anglophone à Ottawa; article. *MD* Sept 9, 1987: p14.
[AUTHORS, CANADIAN]

Writers roll out the barrel; article. *WFP* July 3, 1987: p17.

Alberta publishing developer dies at 55; obituary of Ken McVey. *WFP* July 10, 1987: p21.
[PUBLISHING AND PUBLISHERS IN CANADA]

Billboard: Beausejour stages festivies; notice. *WFP* July 10, 1987: p26.

Billboard: authors group holds meet; column. *WFP* Sept 2, 1987: p20.

Playwrights gather; article. *WFP* Sept 4, 1987: p17.
[DRAMATIC READINGS]

Writers' group upset; article. *WFP* Sept 9, 1987: p37.

Billboard: Jon Sigurdson holds fall tea today; column. *WFP* Sept 26, 1987: p43.
[COMPETITIONS, LITERARY; FICTION READINGS]

Dits et faits; column. *Lettres québec* Autumn 1987; No 47: p6.
[AWARDS, LITERARY; COMPETITIONS, LITERARY; CONFERENCES, LITERARY]

Playwright group marks 25th year; article. *MG* Nov 16, 1987: pC9.
[DRAMATIC READINGS]

UNEQ; article. *Lettres québec* Winter 1986–87; No 44: p7.

Les lectures Skol: pour les dix ans de l'Union des écrivains; article. *MD* Oct 10, 1987: pD8.
[FICTION READINGS]

Week-end; column. *MD* Nov 21, 1987: pA10.
[AWARDS, LITERARY]

Artists blast officials over tax reform; article. *WFP* Oct 2, 1987: p21.
[AUTHORS, CANADIAN]

Ken McVey; obituary. *Quill & Quire* Nov 1987; Vol 53 No 11: p16.

Writers' Union lets off steam; column. Ken Adachi. *TS* June 1, 1987: pD2.

Writers want out of OCO festival; article. Bob Blakey. *CH* March 20, 1987: pC3.
[FESTIVALS, LITERARY]

East coast report: BS is alive and well in Halifax; regional column. Lesley Choyce. *Poetry Can R* Summer 1987; Vol 8 No 4: p16.

Triangular play development; article about Le Centre d'essai des auteurs dramatiques. Hélène Dumas. photo trans · *Can Theatre R* Spring 1987; No 50: p66–69.
[WRITERS' WORKSHOPS]

Anti-smoking message is right on target; column. William French. *G&M* April 14, 1987: pC7.

Promotion ordeal inspires Berton to do even more; column. William French. *G&M* Sept 15, 1987: pA21.
[AUTHORS, CANADIAN]

[Untitled]; letter to the editor. Jean Chapdelaine Gagnon. *MD* Oct 10, 1987: pD4.

Authors group fought for public lending right; letter to the editor. Della Golland-Lui. *TS* April 6, 1987: pA16.
[GOVERNMENT GRANTS FOR WRITERS/PUBLISHERS; LIBRARY SERVICES AND CANADIAN LITERATURE]

Censors, reviews hot topics at Writers Union AGM; article. Christina Hartling. photo · *Quill & Quire* Aug 1987; Vol 53 No 8: p22–23.
[BOOK REVIEWING; CENSORSHIP]

Manitoba writers gather for literary conference; article. Manfred Jager. *WFP* Oct 22, 1987: p46.
[CONFERENCES, LITERARY]

CAA opposes pornography bill; article. Fred Kerner. *Quill & Quire* Aug 1987; Vol 53 No 8: p24.
[AWARDS, LITERARY; CENSORSHIP]

Deneau Publishers seeks reorganization; column. H.J. Kirchhoff. *G&M* Dec 29, 1987: pC8.
[CENSORSHIP; PUBLISHING AND PUBLISHERS IN CANADA]

Un rôle méconnu pour l'Uneq; letter to the editor. Yves Légaré. *MD* Oct 10, 1987: pD4.

Book review editors take the hot seat at writers' conference; article. Liam Lacey. photo · *G&M* May 30, 1987: pC5.
[BOOK REVIEWING; CONFERENCES, LITERARY]

Writers revive censorship-pornography debate; article. Liam Lacey. photo · *G&M* June 1, 1987: pC9.
[AUTHORS, CANADIAN; CENSORSHIP; WOMEN WRITERS]

Les auteurs québécois habillés de cuir . . . ; article. France Lafuste. photo · *MD* June 8, 1987: p9.

La 55e saison du Club musical et littéraire; article. Marie Laurier. photo · *MD* Oct 21, 1987: p14.

Storm brewing in literary heaven; column. Kenneth McGoogan. *CH* Jan 11, 1987: pF4.
[GOVERNMENT GRANTS FOR WRITERS/PUBLISHERS]

Literary extravaganza goes national; column. Kenneth McGoogan. *CH* April 5, 1987: pE5.
[AUTHORS, CANADIAN; FILM ADAPTATIONS OF CANADIAN LITERATURE; WRITERS' WORKSHOPS]

Author interviews hit airwaves; column. Kenneth McGoogan. *CH* April 18, 1987: pE5.
[FESTIVALS, LITERARY; RADIO AND CANADIAN LITERATURE]

Writers' union condemns censorship bill; article. Kenneth McGoogan. photo · *CH* June 2, 1987: pF6.
[BOOK REVIEWING; CENSORSHIP]

Poets help celebrate Dandelion; column. Kenneth McGoogan. *CH* June 28, 1987: pF8.
[AWARDS, LITERARY; CANADIAN LITERARY PERIODICALS; POETRY READINGS]

Festival attracts glitterati; column. Kenneth McGoogan. *CH* Sept 27, 1987: pE6.
[FESTIVALS, LITERARY; FICTION READINGS; POETRY READINGS]

Alberta writers to fight 'censorship' bill; column. Kenneth McGoogan. *CH* Nov 29, 1987: pE6.
[CENSORSHIP; COMPETITIONS, LITERARY; FESTIVALS, LITERARY]

Arts enrich lives as well as pockets; column. Mavor Moore. *G&M* Aug 15, 1987: pC3.
[AUTHORS, CANADIAN]

La vie littéraire; column. Marc Morin. *MD* Oct 31, 1987: pD2.
[COMPETITIONS, LITERARY; POETRY READINGS]

La vie littéraire; column. Marc Morin. *MD* Dec 5, 1987: pD2.
[CANADIAN LITERARY PUBLISHING; CONFERENCES, LITERARY; POETRY READINGS]

L'avenir du français au Québec; article. Dominique Parent. *Lettres québec* Summer 1987; No 46: p9.
[CONFERENCES, LITERARY]

La difficile reconnaissance des gens de lettres; article. Johanne Roy. *MD* May 23, 1987: pD2.
[AUTHORS, CANADIAN; AWARDS, LITERARY]

La vie littéraire; column. Jean Royer. photo · *MD* Jan 3, 1987: pC2.
[CULTURAL IDENTITY; TELEVISION AND CANADIAN LITERATURE]

La vie littéraire; column. Jean Royer. *MD* Feb 21, 1987: pB2.
[CANADIAN LITERARY PUBLISHING; COMPETITIONS, LITERARY; POETRY READINGS; TELEVISION AND CANADIAN LITERATURE]

La vie littéraire; column. Jean Royer. *MD* Feb 28, 1987: pC2.
[AWARDS, LITERARY; CANADIAN LITERARY PERIODICALS; CANADIAN LITERARY PUBLISHING; CONFERENCES, LITERARY; RADIO AND CANADIAN LITERATURE]

La vie littéraire; column. Jean Royer. *MD* March 7, 1987: pB2.
[AWARDS, LITERARY; CANADIAN LITERARY PUBLISHING; POETRY READINGS; RADIO AND CANADIAN LITERATURE; TELEVISION AND CANADIAN LITERATURE]

Les alouettes en colère . . . ; article. Jean Royer. *MD* March 14, 1987: pD1–D2.

"Alliance-Québec fait la guerre avec les mots de la paix"; article. Jean Royer. photo · *MD* March 16, 1987: p11,14.
[CULTURAL IDENTITY]

La vie littéraire; column. Jean Royer. photo · *MD* March 21, 1987: pD2.
[AWARDS, LITERARY; CANADIAN LITERARY PUBLISHING; COMPETITIONS, LITERARY; POETRY READINGS; RADIO AND CANADIAN LITERATURE; TELEVISION AND CANADIAN LITERATURE]

La vie littéraire; column. Jean Royer. *MD* April 25, 1987: pD2.
[AWARDS, LITERARY; CONFERENCES, LITERARY; FESTIVALS, LITERARY; FICTION READINGS; POETRY READINGS; RADIO AND CANADIAN LITERATURE; TELEVISION AND CANADIAN LITERATURE]

La vie littéraire; column. Jean Royer. photo · *MD* May 2, 1987: pD2.
[AWARDS, LITERARY; INTERNATIONAL REVIEWS OF CANADIAN LITERATURE; RADIO AND CANADIAN LITERATURE; TELEVISION AND CANADIAN LITERATURE]

Le Loisir littéraire du Québec fête ses 25 ans; article. Jean Royer. photo · *MD* May 2, 1987: pD2.
[WRITERS' WORKSHOPS]

La vie littéraire; column. Jean Royer. photo · *MD* May 23, 1987: pD2.
[CULTURAL IDENTITY; RADIO AND CANADIAN LITERATURE; TELEVISION AND CANADIAN LITERATURE]

La vie littéraire; column. Jean Royer. photo · *MD* June 6, 1987: pD2.
[GOVERNOR GENERAL'S AWARDS; INTERNATIONAL REVIEWS OF CANADIAN LITERATURE; RADIO AND CANADIAN LITERATURE; TELEVISION AND CANADIAN LITERATURE]

La vie littéraire; column. Jean Royer. photo · *MD* June 13, 1987: pD2.
[AWARDS, LITERARY; COMPETITIONS, LITERARY; POETRY READINGS; RADIO AND CANADIAN LITERATURE; TELEVISION AND CANADIAN LITERATURE]

L'Union des écrivains maintient la sonnerie d'alarme sur la langue; article. Jean Royer. photo · *MD* Sept 3, 1987: p13,15.

La vie littéraire; column. Jean Royer. photo · *MD* Sept 26, 1987: pD2.
[AUDIO-VISUALS AND CANADIAN LITERATURE; CONFERENCES, LITERARY; INTERNATIONAL WRITERS' ORGANIZATIONS; PUBLISHING AND PUBLISHERS IN CANADA]

La vie littéraire; column. Jean Royer. photo · *MD* Oct 17, 1987: pD2.
[CANADIAN LITERARY PERIODICALS; COMPETITIONS, LITERARY; CONFERENCES, LITERARY; FICTION READINGS]

La vie littéraire; column. Jean Royer. *MD* Oct 24, 1987: pD2.
[CONFERENCES, LITERARY; FICTION READINGS; POETRY READINGS]

Here since 1921; letter to the editor. Anita Schmidt. *WFP* Nov 13, 1987: p6.

Tip sheet: . . . writers meet; column. Susan Schwartz. photo · *MG* Oct 14, 1987: pC9.

Poets' league: debt free at last; article. Joseph Sherman. *Quill & Quire* July 1987; Vol 53 No 7: p43.

Book world: adults who love children's books gather at 'Roundtable'; column. Beverley Slopen. *TS* Aug 16, 1987: pA21.
[AGENTS, LITERARY]

De qui se moque Le Devoir?; editorial. Michel Vaïs. photo · *Jeu* 1987; No 45: p7–9.
[AWARDS, LITERARY; CANADIAN LITERARY PERIODICALS]

Bloc-notes; column. Michel Vaïs. photo · *Jeu* 1987; No 45: p227–231.
[AWARDS, LITERARY; GOVERNMENT GRANTS FOR WRITERS/PUBLISHERS]

Prairie Pens — bright talent in small places; article. Gillian Welsh-Vickar. photo · *Can Auth & Book* Winter 1987; Vol 62 No 2: p7.

Poets' club offers sympathetic ears; article. Stephen White. *TS (Neighbours)* March 24, 1987: p25.

WRITERS' WORKSHOPS

Theatre rendezvous resume next week; article. *MG* Jan 29, 1987: pC13.

Billboard: author group plans writing workshop; column. *WFP* Jan 19, 1987: p16.

Billboard: archeology, botany in Greece will be featured in colloquium; column. *WFP* Jan 21, 1987: p30.

Aujourd'hui; column. *MD* Jan 21, 1987: p12.

Aujourd'hui; column. *MD* Feb 10, 1987: p10.
[ETHNIC-CANADIAN WRITING]

Aujourd'hui; column. *MD* Feb 16, 1987: p16.
[FICTION READINGS]

Aujourd'hui; column. *MD* March 10, 1987: p10.

Billboard: cyclo-thon set for Assiniboine; column. *WFP* May 28, 1987: p38.
[WRITERS' ORGANIZATIONS]

Mainstreet Calgary; column. *CH (Neighbors)* April 1, 1987: pA4.
[POETRY READINGS]

Mainstreet Calgary; column. *CH (Neighbors)* May 13, 1987: pA6–A7.
[FICTION READINGS]

What's happening: workshop to help writers; column. *CH* May 15, 1987: pE6–E7.

Mainstreet Calgary; column. *CH (Neighbors)* May 20, 1987: pA10.

Mainstreet Calgary; column. *CH (Neighbors)* May 27, 1987: pA8

Laurentian retreat for women writers; article. *Quill & Quire* May 1987; Vol 53 No 5: p12.

Canadian Studies news and notes; column. *J of Can Studies* Spring 1987; Vol 22 No 1: p161–163.
[CONFERENCES, LITERARY]

Markets & events; column. *Cross Can Writ Q* 1987; Vol 9 No 2: p31–32.
[CANADIAN LITERARY PERIODICALS]

French playwrights' workshop scheduled; article. *WFP* Aug 12, 1987: p5.

Billboard: theatre group stages unemployment revue; column. *WFP* Aug 22, 1987: p34.

Workshop planned; article. *WFP* Aug 26, 1987: p40.

Writers' retreat; notice. *Quill & Quire* Jan 1987; Vol 53 No 1: p20.

Mainstreet Calgary; column. *CH (Neighbors)* Oct 28, 1987: pA22–A23.
[FICTION READINGS]

Mainstreet Calgary; column. *CH (Neighbors)* Nov 4, 1987: pA12.

CANSCAIP workshop at Ryerson; article. *Quill & Quire (Books for Young People)* Oct 1987; Vol 53 No 10: p21.

Canadian Women's Writing Retreat; notice. *Capilano R* 1987; No 42: p66.

Check out drama fest for new theatre talent; article. Marianne Ackerman. photo · *MG* April 25, 1987: H7.
[FESTIVALS, DRAMA]

Writing program a splendid notion; column. Ken Adachi. photo · *TS* July 6, 1987: pD5.

In the neighbourhood of my heart; essay. Don Bouzek. photo · *Can Theatre R* Winter 1987; No 53: p20–25.
[POLITICAL WRITING]

Theatre notes; column. Brian Brennan. *CH* May 11, 1987: pC6.
[DRAMATIC ADAPTATIONS OF CANADIAN LITERATURE]

Chorus of many voices; essay. Beverley Daurio. *Cross Can Writ Q* 1987; Vol 9 No 1: p7,28–29.

Triangular play development; article about Le Centre d'essai des auteurs dramatiques. Hélène Dumas. photo trans · *Can Theatre R* Spring 1987; No 50: p66–69.
[WRITERS' ORGANIZATIONS]

Colonial imperative; essay. Phil Hall. *Books in Can* Oct 1987; Vol 16 No 7: p4–5.

Creative writing teachers — reflections and advice; article. Bruce Hunter. photo · *Cross Can Writ Q* 1987; Vol 9 No 1: p3–4.

Arts Scarborough will sponsor workshop for novice writers; article. Paul Irish. *TS (Neighbours)* May 12, 1987: p10.

Course helps teenagers hone writing skills; article. Dan Lett. photo · *WFP* July 22, 1987: p32.

Border voices speak language of literature; article. Marion McCormick. illus · *MG* July 10, 1987: J5.

Banff Centre lands novelist; column. Kenneth McGoogan. *CH* Feb 22, 1987: pE6.
[CANADIAN LITERARY PERIODICALS; PUBLISHING AND PUBLISHERS IN CANADA]

Writers' event grows on young people; column. Kenneth McGoogan. *CH* March 29, 1987: pE5.
[CONFERENCES, LITERARY]

Literary extravaganza goes national; column. Kenneth McGoogan. *CH* April 5, 1987: pE5.
[AUTHORS, CANADIAN; FILM ADAPTATIONS OF CANADIAN LITERATURE; WRITERS' ORGANIZATIONS]

Fine art of writing: Banff Centre nurtures authors, playwrights, screenwriters; article. Kenneth McGoogan. photo · *CH* May 16, 1987: pC1.

Literary world loses a champion; column. Kenneth McGoogan. *CH* July 12, 1987: pE4.
[AWARDS, LITERARY; CONFERENCES, LITERARY; PUBLISHING AND PUBLISHERS IN CANADA; SCIENCE FICTION]

La vie littéraire; column. Jean Royer. photo · *MD* Jan 10, 1987: pB2.
[AWARDS, LITERARY; POETRY READINGS; RADIO AND CANADIAN LITERATURE; TELEVISION AND CANADIAN LITERATURE]

La vie littéraire; column. Jean Royer. photo · *MD* Jan 24, 1987: pB2.
[AWARDS, LITERARY; POETRY READINGS; PUBLISHING AND PUBLISHERS IN CANADA; RADIO AND CANADIAN LITERATURE]

La vie littéraire; column. Jean Royer. *MD* Feb 7, 1987: pB2.
[COMPETITIONS, LITERARY; CONFERENCES, LITERARY; POETRY READINGS; PUBLISHING AND PUBLISHERS IN CANADA; TELEVISION AND CANADIAN LITERATURE]

La vie littéraire; column. Jean Royer. *MD* March 7, 1987: pB2.
[AWARDS, LITERARY; CANADIAN LITERARY PUBLISHING; POETRY READINGS; RADIO AND CANADIAN LITERATURE; TELEVISION AND CANADIAN LITERATURE]

Le Loisir littéraire du Québec fête ses 25 ans; article. Jean Royer. photo · *MD* May 2, 1987: pD2.
[WRITERS' ORGANIZATIONS]

La vie littéraire; column. Jean Royer. photo · *MD* June 6, 1987: pD2.
[GOVERNOR GENERAL'S AWARDS; INTERNATIONAL REVIEWS OF CANADIAN LITERATURE; RADIO AND CANADIAN LITERATURE; TELEVISION AND CANADIAN LITERATURE]

La vie littéraire; column. Jean Royer. *MD* Oct 3, 1987: pD2.
[AWARDS, LITERARY; CANADIAN LITERARY PUBLISHING; POETRY READINGS]

Students blitz stage in weekend workshop; article. Laura Shutiak. *CH* Feb 13, 1987: pF11.

Blitz immerses students in theatre; article. Laura Shutiak. photo · *CH* Feb 16, 1987: pE5.

Les artistes doivent veiller au grain; essay. Serge Turgeon. *MD* March 11, 1987: p11.
[CULTURAL IDENTITY; WRITERS' ORGANIZATIONS]

The KSW student view; article. Calvin Wharton. *Cross Can Writ Q* 1987; Vol 9 No 1: p9.

WRITERS-IN-RESIDENCE

After 8 years, W.O. Mitchell is heading west; article. *G&M* May 21, 1987: pD1.

City approves writer residency for poet-author; article. *WFP* Sept 10, 1987: p3.

Why writers in residence?; editorial. *WFP* Sept 21, 1987: p6.

Di Michele in residence in Regina; article. *Quill & Quire* Oct 1987; Vol 53 No 10: p20.

Professional writers aid aspiring authors from Ontario libraries; article. Ian Bailey. *WFP* Nov 20, 1987: p38.
[LIBRARY SERVICES AND CANADIAN LITERATURE]

Writers' forum; letter to the editor. Pierre Berton. *WFP* Nov 29, 1987: p6.

Funding fuss shocks writer-in-residence; article. Donald Campbell. photo · *WFP* Oct 6, 1987: p32.

Chit chat; column. Maria Casas. *Quill & Quire (Books for Young People)* April 1987; Vol 53 No 4: p3.
[CHILDREN'S LITERATURE; CHINA-CANADA LITERARY RELATIONS]

Writers lend their expertise; column. William French. *G&M* June 23, 1987: pD5.
[LIBRARY SERVICES AND CANADIAN LITERATURE]

New award celebrates Commonwealth writers; column. William French. photo · *G&M* Nov 17, 1987: pD7.
[AWARDS, LITERARY]

Aspiring writers take their books to the library; article. Phil Johnson. photo · *TS (Neighbors)* Sept 22, 1987: p20.

Writers must be critical of own work, novelist says; article. Phil Johnson. photo · *TS (Neighbors)* Sept 22, 1987: p20.

Author-playwright shares wealth of experience; article. Phil Johnson. photo · *TS (Neighbors)* Sept 29, 1987: p14.

Author's ready to hand out advice; article. H.J. Kirchhoff. photo · *G&M* May 6, 1987: pC6.

David Suzuki set to tell his story in Metamorphosis; column. Henry Mietkiewicz. *TS* April 12, 1987: pC3.

Not so easy; letter to the editor. Harry Nelken. *WFP* Oct 18, 1987: p6.

Writer's earnings questioned; article. David Roberts. *WFP* Sept 9, 1987: p1,4.

Not overpaid; letter to the editor. Anita Schmidt. Kevin Longfield. *WFP* Sept 19, 1987: p7.

Book world: where the $$$ land — legally; column. Beverley Slopen. *TS* March 1, 1987: pA15.
[PUBLISHING AND PUBLISHERS IN CANADA]

Inside the Kootenay School of Writing; article. Calvin Wharton. photo · *Cross Can Writ Q* 1987; Vol 9 No 1: p8–9,29.

Writer-in-residence is worthwhile project; letter to the editor. David Williamson. *WFP* Sept 19, 1987: p7.

Who is muddled?; letter to the editor. David Williamson. *WFP* Sept 29, 1987: p6

WURST, BONNIE R.

Montreal needle trade is setting for comic tale about working girl; review of *Damaged Goods,* includes profile. Barbara Black. photo · *MG* July 18, 1987: J9.
[FIRST NOVELS: BOOK REVIEWS]

WYATT, RACHEL

Up in the air; review of *Time in the Air.* Coral Ann Howells. *Can Lit* Winter 1987; No 115: p150–152.

[Untitled]; review of *Time in the Air.* Kathy Kelly. *Quarry* Winter 1987; Vol 36 No 1: p133–135.

[Untitled]; review of *Time in the Air.* Debra Martens. *Room of One's Own* Sept 1987; Vol 11 No 4: p115–118.

[Untitled]; review of *Time in the Air.* Marcienne Rocard. *Études can* June 1987; No 22: p138–139.

Perils of a double life; review of *Time in the Air.* Norman Sigurdson. *WFP* Jan 10, 1987: p66.

WYCZYNSKI, PAUL

Le Nelligan de Wyczynski: un si beau cadeau; review. Jean Éthier-Blais. photo · *MD* Dec 24, 1987: pC13.

Paul Wyczynski signe une "somme nelliganienne"; review of *Nelligan.* Marie Laurier. photo · *MD* Nov 28, 1987: pD11.

WYLIE, BETTY JANE

Author-playwright shares wealth of experience; article. Phil Johnson. photo · *TS (Neighbors)* Sept 29, 1987: p14.
[WRITERS-IN-RESIDENCE]

WYNNE-JONES, TIM

The big menace; reviews of *I'll Make You Small* and *Mischief City.* Sandra Martin. *G&M* Jan 17, 1987: pE18.

Thrills and chills: hints for Hallowe'en reading; reviews of children's books. Joan McGrath. illus · *Quill & Quire (Books for Young People)* Oct 1987; Vol 53 No 10: p8.
[ANTHOLOGIES: BOOK REVIEWS]

Asimov robotics . . . orchestral overtures . . . marvellous Munsch; reviews of tape versions of children's books. Richard Perry. photo · *Quill & Quire (Books for Young People)* Aug 1987; Vol 53 No 8: p10.
[AUDIO-VISUALS AND CANADIAN LITERATURE]

Picture-power; reviews of *Very Last First Time* and *Zoom Away.* Jon C. Scott. *Can Lit* Spring 1987; No 112: p159–162.

XYZ/Periodical

Littérature sur mesure: de la nouvelle à la page; review of *XYZ.* Jean-Roch Boivin. *MD* Oct 10, 1987: pD2–D3.
[CANADIAN LITERARY PERIODICALS]

La nouvelle, le clip de l'écriture; review of *XYZ.* Carole David. *MD* March 7, 1987: pB2.
[CANADIAN LITERARY PERIODICALS]

La vitrine du livre; reviews of *Le Je(u) illocutoire* and *XYZ.* Guy Ferland. *MD* Aug 1, 1987: pC6.
[CANADIAN LITERARY PERIODICALS]

Ding et Dong; reviews of periodicals. Robert Melançon. *Liberté* Dec 1987; Vol 29 No 6: p122–129.
[CANADIAN LITERARY PERIODICALS]

Photo de famille; article. Jean Royer. photo · *MD* Sept 28, 1987: p9.
[AUTHORS, CANADIAN; CANADIAN LITERARY PERIODICALS]

YANCE, CLAUDE-EMMANUELLE

Mourir comme un chat?; reviews of *Mourir comme un chat* and *Facéties.* Madeleine Ouellette-Michalska. *MD* July 4, 1987: pC6.

Deux livres pour partir en voyage; reviews of *Mourir comme un chat* and *Banc de Brume.* Marie José Thériault. photo · *Lettres québec* Autumn 1987; No 47: p31–32.

YATES, J. MICHAEL

The reader's duties; review of *Schedules of Silence.* Fraser Sutherland. *G&M* June 6, 1987: pC19.

THE YEAR OF FEARS/Novel by David Watmough

The gaucherie and confusion of early manhood; review of *The Year of Fears.* Pauline Carey. *G&M* Oct 17, 1987: pE4.

YELIN, SHULAMIS

[Untitled]; reviews of poetry books. Shaunt Basmajian. *Cross Can Writ Q* 1987; Vol 9 No 2: p22.

[Untitled]; reviews of poetry books. Andrew Parkin. *Poetry Can R* Fall 1987; Vol 9 No 1: p37.
[ANTHOLOGIES: BOOK REVIEWS]

YERGEAU, ROBERT

[Untitled]; review of *L'Usage du réel*. Hélène Dorion. *Estuaire* Winter 1986–87; No 43: p79.

Écrire sur l'écrire; review of *L'Usage du réel*. Régis Normandeau. *Lettres québec* Spring 1987; No 45: p64.

Mort, vie et écriture; review of *Le Tombeau d'Adélina Albert*. Régis Normandeau. photo · *Lettres québec* Autumn 1987; No 47: p69.

La poésie n'est pas une science mais une parole; reviews of *Le Tombeau d'Adélina Albert* and *Qu'en carapaces de mes propres ailes*. Jean Royer. *MD* April 25, 1987: pD4

[Untitled]; reviews of poetry books. Jacques St-Pierre. *Moebius* Winter 1987; No 31: p137–139.

YESTERDAY, TODAY AND TOMORROW/Poetry anthology

Poets, 66–88, publish their own book; article. Suzanne Wintrob. *TS (Neighbours)* March 10, 1987: p18.

YOKEN, MEL B.

[Untitled]; letter to the editor. Roger Dubois. *Lettres québec* Spring 1987; No 45: p7.

YOST, ELWY

Tales that will tempt tots of all ages; review of *Mad Queen of Mordra*. Joan McGrath. *TS* Sept 19, 1987: M6.

YOU CAN'T CATCH ME!/Children's story by Joanne Oppenheim

[Untitled]; review of *You Can't Catch Me!*. Maeve Binchy. *NYT Book R* March 1, 1987: p31.

YOUNG ART/Play by Brad Fraser

Young writer explores time-honored themes; theatre review of *Young Art*. John Fitzgerald. photo · *G&M* Jan 17, 1987: pE13.

Tale hampered by small stage; theatre review of *Young Art*. Henry Mietkiewicz. photo · *TS* Jan 18, 1987: pG3.

YOUNG, DAVID

[Untitled]; theatre review of *Fire*. Mark Abley. photo · *Maclean's* Jan 26, 1987; Vol 100 No 4: p55.

Musical Fire is a damp sparkler; theatre review. Brian Brennan. photo · *CH* Feb 14, 1987: pG4.

Rollicking rock and old-time religion stoke Fire; theatre review. Ray Conlogue. photo · *G&M* Jan 13, 1987: pC7.

Raising two worthy books from the dead; reviews of *Kicking Against the Pricks* and *Incognito*. William French. photo · *G&M* Feb 24, 1987: pD7.

Fire bites off a lot, chews most of it; theatre review of *Fire*. Wayne Grigsby. *MG* Jan 10, 1987: H7.

[Untitled]; theatre reviews of *Fire* and *Opium*. Wayne Grigsby. *MG* Jan 16, 1987: pD10.

[Fire]; theatre review. Susan Minsos. *NeWest R* April 1987; Vol 12 No 8: p17.

YOUNG, PATRICIA

[Untitled]; review of *Melancholy Ain't No Baby*. Maurice Mierau. *Rubicon* Spring 1987; No 8: p220–221.

[Untitled]; review of *Melancholy Ain't No Baby*. Jane Munro. *Poetry Can R* Summer 1987; Vol 8 No 4: p34.

Frost shadows; reviews of poetry books. Andrew Taylor. *Can Lit* Winter 1987; No 115: p197–199.

YVON, JOSE

La fiction du réel / le réel de la fiction; reviews of poetry books. André Brochu. *Voix et images* Winter 1987; No 35: p322–330.

ZANU/Novel by Carol Matas

[Untitled]; reviews of *The Fusion Factor* and *Zanu*. Leslie McGrath. *Quill & Quire (Books for Young People)* June 1987; Vol 53 No 6: p9–10.

[Untitled]; reviews of *The Fusion Factor* and *Zanu*. Mavis Reimer. *Border Cross* Spring 1987; Vol 6 No 2: p25.

How suspense dies when it is misused; reviews of young adult novels. Tim Wynne-Jones. *G&M* Aug 8, 1987: pC19.

ZAREMBA, EVE

Three new faces deserving discovery; reviews of crime novels. Margaret Cannon. photo · *G&M* Oct 17, 1987: pE4.

ZASTROZZI: THE MASTER OF DISCIPLINE/Play by George F. Walker

Satan with a sword; article. John Bemrose. photo · *Maclean's* May 25, 1987; Vol 100 No 21: p55.

A triumph of Gothic comedy; theatre review of *Zastrozzi*. Ray Conlogue. photo · *G&M* May 14, 1987: pC3.

Zastrozzi returns in splended form; theatre review. Robert Crew. photo · *TS* May 14, 1987: pF3.

Chain letter; article. Martin Knelman. illus · *Tor Life* May 1987; Vol 21 No 7: p11.

[Untitled]; theatre review of *Zastrozzi*. Martin Knelman. *Tor Life* June 1987; Vol 21 No 9: p115.

Sword plays: it's fight for the right to parry; article. Henry Mietkiewicz. photo · *TS* May 8, 1987: pD3.

ZAYDOK/Play by Dennis Foon

Contrived character flaws Zaydok; theatre review. Stephen Godfrey. photo · *G&M* Oct 28, 1987: pC5.

ZEKE AND THE INDOOR PLANTS/Children's play by Ruth Smiley

Audience plays out dilemmas in drama; article. Shannon Hall. photo · *CH* Nov 22, 1987: pG8.

ZELLER, LUDWIG

Translators feast on Pheasant; column. William French. illus · *G&M* Sept 22, 1987: pD5.

[Untitled]; reviews of poetry books. Stephen Morrissey. *Poetry Can R* Fall 1987; Vol 9 No 1: p32.

ZEMBLA'S ROCKS/Poems by Louis Dudek

Montreal poets inspired by travel in hot countries; reviews of poetry books. Barbara Black. *MG* March 28, 1987: pE9.

Flashes of mortality; review of *Zembla's Rocks*. Ray Filip. *Books in Can* April 1987; Vol 16 No 3: p36

Some beautiful moments but all too fleeting; reviews of poetry books. Maggie Helwig. *TS* Aug 15, 1987: M6.

Poetry: packing all the power into two of seven titles; reviews of poetry books. Robin Skelton. photo · *Quill & Quire* May 1987; Vol 53 No 5: p24.

The virtuous poet; review of *Zembla's Rocks*. Fraser Sutherland. *G&M* April 18, 1987: pC18.

ZEND, ROBERT

Zendmark; review of *Oab 1*. Karl Jirgens. *Can Lit* Summer-Fall 1987; No 113–114: p217–219.

[Untitled]; reviews of poetry books. Douglas Smith. *Poetry Can R* Spring 1987; Vol 8 No 2–3: p39–40.
[ANTHOLOGIES: BOOK REVIEWS]

ZIEROTH, DALE

A choice of codes; reviews of poetry books. Thomas Gerry. illus · *NeWest R* Nov 1987; Vol 13 No 3: p16 17.

Frost shadows; reviews of poetry books. Andrew Taylor. *Can Lit* Winter 1987; No 115: p197–199.

ZOLA, MEGUIDO

Youngsters get choice of beautiful books; reviews. Helen Norrie. *WFP* Dec 5, 1987: p57.

ZONAILO, CAROLYN

[Untitled]; reviews of poetry books. Lavinia Inbar. illus · *Poetry Can R* Spring 1987; Vol 8 No 2–3: p51–53.

ZOOM AT SEA/Children's story by Tim Wynne-Jones

Asimov robotics . . . orchestral overtures . . . marvellous Munsch; reviews of tape versions of children's books. Richard Perry. photo · *Quill & Quire (Books for Young People)* Aug 1987; Vol 53 No 8: p10.
[AUDIO-VISUALS AND CANADIAN LITERATURE]

ZOOM AWAY/Children's story by Tim Wynne-Jones

Picture-power; reviews of *Very Last First Time* and *Zoom Away*. Jon C. Scott. *Can Lit* Spring 1987; No 112: p159–162.

ZUMTHOR, PAUL

Un sens de la voix à retrouver; interview with Paul Zumthor. Gérald Gaudet. photo · *Estuaire* Winter 1986–87; No 43: p65–73.

ZUNIK DANS LE CHOUCHOU/Children's story by Bertrand Gauthier

Littérature jeunesse; reviews of children's books. Domique Demers. *MD* Oct 10, 1987: pD6.

ZWICKER, LINDA

Playwright finds fodder in crisis-centre duty; article. Bob Blakey. photo · *CH* Jan 16, 1987: pF1.

Playwright's debut shows promise; theatre review of *Penumbra*. Brian Brennan. photo · *CH* Jan 20, 1987: pA10.

Three Toronto plays premiere at Calgary fest; article, includes theatre reviews. Robert Crew. photo · *TS* Feb 10, 1987: pB4.
[FESTIVALS, DRAMA]

New-play festival deserves a curtain call; theatre reviews. Stephen Godfrey. photo · *G&M* Feb 10, 1987: pC5.
[FESTIVALS, DRAMA]

ZWICKY, JAN

[Untitled]; review of *Wittgenstein Elegies*. Anne Burke. *Poetry Can R* Spring 1987; Vol 8 No 2–3: p47.

Confident voices heard through poetry collections; reviews of poetry books. Christopher Wiseman. *CH* Feb 8, 1987: pE5.

ZYGAL: A BOOK OF MYSTERIES AND TRANSLATIONS/Poems by bpNichol

[Untitled]; reviews of *Canada Gees Mate for Life* and *Zygal*. Phil Hall. *Poetry Can R* Fall 1987; Vol 9 No 1: p34.

Subscription Information and Inter-Library Loan Codes

CANADIAN PERIODICALS (ENGLISH)

ALPHA
Occasional.
Acadia Students' Union
P.O. Box 1269
Wolfville, N.S.
BOP IXO
Locations: ACU NBFU NBSAM NBSU NSCS NSHP NSWA
OHM OONL OTU

THE ANTIGONISH REVIEW
$16/yr. Quarterly.
St. Francis Xavier University
Antigonish, N.S.
B2G ICO
ISSN: 0003-5661
Locations: AEU BVA BVAS MWUC NBFU NBSAM NSAS
NSCS NSHD NSHPL NSHS NSTT NSWA OHM OKQ OLU
OOCC OONL OOU OPAL OPET OTMCL OTSTM OTU OTY
OWA OWTU QMG QMM QMU QSHERU SS SSU

ARC
$10 2/yrs. Semi-annual.
Department of English
Carleton University
Ottawa, Ont.
KIS 5B6
ISSN: 0-7709-0178-6
Locations: NSHD OHM OLU OOCC OONL OOU OTU

ARIEL
Ind $12/yr, inst $18/yr. Quarterly.
c / o Mavis Page, Business Manager
University of Calgary
Calgary, Alberta
T2N IN4
ISSN: 0004-1327
Locations: ACMR AEU BVA BVAS BVAU BVIV MBC MWU
MWUC NBFU NBSAM NBSU NSHK NSWA OGU OHM
OKQ OKR OLH OLU OOCC OONL OOU OPAL OPET
OTMCL OTU OTY OWA OWTU QMG QML QMU SRU SSM
SSU

ATLANTIC INSIGHT
$22/yr, $38/2 yrs. U.S. $35/yr. Overseas $45/yr. Monthly.
Insight Publishing Ltd.
1668 Barrington St.
Halifax, N.S.
B3J 2A2
ISSN: 0708-5400

Locations: BVA NBFU NBSAM NSCS NSHD NSHDL
NSHMS NSHP NSHS NSSCG NSTT OOAG OOB OOCC
OOCM OOF OONL OONM OOP OPAL OTU OWA OWTU
SSU

ATLANTIC PROVINCES BOOK REVIEW
No charge. Quarterly.
Saint Mary's University
Halifax, N.S.
B3H 3C3
ISSN: 0316-5981
Locations: AEU BVAU MWUC NBFU NBSAM NSH NSHD
NSHK NSHP NSHS OONL OTMCL OTU OTULS

ATLANTIS
Ind $15/yr, inst $25/yr. U.S. add $6. Overseas add $12.
Semi-annual.
Mount Saint Vincent University
166 Bedford Highway
Halifax, N.S.
B3M 2J6
ISSN: 0702-7818
Locations: ACMR ACU AEU BVA BVAS BVAU MWUC
NBFU NBSAM NSCS NSHD NSHP NSHS NSHV NSTT
NSWA OHM OLU OOCC OOLWB OONL OONM OOP
OPAL OPET OSUL OTDL OTER OTU OTY OWA OWTU
QMG QMHE QMU SRAW SRP SRRI SRU SSU

BOOKS IN CANADA
Ind $15/yr, $28/2 yrs, inst $20/yr, $38/2 yrs. U.S. add $3
surface, $11 airmail. Overseas add $15. Monthly.
Canadian Review of Books Ltd.
366 Adelaide St. East, Suite 432
Toronto, Ont.
M5A 3X9
ISSN: 0045-2564
Locations: ACMR AE AEU BRC BVA BVAS BVAU BVIV MSC
MWP MWU MWUC NBFU NBSAM NFSM NSCS NSHD
NSHS NSHV NSSCG NSTT OHM OKQ OKR OLH OLU
OOAG OOB OOC OOCC OOE OOFF OOL OON OONL
OOP OPET OSUL OTEPL OTER OTEY OTMCL OTNY OTP
OTU OTV OWA OWTU QMBM QMG QML QMM QMMLS
QMU QSHERU SCR SMJT SNB SPANC SR SRCB SRED SRL
SRP SRRI SRU SS SSU SSW SWSE SYP

BORDER CROSSINGS
Ind $15/yr, $27/2 yrs, inst $20/yr, $35/2 yrs. U.S. $19/yr.
Quarterly.
301-160 Princess Street
Winnipeg, Manitoba
R3B IK9

ISSN: 0702-7427
Locations: ACU BVAU MWP MWU MWUC NBSAM OHM
OLU OONL OPAL OTAG OTMCL OTU QMFA QMG SPANC
SRP SS SSU

BRICK
Ind $6/yr, $12/2 yrs, $18/3 yrs, inst $12/yr. Tri-annual.
P.O Box 537
Station Q
Toronto, Ont.
M4T 2M5
ISSN: 0382-8565
Locations: ACMR ACU AEU BVA BVAS MWU MWUC
NBFU NBSAM NBSU NFSM NSCS NSHD OHM OLU
OONL OOU OPET OSUL OTU OTY OWA OWTU QMM
QSHERU SSU

CANADIAN AUTHOR & BOOKMAN
Ind $12.50/yr, $23/2 yrs, $33/3 yrs, inst $20/yr, $32.50/2
yrs, $45/3 yrs. Quarterly.
Canadian Authors Association Business Office
Suite 104-121 Avenue Road
Toronto, Ont.
M5R 2G3
ISSN: 0008-2937
Locations: AE AEP AEU BRC BVA BVAU BVIV MBC MW
MWP MWUC NBFU NBSAM NBSU NFSM NSAS NSHD
NSHP NSHPL OGU OHM OKQ OLU OOCC OONL OOP
OOS OOU OPAL OPET OSUL OTC OTER OTMCL OTP
OTSTM OTU OTULS OTV OTY OW OWA OWTU QMBM
QMBN QMU SRL SRP SRU SSU

CANADIAN CHILDREN'S LITERATURE
$16/yr. Non-Canadian add $1. Quarterly.
Canadian Children's Literature Association
Department of English
University of Guelph
 Guelph, Ont.
N1G 2W1
ISSN: 0319-0080
Locations: ACMR ACU AEU BVAS BVAU MBC MWU
MWUC NBFU NBSAM NSCS NSH NSHD NSHS NSHV
NSTT OHM OKQ OKQM OLU OOCC OONL OPAL OPET
OSUL OTEPL OTER OTEY OTMCL OTNY OTP OTSP OTU
OTULS OWA OWTU QMG QMM QMMLS QMU SMJ SR
SRED SRP SRU SST SWSE SYP

CANADIAN DRAMA
Ind $10/yr, inst $15/yr. Semi-annual.
Department of English
University of Guelph
Guelph, Ont.
N1G 2W1
ISSN: 0317-9044
Locations: ACU AEU BVA BVAS BVAU BVIV MBC MWU
MWUC NBFU NBSAM NBSU NSCS NSHD NSHS NSHV
OHM OKQ OLU OOCC OONL OOU OPET OTMCL OTU
OTY OWA OWTU QQLA QMG QMM QMU SRU SSU

CANADIAN FICTION MAGAZINE
Ind $24/yr, inst $30/yr. U.S. $30/yr. Quarterly.
P.O. Box 946
Station F
Toronto, Ont.
M4Y 2N9
ISSN: 0045-477-X
Locations: ACMR ACU AEU BVA BVAS BVAU BVIV MWU
MWUC NBFU NBSAM NBSU NSCS NSHD NSHK NSHS
NSHV NSWA OHM OKQ OKR OLH OLU OOCC OONL
OOU OPAL OPET OSUL OTMCL OTNY OTP OTU OTY
OWA OWTU QMG QMM QMU QSHERU SR SRP SRU SS
SSU

CANADIAN FORUM
Ind $18/yr, $34/2 yrs, $49/3 yrs, inst #30/yr, $58/2 yrs,
$85/3 yrs. Overseas add $5. Monthly.
70 The Esplanade, Third Floor
Toronto, Ont.
M5E 1R2
ISSN: 0008-3631
Locations: ACMR AE AEP AEU BRC BVA BVAS BVAU
BVAVA BVIP BVIV MBC MW MWP MWU NBFU NBSAM
NBSU NFSM NSAS NSCS NSHD NSHK NSHP NSHS
NSSCG NSTT OCHA OGU OHM OKQ OL OLH OLU OOB
OOC OOCC OOE OOEC OOF OOFF OOL OON OONG
OONL OOP OORT OOS OOU OOV OPAL OPET OS OSUL
OTC OTCIA OTDL OTER OTL OTP OTSTM OTTC OTU
OTULS OTV OTY OW OWA OWTU QMB QMBM QMBN
QMG QMM QMMLS QMMN QMU QQL QSHERU SCR SMJ
SMJT SNB SPANC SR SRL SRP SRU SS SSM SSSA SSU SSW
SYP

CANADIAN LITERATURE
Ind $20/yr, inst $25/yr. Non-Canadian add $5. Quarterly.
c / o Circulation Manager
2029 West Mall
University of British Columbia
Vancouver, B.C.
V6T 1W5
ISSN: 0008-4360
Locations: ACMR ACU AE AEU BRC BVA BVAS BVAU BVIV
MSC MWP MWU MWUC NBFL NBFU NBSAM NBSU
NFSM NSAS NSCS NSHD NSHK NSHL NSHPL NSHS
NSHV NSTT NSWA OCHA OGU OHM OKQ OKR OLH
OLU OOB OOCC OOE OONL OOSH OOU OPAL OPET OS
OSUL OTB OTER OTP OTSTM OTTC OTU OTULS OTU
OTY OW QMBM QMBN QMG QMM QMU QQL QSHERU
QSTJ SCA SMJ SPANC SR SRP SS SSU SSW

CANADIAN POETRY
Ind $12/yr, inst $15/yr. Semi-annual.
Department of English
University of Western Ontario
 London, Ont.
N6A 3K7
ISSN: 0704-5646
Locations: AEU BVAS BVAU MBC MWU MWUC NBSAM
NBSU NSHD OHM OKR OLU OOCC OONL OOU OPAL
OTU OTY OWA OWTU QMG SRU SSU

CANADIAN THEATRE REVIEW
Ind $27.50/yr, inst $37.50/yr, student $22/yr. Non-Canadian
add $3. Quarterly.
Journals Department
University of Toronto Press
5201 Dufferin Street
Downsview, Ont.
M3H 5T8
ISSN: 0315-0836
Locations: ACMR ACU AE AEU BRC BVA BVAS BVAU BVI
BVIPA MBC MSC MWU MWUC NBFU NBSAM NBSU
NSCS NSH NSHD NSHS NSHV NSWA OHM OKQ OKQM
OKR OLU OOCC OOE OONL OONMM OOU OPAL OPET
OTIM OTU OTY OWA OWTU QMG QMM QMU QQLA
QSHERU SR SRP SRU SS SSSI SSU

THE CAPILANO REVIEW
$12/yr, $22/2 yrs.
Capilano College
2055 Purcell Way
North Vancouver, B.C.
V7J 3H5
ISSN: 0315-3754
Locations: ACMR ACU AEU BVA BVAS BVAU BVAVA BVIV
MBC MWU NBFU NBSAM NSCS NSHD OHM OOCC
OONL OOU OPET OTMCL OTU OWA OWTU QMG
QMM SRP SS SSU

CHATELAINE
$15/yr. U.S. $30 (regular), $50 (first-class). Monthly.
Subscription Department
P.O. Box 1600
Postal Station A
Toronto, Ont.
M5W 2B8
ISSN: 0009-1995
Locations: ACMR BVA BVAU MBC MW MWP NBFU
NBSAM NSCS NSHD NSHS NSSCG NSTT OCHA OHM
OKQ OLU OOCS OOE OOEDC OOLWB OONL OOP OOU
OPAL OS OSUL OTDL OTP OTU OW OWA OWTU QMBM
QMG SCA SCR SMJ SMJT SNB SPANC SR SRL SRP SRRI
SSC SSSI SSW SWSE SYP

CONTEMPORARY VERSE 2
Ind $16/yr, $28/2 yrs, inst $20/yr, $36/2 yrs. Non-Canadian
$16(U.S.) / yr. Quarterly.
P.O. Box 32
University Centre
University of Manitoba
Winnipeg, Manitoba
R3T IE0
ISSN: 0319-6879
Locations: ACMR ACU AE AEU BRC BVA BVAS BVAU
BVIPA MBC MWU MWUC NBFU NBSAM NSCS NSHD
NSHK NSHP NSWA OHM OKQ OLU OOCC OONL OOU
OPET OSUL OTU OTY OWA OWTU QMG QML QMM
QMU SRP SS SSU

CROSS-CANADA WRITER'S QUARTERLY
Ind $11/yr, inst $18/yr. Non-Canadian inst $21/yr. Quarterly.
P.O. Box 277
Station F
Toronto, Ont.
M4Y 2L7
ISSN: 0227-2652
Locations: ACU NBSAM NSHD OHM OLU OONL OW OWA

DALHOUSIE REVIEW
$10/yr, $24/3 yrs. Quarterly.
Business Manager
Dalhousie University
Halifax, N.S.
B3H 3J5
ISSN: 0011-5827
Locations: ACMR ACU AE AEP AEU BRC BVA BVAS BVAU
BVIP BVIV MBC MW MWP MWU MWUC NBFL NBFU NBS
NBSAM NBSM NBSU NFSG NFSM NSAS NSCS NSHD
NSHK NSHP NSHPL NSHS NSTT OGU OHM OKF OL OLU
OOA OOB OOC OOCC OOE OOFF OON OONL OOP OOU
OPAL OPET OSUL OTCIA OTER OTL OTLS OTP OTSTM
OTTC OTU OTV OTY OW OWA OWTU QLB QMBM QMBN
QMG QMU QQL QSHERU SR SRL SRP SRU SS SSU SSW

DANDELION MAGAZINE
$8/yr, $15/2 yrs, inst $12/yr. Semi-annual.
The Alexandra Centre
922 - 9th Ave. S.E.
Calgary, Alberta
T2G 0S4
ISSN: 0385-9575
Locations: ACMR ACU AE AEU BVA BVAS NBFU NSHD
OHM OKQ OLU OONL OTU SR SS

DESCANT
Ind $18/yr, inst $26/yr. Quarterly.
P.O. Box 314
Station P
Toronto, Ont.
M5S 2S8
ISSN: 0382-909-X
Locations: ACU AEU BVA BVAU BVAVA BVIPA MBC MWU
NBFU NBSAM NBSU OHM OKQ OKR OLU OOCC OONG
OONL OOU OPET OSUL OTEPL OTIM OTMCL OTNY OTP
OTU OTY OWA QMBM QMG QMM QMU QSHERU SR SRP
SRU SS SSU

THE DINOSAUR REVIEW
$8/yr, $15/2 yrs. Quarterly.
P.O. Box 294
Drumheller, Alberta
T0J 0Y0
ISSN: 0828-0983
Locations: AEU BVAS OLU OONL OTU

ENGLISH STUDIES IN CANADA
Inst $20/yr. Quarterly.
Department of English
University of Alberta
Edmonton, Alberta
T6G 2E5
ISSN: 0317-0802
Locations: ACU AEU BRC BVA BVAS BVAU MBC MWU
MWUC NBFU NBSAM NSCS NSHD NSHK NSHS OHM
OKR OLU OOCC OONL OOU OPAL OPET OSUL OTMCL
OTU OTY OWA OWTU QMG QMM QMU QSHERU SRU
SSM SSU

ESSAYS ON CANADIAN WRITING
Ind $18/4 issues, inst $36/4 issues. Occasional.
307 Coxwell Ave.
Toronto, Ont.
M4L 3B5
ISSN: 0313-0300
Locations: ABA ACMR ACU AE AEU BRC BVA BVAS BVAU
MBC MW MWU MWUC NBFU NBSAM NBSU NSCS NSHK
NSHPC NSHS NSHV NSWA OHM OKQ OLH OLU OOCC
OONF OONL OOU OPAL OPET OSUL OTEPL OTMCL OTP
OTSP OTSTM OTU OWA OWTU QMG QMJ QMM QMU
QSHERU SRU SSU

EVENT
Ind $9/yr, $17/2 yrs, inst $17/2 yrs. Semi-annual.
Douglas College
P.O. Box 2503
New Westminster, B.C.
V3L 5B2
ISSN: 0315-3770
Locations: ACMR ACU AEU BVA BVAS BVAU BVIPA BVIV
NBFU NBSAM NSHD NSHS NSHV OHM OLU OOCC
OONL OOU OPET OTMCL OTU OTY OWA QMG QMM
QSHERU SSU

EXILE
$18/yr, $30/2 yrs, $55/4 yrs. Quarterly.
P.O. Box 67
Station B
Toronto, Ont.
M5T 2C0
ISSN: 0380-6596
Locations: AC ACU AE AEU BVA BVAS BVAU BVIV MBC
MWU MWUC NBSAM NFSM NSCS NSHD NSHK NSHS
NSHV OGU OHM OKQ OKR OLU OOC OOCC OONL
OOU OPET OSUL OTMCL OTSTM OTU OTY OWA OWTU
QMFA QMG QML SR SRP SRU SS SSU

THE FIDDLEHEAD
$14/yr. Non-Canadian $15/yr. Quarterly.
University of New Brunswick
P.O. Box 4400
Fredericton, N.B.
E3B 5A3
ISSN: 0015-0630

Locations: ACMR ACU BRC BVA BVAS BVAU BVIV MBC
MWU MWUC NBFU NBSAM NBSU NFSM NSAS NSCS
NSHD NSHK NSHP NSHS NSHV NSTT NSWA OCHA OGU
OHM OKQ OKQM OKR OLH OLU OOCC OONL OOU
OPAL OPET OSUL OTMCL OTP OTSTM OTU OTV OW
OWA OWTU QMBM QMG QMU QSHERU SRU

THE FINANCIAL POST
$39.95/yr, $69.95/2 yrs, $89.95/3 yrs. U.S. $59.95/yr. U.K.
and Europe $175/yr. Elsewhere &275/yr. Weekly.
Financial Post Circulation
777 Bay Street
Toronto, Ont.
M5W 1A7
ISSN: 0015-2021
Locations: ACM ACMR ACSO ACU MWU MWUC NBFU
NBS NFSCT NFSM NSCS NSHD NSHPC OCHA OGU OHM
OOB OOCC OOCS OOFF OOFP OOL OOMI OONL OORT
OOS OOSM OOU OPAL OS OTDL OTMCL OTP OTULS
OTU OTY OW OWTU QMM QMMSC QMU QQLA SRU SSU

FIREWEED
Ind $12/yr, inst $18/yr. Non-Canadian add $3. Quarterly.
P.O. Box 279
Station B
Toronto, Ont.
M5T 2W2
ISSN: 0706-3857
Locations: AEU MWU MWUC OHM OLU OONL OPET
OTMCL OTU OWTU QMU

GERMINATION
Ind $6/yr, inst $8/yr. Semi-annual.
428 Yale Avenue
Riverview, N.B.
E1B 2B5
ISSN: 0704-6286
Locations: NBFU NBSAM NSHD NSHP OLU OONL OTU

GRAIN
$12/yr, $20/2 yrs. Quarterly.
P.O. Box 1154
Regina, Sask.
S4P 3B4
ISSN: 0315-7423
Locations: ACMR AEU BVA BVAU BVIPA MWUC NBFU
NBSAM NBSU NSHD OGU OHM OLU OOCC OONL OOU
OPET OTU OTY OWA OWTU QMG QMM QMU
QSHERU SRU SSM SSU

THE IDLER
$18/yr, $33/2 yrs, $60/4 yrs. U.S. same rates in $U.S.
Overseas $21(U.S.) / yr surface, $30(U.S.) / yr airmail.
Monthly.
255 Davenport Road
Toronto, Ont.
M5R 1J9
ISSN: 0828-1289
Locations: MWU MWUC NSHK OHM OLU OONL OTU

ISLAND
Ind $12/yr, inst $15/yr. Non-Canadian add $2. Semi-annual.
c / o John Marshall
P.O. Box 256
Lantzville, B.C.
VOR 2H0
ISSN: 0227-0773
Locations: BVAS BVIPA NBFU NBSAM NSHD NSHS OLU
OOCC OONL OTU

JOURNAL OF CANADIAN FICTION
Ind $15/yr, inst $18/yr. Non-Canadian add $0.50/issue
($2/yr). Occasional.
JCF Press
2050 MacKay Street
Montreal, Que.
H3G 2J1
ISSN: 0047-2255
Locations: ACMR ACU AEU MRC BVA BVAU BVIV MBC
MWU MWUC NBFU NBSAM NBSU NFSG NSCS NSHD
NSHPL NSHS NSHV OGU OHM OKQ OKR OLU OOB
OOCC OONL OOU OPAL OPET OSUL OTEPL OTMCL OTP
OTSTM OTU OTV OTY OWA OWTU QMG QML QMM
QMU QRUQR QSHERU QTU SRU SSU

JOURNAL OF CANADIAN POETRY
$12.50/yr, $23.50/2 yrs, $33/3 yrs. Annual.
9 Ashburn Drive
Nepean, Ont.
K2E 6N4
ISSN: 0705-1328
Locations: ACU AEU BVAS BVAU MWU NBFU NBSAM
NSHD OHM OLU OOCC
OONL OOU OPAL OTMCL OTU OWTU QSHERU

JOURNAL OF CANADIAN STUDIES
Ind $16/yr, $30/2 yrs, inst $30/yr, $45/2 yrs, student $10.
Non-Canadian add $3. Quarterly.
Trent University
P.O. Box 4800
Peterborough, Ont.
K9J 7B8
ISSN: 0021-9495
Locations: ACMR AE BRC BVA BVAS BVAU BVIPA BVIV
MBC MWP MWU MWUC NBFU NBSAM NBSU NSCS
NSHD NSHK NSH NSHV NSTT NSWA OGU OHM OKQ
OKR OLH OLU OOB OOC OOCC OOCS OOE OOEC OOF
OOFF OONF OONG OONL OONM OOP OORT OOS OOTC
OOU OPAL OPET OSUL OTER OTP OTRM OTSTM OTU
OTV OTY OW OWA OWTU QMAC QMB QMFA QMG QML
QMM QMML QMU QSHERU SRU SSM SSU

MACLEAN'S MAGAZINE
$45.50/yr. U.S. $60.50/yr surface, $126.50/yr first-class.
Others $101.50/yr surface, $212.50/yr airmail. Weekly.
Maclean Hunter Ltd.
777 Bay Street
Toronto, Ont.
M5W IA7
ISSN: 0024-9262

Locations: ACMR AR BRC BVA BVAC BVAU BVIV MBC
MWP MWU MWUC NBFU NBSAM NBSU NFSM NSCS
NSHD NSHDL NSHPL NSSCG NSTT OCHA OGU OHM
OKQ OOAG OOB OOC OOCC OOCN OOCS OOE OOEDC
OOF OOL OONL OONMM OOP OORT OOS OOTC OOU
OOV OS OSUL OTC OTDL OTER OTMCL OTSTM OTU
OTULS OTV OTY OW OWA OWTU QMHE QML QQLA
QSTJ SRL SRU

THE MALAHAT REVIEW
$15/yr, $40/3 yrs. Quarterly
University of Victoria
P.O. Box 1700
Victoria, B.C.
V8W 2Y2
ISSN: 0025-1216
Locations: ACMR ACU AE AEU BRC BVA BVAS BVAU BVIV
MBC MWU MWUC NBFU NBSAM NFSM NSCS NSWA
OGU OHM OKQ OLU OOCC OONG OONL OOP OOU
OPAL OPET OSUL OTMCL OTSTM OTU OTV OTY OWA
OWTU QMG QMU QQL QSHERU SRU SSU

MATRIX
Ind $7.50/yr, $14/2 yrs, inst $10/yr. Semi-annual.
P.O. Box 510
Lennoxville, Que.
JIM 1Z6
ISSN: 0318-3160
Locations: ACU AEU BVAS BVAU NBFU NBSAM NSCS
NSHD NSWA OHM OLU OOCC OONL OOU OSUL
OTMCL OTU OTY OWA QMG QMM QMU QSHERU SRU
SSU

MOSAIC
Ind $19.50/yr, $48.50/3 yrs, inst $29/yr, $73/3 yrs. Non-
Canadian add $5. Quarterly.
c / o Business Manager
208 Tier Building
University of Manitoba
Winnipeg, Manitoba
R3T 2N2
ISSN: 0027-1276
Locations: AEU BRC BVA BVAS BVAU BVIV MBC MSC
MWP MWU MWUC NBFU NBSAM NBSU NSCS NSHK
NSHPL OGU OHM OKQ OOB OOCC OONL OOU OPAL
OPET OSUL OTP OTSTM OTU OTULS OTV OTY OW OWA
OWTU QMG
QML QMU SRU SSU

THE NEW QUARTERLY
Ind $12/yr, inst $16/yr. Non-Canadian add $1. Quarterly.
English Language Proficiency Program
University of Waterloo
Waterloo, Ont.
N2L 3GI
ISSN: 0227-0455
Locations: MWU NBSAM NSHD OHM OLU OONL OTU
OWTU

THE NEWEST REVIEW
Ind $12/yr, $20/2 yrs, inst $18/yr. Monthly.
P.O. Box 394
Sub P.O. 6
Saskatoon, Sask.
S7N 0W0
ISSN: 0390-2917
Locations: ACMR ACU BVA BVAU MWP MWUC NSHD
OHM OLU OONL OOP OPET OTMCL OTU OTY QMM SSU

NORTHERN LIGHT
$7/yr. Semi-annual.
P.O. Box 162
St. Francis Xavier University
Antigonish, N.S.
B2G 1C0
ISSN: 0317-0586
Locations: ACU AEU BVAS BVAU MWP MWU MWUC
NBFU NBSAM NBSU NSHD OHM OOCC OONL OPAL
OPET OTU OTY OWA OWTU QMM SSU

NORTHWARD JOURNAL
$20/yr, $38/2 yrs. Non-Canadian add $2. Quarterly.
P.O. Box 248
Kapuskasing, Ont.
P5N 2Y4
ISSN: 0706-0955
Locations: ACU BVAS NBFU NBSAM NSHD OHM OLU
OONL OORD OOU OPAL OPET OSUL OSUU OTAG OTU
OWA OWTU QLB QMG

OPEN LETTER
$13.50/3 issues. Non-Canadian $16/3 issues. Occasional.
104 Lyndhurst Avenue
Toronto, Ont.
M5R 2Z7
ISSN:0048-1939
Locations: ACMR ACU AE AEU BRC BVA BVAS BVAU BVIV
MWUC NBFU NBSAM NFSM NSHD NSHV OHM OKQ
OLU OOCC OONL OOU OPAL OPET OSUL OTAG OTEPL
OTMCL OTP OTSP OTU OTY OWA OWTU QMG QMM
QSHERU SRP SS SSU

POETRY CANADA REVIEW
Ind $14/yr, $26/2 yrs, inst $30/yr, $56/2 yrs. Non-Canadian
ind $14(U.S.) / yr, $26(U.S.) / 2 yrs, inst $30(U.S.) / yr,
$56(U.S.) / 2 yrs. Quarterly.
307 Coxwell Avenue
Toronto, Ont.
M4L 3B5
ISSN: 0709-3373
Locations: ACU AEU MWU MWUC NBSAM NBSU NSHD
OHM OLU OONL OOU OPET SSU

POTTERSFIELD PORTFOLIO
Ind $12/3 yrs, inst $15/3 yrs. Non-Canadian ind $15/3 yrs,
inst $18/3 yrs. Annual.
19 Oakhill Drive
Halifax, N.S.
B3M 2V3
ISSN: 0226-0840
Locations: AEU BVA BVAS NBFL NBFU NBS NBSAM NBSU
NSAS NSHD OOCC OONL OOU OTU OWA OWTU
QSHERU SSU

PRAIRIE FIRE
Ind $18/yr, inst $24/yr. Non-Canadian add $4. Quarterly.
208-100 Arthur Street
Winnipeg, Manitoba
R3B 2J2
ISSN: 0821-1124
Locations: MBC MWP MSHD OLU OONL

PRAIRIE JOURNAL OF CANADIAN LITERATURE
Ind $6/yr, inst $12/yr. Semi-annual.
P.O. Box 997
Station G
Calgary, Alberta
T3A 3G2
ISSN: 0827-2921
Locations: ACU OHM OLU OONL OTU

PRISM INTERNATIONAL
Ind $12/yr, $20/2 yrs, inst $18/yr, $24/2 yrs. Quarterly.
Department of Creative Writing
University of British Columbia
Vancouver, B.C.
V6T 1W5
ISSN: 0032-8790
Locations: ACMR ACU AEU BRC BVA BVAS BVAU BVAVA
BVIPA BVIV MBC MWUC NBSAM NBSU NFSM NSCS
NSHD NSHPL NSWA OHM OKQ OLU OOCC OONL OOP
OOU OPAL OPET OSUL OTP OTSTM OTU OTY OWA
OWTU QML QMM QMU QSHERU SSU

QUARRY
$18/yr, $30/2 yrs. Quarterly.
P.O. Box 1061
Kingston, Ont.
K7L 4Y5
ISSN: 0033-5266
Locations: ACMR AEU BVA BVAS BVAU BVIP BVIV MBC
MWU MWUC NBFU NBSAM NBSU NSCS NSHD NSHPL
NSHV OHM OKR OLU OOB OOCC OONL OOU OPAL
OPET OSUL OTP OTSTM OTU OTV OTY OWA OWTU QML
QMU QSHERU SRL

QUEEN'S QUARTERLY
Ind $18/yr, $45/3 yrs, inst $25/yr. Non-Canadian $20(U.S) /
yr,
$50(U.S.) / 3 yrs, inst $25(U.S.) / yr. Quarterly.
Business Manager
Queen's University
Kingston, Ont.
K7L 3N6
ISSN: 0033-6041
Locations: ACMR AE AEP AEU BRC BVA BVAS BVAU BVIP
BVIV MBC MSC MW MWP MWU MWUC NBFL NBFU
NBSAM NBSU NFSM NSAS NSCS NSHD NSHK NSHPL
NSHS NSTT OGU OHM OKF OKQ OL OLH OLU OLUM
OOB OOC OOCC OOCS OOG OON OONL OONM OOP
OOU OOV OPAL OPET OSUL OTER OTK OTL OTMCL OTP
OTSTM OTTC OTU OTV OW OWA OWTU QMBM QMBN
QMU QQL QSHERU SRL SRU SSU

QUILL & QUIRE
$40/yr, $72/2 yrs. Monthly.
56 The Esplanade
Toronto, Ont.
M5E 1A7
ISSN: 0033-6491
Locations: ACMR ACU AE AEU BRC BVA BVAS BVAST
BVAU BVAVA BVIV MBC MWP MWUC NBFU NBSAM
NBSU NSAS NSH NSHD NSHDL NSHP NSHPL NSSCG
NSTT OCKA OGU OHM OKQM OKR OLU OOA OOAECB
OOAG OOB OOCC OOCN OOCS OOFF OOL OON OOND
OONG OONL OOP OOPW OOREX OORT OOS OOSM
OOU OOV OPET OSUL OTAG OTC OTDL OTDT OTEPL
OTK OTMCL OTNY OTP OTSP OTSTM OTUDP OTULS
OTV OTY OW OWA OWAL OWTU QCU QMB QMBM QMG
QMHE QML QMU QMUQ QQL QSTJ QTU SMJ SMJT SNB
SR SRL SRP SRU SS SSAR SSR SSU SWSE

ROOM OF ONE'S OWN
Ind $10/yr, inst $14/yr. Non-Canadian ind $11/yr. Quarterly.
P.O. Box 46160
Station G
Vancouver, B.C.
V6R 4G5
ISSN: 0316-1609
Locations: ACU AEU BVA BVAS BVAU BVAVA BVIPA MSC
MWU MWUC NBFU NSHD NSHV NSWA OHM OLU
OOLWB OONL OOU OS OTMCL OTU OTY OWA OWTU
QMG QMM QMU SSU

RUBICON
Ind $12/yr, $20/2 yrs, inst $16/yr, $25/2 yrs. Semi-annual.
McGill University
853 rue Sherbrooke ouest
Montreal, Que.
H3A 2T6
ISSN: 0715-8610
Locations: AEU BVAU BNFU NSHD OHM OLU OONL OOU
OTU OWA QMG QMM

SATURDAY NIGHT
$28/yr. Non-Canadian add $7.50/yr, $42/yr airmail.
Monthly.
36 Toronto Street, Suite 1160
Toronto, Ont.
M5C 2C5
ISSN: 0036-4975
Locations: ACMR AE AEU BVA BVAU BVIV MBC MW
MWLS MWP MWUC NBFU NBSU NFSM NSAS NSCS
NSHD NSHK NSSCG NSTT OGU OHM OKQ OLU OOB
OOCC OOCS OOEDC OOF OOFF OONL OOP OOREX
OORT OOS OOTC OOV OPAL OTER OTMCL OTP OTSTM
OTU OTULS OTV OTY OW OWA QMU QSTJ SRL SRPS SRU
SSU

STUDIES IN CANADIAN LITERATURE
Ind $9/yr, $17/2 yrs, inst $12/yr, $22/2 yrs. Non-Canadian
$10/yr, $19/2 yrs. Semi-annual.
Department of English
University of New Brunswick
Fredericton, N.B.
E3B 5A3
ISSN: 0380-6995
Locations: ACMR ACU AEU BVA BVAS BVAU MBC MWUC
NBSAM NBSU NSCS NSHD NSHV NSTT OHM OKQ OLU
OOCC OONL OOU OPAL OPET OSUL OTEPL OTMCL
OTNY OTU OTY OWA OWTU QMG QMM QMU SRU SSU

THEATRE HISTORY IN CANADA
Ind $15/yr, inst $22/yr, student $12/yr. Non-Canadian add
$2.50. Semi-annual.
Graduate Centre for Study of Drama
214 College Street
University of Toronto
Toronto, Ont.
M5S 1A1
ISSN: 0226-5751
Locations: ACU AEU ALU BVAS BVAU MSC MWUC
NBSAM NBSU NSHD OHM OLU OOCC OOFF OONL OWA
OWTU SRU SSU

TORONTO LIFE
$22/yr. Non-Canadian add $15. Monthly, plus supplements.
59 Front Street East
Toronto, Ont.
M5E 1B3
ISSN: 0049-4194
Locations: AEU BVA NSH OGU OKQ OLU OONL OOP
OTDL OTDU OTEPL OTET OTL OTNY OTSP OTU OTY
OTYP OWTL QQIAS QQL SSU

THE TORONTO SOUTH ASIAN REVIEW
$15/yr. Tri-annual.
P.O. Box 6996
Station A
Toronto, Ont.
M5W 1X7
ISSN: 0714-3508
Locations: ACU NBSAM OONL OTU

UNIVERSITY OF TORONTO QUARTERLY
Ind $20/yr, inst $37.50/yr, student $12.50/yr. Non-Canadian add $4. Quarterly.
University of Toronto Press
5201 Dufferin Street
Downsview, Ont.
M3H 5T8
ISSN: 0042-0247
Locations: ACMR AE AEU BRC BVA BVAS BVAU BVIP BVIV MBC MW MWP MWU MWUC NBFL NBFU NBSAM NBSU NFSM NSAS NSCS NSH NSHD NSHK NSHP NSHPL NSHS NSTT OGU OHM OKQ OL OLH OLU OOAG OOB OOC OOCC OOL OONL OOP OOU OPAL OPET OSUL OTA OTAR OTEPL OTER OTL OTMCL OTNY OTP OTREC OTSTM OTTC OTU OTUD OTV OTY OW OWA OWTU QMBM QMBN QMU QQL QQLA QSHERU SRL SRU SSU

UNIVERSITY OF WINDSOR REVIEW
$10/yr. Semi-annual.
Department of English
University of Windsor
Windsor, Ont.
N9B 3P4
ISSN: 0042-0352
Locations: ACMR AE AEU BVA BVAS BVAU BVIV MBC MWU MWUC NBFU NBSAM NSCS NSHD NSHS NSHV NSWA OHM OKQ OKR OLU OOCC OONL OOP OOU OPAL OPET OSUL OTMCL OTSTM OTU OTY OW OWA OWTU QMM QMU SRU

WASCANA REVIEW
Ind $7/yr, $18/3 yrs. Non-Canadian $8/yr, $20/3 yrs. Semi-annual.
English Department
University of Regina
Regina, Sask.
S4S 0A2
ISSN: 0043-0412
Locations: BVA BVAS BVAU BVIV MWU MWUC NBFU NBSAM NSHD NSWA OHM OKQ OKR OLU OOCC OONL OOP OOU OPAL OPET OSUL OTAG OTP OTSTM OTU OTY OW OWA OWTU QMG QMU QSHERU SRU

WAVES
79 Denham Drive
Richmond Hill, Ont.
L4C 6H9
ISSN: 0315-3932
Locations: ACU AEU BVA BVAS BVAU BVIPA BVIV NBFU NFSM NSCS NSHD NSWA OGU OHM OKQ OLU OOCC OONL OOU OPET OTEPL OTEY OTMCL OTNY OTP OTU OTY OWA OWTU QMG QMM QMU QSHERU SMJ SRP SSU

WEST COAST REVIEW
Ind $14/yr, inst $18/yr. Quarterly.
c/o English Department
Simon Fraser University
Burnaby, B.C.
V5A 1S6
ISSN: 0043-311-X

Locations: ACMR AEU BRC BVA BVAS BVAU BVIPA BVIV MBC MWU NBFU NBSAM NSCS NSHD NSHS NSWA OGU OHM OKQ OLU OOCC OONL OOP OOU OPAL OPET OSUL OTP OTSTM OTU OWA OWTU QMG QMM QSHERU SRU SSU

WORLD LITERATURE WRITTEN IN ENGLISH
Ind $14/yr, inst $18/yr, student $10/yr. Non-Canadian $15/yr, inst $19/yr. Semi-annual.
University of Toronto Press
5201 Dufferin Street
Downsview, Ont.
M3H 5T8
ISSN: 0093-1705
Locations: BVAS BVAU MWU NBFU NBSAM NFSM NSHD OGU OHM OKQ OKR OLU OOCC OONL OOU OPAL OSUL OTMCL OTP OTU OWA OWTL OWTU QMM QMU QQLA SRU SSU

WRITING
$12/yr, inst $16/yr. Quarterly.
P.O. Box 69609
Station K
Vancouver, B.C.
V5K 4W7
ISSN: 0706-1889
Locations: BVAS BVAU NSHD OHM OLU OONL

CANADIAN PERIODICALS (FRENCH)

ELLIPSE
$10/yr. Semi-annual.
c.p. 10
Faculte des lettres et sciences humaines
Universite de Sherbrooke
Sherbrooke, Que.
J1K 2R1
ISSN: 0046-1830
Locations: ACMR ACU AEU BVAI BVAU BVIV MWU MWUC NBFU NBSAM NBSU NSCS NSHD OHM OKQ OLU OOCC OONL OOP OOU OPET OTEPL OTMCL OTNY OTP OTTC OTU OTV OTY OWA OWTU QCU QMBM QMBN QMG QMU QMUQ QQL QRU QSHERU QTU SRU

ESTUAIRE
Ind $18/yr, inst #30/yr. Non-Canadian $35/yr. Quarterly.
Diffusion Dimedia
539 boul. Lebeau
Saint Laurent, Que.
H4N 1S1
ISSN: 0700-365-X
Locations: ACU AEU BVAU BVIV OLU OOCC OONL OOU OTU OTY OWA OWTU QMFA QMU QSHERU

ÉTUDES FRANCAISES

Ind $15/yr, inst $30/yr, student $11.25/yr. Non-Canadian
$18/yr. Tri-annual.
Presses de l'Universite de Montreal
c.p. 6128, succ A
Montreal, Que.
H3C 3J7
ISSN: 0700-365-X
Locations: ACU AEU BRC BVAS BVAU BVIV MWU MWUC
NBFU NBSAM NFSM NSCS NSHD NSHV OGU OHM OKQ
OLU OOC OOCC OOCS OOE OONL OOP OOU OPAL
OPET OSTCB OSUL OTMCL OTSTM OTTC OTU OTV OTY
OW OWA OWTL OWTU QCU QHU QMBM QMBN QMG
QMHE QMM QMU QQL QQLA QRC QRU QRUQR
QSHERU QSTJ QT QTCE QTCL QTU SRU SSU

ÉTUDES LITTERAIRES

Ind $15/yr, inst $26/yr, student $10/yr. Non-Canadian $18/yr.
Tri-annual.
Les Presses de l'Universite Laval
c.p. 2447
Quebec 2, Que.
G1K 7P4
ISSN: 0014-214-X
Locations: ACU AE AEU BVA BVAS BVAU BVIV MWU
MWUC NBFU NBSAM NFSM NSCS NSHD OGU OHM
OKQ OLH OLU OOC OOCC OONL OOP OOU OPAL
OSTCB OSUL OTMCL OTNY OTP OTSTM OTU OTV OTY
OW OWA OWTL OWTU QCU QHU QMBM QMBN QMG
QML QMU QMUQ QQL QQLA QRU QSHERU QT QTCE
QTCL QTU SRU SSU

JEU: CAHIERS DE THEATRE

Ind $30/yr, $55/2 yrs, inst $40/yr, $75/2 yrs, student
$26/yr. Non-Canadian ind $38/yr surface, $58/yr airmail,
inst
$50/yr surface, $70/yr airmail, student $34/yr. Quarterly.
426 rue Sherbrooke est, bureau 102
Montreal, Que.
H2L 1J6
ISSN: 0382-0335
Locations: ACU AEU BVA BVAU NBFU NBSAM NSCS NSSX
OHM OLU OONL OOU OTU OTY QMG QMM QMU SRU
SSU

LETTRES QUEBECOISES

Ind $12/yr, inst $15/yr. U.S. $12(U.S.) / yr. Overseas $18/yr.
Quarterly.
c.p. 1840, succ B
Montreal, Que.
H3B 3L4
ISSN: 0382-084-X
Locations: ACU AEU BRC BVA BVAS BVAU MBC MSC
MWUC NBFU NSCS NSHD NSSCG OKQ OLU OOCC
OOCS OOE OONL OOP OOU OPET OSUL OTMCL OTSTM
OTU OTY OWA OWTU QSHERU SSU

LIBERTE

$20/yr. 6 issues / yr.
c.p. 399, succ Outremont
Montreal, Que.

H2V 4N3
ISSN: 0024-2020
Locations: AEU BRC BVA BVAS BVAU BVIV MSC MWP
MWU MWUC NBFU NBSAM NSCS NSHD NSHP OGU
OHM OKQ OLU OOCC OONG OONL OOU OPAL OPET
OSUL OTMCL OTP OTSTM OTU OTV OTY OWA OWTU
QMBM QMBN QMHE QMM QMU QQL QRU QSHERU SSM

MOEBIUS

Ind $18/yr, $35/2 yrs, inst $25/yr, $48/2 yrs. Non-Canadian
ind $22/yr, $42/2 yrs, inst $30/yr, $58/2 yrs. Quarterly.
Editions Triptyque
c.p. 670, succ N
Montreal, Que.
H2X 3N4
ISSN: 0225-1582
Locations: AEU OONL OOU QMU QSHERU

LA NOUVELLE BARRE DU JOUR

$45/yr, student / writer $39/yr. Non-Canadian $55/yr.
Occasional.
Diffusion Dimedia
539 boul. Lebeau
Saint Laurent, Que.
H4N 1S2
ISSN: 0704-1888
Locations: ACU AEU BRC BVAS BVAU BVIV MWU NBFU
NSAS NSHD OHM OKQ OKR OLU OOC OOCC OONL
OOU OPET OSUL OTU OTY OWA OWTU QMBM QMBN
QMG QMM QMU QQMC QSHERU SRU

VOIX ET IMAGES

Ind $40/2 yrs, $60/3 yrs, student $30/2 yrs, $45/3 yrs. Non-
Canadian $42/2 yrs, $62/3yrs.
Service des publications
Universite du Quebec a Montreal
c.p. 8888, succ A
Montreal, Que.
H3C 3P8
ISSN: 0318-9201
Locations: ACU AEU BVA BVAS BVAU MBC MWUC NBFU
NBSAM NSCS NSHD NSHV OHM OKQ OLU OOCC OONL
OOP OOU OPET OSUL OTU OTY OWA OWTU QMG QMM
QMU SRU SSU

INTERNATIONAL

INTERNATIONAL

UNITED STATES

AMERICAN REVIEW OF CANADIAN STUDIES
Ind $30/yr, $15/yr student / retired, inst $50/yr. Quarterly.
The Association for Canadian Studies in the United States
One Dupont Circle, Suite 620
Washington, D.C.
U.S.A. 20036
ISSN: 0272-2011
Locations: ACU AEU BVAS BVAU MBC MWU MWUC
NBFU NBSAM NSHD NSHS NSWA OHM OOCC OOE
OOFF OONL OONMM OOP OORT OOU OPAL OPET OSUL
OTER OTU OTY OWA QMU SRU

THE ATLANTIC
$14.95/yr, $27.95/2 yrs, $39.95/3 years. In Canada add $4.
Overseas add $6. Monthly.
Atlantic Subscription Processing Center
P.O. Box 52661
Boulder, Colorado
U.S.A. 80322
ISSN: 0267-9077
Llocations: ACMR ACU AE AEP AEU BRC BVA BVAS BVAU
BVIP BVIV MSC MW MWP MWU NBS NBSAM NBSU
NFSG NFSM NSHD NSHPL NSWA OGU OHM OKF OKQ
OKQM OL OLU OOB OOC OOCC OOCS OOE OOEDC
OOND OONG OONL OOP OORT OOU OOUSI OPAL OPET
OSUL OTER OTK OTL OTMCL OTP OTRC OTTC OTU OTV
OTY OW OWA OWTU QMBM QMBN QMG QMH QML
QMOCP QMU QSHERU QSTJ SCR SMJ SMJT SPANC SR
SRCU SRL SRP SRU SS SSSI SSU SSW SYP

JOURNAL OF CANADIAN CULTURE
$12.50(U.S.) / yr.
Bowling Green University Popular Press
Bowling Green, Ohio
U.S.A. 43403
Locations: BVAS BVAU NBSAM NSHD OHM OLU OTU
OWTU

THE NEW YORK REVIEW OF BOOKS
$34(U.S.) / yr. 24 issues / yr.
Subscription Service Department
P.O. Box 940
Farmingdale, N.Y.
U.S.A. 11737
ISSN: 0028-7504
Locations: ACMR ACU AE AEU BRC BVA BVAS BVAU BVIV
MBC MWU MWUC NBFU NBSAM NBSU NFSM NSH
NSHD NSHPL NSHS NSHV NSTT NSWA OGU OHM OKQ
OKQM OLU OOB OOCC OONL OONMC OOP OORT OOS
OOUSI OPAL OPET OSUL OTER OTMCL OTNY OTSTM
OTU OTV OTY OW OWA OWTU PC QMG QML QSHERU
QSTJ SRL SRP SRU SSM SSU

THE NEW YORK TIMES BOOK REVIEW
$30(U.S.) / yr. U.S. $26(U.S.) / yr. Overseas $30(U.S.) / yr.
Weekly.
Subscription Sales
P.O. Box 492
Hackensack, N.J.
U.S.A. 07602
ISSN: 0028-7806
Locations: ACMR ACU AE BVA BVAS BVAU BVIV MW
MWU MWUC NBFU NBSAM NFSM NSHD NSHS NSTT
OGU OHM OLLE OLU OOB OOCC OON OONL OOP OOU
OPAL OPET OSUL OTDL OTEPL OTEY OTMCL OTNY OTP
OTSP OTU OTULS OTY OTYP OW OWA OWTL OWTU
QMG QML QMU QQLA QSTJ SMJT SR SRL SRP SRU SS
SSM SSUL

THE NEW YORKER
$50(U.S.) / yr. U.S. $32(U.S.) / yr, $52(U.S.) / 2 yrs. Overseas
$56(U.S.) / yr. Weekly.
P.O. Box 56447
Boulder, Colorado
U.S.A. 80322
ISSN: 0028-792X
Locations: ACMR AE BRC BVA BVAU BVIV MW MWP
MWU MWUC NBFU NBSAM NBSU NFSM NSAS NSHD
NSHPL NSWA OHM OKQ OKR OLU OOCC OOCS OOE
OONL OOP OOU OPAL OPET OSUL OTMCL OTSTM OTU
OTV OTY OW OWA OWTU QMBM QML QMM QMU SRU
SSU

YALE FRENCH STUDIES
Yale University Press
92 A Yale Station
New Haven, Connecticut
U.S.A. 06520
ISSN: 0044-0078
Locations: ACU AEU BRC BVA BVAS BVAU BVIV MBC
MWU NBFU NBSAM NBSU NFSM NSAS NSHD NSHV
NSTT NSWA OHM OKQ OLH OLU OOCC OONL OOU
OPET OSUL OTMCL OTSTM OTTC OTY OWA OWTU QMG
QML QMU QQLA
QSHERU SRU SSU

AUSTRALIA

CRNLE REVIEWS JOURNAL
Ind $9(Aust) / yr, $24(Aust) / 3 yrs, inst $12(Aust) / yr,
$32(Aust) / 3 yrs. Airmail add $4(Aust). Semi-annual.
Centre for Research in the New Literatures in English
Flinders University of South Australia
Bedford Park, South Australia 5042
ISSN: 0157-3705
Locations: BVAS NBSAM OHM OLU OOU OTU

GREAT BRITAIN

BRITISH JOURNAL OF CANADIAN STUDIES
Available only to members of The British Assocation for
Canadian Studies. Membership: ind $20, inst $25, student £2.
$20/yr. U.S. $15/yr. Semi-annual.
International Council for Canadian Studies
256 King Edward
Ottawa, Ont.
KIN 7MI
ISSN: 0269-9222
Locations: AEU MWU NBSAM NSHD NSHK OHM OLU
OONL OOP OTU OWTU

JOURNAL OF COMMONWEALTH LITERATURE
Ind $34(U.S.) / yr, inst $40(U.S.) / yr. Airmail add $11(U.S.).
Semi-annual.
Hans Zell Publishers
14 St. Giles, P.O. Box 56
Oxford, U.K.
OXI 3EL
ISSN: 0021-9894
Locations: ACU AEU BVA BVAS BVAU BVIV MBC MWU
MWUC NBFU NBSAM NBSU NFSM NSCS NSHD NSHK
NSHS NSHV NSTT NSWA OGU OH OHM OKQ OLH OLU
OOCC OONL OOU OPAL OS OSTCB OSUL OTB OTEPL
OTMCL OTNY OTP OTR OTSTM OTU OTY OW OWA
OWTL OWTU QMG QML QMU QQLA QSHERU SRU SSM
SSU

TIMES LITERARY SUPPLEMENT
In Canada and U.S. $80(U.S.) / yr. U.K. £50/yr. Europe £72/
yr.
Elsewhere £66 surface, £80 airmail. Weekly.
Priory House
St. John's Lane
London, U.K.
ECIM 4BX
ISSN: 0040-7895
Locations: ACU AE AEU BRC BVAS BVAU BVIV MBC MW
MWU MWUC NBFU NBSU NFSG NFSM NSAS NSWA OKQ
OLLE OLU OOC OOCC OONL OOU OPAL OPET OSUL
OTEPL OTMCL OTNY OTTC OTU OTV OWTL OWTU
QMM QMU QQLA QSHERU SMJT SRP SRU SSU

FRANCE

AFRAM NEWSLETTER
Semi-annual.
c / o Michel Fabre
U.E.R. des Pays Anglophone
5 rue de l'Ecole-de-Medecine
Paris, France 75006

ETUDES CANADIENNES
$30/yr. Semi-annual.
Association Francaise d'Etudes Canadiennes
Maison des Sciences de l'Homme d'Aquitare
Domaine Universitaire
33405 Talence Cedex
France
ISSN: 0153-1700
Locations: ACU AEU BVAS MWUC NBFU NBSAM OHM
OKR OLU OOCC OONL OOP OOU OPET OTER OTU OTY
OWA OWTU QMM QMU QSHERU

GERMANY

ZEITSCHRIFT DER GESELLSCHAFT FUR KANADA-STUDIEN
Karl Wachholtz Verlag
Neumunster, West Germany
ISSN: 0722-849-X
Locations: BVAU OONL OOU OTMCL

NEWSPAPERS

THE CALGARY HERALD

The Herald Building
P.O. Box 2400
Station M
Calgary, Alberta
T2P 0W8
Telephone: (403) 235-0235

LE DEVOIR
$155/yr, $85/6 mos., $45/3 mos.
Messageries Dynamiques
Groupe Quebecor Inc.
775 boul. Lebeau
Saint Laurent, Que.
Telephone: (514) 332-3891

THE GAZETTE
$99/52 wks, $51/26 wks, $25.50/13wks.
250 St. Antoine St. West
Montreal, Que.
H2Y 3R7
Telephone: (514) 282-2222

THE GLOBE AND MAIL
Local rate: $23.40/13 wks, $46.80/26 wks, $93.60/yr.
444 Front St. W.
Toronto, Ont.
M5W 2S9
Telephone: (416) 585-5000

THE TORONTO STAR
$57/3 mos, $112/6 mos, $210/yr. Non-Canadian $150/3 mos,
$290/6 mos, $550/yr.
One Yonge Street
Toronto, Ont.
M5E 1E6
Telephone: (416) 367-2000

THE WINNIPEG FREE PRESS
$88.40/yr.
300 Carlton Street
Winnipeg, Manitoba
R3C 3C1
Telephone: (204) 943-9331

Libraries & Addresses for Inter-Library Loan Codes

ABA	Whyte Museum of the Canadian Rockies, Banff
AC	Calgary Public Library
ACM	Mobil Oil Canada Ltd., Calgary
ACMR	Mount Royal College, Calgary
ACSO	SUNCOR Inc., Calgary
ACU	University of Calgary
AE	Edmonton Public Library
AEP	Alberta Legislature Library, Edmonton
AEU	University of Alberta, Edmonton
AR	Ralston Public Library
BRC	Royal Roads Military College, Victoria
BVA	Vancouver Public Library
BVAI	International North Pacific Fisheries, Vancouver
BVAS	Simon Fraser University, Burnaby
BVAST	Vancouver School of Theology
BVAU	University of British Columbia, Vancouver
BVAVA	Vancouver Art Gallery
BVI	Greater Victoria Public Library
BVIP	Legislative Library, Victoria
BVIPA	Provincial Archives of British Columbia, Victoria
BVIV	University of Victoria
MBC	Brandon University
MSC	College de St-Boniface
MW	Winnipeg Centennial Library
MWLS	Faculty of Law, University of Manitoba, Winnipeg
MWP	Legislative Library of Manitoba, Winnipeg
MWU	University of Manitoba, Winnipeg
MWUC	University of Winnipeg
NBFL	Legislative Library, Fredericton
NBFU	University of New Brunswick, Fredericton
NBS	Saint John Regional Library
NBSAM	Mount Allison University, Sackville
NBSM	New Brunswick Museum, Saint John
NBSU	University of New Brunswick, Saint John
NFSCT	College of Trades and Technology, St. John's
NFSG	Newfoundland Public Library Services, St. John's
NFSM	Queen Elizabeth II Library, Memorial University of Newfoundland, St. John's
NSAS	St. Francis Xavier University, Antigonish
NSCS	Universite Saint-Anne, Church Point
NSH	Halifax City Regional Library
NSHD	Dalhousie University, Halifax
NSHDL	Law School, Dalhousie University, Halifax
NSHK	University of King's College, Halifax
NSHMS	Nova Scotia Museum, Halifax
NSHP	Nova Scotia Public Archives, Halifax
NSHPC	Corporate Research and Information Centre, Nova Scotia Power Corporation, Halifax
NSHPL	Nova Scotia Union Catalogue, Nova Scotia Provincial Library, Halifax
NSHS	St. Mary's University, Halifax
NSHV	Mount St. Vincent University, Halifax
NSSCG	Canadian Coast Guard College, Sydney
NSSX	University College of Cope Breton, Sydney
NSTT	Nova Scotia Teachers' College, Truro
NSWA	Acadia University, Wolfville

OCHA	Chatham Public Library
OCKA	Atomic Energy of Canada, Chalk River
OGU	University of Guelph
OH	Hamilton Public Library
OHM	McMaster University, Hamilton
OKF	Fort Frontenac Library, Canada Dept. of National Defence, Kingston
OKQ	Queen's University, Kingston
OKQM	McArthur College of Education, Queen's University, Kingston
OKR	Royal Military College of Canada, Kingston
OL	London Public Library
OLH	Huron College, London
OLLE	Ontario Library Service - Thames, London
OLU	University of Western Ontario, London
OLUM	Sciences Library, Natural Sciences Centre, University of Western Ontario, London
OOA	National Archives, Ottawa
OOAECB	Atomic Energy Control Board, Ottawa
OOAG	Main Library, Agriculture Canada, Ottawa
OOB	Bank of Canada, Ottawa
OOC	Ottawa Public Library
OOCC	Carleton University, Ottawa
OOCM	Canadian Housing Information Centre, Canada Mortgage and Housing Corporation, Ottawa
OOCN	Canadian Nurses' Association, Ottawa
OOCS	Public Service Commission of Canada, Ottawa
OOE	External Affairs Canada, Ottawa
OOEC	Economic Council of Canada, Ottawa
OOEDC	Export Development Corporation, Ottawa
OOF	Dept. of Finance and Treasury Board of Canada, Ottawa
OOFF	Departmental Library, Environment Canada, Ottawa
OOFP	Forintek Canada Corporation, Ottawa
OOG	Geological Survey of Canada, Ottawa
OOL	Labour Canada, Ottawa
OOLWB	Women's Bureau, Labour Canada, Ottawa
OOMI	Employment and Immigration Canada, Ottawa
OON	Canada Institute for Scientific and Technical Information, National Research Council Canada, Ottawa
OOND	Department of National Defence, Ottawa
OONF	National Film Board, Montreal
OONG	National Gallery of Canada, Ottawa
OONL	National Library of Canada, Ottawa
OONM	National Museums of Canada, Ottawa
OONMC	Canadian War Museum, Ottawa
OONMM	Canadian Museum of Civilization, National Museums of Canada, Ottawa
OOP	Library of Parliament, Ottawa
OOPW	Public Works Canada, Ottawa
OORD	Indian and Northern Affairs Canada, Ottawa
OOREX	Regional Industrial Expansion, Ottawa
OORT	Canadian Radio-Television and Telecommunications Commission, Ottawa
OOS	Statistics Canada, Ottawa
OOSH	Oshawa Public Library
OOSM	Surveys and Mapping Branch, Energy, Mines and Resources Canada, Ottawa
OOTC	Regional Industrial Expansion, Ottawa
OOU	University of Ottawa
OOUSI	United States Information Service, Ottawa
OOV	Veterans Affairs Canada, Charlottetown
OPAL	Lakehead University, Thunder Bay
OPET	Trent University, Peterborough
OS	Sarnia Public Library
OSTCB	Brock Universty, St. Catherines
OSUL	Laurentian University, Sudbury
OSUU	University of Sudbury
OTA	Academy of Medicine, Toronto

OTAG	Art Gallery of Ontario, Toronto
OTAR	Archives of Ontario, Toronto
OTB	Thunder Bay Public Library
OTC	Faculty of Education, University of Toronto
OTCIA	Canadian Institute of International Affairs, Toronto
OTDL	Ontario Ministry of Labour, Toronto
OTDT	Ontario Ministry of Transportation and Communications, Toronto
OTDU	Ontario Ministry of Colleges and Universities, Toronto
OTEPL	Etobicoke Public Library
OTER	Ontario Institute for Studies in Education, Toronto
OTET	TVOntario, Toronto
OTEY	East York Public Library, Toronto
OTIM	Pontifical Institute of Mediaeval Studies, Toronto
OTK	Knox College, University of Toronto
OTL	Legislative Library of Ontario, Toronto
OTLS	Law Society of Upper Canada, Toronto
OTMCL	Metropolitan Toronto Reference Library
OTNY	North York Public Library, Willowdale
OTP	Toronto Public Libraries
OTRC	Canadian Forces College, Toronto
OTREC	Regis College, Toronto
OTRM	Royal Ontario Museum, Toronto
OTSP	Scarborough Public Library
OTSTM	University of St. Michael's College, Toronto
OTTC	University of Trinity College, Toronto
OTU	University of Toronto
OTUD	David Dunlap Observatory, University of Toronto
OTUDP	Clarke Institute of Psychiatry, University of Toronto
OTULS	Faculty of Library Science, University of Toronto
OTV	Victoria University, Toronto
OTY	York University, Toronto
OTYP	York Public Library, Toronto
OW	Windsor Public Library
OWA	University of Windsor
OWAL	Law Library, University of Windsor
OWTL	Wilfrid Laurier University, Waterloo
OWTU	University of Waterloo
PC	Prince Edward Island Provincial Library, Charlottetown
QCU	Universite du Quebec, Chicoutimi
QHU	Universite du Quebec, Hull
QLB	Bishop's University, Lennoxville
QMAC	Macdonald College Library, Ste Anne de Bellevue
QMB	Bell Canada, Montreal
QMBM	Bibliotheque de la ville de Montreal
QMBN	Bibliotheque nationale du Quebec, Montreal
QMFA	Montreal Museum of Fine Arts
QMG	Sir George Williams Campus, Concordia University, Montreal
QMH	Hydro-Quebec, Montreal
QMHE	Ecole des hautes etudes commerciales, Montreal
QML	Loyola Campus, Concordia University, Montreal
QMM	McLennan Library, McGill University, Montreal
QMML	Law Library, McGill University, Montreal
QMMLS	Library and Information Studies Library, McGill University, Montreal
QMMN	Nursing/Social Work Library, McGill University, Montreal
QMMSC	Howard Ross Library of Management, McGill University, Montreal
QMOCP	Canadian Livestock Feed Board, Montreal
QMU	Universite de Montreal
QMUQ	Universite du Quebec, Montreal
QQIAS	Service de documentation, Ministere de la sante et des services sociaux du Quebec, Quebec
QQL	Bibliotheque de l'Assemblee nationale, Quebec
QQLA	Bibliotheque generale, Universite Laval, Quebec

QQMC	Bibliotheque administrative, Ministere des communications du Quebec, Quebec
QRC	College de l'Abitibi-Temiscamingue, Rouyn-Noranda
QRU	Universite du Quebec, Rimouski
QRUQR	Universite du Quebec en Abitibi-Temiscamingue, Rouyn-Noranda
QSHERU	Universite de Sherbrooke
QSTJ	College militaire royal de Saint-Jean
QT	Bibliotheque municipale, Trois-Rivieres
QTCE	Cegep, Trois-Rivieres
QTCL	College Lafleche, Trois-Rivieres
QTU	Universite du Quebec, Trois-Rivieres
SCA	Archibald Library, Caronport
SCR	Chinook Regional Library, Swift Current
SMJ	Moose Jaw Public Library
SMJT	Saskatchewan Techical Institute, Moose Jaw
SNB	Lakeland Library Region, North Battleford
SPANC	Wapiti Regional Library, Prince Albert
SR	Regina Public Library
SRCB	Canadian Bible College, Regina
SRCU	Credit Union Central, Regina
SRED	Saskatchewan Education, Regina
SRL	Legislative Library of Saskatchewan, Regina
SRP	Saskatchewan Library and Union Catalogue, Regina
SRPS	Saskatchewan Public Service Commission, Regina
SRRI	Wascana Institute of Applied Arts & Sciences, Regina
SRU	University of Regina
SS	Saskatoon Public Library
SSAR	Research Station, Agriculture Canada, Saskatoon
SSC	Co-operative College of Canada, Saskatoon
SSM	St. Thomas More College, Saskatoon
SSR	Saskatchewan Research Council, Saskatoon
SSSA	St. Andrew's College, Saskatoon
SSSI	Kelsey Institute of Applied Arts & Sciences, Saskatoon
SST	Saskatchewan Teachers' Federation, Saskatoon
SSU	University of Saskatchewan, Saskatoon
SSUL	Law Library, University of Saskatchewan, Saskatoon
SSW	Wheatland Regional Library, Saskatoon
SWSE	Southeast Regional Library, Weyburn
SYP	Parkland Regional Library, Yorkton